CAMBRIDGE
UNIVERSITY PRESS

Chemistry

for Cambridge International AS & A Level

COURSEBOOK

Lawrie Ryan & Roger Norris

CAMBRIDGE
UNIVERSITY PRESS

University Printing House, Cambridge CB2 8BS, United Kingdom

One Liberty Plaza, 20th Floor, New York, NY 10006, USA

477 Williamstown Road, Port Melbourne, VIC 3207, Australia

314–321, 3rd Floor, Plot 3, Splendor Forum, Jasola District Centre, New Delhi – 110025, India

103 Penang Road, #05-06/07, Visioncrest Commercial, Singapore 238467

Cambridge University Press is part of the University of Cambridge.

It furthers the University's mission by disseminating knowledge in the pursuit of education, learning and research at the highest international levels of excellence.

www.cambridge.org
Information on this title: www.cambridge.org/9781108863193

© Cambridge University Press 2020

First published 2011
Second edition 2014
Third edition 2020

20 19 18 17 16 15 14 13 12 11 10 9 8 7 6 5

Printed in India by Multivista Global Pvt Ltd.

A catalogue record for this publication is available from the British Library

ISBN 978-1-108-86319-3 Coursebook with Digital Access
ISBN 978-1-108-79780-1 Digital Coursebook (2 Years)
ISBN 978-1-108-79781-8 Coursebook eBook

Cambridge University Press has no responsibility for the persistence or accuracy of URLs for external or third-party internet websites referred to in this publication, and does not guarantee that any content on such websites is, or will remain, accurate or appropriate. Information regarding prices, travel timetables, and other factual information given in this work is correct at the time of first printing but Cambridge University Press does not guarantee the accuracy of such information thereafter.

....

....

Exam-style questions and sample answers have been written by the authors. In examinations, the way marks are awarded may be different. References to assessment and/or assessment preparation are the publisher's interpretation of the syllabus requirements and may not fully reflect the approach of Cambridge Assessment International Education.

Cambridge International recommends that teachers consider using a range of teaching and learning resources in preparing learners for assessment, based on their own professional judgement of their students' needs.

Cambridge International copyright material in this publication is reproduced under licence and remains the intellectual property of Cambridge Assessment International Education.

DEDICATED TEACHER AWARDS

Teachers play an important part in shaping futures. Our Dedicated Teacher Awards recognise the hard work that teachers put in every day.

Thank you to everyone who nominated this year, we have been inspired and moved by all of your stories. Well done to all of our nominees for your dedication to learning and for inspiring the next generation of thinkers, leaders and innovators.

Congratulations to our incredible winner and finalists

WINNER

Ahmed Saya
Cordoba School for A-Level,
Pakistan

Sharon Kong Foong
Sunway College,
Malaysia

Abhinandan Bhattacharya
JBCN International School Oshiwara,
India

Anthony Chelliah
Gateway College,
Sri Lanka

Candice Green
St Augustine's College,
Australia

Jimrey Buntas Dapin
University of San Jose-Recoletos,
Philippines

For more information about our dedicated teachers and their stories, go to
dedicatedteacher.cambridge.org

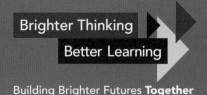

Brighter Thinking
Better Learning

Building Brighter Futures **Together**

> Contents

> How to use this series

This suite of resources supports learners and teachers following the Cambridge International AS & A Level Chemistry syllabus (9701). All of the books in the series work together to help learners develop the necessary knowledge and scientific skills required for this subject.

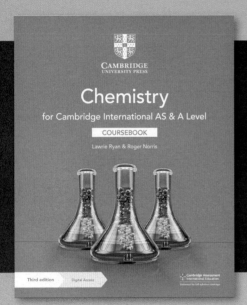

The coursebook provides comprehensive support for the full Cambridge International AS & A Level Chemistry syllabus (9701). It clearly explains facts, concepts and practical techniques, and uses real-world examples of scientific principles. Two chapters provide full guidance to help learners develop investigative skills. Questions within each chapter help them to develop their understanding, while exam-style questions provide essential practice.

The workbook contains over 100 exercises and exam-style questions, carefully constructed to help learners develop the skills that they need as they progress through their Chemistry course.

The exercises also help learners develop understanding of the meaning of various command words used in questions, and provide practice in responding appropriately to these.

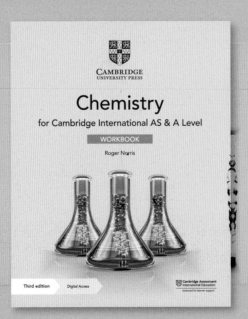

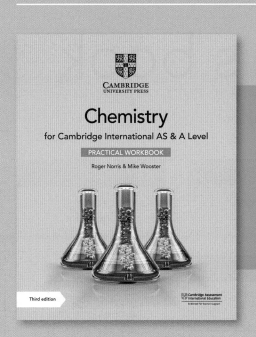

This write-in book provides learners with a wealth of hands-on practical work, giving them full guidance and support that will help them to develop all of the essential investigative skills. These skills include planning investigations, selecting and handling apparatus, creating hypotheses, recording and displaying results, and analysing and evaluating data.

The teacher's resource supports and enhances the materials in the coursebook, workbook and practical workbook. It includes answers for every question and exercise in these three books. It also includes detailed lesson ideas, teaching notes for each topic area including a suggested teaching plan, ideas for active learning and formative assessment, links to resources, ideas for lesson starters and plenaries, differentiation, lists of common misconceptions and ideas for homework activities. The practical teacher's guide, included with this resource, includes detailed support for preparing and carrying out all of the investigations in the practical workbook, including tips for getting things to work well, and a set of sample results that can be used if students cannot do the experiment or fail to collect results.

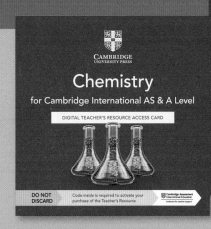

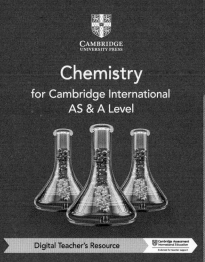

> How to use this book

Throughout this book, you will notice lots of different features that will help your learning. These are explained below.

LEARNING INTENTIONS

These set the scene for each chapter, help with navigation through the coursebook and indicate the important concepts in each topic.

BEFORE YOU START

This feature contains questions and activities on subject knowledge you will need before starting this chapter.

SCIENCE IN CONTEXT

This feature presents real-world examples and applications of the content in a chapter, encouraging you to look further into topics. There are discussion questions at the end which look at some of the benefits and problems of these applications.

PRACTICAL ACTIVITIES

This book does not contain detailed instructions for doing particular experiments, but you will find background information about the practical work you need to do in these boxes. There are also two chapters, P1 and P2, which provide detailed information about the practical skills you need to develop during the course.

Questions

Appearing throughout the text, questions give you a chance to check that you have understood the topic you have just read about. You can find the answers to these questions in the digital version of the coursebook.

KEY DEFINITIONS

Key definitions for important scientific principles, laws and theories are given in the margin and highlighted in the text when it is first introduced. You will also find these definitions in the Glossary at the back of this book.

KEY WORDS

Key vocabulary is highlighted in the text when it is first introduced. Definitions are then given in the margin, which explain the meanings of these words and phrases.

You will also find definitions of these words in the Glossary at the back of this book.

COMMAND WORDS

Command words that appear in the syllabus and might be used in exams are highlighted in the exam-style questions when they are first introduced. In the margin, you will find the Cambridge International definition*.

You will also find the same definitions in the Glossary at the back of this book.

*The information in this section is taken from the Cambridge International syllabus (9701) for examination from 2022. You should always refer to the appropriate syllabus document for the year of your examination to confirm the details and for more information. The syllabus document is available on the Cambridge International website at www.cambridgeinternational.org.

WORKED EXAMPLES

Wherever you need to know how to use a formula to carry out a calculation, there are worked examples boxes to show you how to do this.

REFLECTION

These activities ask you to look back on the topics covered in the chapter and test how well you understand these topics and encourage you to reflect on your learning.

IMPORTANT

Important equations, facts and tips are given in these boxes.

EXAM-STYLE QUESTIONS

These questions provide more demanding exam-style questions, some of which may require use of knowledge from previous chapters. Answers to these questions can be found in the digital version of the coursebook.

SUMMARY CHECKLISTS

There is a summary of key points at the end of each chapter.

SELF-EVALUATION

The summary checklists are followed by 'I can' statements which match the learning intentions at the beginning of the chapter. You might find it helpful to rate how confident you are for each of these statements when you are revising. You should revisit any sections that you rated "Needs more work" or "Almost there".

I can	See section...	Needs more work	Almost there	Ready to move on

These boxes tell you where information in the book is extension content, and is not part of the syllabus.

> Introduction

This book covers the entire syllabus of Cambridge International AS & A Level Chemistry (9701) for examination from 2022. This book is in three parts:

- Chapters 1–18 and P1: the AS Level content, covered in the first year of the course, including a chapter (P1) dedicated to the development of your practical skills

- Chapters 19–30 and P2: the A Level content, including a chapter (P2) dedicated to developing your ability to plan, analyse and evaluate practical investigations

- Appendices: including a Periodic Table, useful formulae and reactions, a glossary and an index.

The main aims of a textbook like this are to explain the various concepts of chemistry that you need to understand, and to provide you with questions that will help you to test your understanding and develop the key skills needed to succeed on this course. The 'How to use this book' pages show the structure of each chapter and the features of this book.

In your study of chemistry, you will find that certain key concepts are repeated, and that these concepts form 'themes' that link the different areas of chemistry together. You will progress and gain confidence in your understanding of chemistry if you take note of these themes. For this coursebook, these key concepts include:

- Atoms and forces

- Experiments and evidence

- Patterns in chemical behaviour and reactions

- Chemical bonds

- Energy changes

Studying chemistry is a stimulating and worthwhile experience. It is an international subject; no single country has a monopoly on the development of the ideas. It can be a rewarding exercise to discover how men and women from many countries have contributed to our knowledge and well-being, through their research into and application of the concepts of chemistry.

We hope not only that this book will help you to succeed in your future studies and career, but also that it will stimulate your curiosity and your imagination. Today's students become the next generation of scientists and engineers, and we hope that you will learn from the past to take chemistry to ever-greater heights.

> # Chapter 1
Atomic structure

LEARNING INTENTIONS

In this chapter you will learn how to:

- describe the structure of the atom as mostly empty space surrounding a very small nucleus that consists of protons and neutrons and state that electrons are found in shells in the space around the nucleus

- describe the position of the electrons in shells in the space around the nucleus

- identify and describe protons, neutrons and electrons in terms of their relative charges and relative masses

- use and understand the terms atomic (proton) number and mass (nucleon) number

- describe the distribution of mass and charges within an atom

- deduce the behaviour of beams of protons, neutrons and electrons moving at the same velocity in an electric field

- understand that ions are formed from atoms or molecules by gain or loss of electrons

- deduce the numbers of protons, neutrons and electrons present in both atoms and ions given atomic (proton) number, mass (nucleon) number and charge

- define the term *isotope* in terms of numbers of protons and neutrons

CONTINUED

- use the notation $^x_y A$ for isotopes, where x is the mass (nucleon) number and y is the atomic (proton) number

- explain why isotopes of the same element have the same chemical properties

- explain why isotopes of the same element have different physical properties (limited to mass and density).

BEFORE YOU START

1   Without looking at the Periodic Table, make a list of the names and symbols for the elements in Periods 1, 2 and 3. Compare your list with another learner then check to see if the symbols are correct.

2   How can you deduce the formula of a simple ion (e.g. a chloride ion or an aluminium ion) by reference to the Periodic Table?

3   Take turns in challenging another learner to write down the formula of a simple ion. Check your answers afterwards using a textbook.

4   Make a list of the subatomic particles in an atom giving their relative mass and relative charges as well as their position in the atom, structure of the atom and isotopes. Compare your answers with those of another learner. Were you in agreement?

5   Write down a definition of the term *isotope*. Put a circle around the three most important words in your definition. Compare your definition to the one in a textbook.

6   What do the terms *mass number* and *proton number* mean? Write down your definitions and compare yours with another learner.

7   Ask another learner to use a data book or the internet to select an isotope. Use this data to deduce the number of protons, neutrons and electrons in an atom or ion of this isotope, e.g. Cr atom or Cr^{3+} ion. If you are unsure, check your answer with someone else in the class or with a teacher.

8   Take a photocopy of the modern Periodic Table and cross out or cut out the group numbers and period numbers. Get another learner to select an element. You then have to state in which period and group that element belongs. Take turns in doing this until you are sure that you can easily identify the group and period of an element.

9   Ask another learner to select an element. You then have to state if the element is a metal, non-metal or metalloid (metalloids have some characteristics of both metals and non-metals). If you are both uncertain, consult a textbook or the internet. Take turns in doing this until you are sure that you can easily identify the position of metals, non-metals and metalloids.

10 Explain to another learner in terms of numbers of electrons and protons why a sodium ion has a single positive charge but an oxide ion has a 2– charge.

11 Explain to another learner what you know about attraction or repulsion of positive and negative charges.

DEVELOPING AN IDEA: NANOMACHINES

Progress in science depends not only on original thinking but also on developing the ideas of other people. The idea of an atom goes back over 2000 years to the Greek philosopher Demokritos. About 350 years ago, Robert Boyle looked again at the idea of small particles but there was no proof. John Dalton moved a step closer to proving that atoms exist: he developed the idea that atoms of the same kind had the same weight, thinking this could explain the results of experiments on combining different substances in terms of rearrangement of the atoms.

At the beginning of the 20th century, J.J. Thomson (see Figure 1.6) suggested three models of the atom. His preferred model was to imagine an atom as a spherical cloud of positive charge in which electrons were placed. A few years later, scientists working under the direction of Ernest Rutherford (see Figure 1.4) fired alpha particles (which we now know are positively charged helium nuclei) at very high speeds at strips of metal only 0.0005 mm thick. Most of the alpha particles went through the strip. This would fit with the idea of atoms being a cloud of charge with very little mass to deflect (change the direction of) the alpha particles. But one alpha particle in every 20 000 was deflected at an angle of more than 90°. From this, Rutherford deduced that there must be something very small and positively charged in the atom. The atomic nucleus had been discovered!

In 1960 Richard Feynman (Figure 1.1) suggested that tiny machines could be made from a few hundred atoms grouped together in clusters. At the time, these ideas seemed like 'science fiction'. But several scientists took up the challenge and the science of nanotechnology was born.

In nanotechnology, scientists design and make objects that may have a thickness of only a few thousand atoms or less. Groups of atoms can be moved around on special surfaces (Figure 1.2). In this way, scientists have started to develop tiny machines that will help deliver medical drugs to exactly where they are needed in the body.

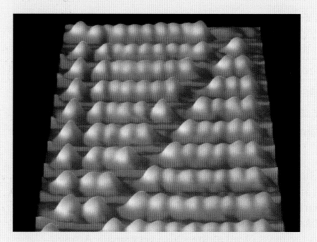

Figure 1.2: Each of the blue peaks in this image is an individual molecule. The molecules can be moved over a copper surface, making this a molecular abacus or counting device.

Questions for discussion

Discuss with another learner or group of learners:

- Why do you think that tiny clusters of atoms are useful for catalysts?

Figure 1.1: Richard Feynman.

- How do you think that you could make tiny clusters of metal atoms on a cold surface?

   Tip: Think about breathing onto a cold surface.

- What other uses could be made of tiny groups / clusters of atoms?

- What advantages and disadvantages could there be in using tiny clusters of atoms to help deliver medical drugs and in cancer treatment?

- What else do you think nanomachines could be used for?

1.1 Elements and atoms

Every substance in our world is made up from chemical elements. These chemical elements cannot be broken down further into simpler substances by chemical means. A few elements, such as nitrogen and gold, are found on their own in nature, not combined with other elements. Most elements, however, are found in combination with other elements as compounds.

Every element has its own chemical symbol. The symbols are often derived from Latin or Greek words. Some examples are shown in Table 1.1.

Element	Symbol
carbon	C
lithium	Li (from Greek 'lithos')
iron	Fe (from Latin 'ferrum')
potassium	K (from Arabic 'al-qualyah' or from the Latin 'kalium')

Table 1.1: Some examples of chemical symbols.

Chemical elements contain only one type of atom. An atom is the smallest part of an element that can take part in a chemical change. Atoms are very small. The diameter of a hydrogen atom is approximately 10^{-10} m, so the mass of an atom is also very small. A single hydrogen atom weighs only 1.67×10^{-27} kg.

1.2 Inside the atom

The structure of an atom

Every atom has nearly all of its mass concentrated in a tiny region in the centre of the atom called the nucleus. The nucleus is made up of particles called nucleons. There are two types of nucleon: protons and neutrons. Atoms of different elements have different numbers of protons.

Outside the nucleus, particles called electrons move around in regions of space called orbitals (see Section 2.3). Chemists often find it convenient to use a simpler model of the atom in which electrons move around the nucleus in electron shells. Each shell is a certain distance from the nucleus at its own particular energy level (see Section 2.3). In a neutral atom, the number of electrons is equal to the number of protons. A simple model of a carbon atom is shown in Figure 1.3.

KEY WORDS

element: a substance containing only one type of atom. All the atoms in an element have the same proton number.

atom: the smallest part of an element that can take part in a chemical change. Every atom contains protons in its nucleus and electrons outside the nucleus. Most atoms have neutrons in the nucleus. The exception is the isotope of hydrogen $^1_1$H.

proton: positively charged particle in the nucleus of the atom.

neutron: uncharged particle in the nucleus of an atom, with the same relative mass as a proton.

electron: negatively charged particle found in orbitals outside the nucleus of an atom. It has negligible mass compared with a proton.

energy levels: the specific distances from the nucleus corresponding to the energy of the electrons. Electrons in energy levels further from the nucleus have more energy than those closer to the nucleus. Energy levels are split up into sub-levels which are given the names s, p, d, etc.

When we use a simple model of the atom we talk about shells (n = 1, n = 2, etc) and sub-shells 2s, 2p, etc. In this model, the electrons are at a fixed distance from the nucleus. This model is useful when we discuss ionisation energies (Chapter 2).

When we discuss where the electrons really are in space, we use the orbital model. In this model, there is a probability of finding a particular electron within certain area of space outside the nucleus. We use this model for discussing bonding and referring to electrons in the sub-shells.

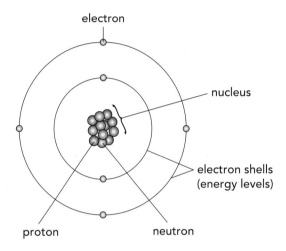

Figure 1.3: A model of a carbon atom. This model is not very accurate but it is useful for understanding what happens to the electrons during chemical reactions.

Atoms are tiny, but the nucleus of an atom is much smaller. If the diameter of an atom were the size of a football stadium, the nucleus would only be the size of a pea. This means that most of the atom is empty space! Electrons are even smaller than protons and neutrons.

Figure 1.4: Ernest Rutherford (left) and Hans Geiger (right) using their alpha particle apparatus. Interpretation of the results led to Rutherford proposing the nuclear model for atoms.

PRACTICAL ACTIVITY 1.1

Experiments with subatomic particles

We can deduce the electric charge of subatomic particles by showing how beams of electrons, protons and neutrons behave in electric fields. If we fire a beam of electrons past electrically charged plates, the electrons are deflected (change direction) away from the negative plate and towards the positive plate (Figure 1.5a). This shows us that the electrons are negatively charged because opposite charges attract each other and like charges repel each other.

A cathode-ray tube (Figure 1.5b) can be used to produce beams of electrons. At one end of the tube is a metal wire (cathode), which is heated to a high temperature when a low voltage is applied to it. At the other end of the tube is a fluorescent screen, which glows when electrons hit it.

The electrons are given off from the heated wire and are attracted towards two metal plates, which are positively charged. As they pass through the metal plates, the electrons form a beam. When the electron beam hits the screen a spot of light is produced. When an electric field is applied across this beam the electrons are deflected. The fact

CONTINUED

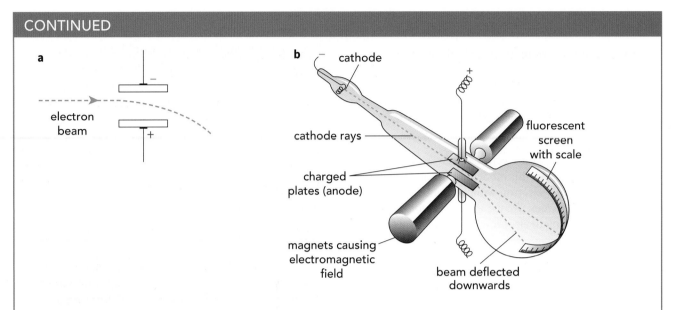

Figure 1.5: a The beam of electrons is deflected away from a negatively charged plate and towards a positively charged plate. **b** The electron beam in a cathode-ray tube is deflected by an electromagnetic field. The direction of the deflection shows us that the electron is negatively charged.

that the electrons are so easily attracted to the positively charged **anode** and that they are easily deflected by an electric field shows us that:

* electrons have a negative charge
* electrons have a very small mass.

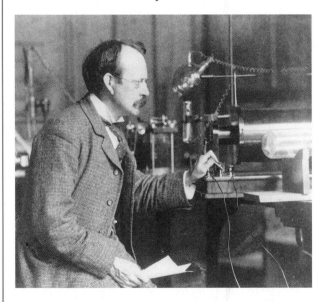

Figure 1.6: J. J. Thomson calculated the charge to mass ratio of electrons. He used results from experiments with electrons in cathode-ray tubes.

> **KEY WORD**
>
> **anode:** the positive electrode (where oxidation reactions occur).

In recent years, experiments have been carried out with beams of electrons, protons and neutrons moving at the same velocity in an electric field.

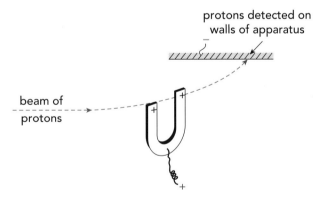

Figure 1.7: A beam of protons is deflected away from a positively charged area. This shows us that protons have a positive charge.

CONTINUED

The results of these experiments show that:

- a proton beam is deflected away from a positively charged plate; as like charges repel, the protons must have a positive charge (Figure 1.7)
- an electron beam is deflected towards a positively charged plate; as opposite charges attract, the electrons must have a negative charge
- a beam of neutrons is not deflected; this shows that they are uncharged.

In these experiments, huge voltages have to be used to deflect the proton beam. This contrasts with the very low voltages needed to deflect an electron beam. These experiments show us that protons are much heavier than electrons. If we used the same voltage to deflect electrons and protons, the beam of electrons would have a far greater deflection than the beam of protons. This is because a proton is about 2000 times heavier than an electron.

IMPORTANT

Remember that like charges repel each other and unlike charges attract each other.

Question

1   A beam of electrons is passing close to a highly negatively charged plate. When the electrons pass close to the plate, they are deflected away from the plate.

    a   What deflection would you expect, if any, when the experiment is repeated with beams of **i** protons and **ii** neutrons? Explain your answers.

    b   Which subatomic particle (electron, proton or neutron) would deviate the most? Explain your answer.

Masses and charges: a summary

Electrons, protons and neutrons have characteristic charges and masses. The values of these are too small to be very useful when discussing general chemical properties. For example, the charge on a single electron is -1.602×10^{-19} coulombs. We therefore compare their masses and charges by using their relative charges and masses. These are not the actual charges and masses. They are the charges and masses compared with each other in a simple ratio. These are shown in Table 1.2.

1.3 Numbers of nucleons

Atomic (proton) number and mass (nucleon) number

The number of protons in the nucleus of an atom is called the atomic number (proton number) (Z). Every atom of the same element has the same number of protons in its nucleus. It is the atomic number that makes an atom what it is. For example, an atom with an **atomic number** of 11 must be an atom of the element sodium. No other element can have 11 protons in its nucleus. The Periodic Table of elements is arranged in order of the atomic numbers of the individual elements (see Appendix 1).

The mass number (nucleon number) (A) is the number of protons plus neutrons in the nucleus of an atom.

Subatomic particle	Symbol	Relative mass	Relative charge
electron	e	$\frac{1}{1836}$	−1
neutron	n	1	0
proton	p	1	+1

Table 1.2: Comparing electrons, neutrons and protons.

KEY DEFINITION

atomic number: the number of protons in the nucleus of an atom. Also called the proton number. Remember that in writing isotopic symbols, $_y^x A$, this is the figure which is subscript.

How many neutrons?

We can use the mass number and atomic number to find the number of neutrons in an atom. As:

mass number = number of protons + number of neutrons

Then:

number of neutrons = mass number – atomic number
$$= A - Z$$

For example, an atom of aluminium has a mass number of 27 and an atomic number of 13. So an aluminium atom has 27 – 13 = 14 neutrons.

Question

2   Use the information in Table 1.3 to deduce the number of electrons and neutrons in a neutral atom of:

   a   vanadium

   b   strontium

   c   phosphorus

Atom	Mass number	Proton number
vanadium	51	23
strontium	88	38
phosphorus	31	15

Table 1.3: Information table for Question 2

Isotopes

All atoms of the same element have the same number of protons. However, they may have different numbers of neutrons. Atoms of the same element that have different numbers of neutrons are called isotopes.

Isotopes are atoms of the same element with different **mass numbers**.

Isotopes of a particular element have the same chemical properties because they have the same number of electrons. They have slightly different physical properties, such as small differences in density or small differences in mass, because they have different numbers of neutrons.

We can write symbols for isotopes. We write the nucleon number at the top left of the chemical symbol and the proton number at the bottom left.

The symbol for the isotope of boron with 5 protons and 11 nucleons is written $^{11}_{5}B$:

nucleon number $\longrightarrow$ $^{11}_{5}B$
proton number $\longrightarrow$

Hydrogen has three isotopes. The atomic structure and isotopic symbols for the three isotopes of hydrogen are shown in Figure 1.8.

When writing generally about isotopes, chemists also name them by leaving out the proton number and placing the mass number after the name. For example, the isotopes of hydrogen can be called hydrogen-1, hydrogen-2 and hydrogen-3.

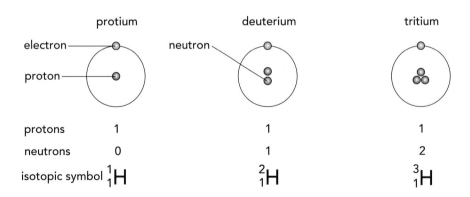

	protium	deuterium	tritium
protons	1	1	1
neutrons	0	1	2
isotopic symbol	$^{1}_{1}H$	$^{2}_{1}H$	$^{3}_{1}H$

Figure 1.8: The atomic structure and isotopic symbols for the three isotopes of hydrogen.

Remember that in writing isotopes, mass number is the figure which is superscript.

Isotopes can be radioactive or non-radioactive. Specific radioisotopes (radioactive isotopes) can be used to check for leaks in oil or gas pipelines and to check the thickness of paper. They are also used in medicine to treat some types of cancer and to check the activity of the thyroid gland in the throat.

Question

3   Use the Periodic Table in Appendix 1 to help you. Write isotopic symbols for the following neutral atoms:

a   bromine-81

b   calcium-44

c   iron-58

d   palladium-110

How many protons, neutrons and electrons?

In a neutral atom the number of positively charged protons in the nucleus equals the number of negatively charged electrons outside the nucleus. When an atom gains or loses electrons, ions are formed, which are electrically charged. For example:

Cl	+	e^-	→	Cl^-
chlorine atom		1 electron gained		chloride ion
17 protons				17 protons
17 electrons				18 electrons

The chloride ion has a single negative charge because there are 17 protons (+) and 18 electrons (−).

Mg	→	Mg^{2+}	+	$2e^-$
magnesium atom		magnesium ion		2 electrons removed
12 protons		12 protons		
12 electrons		10 electrons		

The magnesium ion has a charge of 2+ because it has 12 protons (+) but only 10 electrons (−).

The isotopic symbol for an ion derived from sulfur-33 is $^{33}_{16}S^{2-}$. This sulfide ion has 16 protons, 17 neutrons (because $33 - 16 = 17$) and 18 electrons (because $16 + 2 = 18$).

IMPORTANT

Ions: charged particles formed by the loss or gain of electrons from an atom or group of covalently bonded atoms. Remember that positive ions are formed when one or more electrons are *lost* by an atom and that negative ions are formed when one or more electrons are *gained* by an atom.

WORKED EXAMPLE

1   Deduce the number of electrons in the ion $^{52}_{24}Cr^{2+}$.

Solution

Step 1: Work out the number of protons. This is the subscripted number 24.

Step 2: Number of protons = number of electrons in the neutral atom. So number of electrons in the atom is 24.

Step 3: For a positive ion subtract the number of charges (because electrons have been lost from the atom). For a negative ion add the number of charges (because electrons have been gained).
So for Cr^{2+}, $24 - 2 = 22$ electrons.

Questions

4   Deduce the number of electrons in each of these ions.

a $^{40}_{19}K^+$

b $^{15}_{7}N^{3-}$

c $^{18}_{8}O^{2-}$

d $^{71}_{31}Ga^{3+}$

5   In which one of the following ways are isotopes of the same element exactly the same?

A   The sum of the number of electrons and the number of neutrons in each atom.

B   The mass of the nucleus in each atom.

C   The number of electrons in each atom.

D   The sum of the number of protons and the number of neutrons in each atom.

6 Deduce the number of electrons, protons and neutrons in each of these ions:

   a $_{35}^{81}\text{Br}^-$

   b $_{38}^{58}\text{Ce}^{3+}$

REFLECTION

Read the paragraph in 'Developing an idea: Nanomachines' at the beginning of this chapter about Rutherford's work in discovering the nucleus. Discuss these questions with another learner:

1   Why, in Rutherford's experiments, did most of the alpha particles go straight through the metal foil and so few bounced back?

2   Suggest what happened to the alpha particles that went a little way from the nucleus. Use ideas of attractive or repulsive forces.

3   Use your knowledge of what you have learned in this chapter to think about any other experiments that could have been used.

How much did you contribute to the discussion? Could you have contributed more?

SUMMARY

Beams of protons and electrons are deflected by electric fields but neutrons are not.

The atom consists of positively charged protons and neutral neutrons in the nucleus, surrounded by negatively charged electrons arranged in energy levels (shells).

Isotopes are atoms with the same atomic number but different mass numbers. They only differ in the number of neutrons they contain.

EXAM-STYLE QUESTIONS

1   Boron is an element in Group 13 of the Periodic Table.

   Boron has two isotopes.

   a   **Deduce** the number of **i** protons, **ii** neutrons and **iii** electrons in one neutral atom of the isotope $_{5}^{11}\text{B}$.   **[3]**

   b   What do you understand by the term *isotope*?   **[1]**

   c   **State** the relative masses and charges of:

      i   an electron   **[2]**

      ii   a neutron   **[2]**

      iii   a proton   **[2]**

                          [Total: 10]

COMMAND WORDS

Deduce: conclude from available information.

State: express in clear terms.

2 Zirconium, Zr, and hafnium, Hf, are metals.

An isotope of zirconium has 40 protons and 91 nucleons.

a i Write the isotopic symbol for this isotope of zirconium. [1]

ii State the number of neutrons present in one atom of this isotope. [1]

b The symbol for a particular ion of hafnium ion is $^{180}_{72}Hf^{2+}$.

Deduce the number of electrons that are present in one of these hafnium ions. [1]

c The subatomic particles present in zirconium and hafnium are electrons, neutrons and protons. A beam of protons is fired into an electric field produced by two charged plates, as shown in the diagram.

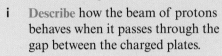

i **Describe** how the beam of protons behaves when it passes through the gap between the charged plates. [1]

ii **Explain** your answer. [1]

d Describe and explain what happens when a beam of neutrons passes through the gap between the charged plates. [2]

[Total: 7]

3 a Describe the structure of an atom, giving details of the subatomic particles present. [6]

b Explain the terms *atomic number* and *nucleon number*. [2]

c Copy and complete the table: [2]

Neutral atom	Atomic number	Nucleon number	Numbers of each subatomic particle present
Mg	12	24	
Al	13	27	

d Explain why atoms are neutral. [1]

e An oxygen atom has 8 protons in its nucleus. Explain why it cannot have 9 protons. [1]

f When deducing the relative mass of an atom, the electrons are not used in the calculation. Explain why not. [1]

[Total: 13]

4 The symbols below describe two isotopes of the element uranium.

$$^{235}_{92}U \quad ^{238}_{92}U$$

a State the meaning of the term *isotope*. [1]

b State two ways in which these two isotopes of uranium are identical. [2]

c State how these isotopes differ. [2]

d State the number of electrons present in one U^{2+} ion. [1]

[Total: 6]

COMMAND WORDS

Describe: state the points of a topic / give characteristics and main features.

Explain: set out purposes or reasons / make the relationships between things evident / provide why and / or how and support with relevant evidence.

CONTINUED

5 The table below shows the two naturally occurring isotopes of chlorine.

   a Copy and complete the table.

	$^{35}_{17}Cl$	$^{37}_{17}Cl$
number of protons		
number of electrons		
number of neutrons		

[3]

   b The relative atomic mass of chlorine is 35.5. What does this tell you about the relative abundance of the two naturally occurring isotopes of chlorine? [2]

   c Magnesium chloride contains magnesium ions, Mg^{2+}, and chloride ions, Cl^-.

     i Explain why a magnesium ion is positively charged. [1]

     ii Explain why a chloride ion has a single negative charge. [2]

[Total: 8]

SELF-EVALUATION

After studying this chapter, complete a table like this:

I can	See section...	Needs more work	Almost there	Ready to move on
understand that every atom has an internal structure with a nucleus in the centre and the negatively charged electrons arranged in 'shells' outside the nucleus	1.2			
understand that most of the mass of the atom is in the nucleus, which contains protons (positively charged) and neutrons (uncharged)	1.2			
understand that beams of protons and electrons are deflected by electric fields but neutrons are not	1.2			
understand that atoms of the same element have the same number of protons; this is called the atomic (proton) number (Z)	1.3			
understand that the mass (nucleon) number (A), is the total number of protons and neutrons in an atom	1.3			

CONTINUED

I can	See section...	Needs more work	Almost there	Ready to move on
deduce the number of neutrons in an atom by subtracting the atomic number from the mass number ($A-Z$)	1.3			
understand that in a neutral atom, the number of electrons equals the number of protons: when there are more protons than electrons, the atom becomes a positive ion; when there are more electrons than protons, a negatively charged ion is formed	1.3			
understand that isotopes are atoms with the same atomic number but different mass numbers; they only differ in the number of neutrons they contain.	1.3			

> Chapter 2

Electrons in atoms

CONTINUED

- use and understand the 'electrons in boxes' notation, e.g.

for Fe: [Ar] ↑↓ | ↑ | ↑ | ↑ | ↑   ↑↓

- describe and sketch the shapes of s and p orbitals

- describe a free radical as a species with one or more unpaired electrons

- define the term *first ionisation energy*

- construct equations to represent first, second and subsequent ionisation energies

- identify and explain the trend in ionisation energies across a period and down a group of the Periodic Table

- identify and explain the variation in successive ionisation energies of an element

- describe and understand that ionisation energies are due to the attraction between the nucleus and the outer electron

- explain the factors influencing the ionisation energies of the elements (in terms of nuclear charge, atomic / ionic radius, shielding by inner shells and sub-shells, and spin-pair repulsion)

- deduce the electronic configurations of elements using successive ionisation energy data

- deduce the position of an element in the Periodic Table using successive ionisation energy data

- explain qualitatively the variations in atomic radius and ionic radius across a period and down a group.

BEFORE YOU START

1   What are the relative masses and relative charges of a proton and an electron?

2   Explain to another learner:

   a   what is meant by the terms *electron shell* and *electronic configuration*

   b   why, in terms of electronic configuration, the gases helium, neon and argon are relatively unreactive.

3   Draw a labelled diagram to show the structure of a calcium atom. Compare your drawing with that of another learner.

4   Ask another learner to select one of the first 20 elements in the Periodic Table. Can you deduce the simple electronic configuration for an atom of this element? Take turns in doing this until you are sure that you can write simple electronic configurations.

5   Ask another learner to select one of the first 20 elements in the Periodic Table. Then ask them to state the charge on the ion. This time, deduce the simple electronic configuration for the ion of this element. Take turns in doing this until you are sure that you can write the electronic configurations for the ions.

6   Ask another learner to select any element in the Periodic Table. Write an ion–electron equation such as $Mg \rightarrow Mg^{2+} + 2e^-$ for this element, making sure that the charges balance. Take turns in doing this until you are sure that you can write this type of equation.

CONTINUED

7 What prefixes do you know that can be placed before the basic unit and what is their relationship to the basic unit? For example, a centimetre (cm) is one-hundredth of a metre (m).

8 Practise writing units in standard form, e.g. g / cm³ becomes $g\ cm^{-3}$ (the negative 3 shows that the cm³ is the divisor). Try changing the following into standard form:

a mol / dm³

b kJ / mol.

Compare your answers with those of another learner.

SEEING MORE DETAIL

If we try to study materials using an ordinary microscope with glass lenses, we find that there is a limit to how much we can magnify something. For example, we cannot see the tiny pores in some types of polymers (long-chain molecules). If, instead of light, we use a beam of electrons as a source of illumination, we can increase the magnification of an object up to a million times. This is because the wavelength of electrons can be 100 000 times shorter than the wavelength of visible light. (The wavelength is the distance between the crests of two waves). In Section 1.2, we saw how beams of electrons can be produced by a cathode-ray tube. We use an 'electron gun' similar to this to fire a beam of electrons at a sample. In 1926, Hans Busch developed an electromagnetic lens. Other scientists encouraged him to develop an electron microscope but it was not until 1931 that Ernst Ruska and Max Knoll produced the first electron microscope.

In the modern electron transmission microscope, a beam of electrons is accelerated in an electric field and focused on a specimen by an electromagnetic lens. Some electrons are transmitted through the specimen, others are absorbed and reflected as various types of radiation. The transmitted and reflected radiation can be absorbed onto a fluorescent screen to give an image (Figure 2.1).

The electron microscope can be used to calculate the size of pores in polymers and investigate the surfaces of metals (see Figure 2.2) and other materials. The radiation reflected in a scanning electron microscope can be used to identify chemical elements.

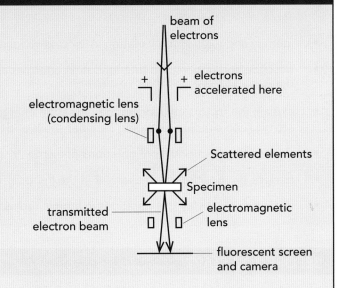

Figure 2.1: Processes occurring in a simplified transmission electron microscope.

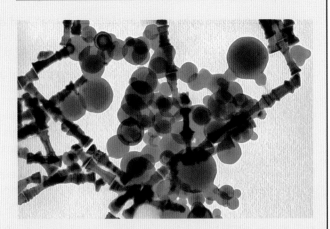

Figure 2.2: Coloured scanning electron micrograph of metal nanoparticles.

CONTINUED

Questions for discussion

Discuss with another learner or group of learners:

- Why must the inside of the electron microscope be at a very low pressure so that there is hardly any air present?

- Why must the specimens studied using an electron microscope have dry surfaces?

- Why might it be useful to be able to look at a substance in more detail?

2.1 Simple electronic structure

In Section 1.2 we saw that electrons are arranged outside the nucleus in **energy levels** or quantum shells. These principal energy levels or principal quantum shells (symbol n) are numbered according to how far they are from the nucleus. The lowest energy level, n = 1, is closest to the nucleus, the energy level n = 2 is further out, and so on. The electrons in quantum shells further away from the nucleus have more energy and are held less tightly to the nucleus.

The arrangement of electrons in an atom is called its electronic structure or **electronic configuration**. The electronic configurations of lithium, neon and chlorine are shown in Figure 2.3, together with a shorthand way of writing this structure.

KEY DEFINITION

energy levels: each electron in an atom has its particular average amount of energy. The further away the electron is from the nucleus, the more energy it has. Each principal energy level (symbol n) corresponds to an electron shell at a certain distance from the nucleus. Energy levels are split up into sub-levels which are given the names s, p, d, etc.

electronic configuration: a way of representing the arrangement of the electrons in atoms showing the principal quantum shells, the sub-shells and the number of electrons present, e.g. $1s^2\, 2s^2\, 2p^3$. The electrons may also be shown in boxes.

| lithium | neon | chlorine |
| 2,1 | 2,8 | 2,8,7 |

Figure 2.3: The simple electronic structures of lithium, neon and chlorine. The nuclei of the atoms are not shown.

Table 2.1 shows the number of electrons in each of the principal quantum shells (principal energy levels) for the first 11 elements in the Periodic Table.

Each principal quantum shell can hold a maximum number of electrons:

- shell 1: up to 2 electrons
- shell 2: up to 8 electrons
- shell 3: up to 18 electrons
- shell 4: up to 32 electrons.

	Atomic number	Number of electrons in shell		
		n = 1	n = 2	n = 3
H	1	1		
He	2	2		
Li	3	2	1	
Be	4	2	2	
B	5	2	3	
C	6	2	4	
N	7	2	5	
O	8	2	6	
F	9	2	7	
Ne	10	2	8	
Na	11	2	8	1

Table 2.1: Simple electronic configurations of the first 11 elements in the Periodic Table.

Question

1 Write the simple electronic configurations of the following atoms, showing the principal quantum shells only:

a sulfur; the atomic number of sulfur, $Z = 16$

b magnesium, $Z = 12$

c fluorine, $Z = 9$

d potassium, $Z = 19$

e carbon, $Z = 6$

2.2 Evidence for electronic structure

Ionisation energy, IE

By firing high-speed electrons at atoms, scientists can work out how much energy has to be supplied to form an ion by knocking out one electron from each atom.

The energy change that accompanies this process is called the *ionisation energy* (Figure 2.4).

The **first ionisation energy** of an element is the energy needed to remove one electron from each atom in one mole of atoms of the element in the gaseous state to form one mole of gaseous 1+ ions.

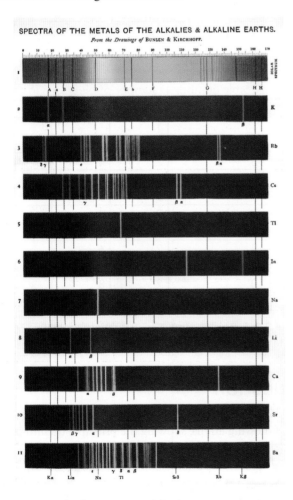

SPECTRA OF THE METALS OF THE ALKALIES & ALKALINE EARTHS.
From the Drawings of Bunsen & Kirchhoff.

Figure 2.4: The frequencies of the lines in an atomic emission spectrum can be used to calculate a value for the ionisation energy.

IMPORTANT

When writing definitions, look for the key words and try to remember these. In the definition above, look out for where it says one mole of atoms and one mole of 1+ ions and the gaseous states. One way of helping you to learn definitions is to write out the definition and circle the important parts.

Ionisation energies are measured under standard conditions. The general symbol for ionisation energy is IE. Its units are kJ mol^{-1}.

The symbol for the first ionisation energy is IE_1. Using calcium as an example:

1st ionisation energy: $Ca(g) \rightarrow Ca^+(g) + e^-$

$IE_1 = 590$ kJ mol^{-1}

If a second electron is removed from each ion in a mole of gaseous 1+ ions, we call it the *second ionisation energy*, IE_2. Again, using calcium as an example:

2nd ionisation energy: $Ca^+(g) \rightarrow Ca^{2+}(g) + e^-$

$IE_2 = 1150$ kJ mol^{-1}

Removal of a third electron from each ion in a mole of gaseous 2+ ions is called the *third ionisation energy*. Again, using calcium as an example:

3rd ionisation energy: $Ca^{2+}(g) \rightarrow Ca^{3+}(g) + e^-$

$IE_3 = 4940$ kJ mol^{-1}

We can continue to remove electrons from an atom until only the nucleus is left. We call this sequence of ionisation energies **successive ionisation energies**.

IMPORTANT

When you write equations for successive ionisation energies, remember that:

- the atoms and ions are in the gaseous state
- the charge on the ion on the right-hand side gives the number of the ionisation energy (1st, 2nd, 3rd, etc.)

KEY WORD

successive ionisation energies: the energy required in each step to remove the first electron, then the second, then the third, and so on, from a gaseous atom. Note: you should be able to write equations for each of these steps, e.g.

1st ionisation energy: $Li(g) \rightarrow Li^+(g) + e^-$

2nd ionisation energy: $Li^+(g) \rightarrow Li^{2+}(g) + e^-$

3rd ionisation energy: $Li^{2+}(g) \rightarrow Li^{3+}(g) + e^-$

The successive ionisation energies for the first 11 elements in the Periodic Table are shown in Table 2.2.

The data in Table 2.2 shows us that:

- For each element, the successive ionisation energies increase. This is because the net positive charge on the ion gets greater as each electron is removed. As each electron is removed there is a greater attractive force between the positively charged protons in the nucleus and the remaining negatively charged electrons. Therefore, more energy is needed to overcome these attractive forces.

- There is a big difference between some successive ionisation energies. For nitrogen, this occurs between the 5th and 6th ionisation energies. For sodium, the first big difference occurs between the 1st and 2nd ionisation energies. These large changes indicate that for the second of these two ionisation energies the electron is being removed from a principal quantum shell closer to the nucleus.

For example, for the 5th ionisation energy of nitrogen, the electron being removed is from the 2nd principal quantum shell. For the 6th ionisation energy of nitrogen, the electron being removed is from the 1st principal quantum shell.

Question

2   **a**   Write equations that describe:

    i   the 1st ionisation energy of calcium

    ii   the 3rd ionisation energy of potassium

    iii   the 2nd ionisation energy of lithium

    iv   the 5th ionisation energy of sulfur.

    b   The 2nd ionisation energy of nitrogen is 2860 kJ mol^{-1}. The 3rd ionisation energy of nitrogen is 4580 kJ mol^{-1}. Explain why the 3rd ionisation energy is higher.

Element		Electrons removed										
		1	2	3	4	5	6	7	8	9	10	11
1	H	1310										
2	He	2370	5250									
3	Li	519	7300	11800								
4	Be	900	1760	14850	21000							
5	B	799	2420	3660	25000	32800						
6	C	1090	2350	4620	6220	37800	47300					
7	N	1400	2860	4580	7480	9450	53300	64400				
8	O	1310	3390	5320	7450	11000	13300	71300	84100			
9	F	1680	3370	6040	8410	11000	15200	17900	92000	106000		
10	Ne	2080	3950	6150	9290	12200	15200	20000	23000	117000	131400	
11	Na	494	4560	6940	9540	13400	16600	20100	25500	28900	141000	158700

Table 2.2: Successive ionisation energies for the first 11 elements in the Periodic Table (values in kJ mol^{-1}).

Factors that influence ionisation energy

Four factors that influence ionisation energy are:

- The size of the nuclear charge: as the atomic number (number of protons) increases, the positive nuclear charge in the nucleus increases. The bigger the positive charge, the greater the attractive force between the nucleus and the electrons. So, more energy is needed to overcome these attractive forces if an electron is to be removed.

    In general, ionisation energy increases as the proton number increases.

- Distance of outer electrons from the nucleus: the force of attraction between positive and negative charges decreases rapidly as the distance between them increases. So, electrons in shells further away from the nucleus are less attracted to the nucleus than those closer to the nucleus.

    In general, the further the outer electron shell is from the nucleus, the lower the ionisation energy.

- Shielding effect of inner electrons: as all electrons are negatively charged, they repel each other. Electrons in full inner shells repel electrons in outer shells. Full inner shells of electrons prevent the outer electrons feeling the full nuclear charge. This is called **shielding**. The greater the shielding of outer electrons by the inner electron shells, the lower the attractive forces between the nucleus and the outer electrons. See Section 2.2 for information on sub-shells and how they affect shielding.

    In general, the ionisation energy is lower as the number of full electron shells between the outer electrons and the nucleus increases.

- Spin-pair repulsion: electrons in the same atomic orbital in a sub-shell (see Section 2.3) repel each other more than electrons in different atomic orbitals. This increased repulsion makes it easier to remove an electron. So first ionisation energy is decreased.

KEY WORD

shielding: the ability of inner shell electrons to reduce the effect of the nuclear charge on outer shell electrons.

Interpreting successive ionisation energies

Figure 2.5 shows a graph of successive ionisation energies against the number of electrons removed for sodium. A logarithmic scale (to the base 10) is used because the values of successive ionisation energies have such a large range.

We can deduce the following about sodium from Figure 2.5:

- The first electron removed has a low first ionisation energy, when compared with the rest of the data. It is very easily removed from the atom. It is therefore likely to be a long way from the nucleus and well shielded by inner electron shells.

- The second electron is much more difficult to remove than the first electron. There is a big jump in the value of the ionisation energy. This suggests that the second electron is in a shell closer to the nucleus than the first electron. Taken together, the 1st and 2nd ionisation energies suggest that sodium has one electron in its outer shell.

- From the second to the ninth electrons removed, there is only a gradual change in successive ionisation energies. This suggests that all these eight electrons are in the same shell.

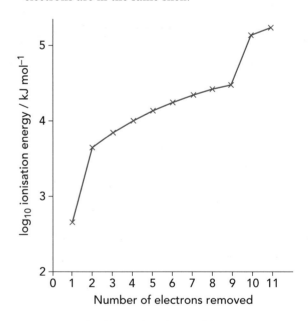

Figure 2.5: Graph of logarithm ($\log_{10}$) of the ionisation energy of sodium against the number of electrons removed.

- The 10th and 11th electrons have extremely high ionisation energies, when compared with the rest of the data. This suggests that they are very close to the nucleus. There must be a very great force of attraction between the nucleus and these electrons and there are no inner electrons to shield them. The large increase in ionisation energy between the 9th and 10th electrons confirms that the 10th electron is in a shell closer to the nucleus than the 9th electron.

Figure 2.6 shows this arrangement of electrons.

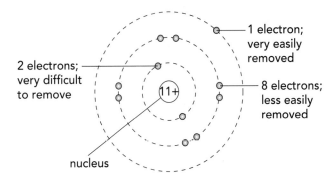

Figure 2.6: The arrangement of electrons in an atom of sodium can be deduced from the values of successive ionisation energies.

WORKED EXAMPLE

1 The successive ionisation energies, IE, of an element X are shown in Table 2.3. Which group in the Periodic Table does X belong to?

Solution

Step 1: We look for a large jump in the value of the ionisation energy. This occurs between the removal of the 6th and 7th electrons.

Step 2: Take the lower number (this represents the number of electrons that are relatively easily removed). This number is the number of electrons in the outer shell of X. In this case 6.

Step 3: Relate number of outer shell electrons to the group number. So, element X must be in Group 16 of the Periodic Table.

Number of electrons removed	1	2	3	4	5	6	7	8	9	10
IE / kJ mol⁻¹	1000	2260	3390	4540	7010	8500	27 100	31 670	36 580	43 140

Table 2.3: The successive ionisation energies of an element X.

Question

3 a The successive ionisation energies of boron are shown in Table 2.4.

Ionisation	1st	2nd	3rd	4th	5th
Ionisation energy / kJ mol⁻¹	799	2420	3660	25 000	32 800

Table 2.4: Successive ionisation energies of boron.

  i Why is there a large increase between the third and fourth ionisation energies?

  ii Explain how these figures confirm that the electronic structure of boron is 2, 3.

b For the element aluminium ($Z = 13$), sketch a graph to predict the $\log_{10}$ of the successive ionisation energies (y-axis) against the number of electrons removed (x-axis).

We can use successive ionisation energies in this way to:

- predict or confirm the simple electronic configuration of elements

- confirm the number of electrons in the outer shell of an element and hence the group to which the element belongs

- deduce which group an element belongs to in the Periodic Table.

Question

4   a   The first six ionisation energies of an element are 1090, 2350, 4610, 6220, 37 800 and 47 300 kJ mol^{-1}.

Which group in the Periodic Table does this element belong to? Explain your decision.

b   Sketch a graph to show the $\log_{10}$ values of the first four successive ionisation energies of a Group 2 element.

2.3 Sub-shells and atomic orbitals

Quantum sub-shells

KEY WORD

sub-shells (subsidiary quantum shells): regions of the principal quantum shells where electrons exist in defined areas associated with particular amounts of energy. They are named s, p, d, etc.

The principal quantum shells, apart from the first, are split into sub-shells (sub-levels). Each principal quantum shell contains a different number of sub-shells. The sub-shells are distinguished by the letters s, p or d. There are also f sub-shells for elements with more than 57 electrons. Figure 2.7 shows the sub-shells for the first four principal quantum levels. In any principal quantum shell, the energy of the electrons in the sub-shells increases in the order s < p < d.

- The first principal quantum level, n = 1, can hold a maximum of 2 electrons in an s sub-shell.

- The second principal quantum level, n = 2, can hold a maximum of 8 electrons: 2 electrons in the s sub-shell and 6 electrons in the p sub-shell.

- The third principal quantum level, n = 3, can hold a maximum of 18 electrons: 2 electrons in the s sub-shell, 6 electrons in the p sub-shell and 10 electrons in the d sub-shell.

You will also notice from Figure 2.7 that the order of the sub-shells in terms of increasing energy does not follow a regular pattern of s then p then d after the element argon. The order of sub-shells after argon

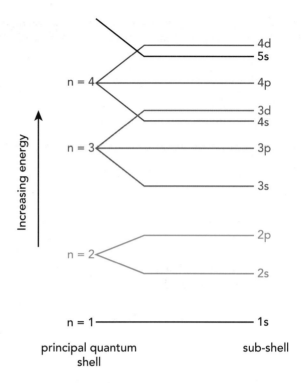

Figure 2.7: The sub-shells for the first four principal quantum shells. The maximum number of electrons that are allowed in each sub-shell is: s = 2 electrons, p = 6 electrons, d = 10 electrons.

appears to overlap. The next element after argon is potassium. Potassium's outer electron is in the 4s, not in the 3d, sub-shell. The first element with an electron in the 3d sub-shell is element 21, scandium.

When high-speed electrons hit gas particles at low pressure, coloured lines are seen through an instrument called a spectroscope (see Figure 2.4). The letters s, p and d come from the terms used to describe these lines: 's' for 'sharp', 'p' for 'principal' and 'd' for 'diffuse'.

Atomic orbitals

Each sub-shell contains one or more atomic orbitals.

An atomic orbital is a region of space around the nucleus of an atom that can be occupied by one or two electrons.

KEY WORD

atomic orbitals: regions of space outside the nucleus that can be occupied by a maximum of two electrons. Orbitals are named s, p, d and f. They have different shapes.

As each orbital can only hold a maximum of two electrons, the number of orbitals in each sub-shell must be:

- s – one orbital
- p – three orbitals
- d – five orbitals

Shapes of the orbitals

Each orbital has a three-dimensional shape. Within this shape there is a high probability of finding the electron or electrons in the orbital. Figure 2.8 shows how we represent the s and p orbitals.

An s orbital has a spherical shape. The 2s orbital in the second principal quantum shell has the same shape as the 1s orbital in the first quantum shell. They are both spherical, but electrons in the 2s orbital have more energy than electrons in the 1s orbital. There are three 2p orbitals in the second quantum shell. Each of these has the same shape. The shape is like an hourglass with two 'lobes'. The three sets of 'lobes' are arranged at right angles to each other along the x, y and z axes. Hence the three 2p orbitals are named $2p_x$, $2p_y$ and $2p_z$. The three 2p orbitals have the same energy as each other. There are also three 3p orbitals in the third quantum shell. Their shapes are similar to the shapes of the 2p orbitals but, again, their energies are higher.

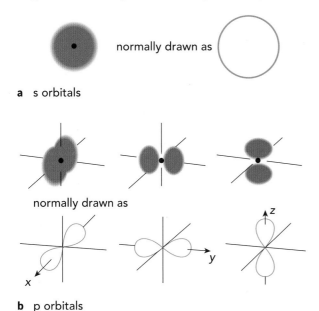

a s orbitals

normally drawn as

b p orbitals

Figure 2.8: Representations of orbitals (the position of the nucleus is shown by the black dot). **a** s orbitals are spherical. **b** p orbitals, p_x, p_y and p_z, have 'lobes' along the x, y and z axes.

Figure 2.9: The shape of a dz^2 orbital.

The d orbitals are more complex in shape and arrangement in space. In 1925 Louis de Broglie suggested that electrons behaved like waves. This led to the idea of electron probability clouds. The electron probability cloud for one type of d orbital has two pieces: it is like a modified p orbital with a ring around the middle (Figure 2.9). You will not need to know the d-orbital shapes at AS Level, but you will for A Level when studying the transition elements (see Chapter 24).

Filling the shells and orbitals

The most stable electronic configuration of an atom is the one that has the lowest amount of energy. The order in which the sub-shells are filled depends on their relative energy. The sub-shell with the lowest energy, the 1s, is therefore filled first, followed by those that are successively higher in energy. As we noted in Figure 2.7, the order of the sub-shells in terms of increasing energy does *not* follow a regular pattern of s then p then d after argon, where the 3p sub-shell is full. Figure 2.10 shows the order of filling the sub-shells.

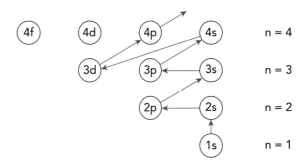

Figure 2.10: Diagram to show the order in which orbitals are filled up to shell n = 4.

Question

5 **a** Give the three types of orbital present in the third principal quantum shell.

b State the maximum number of electrons that can be found in each sub-shell of the third quantum shell.

2.4 Electronic configurations

Representing electronic configurations

Here is a detailed way of writing the electronic configuration of an atom of hydrogen, that includes information about the number of electrons in each sub-shell.

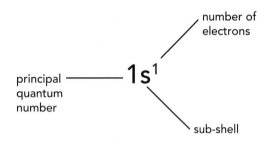

- Helium has two electrons. Both electrons can go into the 1s orbital, as this can hold a maximum of two electrons. So, the electronic structure of helium is $1s^2$.

- Lithium has three electrons. The 1s orbital can only hold a maximum of two electrons so the third electron must go into the next highest sub-shell, the 2s. So, the electronic structure of lithium is $1s^2 2s^1$.

Electrons are added one by one for successive elements, filling each sub-shell in order of increasing energy. You can see the electronic configurations of the first 18 elements in Table 2.5.

A question about this type of detailed notation will often be stated like this: 'Use $1s^2$ notation to give the electronic configuration …' as in Question 6.

Question

6 Use $1s^2$ notation to give the electronic configurations of the atoms with the following atomic numbers:

 a 16

 b 9

 c 20

The electronic configurations of some of the elements after argon are shown in Table 2.6. In this table, part of the electronic configuration of each element is represented by [Ar]. This 'noble gas core' represents the

electronic configuration of argon: $1s^2 2s^2 2p^6 3s^2 3p^6$. This method is a shorthand way of writing electronic structures of atoms with many electrons. However, in an exam you should be prepared to write out the full electronic configuration.

You should note the following:

Electronic configuration of potassium

Potassium has the electronic configuration $1s^2 2s^2 2p^6 3s^2 3p^6 4s^1$. The outer electron goes into the 4s sub-shell rather than the 3d sub-shell because the 4s is below the 3d in terms of its energy.

Filling the 3d sub-shell

After calcium, a new sub-shell becomes occupied. The next electron goes into a 3d sub-shell rather than a 4p sub-shell. So, scandium has the electronic configuration [Ar] $3d^1 4s^2$. This is because electrons occupy the orbitals with the lowest energy: the 3d sub-shell is just above the 4s sub-shell but below the 4p sub-shell. This begins a pattern of filling the 3d sub-shell ending with zinc. Zinc has the electronic configuration [Ar] $3d^{10} 4s^2$.

Proton number	Symbol	Electronic configuration
1	H	$1s^1$
2	He	$1s^2$
3	Li	$1s^2 2s^1$
4	Be	$1s^2 2s^2$
5	B	$1s^2 2s^2 2p^1$
6	C	$1s^2 2s^2 2p^2$
7	N	$1s^2 2s^2 2p^3$
8	O	$1s^2 2s^2 2p^4$
9	F	$1s^2 2s^2 2p^5$
10	Ne	$1s^2 2s^2 2p^6$
11	Na	$1s^2 2s^2 2p^6 3s^1$
12	Mg	$1s^2 2s^2 2p^6 3s^2$
13	Al	$1s^2 2s^2 2p^6 3s^2 3p^1$
14	Si	$1s^2 2s^2 2p^6 3s^2 3p^2$
15	P	$1s^2 2s^2 2p^6 3s^2 3p^3$
16	S	$1s^2 2s^2 2p^6 3s^2 3p^4$
17	Cl	$1s^2 2s^2 2p^6 3s^2 3p^5$
18	Ar	$1s^2 2s^2 2p^6 3s^2 3p^6$

Table 2.5: Electronic configurations for the first 18 elements in the Periodic Table.

Chromium and copper

The electronic configurations of chromium and copper do not follow the expected pattern. Chromium has the electronic configuration [Ar] $3d^5$ $4s^1$ (rather than the expected [Ar] $3d^4$ $4s^2$). Copper has the electronic configuration [Ar] $3d^{10}$ $4s^1$ (rather than the expected [Ar] $3d^9$ $4s^2$). This is because the $3d^5 4s^1$ and $3d^{10}4s^1$ electron arrangements are more energetically stable. You will have to learn that these two elements are exceptions to the pattern.

Gallium to krypton

The electrons then add to the 4p sub-shell because this is the next highest energy level above the 3d.

Proton number	Name (Symbol)	Electronic configuration
19	potassium (K)	[Ar] $4s^1$
20	calcium (Ca)	[Ar] $4s^2$
21	scandium (Sc)	[Ar] $3d^1$ $4s^2$
24	chromium (Cr)	[Ar] $3d^5$ $4s^1$
25	manganese (Mn)	[Ar] $3d^5$ $4s^2$
29	copper (Cu)	[Ar] $3d^{10}$ $4s^1$
30	zinc (Zn)	[Ar] $3d^{10}$ $4s^2$
31	gallium (Ga)	[Ar] $3d^{10}$ $4s^2$ $4p^1$
35	bromine (Br)	[Ar] $3d^{10}$ $4s^2$ $4p^5$
36	krypton (Kr)	[Ar] $3d^{10}$ $4s^2$ $4p^6$

Table 2.6: Electronic configurations for some of the elements 19 to 36, where [Ar] is the electronic structure of argon $1s^2$ $2s^2$ $2p^6$ $3s^2$ $3p^6$.

Question

7   Use $1s^2$ notation to give the electronic configurations for the following elements:

a   vanadium ($Z = 23$)

b   copper ($Z = 29$)

c   selenium ($Z = 34$)

Orbitals and the Periodic Table

The arrangement of elements in the Periodic Table reflects the electronic structure of the elements. The Periodic Table can be split into blocks of elements (Figure 2.11).

- Elements in Groups 1 and 2 have outer electrons in an s sub-shell. These are therefore together called the s-block.

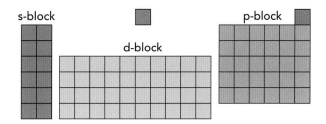

Figure 2.11: Some of the blocks of elements in the Periodic Table.

- Elements in Groups 13 to 18 (apart from He) have outer electrons in a p sub-shell. These are therefore together called the p-block.

- Elements that add electrons to the d sub-shells are called the d-block elements. Most of these are transition elements.

Questions

8   a   An element has the electronic configuration $1s^2$ $2s^2$ $2p^6$ $3s^2$ $3p^6$ $3d^{10}$ $4s^2$ $4p^6$ $4d^{10}$ $5s^2$ $5p^5$.

   i   Which block in the Periodic Table does this element belong to?

   ii Which group does it belong to?

   iii Identify this element.

   b   Which block in the Periodic Table does the element with the electronic configuration $1s^2$ $2s^2$ $2p^6$ $3s^2$ $3p^6$ $3d^5$ $4s^1$ belong to?

9   Which one of these statements about the electrons in the outermost principal quantum shell of phosphorus (atomic number 15) is true?

   A   There are five p-type electrons and no s-type electrons

   B   There are three p-type electrons and two s-type electrons

   C   There are two p-type electrons and two s-type electrons

   D   There are five s-type electrons and no p-type electrons

Filling the orbitals

A useful way of representing electronic configurations is a diagram that places electrons in boxes (Figure 2.12).

- Each box represents an atomic orbital.

- The boxes (orbitals) can be arranged in order of increasing energy from bottom to top.

- An electron is represented by an arrow.

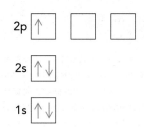

Figure 2.12: The electronic configuration of boron in box form.

- The direction of the arrow represents the 'spin' of the electron. (We imagine an electron rotating around its own axis either in a clockwise or anticlockwise direction.)

- When there are two electrons in an orbital, the 'spins' of the electrons are opposite, so the two arrows in this box point in opposite directions.

Electrons in the same region of space repel each other because they have the same charge. This is called **spin-pair repulsion**. Wherever possible, electrons will occupy separate orbitals in the same sub-shell to minimise this repulsion, so these electrons have their 'spin' in the same direction. Electrons are only paired when there are no more empty orbitals available within a sub-shell. The spins are then opposite to minimise repulsion. Figure 2.13 shows the electronic structures of carbon, nitrogen and oxygen to illustrate these points.

> **KEY WORD**
>
> **spin-pair repulsion:** a pair of electrons in the same orbital repel each other because they have the same charge. Pairing the spinning electrons so they spin in opposite directions reduces the repulsion. The repulsion is more than that of single electrons in separate orbitals. That is why the electrons in the p and d orbitals go into separate orbitals before being paired up.

Free radicals

A **free radical** is a species with one or more unpaired electrons. An example of a free radical is an isolated chlorine atom, which has the electronic configuration $1s^2 2s^2 2p^6 3s^2 3p^5$. In the 3p orbitals, two of the orbitals have paired electrons and the remaining orbital has an unpaired electron. The unpaired electron in a free radical is shown as a dot ·, e.g. Cl·. Groups of atoms can also be free radicals. For example, the $H_3C·$ radical has a carbon atom with an unpaired electron.

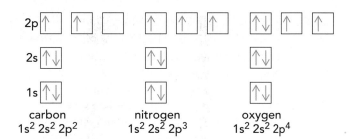

Figure 2.13: When adding electrons to a particular sub-shell, the electrons are only paired when no more empty orbitals are available.

> **KEY WORD**
>
> **free radical:** a species with one (or sometimes more than one) unpaired electron.

> **IMPORTANT**
>
> The word *species* refers to different particles such as atoms, ions, molecules, free radicals or electrons when we want to write in general terms or about more than one type of particle.

Electronic configuration of ions

Positive ions are formed when electrons are removed from atoms. The sodium ion, Na^+ (proton number = 11), has 10 electrons so its electronic configuration is $1s^2 2s^2 2p^6$. Note that this is the same as the electronic configuration of neon, the element with 10 electrons in each atom.

Negative ions are formed when atoms gain electrons. The sulfide ion, S^{2-} (proton number = 16), has 18 electrons. Its electronic configuration is $1s^2 2s^2 2p^6 3s^2 3p^6$, which is the same as argon, the element with 18 electrons in each atom.

Note that, in general, electrons in the outer sub-shell are removed when metal ions form their positive ions. However, the d-block elements behave slightly differently. Reading across the Periodic Table from potassium to zinc, the 4s sub-shell fills before the 3d sub-shell. But when atoms of a d-block element lose electrons to form ions, the 4s electrons are lost first.

For example:

Ti atom: $1s^2 2s^2 2p^6 3s^2 3p^6 3d^2 4s^2 \rightarrow$
$\qquad$ Ti^{2+} ion: $1s^2 2s^2 2p^6 3s^2 3p^6 3d^2$
Cr atom: $1s^2 2s^2 2p^6 3s^2 3p^6 3d^5 4s^1 \rightarrow$
$\qquad$ Cr^{3+} ion: $1s^2 2s^2 2p^6 3s^2 3p^6 3d^3$

2   Use $1s^2$ notation to deduce the electronic configuration of an Fe^{3+} ion.

Solution

Step 1: Deduce the number of electrons in an iron atom (= number of protons shown in the Periodic Table for iron) = 26

Step 2: Deduce the electronic configuration of an iron atom by adding the electrons to the orbitals in order. Remember to fill the 4s before the 3d.
= $1s^2 \, 2s^2 \, 2p^6 \, 3s^2 \, 3p^6 \, 4s^2 \, 3d^6$

Step 3: For a 3+ ion, we remove three electrons.
- the 2 outer s-electrons are removed first: $1s^2 \, 2s^2 \, 2p^6 \, 3s^2 \, 3p^6 \, 4s^2 3d^6 \rightarrow$ $1s^2 2s^2 \, 2p^6 \, 3s^2 \, 3p^6 \, 3d^6$
- an outer d-electron is then removed: $1s^2 \, 2s^2 \, 2p^6 \, 3s^2 \, 3p^6 \, 3d^6 \rightarrow$ $1s^2 2s^2 \, 2p^6 \, 3s^2 \, 3p^6 \, 3d^5$

Question

10   Write electronic configurations for the following ions:

a Al^{3+} ($Z = 13$)

b O^{2-} ($Z = 8$)

c Fe^{2+} ($Z = 26$)

d Cu^{2+} ($Z = 29$)

e Cu^+ ($Z = 29$)

2.5 Periodic patterns of atomic and ionic radii

atomic radius: the covalent atomic radius is half the distance between the nuclei of two covalently bonded atoms of the same type. This is not the only type of atomic radius but it gives us the best data when comparing the elements across a period.

Stable metal ions are smaller than metal atoms because the atoms have lost their outer shell electrons, so the attractive forces between the nucleus and outer electrons is larger. Stable non-metal ions are larger than metal atoms because the atoms have gained electrons to complete their outer shells, so the attractive forces between the nucleus and outer electrons is smaller.

Atomic radius

The atomic radius increases down any group. This is because, going down the group, each successive element has one more shell of electrons which is further from the nucleus. Although there is also an increasing nuclear charge going down the group, the increased effect of inner shell electrons shielding the outer shell electrons is more important.

The atomic radius decreases across any period. This is because the number of protons, and therefore the nuclear charge, increases by one with each successive element. The number of electrons also increases by one but the extra electron added goes into the same (outer) energy level. This means that the shielding does not change significantly. The greater attractive force of the increased nuclear charge on the outer shell electrons pulls them closer to the nucleus.

Ionic radius

The ionic radius increases down any group (for ions with the same charge). In each group the number of electrons lost or gained by each element in the group is generally the same. For example, Group 2 elements form 2+ ions and atoms of Group 17 elements form ions with a charge of −1. The reason for the increase in ionic radius is similar to that for the atoms. Going down the group, each successive element has one more shell of electrons which is further from the nucleus. The increased effect of inner shell electrons shielding the outer shell electrons is more important than the effect of increased nuclear charge.

Going across a period from Group 1 to Group 14, the ionic radius decreases. This is for similar reasons to those for decreasing atomic radii across a period. The increasing nuclear charge attracts the electrons in the outer electron shell closer to the nucleus with increasing atomic number. The shielding is approximately the same, so has less effect than the increase in nuclear charge. Positively charged ions are smaller than their original atoms because they have lost their outer shell electrons. The change is generally greater than that for the atomic radius due to the increase in charge as we go from Groups 1 to 14. Negatively charged ions in Groups 15 to 18 are larger than their original atoms because each atom will have gained one or more extra electrons into their outer energy level. From Group 15 to Group 18, the ionic radius decreases. This is for similar reasons to those for decreasing atomic radii across a period and due to the normal charge on the ions decreasing.

Question

11 a Explain why the values for the ionic radii for the negative ions in Period 3 are higher than the ionic radii for the positive ions.

b Sketch a graph to show how the ionic radius changes across Period 3.

2.6 Patterns in ionisation energies in the Periodic Table

Patterns across a period

Figure 2.14 shows how the first ionisation energy, IE_1, changes across the first two periods. We can explain the form of the graph mainly by referring to the factors that influence ionisation energies (see Section 2.2).

> **IMPORTANT**
>
> The variation in the values of first ionisation energy is a periodic property because when plotted against atomic number it shows a repeating pattern. The same goes for the variation of atomic and ionic radii (see Chapter 10, Section 10.2).

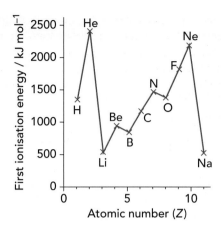

Figure 2.14: A graph of the first ionisation energies of the elements hydrogen to sodium plotted against atomic number.

1 There is a general increase in IE_1 across a period. This applies to Period 1 (hydrogen and helium), Period 2 (lithium to neon) and also to other periods. As you go across a period the nuclear charge increases. But the electron removed comes from the same shell. The force of attraction between the positive nucleus and the outer negative electrons increases across the period because:

- the nuclear charge increases

- the distance between the nucleus and the outer electron remains reasonably constant

- the shielding by inner shells remains reasonably constant.

2 There is a rapid decrease in ionisation energy between the last element in one period and the first element in the next period. The IE_1 for lithium is much smaller than the IE_1 for helium. Helium has two electrons. These are in the first quantum shell. But lithium has three electrons. The third electron must go into the next quantum shell further away from the nucleus. The force of attraction between the positive nucleus and the outer negative electrons decreases because:

- the distance between the nucleus and the outer electron increases

- the shielding by inner shells increases

- these two factors outweigh the increased nuclear charge.

3 There is a slight decrease in IE_1 between beryllium and boron. Although boron has one more proton than beryllium, there is a slight decrease in IE_1 on removal of the outer electron. Beryllium has the electronic structure $1s^2 2s^2$ and boron has the electronic structure $1s^2 2s^2 2p^1$. The fifth electron in boron must be in the 2p sub-shell, which is slightly further away from the nucleus than the 2s sub-shell. There is less attraction between the fifth electron in boron and the nucleus because:

- the distance between the nucleus and the outer electron increases slightly
- the shielding by inner shells increases slightly
- these two factors outweigh the increased nuclear charge.

4 There is a slight decrease in IE_1 between nitrogen and oxygen. Oxygen has one more proton than nitrogen and the electron removed is in the same 2p sub-shell. So, you might think that IE_1 would increase. However, the spin-pairing of the electrons plays a part here. If you look back at Figure 2.13, you will see that the electron removed from the nitrogen is from an orbital that contains an unpaired electron. The electron removed from the oxygen is from the orbital that contains a pair of electrons. The extra repulsion between the pair of electrons in this orbital results in less energy being needed to remove an electron. So, IE_1 for oxygen is lower, because of spin-pair repulsion.

These patterns repeat themselves across the third period. However, the presence of the d-block elements in Period 4 disrupts the pattern, as d-block elements have first ionisation energies that are relatively similar and fairly high.

Patterns down a group

The first ionisation energy decreases as you go down a group in the Periodic Table. For example, in Group 1 the values of IE_1 are:

- Li = 519 kJ mol^{-1}
- Na = 494 kJ mol^{-1}
- K = 418 kJ mol^{-1}
- Rb = 403 kJ mol^{-1}

As you go down the group, the outer electron removed is from the same type of orbital but from a successively higher principal quantum level: 2s for lithium, 3s for sodium and 4s for potassium. Although the nuclear charge is increasing down the group there is less attraction between the outer electron and the nucleus because:

- the distance between the nucleus and the outer electron increases
- the shielding by complete inner shells increases
- these two factors outweigh the increased nuclear charge.

Questions

12 a The first ionisation energies of four consecutive elements in the Periodic Table are:

sodium = 494 kJ mol^{-1}

magnesium = 736 kJ mol^{-1}

aluminium = 577 kJ mol^{-1}

silicon = 786 kJ mol^{-1}

    i Explain the general increase in ionisation energies from sodium to silicon.

    ii Explain why aluminium has a lower first ionisation energy than magnesium.

b The first ionisation energy of fluorine is 1680 kJ mol^{-1} whereas the first ionisation energy of iodine is 1010 kJ mol^{-1}. Explain why fluorine has a higher first ionisation energy than iodine despite fluorine having a smaller nuclear charge.

13 Which one of the diagrams in Figure 2.15 could be the graph of first ionisation energies for a series of elements consecutive in atomic number and beginning with an element in Group 15?

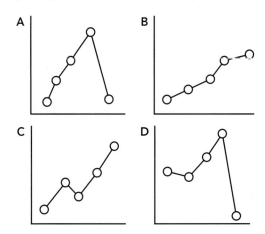

Figure 2.15: Four graphs of first ionisation energy against atomic number.

REFLECTION

1   Think what you have learned about the following and write a paragraph to explain the trends:

   a   the variation of atomic or ionic radius across a period and down a group

   b   the variation of first ionisation energy across a period and down a group

   c   the variation of successive ionisation energies of an element in Period 3 of the Periodic Table.

2   Share your ideas with the class or another learner. If you were the teacher, what comments would you make about your paragraph?

SUMMARY

Electron shells can be divided into s, p and d sub-shells which can hold a maximum of 2, 6 and 10 electrons respectively, and each sub-shell has a specific number of orbitals which can each hold a maximum of two electrons.

The first ionisation energy of an element is the energy needed to remove one electron from each atom in one mole of atoms of the element in the gaseous state (to form gaseous 1+ ions).

The magnitude (how big the value is) of the ionisation energy depends on four things:
•   the distance of the electron from the nucleus
•   the number of positive charges in the nucleus
•   the degree of shielding of outer electrons by inner electron shells
•   spin-pair repulsion.

The electronic configuration of the outer shell electrons and the position of an element in the Periodic Table can be deduced using successive ionisation energy data.

EXAM-STYLE QUESTIONS

1   The sketch graph shows the 13 successive ionisation energies of aluminium.

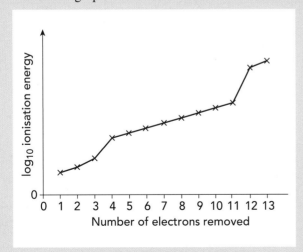

CONTINUED

COMMAND WORD

Define: give precise meaning.

    a   **Define** the term *first ionisation energy*.   **[3]**

    b   Explain how the graph provides evidence for the existence of three electron shells in an aluminium atom.   **[6]**

    c   Write an equation, including state symbols, to represent the 2nd ionisation energy of aluminium.   **[2]**

    d   Write the electronic configuration of an aluminium ion, Al^{3+}, using $1s^2$ notation.   **[1]**

                                      [Total: 12]

2   The table shows the first ionisation energies, IE_1, in kJ mol^{-1}, of the elements in Period 3 of the Periodic Table.

Element	Na	Mg	Al	Si	P	S	Cl	Ar
IE_1	494	736	577	786	1060	1000	1260	1520

    a   Explain why there is a general increase in the value of IE_1 across the period.   **[4]**

    b   Explain why aluminium has a lower value of IE_1 than magnesium.   **[4]**

    c   Write the electronic configuration for argon ($Z = 18$) using $1s^2$ notation.   **[1]**

    d   Copy and complete the diagram below for the 15 electrons in phosphorus by:

        i   adding labels for the other sub-shells   **[1]**

        ii   showing how the electrons are arranged.   **[3]**

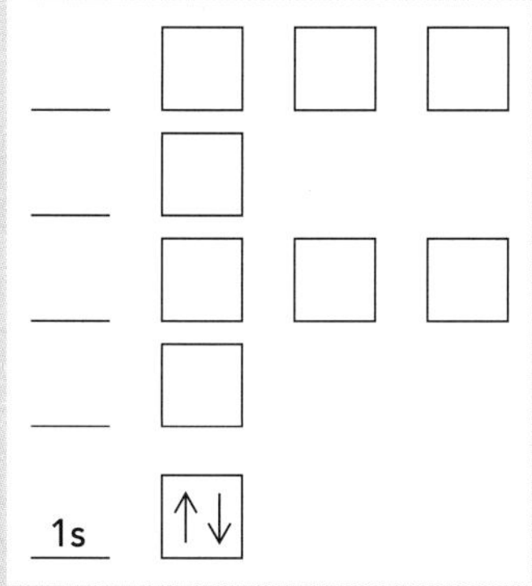

COMMAND WORD

Predict: suggest what may happen based on available information.

    e   **Predict** a value for the first ionisation energy for potassium, which has one more proton than argon.   **[1]**

                                        [Total: 14]

3   **a**   State the meaning of the term atomic orbital.   **[1]**

    b   Draw diagrams to show the shape of:

        i   an s orbital   **[1]**

        ii   a p orbital.   **[1]**

CONTINUED

c Element X has the electronic configuration $1s^2\ 2s^2\ 2p^6\ 3s^2\ 3p^6\ 3d^8\ 4s^2$.

   i State which block in the Periodic Table element X belongs to. **[1]**

   ii State the maximum number of electrons in a d sub-shell. **[1]**

d Element X forms an ion of type X^{2+}.

   i Write the full electronic configuration for this ion using $1s^2$ notation. **[1]**

   ii Write the symbol for the sub-shell that begins to fill after the 3d and 4s are completely full. **[1]**

[Total: 7]

4 The first ionisation energies of several elements with consecutive atomic numbers are shown in the graph.

   The letters are *not* the symbols of the elements.

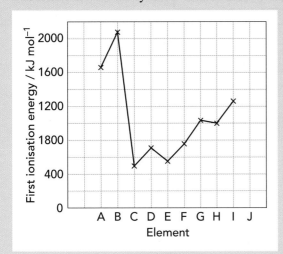

a **Suggest** which of the elements A to I belong to Group 1 in the Periodic Table. Explain your answer. **[3]**

b Suggest which of the elements A to I could have the electronic configuration $1s^2\ 2s^2\ 2p^6\ 3s^2$. **[1]**

c Explain the rise in first ionisation energy between element E and element G. **[4]**

d Estimate the 1st ionisation energy of element J. **[2]**

e The successive ionisation energies of element A are shown in the next sketch graph.

COMMAND WORD

Suggest: apply knowledge and understanding to situations where there is a range of valid responses in order to make proposals / put forward considerations.

CONTINUED

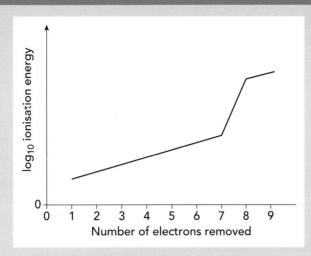

Explain what information this graph gives about how the electrons are arranged in shells for element A. [3]

[Total: 13]

5   a   Define the following:

   i   1st ionisation energy [3]

   ii   3rd ionisation energy. [3]

   b   Give the equations representing:

   i   the 1st ionisation energy of magnesium [2]

   ii   the 3rd ionisation energy of magnesium. [2]

   c   State which ionisation energies are represented by the equations below.

   i $Mg^{3+}(g) \rightarrow Mg^{4+}(g) + e^-$ [1]

   ii $Al^{5+}(g) \rightarrow Al^{6+}(g) + e^-$ [1]

[Total: 12]

6   The graph shows a sketch of $\log_{10}$ (ionisation energy) against number of electrons removed for magnesium.

Use this graph to answer the following questions.

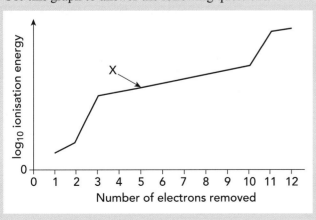

CONTINUED

a Explain why the first two electrons are relatively easy to remove. **[3]**

b Explain why there is a sharp rise in ionisation energy when the third electron is removed. **[3]**

c Explain what information the graph gives about the electron arrangement of magnesium. **[3]**

d Construct the equation for the ionisation energy marked X (the 5th ionisation energy). **[2]**

[Total: 11]

7 a The table shows the first five ionisation energies for five elements (A to E). For each one, state which group the element belongs to. **[5]**

Element	Ionisation energy / kJ mol⁻¹				
	1st	2nd	3rd	4th	5th
A	786.5	1577.1	3231.6	4355.5	16 091
B	598.8	1145.4	4912	6491	8153
C	496	4562	6910	9543	13 354
D	1087	2353	4621	6223	37 831
E	578	1817	2744	11 577	14 842

b Explain your reasoning behind your answer for element E. **[1]**

c Sketch a graph to show how $\log_{10}$ (ionisation energy) for phosphorus (atomic number 15) varies when plotted against number of electrons removed. **[6]**

[Total: 12]

8 a Define the term *first ionisation energy*. **[3]**

b Sketch a graph to show how $\log_{10}$ (ionisation energy) for chlorine (atomic number 17) varies when plotted against number of electrons removed. **[6]**

c Explain the shape of the graph you have drawn. **[6]**

[Total: 15]

SELF-EVALUATION

I can	See section...	Needs more work	Almost there	Ready to move on
understand that electrons in an atom can exist only in certain energy levels (shells) outside the nucleus	2.1			
understand that main energy levels (shells) are given principal quantum numbers n = 1, 2, 3, 4, etc.; the lowest energy level (n = 1) is closest to the nucleus	2.1			

CONTINUED

I can	See section...	Needs more work	Almost there	Ready to move on
understand that shells may be divided into sub-shells known as s, p and d sub-shells, which can hold a maximum of 2, 6 and 10 electrons, respectively	2.1, 2.3			
understand that the region of space in which an electron is likely to be found is called an orbital: each sub-shell has a number of orbitals which can each hold a maximum of two electrons; sub-shells s, p and d have 1, 3 and 5 orbitals, respectively	2.3			
understand that s orbitals are spherical in shape and p orbitals have two 'lobes'	2.3			
understand that when two electrons are present in an orbital they spin in opposite directions and are said to be paired	2.3			
deduce the electronic configuration of atoms by adding electrons to each orbital starting from those in the lowest energy level	2.4			
understand that when electrons are added to orbitals in the same sub-shell they go into separate orbitals if possible; electrons pair up where this is not possible	2.4			
understand that a free radical is a species with one or more unpaired electrons	2.4			
understand that the first ionisation energy of an element is the energy needed to remove one electron from each atom in one mole of atoms of the element in the gaseous state (to form gaseous 1+ ions)	2.2			
understand that the magnitude of the ionisation energy depends on four factors: a the distance of the electron from the nucleus b the number of positive charges in the nucleus c the degree of shielding of outer electrons by inner shells and sub-shells d spin-pair repulsion	2.2, 2.6			
deduce trends in first ionisation energy of the elements across a period and down a group using the four factors above	2.2, 2.6			
explain trends in atomic and ionic radius of the elements across a period and down a group using the four factors listed above	2.5			
understand that the ionisation energies needed to remove the first, second, third, fourth, etc. electrons from each atom or ion in a mole of gaseous atoms are called *successive ionisation energies*	2.2			
deduce electronic configuration and the position of an element in the Periodic Table (which group the element belongs to) using successive ionisation energy data.	2.2, 2.6			

> Chapter 3

Atoms, molecules and stoichiometry

LEARNING INTENTIONS

In this chapter you will learn how to:

*   define *unified atomic mass unit* as one twelfth of the mass of a carbon-12 atom

*   define and use the terms *relative atomic mass*, *isotopic mass* and *formula mass* in terms of unified atomic mass unit

*   define and use the term *mole* in terms of the Avogadro constant

*   write formulae of ionic compounds from ionic charges and oxidation numbers, including:

    *   the prediction of ionic charge from the position of an element in the Periodic Table

    *   recall of the names and formulae for the ions NO_3^-, CO_3^{2-}, SO_4^{2-}, OH^-, NH_4^+, Zn^{2+}, Ag^+, HCO_3^- and PO_4^{3-}

CONTINUED

- analyse mass spectra in terms of isotopic abundances

- calculate the relative atomic mass of an element given the relative abundances of its isotopes or its mass spectrum

- find the molecular mass of an organic molecule from the molecular ion peak in a mass spectrum

- suggest the identity of molecules using information from simple fragmentation patterns in a given mass spectrum

- deduce the number of carbon atoms in a compound using the [M + 1] peak and the relevant formula

- deduce the presence of chlorine and bromine atoms in a compound using the [M + 2] peak

- write and construct balanced equations, including ionic equations (not including spectator ions)

- use the correct state symbols in equations

- define and use the terms *empirical formula* and *molecular formula*

- calculate empirical and molecular formulae using given data

- understand and use the terms *anhydrous*, *hydrated* and *water of crystallisation*

- perform calculations, including use of the mole concept involving:

  - reacting masses (from formulae and equations) including percentage yield calculations

  - volumes of gases (e.g. in the burning of hydrocarbons)

  - volumes and concentrations of solutions

  - limiting reagents and excess reagent

- deduce stoichiometric relationships from calculations involving reacting masses, volumes of gases and volumes and concentrations of solutions.

BEFORE YOU START

1   Compound ions have more than one type of atom in them, e.g. a sulfate ion. Write down the names and give the formulae of as many compound ions as you can. Compare your answers with the rest of the class.

2   Take turns in challenging another learner to write down the formula of a simple compound by balancing the charges on the positive and negative ions. Check your answers afterwards using a textbook or the internet.

3   What is meant by the term *diatomic*? Make a list of diatomic molecules. When you think your list is complete, compare it with the list made by others in the class. Were there any molecules that you forgot about?

4   What do you understand by the chemical terms *salt*, *anhydrous*, *hydrated* and *water of crystallisation*?

CONTINUED

5   Take turns to challenge a partner to balance simple equations. Your partner looks in a textbook for an equation, then writes the equation down without the large numbers in front of each element or compound. You then try to balance the equation. How well did you do? Take turns in doing this until you are sure that you can balance simple equations.

6   Explain to another learner how you change the units dm^3 into cm^3 and cm^3 into dm^3? Does the other learner agree with you?

7   Make a list of other units that you know about. What do the units refer to (e.g. pressure, temperature)?

8   Work with another learner to write down the meaning of each of the chemical terms *mole*, *relative atomic mass*, *concentration*, *molar gas volume*, *standard temperature and pressure*. Compare your definitions with those in a textbook.

9   Explain to another learner how to change the form of an equation of type $z = \frac{y}{x}$ to make y or x the subject. Use the expression $\text{moles} = \frac{\text{mass}}{\text{relative atomic mass}}$ as an example.

10 Work with another learner to make a list of other examples of equations of type $z = \frac{y}{x}$.

11 What is the meaning of the terms *standard form* and *significant figures* when applied to numbers? If you are not sure, ask another learner, or a teacher, or look on the internet.

12 Take turns in challenging a partner to convert figures into standard form. Your partner thinks of a number from 0.0001 to 100 000, e.g. 0.025 or 37 500, and asks you to change this into standard form. Take turns to do this until you are sure that you understand the use of standard form.

GETTING OUT THE GOLD!

For thousands of years, people have heated rocks to extract materials. The remains of charcoal kilns for extracting metals dating back thousands of years have been found in Africa. Recently, chemists have learnt more about how to get materials from the rocks, from the sea, and from plants.

A lot of gold is present as microscopic particles in the rocks. The gold is obtained by crushing and grinding the rocks from mines that are open to the air (Figure 3.1). Scientists use a method called froth flotation to produce a 'sulfide concentrate' which contains gold, FeS_2, $CuFeS_2$ and SiO_2 (sand). This is heated strongly in a furnace, then treated with a solution of sodium cyanide. This makes the gold into soluble gold cyanide which is then reacted with zinc to form gold. The impurities remain in solution. A problem with this method is that the need for strong heating makes it difficult to extract the gold using sodium cyanide.

Figure 3.1: An open-cast gold mine.

Recently, scientists have used bacteria to extract the gold. Strong heating is not needed. The bacteria are mixed with the 'sulfide concentrate' and water which contains dissolved oxygen. The bacteria catalyse

CONTINUED

the oxidation of the sulfides and also help to make the products of this oxidation water-soluble. After oxidation, the pH of the mixture is first adjusted by adding just the right amount of lime, and then treated with sodium cyanide.

Questions for discussion

Discuss with another learner or group of learners:

- Look at Figure 3.1. What are the problems with mines which are open to the air, in terms of health, pollution and other factors?

- Why is heating the sulfide concentrate in the open air bad for the environment? How can you reduce these harmful effects?

- Suggest why, when extracting materials, it is important to mix the materials in the right amounts?

- What are the advantages and disadvantages of using bacteria to extract gold compared with the old method?

3.1 Masses of atoms and molecules

Unified atomic mass unit

Atoms of different elements have different masses. When we perform chemical calculations, we need to know how heavy one atom is compared with another. The mass of a single atom is so small that it is impossible to weigh it directly. To overcome this problem, we have to weigh a lot of atoms. We then compare this mass with the mass of the same number of 'standard' atoms. We define atomic mass in terms of a 'standard' atom. We call this standard the **unified atomic mass unit**. Scientists have defined unified atomic mass in terms of the isotope of carbon-12.

The formal definition of a unified atomic mass unit is: one twelfth of an unbound neutral atom of the carbon-12 isotope in its ground state. (Unbound means an isolated carbon atom and the ground state is the lowest energy state.) The simplified definition, which you can use for exams, is: one twelfth of the mass of a carbon-12 atom. The symbol for the unit of unified atomic mass is u. You will also see the symbol Da used (abbreviation for Dalton).

1 unified atomic mass unit = 1 u = 1.66×10^{-27} kg

KEY WORD

unified atomic mass unit: one twelfth of the mass of a carbon-12 atom.

Relative atomic mass, A_r

The relative atomic mass is the ratio of the average mass of the atoms of an element to the unified atomic mass unit. The values of the relative atomic mass in the Periodic Table are determined by using the weighted average mass of the atoms of a particular element. This is because most elements are mixtures of isotopes. The definition specifies a particular sample because the proportion of different isotopes can vary slightly according to the location where the element has been extracted. But this difference is usually so small that for practical purposes we can use the values given in the Periodic Table.

$$A_r = \frac{\text{weighted average mass of atoms in a given sample of an element}}{\text{unified atomic mass unit}}$$

Note that relative atomic mass has no units because it is a ratio and the units cancel.

The exact A_r of hydrogen is 1.0079. This is very close to 1 and most Periodic Tables give the A_r of hydrogen as 1.0. However, some elements in the Periodic Table have values that are not whole numbers. For example, the A_r for chlorine is 35.5. This is because chlorine has two main isotopes. In a sample of chlorine, chlorine-35 makes up about three-quarters of the chlorine atoms and chlorine-37 makes up about a quarter.

Relative isotopic mass

Isotopes are atoms that have the same number of protons but different numbers of neutrons (see Section 1.3). We represent the mass number (the total number of neutrons plus protons in an atom) by a number written at the top left-hand corner of the atom's symbol, e.g. ^{20}Ne, or by a number written after the atom's name or symbol, e.g. neon-20 or Ne-20.

We use the term **relative isotopic mass** for the mass of a particular isotope of an element which has the Avogadro number of atoms (6.02×10^{23}). For example, the relative isotopic mass of carbon-13 is exactly 13.

Masses of compounds

We find the relative molecular mass (M_r) by adding up the **relative atomic masses** of all the atoms present in one molecule.

For example, for methane:

formula: CH_4

atoms present: $1 \times C; 4 \times H$

add A_r values: $(1 \times A_r[C]) + (4 \times A_r[H]) = M_r$ of methane

$$= (1 \times 12.0) + (4 \times 1.0) = 16.0$$

When calculating relative molecular masses, we use the simplest formula for the compound. For silicon dioxide, which has a giant covalent structure of silicon and oxygen atoms joined together, the simplest formula is SiO_2. We say that SiO_2 is the **formula unit** of silicon dioxide.

Relative molecular mass, M_r

The **relative molecular mass**, M_r is the ratio of the weighted average mass of a molecule of a molecular compound to the unified atomic mass unit. The relative molecular mass has no units.

$$M_r = \frac{\text{weighted average mass of molecules in a given sample of a molecular compound}}{\text{unified atomic mass unit}}$$

Relative formula mass

For compounds containing ions we use the term **relative formula mass**. This is calculated in the same way as for relative molecular mass. It is also given the same symbol, M_r. For example, for magnesium hydroxide:

formula: $Mg(OH)_2$

ions present: $1 \times Mg^{2+}; 2 \times (OH^-)$

add A_r values: $(1 \times A_r[Mg]) + (2 \times (A_r[O] + A_r[H]))$

M_r of magnesium
hydroxide: $= (1 \times 24.3) + (2 \times (16.0 + 1.0)) = 58.3$

3.2 Hydrated and anhydrous compounds

Some compounds can form crystals which have water as part of their structure. This water is called the **water of crystallisation**.

- A compound containing water of crystallisation is called a **hydrated compound**, e.g. hydrated copper(II) sulfate, $CuSO_4 \cdot 5H_2O$

- A compound which does not contain water of crystallisation is called an **anhydrous** compound e.g. anhydrous copper(II) sulfate, $CuSO_4$

- There can be different degrees of hydration of a compound, e.g. cobalt(II) chloride-6-water $CoCl_2 \cdot 6H_2O$ and cobalt(II) chloride-2-water $CoCl_2 \cdot 2H_2O$

- When writing chemical formulae for hydrated compounds, we show water of crystallisation separated from the main formula by a dot. Note that the number of moles of water of crystallisation is usually a whole number.

Anhydrous compounds can be converted to hydrated compounds by adding water:

e.g. $CuSO_4 + 5H_2O \rightarrow CuSO_4 \cdot 5H_2O$

The reaction can be reversed by heating:

e.g. $CuSO_4 \cdot 5H_2O \rightarrow CuSO_4 + 5H_2O$

KEY WORDS

water of crystallisation: a specific number of moles of water associated with a crystal structure.

hydrated compound: compound which contains a definite number of moles of water in their structure (water of crystallisation).

anhydrous: containing no water of crystallisation.

IMPORTANT

To calculate the relative molecular mass, M_r, of a hydrated salt such as $CuSO_4 \cdot 5H_2O$, you first calculate the M_r of $CuSO_4$ and $5H_2O$ separately, then add these together.

Note that in some textbooks you will see the formulae for hydrated salts written with the dot at the bottom e.g. $CuSO_4.5H_2O$.

PRACTICAL ACTIVITY 3.1

Can you reverse the reaction?

SAFETY: Only carry out this activity in the presence of a teacher, after they have explained safety aspects.

1   Put one spatulaful of hydrated copper(II) sulfate into a boiling tube.
2   Heat the tube strongly. Record your observations.
3   Let the tube cool for a few minutes.
4   Add a few drops of water to the tube. Record your observations.

Explain your observations using the terms *anhydrous*, *hydrated* and *water of crystallisation*.

Question

1   Use the Periodic Table in Appendix 1 to calculate the relative formula masses of the following:
    a   calcium chloride, $CaCl_2$
    b   copper(II) sulfate, $CuSO_4$
    c   ammonium sulfate, $(NH_4)_2SO_4$
    d   magnesium nitrate-6-water, $Mg(NO_3)_2 \cdot 6H_2O$

Tip: for part **d** you need to calculate the mass of water separately and then add it to the M_r of $Mg(NO_3)_2$.

3.3 Accurate relative atomic masses

Mass spectrometry

A mass spectrometer (Figure 3.2) can be used to measure the mass of each isotope present in an element. It also compares how much of each isotope is present: the relative abundance (**relative isotopic abundance**). A simplified diagram of a mass spectrometer is shown in Figure 3.3. You will not be expected to know the details of how a mass spectrometer works, but it is useful to understand how the results are obtained.

KEY WORD

relative isotopic abundance: the proportion of one particular isotope in a mixture of isotopes, usually expressed as a percentage. The heights of the peaks in a mass spectrum show the proportion of each isotope present.

Figure 3.2: A mass spectrometer is a large and complex instrument.

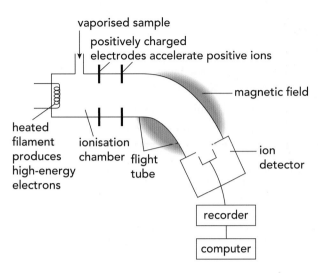

Figure 3.3: Simplified diagram of a mass spectrometer.

The atoms of the element in the vaporised sample are converted into ions. The stream of ions travels to a detector after being deflected by a strong magnetic field. As the magnetic field is increased, the ions of heavier and heavier isotopes move towards the detector. The detector is connected to a computer, which displays the mass spectrum.

The mass spectrum produced shows the relative abundance (isotopic abundance) on the vertical axis and the mass to ion charge ratio (m / e) on the horizontal axis. Figure 3.4 shows a typical mass spectrum for a sample of lead. Table 3.1 shows how the data is interpreted.

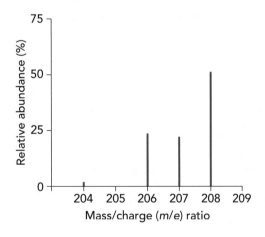

Figure 3.4: The mass spectrum of a sample of lead.

For singly positively charged ions, the (m / e) values give the nucleon number of the isotopes detected. In the case of lead, Table 3.1 shows that 52% of the lead is the

isotope with an isotopic mass of 208. The rest is lead-204 (2%), lead-206 (24%) and lead-207 (22%).

Isotopic mass	Relative abundance / %
204	2
206	24
207	22
208	52
total	100

Table 3.1: The data from Figure 3.4.

Determination of A_r from mass spectra

> **IMPORTANT**
>
> You do *not* need to know the exact working of the mass spectrometer.

We can use the data obtained from a mass spectrometer to calculate the relative atomic mass of an element very accurately. To calculate the relative atomic mass, we follow this method:

- multiply each isotopic mass by its percentage abundance
- add the figures together
- divide by 100.

We can use this method to calculate the relative atomic mass of neon from its mass spectrum, shown in Figure 3.5.

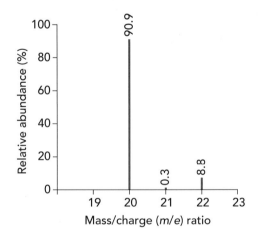

Figure 3.5: The mass spectrum of neon, Ne.

The mass spectrum of neon has three peaks: ^{20}Ne (90.9%), ^{21}Ne (0.3%) and ^{22}Ne (8.8%).

$$A_r \text{ of neon} = \frac{(20 \times 90.9) + (21.0 \times 0.3) + (22 \times 8.8)}{100} = 20.2$$

Note that this answer is given to 3 significant figures, which is consistent with the data given.

A high-resolution mass spectrometer can give very accurate relative isotopic masses. For example, ^{16}O = 15.995 and ^{32}S = 31.972. Because of this high level of precision, chemists can distinguish between molecules such as SO_2 and S_2, which appear to have the same relative molecular mass.

Question

2   Look at the mass spectrum of germanium, Ge.

   a   Write isotopic formula for the heaviest isotope of germanium.

   b   Use the % abundance of each isotope to calculate the relative atomic mass of germanium.

Identification of an organic compound using mass spectrometry

The main use of mass spectrometry is in the identification of organic compounds. As in other forms of spectroscopy, a substance can be identified by matching its spectrum against the spectra of known substances stored in a database. This technique is known as 'fingerprinting'.

The high energy electrons knock electrons from the molecules and break covalent bonds, fragmenting the molecule. Figure 3.6 shows the mass spectrum produced by propanone, CH_3COCH_3.

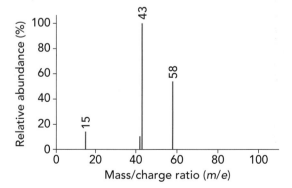

Figure 3.6: The mass spectrum of propanone, CH_3COCH_3.

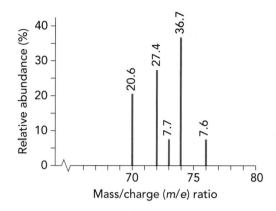

Figure 3.7: The mass spectrum of germanium, Ge.

The peak at the highest mass-to-charge ratio is caused by the molecular ion (M^+). This ion is formed by the sample molecule with one electron knocked out. It gives us the relative molecular mass of the sample. We can assume the ions detected carry a single positive charge, so the reading on the horizontal axis gives us the mass. In the case of propanone, CH_3COCH_3, the molecular ion has a relative mass of 58.0. This corresponds to $CH_3COCH_3^+$, with a mass of $(3 \times 12.0) + (1 \times 16.0) + (6 \times 1.0)$.

We also get large peaks at 15 and 43 on the mass spectrum. These peaks are due to fragments that are produced when propanone molecules are broken apart by the electron bombardment. Knowing the structure of propanone, we should be able to identify the fragment responsible for each peak (Figure 3.8).

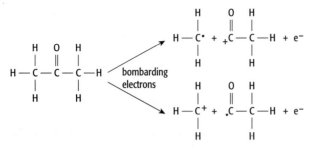

Figure 3.8: The fragmentation of propanone: $^+CH_3$ causes the peak at 15 and CH_3CO^+ causes the peak at 43.

Remember that fragmentation (breaking apart) of a compound in a mass spectrometer causes certain bonds to break. You can deduce what the fragment is by adding up the atomic masses of carbon, hydrogen and / or other atoms. So a fragment of m/e 15 is $C + 3H = 12 + (3 \times 1)$ which is $^+CH_3$ and a fragment of m/e 43 could be $^+C_3H_7$ or CH_3CO^+.

The electron bombardment has caused the C—C single bonds in the propanone molecules to break. This has resulted in the fragments at m/e 15 and 43 that are observed in Figure 3.6. The breaking of single bonds, such as C—C, C—O or C—N, is the most common cause of **fragmentation**.

These fragments are very common in mass spectra of organic compounds.

Mass	Fragment
15	$^+CH_3$
28	^+CO or $C_2H_4^+$
29	$CH_3CH_2^+$
43	$C_3H_7^+$ or CH_3CO^+

Table 3.2: Common fragments in the mass spectra of organic compounds.

Question

3 Look at Figure 3.10, which shows the mass spectrum of ethanol, C_2H_5OH. A structural isomer of ethanol is methoxymethane, an ether with the formula CH_3OCH_3.

a Predict the mass-to-charge ratio of a fragment that would appear on the mass spectrum of methoxymethane but does not appear on ethanol's mass spectrum.

b Give the formula of the ion responsible for the peak in your answer to part **a**.

c Look at the mass spectrum of ethanoic acid:

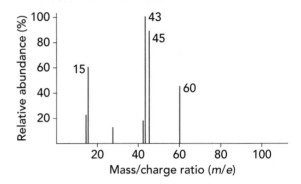

Figure 3.9: Mass spectrum of ethanoic acid.

Identify the fragments with mass-to-charge ratios of:

i   15
ii 43
iii 45
iv 60.

High-resolution mass spectra

High-resolution mass spectrometers can distinguish between ions that appear to have the same mass on a low-resolution mass spectrum. Table 3.3 shows the accurate relative isotopic masses of the most common atoms found in organic molecules.

Isotope	Relative isotopic mass
^1H	1.007 824 6
^{12}C	12.000 000 0
^{14}N	14.003 073 8
^{16}O	15.994 914 1

Table 3.3: Accurate masses of isotopes.

molecular formula: the formula that shows the number and type of each atom in a molecule, e.g. the molecular formula for ethanol is C_2H_6O.

These accurate isotopic masses allow us to measure the mass of the molecular ion so accurately that it can only correspond to one possible molecular formula. For example, a molecular ion peak at 45 could be caused by C_2H_7N or CH_3NO. However, a high-resolution mass spectrum would show the $C_2H_7N^+$ peak at 45.057846 and the CH_3NO^+ peak at 45.021462. We can, therefore, be sure which molecule is being analysed.

Using the [M + 1] peak

There will always be a very small peak just beyond the molecular ion peak at a mass of [M + 1]. This is caused by molecules in which one of the carbon atoms is the ^{13}C isotope. This is shown in the mass spectrum of ethanol in Figure 3.10.

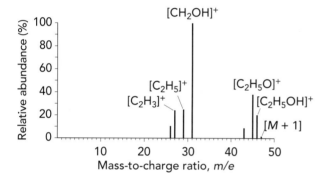

Figure 3.10: The mass spectrum of ethanol, showing the [M + 1] peak.

In any organic compound there will be 1.10% carbon-13. We can use this fact to work out the number of carbon atoms (n) in a molecule. We apply the equation:

$$n = \frac{100}{1.1} \times \frac{\text{abundance of } [M+1]^+ \text{ ion}}{\text{abundance of } M^+ \text{ ion}}$$

WORKED EXAMPLE

1 An unknown compound has a molecular ion peak, M^+, with a relative abundance of 54.5% and has an [M + 1]$^+$ peak with a relative abundance of 3.6%. How many carbon atoms does the unknown compound contain?

Solution

Substituting the values of relative abundance into the equation:

$$n = \frac{100}{1.1} \times \frac{\text{abundance of } [M+1]^+ \text{ ion}}{\text{abundance of } M^+ \text{ ion}}$$

CONTINUED

we get:

$$n = \frac{100}{1.1} \times \frac{3.6}{54.5} = 6.0$$

There are 6 carbon atoms in each molecule.

Question

4 A hydrocarbon has a molecular ion peak at a mass-to-charge ratio of 84 (relative abundance of 62.0%) and an [M + 1] peak with a relative abundance of 4.1%.

How many carbon atoms are in the hydrocarbon?

Using [M + 2] and [M + 4] peaks

Note: Material relating to [M + 4] peaks is extension content. It is not part of the syllabus.

IMPORTANT

We can tell whether there is chlorine or bromine in an organic compound by comparing the relative heights of the M and [M + 2] peaks. If the peak heights are equal, there is one atom of bromine per molecule. If the peak heights are in the ratio 3 [M] to 1 [M + 2], there is one atom of chlorine per molecule.

If the sample compound contains chlorine or bromine atoms, we also get peaks beyond the molecular ion peak because of isotopes of chlorine and bromine. Chlorine has two isotopes, ^{35}Cl and ^{37}Cl, as does bromine, ^{79}Br and ^{81}Br. Table 3.4 shows the approximate percentage of each isotope in naturally occurring samples.

Isotope	Approximate %
^{35}Cl	75
^{37}Cl	25
^{79}Br	50
^{81}Br	50

Table 3.4: Naturally occurring isotopes of chlorine and bromine.

One Cl or Br atom per molecule

Imagine a sample of chloromethane, CH_3Cl. We will have molecules of $CH_3{}^{35}Cl$ (75%) and molecules of

$CH_3^{37}Cl$ (25%). The molecular ion will be $CH_3^{35}Cl^+$, and two units beyond that on the mass spectrum will be the peak for $CH_3^{37}Cl^+$. The peak for $CH_3^{37}Cl^+$ will be one-third the height of the molecular ion. This is the $[M + 2]$ peak.

In the mass spectrum of bromomethane, CH_3Br, we will have two molecular ion peaks of approximately the same height: one for $CH_3^{79}Br^+$ and the other for $CH_3^{81}Br^+$ (the $[M + 2]$ peak).

You should look out for the relative heights mentioned here when interpreting mass spectra.

- If the $[M + 2]$ peak is one-third the height of the M peak, this suggests the presence of one chlorine atom per molecule.

- If the $[M + 2]$ peak is the same as the height of the M peak, this suggests the presence of one bromine atom per molecule.

An example of the $[M + 2]$ peak is shown on the mass spectrum of chlorobenzene (Figure 3.11).

Two Cl or Br atoms per molecule

The situation is a little more complex with two chlorine atoms in a molecule, as there are three possibilities. Considering dichloromethane, CH_2Cl_2, we have:

$^{35}ClCH_2^{35}Cl^+$	the M peak
$^{35}ClCH_2^{37}Cl^+$	the $[M + 2]$ peak
$^{37}ClCH_2^{35}Cl^+$	the $[M + 2]$ peak
$^{37}ClCH_2^{37}Cl^+$	the $[M + 4]$ peak

The relative heights of the peaks must take into account the natural abundances: it works out as 9 : 6 : 1 for molecules with two Cl atoms.

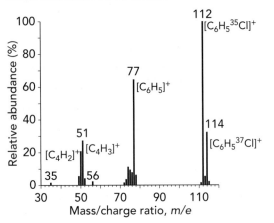

Figure 3.11: The mass spectrum of chlorobenzene, showing the $[M + 2]$ peak. (Note that there are also tiny $[M + 1]$ and $[M + 3]$ peaks corresponding to ^{13}C in the molecule.)

The M, $[M + 2]$ and $[M + 4]$ peaks also occur in dibromomethane but the relative heights of peaks are easier to work out. Because the ratio ^{79}Br : ^{81}Br is 1 : 1, the M : $[M + 2]$: $[M + 4]$ height ratio is 1 : 2 : 1.

Question

Note: Question 5 contains extension content as $[M + 4]$ peaks are not included in the syllabus.

5 a List the ions responsible for the M, $[M + 2]$ and $[M + 4]$ peaks in a mass spectrum of dibromomethane.

b What would be the mass-to-charge ratio and relative abundances of the major peaks with the highest charge-to-mass ratios in the mass spectrum of chloroethane?

c How many peaks would you see beyond the molecular ion peak in 1,1-dibromoethane? What would be their mass-to-charge ratios and abundances relative to the molecular ion? (Ignore peaks due to ^{13}C.)

3.4 Amount of substance

The mole and the Avogadro constant

The formula of a compound shows us the number of atoms of each element present in one formula unit or one molecule of the compound. We know that two atoms of hydrogen ($A_r = 1.0$) combine with one atom of oxygen ($A_r = 16.0$) in water, so the ratio of mass of hydrogen atoms to oxygen atoms in a water molecule is 2 : 16. No matter how many molecules of water we have, this ratio will always be the same. But the mass of even 1000 atoms is far too small to be weighed. We have to scale up much more than this to get an amount of substance that is easy to weigh.

The number of particles equivalent to the relative atomic mass or relative molecular mass of a substance in grams is called the Avogadro constant (or Avogadro number). The symbol for the Avogadro constant is L (the symbol N_A may also be used). The numerical value of the Avogadro constant is 6.02×10^{23}. The mass of substance with this number of particles is called a **mole**.

The Avogadro constant is chosen so that the mass of one mole in grams equals the average mass of an atom of an element in unified atomic mass units. So a mole of sodium ($A_r = 23.0$) contains 6.02×10^{23} atoms and has a mass of 23.0 g. The abbreviation for a mole is mol.

KEY DEFINITION

mole: the amount of substance which contains 6.02×10^{23} specified particles (atoms, molecules, ions or electrons).

We can define the mole in terms of the **Avogadro constant**: A mole is the amount of substance which contains 6.02×10^{23} specified particles. The particles can be atoms, molecules, ions or electrons.

IMPORTANT

In many books you will see an alternative definition of the mole based on the carbon-12 isotope: one mole of a substance is the amount of that substance that has the same number of specific particles (atoms, molecules or ions) as there are atoms in exactly 12 g of the carbon-12 isotope. This definition is now out of date.

KEY WORDS

Avogadro constant, L: the number of specified particles (atoms, ions, molecules or electrons) in a mole of those particles. Its numerical value is 6.02×10^{23}.

molar mass: the mass of a mole of substance in grams.

The Avogadro constant applies to atoms, molecules, ions and electrons. So in 1 mole of sodium there are 6.02×10^{23} sodium atoms and in 1 mole of sodium chloride (NaCl) there are 6.02×10^{23} sodium ions and 6.02×10^{23} chloride ions.

It is important to make clear what type of particles we are referring to. If we just state 'moles of chlorine', it is not clear whether we are thinking about chlorine atoms or chlorine molecules. A mole of chlorine molecules, Cl_2, contains 6.02×10^{23} chlorine molecules but twice as many chlorine atoms, as there are two chlorine atoms in every chlorine molecule.

IMPORTANT

Molar mass is a general term used for the mass in grams of 1 mole of a compound, whether ionic, simple molecules or giant covalent structures. 'Relative molecular mass' refers only to molecules.

Figure 3.12: Amedeo Avogadro (1776–1856) was an Italian scientist, who first deduced that equal volumes of gases contain equal numbers of molecules. Although the Avogadro constant is named after him, it was left to other scientists to calculate the number of particles in a mole.

We often refer to the mass of a mole of substance as its **molar mass** (abbreviation M). The units of molar mass are g mol^{-1}.

Moles and mass

The Système International (SI) base unit for mass is the kilogram. But this is a rather large mass to use for general laboratory work in chemistry, so chemists prefer to use the relative molecular mass or formula mass in grams (1000 g = 1 kg). You can find the number of moles of a substance by using the mass of substance and mass of one mole of that substance (the molar mass)

$$\text{number of moles (mol)} = \frac{\text{mass of substance in grams (g)}}{\text{molar mass (g mol}^{-1})}$$

Some students find it helpful to use a triangle such as that shown to work out mass from molar mass and number of moles. By covering the quantity you want to find, you will see the correct form of the equation to use.

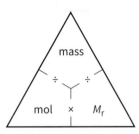

Figure 3.13: Triangle diagram for mole calculations.

However, it is far *better to learn how to cross multiply* because such triangles will not work with more complex equations: ask another learner or a teacher to help you.

WORKED EXAMPLES

2   How many moles of sodium chloride are present in 117.0 g of sodium chloride, NaCl?

(A_r values: Na = 23.0, Cl = 35.5)

Solution

Step 1: molar mass of NaCl = 23.0 + 35.5
= 58.5 g mol^{-1}

Step 2: number of moles $= \dfrac{\text{mass}}{\text{molar mass}} = \dfrac{117.0}{58.5}$

= 2.0 mol

3   What mass of sodium hydroxide, NaOH, is present in 0.25 mol of sodium hydroxide?

(A_r values: H = 1.0, Na = 23.0, O = 16.0)

Solution

Step 1: molar mass of NaOH = 23.0 + 16.0
+ 1.0 = 40.0 g mol^{-1}

Step 2: mass = number of moles × molar mass
= 0.25 × 40.0 g = 10.0 g NaOH

When dealing with moles, it is important to be clear about the type of particle referred to. For example: 32.0 grams of oxygen O_2 contains 1 mole of oxygen molecules but 2 moles of oxygen atoms and 1 mole of $MgCl_2$ contains 1 mol of Mg^{2+} ions but 2 moles of Cl^- ions.

Question

6   **a**   Use these A_r values (Fe = 55.8, N = 14.0, O = 16.0, S = 32.1) to calculate the amount of substance in moles in each of the following:

   i   10.7 g of sulfur atoms

   ii   64.2 g of sulfur molecules (S_8)

   iii   60.45 g of anhydrous iron(III) nitrate, $Fe(NO_3)_3$

   b   Use the value of the Avogadro constant (6.02×10^{23} mol^{-1}) to calculate the total number of atoms in 7.10 g of chlorine atoms. (A_r value: Cl = 35.5)

To find the mass of a substance present in a given number of moles, you need to rearrange the equation

$$\text{number of moles (mol)} = \frac{\text{mass of substance in grams (g)}}{\text{molar mass (g mol}^{-1})}$$

mass of substance (g) =
   number of moles (mol) × molar mass (g mol^{-1})

Figure 3.14 shows what the molar mass of six elements looks like.

Figure 3.14: One mole quantities of common elements. The cylinders from left to right hold mercury, lead and copper. Sulfur is in the left flask, magnesium in the right and chromium on the watch-glass.

Question

7 Use these A_r values: C = 12.0, Fe = 55.8, H = 1.0, O = 16.0, Na = 23.0.

Calculate the mass of the following:

a 20 moles of carbon dioxide, CO_2

b 0.050 moles of sodium carbonate, Na_2CO_3

c 5.00 moles of iron(II) hydroxide, $Fe(OH)_2$

3.5 Mole calculations

Reacting masses

Figure 3.15: Iron reacting with sulfur to produce iron sulfide. We can calculate exactly how much iron is needed to react with sulfur and the mass of the products formed by knowing the molar mass of each reactant and the balanced chemical equation.

KEY WORD

stoichiometry: the mole ratios of reactants and products shown in the balanced equation. For the equation: $2Na + Cl_2 \rightarrow 2NaCl$, the stoichiometry is $2(Na) : 1(Cl_2) : 2(NaCl)$.

When reacting chemicals together, we may need to know what mass of each reactant to use so that they react exactly and there is no waste (Figure 3.15). To calculate this, we need to know the chemical equation. This shows us the ratio of moles of the reactants and products: the **stoichiometry** of the equation. The balanced equation shows this stoichiometry. For example, in the reaction

$$Fe_2O_3 + 3CO \rightarrow 2Fe + 3CO_2$$

1 mole of iron(III) oxide reacts with 3 moles of carbon monoxide to form 2 moles of iron and 3 moles of carbon dioxide. The stoichiometry of the equation is 1 : 3 : 2 : 3. The large numbers that are included in the equation (3, 2 and 3) are called *stoichiometric numbers*.

In order to find the mass of products formed in a chemical reaction we use:

- the mass of the reactants

- the molar mass of the reactants

- the balanced equation.

WORKED EXAMPLE

4 Magnesium burns in oxygen to form magnesium oxide.

$$2Mg + O_2 \rightarrow 2MgO$$

Calculate the mass of oxygen needed to react with 1 mole of magnesium. What is the mass of the magnesium oxide formed?.

Solution

Step 1: Write the balanced equation.
$$2Mg + O_2 \rightarrow 2MgO$$

Step 2: Multiply each formula mass in g by the relevant stoichiometric number in the equation.

2×24.3 g	1×32.0 g	$2 \times (24.3$ g $+ 16.0$ g$)$
48.6 g	32.0 g	80.6 g

From this calculation we can deduce that:

- 32.0 g of oxygen are needed to react exactly with

- 48.6 g of magnesium

- 80.6 g of magnesium oxide are formed.

If we burn 12.15 g of magnesium (0.5 mol) we get 20.15 g of magnesium oxide. This is because the stoichiometry of the reaction shows us that for each mole (or part of mole) of magnesium burnt, we get the same number of moles of magnesium oxide. This means that for every 0.5 mole burnt, we get 0.5 mole of product.

In this type of calculation we do not always need to know the molar mass of each of the reactants. If one or more of the reactants is in excess, we need only know the mass in grams and the molar mass of the reactant that is *not* in excess.

- The reactant which has the number of moles in excess is called the *excess reagent*.

- The reactant which is not in excess is called the *limiting reagent*.

IMPORTANT

Remember that in calculating which reactant is limiting, you must:
- work out the number of moles of the reactant
- take into account the ratio of the reactants shown in the equation (the stoichiometry).

WORKED EXAMPLE

5   A sample of 79.8 g of iron(III) oxide is mixed with 9.36 g of carbon and heated. A reaction occurs.

$$2Fe_2O_3 + 3C \rightarrow 4Fe + 3CO_2$$

Show by calculation that iron(III) oxide is the limiting reactant.

(A_r values: Fe = 55.8, O = 16.0, C = 12.0)

Solution

Step 1: Calculate the moles of each reagent.

$$\text{moles of } Fe_2O_3 = \frac{79.8}{(2 \times 55.8) + (3 \times 16.0)}$$
$$= 0.50 \text{ mol}$$

$$\text{moles of } C = \frac{9.36}{12} = 0.78 \text{ mol}$$

Step 2: Refer to the stoichiometry of the equation:

For every 2 Fe_2O_3 which react, 3 C are needed

So for 0.5 mol Fe_2O_3 we need $0.5 \times \frac{3}{2} =$ 0.75 mol C

Step 3: Determine which is in excess.

number of moles C required = 0.75
number of moles C from step 1 = 0.78
So C is in excess by 0.78 − 0.75 = 0.03 mol and iron(III) oxide is limiting.

WORKED EXAMPLE

6   Iron(III) oxide reacts with carbon monoxide to form iron and carbon dioxide.

$$Fe_2O_3 + 3CO \rightarrow 2Fe + 3CO_2$$

Calculate the maximum mass of iron produced when 798 g of iron(III) oxide is reduced by excess carbon monoxide. (A_r values: Fe – 55.8, O – 16.0)

Solution

Step 1: Write the balanced equation.

$$Fe_2O_3 + 3CO \rightarrow 2Fe + 3CO_2$$

Step 2: Calculate molar masses taking into account the number of moles in the equation.

1 mole iron(III) oxide	$\rightarrow$	2 moles iron
$(2 \times 55.8) + (3 \times 16.0)$	$\rightarrow$	2×55.8
159.6 g Fe_2O_3	$\rightarrow$	111.6 g Fe

Step 3: Calculate mass of Fe in 798 g Fe_2O_3

$$\frac{111.6}{159.6} \times 798$$
$$= 558 \text{ g Fe}$$

You can see that in step 3, we have simply used ratios to calculate the amount of iron produced from 798 g of iron(III) oxide.

Question

8   a   Sodium reacts with excess oxygen to form sodium peroxide, Na_2O_2.

$$2Na + O_2 \rightarrow Na_2O_2$$

Calculate the maximum mass of sodium peroxide formed when 4.60 g of sodium is burnt in excess oxygen. (A_r values: Na = 23.0, O = 16.0)

b   Tin(IV) oxide is reduced to tin by carbon. Carbon monoxide is also formed.

$$SnO_2 + 2C \rightarrow Sn + 2CO$$

Calculate the mass of carbon that exactly reacts with 14.0 g of tin(IV) oxide. Give your answer to 3 significant figures.
(A_r values: C = 12.0, O = 16.0, Sn = 118.7)

The stoichiometry of a reaction

We can find the stoichiometry of a reaction if we know the amounts of each reactant that exactly react together and the amounts of each product formed.

For example, if we react 4.0 g of hydrogen with 32.0 g of oxygen we get 36.0 g of water. (A_r values: H = 1.0, O = 16.0) hydrogen (H_2) + oxygen (O_2) → water (H_2O)

$$\frac{4.0}{2 \times 1.0} \qquad \frac{32.0}{2 \times 16.0} \qquad \frac{36.0}{(2 \times 1.0) + 16.0}$$

$$= 2 \text{ mol} \qquad = 1 \text{ mol} \qquad = 2 \text{ mol}$$

This ratio is the ratio of stoichiometric numbers in the equation. So the equation is:

$$2H_2 + O_2 \rightarrow 2H_2O$$

We can still deduce the stoichiometry of this reaction even if we do not know the mass of oxygen that reacted. The ratio of hydrogen to water is 1 : 1. But there is only one atom of oxygen in a molecule of water: half the amount in an oxygen molecule. So the mole ratio of oxygen to water in the equation must be 1 : 2.

Question

9 56.2 g of silicon, Si, reacts exactly with 284.0 g of chlorine, Cl_2, to form 340.2 g of silicon(IV) chloride, $SiCl_4$. Use this information to calculate the stoichiometry of the reaction.
(A_r values: Cl = 35.5, Si = 28.1)

Significant figures

When we perform chemical calculations it is important that we give the answer to the number of significant figures that fits with the data provided. The examples here show the number 526.84 rounded up to varying numbers of significant figures.

rounded to 4 significant figures = 526.8

rounded to 3 significant figures = 527

rounded to 2 significant figures = 530

IMPORTANT

When you are writing an answer to a calculation, the answer should be to the same number of significant figures as the least number of significant figures in the data.

Do not round numbers to the correct number of significant figures until the end of a calculation or you risk introducing errors.

Percentage composition by mass

We can use the formula of a compound and relative atomic masses to calculate the percentage by mass of a particular element in a compound.

$$\% \text{ by mass} = \frac{\text{atomic mass} \times \text{number of moles of particular element in a compound}}{\text{molar mass of compound}}$$

WORKED EXAMPLES

7 How many moles of calcium oxide are there in 2.9 g of calcium oxide?
(A_r values: Ca = 40.1, O = 16.0)

Solution

If you divide 2.9 by 56.1, your calculator shows 0.051 693 … The least number of significant figures in the data, however, is 2 (the mass is 2.9 g). So your answer should be expressed to 2 significant figures, as 0.052 mol.

Note:

1 Zeros before a number are not significant figures. For example, 0.004 is only to 1 significant figure.

2 After the decimal point, zeros after a number are significant figures. 0.0040 has 2 significant figures and 0.004 00 has 3 significant figures.

3 If you are performing a calculation with several steps, do not round up in between steps. Round up at the end.

8 Calculate the percentage by mass of iron in iron(III) oxide, Fe_2O_3.
(A_r values: Fe = 55.8, O = 16.0)

Solution

$$\% \text{ mass of iron} = \frac{2 \times 55.8}{(2 \times 55.8) + (3 \times 16.0)} \times 100$$
$$= 69.9 \%$$

Figure 3.16: This iron ore is impure Fe_2O_3. We can calculate the mass of iron that can be obtained from Fe_2O_3 by using molar masses.

Question

10 Calculate the percentage by mass of carbon in ethanol, C_2H_5OH.

(A_r values: C = 12.0, H = 1.0, O = 16.0)

Percentage yield

In many chemical reactions, especially organic reactions, not all the reactants are changed to the products you want. This is because there are other reactions going on at the same time; reactants or products are lost to the atmosphere; or the reaction does not go to completion. The percentage yield tells you how much of a particular product you get from the reactants compared with the maximum theoretical amount that you can get.

$$\text{percentage yield} = \frac{\text{actual yield}}{\text{predicted yield (theoretical yield)}} \times 100$$

The *actual yield* is the moles or mass of product obtained by experiment.

The *predicted yield* is the moles or mass of product obtained by calculation if no side products are formed and all of a specific reactant is converted to a specific product.

WORKED EXAMPLE

9 A sample of aluminium chloride, $AlCl_3$, is made by reacting 18 g of aluminium powder with excess chlorine. The mass of aluminium chloride produced is 71.0 g. Calculate the percentage yield of aluminium oxide. (A_r values: Al = 27.0, Cl = 35.5)

$2Al + 3Cl_2 \rightarrow 2AlCl_3$

Solution

Step 1: Calculate the predicted mass from the stoichiometry of the equation if all the aluminium is converted to aluminium chloride.

2×27 g Al produces
$2 \times (27 + (3 \times 35.5))$ g $AlCl_3$
54 g Al produces 267 g $AlCl_3$

Step 2: Calculate the mass of aluminium chloride formed from the given amount of aluminium using simple proportion.

18 g Al produces $267 \times \frac{18}{54} = 89.0$ g $AlCl_3$

Step 3: Calculate the percentage yield.

$\frac{71.0}{89.0} \times 100 = 79.8\%$

Empirical formulae

The **empirical formula** of a compound is the simplest whole number ratio of the elements present in one molecule or formula unit of the compound. The molecular formula of a compound shows the number of atoms of each element present in a molecule.

Table 3.5 shows the empirical and molecular formulae for a number of compounds.

- The formula for an ionic compound is always its empirical formula.

- The empirical formula and molecular formula for simple inorganic molecules are often the same.

- Organic molecules often have different empirical and molecular formulae.

KEY WORD

empirical formula: the simplest whole number ratio of the elements present in one molecule or formula unit of the compound, e.g. the empirical formula of ethanoic acid is CH_3O.

Compound	Empirical formula	Molecular formula
water	H_2O	H_2O
hydrogen peroxide	HO	H_2O_2
sulfur dioxide	SO_2	SO_2
butane	C_2H_5	C_4H_{10}
cyclohexane	CH_2	C_6H_{12}

Table 3.5: Some empirical and molecular formulae.

Question

11 Deduce the empirical formula of:

    a hydrazine, N_2H_4

    b octane, C_8H_{18}

    c benzene, C_6H_6

    d ammonia, NH_3

The empirical formula can be found by determining the mass of each element present in a sample of the compound. For some compounds this can be done by combustion. An organic compound must be very pure in order to calculate its empirical formula.

WORKED EXAMPLES

10 Deduce the formula of magnesium oxide.

Solution

This can be found as follows:

- burn a known mass of magnesium (0.486 g) in excess oxygen

- record the mass of magnesium oxide formed (0.806 g)

- calculate the mass of oxygen that has combined with the magnesium (0.806 − 0.486 g) = 0.320 g

- calculate the mole ratio of magnesium to oxygen

- (A_r values: Mg = 24.3, O = 16.0)

$$\text{moles of Mg} = \frac{0.486\ \text{g}}{24.3\ \text{g mol}^{-1}} = 0.0200\ \text{mol}$$

$$\text{moles of oxygen} = \frac{0.320\ \text{g}}{16.0\ \text{g mol}^{-1}} = 0.0200\ \text{mol}$$

The simplest ratio of magnesium : oxygen is 1 : 1. So the empirical formula of magnesium oxide is MgO.

11 When 1.55 g of phosphorus is completely combusted 3.55 g of an oxide of phosphorus is produced. Deduce the empirical formula of this oxide of phosphorus.
(A_r values: O = 16.0, P = 31.0)

Solution

	P	O
Step 1: note the mass of each element	1.55 g	3.55 − 1.55 = 2.00 g
Step 2: divide by atomic masses	$\dfrac{1.55\ \text{g}}{31.0\ \text{g mol}^{-1}}$ = 0.05 mol	$\dfrac{2.00\ \text{g}}{16.0\ \text{g mol}^{-1}}$ = 0.125 mol
Step 3: divide by the lowest figure	$\dfrac{0.05}{0.05}$ = 1	$\dfrac{0.125}{0.05}$ = 2.5
Step 4: if needed, obtain the lowest whole number ratio to get empirical formula	P_2O_5	

Table 3.6: Steps to deduce an empirical formula.

An empirical formula can also be deduced from data that give the percentage composition by mass of the elements in a compound.

WORKED EXAMPLE

12 A compound of carbon and hydrogen contains 85.7% carbon and 14.3% hydrogen by mass. Deduce the empirical formula of this hydrocarbon.
(A_r values: C = 12.0, H = 1.0)

Solution

	C	H
Step 1: note the % by mass	85.7	14.3
Step 2: divide by A_r values	$\dfrac{85.7}{12.0}$ = 7.142	$\dfrac{14.3}{1.0}$ = 14.3
Step 3: divide by the lowest figure	$\dfrac{7.142}{7.142}$ = 1	$\dfrac{14.3}{7.142}$ = 2

Empirical formula is CH_2.

Question

12 The composition by mass of a hydrocarbon is 10% hydrogen and 90% carbon. Deduce the empirical formula of this hydrocarbon.
(A_r values: C = 12.0, H = 1.0)

Molecular formulae

The molecular formula shows the actual number of each of the different atoms present in a molecule. We use the molecular formula to write balanced equations and to calculate molar masses. The molecular formula is always a multiple of the empirical formula. For example, the molecular formula of ethane, C_2H_6, is twice the empirical formula, CH_3.

In order to deduce the molecular formula we need to know:

- the relative formula mass of the compound

- the empirical formula.

WORKED EXAMPLE

13 A compound has the empirical formula CH_2Br. Its relative molecular mass is 187.8. Deduce the molecular formula of this compound.

(A_r values: Br = 79.9, C = 12.0, H = 1.0)

Solution

Step 1: Find the empirical formula mass:
$12.0 + (2 \times 1.0) + 79.9 = 93.9$

Step 2: Divide the relative molecular mass by the empirical formula mass: $\dfrac{187.8}{93.9} = 2$

Step 3: Multiply the number of atoms in the empirical formula by the number in step 2:
$2 \times CH_2Br$, so molecular formula is $C_2H_4Br_2$.

Question

13 The empirical formulae and molar masses of three compounds, A, B and C, are shown in Table 3.7. Calculate the molecular formula of each of these compounds.

(A_r values: C = 12.0, Cl = 35.5, H = 1.0)

Compound	Empirical formula	M_r
A	C_3H_5	82
B	CCl_3	237
C	CH_2	112

Table 3.7: Information table for Question 13.

3.6 Chemical formulae and chemical equations

Deducing the formula for ionic and covalent compounds

Ionic compounds

The electronic structure of the individual elements in a compound determines the formula of a compound (see Section 2.1). The formula of an ionic compound is determined by the charges on each of the ions present. The number of positive charges is balanced by the number of negative charges so that the total charge on the compound is zero. We can work out the formula for a compound if we know the charges on the ions. Figure 3.17 shows the charges on some ions related to the position of the elements in the Periodic Table. The form of the Periodic Table that we shall be using has 18 groups because the transition elements are numbered as Groups 3 to 12. So, aluminium is in Group 13 and chlorine is in Group 17.

For simple metal ions in Groups 1 and 2, the value of the positive charge is the same as the group number. For a simple metal ion in Group 13, the value of the positive charge is 3+. For a simple non-metal ion in Groups 15 to 17, the value of the negative charge is 18 minus the group number. The charge on the ions of transition elements can vary. For example, iron forms two types of ions, Fe^{2+} and Fe^{3+} (Figure 3.18).

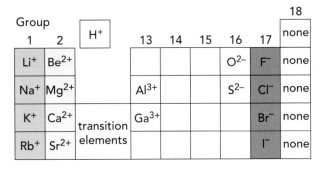

Figure 3.17: The charge on some simple ions is related to their position in the Periodic Table.

Figure 3.18: Iron(II) chloride (left) and iron(III) chloride (right). These two chlorides of iron both contain iron and chlorine, but they have different formulae.

KEY DEFINITION

oxidation number (oxidation state): a number given to an atom or ion in a compound that describes how oxidised or reduced it is.

The roman numerals after the ions are called oxidation numbers.

There are rules for deducing oxidation numbers (see Section 7.2):

- For most metal ions in Groups 1 to 3, the oxidation numbers are equal to the positive charge on the ion, e.g. an Al^{3+} ion has an oxidation number of +3. When naming compounds containing these ions, we do not include the oxidation number of the positive ion, e.g. magnesium oxide (*not* magnesium(II) oxide).

- Simple negative ions have oxidation numbers which are the same as the charge on the ion, e.g. O^{2-} has an oxidation number of −2 and Cl^{-} has an oxidation number of −1. When naming compounds containing these ions we do not include the oxidation number of the negative ion as these do not generally vary.

- For transition elements, the oxidation numbers do vary. They show the charge on the ion, e.g. chromium(II) chloride contains a Cr^{2+} ion and chromium(III) chloride contains a Cr^{3+} ion. When naming these compounds we must include the oxidation number to avoid confusion.

Ions that contain more than one type of atom are called **compound ions**. Some common compound ions and two metal ions that you should learn are listed in Table 3.8. The formula for an ionic compound is obtained by balancing the charges of the ions.

Ion	Formula
ammonium	NH_4^+
carbonate	CO_3^{2-}
hydrogencarbonate	HCO_3^-
hydroxide	OH^-
nitrate	NO_3^-
phosphate	PO_4^{3-}
sulfate	SO_4^{2-}
zinc	Zn^{2+}
silver	Ag^+

Table 3.8: The formulae of some common ions.

KEY WORD

compound ion: an ion containing more than one type of element, e.g. OH^-, and PO_4^{3-}.

WORKED EXAMPLES

14 Deduce the formula of magnesium chloride.

Solution

Ions present: Mg^{2+} and Cl^-.

For electrical neutrality, we need two Cl^- ions for every Mg^{2+} ion.

$(2 \times 1-) + (1 \times 2+) = 0$

So the formula is $MgCl_2$.

15 Deduce the formula of aluminium oxide.
Ions present: Al^{3+} and O^{2-}.

For electrical neutrality, we need three O^{2-} ions for every two Al^{3+} ions.

$(3 \times 2-) + (2 \times 3+) = 0$

So the formula is Al_2O_3.

Covalent compounds

You can work out the formula of a covalent compound from the number of electrons needed to achieve the stable electronic configuration of a noble gas (see Section 4.1). In general, carbon atoms form four bonds with other atoms, hydrogen and halogen atoms form one bond and oxygen atoms form two bonds. So the formula of water, H_2O, follows these rules. The formula for methane is CH_4, with each carbon atom bonding with four hydrogen atoms. However, there are many exceptions to these rules.

Compounds containing a simple metal ion and non-metal ion are named by changing the end of the name of the non-metal element to '-ide'.

sodium + chlorine → sodium chloride

zinc + sulfur → zinc sulfide

The names of compound ions containing oxygen often end in '-ate'. Sometimes they end in '-ite'. For example, the sulfate ion contains sulfur and four oxygen atoms, the phosphate ion contains phosphorus and oxygen.

Question

14 a Write down the formula of each of the following compounds:

   i magnesium nitrate

   ii calcium sulfate

   iii sodium iodide

   iv hydrogen bromide

   v sodium sulfide

b Name each of the following compounds:

   i Na_3PO_4

   ii $(NH_4)_2SO_4$

   iii $AlCl_3$

   iv $Ca(NO_3)_2$

Balancing chemical equations

When chemicals react, atoms cannot be either created or destroyed. So there must be the same number of each type of atom on the reactants side of a chemical equation as there are on the products side. A symbol equation is a shorthand way of describing a chemical reaction. It shows the number and type of the atoms in the reactants and the number and type of atoms in the products. If this number of each type of atom is the same on both sides, we say the equation is *balanced*. Follow these examples to see how we balance an equation.

IMPORTANT

When balancing chemical equations remember:

- Do not change any of the formulae.

- The numbers used to balance are put in front of the formulae.

- In equations involving combustion reactions of organic compounds, balance the carbon first and then the hydrogen. Balance the oxygen last.

WORKED EXAMPLES

16 Write a balanced equation for the reaction of hydrogen and oxygen to form water.

Solution

Step 1: Write down the formulae of all the reactants and products. For example:

$$H_2 + O_2 \rightarrow H_2O$$

Step 2: Count the number of atoms of each reactant and product.

$$H_2 + O_2 \rightarrow H_2O$$
2[H] 2[O]   2[H] + 1[O]

Step 3: Balance one of the atoms by placing a number in front of one of the reactants or products. In this case the oxygen atoms on the right-hand side need to be balanced, so that they are equal in number to those on the left-hand side. Remember that the number in front multiplies everything in the formula. For example, $2H_2O$ has 4 hydrogen atoms and 2 oxygen atoms.

$$H_2 + O_2 \rightarrow 2H_2O$$
2[H] 2[O]   4[H] + 2[O]

Step 4: Keep balancing in this way, one type of atom at a time until all the atoms are balanced.

$$2H_2 + O_2 \rightarrow 2H_2O$$
4[H] 2[O]   4[H] + 2[O]

Note that when you balance an equation you must not change the formulae of any of the reactants or products.

17 Write a balanced equation for the reaction of iron(III) oxide with carbon monoxide to form iron and carbon dioxide.

Solution

Step 1: Formulae:

$$Fe_2O_3 + CO \rightarrow Fe + CO_2$$

Step 2: Count the number of atoms.

$$Fe_2O_3 + CO \rightarrow Fe + CO_2$$
2[Fe]   1[C]   1[Fe]   1[C]
3[O]   1[O]   2[O]

Step 3: Balance the iron.

$$Fe_2O_3 + CO \rightarrow 2Fe + CO_2$$
2[Fe]   1[C]   2[Fe] + 1[C]
3[O]   1[O]   2[O]

Step 4: Balance the oxygen.

$$Fe_2O_3 + 3CO \rightarrow 2Fe + 3CO_2$$
2[Fe]   3[C]   2[Fe]   3[C]
3[O]   3[O]   6[O]

In step 4, the oxygen in the CO_2 comes from two places, the Fe_2O_3 and the CO. Note that trial and error is involved here as the carbon also needs to be balanced.

In this particular case, in order to balance the equation, three oxygen atoms come from the iron oxide and three oxygen atoms come from the carbon monoxide.

IMPORTANT

When balancing chemical equations follow these steps:

* Write the formulae of the reactants and products

* Count the numbers of atoms in each reactant and product

* Balance the atoms one at a time until all the atoms are balanced.

Question

15 Write balanced equations for the following reactions.

a Iron reacts with hydrochloric acid to form iron(II) chloride, $FeCl_2$, and hydrogen.

b Aluminium hydroxide, $Al(OH)_3$, breaks down on heating to form aluminium oxide, Al_2O_3, and water.

c Hexane, C_6H_{14}, burns in oxygen to form carbon dioxide and water.

Using state symbols

We sometimes find it useful to specify the physical states of the reactants and products in a chemical reaction. This is especially important where chemical equilibria and rates of reaction are being discussed (see Chapter 8 and Chapter 9). We use the following state symbols:

- (s) solid
- (l) liquid
- (g) gas
- (aq) aqueous (a solution in water).

State symbols are written after the formula of each reactant and product. For example:

$$ZnCO_3(s) + H_2SO_4(aq) \rightarrow ZnSO_4(aq) + H_2O(l) + CO_2(g)$$

KEY WORD

state symbol: in a chemical equation a symbol (sign) placed after each reactant and product in a chemical equation to indicate whether they are solid (s), liquid (l), gas (g) or in aqueous solution (aq).

Question

16 Write balanced equations, including state symbols, for the following reactions.

a Solid calcium carbonate reacts with aqueous hydrochloric acid to form water, carbon dioxide and an aqueous solution of calcium chloride.

b An aqueous solution of zinc sulfate, $ZnSO_4$, reacts with an aqueous solution of sodium hydroxide.

The products are a precipitate of zinc hydroxide, $Zn(OH)_2$, and an aqueous solution of sodium sulfate.

Figure 3.19: The reaction between calcium carbonate and hydrochloric acid.

The equation for the reaction shown in Figure 3.19, with all the state symbols, is:

$$CaCO_3(s) + 2HCl(aq) \rightarrow CaCl_2(aq) + CO_2(g) + H_2O(l)$$

Question

17 Which is the correct equation for the reaction between iron(III) oxide and carbon monoxide?

A $Fe_2O_3(g) + 3CO(g) \rightarrow 2Fe(s) + 3CO_2(l)$

B $2FeO(s) + 2CO(g) \rightarrow 2Fe(s) + 2CO_2(l)$

C $Fe_2O_3(g) + 3CO(g) \rightarrow 2Fe(s) + 3CO_2(g)$

D $2Fe_2O_3(g) + 3CO(g) \rightarrow 4Fe(s) + 3CO_2(g)$

Balancing ionic equations

When ionic compounds dissolve in water, the ions separate from each other. For example:

$$NaCl(s) + aq \rightarrow Na^+(aq) + Cl^-(aq)$$

Ionic compounds include salts such as sodium bromide, magnesium sulfate and ammonium nitrate. Acids and alkalis also contain ions. For example, $H^+(aq)$ and $Cl^-(aq)$ ions are present in hydrochloric acid and $Na^+(aq)$ and $OH^-(aq)$ ions are present in sodium hydroxide.

Many chemical reactions in aqueous solution involve ionic compounds. Only some of the ions in solution take part in these reactions.

spectator ions: ions present in a reaction mixture which do not take part in the reaction.

ionic equation: a balanced equation showing only those ions, atoms or molecules taking part in the reaction. Spectator ions are not shown. Ionic equations are often written for reactions involving a change in oxidation state.

The ions that play no part in the reaction are called spectator ions.

An **ionic equation** is simpler than a full chemical equation. It shows only the ions or other particles taking part in a reaction. Spectator ions are omitted (left out). Ionic equations are often written for reactions involving a change in oxidation state. Compare the full equation for the reaction of zinc with aqueous copper(II) sulfate with the ionic equation.

full chemical equation:
$$Zn(s) + CuSO_4(aq) \rightarrow ZnSO_4(aq) + Cu(s)$$

with charges:
$$Zn(s) + Cu^{2+}SO_4^{2-}(aq) \rightarrow Zn^{2+}SO_4^{2-}(aq) + Cu(s)$$

cancelling spectator ions:
$$Zn(s) + Cu^{2+}\cancel{SO_4^{2-}(aq)} \rightarrow Zn^{2+}\cancel{SO_4^{2-}(aq)} + Cu(s)$$

ionic equation:
$$Zn(s) + Cu^{2+}(aq) \rightarrow Zn^{2+}(aq) + Cu(s)$$

In the ionic equation you will notice that:

- there are no sulfate ions: these are the spectator ions as they have not changed

- both the charges and the atoms are balanced.

IMPORTANT

When writing an ionic equation remember:

- The product(s) will often include a precipitate or simple molecules such as iodine or water e.g. $Cl_2(aq) + 2I^-(aq) \rightarrow I_2(aq) + 2Cl^-(aq)$

- Acids are represented by H^+ ions, e.g. $ZnO(s) + 2H^+(aq) \rightarrow Zn^{2+}(aq) + H_2O(l)$

The next examples show how we can change a full equation into an ionic equation.

WORKED EXAMPLE

18 Writing an ionic equation:

Solution

Step 1: Write down the full balanced equation.
$$Mg(s) + 2HCl(aq) \rightarrow MgCl_2(aq) + H_2(g)$$

Step 2: Write down all the ions present. Any reactant or product that has a state symbol (s), (l) or (g) or is a covalent molecule in solution such as chlorine, $Cl_2(aq)$, does not split into ions.
$$Mg(s) + 2H^+(aq) + 2Cl^-(aq) \rightarrow$$
$$Mg^{2+}(aq) + 2Cl^-(aq) + H_2(g)$$

Step 3: Cancel the ions that appear on both sides of the equation (the spectator ions).
$$Mg(s) + 2H^+(aq) + 2\cancel{Cl^-(aq)} \rightarrow$$
$$Mg^{2+}(aq) + 2\cancel{Cl^-(aq)} + H_2(g)$$

Step 4: Write down the equation omitting the spectator ions.
$$Mg(s) + 2H^+(aq) \rightarrow Mg^{2+}(aq) + H_2(g)$$

19 Write the ionic equation for the reaction of aqueous chlorine with aqueous potassium bromide. The products are aqueous bromine and aqueous potassium chloride.

Solution

Step 1: The full balanced equation is:
$$Cl_2(aq) + 2KBr(aq) \rightarrow$$
$$Br_2(aq) + 2KCl(aq)$$

Step 2: The ions present are:
$$Cl_2(aq) + 2K^+(aq) + 2Br^-(aq) \rightarrow$$
$$Br_2(aq) + 2K^+(aq) + 2Cl^-(aq)$$

Step 3: Cancel the spectator ions:
$$Cl_2(aq) + 2\cancel{K^+(aq)} + 2Br^-(aq) \rightarrow$$
$$Br_2(aq) + 2\cancel{K^+(aq)} + 2Cl^-(aq)$$

Step 4: Write the final ionic equation:
$$Cl_2(aq) + 2Br^-(aq) \rightarrow Br_2(aq) + 2Cl^-(aq)$$

Questions

18 Change these full equations to ionic equations.

a $H_2SO_4(aq) + 2NaOH(aq) \rightarrow Na_2SO_4(aq) + 2H_2O(l)$

b $Br_2(aq) + KI(aq) \rightarrow 2KBr(aq) + I_2$

19 Write ionic equations for these precipitation reactions.

a $CuSO_4(aq) + 2NaOH(aq) \rightarrow Cu(OH)_2(s) + Na_2SO_4(aq)$

b $Pb(NO_3)_2(aq) + 2KI(aq) \rightarrow PbI_2(s) + 2KNO_3(aq)$

Chemists usually prefer to write ionic equations for precipitation reactions. A precipitation reaction is a reaction where two aqueous solutions react to form a solid: the precipitate. For these reactions the method of writing the ionic equation can be simplified. All you have to do is:

- write the formula of the precipitate as the product

- write the ions that go to make up the precipitate as the reactants.

WORKED EXAMPLE

20 An aqueous solution of iron(II) sulfate reacts with an aqueous solution of sodium hydroxide. A precipitate of iron(II) hydroxide is formed, together with an aqueous solution of sodium sulfate.

Solution

Step 1: Write the full balanced equation

$FeSO_4(aq) + 2NaOH(aq) \rightarrow Fe(OH)_2(s) + Na_2SO_4(aq)$

Step 2: Identify the precipitate formed: $Fe(OH)_2(s)$

Step 3: Identify the ions which form the precipitate:

$Fe^{2+}(aq)$ and $OH^-(aq)$

Step 4: Write the ionic equation:

$Fe^{2+}(aq) + 2OH^-(aq) \rightarrow Fe(OH)_2(s)$

REFLECTION

1 Work with another learner to discuss these points:

a What are the stages in balancing a chemical equation?

b What sort of problems have you found when trying to write ionic equations?

c How do you know which species to include in the equation?

2 Make a list of the key words in this chapter so far, e.g. mole, and see if you can explain their meaning to another learner.

3 Work with another learner to discuss an activity (it could be memory aid or a game) to help you learn how to write formulae or do mole calculations. Can you teach this to someone else in your class?

3.7 Solutions and concentration

Calculating the concentration of a solution

The concentration of a solution is the amount of **solute** dissolved in a solvent to make 1 dm^3 (one cubic decimetre) of solution. The **solvent** is usually water. There are 1000 cm^3 in a cubic decimetre. When 1 mole of a compound is dissolved to make 1 dm^3 of solution the concentration is 1 mol dm^{-3}.

$$\text{concentration (mol dm}^{-3}) = \frac{\text{number of moles of solute (mol)}}{\text{volume of solution (dm}^3)}$$

We use the terms 'concentrated' and 'dilute' to refer to the relative amount of solute in the solution. A solution with a low concentration of solute is a dilute solution. If there is a high concentration of solute, the solution is concentrated.

When performing calculations involving concentrations in mol dm^{-3} you need to:

- change mass in grams to moles

- change cm^3 to dm^3 (by dividing the number of cm^3 by 1000).

KEY WORDS

solute: a substance which dissolves in a solvent to form a solution.

solvent: a substance which dissolves a solute to form a solution.

IMPORTANT

When making solutions of known concentration, you dissolve a weighed amount of solute in a small amount of solvent. Then you make it up to the required volume by adding more solvent. You do *not* add the solute to the required final volume of solvent because the total volume of the solution may then change.

WORKED EXAMPLE

21 Calculate the concentration in mol dm^{-3} of sodium hydroxide, NaOH, if 250 cm^3 of a solution contains 2.0 g of sodium hydroxide.

Solution

(M_r value: NaOH = 40.0)

Step 1: Change grams to moles.

$$\frac{2.0}{40.0} = 0.050 \text{ mol NaOH}$$

Step 2: Change cm^3 to dm^3.

$$250 \text{ cm}^3 = 0.25 \text{ dm}^3$$

Step 3: Calculate concentration.

$$\frac{0.050 \text{ (mol)}}{0.25 \text{ (dm}^3)} = 0.20 \text{ mol dm}^{-3}$$

Figure 3.20: The concentration of chlorine in the water in a swimming pool must be carefully controlled.

We often need to calculate the mass of a substance present in a solution of known concentration and volume. To do this we:

- rearrange the concentration equation to:

    number of moles (mol) = concentration (mol dm^{-3}) × volume (dm^3)

- multiply the moles of solute by its molar mass

    mass of solute (g) = number of moles (mol) × molar mass (g mol^{-1})

WORKED EXAMPLE

22 Calculate the mass of anhydrous copper(II) sulfate in 55 cm³ of a 0.20 mol dm⁻³ solution of copper(II) sulfate. (A_r values: Cu = 63.5, O = 16.0, S = 32.1)

Solution

Step 1: Change cm³ to dm³.

$$\frac{55}{1000} = 0.055 \text{ dm}^3$$

Step 2: moles = concentration (mol dm⁻³) × volume of solution (dm³)

$$= 0.20 \times 0.055 = 0.011 \text{ mol}$$

Step 3: mass (g) = moles × M

$$= 0.011 \times (63.5 + 32.1 + (4 \times 16.0))$$

$$= 1.8 \text{ g (to 2 significant figures)}$$

Question

20 a Calculate the concentration, in mol dm⁻³, of the following solutions: (A_r values: C = 12.0, H = 1.0, Na = 23.0, O = 16.0)

　i a solution of sodium hydroxide, NaOH, containing 2.0 g of sodium hydroxide in 50 cm³ of solution

　ii a solution of ethanoic acid, CH_3CO_2H, containing 12.0 g of ethanoic acid in 250 cm³ of solution.

　b Calculate the number of moles of solute dissolved in each of the following:

　i 40 cm³ of aqueous nitric acid of concentration 0.2 mol dm⁻³

　ii 50 cm³ of calcium hydroxide solution of concentration 0.01 mol dm⁻³.

PRACTICAL ACTIVITY 3.2

Carrying out a titration

A procedure called a titration is used to determine the amount of substance present in a solution of unknown concentration. There are several different kinds of titration. One of the commonest involves the exact neutralisation of an alkali by an acid (Figure 3.21).

If we want to determine the concentration of a solution of sodium hydroxide of unknown concentration we use the following procedure.

- Use a volumetric pipette to place a given volume (usually 10 cm³ or 25 cm³) of sodium hydroxide of unknown concentration into a flask.

- Get some of acid of known concentration, e.g. hydrochloric acid of concentration 1.00 mol dm⁻³

- Fill a clean burette with the acid (after having washed the burette with a little of the acid).

- Record the initial burette reading.

- Add a few drops of an indicator solution to the alkali in the flask, e.g. methyl orange.

- Slowly add the acid from the burette to the flask, swirling the flask all the time until the indicator changes colour (the end-point).

- Record the final burette reading. The final reading minus the initial reading is called the **titre**. This first titre is normally known as a 'rough' value.

- Repeat this process, adding the acid drop by drop near the end-point.

KEY WORD

titre: in a titration, the final burette reading minus the initial burette reading.

CONTINUED

- Repeat again, until you have two titres that are no more than 0.10 cm³ apart.

- Take the average of these two titre values.

Your results should be recorded in a table, looking like this:

	Rough	1	2	3
Final burette reading / cm³	37.60	38.65	36.40	34.75
Initial burette reading / cm³	2.40	4.00	1.40	0.00
Titre / cm³	35.20	34.65	35.00	34.75

Table 3.9: Example results table.

You should note:

- all burette readings are given to an accuracy of 0.05 cm³

- the units are shown like this: / cm³

- the two titres that are no more than 0.10 cm³ apart are 1 and 3, so they would be averaged

- the average titre is 34.70 cm³.

In every titration there are five important things you need to know or work out:

1. the balanced equation for the reaction
2. the volume of the solution from the burette (in this example this is hydrochloric acid)
3. the concentration of the solution in the burette
4. the volume of the solution in the titration flask (in this example this is sodium hydroxide)
5. the concentration of the solution in the titration flask.

If we know four of these five things, we can calculate the fifth. So, in order to calculate the concentration of sodium hydroxide in the flask, we need to know the first four of these points.

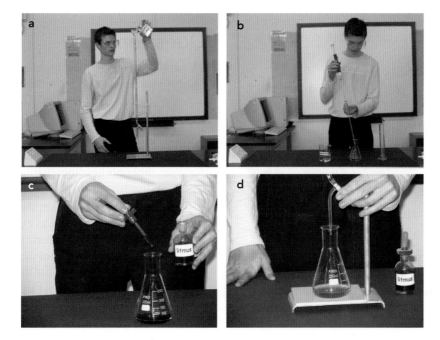

Figure 3.21: a A funnel is used to fill the burette with hydrochloric acid. **b** A graduated pipette is used to measure 25.0 cm³ of sodium hydroxide solution into a conical flask. **c** An indicator called litmus is added to the sodium hydroxide solution, which turns blue. **d** 12.5 cm³ of hydrochloric acid from the burette have been added to the 25.0 cm³ of alkali in the conical flask. The litmus has gone red, showing that this volume of acid was just enough to neutralise the alkali.

Calculating solution concentration by titration

A titration is often used to find the exact concentration of a solution. Worked example 23 shows the steps used to calculate the concentration of a solution of sodium hydroxide when it is neutralised by aqueous sulfuric acid of known concentration and volume.

WORKED EXAMPLE

23 25.0 cm^3 of a solution of sodium hydroxide is exactly neutralised by 15.10 cm^3 of sulfuric acid of concentration $0.200 \text{ mol dm}^{-3}$.

$$2NaOH + H_2SO_4 \rightarrow Na_2SO_4 + 2H_2O$$

Calculate the concentration, in mol dm^{-3}, of the sodium hydroxide solution.

Solution

Step 1: Calculate how many moles of acid.

moles = concentration $(\text{mol dm}^{-3}) \times$
volume of solution (dm^3)

$0.200 \times \frac{15.10}{1000} = 0.00302 \text{ mol } H_2SO_4$

Step 2: Use the stoichiometry of the balanced equation to calculate how many moles of NaOH.

moles of NaOH =
moles of acid (from step 1) $\times 2$
$= 0.00604 \text{ mol}$

Step 3: Calculate the concentration of NaOH.

concentration $(\text{mol dm}^{-3}) =$

$\dfrac{\text{number of moles of solute (mol)}}{\text{volume of solution (dm}^3)}$

$= \dfrac{0.00604}{0.0250}$

$= 0.242 \text{ mol dm}^{-3}$

Note:

- In the first step we use the reagent for which the concentration and volume are both known.

- In step 2, we multiply by 2 because the balanced equation shows that 2 mol of NaOH reacts with every 1 mol of H_2SO_4.

CONTINUED

- In step 3, we divide by 0.0250 because we have changed cm^3 to dm^3 $0.0250 = \frac{25.0}{1000}$

- The answer is given to 3 significant figures because the smallest number of significant figures in the data is 3.

IMPORTANT

When doing calculations from the results of titrations, remember:
- average only those titres which are very close to each other, e.g. within 0.1–0.2 cm^3 of each other, *and* ignore the rough (rangefinder) titration.

- keep the units the same. It is often easier to convert volumes in cm^3 to dm^3 because **solution concentration** is usually given in mol dm^{-3}.

Note that in some older books M is sometimes used in place of mol dm^{-3}.

Question

21 a The equation for the reaction of strontium hydroxide with hydrochloric acid is shown below.

$$Sr(OH)_2 + 2HCl \rightarrow SrCl_2 + 2H_2O$$

25.0 cm^3 of a solution of strontium hydroxide was exactly neutralised by 15.00 cm^3 of $0.100 \text{ mol dm}^{-3}$ hydrochloric acid. Calculate the concentration, in mol dm^{-3}, of the strontium hydroxide solution.

b 20.0 cm^3 of a $0.400 \text{ mol dm}^{-3}$ solution of sodium hydroxide was exactly neutralised by 25.25 cm^3 of sulfuric acid. Calculate the concentration, in mol dm^{-3}, of the sulfuric acid. The equation for the reaction is:

$$H_2SO_4 + 2NaOH \rightarrow Na_2SO_4 + 2H_2O$$

Deducing stoichiometry by titration

We can use titration results to find the stoichiometry of a reaction. In order to do this, we need to know the concentrations and the volumes of both the reactants. Worked example 24 shows how to determine the stoichiometry of the reaction between a metal hydroxide and an acid.

WORKED EXAMPLE

24 25.0 cm^3 of a $0.0500 \text{ mol dm}^{-3}$ solution of a metal hydroxide was titrated against a solution of $0.200 \text{ mol dm}^{-3}$ hydrochloric acid. It required 12.50 cm^3 of hydrochloric acid to exactly neutralise the metal hydroxide. Deduce the stoichiometry of this reaction.

Solution

Step 1: Calculate the number of moles of each reagent.

moles of metal hydroxide = concentration (mol dm^{-3}) × volume of solution (dm^3)

$$= 0.0500 \times \frac{25.0}{1000} = 1.25 \times 10^{-3} \text{ mol}$$

moles of hydrochloric acid = concentration (mol dm^{-3}) × volume of solution (dm^3)

$$= 0.200 \times \frac{12.50}{1000} = 2.50 \times 10^{-3} \text{ mol}$$

Step 2: Deduce the simplest mole ratio of metal hydroxide to hydrochloric acid.

1.25×10^{-3} moles of hydroxide : 2.50×10^{-3} moles of acid = 1 hydroxide : 2 acid

Step 3: Write the equation.

$$M(OH)_2 + 2HCl \rightarrow MCl_2 + 2H_2O$$

One mole of hydroxide ions neutralises one mole of hydrogen ions. As one mole of the metal hydroxide neutralises two moles of hydrochloric acid, the metal hydroxide must contain two hydroxide ions in each formula unit.

KEY WORD

solution concentration: the amount of solute (in moles) dissolved in a stated volume of solution (usually in 1.00 dm^3).

Questions

22 20.0 cm^3 of a metal hydroxide of concentration $0.0600 \text{ mol dm}^{-3}$ was titrated with $0.100 \text{ mol dm}^{-3}$ hydrochloric acid. It required 24.00 cm^3 of the hydrochloric acid to exactly neutralise the metal hydroxide.

a Calculate the number of moles of metal hydroxide used.

b Calculate the number of moles of hydrochloric acid used.

c What is the simplest mole ratio of metal hydroxide to hydrochloric acid?

d Write a balanced equation for this reaction using your answers to parts **a**, **b** and **c** to help you. Use the symbol M for the metal.

23 0.4 moles of aluminium sulfate, $Al_2(SO_4)_3$, are dissolved in water and the volume of the solution was made up to 500 cm^3. Which one of these statements is correct?

A The solution contains a total of 2 moles of ions.

B The concentration of aluminium ions is 0.8 mol dm^{-3}.

C The concentration of sulfate ions in solution is 1.2 mol dm^{-3}.

D The solution contains a total of 4 moles of ions.

3.8 Calculations involving gas volumes

Using the molar gas volume

In 1811 the Italian scientist Amedeo Avogadro suggested that equal volumes of all gases contain the same number of molecules. This is called *Avogadro's hypothesis*. This idea is approximately true as long as the pressure is not too high or the temperature too low. It is convenient to measure volumes of gases at room temperature (20 °C) and pressure (1 atmosphere). At room temperature and pressure (r.t.p.) one mole of any gas has a volume of 24.0 dm^3. So, 24.0 dm^3 of carbon dioxide and 24.0 dm^3 of hydrogen both contain one mole of gas molecules.

We can use the **molar gas volume** of 24.0 dm³ at r.t.p. to find:

- the volume of a given mass or number of moles of gas
- the mass or number of moles of a given volume of gas.

KEY WORD

molar gas volume: the volume occupied by one mole of any gas at room temperature and pressure (r.t.p.). One mole of gas occupies 24.0 dm³ at r.t.p.

WORKED EXAMPLES

25 Calculate the volume of 0.40 mol of nitrogen at r.t.p.

Solution

volume (in dm³) = 24.0 × number of moles of gas
= 24.0 × 0.40 = 9.6 dm³

26 Calculate the mass of methane, CH_4, present in 120 cm³ of methane. (M_r value: methane = 16.0)

Solution

120 cm³ is 0.120 dm³ $\left(\dfrac{120}{1000} = 0.120 \right)$

moles of methane = $\dfrac{\text{volume of methane (dm}^3\text{)}}{24.0}$

$= \dfrac{0.120}{24.0} = 5 \times 10^{-3}$ mol

mass of methane $= 5 \times 10^{-3} \times 16.0$
$= 0.080$ g methane

Question

24 a Calculate the volume, in dm³, occupied by 26.4 g of carbon dioxide at r.t.p.
(A_r values: C = 12.0, O = 16.0)

b A flask of volume 120 cm³ is filled with helium gas at r.t.p. Calculate the mass of helium present in the flask. (A_r value: He = 4.0)

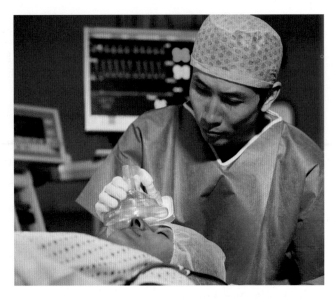

Figure 3.22: Anaesthetists have to know about gas volumes so that patients remain unconscious during major operations.

Gas volumes and stoichiometry

We can use the ratio of reacting volumes of gases to deduce the stoichiometry of a reaction. If we mix 20 cm³ of hydrogen with 10 cm³ of oxygen and explode the mixture, we will find that the gases have exactly reacted together and no hydrogen or oxygen remains. According to Avogadro's hypothesis, equal volumes of gases contain equal numbers of molecules and therefore equal numbers of moles of gases. So the mole ratio of hydrogen to oxygen is 2 : 1. We can summarise this as:

	hydrogen	+	oxygen	→	water
	(H_2)		(O_2)		(H_2O)
	20 cm³		10 cm³		
ratio of moles	2	:	1		
equation	$2H_2$	+	O_2	→	$2H_2O$

We can extend this idea to experiments involving combustion data of hydrocarbons. Worked example 27 shows how the formula of propane and the stoichiometry of the equation can be deduced. Propane is a hydrocarbon: a compound of carbon and hydrogen only.

WORKED EXAMPLE

27 When 50 cm³ of propane reacts exactly with 250 cm³ of oxygen, 150 cm³ of carbon dioxide is formed.

propane + oxygen → carbon dioxide + water

$$C_xH_y \qquad (O_2) \qquad (CO_2) \qquad (H_2O)$$

50 cm³   250 cm³   150 cm³

Solution

ratio of moles:

   1   5   3

As 1 mole of propane produces 3 moles of carbon dioxide, there must be 3 moles of carbon atoms in one mole of propane, $x = 3$.

$$C_3H_y + 5O_2 \rightarrow 3CO_2 + zH_2O$$

The 5 moles of oxygen molecules are used to react with both the carbon and the hydrogen in the propane. 3 moles of these oxygen molecules have been used in forming carbon dioxide.
So $5 - 3 = 2$ moles of oxygen molecules must be used in reacting with the hydrogen to form water. There are 4 moles of atoms in 2 moles of oxygen molecules, so there must be 4 moles of water formed.

$$C_3H_y + 5O_2 \rightarrow 3CO_2 + 4H_2O$$

So there must be 8 hydrogen atoms in 1 molecule of propane.

$$C_3H_8 + 5O_2 \rightarrow 3CO_2 + 4H_2O$$

Questions

25 50 cm³ of a gaseous hydride of phosphorus, PH_n reacts with exactly 150 cm³ of chlorine, Cl_2, to form liquid phosphorus trichloride and 150 cm³ of hydrogen chloride gas, HCl.

   a How many moles of chlorine react with 1 mole of the gaseous hydride?

   b Deduce the formula of the phosphorus hydride.

   c Write a balanced equation for the reaction.

26 What is the volume of carbon dioxide produced when 14 g of ethene, C_2H_4, reacts with excess oxygen? (M_r ethene = 28)

$$C_2H_4(g) + 3O_2(g) \rightarrow 2CO_2(g) + 2H_2O(l)$$

   A 96.0 dm³

   B 24.0 dm³

   C 0.0467 dm³

   D 12.0 dm³

REFLECTION

1 Make a list of the chemical expressions that you have learned during this chapter, e.g. the relationship between moles, mass and relative molecular mass.

2 Compare your list with another learner then write the expressions out in as many different ways as you can, e.g. the expression $density = \frac{mass}{volume}$ could be rewritten as $mass = density \times volume$

What problems did you come across? How did you solve them?

SUMMARY

Unified atomic mass unit is one twelfth of the mass of a carbon-12 atom.
Relative atomic mass is the ratio of the weighted average mass of atoms in a given sample of an element to the unified atomic mass unit.
The mass spectrometer can be used to determine atomic masses and isotopic abundances, to deduce the molecular mass of an organic compound and to deduce the formula of an organic molecule from its fragmentation pattern and isotopic ratios.
One mole of a substance is the amount of substance that has the Avogadro number of specified particles (6.02×10^{23}). The particles can be atoms, molecules, ions or electrons.
Molecular formulae show the total number of atoms of each element present in one molecule or one formula unit of the compound. Empirical formulae show the simplest whole number ratio of atoms in a compound.
The mole concept can be used to calculate: • reacting masses   • volumes of gases   • volumes and concentrations of solutions.
The stoichiometry of a reaction can be obtained from calculations involving reacting masses, gas volumes, and volumes and concentrations of solutions.

EXAM-STYLE QUESTIONS

1   a   i   State the meaning of the term *relative atomic mass*.   [1]

   ii   A sample of boron was found to have the following % composition by mass: $_{5}^{10}B$ (18.7%), $_{5}^{11}B$ (81.3%)

   Calculate a value for the relative atomic mass of boron.
   Give your answer to 3 significant figures.   [2]

   b   Boron ions, B^{3+}, can be formed by bombarding gaseous boron with high-energy electrons. Deduce the number of electrons in one B^{3+} ion.   [1]

   c   Boron is present in compounds called *borates*.

   i   Use the A_r values below to calculate the relative molecular mass of iron(III) borate, $Fe(BO_2)_3$.
   (A_r values: Fe = 55.8, B = 10.8, O = 16.0)   [1]

   ii   The accurate relative atomic mass of iron, Fe, is 55.8. Explain why the accurate relative atomic mass is not a whole number.   [1]

   [Total: 6]

2   This question is about some metals and metal compounds.

   a   i   Hafnium, Hf, forms a hydrated peroxide whose formula can be written as $HfO_3 \cdot 2H_2O$. Use the A_r values below to calculate the relative molecular mass of hydrated hafnium peroxide.
   (A_r values: Hf = 178.5, H = 1.0, O = 16.0)   [1]

   ii   What is meant by the term *hydrated salt*?   [1]

COMMAND WORD

Calculate: work out from given facts, figures or information

CONTINUED

b A particular isotope of hafnium has 72 protons and a nucleon number of 180. Write the isotopic symbol for this isotope, showing this information. [1]

c The mass spectrum of zirconium is shown below.

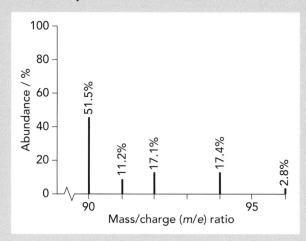

i Give the isotopic symbol for the most abundant isotope of zirconium. [1]

ii Use the information from this mass spectrum to calculate the relative atomic mass of zirconium. Give your answer to 3 significant figures. [2]

iii High-resolution mass spectra show accurate relative isotopic masses. State the meaning of the term *relative isotopic mass*? [1]

d A sample of 15.2 g of tin(IV) oxide is mixed with 2.41 g of carbon and heated. A reaction occurs.

$$SnO_2 + 2C \rightarrow Sn + 2CO$$

Show by calculation that the reagent in excess is tin(IV) oxide. (A_r values: Sn = 118.7, C = 12.0, O = 16.0). [2]

e A sample of zirconium is made by reacting 58.30 g of zirconium tetrachloride, $ZrCl_4$, with excess magnesium.

$$ZrCl_4 + 2Mg \rightarrow Zr + 2MgCl_2$$

The mass of zirconium produced is 20.52 g. Calculate the percentage yield of zirconium. (A_r values: Zr = 91.2, Cl = 35.5, Mg = 24.3) [2]

[Total: 11]

3 Solid sodium carbonate reacts with aqueous hydrochloric acid to form aqueous sodium chloride, carbon dioxide and water.

$$Na_2CO_3 + 2HCl \rightarrow 2NaCl + CO_2 + H_2O$$

a Rewrite this equation to include state symbols. [1]

b Calculate the number of moles of hydrochloric acid required to react exactly with 4.15 g of sodium carbonate. (A_r values: C = 12.0, Na = 23.0, O = 16.0, H = 1.0, Cl = 35.5) [3]

CONTINUED

c   Define the term *mole*. [1]

d   An aqueous solution of 25.0 cm³ sodium carbonate of concentration 0.0200 mol dm⁻³ is titrated with hydrochloric acid. The volume of hydrochloric acid required to exactly react with the sodium carbonate is 12.50 cm³.

   i   Calculate the number of moles of sodium carbonate present in the solution of sodium carbonate. [1]

   ii Calculate the concentration of the hydrochloric acid. [2]

e   How many moles of carbon dioxide are produced when 0.2 mol of sodium carbonate reacts with excess hydrochloric acid? [1]

f   Calculate the volume of this number of moles of carbon dioxide at r.t.p. (1 mol of gas occupies 24 dm³ at r.t.p.) [1]

[Total: 10]

4   Hydrocarbons are compounds of carbon and hydrogen only. Hydrocarbon Z is composed of 80% carbon and 20% hydrogen.

a   Calculate the empirical formula of hydrocarbon Z. (A_r values: C = 12.0, H = 1.0) [3]

b   The molar mass of hydrocarbon Z is 30.0 g mol⁻¹. Deduce the molecular formula of this hydrocarbon. [1]

c   When 50 cm³ of hydrocarbon Y is burnt, it reacts with exactly 300 cm³ of oxygen to form 200 cm³ of carbon dioxide. Water is also formed in the reaction. Construct the equation for this reaction. Explain your reasoning. [4]

d   Propane has the molecular formula C_3H_8. Calculate the mass of 600 cm³ of propane at r.t.p. (1 mol of gas occupies 24 dm³ at r.t.p.) (A_r values: C = 12.0, H = 1.0) [2]

[Total: 10]

5   When sodium reacts with titanium chloride ($TiCl_4$), sodium chloride (NaCl) and titanium (Ti) are produced.

a   Construct the balanced symbol equation for the reaction. [2]

b   Calculate the mass of titanium produced from 380 g of titanium chloride. Give your answer to 3 significant figures. (A_r values: Ti = 47.9, Cl = 35.5) [2]

c   Calculate the mass of titanium produced using 46.0 g of sodium. Give your answer to 3 significant figures. (A_r value: Na = 23.0) [2]

[Total: 6]

6   In this question give all answers to 3 significant figures.

The reaction between NaOH and HCl can be written as:

$HCl + NaOH \rightarrow NaCl + H_2O$

CONTINUED

In this reaction, 15.0 cm³ of hydrochloric acid was neutralised by 20.0 cm³ of 0.0500 mol dm⁻³ sodium hydroxide.

a   Calculate the volume in dm³ of:

   i   the acid [1]

   ii   the alkali [1]

b   Calculate the number of moles of alkali. [1]

c   Calculate the number of moles of acid and then its concentration. [2]

[Total: 5]

7   Give all answers to 3 significant figures.

Ammonium nitrate decomposes on heating to give nitrogen(II) oxide and water as follows:

$$NH_4NO_3(s) \rightarrow N_2O(g) + 2H_2O(l)$$

(A_r values: N = 14.0; H = 1.0; O = 16.0)

a   Deduce the formula mass of ammonium nitrate. [1]

b   How many moles of ammonium nitrate are present in 0.800 g of the solid? [2]

c   Calculate the volume of N_2O gas that would be produced from this mass of ammonium nitrate? [2]

[Total: 5]

8   Give all answers to 3 significant figures.

a   1.20 dm³ of hydrogen chloride gas was dissolved in 100 cm³ of water.

   i   Calculate the number of moles of hydrogen chloride gas present. [1]

   ii   Calculate the concentration of the hydrochloric acid formed. [2]

b   25.0 cm³ of the acid was then titrated against sodium hydroxide of concentration 0.200 mol dm⁻³ to form NaCl and water:

$$NaOH + HCl \rightarrow H_2O + NaCl$$

   i   Calculate the number of moles of acid used. [2]

   ii   Calculate the volume of sodium hydroxide used. [2]

[Total: 7]

9   Give all answers to 3 significant figures.

4.80 dm³ of chlorine gas was reacted with sodium hydroxide solution. The reaction taking place was as follows:

$$Cl_2(g) + 2NaOH(aq) \rightarrow NaCl(aq) + NaOCl(aq) + H_2O(l)$$

(A_r values: Na = 23.0; Cl = 35.5; O = 16.0)

a   Calculate the number of moles of Cl_2 reacted. [1]

b   Calculate the mass of NaOCl formed. [2]

c   The concentration of the NaOH was 2.00 mol dm⁻³. Calculate the volume of sodium hydroxide solution required. [2]

d   Write an ionic equation for this reaction. [1]

[Total: 6]

CONTINUED

10 Calcium oxide reacts with hydrochloric acid according to the equation:

$$CaO + 2HCl \rightarrow CaCl_2 + H_2O$$

A_r values: H = 1.0; O = 16.0; Cl = 35.5; Ca = 40.1

a Calculate the mass of calcium chloride formed when 28.05 g of calcium oxide reacts with excess hydrochloric acid. [2]

b Calculate the mass of hydrochloric acid that reacts with 28.05 g of calcium oxide. [2]

c Calculate the mass of water produced. [1]

[Total: 5]

11 When ammonia gas and hydrogen chloride gas mix together, they react to form a solid called ammonium chloride.

A_r values: H = 1.0; N = 14.0; Cl = 35.5

a Write a balanced equation for this reaction, including state symbols. [2]

b Calculate the molar masses of ammonia, hydrogen chloride and ammonium chloride. [3]

c Calculate the volumes of ammonia and hydrogen chloride gases that must react at r.t.p. in order to produce 10.7 g of ammonium chloride? (1 mol of gas occupies 24 dm³ at r.t.p.) [3]

[Total: 8]

12 The mass spectrum of an organic compound with the structure $CH_3CH_2CH_2CH_3$ is shown.

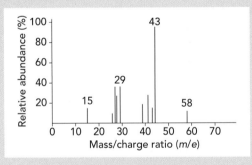

a Identify the fragments with mass/charge ratios of

i 15 **ii** 29 **iii** 43 **iv** 58 [4]

b An organic compound, Z, has a molecular ion peak, M, with a relative abundance of 36.4% and an [$M + 1$] peak with a relative abundance of 4.8 %. Deduce the number of carbon atoms this compound contains. [2]

c The mass spectrum of chlorobutane shows an [$M + 2$] peak beyond the M_r peak. Explain why there is an [$M + 2$] peak. [1]

d The relative height of the [$M + 2$] peak in organic compound T is the same as that of the M_r peak. Explain how this shows that the compound contains one atom of bromine and not one atom of chlorine. [3]

[Total: 10]

SELF-EVALUATION

After studying this chapter, complete a table like this:

I can	See section...	Needs more work	Almost there	Ready to move on
define and use the terms *unified atomic mass unit, relative atomic mass, relative isotopic mass* and *relative formula mass*	3.1			
analyse mass spectra in terms of isotopic abundances	3.3			
deduce the accurate relative atomic mass of an element using data from a mass spectrum	3.3			
deduce the molecular mass of an organic molecule from the molecular ion peak in a mass spectrum	3.3			
suggest the identity of molecules formed by simple fragmentation in a given mass spectrum	3.3			
deduce the number of carbon atoms in a compound using the $[M + 1]$ peak and the relevant formula: $n = \dfrac{100}{1.1} \times \dfrac{\text{abundance of } [M+1]^+ \text{ ion}}{\text{abundance of } M^+ \text{ ion}}$	3.3			
deduce the presence of chlorine and bromine atoms in a compound using the $[M + 2]$ peak	3.3			
define and use the terms *mole* and *Avogadro constant*	3.4			
understand the meaning of the terms *anhydrous, hydrated* and *water of crystallisation*	3.2			
write formulae of ionic compounds from ionic charges and oxidation numbers including: **a** the prediction of ionic charge from the position of an element in the Periodic Table **b** recall of the names and formulae for the ions NO_3^-, CO_3^{2-}, SO_4^{2-}, OH^-, NH_4^+, Zn^{2+}, Ag^+, HCO_3^- and PO_4^{3-}	3.6			
write and construct balanced equations, including ionic equations	3.6			
use the correct state symbols in equations	3.6			
define and use the terms *empirical formula* and *molecular formula*	3.5			
calculate empirical and molecular formulae using given data	3.5			
perform calculations using the mole concept involving reacting masses	3.5			
understand the terms *excess reactant* and *limiting reactant*	3.5			
perform calculations using mole concept involving **a** percentage yield **b** volumes of gases **c** concentrations of solutions **d** limiting reagents and excess reagent	3.5, 3.7, 3.8			
deduce stoichiometry of a reaction using reacting masses, volumes of gases and volumes and concentrations of solutions.	3.5			

› Chapter 4
Chemical bonding

LEARNING INTENTIONS

In this chapter you will learn how to:

- define *electronegativity* and explain the factors influencing the electronegativity values of the elements

- explain the trends in electronegativity across a period and down a group in the Periodic Table

- use differences in the Pauling electronegativity values to predict if a compound has ionic or covalent bonds

- define *ionic bonding* and describe ionic bonding in compounds such as sodium chloride, magnesium oxide and calcium fluoride

- define *covalent bonding* and describe covalent bonding in molecules such as hydrogen, oxygen, nitrogen, chlorine, hydrogen chloride, carbon dioxide, ammonia, methane, ethane and ethene

- describe how some atoms in Period 3 can expand their octet of electrons to form compounds such as sulfur dioxide, phosphorus pentachloride and sulfur hexafluoride

- describe co-ordinate bonding (dative covalent bonding) in ions such as NH_4^+ and molecules such as Al_2Cl_6

CONTINUED

- use dot-and-cross diagrams to show the arrangement of electrons in compounds with ionic, covalent and co-ordinate bonding

- describe covalent bonding in terms of orbital overlap giving sigma (σ) and pi (π) bonds

- describe how sigma and pi bonds form in molecules such as H_2, C_2H_6, C_2H_4, HCN and N_2

- describe hybridisation of atomic orbitals to form sp, sp^2 and sp^3 orbitals

- define the terms *bond energy* and *bond length* and use these to compare the reactions of covalent molecules

- describe and explain the shapes and bond angles in simple molecules (such as BF_3, CO_2, CH_4, NH_3, H_2O, SF_6 and PF_5) using 'valence shell electron pair repulsion' theory (VSEPR)

- predict the shapes and bond angles in other molecules and ions similar to those above

- describe hydrogen bonding and explain, in terms of hydrogen bonding, why some physical properties of water are unusual for a molecular compound

- use electronegativity values to explain bond polarity and dipole moments in molecules

- describe and understand the different types of intermolecular forces (van der Waals' forces) as either instantaneous dipoles or permanent dipoles

- describe metallic bonding

- describe the relative bond strengths of ionic, covalent and metallic bonds compared with intermolecular forces.

BEFORE YOU START

1   Take it in turns to explain to another learner what is meant by each of the following:

    a   covalent bonding

    b   ionic bonding

    c   metallic bonding

    d   intermolecular forces

    Mention the types of particles that are responsible for the attractive forces between the atoms or ions.

2   Draw a labelled diagram of an ionic compound and a simple covalent compound. Compare your diagrams with those of another learner.

3   Make a list of the typical physical properties of metals such as iron and non-meals such as sulfur. Compare your list with the list made by others in the class.

4   Ask another learner to select one of the first 20 elements in the Periodic Table. Can you deduce the simple electronic configuration for an atom of this element? Take turns in doing this until you are sure that you can write simple electronic configurations.

CONTINUED

5   Explain to another learner how to work out the number of electrons in the outer principal energy level of atoms in Groups 1 and 2 and in Groups 13–18 (you may know Groups 13 to 18 as Groups 3 to 8)

6   Ask another learner to select one of the positive ions: sodium, magnesium or calcium, and one of the negative ions: oxygen, chlorine or bromine. Draw the simple electronic configuration for the positive and negative ions selected and then draw a dot-and-cross diagram for the compound formed from these ions.

7   How confident are you in drawing dot-and-cross diagrams for molecules? Without looking at a textbook, work with a partner to draw dot-and-cross diagrams for the following molecules:

   a   hydrogen

   b   chlorine

   c   hydrogen chloride

   d   methane (CH_4)

   e   water

   f   ammonia

   g   oxygen

   Show only the outer shell electrons.

8   Try this problem by yourself and then discuss your ideas with a partner.

   Lone pairs of electrons repel each other more than a pair of electrons in a bond. Draw the electronic structure of a methane molecule and a water molecule and suggest why the methane molecule has an H—C—H bond angle of about 109.5° but a water molecule has an H—O—H bond angle of 104.5°.

SKATING ON WATER

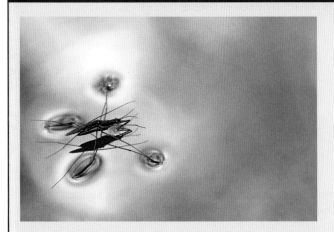

Figure 4.1: The intermolecular forces in water allow some insects to skate over its surface.

Some insects can skate across the surface of a pond (Figure 4.1). How do they do this? Part of the answer is that water has unusual physical properties due to the strong forces of attraction (intermolecular forces) between the water molecules. The unusually strong intermolecular forces in water are due to hydrogen bonding. These attractive forces make it more difficult for water molecules to slide over each other compared with most other liquids. A water molecule below the surface is attracted equally in all directions to other water molecules. At the surface, where water and air meet, there is hardly any attraction between the molecules in the air and the water molecules. But the water molecules at the surface are strongly attracted to each other. So there is a

CONTINUED

downward force at the surface of the liquid which pulls the surface inwards. This surface tension causes the surface of the water to appear to have an elastic skin. You can float a paper clip on water to demonstrate surface tension:

- Fill a glass right up to the top with water.

- Take a paper clip and lower it gently onto the surface of the water using a fork.

Skating insects take advantage of the high surface tension of water by having special features such as wide feet. These feet are also covered in a hard layer which repels water.

Questions for discussion

Discuss with another learner or group of learners:

- Suggest why skating insects have wide feet and not narrow feet.

- Can you think of any liquids that do not mix with water and are lighter than water?

- Suggest why a soft paper-like layer on insect's feet would not allow them to stay on the surface of the water.

- Imagine that you are designing an insect that can skate perfectly on water. What other features would be useful?

4.1 Types of chemical bonding

IMPORTANT

When elements form compounds, they either gain, lose or share electrons to get to the nearest stable noble gas electronic configuration. There are exceptions to this rule for some Group 15, 16 and 17 elements.

Ionic bonding is the electrostatic attraction between positive ions (**cations**) and negative ions (**anions**) in an ionic crystal **lattice**. Covalent bonds are formed when the outer electrons of two atoms are shared. The ionic or covalent bonds formed are usually very strong: it takes a lot of energy to break them. There is also a third form of strong bonding: metallic bonding.

Although the atoms within molecules are kept together by strong covalent bonds, the forces between molecules are weak. We call these weak forces between molecules **van der Waals' forces**. The term van der Waals' forces is a general term used to describe all **intermolecular forces**.

There are several types of van der Waals forces:

- dipole (instantaneous dipole–induced dipole (id–id) forces. These are also called *London dispersion forces*.

- permanent dipole–permanent dipole (pd–pd) forces.

- hydrogen bonding, which is a stronger form of permanent dipole–permanent dipole force.

If you understand these different types of chemical bonding and understand intermolecular forces, this will help you to explain the structure and some physical properties of elements and compounds.

KEY WORDS

anion: a negatively charged ion.

cation: a positively charged ion.

lattice: a regularly repeating arrangement of atoms, molecules or ions in three dimensions throughout the whole crystal structure.

van der Waals' forces: weak forces of attraction between molecules involving either instantaneous (id–id) or permanent dipole–permanent dipole forces (pd–pd) (including hydrogen bonding). The expression covers all types of intermolecular forces.

intermolecular forces: the weak forces between molecules.

4.2 Ionic bonding

How are ions formed?

One way of forming ions is for atoms to gain or lose one or more electrons.

- Positive ions are formed when an atom loses one or more electrons. Metal atoms usually lose electrons and form positive ions.

- Negative ions are formed when an atom gains one or more electrons. Non-metal atoms usually gain electrons and form negative ions.

The charge on the ion depends on the number of electrons lost or gained (see Section 2.4).

When metals combine with non-metals, the electrons in the outer shell of the metal atoms are transferred to the non-metal atoms. Each non-metal atom usually gains enough electrons to fill its outer shell. As a result of this, the metal atoms and non-metal atoms usually end up with outer electron shells that are complete: they have the electronic configuration of a noble gas.

In Figure 4.2 we can see that:

- the sodium ion has the same electronic structure as neon: $[2,8]^+$

- the chloride ion has the same electronic structure as argon: $[2,8,8]^-$.

The strong force of attraction between the positive ions and negative ions in the ionic crystal lattice results in an **ionic bond**. An ionic bond is sometimes called an **electrovalent bond**. In an ionic structure such as sodium chloride crystals (Figure 4.3), the ions are arranged in a regular repeating pattern (see Chapter 5). As a result of this, the force between one ion and the ions of opposite charge that surround it is very great. In other words, ionic bonding is very strong.

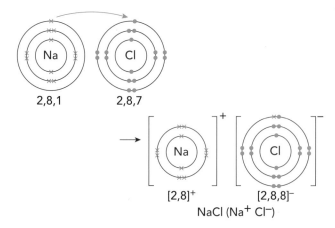

Figure 4.2: The formation of a sodium ion and chloride ion by electron transfer.

Figure 4.3: These crystals of salt are made up of millions of sodium ions and chloride ions.

KEY DEFINITION

ionic bonding: the electrostatic attraction between oppositely charged ions (cations and anions).

KEY WORDS

electrovalent bond: another name for an ionic bond.

dot-and-cross diagram: a diagram showing the arrangement of the outer-shell electrons in an ionic or covalent element or compound. The electrons are shown as dots or crosses to show their origin.

Dot-and-cross diagrams

You will notice that in Figure 4.2 we use dots and crosses to show the electronic configuration of the chloride and sodium ions. This helps us keep track of where the electrons have come from. It does not mean that the electron transferred is any different from the others. Diagrams like this are called **dot-and-cross diagrams**.

When drawing a dot-and-cross diagram for an ionic compound it is usually acceptable to draw the outer electron shell of the metal ion without any electrons. This is because it has transferred these electrons to the negative ion. Figure 4.4 shows the outer shell dot-and-cross diagram for sodium chloride.

A dot-and-cross diagram shows:

- the outer electron shells only
- the charge of the ion is spread evenly, by using square brackets
- the charge on each ion, written at the top right-hand corner.

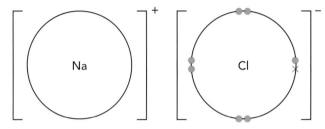

Figure 4.4: Dot-and-cross diagram for sodium chloride.

Some examples of dot-and-cross diagrams

Magnesium oxide

When magnesium reacts with oxygen to form magnesium oxide, the two electrons in the outer shell of each magnesium atom are transferred to the incompletely filled orbitals of an oxygen atom. By losing two electrons, each magnesium atom achieves the electronic configuration [2,8] (Figure 4.5). By gaining two electrons, each oxygen atom achieves the electronic configuration [2,8]. [2,8] is the electronic configuration of neon. It is sometimes called a *noble-gas configuration*. When ions or atoms have 8 electrons in their outer shell like this it is called an *octet of electrons* (the prefix oct means 8).

Figure 4.5: Dot-and-cross diagram for magnesium oxide.

Calcium fluoride

Each calcium atom has two electrons in its outer shell, and these can be transferred to two fluorine atoms. By losing two electrons, each calcium atom achieves the electronic configuration [2,8,8] (Figure 4.6). The two fluorine atoms each gain one electron to achieve

the electronic configuration [2,8]. [2,8] is the electronic configuration of neon; it is a 'noble-gas configuration'.

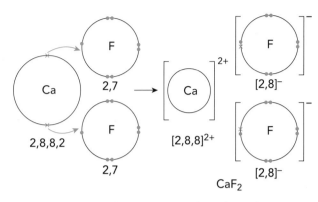

Figure 4.6: Dot-and-cross diagram for calcium fluoride.

Question

1   Draw dot-and-cross diagrams for the ions in the following ionic compounds. Show only the outer electron shells.
    a   Potassium chloride, KCl
    b   Sodium oxide, Na_2O
    c   Calcium oxide, CaO
    d   Magnesium chloride, $MgCl_2$

4.3 Covalent bonding

Single covalent bonds

When two non-metal atoms combine, they share one or more pairs of electrons. A shared pair of electrons is called a *single covalent bond*, or a *bond pair*. A single **covalent bond** is represented by a single line between the atoms: for example, Cl—Cl.

> **KEY DEFINITIONS**
>
> **covalent bonding:** the electrostatic attraction between the nuclei of two atoms and a shared pair of electrons.
>
> **lone pairs (of electrons):** pairs of electrons in the outer shell of an atom that are not involved in bonding.

You can see that when chlorine atoms combine not all the electrons are used in bonding. The pairs of outer-shell electrons not used in bonding are called **lone pairs**.

Figure 4.7: a Bromine and **b** iodine are elements. They both have simple covalent molecules.

Each atom in a chlorine molecule has three lone pairs of electrons and shares one bonding pair of electrons (Figure 4.8).

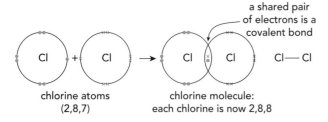

Figure 4.8: Atoms of chlorine share electrons to form a single covalent bond.

IMPORTANT

A dot-and-cross diagram shows the arrangement of the electrons in the main energy levels. We generally only show the outer energy level when we draw dot-and-cross diagrams. Remember that we only draw the electrons as dots and crosses to show us which atoms the electrons come from.

When drawing the arrangement of electrons in a molecule:

- use a 'dot' for electrons from one of the atoms and a 'cross' for the electrons from the other atom

- if there are more than two types of atom, use additional symbols such as a small circle or a small triangle

- draw the outer electrons in pairs, to show the number of bond pairs and the number of lone pairs.

Some examples of dot-and-cross diagrams for simple covalently bonded molecules are shown in Figure 4.9.

There are some cases in which the electrons around a central atom may not have a noble gas configuration (an octet of electrons). For example:

- boron trifluoride, BF_3, has only six electrons around the boron atom. We say that the boron atom is 'electron deficient'.

- sulfur hexafluoride, SF_6, has twelve electrons around the central sulfur atom. We say that the sulfur atom has an 'expanded octet' (Figure 4.10).

- phosphorus(V) chloride, PCl_5, has 10 electrons around the central phosphorus atom. Phosphorus has expanded its octet (Figure 4.10).

- sulfur dioxide, SO_2, the sulfur atom forms a double bond with each oxygen atom. This leaves a pair of non-bonding electrons on the sulfur atom. There are 10 electrons around the sulfur atom. Sulfur has expanded its octet (Figure 4.10).

Some elements in Periods 15, 16 and 17 have more than 8 electrons in their outer shell when they form compounds. According to one theory they use unfilled p-orbitals or d-orbitals in the third main energy level for the extra electrons. Some common examples of this expansion of the octet are seen in compounds of phosphorus, sulfur and chlorine with oxygen or fluorine.

Question

2 Draw dot-and-cross diagrams for the following covalently bonded molecules. Show only the outer electron shells. Note that in part **d** the beryllium atom is electron deficient and in part **e** the antimony atom has an expanded octet.

   a tetrachloromethane, CCl_4

   b phosphorus(III) chloride

   c bromine, Br_2

   d beryllium chloride, $BeCl_2$

   e antimony pentafluoride, $SbFl_5$

a hydrogen

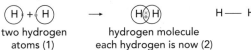

two hydrogen atoms (1)

hydrogen molecule each hydrogen is now (2)

b methane

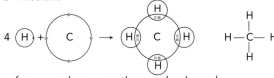

four hydrogen atoms (1)

carbon atom (2,4)

methane molecule: each hydrogen now shares two electrons with carbon

c water

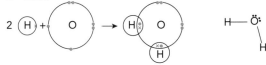

two hydrogen atoms (1)

oxygen atom (2,6)

water molecule: hydrogen and oxygen both fill their outer shells by sharing electrons

d ammonia

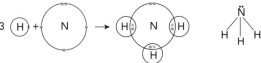

three hydrogen atoms (1)

nitrogen atom (2,5)

ammonia molecule: hydrogen and nitrogen both fill their outer shells by sharing electrons

e hydrogen chloride

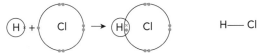

hydrogen atom (1)

chlorine atom (2,8,7)

hydrogen chloride molecule: hydrogen and chlorine both fill their outer shells by sharing electrons

f ethane

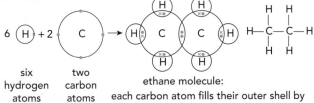

six hydrogen atoms (1)

two carbon atoms (2,4)

ethane molecule: each carbon atom fills their outer shell by sharing electrons with one other carbon atom and some hydrogen atoms

Figure 4.9: Dot-and-cross diagrams for some covalent compounds: **a** hydrogen, H_2, **b** methane, CH_4, **c** water, H_2O, **d** ammonia, NH_3, **e** hydrogen chloride, HCl and **f** ethane, C_2H_6.

a boron trifluoride

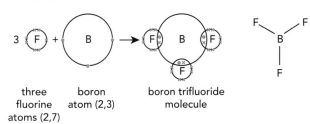

three fluorine atoms (2,7)

boron atom (2,3)

boron trifluoride molecule

b sulfur hexafluoride

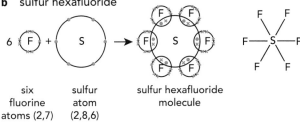

six fluorine atoms (2,7)

sulfur atom (2,8,6)

sulfur hexafluoride molecule

c phosphorus(V) chloride, PCl_5

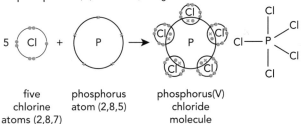

five chlorine atoms (2,8,7)

phosphorus atom (2,8,5)

phosphorus(V) chloride molecule

d sulfur dioxide, SO_2

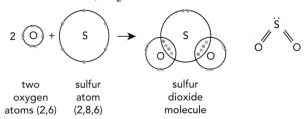

two oxygen atoms (2,6)

sulfur atom (2,8,6)

sulfur dioxide molecule

Figure 4.10: Dot-and-cross diagrams for **a** boron trifluoride, BF_3, **b** sulfur hexafluoride, SF_6, **c** phosphorus(V) chloride, PCl_5 and **d** sulfur dioxide, SO_2.

Multiple covalent bonds

Some atoms can bond together by sharing two pairs of electrons. We call this a double covalent bond. A **double covalent bond** is represented by a double line between the

KEY WORD

double covalent bond: two shared pairs of electrons bonding two atoms together.

atoms: for example, O=O. The dot-and-cross diagrams for oxygen, carbon dioxide and ethene, all of which have double covalent bonds, are shown in Figure 4.11.

- In order to form an oxygen molecule, each oxygen atom needs to gain two electrons to complete its outer shell so two pairs of electrons are shared and two covalent bonds are formed.

- For carbon dioxide, each oxygen atom needs to gain two electrons as before. But the carbon atom needs to gain four electrons to complete its outer shell. So two oxygen atoms each form two bonds with carbon, so that the carbon atom has eight electrons around it.

- In ethene, two hydrogen atoms share a pair of electrons with each carbon atom. This leaves each carbon atom with two outer shell electrons for bonding with each other. A double bond is formed between the two carbon atoms.

a Oxygen

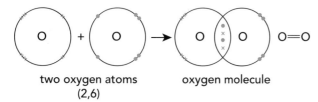

two oxygen atoms
(2,6)

oxygen molecule

b Carbon dioxide

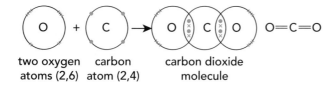

two oxygen   carbon
atoms (2,6)   atom (2,4)

carbon dioxide
molecule

c Ethene

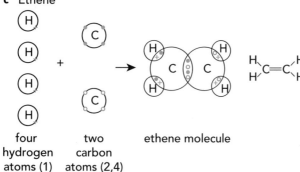

four
hydrogen
atoms (1)

two
carbon
atoms (2,4)

ethene molecule

Figure 4.11: Dot-and-cross diagrams for **a** oxygen, O_2, **b** carbon dioxide, CO_2, and **c** ethene, C_2H_4.

> **KEY WORD**
>
> **triple covalent bond:** three shared pairs of electrons bonding two atoms together.

Atoms can also bond together by sharing three pairs of electrons. We call this a **triple covalent bond**. Figure 4.12 shows a dot-and-cross diagram for the triple-bonded nitrogen molecule.

In order to form a nitrogen molecule, each nitrogen atom needs to gain three electrons to complete its outer shell. So three pairs of electrons are shared and three covalent bonds are formed.

Nitrogen

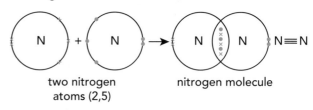

two nitrogen
atoms (2,5)

nitrogen molecule

Figure 4.12: Dot-and-cross diagram for a nitrogen molecule, N_2.

Question

3   Draw dot-and-cross diagrams for the following covalently bonded molecules. Show only the outer electron shells:

   a   carbonyl chloride O=CCl$_2$

   b   carbon disulfide, CS_2.

Co-ordinate bonding (dative covalent bonding)

A **co-ordinate bond** (or dative covalent bond) is formed when one atom provides both the electrons needed for a covalent bond.

> **KEY WORD**
>
> **co-ordinate bond:** the sharing of a pair of electrons between two atoms where both the electrons in the bond come from the same atom. Also called a dative covalent bond.

For dative covalent bonding we need:

- one atom to have a lone pair of electrons

- a second atom to have an unfilled orbital to accept the lone pair. In other words, an electron-deficient compound.

KEY WORD

electron deficient: an atom or molecule that has less than its usual share of electrons.

An example of this is the ammonium ion, NH_4^+, formed when ammonia combines with a hydrogen ion, H^+. The hydrogen ion is **electron deficient**. It has space for two electrons in its shell. The nitrogen atom in the ammonia molecule has a lone pair of electrons. The lone pair on the nitrogen atom provides both electrons for the bond (Figure 4.13).

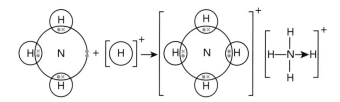

Figure 4.13: The formation of a co-ordinate bond in the ammonium ion.

In a displayed formula (which shows all atoms and bonds), a co-ordinate bond is represented by an arrow. The head of the arrow points away from the lone pair that forms the bond.

Another molecule that has co-ordinate bonds is aluminium chloride. At high temperatures aluminium chloride exists as molecules with the formula $AlCl_3$. This molecule is electron deficient. It still needs two electrons to complete the outer shell of the aluminium atom. At lower temperatures two molecules of $AlCl_3$ combine to form a molecule with the formula Al_2Cl_6. The $AlCl_3$ molecules are able to combine because lone pairs of electrons on two of the chlorine atoms form co-ordinate bonds with the aluminium atoms, as shown in Figure 4.14.

IMPORTANT

A displayed formula shows all of the atoms and all of the bonds. You do not have to show the correct bond angles in a displayed formula.

Question

4 a Draw dot-and-cross diagrams to show the formation of a co-ordinate bond between the following:

  i boron trifluoride, BF_3, and ammonia, NH_3, to form the compound F_3BNH_3

  ii phosphine, PH_3, and a hydrogen ion, H^+, to form the ion PH_4^+.

  b Draw the displayed formulae of the products formed in part **a**. Show the co-ordinate bond by an arrow.

Bond length and bond energy

In general, double bonds are shorter than single bonds. This is because double bonds have a greater quantity of negative charge between the two atomic nuclei. The greater force of attraction between the electrons and the nuclei pulls the atoms closer together. This results in a stronger bond. We measure the strength of a bond by its **bond energy**. This is the energy needed to break one mole of a given covalent bond in the gaseous state (see also Chapter 6). The distance from the nucleus of one

KEY DEFINITION

bond energy: the energy required to break one mole of a particular covalent bond in the gaseous state. The units of bond energy are kilojoules per mole, kJ mol⁻¹.

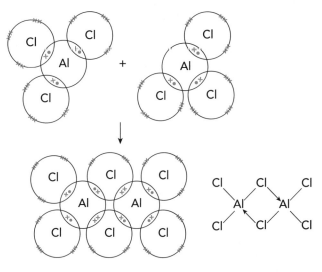

Figure 4.14: A dot-and-cross diagram for an aluminium chloride molecule, Al_2Cl_6.

KEY DEFINITION

bond length: the distance between the nuclei of two covalently bonded atoms.

atom to another depends on the two atoms forming the bond. The internuclear distance between two covalently bonded atoms is called the **bond length**. Table 4.1 shows some values of bond lengths and bond energies.

Bond	Bond energy / kJ mol^{-1}	Bond length / nm
C—C	350	0.154
C=C	610	0.134
C—O	360	0.143
C=O	740	0.116

Table 4.1: Examples of values for bond energies and bond lengths.

Bond strength can influence the reactivity of a compound. The molecules in liquids and gases are in random motion so they are constantly colliding with each other. A reaction only happens between molecules when a collision occurs with enough energy to break bonds in either or both molecules. Nitrogen is unreactive because it has a triple bond, N≡N. It takes a lot of energy to break the nitrogen atoms apart. The bond energy required is 994 kJ mol^{-1}. Oxygen is much more reactive. Although it has a double bond, it only takes 496 kJ to break a mole of O=O bonds. However, bond strength is only one factor that influences the reactivity of a molecule. The polarity of the bond (see Section 4.7) and whether the bond is a σ bond (sigma bond) or a π bond (pi bond) (see Section 4.5) both play a large part in determining chemical reactivity.

Question

5 The table lists bond lengths and bond energies of some hydrogen halides.

Hydrogen halide	Bond length / nm	Bond energy / kJ mol^{-1}
HCl	0.127	431
HBr	0.141	366
HI	0.161	299

Table 4.2: Information table for Question 5.

a Describe the relationship between the bond length and the bond energy for these hydrogen halides.

b Suggest why the bond energy values decrease in the order HCl > HBr > HI.

c Suggest a value for the bond length in hydrogen fluoride, HF.

4.4 Shapes of molecules
Valence shell electron pair repulsion theory (VSEPR)

Because all electrons have the same (negative) charge, they repel each other when they are close together. So, a pair of electrons in the bonds surrounding the central atom in a molecule will repel other electron pairs. This repulsion forces the pairs of electrons apart until the repulsive forces are minimised.

The shape and bond angles of a covalently bonded molecule depend on:

- the number of pairs of electrons around each atom
- whether these pairs are lone pairs or bonding pairs.

IMPORTANT

VSEPR:

- The valence shell electrons are the electrons in the main outer shell.
- Pairs of electrons repel each other because they have the same charge.
- A lone pair of electrons repel each other more than a bonded pair of electrons.
- Repulsion between multiple and single bonds is treated the same as for repulsion between single bonds. Repulsions between pairs of double bonds are greater.
- The shape of a molecule can be deduced using this theory, with the most stable shape being that which minimises the forces of repulsion.

Lone pairs of electrons have a more concentrated electron charge cloud than bonding pairs of electrons. Their cloud charges are wider and slightly closer to the nucleus of the central atom. This results in a different amount of repulsion between different types of electron pairs. The order of repulsion is lone pair–lone pair (most repulsion) > lone pair–bond pair > bond pair–bond pair (least repulsion).

Figure 4.15 shows the repulsions between lone pairs (pink) and bonding pairs (white) in a water molecule.

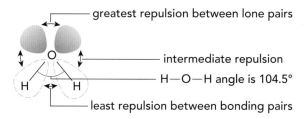

Figure 4.15: Repulsion between lone and bonding electron pairs in water.

Working out the shapes of molecules

The differences in electron-pair repulsion determine the shape and bond angles in a molecule. Figure 4.16 compares the shapes and bond angles of methane, ammonia and water. Space-filling models of these molecules are shown in Figure 4.17. Each of these molecules has four pairs of electrons surrounding the central atom. Note that in drawing three-dimensional diagrams, the triangular 'wedge' is the bond coming towards you and the dashed black line is the bond going away from you.

- Methane has four bonding pairs of electrons surrounding the central carbon atom. The equal repulsive forces of each bonding pair of electrons results in a structure with all H—C—H bond angles being 109.5°. We call this a *tetrahedral* structure.

- In ammonia and water, the tetrahedral arrangement of the electron pairs around the central atom becomes distorted.

- Ammonia has three bonding pairs of electrons and one lone pair. As lone pair–bond pair repulsion is greater than bond pair–bond pair repulsion, the bonding pairs of electrons are pushed closer together. This gives the ammonia molecule a pyramidal shape. The H—N—H bond angle is about 107°. We call this a *pyramidal* structure.

- Water has two bonding pairs of electrons and two lone pairs. The greatest force is between the two lone pairs. This results in the bonds being pushed even closer together. The shape of the water molecule is a non-linear V shape. The H—O—H bond angle is 104.5°.

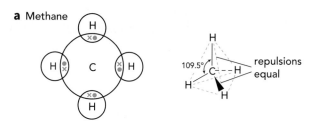

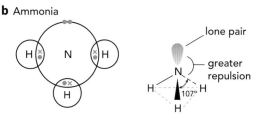

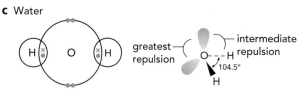

Figure 4.16: The bond angles in **a** methane, **b** ammonia, and **c** water depend on the type of electron-pair repulsion.

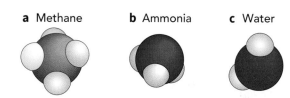

Figure 4.17: Shapes of molecules. These space-filling models show the molecular shapes of **a** methane, CH_4, **b** ammonia, NH_3, and **c** water, H_2O.

Question

6   a   Predict, using VSEPR theory, the shapes of the following molecules, which you drew in question 2 in Section 4.3:

      i   tetrachloromethane, CCl_4

      ii   beryllium chloride, $BeCl_2$

      iii   phosphorus(III) chloride.

   b   Draw dot-and-cross diagrams for the following molecules and then predict their shapes:

      i   hydrogen sulfide, H_2S

      ii   phosphine, PH_3.

WORKED EXAMPLE

1 Predict the shape and bond angles in a molecule of stibine, SbH_3. Explain how you arrived at your conclusions.

Solution

Step 1: Use the Periodic Table to find to which groups the atoms belong.
Sb = 15

Step 2: Deduce the number of electrons in the outer principal quantum shell.
Sb = 5, H = 1

Step 3: Draw a dot-and-cross diagram for the molecule.
In this case you should recognise the similarity to structure of ammonia. So there will be 3 bonding pairs of electrons and 1 lone pair.

Step 4: Use VSEPR theory to work out approximate bond angles.
Repulsion between lone pair and bond pair electrons is greater than repulsions between a bonding pair and a bonding pair. So for four pairs of electrons, the H—Sb—H bond angle is reduced from the tetrahedral bond angle to lower than 109.5° (the tetrahedral bond angle). Any suitable value lower than about 107° (the value of ammonia is a suitable estimate). But the value should be above 90°. (The actual value is 91.7°. The low value is related to the large size of the Sb atom).

Step 5: Deduce the shape.
You should recognise the similarity with the shape of ammonia which is pyramidal.

More molecular shapes

We can work out the shapes of other molecules by following the rules for electron-pair repulsion.

Boron trifluoride

Boron trifluoride is an electron-deficient molecule. It has only six electrons in its outer shell. The three bonding pairs of electrons repel each other equally, so the F—B—F bond angles are 120° (Figure 4.18). We describe the shape of the molecule as *trigonal planar*. Trigonal means having three angles.

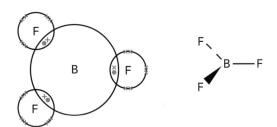

Figure 4.18: Boron trifluoride.

Carbon dioxide

Carbon dioxide has two carbon–oxygen double bonds and no lone pairs. The four electrons in each double bond repel other electrons in a similar way to the two electrons in a single bond (Figure 4.19). So, the O=C=O bond angle is 180°. We describe the shape of the carbon dioxide molecule as *linear*.

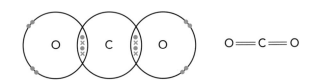

Figure 4.19: Carbon dioxide.

Phosphorus pentafluoride

Phosphorus pentafluoride has five bonding pairs of electrons and no lone pairs. The repulsion between the electron pairs results in the most stable structure being one where two pyramids with bases of three angles are joined (Figure 4.20). We call this structure *trigonal bipyramidal*. Three of the fluorine atoms lie in the same plane as the phosphorus atom. The bond angles F—P—F within this plane are 120°. Two of the fluorine atoms lie above and below this plane, at 90° to it.

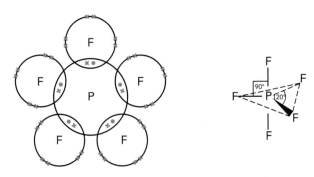

Figure 4.20: Phosphorus pentafluoride.

Sulfur hexafluoride

Sulfur hexafluoride has six bonding pairs of electrons and no lone pairs. The equal repulsion between the electron pairs results in the structure shown in Figure 4.21. All F—S—F bond angles are 90°. We describe the shape as *octahedral*.

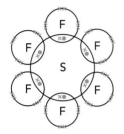 

Figure 4.21: Sulfur hexafluoride.

Questions

7 **a** Draw a dot-and-cross diagram for a molecule of selenium hexafluoride, SeF_6. A single selenium atom has six electrons in its outer shell.

b Predict the shape of selenium hexafluoride.

c Draw the shape of the phosphorus(V) chloride molecule that you drew as a dot-and-cross diagram in question 2 in Section 4.3.

8 In trimethylamine, $(CH_3)_3N$: three CH_3 groups are attached to the nitrogen by C—N bonds. The repulsion of the CH_3 groups is slightly greater than the repulsion of the H atoms in ammonia.

Which one of these bond angles for the C—N—C bond in trimethylamine, is correct?

A about 90°   **C** about 109.5°

B about 107°   **D** about 120°

4.5 σ bonds and π bonds

A single covalent bond is formed when two non-metal atoms combine. Each atom that combines has an atomic orbital containing a single unpaired electron. In the formation of a covalent bond the atomic orbitals overlap so that a combined orbital is formed, containing two electrons. We call this combined orbital a *molecular orbital*. The

> **IMPORTANT**
>
> Covalent bonds are formed when atomic orbitals overlap.

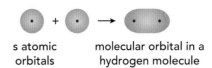

Figure 4.22: Two 1s atomic orbitals in hydrogen overlap to form a covalent bond.

amount of overlap of the atomic orbitals determines the strength of the bond: the greater the overlap, the stronger the bond. Figure 4.22 shows how the s atomic orbitals of two hydrogen atoms overlap to form a covalent bond.

- The greater the overlap, the stronger the bond.

- The mixing of atomic orbitals is called hybridisation. Mixing an s with three, two or one p-type orbitals forms sp³, sp² and sp hybrid orbitals.

- Sigma bonds (σ bonds) are formed from end-on overlap of atomic orbitals. Pi bonds (π bonds) are formed from sideways overlap of atomic orbitals.

The p atomic orbitals can also overlap linearly (end-on) to form covalent bonds. When p orbitals are involved in forming single bonds, they become modified to include some s orbital character. The orbital is slightly altered in shape to make one of the lobes of the p orbital bigger. The process of mixing atomic orbitals (for example, one s orbital and three p orbitals) in this way is called hybridisation. The hybrids are called *sp³ hybrids*. In sp³ hybrids, each orbital has $\frac{1}{4}$ s character and $\frac{3}{4}$ p character. When one s orbital and two p orbitals are hybridised, the hybrids are called *sp² hybrids*. When one s orbital and one p orbital are hybridised, the hybrids are called *sp orbitals*. When hybridised orbitals overlap linearly (end-on) we call the bond a σ *bond* (sigma bond). Figure 4.23 shows the formation of σ bonds.

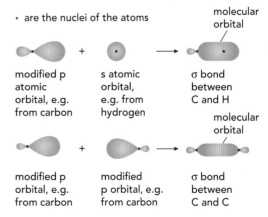

Figure 4.23: Bonds are formed by the linear (end-on) overlap of atomic orbitals.

The electron density of each σ bond is symmetrical about a line joining the nuclei of the atoms forming the bond.

Bonds formed by the sideways overlap of p orbitals are called π bonds (pi bonds). A π bond is not symmetrical about the axes joining the nuclei of the atoms forming the bond. Figure 4.24 shows how a π bond is formed from two p orbitals overlapping sideways.

We often draw a single π bond as two electron clouds, one arising from each lobe of the p orbitals. You must remember, though, that the two clouds of electrons in a π bond represent *one* bond consisting of a total of two electrons.

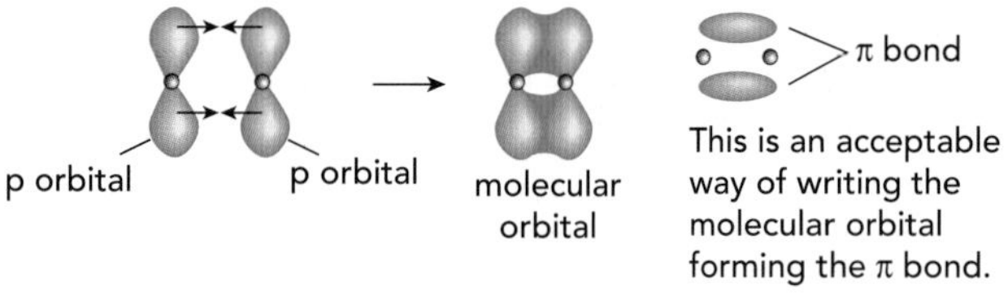

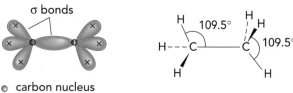

Figure 4.24: π bonds are formed by the sideways overlap of atomic orbitals.

The shape of some organic molecules

We can explain the shapes of molecules in terms of the patterns of electron density found in σ bonds and π bonds.

Ethane

The displayed formula for ethane is:

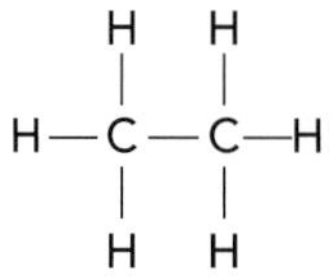

All the bonds in ethane are formed by linear overlap of atomic orbitals. They are all σ bonds.

Figure 4.25 shows the electron density distribution in ethane formed by these σ bonds. All the areas of electron density repel each other equally. This makes the H—C—H bond angles all the same (109.5°).

σ bonds

○ carbon nucleus
× hydrogen nucleus

Figure 4.25: The electron density distribution in ethane.

Ethene

The displayed formula for ethene is:

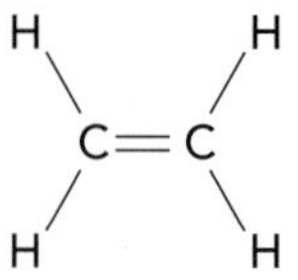

Each carbon atom in ethene uses three of its four outer electrons to form σ bonds. Two σ bonds are formed with the hydrogen atoms and one σ bond is formed with the other carbon atom.

The fourth electron from each carbon atom occupies a p orbital, which overlaps sideways with a similar p orbital on the other carbon atom. This forms a π bond. Figure 4.26 shows how this occurs.

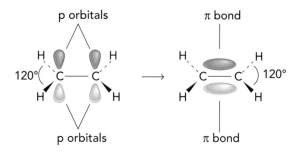

Figure 4.26: Overlap of p orbitals to produce a π bond in ethene.

The electron density distribution of both the σ and π bonds in ethene is shown in Figure 4.27.

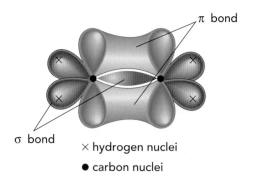

× hydrogen nuclei
● carbon nuclei

Figure 4.27: The electron density distribution in ethene.

Ethene is a planar molecule because this ensures the maximum overlap of the p orbitals that form the π bond. You will notice that the electron clouds that make up the π bond lie above and below the plane of the carbon and hydrogen nuclei. We would expect the H—C—H bond angle in ethene to be about 120° because the three areas of electron density of the σ bonds are equally distributed. However, because of the position of the π bond, this bond angle is actually 117°. This minimises the repulsive forces.

Triple bonds

In the nitrogen molecule, N≡N, hydrogen cyanide, H—C≡N and ethyne, H—C≡C—H, there are triple bonds. The triple bond is formed from two π bonds (pi bonds) and one σ bond (sigma bond). The two π bonds are at right angles to each other.

In hydrogen cyanide one σ bond is formed between the hydrogen atom and the carbon atom (by overlap of an sp carbon hybrid orbital with the 1s hydrogen orbital). A second σ bond is formed between the carbon and the nitrogen atom (by overlap of an sp carbon hybrid orbital with a p orbital on the nitrogen). This leaves the remaining p orbitals on each nitrogen atom to form two π bonds at right angles to each other.

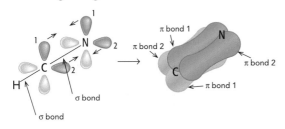

Figure 4.28: Overlap of two sets of p orbitals of nitrogen and carbon to produce two π bonds in hydrogen cyanide.

4.6 Metallic bonding

What is a metallic bond?

In a metal, the atoms are packed closely together in a regular arrangement called a *lattice*. Metal atoms in a lattice tend to lose their outer shell electrons and become positive ions. The outer shell electrons occupy new energy levels and are free to move throughout the metal lattice. We call these electrons **delocalised electrons** (mobile electrons). Delocalised electrons are electrons that are not associated with any one particular atom or bond.

Metallic bonding is strong. This is because the ions are held together by the strong electrostatic attraction between their positive charges and the negative charges of the delocalised electrons (Figures 4.29 and 4.30).

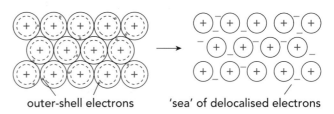

outer-shell electrons 'sea' of delocalised electrons

Figure 4.30: Metallic bonding: there are strong attractive forces between the positively charged ions and the delocalised electrons.

KEY WORDS

delocalised electrons: electrons that are not associated with any particular atom. In metals, the delocalised electrons move throughout the metallic structure between the metal ions when a voltage is applied. (In the molecule benzene, the delocalised electrons have a more limited movement.)

metallic bonding: the electrostatic attraction between positive ions and delocalised electrons.

Figure 4.29: Metals: **a** sodium, **b** gold, **c** mercury, **d** magnesium and **e** copper.

This electrostatic attraction acts in all directions. The strength of metallic bonding increases with:

- increasing positive charge on the ions in the metal lattice

- decreasing size of metal ions in the lattice

- increasing number of mobile electrons per atom.

Metallic bonding and the properties of metals

We can use our model of metallic bonding to explain many of the properties of metals.

Most metals have high melting points and high boiling points

It takes a lot of energy to weaken the strong attractive forces between the metal ions and the delocalised electrons. These attractive forces can only be overcome at high temperatures. However, mercury is a liquid at room temperature (Figure 4.31). This is because some of the electrons in a mercury atom are bound more tightly than usual to the nucleus, weakening the metallic bonds between atoms.

Figure 4.31: Mercury is a liquid at room temperature.

Metals conduct electricity

When a voltage is applied to a piece of metal, an electric current flows in it because the delocalised electrons (mobile electrons) are free to move. Metallic bonding is the only type of bonding that allows us to predict reliably that a solid will conduct electricity. Covalent solids cannot conduct electricity because none of their electrons are free to move throughout the structure, although graphite is an exception to this. Ionic solids cannot conduct because neither their electrons nor their ions are free to move from place to place.

Question

9 Answer the following, giving a full explanation in terms of metallic bonding.

a Explain why aluminium has a higher melting point than sodium.

b The thermal conductivity of stainless steel is 82 W m^{-1} K^{-1}. The thermal conductivity of copper is 400 W m^{-1} K^{-1}. Why do some stainless steel saucepans have a copper base?

c Why does aluminium conduct electricity better than sodium?

Metals conduct heat

The conduction of heat is partly due to the movement of the delocalised electrons but mainly due to the vibrations passed on from one metal ion to the next.

4.7 Intermolecular forces

The forces within molecules due to covalent bonding are strong. However, the forces between molecules are much weaker. We call these forces van der Waals' forces (intermolecular forces).

There are two types of van der Waals' (intermolecular) force:

- instantaneous (temporary) dipole–induced dipole forces (id–id) forces. These are also called *London dispersion forces*.

- permanent dipole–permanent dipole (pd–pd) forces (including hydrogen bonding).

A special case of permanent dipole–permanent dipole forces is hydrogen bonding. This occurs between molecules where hydrogen is bonded to a highly electronegative atom.

> **IMPORTANT**
>
> Remember that 'van der Waals' forces' is a general term used for all intermolecular forces including id–id forces, pd–pd forces and hydrogen bonding.

Table 4.2 compares the relative strength of these intermolecular forces and other bonds.

Type of bond or force	Bond strength / kJ mol⁻¹
ionic bonding in sodium chloride	760
O—H covalent bond in water	464
hydrogen bonding	20–50
permanent dipole–permanent dipole force	5–20
id–id forces	1–20

Table 4.2: Strengths of different types of bond and intermolecular force.

In order to understand how intermolecular forces work, we first have to know about **electronegativity** and bond polarity.

KEY DEFINITION

electronegativity: the power of a particular atom that is covalently bonded to another atom to attract the bonding pair of electrons towards itself.

Electronegativity

Electronegativity is the power of a particular atom that is covalently bonded to another atom to attract the bonding pair of electrons towards itself.

The greater the value of the electronegativity, the greater the power of an atom to attract the electrons in a covalent bond towards itself. For Groups 1 to 17 the pattern of electronegativity is:

• electronegativity increases across a period from Group 1 to Group 17

• electronegativity increases up each group.

This means that fluorine is the most electronegative element.

For the most electronegative elements, the order of electronegativity is:

$$\xrightarrow{\text{increasing electronegativity}}$$
$$Br < Cl < N < O < F$$

Carbon and hydrogen have electronegativities that are lower than those of most other non-metallic elements.

Factors influencing electronegativity

The value of the electronegativity depends on:

• nuclear charge: atoms in the same period with a greater (positive) nuclear charge are more likely to attract the bonding pair of electrons.

• atomic radius: atoms in the same group in which the outer electrons are further from the nucleus are less likely to attract the bonding pair of electrons because the pull of the positive nucleus on the electron pair is lower.

• shielding: the greater the number of inner electron shells and sub-shells, the lower the effective nuclear charge on the bonding electrons.

Ionic or covalent?

The most commonly used scale of electronegativity values is called the Pauling electronegativity scale, N_p. Table 4.3 shows some Pauling electronegativity values.

Li	Be	B	C	N	O	F
1.0	1.5	2.0	2.5	3.0	3.5	4.0
Na	Mg	Al	Si	P	S	Cl
0.9	1.2	1.5	1.8	2.1	2.5	3.0

Table 4.3: Some Pauling electronegativity values.

Note:

• carbon ($N_p = 2.5$) and hydrogen ($N_p = 2.1$) have electronegativities that are lower than those of many other non-metallic elements

• Pauling electronegativity has no units.

Differences in electronegativity values can be used to predict whether a simple compound has ionic or covalent bonds.

• If the electronegativity difference is high, e.g. 2.0 or more, the compound is likely to be ionic. E.g. sodium chloride: Na = 0.9, Cl = 3.0. Difference = 2.1.

• If the electronegativity difference is lower, e.g. below 1.0, the compound is likely to be covalent. E.g. methane: C = 2.5, H = 2.1. Difference = 0.4.

• A zero value shows that there is no ionic character in the bond, e.g. Cl—Cl.

• Some compounds are not entirely covalent and have some ionic character in them. These have intermediate electronegativity differences, e.g. 1.0.

Polarity in molecules

When the electronegativity values of the two atoms forming a covalent bond are the same, the pair of electrons is equally shared. We say that the covalent bond is *non-polar*. For example, hydrogen (H_2), chlorine (Cl_2) and bromine (Br_2) are non-polar molecules.

When a covalent bond is formed between two atoms having different electronegativity values, the more electronegative atom attracts the pair of electrons in the bond towards it.

As a result:

- the centre of positive charge does not coincide with the centre of negative charge

- we say that the electron distribution is asymmetric

- the two atoms are partially charged

- we show:

    - the less electronegative atom with the partial charge δ+ ('delta positive')

    - the more electronegative atom with the partial charge δ– ('delta negative')

- we say that the bond is *polar* (or that it has a dipole).

Figure 4.32 shows the polar bond in a hydrogen chloride molecule.

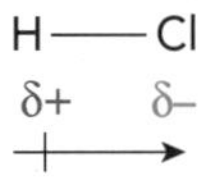

H ——— Cl
δ+   δ–
+———→

Figure 4.32: Hydrogen chloride is a polar molecule.

As the difference in electronegativity values of the atoms in a covalent bond increases, the bond becomes more polar. The degree of polarity of a molecule is measured as a dipole moment. The direction of the dipole is shown by the sign +———→. The arrow points to the partially negatively charged end of the dipole.

In molecules containing more than two atoms, we have to take into account:

- the polarity of each bond

- the arrangement of the bonds in the molecule.

Trichloromethane, $CHCl_3$, is a polar molecule. The three C—Cl dipoles point in a similar direction. Their combined effect is not cancelled out by the polarity of the C—H bond. This is because the C—H bond

is virtually non-polar. The electron distribution is asymmetric. The molecule is polar, with the negative end towards the chlorine atoms. This is shown in Figure 4.33a.

Some molecules contain **polar bonds** but have no overall polarity. This is because the polar bonds in these molecules are arranged in such a fashion that the dipole moments cancel each other out. An example is tetrachloromethane, CCl_4 (Figure 4.33b). Tetrachloromethane has four polar C—Cl bonds pointing towards the four corners of a tetrahedron. The dipoles in each bond cancel each other, so tetrachloromethane is non-polar.

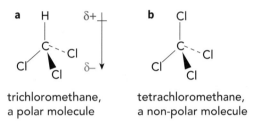

Figure 4.33: The polarity of **a** trichloromethane and **b** tetrachloromethane.

We can determine the charge distribution in molecules and ions by a method called *X-ray spectroscopy*. One method involves firing X-rays at molecules and measuring the energy of the electrons given off. Using this method, scientists have found that in a sulfate ion, the sulfur atom has a charge of +1.12 units and the four oxygen atoms each have a charge of –0.78 units.

KEY WORDS

polar bonds: the electron pair in the bond is drawn towards the atom with the larger electronegativity, making one end of the molecule slightly positive compared with the other.

bond polarity: the partial separation of charge when two different atoms are joined by a covalent bond. This results in an unequal attraction for the bonding pair of electrons.

Question

10 Are the following molecules polar or non-polar? In each case give a reason for your answer.

(Electronegativity values: F = 4.0, Cl = 3.0, Br = 2.8, S = 2.5, C = 2.5, H = 2.1)

a   chlorine, Cl_2

b   hydrogen fluoride, HF

c   the V-shaped molecule, sulfur dichloride, SCl_2

d   the tetrahedral molecule, chloromethane, CH_3Cl

e   the tetrahedral molecule, tetrabromomethane, CBr_4

Polarity and chemical reactivity

Bond polarity influences chemical reactivity. For example, both nitrogen, N≡N, and carbon monoxide, C≡O, have triple bonds requiring a similar amount of energy to break them. Nitrogen is a non-polar molecule and is fairly unreactive. But carbon monoxide is a polar molecule, and this explains its reactivity with oxygen and its use as a reducing agent. Many chemical reactions are started by a reagent attacking one of the electrically charged ends of a polar molecule. For example, chloroethane, C_2H_5Cl, is far more reactive than ethane, C_2H_6. This is because reagents such as OH⁻ ions can attack the delta-positive carbon atom of the polarised C—Cl bond (see also Section 16.2).

$$
\begin{array}{c}
\quad\; H \quad\; H \\
\quad\; | \qquad | \\
H - C - \overset{\delta+}{C} - \overset{\delta-}{Cl} \\
\quad\; | \qquad | \\
\quad\; H \quad\; H
\end{array}
$$

Such an attack is not possible with ethane because the C—H bond is virtually non-polar. This helps to explain why alkanes such as ethane are not very reactive.

Instantaneous dipole–induced dipole (id–id) forces

Noble gases such as neon and argon exist as isolated atoms. Noble gases can be liquefied, but at very low temperatures, so there must be very weak forces of attraction between their atoms. These weak forces keep the atoms together in the liquid state.

Bromine is a non-polar molecule that is liquid at room temperature. The weak forces of attraction are keeping the bromine molecules together at room temperature. These very weak forces of attraction are called instantaneous dipole–induced dipole (id–id) forces, or London dispersion forces. These forces exist between all atoms or molecules. So, how do these forces arise?

The electron charge clouds in a non-polar molecule (or atom) are constantly moving. It often happens that more of the charge cloud is on one side of the molecule than the other. This means that one end of the molecule has, for a short time, more negative charge than the other. A temporary dipole is set up. This dipole can set up (induce) a dipole on neighbouring molecules. As a result of this, there are forces of attraction between the δ+ end of the dipole in one molecule and the δ– end of the dipole in a neighbouring molecule (Figure 4.34). These dipoles are always temporary because the electrons clouds are always moving. **Instantaneous dipole–induced dipole forces** are sometimes called *temporary dipole–induced dipole forces*.

Instantaneous dipole–induced dipole forces increase with:

- increasing number of electrons (and protons) in the molecule
- increasing the number of contact points between the molecules: contact points are places where the molecules come close together.

Differences in the size of the instantaneous dipole–induced dipole (id–id) forces can be used to explain the trend in the enthalpy change of vaporisation and boiling points of the noble gases. Figure 4.35 shows how these vary with the number of electrons present. (The enthalpy change of vaporisation is the energy required to convert a mole of liquid into a mole of gas.)

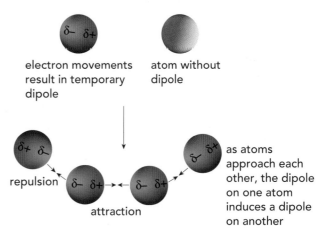

Figure 4.34: How instantaneous dipole–induced dipole forces arise.

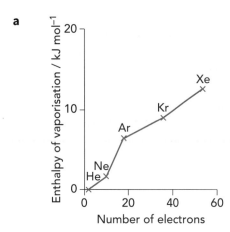

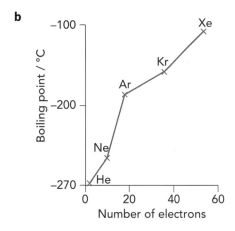

Figure 4.35: a Enthalpy changes of vaporisation and **b** boiling points of the noble gases plotted against the number of electrons present.

You can see that both the enthalpy change of vaporisation and the boiling points of the noble gases increase as the number of electrons increases (Figure 4.35). This is because the id–id forces between the atoms are increased with an increasing number of electrons. So, more energy is needed to change the liquid into vapour and the boiling point is higher.

The effect of increasing the number of contact points can be seen by comparing the boiling points of pentane (boiling point 36 °C) and 2,2-dimethylpropane (boiling point 10 °C) (Figure 4.36). These compounds have equal numbers of electrons in their molecules.

The molecules in pentane can line up beside each other so there is a large number of contact points. The id–id forces are higher, so the boiling point is higher. The molecules of 2,2-dimethylpropane are more compact. The surface area available for coming into contact with neighbouring molecules is smaller. The id–id forces are relatively lower, so the boiling point is lower.

The id–id forces between individual atoms are very small. However, the total id–id forces between very long non-polar molecules such as poly(ethene) molecules (see Section 15.5) can be much larger. That is why poly(ethene) is a solid at room temperature.

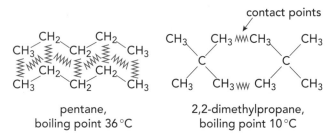

pentane, boiling point 36 °C

2,2-dimethylpropane, boiling point 10 °C

Figure 4.36: The difference in boiling points of pentane and 2,2-dimethylpropane can be explained by the strength of the instantaneous dipole–induced dipole forces.

Two types of poly(ethene) are low-density poly(ethene), LDPE, and high-density poly(ethene), HDPE. Both have crystalline and non-crystalline regions in them (Figure 4.37).

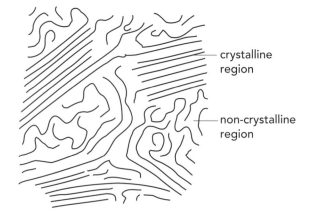

Figure 4.37: Crystalline and non-crystalline regions in poly(ethene).

HDPE has more crystalline regions where the molecules are closer together than LDPE. The total id–id forces are greater, so HDPE is the stronger of the two.

Question

11 **a** The boiling points of the halogens are:

fluorine	–188 °C	chlorine	–35 °C
bromine	+59 °C	iodine	+184 °C

   i Describe the trend in these boiling points going down Group 17.

   ii Explain the trend in these boiling points.

   b The table lists the formulae and boiling points of some alkanes. Explain the trend in terms of instantaneous dipole–induced dipole forces.

Alkane	Structural formula	Boiling point /°C
methane	CH_4	–164
ethane	CH_3CH_3	–88
propane	$CH_3CH_2CH_3$	–42
butane	$CH_3CH_2CH_2CH_3$	0

Permanent dipole–permanent dipole (pd–pd) forces

In some molecules, the dipole is permanent. Molecules with a permanent dipole are called *polar molecules*. A fine jet of polar molecules will be attracted towards an electrically charged plastic rod or comb. (The rod can be charged by rubbing it with a woollen cloth.) Figure 4.38 shows the result of this experiment.

Figure 4.38: The deflection of water by an electrically charged nylon comb.

The molecules are always attracted to the charged rod, whether the rod is positively or negatively charged. This is because the molecules have both negatively and positively charged ends.

The forces between two molecules having permanent dipoles are called **permanent dipole–permanent dipole (pd–pd) forces**. The attractive force between the δ+ charge on one molecule and the δ– charge on a neighbouring molecule causes a weak attractive force between the molecules (Figure 4.39).

> **KEY WORD**
>
> **permanent dipole–permanent dipole forces (pd–pd forces):** attractive intermolecular forces which result from permanent dipoles in molecules.

weak permanent
dipole–permanent dipole force

$$
\begin{array}{ccc}
CH_3 & & CH_3 \\
\diagdown & \delta- & \diagdown \quad \delta- \\
\delta+ \; C = O & \bigg| & \delta+ \; C = O \\
\diagup & & \diagup \\
CH_3 & & CH_3
\end{array}
$$

Figure 4.39: Permanent dipole–permanent dipole forces in propanone.

For small molecules with the same number of electrons, permanent dipole–permanent dipole forces are often stronger than instantaneous dipole–induced dipole forces. For example, propanone (CH_3COCH_3, $M_r = 58$) has a higher boiling point than butane ($CH_3CH_2CH_2CH_3$, $M_r = 58$). This means that more energy is needed to break the intermolecular forces between propanone molecules than between butane molecules) (Figure 4.40).

butane,
boiling point 0 °C

propanone,
boiling point 56 °C

Figure 4.40: The difference in the boiling points of propanone and butane can be explained by the different types of intermolecular force between the molecules.

The permanent dipole–permanent dipole forces between propanone molecules are strong enough to make this substance a liquid at room temperature. There are only instantaneous dipole–induced dipole forces between butane molecules. These forces are comparatively weak, so butane is a gas at room temperature.

Question

12 Bromine, Br_2, and iodine monochloride, ICl, have the same number of electrons. But the boiling point of iodine monochloride is nearly 40 °C higher than the boiling point of bromine. Explain this difference.

4.8 Hydrogen bonding

> **Note:** Learners are only expected to describe hydrogen bonding in relation to molecules containing N—H and O—H. The material in this section relating to the F—H group is extension material, and is not on the syllabus.

Hydrogen bonding is the strongest form of intermolecular bonding. It is a type of permanent dipole–permanent dipole bonding.

For hydrogen bonding to occur between two molecules we need:

- one molecule to have a hydrogen atom covalently bonded to F, O or N (the three most electronegative atoms)

- a second molecule to have an F, O or N atom with an available lone pair of electrons.

> ### KEY WORD
>
> **hydrogen bond:** the strongest type of intermolecular force but weaker than covalent bonds. It is a strong type of pd-pd force.

For hydrogen bonding to happen the molecules must have:

- a H atom covalently bonded to a highly electronegative atom, e.g. N, O or F

- another highly electronegative atom with a lone pair of electrons.

When a hydrogen atom is covalently bonded to a very electronegative atom, the bond is very highly polarised. The $\delta+$ charge on the hydrogen atom is high enough for a bond to be formed with a lone pair of electrons on the F, O or N atom of a neighbouring molecule (Figure 4.41).

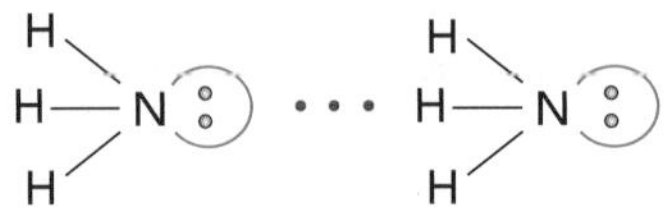

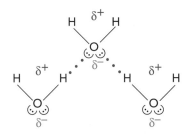

Figure 4.41: Hydrogen bonding between two ammonia molecules. A hydrogen bond is represented by a line of dots.

The force of attraction is about one-tenth of the strength of a normal covalent bond. For maximum bond strength, the angle between the covalent bond to the hydrogen atom and the **hydrogen bond** is usually 180°.

The average number of hydrogen bonds formed per molecule depends on:

- the number of hydrogen atoms attached to F, O or N in the molecule

- the number of lone pairs present on the F, O or N.

Water has two hydrogen atoms and two lone pairs per molecule (Figure 4.42). So water is extensively hydrogen bonded with other water molecules. It has an average of two hydrogen bonds per molecule.

Figure 4.42: Water can form, on average, two hydrogen bonds per molecule.

Ammonia is less extensively hydrogen bonded than water (see Figure 4.41). It can form, on average, only one hydrogen bond per molecule. Although each ammonia molecule has three hydrogen atoms attached to the nitrogen atom, it has only one lone pair of electrons that can be involved in hydrogen bond formation.

REFLECTION

Take an A4 sheet of paper and divide it into two columns. In the left-hand column write down, one under another, the key words, phrases and definitions that you have come across in this chapter in any order. There are at least 15! Do this without looking at the book.

Work with another learner:

a   Ask another learner to define the first term that you have chosen.

b   Write the definition next to the term in the second column.

c   After each turn, check your explanation or definition with that given in the book

    and rewrite if necessary.

d   Take it in turns to ask each other to explain the terms or give definitions.

How many of these key words, phrases and definitions did you know before studying this chapter?

Questions

Note: Questions **13 c** and **14** are extension material.

13   Draw diagrams to show hydrogen bonding between the following molecules:

a   ethanol, C_2H_5OH, and water

b   ammonia and water

c   two hydrogen fluoride molecules.

14   The boiling points of the hydrogen halides are shown in the table.

Hydrogen halide	HF	HCl	HBr	HI
Boiling point / °C	+20	–85	–67	–35

Table 4.4: Information table for Question 14.

a   Explain the trend in boiling points from HCl to HI.

b   Explain why the boiling point of HF is so much higher than the boiling point of HCl.

How does hydrogen bonding affect boiling point?

Some compounds have higher boiling points than expected. This can be due to hydrogen bonding. Figure 4.43 shows a graph of the boiling points of the hydrogen halides, HF, HCl, HBr and HI, plotted against the position of the halogen in the Periodic Table.

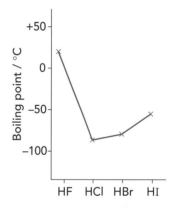

Figure 4.43: The boiling points of the hydrogen halides.

The rise in boiling point from HCl to HI is due to the increasing number of electrons in the halogen atoms as we go down the group. This leads to increased instantaneous dipole–induced dipole forces as the molecules get bigger. If hydrogen fluoride only had instantaneous dipole–induced dipole forces between its molecules, we would expect its boiling point to be about –90 °C. However, the boiling point of hydrogen fluoride is +20 °C, which is much higher. This is because of the stronger intermolecular forces of hydrogen bonding between the HF molecules.

Question

15 The table lists the boiling points of some Group 15 hydrides.

Hydride	Boiling point / °C
ammonia, NH_3	−33
phosphine, PH_3	−88
arsine, AsH_3	−55
stibine, SbH_3	−17

Table 4.5: Information table for Question 15.

a Explain the trend in the boiling points from phosphine to stibine.

b Explain why the boiling point of ammonia does not follow this trend.

The peculiar properties of water

Enthalpy change of vaporisation and boiling point

Water has a much higher enthalpy change of vaporisation and boiling point than expected. This is due to its extensive hydrogen bonding. Figure 4.44 shows the enthalpy changes of vaporisation of water and other Group 16 hydrides.

The rise in enthalpy change of vaporisation from H_2S to H_2Te is due to the increasing number of electrons in the Group 16 atoms as we go down the group. This leads to increased instantaneous dipole–induced dipole forces as the molecules get bigger. If water only had instantaneous dipole–induced dipole forces between its molecules, we would expect its enthalpy change to be about 17 kJ mol⁻¹. But the enthalpy change of vaporisation of water is much higher. This is because water is extensively hydrogen bonded. The boiling point of water is also much higher than predicted by the trend in boiling points for the other Group 16 hydrides. This also indicates that we need much more energy to break the bonds between water molecules compared with other hydrides of Group 16 elements.

Surface tension and viscosity

Water has a high surface tension and high viscosity.

Hydrogen bonding reduces the ability of water molecules to slide over each other, so the viscosity of water is high. The hydrogen bonds in water also exert a significant downward force at the surface of the liquid. This causes the surface tension of water to be higher than for most liquids.

Ice is less dense than water

Most solids are denser than their liquids. This is because the molecules are more closely packed in the solid state. But this is not true of water. In ice, there is a three-dimensional hydrogen-bonded network of water molecules. This produces a rigid lattice in which each oxygen atom is surrounded by a tetrahedron of hydrogen atoms. This 'more open' arrangement, due to the relatively long bond lengths of the hydrogen bonds, allows the water molecules to be slightly further apart than in the liquid (Figures 4.45 and 4.46). So the density of ice is less than that of liquid water.

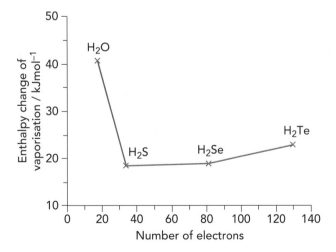

Figure 4.44: Enthalpy changes of vaporisation for Group 16 hydrides plotted against number of electrons present.

Figure 4.45: Ice floats on water.

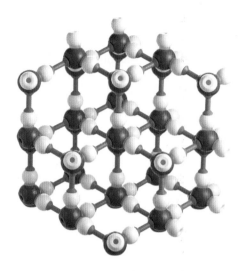

Figure 4.46: A model of ice. Oxygen atoms are red, hydrogen atoms are white, hydrogen bonds are lilac. This hydrogen-bonded arrangement makes ice less dense than water.

Question

16 Which pair of liquids when mixed has the strongest van der Waals' forces?

A H_3C—CO—CH_3 and H_3C—CO—CH_2—CH_3

B H_3C—CH_2—Cl and H_3C—O—H

C H_3C—CH_2—CH_2—CH_2—CH_2—CH_2—CH_3 and H_3C—CH_2—CH_2—CH_2—CH_2—CH_3

D H_3C—O—H and H_3C—CH_2—CH_2—NH_2

4.9 Bonding and physical properties

The type of bonding between atoms, ions or molecules influences the physical properties of a substance.

> **IMPORTANT**
>
> Giant structures such as ionic structures, metals and carbon (graphite and diamond) generally have high melting points but this does not give evidence about the type of bonding. If a substance has a low melting point, it is a better indication that the bonding is covalent within the molecule and there are weak van der Waals' forces of attraction between the molecules (intermolecular forces).

Physical state at room temperature and pressure

Ionic compounds

Ionic compounds are solids at room temperature and pressure. This is because:

- there are strong electrostatic forces (ionic bonds) holding the positive and negative ions together

- the ions are regularly arranged in a lattice (see Chapter 5), with the oppositely charged ions close to each other.

Ionic compounds have high melting points, high boiling points and high enthalpy changes of vaporisation. It takes a lot of energy to overcome the strong electrostatic attractive forces.

Metals

Metals, apart from mercury, are solids. Many metals have high melting points, high boiling points and high enthalpy changes of vaporisation. This is because it takes a lot of energy to overcome the strong attractive forces between the positive ions and the 'sea' of delocalised electrons.

> **IMPORTANT**
>
> Remember that not all metals have high melting points. Group 1 metals and mercury have lower boiling points than some non-metals, so do not use high melting point as a characteristic of metals unless you are only referring to transition elements.

Covalent compounds

Covalently bonded substances with simple molecular structures, for example, water and ammonia, are usually liquids or gases. This is because the intermolecular forces are weak. It does not take much energy to overcome these intermolecular forces. So these substances have low melting points, low boiling points and low enthalpy changes of vaporisation compared with ionic compounds. Some substances that have covalently bonded molecules may be solids at room temperature: for example, iodine and poly(ethene). These are usually molecules where the total instantaneous dipole–induced dipole forces are considerable. However, the melting points of these substances are still fairly low compared with ionic compounds or most metals.

Solubility

Ionic compounds

Most ionic compounds are soluble in water. This is because water molecules are polar and they are attracted to the ions on the surface of the ionic solid. These attractions are called ion–dipole attractions (see Section 19.4). These attractions replace the electrostatic forces between the ions and so the ions go into solution.

Metals

Metals do not dissolve in water. The force of attraction between the ions and the delocalised electrons is too great for water molecules to disrupt the structure and form bonds with the ions. However, some metals, for example sodium and calcium, react with water rather than dissolving in water.

Covalent compounds

Covalently bonded substances with simple molecular structures fall into two groups.

- Those that are insoluble in water. Most covalently bonded molecules are non-polar. Water molecules are not attracted to them so they are insoluble. An example is iodine.

- Those that are soluble in water. Small molecules that can form hydrogen bonds with water are generally soluble. An example is ethanol, C_2H_5OH.

Some covalently bonded substances react with water rather than dissolving in it. For example, hydrogen chloride reacts with water to form hydrogen ions and chloride ions, and the ions are soluble. Silicon chloride reacts with water to form hydrogen ions, chloride ions and silicon dioxide. This reaction is called a **hydrolysis** reaction.

> ### KEY WORD
>
> **hydrolysis:** the breakdown of a compound by water. Hydrolysis is also used to describe the breakdown of a substance by dilute acids or alkali.

Electrical conductivity

> ### IMPORTANT
>
> Remember that electrical conductivity in molten or aqueous ionic compounds is due to mobile ions. Electrical conductivity in metals is due to mobile electrons.

Ionic compounds

Ionic compounds do not conduct electricity when in the solid state. This is because the ions are fixed in the lattice and can only vibrate around a fixed point. When molten, an ionic compound conducts electricity because the ions are mobile.

Metals

Metals conduct electricity both when solid and when molten. This is because the delocalised electrons move throughout the structure when a voltage is applied.

Covalent compounds

Covalently bonded substances with simple molecular structures do not conduct electricity. This is because they have neither ions nor electrons that are mobile.

> ### PRACTICAL ACTIVITY 4.1
>
> **Ionic, covalent or metallic?**
>
> SAFETY: Only carry out this activity in the presence of a teacher after safety aspects have been explained.
>
> You are given several solid substances and have to decide whether the bonding is ionic, covalent or metallic. Carry out these investigations and record your observations.
>
> **Procedure**
>
> 1 Set up an electrical circuit containing batteries, connecting leads, a lamp (bulb) and crocodile clips. This may already be set up for you.
>
> 2 Place one of the solids between the crocodile clips. Does the lamp (bulb) light?
>
> 3 Add a small amount of the solid to 20 cm³ of water in a beaker and stir with a glass rod.
>
>   Does the solid dissolve? If the solid dissolves, keep the solution.
>
> 4 Dip a clean conductivity probe into the solution from step 3. Does the solution conduct electricity?
>
> Which solids are ionic, which are covalent and which are metallic? Explain your answers.

Question

17 Explain the following differences in terms of the type of bonding present.

a Aluminium oxide has a melting point of 2980 °C but aluminium chloride changes to a vapour at 178 °C.

b Magnesium chloride conducts electricity when molten but not when solid.

c Iron conducts electricity when solid but the ionic solid iron(II) chloride does not conduct when solid.

d Sodium sulfate dissolves in water but sulfur does not.

e Propanol, $CH_3CH_2CH_2OH$, is soluble in water but propane, $CH_3CH_2CH_3$, is not.

f A solution of hydrogen chloride in water conducts electricity.

REFLECTION

Work with another learner to make a mind map (spider diagram) of the different types of bonding that you have learned about in this chapter. On your mind map include information about how different types of bonding affect the physical properties of substances. Reflect on any ideas you both might have on how you could improve your mind map.

SUMMARY

Ionic bonding is the electrostatic attraction between oppositely charged ions. Covalent bonding is the electrostatic attraction between the nuclei of two atoms and a shared pair of electrons.
Electronegativity is the power of a particular atom that is covalently bonded to another atom to attract the bonding pair of electrons towards itself.
Bond energy is the energy required to break one mole of a particular covalent bond in the gaseous state. The units of bond energy are kilojoules per mole, $kJ\,mol^{-1}$.
The bond angles within molecules and the shapes of molecules can be predicted by VSEPR theory (lone pairs of electrons repel each other more than bonding pairs of electrons).
Bonding can be described in terms of hybridisation of atomic orbitals and sigma (σ) bonds and pi (π) bonds.
Van der Waals' forces can be classified as instantaneous dipole–induced dipole forces (very weak), permanent dipole–permanent dipole forces (slightly stronger) and hydrogen bonding (the strongest). Van der Waals' forces are weaker than covalent, ionic or metallic bonding.
Metallic bonding is the electrostatic attraction between positive ions and delocalised electrons.
Some of the physical properties of ionic, simple covalent molecules and metals can be related to the type of bonding present.

EXAM-STYLE QUESTIONS

1   The table shows the atomic number and boiling points of some noble gases.

Gas	helium	neon	argon	krypton	xenon
Atomic number	2	10	18	36	54
Boiling point / °C	−269	−246	−186	−153	−107

a   Use ideas about forces between atoms to explain this trend in
    boiling points.   [2]

b   Xenon forms a number of covalently bonded compounds with fluorine.

   i   Define the term *covalent bond*.   [1]

   ii   Draw a dot-and-cross diagram for xenon tetrafluoride, XeF_4 [1]

   iii Suggest a shape for XeF_4. Explain your answer.   [3]

c   The structure of xenon trioxide is shown below.

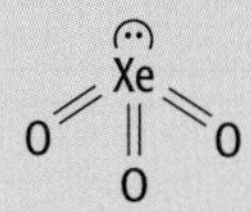

$$O = Xe = O$$
$$\|$$
$$O$$

   i   By referring to electron pairs, explain why xenon trioxide has
        this shape.   [2]

   ii   Draw the structure of xenon trioxide to show the partial charges
        on the atoms and the direction of the dipole in the molecule.   [2]

                                                                 [Total: 11]

2   Aluminium chloride, $AlCl_3$, and ammonia, NH_3, are both covalent molecules.

   a   i   Draw a diagram of an ammonia molecule, showing its shape.
            Show any lone pairs of electrons.   [3]

       ii   State the bond angle $\underset{H}{\overset{N}{\diagdown}}$ in the ammonia molecule.   [1]

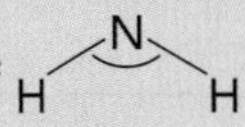

   b   Explain why ammonia is a polar molecule.   [2]

   c   An ammonia molecule and an aluminium chloride molecule can join
       together by forming a co-ordinate bond.

       i   Explain how a co-ordinate bond is formed.   [1]

       ii   Draw a dot-and-cross diagram to show the bonding in the
            compound formed between ammonia and aluminium chloride,
            H_3NAlCl_3. (Use • for a nitrogen electron, o for an aluminium
            electron and × for the hydrogen and chlorine electrons.)   [3]

   d   Aluminium chloride molecules join together to form a compound with
       the formula Al_2Cl_6. Draw a displayed formula (showing all atoms and
       bonds) to show the bonding in one Al_2Cl_6 molecule.
       Show the dative covalent bonds by arrows.   [2]

                                                                 [Total: 12]

CONTINUED

3 Electronegativity values can be used to predict the polarity of bonds.

a Define the term *electronegativity*. [2]

b The electronegativity values for some atoms are given below:

H = 2.1, C = 2.5, F = 4.0, Cl = 3.0, I = 2.5

Use these values to predict the polarity of each of the following bonds by copying the bonded atoms shown below and adding δ+ or δ− above each atom.

    i   H—I [1]

    ii   F—I [1]

    iii   C—Cl [1]

c The shape of iodine trichloride, ICl_3, is shown below.

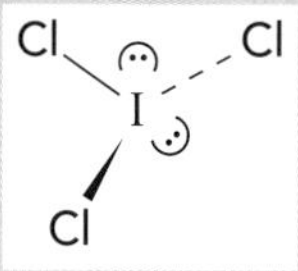

    i   Use the electronegativity values above to explain how you know that iodine trichloride is a covalent compound. [2]

    ii   Describe the shape of this molecule. [2]

    iii   Explain why the ICl_3 molecule has this shape. [2]

    iv   Suggest a value for the Cl—I—Cl bond angle. [1]

d Tetrachloromethane, CCl_4, is a non-polar molecule.

    i   Draw a diagram to show the shape of this molecule. [2]

    ii   Explain why this molecule is non-polar. [1]

[Total: 15]

4 The diagram below shows part of a giant metallic structure.

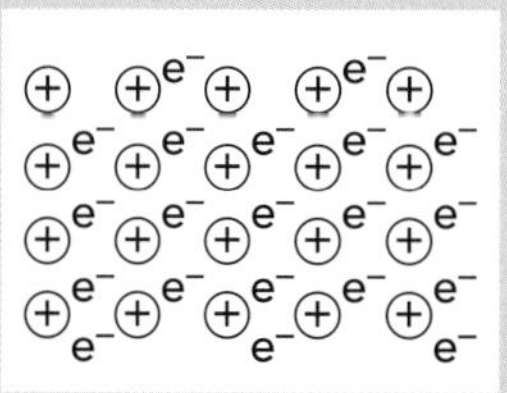

a Use this diagram to explain the main features of metallic bonding. [3]

b Explain why metals are good conductors of electricity. [2]

c Explain why, in general, metals have high melting points. [2]

d Suggest why potassium is a better conductor of electricity than lithium. [4]

[Total: 11]

CONTINUED

5   Methane, CH_4, is a gas at room temperature.

   a   Explain why methane is a gas at room temperature.   [2]

   b   Draw a diagram to show the shape of a molecule of methane. On your
       diagram show a value for the HCH bond angle.   [3]

   c   Perfumes often contain molecules that have simple molecular structures.
       Explain why.   [2]

   d   When a negatively charged rod is held next to a stream of propanone,
       CH_3COCH_3, the stream of propanone is attracted to the rod.

       Draw the full structure of a molecule of propanone and use your diagram
       to explain why the stream of propanone is attracted to the rod.   [3]

                                                                    [Total: 10]

6   Sodium iodide and magnesium oxide are ionic compounds. Iodine and oxygen
    are covalent molecules.

   a   Draw dot-and-cross diagrams for:

       i   magnesium oxide   [1]

       ii   oxygen   [1]

   b   Describe how sodium iodide and iodine differ in their solubility in
       water. Explain your answer.   [3]

   c   Explain why molten sodium iodide conducts electricity but molten
       iodine does not.   [2]

   d   The boiling point of sodium iodide is 1304 °C. The boiling point of
       iodine is 184 °C. Explain this difference.   [5]

   e   The Pauling electronegativities of Na and iodine are shown.

       sodium = 0.9, iodine = 2.5

       Use these electronegativity values to explain why sodium iodide is an
       ionic compound and not a covalent compound.   [2]

                                                                    [Total: 14]

7   Hydrogen sulfide, H_2S, is a covalent compound.

   a   Draw a dot-and-cross diagram for hydrogen sulfide.   [2]

   b   Draw a diagram of a hydrogen sulfide molecule to show its shape.
       Show on your diagram:

       i   the value of the HSH bond angle   [2]

       ii   the partial charges on each atom as $\delta+$ or $\delta-$ [1]

       iii an arrow showing the exact direction of the dipole in the
            molecule as a whole.   [1]

CONTINUED

c   Oxygen, O, sulfur, S, and selenium, Se, are in the same group in the Periodic Table.

    i   Explain why hydrogen selenide, H_2Se, has a higher boiling point than hydrogen sulfide, H_2S.   **[2]**

    ii   Explain why the boiling point of water is so much higher than the boiling point of hydrogen sulfide.   **[5]**

[Total: 13]

8   The table shows the type of bonding in a number of elements and compounds.

Element or compound	Type of bonding
Fe, Na	metallic
NaCl, $MgCl_2$	ionic
CO_2, Br_2	covalent within the molecules

a   Draw a labelled diagram to show metallic bonding.   **[2]**

b   Explain why magnesium chloride has a high melting point but bromine has a low melting point.   **[5]**

c   Explain why solid sodium conducts electricity but solid sodium chloride does not conduct electricity.   **[2]**

d   **i**   Draw a dot-and-cross diagram for carbon dioxide.   **[1]**

    ii   Describe the shape of the carbon dioxide molecule.   **[1]**

    iii   Explain why a carbon dioxide molecule has this shape.   **[2]**

e   Bromine is a liquid at room temperature. Weak instantaneous dipole–induced dipole forces hold the bromine molecules together. Describe how these forces arise.   **[5]**

[Total: 18]

9   **a**   Water is extensively hydrogen bonded. This gives it anomalous (peculiar) properties.

    i   Explain why ice is less dense than liquid water.   **[3]**

    ii   State two other anomalous properties of water.   **[2]**

b   Propanone has the structure shown below.

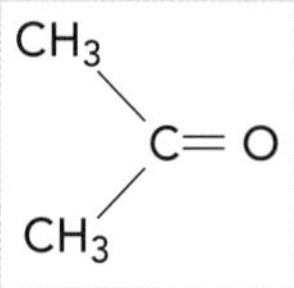

When propanone dissolves in water, it forms a hydrogen bond with water.

Describe the features water and propanone molecules have in order to form a hydrogen bond.   **[2]**

c   Draw a diagram to show a propanone molecule and a water molecule forming a hydrogen bond.   **[2]**

CONTINUED

d Propanone has a double bond. One of the bonds is a σ bond (sigma bond). The other is a π bond (pi bond).

Explain the difference between a σ bond and a π bond in terms of how they are formed. [3]

e Copy the diagram, then complete it to show the shapes of the electron clouds in the σ bond and the π bond between the carbon atoms in ethene. Label your diagram. [3]

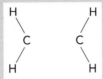

[Total: 15]

SELF-EVALUATION

After studying this chapter, complete a table like this:

I can	See section...	Needs more work	Almost there	Ready to move on
define electronegativity and explain the factors influencing the electronegativity values of the elements	4.7			
explain the trends in electronegativity across a period and down a group in the Periodic Table	4.7			
use differences in the Pauling electronegativity values to predict if a compound has ionic or covalent bonds	4.7			
define ionic bonding and describe ion bonding in **a** sodium chloride **b** magnesium oxide **c** calcium fluoride	4.2			

CONTINUED

I can	See section...	Needs more work	Almost there	Ready to move on
define covalent bonding and describe covalent bonding in a hydrogen e hydrogen chloride b oxygen f carbon dioxide c nitrogen g ammonia i ethane d chlorine h methane j ethene	4.3			
describe how some atoms in Period 3 can expand their octet of electrons to form compounds such as sulfur dioxide, phosphorus pentachloride and sulfur hexafluoride	4.3			
describe co-ordinate bonding (dative covalent bonding) in ions such as NH_4^+ and molecules such as Al_2Cl_6	4.3			
use dot-and-cross diagrams to show the arrangement of electrons in compounds with ionic, covalent and co-ordinate bonding	4.3			
describe covalent bonding in terms of orbital overlap giving sigma (σ) and pi (π) bonds	4.5			
describe how sigma and pi bonds form in a H_2 b C_2H_6 c C_2H_4 d HCN e N_2	4.5			
describe hybridisation of atomic orbitals to form sp, sp^2 and sp^3 orbitals	4.5			
define the terms *bond energy* and *bond length* and use these to compare the reactions of covalent molecules	4.3			
using 'valence shell electron pair repulsion' (VSEPR) theory, describe and explain the shapes and bond angles in: a BF_3 b CO_2 c CH_4 d NH_3 e H_2O f SF_6 g PF_5	4.4, 4.5			
predict the shapes and bond angles in other molecules and ions similar to those above	4.4			

CONTINUED

I can	See section...	Needs more work	Almost there	Ready to move on
describe hydrogen bonding	4.8			
explain, in terms of hydrogen bonding, the unusual properties of water (relatively low density of ice, relatively high melting point, relatively high surface tension)	4.8			
describe and understand the different types of intermolecular forces (van der Waals' forces) as either instantaneous dipoles or permanent dipoles	4.7			
describe metallic bonding	4.6			
describe the relative bond strengths of ionic, covalent and metallic bonds compared with intermolecular forces.	4.9			

States of matter

CONTINUED

- giant molecular structures including silicon(IV) oxide, graphite and diamond

- giant metallic structures including copper

- describe, interpret and predict the effect of different types of structure and bonding on the physical properties of substances, e.g. effect on melting point, boiling point, electrical conductivity and solubility

- deduce the type of structure and bonding present in a substance from given information.

BEFORE YOU START

1   Describe the states of matter (solids, liquids and gases) in terms of the proximity (closeness), arrangement and motion of particles. Compare your answers with those of another learner. How well did they compare?

2   How does the volume of a gas change when the temperature is changed at constant pressure and the pressure is changed at constant temperature? Discuss with another learner the reasons for these changes, using ideas about moving particles.

3   Draw a diagram of a giant covalent structure such as diamond or graphite. Compare your drawing with one in a textbook. How could your drawing be improved?

4   Discuss these questions with another learner.

   a   Why does diamond have a very high melting point but sulfur has a low melting point?

   b   Why does graphite conduct electricity but diamond does not?

   c   Explain how metals are able to conduct electricity.

   d   Use your knowledge of the structure of metals to explain why metals are malleable.

   Be prepared to share your ideas with the rest of the class.

5   Try this problem by yourself and then discuss with another learner.

   A substance, Y, is soluble in water. Y does not conduct electricity either when solid or in solution. Y has a melting point of 185°C.

   Describe the structure and bonding in Y, giving reasons for your answer.

6   Phosphorus has a simple molecular structure. Work with another learner to make a list of the physical properties of phosphorus.

LIQUID CRYSTALS: THE FOURTH STATE OF MATTER?

Figure 5.1: A liquid crystal display in action in a mobile phone.

Liquid crystal displays (LCDs) in mobile phones and computers are now part of everyday life (Figure 5.1). But how do they work?

When you heat crystals of cholesteryl benzoate to 147 °C, they melt to form a cloudy liquid. At 180 °C the liquid becomes transparent. The cloudy state between the liquid and solid is called a *liquid crystal metaphase*. Many substances with rod-shaped molecules form a metaphase. In the metaphase, the molecules can move slightly. They have lost their regular arrangement but there is still some structure. For example, they point in about the same direction or are twisted into a helix. The direction in which the molecules face can be changed by small electric fields.

LCDs have a thin film of liquid crystal between two transparent plates. The plates are treated chemically so that the liquid crystals arrange themselves in a particular way. The plates have an electrically conducting coating on their inner surface. Light that enters the display unit goes through a polariser, which makes the light vibrate in one plane. When the polarised light passes through the liquid crystal it turns through 90°. The light then passes through a second polariser set at 90° to the first. The display unit appears bright (Figure 5.2).

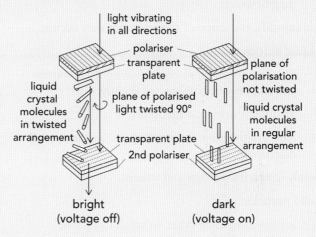

Figure 5.2: The bright and dark states of a liquid crystal (LCD) display.

When you apply a small voltage. the direction of the molecules changes so they no longer rotate in the plane of the polarised light. The unit appears dark.

When the voltage is switched off the molecules go back to their original arrangement. By making the conductive layer as separate small areas any pattern can be displayed and switched on or off by a small voltage.

Questions for discussion

Discuss with another learner or group of learners:

- Compare the structures of a metaphase with a liquid and a solid. Is a metaphase another state of matter or not?

- How many hours a day do you spend looking at LCD screens (phone, computer, etc)? Do you think this is good for you or not? Why do some people think that too much time spent on looking mobile phone screens is a bad thing?

5.1 States of matter

Gases have no fixed shape or volume.

Gas particles:

- are far apart, therefore gases can be compressed

- are randomly arranged

- can move freely from place to place, in all directions.

Liquids take the shape of the container they occupy.

Liquid particles:

- are close together, so liquids have a fixed volume and can only be compressed slightly

- are mostly arranged randomly

- have limited movement from place to place, in all directions.

Solids have a fixed shape and volume.

Solid particles:

- are touching each other, so solids cannot be compressed

- are usually in a regular arrangement

- cannot change positions with each other: they can only vibrate.

Question

1   Describe the changes that occur in the closeness and motion of the particles when:

   a   a solid changes to a liquid

   b   a liquid changes to a gas.

The state of a substance at room temperature and pressure depends on its structure and bonding. Four types of structure are found in elements and compounds:

- simple molecular or simple atomic, e.g. carbon dioxide, argon

- giant ionic, e.g. sodium chloride

- giant metallic, e.g. iron, copper

- giant molecular, e.g. silicon(IV) oxide.

The simple atomic structures found in the noble gases generally have similar physical properties to simple molecular gases. Although noble gases exist as isolated atoms, they can be thought of as having a molecular structure.

5.2 The gaseous state

The kinetic theory of gases

The idea that molecules in gases are in constant movement is called the **kinetic theory of gases**. This theory makes certain assumptions:

- the gas molecules move rapidly and randomly

- the distance between the gas molecules is much greater than the diameter of the molecules, so the volume of the molecules is negligible (hardly any volume).

- there are no intermolecular forces of attraction or repulsion between the molecules

- all collisions between particles are elastic: this means no kinetic energy is lost in collisions (kinetic energy is the energy associated with moving particles)

- the temperature of the gas is related to the average kinetic energy of the molecules.

A theoretical gas that fits this description is called an **ideal gas**. In reality, the gases you are learning about don't fit this description exactly, although they may come very close. We call these gases **real gases**.

Noble gases with small atoms, such as helium and neon, come close to ideal gas behaviour. This is because the intermolecular forces are so small.

KEY WORDS

kinetic theory: the theory that particles in gases and liquids are in constant movement. The kinetic theory can be used to explain the effect of temperature and pressure on the volume of a gas as well as rates of chemical reactions.

real gas: a gas that does not obey the ideal gas law, especially at low temperatures and high pressures.

KEY DEFINITION

ideal gas: a gas whose volume varies in proportion to the temperature and in inverse proportion to the pressure. Noble gases such as helium and neon approach ideal behaviour because of their low intermolecular forces.

Question

2   Explain why the intermolecular forces in a sample of helium and neon are very small.

> **IMPORTANT**
>
> Ideal gases have zero particle volume and no intermolecular forces of attraction.

Ideal gases

The volume that a gas occupies depends on:

- its pressure; we measure pressure in pascals, Pa

- its temperature; we measure temperatures of gases in kelvin, K.

The kelvin temperature equals the Celsius temperature plus 273. For example, 100 °C is 100 + 273 = 373 K.

Question

3   **a**   Convert the following temperatures into the kelvin temperature:

   i   245 °C

   ii   −45 °C

   b   How many pascals are there in 15 kPa?

> **IMPORTANT**
>
> The pressure of a gas is due to collisions between the gas molecules and the walls of the container.

Gases in a container exert a pressure. This is because the gas molecules are constantly hitting the walls of the container. If we decrease the volume of a gas (at constant temperature) the molecules are squashed closer together and hit the walls of the container more often.

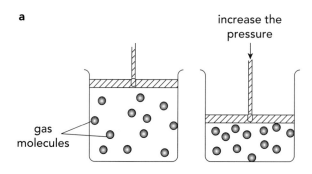

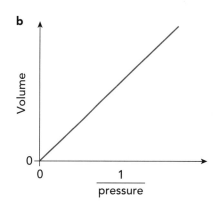

Figure 5.3: **a** As the volume of a gas decreases, at constant temperature, its pressure increases due to the increased frequency of the gas molecules hitting the walls of the container. **b** For an ideal gas a plot of the volume of gas against $\frac{1}{pressure}$ shows a proportional relationship

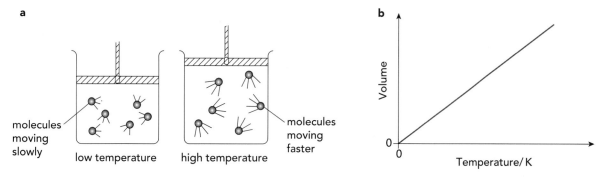

Figure 5.4: **a** As the temperature increases, at constant pressure, the volume of a gas increases. Molecules hit the walls with increased force. **b** For an ideal gas, the volume of a gas is proportional to its kelvin temperature.

So the pressure of the gas increases (Figure 5.3a). A graph of volume of gas plotted against $\dfrac{1}{\text{pressure}}$ gives a proportional relationship (as shown by the straight line in Figure 5.3b). We say that the volume is *inversely proportional* to the pressure.

> **IMPORTANT**
>
> Two variables are proportional if there is a constant ratio between them. Look at the figures for temperature and gas volume in the table below:
>
> | Temperature / K | 136.5 | 273 | 546 |
> |---|---|---|---|
> | Gas volume / dm³ | 11.2 | 22.4 | 44.8 |
>
> **Table 5.1:** Data table showing temperature against gas volume.

When a gas is heated at constant pressure its volume increases (Figure 5.4a). This is because the particles move faster and hit the walls of the container with greater force. For the pressure to be constant, the molecules must get further apart. The volume of a gas at constant pressure is proportional to its temperature measured in kelvin (Figure 5.4b).

An ideal gas will have a volume that varies exactly in proportion to its temperature and exactly in inverse proportion to its pressure.

Question

4   Some chemical reactions involving gases are performed in sealed glass tubes that do not melt at high temperatures. If the tubes have walls that are too thin, the tubes can easily break. Use the kinetic theory of gases to explain why these tubes should not be heated to high temperatures.

Limitations of the ideal gas laws

Scientists have taken accurate measurements to show how the volumes of gases change with temperature and pressure. These show us that gases do not always behave exactly as we expect an ideal gas to behave. This is because real gases do not always obey the kinetic theory in two ways:

*   there is not zero attraction between the molecules

*   we cannot ignore the volume of the molecules themselves.

These differences are especially noticeable at very high pressures and very low temperatures. Under these conditions:

*   the molecules are close to each other

*   the volume of the molecules is not negligible compared with the volume of the container

*   there are instantaneous dipole–induced dipole forces or permanent dipole–permanent dipole forces of attraction between the molecules

*   attractive forces pull the molecules towards each other and away from the walls of the container

*   the pressure is lower than expected for an ideal gas

*   the effective volume of the gas is smaller than expected for an ideal gas.

Question

5   a   What is meant by the term *ideal gas*?

b   Under what conditions do real gases differ from ideal gases? Explain your answer.

The general gas equation

> **IMPORTANT**
>
> The ideal gas equation $pV = nRT$ shows the relationship between pressure, volume, temperature and number of moles of gas. Make sure that you can rearrange this equation to make any of these values the subject of the expression, e.g. $n = \dfrac{pV}{RT}$

For an ideal gas, we can combine the laws about how the volume of a gas depends on temperature and pressure. We also know from Section 3.8 that the volume of a gas is proportional to the number of moles present. Putting all these together, gives us the ideal gas equation:

$$pV = nRT$$

p is the pressure in pascals, Pa

V is the volume of gas in cubic metres, m^3
(1 m^3 = 1000 dm^3)

n is the number of moles of gas $\left(n = \dfrac{m}{M_r} \right)$

R is the gas constant, which has a value of
8.31 J K^{-1} mol^{-1}

T is the temperature in kelvin, K.

Calculations using the general gas equation

If we know any four of the five physical quantities in the general gas equation, we can calculate the fifth.

> **IMPORTANT**
>
> To change °C to kelvin, add 273 to the Celsius (°C) temperature.
>
> A pressure of 101 325 pascals = 1.0 atmosphere pressure.

WORKED EXAMPLES

1 Calculate the volume occupied by 0.500 mol of carbon dioxide at a pressure of 150 kPa and a temperature of 19 °C.

$(R = 8.31$ J K^{-1} $mol^{-1})$

Solution

Step 1: Change pressure and temperature to their correct units:

150 kPa = 150 000 Pa;
19 °C = 19 + 273 = 292 K

Step 2: Rearrange the general gas equation to the form you need:

$pV = nRT$ so $V = \dfrac{nRT}{p}$

Step 3: Substitute the figures:

$V = \dfrac{nRT}{p}$

$= \dfrac{0.500 \times 8.31 \times 292}{150\ 000}$

$= 8.09 \times 10^{-3}$ m^3

$= 8.09$ dm^3

2 A flask of volume 5.00 dm^3 contained 4.00 g of oxygen.

Calculate the pressure exerted by the gas at a temperature of 127 °C.

$(R = 8.31$ J K^{-1} mol^{-1}; M_r oxygen = 32.0$)$

Solution

Step 1: Change temperature and volume to their correct units and calculate the number of moles of oxygen.

127 °C = 127 + 273 = 400 K

5 dm^3 = $\dfrac{5.00}{1000}$ m^3 = 5.00 × 10^{-3} m^3

$n = \dfrac{m}{M_r}$

$= \dfrac{4.00}{32.0}$

$= 0.125$ mol

Step 2: Rearrange the general gas equation to the form you need:

$pV = nRT$ so $p = \dfrac{nRT}{V}$

Step 3: Substitute the figures:

$p = \dfrac{nRT}{V}$

$p = \dfrac{0.125 \times 8.31 \times 400}{5 \times 10^3}$

$p = 8.31 \times 10^4$ Pa

Note:

If you are given the pressure in kPa and the volume in dm^3, you can insert these figures directly into the equation without having to convert into Pa and m^3. This is because by changing kPa to Pa you are multiplying by 1000 and by changing dm^3 to m^3 you are dividing by 1000. Because p and V are on the same side of the equation $pV = nRT$, the × 1000 and ÷ 1000 cancel each other.

Remember that if you substitute the pressure in kPa in the equation $pV = nRT$, the volume of gas calculated will be in dm^3. If you substitute the pressure in Pa in the equation $pV = nRT$, the volume of gas calculated will be in m^3.

Calculating relative molecular masses

An accurate method of finding the relative molecular mass of a substance is to use a mass spectrometer (see Chapter 3).

A less accurate method, but one that is suitable for a school laboratory, is to use the general gas equation to find the mass of gas in a large flask. As the number of moles is the mass of a substance divided by its relative molecular mass, we can find the relative molecular mass of a gas by simply substituting in the general gas equation. Although weighing gases is a difficult process because they are so light and you have to consider the buoyancy of the air, the method can give reasonable results.

You can apply this method to find the relative molecular mass of a volatile liquid. The volatile liquid is injected into a gas syringe placed in a syringe oven (Figure 5.5). The liquid vaporises and the volume of the vapour is recorded.

WORKED EXAMPLE

3   A flask of volume 2.00 dm^3 was found to contain 5.28 g of a gas. The pressure in the flask was 200 kPa and the temperature was 20 °C. Calculate the relative molecular mass of the gas.

   ($R = 8.31$ J K^{-1} mol^{-1})

   Solution

   Step 1: Change pressure, temperature and volume to their correct units.

   $200 \text{ kPa} = 2.00 \times 10^5 \text{ Pa}$

   $20 \text{ °C} = 20 + 273 = 293 \text{ K}$

   $2.00 \text{ dm}^3 = \frac{2.00}{1000} \text{ m}^3 = 2.00 \times 10^{-3} \text{ m}^3$

   Step 2: Rearrange the general gas equation to the form you need:

   $$pV = nRT \quad \text{and} \quad n = \frac{m}{M_r}$$

   $$\text{so } pV = \frac{m}{M_r} RT,$$

   which gives $M_r = \frac{mRT}{pV}$

   Step 3: Substitute the figures:

   $$M_r = \frac{mRT}{pV} = \frac{5.28 \times 8.31 \times 293}{(2.00 \times 10^5) \times (2.0 \times 10^{-3})}$$

   $$= 32.14$$

   $$= 32 \text{ g mol}^{-1}$$

Question

6   **a**   Calculate the volume occupied by 272 g of methane at a pressure of 250 kPa and a temperature of 54 °C.
      ($R = 8.31$ J K^{-1} mol^{-1}; M_r methane = 16.0)

   b   The pressure exerted by 0.25 mol of carbon monoxide in a 10 dm^3 flask is 120 kPa. Calculate the temperature in the flask in kelvin.

PRACTICAL ACTIVITY 5.1

Determining relative molecular mass

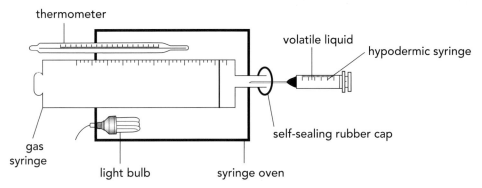

Figure 5.5: The relative molecular mass of a volatile liquid can be found using a syringe oven.

SAFETY: Only carry out this activity in the presence of a teacher after safety aspects have been explained.

1 Put a gas syringe in the syringe oven and leave until the temperature is constant.

2 Record the volume of air in the gas syringe.

3 Fill a hypodermic syringe with the volatile liquid and find its total mass.

4 Inject a little of the liquid into the gas syringe then find the total mass of the hypodermic syringe again.

5 Allow the liquid to vaporise in the gas syringe.

6 Record the final volume of vapour + air in the gas syringe.

7 Record the atmospheric temperature and pressure.

The calculation is carried out in the same way as Worked example 3.

The volume of vapour produced is:

final gas syringe volume
　　　　　　　　　　－ initial gas syringe volume

The mass used in the calculation is:

initial mass of hypodermic syringe + liquid
　　　　　－ final mass of hypodermic syringe + liquid

Questions

7 When 0.08 g of liquid X was vaporised at 100 °C, 23 cm³ of vapour was formed. The atmospheric pressure was 1.02×10^5 Pa. Calculate the relative molecular mass of liquid X. ($R = 8.31$ J K^{-1} mol^{-1})

8 A flask of volume 2×10^{-3} m³ contains 4.19 g of a gas. The pressure in the flask is 300 kPa and the temperature is 20 °C. $R = 8.31$ J K^{-1} mol^{-1}.

You can find the relative molecular mass using the expression:

$$M_r = \frac{mRT}{pV}$$

Which one of the following gives the correct value for the relative molecular mass of the gas?

A $\dfrac{4.19 \times 8.31 \times 293}{(300 \times 10^3) \times (2 \times 10^{-3})}$

B $\dfrac{4.19 \times 8.31 \times 20}{(300 \times 10^3) \times (2 \times 10^{-3})}$

C $\dfrac{4.19 \times 8.31 \times 293}{(300) \times (2 \times 10^{-3})}$

D $\dfrac{(300 \times 10^3) \times (2 \times 10^{-3})}{4.19 \times 8.31 \times 293}$

5.3 The liquid state

The behaviour of liquids

When we heat a solid:

- the energy transferred to the solid makes the particles vibrate more vigorously

- the forces of attraction between the particles weaken

- the solid changes to a liquid at its melting point.

> **IMPORTANT**
>
> The melting point of a solid is the temperature at which it changes to a liquid at 1 atmosphere pressure.

We call this change of state *melting*.

For ionic compounds, we need a high temperature to melt the substance because ionic bonding is very strong. For molecular solids, we need a lower temperature, just enough to overcome the weak intermolecular forces between the particles.

The particles in a liquid are still close to each other but they have enough kinetic energy to keep sliding past each other in a fairly random way. They do not move freely as gas particles do. For brief periods, the particles in liquids are arranged in a slightly ordered way. But this order is always being broken up when the particles gain kinetic energy from neighbouring particles.

When we cool a liquid, the particles:

- lose kinetic energy so they do not move around so readily

- experience increasing forces of attraction

- stop sliding past each other when the temperature is sufficiently low; the liquid solidifies.

We call this change of state *freezing*.

Vaporisation and vapour pressure

When we heat a liquid:

- the energy transferred to the liquid makes the particles move faster

- the forces of attraction between the particles weaken

- the particles with most energy are the first to escape from the forces holding them together in the liquid

- the liquid evaporates: this happens at a temperature below the boiling point

- the forces weaken enough for all the particles to become completely free from each other; they move fast and randomly and they spread out

- the liquid boils; this happens at the boiling point.

This change from the liquid state to the gas state is called **vaporisation**. The energy required to change one mole of liquid to one mole of gas is called the *enthalpy change of vaporisation*.

When we cool a vapour, the particles:

- lose kinetic energy so the molecules move around less quickly

- experience increasing forces of attraction

- move more slowly and become closer together when the temperature is sufficiently low; the gas liquefies.

We call this change of state **condensation**.

These changes in state are *reversible*. Water can be boiled to form steam, and steam can be condensed to form liquid water. These changes involve opposite energy transfers. For example: energy has to be transferred to water to boil it to form steam. But when steam condenses to form water, energy is transferred from the steam.

If we put some water in an open beaker, it evaporates until none is left. But what happens when we allow water to evaporate in a closed container?

> **KEY WORDS**
>
> **vaporisation**: the change in state when a liquid changes to vapour.
>
> **condensation**: the change in state when a vapour changes to a liquid.

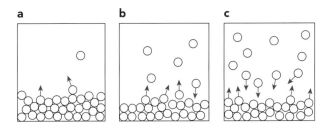

Figure 5.6: a Water molecules move from liquid to vapour. **b** As more molecules move from liquid to vapour, some begin to move back to the liquid. **c** An equilibrium is reached with molecules going from liquid to vapour at the same rate as from vapour to liquid.

At first, water molecules escape from the surface of the liquid to become vapour (Figure 5.6a). As more and more molecules escape, the molecules in the vapour become closer together. Eventually the molecules with lower kinetic energy will not be able to overcome the attractive forces of neighbouring molecules. The vapour begins to condense. So some water molecules return to the liquid (Figure 5.6b). Eventually, water molecules return to the liquid at the same rate as water molecules escape to the vapour. A position of equilibrium is reached (Figure 5.6c; see Chapter 8).

At equilibrium the concentration of water molecules in the vapour remains constant.

$$\text{water molecules in liquid} \underset{\xrightarrow{\hspace{2cm}}}{\overset{\text{equal rate of movement}}{\xleftarrow{\hspace{2cm}}}} \text{water molecules in vapour}$$

In this situation the pressure exerted by a vapour in equilibrium with its liquid is called its **vapour pressure**. The vapour pressure is caused by the gas particles hitting the walls of the container. Vapour pressure will increase when the temperature increases because:

- the gas particles have more kinetic energy
- the gas particles move faster, so they are able to overcome intermolecular forces of attraction more easily.

> **IMPORTANT**
>
> The boiling point of a liquid is the temperature at which it changes to a gas at 1 atmosphere (101 325 Pa) pressure. A more exact definition is the temperature at which the vapour pressure is equal to the atmospheric pressure.

Question

9 Bromine is a reddish-brown liquid. Some liquid bromine is placed in a closed jar. The bromine starts to evaporate. The colour of the vapour above the liquid bromine becomes darker and darker. After a time the bromine vapour does not get any darker.

Use ideas about moving particles to explain these observations.

5.4 The solid state

Many ionic, metallic and covalent compounds are crystalline. The regular structure of crystals is due to the regular packing of the particles within the crystal. We call this regularly repeating arrangement of ions, atoms or molecules a *crystal lattice*.

Ionic lattices

Ionic lattices have three-dimensional arrangements of alternating positive and negative ions. Compounds with ionic lattices are sometimes called *giant ionic structures*.

The type of **lattice** formed depends on the relative sizes of the ions present. The ionic lattices for sodium chloride and magnesium oxide are cubic. In sodium chloride, each sodium ion is surrounded by six oppositely charged chloride ions. The chloride ions are much larger than the sodium ions. The sodium ions fit into the spaces between the chloride ions so that they are as close as possible to them (Figure 5.7).

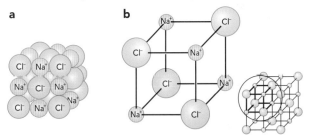

Figure 5.7: The arrangement of the ions in sodium chloride: **a** the actual packing of the ions, **b** an 'exploded' view so that you can see the arrangement of the ions clearly.

> **KEY WORDS**
>
> **vapour pressure:** the pressure exerted by a vapour in equilibrium with a liquid.
>
> **lattice:** a regularly repeating arrangement of ions, atoms or molecules in three dimensions.

Magnesium oxide has the same lattice structure as sodium chloride. Magnesium ions replace sodium ions and the oxide ions replace the chloride ions.

The properties of ionic compounds reflect their structure as well as their bonding:

- They are hard. It takes a lot of energy to scratch the surface because of the strong attractive forces keeping the ions together.

- They are brittle. Ionic crystals may split apart when hit in the same direction as the layers of ions (Figure 5.8). The layers of ions may be displaced by the force of the blow so that ions with the same charge come together. The repulsions between thousands of ions in the layers, all with the same charge, cause the crystals to split along these cleavage planes.

- They have high melting points and high boiling points. This is because the attraction between the large numbers of oppositely charged ions in the lattice acts in all directions and bonds them strongly together. The melting points and boiling points increase with the charge density on the ions. So magnesium oxide, $Mg^{2+}O^{2-}$, has a higher melting point (2852 °C) than sodium chloride, Na^+Cl^- (801 °C). This is because there is a greater electrostatic attraction between doubly charged positive and negative ions than between singly charged ions of similar size.

- Many ionic compounds are soluble in water because they can form ion–dipole bonds (see Section 19.4).

- They only conduct electricity when molten or in solution (see Section 4.9).

Metallic lattices

> **IMPORTANT**
>
> Remember that metals conduct electricity when solid or liquid due to mobile delocalised *electrons* but ionic giant structures only conduct when liquid (molten) or when in aqueous solution due to mobile *ions*.

In Chapter 4, we learnt that a metallic lattice consists of ions surrounded by a sea of electrons. The ions are often packed in hexagonal layers or in a cubic arrangement. Figure 5.9 shows part of a lattice of copper ions arranged in layers. When a force is applied, the layers can slide over each other. But in a metallic bond, the attractive forces between the metal ions and the delocalised electrons act in all directions. So when the layers slide, new metallic bonds are easily re-formed between ions in new lattice positions and the delocalised electrons (Figure 5.11). The delocalised electrons continue to hold the ions in the lattice together. The metal now has a different shape. This explains why metals are malleable (they can be hammered into different shapes) and ductile (they can be drawn into wires). The high tensile strength and hardness of most metals is also due to the strong attractive forces between the metal ions and the delocalised electrons.

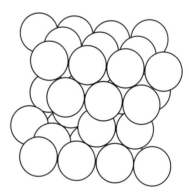

Figure 5.9: Layers of copper ions.

Figure 5.10: You can clearly see the metal crystals or 'grains' in this metal plate.

Figure 5.8: Sapphires sparkle in the light when polished. They are cut by exerting a force on the cleavage planes between layers of ions in the crystal.

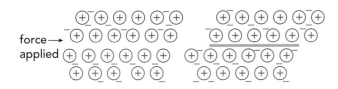

Figure 5.11: When a force is applied to a metallic structure, the layers slide over each other and re-form in new lattice positions.

Alloys and their properties

An **alloy** is a mixture of two or more metals or a metal with a non-metal. The metal added to create the alloy becomes part of the crystal lattice of the other metal.

KEY WORD

alloy: a mixture of two or more metals or a metal with a non-metal.

Brass is an alloy of copper (70%) with zinc (30%). It is stronger than copper but still malleable. For these reasons, it is used for musical instruments, ornaments and household items such as door handles.

But *why* is brass stronger than pure copper?

Zinc ions are larger than copper ions. The presence of different-sized metal ions makes the arrangement of the lattice less regular. This stops the layers of ions from sliding over each other so easily when a force is applied (Figure 5.12).

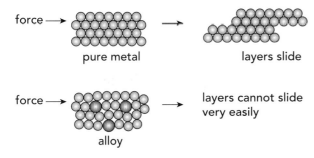

Figure 5.12: The layers of ions in an alloy slide less easily than in a pure metal because the structure of the lattice is less regular.

Pure aluminium is softer than many metals. It is ductile and has high electrical and thermal conductivity. Because of its low strength, pure aluminium is of little use in engineering. But its strength can be increased by adding other elements such as copper, magnesium, silicon and manganese. Many alloys of aluminium are lightweight, strong and resistant to corrosion. These are used for the bodies of aircraft, for the cylinder blocks of car engines and for bicycle frames, all situations where low density combined with strength and corrosion resistance is important.

Bronze is an alloy of copper and tin. A 33-metre high bronze statue was built near the harbour in Rhodes (Greece) over 2000 years ago. The statue fell down after an earthquake and was eventually bought by a Syrian merchant. The bronze was recycled to make useful implements.

Question

10 Explain the following:

  a   why are most metals strong, but ionic solids are brittle?

  b   why is an alloy of copper and tin stronger than either copper or tin alone?

Simple molecular lattices

Substances with a simple molecular structure, such as iodine, can also form crystals (Figure 5.13). This reflects the regular packing of the molecules in a lattice structure.

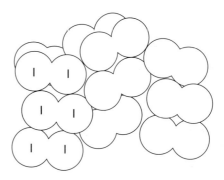

Figure 5.13: Iodine molecules are arranged in a lattice structure.

Ice also forms a crystalline lattice. Ice and water have peculiar properties because of hydrogen bonding (see Section 4.8).

The distance between the nuclei of neighbouring iodine molecules is greater than the distance between the nuclei within the iodine molecule. This is because the forces between the molecules are weak intermolecular forces, whereas the forces between the atoms within the molecule are strong covalent bonds. Very little energy is needed to overcome the weak intermolecular forces between the molecules. The lattice is easily broken down when iodine crystals are heated, so iodine has a low melting point.

Question

11 The table shows some properties of four elements. Use the data to answer the following questions.

Element	Density / g cm^{-3}	Tensile strength / 10^{10} Pa	Electrical conductivity / 10^8 S m^{-1}
aluminium	2.70	7.0	0.38
iron / steel	7.86	21.1	0.10
copper	8.92	13.0	0.59
sulfur	2.07	breaks easily	1×10^{-23}

Table 5.2: Information table for Question 11.

a Why is aluminium with a steel core used for overhead electricity cables in preference to copper?

b Suggest why many car engine blocks are made from aluminium alloys rather than from steel.

c Explain the differences in tensile strength and electrical conductivity of iron and sulfur.

Giant molecular structures

IMPORTANT

GIANT STRUCTURE: Most giant structures have a network of either covalent bonds (molecular giant structure), metallic bonds (metallic giant structure) or ionic bonds (ionic giant structure). The network of strong bonds is hard to break and so the melting and boiling points of these structures are generally very high.

Some covalently bonded structures have a three-dimensional network of covalent bonds throughout the whole structure. We call these structures giant molecular structures or giant covalent structures.

They have high melting and boiling points because of the large number of strong covalent bonds linking the whole structure. Elements such as carbon (graphite and diamond), and compounds such as silicon dioxide, can be giant molecular structures. Diamond and graphite are different forms of the same element. Different crystalline or molecular forms of the same element are called allotropes.

KEY WORDS

giant molecular structure / giant covalent structure: structures having a three-dimensional network of covalent bonds throughout the whole structure.

allotrope: different crystalline or molecular forms of the same element. Graphite and diamond are allotropes of carbon.

IMPORTANT

Allotropes are different crystalline forms of the same element. The term only applies to solids. Diamond, graphite and buckminsterfullerene are allotropes of carbon.

Graphite

In graphite, the carbon atoms are arranged in planar layers. Within the layers, the carbon atoms are arranged in hexagons. Each carbon atom is joined to three other carbon atoms by strong covalent bonds (Figure 5.14). The fourth electron of each carbon atom occupies a p orbital. These p orbitals on every carbon atom in each planar layer overlap sideways. A cloud of delocalised electrons is formed above and below the plane of the carbon rings. These electron clouds join up to form extended delocalised rings of electrons.

The layers of carbon atoms are kept next to each other by weak instantaneous dipole–induced dipole forces.

The properties of graphite are related to its structure.

- **High melting and boiling points:** there is strong covalent bonding throughout the layers of carbon atoms. A lot of energy is needed to overcome these strong bonds.

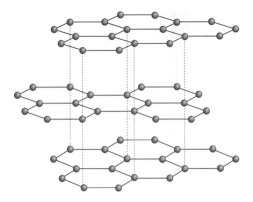

Figure 5.14: The structure of graphite.

- **Softness:** graphite is easily scratched. The forces between the layers of carbon atoms are weak. The layers of graphite can slide over each other when a force is applied. The layers readily flake off. This 'flakiness' is why graphite is used in pencil 'leads' and feels slippery.

- **Good conductor of electricity:** when a voltage is applied, the delocalised electrons (mobile electrons) can move along the layers.

Diamond

In diamond, each carbon atom forms four covalent bonds with other carbon atoms (Figure 5.15). The carbon atoms are positioned around each other in a tetrahedral arrangement. The network of carbon atoms extends almost unbroken throughout the whole structure. The regular arrangement of the atoms gives diamond a crystalline structure.

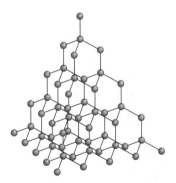

Figure 5.15: The structure of diamond.

The properties of diamond are related to its structure.

- **High melting and boiling points:** there is strong covalent bonding throughout the whole structure. A lot of energy is needed to break these strong bonds and separate the atoms.

- **Hardness:** diamond cannot be scratched easily because it is difficult to break the three-dimensional network of strong covalent bonds.

- **Does not conduct electricity:** all of the four outer electrons on every carbon atom are involved in covalent bonding. This means that there are no free electrons available to carry the electric current.

Most of the diamonds used around the world have been mined from the Earth's crust. However, artificial diamonds can be made by heating other forms of carbon under high pressure. Artificial diamonds are too small to be used for jewellery but they can be used for drill tips.

Silicon(IV) oxide

There are several forms of silicon(IV) oxide. The silicon(IV) oxide found in the mineral quartz (Figure 5.16) has a structure similar to diamond (Figure 5.17).

Figure 5.16: The shape of these quartz crystals reflects the regular arrangement of the silicon and oxygen atoms.

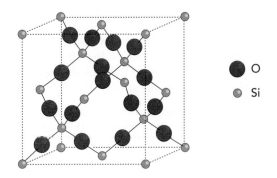

	O
	Si

Figure 5.17: The structure of silicon(IV) oxide.

Each silicon atom is bonded to four oxygen atoms but each oxygen atom is bonded to only two silicon atoms. So the formula for silicon(IV) oxide is SiO_2. Silicon dioxide has properties similar to that of diamond. It forms hard, colourless crystals with high melting and boiling points and it does not conduct electricity.

Sand is largely silicon(IV) oxide.

> **IMPORTANT**
>
> Remember that most giant molecular structures do not conduct electricity. One exception is graphite. Most do not conduct heat but diamond is a good conductor of heat.

Questions

12 Explain the following properties of silicon(IV) oxide by referring to its structure and bonding.

   a   It has a high melting point.

   b   It does not conduct electricity.

   c   It is a crystalline solid.

   d   It is hard.

13 Copy and complete the table below to compare the properties of giant ionic, giant molecular, giant metallic and simple molecular structures.

	Giant ionic	Giant molecular	Metallic	Simple molecular
Two examples				
Particles present				
Forces keeping particles together				
Hardness				
Melting points and boiling points				
Electrical conductivity				
Solubility in water				

Table 5.3: Table template for Question 13.

14 The table shows some physical properties of three substances X, Y and Z.

Substance	Melting point / °C	Electrical conductivity when molten	Solubility in water
X	747	good	soluble
Y	114	very poor	almost insoluble
Z	1495	good	insoluble

Table 5.4: Information table for Question 14.

Which one of these statements about X, Y and Z is completely true?

A   X has a giant ionic structure, Y has a giant molecular structure, Z is a metal.

B   X is a metal, Y has a simple molecular structure, Z has a giant molecular structure.

C   X is a metal, Y has a simple molecular structure, Z has a giant ionic structure.

D   X has a giant ionic structure, Y has a simple molecular structure, Z is a metal.

5.5 Fullerenes

Graphite and diamond are not the only allotropes of carbon. In recent years, substances called *fullerenes* have been made. The structure of many fullerenes is based on rings of carbon atoms, as is the structure of graphite. But many fullerenes exhibit properties unlike those of graphite. The individual particles in fullerenes may have one of their dimensions between 0.1 and 100 nanometres (1 nanometre = 10^{-9} m). Particles of this size are called *nanoparticles*. Another form of carbon, *graphene*, can be regarded as a single layer of graphite.

Fullerenes are allotropes of carbon in the form of hollow spheres or tubes. They are similar in structure to graphite, in that each carbon atom is bonded to three other carbon atoms. They contain rings of carbon atoms arranged in hexagons and in addition many contain rings of carbon atoms arranged in pentagons.

Buckminsterfullerene

The first fullerene discovered was called **buckminsterfullerene, C_{60}** (Figure 5.18). Buckminsterfullerene is a simple molecular structure. The C_{60} molecule has the shape of a football (soccer ball). The carbon atoms are arranged at the corners of 20 hexagons and 12 pentagons. The bonds where two hexagons join are shorter than the bonds between the hexagons and the pentagons. As in graphite, some of the electrons in C_{60} are delocalised, but to a lesser extent than in graphite. Since the discovery of the C_{60} molecule, many types of buckminsterfullerene have

KEY WORD

buckminsterfullerene: a simple molecular structure of carbon, with formula C_{60}. The molecule has the shape of a football (soccer ball). The carbon atoms are arranged at the corners of 20 hexagons and 12 pentagons. The bonds where two hexagons join are shorter than the bonds between the hexagons and the pentagons.

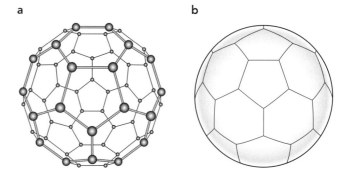

a   b

Figure 5.18: The shape of a buckminsterfullerene molecule, C_{60}, **a** is similar to that of a football, **b**.

been discovered. Some are ball-shaped molecules that are multiples of C_{60}, e.g. C_{120}. Other fullerene molecules include C_{20}, C_{70} and C_{72}.

The properties of buckminsterfullerene are significantly different from those of graphite and diamond.

- It has a relatively low sublimation point. It turns directly from the solid to the vapour state when heated to about 600 °C. (Graphite only turns from the solid to the vapour state at about 3700 °C.) This is because there are weak intermolecular forces between each buckminsterfullerene molecule and no continuous layered giant structure as in graphite.

- It is relatively soft because it does not require much energy to overcome the weak intermolecular forces.

- It is a poor conductor of electricity compared with graphite because the extent of electron delocalisation is lower.

- It is slightly soluble in solvents such as carbon disulfide and methylbenzene. Neither diamond nor graphite is soluble in common solvents.

- It is more reactive than graphite or diamond. Buckminsterfullerene reacts with hydrogen, fluorine, chlorine, bromine and oxygen. This is due to the relatively high electron density in certain parts of the molecule (see electrophilic addition in Section 15.1).

Nanotubes

> **Note:** Nanotubes and graphene are not part of the syllabus, but you may be asked questions about the structure and related properties of an unfamiliar substance from given information, e.g. a diagram of the structure.

A second type of fullerene is a class of molecules described as **nanotubes**. Nanotubes are fullerenes of hexagonally arranged carbon atoms like a single layer of graphite bent into the form of a cylinder (Figure 5.19). The first nanotubes to be made were one layer of carbon atoms in thickness. More recently, nanotubes have been made with thicker walls with several tubes inside one another.

Although the diameter of a nanotube is very small, it can be made relatively long. The length of the nanotube cylinder can be a million times greater than its diameter.

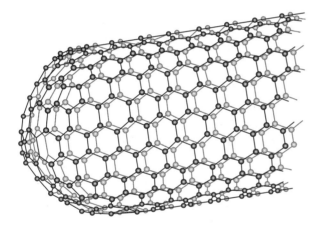

Figure 5.19: Part of the structure of a nanotube. The ends of the cylinder are often closed.

Nanotubes have characteristic properties:

- They have high electrical conductivity along the long axis of the cylinder. This is because, like graphite, some of the electrons are delocalised and are able to move along the cylinder when a voltage is applied.

KEY WORD

nanotube: fullerene of hexagonally arranged carbon atoms like a single layer of graphite bent into the form of a cylinder.

- They have a very high tensile strength when a force is applied along the long axis of the cylinder. They can be up to 100 times stronger than steel of the same thickness.

- They have very high melting points (typically about 3500 °C). This is because there is strong covalent bonding throughout the structure.

Fullerenes have a large range of potential uses. Scientists can attach reactive groups to their surfaces and metal complexes (see Section 24.3) can also be formed. Small molecules or atoms can be trapped in the cages of buckminsterfullerenes. Possible medical uses include delivering drugs to specific places in the body. Nanotubes are used in tiny electrical circuits as 'wires' and as electrodes in paper-thin batteries. They can be incorporated into clothing and sports equipment for added strength. They have also been used in the treatment of certain types of cancer.

Graphene

Graphene is a single isolated layer of graphite (Figure 5.20). The hexagonally arranged sheet of carbon atoms is not completely rigid and it can be distorted.

Graphene has some of the properties of graphite, but they are more exaggerated. For example:

- Graphene is the most chemically reactive form of carbon.

- Single sheets of graphene burn at very low temperatures and are much more reactive than graphite.

- Graphene is extremely strong for its mass.

- For a given amount of material, graphene conducts electricity and heat much better than graphite.

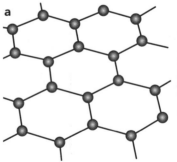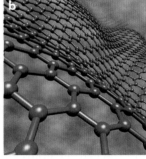

Figure 5.20: a Part of a graphene sheet. **b** 'Waves' in a sheet of graphene.

It has been said that 'a one square metre hammock made of graphene could support a 4 kg cat but would weigh only as much as the cat's whisker'. Potential applications of graphene include use in tiny electrical circuits and for tiny transistors, touchscreens, solar cells and other energy storage devices.

Question

15 Suggest, using ideas of structure and bonding, why:

   a   buckminsterfullerene, C_{60}, is converted from a solid to a gas at a relatively low temperature

   b   graphene is a good conductor of electricity

   c   buckminsterfullerene, C_{60}, is relatively soft.

REFLECTION

1   Work with another learner to draw up a mind map (spider diagram) to show different types of chemical structure. For each structure, include the types of bonding and show how its physical properties relate to either structure or bonding or both. For example, starting from the centre, you might have: all substances → type of structure → type of bonding → melting point high because…

   How would you improve the mind map?

2   Work with another learner to write a list of scientific words that are new to you in this chapter (they don't have to be key words). Then ask the other learner to explain one of the words to you. It is then your turn to explain a word that the other learner has chosen from the list.

   What was the most challenging word for you to explain?

SUMMARY

Ideal gases have zero particle volume and no intermolecular forces of attraction.
The volume of a gas under different conditions of temperature and pressure can be calculated using the ideal gas equation $pV = nRT$.
The ideal gas equation can be used to determine the relative molecular mass of simple molecules.
Ionic compounds form a giant three-dimensional lattice structure containing ions in a regularly repeating pattern. The high melting points of ionic substances are due to strong ionic forces acting in all directions between the ions.
The low melting points of simple molecular structures such as iodine are due to weak intermolecular forces between the molecules.
The high melting points of giant molecular structures such as diamond are due to the large number of strong covalent bonds arranged in a regularly repeating pattern.

EXAM-STYLE QUESTIONS

COMMAND WORD

Give: produce an answer from a given source or recall / memory.

1   Four types of structure are:
   - giant molecular
   - giant ionic
   - giant metallic
   - simple molecular

   a   **Give** two examples of a giant ionic structure and two examples of a simple molecular structure.   [4]

   b   Explain why substances with giant ionic structures are often brittle, but metallic structures are malleable.   [6]

   c   Explain why giant molecular structures have higher melting points than simple molecular structures.   [6]

   d   Diamond and graphite are two forms of carbon with giant molecular structures. Explain why graphite conducts electricity but diamond does not.   [5]

   [Total: 21]

2   The structures of carbon dioxide and silicon dioxide are shown in the diagram below.

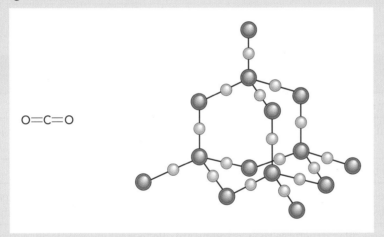

   O=C=O

   Use your knowledge of structure and bonding to explain the following:

   a   carbon dioxide is a gas at room temperature   [3]

   b   silicon(IV) oxide is a solid with a high melting point   [3]

   c   neither carbon dioxide nor silicon(IV) oxide conducts electricity.   [2]

   [Total: 8]

3   This question is about gases.

   a   What is meant by the term *ideal gas*?   [1]

   b   Under what conditions does a gas not behave ideally? Explain your answer for one of these conditions.   [4]

CONTINUED

c Helium is a noble gas. It exists as single atoms. Explain why:

   i helium has a very low boiling point [2]

   ii helium does not conduct electricity. [1]

d A weather balloon contains 0.500 kg of helium. Calculate the volume of the gas in the balloon at a pressure of 0.500×10^5 Pa and a temperature of −20.0 °C.

   ($R = 8.31$ J K^{-1} mol^{-1}; A_r He = 4.0) [5]

[Total: 13]

4 Water and bromine are both simple molecular substances.

a Both water and bromine form a lattice structure in the solid state. What is the meaning of the term *lattice*? [2]

b The boiling point of water is 100 °C. The boiling point of bromine is 59 °C. Explain the reason for this difference in terms of intermolecular forces. [4]

c Use ideas about the kinetic theory to explain what happens when liquid bromine evaporates to form bromine vapour. [4]

d When 0.20 g of a liquid, Y, with a simple molecular structure was evaporated it produced 80 cm^3 of vapour.

   The temperature was 98 °C and the pressure 1.1×10^5 Pa. Calculate the relative molecular mass of Y.

   ($R = 8.31$ J K^{-1} mol^{-1}) [5]

[Total: 15]

5 The table gives data on the physical properties of five substances, A to E.

a Copy the table and fill in the gaps. [7]

Substance	Melting point	Electrical conductivity		Type of structure
		as a solid	as a liquid	
A	high	poor	good	i
B	very low	ii	iii	iv
C	high	poor	poor	v
D	high	good	vi	giant metallic
E	high	poor	vii	giant covalent

b Explain the magnitude (how high or low) of the melting point and electrical conductivity of substance A. [6]

c Explain the magnitude of the melting point and electrical conductivity of substance B. [5]

[Total: 18]

6 The uses of metals are often related to their properties.

   a Describe the structure of a typical metal. [2]

   b Explain why metals are malleable. [4]

   c Consider the information in the table below to answer the questions that follow.

Element	Density / g cm^{-3}	Tensile strength / 10^{10} Pa	Electrical conductivity / 10^8 S m^{-1}
aluminium	2.70	7.0	0.38
copper	8.92	13.0	0.59
steel	7.86	21.1	0.10

   i Suggest why aluminium is more suitable than steel for building aeroplane bodies. [1]

   ii Explain why overhead electricity cables are made from aluminium with a steel core rather than just from copper. [5]

   d The effect of alloying copper with zinc on the strength of the alloy is shown in the table below.

% copper	% zinc	Tensile strength / 10^8 Pa
100	0	2.3
80	20	3.0
60	40	3.6
0	100	1.4

   Describe and explain the change in tensile strength as the percentage of zinc increases from 0% to 40%. [5]

   e State the name of the alloy of copper with zinc. [1]

   [Total: 18]

7 The diagram shows the structures of graphite and diamond.

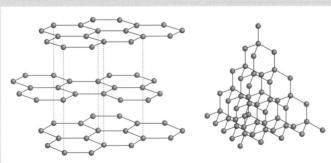

CONTINUED

Use the diagrams and your knowledge of structure and bonding to answer the following questions.

a   Explain why both diamond and graphite have high melting points.   **[2]**

b   i   Explain why graphite is used in making handles for tennis racquets.   **[3]**

   ii   Explain why graphite is used in pencil 'leads' for writing.   **[4]**

c   Explain why diamond is used on the tips of high-speed drills.   **[5]**

[Total: 14]

8   Crystals of sodium chloride have a lattice structure.

a   Describe a sodium chloride lattice.   **[3]**

b   Explain the following properties of sodium chloride.

   i   Sodium chloride has a high melting point.   **[3]**

   ii   Sodium chloride conducts electricity when molten but not when solid.   **[3]**

   iii   Sodium chloride is hard but brittle.   **[5]**

[Total: 14]

9   The diagram shows some allotropes of carbon.

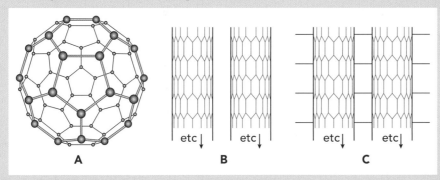

a   Give the name of allotrope A, which has the formula C_{60}.   **[1]**

b   Explain in terms of structure and bonding why structure A is gaseous at 800 °C but diamond is not.   **[6]**

c   Structure B shows an allotrope of carbon in the form of tubes.

   Describe the similarities and differences between structure B and graphite.   **[4]**

d   Structure C is stronger than structure B when a force is applied in the same direction as the long axis of the tube.

   Explain why structure C is stronger.   **[5]**

[Total: 16]

SELF-EVALUATION

After studying this chapter, complete a table like this:

I can	See section...	Needs more work	Almost there	Ready to move on
explain the origin of pressure in a gas in terms of collisions between gas molecules and the walls of the container	5.2			
explain that ideal gases have zero particle volume and no intermolecular forces of attraction	5.2			
use the ideal gas equation, $pV = nRT$, in calculations, including the determination of relative molecular mass	5.2			
describe the lattice structure of giant ionic structures including sodium chloride and magnesium oxide	5.4			
describe the lattice structure of simple molecular structures including iodine, buckminsterfullerene and ice	5.4, 5.5			
describe the lattice structure of giant molecular structures including silicon(IV) oxide, graphite and diamond	5.4			
describe the lattice structure of giant metallic structures including copper	5.4			
describe, interpret and predict the effect of different types of structure and bonding on the physical properties of substances such as: a effect on melting point b effect boiling point c effect on electrical conductivity d effect on solubility	5.3, 5.4, 5.5			
deduce the type of structure and bonding present in a substance from given information.	5.3, 5.4, 5.5			

> ## Chapter 6
Enthalpy changes

LEARNING INTENTIONS

In this chapter you will learn how to:

* explain and use the term *enthalpy change* (ΔH) and apply it to exothermic (ΔH is negative) and endothermic (ΔH is positive) chemical reactions

* construct and interpret reaction pathway diagrams in terms of enthalpy changes and activation energy

* define and use the term *standard conditions*

* define and use the term *enthalpy change* with particular reference to enthalpy changes of reaction, formation, combustion and neutralisation

* explain energy transfers during chemical reactions in terms of breaking and making chemical bonds

* use bond energies to calculate enthalpy change of reaction

* understand that some bond energies are exact and some bond energies are averages

* calculate enthalpy changes from experimental results, including the use of the relationships: $q = mc\Delta T$ and $\Delta H = -mc\Delta T$

CONTINUED

- use Hess's law to construct simple energy cycles

- carry out calculations using energy cycles to determine enthalpy changes that cannot be found by direct experiment

- carry out calculations using bond energy data.

BEFORE YOU START

1 Make a list of reactions that are definitely exothermic and another list of reactions that you know are endothermic. Explain to another learner how you know that these reactions are either exothermic or endothermic.

2 Work with another learner to draw a fully labelled reaction pathway diagram (energy profile diagram) for an endothermic reaction.
   Explain to another learner how this diagram shows that the reaction is endothermic.

3 Take it in turns to explain these terms to another learner: *bond energy*; *enthalpy change*; *activation energy*; *standard conditions*.

4 Write the displayed formulae (structures showing all atoms and all bonds) of the following: CO_2, H_2O, C_2H_6, NH_3, C_2H_5OH. Check your answers with those in a textbook.

5 Work with another learner to describe how to calculate the energy change in the reaction $C_2H_4 + 3O_2 \rightarrow 2CO_2 + 2H_2O$ by using bond energies. You can do this in the form of a table if you wish.

ENERGY IN OUR WORLD

Will some countries disappear?

The transfer of energy to or from substances plays a great part in industry and everyday life. At present, most vehicles, aircraft and power stations depend on the combustion of fossil fuels such as petrol, kerosene or natural gas. The downside to this is that when fossil fuels are burned, carbon dioxide is produced. Carbon dioxide is a greenhouse gas which, with other greenhouse gases, is responsible for the enhanced global warming of the Earth's atmosphere.

Although the concentration of carbon dioxide in the air is very low, in the last 150 years its concentration has increased from 280 parts per million parts of air to 400 parts per million. This has caused the temperature of the Earth's surface to rise by 0.9 °C over the past 150 years. Most of this increase has happened in the last 35 years. This has resulted in enough melting of the ice caps in the Arctic and Antarctic to make

the sea level rise by nearly 20 cm. If this carries on at the present rate, low-lying islands such the Maldives (Figure 6.1) in the Indian Ocean (maximum height 5 m above sea level) and Vanuatu, Kiribati and the Solomon Islands in the Pacific Ocean will disappear under the sea. Their populations will have to move elsewhere. Low-lying areas in many other countries will also be affected.

Carbon dioxide also dissolves in the oceans causing the water to become slightly acidic. Acidification of the oceans has increased by 30% over the last 150 years and is presently increasing by 2 billion tonnes each year. This is having an effect on organisms such as corals, which are very sensitive to small changes in pH.

Scientists and engineers have responded to this problem by trying to reduce our dependence on burning fossil fuels. The rise in the use of solar

CONTINUED

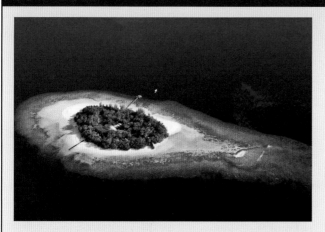

Figure 6.1: The islands of the Maldives may disappear below the sea in the next century if the rate of enhanced global warming does not decrease.

energy, wind energy and battery-powered vehicles, however, is slow. So scientists have recently been

trying to think of ideas such as capturing and solidifying carbon dioxide in order to reduce the amount escaping into the atmosphere.

Questions for discussion

Discuss with another learner or group of learners:

- As consumers we have a choice of what car to buy or how to heat or cool our homes. How can individual people help to reduce the amount of carbon dioxide that is going into the atmosphere?

- Why do you think that the governments of many countries are not taking more steps to deal with enhanced global warming?

- The chemical industry is often accused of causing environmental problems. Do you think this is fair? Or are we too ready to blame others for environmental problems that we are responsible for?

6.1 What are enthalpy changes?

Exothermic or endothermic?

Chemical reactions that transfer heat energy to the surroundings are described as exothermic. In an exothermic reaction, the temperature of the surroundings increases. For example, when magnesium reacts with sulfuric acid in a test-tube, the energy released is transferred to the surroundings and the temperature of the reaction mixture in the tube increases.

$$Mg(s) + H_2SO_4(aq) \rightarrow$$
$$MgSO_4(aq) + H_2(g) \text{ (energy released)}$$

The surroundings include:

- the solvent (in this case water)
- the air around the test-tube
- the test-tube itself
- anything dipping into the test-tube (e.g. a thermometer).

Other examples of exothermic reactions include:

- the combustion of fuels
- the oxidation of carbohydrates in the bodies of animals and plants (respiration)
- the reaction of water with quicklime (calcium oxide) (see Section 11.4).

We describe chemical reactions that absorb heat energy from the surroundings as endothermic. In an endothermic reaction, the temperature of the surroundings decreases (Figure 6.2). For example, when sodium hydrogencarbonate reacts with an aqueous solution of citric acid in a test-tube, the temperature of the reaction mixture in the tube decreases because the citric acid and sodium hydrogencarbonate are absorbing the heat energy from the solvent, the test-tube and the air.

KEY WORDS

exothermic reaction: heat energy is released during a reaction. The value of ΔH is negative.

endothermic reaction: heat energy is absorbed during a reaction. The value of ΔH is positive.

Figure 6.2: Using a cooling pack to treat a sports injury. When you rub or press the pack, water and ammonium chloride crystals mix. As the crystals dissolve, energy is transferred from the surroundings, cooling the injury.

Other examples of endothermic reactions include:

- the decomposition of limestone by heating (all thermal decomposition reactions are endothermic)

- photosynthesis (in which the energy is supplied by sunlight)

- dissolving certain ammonium salts in water

$$NH_4Cl(s) + aq \rightarrow NH^+(aq) + Cl^-(aq)$$
ammonium   water   ammonium   chloride
chloride   ions   ions

Question

1 Classify each process as exothermic or endothermic:

    a   the burning of magnesium in air

    b   the crystallisation of copper(II) sulfate from a saturated solution

    c   the thermal decomposition of magnesium nitrate

    d   the fermentation of glucose by yeast

    e   the evaporation of sea water.

Enthalpy changes and enthalpy profile diagrams

The energy exchange between a chemical reaction and its surroundings at constant pressure is called the enthalpy change. Enthalpy is the total energy associated with the materials that react. The symbol for enthalpy is H. We cannot measure enthalpy, but we can measure an enthalpy change when heat energy is exchanged with the surroundings. We can write this as:

$$\Delta H = H_{products} - H_{reactants}$$
enthalpy = enthalpy of − enthalpy of
change   products   reactants

The symbol Δ is the upper case Greek letter 'delta'. This symbol is often used to mean a change in a quantity.

For example, ΔT means a change in temperature and ΔH means the enthalpy change.

The units of enthalpy change are kilojoules per mole (kJ mol^{-1}).

We can draw reaction pathway diagrams (also known as enthalpy profile diagrams) to show enthalpy changes. The enthalpy of the reactants and products is shown on the y-axis. The x-axis shows the reaction pathway, with reactants on the left and products on the right. Reaction pathway diagrams usually also show the activation energy, E_A, as a hump (up and down curve) between the reactants and the products. The activation energy is the minimum energy that colliding particles must possess for a reaction to happen. Activation energy always has a positive value of ΔH because enough energy has to be absorbed to increase the kinetic energy of the reactant molecules so that they collide with enough force to break bonds (see Section 6.5).

KEY DEFINITIONS

enthalpy change, ΔH: the heat energy transferred during a chemical reaction.

reaction pathway diagram: shows the relative enthalpies of the reactants (on the left) and the products (on the right) and the enthalpy change as an arrow. It may also include the activation energy.

activation energy, E_A: the minimum energy that colliding particles must possess to break bonds to start a chemical reaction.

For an exothermic reaction, energy is released to the surroundings. So the enthalpy of the reactants must be greater than the enthalpy of the products. We can see from the reaction pathway diagram for the combustion of methane (Figure 6.3) that $H_{products} - H_{reactants}$ is negative.

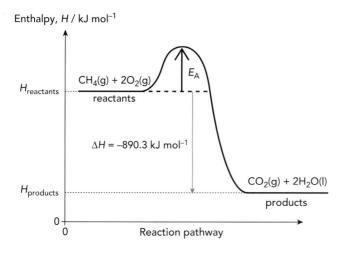

Enthalpy, H / kJ mol^{-1}

Figure 6.3: Reaction pathway diagram for the combustion of methane.

We can include this information in the equation for the reaction:

$$CH_4(g) + 2O_2(g) \rightarrow CO_2(g) + 2H_2O(l)$$
$$\Delta H = -890.3 \text{ kJ mol}^{-1}$$

The negative sign shows that the reaction is *exothermic*.

For an endothermic reaction, energy is absorbed from the surroundings by the substances in the reaction. So the enthalpy of the products must be greater than the enthalpy of the reactants. We can see from the reaction pathway diagram for the thermal decomposition of calcium carbonate (Figure 6.4) that $H_{products} - H_{reactants}$ is positive.

$$CaCO_3(s) \rightarrow CaO(s) + CO_2(g) \quad \Delta H = +572 \text{ kJ mol}^{-1}$$

The positive sign shows that the reaction is *endothermic*.

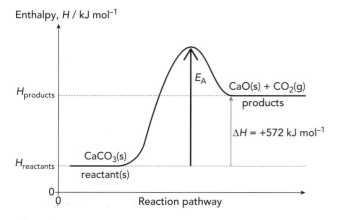

Enthalpy, H / kJ mol^{-1}

Figure 6.4: Reaction pathway diagram for the decomposition of calcium carbonate

---

Question

2   Draw full reaction pathway diagrams including activation energy for:

a   the combustion of sulfur to form sulfur dioxide

b   the endothermic reaction
   $$H_2O(g) + C(s) \rightarrow H_2(g) + CO(g)$$

6.2 Standard enthalpy changes

Standard conditions

To make any comparison of enthalpy changes a fair comparison, we must use the same conditions, called **standard conditions**. These are:

- a pressure of 101 kPa (1.01×10^5 Pa, approximately normal atmospheric pressure)

- a temperature of 298 K (25 °C) (add 273 to the Celsius temperature to convert a temperature into kelvin)

- each substance involved in the reaction is in its normal physical state (solid, liquid or gas) at 101 kPa and 298 K.

The symbol $\ominus$ is used to indicate that the enthalpy change refers to a reaction carried out under standard conditions.

The information in the equation:

$$CH_4(g) + 2O_2(g) \rightarrow CO_2(g) + 2H_2O(l) \quad \Delta H^{\ominus} = -890.3 \text{ kJ mol}^{-1}$$

shows us that when one mole of methane gas reacts with two moles of oxygen gas to form one mole of carbon dioxide gas and two moles of water in the liquid state, the standard enthalpy change is -890.3 kJ mol^{-1}.

A variety of enthalpy changes

We can describe enthalpy changes according to the type of chemical reaction taking place. For example:

- enthalpy change of formation

- enthalpy change of combustion

- enthalpy change of neutralisation.

In more general cases we can use the term:

- enthalpy change of reaction.

Standard enthalpy change of reaction, $\Delta H_r^{\ominus}$

The **standard enthalpy change of reaction**, $\Delta H_r^{\ominus}$ is the enthalpy change when the amounts of reactants shown in the stoichiometric equation react to give products under standard conditions. The reactants and products must be in their standard states.

The symbol for standard enthalpy change of reaction is $\Delta H_r^{\ominus}$. Enthalpy changes of reaction can be exothermic or endothermic.

The equation that describes the reaction must be given. For example, the equation:

$$H_2(g) + \frac{1}{2}O_2(g) \rightarrow H_2O(l) \quad \Delta H_r^{\ominus} = -286 \text{ kJ mol}^{-1}$$

shows us the enthalpy change when one mole of water is formed from hydrogen and oxygen. In this case, 286 kJ of energy is released.

However, if we write the equation as:

$$2H_2(g) + O_2(g) \rightarrow 2H_2O(l) \quad \Delta H_r^{\ominus} = -572 \text{ kJ}$$

two moles of water are formed from hydrogen and oxygen. In this case, 572 kJ of energy is released.

Standard enthalpy change of formation, $\Delta H_f^{\ominus}$

The **standard enthalpy change of formation**, $\Delta H_f^{\ominus}$ is the enthalpy change when one mole of a compound is formed from its elements under standard conditions. The reactants and products must be in their standard states.

The symbol for standard enthalpy change of formation is $\Delta H_f^{\ominus}$. Enthalpy changes of formation can be exothermic or endothermic. We write the formula of the compound in square brackets after $\Delta H_f^{\ominus}$ to help us when we do calculations involving enthalpy changes. Examples are:

$$2Fe(s) + 1\frac{1}{2}O_2(g) \rightarrow Fe_2O_3(s)$$
$$\Delta H_f^{\ominus} [Fe_2O_3(s)] = -824.2 \text{ kJ mol}^{-1}$$

$$C(graphite) + 2S(s) \rightarrow CS_2(l)$$
$$\Delta H_f^{\ominus} [CS_2(l)] = +98.7 \text{ kJ mol}^{-1}$$

Note that the state symbol for carbon is shown as 'graphite'. This is because there are several forms of carbon but the most stable is graphite. We choose the most stable form when writing equations where enthalpy changes are shown.

By definition, the standard enthalpy change of formation of any element in its standard state is zero.

Standard enthalpy change of combustion, $\Delta H_c^{\ominus}$

The **standard enthalpy change of combustion**, $\Delta H_c^{\ominus}$ is the enthalpy change when one mole of a substance is burnt in excess oxygen under standard conditions. The reactants and products must be in their standard states.

KEY DEFINITIONS

standard enthalpy change of reaction, $\Delta H_r^{\ominus}$: the enthalpy change when the amounts of reactants shown in the stoichiometric equation react to give products under standard conditions.

standard enthalpy change of formation, $\Delta H_f^{\ominus}$: the enthalpy change when one mole of a compound is formed from its elements under standard conditions.

standard enthalpy change of combustion, $\Delta H_c^{\ominus}$: the enthalpy change when one mole of a substance is burnt in excess oxygen under standard conditions.

The symbol for standard enthalpy change of combustion is $\Delta H_c^{\ominus}$. Enthalpy changes of combustion are always exothermic. The substances combusted can be either elements or compounds.

$$S(s) + O_2(g) \rightarrow SO_2(g)$$
$$\Delta H_c^{\ominus}[S(s)] = -296.8 \text{ kJ mol}^{-1}$$

$$CH_4(g) + 2O_2(g) \rightarrow CO_2(g) + 2H_2O(l)$$
$$\Delta H_c^{\ominus}[CH_4(g)] = -890.3 \text{ kJ mol}^{-1}$$

Note that the first equation can be considered as either the enthalpy change of combustion of sulfur or the enthalpy change of formation of sulfur dioxide.

Question

3 Identify each of the following reactions as $\Delta H_r^{\ominus}$, $\Delta H_f^{\ominus}$ or $\Delta H_c^{\ominus}$:

a $MgCO_3(s) \rightarrow MgO(s) + CO_2(g)$

b $C(graphite) + O_2(g) \rightarrow CO_2(g)$

c $HCl(g) + NH_3(g) \rightarrow NH_4Cl(s)$

d $H_2(g) + \frac{1}{2}O_2(g) \rightarrow H_2O(l)$

Standard enthalpy change of neutralisation, $\Delta H_{neut}^{\ominus}$

The **standard enthalpy change of neutralisation**, $\Delta H_{neut}^{\ominus}$ is the enthalpy change when one mole of water is formed by the reaction of an acid with an alkali under standard conditions.

For example:

$$HCl(aq) + NaOH(aq) \rightarrow NaCl(aq) + H_2O(l)$$
$$\Delta H_{neut}^{\ominus} = -57.1 \text{ kJ mol}^{-1}$$

For any acid–alkali reaction the ionic equation is:

$$H^+(aq) + OH^-(aq) \rightarrow H_2O(l)$$

The other ions in solution (Cl⁻ and Na⁺) are spectator ions and take no part in the reaction (see Section 3.6).

6.3 Measuring enthalpy changes

We can measure the enthalpy change of some reactions by different techniques.

We can measure the enthalpy change of some reactions by a technique called *calorimetry*. The apparatus used is called a *calorimeter*. A simple calorimeter can be a polystyrene drinking cup (Figure 6.5), a vacuum flask or a metal can.

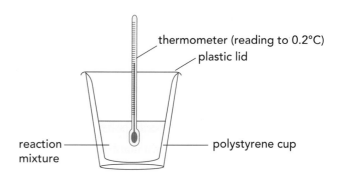

Figure 6.5: A polystyrene cup can act as a calorimeter for finding some enthalpy changes.

When carrying out experiments in calorimeters, we use known amounts of reactants and known volumes of liquids. We also measure the temperature change of the liquid in the calorimeter as the reaction occurs. The thermometer should be accurate to 0.1 or 0.2 °C.

Calorimetry relies on the fact that it takes 4.18 J of energy to increase the temperature of 1 g of water by 1 °C. The energy required to raise the temperature of 1 g of a substance by 1 °C (1 K) is called the **specific heat capacity**, c, of the liquid. So, the specific heat capacity of water is 4.18 J g⁻¹ °C⁻¹.

The energy transferred as heat is given by the relationship:

$$q = mc\Delta T$$

where:

q is the heat transferred, in J

m is the mass of water, in g

c is the specific heat capacity, in J g⁻¹ °C⁻¹

ΔT is the temperature change, in °C

KEY DEFINITION

standard enthalpy change of neutralisation, $\Delta H_{neut}^{\ominus}$: the enthalpy change when one mole of water is formed by the reaction of an acid with an alkali under standard conditions.

KEY WORD

specific heat capacity, c: the energy needed to raise the temperature of 1 g of a substance by 1 °C (by 1 K).

As 1 cm^3 of water weighs 1 g, we can substitute volume of water in cm^3 of water for mass of water in g in the equation. Aqueous solutions of acids, alkalis and salts are assumed to be largely water.

With solutions we make the assumptions that:

- 1 cm^3 of solution has a mass of 1 g
- the solution has the same specific heat capacity as water.

The heat transferred for a known number of moles of reactants in the calorimeter is given by

$$q = mc\Delta T$$

We can scale this up to get the enthalpy change per mole of defined reactant or product. The relationship we then use is

$$\Delta H = -mc\Delta T$$

Note: A rise in temperature is given a positive sign. So the value of ΔH is negative for an exothermic reaction. A fall in temperature is given a negative sign. So the value of ΔH is positive for an endothermic reaction.

> ## IMPORTANT
>
> The energy released in calorimetry experiments for a known number of moles of a specified reactant is given by $q = mc\Delta T$.
>
> When we multiply this up to 1 mole of a stated product or reactant, the equation we use is
> $$\Delta H = -mc\Delta T$$
> The negative sign shows that the reaction is exothermic.

PRACTICAL ACTIVITY 6.1

The enthalpy change of neutralisation by experiment

SAFETY: Only carry out this activity in the presence of a teacher after safety aspects have been explained.

We can find the enthalpy change of neutralisation of sodium hydroxide with hydrochloric acid by mixing equal volumes of known equimolar concentrations of acid and alkali together in a polystyrene cup.

Procedure

1. Place 50 cm^3 of 1.0 mol dm^{-3} hydrochloric acid in the cup and record its temperature.

2. Add 50 cm^3 of 1.0 mol dm^{-3} sodium hydroxide (at the same temperature) to the acid in the cup.

3. Stir the reaction mixture with the thermometer and record the highest temperature.

In this experiment most of the heat is transferred to the solution, as the polystyrene cup is a good insulator. Cooling of the warm solution is not a great problem: the reaction is rapid so the maximum temperature is reached before much cooling of the warm solution has occurred. However, there are still heat losses to the air and to the thermometer, which make the result less exothermic than the data book value of -57.1 kJ mol^{-1}.

Specimen results and calculation

mass of solution = 100 g
(50 cm^3 of acid plus 50 cm^3 of alkali and assuming that 1.0 cm^3 of solution has a mass of 1.0 g)

specific heat capacity = 4.18 J g^{-1} °C^{-1}
(assuming that the heat capacity of the solution is the same as the heat capacity of water)

starting temperature = 21.3 °C reactant solutions

final temperature = 27.8 °C product solution

temperature rise = +6.5 °C
(use the relationship $q = mc\Delta T$)

heat energy released = 100 × 4.18 × 6.5
= 2717 J

At the start, the reaction mixture contained 50 cm^3 of 1.0 mol dm^{-3} hydrochloric acid and 50 cm^3 of 1.0 mol dm^{-3} sodium hydroxide. The number of moles of each (and of the water formed) is calculated using

$$\frac{\text{concentration} \times \text{volume (in cm}^3\text{)}}{1000} = \frac{1.0 \times 50}{1000}$$

$$= 0.050 \text{ moles}$$

So 2717 J of energy was released by 0.050 moles of acid.

Therefore, for one mole of acid (forming one mole of water) the energy released was

$$\frac{2717}{0.050} = \Delta H^\ominus_{\text{neut}} = 54\,340 \text{ J mol}^{-1}$$

$$\Delta H^\ominus_{\text{neut}} = -54 \text{ kJ mol}^{-1} \text{ (to 2 significant figures)}$$

The negative sign shows that the reaction is exothermic.

PRACTICAL ACTIVITY 6.2

Finding the enthalpy change of combustion of propan-1-ol

SAFETY: Only carry out this activity in the presence of a teacher after safety aspects have been explained.

We can find the enthalpy change of combustion by burning a known mass of substance and using the heat released to raise the temperature of a known mass of water. The apparatus used for this consists of a spirit burner and a metal calorimeter (Figure 6.6).

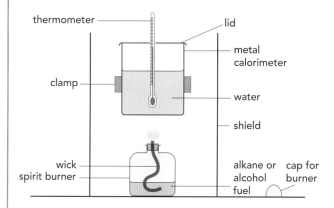

Figure 6.6: A simple apparatus used to find the enthalpy change of combustion of fuels.

Procedure

Weigh the spirit burner containing propan-1-ol. The cap on the burner must be kept on when the burner is not lit to avoid evaporation of the fuel.

Pour 100 cm³ (100 g) of water into the calorimeter. For greater accuracy this should be weighed out.

Stir the water and record its temperature with a thermometer reading to at least the nearest 0.1 °C.

Place the spirit burner beneath the calorimeter, remove the cap and light the wick. The length of the wick should have been previously adjusted so that the material of the wick does not burn and the flame just touches the bottom of the calorimeter.

Keep stirring the water with the thermometer until there is a temperature rise of about 10 °C. Record this temperature.

Remove the spirit burner, place the cap on it and reweigh it.

To find the standard enthalpy change of combustion we need to know:

- the mass of fuel burnt
- the temperature rise of the water
- the mass of the water
- the relative molecular mass of the fuel (propan-1-ol).

Specimen results and calculation

mass of water in calorimeter	= 100 g
mass of spirit burner and propan-1-ol at start	= 86.27 g
mass of spirit burner and propan-1-ol at end	= 86.06 g
mass of propan-1-ol burnt	= 0.21 g
initial temperature of water	= 20.2 °C
final temperature of water	= 30.9 °C
temperature change of the water	= +10.7 °C

Using the relationship $q = mc\Delta T$ (mass of water × specific heat capacity of water × temperature change):

energy released by burning 0.21 g propanol
$- -(100 \times 4.18 \times 10.7) = 4472.6$ J

the mass of 1 mole of propan-1-ol, C_3H_7OH, is 60 g

so for 60 g propan-1-ol the energy released $\Delta H_c^\ominus$ is

$$-4472.6 \times \frac{60}{0.21} = -1\ 277\ 885.7 \text{ J mol}^{-1}$$

$\Delta H_c^\ominus = -1300$ kJ mol⁻¹ (to 2 significant figures)

This is much less than the data book value of −2021 kJ mol⁻¹, mainly due to heat losses to the surroundings.

Questions

4 a Calculate the energy transferred when the temperature of 75 cm³ of water rises from 23 °C to 54 °C.

b When 8 g of sodium chloride is dissolved in 40 cm³ of water, the temperature falls from 22 °C to 20.5 °C. Calculate the energy absorbed by the solution when sodium chloride dissolves.

c A student added 50 cm³ of sodium hydroxide to 50 cm³ of hydrochloric acid. Both solutions were at 18 °C to start with. When the solutions were mixed a reaction occurred. The temperature rose to 33 °C. How much energy is released in this reaction?

5 Explain why the enthalpy change of neutralisation of one mole of sulfuric acid, H_2SO_4, is not the standard enthalpy change of neutralisation in kJ mol^{-1}.

6 A student added 10 g (0.25 mol) of sodium hydroxide to 40 cm³ of water to make a concentrated solution. All the sodium hydroxide dissolved. The student measured the maximum temperature rise. The student suggested that these results would give an accurate value for the standard enthalpy change of solution. Give two reasons why the student is incorrect.

7 A student calculated the standard enthalpy change of combustion of ethanol $\Delta H_c^{\ominus}$ [C_2H_5OH] by calorimetry as −870 kJ mol^{-1}. The data book value is −1367 kJ mol^{-1}. Explain why there is a difference between these values.

6.4 Hess's law

Conserving energy

The law of conservation of energy states that 'energy cannot be created or destroyed'. This is also called the *first law of thermodynamics*.

The first law of thermodynamics also applies to chemical reactions: the total energy of the chemicals and their surroundings must remain constant. In 1840, Germain Hess applied the law of conservation of energy to enthalpy changes.

Hess's law states that 'the total enthalpy change in a chemical reaction is independent of the route by which the chemical reaction takes place as long as the initial and final conditions are the same'. The states of the reactants and products must also be the same whichever route is followed.

KEY WORD

Hess's law: the enthalpy change in a chemical reaction is independent of the route by which the chemical reaction takes place as long as the initial and final conditions and states of reactants and products are the same for each route.

Enthalpy cycles (Energy cycles)

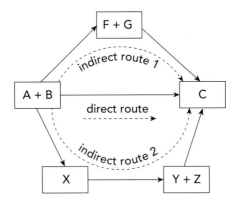

Figure 6.7: The enthalpy change is the same no matter which route is followed.

We can illustrate Hess's law by drawing enthalpy cycles. These are often called *energy cycles* or *Hess cycles*. In Figure 6.7, the reactants A and B combine directly to form C. This is the direct route.

Two indirect routes are also shown. One other way of changing A + B to C is to convert A + B into different substances F + G (intermediates), which then combine to form C.

Hess's law tells us that the enthalpy change of reaction for the direct route is the same as for the indirect route. It does not matter how many steps there are in the indirect route. We can still use Hess's law.

We can use Hess's law to calculate enthalpy changes that cannot be found by experiments using calorimetry. For example, the enthalpy change of formation of propane cannot be found by direct experiment because hydrogen does not react with carbon under standard conditions.

IMPORTANT

You may be asked to draw an energy cycle. This is just another way of describing an enthalpy cycle or Hess cycle. Energy cycle is the more general term.

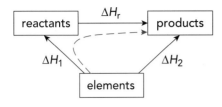

Figure 6.8: An enthalpy cycle (energy cycle) for calculating an enthalpy change of reaction. The dashed line shows the indirect (two-step) route.

Enthalpy change of reaction from enthalpy changes of formation

We can calculate the enthalpy change of reaction by using the type of enthalpy cycle (energy cycle) shown in Figure 6.8.

We use the enthalpy changes of formation of the reactants and products to calculate the enthalpy change of the reaction. We take note of the directions of the arrows to find the one-stage (direct) and two-stage (indirect) routes. When we use Hess's law we see that:

$$\Delta H_2 = \Delta H_1 + \Delta H_r$$
direct route   indirect route

So $\Delta H_r = \Delta H_2 - \Delta H_1$

To calculate the enthalpy change of reaction using this type of enthalpy cycle, we use the following procedure:

- write the balanced equation at the top

- draw the cycle with elements at the bottom

- draw in all arrows, making sure they go in the correct directions

- apply Hess's law, taking into account the number of moles of each reactant and product.

If there are 3 moles of a product, e.g. $3CO_2(g)$, we must multiply the enthalpy change of formation by 3. Also remember that the standard enthalpy change of formation of an element in its standard state is zero.

WORKED EXAMPLE

1 Calculate the standard enthalpy change for the reaction:

$$2NaHCO_3(s) \rightarrow Na_2CO_3(s) + CO_2(g) + H_2O(l)$$

Solution

The relevant enthalpy changes of formation are:

$\Delta H_f^\ominus [NaHCO_3(s)] = -950.8 \text{ kJ mol}^{-1}$

$\Delta H_f^\ominus [Na_2CO_3(s)] = -1130.7 \text{ kJ mol}^{-1}$

$\Delta H_f^\ominus [CO_2(g)] = -393.5 \text{ kJ mol}^{-1}$

$\Delta H_f^\ominus [H_2O(l)] = -285.8 \text{ kJ mol}^{-1}$

The enthalpy cycle is shown in Figure 6.9.

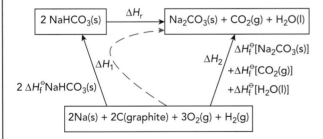

Figure 6.9: The enthalpy cycle for the decomposition of sodium hydrogencarbonate. The dashed line shows the two-step route.

Step 1: Apply Hess's law.

$\Delta H_2 = \Delta H_1 + \Delta H_r$

$\quad = \Delta H_f^\ominus [Na_2CO_3(s)] + \Delta H_f^\ominus [CO_2(g)] + \Delta H_f^\ominus [H_2O(l)]$

$\quad = 2\Delta H_f^\ominus [NaHCO(s)] + \Delta H_r^\ominus$

Step 2: Insert the values of ΔH taking care to multiply by the correct number of moles.

$(-1130.7) + (-393.5) + (-285.8) = 2(-950.8) + \Delta H_r^\ominus$

$-1810.0 = -1901.6 + \Delta H_r$

Step 3: Rearrange the figures to make ΔH_r the subject.

So $\Delta H_r^\ominus = (-1810.0) - (-1901.6)$

$\Delta H_r^\ominus = +91.6 \text{ kJ mol}^{-1}$ (for the equation shown)

Note:

- the value for $\Delta H_f^\ominus [NaHCO(s)]$ is multiplied by 2 because 2 moles of $NaHCO_3$ appear in the equation

- the values for $\Delta H_f^\ominus [Na_2CO_3(s)]$, $\Delta H_f^\ominus [CO_2(g)]$ and $\Delta H_f^\ominus [H_2O(l)]$ are added together to give ΔH_2. Take care to account for the fact that some values may be positive and some negative.

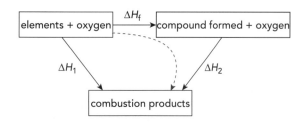

Figure 6.10: An enthalpy cycle for calculating an enthalpy change of formation from enthalpy changes of combustion.

> **IMPORTANT**
>
> When doing enthalpy cycle (energy cycle) calculations remember that:
>
> 1 the enthalpy change of an element in its normal state is zero
> 2 you must take into account the number of moles of reactants and products in each part of the energy cycle.

WORKED EXAMPLE

2 Calculate the standard enthalpy change of formation of ethane, C_2H_6.

Solution

The relevant enthalpy changes of combustion are:

$C(graphite) + O_2(g) \rightarrow CO_2(g)$

$\Delta H_c^{\ominus} [C(graphite)] = -393.5 \text{ kJ mol}^{-1}$

$H_2(g) + \frac{1}{2}O_2(g) \rightarrow H_2O(l)$

$\Delta H_c^{\ominus} [H_2(g)] = -285.8 \text{ kJ mol}^{-1}$

$C_2H_6(g) + 3\frac{1}{2}O_2(g) \rightarrow 2CO_2(g) + 3H_2O(l)$

$\Delta H_c^{\ominus} [C_2H_6(g)] = -1559.7 \text{ kJ mol}^{-1}$

Step 1: Write the enthalpy change of formation at the top and then draw the energy cycle with the combustion products at the bottom. Make sure the arrows are in the correct direction.

The enthalpy cycle is shown in Figure 6.11.

Step 2: Apply Hess's law.

$\Delta H_1 = \Delta H_f + \Delta H_2$

Step 3: Insert the values of ΔH taking care to multiply by the correct number of moles.

$\Delta H_1 \qquad\qquad = \Delta H_f + \Delta H_2$

$2(-393.5) + 3(-285.8) = \Delta H_f + (-1559.7)$

$-1644.4 \qquad\qquad = \Delta H_f + (-1559.7)$

Step 4: Rearrange the figures to make ΔH_f the subject.

$\Delta H_f = -1644.4 - (-1559.7) =$

$\qquad\qquad\qquad -84.7 \text{ kJ mol}^{-1}$

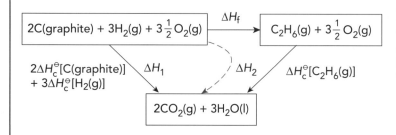

Figure 6.11: The enthalpy cycle to find the enthalpy change of formation of ethane using enthalpy changes of combustion. The dashed line shows the two-step route.

Question

8 a Draw an enthalpy cycle to calculate $\Delta H_r^{\ominus}$ for the reaction

$2Al(s) + Fe_2O_3(s) \rightarrow 2Fe(s) + Al_2O_3(s)$

b Calculate ΔH_r using the following information:

$\Delta H_f^{\ominus} [Fe_2O_3(s)] = -824.2 \text{ kJ mol}^{-1}$

$\Delta H_f^{\ominus} [Al_2O_3(s)] = -1675.7 \text{ kJ mol}^{-1}$

Enthalpy change of formation from enthalpy changes of combustion

We can calculate the enthalpy change of formation of many compounds by using the type of enthalpy cycle shown in Figure 6.10.

We use the enthalpy changes of combustion of the reactants and products to calculate the enthalpy change of formation. When we take note of the direction of the arrows to find the one-stage (direct) and two-stage (indirect) routes and use Hess's law we see that:

$$\Delta H_1 = \Delta H_f + \Delta H_2$$
$$\text{direct route} \qquad \text{indirect route}$$

So $\Delta H_f = \Delta H_1 - \Delta H_2$

To calculate the enthalpy change of formation using this type of cycle:

- write the equation for enthalpy change of formation at the top; add oxygen on both sides of the equation to balance the combustion reactions

- draw the cycle with the combustion products at the bottom

- draw in all arrows, making sure they go in the correct directions

- apply Hess's law, taking into account the number of moles of each reactant and product.

IMPORTANT

Remember that in constructing enthalpy cycles (energy cycles) to calculate ΔH_f, ΔH_c or ΔH_{neut}, the reaction required is put at the top of the energy cycle triangle.

Questions

9 a Draw an enthalpy cycle to calculate the enthalpy change of formation of ethanol, C_2H_5OH, using enthalpy changes of combustion.

   b Calculate a value for $\Delta H_f [C_2H_5OH(l)]$ using the following data:

   $\Delta H_c^\ominus [C(\text{graphite})] = -393.5 \text{ kJ mol}^{-1}$

   $\Delta H_c^\ominus [H_2(g)] = -285.8 \text{ kJ mol}^{-1}$

   $\Delta H_c^\ominus [C_2H_5OH(l)] = -1367.3 \text{ kJ mol}^{-1}$

10 Look at this equation.

   $3Mg(s) + Fe_2O_3(s) \rightarrow 2Fe(s) + 3MgO(s)$

   Which one of the following gives the correct value for the enthalpy change of this reaction?

   A $\Delta H_r = \Delta H_f [Fe_2O_3(s)] - 3\Delta H_f [MgO(s)]$

   B $\Delta H_r = \Delta H_f [MgO(s)] - \Delta H_f [Fe_2O_3(s)]$

   C $\Delta H_r = 2\Delta H_f [Fe(g)] + 3\Delta H_f [MgO(g)] -$
   $\qquad\qquad 3\Delta H_f [Mg(g)] + \Delta H_f [Fe_2O_3(g)]$

   D $\Delta H_r = 3\Delta H_f [MgO(s)] - \Delta H_f [Fe_2O_3(s)]$

6.5 Bond energies and enthalpy changes

IMPORTANT

Remember that bond breaking is endothermic and bond making is exothermic.

Bond breaking and bond making

Enthalpy changes are due to the breaking and forming of bonds. Breaking bonds requires energy. The energy is needed to overcome the attractive forces joining the atoms together. Energy is released when new bonds are formed. Bond breaking is endothermic and bond forming is exothermic.

In a chemical reaction:

- if the energy needed to break bonds is *less* than the energy released when new bonds are formed, the reaction will release energy and is exothermic.

- if the energy needed to break bonds is *more* than the energy released when new bonds are formed, the reaction will absorb energy and is endothermic.

We can draw reaction pathway diagrams to show these changes (Figure 6.12). In reality, not all the bonds in a compound are broken and then re-formed during a reaction. In most reactions only some of the bonds in the reactants are broken and then new bonds are formed in a specific sequence.

Bond energy

The amount of energy needed to break a specific covalent bond is called the *bond dissociation energy*. We sometimes call this the **exact bond energy** or *bond enthalpy*.

KEY WORD

exact bond energy: the energy needed to break a specific covalent bond in a named molecule in the gaseous state, e.g. the O—H bond in water. Also called the bond dissociation energy or bond enthalpy.

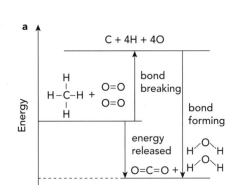
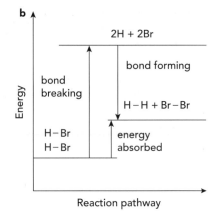

Figure 6.12: a An energy level diagram showing bond breaking and bond forming for the combustion of methane (exothermic). **b** An energy level diagram showing bond breaking and bond forming for the decomposition of hydrogen bromide (endothermic).

The symbol for bond energy is E. We put the type of bond broken in brackets after the symbol.

So $E(C—H)$ refers to the bond energy of a mole of single bonds between carbon and hydrogen atoms.

The bond energy for double and triple bonds refers to a mole of double or triple bonds. Two examples of equations relating to bond energies are:

$$Br_2(g) \rightarrow 2Br(g) \qquad E(Br—Br) = +193 \text{ kJ mol}^{-1}$$

$$O{=}O(g) \rightarrow 2O(g) \qquad E(O{=}O) = +498 \text{ kJ mol}^{-1}$$

The values of bond energies are always positive (endothermic) because they refer to bonds being broken.

When new bonds are formed the amount of energy released is the same as the amount of energy absorbed when the same type of bond is broken. So, for the formation of oxygen molecules from oxygen atoms:

$$2O(g) \rightarrow O_2(g) \qquad E(O{=}O) = -498 \text{ kJ mol}^{-1}$$

Average bond energy

Bond energy is affected by other atoms in the molecule. The O—H bond in water has a slightly different bond energy value to the O—H bond in ethanol. In ethanol, the oxygen is connected to a carbon atom rather than another hydrogen atom. We call these bond energies *exact bond energies*. The O—H bond is in a different environment. Identical bonds in molecules with two

(or more) types of bond have different bond energies when we measure them. It takes more energy to break the first O—H bond in water than to break the second. For these reasons we use average bond energies taken from a number of bonds of the same type but in different environments.

We cannot usually find the value of bond energies directly, so we have to use an enthalpy cycle. The **average bond energy** of the C—H bond in methane can be found using the enthalpy changes of atomisation of carbon and hydrogen and the enthalpy change of combustion or formation of methane.

IMPORTANT

The standard enthalpy change of atomisation, $\Delta H_{at}^{\ominus}$, is the enthalpy change when one mole of gaseous atoms is formed from its element under standard conditions. So, $\Delta H_{at}^{\ominus}$ [H_2] relates to the equation $\frac{1}{2}H_2(g) \rightarrow H(g)$

KEY WORD

average bond energy: the average energy needed to break a specific covalent bond averaged from a variety of molecules in the gaseous state, e.g. the average O—H bond energy in ethanol, water and other compounds.

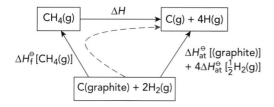

Figure 6.13: An enthalpy cycle to find the average bond energy of the C—H bond. The dashed line shows the two-step route.

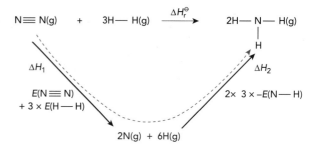

Figure 6.14: The enthalpy cycle for ammonia synthesis. The dashed line shows the two-step route.

The enthalpy cycle for calculating the average C—H bond energy is shown in Figure 6.13. Using the enthalpy cycle shown in Figure 6.13, the average C—H bond energy can be found by dividing the value of ΔH on the diagram by four (because there are four C—H bonds in a molecule of methane).

Question

11 Use the information in Figure 6.13 and the information below to demonstrate that the average bond energy of the C—H bond is 415.9 kJ mol^{-1}.

$$\Delta H_f^\ominus [CH_4] = -74.8 \text{ kJ mol}$$

$$\Delta H_{at}^\ominus [\tfrac{1}{2} H] = +218 \text{ kJ mol}^{-1}$$

$$\Delta H_{at}^\ominus [C(graphite)] = +716.7 \text{ kJ mol}^{-1}$$

6.6 Calculating enthalpy changes using bond energies

We can use bond energies to calculate the enthalpy change of a reaction that we cannot measure directly. For example, the reaction for the Haber process (see Section 8.5):

$$N_2(g) + 3H_2(g) \rightleftharpoons 2NH_3(g)$$

The enthalpy cycle for this reaction is shown in Figure 6.14. The relevant bond energies are:

$$E(N \equiv N) = 945 \text{ kJ mol}^{-1}$$

$$E(H - H) = 436 \text{ kJ mol}^{-1}$$

$$E(N - H) = 391 \text{ kJ mol}^{-1}$$

It is often easier to set out the calculation as a balance sheet, as shown below:

Bonds broken ΔH_1 (kJ)	Bonds formed ΔH_2 (kJ)
$1 \times N \equiv N = 1 \times 945 = 945$	$6 \times N - H = 6 \times 391$
$3 \times H - H - 3 \times 436 = 1308$	
total = +2253	total = −2346

Note in these calculations that:

- one triple bond in nitrogen is broken

- three single bonds in hydrogen are broken

- six single N—H bonds in hydrogen are formed (because each of the two ammonia molecules has three N—H bonds)

- values for bond breaking are positive, as these are endothermic, and values for bond forming are negative, as these are exothermic.

From the enthalpy cycle in Figure 6.14:

$$\Delta H_r = \Delta H_1 + \Delta H_2$$

ΔH_r = enthalpy change for bonds broken
          + enthalpy change for bonds formed

$$\Delta H_r = 2253 + (-2346) = -93 \text{ kJ mol}^{-1}$$

Questions

12 The equation for the combustion of ethanol is:

$$C_2H_5OH(l) + 3O_2(g) \rightarrow 2CO_2(g) + 3H_2O(l)$$

a Rewrite this equation to show all the bonds in the reactants and products.

b Use the following bond energies (in kJ mol⁻¹) to calculate a value for the standard enthalpy change of this reaction:

    i $E(C—C) = +347$

    ii $E(C—H) = +410$

    iii $E(C—O) = +336$

    iv $E(O{=}O) = +496$

    v $E(C{=}O) = +805$

    vi $E(O—H) = +465$

c The standard enthalpy change of combustion of ethanol is −1367.3 kJ mol⁻¹. Suggest why this value differs from the value obtained using bond energies.

13 Look at this equation.

$$CH_4(g) + 2O_2(g) \rightarrow CO_2(g) + 2H_2O(g)$$

Which one of the following statements is completely correct?

A four C—H bonds and two O=O bonds are broken (exothermic) reaction and two C=O bonds and four O—H bonds are formed (endothermic)

B four C—H bonds and two O=O bonds are broken (endothermic) and two C=O bonds and four O—H bonds are formed (exothermic)

C four C—H bonds and two O—O bonds are broken (endothermic) and two C—O bonds and four O—H bonds are formed (exothermic)

D four C—H bonds and two O=O bonds are broken (endothermic) and two C=O bonds and two O—H bonds are formed (exothermic)

REFLECTION

1 Work with another learner to make a list of differences between the definitions of the standard enthalpy changes of formation, reaction, combustion and neutralisation as well as any differences in the way that you draw the energy cycle diagrams.

2 Work with another learner to describe the sequence of operations in one of the experiments that appear in this chapter, e.g. deducing enthalpy change of combustion or deducing the enthalpy change of reaction. Think about what you would need to measure and the variables you would need to control. What equations would you need to use when processing the results? What would you change if you had to do this again?

SUMMARY

Exothermic enthalpy changes have negative ΔH values. Endothermic enthalpy changes have positive ΔH values.

Enthalpy changes can be calculated experimentally using the relationship:

    enthalpy change, q = mass of liquid × specific heat capacity × temperature change.

For a mole of defined substance this is written $\Delta H = -mc\Delta T$

Standard enthalpy change of formation relates to the enthalpy change when one mole of a compound is formed from its elements under standard conditions. Similar definitions can be written for standard enthalpy changes of combustion and reaction.

Hess's law can be used to calculate enthalpy changes for reactions that do not occur directly or cannot be found by experiment.

Bond breaking is endothermic; bond making is exothermic.

Average bond energies are often used because the strength of a bond between two particular types of atom is slightly different in different compounds.

EXAM-STYLE QUESTIONS

COMMAND WORD

Sketch: make a simple drawing showing the key features.

1   Copper(II) nitrate decomposes on heating. The reaction is endothermic.

$$2Cu(NO_3)_2(s) \rightarrow 2CuO(s) + 4NO_2(g) + O_2(g)$$

   a   Sketch a reaction pathway diagram for this reaction to include the activation energy. [3]

   b   Draw an energy cycle to calculate the standard enthalpy change for this reaction, using enthalpy changes of formation. [3]

   c   Calculate the enthalpy change for this reaction using the following enthalpy changes of formation.

$$\Delta H_f^{\ominus} [Cu(NO_3)_2(s)] = -302.9 \text{ kJ mol}^{-1}$$
$$\Delta H_f^{\ominus} [CuO(s)] = -157.3 \text{ kJ mol}^{-1}$$
$$\Delta H_f^{\ominus} [NO_2(g)] = +33.2 \text{ kJ mol}^{-1}$$
[3]

   d   Copper(II) sulfate is soluble in water. A student dissolved 25.0 g of copper(II) sulfate in 100 cm³ of water in a polystyrene beaker stirring all the time. The temperature of the water fell by 2.9 °C.

   i   Calculate the enthalpy change of solution of copper(II) sulfate. (specific heat capacity of water = 4.18 J g⁻¹ °C⁻¹; relative molecular mass of copper(II) sulfate = 249.7 g mol⁻¹) [3]

   ii   Suggest one source of error in this experiment and explain how the error affects the results. [2]

[Total: 14]

2   Propanone is a liquid. It has the structure

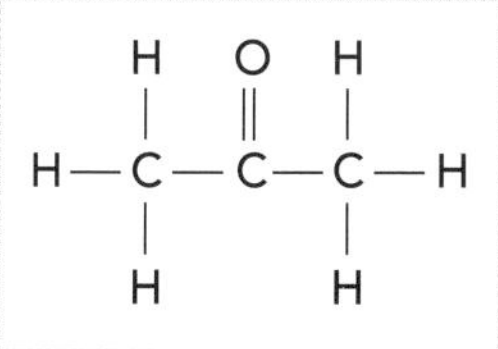

   The equation for the complete combustion of propanone is:

$$CH_3COCH_3(l) + 4O_2(g) \rightarrow 3CO_2(g) + 3H_2O(l)$$

   a   Use the following bond energies (in kJ mol⁻¹) to calculate a value for the standard enthalpy change of this reaction:

$$E(C—C) = +347$$
$$E(C—H) = +413$$
$$E(O=O) = +496$$
$$E(C=O) = +805$$
$$E(O—H) = +465$$
[4]

   b   Explain why it would be more accurate to use exact bond energies rather than average bond energies in this calculation. [2]

   c   The standard enthalpy change of combustion of propanone is −1816.5 kJ mol⁻¹. Suggest why this value differs from the value obtained using bond energies. [2]

d The standard enthalpy change of formation of propanone is -248 kJ mol^{-1}.

    i Define the term *standard enthalpy change of formation*. [3]

    ii Write the equation that describes the standard enthalpy change of formation of propanone. [2]

    iii Explain why the enthalpy change of formation of propanone cannot be found by a single experiment. [1]

                                                                  [Total: 14]

3 240 cm^3 of ethane (C_2H_6) was burnt in a controlled way and found to raise the temperature of 100 cm^3 of water by 33.5 °C. (specific heat capacity of water $= 4.18$ J g^{-1} K^{-1}; 1 mol of gas molecules occupies 24.0 dm^3 at r.t.p.)

    a Calculate the number of moles of ethane that were burned. [1]

    b Calculate the heat change, q, for the experiment. [2]

    c Calculate the molar enthalpy change of combustion for ethane, as measured by this experiment. [2]

    d Use the values below to calculate the standard molar enthalpy change for the complete combustion of ethane.

$$\Delta H_f^\ominus \,[CO_2] = -394 \text{ kJ mol}^{-1}$$
$$\Delta H_f^\ominus \,[H_2O] = -286 \text{ kJ mol}^{-1}$$
$$\Delta H_f^\ominus \,[C_2H_6] = -85 \text{ kJ mol}^{-1} \quad [4]$$

    e Give possible reasons for the difference between the two results. [2]

                                                                  [Total: 11]

4 **a** Define *standard enthalpy change of combustion*. [3]

    b **i** When red phosphorus burns in oxygen the enthalpy change is -2967 kJ mol^{-1}. For white phosphorus the enthalpy change is -2984 kJ mol^{-1}. For both forms of phosphorus the reaction taking place is:

$$P_4(s) + 5O_2(g) \rightarrow P_4O_{10}(s)$$

          Use this information to calculate the enthalpy change for the transformation: $P_4(\text{white}) \rightarrow P_4(\text{red})$ [5]

      ii Represent these changes on an energy level diagram. [3]

                                                                    [Total: 11]

5 **a** Define *standard enthalpy change of formation*. [3]

    b Calculate the standard enthalpy change of formation of methane from the following standard enthalpy changes of combustion:

        carbon $= -394$ kJ mol^{-1}

        hydrogen $= -286$ kJ mol^{-1}

        methane $= -891$ kJ mol^{-1} [4]

c   Calculate the standard enthalpy change of combustion of methane using the following bond energies:

E(C—H) = +412 kJ mol^{-1}

E(O=O) = +496 kJ mol^{-1}

E(C=O) = +805 kJ mol^{-1}

E(O—H) = +463 kJ mol^{-1} [4]

[Total: 11]

6   a   Define *average bond energy*.   [2]

b   Use the average bond energies that follow to calculate a value for the enthalpy change for the reaction:

$H_2 + I_2 \rightarrow 2HI$

E(H—H) = +436 kJ mol^{-1}

E(I—I) = +151 kJ mol^{-1}

E(H—I) = +299 kJ mol^{-1} [3]

c   Represent these changes on an energy level diagram.   [3]

[Total: 8]

7   a   Define *standard enthalpy change of reaction*.   [3]

b   Given the enthalpy changes ΔH_1 and ΔH_2 below, construct a Hess's cycle that will enable you to find the enthalpy change, ΔH_r, for the reaction:

$MgCO_3(s) \rightarrow MgO(s) + CO_2(g)$ ΔH_r

$MgCO_3(s) + 2HCl(aq) \rightarrow MgCl_2(aq) + CO_2(g) + H_2O(l)$ ΔH_1

$MgO(s) + 2HCl(aq) \rightarrow MgCl_2(aq) + H_2O(l)$ ΔH_2 [4]

[Total: 7]

8   In an experiment, a spirit burner is used to heat 250 cm^3 of water by burning methanol (CH_3OH). (A_r values: C = 12.0, H = 1.0, O = 16.0; specific heat capacity of water = 4.18 J g^{-1} °C^{-1})

Results:

starting temperature of water = 20.0 °C

starting mass of burner + fuel = 248.8 g

final temperature of water = 43.0 °C

final mass of burner + fuel = 245.9 g

a   Calculate the energy in joules that went into heating the water.   [2]

b   Calculate the number of moles of fuel burned.   [2]

c   Calculate an experimental value for the enthalpy change of combustion of methanol from these results.   [2]

d   Suggest three reasons why your answer is much smaller than the accepted standard enthalpy of combustion of methanol.   [3]

[Total: 9]

SELF-EVALUATION

After studying this chapter, complete a table like this:

I can	See section...	Needs more work	Almost there	Ready to move on
explain and use the term *enthalpy change* (ΔH) and apply it to exothermic chemical reactions (ΔH is negative) and endothermic chemical reactions (ΔH is positive)	6.1			
construct and interpret a reaction pathway diagram in terms of enthalpy changes and activation energy	6.1			
define and use the term *standard conditions*	6.2			
define and use the term *enthalpy change of formation*	6.2			
define and use the term *enthalpy change of combustion*	6.2			
define and use the term *enthalpy change of neutralisation*	6.2			
explain energy transfers during chemical reactions in terms of bond breaking (endothermic) and bond making (exothermic)	6.3, 6.5			
use bond energies to calculate enthalpy change of reaction	6.5, 6.6			
understand that some bond energies are exact and some bond energies are averages	6.5, 6.6			
calculate enthalpy changes from experimental results, including the use of the relationships: $q = mc\Delta T$ and $\Delta H = -mc\Delta T$	6.3			
use Hess's law to construct simple energy cycles	6.4			
carry out calculations using energy cycles to determine enthalpy changes that cannot be found by direct experiment	6.6			
carry out calculations using bond energy data.	6.6			

> Chapter 7

Redox reactions

BEFORE YOU START

1   Write down as many definitions of oxidation and reduction as you can. Compare your definitions with other learners. Were there any definitions that you left out? Discuss with another learner which definitions of oxidations and reduction are generally most useful.

2   Get another learner to select an oxidation–reduction (redox) equation from a textbook. Explain to the other learner how you know which compound or element has been oxidised and which has been reduced. Then reverse the process: you choose and the other learner explains.

3   Make a list of oxidising agents and reducing agents. Compare your list with others in the class. Were there any obvious ones that you missed out?

4   Do you know any qualitative tests for oxidising agents and reducing agents? Write them down and compare your ideas with the rest of the class. Check in a textbook to confirm the tests.

5   Take turns in challenging a partner to balance some of the equations from Chapter 3 in this coursebook. Your partner looks in the book for an equation then writes the equation down without the large numbers in front of each element or compound. You then try to balance the equation. How well did you do? Take turns in doing this until you are sure that you can balance these equations.

6   Now try a similar thing to the challenge directly above but select ionic equations.

7   Write down a list of compounds that include oxidation numbers as roman numerals, e.g. (II), (IV). Compare your list with the others in the class.

SELF-DARKENING LENSES

Figure 7.1: These photochromic lenses darken in strong light.

Glass has an open network structure of covalently bonded silicon and oxygen atoms. If we add a very small amount of silver chloride and copper(I) chloride to the glass, we can alter its properties so that it remains transparent in weak light but darkens in strong light. This photochromic glass can be used to make spectacle lenses that get darker and darker when more and more ultraviolet light is absorbed (Figure 7.1). The silver chloride and copper(I) chloride are present at such a low concentration that the glass is transparent to light.

When the light is strong, the ultraviolet radiation causes a redox reaction between the silver ions and the copper(I) ions.

$$Ag^+(s) + Cu^+(s) \rightarrow Ag(s) + Cu^{2+}(s)$$

The silver produced reflects the light from the glass so less light is transmitted and the lenses darken. Less ultraviolet light gets to the eyes. This is important because too much ultraviolet light has been linked to damage to the retina of the eye, cataracts (cloudiness of the lens of the eye) and skin cancer. When we move back into the shade, the copper(II) ions oxidise the silver back to silver ions and the lenses become transparent again. The darkening process in bright light takes less than one minute but the reverse process takes from 2–5 minutes. The speed of this

CONTINUED

redox reaction depends on the temperature. At very high temperatures the glasses darken more quickly but do not achieve the full protection of ordinary sunglasses. At very low temperatures the lenses darken more slowly but become relatively darker. However, they take a longer time to go clear again.

More recently, photochromic plastic lenses have been introduced that depend on the change in structure of complex molecules instead of redox reactions.

Questions for discussion

Discuss with another learner or group of learners:

* What are the advantages and disadvantages of photochromic lenses made of glass compared with sunglasses?

* Give some the advantages and disadvantages of using photochromic glasses

    * in cold weather

    * in hot weather

7.1 What is a redox reaction?

A simple definition of **oxidation** is 'gain of oxygen by an element'. For example, when magnesium reacts with oxygen, the magnesium combines with oxygen to form magnesium oxide. Magnesium has been oxidised.

$$2Mg(s) + O_2(g) \rightarrow 2MgO(s)$$

A simple definition of **reduction** is 'loss of oxygen'. When copper(II) oxide reacts with hydrogen, this is the equation for the reaction:

$$CuO(s) + H_2(g) \rightarrow Cu(s) + H_2O(l)$$

Copper(II) oxide loses its oxygen. Copper(II) oxide has been reduced.

But if we look carefully at the copper oxide / hydrogen equation, we can see that oxidation is also taking place. The hydrogen is gaining oxygen to form water. The hydrogen has been oxidised. We can see that reduction and oxidation have taken place together.

Oxidation **I**s **L**oss of electrons.

Reduction **I**s **G**ain of electrons.

The initial letters shown in bold capitals spell OIL RIG. This may help you to remember these two definitions!

Oxidation and reduction always take place together. We call the reactions in which this happens **redox reactions**. Redox reactions are very important. For example, one redox reaction – photosynthesis – provides food for the entire planet, and another one – respiration – keeps you alive.

We can also define reduction as addition of hydrogen to a compound and oxidation as removal of hydrogen from a compound. This is often seen in the reaction of organic compounds (see Chapter 14).

There are two other ways of finding out whether or not a substance has been oxidised or reduced during a chemical reaction:

* electron transfer

* changes in oxidation number.

KEY DEFINITIONS

oxidation: the loss of electrons from an atom, ion or molecule.

reduction: the gain of electrons by an atom, ion or molecule.

redox reaction: a reaction in which oxidation and reduction take place at the same time.

Question

1   a   In each of the following equations, state which reactant has been oxidised:

   i $PbO + H_2 \rightarrow Pb + H_2O$

   ii $CO + Ag_2O \rightarrow 2Ag + CO_2$

   iii $2Mg + CO_2 \rightarrow 2MgO + C$

   b   In each of the following equations, state which reactant has been reduced:

   i $5CO + I_2O_5 \rightarrow 5CO_2 + I_2$

   ii $2H_2S + SO_2 \rightarrow 3S + 2H_2O$

   iii $CH_2{=}CH_2 + H_2 \rightarrow CH_3CH_3$

Redox and electron transfer

Half-equations

We can extend our definition of redox to include reactions involving ions.

Sodium reacts with chlorine to form the ionic compound sodium chloride.

$$2Na(s) + Cl_2(g) \rightarrow 2NaCl(s)$$

We can divide this reaction into two separate equations, one showing oxidation and the other showing reduction. We call these **half-equations**.

When sodium reacts with chlorine:

- Each sodium atom loses one electron from its outer shell. Oxidation is loss of electrons (OIL). The sodium atoms have been oxidised.

  $Na \rightarrow Na^+ + e^-$

  This half-equation shows that sodium is oxidised.

We could also write this half-equation as:

$Na - e^- \rightarrow Na^+$

- Each chlorine atom gains one electron to complete its outer shell. Reduction is gain of electrons (RIG). The chlorine atoms have been reduced.

  $Cl_2 + 2e^- \rightarrow 2Cl^-$

  This half-equation shows chlorine being reduced. There are two chlorine atoms in a chlorine molecule, so two electrons are gained.

In another example, iron reacts with copper(II) ions, Cu^{2+}, in solution to form iron(II) ions, Fe^{2+}, and copper.

$$Fe(s) + Cu^{2+}(aq) \rightarrow Fe^{2+}(aq) + Cu(s)$$

- Each iron atom loses two electrons to form an Fe^{2+} ion. The iron atoms have been oxidised.

  $Fe \rightarrow Fe^{2+} + 2e^-$

  We could also write this half-equation as:

  $Fe - 2e^- \rightarrow Fe^{2+}$

- Each copper(II) ion gains two electrons. The copper ions have been reduced.

  $Cu^{2+} + 2e^- \rightarrow Cu$

Balancing half-equations

We can construct a balanced ionic equation from two half-equations by balancing the numbers of electrons lost and gained and then adding the two half-equations together. The numbers of electrons lost and gained in a redox reaction must be equal.

WORKED EXAMPLES

1   Construct the balanced ionic equation for the reaction between nickel and iron(III) ions, Fe^{3+}, from the half-equations:

   Solution

   $Ni(s) \rightarrow Ni^{2+}(aq) + 2e^-$

   $Fe^{3+}(aq) + e^- \rightarrow Fe^{2+}(aq)$

   - Each Ni atom loses two electrons when it is oxidised. Each Fe^{3+} ion gains one electron when it is reduced.

   - So two Fe^{3+} ions are needed to gain the two electrons lost when each Ni^{2+} ion is formed

     $2Fe^{3+}(aq) + 2e^- \rightarrow 2Fe^{2+}(aq)$

     $Ni(s) \rightarrow Ni^{2+}(aq) + 2e^-$

   - The balanced ionic equation is:

     $Ni(s) + 2Fe^{3+}(aq) \rightarrow Ni^{2+}(aq) + 2Fe^{2+}(aq)$

     Note how the electrons have cancelled out.

CONTINUED

2 Construct the balanced ionic equation for the reaction of iodide ions (I^-) with manganate(VII) ions (MnO_4^-) in the presence of hydrogen ions (H^+). Use the following two half-equations to help you:

$$2I^-(aq) \rightarrow I_2(aq) + 2e^- \tag{i}$$

$$MnO^-(aq) + 8H^+(aq) + 5e^- \rightarrow Mn^{2+}(aq) + 4H_2O(l) \tag{ii}$$

Solution

- When two iodide ions are oxidised, they lose two electrons. Each MnO_4^- ion gains five electrons when it is reduced.

- So we must multiply equation i by 5 and equation ii by 2 to balance the number of electrons:

$$10I^-(aq) \rightarrow 5I_2(aq) + 10e^-$$

$$2MnO_4^-(aq) + 16H^+(aq) + 10e^- \rightarrow$$
$$2Mn^{2+}(aq) + 8H_2O(l)$$

- The balanced ionic equation is:

$$2MnO_4^-(aq) + 10I^-(aq) + 16H^+(aq) \rightarrow$$
$$2Mn^{2+}(aq) + 5I_2(aq) + 8H_2O$$

KEY WORD

half-equation: an equation which shows either oxidation or reduction only. These are sometimes called ion–electron equations, because you need to balance the equation by including the correct number of electrons. Example: $Al^{3+} + 3e^- \rightarrow Al$.

Question

2 a Write two half-equations for the following reactions. For each half-equation state whether oxidation or reduction is occurring.

    i $Cl_2 + 2I^- \rightarrow I_2 + 2Cl^-$

    ii $2Mg + O_2 \rightarrow 2MgO$

    iii $4Fe + 3O_2 \rightarrow 2Fe_2O_3$

  b Zinc metal reacts with IO_3^- ions in acidic solution. Construct a balanced ionic equation for this reaction, using the two half-equations below:

    $2IO_3^- + 12H^+ + 10e^- \rightarrow I_2 + 6H_2O$

    $Zn \rightarrow Zn^{2+} + 2e^-$

7.2 Oxidation numbers

What are oxidation numbers?

We can extend our definition of redox even further to include oxidation and reduction in reactions involving covalent compounds. We do this by using

Figure 7.2: This is part of a ship's hull. It is made of iron protected by bars of magnesium metal. The magnesium atoms (oxidation number = 0) are oxidised to Mg^{2+} ions (oxidation number = +2) in preference to iron atoms changing to Fe^{3+}. This is called *sacrificial protection*.

oxidation numbers (oxidation numbers are also called *oxidation states*). An oxidation number is a number given to each atom or ion in a compound that shows us its degree of oxidation. Oxidation numbers can be positive, negative or zero. The + or − sign must always be included. Higher positive oxidation numbers mean that an atom or ion is more oxidised. Higher negative oxidation numbers mean that an atom or ion is more reduced. Figure 7.2 shows magnesium (oxidation number 0) attached to the hull of a ship. It prevents the hull rusting by sacrificial protection when it releases electrons. During this process, the oxidation number of magnesium changes from 0 (in Mg metal) to +2 in the Mg^{2+} ion.

Oxidation number rules

> **IMPORTANT**
>
> The more positive (or less negative) the oxidation number, the more oxidised a substance is. The less positive (or more negative) the oxidation number, the more reduced a substance is. Take care with negative oxidation numbers: Remember that an ox. no. of -3 is less oxidised / more reduced than an ox. no. of -2.

We can deduce the oxidation number of any atom or ion by oxidation number rules. It is important to note that an oxidation number refers to a *single atom* in a compound.

1 The oxidation number of any uncombined element is zero. For example, the oxidation numbers of each atom in S_8, Cl_2 and Zn is zero.

2 In compounds many atoms or ions have fixed oxidation numbers:
   - Group 1 elements are always $+1$
   - Group 2 elements are always $+2$
   - fluorine is always -1
   - hydrogen is $+1$ (except in metal hydrides such as NaH, where it is -1)
   - oxygen is -2 (except in peroxides, where it is -1, and in F_2O, where it is $+2$).

3 The oxidation number of an element in a monatomic ion is always the same as the charge. For example, Cl^- is -1, Al^{3+} is $+3$.

4 The sum of the oxidation numbers in a compound is zero.

5 The sum of the oxidation numbers in an ion is equal to the charge on the ion.

6 In either a compound or an ion, the more electronegative element is given the negative oxidation number.

7.3 Applying the oxidation number rules

In the rest of this chapter we shall use 'ox. no.' as an abbreviation for oxidation number.

Compounds of a metal with a non-metal

The metal always has the positive ox. no. and the non-metal has the negative ox. no. For example, in sodium oxide, Na_2O, $Na = +1$ and $O = -2$.

If we do not know the ox. no. of one of the atoms, we can often work it out using the invariable ox. nos. in rule 2. For example in sodium sulfide:

> ox. no. of each Na atom $= +1$
>
> for two sodium atoms $= +2$
>
> Na_2S has no overall charge, so the total ox. no. is zero (rule 4)
>
> ox. no. of S $= -2$

Compounds of a non-metal with a non-metal

In compounds containing two different non-metals, the sign of the ox. no. depends on the electronegativity of each atom (see Section 10.5). The most electronegative element is given the negative sign (rule 6).

Sulfur dioxide, SO_2

ox. no. of each O atom $= -2$

for two oxygen atoms $= 2 \times (-2) = -4$

SO_2 has no charge, so the total ox. no. is zero (rule 4)

ox. no. of S $= +4$

Iodine trichloride, ICl_3

chlorine is more electronegative than iodine, so chlorine is $-$ and iodine is $+$

ox. no. of each Cl atom $= -1$

for three chlorine atoms $= 3 \times (-1) = -3$

ICl_3 has no charge, so the total ox. no. is zero (rule 4)

ox. no. of I $= +3$

Hydrazine, N_2H_4

nitrogen is more electronegative than hydrogen, so nitrogen is $-$ and hydrogen is $+$

ox. no. of each H atom $= +1$ (rule 2)

for four hydrogen atoms $= 4 \times (+1) = +4$

N_2H_4 has no charge, so the total ox. no. is zero (rule 4)

ox. no. of two N atoms $= -4$

ox. no. of each N atom $= -2$

Compound ions

Compound ions are ions with two or more different atoms. Examples are the sulfate ion, SO_4^{2-}, and the nitrate ion, NO_3^-. We use rule 5 to work out the ox. no. that we do not know.

Nitrate ion, NO_3^-

ox. no. of each O atom = −2

for three oxygen atoms = $3 \times (-2) = -6$

NO_3^- has a charge of 1−, so the total ox. no. of N and O atoms is −1 (rule 5)

ox. no. of the nitrogen atom plus ox. no. of the three oxygen atoms (−6) = −1

ox. no. of N = +5

IMPORTANT

Remember:

1   the oxidation number refers to a single atom or ion in a compound

2   the oxidation number of an element is zero, e.g. for Al, Si, Cl_2, P_4 ox. no.= 0

3   oxidation numbers are usually whole numbers. In cases where they appear to be fractions it is because the structure of the compound has not been taken into account.

Question

3   State the ox. no. of the bold atoms in these compounds or ions:

   a   **P**$_2$O$_5$ e   N**H**$_3$

   b   **S**O$_4^{2-}$ f   **Cl**O$_2^-$

   c   H$_2$**S**   g   Ca**C**O$_3$

   d   **Al**$_2$Cl$_6$

7.4 Redox and oxidation number

We can define oxidation and reduction in terms of the oxidation number changes of particular atoms during a reaction:

   Oxidation is an increase in oxidation number.

   Reduction is a decrease in oxidation number.

Figure 7.3 shows a redox reaction between copper and silver nitrate.

Figure 7.3: Copper reacts with silver nitrate to form silver and copper(II) nitrate. The ox. no. of each copper atom has increased by two. The ox. no. of each silver ion decreases by one.

When tin reacts with nitric acid, the oxidation numbers of each atom of tin and nitrogen change as shown below.

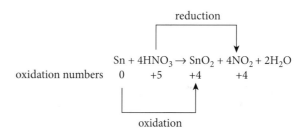

Each tin atom (Sn) has increased in ox. no. by +4: tin has been oxidised. Each nitrogen atom has decreased in ox. no. by −1: nitrogen has been reduced. The ox. no. of each oxygen atom is unchanged at −2. The ox. no. of each hydrogen atom is unchanged at +1. Oxygen and hydrogen are neither oxidised nor reduced.

- In this reaction, nitric acid is acting as an oxidising agent because it increases the oxidation number of another atom.

- In this reaction, tin is acting as a reducing agent because it decreases the oxidation number of another atom.

7.5 Oxidising agents and reducing agents

> **KEY DEFINITIONS**
>
> **oxidising agent:** a substance which brings about oxidation by removing electrons from another atom or ion.
>
> **reducing agent:** a substance which brings about reduction by donating (giving) electrons to another atom or ion.

An **oxidising agent (oxidant)** is a substance which brings about oxidation by removing electrons from another atom or ion.

- An oxidising agent increases the oxidation number of another atom or ion.

- When this happens, the oxidation number of the oxidising agent decreases.

- Typical oxidising agents are oxygen, chlorine and potassium manganate(VII).

A **reducing agent (reductant)** is a substance that brings about reduction by donating (giving) electrons to another atom or ion.

- A reducing agent decreases the oxidation number of another atom or ion.

- When this happens, the oxidation number of the reducing agent increases.

- Typical reducing agents are hydrogen, potassium iodide and reactive metals such as aluminium.

Since oxidation and reduction occur together, in every redox reaction there must be an oxidising agent and a reducing agent.

For example, in the reaction given by the equation:

$$MnO_4^- + 5Fe^{2+} + 8H^+ \rightarrow Mn^{2+} + 5Fe^{3+} + 4H_2O$$

- MnO_4^- is the oxidising agent because the oxidation number of Mn decreases from +7 to +2

- MnO_4^- has increased the oxidation state of iron from +2 to +3

- Fe^{2+} is the reducing agent because the oxidation number of Fe increases from +2 to +3

- Fe^{2+} has decreased the oxidation state of Mn in MnO_4^- from +7 to +2

The ability of a substance to act as a good oxidising or reducing agent depends on its standard electrode potential (see Section 20.4). Many substances can act as either oxidising or reducing agents depending on the substances they are reacting with as well as the conditions.

For example, hydrogen peroxide can act as an oxidising agent or a reducing agent.

Oxidising agent

ox. no.
$$2Fe^{2+} + H_2O_2 + 2H^+ \rightarrow 2Fe^{3+} + H_2O$$
$$\phantom{2Fe^{2}}+2 -1 +3 \phantom{Fe^{3+}+}-2$$

Reducing agent

ox. no.
$$2Fe^{3+} + H_2O_2 + 2OH^- \rightarrow 2Fe^{2+} + 2H_2O + O_2$$
$$\phantom{2Fe^{2}}+3 -1 +2 \phantom{Fe^{2+}+2H_2O+}0$$

Question

4 a Deduce the change in ox. no. for the bold atoms or ions in each of the following equations. In each case, state whether oxidation or reduction has taken place.

   i $2I^- + \mathbf{Br_2} \rightarrow I_2 + \mathbf{2Br^-}$

   ii $(NH_4)_2Cr_2O_7 \rightarrow N_2 + 4H_2O + Cr_2O_3$

   iii $\mathbf{As_2O_3} + 2I_2 + 2H_2O \rightarrow \mathbf{As_2O_5} + 4H^+ + 4I^-$

b Identify the oxidising agent and the reducing agent in parts **a i** and **a iii**.

7.6 Naming compounds

We sometimes use Roman numbers, in brackets, to name compounds. We use these systematic names to distinguish different compounds made of the same elements. For example, there are two types of iron chloride. We show the difference by naming them iron(II) chloride and iron(III) chloride. The numbers in brackets are the oxidation numbers of the iron.

- In iron(II) chloride, the ox. no. of the iron is +2. The compound contains Fe^{2+} ions. The formula is $FeCl_2$.

- In iron(III) chloride, the ox. no. of the iron is +3. The compound contains Fe^{3+} ions. The formula is $FeCl_3$.

We can also use oxidation numbers to distinguish between non-metal atoms in molecules and ions.

Oxides of nitrogen

There are several oxides of nitrogen, including N_2O, NO and NO_2. We distinguish between these according to the ox. no. of the nitrogen atom. (The ox. no. of oxygen is generally −2.)

> The ox. no. of N in N_2O is +1. So this compound is nitrogen(I) oxide.
>
> The ox. no. of N in NO is +2. So this compound is nitrogen(II) oxide.
>
> The ox. no. of N in NO_2 is +4. So this compound is nitrogen(IV) oxide.

Nitrate ions

Sodium, nitrogen and oxygen can form two different compounds $Na^+NO_2^-$ and $Na^+NO_3^-$ (Figure 7.4). The ox. no. of sodium is +1 and the ox. no. of oxygen is −2. So it is the ox. no. of nitrogen that varies.

- The ox. no. of N in the NO_2^- ion is +3. So NaNO is sodium nitrate(III).

- The ox. no. of N in the NO_3^- ion is +5. So $NaNO_3$ is sodium nitrate(V).

Note that the ox. no. comes *after* the ion it refers to.

The names of ions containing oxygen and one other element end in '-ate' (but hydroxide ions, OH^-, are an exception to this rule). For example, ions containing chlorine and oxygen are chlorates and ions containing sulfur and oxygen are sulfates.

The names of inorganic acids containing oxygen end in '-ic'. The Roman number goes directly after the ion that contains the oxygen and another element.

H_3PO_3 is called phosphoric(III) acid because the ox. no. of phosphorus is +3.

$HClO_4$ is called chloric(VII) acid because the ox. no. of chlorine is +7. Salts of the common acids are usually

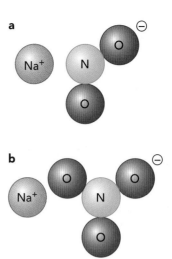

Figure 7.4: a One formula unit of 'sodium nitrate(III)'. **b** One formula unit of 'sodium nitrate(V)'.

named without including the ox. no. of the non-metal ion. For example, $Mg(NO_3)_2$ is magnesium nitrate not magnesium nitrate(V), and K_2SO_4 is potassium sulfate not potassium sulfate(VI). Note also that we do not state the ox. no. of the metal if it has only one oxidation state.

Question

5 Give the full systematic names of the following:

    a Na_2SO_3

    b Na_2SO_4

    c $Fe(NO_3)_2$

    d $Fe(NO_3)_3$

    e $FeSO_4$

    f Cu_2O

    g H_2SO_3

    h Mn_2O_7

REFLECTION

Work with another learner to work out the oxidation number of M in oxides with the general formula M_xO_y, where x can be any number from 1 to 3 and y can be any number from 1 to 4.

One learner writes the formula for an imaginary oxide using these rules, e.g. M_2O_4, MO_3. Both then work together to deduce the ox. no. for M.

Don't worry if the ox. no. comes out as a fraction: this is only for practice at deducing oxidation numbers!

What resources did you use? Which were the most helpful?

7.7 From name to formula

You can work out the formula of a compound from its name.

WORKED EXAMPLE

3   Each formula unit of sodium chlorate(V) contains one sodium ion. What is the formula of sodium chlorate(V)?

Solution

We know that:

sodium has an ox. no. of +1

oxygen has an ox. no. of −2

the ox. no. of chlorine is +5

the chlorate(V) ion has a charge of 1− (to balance the 1+ charge of the sodium).

We can work out the formula of the chlorate(V) ion from the oxidation numbers of oxygen and chlorine (let n be the number of oxygen atoms):

$$\text{ox. no. (Cl)} + \text{ox. no. (O)} = -1$$
$$+5 + n \times (-2) \qquad = -1$$
$$n \qquad\qquad = 3$$

So the chlorate(V) ion is ClO_3^- and sodium chlorate(V) is $NaClO_3$.

Question

6   Give the formulae of:

a   sodium chlorate(I)

b   iron(III) oxide

c   potassium nitrate(III)

d   phosphorus(III) chloride.

PRACTICAL ACTIVITY 7.1

Demonstrating a redox reaction

SAFETY: Only carry out this activity in the presence of a teacher after safety aspects have been explained.

We can demonstrate the redox reaction between iron(II) chloride and potassium manganate(VII) using qualitative chemical tests. Aqueous potassium manganate(VII) is purple in colour. When it reacts with iron(II) ions in the presence of excess acid it is usually converted to manganese(II) ions, which appear colourless at low concentrations.

Procedure

You will need three clean test-tubes and separate dropping pipettes for each solution.

1   In the first test-tube, put 1 cm depth of aqueous iron(II) chloride.

2   Using a dropping pipette, add aqueous sodium hydroxide dropwise until you see a definite change. Record your observations.

3   In the second test-tube, put 1 cm depth of aqueous iron(III) chloride.

4   Using a dropping pipette, add aqueous sodium hydroxide dropwise until you see a definite change. Record your observations.

5   In the third test-tube, put 2 cm depth of aqueous iron(II) chloride.

6   Using a dropping pipette, add aqueous acidified potassium manganate(VII) to the solution of iron(II) chloride dropwise until you see a definite colour change. Record your observations.

7   Now add aqueous sodium hydroxide to the contents of this tube until you see a further change. Record your observations.

Use your results to explain how you know that a redox reaction has taken place. Name the oxidising agent and the reducing agent.

7.8 Balancing chemical equations using oxidation numbers

We can use oxidation numbers to balance equations involving redox reactions. This method is especially useful where compound ions such as nitrate(V) or manganate(VII) are involved.

WORKED EXAMPLES

4   Copper(II) oxide (CuO) reacts with ammonia (NH_3) to form copper, nitrogen (N_2) and water. Deduce the balanced equation for this reaction.

Solution

Step 1: Write the unbalanced equation and identify the atoms which change in ox. no. (shown here in red).

$$CuO + NH_3 \rightarrow Cu + N_2 + H_2O$$
$$+2 -2 \quad -3 +1 \quad 0 \quad 0 \quad +1 -2$$

Step 2: Deduce the ox. no. changes.

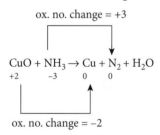

ox. no. change = +3

$$CuO + NH_3 \rightarrow Cu + N_2 + H_2O$$
$$+2 \quad -3 \quad 0 \quad 0$$

ox. no. change = −2

Step 3: Balance the ox. no. changes.

ox. no. change = 2 × (+3) = +6

$$3CuO + 2NH_3 \rightarrow 3Cu + N_2 + H_2O$$
$$3 × (+2) \quad 2 × (-3) \quad 0 \quad 0$$

ox. no. change = 3 × (−2) = −6

The change in ox. nos. are −2 for the copper and +3 for the nitrogen. To balance the ox. no. changes, we need to multiply the copper by 3 and the nitrogen in the ammonia by 2. The total ox. no. changes are then balanced (−6 and +6). Note that we do not multiply the N_2 by 2 because there are already two atoms of

nitrogen present. Once these ratios have been fixed, you must not change them.

Step 4: Balance the atoms.

There are six hydrogen atoms in the $2NH_3$ on the left. These are balanced with six on the right (as $3H_2O$). This also balances the number of oxygen atoms. The final equation is:

$$3CuO + 2NH_3 \rightarrow 3Cu + N_2 + 3H_2O$$

5   Manganate(VII) ions (MnO_4^-) react with Fe^{2+} ions in the presence of acid (H^+) to form Mn^{2+} ions, Fe^{3+} ions and water.

Step 1: Write the unbalanced equation and identify the atoms that change in ox. no.

$$MnO_4^- + Fe^{2+} + H^+ \rightarrow Mn^{2+} + Fe^{3+} + H_2O$$
$$+7 -2 \quad +2 \quad +1 \quad +2 \quad +3 \quad +1 -2$$

Step 2: Deduce the ox. no. changes.

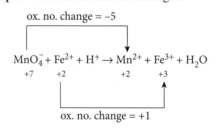

ox. no. change = −5

$$MnO_4^- + Fe^{2+} + H^+ \rightarrow Mn^{2+} + Fe^{3+} + H_2O$$
$$+7 \quad +2 \quad +2 \quad +3$$

ox. no. change = +1

Step 3: Balance the ox. no. changes.

ox. no. change = 1 × (−5) = −5

$$MnO_4^- + 5Fe^{2+} + H^+ \rightarrow Mn^{2+} + 5Fe^{3+} + H_2O$$
$$+7 \quad +2 \quad +2 \quad +3$$

ox. no. change = 5 × (+1) = +5

$$MnO_4 + 5Fe^{2+} + H^+ \rightarrow Mn^{2+} + 5Fe^{3+} + H_2O$$

CONTINUED

Step 4: Balance the charges.

Initially ignore the hydrogen ions, as these will be used to balance the charges.

The total charge on the other reactants is:
$(1-)$ (from MnO_4^-) + $(5 \times 2+)$ (from $5Fe^{2+}$)
$= 9+$

The total charge on the products is:
$(2+)$ (from Mn^{2+}) + $(5 \times 3+)$ (from $5Fe^{3+}$)
$= 17+$

To balance the charges we need 8 H^+ ions on the left.

$$MnO_4^- + 5Fe^{2+} + 8H^+ \rightarrow Mn^{2+} + 5Fe^{3+} + H_2O$$

Step 5: Balance the hydrogen atoms in the water.

$$MnO_4^- + 5Fe^{2+} + 8H^+ \rightarrow Mn^{2+} + 5Fe^{3+} + 4H_2O$$

Question

7 Use the oxidation number method to balance these equations.

a $H_2SO_4 + HI \rightarrow S + I_2 + H_2O$

b $HBr + H_2SO_4 \rightarrow Br_2 + SO_2 + H_2O$

c $V^{3+} + I_2 + H_2O \rightarrow VO^{2+} + I^- + H^+$

7.9 Disproportionation

KEY DEFINITION

disproportionation: the simultaneous oxidation and reduction of the same species in a chemical reaction

The element chlorine (Cl_2, oxidation number = 0) undergoes a type of redox reaction called **disproportionation** when it reacts with alkali. Disproportionation can be thought of as a 'self-reduction / oxidation' reaction. When chlorine reacts with dilute alkali, some chlorine atoms are reduced and some are oxidised in the same reaction. The actual reaction that takes place depends on the temperature.

When we add chlorine to cold aqueous sodium hydroxide the following disproportionation reaction takes place:

$$Cl_2(aq) + 2NaOH(aq) \rightarrow NaCl(aq) + NaClO(aq) + H_2O(l)$$
$$\text{sodium chlorate(I)}$$

The ionic equation for this redox reaction can be split into two half-equations, showing the reduction and oxidation.

- The reduction reaction is:

$$\tfrac{1}{2}Cl_2 + e^- \rightarrow Cl^-$$
ox. no.   0 -1

The change in oxidation number of chlorine is -1.

- The oxidation reaction is:

$$\tfrac{1}{2}Cl_2 + 2OH^- \rightarrow ClO^- + H_2O + e^-$$
ox. no.   0 $+1$

The change in oxidation number of chlorine is $+1$.

The oxidation numbers are balanced so there are equal numbers of moles of Cl^- and ClO^- in the equation.

Balancing equations involving disproportionation

When we add chlorine and hot concentrated aqueous sodium hydroxide a different disproportionation reaction takes place. The products are chloride ions, Cl^-, chlorate(V) ions, ClO_3^- and water. Worked example 6 shows how to balance this disproportionation reaction.

WORKED EXAMPLE

6 Balance the disproportionation reaction which takes place when chlorine is added to hot concentrated aqueous sodium hydroxide. The products are chloride ions, Cl^-, chlorate(V) ions, ClO_3^- and water.

Solution

Step 1: Write the unbalanced equation and identify the atoms that change in ox. no.

$$\tfrac{1}{2}Cl_2 + OH^- \rightarrow Cl^- + ClO_3^- + H_2O$$

ox. no.   0   −1   +5

Step 2: Deduce the ox. no. changes.

$$\tfrac{1}{2}Cl_2 \rightarrow Cl^- \text{ is } -1$$

$$\tfrac{1}{2}Cl_2 \rightarrow ClO_3^- \text{ is } +5$$

Step 3: Balance the ox. no. changes.

For each ClO_3^- ion formed we need 5 Cl^- to balance.

$$3Cl_2 + OH^- \rightarrow 5Cl^- + ClO_3^- + H_2O$$

Step 4: Balance the charges.

$$3Cl_2 + 6OH^- \rightarrow 5Cl^- + ClO_3^- + H_2O$$

Step 5: Balance the chlorine molecules and the water.

$$3Cl_2 + 6OH^- \rightarrow 5Cl^- + ClO_3^- + 3H_2O$$

Question

8 Look at the equation:

$$Cr_2O_7^{2-} + 2H^+ + 3SO_2 \rightarrow 2Cr^{3+} + H_2O + 3SO_4^{2-}$$

Which one of these statements about the oxidation number changes is correct?

A The ox. no. of each Cr atom changes from +12 to +3

B The ox. no. of each sulfur atom changes from + 4 to +6

C The ox. no. of each hydrogen atom changes from +1 to 0

D The ox. no. of each Cr atom changes from +7 to +3

REFLECTION

Work with another learner or group of learners.

Each member of the group looks in this coursebook or another textbook for one or two equations involving redox reactions. You write the equation down but unbalanced. When you have a number of equations, try balancing them (using the ox. no. method) by working together as a group. You might start by selecting the equations that seem easier.

How easy was it to balance these equations? Which steps in the balancing do you need to improve?
Did any of your equations turn out not to be redox equations?

SUMMARY

In a redox reaction, both oxidation (increase in oxidation number) and reduction (decrease in oxidation number) are taking place.
Redox reactions can be explained in terms of electron loss (oxidation) and electron gain (reduction).
Oxidation numbers are used to name compounds and balance equations.
An oxidising agent brings about oxidation by removing electrons from another atom or ion.
A reducing agent brings about reduction by donating electrons to another atom or ion.

EXAM-STYLE QUESTIONS

1 In the industrial production of nitric acid the following changes take place to the nitrogen.

$$N_2 \xrightarrow{\text{stage 1}} NH_3 \xrightarrow{\text{stage 2}} NO \xrightarrow{\text{stage 3}} NO_2 \xrightarrow{\text{stage 4}} HNO_3$$

   a Deduce the oxidation number of the nitrogen atom in each molecule. [5]

   b For each stage, state whether oxidation or reduction has taken place. In each case explain your answer. [2]

   c Give the full systematic name for NO_2. [1]

   d Nitric acid, HNO_3, reacts with red phosphorus.

$$P + 5HNO_3 \rightarrow H_3PO_4 + 5NO_2 + H_2O$$

By referring to oxidation number changes, explain why this is a redox reaction. [5]

   e Explain why nitric acid can be described as an oxidising agent in this reaction. [1]

[Total: 14]

2 Calcium reacts with cold water to form calcium hydroxide, $Ca(OH)_2$, and hydrogen, H_2.

   a State the oxidation number of calcium in:

   i calcium metal [1]

   ii calcium hydroxide. [1]

   b State the oxidation number of hydrogen in:

   i water [1]

   ii hydrogen gas. [1]

   c Write two half-equations for the reaction between water and calcium hydroxide to show:

   i the change from calcium to calcium ions [1]

   ii the change from water to hydroxide ions and hydrogen. [1]

   d State the half-equations in part c in which reduction is occurring. Give a reason for your answer. [1]

   e Write a balanced equation for the reaction of calcium with water. [1]

   f Explain the role played by water in this reaction. [1]

[Total: 9]

3 The unbalanced equation for the reaction of sulfur dioxide with bromine is shown below.

$$SO_2 + Br_2 + H_2O \rightarrow SO_4^{2-} + Br^- + H^+$$

   a State the oxidation number of sulfur in:

   i SO_2 [1]

   ii SO_4^{2-} [1]

   b State the oxidation number of bromine in:

   i Br_2 [1]

   ii Br^- [1]

c Identify the reducing agent in this reaction. Give a reason for your answer. [1]

d State the change in oxidation number for:

 i each S atom [1]

 ii each bromine atom. [1]

e Construct a balanced equation for this reaction. [2]

[Total: 9]

4 Aluminium reacts with hydrochloric acid to form aluminium chloride, $AlCl_3$, and hydrogen. This is a redox reaction.

a Explain in term of electrons, what is meant by a redox reaction. [3]

b **i** Write a half-equation to show aluminium changing to aluminium ions. [1]

 ii Write a second half-equation to show what happens to the hydrogen ions from the acid. [1]

 iii Deduce the change in oxidation number when a hydrogen ion turns into a hydrogen atom. [1]

c Construct a balanced ionic equation for the reaction between aluminium atoms and hydrogen ions. [1]

[Total: 7]

5 Iodine, I_2, reacts with thiosulfate ions, $S_2O_3^{2-}$ to form iodide ions, I^-, and tetrathionate ions, S_4O_6

$$I_2 + 2S_2O_3^{2-} \rightarrow 2I^- + S_4O_6^{2-}$$

a State the oxidation number of each sulfur atom in:

 i a $S_2O_3^{2-}$ ion [1]

 ii a $S_4O_6^{2-}$ ion. [1]

b Explain in terms of electron transfer why the conversion of iodine to iodide ions is a reduction reaction. [1]

c When a salt containing iodide ions is warmed with concentrated sulfuric acid and MnO_2, iodine is evolved:

$$2I^- + MnO_2 + 6H^+ + 2SO_4^{2-} \rightarrow I_2 + Mn^{2+} + 2HSO_4^- + 2H_2O$$

 i State the systematic name for MnO_2. [1]

 ii Deduce the oxidation number of S in the SO_4^{2-} ion. [1]

 iii State which reactant gets oxidised in this reaction. Explain your answer by using oxidation numbers. [1]

 iv State which substance is the oxidising agent. Explain your answer. [1]

[Total: 7]

6 The compound $KBrO_3$ decomposes when heated:

$$2KBrO_3 \rightarrow 2KBr + 3O_2$$

a State the oxidation numbers of bromine in:

 i $KBrO_3$ [1]

 ii KBr [1]

CONTINUED

b Explain, using oxidation numbers, why this reaction is a redox reaction. [3]

c State the systematic name of $KBrO_3$. [1]

d When $KBrO_3$ reacts with hydrazine, N_2H_4, nitrogen gas is evolved:

$$2KBrO_3 + 3N_2H_4 \rightarrow 2KBr + 3N_2 + 6H_2O$$

   i Deduce the oxidation number change of the bromine atom when $KBrO_3$ is converted to KBr. [1]

   ii Deduce the oxidation number change for each nitrogen atom when N_2H_4 is converted to N_2. [2]

   iii Use your answers to **i** and **ii** to explain why 2 moles of $KBrO_3$ react with 3 moles of N_2H_4. [3]

[Total: 12]

SELF-EVALUATION

After studying this chapter, complete a table like this:

I can	See section...	Needs more work	Almost there	Ready to move on
deduce oxidation numbers of elements in compounds and ions	7.2, 7.3, 7.4			
explain and use the terms *redox*, *oxidation* and *reduction* in terms of electron transfer and changes in oxidation number	7.1			
explain and use the term *disproportionation* in terms of electron transfer and changes in oxidation number	7.9			
explain and use the terms *oxidising agent* and *reducing agent*	7.5			
use changes in oxidation numbers to help balance chemical equations	7.5, 7.8			
use Roman numerals to indicate the degree of oxidation or reduction of an element in a compound.	7.6			

> Chapter 8
Equilibria

LEARNING INTENTIONS

In this chapter you will learn how to:

- explain what is meant by a *reversible reaction*

- explain what is meant by *dynamic equilibrium* in terms of the rate of forward and backward reactions being equal and concentration of reactants and products remaining constant

- explain why a closed system is needed for equilibrium to be established

- define Le Chatelier's principle as: 'if a change is made to a system at dynamic equilibrium the position of equilibrium moves to minimise this change'

- use Le Chatelier's principle to deduce qualitatively the effects of changes in temperature, concentration, pressure or presence of a catalyst on a reaction at equilibrium

CONTINUED

- deduce expressions for equilibrium constants in terms of concentrations, K_c

- use the terms *mole fraction* and *partial pressure*

- deduce expressions for equilibrium constants in terms of partial pressures, K_p

- Use K_c and K_p expressions to carry out equilibrium calculations

- calculate the quantities present at equilibrium from given data

- understand which factors affect the value of the equilibrium constant

- describe and explain the conditions used in the Haber process and the Contact process

- write the formula and give the names of common acids and alkalis (HCl, H_2SO_4, HNO_3, CH_3COOH, $NaOH$, KOH, NH_3)

- describe the Brønsted–Lowry theory of acids and bases

- describe strong acids and strong bases and weak acids and weak bases in terms of being fully dissociated or partially dissociated

- describe acid, alkaline and neutral solutions in terms of pH

- explain qualitatively the differences in behaviour of strong and weak acids in terms of electrical conductivity, universal indicator, pH and reactivity with reactive metals

- describe neutralisation reactions in terms of H^+ (aq) + OH^- (aq) $\rightarrow$ H_2O (l)

- sketch pH titration curves using combinations of strong and weak acids with strong and weak alkalis

- select suitable indicators for acid–alkali titrations using data provided.

BEFORE YOU START

1 Take it in turn to explain these chemical terms to another learner:

    a stoichiometry

    b state symbols

    c mole

    d r.t.p.

    e standard form

    f reversible reaction

    g position of equilibrium.

2 Write all that you know about a reaction that is in equilibrium and the factors that affect equilibrium. Compare your answers with other learners in the class.

3 In Chapter 3 you did mole calculations, including calculations involving solution concentrations and gas volumes. Write down all the expressions that you know which connect these things to the number of moles. Be ready to share your answers with others in the class.

CONTINUED

4   What are the units of volume, pressure and temperature? What a smaller or larger units of these basic units are commonly used?

5   Take turns in challenging a partner to convert figures into standard form. Your partner thinks of a number from 0.00001 to 1 000 000, e.g. 0.0063 or 675 000, and asks you to change this into standard form. Take turns in doing this until you are sure that you understand the use of standard form.

6   Work with another learner to describe and explain what you know about the manufacture of either ammonia or sulfuric acid and the factors which affect the yield. Be ready to share this with the class.

7   Make a list of acids and alkalis together with their formulae. Share your list and formulae with the rest of the class.

8   Write down the main points about the pH scale and the colour changes of named indicators in acidic and alkaline conditions. Compare your answers with other learners in the class.

9   Discuss these questions with another learner:

a   What are the differences between a concentrated weak acid and a dilute strong acid?

b   What is the meaning of the terms *neutralisation*, *indicator*, *salt*, *titration*?

10   Work with another learner to describe how you would carry out an acid–alkali titration and process the results.

IMPROVING THE EFFICIENCY!

Figure 8.1: Ammonia plant in Western Australia.

Millions of tonnes of ammonia are produced throughout the world every year (Figure 8.1).

Ammonia is used to make fertilisers, nitric acid and nylon.

Ammonia is now made using the Haber process, by combining hydrogen and nitrogen in the presence of a catalyst. The reaction does not go to completion. It reaches equilibrium when the rates of the forward and backward reactions are equal. The amount of energy needed to run a complex plant for making ammonia is huge and over the last 100 years, chemists have been working to bring down the energy costs and reduce pollution.

Before the Haber process was invented, ammonia was produced by the electric arc processes, which used cheap hydroelectricity but required a temperature of 3000 °C to work. The energy required per tonne of ammonia formed was

Country	China	India	Russia	USA	Indonesia
Tonnes of NH_3 / year	45 500 000	12 000 000	10 000 000	8 800 000	5 000 000

Table 8.1: The countries producing the greatest amount of ammonia.

CONTINUED

500 gigajoules (1 gigajoule = 10^9 J). This and the cyanamide process for making ammonia produced a lot of polluting waste products. The inefficiency of these processes encouraged the development of the Haber process for the direct synthesis of ammonia from hydrogen and nitrogen. This has the advantage of producing pure ammonia but high temperatures and pressures are still needed. The essential part of this process was to find a suitable catalyst. At first, osmium was used but this was too difficult to obtain. A catalyst of iron-coated iron oxides was then developed. This reduced the energy requirement for the process to about 90 gigajoules per tonne of ammonia. But there were still problems, including pollution problems, because of the use of coal to provide energy and hydrogen. In addition, energy-inefficient electrolysis was used to produce hydrogen. By 1960, many ammonia plants had switched to natural gas and used petroleum fractions to produce hydrogen. This increased the energy efficiency of the whole process even more. In modern ammonia plants, the efficiency has been further increased so that only about 40 gigajoules are needed to produce a tonne of ammonia. These plants use ruthenium as a catalyst, which decreases the operating temperature.

Questions for discussion

Discuss with another learner or group of learners:

- Many chemists are trying to develop 'greener' manufacturing processes. Use some of the ideas in the passage above and any other things you can think of to make a list of things that chemists could do to develop 'greener' manufacturing processes.

- Chemists have sometimes been blamed for polluting the environment and using up natural resources. Is this fair?

8.1 Reversible reactions and equilibrium

Reversible reactions

Some reactions can be reversed. For example, when blue, hydrated copper(II) sulfate is heated, it loses its water of crystallisation and changes to white anhydrous copper(II) sulfate (see Figure 8.2).

$$CuSO_4 \cdot 5H_2O(s) \quad \rightarrow \quad CuSO_4(s) \quad + 5H_2O(l)$$
$$\text{hydrated} \qquad\qquad \text{anhydrous}$$
$$\text{copper(II) sulfate} \qquad \text{copper(II) sulfate}$$

This is called the *forward* reaction.

When water is added to anhydrous copper(II) sulfate, the reaction is reversed.

$$CuSO_4(s) + 5H_2O(l) \rightarrow CuSO_4 \cdot 5H_2O(s)$$

This is called the *backward* (or *reverse*) reaction.

We show these two reactions in the same equation by using two half arrows: $\rightleftharpoons$

$$CuSO_4 \cdot 5H_2O(s) \rightleftharpoons CuSO_4(s) + 5H_2O(l)$$

Figure 8.2: Hydrated copper(II) sulfate (left) and anhydrous copper(II) sulfate (right).

KEY WORD

reversible reaction: a reaction in which products can be changed back to reactants by reversing the conditions.

A reaction in which the products can react to re-form the original reactants is called a **reversible reaction**. In this case, heating and adding water are not being carried out at the same time. However, there is a type of chemical reaction in which the forward reaction and the backward reaction take place at the same time.

In many chemical reactions, the reactants are not used up completely. Some products are formed but the maximum theoretical yield is not obtained. A mixture of products and reactants is formed. The products react together to re-form reactants at the same time as the reactants are forming products. This type of reversible reaction is called an **equilibrium reaction**. We use the sign ⇌ in equilibrium reactions to show that they are reversible.

For example, consider the reaction between hydrogen and iodine carried out in a sealed glass tube at 400 °C:

$$H_2(g) + I_2(g) \rightleftharpoons 2HI(g)$$

Molecules of hydrogen iodide are breaking down to hydrogen and iodine at the same rate as hydrogen and iodine molecules are reacting together to form hydrogen iodide (see Figure 8.3).

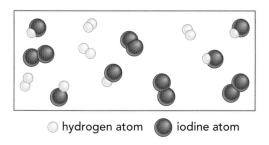

○ hydrogen atom   ● iodine atom

Figure 8.3: A snapshot of the dynamic equilibrium between hydrogen gas, iodine gas and hydrogen iodide gas.

When fizzy drinks are made, carbon dioxide gas is dissolved in the drink under pressure. When you take the lid off a bottle of fizzy drink, bubbles of carbon dioxide suddenly appear. When you put the lid back on, the bubbles stop. This is because of the equilibrium reaction $CO_2(g) \rightleftharpoons CO_2(aq)$

The forward reaction happens during manufacture and the backward reaction happens on opening.

Characteristics of equilibrium

An equilibrium reaction has four particular features under constant conditions:

1 it is dynamic
2 the forward and reverse reactions occur at the same rate
3 the concentrations of reactants and products remain constant at equilibrium
4 it requires a **closed system**.

It is dynamic

The phrase **dynamic equilibrium** means that the molecules or ions of reactants and products are continuously reacting. Reactants are continuously being changed to products and products are continuously being changed back to reactants.

> ### KEY WORDS
>
> **equilibrium reaction:** a reaction that does not go to completion and in which reactants and products are present in fixed concentration ratios.
>
> **dynamic equilibrium:** reactants are being converted to products at the same rate as products are being converted back to reactants.
>
> **closed system:** a system in which matter is not lost or gained, e.g. gases in a closed jar.

The forward and backward reactions occur at the same rate

At equilibrium, the rate of the forward reaction equals the rate of the backward reaction. Molecules or ions of reactants are becoming products, and those in the products are becoming reactants at the same rate.

> ### IMPORTANT
>
> - We can get to the equilibrium state by starting from only the reactants or only the products.
> - At equilibrium, the concentration of products and reactants is constant.
> - At equilibrium, molecules of reactants are reacting to form molecules of products at the same rate as molecules of products are reacting to form molecules of reactants.

The concentrations of reactants and products remain constant at equilibrium

The concentrations remain constant because, at equilibrium, the rates of the forward and backward reactions are equal. The equilibrium can be approached from two directions. For example, in the reaction:

$$H_2(g) + I_2(g) \rightleftharpoons 2HI(g)$$

we can start by either:

- using a mixture of colourless hydrogen gas and purple iodine vapour, or

- using only colourless hydrogen iodide gas.

Figure 8.4 shows what happens when 5.00×10^{-3} mol of hydrogen molecules and 5.00×10^{-3} mol of iodine molecules react at 500 K in a vessel of volume 1 dm³. As time passes, the purple colour of the iodine vapour fades until equilibrium is reached. At equilibrium the mixture contains 0.68×10^{-3} mol of iodine, 0.68×10^{-3} mol of hydrogen and 8.64×10^{-3} mol of hydrogen iodide.

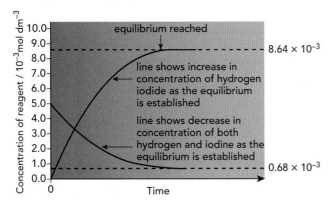

Figure 8.4: The changes in the concentrations of reagents as 5.00×10^{-3} mol of each of hydrogen and iodine react to form an equilibrium mixture with hydrogen iodide in a vessel of volume 1 dm³.

Figure 8.5 shows that the same equilibrium can be achieved when 10.00×10^{-3} mol of hydrogen iodide molecules decompose to iodine and hydrogen. You can see that the same equilibrium concentrations of all three molecules are achieved.

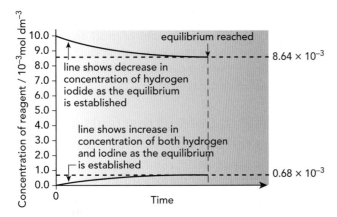

Figure 8.5: The changes in the concentrations of reagents as 10.00×10^{-3} mol of hydrogen iodide react to form an equilibrium mixture with hydrogen and iodine gases in a vessel of 1 dm³.

Question

1   These questions relate to the information in Figure 8.5.

   a   Why are the concentrations of iodine and hydrogen at equilibrium the same?

   b   Describe how the depth of colour of the reaction mixture changes as time progresses.

   c   Explain why there must be 8.64×10^{-3} mol of hydrogen iodide molecules in the equilibrium mixture if 0.68×10^{-3} mol of iodine are present.

Equilibrium requires a closed system

A *closed system* is one in which none of the reactants or products escapes from the reaction mixture. In an *open system* some matter is lost to the surroundings. Figure 8.6 shows the difference between a closed system and an open system when calcium carbonate is heated at a high temperature in a strong container.

Many chemical reactions can be studied without placing them in closed containers. They can reach equilibrium in open flasks if the reaction takes place entirely in solution and no gas is lost.

a

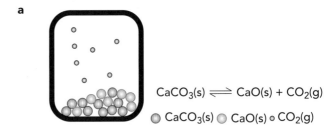

b

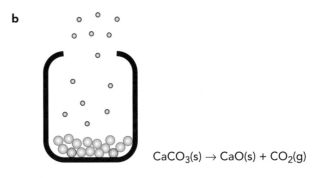

Figure 8.6: a A closed system. No carbon dioxide escapes. The calcium carbonate is in equilibrium with calcium oxide and carbon dioxide. **b** An open system. The calcium carbonate is continually decomposing as the carbon dioxide is lost. The reaction eventually goes to completion.

Question

2 A beaker contains saturated aqueous sodium chloride solution in contact with undissolved solid sodium chloride. Sodium ions and chloride ions are constantly moving from solid to solution and from solution to solid.

a i Explain why this is a closed system.

ii Explain why the concentration of the saturated sodium chloride solution does not change, even though ions are still moving into the solution from the solid.

b Bromine is a reddish-brown liquid that vaporises at room temperature. Some liquid bromine is put in a closed jar. The colour of the bromine vapour above the liquid gets darker and darker until the depth of colour remains constant. Bromine liquid still remains in the jar. Explain what is happening in terms of changes in concentration of the bromine molecules in the vapour.

8.2 Changing the position of equilibrium

IMPORTANT

- Remember that although the concentration of reactants and products are constant at equilibrium, this does *not* mean that they are equal to each other.
- The position of equilibrium tells us how far the reaction goes to the products or reactants.
- If the concentration of products is greater than the concentration of reactants, the position of equilibrium is to the right (towards the product side).
- If the concentration of products is far less than the concentration of reactants, the position of equilibrium is to the left (towards the reactants side).
- Remember that for equilibrium reactions, you always have to refer to the equation written. If you write it the other way round, the reactants are the products!

Position of equilibrium

The position of equilibrium refers to the relative amounts of products and reactants present in an equilibrium mixture.

If a system in equilibrium is disturbed (e.g. by a change in temperature) and the concentration of products increases relative to the reactants, we say that the position of equilibrium has shifted to the right.

If the concentration of products decreases relative to the reactants, we say that the position of equilibrium has shifted to the left.

Le Chatelier's principle

Changes in both concentration and temperature affect the position of equilibrium. When any of the reactants or products are gases, changes in pressure may also affect the position of equilibrium. French chemist Henri Le Chatelier (1850–1936) observed how these factors affect the position of equilibrium. He put forward a general rule, known as **Le Chatelier's principle**.

If one or more factors that affect a dynamic equilibrium is changed, the position of equilibrium moves to minimise this change.

We can predict the effect of changing concentration and pressure by referring to the stoichiometric equation for the reaction. We can predict the effect of changing the temperature by referring to the enthalpy change of the reaction.

KEY DEFINITION

Le Chatelier's principle: if one or more factors that affect a dynamic equilibrium is changed, the position of equilibrium moves to minimise this change.

How does change in concentration affect the position of equilibrium?

When the concentration of one or more of the reactants is increased:

- the system is no longer in equilibrium
- the position of equilibrium moves to the right to reduce the effect of the increase in concentration of reactant
- more products are formed until equilibrium is restored.

When the concentration of one or more of the products is increased:

- the system is no longer in equilibrium
- the position of equilibrium moves to the left to reduce the effect of the increase in concentration of product
- more reactants are formed until equilibrium is restored.

For example, look at the reaction:

$$CH_3COOH(l) + C_2H_5OH(l) \rightleftharpoons CH_3COOC_2H_5(l) + H_2O(l)$$

   ethanoic acid   ethanol   ethyl ethanoate   water

What happens when we add more ethanol?

The concentration of ethanol is increased.

According to Le Chatelier's principle, some of the ethanol must be removed to reduce the concentration of the added ethanol.

The position of equilibrium shifts to the right.

More ethanol reacts with ethanoic acid and more ethyl ethanoate and water are formed.

What happens when we add more water?

The concentration of water is increased.

According to Le Chatelier's principle, some of the water must be removed to reduce the concentration of the added water.

The position of equilibrium shifts to the left.

So more water reacts with ethyl ethanoate and more ethanoic acid and ethanol are formed.

What happens when we remove some water?

The concentration of water is decreased.

According to Le Chatelier's principle, some water must be added to increase its concentration.

The position of equilibrium shifts to the right.

So more ethanoic acid reacts with ethanol and more water and ethyl ethanoate are formed.

A natural effect of how change in concentration affects the position of equilibrium is shown by the formation of stalactites and stalagmites (Figure 8.7).

PRACTICAL ACTIVITY 8.1

An equilibrium involving iodine, acid and alkali

SAFETY: Only carry out this activity in the presence of a teacher after safety aspects have been explained.

Iodine dissolves in aqueous potassium iodide. We shall call this 'iodine solution'. Iodine is also soluble in aqueous sodium hydroxide. In this activity, you will see how you can reverse the reaction by changing the concentration of acid or alkali.

You will need two test-tubes and three dropping pipettes for this experiment.

Procedure

1   Using a dropping pipette, put 1 cm depth of 'iodine solution' into two separate test-tubes.

2   To the first test-tube add dilute sulfuric acid (use a fresh dropping pipette). Record any observations

3   To the second test-tube add dilute sodium hydroxide (use a fresh dropping pipette). Record any observations.

4   To the first test-tube add sodium hydroxide until it is in excess. Record any observations.

5   To the second test-tube add sulfuric acid until it is in excess. Record any observations.

How do you know that the reaction is reversible?

Explain the results in terms of H$^+$ ions from the acid and OH$^-$ ions from the alkali.

Figure 8.7: Stalactites and stalagmites are formed as a result of water passing through rocks containing calcium carbonate. The solution running through these rocks contains water, dissolved carbon dioxide and calcium hydrogencarbonate:

$CaCO_3(s) + H_2O(l) + CO_2(aq) \rightleftharpoons Ca(HCO_3)_2(aq)$

When droplets of this mixture are formed on the roof of the cave, some of the carbon dioxide in the droplets escapes into the air. The position of equilibrium shifts to the left and calcium carbonate is deposited.

Question

3 a Use this reaction:

$CH_3COOH(l) + C_2H_5OH(l) \rightleftharpoons$
$CH_3COOC_2H_5(l) + H_2O(l)$

Explain what happens to the position of equilibrium when:

i   more $CH_3COOC_2H_5(l)$ is added

ii some $C_2H_5OH(l)$ is removed.

b Use this reaction:

$Ce^{4+}(aq) + Fe^{2+}(aq) \rightleftharpoons Ce^{3+}(aq) + Fe^{3+}(aq)$

Explain what happens to the position of equilibrium when:

i   the concentration of $Fe^{2+}(aq)$ ions is increased

ii water is added to the equilibrium mixture.

The effect of pressure on the position of equilibrium

Change in pressure only affects reactions where gases are reactants or products. The molecules or ions in solids and liquids are packed closely together and cannot be compressed very easily. In gases, the molecules are far apart (Figure 8.8).

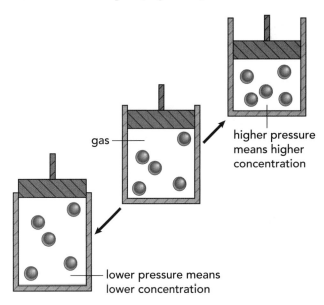

gas

higher pressure means higher concentration

lower pressure means lower concentration

Figure 8.8: Pressure has a considerable effect on the concentration of gases.

The pressure of a gas is caused by the molecules hitting the walls of the container. Each molecule in a mixture of gases contributes towards the total pressure. So, at constant temperature, the more gas molecules there are in a given volume, the higher the pressure.

Figure 8.9 shows what happens when we increase the pressure on the reaction represented by:

X(g)	+	Y(g)	⇌	Z(g)
1 mol		1 mol		1 mol

In this reaction there are two moles of gas on the left and one on the right. When the pressure is increased at constant temperature:

- the molecules are closer together, because the pressure has increased

- the position of equilibrium shifts to minimise this increase

- it shifts in the direction of fewer gas molecules (in the direction that opposes the increase in pressure)

- more product, Z, is formed from X and Y until equilibrium is re-established.

a Initial pressure

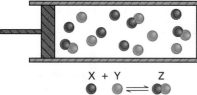

13 molecules contributing to the pressure.

b Pressure is increased

More molecules of Z are formed, reducing the total number of molecules from 13 to 11.

Figure 8.9: An increase in pressure in this case causes the equilibrium to shift to the right, to produce more molecules of Z than before, but fewer molecules in the reaction vessel overall.

For example, consider the reaction:

$$2SO_2(g) + O_2(g) \rightleftharpoons 2SO_3(g)$$

There are three moles of gas molecules on the left of the equation and two on the right.

What happens when we increase the pressure?

The molecules are closer together, because the pressure is higher.

According to Le Chatelier's principle, the reaction must shift in the direction that reduces the number of molecules of gas.

The position of equilibrium shifts to the right.

So more SO_2 reacts with O_2 to form SO_3.

What happens when we decrease the pressure?

The molecules are further apart, because the pressure is lower.

According to Le Chatelier's principle, the reaction must shift in the direction that increases the number of molecules of gas.

The position of equilibrium shifts to the left.

So more SO_2 and O_2 molecules are formed by the decomposition of SO_3 molecules.

Table 8.2 summarises the effect of changes in pressure on two other gas reactions.

Note that:

- if there are equal numbers of molecules of gas on each side of the equation, the position of equilibrium is not affected by a change in pressure.

- in a reaction involving gases and solids (or liquids), it is only the molecules of gases that count when determining how pressure affects the position of equilibrium.

Change in pressure	Fewer molecules of gas on right $N_2(g) + 3H_2(g) \rightleftharpoons 2NH_3(g)$	More molecules of gas on right $N_2O_4(g) \rightleftharpoons 2NO_2(g)$
pressure increase	equilibrium position shifts towards product: more NH_3 forms	equilibrium position shifts towards reactant: more N_2O_4 forms
pressure decrease	equilibrium position shifts towards reactants: more N_2 and H_2 form	equilibrium position shifts towards product: more NO_2 forms

Table 8.2: The effect of changes in pressure on gas reactions.

Question

4 **a** Predict the effect of increasing the pressure on the following reactions:

    i $N_2O_4(g) \rightleftharpoons 2NO_2(g)$

    ii $CaCO_3(s) \rightleftharpoons CaO(s) + CO_2(g)$

b Predict the effect of decreasing the pressure on the reaction:

$$2NO_2(g) \rightleftharpoons 2NO(g) + O_2(g)$$

The effect of temperature on the position of equilibrium

The decomposition of hydrogen iodide is an endothermic reaction.

$$2HI(g) \rightleftharpoons H_2(g) + I_2(g) \qquad \Delta H_r = +9.6 \text{ kJ mol}^{-1}$$

The effect of temperature on the equilibrium concentration of hydrogen iodide and hydrogen at equilibrium for the forward reaction is shown in Table 8.3.

Temperature / °C	Equilibrium concentration of HI / mol dm^{-3}	Equilibrium concentration of H$_2$ (or I$_2$) / mol dm^{-3}
25	0.934	0.033
230	0.864	0.068
430	0.786	0.107
490	0.773	0.114

Table 8.3: Effect of temperature on the decomposition of hydrogen iodide.

You can see from Table 8.3 that, as the temperature increases, the concentration of product increases. The position of equilibrium shifts to the right. We can explain this using Le Chatelier's principle:

- an increase in temperature increases the energy of the surroundings

- according to Le Chatelier's principle, the reaction will go in the direction that opposes the increase in energy

- the reaction will go in the direction in which energy is absorbed, which is the endothermic reaction

- the position of equilibrium shifts to the right, producing more H$_2$ and I$_2$.

If an increase of temperature favours an endothermic reaction, a decrease of temperature favours an exothermic reaction. This means that:

- a decrease in temperature decreases the energy of the surroundings

- according to Le Chatelier's principle, the reaction will go in the direction that opposes the decrease in energy

- so the reaction will go in the direction in which energy is released, which is the exothermic reaction.

Table 8.4 summarises the effect of temperature changes on the position of equilibrium for endothermic and exothermic reactions.

Temperature change	Endothermic reaction 2HI(g) $\rightleftharpoons$ H$_2$(g) + I$_2$(g)	Exothermic reaction 2SO$_2$(g) + O$_2$(g) $\rightleftharpoons$ 2SO$_3$(g)
temperature increase	position of equilibrium shifts towards products: more H$_2$ and I$_2$ formed	position of equilibrium shifts towards reactants: more SO$_2$ and O$_2$ formed
temperature decrease	position of equilibrium shifts towards reactant: more HI formed	position of equilibrium shifts towards product: more SO$_3$ formed

Table 8.4: Effect of temperature on endothermic and exothermic reactions.

Question

5 **a** Predict the effect of increasing the temperature on the reaction:

$$H_2(g) + CO_2(g) \rightleftharpoons H_2O(g) + CO(g)$$
$$\Delta H_r = +41.2 \text{ kJ mol}^{-1}$$

b In the reaction

$$Ag_2CO_3(s) \rightleftharpoons Ag_2O(s) + CO_2(g)$$

increasing the temperature increases the amount of carbon dioxide formed at constant pressure. Is this reaction exothermic or endothermic? Explain your answer.

Do catalysts have any effect on the position of equilibrium?

A catalyst is a substance that increases the rate of a chemical reaction. Catalysts reduce the time taken to reach equilibrium, but they have no effect on the position of equilibrium once this is reached. This is because they increase the rate of the forward and reverse reactions equally.

> **IMPORTANT**
>
> Remember that:
>
> - The equilibrium constant, K_c or K_p, remains the same value even when we change the concentration or pressure or add a catalyst.
> - Only change in temperature affects the value of the equilibrium constant K_c or K_p.

8.3 Equilibrium expressions and the equilibrium constant, K_c

> **IMPORTANT**
>
> - Remember square brackets, e.g. $[Cl_2]$, are used here to show the *concentration* of the substance inside the brackets. Don't get them muddled with the square brackets used for complex ions (see Chapter 24).
> - When writing equilibrium expressions we assume that $[X][Y]$ means $[X] \times [Y]$.
> - If we are being very accurate, we should include the subscript eqm after the square brackets e.g. $[Cl_2]_{eqm}$ but this is usually omitted.

Equilibrium expressions

When hydrogen reacts with iodine in a closed tube at 500 K, the following equilibrium is set up:

$$H_2(g) + I_2(g) \rightleftharpoons 2HI(g)$$

Table 8.5 shows the relationship between the equilibrium concentrations of H_2, I_2 and HI. The square brackets in the last column refer to the concentration, in mol dm^{-3}, of the substance inside the brackets. The results are obtained as follows:

- several tubes are set up with different starting concentrations of hydrogen and iodine

- the contents of the tubes are allowed to reach equilibrium at 500 K

- the concentrations of hydrogen, iodine and hydrogen iodide at equilibrium are determined.

The last column in Table 8.5 shows the number we get by arranging the concentrations of H_2, I_2 and HI in a particular way. We get this expression by taking the square of the concentration of hydrogen iodide and dividing it by the concentrations of hydrogen and iodine at equilibrium. So for the first line of data in Table 8.5:

$$\frac{[HI]^2}{[H_2][I_2]} = \frac{(8.64 \times 10^{-3})^2}{(0.68 \times 10^{-3})(0.68 \times 10^{-3})} = 161$$

You can see that this expression gives an approximately constant value close to about 160 whatever the starting concentrations of H_2, I_2 and HI.

We call this constant the **equilibrium constant, K_c**. The subscript 'c' refers to the fact that concentrations have been used in the calculations.

There is a simple relationship that links K_c to the equilibrium concentrations of reactants and products and the stoichiometry of the equation. This is called an **equilibrium expression**.

> **IMPORTANT**
>
> - Remember that the concentrations of products go at the top of an equilibrium expression and the concentrations of the reactants go at the bottom.
> - Solids and liquids that appear in the balanced equation are NOT included in the equilibrium expression.

For a general reaction:

$$mA + nB \rightleftharpoons pC + qD$$

(where m, n, p and q are the number of moles in the stoichiometric equation)

$$K_c = \frac{[C]^p[D]^q}{[A]^m[B]^n}$$

> **KEY WORDS**
>
> **equilibrium constant, K_c or K_p:** a constant calculated from the equilibrium expression for a reaction. It can be in terms of concentrations, K_c, or partial pressures, K_p.
>
> **equilibrium expression:** a simple relationship that links K_c to the equilibrium concentrations, or K_p to the equilibrium partial pressures, of reactants and products and the stoichiometric equation.

concentration of product D

$$K_c = \frac{[C]^p [D]^q}{[A]^m [B]^n}$$

← number of moles of product D

← number of moles of reactant B

concentration of reactant B

In equilibrium expressions involving a solid, we ignore the solid. This is because its concentration remains constant, however much solid is present. For example:

$$Ag^+(aq) + Fe^{2+}(aq) \rightleftharpoons Ag(s) + Fe^{3+}(aq)$$

The equilibrium expression for this reaction is:

$$K_c = \frac{[Fe^{3+}(aq)]}{[Ag^+(aq)][Fe^{2+}(aq)]}$$

Concentration of H_2 at equilibrium / mol dm⁻³	Concentration of I_2 at equilibrium / mol dm⁻³	Concentration of HI at equilibrium / mol dm⁻³	$\frac{[HI]^2}{[H_2][I_2]}$
0.68×10^{-3}	0.68×10^{-3}	8.64×10^{-3}	161
0.50×10^{-3}	0.50×10^{-3}	6.30×10^{-3}	159
1.10×10^{-3}	2.00×10^{-3}	18.8×10^{-3}	161
2.50×10^{-3}	0.65×10^{-3}	16.1×10^{-3}	160

Table 8.5: The relationship between the equilibrium concentrations of H_2, I_2 and HI in the reaction $H_2 + I_2 \rightleftharpoons 2HI$

What are the units of K_c?

In the equilibrium expression, each figure within a square bracket represents the concentration in mol dm⁻³. The units of K_c therefore depend on the form of the equilibrium expression.

WORKED EXAMPLES

1 a Write an expression for K_c:

$$N_2(g) + 3H_2(g) \rightleftharpoons 2NH_3(g)$$

Solution

$$K_c = \frac{[NH_3]^2}{[N_2][H_2]^3}$$

b Write an expression for K_c:

$$2SO_2(g) + O_2(g) \rightleftharpoons 2SO_3(g)$$

Solution

$$K_c = \frac{[SO_3]^2}{[SO_2]^2[O_2]}$$

CONTINUED

2 State the units of K_c for the reaction:

$$H_2 + I_2 \rightleftharpoons 2HI$$

Solution

$$K_c = \frac{[HI]^2}{[H_2][I_2]}$$

Units of $K_c = \dfrac{\cancel{(mol\,dm^{-3})} \times \cancel{(mol\,dm^{-3})}}{\cancel{(mol\,dm^{-3})} \times \cancel{(mol\,dm^{-3})}}$

The units of mol dm⁻³ cancel, so K_c has no units.

3 State the units of K_c for the reaction:

$$2SO_2(g) + O_2(g) \rightleftharpoons 2SO_3(g)$$

Solution

Units of K_c

$$= \frac{\cancel{(mol\,dm^{-3})} \times \cancel{(mol\,dm^{-3})}}{\cancel{(mol\,dm^{-3})} \times \cancel{(mol\,dm^{-3})} \times (mol\,dm^{-3})}$$

$$= \frac{1}{(mol\,dm^{-3})} = dm^3\,mol^{-1}$$

Question

6 Write equilibrium expressions for the following reactions and state the units of K_c.

a $CO(g) + 2H_2(g) \rightleftharpoons CH_3OH(g)$

b $4HCl(g) + O_2(g) \rightleftharpoons 2H_2O(g) + 2Cl_2(g)$

Some examples of equilibrium calculations

WORKED EXAMPLES

4 In this calculation we are given the number of moles of each of the reactants and products at equilibrium together with the volume of the reaction mixture.

Ethanol reacts with ethanoic acid to form ethyl ethanoate and water.

$$CH_3COOH(l) + C_2H_5OH(l) \rightleftharpoons CH_3COOC_2H_5(l) + H_2O(l)$$
ethanoic acid   ethanol   ethyl ethanoate   water

500 cm³ of the reaction mixture at equilibrium contained 0.235 mol of ethanoic acid and 0.0350 mol of ethanol together with 0.182 mol of ethyl ethanoate and 0.182 mol of water. Use this data to calculate a value of K_c for this reaction.

Solution

Step 1: Write out the balanced chemical equation with the concentrations beneath each substance.

$$CH_3COOH(l) \quad + \quad C_2H_5OH(l) \quad \rightleftharpoons \quad CH_3COOC_2H_5(l) \quad + \quad H_2O(l)$$

$$\dfrac{0.235 \times 1000}{500} \qquad\qquad \dfrac{0.035 \times 1000}{500} \qquad\qquad \dfrac{0.182 \times 1000}{500} \qquad\qquad \dfrac{0.182 \times 1000}{500}$$

0.470 mol dm⁻³   0.070 mol dm⁻³   0.364 mol dm⁻³   0.364 mol dm⁻³

Step 2: Write the equilibrium constant for this reaction in terms of concentration.

$$K_c = \frac{[CH_3COOC_2H_5][H_2O]}{[CH_3COOH][C_2H_5OH]}$$

Step 3: Substitute the equilibrium concentrations into the expression.

$$K_c = \frac{(0.364) \times (0.364)}{(0.470) \times (0.070)} = 4.03 \text{ (to 3 significant figures)}$$

Step 4: Add the correct units by referring back to the equilibrium expression:

The units of mol dm⁻³ cancel, so K_c has no units.

Therefore $K_c = 4.03$.

Note: If there are equal numbers of moles on the top and bottom of the equilibrium expression, you can use moles rather than concentration in mol dm⁻³ in the calculation. In all other cases, if volumes are given, the concentrations must be calculated before they are substituted into the equilibrium expression.

5 In this example we are only given the initial concentrations of the reactants and the equilibrium concentration of the product.

Propanone reacts with hydrogen cyanide as follows:

$$CH_3COCH_3 \quad + \quad HCN \quad \rightleftharpoons \quad CH_3C(OH)(CN)CH_3$$
propanone   hydrogen cyanide   product

A mixture of 0.0500 mol dm^{-3} propanone and 0.0500 mol dm^{-3} hydrogen cyanide is left to reach equilibrium at room temperature. At equilibrium the concentration of the product is 0.0233 mol dm^{-3}. Calculate K_c for this reaction.

Solution

Step 1: Write out the balanced chemical equation with all the data underneath:

$$CH_3COCH_3 \quad + \quad HCN \quad \rightleftharpoons \quad CH_3C(OH)(CN)CH_3$$

initial conc.:	0.0500 mol dm^{-3}	0500 mol dm^{-3}	0 mol dm^{-3}
Conc. at equilibrium:	to be calculated	to be calculated	0.0233 mol dm^{-3}

Step 2: Calculate the equilibrium concentrations of the reactants.

The chemical equation shows that for every mole of product formed, 1 mole of CH_3COCH_3 and 1 mole of HCN are consumed. So the equilibrium concentrations are as follows:

CH_3COCH_3; $0.0500 - 0.0233 = 0.0267$ mol dm^{-3}

HCN; $0.0500 - 0.0233 = 0.0267$ mol dm^{-3}

Step 3: Write the equilibrium constant for this reaction in terms of concentrations:

$$K_c = \frac{[CH_3C(OH)(CN)CH_3]}{[CH_3COCH_3][HCN]}$$

Step 4: Substitute the equilibrium concentrations into the expression

$$K_c = \frac{(0.0233)}{(0.0267)\times(0.0267)} = 32.7 \text{ (to 3 significant figures)}$$

Step 5: Add the correct units by referring back to the equilibrium expression.

$$\frac{(\text{mol dm}^{-3})}{(\text{mol dm}^{-3})(\text{mol dm}^{-3})} = \frac{1}{(\text{mol dm}^{-3})} = \text{dm}^3\,\text{mol}^{-1}$$

So $K_c = 32.7$ dm^3 mol^{-1}

6 In this example we are given the initial and equilibrium concentrations of the reactants but not the products. Ethyl ethanoate is hydrolysed by water:

$$CH_3COOC_2H_5 + H_2O \rightleftharpoons CH_3COOH + C_2H_5OH$$

ethyl ethanoate   water   ethanoic acid   ethanol

0.1000 mol of ethyl ethanoate are added to 0.1000 mol of water. A little acid catalyst is added and the mixture made up to 1 dm^3 with an inert solvent. At equilibrium 0.0654 mol of water are present. Calculate K_c for this reaction.

Solution

Step 1: Write out the balanced chemical equation with all the data underneath.

$$CH_3COOC_2H_5 \quad + \quad H_2O \quad \rightleftharpoons \quad CH_3COOH \quad + \quad C_2H_5OH$$

initial conc.:	0.1000 mol dm^{-3}	0.1000 mol dm^{-3}	0	0
conc. at equilibrium:		0.0654 mol dm^{-3}		

Step 2: Calculate the unknown concentrations:

- the chemical equation shows that 1 mole of $CH_3COOC_2H_5$ reacts with 1 mole water, so the equilibrium concentration of $CH_3COOC_2H_5$ is also 0.0654 mol dm^{-3} (as we started with the same initial concentrations of ethyl ethanoate and water)

- the amount of water used in forming the products is $(0.1000 - 0.0654) = 0.0346$ mol dm^{-3}.

CONTINUED

The chemical equation shows that 1 mole of water formed 1 mole of ethanoic acid and 1 mole of ethanol. So the concentrations of both the products at equilibrium is 0.0346 mol dm⁻³

$$CH_3COOC_2H_5 \ + \ H_2O \ \rightleftharpoons \ CH_3COOH \ + \ C_2H_5OH$$

conc. at equilibrium / mol dm⁻³: 0.0654   0.0654   0.0346   0.0346

Step 3: Write the equilibrium constant for this reaction in terms of concentrations:

$$K_c = \frac{[CH_3COOH][C_2H_5OH]}{[CH_3COOC_2H_5][H_2O]}$$

Step 4: Substitute the equilibrium concentrations into the expression:

$$K_c = \frac{(0.0346) \times (0.0346)}{(0.0645) \times (0.0645)} = 0.288$$

(to 3 significant figures)

Step 5: Add the correct units by referring back to the equilibrium expression.

$$\frac{(\text{mol dm}^{-3}) \times (\text{mol dm}^{-3})}{(\text{mol dm}^{-3}) \times (\text{mol dm}^{-3})}$$

The units of mol dm⁻³ cancel, so K_c has no units. Therefore $K_c = 0.288$.

Questions

7 Calculate the value of K_c for the following reaction using the information below:

$$H_2(g) + CO_2(g) \rightleftharpoons H_2O(g) + CO(g)$$

initial concentration of $H_2(g)$ = 10.00 mol dm⁻³.

initial concentration of $CO_2(g)$ = 10.00 mol dm⁻³.

equilibrium concentration of $CO(g)$ = 9.47 mol dm⁻³.

8 Nitrogen and hydrogen react together to form ammonia.

$$N_2(g) + 3H_2(g) \rightleftharpoons 2NH_3(g)$$

0.1 mol of nitrogen and 0.1 mol of hydrogen were mixed in a closed container of volume 1 dm³.

At equilibrium n mol ammonia is formed. What is the concentration of hydrogen at equilibrium?

A $0.1 - n$ C $0.1 - 1.5n$

B $0.1 - 0.667n$ D $0.1 - 0.5n$

IMPORTANT

The key stages in equilibrium calculations are:

1 Write the equation.
2 Write down the information about the concentrations given below each reactant / product.
3 Deduce the concentrations at equilibrium.
4 Write the equilibrium expression.
5 Substitute the values to find either K_c or the concentration of a particular reactant / product.

REFLECTION

Work with another learner to draw a spider diagram (mind map) of what you have learned so far about equilibrium. For example, one arm of your diagram could be equilibrium (in the centre of the diagram) → effect of different factors → X, Y, Z.

Another arm could be equilibrium (in the centre of the diagram) → equilibrium expressions → how you write them / what not to include.

How would you improve your spider diagram?

K_c and concentration changes

If all other conditions remain constant, the value of K_c does not change when the concentration of reactants or products is altered.

Take the example of the decomposition of hydrogen iodide.

$$2HI \rightleftharpoons H_2 + I_2$$

The equilibrium constant at 500 K for this reaction is 6.25×10^{-3}.

$$K_c = \frac{[H_2][I_2]}{[HI]^2} = 6.25 \times 10^{-3}$$

When more hydrogen iodide is added to the equilibrium mixture, the equilibrium is disturbed.

The ratio of concentrations of products to reactants in the equilibrium expression decreases.

To restore equilibrium, both $[H_2]$ and $[I_2]$ increase and $[HI]$ decreases.

Equilibrium is restored when the values of the concentrations in the equilibrium expression are such that the value of K_c is once again 6.25×10^{-3}.

K_c and pressure changes

Where there are different numbers of gas molecules on each side of a chemical equation, a change in pressure alters the position of equilibrium. It is shifted in the direction that results in fewer gas molecules being formed. However, if all other conditions remain constant, the value of K_c does not change when the pressure is altered.

K_c and temperature changes

We have seen in Section 8.2 that for an endothermic reaction, an increase in temperature shifts the reaction in the direction of more products.

So for the endothermic reaction:

$$2HI \rightleftharpoons H_2 + I_2$$

- the concentrations of H_2 and I_2 increase as the temperature increases
- the concentration of HI falls as the temperature increases.

Look at how these changes affect the equilibrium expression:

$$K_c = \frac{[H_2][I_2]}{[HI]^2}$$

We see that the equilibrium constant must increase with increasing temperature. This is because $[H_2]$ and $[I_2]$ are increasing and $[HI]$ is decreasing. Table 8.6 shows how the value of K_c for this reaction changes with temperature.

Temperature / K	K_c (no units)
300	1.26×10^{-3}
500	6.25×10^{-3}
1000	18.5×10^{-3}

Table 8.6: Variation of K_c for the reaction $2HI \rightleftharpoons H_2 + I_2$ with temperature.

For an exothermic reaction, an increase in temperature shifts the reaction in favour of more reactants.

Now look at the exothermic reaction:

$$2SO_2 + O_2 \rightleftharpoons 2SO_3$$

- The concentrations of SO_2 and O_2 increase as the temperature increases.
- The concentration of SO_3 falls as the temperature increases.

How do these changes affect the equilibrium expression?

$$K_c = \frac{[SO_3]^2}{[SO_2]^2[O_2]}$$

We see that the equilibrium constant must decrease with increasing temperature. This is because $[SO_2]$ and $[O_2]$ are increasing and $[SO_3]$ is decreasing.

Question

9 a   Deduce the effect of increase in temperature on the value of K_c for the reaction:

$$2NO_2(g) + O_2(g) \rightleftharpoons 2NO(g) \quad \Delta H_r = -115 \text{ kJ mol}^{-1}$$

   b   Explain why increasing the concentration of oxygen in this reaction does not affect the value of K_c.

8.4 Equilibria in gas reactions: the equilibrium constant, K_p

Partial pressure

For reactions involving mixtures of gases, it is easier to measure the pressure than to measure concentrations. The total pressure in a mixture of gases is due to each molecule bombarding the walls of the container. At constant temperature, each gas in the mixture contributes to the total pressure in proportion to the number of moles present (Figure 8.10). The pressure exerted by any one gas in the mixture is called its **partial pressure**.

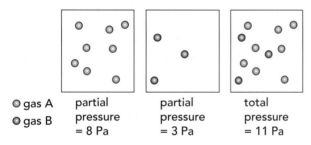

◎ gas A	partial	partial	total
◉ gas B	pressure	pressure	pressure
	= 8 Pa	= 3 Pa	= 11 Pa

the volumes of the containers are the same

Figure 8.10: Each gas in this mixture contributes to the pressure in proportion to the number of moles present.

The total pressure of a gas equals the sum of the partial pressures of the individual gases.

$$p_{total} = p_A + p_B + p_C \dots$$

where p_A, p_B, p_C are the partial pressures of the individual gases in the mixture.

Equilibrium expressions involving partial pressures

We write equilibrium expressions in terms of partial pressures in a similar way to equilibrium expressions in terms of concentrations. But there are some differences:

- we use p for partial pressure

- the reactants and products are written as subscripts after the p

- the number of moles of particular reactants or products is written as a power after the p

- square brackets are *not* used

- we give the equilibrium constant the symbol K_p (the equilibrium constant in terms of partial pressures).

For example, the equilibrium expression for the reaction:

$$N_2(g) + 3H_2(g) \rightleftharpoons 2NH_3(g)$$

is written as $K_p = \dfrac{p_{NH_3}^2}{p_{N_2} \times p_{H_2}^3}$

WORKED EXAMPLES

7 Deduce the units of K_p for the following reaction:
   $$N_2O_4(g) \rightleftharpoons 2NO_2(g)$$

   Solution

   The equilibrium expression is:

   $$K_p = \dfrac{p_{NO_2}^2}{p_{N_2O_4}}$$

   The units are $\dfrac{\cancel{Pa} \times Pa}{\cancel{Pa}} = Pa$

8 Deduce the units of K_p for the following reaction:
   $$2SO_2(g) + O_2(g) \rightleftharpoons 2SO_3(g)$$

   Solution

   The equilibrium expression is:

   $$K_p = \dfrac{p_{SO_3}^2}{p_{SO_2}^2 \times p_{O_2}}$$

   The units are $\dfrac{\cancel{Pa} \times \cancel{Pa}}{\cancel{Pa} \times \cancel{Pa} \times Pa} = \dfrac{1}{Pa} = Pa^{-1}$

What are the units of K_p?

The units of pressure are pascals, Pa. The units of K_p depend on the form of the equilibrium expression.

Although the standard unit of pressure is the pascal, many chemists in industry use the atmosphere as the unit of pressure. 1 atmosphere $= 1.01 \times 10^5$ Pa. Using 'atmospheres' as units simplifies calculations because the numbers used are not as large.

Questions

10 The reaction below was carried out at a pressure of 10.00×10^4 Pa and at constant temperature.

$$N_2(g) + O_2(g) \rightleftharpoons 2NO(g)$$

The partial pressures of nitrogen and oxygen are both 4.85×10^4 Pa.

Calculate the partial pressure of the nitrogen(II) oxide, NO(g), at equilibrium.

11 Deduce the units of K_p for the following reactions:

a $PCl_5(g) \rightleftharpoons PCl_3(g) + Cl_2(g)$

b $N_2(g) + 3H_2(g) \rightleftharpoons 2NH_3(g)$

c $3Fe(s) + 4H_2O(g) \rightleftharpoons Fe_3O_4(s) + 4H_2(g)$

Calculations using partial pressures

WORKED EXAMPLES

9 In this example we are given the partial pressure of each gas in the mixture.

In the reaction:

$$2SO_2(g) + O_2(g) \rightleftharpoons 2SO_3(g)$$

the equilibrium partial pressures at constant temperature are $SO_2 = 1.0 \times 10^6$ Pa, $O_2 = 7.0 \times 10^6$ Pa, $SO_3 = 8.0 \times 10^6$ Pa. Calculate the value of K_p for this reaction.

Solution

Step 1: Write the equilibrium expression for the reaction in terms of partial pressures.

$$K_p = \frac{p_{SO_3}^2}{p_{SO_2}^2 \times p_{O_2}}$$

Step 2: Substitute the equilibrium concentrations into the expression.

$$K_p = \frac{\left(8.0 \times 10^6\right)^2}{\left(1.0 \times 10^6\right)^2 \times 7.0 \times 10^6} = 9.1 \times 10^{-6}\ \text{Pa}^{-1}$$

Step 3: Add the correct units.

The units are $\dfrac{\cancel{Pa} \times \cancel{Pa}}{\cancel{Pa} \times \cancel{Pa} \times Pa} = \dfrac{1}{Pa} = Pa^{-1}$

$K_p = 9.1 \times 10^{-6}\ \text{Pa}^{-1}$

10 In this calculation we are given the partial pressure of two of the three gases in the mixture as well as the total pressure.

Nitrogen reacts with hydrogen to form ammonia.

$$N_2(g) + 3H_2(g) \rightleftharpoons 2NH_3(g)$$

The pressure exerted by this mixture of hydrogen, nitrogen and ammonia at constant temperature is 2.000×10^7 Pa. Under these conditions, the partial pressure of nitrogen is 1.490×10^7 Pa and the partial pressure of hydrogen is 0.400×10^7 Pa. Calculate the value of K_p for this reaction.

Solution

Step 1: Calculate the partial pressure of ammonia. We know that the total pressure is the sum of the partial pressures.

$$p_{total} = p_{N_2} + p_{H_2} + p_{NH_3}$$

$$2.00 \times 10^7 = (1.49 \times 10^7) + (0.400 \times 10^7) + p_{NH_3}$$

Partial pressure of $NH_3 = 0.110 \times 10^7$ Pa

Step 2: Write the equilibrium expression for the reaction in terms of partial pressures.

$$K_p = \frac{p_{NH_3}^2}{p_{N_2} \times p_{H_2}^3}$$

Step 3: Substitute the equilibrium concentrations into the expression.

$$K_p = \frac{\left(0.110 \times 10^7\right)^2}{\left(1.490 \times 10^7\right) \times \left(0.400 \times 10^7\right)^3}$$

$$K_p = 1.27 \times 10^{-15}$$

Step 4: Add the correct units.

The units $= \dfrac{\cancel{Pa} \times \cancel{Pa}}{\cancel{Pa} \times \cancel{Pa} \times Pa \times Pa} = \dfrac{1}{Pa^2} = Pa^{-2}$

$K_p = 1.27 \times 10^{-15}\ \text{Pa}^{-2}$

Questions

12 The information below gives the data for the reaction of hydrogen with iodine at 500 °C.

$$H_2(g) + I_2(g) \rightleftharpoons 2HI(g)$$

The table shows the initial partial pressures and the partial pressures at equilibrium of hydrogen, iodine and hydrogen iodide. The total pressure was constant throughout the experiment.

	Partial pressures / Pa		
	hydrogen	iodine	hydrogen iodide
Initially	7.27×10^6	4.22×10^6	0
At equilibrium	3.41×10^6		7.72×10^6

Table 8.7: Table for Question 12.

a Deduce the partial pressure of the iodine at equilibrium.

b Calculate the value of K_p for this reaction, including the units.

13 When metallic mercury is shaken with a solution of mercury(II) nitrate a solution of mercury(I) nitrate is formed.

$$Hg(l) + Hg^{2+}(aq) \rightleftharpoons Hg_2^{2+}(aq)$$

What is the correct equilibrium expression for this reaction?

A $\dfrac{[Hg_2^{2+}]}{[Hg^{2+}]}$

B $\dfrac{[Hg_2^{2+}]}{[Hg^{2+}][Hg]}$

C $\dfrac{[Hg_2^{2+}]^2}{[Hg^{2+}]}$

D $\dfrac{p_{Hg_2^{2+}}}{p_{Hg^{2+}}}$

Partial pressure and mole fractions

The number of moles of gas is proportional to the volume of the gas at constant temperature. So it follows that the partial pressure of a gas is proportional to its concentration. The **mole fraction** of a gas is given by the relationship:

$$\text{mole fraction} = \frac{\text{number of moles of a particular gas}}{\text{total number of moles of all the gases in a mixture}}$$

So the mole fraction of ammonia in a mixture containing 0.5 mol ammonia, 0.9 mol hydrogen and 0.6 mol of nitrogen is:

$$\frac{0.5}{0.5 + 0.9 + 0.6} = 0.25 \text{ (no units)}$$

The partial pressure is related to the mole fraction by the relationship:

partial pressure = mole fraction × total pressure (of all the gases in the mixture)

We can therefore use the number of moles of each reactant and product in a mixture together with the total pressure to calculate a value for K_p.

WORKED EXAMPLE

11 The equilibrium between hydrogen, iodine and hydrogen iodide at 600 K is shown.

$$H_2(g) + I_2(g) \rightleftharpoons 2HI(g)$$

At equilibrium the number of moles present are:

$H_2 = 1.71 \times 10^{-3}$, $I_2 = 2.91 \times 10^{-3}$, $HI = 1.65 \times 10^{-2}$

The total pressure is 100 kPa.
Calculate the value of K_p for this reaction.

Solution

Step 1: Calculate the total number of moles
$(1.71 \times 10^{-3}) + (2.91 \times 10^{-3}) + (1.65 \times 10^{-2})$
$= 2.112 \times 10^{-2}$

Step 2: Calculate the mole fraction of each gas

$$H_2 = \frac{1.71 \times 10^{-3}}{2.112 \times 10^{-2}} = 0.0810$$

$$I_2 = \frac{2.91 \times 10^{-3}}{2.112 \times 10^{-2}} = 0.1378$$

$$HI = \frac{1.65 \times 10^{-2}}{2.112 \times 10^{-2}} = 0.7813$$

Step 3: Calculate the partial pressure of each gas
$H_2 = 0.0810 \times 100 = 8.10$ kPa
$I_2 = 0.1378 \times 100 = 13.78$ kPa
$HI = 0.7813 \times 100 = 78.13$ kPa

Step 4: Write the equilibrium expression and substitute the values

$$K_p = \frac{p_{HI}^2}{p_{H_2} \times p_{I_2}}$$

$$K_p = \frac{78.13 \times 78.13}{8.10 \times 13.78} = 54.7 \text{ (no units)}$$

8.5 Equilibria and the chemical industry

An understanding of equilibrium is important in the chemical industry. Equilibrium reactions are involved in some of the stages in the large-scale production of ammonia, sulfuric acid and many other chemicals.

Equilibrium and ammonia production

The synthesis of ammonia is carried out by the Haber process. The equilibrium reaction involved is:

$$N_2(g) + 3H_2(g) \rightleftharpoons 2NH_3(g) \qquad \Delta H_r = -92 \text{ kJ mol}^{-1}$$

We can use Le Chatelier's principle to show how to get the best yield of ammonia. At high temperatures, when the reaction is faster, the position of equilibrium is to the left because the reaction is exothermic (ΔH is negative).

What happens if we increase the pressure?

When we increase the pressure, the reaction goes in the direction that results in fewer molecules of gas being formed.

The equilibrium shifts in the direction that reduces the pressure.

In this case there are four molecules of gas on the left-hand side and two on the right-hand side. So the equilibrium shifts towards the right.

The yield of ammonia increases.

What happens if we decrease the temperature?

A decrease in temperature decreases the energy of the surroundings.

The reaction will go in the direction in which energy is released.

Energy is released in the exothermic reaction, in which the position of equilibrium favours ammonia production.

This shifts the position of equilibrium to the right.

The value of K_p increases.

What happens if we remove ammonia by condensing it to a liquid?

We can do this because ammonia has a much higher boiling point than hydrogen and nitrogen.

The position of equilibrium shifts to the right to replace the ammonia that has been removed.

More ammonia is formed from hydrogen and nitrogen to keep the value of K_p constant.

Equilibrium and the production of sulfuric acid

The synthesis of sulfuric acid is carried out by the Contact process. The main equilibrium reaction involved is:

$$2SO_2(g) + O_2(g) \rightleftharpoons 2SO_3(g) \qquad \Delta H_r = -197 \text{ kJ mol}^{-1}$$

We can use Le Chatelier's principle to show how to get the best yield of sulfur trioxide.

What happens when we increase the pressure?

When we increase the pressure, the reaction goes in the direction that results in fewer molecules of gas being formed, to reduce the pressure.

There are three molecules of gas on the left-hand side and two on the right-hand side, so the equilibrium shifts towards the right.

However, in practice, the reaction is carried out at just above atmospheric pressure. This is because the value of K_p is very high.

The position of equilibrium is far over to the right even at atmospheric pressure. Very high pressure is unnecessary, and is not used as it is expensive.

What happens if we decrease the temperature?

Decreasing the temperature shifts the position of equilibrium to the right.

A decrease in temperature decreases the energy of the surroundings so the reaction will go in the direction in which energy is released.

This is the exothermic reaction, in which the position of equilibrium favours SO_3 production. The value of K_p increases.

SO_3 is removed by absorbing it in 98% sulfuric acid. The SO_3 reacts with the solution and eventually more H_2SO_4 is formed. Although the SO_3 is absorbed in a continuous process, this does not affect the equilibrium significantly because the position of equilibrium is already far over to the right.

Question

14 The Haber process for the synthesis of ammonia may operate at a temperature of 450 °C and pressure of 1.50×10^7 Pa using an iron catalyst.

$$N_2(g) + 3H_2(g) \rightleftharpoons 2NH_3(g) \qquad \Delta H_r = -92 \text{ kJ mol}^{-1}$$

a   Suggest why a temperature of more than 450 °C is not used even though the rate of reaction would be faster.

b   Suggest why the reaction is carried out at a high pressure rather than at normal atmospheric pressure. Explain your answer.

c   Explain why the removal of ammonia as soon as it is formed is an important part of this industrial process.

d   When the ammonia has been removed, why doesn't it decompose back to nitrogen and hydrogen?

8.6 Acid–base equilibria

pH values and neutralisation

pH values

We can use universal indicator or a pH meter to deduce whether a substance is acidic, alkaline or neutral.

- acids have pH values below pH 7
- alkalis have pH values above pH 7
- a neutral solution has a pH value of exactly 7.

Neutralisation

> **KEY WORD**
>
> **neutralisation:** the reaction of an acid with an alkali to form a salt and water.

A salt is a compound formed when an acid reacts with a base (or alkali). This type of reaction is called a **neutralisation** reaction.

Examples are:

$$\underset{\text{sulfuric acid}}{H_2SO_4(aq)} + \underset{\text{sodium hydroxide}}{2NaOH(aq)} \rightarrow \underset{\text{sodium sulfate}}{Na_2SO_4(aq)} + \underset{\text{water}}{2H_2O(l)}$$

$$2HCl(aq) + Ba(OH)_2(aq) \rightarrow BaCl_2(aq) + 2H_2O(l)$$
hydrochloric acid   barium hydroxide   barium chloride   water

From these equations we can see that:

- acid + alkali → salt + water

- sodium sulfate and barium chloride are salts

- the simplest ionic equation for a neutralisation reaction is:

$$H^+(aq) + OH^-(aq) \rightarrow H_2O(l)$$

Some simple definitions of acids and bases

A very simple definition of an **acid** is that it is a substance that neutralises a **base**. A **salt** and water are formed.

KEY WORDS

acid: a proton (H^+ ion) donor.

base: a proton (H^+ ion) acceptor.

salt: a substance formed when an acid reacts with a salt, an alkali, a metal oxide or a carbonate.

$$2HCl(aq) + CaO(s) \rightleftharpoons CaCl_2(aq) + H_2O(l)$$
acid   base

The equation above also shows us a very simple definition of a base. A base is a substance that neutralises an acid.

IMPORTANT

A base is a compound that contains oxide or hydroxide ions and reacts with an acid to form a salt and water. Alkalis are bases which are soluble in water.

If we look at the formulae for some acids in Table 8.8, we see that they all contain hydrogen atoms. When the acid dissolves in water, it ionises and forms hydrogen ions. Note that in organic acids such as carboxylic acids (see Section 14.3), only some of the hydrogen atoms are capable of forming ions (see Figure 8.11).

Figure 8.11: The sour taste of lemons is due to citric acid and that of vinegar is due to ethanoic acid. Baking soda is basic and is used to make bread dough rise.

Acid–base equilibria are important in the human body (Figure 8.12).

Figure 8.12: Many foods have high quantities of sugar in them. The sugar is converted to acid by bacteria in your mouth. This acid can attack the enamel on your teeth. By chewing sugar-free gum, more saliva is produced. Saliva is slightly alkaline. It neutralises the acid.

Name of acid	Formula	Ions formed in water
hydrochloric acid	HCl	$H^+ + Cl^-$
nitric acid	HNO_3	$H^+ + NO_3^-$
sulfuric acid	H_2SO_4	$2H^+ + SO_4^{2-}$
ethanoic acid	CH_3COOH	$CH_3COO^- + H^+$
benzoic acid	C_6H_5COOH	$C_6H_5COO^- + H^+$

Table 8.8: Formulae and ions of some common acids.

IMPORTANT

You must know the names and formulae of the first four acids in Table 8.8.

A better definition of an acid is a substance that releases hydrogen ions when it dissolves in water. For example:

$$HCl(g) + aq \rightarrow H^+(aq) + Cl^-(aq)$$

The formulae for some bases are given in Table 8.9. Many metal oxides or hydroxides are bases. Some bases dissolve in water to form hydroxide ions in solution. A base that is soluble in water is called an alkali. For example:

$$NaOH(s) + aq \rightarrow Na^+(aq) + OH^-(aq)$$

Some alkalis are formed by the reaction of a base with water. When ammonia gas dissolves in water, some of the ammonia molecules react with water molecules. Hydroxide ions are released in this reaction.

$$NH_3(g) + H_2O(l) \rightarrow NH_4^+(aq) + OH^-(aq)$$

Aqueous ammonia is therefore an alkali. We can also see from the equation above that the ammonia has accepted a hydrogen ion to become NH_4^+. So a wider definition of a base is a substance that accepts hydrogen ions.

IMPORTANT

Common alkalis that you must know are: sodium hydroxide (NaOH), potassium hydroxide (KOH) and ammonia (NH_3)

Name of base	Formula
calcium oxide	CaO
copper(II) oxide	CuO
sodium hydroxide	NaOH
calcium hydroxide	$Ca(OH)_2$
ammonia	NH_3

Table 8.9: The formulae of some common bases.

Question

15 a Write an equation to show potassium hydroxide dissolving in water.

b Write an equation for liquid nitric acid dissolving in water.

c Write ionic equations for:

i the reaction in aqueous solution between sodium hydroxide and nitric acid

ii the reaction in aqueous solution between potassium hydroxide and hydrochloric acid.

The Brønsted–Lowry theory of acids and bases

The definitions of acids and bases given earlier are limited to reactions taking place in water. In 1923 the Danish chemist J. Brønsted and the English chemist T. Lowry suggested a more general definition of acids and bases. This definition is based on the idea that in an acid–base reaction, a proton is transferred from an acid to a base (a hydrogen ion, H^+, is a proton).

A **Brønsted–Lowry acid** is a proton donor.

A **Brønsted–Lowry base** is a proton acceptor.

When hydrochloric acid is formed, hydrogen chloride gas dissolves in water and reacts to form hydroxonium ions, H_3O^+, and chloride ions (Figure 8.13). You can see that the water is involved in the reaction.

$$HCl(g) + H_2O(l) \rightarrow H_3O^+(aq) + Cl^-(aq)$$

Hydrochloric acid is an acid because it donates a proton to water. This means that water is acting as a Brønsted–Lowry base. The water is accepting a proton:

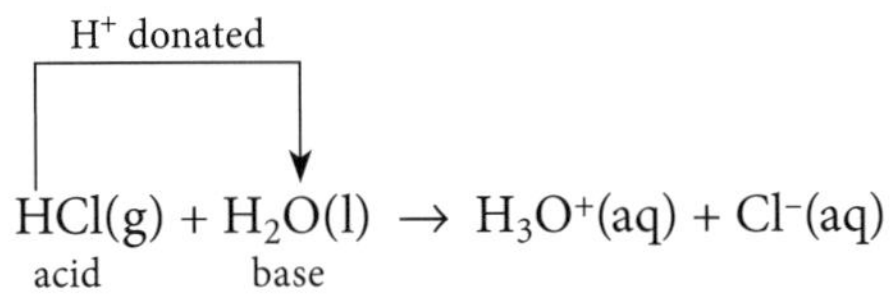

Water can also act as an acid. When ammonia reacts with water, it accepts a proton from the water and becomes an NH_4^+ ion (Figure 8.14).

KEY DEFINITIONS

Brønsted–Lowry acid: a proton (H^+ ion) donor.

Brønsted–Lowry base: a proton (H^+ ion) acceptor.

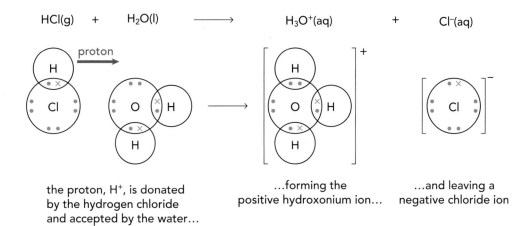

$HCl(g)$ + $H_2O(l)$ $\longrightarrow$ $H_3O^+(aq)$ + $Cl^-(aq)$

the proton, H^+, is donated by the hydrogen chloride and accepted by the water...

...forming the positive hydroxonium ion...

...and leaving a negative chloride ion

Figure 8.13: An acid is a proton donor. Hydrogen chloride is the acid in this reaction. A base is a proton acceptor. Water is the base in this reaction. Remember that a proton is a hydrogen ion, H^+.

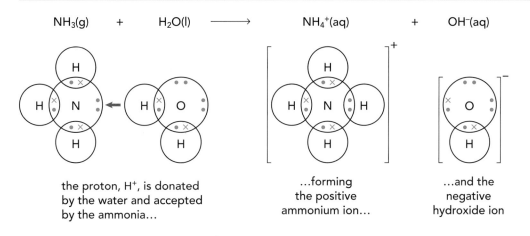

$NH_3(g)$ + $H_2O(l)$ $\longrightarrow$ $NH_4^+(aq)$ + $OH^-(aq)$

the proton, H^+, is donated by the water and accepted by the ammonia...

...forming the positive ammonium ion...

...and the negative hydroxide ion

Figure 8.14: Water is the proton donor (it is the acid); ammonia is the proton acceptor (it is the base).

$$\overset{\text{H}^+ \text{ donated}}{\overbrace{NH_3(g) + H_2O(l)}} \rightleftharpoons NH_4^+(aq) + OH^-(aq)$$
base   acid

Substances like water, which can act as either acids or bases, are described as *amphoteric*.

Brønsted–Lowry acids and bases do not have to involve aqueous solutions. For example, when chloric(VII) acid ($HClO_4$) reacts with ethanoic acid (CH_3COOH) in an inert solvent, the following equilibrium is set up:

$$\overset{\text{H}^+ \text{ donated}}{\overbrace{HClO_4 + CH_3COOH}} \rightleftharpoons ClO_4^- + CH_3COOH_2^+$$
acid   base

In this reaction, $HClO_4$ is the acid because it is donating a proton to CH_3COOH. CH_3COOH is the base because it is a proton acceptor.

When an acid or base reacts with water, an equilibrium mixture is formed. For acids such as hydrochloric acid, the position of equilibrium is almost entirely in favour of the products. But for ammonia, the position of equilibrium favours the reactants. The equations can be written to show this. For example:

$$HCl(g) + aq \rightarrow H^+(aq) + Cl^-(aq)$$

A forward arrow is used as this reaction goes to completion.

$$NH_3(g) + H_2O(l) \rightleftharpoons NH_4^+(aq) + OH^-(aq)$$

An equilibrium arrow is used as this reaction does not go to completion.

Questions

16 Identify which reactants are acids and which are bases in the following reactions:

a $NH_4^+ + H_2O \rightleftharpoons NH_3 + H_3O^+$

b $HCOOH + HClO_2 \rightleftharpoons HCOOH_2^+ + ClO_2^-$

17 Identify the acid and the base on the right-hand side of these equilibria.

a $HClO_2 + HCOOH \rightleftharpoons ClO_2^- + HCOOH_2^+$

b $H_2S + H_2O \rightleftharpoons HS^- + H_3O^+$

Strong and weak acids and bases

Strong acids

> ### IMPORTANT
>
> When referring to acids and bases remember that **weak** and **strong** have to do with degree of dissociation and *not* concentration. Concentration is to do with the number of moles per dm³. The words to use here are 'concentrated' and 'dilute'.

When hydrogen chloride dissolves in water to form a solution of concentration 0.1 mol dm⁻³, it ionises almost completely. We say that the acid is almost completely dissociated.

$$HCl(g) + H_2O(l) \rightarrow H_3O^+(aq) + Cl^-(aq)$$

The position of equilibrium is so far over to the right that we can show this as an irreversible reaction. The pH of this 0.1 mol dm⁻³ solution is pH 1. The pH of a solution depends on the concentration of hydroxonium ions, H_3O^+. The higher the concentration of hydroxonium ions, the lower the pH.

> ### KEY WORDS
>
> **degree of dissociation:** the extent to which a molecule of an acid ionises in a solvent to produce H⁺ ions or the extent to which a base produces OH⁻ ions in a solvent.
>
> **strong acids and bases:** acid and bases which dissociate completely in solution.
>
> **weak acids and bases:** acid and bases which dissociate partially (incompletely) in solution.

The low pH shows that there is a high concentration of hydroxonium ions in solution.

Acids that dissociate almost completely in aqueous solution are called *strong acids*.

The mineral acids, hydrochloric acid, sulfuric acid and nitric acid, are all strong acids.

> ### IMPORTANT
>
> Hydrogen ions in aqueous solution are correctly written as H_3O^+ (hydroxonium or oxonium ion). It is often acceptable to simplify its structure as H⁺. For example:
> Ionisation of a strong acid: $HCl \rightarrow H^+ + Cl^-$
> Ionisation of a weak acid:
> $\quad CH_3COOH \rightleftharpoons CH_3COO^- + H^+$

Weak acids

When ethanoic acid dissolves in water to form a solution of concentration 0.1 mol dm⁻³, it is only slightly ionised. There are many more molecules of ethanoic acid in solution than ethanoate ions and hydroxonium ions. We say that the acid is partially (or incompletely) dissociated.

$$\underset{\text{ethanoic acid}}{CH_3COOH(l)} + H_2O(l) \rightleftharpoons \underset{\text{ethanoate ion}}{CH_3COO^-(aq)} + \underset{\text{hydroxonium ion}}{H_3O^+(aq)}$$

The position of equilibrium is well over to the left. The pH of this 0.1 mol dm⁻³ solution is pH 2.9. The pH is much higher compared with a solution of hydrochloric acid of the same concentration. This is because the concentration of hydroxonium ions in solution is far lower.

Acids that are only partially dissociated in solution are called *weak acids*.

Weak acids include most organic acids, hydrocyanic acid (HCN), hydrogen sulfide and 'carbonic acid'.

Although we sometimes talk about the weak acid carbonic acid, you will never see a bottle of it. The acid is really an equilibrium mixture of carbon dioxide dissolved in water. The following equilibrium is set up:

$$CO_2(g) + H_2O(l) \rightleftharpoons HCO_3^-(aq) + H^+(aq)$$

The amount of CO_2 that forms undissociated carbonic acid, H_2CO_3, is very small as H_2CO_3 ionises readily.

> **IMPORTANT**
>
> Sulfuric acid has two hydrogen ions that can ionise. The first hydrogen to ionise dissociates almost completely:
> $H_2SO_4 \rightarrow H^+ + HSO_4^-$.
> HSO_4^-, however, behaves as a weak acid:
> $HSO_4^- \rightleftharpoons H^+ + HSO_4^-$

Strong bases

When sodium hydroxide dissolves in water to form a solution of concentration 0.1 mol dm^{-3}, it ionises completely.

$$NaOH(s) + aq \rightarrow Na^+(aq) + OH^-(aq)$$

The position of equilibrium is far over to the right.

The solution formed is highly alkaline due to the high concentration of hydroxide ions present. The pH of this 0.1 mol dm^{-3} solution is pH 13.

Bases that dissociate almost completely in solution are called *strong bases*.

The Group 1 metal hydroxides are strong bases.

Weak bases

When ammonia dissolves and reacts in water to form a solution of concentration 0.1 mol dm^{-3}, it is only slightly ionised. There are many more molecules of ammonia in solution than ammonium ions and hydroxide ions.

$$NH_3(g) + H_2O(l) \rightleftharpoons NH_4^+(aq) + OH^-(aq)$$

The position of equilibrium is well over to the left. The pH of this 0.1 mol dm^{-3} solution is pH 11.1. The pH is much lower compared with a solution of sodium hydroxide of the same concentration. This is because the concentration of hydroxide ions in solution is far lower.

Bases which dissociate to only a small extent in solution are called *weak bases*.

Ammonia, amines (see Section 16.2) and some hydroxides of transition metals are weak bases.

Questions

18 Nitric acid is a strong acid but chloric(I) acid, HClO, is a weak acid.

    a Explain the difference between a strong acid and a weak acid.

    b Write equations showing the ionisation of each of these acids in water.

    c Suggest relative pH values for 0.1 mol dm^{-3} aqueous solutions of:

        i chloric(I) acid

        ii nitric acid

    d Hydrazine, N_2H_4, is a weak base.

        i Write a chemical equation to show the equilibrium reaction of hydrazine with water.

        ii State the relative concentrations (high or low) of the N_2H_4 molecules and the products.

19 **a** The pH of a solution depends on the hydrogen ion (hydroxonium ion) concentration. Which concentration of ethanoic acid in Table 8.10 has the highest concentration of hydrogen ions in solution?

    b Which acid or alkali in Table 8.10 has the highest concentration of hydroxide ions?

    c Explain why a solution of 0.1 mol dm^{-3} ethanoic acid has a lower electrical conductivity than a solution of 0.1 mol dm^{-3} hydrochloric acid.

    d Both hydrochloric acid and ethanoic acid react with magnesium. The rate of reaction of 1.0 mol dm^{-3} hydrochloric acid with magnesium is much faster than the rate of reaction of 1.0 mol dm^{-3} ethanoic acid. Explain why.

Distinguishing a weak acid from a strong acid

We can distinguish between a strong and weak acid by their pH values, electrical conductivity and reactivity. When making these comparisons, we must use dilute solutions of strong and weak acids of the same concentration.

pH values

Dilute solutions of a strong acids have lower pH values than those of weak acids of the same concentration. This is because the concentration of hydrogen ions is greater in strong acids.

Acid or base	pH of 1.0 mol dm^{-3} solution	pH of 0.1 mol dm^{-3} solution	pH of 0.01 mol dm^{-3} solution
hydrochloric acid (strong acid)	0	1	2
ethanoic acid (weak acid)	2.4	2.9	3.4
sodium hydroxide (strong base)	14	13	12
ammonia (weak base)	11.6	11.1	10.6

Table 8.10: pH values of some typical strong and weak acids and bases.

We can determine pH by;

- Dipping a pH electrode into a solution of the acid: a pH meter connected to the pH electrode shows the pH value.

- Dipping universal indicator paper into a solution of the acid and noting the colour change. We then compare the colour with that on a chart which shows the colours at different pH values.

Table 8.10 compares the pH values of some typical strong and weak acids and bases.

Electrical conductivity

Dilute solutions of a strong acids have greater electrical conductivity than those of weak acids of the same concentration. This is because the concentration of hydrogen ions (and other ions) is greater in strong acids.

We can determine electrical conductivity by dipping a conductivity electrode into a solution of the acid: a conductivity meter connected to the electrode shows the conductivity.

Reaction with reactive metals

Dilute solutions of weak and strong acids of the same concentration have different reactivity with reactive metals such as magnesium. When a piece of magnesium ribbon is added to a strong acid, a steady stream of hydrogen bubbles is observed.

$$Mg(s) + 2HCl \rightarrow MgCl_2(aq) + H_2(g)$$

When we add a piece of magnesium ribbon to a weak acid of the same concentration, only a few bubbles are observed. This is because the concentration of hydrogen ions is greater in strong acids.

8.7 Indicators and acid–base titrations

In Chapter 3 we learned that indicators are used to detect the end-point in acid–alkali titrations. You may also have used indicators such as litmus to test whether a substance is acidic or alkaline. In this section, we shall look more closely at how specific indicators are used in titrations involving strong and weak acids and bases.

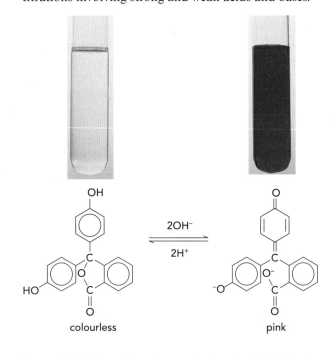

Figure 8.15: The colour change in phenolphthalein is due to small differences in the structure of its molecule when hydrogen ions or hydroxide ions are added.

Introducing indicators

An **acid–base indicator** is a dye or mixture of dyes that changes colour over a specific pH range (Figures 8.15 and 8.16). In simple terms, many indicators can be considered as weak acids in which the acid (HIn) and its conjugate base (In⁻) have different colours.

> **IMPORTANT**
>
> An acid and base on different sides of the equation are said to be conjugate with each other if one can be converted to the other by gain or loss of a hydrogen ion (see Chapter 21).

$$HIn \rightleftharpoons H^+ + In^-$$

un-ionised   conjugate base
indicator   colour B
colour A

- Adding an acid to this indicator solution shifts the position of equilibrium to the left. There are now more molecules of colour A.

- Adding an alkali shifts the position of equilibrium to the right. There are now more ions of colour B.

- The colour of the indicator depends on the relative concentrations of HIn and In⁻. The colour of the indicator during a titration depends on the concentration of H⁺ ions present.

Indicators usually change colour over a pH range of between 1 and 2 pH units. In the middle of the range there is a recognisable end-point where the indicator

> **KEY WORD**
>
> **acid–base indicator:** a compound that has two different ranges of colours depending on the pH of the solution in which it is placed. It changes colour over a narrow range of pH values.

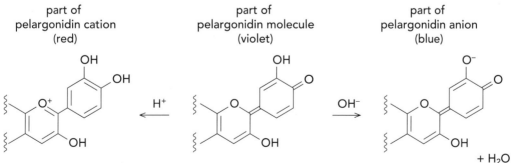

Figure 8.16: The red petals of pelargonium (geranium) contain the dye pelargonidin. Hydrogen ions or hydroxide ions can make small changes in its molecular structure to produce different colours.

has a colour in between the two extremes of colour. For example, bromothymol blue is yellow in acidic solution and blue in alkaline solution. The colour change takes place between pH 6.0 and pH 7.6. The end-point, which is a greyish-green colour, occurs when the pH is 7.0.

The pH at which indicators begin to change colour varies considerably. Table 8.11 shows the colours, ranges and end-points of some indicators.

Name of dye	Colour at lower pH	pH range	End-point	Colour at higher pH
methyl violet	yellow	0.0–1.6	0.8	blue
methyl yellow	red	2.9–4.0	3.5	yellow
methyl orange	red	3.2–4.4	3.7	yellow
bromophenol blue	yellow	2.8–4.6	4.0	blue
bromocresol green	yellow	3.8–5.4	4.7	blue
methyl red	red	4.2–6.3	5.1	yellow
bromothymol	yellow	6.0–7.6	7.0	blue
phenolphthalein	colourless	8.2–10.0	9.3	pink/violet
alizarin yellow	yellow	10.1–13.0	12.5	orange/red

Table 8.11: Some of the chemical indicators used to monitor pH, with their pH ranges of use and pH of end-point.

PRACTICAL ACTIVITY 8.2

Monitoring pH change

In Section 3.7 we described the titration procedure for determining the amount of acid required to neutralise an alkali. Figure 8.17 shows the apparatus used to follow the changes in pH when a base is titrated with an acid.

Procedure

- set up the apparatus with the pH electrode connected to the computer via a data logger
- switch on the magnetic stirrer
- deliver the acid at a constant slow rate from the burette into the alkali in the flask
- stop when the pH has reached a nearly constant low value.

The pH of the reaction mixture can also be monitored manually. You record the pH after fixed volumes of acid samples have been added to the flask, e.g. add one 1 cm³ sample at a time until the pH starts changing rapidly, then add 0.5 cm³ samples.

The graphs recorded on the computer or drawn by hand show how pH varies with the volume of acid added. The shapes of these graphs are characteristic and depend on whether the acid and base used in the titration are strong or weak.

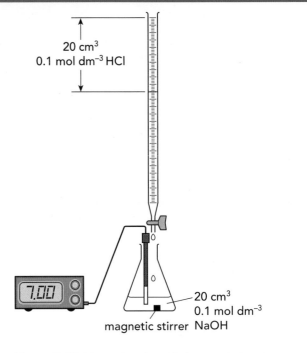

20 cm³
0.1 mol dm⁻³ HCl

7.00

20 cm³
0.1 mol dm⁻³
magnetic stirrer   NaOH

Figure 8.17: Measuring the pH change during the titration of sodium hydroxide with hydrochloric acid.

Strong acids with strong bases

Figure 8.18 shows how the pH changes when 0.100 mol dm⁻³ sodium hydroxide (a strong base) is titrated with 0.100 mol dm⁻³ hydrochloric acid (a strong acid) in the presence of bromothymol blue indicator.

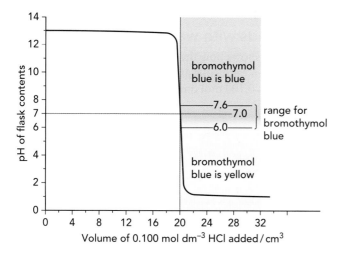

Figure 8.18: A strong acid–strong base titration with bromothymol blue as indicator.

These results show:

- a sharp fall in the graph line between pH 10.5 and pH 3.5; in this region tiny additions of H⁺ ions result in a rapid change in pH

- a midpoint of the steep slope at pH 7

- the midpoint of the sharp fall corresponds to the point at which the H⁺ ions in the acid have exactly reacted with the OH⁻ ions in the alkali; this is the end-point of the titration

- bromothymol blue indicator changed from blue to yellow over the range 7.6 to 6.0 where the slope is steepest.

Because there is a sharp change in pH over the region pH 3.5 to 10.5 we can use other indicators that change colour within this region. For example, phenolphthalein changes colour in the pH range 8.2 to 10.0 (Figure 8.19).

Because the sharp pH change occurs over such a wide pH range, there are many indicators that can be used to determine the end-point of the reaction of a strong acid with a strong base.

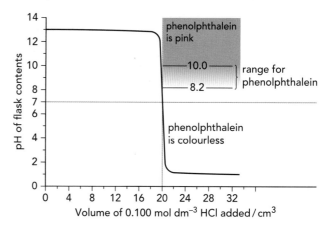

Figure 8.19: A strong acid–strong base titration with phenolphthalein as indicator.

Question

20 Use Table 8.11 to identify:

a those indicators which could be used for a strong acid–strong base titration like the one in Figure 8.18.

b those indicators that could not be used.

Strong acids with weak bases

Figure 8.20 shows how the pH changes when 0.100 mol dm⁻³ aqueous ammonia (a weak base) is titrated with 0.100 mol dm⁻³ nitric acid (a strong acid).

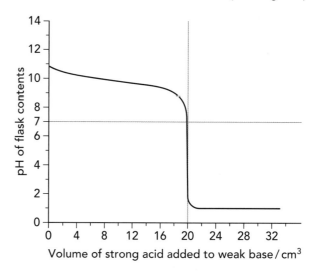

Figure 8.20: A typical strong acid–weak base titration.

These results show:

- a sharp fall in the graph line between pH 7.5 and pH 3.5

- that the midpoint of the steep slope is at about pH 5.

Because there is a sharp change in pH over the region 3.5 to 7.5, we can use methyl red as an indicator for this titration. This is because methyl red changes colour between pH 4.2 and pH 6.3, values that correspond with the region of sharpest pH change. Phenolphthalein would not be a suitable indicator to use because it only changes colour in alkaline regions (pH 8.2–10) that do not correspond to the sharp pH change. The phenolphthalein would change colour only gradually as more and more acid is added, instead of changing suddenly on the addition of a single drop at the end-point.

Weak acids with strong bases

Figure 8.21 shows how the pH changes when $0.100 \ mol \ dm^{-3}$ aqueous sodium hydroxide (a strong base) is titrated with $0.100 \ mol \ dm^{-3}$ benzoic acid (a weak acid).

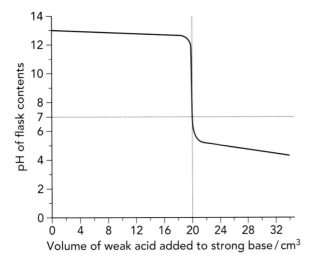

Figure 8.21: A typical weak acid–strong base titration.

These results show:

- a sharp fall in the graph line between pH 11 and pH 7.5

- that the midpoint of the steep slope is at about pH 9.

Because there is a sharp change in pH over the region pH 7.5 to 11 we can use phenolphthalein as an indicator

for this titration. This is because phenolphthalein changes colour between pH 8.2 and pH 10, values that correspond with the region of sharpest pH change. Methyl orange would not be a suitable indicator to use because it only changes colour in acidic regions that do not correspond to the sharp pH change.

Weak acids with weak bases

Figure 8.22 shows how the pH changes when $0.100 \ mol \ dm^{-3}$ aqueous ammonia (a weak base) is titrated with $0.100 \ mol \ dm^{-3}$ aqueous benzoic acid (a weak acid).

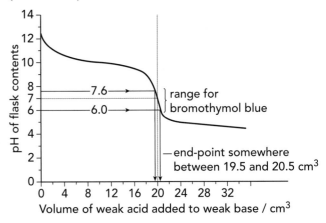

Figure 8.22: A typical weak acid–weak base titration.

These results show that there is no sharp fall in the graph line. No acid–base indicator is suitable to determine the end-point of this reaction. In the example shown, bromothymol blue:

- starts changing colour when $19.50 \ cm^3$ of acid have been added

- finishes changing colour when $20.50 \ cm^3$ of acid have been added.

Such a gradual colour change on addition of acid is not good enough when you need to be able to read the end-point to the nearest $0.05 \ cm^3$.

Questions

21 a Suggest a suitable indicator to find the end-points of the reactions between:

    i $0.0500 \ mol \ dm^{-3}$ nitric acid and $0.0500 \ mol \ dm^{-3}$ aqueous ammonia

    ii $2.00 \ mol \ dm^{-3}$ aqueous sodium hydroxide and $1.00 \ mol \ dm^{-3}$ sulfuric acid

iii 0.00500 mol dm⁻³ aqueous potassium hydroxide and 0.00500 mol dm⁻³ butanoic acid.

b Suggest why phenolphthalein would not be a suitable indicator to use to find the end-point when 0.0100 mol dm⁻³ hydrochloric acid is titrated against 0.0100 mol dm⁻³ urea, a weak base.

22 The sketch graph (Figure 8.23) shows the change in pH when an acid and an alkali react with one being added slowly to the other. Both acid and alkali have a concentration 0.1 mol dm⁻³.

Which one of these statements is correct?

A Weak alkali is being added to a weak acid.

B Strong alkali is being added to a strong acid.

C Strong acid is being added to a weak alkali.

D Strong alkali is being added to a weak acid.

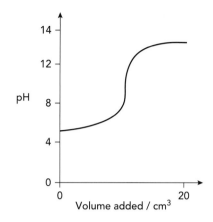

Figure 8.23: Sketch graph for Question 22.

REFLECTION

Think about what you have learned about acids and bases. Write a paragraph about the difference between strong and weak acids and bases. Then sketch one graph to show how the pH changes when a weak or strong acid is added slowly to a weak or strong base: choose your own combination! Share these ideas with another learner.

What problems did you come across? How did you solve them?

SUMMARY

For some chemical reactions, dynamic equilibrium is reached when the rates of the forward and reverse reactions are equal so the concentrations of reactants and products remain constant.
Le Chatelier's principle states that, if a change is made to a system at dynamic equilibrium, the position of equilibrium moves to minimise this change.
Changes in temperature, pressure and concentration of reactants and products affect the position of equilibrium, but the value of equilibrium constant is only affected by a change in temperature.
For an equilibrium reaction, there is a relationship between the concentrations of the reactants and products which is given by the equilibrium constant in terms of concentrations, K_c, and / or partial pressure, K_p.
Equilibrium constants in terms of concentrations, K_c, and partial pressure, K_p, can be deduced from appropriate data.
The Brønsted–Lowry theory of acids and bases states that acids are proton donors and bases are proton acceptors.
Strong acids and bases are completely dissociated in aqueous solution whereas weak acids and bases are only slightly dissociated.

EXAM-STYLE QUESTIONS

1   The reaction $2SO_2(g) + O_2(g) \rightleftharpoons 2SO_3(g)$ reaches dynamic equilibrium in a closed vessel. The forward reaction is exothermic. The reaction is catalysed by V_2O_5.

    a State what is meant by the term *dynamic equilibrium*. [2]

    b Deduce what will happen to the position of equilibrium when:

        i some sulfur trioxide, SO_3, is removed from the vessel [1]

        ii the pressure in the vessel is lowered [1]

        iii more V_2O_5 is added [1]

        iv the temperature of the vessel is increased. [1]

    c Define *Le Chatelier's principle*. [2]

    d Use Le Chatelier's principle to explain what will happen to the position of equilibrium in the reaction
$H_2(g) + CO_2(g) \rightleftharpoons H_2O(g) + CO(g)$
when the concentration of hydrogen is increased. [5]

                                                                      [Total: 13]

2   Hydrogen, iodine and hydrogen iodide are in equilibrium in a sealed tube at constant temperature.

The equation for the reaction is:

$$H_2(g) + I_2(g) \rightleftharpoons 2HI(g) \qquad \Delta H_r = -96 \text{ kJ mol}^{-1}$$

The partial pressures of each gas are shown in the table below.

Gas	Partial pressure / Pa
H_2	2.330×10^6
I_2	0.925×10^6
HI	10.200×10^6

    a Explain the meaning of the term *partial pressure*. [2]

    b Calculate the total pressure of the three gases in this mixture. [1]

    c Deduce an equilibrium expression for this reaction in terms of partial pressures. [1]

    d Calculate a value for K_p for this reaction, including the units. [1]

    e Use Le Chatelier's principle to explain what happens to the position of equilibrium in this reaction when:

        i the temperature is increased [5]

        ii some iodine is removed. [5]

                                                                        [Total: 15]

CONTINUED

3   The equilibrium between three substances, A, B and C, is shown below.

$A(g) + B(g) \rightleftharpoons C(g)$

Initially there were 0.1 mol of A and 0.2 mol of B in the reaction mixture.
A and B reacted together to produce an equilibrium mixture containing
0.04 mol of C. The total volume of the mixture was 2.00 dm³.

a   Calculate the number of moles of A and B at equilibrium.   [2]

b   Calculate the concentrations of A, B and C at equilibrium.   [3]

c   i   Write the equilibrium expression for K_c.   [1]

    ii Calculate the value of K_c and give the units.   [2]

[Total: 8]

4   Gaseous hydrogen and gaseous iodine react together to form hydrogen iodide.

$H_2 + I_2 \rightleftharpoons 2HI$

a   The graph shows how the amount of hydrogen iodide varies with
    time in a 1.00 dm³ container.

    The initial amounts of hydrogen and iodine were 1.00 mol H_2 and
    1.00 mol I_2.

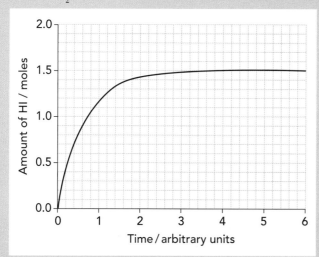

    Sketch a similar graph to show how the number of moles of
    hydrogen varies with time.   [5]

b   Calculate the number of moles of iodine present at equilibrium.   [1]

c   i   Write the equilibrium expression for K_c for the reaction
        between gaseous hydrogen and iodine.   [1]

    ii Calculate the value of K_c and give the units.   [2]

[Total: 9]

5   a   Describe three characteristic features of chemical equilibrium.   [3]

CONTINUED

b When 1 mol of N_2O_4 gas is allowed to come to equilibrium with NO_2 gas under standard conditions, only 20% of the N_2O_4 is converted to NO_2.

$$N_2O_4 \rightleftharpoons 2NO_2 \qquad \Delta H_r = +58 \text{ kJ mol}^{-1}$$

   i Give the equilibrium expression for this reaction. [1]

   ii Calculate the value of K_c for the reaction. Assume that the volume of the reaction mixture is 1 dm^3. [4]

c Explain the effect on K_c of an increase in:

   i pressure [2]

   ii temperature. [2]

[Total: 12]

6 This question is about the following reaction:

$$CH_3COOH(l) + C_2H_5OH(l) \rightleftharpoons CH_3COOC_2H_5(l) + H_2O(l)$$

  ethanoic acid   ethanol   ethyl ethanoate   water

9.20 g of ethanol are mixed with 12.00 g of ethanoic acid in an inert solvent. The total volume of solution is 250 cm^3. The mixture is left to equilibrate for several days. At equilibrium 70% of the reactants are converted to products.

a Calculate the concentration of each reactant at the start [2]

b Calculate the concentration of each reactant at equilibrium. [2]

c Calculate the concentration of each product at equilibrium. [2]

d **i** Write the equilibrium expression for this reaction. [1]

   ii Calculate the value of K_c for the reaction. [1]

   iii Explain why there are no units for K_c for this reaction. [1]

e Deduce what will happen to the numerical value of K_c if 100 cm^3 of water is added to the equilibrium mixture. [1]

f Deduce what will happen to the yield of ethyl ethanoate if 100 cm^3 of water is added to the equilibrium mixture. Explain your answer. [2]

[Total: 12]

7 **a** Hydrogen chloride and ammonia both ionise in water:

$$HCl + H_2O \rightleftharpoons H_3O^+ + Cl^- \qquad \text{equation 1}$$

$$NH_3 + H_2O \rightleftharpoons NH_4^+ + OH^- \qquad \text{equation 2}$$

   i State the name of the ion H_3O^+. [1]

   ii Identify the acid and the base on the left-hand side of each equation. [2]

   iii By referring to equation 1 and equation 2, explain why water is described as being *amphoteric*. [5]

b When dissolved in an organic solvent, hydrogen chloride reacts with hydrogen iodide as follows:

$$HCl + HI \rightleftharpoons H_2Cl^+ + I^-$$

Use the Brønsted–Lowry theory of acids and bases to explain which reactant is the acid, and which reactant is the base. [2]

CONTINUED

c   Hydrochloric acid is a strong acid but ethanoic acid, CH_3COOH, is a weak acid.

   i   Explain the difference between a strong acid and a weak acid. [2]

   ii   Suggest a value of the pH for a 0.1 mol dm^{-3} solution of ethanoic acid in water. [1]

   iii   Write a chemical equation to show the reaction when ethanoic acid donates a proton to water. [2]

[Total: 15]

8   This question is about the reaction:

$$N_2(g) + 3H_2(g) \rightleftharpoons 2NH_3(g) \qquad \Delta H_r = -92 \text{ kJ mol}^{-1}$$

120.0 mol of hydrogen gas are mixed with 40.0 mol of nitrogen gas then pressurised. The mixture of gases is passed at constant pressure over an iron catalyst at 450 °C until the mixture reaches equilibrium.

The total volume of the mixture is 1.0 dm^3. 20% of the reactants are converted to ammonia.

a   Calculate the number of moles of nitrogen and hydrogen remaining at equilibrium. [2]

b   Calculate the number of moles of ammonia formed. [1]

c   Write an equilibrium expression for K_c. [1]

d   Calculate a value for K_c, including units. [2]

e   State what will happen to the numerical value of K_c when the pressure is raised. [1]

f   State what will happen to the numerical value of K_c when the temperature is raised. [1]

[Total: 8]

9   Ethanol can be manufactured by reacting ethene, C_2H_4, with steam.

$$C_2H_4(g) + H_2O(g) \rightleftharpoons C_2H_5OH(g)$$

a   Write the equilibrium expression in terms of partial pressures, K_p, for this reaction. [1]

b   State the units of K_p for this reaction. [1]

c   The reaction is at equilibrium at 290 °C and 7.00×10^6 Pa pressure. Under these conditions the partial pressure of ethene is 1.50×10^6 Pa and the partial pressure of steam is 4.20×10^6 Pa.

   i   Calculate the partial pressure of ethanol. [1]

   ii   Calculate the value of the equilibrium constant, K_p, under these conditions. [1]

d   The reaction is carried out in a closed system. Explain the meaning of the term *closed system*. [1]

e   Use Le Chatelier's principle to explain what will happen to the position of equilibrium in this reaction when the pressure is increased. [3]

CONTINUED

f   The results in the table below show the effect of temperature on the percentage of ethene converted to ethanol at constant pressure. Use this information to deduce the sign of the enthalpy change for this reaction. Explain your answer.

Temperature / °C	% of ethene converted
260	40
290	38
320	36

[4]

[Total: 12]

10 a   Sketch the graph of pH that would be obtained when 10.0 cm^3 of $0.200 \text{ mol dm}^{-3}$ HCl is titrated against $0.200 \text{ mol dm}^{-3}$ aqueous ammonia. [3]

   b   Explain why methyl orange is a suitable indicator for this titration but phenolphthalein is not. [2]

   c   Sketch the graph that would be obtained if 25.0 cm^3 of $0.200 \text{ mol dm}^{-3}$ sodium hydroxide is titrated against $0.100 \text{ mol dm}^{-3}$ ethanoic acid solution. [3]

   d   Explain why phenolphthalein is a suitable indicator for this titration but methyl orange is not. [2]

   e   Bromocresol green and bromothymol blue are indicators. Bromocresol green has a pH range of 3.8 to 5.4 and bromothymol blue has a pH range of 6 to 7.6. Would either of these indicators be suitable for the titration in part **a** or the titration in part **c**? Explain your answer. [4]

[Total: 14]

IMPORTANT

In Question 10 a, the command word 'sketch' requires a bit more than just drawing the line and labelling the axes. You must include some pH values.

SELF-EVALUATION

After studying this chapter, complete a table like this:

I can	See section...	Needs more work	Almost there	Ready to move on
explain what is meant by a *reversible reaction*	8.1			
explain what is meant by *dynamic equilibrium* in terms of the rate of forward and backward reactions being equal and concentration of reactants and products remaining constant	8.1			
explain why a closed system is needed for equilibrium to be established	8.1			
define Le Chatelier's principle as: if a change is made to a system at dynamic equilibrium the position of equilibrium moves to minimise this change	8.2			

CONTINUED

I can	See section...	Needs more work	Almost there	Ready to move on
use Le Chatelier's principle to deduce qualitatively the effects of changes in temperature, concentration, pressure or presence of a catalyst on a reaction at equilibrium	8.2			
deduce expressions for equilibrium constants in terms of concentrations, K_c	8.2, 8.3			
use the terms *mole fraction* and *partial pressure*	8.4			
deduce expressions for equilibrium constants in terms of partial pressures, K_p	8.4			
Use K_c and K_p expressions to carry out equilibrium calculations	8.3, 8.4			
calculate the quantities present at equilibrium from given data	8.3			
understand which factors affect the value of the equilibrium constant	8.3			
describe and explain the conditions used in the Haber process and the Contact process	8.5			
write the formula and give the names of common acids and alkalis (HCl, H_2SO_4, HNO_3, CH_3COOH, NaOH, KOH, NH_3)	8.6			
describe the Brønsted–Lowry theory of acids and bases	8.6			
describe strong acids and strong bases and weak acids and weak bases in terms of fully dissociated or partially dissociated	8.6			
describe acidic, alkaline and neutral solutions in terms of pH	8.6			
explain qualitatively the differences in behaviour of strong and weak acids in terms of electrical conductivity, universal indicator, pH and reactivity with reactive metals	8.6			
describe neutralisation reactions in terms of $H^+(aq) + OH^-(aq) \rightarrow H_2O(l)$	8.6			
sketch pH titration curves using combinations of strong and weak acids with strong and weak alkalis	8.6			
select suitable indicators for acid-alkali titrations using data provided.	8.7			

Chapter 9

Rates of reaction

LEARNING INTENTIONS

In this chapter you will learn how to:

- explain and use the terms:
  - rate of reaction
  - frequency of collisions
  - effective and non-effective collisions
- explain, in terms of frequency of effective collisions, the effect of changes of concentration and pressure on the rate of reaction
- use experimental data to calculate the rate of a reaction
- define *activation energy*, E_A
- sketch and use the Boltzmann distribution curve to explain the importance of activation energy
- explain the effect of temperature change on rate of reaction in terms of the Boltzmann distribution and the frequency of effective collisions
- explain and use the terms *catalyst* and *catalysis*

CONTINUED

- explain how a catalyst works in terms of difference in activation energy and difference in mechanism
- explain the effect of catalysts in terms of the Boltzmann distribution
- construct and interpret a reaction pathway diagram in the presence and absence of a catalyst.

BEFORE YOU START

1 Discuss with another learner how to measure the course of a chemical reaction where a gas is produced. Give at least two different methods. Which one of these is better and why?

2 Take it in turn to explain these chemical terms to another learner:

a catalyst

b rate of reaction

c collision theory

d limiting reactant

e activation energy

f kinetic energy

g frequency of collisions

3 Discuss these questions with another learner:

a Why does increasing the pressure in a chemical reaction involving gases increase the rate of reaction?

b Why does a decrease in temperature lead to a decrease in the rate of a chemical reaction?

c When reacted with 20 cm³ of 1.0 mol dm⁻³ hydrochloric acid, why does 5 g of zinc powder react faster than a single 5 g piece of zinc?

4 How confident are you at sketching and interpreting graphs showing how the volume of gas produced in a reaction changes with time?

Sketch a graph to show how the volume of carbon dioxide gas changes with time when excess calcium carbonate reacts with hydrochloric acid of two different concentrations (1.0 mol dm⁻³ and 2.0 mol dm⁻³). Compare your graph with other members of the class.

5 How confident are you at plotting a graph and determining the gradient?
Try this: Plot a graph of volume of gas against time using this data.

Volume / cm³	0	3.5	5	8	10	15
Time / s	0	21	30	47	59	91

Table 9.1: Information table for Question 5.

Then calculate the initial gradient ($\frac{y}{x}$) of this graph. Compare the value of your gradient with other learners.

SLOWING THE RATE CAN BE IMPORTANT

Figure 9.1: a The reactions that produce firework explosions need to take place in a fraction of a second. **b** Corrosion of some metals, such as the rusting of iron, is a much slower reaction.

As Figure 9.1 shows, some chemical reactions are very fast (they have a high rate of reaction) and others are much slower. Some reactions are not very useful to us: for example, rusting of iron, decomposition of wood, and browning of foodstuffs. The rate of a chemical reaction depends on many things. Rusting takes place very slowly in dry air. It takes much longer for iron to rust in the dry desert compared with the much faster rusting which takes place in seawater. The rate of rusting also depends on pH: faster rusting occurs at low pH values (green rust) and high pH values (red rust). There are several other things that speed up

or slow down chemical reactions. One of the most obvious is the effect of temperature. Unwanted oxidation reactions such as the browning of foods can be slowed down by reducing the temperature.

Change in temperature has a great effect on biological and chemical molecules in plants and animals. Increasing the temperature makes respiration faster and the chemical reactions in our body (metabolism) also speed up. But if the temperature is too high (over about 40 °C) the rate of enzyme-catalysed reactions in our bodies starts to decrease because the structure of the enzymes and other proteins in the body is changed. If the temperature is too low, the rate of metabolism gets too low and we may get hypothermia, where the body temperature drops to a dangerously low level.

But in some cases, low body temperatures can be useful. During some surgical operations patients are cooled down to help lower the rate of respiration and rate of blood flow. Lowering the temperature of the blood improves the chances of survival in complex heart operations such as cardiac bypass surgery. The cooled blood is passed through a heart–lung machine which keeps the blood flowing through the body. The temperature of the body is gradually lowered from 37 °C to 30–32 °C. This lowers the rate of reactions in the body and protects the brain and other organs from damage while the heart is stopped during surgery.

Questions for discussion

Discuss with another learner or group of learners:

- If left in the open, food usually goes bad because of oxidation or decomposition reactions. Which foods go bad quickly? What can we do to stop food going bad?

- In places that have seasons which are very cold, some animals lower their body temperature. What is the advantage of this?

- Make a list of other reactions that are very fast or very slow. Compare your answers with other groups.

9.1 Rate of reaction

The study of rates of chemical reactions is called **reaction kinetics**. The data we gather from rate experiments can tell us a lot about how reactions take place. We can then make deductions about the mechanism of a reaction. The balanced chemical equation gives us no information about the rate of a reaction. Experiments are needed to measure the rate at which reactants are used up or products are formed.

The rate of a reaction can be defined as follows:

$$\text{rate} = \frac{\text{change in amount of reactants or products}}{\text{time}}$$

Units of concentration are usually expressed in $mol\ dm^{-3}$. Units of time are usually expressed in seconds. So, the units of **rate of reaction** are normally $mol\ dm^{-3}\ s^{-1}$. For very slow reactions, you may see the units of rates expressed as $mol\ dm^{-3}\ min^{-1}$ or $mol\ dm^{-3}\ h^{-1}$.

Question

1   Convert the following rates into the units of $mol\ dm^{-3}\ s^{-1}$:

   a   0.254 g of I_2 consumed in 1.00 h in a reaction mixture of volume 1 dm^3. ($A_r[I] = 127$)

   b   0.0440 g ethyl ethanoate formed in 1.00 min from a reaction mixture of volume 400 cm^3. ($M_r[CH_3COOC_2H_5] = 88.0$)

PRACTICAL ACTIVITY 9.1

Methods for following the course of a reaction

In order to find out how the rate of reaction changes with time, we need to select a suitable method to follow the progress of a reaction. This method will measure either the rate of disappearance of a reactant, or the rate of appearance of a product. There are two main types of method: *sampling* and *continuous*.

1   Sampling

This method involves taking small samples of the reaction mixture at various times and then carrying out a chemical analysis on each sample. An example is the alkaline hydrolysis of bromobutane:

$$C_4H_9Br + OH^- \rightarrow C_4H_9OH + Br^-$$

Samples are removed at various times and 'quenched' to stop or slow down the reaction, e.g. by cooling the sample in ice. The hydroxide ion concentration can be found by titration with a standard solution of a strong acid.

2   Continuous

In this method a physical property of the reaction mixture is monitored over a period of time. Some examples are using colorimetry, a conductivity meter or measuring changes in gas volume or gas pressure.

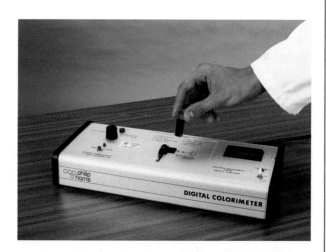

Figure 9.2: We can use a colorimeter to monitor the progress of a reaction. It measures the transmission of light through a 'cell' containing the reaction mixture. The less concentrated the colour of the reaction mixture, the more light is transmitted through the 'cell'.

CONTINUED

Colorimetry can be used to monitor the change in colour of a particular reactant (Figure 9.2). For example, we can use this method to follow the reaction of iodine with propanone:

$$CH_3COCH_3 + I_2 \rightarrow CH_3COCH_2I + HI$$

As the reaction proceeds, the colour of the iodine fades.

Changes in electrical conductivity of a solution can also be measured. For example, we can use this method to follow the reaction:

$$(CH_3)_3CBr + H_2O \rightarrow (CH_3)_3COH + H^+ + Br^-$$

As the reaction proceeds, the electrical conductivity of the solution increases because ions are being formed in the reaction. This method can sometimes be used even if there are ions on both sides of the equation, because ions vary in their conductivities. For example, the small H^+ and OH^- ions have very high conductivities but Br^- ions have a low conductivity.

We can measure changes in gas volume or gas pressure. For example, we can use this method to follow the reaction of benzenediazonium chloride, $C_6H_5N\equiv N^+Cl^-$, with water.

$$C_6H_5N\equiv N^+Cl^-(aq) + H_2O(l) \rightarrow$$
$$C_6H_5OH(aq) + N_2(g) + HCl(aq)$$

We can monitor the reaction by measuring the change in volume of gas released with time. You may have used this method to follow the rate of the reaction between calcium carbonate and hydrochloric acid. If you did, you will have measured the change in volume of carbon dioxide gas released with time (Figure 9.3).

The progress of some reactions can be followed by measuring small changes in the volume of the reaction mixture. For example, during the hydration of methylpropene, the volume decreases.

$$(CH_3)_2C\!=\!CH_2 + H_2O \xrightarrow{H^+} (CH_3)_3COH + H^+$$

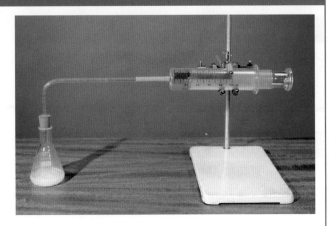

Figure 9.3: We can follow the rate of reaction by measuring the change in volume of a gas given off in a reaction. In this experiment, CO_2 is being given off when $CaCO_3$ reacts with HCl.

An instrument called a dilatometer (Figure 9.4) is used to measure the small changes in volume. The temperature has to be controlled to an accuracy of ±0.001 °C. Can you think why?

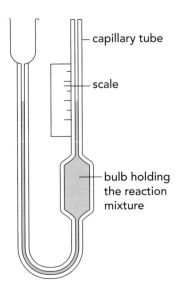

Figure 9.4: A dilatometer.

Question

2 a Suggest a suitable method for following the progress of each of these reactions:

    i $H_2O_2(aq) + 2I^-(aq) + 2H^+(aq) \rightarrow$
$$2H_2O(l) + I_2(aq)$$

    ii $HCOOCH_3(aq) + H_2O(l) \rightarrow$
$$HCOOH(aq) + CH_3OH(aq)$$

    iii $2H_2O_2(aq) \rightarrow 2H_2O(l) + O_2(g)$

    iv $BrO_3^-(aq) + 5Br^-(aq) + 6H^+(aq) \rightarrow$
$$3Br_2(aq) + 3H_2O(l)$$

b Why is it essential to keep the temperature constant when measuring the progress of a reaction?

Calculating rate of reaction graphically

Rate of reaction usually changes as the reaction proceeds. This is because the concentration of reactants is decreasing. Taking the isomerisation of cyclopropane to propene as an example:

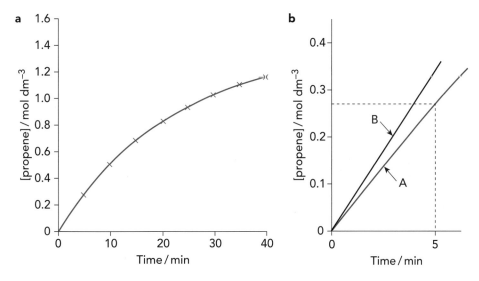

cyclopropane   propene

We can follow the progress of this reaction by measuring the decrease in concentration of cyclopropane or increase in concentration of propene. Table 9.2 shows these changes at 500 °C. The measurements were all made at the same temperature because reaction rate is greatly affected by temperature.

Time / min	[cyclopropane] / mol dm^{-3}	[propene] / mol dm^{-3}
0	1.50	0.00
5	1.23	0.27
10	1.00	0.50
15	0.82	0.68
20	0.67	0.83
25	0.55	0.95
30	0.45	1.05
35	0.37	1.13
40	0.33	1.17

Table 9.2: Concentrations of reactant (cyclopropane) and product (propene) at 5-minute intervals (temperature = 500 °C (773 K)).

Note that we put square brackets, [ ], around the cyclopropane and propene to indicate *concentration*: [propene] means 'concentration of propene'.

Figure 9.5 shows how the concentration of propene changes with time.

Figure 9.5: How the concentration of propene changes with time in the reaction cyclopropane → propene. **a** the whole curve. **b** The first part of the curve magnified. Line A shows the average rate over the first 5 minutes. Line B shows the actual initial rate found by drawing a tangent at the start of the curve.

We can see from Figure 9.5b that the concentration of propene increases from 0.00 to 0.27 mol dm⁻³ in the first 5 minutes. In Section 6.1 we used the symbol Δ (Greek capital 'delta') to represent a *change* in a particular quantity. So we can write:

$$\text{rate of reaction} = \frac{\Delta[\text{propene}]}{\Delta\,\text{time}} = \frac{0.27}{5}$$

$$= 0.054 \text{ mol dm}^{-3} \text{ min}^{-1}$$

This gives the average rate of reaction over the first 5 minutes. You will notice, however, that the graph is a curve which becomes shallower with time. So the rate decreases with time. By measuring the change in concentration over shorter and shorter time intervals we get an increasingly accurate value of the reaction rate. If we make the time interval over which we measure the reaction almost zero, we obtain a reaction rate at a particular instant. We do this by drawing tangents at particular points on the curve. Line B in Figure 9.5b shows a tangent drawn at the start of the curve. This gives a much more accurate value of the initial rate of reaction.

WORKED EXAMPLE

1   Figure 9.6 shows how to draw a tangent and calculate the rate at a particular point on a curve. In this case, we are using a graph of concentration of cyclopropane against time.

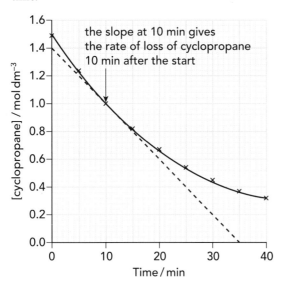

Figure 9.6: The rate of decrease of cyclopropane concentration over time as the reaction proceeds. The rate of reaction at a given time can be found by drawing a tangent and measuring the gradient.

Procedure

Step 1: Select a point on the graph corresponding to a particular time (10 minutes in this example).

Step 2: Draw a straight line at this point so that it just touches the line. The two angles between the straight line and the curve should look very similar.

Step 3: Extend the tangent to meet the axes of the graph.

Step 4: Calculate the gradient (slope) of the tangent. This is a measure of the rate of reaction. In this example the slope is:

$$\text{slope} = \frac{0.00 - 1.40}{35 \times 60}$$

$$= -6.67 \times 10^{-4} \text{ mol dm}^{-3} \text{ s}^{-1}$$

Note:

- we convert the minutes to seconds by multiplying by 60

- the sign of the gradient is negative because the reactant concentration is decreasing

- the value of -6.67×10^{-4} mol dm⁻³ s⁻¹ refers to the rate of change of cyclopropane concentration

- this is the rate of reaction when the cyclopropane concentration is 1.00 mol dm⁻³.

Changes in rate as the reaction proceeds

As time passes, the concentration of cyclopropane falls. We can find the rate at different concentrations of cyclopropane by drawing tangents at several points on the graph. Figure 9.7 shows how this is done for cyclopropane concentrations of 1.50 mol dm^{-3} (the initial rate), 1.00 mol dm^{-3} and 0.50 mol dm^{-3}. The data is summarised in Table 9.3.

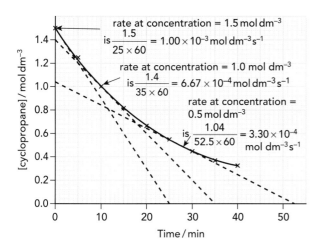

rate at concentration = 1.5 mol dm^{-3}
is $\dfrac{1.5}{25 \times 60}$ = 1.00×10^{-3} mol dm^{-3} s^{-1}

rate at concentration = 1.0 mol dm^{-3}
is $\dfrac{1.4}{35 \times 60}$ = 6.67×10^{-4} mol dm^{-3} s^{-1}

rate at concentration = 0.5 mol dm^{-3}
is $\dfrac{1.04}{52.5 \times 60}$ = 3.30×10^{-4} mol dm^{-3} s^{-1}

Figure 9.7: Calculation of the rate of decrease of cyclopropane concentration, made at regular intervals.

[cyclopropane] / mol dm^{-3}	Rate / mol dm^{-3} s^{-1}	Rate divided by [cyclopropane] / s^{-1}
1.50	1.00×10^{-3}	6.67×10^{-4}
1.00	6.67×10^{-4}	6.67×10^{-4}
0.50	3.30×10^{-4}	6.60×10^{-4}

Table 9.3: Rates of decrease for cyclopropane at different concentrations, calculated from Figure 9.7.

A graph of rate of reaction against concentration of cyclopropane (Figure 9.8) shows us that the rate is directly proportional to the concentration of cyclopropane. So, if the concentration of cyclopropane is doubled the rate of reaction is doubled. If the concentration of cyclopropane falls by one-third, the rate of reaction falls by one-third.

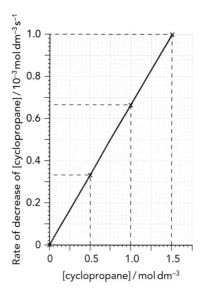

Figure 9.8: The rate of decrease of cyclopropane. Note how the gradient (rate / concentration) is constant.

Question

3 a i Plot the data in Table 9.2 for increase in propene concentration with time.

   ii Calculate the rate after 10 minutes (when the propene concentration is 0.50 mol dm^{-3}) by drawing a tangent.

   b Use the same method to calculate the rate of reaction at propene concentrations of 0.00 mol dm^{-3}, 0.30 mol dm^{-3} and 0.90 mol dm^{-3}.

   c i Calculate the concentration of cyclopropane when the concentration of propene is 0.00, 0.30, 0.50 and 0.90 mol dm^{-3}.

   ii Plot a graph of rate of reaction against [cyclopropane]. Note that the graph is for cyclopropane concentration *not* [propene] as it is the concentration of the reactant that is affecting the rate, not the product.

PRACTICAL ACTIVITY 9.2

The reaction between calcium carbonate and hydrochloric acid

By collecting data and then analysing it, we can work out the relationship between the rate of reaction and concentration of reactant. In this case we are going to use the apparatus shown in Figure 9.9 to collect data about the reaction between marble chips (calcium carbonate) and hydrochloric acid. The marble chips are in excess.

$$CaCO_3(s) + 2HCl(aq) \rightarrow$$
$$CaCl_2(aq) + CO_2(g) + H_2O(l)$$

Procedure

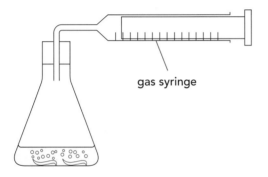

gas syringe

Figure 9.9: Apparatus needed to measure the volume of gas given off in the reaction.

1. Set up the apparatus as shown in Figure 9.9 but remove the stopper from the flask and set the syringe to zero.

2. Put about 10 g of large marble chips into the flask. Each marble chip should be about the same size and weigh 1.5–1.8 g.

3. Put 20 cm³ of acid into the flask and leave for two seconds for the solution to become saturated with carbon dioxide.

4. Put the stopper on the flask and immediately start a stopclock.

5. Record the volume of the gas in the syringe every 30 s until there is no further change in volume.

Record your results in a table with these headings:

- time / s
- volume of gas (V_t) / cm³
- final volume of gas – volume of gas at time t ($V_f - V_t$) / cm³

The hydrochloric acid is the limiting reactant. As the reaction proceeds, the concentration of the hydrochloric acid decreases. $V_f - V_t$ is proportional to the concentration of hydrochloric acid at each time, t.

Plot a graph of $V_f - V_t$ against time, t, and look at its shape. This will give us information about the kinetics of the reaction (see Chapter 22).

REFLECTION

1. Think about what you have learned so far. Explain to another learner how you can determine the initial rate of reaction from the experimental results of a reaction which produces a gas.

2. Work with another learner to list the different ways of following the rate of reaction.

   What obstacles did your partner help you overcome?

Collision theory

When we explain the effects of concentration, temperature, surface area and catalysts on rates of reaction, we use the **collision theory**. Collision theory states that in order to react with each other, particles must collide in the correct orientation and with sufficient energy. The particles might be atoms, ions or molecules.

KEY WORD

collision theory: in order for particles to react when they collide, they must have sufficient energy and collide in the correct orientation.

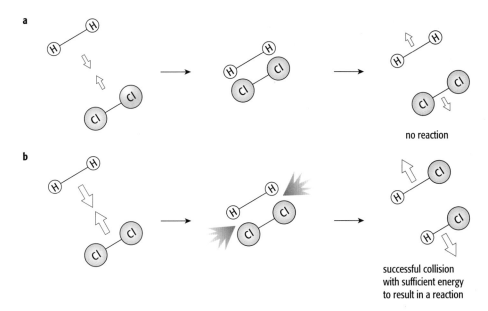

Figure 9.10: **a** Ineffective (unsuccessful) and **b** effective (successful) collisions.

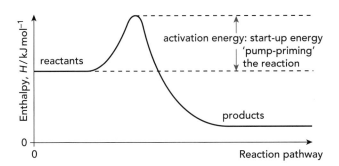

Figure 9.11: The activation energy in an exothermic reaction.

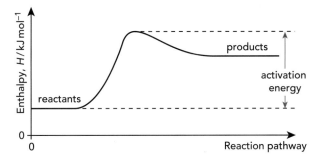

Figure 9.12: The activation energy in an endothermic reaction.

When reactant particles collide they may simply bounce off each other, without changing. This is called an **ineffective collision**. An ineffective collision takes place if the colliding particles do not have enough energy to react. No reaction occurs. If the reactant particles *do* have enough energy to react, they may change into product particles when they collide. This is called an **effective collision** (or successful collision) (Figure 9.10).

The minimum energy that colliding particles must possess for a collision to be effective is called the activation energy, E_A, for that particular reaction.

We can show the activation energy for an exothermic reaction and an endothermic reaction on reaction pathway diagrams, as in Figures 9.11 and 9.12.

According to the collision theory, a reaction will speed up if:

- the frequency of collisions increases

- the proportion of particles with energy greater than the activation energy increases.

The *frequency* of collisions is the number of collisions per unit time, e.g. number of collisions per second.

> **KEY WORDS**
>
> **ineffective collisions:** the particles collide without sufficient kinetic energy to react. Collisions may also be ineffective because, although the molecules collide with enough energy, the reactive parts of the molecules are not close enough to each other.
>
> **effective collisions:** collisions of particles which lead to bond breaking and a chemical reaction.

A **catalyst** is a substance that increases the rate of a reaction but remains chemically unchanged itself at the end of the reaction. A catalyst does this by making it possible for the particles to react by an alternative mechanism. This alternative mechanism has a lower activation energy (see Figure 9.13). You can read more about catalysts in Section 9.4.

> ### KEY WORD
>
> **catalyst:** a substance that increases the rate of a chemical reaction but is chemically unchanged at the end of the reaction. It provides a different mechanism of reaction which has a lower activation energy.

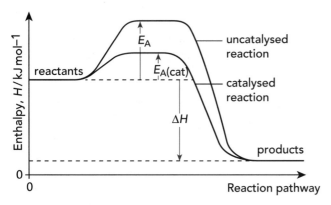

Figure 9.13: The effect of a catalyst on the activation energy in an exothermic reaction.

Question

4 **a** Draw a different set of apparatus that could be used to follow the course of the reaction shown in Figure 9.9.

b What do we mean by:

i the activation energy of a reaction?

ii a catalyst?

c How does a catalyst work? Select the correct answer from the list below.

A by increasing the frequency of collisions

B by decreasing the activation energy

C by increasing the activation energy.

d Use the collision theory to explain how increasing the surface area of a solid reactant increases the rate of reaction.

9.2 The effect of concentration on rate of reaction

> ### IMPORTANT
>
> Remember that increase in concentration of a reactant increases rate because it increases the *frequency* of the collisions. It is not enough to write 'there are more collisions'. You must include an idea of collisions per second. Frequency is a number (of something) per second.

In chemistry, we usually measure the concentration of solutions in moles per decimetre cubed: $mol\ dm^{-3}$. The more concentrated a solution, the greater the number of particles of solute dissolved in a given volume of solvent. In reactions involving solutions, more concentrated reactants have a faster rate of reaction. This is because the random motion of the particles in solution results in more frequent collisions between reacting particles. This is shown in Figure 9.14.

The effect of pressure in reactions involving gases is similar to the effect of concentration in solutions. As we increase the pressure of reacting gases, there are more gas molecules in a given volume. This results in more collisions in any given time, and a faster rate of reaction.

a   b

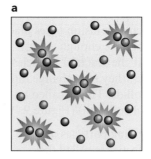 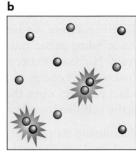

Figure 9.14: The particles in box **a** are closer together than those in box **b**. There are more particles in the same volume, so the chances and frequency of collisions between reacting particles are increased. Therefore, the rate of reaction is greater in box **a** than in box **b**.

Questions

5 **a** Dilute hydrochloric acid reacts with marble chips (calcium carbonate), giving off carbon dioxide gas. Which solution of acid will have the fastest initial rate of reaction?

    A 50 cm³ of 0.5 mol dm⁻³

    B 10 cm³ of 1.0 mol dm⁻³

    C 25 cm³ of 0.5 mol dm⁻³

   b Explain your answer to part **a**.

6 Which one of these explanations about the effect of increasing the concentration of the reactants on the rate of reaction is completely correct?

    A The particles have more energy and collide with a greater frequency

    B The particles are closer together and there are more collisions.

    C The particles are closer together and collide more frequently.

    D The particles have a greater collision rate because they collide more effectively.

9.3 The effect of temperature on rate of reaction

To fully understand rates of reaction, we need to look more closely at the energy possessed by the reactant particles.

In a sample of any substance, at a given temperature, the particles will not all possess the same amount of energy as each other. A few particles will have a relatively small amount of energy. A few particles will have a relatively large amount of energy. Most particles will have an amount of energy somewhere in between. The distribution of energies at a given temperature can be shown on a graph (see Figure 9.15). This is called the **Boltzmann distribution**.

KEY WORD

Boltzmann distribution: a graph showing the number of molecules with a particular kinetic energy plotted against the kinetic energy. The exact shape of the curve varies with temperature. The curve shows that only a very small proportion of the molecules have very high energies.

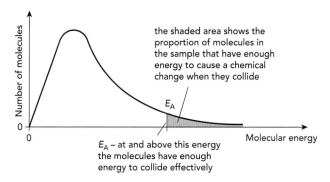

Figure 9.15: The Boltzmann distribution of molecular energies, showing the activation energy.

In Figure 9.15, the activation energy, E_A, is labelled. We have seen that the activation energy is defined as the minimum energy required for colliding particles to react. When we raise the temperature of a reaction mixture, the average kinetic (movement) energy of the particles increases. Particles in solution and in gases will move around more quickly at a higher temperature, resulting in more frequent collisions. However, experiments show us that the effect of temperature on rate of reaction cannot be totally explained by more frequent collisions. The key factor is that the proportion of *successful* collisions increases greatly as we increase the temperature. The distribution of molecular energies changes as we raise the temperature, as shown in Figure 9.16. The curve showing the Boltzmann distribution at the higher temperature flattens and the peak shifts to the right.

The area under the curve represents the number of particles. The shaded area shows the number of particles with energy greater than the activation energy, E_A. For a 10 °C rise in temperature this area under the curve approximately doubles, as does the rate of many reactions.

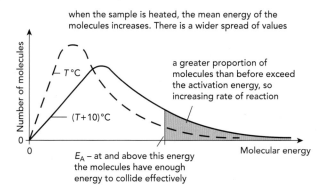

Figure 9.16: The Boltzmann distribution of molecular energies at temperatures T °C and $(T + 10)$ °C, showing the activation energy.

Therefore, increasing the temperature increases the rate of reaction because:

- the increased energy results in particles moving around more quickly, which increases the frequency of collisions

- the proportion of successful collisions (i.e. those that result in a reaction) increases because the proportion of particles exceeding the activation energy increases. This is the more important factor.

> **IMPORTANT**
>
> Remember that increasing temperature increases the rate of reaction because of two factors:
>
> 1 The frequency of effective collisions is greater because of the greater kinetic energy of the molecules
>
> 2 A greater proportion of the molecules have kinetic energy greater than the activation energy.
>
> The second reason has a far greater effect.

Question

7 a What is the Boltzmann distribution?

  b Explain why a 10 °C rise in temperature can approximately double the rate of a reaction.

9.4 Catalysis

> **IMPORTANT**
>
> Catalysts increase the rate because they make the reaction go by a different reaction pathway (mechanism) that has a lower activation energy than the uncatalysed reaction.

In Figure 9.13 we saw how a catalyst works by providing an alternative mechanism (or reaction pathway) with a lower activation energy. We can show this on a Boltzmann distribution (see Figure 9.17).

Note that the presence of a catalyst does *not* affect the shape of the Boltzmann distribution. However, by providing a lower activation energy, a greater proportion of molecules in the reaction mixture have sufficient energy to react. The shaded area under the curve represents the numbers of molecules that have energy greater than the activation energy of the reaction. The total shaded area (including both the light and dark shading) under the curve shows the number of particles with energy greater than the activation energy with the catalyst present ($E_{A(cat)}$). This area is much larger than the dark shaded area for the reaction without a catalyst. Therefore, the rate at which effective collisions occur, and so the rate of the catalysed reaction, is greatly increased compared with the rate of the uncatalysed reaction.

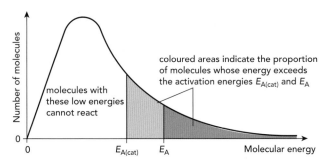

Figure 9.17: The Boltzmann distribution of molecular energies, showing the change in activation energy with and without a catalyst.

Question

8 Which one of these statements about the Boltzmann curve is correct?

  A The Boltzmann curve shows that for most reactions, most particles have energies greater than the activation energy.

  B The Boltzmann curve shows the total number of particles on the y-axis and the activation energy on the x-axis.

  C When the temperature of a chemical reaction is increased the highest point on the Boltzmann curve is still the same.

  D At constant temperature, the area under the Boltzmann curve above the activation energy is greater for a catalysed reaction than for the same uncatalysed reaction.

Homogeneous and heterogeneous catalysts

When a catalyst and the reactants in a catalysed reaction are in the same phase, we describe the catalyst as a *homogeneous* catalyst. For example, we can describe a catalyst as homogeneous if it is dissolved in water and the reactants are also present as an aqueous solution.

If the catalyst is in a different phase to the reactants, we describe the catalyst as a *heterogeneous* catalyst. You have probably met an example of heterogeneous catalysis when making oxygen gas. The reaction commonly used in the laboratory is the decomposition of hydrogen peroxide solution:

$$2H_2O_2(aq) \rightarrow 2H_2O(l) + O_2(g) \qquad \text{slow reaction}$$

This is a very slow reaction at room temperature. However, when a little of the insoluble solid manganese(IV) oxide powder, $MnO_2(s)$, is added, oxygen is given off quickly (Figure 9.18).

$$2H_2O_2(aq) \xrightarrow{MnO_2(s)} 2H_2O(l) + O_2(g) \qquad \text{fast reaction}$$

At the end of the reaction, when no more gas is being released, you can recover the solid catalyst by filtering off the water and drying the black powder of manganese(IV) oxide.

Many heterogeneous catalysts are solids that catalyse gaseous reactants. The reactions take place on the surface of the solid catalyst. There are many examples in industry, including the iron catalyst used in the manufacture of ammonia from nitrogen

Figure 9.18: a A solution of hydrogen peroxide at room temperature. **b** The solution of hydrogen peroxide with a little manganese(IV) oxide added.

gas and hydrogen gas, and the nickel catalyst used when adding hydrogen gas to vegetable oils to make margarine.

Question

9   **a**   **i**   Explain whether the reaction below is an example of heterogeneous catalysis or homogeneous catalysis:

$$2SO_2(g) + O_2(g) \underset{V_2O_5(s)}{\rightleftharpoons} 2SO_3(g)$$

   ii   Explain how a catalyst increases the rate of reaction in terms of activation energy and the distribution of molecular energies in a sample of reactants.

   b   Draw a reaction profile diagram to show a typical uncatalysed reaction and the catalysed version of the reaction. On your diagram show the activation energy for the catalysed and uncatalysed reactions.

KEY WORD

catalysis: the increase in rate of a chemical reaction brought about by the addition of particular substances which are not used up in the reaction.

SUMMARY

The rate of reaction can be found by drawing tangents to a curve of extent of reaction against time.
At higher concentration (or higher pressure), more frequent collisions occur between reactant molecules. This increases the rate of reaction.
The activation energy of a reaction, E_A, is the minimum energy required by colliding particles for a collision to be effective. Reaction pathway diagrams show how the activation energy provides a barrier to reaction.
At higher temperature, molecules have more kinetic energy, so a higher percentage of successful collisions occur between reactant molecules.
The Boltzmann distribution represents the numbers of molecules in a sample with particular energies. The change in the Boltzmann distribution as temperature is increased shows how more molecules have energy greater than the activation energy. This in turn leads to an increase in reaction rate.
A catalyst increases the rate of a reaction by providing an alternative reaction pathway with lower activation energy. More molecules have sufficient energy to react, so the rate of reaction is increased. The catalyst is not used up in the reaction.

EXAM-STYLE QUESTIONS

1 Calcium carbonate reacts with dilute hydrochloric acid.

$$CaCO_3(s) + 2HCl(aq) \rightarrow CaCl_2(aq) + CO_2(g) + H_2O(l)$$

The progress of the reaction was followed by measuring the volume of gas produced at particular time intervals. The results are shown.

Time / s	0	10	20	30	40	50	60	70	80	100	120
Volume of gas / cm³	0	9	16	22	27.5	32	36	39.5	42	45	45

a Plot a suitable graph of these results. Label the axes. [3]

b Calculate the initial rate of reaction by drawing a tangent. Show how you worked out your answer on the graph. Include the correct units. [3]

c Describe how the rate of reaction changes with time and explain how you know this by referring to the line of the graph. [2]

d Describe how to calculate the rate of reaction at 40 s. [2]

e The mass of calcium carbonate used was 0.1875 g. The volume of 0.100 mol dm⁻³ hydrochloric acid used was 40 cm³. M_r CaCO₃ = 100.1

Demonstrate by calculation that the calcium carbonate was the limiting reagent. [4]

f The concentration of hydrochloric acid was doubled. On your graph draw a line to show how the rate of reaction changes with time. [2]

[Total: 16]

COMMAND WORD

Demonstrate: show how or give an example.

CONTINUED

2 **a** Explain why gases react together faster at higher pressure. [2]

  b Explain why reactants in solution react faster at higher concentration. [1]

  c Explain why finely divided solids react more quickly than solid lumps. [2]

  d Explain why raising the temperature increases the rate of reaction. [4]

  [Total: 9]

3 **a** Sketch a graph to show the Boltzmann distribution of molecular energies. Label the axes. [4]

  b Define *activation energy*. [2]

  c Shade an area on the graph to show the number of molecules capable of reacting. [2]

  d Mark on your graph a possible activation energy for the same reaction in the presence of a catalyst. [1]

  e Shade an area on the graph to show the additional number of molecules capable of reacting because of the presence of a catalyst. [1]

  f Draw a second curve on your graph to show the Boltzmann distribution of molecular energies at a slightly higher temperature. [2]

  [Total: 12]

4 The Haber process is used in industry to convert nitrogen and hydrogen to ammonia. The formation of ammonia gas is exothermic.

  a Sketch the enthalpy profile for the Haber process in the absence of a catalyst. [1]

  b On the same diagram, sketch the enthalpy profile for the Haber process in the presence of a catalyst. [1]

  c Label the activation energy on one of the profiles. [1]

  [Total: 3]

5 The activation energy for the uncatalysed decomposition of ammonia to its elements is $+335 \text{ kJ mol}^{-1}$.

  a Write the equation for this reaction, including state symbols. [3]

  b The enthalpy of reaction for this decomposition is $+92 \text{ kJ mol}^{-1}$. Calculate the activation energy for the uncatalysed formation of ammonia from nitrogen and hydrogen. [3]

  c If tungsten is used as a catalyst, the activation energy changes. Explain how it will change. [1]

  [Total: 7]

> **IMPORTANT**
>
> Remember that when writing questions about how rate of reaction changes with concentration or temperature, it is important to use words like *greater* rate, *faster* reaction, *increased* rate. Do *not* just write 'it is fast', 'it is slow'.

SELF-EVALUATION

After studying this chapter, complete a table like this:

I can	See section...	Needs more work	Almost there	Ready to move on
explain and use the terms: **a** rate of reaction **b** frequency of collisions **c** effective and non-effective collisions	9.1			
explain, in terms of frequency of effective collisions, the effect of changes of concentration and pressure on the rate of reaction	9.1, 9.2, 9.3			
use experimental data to calculate the rate of a reaction	9.1			
define *activation energy*	9.1			
sketch and use the Boltzmann distribution curve to explain the importance of activation energy	9.4			
explain the effect of temperature change on rate of reaction in terms of frequency of the Boltzmann distribution and the frequency of effective collisions	9.4			
explain and use the terms *catalyst* and *catalysis*	9.4			
explain how a catalyst works in terms of difference in activation energy and difference in mechanism	9.4			
explain the effect of catalysts in terms of the Boltzmann distribution	9.4			
construct and interpret a reaction pathway diagram in the presence and absence of a catalyst.	9.4			

Chapter 10

Periodicity

LEARNING INTENTIONS

In this chapter you will learn how to:

- describe and explain the periodicity in the variation of atomic radius, ionic radius, melting point and electrical conductivity of the elements

- describe and write equations for the reactions of the elements with oxygen to give Na_2O, MgO, Al_2O_3, P_4O_{10} and SO_2

- describe and write equations for the reactions of the elements with chlorine to give $NaCl$, $MgCl_2$, $AlCl_3$, $SiCl_4$ and PCl_5

- describe and write equations for the reactions of Na and Mg with water

- describe and explain the variation in the oxidation number of the oxides Na_2O, MgO, Al_2O_3, P_4O_{10}, SO_2 and SO_3 and the chlorides $NaCl$, $MgCl_2$, $AlCl_3$, $SiCl_4$ and PCl_5 in terms of their outer shell electrons

- describe and write equations for the reactions, if any, of Na_2O, MgO, Al_2O_3, SiO_2, P_4O_{10}, SO_2 and SO_3 with water, including the likely pH of the solutions obtained

- describe, explain and write equations for the acid / base behaviour of Na_2O, MgO, Al_2O_3, P_4O_{10}, SO_2, SO_3, $NaOH$, $Mg(OH)_2$ and $Al(OH)_3$

- describe the amphoteric behaviour of Al_2O_3 and $Al(OH)_3$

- describe and write equations for the reactions, if any, of $NaCl$, $MgCl_2$, $AlCl_3$, $SiCl_4$ and PCl_5 with water, including the likely pH of the solutions obtained

CONTINUED

- explain the variations in the trends in reactivity of the oxides and chloride above in terms of bonding and electronegativity

- deduce the types of bonding present in oxides and chlorides of Period 3 from their chemical and physical properties

- predict the characteristic properties of an element in a given group using knowledge of periodicity

- deduce the nature, position in the Periodic Table and identity of unknown elements from given information.

BEFORE YOU START

1 Discuss these questions with another learner.

   a Substance X does not conduct electricity when solid but conducts when molten. What type of bonding is present in this structure? Suggest two other physical properties of X, giving reasons for your answers.

   b Substance Y has a very high melting point and does not conduct electricity when molten. What type of structure is Y? Suggest one other physical property of Y, giving reasons for your answer.

2 In Chapter 2 you learned about first ionisation energy. Discuss with another learner how first ionisation energy changes across Period 2 and the reasons for this. Be prepared to explain your answers to the class.

3 In Chapter 2 you also learned about how atomic radius changes across a period and down a group. Describe and explain these patterns to another learner. In return, get the other learner to describe and explain how ionic radius changes across a period and down a group.

4 In Chapter 7 you learned about oxidation numbers. Describe and explain to another learner the change in oxidation numbers of the elements in their oxides belonging to Groups 1, 2 and 13 to 17. In return, get the other learner to describe and explain the variation in oxidation numbers of the chlorides in Groups 13 to 17.

5 Take it in turn to explain these chemical terms to another learner:

   a Brønsted–Lowry acid

   b Brønsted–Lowry base

   c electronegativity

   d amphoteric oxide

6 Make a list of acidic, basic and amphoteric oxides. Compare your list with other members of the class.

ARRANGING THE ELEMENTS

The chemical elements that we know were gradually discovered over many thousands of years. The first metal elements used by early humans, e.g. copper, gold, were found naturally. Evidence from the Middle East and Africa suggests that copper was extracted by heating with charcoal over 7000 years ago. Humans were extracting lead in Africa over 6000 years ago and over 5000 years ago, people were extracting iron from iron ore in Egypt. The progress in extracting other elements was slow until about 260–220 years ago when there was a sudden increase in the 'discovery' of new elements. Elements such as hydrogen, chlorine and manganese were 'discovered' in this period. A little later (1807), sodium and potassium were isolated by electrolysis.

Because so many elements were then known, chemists started to group them together and link them to their 'atomic weights'. Johann Döbereiner and John Newlands produced tables which showed that there was a relationship between the properties of some elements and their 'atomic weights'. It was not until 1869 that the Russian chemist Dmitri Mendeleev arranged the elements into the Periodic Table that we know today (Figure 10.1). He organised the elements known at that time in order of their atomic mass, arranging elements with similar properties into vertical columns. He left gaps where the pattern broke down, arguing that these spaces would eventually be filled by as yet undiscovered elements. For example, he left a space below silicon, and he made predictions of how the 'new' element would behave when it was discovered. He also changed the order of elements in places where similar elements did not quite line up in columns based on atomic mass. These apparent inconsistencies resulted in some of his fellow chemists doubting the importance of his table, but they were convinced following the discovery of germanium in 1886. Germanium closely matched the properties that Mendeleev had predicted for the 'new' element below silicon, using his Periodic Table.

Figure 10.1: a Dmitri Mendeleev (1834–1907). b This version of Mendeleev's Periodic Table is on the building in St Petersburg where he worked.

In the 20th and 21st centuries, further elements, many of which exist for only a few seconds because they are radioactively unstable, have been added to the Periodic Table. Many of these have been discovered by female scientists such as Marie Curie (radium and polonium), Lisa Meitner (protactinium) and Marguerite Perey (francium). One of the latest elements to be discovered is tennessine, which has an atomic number of 117. Which group is this in?

Questions for discussion

Discuss with another learner or group of learners:

- Why do you think that elements such as copper and lead were the first to be extracted but it was not until about 200 years ago that sodium and potassium were extracted?

- Neither the noble gases nor the radioactive elements in Period 7 appear in Mendeleev's table because they had not been discovered. What features of these elements do you think made their discovery difficult?

10.1 Structure of the Periodic Table

We now know that the chemical elements are arranged in the Periodic Table in order of atomic number, not atomic mass as first thought. This explains why Mendeleev had to re-order some elements in his table (which was developed before scientists knew about the structure of the atom). The modern Periodic Table is shown in Figure 10.3 in Section 10.2. There are 18 groups (vertical columns) in the Periodic Table. The rows across the table are called periods. In this chapter we will be looking for patterns going across the third period, from sodium (Na) to argon (Ar). The patterns seen across Period 3 are seen across other periods, too. This recurrence of the same pattern is called **periodicity**.

> **KEY WORD**
>
> **periodicity:** the repeating patterns in the physical and chemical properties of the elements across the periods of the Periodic Table.

> **IMPORTANT**
>
> The latest accepted form of the Periodic Table has groups numbered from 1 to 18. The transition elements are given group numbers. It is easy to change the old Groups III to VIII into the modern form. You just add 10. So Group III becomes Group 13 and Group VII becomes 17.

Question

1   Look at the Periodic Table in Figure 10.3.

   a   Which element is found in Period 4, Group 17?

   b   The relative atomic masses of tellurium (Te) and iodine (I) are 128 and 127, respectively. Why did this present a problem to Mendeleev when he was constructing his Periodic Table?

   c   Why are the elements in Groups 1 and 2 known as 's-block elements', whereas those in Group 17 are called 'p-block elements'?

10.2 Periodicity of physical properties

Periodic patterns of atomic radii

We can compare the size of different atoms using their atomic radii. The data for these measurements can come from an element's single covalent radius (Figure 10.2).

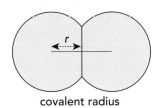

covalent radius

Figure 10.2: The distance between the two nuclei of the same type of atom can be determined and then divided by two to arrive at the atomic (single covalent) radius.

There are other measures of atomic radii, such as metallic radii and van der Waals' radii. However, covalent radii can be obtained for most elements, so these provide the best data for comparison purposes across a period.

The values of the atomic radii of the elements in Period 3 are given in Table 10.1. We can see the pattern across the period more clearly on a graph (Figure 10.4).

> **IMPORTANT**
>
> The atomic radius decreases across a period because the increasingly positive nuclear charge pulls the electrons in the outer shell closer to the nucleus.

The atoms of the noble gases in Group 18, such as argon in Period 3, do not have a covalent radius, as they do not form bonds with each other. Their atomic radii can be determined from their van der Waals' radius. This is found by measuring the distance between the nuclei of two neighbouring, touching atoms which are not chemically bonded together. This distance is divided

key: atomic number / atomic symbol / name / relative atomic mass

Period	1	2	3	4	5	6	7	8	9	10	11	12	13	14	15	16	17	18
1								1 H hydrogen 1.0										2 He helium 4.0
2	3 Li lithium 6.9	4 Be beryllium 9.0											5 B boron 10.8	6 C carbon 12.0	7 N nitrogen 14.0	8 O oxygen 16.0	9 F fluorine 19.0	10 Ne neon 20.2
3	11 Na sodium 23.0	12 Mg magnesium 24.3											13 Al aluminium 27.0	14 Si silicon 28.1	15 P phosphorus 31.0	16 S sulfur 32.1	17 Cl chlorine 35.5	18 Ar argon 39.9
4	19 K potassium 39.1	20 Ca calcium 40.1	21 Sc scandium 45.0	22 Ti titanium 47.9	23 V vanadium 50.9	24 Cr chromium 52.0	25 Mn manganese 54.9	26 Fe iron 55.8	27 Co cobalt 58.9	28 Ni nickel 58.7	29 Cu copper 63.5	30 Zn zinc 65.4	31 Ga gallium 69.7	32 Ge germanium 72.6	33 As arsenic 74.9	34 Se selenium 79.0	35 Br bromine 79.9	36 Kr krypton 83.8
5	37 Rb rubidum 85.5	38 Sr strontium 87.6	39 Y yttrium 88.9	40 Zr zirconium 91.2	41 Nb niobium 92.9	42 Mo molybdenum 95.9	43 Tc technetium –	44 Ru ruthenium 101.1	45 Rh rhodium 102.9	46 Pd palladium 106.4	47 Ag silver 107.9	48 Cd cadmium 112.4	49 In indium 114.8	50 Sn tin 118.7	51 Sb antimony 121.8	52 Te tellurium 127.6	53 I iodine 126.9	54 Xe xenon 131.3
6	55 Cs caesium 132.9	56 Ba barium 137.3	57–71 lanthanoids	72 Hf hafnium 178.5	73 Ta tantalum 180.9	74 W tungsten 183.8	75 Re rhenium 186.2	76 Os osmium 190.2	77 Ir iridium 192.2	78 Pt platinum 195.1	79 Au gold 197.0	80 Hg mercury 200.6	81 Tl thallium 204.4	82 Pb lead 207.2	83 Bi bismuth 209.0	84 Po polonium –	85 At astatine –	86 Rn radon –
7	87 Fr francium –	88 Ra radium –	89–103 actinoids	104 Rf rutherfordium –	105 Db dubnium –	106 Sg seaborgium –	107 Bh bohrium –	108 Hs hassium –	109 Mt meitnerium –	110 Ds darmstadtium –	111 Rg roentgenium –	112 Cn copernicium –	113 Nh nihonium –	114 Fl flerovium –	115 Mc moscovium –	116 Lv livermorium –	117 Ts tennessine –	118 Og oganesson –

lanthanoids	57 La lanthanum 138.9	58 Ce cerium 140.1	59 Pr praseodymium 140.9	60 Nd neodymium 144.4	61 Pm promethium –	62 Sm samarium 150.4	63 Eu europium 152.0	64 Gd gadolinium 157.3	65 Tb terbium 158.9	66 Dy dysprosium 162.5	67 Ho holmium 164.9	68 Er erbium 167.3	69 Tm thullum 168.9	70 Yb ytterbium 173.1	71 Lu lutetium 175.0
actinoids	89 Ac actinium –	90 Th thorium 232.0	91 Pa protactinium 231.0	92 U uranium 238.0	93 Np neptunium –	94 Pu plutonium –	95 Am americium –	96 Cm curium –	97 Bk berkelium –	98 Cf californium –	99 Es einsteinium –	100 Fm fermium –	101 Md mendelevium –	102 No nobelium –	103 Lr lawrencium –

Figure 10.3: The Periodic Table of the elements. A larger version of the Periodic Table can be found in Appendix 1.

Period 3 element	Na	Mg	Al	Si	P	S	Cl	Ar
Atomic radius / nm	0.157	0.136	0.125	0.117	0.110	0.104	0.099	–

Table 10.1: The atomic (single covalent) radii of Period 3 elements (no data are available for argon). The units are nanometres, where 1 nm = 10^{-9} m.

by two to give the van der Waals' radius. This figure will be higher than the single covalent radius of any given element, as there is no overlap of electron clouds involved in the van der Waals' radius.

The atomic radius decreases across Period 3, as shown in Figure 10.4. The same pattern is also found in other periods. Across a period, the number of protons (and so the nuclear charge) and the number of electrons increases by one with each successive element. The extra electron added to the atoms of each successive element occupies the same principal quantum shell (energy level). This means that the shielding effect remains roughly constant (see Section 2.2), so the greater attractive force exerted by the increasing positive nuclear charge on the outer (valence) shell electrons pulls them in closer to the nucleus. For this reason, the atomic radius decreases across the period.

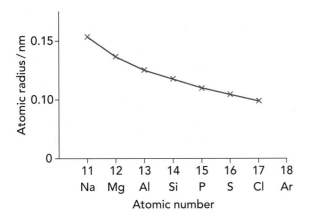

Figure 10.4: Plotting the atomic radii (single covalent radii) against atomic number for the elements in Period 3 (argon not included).

Periodic patterns of ionic radii

> **IMPORTANT**
>
> The ionic radius decreases across a period as the positive charge on the ion increases and the negative charge on the ion decreases. This is because the increasingly positive nuclear charge pulls the electrons in the outer shell closer to the nucleus. In the same period, the negative ions have larger ionic radii than the positive ions because they have one more electron shell, so the outer electrons are further from the nucleus and there is more shielding.

From your work in Chapter 4, you will know that the atoms of metallic elements produce positively charged ions (called cations), such as Na^+. By contrast, the atoms of non-metallic elements form negatively charged ions (called anions), such as Cl^-. What pattern in ionic radii do we see going across Period 3? The data are shown in Table 10.2 and are displayed graphically in Figure 10.5.

The positively charged ions have effectively lost their outer shell of electrons (the third principal quantum shell or energy level) from their original atoms. For this reason, the cations are much smaller than their atoms. To add to this effect, there is also less shielding of the outer electrons in these cations compared with their original atoms.

Going across the period, from Na^+ to Si^{4+}, the ions get smaller for reasons similar to those for the decreasing atomic radii across a period. The increasing nuclear charge attracts the outermost (valence-shell) electrons in the second principal quantum shell (energy level) closer to the nucleus with increasing atomic number.

The negatively charged ions are larger than their original atoms. This is because each atom will have gained one or more extra electrons into their third principal quantum shell. This increases the repulsion between its electrons, while the nuclear charge remains constant. This increases the size of any anion compared with its atom.

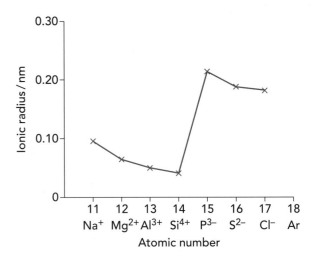

Figure 10.5: Plotting the ionic radii against atomic number for the elements in Period 3 (argon not included).

The anions decrease in size, going from P^{3-} to Cl^-, as the nuclear charge increases across the period.

Ions of Period 3 elements	Na^+	Mg^{2+}	Al^{3+}	Si^{4+}	P^{3-}	S^{2-}	Cl^-	Ar
Ionic radius / nm	0.095	0.065	0.050	0.041	0.212	0.184	0.181	–

Table 10.2: The ionic radii of Period 3 elements (no data are available for argon).

Question

2 Look at the elements in Period 2 of the Periodic Table in Appendix 1. Using your knowledge of Period 3 elements, predict and explain the relative sizes of:

a the atomic radii of lithium and fluorine

b a lithium atom and its ion, Li^+

c an oxygen atom and its ion, O^{2-}

d a nitride ion, N^{3-}, and a fluoride ion, F^-.

Periodic patterns of melting points and electrical conductivity

Physical properties, such as the melting point and electrical conductivity of the elements, also show trends across a period. Again, using Period 3 as an example, we can show the data in tables and on graphs (see Tables 10.3 and 10.4 and the graph in Figure 10.6).

The electrical conductivity increases across the metals of Period 3 from sodium (Group 1) to aluminium (Group 13). The electrical conductivity then drops dramatically to silicon, which is described as a semiconductor, and falls even further to the non-metallic insulators phosphorus and sulfur.

To explain the trend in melting points and electrical conductivity across a period, we have to consider the bonding and structure of the elements (see Table 10.5).

Sodium, magnesium and aluminium, at the start of Period 3, are all metallic elements. As you saw in Section 4.6, their metallic bonding can be described as positive ions arranged in a giant lattice held together by a 'sea' of delocalised electrons. The delocalised electrons are those from the outermost (valence) shell. These delocalised electrons are free to move around within the structure of the metal. When a potential difference is applied, the delocalised electrons drift through the metal towards the positive terminal. Both the melting point and the electrical conductivity increase from sodium to magnesium to aluminium. This can be explained by the number of electrons each metal donates into the 'sea' of delocalised electrons and the increasing charge on the metal ions in the giant metallic lattice. Each sodium atom donates just one electron,

forming Na^+ ions in the lattice, whereas each aluminium atom donates three electrons, forming Al^{3+} ions. This makes the metallic bonding in aluminium stronger, as the electrostatic forces of attraction between its 3+ ions and the larger number of negatively charged delocalised electrons holding the giant structure together are stronger. There are also more delocalised electrons available to drift through the structure when aluminium metal conducts an electric current, making aluminium a better electrical conductor than sodium.

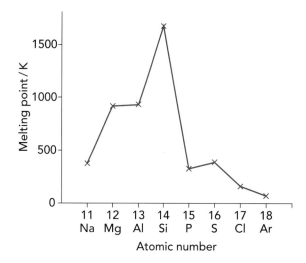

Figure 10.6: Plotting the melting point against atomic number for the elements in Period 3.

> **IMPORTANT**
>
> The change in melting point across a period reflects the type of structure and bonding. As we go across a period, the metals have increasingly strong metallic bonding and their melting points increase. In Period 2 and Period 3, the Group 14 elements have giant covalent structures so have very high melting points. In Groups 15 to 18, most of the elements have simple molecular structures so have relatively low melting points.

The element in the centre of Period 3, silicon, has the highest melting point because of its giant molecular structure (also called a giant covalent structure). Every silicon atom is held to its neighbouring silicon atoms by strong covalent bonds. However, its electrical

Period 3 element	sodium (Na)	magnesium (Mg)	aluminium (Al)	silicon (Si)	phosphorus (P)	sulfur (S)	chlorine (Cl)	argon (Ar)
Melting point / K	371	923	932	1683	317	392	172	84

Table 10.3: The melting points of Period 3 elements (measured in kelvin, K, where 0 °C = 273 K).

Period 3 element	sodium (Na)	magnesium (Mg)	aluminium (Al)	silicon (Si)	phosphorus (P)	sulfur (S)	chlorine (Cl)	argon (Ar)
Electrical conductivity / S m^{-1}	0.218	0.224	0.382	2×10^{-10}	10^{-17}	10^{-23}	–	–

Table 10.4: The electrical conductivity of Period 3 elements (measured in siemens per metre, S m^{-1}, where siemens are proportional to the ease with which electrons can pass through a material).

Period 3 element	sodium (Na)	magnesium (Mg)	aluminium (Al)	silicon (Si)	phosphorus (P)	sulfur (S)	chlorine (Cl)	argon (Ar)
Bonding	metallic	metallic	metallic	covalent	covalent	covalent	covalent	–
Structure	giant metallic	giant metallic	giant metallic	giant molecular	simple molecular	simple molecular	simple molecular	simple molecular

Table 10.5: The bonding and structures of Period 3 elements.

conductivity is much lower than the metals at the start of the period because there are no delocalised electrons free to move around within its structure. Silicon is classed as a semimetal, or *metalloid*.

The elements to the right of silicon are all non-metallic elements. They exist as relatively small molecules. Sulfur exists as S_8 molecules, phosphorus as P_4 molecules and chlorine as Cl_2 molecules. Although the covalent bonds within each molecule are strong, there are only relatively weak instantaneous dipole–induced dipole forces between their molecules (see Section 4.7). Therefore, it does not take much energy to break these weak intermolecular forces and melt the elements. At room temperature, phosphorus and sulfur are solids with low melting points and chlorine is a gas.

Argon gas exists as single atoms with very weak instantaneous dipole–induced dipole forces between these atoms.

Question

3   a   Why does sulfur have a lower melting point than silicon?

b   Why does sulfur have a higher melting point than chlorine?

c   Why is magnesium a better electrical conductor than:

i   phosphorus?

ii   sodium?

Periodic patterns of first ionisation energies

You have looked at the pattern in first ionisation energies for the first two periods in Section 2.6. In Period 3 the pattern is the same as in Period 2. This is shown by the data in Table 10.6 and the graph in Figure 10.7.

Period 3 element	First ionisation energy / kJ mol⁻¹
sodium (Na)	494
magnesium (Mg)	736
aluminium (Al)	577
silicon (Si)	786
phosphorus (P)	1060
sulfur (S)	1000
chlorine (Cl)	1260
argon (Ar)	1520

Table 10.6: The first ionisation energy $(X(g) \rightarrow X^+(g) + e^-)$ of Period 3 elements in kilojoules per mole (kJ mol⁻¹).

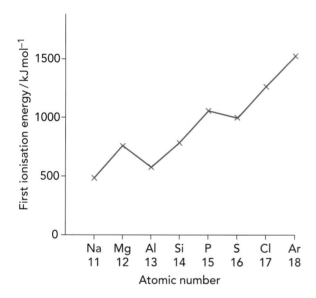

Figure 10.7: Plotting the first ionisation energy $(X(g) \rightarrow X^+(g) + e^-)$ against atomic number for the elements in Period 3.

IMPORTANT

There is a general increase in first ionisation energy across a period because the increasing nuclear charge and decreasing atomic radius makes the attractive forces between the nucleus and outer electrons greater. Remember that Group 13 and Group 16 elements may not obey this general rule (see Chapter 2).

In general, the first ionisation energy increases across Period 3 as the positive nuclear charge increases and electrons successively fill the third quantum shell. As electrons are in the same shell, the shielding effect is similar in atoms of each element. There are small 'dips' in the general trend across the period between Mg and Al, and between P and S. The same pattern appears in Period 2 for Be and B, and N and O. The explanation given in Section 2.6 also applies here in Period 3.

Questions

4 **a** What is the general trend in first ionisation energies across Period 3?

   b Explain why aluminium has a lower first ionisation energy than magnesium.

   c Explain why sulfur has a lower first ionisation energy than phosphorus.

   d Look at Period 4 in the Periodic Table (Appendix 1).

   The first ionisation energies of the p-block elements are given in the table below.

   Predict the missing value for the first ionisation energy of selenium.

p-block element of Period 4	Atomic number	First ionisation energy / kJ mol⁻¹
gallium (Ga)	31	577
germanium (Ge)	32	762
arsenic (As)	33	966
selenium (Se)	34	
bromine (Br)	35	1140
krypton (Kr)	36	1350

Table 10.7: Information table for Question 4.

5 Which one of these statements about the periodicity of the Period 3 elements is correct?

   A The melting points increase to Group 13 then decrease suddenly to low values for Groups 14–18.

   B The bonding of the elements changes from metallic in Groups 1, 2 and 13 to covalent in Groups 14 to 17.

   C The ionic radius decreases steadily from sodium to argon.

   D The structure of the elements changes from metallic in Groups 1, 2 and 13 to simple molecular in Groups 14 to 17.

> **REFLECTION**
>
> 1   Work with another learner. Write down a list of the physical properties of the elements in Period 3 (Groups 1, 2 and 13–17 only) that helps distinguish them from some of the other elements in Period 3.
>
> 2   Ask another learner to select one of these properties and one of the elements in Period 3.
>
> 3   Both of you write down how the value of this physical property compares with other elements in the same period. Compare your answers.
>
> 4   Check how well did you did by comparing your answers with the information in the coursebook.

10.3 Periodicity of chemical properties

We will now look at the chemistry of some of the elements of Period 3 and their compounds, focusing on the oxides and chlorides.

PRACTICAL ACTIVITY 10.1

Reactions of Period 3 elements with oxygen

Some of these experiments may be demonstrated by your teacher. Watch carefully to see what happens and note down your observations.

1   Sodium reacts vigorously when heated and placed in a gas jar of oxygen. The sodium burns with a bright yellow flame (Figure 10.8). The main product when sodium burns in a limited amount of oxygen is a white solid, sodium oxide:

$$4Na(s) + O_2(g) \rightarrow 2Na_2O(s)$$

2   Magnesium also reacts vigorously when heated in oxygen, forming magnesium oxide. Aluminium metal is protected by a layer of aluminium oxide, but powdered aluminium does react well with oxygen. Both metals burn with bright white flames.

$$2Mg(s) + O_2(g) \rightarrow 2MgO(s)$$

$$4Al(s) + 3O_2(g) \rightarrow 2Al_2O_3(s)$$

Figure 10.8: Sodium reacts vigorously with oxygen gas.

CONTINUED

3   Silicon reacts slowly with oxygen to form silicon(IV) oxide (silicon dioxide):

$$Si(s) + O_2(g) \rightarrow SiO_2(s)$$

4   Phosphorus reacts vigorously with oxygen. A yellow or white flame is seen, and clouds of white phosphorus(V) oxide are produced:

$$4P(s) + 5O_2(g) \rightarrow P_4O_{10}(s)$$

5   Sulfur powder, once ignited, burns gently with a blue flame in a gas jar of oxygen gas. Toxic fumes of sulfur dioxide gas are produced (Figure 10.9):

$$S(s) + O_2(g) \rightarrow SO_2(g)$$

Further oxidation of sulfur dioxide gives sulfur trioxide. Their systematic names are sulfur(IV) oxide and sulfur(VI) oxide, respectively.

$$2SO_2(g) + O_2(g) \xrightleftharpoons{V_2O_2 \text{catalyst}} 2SO_3(g)$$

6   Chlorine and argon do not react with oxygen.

Figure 10.9: Sulfur burns gently in oxygen gas.

Reactions of Period 3 elements with chlorine

When sodium metal is heated then plunged into a gas jar of chlorine there is a vigorous reaction, forming sodium chloride:

$$2Na(s) + Cl_2(g) \rightarrow 2NaCl(s)$$

Magnesium and aluminium also react vigorously with chlorine gas:

$$Mg(s) + Cl_2(g) \rightarrow MgCl_2(s)$$

$$2Al(s) + 3Cl_2(g) \rightarrow Al_2Cl_6(s)$$

Silicon reacts slowly with chlorine, as it does with oxygen, giving silicon(IV) chloride:

$$Si(s) + 2Cl_2(g) \rightarrow SiCl_4(l)$$

Phosphorus also reacts slowly with excess chlorine gas:

$$2P(s) + 5Cl_2(g) \rightarrow 2PCl_5(l)$$

Sulfur does form chlorides, such as SCl_2 and S_2Cl_2, but you do not need to cover these for your examination.

Argon does not form a chloride.

Reactions of sodium and magnesium with water

PRACTICAL ACTIVITY 10.2

Reaction of sodium and magnesium with water

Some of these experiments may be demonstrated by your teacher. Watch carefully to see what happens and note down your observations.

1   Sodium reacts vigorously with cold water, melting into a ball of molten metal (Figure 10.10). It moves across the surface of the water, giving off hydrogen gas. It quickly gets smaller and smaller until it disappears, leaving a strongly alkaline solution (e.g. pH 14) of sodium hydroxide behind:

$$2Na(s) + 2H_2O(l) \rightarrow 2NaOH(aq) + H_2(g)$$

CONTINUED

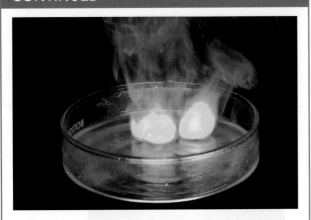

Figure 10.10: There is a violent reaction when sodium is placed on a piece of filter paper floating on the surface of water.

2 By contrast, fresh magnesium reacts extremely slowly with cold water, taking several days to produce a test-tube of hydrogen gas. The solution formed is very weakly alkaline (e.g. pH 11), as any magnesium hydroxide formed is only slightly soluble. Therefore, a lower concentration of $OH^-(aq)$ ions enters the solution compared with the result when sodium is added to water. This is because sodium hydroxide is much more soluble in water than magnesium hydroxide.

$$Mg(s) + 2H_2O(l) \xrightarrow{\text{slow reaction}} Mg(OH)_2(aq) + H_2(g)$$

When heated, magnesium does react vigorously with water in the form of steam to make magnesium oxide and hydrogen gas:

$$Mg(s) + H_2O(g) \rightarrow MgO(s) + H_2(g)$$

Question

6 a i The Group 1 metal lithium reacts in a similar way to sodium. It reacts with oxygen, producing lithium oxide. Write the balanced symbol equation, including state symbols, for this reaction.

ii Lithium also reacts with chlorine. Write the balanced symbol equation, including state symbols, for this reaction.

b i The Group 2 metal calcium reacts more vigorously with cold water than magnesium does, forming an alkaline solution. Write the balanced symbol equation, including state symbols, for this reaction.

ii The solution formed when 0.01 mol of calcium react completely with 1 dm^3 of water is more alkaline than the solution formed when 0.01 mol of magnesium react completely with 1 dm^3 of water. Explain why.

10.4 Oxides of Period 3 elements

Oxidation numbers of oxides

Table 10.8 shows the formulae of some of the common oxides of the Period 3 elements.

The maximum oxidation number of each element rises as we cross the period. This happens because the Period 3 element in each oxide can use all the electrons in its outermost shell in bonding to oxygen (ox. no. = −2). They all exist in positive oxidation states because oxygen has a higher electronegativity than any of the Period 3 elements. See Section 12.2 for more about electronegativity.

Period 3 element	Na	Mg	Al	Si	P	S	Cl	Ar
Formula of oxide	Na_2O	MgO	Al_2O_3	SiO_2	P_4O_{10}	SO_2, SO_3	Cl_2O_7	–
Oxidation number of Period 3 element	+1	+2	+3	+4	+5	+4, +6	+4, +6, +7	–

Table 10.8: Oxidation numbers of the Period 3 elements in some common oxides. Chlorine has other oxides, such as Cl_2O, in which its oxidation number is +1, and Cl_2O_5, in which its oxidation number is +5.

10.5 Effect of water on oxides and hydroxides of Period 3 elements

The oxides of sodium and magnesium react with water to form hydroxides. The presence of excess aqueous hydroxide ions, OH⁻(aq), makes these solutions alkaline:

$$Na_2O(s) + H_2O(l) \rightarrow 2NaOH(aq)$$

strongly alkaline solution, e.g. pH 14

$$MgO(s) + H_2O(l) \rightarrow Mg(OH)_2(aq)$$

weakly alkaline solution, e.g. pH 10

Figure 10.11: The basic magnesium oxide or hydroxide reacts with acid in the stomach to form a salt plus water.

Magnesium oxide and magnesium hydroxide are commonly used in indigestion remedies (Figure 10.11). These basic compounds neutralise excess acid in the stomach, relieving the pain:

$$MgO(s) + 2HCl(aq) \rightarrow MgCl_2(aq) + H_2O(l)$$

$$Mg(OH)_2(s) + 2HCl(aq) \rightarrow MgCl_2(aq) + 2H_2O(l)$$

Aluminium oxide does not react or dissolve in water, which is why an oxide layer can protect aluminium metal from corrosion. However, it does react and dissolve when added to acidic or alkaline solutions.

- With acid:

$$Al_2O_3(s) + 3H_2SO_4(aq) \rightarrow Al_2(SO_4)_3(aq) + 3H_2O(l)$$

- With hot, concentrated alkali:

$$Al_2O_3(s) + 2NaOH(aq) + 3H_2O(l) \rightarrow$$
$$2NaAl(OH)_4(aq)$$

When aluminium oxide reacts with an acid it behaves like a base: it forms a salt (aluminium sulfate in the example with dilute sulfuric acid above) plus water.

When it reacts with an alkali it behaves like an acid: reacting to form a salt (sodium tetrahydroxoaluminate in the example with sodium hydroxide above).

Compounds that can act as both acids and bases, such as aluminium oxide, are called **amphoteric**.

> **KEY WORD**
>
> **amphoteric:** able to behave as both an acid and as a base. Aluminium oxide is an amphoteric oxide because it reacts with both acids such as hydrochloric acid and bases such as sodium hydroxide to form salts.

Silicon dioxide is also insoluble in water. Water cannot break down its giant molecular structure. However, it will react with and dissolve in hot, concentrated alkali:

$$SiO_2(s) + 2NaOH(aq) \rightarrow Na_2SiO_3(aq) + H_2O(l)$$

Silicon dioxide acts as an acid when it reacts with sodium hydroxide, forming a salt (sodium silicate) plus water. It does not react with acids, so it is classed as an acidic oxide.

Phosphorus(V) oxide reacts vigorously and dissolves in water to form an acidic solution of phosphoric(V) acid (pH 2):

$$P_4O_{10}(s) + 6H_2O(l) \rightarrow 4H_3PO_4(aq)$$

phosphoric(V) acid

The oxides of sulfur, SO_2 and SO_3, both react and dissolve in water, forming acidic solutions (pH 1):

$$SO_2(g) + H_2O(l) \rightarrow H_2SO_3(aq)$$

sulfurous acid (also known as sulfuric(IV) acid)

$$SO_3(g) + H_2O(l) \rightarrow H_2SO_4(aq)$$

sulfuric(VI) acid

The effect of bonding and electronegativity on the structure and acidic / basic nature of Period 3 oxides

Table 10.9 shows a summary of the acidic / basic nature of the Period 3 oxides. You need to know this summary for your examination. We can explain the behaviour of the oxides by looking at their structure and bonding (Table 10.10 and Figure 10.12).

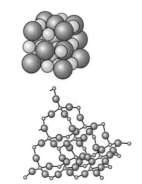

the giant ionic structure of magnesium oxide

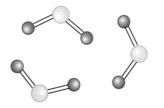

the giant covalent structure of silicon dioxide

> ### IMPORTANT
>
> Remember that electronegativity is the power of an atom to attract the electrons in a covalent bond towards itself. Electronegativity increases across a period and decreases down a group (ignoring the Group 18 elements).

the simple molecular structure of sulfur dioxide

Going across a period, the elements get more electronegative as electrons are more strongly attracted by the increasing positive nuclear charge (see Section 4.7). The electronegativity values, which indicate the strength of the attraction of an atom for the electrons in a bond, are shown in Table 10.11.

Figure 10.12: The structures of some Period 3 oxides.

Period 3 oxide	Na_2O	MgO	Al_2O_3	SiO_2	P_4O_{10}	SO_2, SO_3
Acid / base nature	basic	basic	amphoteric	acidic	acidic	acidic

Table 10.9: The acid / base nature of some Period 3 oxides.

Period 3 oxide	Na_2O	MgO	Al_2O_3	SiO_2	P_4O_{10}	SO_2, SO_3
Relative melting point	high	high	very high	very high	low	low
Electrical conductivity when in liquid state	good	good	good	none	none	none
Chemical bonding	ionic	ionic	ionic (with a degree of covalent character)	covalent	covalent	covalent
Structure	giant ionic	giant ionic	giant ionic	giant covalent	simple molecular	simple molecular

Table 10.10: Some properties, chemical bonding and structure of some Period 3 oxides.

Period 3 element	Na	Mg	Al	Si	P	S	Cl	Ar
Electronegativity	0.9	1.2	1.5	1.8	2.1	2.5	3.0	–

Table 10.11: Electronegativity values for some Period 3 oxides (no data are available for argon).

IMPORTANT

As we go across Period 3, the structure of the oxides changes from ionic metal oxides (which are basic oxides) to giant covalent oxides to simple molecular oxides (which are acidic oxides).

The electronegativity of oxygen is 3.5. The greater the difference in electronegativity between the Period 3 element and oxygen, the more likely it is that the oxide will have ionic bonding. Electrons will be transferred from sodium, magnesium and aluminium atoms (forming positively charged ions) to oxygen atoms (forming O^{2-} ions) when their oxides are formed. The other Period 3 elements will form covalently bonded oxides in which bonding electrons are shared.

Notice the high melting points of the giant ionic and giant covalent structures, leading to the use of:

- magnesium oxide to line the inside of furnaces

- aluminium oxide and silicon dioxide to make ceramics, with giant covalent structures designed to withstand high temperatures and provide electrical insulation.

The oxides of the metals sodium and magnesium, with purely ionic bonding, produce alkaline solutions with water as their oxide ions, $O^{2-}(aq)$, become hydroxide ions, $OH^-(aq)$. The oxide ions behave as bases by accepting H^+ ions from water molecules:

$$O^{2-}(aq) + H_2O(l) \rightarrow 2OH^-(aq)$$

By contrast, the covalently bonded non-metal oxides of phosphorus and sulfur dissolve and react in water to form acidic solutions. The acid molecules formed donate H^+ ions to water molecules, behaving as typical acids. For example, sulfuric(VI) acid:

$$H_2SO_4(aq) + H_2O(l) \rightarrow H_3O^+(aq) + HSO_4^-(aq)$$

The insoluble oxides of aluminium and silicon show their acidic nature by reacting and dissolving in an alkaline solution, such as hot, concentrated sodium hydroxide solution, forming a soluble salt. This behaviour is typical of a covalently bonded oxide. However, aluminium oxide also reacts and dissolves in acidic solutions, forming a soluble salt: behaviour typical of a basic metal oxide with ionic bonding. Because aluminium oxide behaves in these two ways, this provides evidence that the chemical bonding in aluminium oxide is not purely ionic nor purely covalent. It is amphoteric.

Question

7 a The element germanium is in Group 14, in Period 4. It is classed as a semimetal or metalloid, as is silicon in Period 3.

   i Predict the chemical bonding and structure of the element germanium.

   ii Germanium(IV) oxide has properties similar to silicon dioxide. It is an acidic oxide. Write a balanced symbol equation, including state symbols, to show the reaction of germanium(IV) oxide with hot, concentrated sodium hydroxide solution.

   iii What would you expect to happen if germanium(IV) oxide was added to $2.0\ mol\ dm^{-3}$ hydrochloric acid?

   b Potassium oxide (K_2O) is a basic oxide. It reacts and dissolves in water, forming an alkaline solution.

   i Write a balanced symbol equation, including state symbols, to show the reaction of potassium oxide with water.

   ii Write a balanced symbol equation, including state symbols, to show the reaction of potassium oxide with dilute nitric acid.

   iii Predict the chemical bonding and structure of potassium oxide.

10.6 Chlorides of Period 3 elements

Oxidation numbers of the Period 3 chlorides

Table 10.12 shows the formulae of the common chlorides of the Period 3 elements.

The oxidation numbers rise as we cross Period 3, until we reach sulfur in Group 16. This happens because the Period 3 elements from sodium to phosphorus use all the electrons in their outermost shell, their valence electrons, in bonding to chlorine (ox. no. = −1). They all exist in positive oxidation states because chlorine has a higher electronegativity than any of the other Period 3 elements (see Table 10.12).

Period 3 element	sodium (Na)	magnesium (Mg)	aluminium (Al)	silicon (Si)	phosphorus (P)	sulfur (S)	chlorine (Cl)	argon (Ar)
Formula of chloride	NaCl	$MgCl_2$	Al_2Cl_6	$SiCl_4$	PCl_5	SCl_2	–	–
Oxidation number of Period 3 element	+1	+2	+3	+4	+5	+2	–	–

Table 10.12: Oxidation numbers of the Period 3 elements in their chlorides. Phosphorus also has a chloride with the formula PCl_3, in which its oxidation number is +3. Sulfur also has a chloride S_2Cl_2, in which its oxidation number is +1.

10.7 Effect of water on chlorides of Period 3 elements

As with the oxides of Period 3 elements, the chlorides also show characteristic behaviour when we add them to water. Once again, this is linked to their structure and bonding (Table 10.13).

At the start of Period 3, the ionic chlorides of sodium (NaCl) and magnesium ($MgCl_2$) do not react with water. The polar water molecules are attracted to the ions, dissolving the chlorides by breaking down the giant ionic structures. The solutions formed contain the positive metal ions and the negative chloride ions surrounded by water molecules. The metal ions and the chloride ions are called *hydrated* ions:

$$NaCl(s) \xrightarrow{\text{water}} Na^+(aq) + Cl^-(aq)$$

Aluminium chloride is sometimes represented as $AlCl_3$, which suggests that its chemical bonding is likely to be ionic: with Al^{3+} ions and Cl^- ions in a giant lattice. In

solid hydrated aluminium chloride crystals, this is the case. However, without water it exists as Al_2Cl_6. This can be thought of as a *dimer* (two molecules joined together) of $AlCl_3$. Al_2Cl_6 is a covalently bonded molecule (see Figure 10.13).

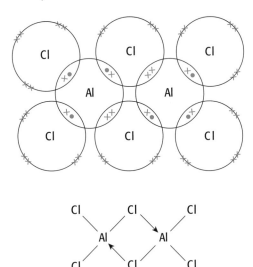

Figure 10.13: The chemical bonding in Al_2Cl_6.

Formula of chloride	NaCl	$MgCl_2$	Al_2Cl_6	$SiCl_4$	PCl_5	SCl_2
Chemical bonding	ionic	ionic	covalent	covalent	covalent	covalent
Structure	giant ionic	giant ionic	simple molecular	simple molecular	simple molecular	simple molecular
Observations when added to water	white solids dissolve to form colourless solutions		chlorides react with water, giving off white fumes of hydrogen chloride gas			
pH of solution formed with water	7	6.5	3	2	2	2

Table 10.13: The structure and bonding of the chlorides of Period 3 elements and the effect of water on these chlorides.

As we go across Period 3, the structures of the chlorides change from ionic metal chlorides (which are neutral) to metallic chlorides (which can be hydrolysed by water to form acids as one of the products) to simple molecular chlorides (which form acids when added to water).

Once we add water, the dimers are broken down and aluminium ions and chloride ions enter the solution. Each relatively small and highly charged Al^{3+} ion is hydrated and causes a water molecule bonded to it to lose an H^+ ion. This turns the solution acidic. We can show this in an equation as follows:

$$[Al(H_2O)_6]^{3+}(aq) \rightarrow [Al(H_2O)_5OH]^{2+}(aq) + H^+(aq)$$

The non-metal chlorides $SiCl_4$ and PCl_5 are hydrolysed in water, releasing white fumes of hydrogen chloride gas in a rapid reaction (Figure 10.14).

$$SiCl_4(l) + 2H_2O(l) \rightarrow SiO_2(s) + 4HCl(g)$$

The SiO_2 is seen as an off-white precipitate. Some of the hydrogen chloride gas produced dissolves in the water, leaving an acidic solution (hydrochloric acid).

Phosphorus(V) chloride also undergoes hydrolysis when added to water:

$$PCl_5(s) + 4H_2O(l) \rightarrow H_3PO_4(aq) + 5HCl(g)$$

Both products are soluble in water and are highly acidic.

Figure 10.14: Solid phosphorus(V) chloride is hydrolysed in water, releasing white fumes of hydrogen chloride gas.

REFLECTION

1   Work with another learner. On separate pieces of paper, write the name of the Period 3 elements from Groups 1, 2 and 13–17. Turn these over so you can't see the names and mix them up.

2   Each of you chooses one of the pieces of paper and writes down all that you know about the reaction of that element with water. Include the pH value of the solution formed and an equation.

3   Compare your answers. Did you do this differently to your partner?

4   Check how well did you did by comparing your answers with the information in the coursebook.

Question

8   Which one of these statements is completely correct?

   A   Aluminium oxide reacts with water to form a solution with a pH of 13–14

   B   Sodium chloride dissolves in water to form a solution of pH 2

   C   Phosphorus pentachloride reacts with water to form a solution of pH 1–2

   D   Magnesium reacts with cold water to form a solution with a pH of 13–14.

10.8 Deducing the position of an element in the Periodic Table

We can deduce the possible position of an element in the Periodic Table by looking at its physical and chemical properties. We can also predict, as Mendeleev did, the physical and chemical properties of an element in a given group if we know its position. In the worked examples given, note there are several ways of arriving at the same conclusion.

WORKED EXAMPLES

1 Element G forms a chloride, which reacts with water to form a solution of pH 1. It forms an oxide which has a melting point of 1610 °C. The oxide does not dissolve in or react with aqueous sodium hydroxide. Deduce the possible position of G in the Periodic Table.

Solution

Step 1: Use the pH data to decide whether G is likely to be a metal or non-metal.

Low pH suggests that it is a metal chloride which undergoes hydrolysis, so is likely to be in Group 13 to 17.

Step 2: Use the solubility data.

The oxide doesn't dissolve in sodium hydroxide. This rules out aluminium oxide because this reacts with sodium hydroxide. So G could be a giant covalent structure or simple molecular structure.

Step 3: Use melting point data.

The melting point is high so it is likely to be a giant covalent structure in Group 14.

Step 4: It cannot be in Period 2 because CO_2 is a gas. So it could be in Period 3 or lower.

2 Selenium is in Group 16 and Period 4 of the Periodic Table. Predict some physical and chemical properties of selenium.

Step 1: Identify the likely structure of selenium from its position in the Periodic Table and comparison with other Group 16 elements.

It's a non-metal in Group 16 so comparing with sulfur it should have a simple molecular structure.

Step 2: Identify the physical properties related to the structure.

Simple molecular structures have (relatively) low melting points, do not conduct electricity and are insoluble in water.

Step 3: Identify the chemical properties related to reaction with water, reaction with chlorine and reaction with oxygen.

Simple molecules do not react with water.

Reacts with chlorine to form simple molecule $SeCl_4$ (which reacts with water vapour in the air to produce hydrogen chloride).

Reacts with oxygen to form an oxide of possible formula SeO_2 (by comparison with sulfur).

Question

9 a The chloride of an unknown element, X, is a liquid at 20 °C. This chloride reacts with water, giving off white fumes and leaving an acidic solution.

   i Does element X belong to Group 1, Group 2 or Group 15 of the Periodic Table?

   ii What type of reaction takes place between X and water?

   iii Identify the white fumes given off when X reacts with water.

   b The chloride of an unknown element Y is a solid at 20 °C. This chloride does not react with water but dissolves to give a neutral solution. Does element Y belong to Group 1, Group 14 or Group 16 of the Periodic Table?

SUMMARY

As you go across a period in the Periodic Table, there are variations in physical properties such as ionisation energies, atomic radii, ionic radii, melting points and electrical conductivities.

Atomic radii decrease across a period due to increasing nuclear charge.

Across the period, the structures of the elements change from giant metallic, through giant molecular to simple molecular. Group 18 elements consist of individual atoms.

Across the period, the oxides of Period 3 elements change from basic compounds with ionic bonding through to giant molecular in the centre of the period (Group 14) with silicon, going on to acidic covalently bonded simple molecules of the non-metal oxides. Aluminium oxide (in Group 13) is amphoteric, exhibiting both basic and acidic behaviour.

Across the period, the chlorides of Period 3 elements change from ionic compounds that dissolve in water to covalent compounds that are hydrolysed by water, releasing fumes of hydrogen chloride and leaving an acidic solution.

EXAM-STYLE QUESTIONS

1 a Explain what is meant by the term 'periodic property'. [2]

   b The graph shows how a periodic property varies when plotted against atomic number for Period 3 (sodium to argon).

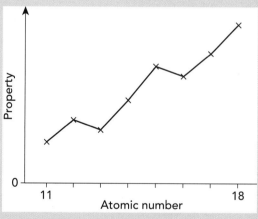

   i   Identify the property. [1]
   ii Explain the overall trend across the period. [4]

[Total: 7]

COMMAND WORD

Identify: name / select / recognise.

CONTINUED

2 The variation of melting point with atomic number for Periods 2 and 3 is shown in the graph below.

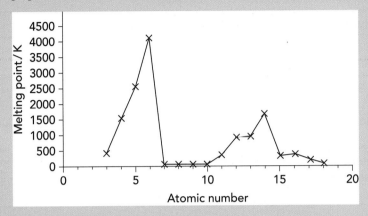

a Explain what we mean when we say melting point is a *periodic* property. [1]

b Explain the following.

   i The melting point of silicon is much greater than that of phosphorus. [4]

   ii The melting point of aluminium is greater than that of sodium. [5]

[Total: 10]

3 a i Describe how the atomic radius varies across Periods 2 and 3. [1]

      ii Explain this trend. [4]

   b i Describe how the atomic radius varies down each group of the Periodic Table. [1]

      ii Explain this trend. [1]

[Total: 7]

4 a Describe the acid–base nature of the solutions obtained when the following compounds are added to water.

      Use equations to illustrate your answers.

      i sodium chloride [2]

      ii sulfur trioxide [2]

      iii sodium oxide [2]

      iv phosphorus(V) chloride. [2]

   b i Write an equation for the reaction of magnesium with cold water. [1]

      ii Predict and explain the pH of the resulting solution. [2]

CONTINUED

c Phosphorus(III) chloride (PCl$_3$) is a liquid that reacts vigorously with water. One of the products of this reaction is H$_3$PO$_3$, which forms in solution.

    i Write an equation, including state symbols, showing the reaction of phosphorus(III) chloride with water. **[1]**

    ii Predict the pH of the solution obtained. **[1]**

    iii State one observation a student watching the reaction would make. **[1]**

[Total: 14]

SELF-EVALUATION

After studying this chapter, complete a table like this:

I can	See section...	Needs more work	Almost there	Ready to move on
describe and explain the periodicity in the variation of atomic radius, ionic radius, melting point and electrical conductivity of the elements	10.2			
describe and write equations for the reactions of the elements with oxygen to give Na$_2$O, MgO, Al$_2$O$_3$, P$_4$O$_{10}$ and SO$_2$	10.3			
describe and write equations for the reactions of the elements with chlorine to give NaCl, MgCl$_2$, AlCl$_3$, SiCl$_4$ and PCl$_5$	10.3			
describe and write equations for the reactions of Na and Mg with water	10.3			
describe and explain the variation in the oxidation number of the oxides Na$_2$O, MgO, Al$_2$O$_3$, P$_4$O$_{10}$, SO$_2$ and SO$_3$ and the chlorides NaCl, MgCl$_2$, AlCl$_3$, SiCl$_4$ and PCl$_5$ in terms of their outer shell electrons	10.4			
describe and write equations for the reactions, if any, of Na$_2$O, MgO, Al$_2$O$_3$, SiO$_2$, P$_4$O$_{10}$, SO$_2$ and SO$_3$ with water, including the likely pH of the solutions obtained	10.5			
describe, explain and write equations for the acid / base behaviour of Na$_2$O, MgO, Al$_2$O$_3$, P$_4$O$_{10}$, SO$_2$, SO$_3$, NaOH, Mg(OH)$_2$ and Al(OH)$_3$	10.5			
describe the amphoteric behaviour of Al$_2$O$_3$ and Al(OH)$_3$	10.5			
describe and write equations for the reactions, if any, of NaCl, MgCl$_2$, AlCl$_3$, SiCl$_4$ and PCl$_5$ with water, including the likely pH of the solutions obtained	10.6			

CONTINUED

I can	See section...	Needs more work	Almost there	Ready to move on
explain the variations in the trends in reactivity of the oxides and chlorides above in terms of bonding and electronegativity	10.6, 10.7			
deduce the types of bonding present in oxides and chlorides of Period 3 from their chemical and physical properties	10.6			
predict the characteristic properties of an element in a given group using knowledge of periodicity	10.8			
deduce the nature, position in the Periodic Table and identity of unknown elements from given information.	10.8			

> # Chapter 11
Group 2

LEARNING INTENTIONS

In this chapter you will learn how to:

- describe and write equations for the reactions of the Group 2 elements with oxygen, water and dilute acids

- describe and write equations for the reactions of the Group 2 oxides, hydroxides and carbonates with water and with dilute acids

- describe and write equations for the thermal decomposition of the Group 2 nitrates and carbonates

- describe, and make predictions from, the trends in properties of the Group 2 elements and their compounds that are covered in this chapter

- state the variation in the solubilities of the Group 2 hydroxides and sulfates.

BEFORE YOU START

Working in your group, answer these questions:

1   Which one of the following electronic configurations correctly describes an atom of calcium?

   A $1s^2\,2s^2\,2p^6\,3s^2$

   B $1s^2\,2s^2\,2p^6\,3s^2\,3p^3\,3d^3\,4s^2$

   C $1s^2\,2s^2\,2p^6\,3s^2\,3p^6\,4s^2$

   D $1s^2\,2s^2\,2p^6\,3s^2\,3d^8$

2   Magnesium powder reacts with dilute hydrochloric acid, giving off hydrogen and leaving a solution of magnesium chloride.

   Write a balanced equation, including state symbols for this reaction.

3   Write down the trend in the reactivity of the Group 1 elements, with increasing atomic number (going down the group).

4   The first ionisation energy of beryllium is 900 kJ mol^{-1}.

   Write down exactly what this statement means in a single sentence.

   Swap your answer with another student. Then discuss each other's answers and revise your sentence if necessary.

5   Working as a pair, one person explains to the other how a magnesium ion is formed from a magnesium atom. Then the other person explains the formation of an oxide ion. Finally discuss together how the ions form ionic bonds in the compound, magnesium oxide.

SOME USES OF GROUP 2 COMPOUNDS

Elements from Group 2 are used in a range of applications. For example, Group 2 metals produce coloured flames when heated, leading to their use in flares and fireworks. Magnesium in its powdered form is used in flares. The large surface area in a fine powder increases the rate of reaction with oxygen.

In military aircraft, the heat given off from decoy magnesium flares confuses the Infrared detection systems in heat-seeking missiles (Figure 11.1). The missiles cannot focus in and target the aircraft.

The compounds of Group 2 elements are used even more widely than the elements themselves. Most useful is calcium carbonate, $CaCO_3$. It is found in the many types of limestone, which provide useful rocks for building. The limestone rock itself can be shaped into blocks that builders can bind to each other using mortar. Marble is another form of calcium carbonate used as a building material, for example to make expensive tiles.

Figure 11.1: A military plane releasing its decoy flares to protect itself from missile attack.

CONTINUED

However, most calcium carbonate is used to make cement. The first stage in the manufacture of cement is the roasting of limestone in a lime kiln (see Figure 11.2).

At the high temperatures in the kiln, calcium carbonate decomposes to form calcium oxide (also called lime or quicklime):

$$CaCO_3(s) \xrightarrow{\text{heat}} \underset{\text{lime}}{CaO(s)} + CO_2(g)$$

The calcium oxide made in the lime kiln is roasted with clay to make cement. Cement can be mixed with sand and small pieces of rock to make concrete, the most widely used building material in the world. Builders improve its strength by including iron rods, which run through the concrete.

Farmers use slaked lime (calcium hydroxide, $Ca(OH)_2$) to raise the pH of acidic soil. Calcium hydroxide is basic, so it will react with and neutralise acid, raising the pH of the soil.

Questions for discussion

1   Limestone rock is mined from huge quarries before being taken to lime kilns to be roasted. In a small group, discuss some environmental impacts of using the world's most common building material, concrete.

Figure 11.2: In a rotating lime kiln, calcium carbonate undergoes thermal decomposition to form calcium oxide and carbon dioxide.

2   When lightning strikes during a thunderstorm, the rain that falls is a dilute solution of nitric acid (HNO_3). Work with a partner to write a balanced chemical equation, including state symbols, to show how slaked lime (calcium hydroxide) added to soil can neutralise nitric acid.

3   Justify which is the more important use of a Group 2 compound: making concrete or raising the pH of soil.

11.1 Physical properties of Group 2 elements

We sometimes refer to the elements in Group 2 of the Periodic Table as the **alkaline earth metals**. As the elements are in Group 2, they have atoms whose electronic configurations end with two electrons in their outermost principal quantum shell. These two outer electrons occupy an s sub-shell.

KEY WORD

alkaline earth metals: elements in Group 2 of the Periodic Table.

Here are the electronic configurations of the first five elements in Group 2:

Beryllium (Be)	$1s^2 2s^2$
Magnesium (Mg)	$1s^2 2s^2 2p^6 3s^2$
Calcium (Ca)	$1s^2 2s^2 2p^6 3s^2 3p^6 4s^2$
Strontium (Sr)	$1s^2 2s^2 2p^6 3s^2 3p^6 3d^{10} 4s^2 4p^6 5s^2$
Barium (Ba)	$1s^2 2s^2 2p^6 3s^2 3p^6 3d^{10} 4s^2 4p^6$ $4d^{10} 5s^2 5p^6 6s^2$

One way of describing the size of an atom is its metallic radius. The metallic radius is half the distance between the nuclei in a giant metallic lattice (Figure 11.3). See Section 10.2 for other measures that describe the size of atoms.

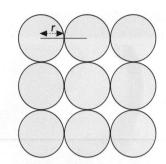

Figure 11.3: The metallic radius gives us a measure of the size of the atoms of metallic elements.

Look at the metallic radii of the Group 2 elements measured in nanometres, shown in Table 11.1.

Group 2 element	Metallic radius / nm
beryllium (Be)	0.122
magnesium (Mg)	0.160
calcium (Ca)	0.197
strontium (Sr)	0.215
barium (Ba)	0.217

Table 11.1: The metallic radii of the Group 2 elements. (1 nm = 1 × 10⁻⁹ m).

Can you see the trend? The atoms of Group 2 elements get larger going down the group. This is because the outer two electrons occupy a new principal quantum shell that is further away from the nucleus.

There are also general trends in other physical properties, such as melting point and density, shown in Table 11.2 and displayed in Figures 11.4 and 11.5.

Group 2 element	Atomic number	Melting point / °C	Density / g cm⁻³
beryllium (Be)	4	1280	1.85
magnesium (Mg)	12	650	1.74
calcium (Ca)	20	838	1.55
strontium (Sr)	38	768	2.6
barium (Ba)	56	714	3.5

Table 11.2: The melting points and densities of the Group 2 elements.

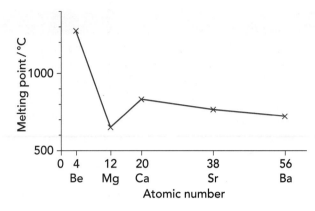

Figure 11.4: Melting points of the Group 2 elements.

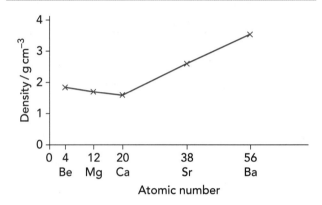

Figure 11.5: Densities of the Group 2 elements.

Question

1   a   Look at Figure 11.4.

Give the *general* trend in the melting points going down Group 2.

Which element breaks the trend?

   b   Explain why the atoms in Group 2, as in any other group, get larger with increasing atomic number.

   c   i   State the charge you would expect the ions of Group 2 elements to carry.

   ii   Predict whether their ions will be larger or smaller than their atoms.

   iii   Compare your answers to parts **i** and **ii** with another student's answers. Then discuss and explain your ideas together.

   d   Radium (Ra) is a radioactive element found below barium at the bottom of Group 2. Working with a partner, apply your knowledge of trends in Group 2 to discuss and predict:

   i   its melting point

   ii   its density

   iii   its metallic radius.

11.2 Reactions of Group 2 elements

The Group 2 metals form ionic compounds. When they react, their atoms lose the two electrons from their outermost s sub-shell and form an ion with the stable electronic configuration of a noble gas. This creates a 2+ ion. For example, in the ionisation of a magnesium atom to a magnesium ion:

$$Mg \rightarrow Mg^{2+} + 2e^-$$

oxidation number   0   +2

The metals act as reducing agents. Their atoms donate (give away) electrons and so they are oxidised themselves as they react to form their 2+ ions. The ionisation energies shown in Table 11.3 show how easily the two outer electrons are removed from the Group 2 atoms.

Group 2 element	First ionisation energy / kJ mol^{-1}	Second ionisation energy / kJ mol^{-1}
beryllium (Be)	900	1760
magnesium (Mg)	736	1450
calcium (Ca)	590	1150
strontium (Sr)	548	1060
barium (Ba)	502	966

Table 11.3: The first and second ionisation energies of the Group 2 elements.

The metals in Group 2 get more reactive as we go down the group. As you can see from Table 11.3, it takes less energy (i.e. it gets easier) to remove the pair of outer electrons going down Group 2. So, although the positive charge on the nucleus increases down the group:

- the greater shielding effect provided by extra inner shells of electrons, and
- the larger distance of the outermost electrons from the nucleus
  outweigh the attraction of the higher nuclear charge.

This helps to explain the increase in reactivity going down the group, as it gets easier for the atoms to form their 2+ ions.

This trend is shown by looking at reactions of the Group 2 metals, magnesium to barium, with dilute hydrochloric acid. The metals react with dilute hydrochloric acid, forming a solution of the metal chloride and giving off hydrogen gas.

For example:

$$Mg(s) + 2HCl(aq) \rightarrow MgCl_2(aq) + H_2(g)$$
$$Ca(s) + 2HCl(aq) \rightarrow CaCl_2(aq) + H_2(g)$$

The reactions get more vigorous descending the group. You can see this by the increasing rate at which bubbles of hydrogen gas are given off.

Magnesium reacts in a similar way with dilute sulfuric acid:

$$Mg(s) + H_2SO_4(aq) \rightarrow MgSO_4(aq) + H_2(g)$$

However, any reaction with calcium, strontium or barium is quickly stopped by the formation of an insoluble sulfate layer on the surface of the metals. For example, you can see a slow stream of hydrogen bubbles for a short time when a pellet (small piece) of calcium metal is dropped into dilute sulfuric acid:

$$Ca(s) + H_2SO_4(aq) \rightarrow CaSO_4(s) + H_2(g)$$

The calcium gets then gets completely covered by a layer sparingly soluble calcium sulfate and the bubbles of hydrogen stop rising from the metal.

Strontium sulfate and barium sulfate are even less soluble than calcium sulfate so will quickly stop any reaction with the metals strontium and barium.

Question

2 **a** **i** Which one of the following electronic configurations correctly describes a calcium ion?

   A $1s^2\,2s^2\,2p^6\,3s^2$

   B $1s^2\,2s^2\,2p^6\,3s^2\,3p^6$

   C $1s^2\,2s^2\,2p^6\,3s^2\,3p^6\,4s^2$

   D $1s^2\,2s^2\,2p^6\,3s^2\,3p^6\,4s^1$

   ii Write a half equation to show the conversion of a calcium atom into a calcium ion.

   iii How does the oxidation number of calcium change in part **ii**? Explain whether the calcium has been oxidised or reduced in this change.

b Add up the first two ionisation energies of the Group 2 elements shown in Table 11.3, and record your results in a table.

c Draw a sketch graph to show the 'sum of the first two ionisation energies' against atomic number for the Group 2 elements beryllium to barium.

d Discuss the trend shown on your graph and how this might affect the reactivity of the Group 2 elements.

11.3 Reactions with oxygen

The Group 2 metals burn in air, and burn more rapidly in oxygen gas. The metals form white solid oxides. For example, magnesium ribbon burns with a bright white flame once it is ignited in a Bunsen flame (Figure 11.6):

$$2Mg(s) + O_2(g) \rightarrow 2MgO(s)$$

The magnesium oxide formed is basic in character, as shown in Section 10.5.

The Group 2 metals get more reactive with oxygen going down the group. The larger atoms lose their outer two electrons more readily than the smaller atoms in the group. The reasons for this are given below Table 11.3.

Figure 11.6: Magnesium ribbon reacting with oxygen in the air.

Barium metal is so highly reactive that it must be stored under oil to keep it out of contact with air.

Some of the Group 2 metals burn with characteristic flame colours. In the heat of the Bunsen burner flame, the metal atoms are oxidised, losing two electrons, and forming their positive ions. The oxidation number of the metal atoms (0) increases to the +2 state in the process. It is the 2+ ions formed in the reaction that cause the characteristic colours you can see in the Bunsen burner flame.

Flame tests

We can test for calcium, strontium and barium ions in compounds using flame tests (Figure 11.7). A nichrome wire, cleaned with concentrated hydrochloric acid, is dipped into a sample of the salt to be tested and heated in a non-luminous Bunsen flame:

- calcium compounds give a brick-red colour

- strontium compounds give a scarlet/red colour

- barium compounds give an apple-green colour.

Figure 11.7: The flame colours of calcium, strontium and barium.

Reactions of oxides with dilute acid

The basic oxides of the Group 2 metals can be neutralised by dilute acid. The general equation for the reaction of a basic oxide is:

basic oxide + dilute acid → a salt + water

For example:

$MgO(s) + 2HCl(aq) \rightarrow MgCl_2(aq) + H_2O(l)$

The white magnesium oxide powder dissolves, forming a colourless solution of magnesium chloride, as it reacts with the dilute acid. The oxides of calcium (CaO), strontium (SrO) and barium (BaO) are also neutralised by dilute hydrochloric acid.

A similar reaction occurs when excess dilute sulfuric acid is added to the Group 2 oxides, but a sulfate solution is formed:

$MgO(s) + H_2SO_4(aq) \rightarrow MgSO_4(aq) + H_2O(l)$

With dilute sulfuric acid, the decreasing solubility of the sulfate formed going down the group will also affect the neutralisation reaction with dilute sulfuric acid. The insoluble sulfates will form at the surface of the oxides, protecting any solid oxide beneath. However, when the oxide is in the form of a powder and stirred, significant neutralisation can occur.

11.4 Reactions with water

We have seen in Section 10.3 how magnesium reacts very slowly with cold water (Figure 11.8). However, if left long enough, the reaction will eventually form a weakly alkaline solution, and give off enough hydrogen to test:

$Mg(s) + 2H_2O(l) \rightarrow Mg(OH)_2(aq) + H_2(g)$

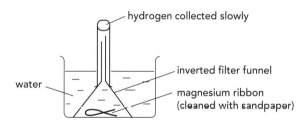

Figure 11.8: Cleaned with sandpaper, magnesium ribbon reacts very, very slowly with water at room temperature.

Hot magnesium does react vigorously with water in the form of steam. The magnesium and steam produce magnesium oxide (a white solid) and hydrogen gas (see Figure 11.9):

$Mg(s) + H_2O(g) \rightarrow MgO(s) + H_2(g)$

Calcium reacts more readily than magnesium with water at room temperature:

$Ca(s) + 2H_2O(l) \rightarrow Ca(OH)_2(aq) + H_2(g)$

This reaction gives off a steady stream of hydrogen gas and forms a cloudy white suspension of slightly soluble calcium hydroxide. The calcium hydroxide that does dissolve forms a solution that we call 'limewater', which makes the solution weakly alkaline.

Going down the group, hydrogen gas is released more and more rapidly by the reaction of the Group 2 metal with water (see Figure 11.10).

Figure 11.9: An experiment showing magnesium reacting with steam. The steam is given off from mineral wool soaked in water at the right-hand end of the test-tube. The white magnesium oxide formed is visible inside the test-tube. The hydrogen gas produced in the reaction has been ignited at the end of the straight tube.

Reactions of Group 2 oxides and water

Magnesium oxide is only slightly soluble in water, and forms a weakly alkaline solution of magnesium hydroxide. A saturated solution of magnesium hydroxide will have a pH value of about 10:

$$MgO(s) + H_2O(l) \rightarrow Mg(OH)_2(aq)$$

Calcium oxide, CaO, reacts with water to form calcium hydroxide. When water is dripped onto the surface of a lump of calcium oxide it causes a vigorous reaction. It releases so much energy that some of the water boils off as the solid lump appears to expand, and cracks open:

$$CaO(s) + H_2O(l) \rightarrow Ca(OH)_2(s)$$

Figure 11.10: Barium reacting vigorously with water, forming alkaline barium hydroxide solution and giving off hydrogen gas.

In excess water, some of the slightly soluble calcium hydroxide dissolves to form a weakly alkaline solution, with a slightly higher pH than magnesium hydroxide. The higher concentration of aqueous hydroxide ions in a saturated solution of calcium hydroxide solution result in its pH of about 11:

$$Ca(OH)_2(s) \xrightarrow{\text{water}} Ca^{2+}(aq) + 2OH^-(aq)$$

In general, the reaction and dissolving of the Group 2 metal oxides in water is described by the following ionic equation:

$$O^{2-}(s) + H_2O(l) \rightarrow 2OH^-(aq)$$

> **IMPORTANT**
>
> The solutions formed from the reactions of the Group 2 metal oxides with water get more alkaline going down the group.

We can explain this increase in alkalinity by looking at the solubility of the Group 2 hydroxides formed (see Table 11.4).

Group 2 hydroxide, general formula $X(OH)_2$	Solubility of hydroxide at 298 K (mol / 100 g of water)
magnesium hydroxide, $Mg(OH)_2$	2.0×10^{-5}
calcium hydroxide, $Ca(OH)_2$	1.5×10^{-3}
strontium hydroxide, $Sr(OH)_2$	3.4×10^{-3}
barium hydroxide, $Ba(OH)_2$	1.5×10^{-2}

Table 11.4: Solubility of the Group 2 hydroxides in water.

IMPORTANT

The solubility of the Group 2 hydroxides increases going down Group 2.

Therefore, when adding and stirring magnesium hydroxide in water to make a saturated solution, then doing the same with barium hydroxide, there will be a higher concentration of hydroxide ions in the saturated barium hydroxide solution. This higher concentration of hydroxide ions results in a higher pH value for the barium hydroxide solution.

KEY WORD

saturated solution: a solution which can dissolve no more solute at a particular temperature (in the presence of undissolved solute).

Reactions of hydroxides with dilute acid

The alkaline hydroxides of the Group 2 metals will all be neutralised by dilute acid:

hydroxide + dilute acid → a salt + water

For example, with magnesium hydroxide powder and dilute hydrochloric acid or sulfuric acid:

$$Mg(OH)_2(s) + 2HCl(aq) \rightarrow MgCl_2(aq) + 2H_2O(l)$$

$$Mg(OH)_2(s) + H_2SO_4(aq) \rightarrow MgSO_4(aq) + 2H_2O(l)$$

or with barium hydroxide solution:

$$Ba(OH)_2(aq) + 2HCl(aq) \rightarrow BaCl_2(aq) + 2H_2O(l)$$

$$Ba(OH)_2(aq) + H_2SO_4(aq) \rightarrow BaSO_4(s) + 2H_2O(l)$$

The barium sulfate forms as a white precipitate, unlike the soluble barium chloride (a colourless solution).

Question

3   a   Write balanced chemical equations, including state symbols, for the reaction of:

  i   strontium with oxygen

  ii   strontium oxide with water.

  b   i   Write a balanced chemical equation, including state symbols, for the reaction of barium with water.

  ii   Predict the pH of the solution formed in part **b i**.

  c   Radium (Ra) is a radioactive element found below barium at the bottom of Group 2.

  Applying your knowledge of Group 2, discuss and predict with a partner:

  i   the formula of the ion formed by radium

  ii   the formulae of its oxide and hydroxide

  iii   its first ionisation energy

  iv   its reactivity compared with barium

  v   the relative pH of its saturated hydroxide solution compared with a saturated solution of calcium hydroxide

  vi   the solubility of its sulfate compared with strontium sulfate

  vii   the equation for the reaction of its solid oxide with dilute hydrochloric acid

  viii   what you would expect to see if you mixed radium hydroxide solution with dilute sulfuric acid.

  d   Using Table 11.4 and the relative atomic mass data (from the Periodic Table at the back of this book), calculate the mass of calcium hydroxide that will dissolve in 50 g of water at 298 K. Write down each step in your working out. Then join another student to explain your answers to each other and discuss who has the better answer.

Reactions of Group 2 carbonates

The Group 2 carbonates have the general formula XCO_3. The carbonates of magnesium, calcium, strontium and barium are all *insoluble in water*.

However, the carbonates all react in dilute acid, forming a salt and water and giving off carbon dioxide gas. For example, with dilute sulfuric acid:

$$MgCO_3(s) + H_2SO_4(aq) \rightarrow MgSO_4(aq) + H_2O(l) + CO_2(g)$$

The magnesium sulfate salt formed in the reaction above is soluble in water. This remains in aqueous solution, and no solid carbonate will remain in excess dilute sulfuric acid.

However, the sulfates of the other Group 2 elements are much less soluble than magnesium sulfate. Remember the decreasing trend in the solubility of the sulfates described in Section 11.2. So the sulfates of calcium, strontium and barium tend to form as an insoluble sulfate layer on their solid carbonates. This stops any further reaction after the initial effervescence (bubbling) of carbon dioxide gas is seen.

For example:

$$BaCO_3(s) + H_2SO_4(aq) \rightarrow BaSO_4(s) + H_2O(l) + CO_2(g)$$

The reactions of the Group 2 carbonates with dilute hydrochloric acid will all form soluble chloride salts, water and carbon dioxide gas.

For example:

$$BaCO_3(s) + 2HCl(aq) \rightarrow BaCl_2(aq) + H_2O(l) + CO_2(g)$$

Thermal decomposition of Group 2 carbonates and nitrates

The carbonates and nitrates of the Group 2 elements decompose when heated. The carbonates break down to form the metal oxide and give off carbon dioxide gas. For example:

$$MgCO_3(s) \xrightarrow{\text{heat}} MgO(s) + CO_2(g)$$

The temperature at which thermal decomposition of the Group 2 carbonates takes place *increases* going down Group 2.

The Group 2 nitrates also undergo **thermal decomposition**.

KEY WORD

thermal decomposition: the breakdown of a compound by heat into two or more different substances.

For example:

$$2Ca(NO_3)_2(s) \xrightarrow{\text{heat}} 2CaO(s) + 4NO_2(g) + O_2(g)$$

A brown gas is observed when a Group 2 nitrate is heated. This is toxic nitrogen dioxide, NO_2 (nitrogen(IV) oxide).

IMPORTANT

As with the carbonates, a higher temperature is needed to thermally decompose the nitrates as Group 2 is descended.

You can read an explanation of the trend in the thermal stability of the Group 2 carbonates and nitrates in Section 19.3.

Questions

4 a i Write the chemical formula of magnesium carbonate.

ii Discuss with a partner why the formula of magnesium carbonate is *not* Mg_2CO_3.

b Write a balanced symbol equation for the reaction of barium carbonate with dilute nitric acid.

c Which one of the three compounds listed will decompose at the lowest temperature?

i A calcium carbonate

B strontium carbonate

C barium carbonate

ii A barium nitrate

B calcium nitrate

C magnesium nitrate

d Write balanced chemical equations, including state symbols, for the thermal decomposition of:

i strontium carbonate

ii barium nitrate.

REFLECTION

Reflect on which parts of this chapter you found easiest to understand.

1 Work with another learner to discuss these points:

a Write word and symbol equations for the reactions of either magnesium, calcium, strontium or barium with:

i oxygen

ii water

iii dilute hydrochloric acid.

b Now try the equations for the oxide, hydroxides and carbonates of a Group 2 element of your choice with water and with dilute sulfuric acid.

c Make a list of the key words in this chapter so far and explain their meaning to another learner.

2 Work with another learner to discuss ways of remembering the trends descending Group 2 in **a** to **d** below. This could even be an illustration, based on stairs or ladders, or a role-play, acting out the rising and falling trends.

a the reactivity of the Group 2 elements

b the solubility of their hydroxides

c the solubility of their sulfates

d the thermal stability of their carbonates and nitrates.

3 Think back to the start of your work on the Group 2 elements and their compounds. Discuss the skills you needed to use, including practical skills, with a partner.

4 Which skills did you enjoy practising most?

SUMMARY

Going down Group 2 from magnesium to barium, the atomic radius increases. This is due to the addition of an extra principal quantum shell of electrons for the atoms of each element as the group is descended.

The Group 2 elements, magnesium to barium, react with water to produce hydrogen gas and the metal hydroxide, which may be only slightly soluble.

The Group 2 elements, magnesium to barium, burn in air to form white solid oxides. These oxides form hydroxides with water. The hydroxides get more soluble in water going down the group so their solutions can become more alkaline.

The sulfates of Group 2 elements get less soluble in water going down the group.

Reactivity of the elements with oxygen or water increases going down Group 2, as the first and second ionisation energies decrease. Therefore it becomes easier to remove electrons from the atoms descending Group 2.

The Group 2 carbonates and nitrates get more resistant to thermal decomposition descending the group.

EXAM-STYLE QUESTIONS

You will need a copy of the Periodic Table (see Appendix 1) to answer some of these questions.

1   Which row of the table is correct, A, B, C or D?   [1]

Row	Trend in reactivity of elements going down Group 2	Trend in solubility of sulfates going down Group 2	Trend in solubility of hydroxides going down Group 2
A	increases	decreases	increases
B	decreases	decreases	increases
C	increases	increases	decreases
D	decreases	increases	decreases

2   Beryllium and radium are both in Group 2.

   a   Write the electronic configuration of beryllium.   [2]

   b   Give the equations for the reactions of beryllium and radium with oxygen.   [4]

   c   Using dot-and-cross diagrams, and showing the outer electrons only, draw the electronic configurations of beryllium and oxygen before and after bonding.   [5]

   d   Draw a diagram to show the metallic bonding in both beryllium and radium.   [3]

   e   Using your diagram, explain why beryllium has a higher melting point than radium.   [4]

[Total: 18]

CONTINUED

3 a Limewater is a solution of calcium hydroxide.

    i Give the formula of calcium hydroxide. [1]

    ii Explain why calcium hydroxide is used in agriculture. [2]

  b Exactly 0.1 moles of each of calcium hydroxide and barium hydroxide are added to separate beakers containing 100 cm³ of water and stirred to form saturated solutions.

    Explain which solution has the higher pH value. [2]

                         [Total: 5]

4 For the following reactions, state which elements are oxidised and which are reduced, and give the changes in oxidation number.

  a $Sr + Cl_2 \rightarrow SrCl_2$ [3]

  b $Sr + 2H_2O \rightarrow Sr(OH)_2 + H_2$ [3]

  c $2Mg + CO_2 \rightarrow 2MgO + C$ [3]

                         [Total: 9]

SELF-EVALUATION

After studying this chapter, complete a table like this:

I can	See section...	Needs more work	Almost there	Ready to move on
describe, and write equations for, the reactions of the Group 2 elements with oxygen, water and dilute acids	11.2, 11.3, 11.4			
describe, and write equations for, the reactions of the Group 2 oxides, hydroxides and carbonates with water and with dilute acids	11.3, 11.4			
describe, and write equations for, the thermal decomposition of the Group 2 nitrates and carbonates	11.4			
describe, and make predictions from, the trends in properties of the Group 2 elements and their compounds that are covered in this chapter	11.1			
state the variation in the solubilities of the Group 2 hydroxides and sulfates.	11.2, 11.3			

Chapter 12

Group 17

LEARNING INTENTIONS

In this chapter you will learn how to:

- describe the colours of, and explain the trend in volatility of, the Group 17 elements chlorine, bromine and iodine

- describe and explain:

  - the relative reactivity of these Group 17 elements as oxidising agents (and the halide ions as reducing agents)

  - the reactions of the elements with hydrogen

  - the relative thermal stabilities of the hydrides (in terms of bond strengths)

- describe and explain the reactions of halide ions with:

  - aqueous silver ions, followed by adding aqueous ammonia

  - concentrated sulfuric acid

- describe and interpret the disproportionation reactions of chlorine with cold, and with hot, aqueous sodium hydroxide

- explain the use of chlorine in water purification.

BEFORE YOU START

Working in a small group:

1 Write down the electronic configuration of a bromine atom.

2 The oxidation number of chlorine can vary. Give its oxidation number in the following compounds:

  a NaCl

  b NaClO

3 Explain which element is oxidised and which is reduced in this reaction:

  $2Fe(s) + 3Cl_2(g) \rightarrow 2FeCl_3(s)$

4 a Draw a dot-and-cross diagram to show the covalent bonding in a chlorine molecule, Cl_2. Only include outer shell electrons.

  b Discuss with a partner what we mean by 'bond energy'. Compare your answer with another pair of learners and write an agreed definition of the term *bond energy*.

  c State the unit that bond energies are expressed in.

USES OF THE HALOGENS AND THEIR COMPOUNDS

People have not always used the halogens and their compounds to benefit society. For example, chlorine was used as the first chemical weapon in the First World War (1914–18). Its compounds can also be used in biological nerve gases, though this use is banned by international agreement.

However, scientists can use chlorine to kill bacteria in drinking water (Figure 12.1). This saves millions of lives around the world. It has greatly reduced the number of cases of cholera, but about 25 000 people still die world-wide every day from diseases spread in water.

Many pesticides containing halogen atoms have reduced deaths caused by disease-carrying insects. Malaria is the main disease. These pesticides also reduce the loss of crops in storage. However, these halogen compounds can have bad effects on other wildlife in the food chain.

Halogen compounds have also damaged the Earth's ozone layer. This thin layer of gas in the upper atmosphere absorbs harmful ultra-violet rays from the Sun. The halogen compounds called CFCs (chlorofluorocarbons) are very unreactive and people once thought they were completely harmless to living things. So CFCs were used in aerosols and as coolants in fridges.

Figure 12.1: Chlorine may be added to drinking water to kill harmful microorganisms.

Then, scientists in the 1980s discovered a hole in our protective ozone layer caused by CFCs reacting with ozone: and the hole was growing. This meant that people would have a greater risk of getting skin cancer and eye cataracts. Because of this, CFCs are now banned, as are other halogen compounds that

CONTINUED

were used in fire extinguishers, flame-proofing and solvents. Scientists are now using new compounds instead of CFCs. There is evidence that the hole in the ozone layer is gradually getting smaller. You can find out more detail on the environmental effect of CFCs at the start of Chapter 16.

Question for discussion

Discuss with another learner or group of learners:

- Do you believe that the uses of halogens and their compounds have had a positive or negative effect on the world, overall?

12.1 Physical properties of Group 17 elements

KEY WORD

halogens: the Group 17 elements.

In this chapter we are looking at the elements in Group 17 of the Periodic Table. These are called the **halogens**. Their atoms all have seven electrons in the outer principal quantum shell.

Here are the electronic configurations of the first four elements in Group 17:

fluorine (F)	$1s^2\,2s^2\,2p^5$
chlorine (Cl)	$1s^2\,2s^2\,2p^6\,3s^2\,3p^5$
bromine (Br)	$1s^2\,2s^2\,2p^6\,3s^2\,3p^6\,3d^{10}\,4s^2\,4p^5$
iodine (I)	$1s^2\,2s^2\,2p^6\,3s^2\,3p^6\,3d^{10}\,4s^2\,4p^6\,4d^{10}\,5s^2\,5p^5$

The Group 17 elements are all non-metals. At room temperature, they exist as diatomic molecules, i.e. molecules made up of two atoms, F_2, Cl_2, Br_2 and I_2. There is a single covalent bond between the two atoms in each molecule. You can see the elements chlorine, bromine and iodine in Figure 12.2.

Figure 12.2: Three of the Group 17 elements, known as the halogens. Notice that the colour of the elements gets darker going down the group.

Table 12.1 shows some of the physical properties of the halogens.

Looking at Table 12.1, you can see that the melting points and boiling points of the halogens *increase* going down the group. The boiling point data gives us an idea of the **volatility** of the halogens, i.e. the ease with which they evaporate. All the values are relatively low because they have simple molecular structures. There are only weak van der Waals' forces between their diatomic molecules, caused by instantaneous dipole–induced

Group 17 element	Atomic radius / nm	Melting point / °C	Boiling point / °C	Colour
fluorine (F_2)	0.072	−220	−188	pale yellow
chlorine (Cl_2)	0.099	−101	−35	green / yellow
bromine (Br_2)	0.114	−7	59	orange / brown
iodine (I_2)	0.133	114	184	grey / black solid, purple vapour

Table 12.1: Some physical properties of the Group 17 elements. The atomic radius value is taken from single covalent data (see Section 4.3).

dipole forces. These forces increase as the number of electrons in the molecules increases with increasing atomic number. The greater the number of electrons, the greater the opportunities for instantaneous dipoles arising within molecules, and for induced dipoles to be produced on neighbouring molecules. The larger the molecules, the stronger the van der Waals' forces between molecules. This makes iodine the least volatile and fluorine the most volatile of the halogens you are learning about.

KEY WORD

volatility: the ease with which a substance evaporates. A volatile substance will evaporate at a low temperature.

You can also see that the colours of the halogens get darker going down the group.

Question

1   a   Describe the trend in volatility you see going down Group 17.

   b   Using Table 12.1, deduce the state of each halogen at 20 °C.

   c   What is the trend in the atomic radii of the halogens? Explain this trend.

   d   Astatine (At) lies below iodine at the bottom of Group 17. Discuss with a partner, and then predict astatine's:

      i   state at 20 °C

      ii   colour

      iii atomic radius.

12.2 Reactions of Group 17 elements

The halogen atoms need to gain just one more electron to achieve the stable electronic configuration of the noble gas atoms to the right of them in the Periodic Table. Therefore, halogens react with metallic elements, with each of their atoms gaining one electron from atoms of the metal, to become ions with a 1− charge.

For example:

$$Ca(s) + Cl_2(g) \rightarrow Ca^{2+}(Cl^-)_2(s)$$

When a halogen reacts with a metal atom, the halogen atom gains one electron. Because of this, the halogen elements are oxidising agents (electron acceptors). In the process of oxidising another substance, the elements themselves are reduced. Their oxidation number is reduced from 0 in the element to −1 in the compound formed.

$$Cl_2 \rightarrow 2Cl^- + 2e^-$$

oxidation number   0   −1

The halogens also react with many non-metals. Each halogen atom shares a pair of electrons with the other non-metal atom in a covalent bond, e.g. in hydrogen chloride, HCl.

$$H_2(g) + Cl_2(g) \rightarrow 2HCl(g)$$

We can repeat the reactions of chlorine with calcium and with hydrogen (shown here) with the other halogens. In these experiments we find that the reactions of fluorine are more **vigorous** than those of chlorine. Bromine reacts less vigorously than chlorine, and iodine is less reactive than bromine.

IMPORTANT

The halogens get less reactive going down Group 17.

KEY WORD

vigorous: a reaction that has a rapid rate of reaction.

Electronegativity is the ability of a covalently bonded atom to attract the bonding pair of electrons towards itself (see Section 4.7). This pattern in reactivity corresponds to the trend in electronegativity going down the group, shown in Table 12.2.

A fluorine atom has the strongest pull on the pair of electrons in a covalent bond, while an iodine atom has the weakest attraction for electrons. We can explain this by looking at the atomic radii data in Table 12.1. The fluorine

Halogen	Electronegativity
fluorine (F)	4.0
chlorine (Cl)	3.0
bromine (Br)	2.8
iodine (I)	2.5

Table 12.2: Electronegativity values of the halogens.

atom is the smallest in the group. Its outer shell is nearer to the attractive force of the nucleus and an electron entering its outer shell will also experience the least shielding from the attraction of the positive nuclear charge.

These factors outweigh the fact that fluorine's nuclear charge is only 9+ compared with iodine's 53+. Therefore, fluorine is a much stronger oxidising agent (acceptor of electrons) than iodine.

Question

2 a In a small group, discuss in detail why chlorine is more reactive than bromine.

b Design and produce a poster to illustrate your answer to part **a** to the rest of the class.

Evidence for the oxidising power of the halogens

We can also judge the relative reactivity (or the oxidising power) of the halogens by looking at their displacement reactions with other halide ions in solution.

> **IMPORTANT**
>
> A more reactive halogen can displace a less reactive halogen from a halide solution of the less reactive halogen.

Let's look at an example. When chlorine water, $Cl_2(aq)$, is added to a solution of sodium bromide containing $Br^-(aq)$ ions, the solution changes to a yellowish-brown colour. The colour is caused by the presence of dissolved bromine molecules, $Br_2(aq)$, as found in bromine water. The displacement reaction that takes place is:

$$Cl_2(aq) + 2NaBr(aq) \rightarrow 2NaCl(aq) + Br_2(aq)$$

We say that chlorine has displaced bromine from solution.

This is summarised in the ionic equation for this displacement reaction:

$$Cl_2(aq) + 2Br^-(aq) \rightarrow 2Cl^-(aq) + Br_2(aq)$$

The chlorine atoms are more electronegative than bromine atoms so are more likely (have a stronger tendency) to form negatively charged ions.

Likewise, bromine will displace iodine from an iodide solution:

$$Br_2(aq) + 2NaI(aq) \rightarrow 2NaBr(aq) + I_2(aq)$$

or as an ionic equation:

$$Br_2(aq) + 2I^-(aq) \rightarrow 2Br^-(aq) + I_2(aq)$$

> **IMPORTANT**
>
> These displacement reactions show that the oxidising power of the halogens (their ability to gain electrons) *decreases* going down Group 17.

The colours of the halogen molecules in solution are difficult to identify positively in these displacement experiments. However, the halogens (Cl_2, Br_2 and I_2) dissolve well in the colourless liquid, cyclohexane (which is **immiscible** in water, forming two separate layers). The halogens dissolved in cyclohexane are clearly different colours.

Therefore, you can add some of this organic solvent after mixing the halogen / halide solutions, shaking the mixture. Then allow the reaction mixture to settle into two layers, showing clearly which halogen is present as its diatomic molecules (see Figure 12.3).

> **KEY WORD**
>
> **immiscible:** two liquids that do not dissolve in each other and so form two separate layers, such as oil and water or cyclohexane and water.

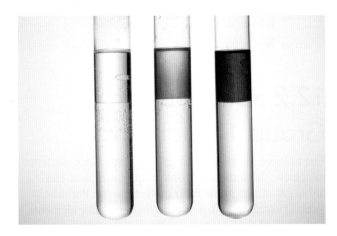

Figure 12.3: Cyclohexane forms a layer on top of water. Dissolved chlorine is very pale green in this upper organic layer, bromine is orange and iodine is purple.

Question

3 Chlorine water is mixed with a solution of potassium iodide in a test-tube, 2 cm³ of cyclohexane is added to the test-tube, which is stoppered and shaken, then allowed to stand.

a Write a balanced symbol equation, including state symbols, for the reaction that occurs.

b Write an ionic equation for this reaction.

c What colour is the cyclohexane layer at the end of the experiment?

REFLECTION

1   Reflect on your work looking at the displacement reactions of the halogens and their halide solutions.

2   Discuss with a partner to decide how confident you are at constructing ionic equations, as in part **b** in Question 3 above.

3   Can you draw conclusions from your observations of the experiments?

4   Now reflect on what you have discussed above and write a series of steps for constructing ionic equations.

Reactions of halogens with hydrogen

The halogens form hydrogen halides when combined with hydrogen gas.

One example of this is the reaction of hydrogen with chlorine to give hydrogen chloride gas. The trend in reactivity is illustrated by their reactions in Table 12.3.

Equation for reaction	Description of reaction
$H_2(g) + F_2(g) \rightarrow 2HF(g)$	reacts explosively even in cool, dark conditions
$H_2(g) + Cl_2(g) \rightarrow 2HCl(g)$	reacts explosively in sunlight
$H_2(g) + Br_2(g) \rightarrow 2HBr(g)$	reacts slowly on heating
$H_2(g) + I_2(g) \rightleftharpoons 2HI(g)$	forms an equilibrium mixture on heating

Table 12.3: The reactions of hydrogen and the halogens, showing decreasing reactivity going down Group 17.

KEY WORD

thermal stability: the resistance of a compound to breakdown by heating.

The hydrogen halides formed differ in their **thermal stability**. Hydrogen iodide can be decomposed by inserting a red-hot wire into a sample of hydrogen iodide gas. The purple fumes seen are iodine vapour:

$$2HI(g) \rightarrow H_2(g) + I_2(g)$$

By contrast, hydrogen fluoride and hydrogen chloride are not decomposed in temperatures up to 1500 °C.

Hydrogen bromide is not as stable as HF and HCl, but it is more resistant to decomposition than hydrogen iodide. At 430 °C in a closed container, 10% of a sample of HBr will decompose, whereas around 20% of HI decomposes at that temperature.

IMPORTANT

The hydrogen halides get less thermally stable going down Group 17.

most thermally stable HF

HCl

HBr

least thermally stable HI

We can explain this trend by looking at the bond strengths as shown by bond energies in Table 12.4.

Hydrogen–halogen bond	Bond energy / kJ mol⁻¹
H—F	562
H—Cl	431
H—Br	366
H—I	299

Table 12.4: Hydrogen–halogen bond energies.

As you can see in Table 12.4, the bond energies decrease going down Group 17, making it easier to break the hydrogen–halogen bond. This is because the iodine atom is the largest atom. The overlap of its outer shell with a hydrogen atom gives a much longer bond length than with the other smaller halogen atoms. The longer the bond, the weaker it is, and the less energy required to break it. For this reason, HI is less thermally stable than HF.

Question

4 **a** Astatine (At) lies below iodine at the bottom of Group 17.

Discuss and predict:

i the equation for its reaction with hydrogen

ii the vigour of its reaction with hydrogen

iii the thermal stability of its hydride.

b Explain why chlorine is a more powerful oxidising agent than bromine.

c Working with a partner, design a picture with labels to illustrate your answer to part **b**. If possible, you could make this into a PowerPoint slide to share your ideas with the rest of the class.

12.3 Reactions of the halide ions

In this section, we consider the reactions of the negatively charged halide ions formed by the halogens.

PRACTICAL ACTIVITY 12.1

Testing for halide ions

We can identify the halide ions, $Cl^-(aq)$, $Br^-(aq)$ and $I^-(aq)$, by using simple chemical tests. If an unknown compound is dissolved in dilute nitric acid and silver nitrate solution is added, a precipitate will form if the unknown solution contains halide ions. The precipitate will be silver chloride (AgCl), silver bromide (AgBr) or silver iodide (AgI) (see Figure 12.4).

These precipitates are similar in colour. We can then use a further test to help us distinguish one precipitate from another. We can add ammonia solution – dilute ammonia solution followed by concentrated ammonia solution – to verify the result. The results of the tests are shown in Table 12.5.

The general equation for the precipitation reaction with silver nitrate solution is:

$$AgNO_3(aq) + X^-(aq) \rightarrow AgX(s) + NO_3^-(aq)$$

where X^- represents the halide ion.

The nitrate ions can be left out to produce the ionic equation. They are called 'spectator ions', i.e. ions that do not get involved in the reaction:

> **IMPORTANT**
>
> $Ag^+(aq) + X^-(aq) \rightarrow AgX(s)$

The ammonia can form complex ions that are soluble in water when added to:

- silver chloride, as it forms soluble complex ions with *dilute* ammonia

- silver bromide, as it forms soluble complex ions with *concentrated* ammonia.

Silver iodide precipitate does not dissolve on adding dilute or concentrated ammonia solution.

Figure 12.4: Colours of the silver halide precipitates: silver chloride (on the left), silver bromide and silver iodide (on the right).

CONTINUED

Halide ion	Colour of silver halide precipitate on addition of silver nitrate solution	Effect on precipitate of adding dilute ammonia solution	Effect on precipitate of adding concentrated ammonia solution
chloride, Cl⁻(aq)	white	dissolves	dissolves
bromide, Br⁻(aq)	cream	remains insoluble	dissolves
iodide, I⁻(aq)	pale yellow	remains insoluble	remains insoluble

Table 12.5: The results of positive tests for halide ions.

Reactions of halide ions with concentrated sulfuric acid

Compounds that contain Cl⁻, Br⁻ or I⁻ ions will react with concentrated sulfuric acid. All of these reactions produce one or more toxic gases, so they must be performed with great care in a fume cupboard.

We can prepare hydrogen chloride gas by dropping concentrated sulfuric acid slowly onto crystals of sodium chloride (see the apparatus in Figure 12.5).

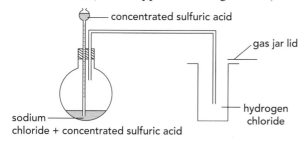

Figure 12.5: Preparing a sample of hydrogen chloride gas. Hydrogen chloride gas is denser than air, so it displaces the air from the gas jar as it collects.

The reaction that takes place is:

$$NaCl(s) + H_2SO_4(l) \rightarrow NaHSO_4(s) + HCl(g)$$

The hydrogen chloride (HCl) gas produced is visible as white fumes.

However, we cannot use the same reaction to prepare samples of pure hydrogen bromide or hydrogen iodide. We saw in Section 12.2 how it gets increasingly easy to decompose the hydrogen halides going down the group.

When the hydrogen halides decompose into their elements, the halide part of the molecule in HBr and HI is oxidised. Concentrated sulfuric acid is a relatively strong oxidising agent. It is not strong enough to oxidise HCl, but concentrated sulfuric acid will oxidise and decompose HBr and HI. So, any HBr or HI formed in the reaction between sodium bromide, or sodium iodide, and concentrated sulfuric acid undergoes further oxidation.

With sodium *bromide,* hydrogen bromide is produced in the initial reaction:

$$NaBr(s) + H_2SO_4(l) \rightarrow NaHSO_4(s) + HBr(g)$$

This is followed by oxidation of HBr(g). The sulfuric acid itself is reduced to sulfur dioxide gas as it oxidises the HBr formed:

$$2HBr(g) + H_2SO_4(l) \rightarrow Br_2(g) + SO_2(g) + 2H_2O(l)$$

A reddish brown gas is seen. This is the element bromine, Br_2.

With sodium *iodide,* the sulfuric acid is reduced to several sulfur products as it oxidises the hydrogen iodide formed to different extents. The products of the oxidation of HI are sulfur dioxide, sulfur and hydrogen sulfide, as shown in the reactions below:

$$NaI(s) + H_2SO_4(l) \rightarrow NaHSO_4(s) + HI(g)$$

followed by oxidation of HI(g):

$$2HI(g) + H_2SO_4(l) \rightarrow I_2(g) + SO_2(g) + 2H_2O(l)$$

and:

$$6HI(g) + H_2SO_4(l) \rightarrow 3I_2(g) + S(s) + 4H_2O(l)$$

and:

$$8HI(g) + H_2SO_4(l) \rightarrow 4I_2(g) + H_2S(g) + 4H_2O(l)$$

Several observations can be made here:

- sulfur is seen as a yellow solid
- hydrogen sulfide has a strong smell of bad eggs
- iodine is produced as a violet / purple vapour.

Therefore, NaBr or NaI produce a mixture of gases when they react with concentrated sulfuric acid, so this is not a good way to prepare a sample of the gases HBr or HI.

> **IMPORTANT**
>
> It gets easier to oxidise the hydrogen halides going down Group 17.

In the reactions above, the bromide ions (Br^-) in HBr, and the iodide ions (I^-) in HI, act as reducing agents. The bromide and iodide ions are electron donors. As they reduce the sulfuric acid, their oxidation numbers increase from -1 to 0 (zero) and bromide and iodide ions are oxidised.

Question

5 a You suspect that a solid compound might be potassium bromide. Describe how you would test your idea. Then describe the positive results you would get if you were correct.

   b i Working with a partner, discuss what you would see in a test-tube in which concentrated sulfuric acid is added dropwise to solid potassium iodide that you would *not* see if the acid was added to potassium chloride.

      ii Write equations, including state symbols, to describe the reactions taking place in the test-tube between concentrated sulfuric acid and potassium iodide. Check your equations against those of another pair of learners. Are the reactants and products and their formulae correct? Are their state symbols correct? Do the equations balance?

   c Decide with your partner which one of the following ions is the strongest reducing agent:

      A fluoride
      B chloride
      C bromide
      D iodide

      Discuss together why that ion would be the best electron donor of the four ions in terms of ionic radius and shielding of the nuclear charge. Then write an answer that also considers the size of the charge carried by the nuclei of the ions.

> **IMPORTANT**
>
> The halide ions are increasingly effective as reducing agents going down Group 17.

12.4 Disproportionation reactions

The element chlorine (Cl_2, oxidation number $= 0$) undergoes a type of redox reaction called *disproportionation* when it reacts with alkali. We can think of disproportionation as a 'self-reduction / oxidation' reaction. When chlorine reacts with dilute alkali, some chlorine atoms are reduced and some are oxidised in the same reaction. The actual reaction that takes place depends on the temperature.

Chlorine in cold alkali (15 °C)

$$Cl_2(aq) + 2NaOH(aq) \rightarrow NaCl(aq) + NaClO(aq) + H_2O(l)$$
$$\text{sodium chlorate(I)}$$

The ionic equation for the reaction is:

$$Cl_2(aq) + 2OH^-(aq) \rightarrow Cl^-(aq) + ClO^-(aq) + H_2O(l)$$
$$\quad\; 0 \qquad\qquad\qquad\qquad\quad -1 \qquad +1$$
oxidation number of Cl

The ionic equation for this redox reaction can be split into two half-equations, showing the reduction and oxidation.

- The reduction reaction (in which chlorine's oxidation number is reduced is):

$$\tfrac{1}{2}Cl_2 + e^- \rightarrow Cl^-$$
oxidation number of Cl $\quad 0 \qquad\qquad -1$

- The oxidation reaction taking place at the same time is:

$$\tfrac{1}{2}Cl_2 + 2OH^- \rightarrow ClO^- + H_2O + e^-$$
oxidation number of Cl $\quad 0 \qquad\qquad\qquad +1$

Chlorine in hot alkali (70 °C)

When we add chlorine and hot concentrated aqueous sodium hydroxide a different disproportionation reaction takes place:

$$3Cl_2(aq) + 6NaOH(aq) \rightarrow 5NaCl(aq) + NaClO_3(aq) + 3H_2O(l)$$
$$\qquad 0 \qquad\qquad\qquad\qquad\qquad -1 \qquad\qquad +5$$

oxidation
number — reduction —
of Cl — oxidation —

Chlorination of water

Adding a small amount of chlorine to a water supply will kill bacteria and make the water safer to drink. The chlorine undergoes disproportionation in water:

$$\underset{\substack{\text{oxidation} \\ \text{number of Cl}}}{} \quad \underset{0}{Cl_2(aq)} + H_2O(l) \rightarrow \underset{-1}{HCl(aq)} + \underset{+1}{HClO(aq)}$$

HClO is called chloric(I) acid. It sterilises water by killing bacteria. Some of the HClO dissociates in water to produce $ClO^-(aq)$, which also acts as a sterilising agent.

REFLECTION

1   Work with another learner to discuss these tasks:

   a   Can you describe the colours of, and explain the trend in volatility of, the Group 17 elements chlorine, bromine and iodine?

   b   Make a list of the key words in this chapter and discuss their meaning with another learner.

2   Work with another learner to reflect on the importance of using oxidation numbers in understanding the reactions of Group 17 elements and their compounds. Try to use changes in oxidation state to judge which species in a redox reaction is oxidised and which is reduced.

3   Discuss which parts of this chapter you enjoyed most, and which, if any, you still feel unsure about. You can use the checklist after the Summary to help you to decide.

SUMMARY

The halogens chlorine, bromine and iodine exist as covalent diatomic molecules. They become increasingly less volatile and more deeply coloured on descending Group 17. Their volatility decreases as instantaneous dipole–induced dipole forces between molecules increase.

All the halogen elements are oxidising agents: they are electron acceptors. Their power as oxidising agents decreases descending Group 17.

All the halide ions can act as reducing agents: they are potential electron donors. Their power as reducing agents increases descending Group 17.

The reactivity of the halogens decreases descending the group.

It gets easier to oxidise the hydrogen halides going down Group 17, as the strength of the hydrogen–halogen bond decreases.

Chlorine reacts with cold hydroxide ions in a disproportionation ('self-reduction–oxidation') reaction.

A different disproportionation reaction takes place between chlorine and hot alkali, producing NaCl(aq), $NaClO_3(aq)$ and water.

An important use of chlorine is in the prevention of disease by chlorination of water supplies. The reaction between chlorine and water also involves disproportionation.

EXAM-STYLE QUESTIONS

You will need a copy of the Periodic Table (see Appendix 1) to answer some of these questions.

1   The table below shows a reactant and a product from different redox reactions involving halogens and their compounds. Use the table to answer both parts of this question.

	Reactant	Product
A	$2Cl^-$	Cl_2
B	Cl^-	ClO^-
C	ClO_3^-	Cl_2
D	ClO^-	ClO_3^-

   a   Which conversion of reactant to product, A to D, involves the greatest change in oxidation state? [1]

   b   How many of the changes in the table are examples of oxidation?

      A 1

      B 2

      C 3

      D 4 [1]

[Total: 2]

2   a   Give the molecular formula of bromine. [1]

   b   List the elements bromine, chlorine and iodine in order of boiling point, starting with the lowest. [2]

   c   Explain the reasons for the trend described in part **b**. [2]

[Total: 5]

3   a   Identify which of these mixtures will result in a chemical reaction:

     i   bromine solution and sodium chloride solution [1]

     ii   iodine solution and sodium bromide solution [1]

     iii chlorine solution and potassium bromide solution [1]

     iv   bromine solution and sodium iodide solution [1]

   b   Write a balanced chemical equation for each reaction that occurs in part **a**. [4]

   c   Name the type of reaction that occurs in part **a**. [1]

   d   Describe the trend that the reactions in part **a** display. [1]

   e   For one of the reactions that occurs in part **a**, identify the substance oxidised and the substance reduced. [2]

   f   For one of the reactions that occurs in part **a**, rewrite the equation as an ionic equation. [1]

   g   The element chlorine is a stronger oxidising agent than bromine. Explain why. [2]

[Total: 15]

CONTINUED

4 a Copy and complete the equations below, including state symbols.

    i $AgNO_3(aq) + NaCl(aq) \rightarrow \ldots$ [2]

    ii $AgNO_3(aq) + NaBr(aq) \rightarrow \ldots$ [2]

    iii $AgNO_3(aq) + NaI(aq) \rightarrow \ldots$ [2]

  b Describe what you would observe in each reaction in part **a**.   [4]

  c Describe what you would observe in each case if dilute ammonia solution were subsequently added.   [1]

  d Describe what you would observe in each case if concentrated ammonia solution were subsequently added.   [1]

                                              [Total: 12]

5 a For the reaction of chlorine with water:

    i write a balanced chemical equation   [2]

    ii give the oxidation numbers of chlorine before and after the reaction   [3]

    iii give one use for the process.   [1]

  b For the reaction of chlorine with cold dilute aqueous sodium hydroxide:

    i write a balanced chemical equation   [2]

    ii give the oxidation numbers of chlorine before and after the reaction.   [3]

  c State the name given to the type of reaction in parts **a** and **b**.   [1]

                                              [Total: 12]

SELF-EVALUATION

After studying this chapter, complete a table like this:

I can	See section...	Needs more work	Almost there	Ready to move on
describe the colours of Group 17 elements	12.1			
explain the trend in volatility of the Group 17 elements chlorine, bromine and iodine	12.1			
explain the relative reactivity of these Group 17 elements as oxidising agents (and the halide ions as reducing agents)	12.2			
explain the reactions of the elements with hydrogen	12.2			
explain the relative thermal stabilities of the hydrides (in terms of bond strengths)	12.2			
explain the reactions of halide ions with aqueous silver ions, followed by adding aqueous ammonia	12.3			
explain the reactions of halide ions with concentrated sulfuric acid	12.3			
explain the disproportionation reactions of chlorine with cold, and with hot, aqueous sodium hydroxide	12.4			
explain the use of chlorine in water purification.	12.4			

> Chapter 13
Nitrogen

BEFORE YOU START

1   Working with a partner, discuss the bonding in an ammonia molecule, NH_3. Then draw a dot-and-cross diagram of the molecule.

2   **a** Give the shape of a methane, CH_4, molecule.

    b Discuss with a partner why a methane molecule is this shape.

3   The oxidation number of nitrogen can vary.
    Give nitrogen's oxidation number in:

    a N_2

    b NO

    c NO_3^-

4   Discuss with a partner which substance is acting as an acid and which is a base this reaction.

    $HCl(aq) + H_2O(l) \rightarrow H_3O^+(aq) + Cl^-(aq)$

5   Draw a reaction pathway diagram that could be used as a PowerPoint slide to explain to the rest of your class how a catalyst works.

FERTILISER ISSUES

Ammonia (NH_3) is a simple compound that can be made using nitrogen gas (N_2). It is used to make ammonium compounds that are very important fertilisers. Ammonium salts commonly used in fertilisers include ammonium chloride (NH_4Cl), ammonium nitrate (NH_4NO_3), ammonium phosphate ($(NH_4)_3PO_4$ and ammonium sulfate ($(NH_4)_2SO_4$.

Nitrogen is removed from the soil when plants absorb nitrates through their roots as they grow. When farmers harvest their crops, the nitrogen is not replaced, as the plants do not die naturally and rot back into the soil. So farmers use fertilisers, mainly ammonium compounds, to replace this essential nitrogen in the soil.

Nitrogen-based fertilisers must be soluble in water for plants to absorb the nitrate ions they provide. This has created an environmental problem. The nitrates can be washed, or leached, out of the soil by rain into groundwater. These nitrates can then end up in rivers and lakes. Once in rivers and lakes, the nitrates promote the growth of algae (a simple water plant) on the surface, causing **eutrophication** (Figure 13.1).

> ### KEY WORD
>
> **eutrophication:** an environmental problem caused by fertilisers leached from fields into rivers and lakes.

Figure 13.1: Fertilisers leached from farmland have caused eutrophication in this river.

CONTINUED

When fertilisers are washed from the soil into rivers:

- A bloom of algae can spread across the surface, blocking out the light for other plant life in the water.

- When the plants and algae die, bacteria in the water feed on them, decomposing the plant material.

- The bacteria multiply rapidly with so much food available, using up the dissolved oxygen in the water.

- Fish extract dissolved oxygen from water, taken in through their gills. Without this dissolved oxygen they die, affecting the whole ecosystem.

Eutrophication isn't the only problem with fertilisers being leached from the soil. Nitrates have also been detected in our drinking water, especially in agricultural areas. People are worried that nitrates in drinking water cause 'blue baby' syndrome (when a newborn baby's blood is starved of oxygen), as well as stomach cancer. But others argue that links between nitrates and diseases have not been proven and that recommended nitrate levels are set unrealistically low.

Farmers can help limit the amount of nitrates in watercourses by adding the most economical amounts of fertilisers at the right time of year. This will minimise the leaching of excess fertiliser from the soil and into our rivers and lakes.

Questions for discussion

Working with another learner or group of learners:

- Discuss the statement 'Nitrogen-based fertilisers do more harm than good.' Then feedback any conclusions you make to the whole group.

- Try to make suggestions that could help reduce any harmful effects caused by the large-scale use of fertilisers.

13.1 Nitrogen gas

Nitrogen is in Group 15 of the Periodic Table. It is a non-metallic element that makes up about 78% of the Earth's atmosphere. It exists as diatomic molecules, N_2.

Nitrogen gas is the main unreactive gas in air that dilutes the effects of the reactive gas, oxygen. To understand the lack of reactivity of nitrogen gas, we have to look at the bonding within its molecules.

The electronic configuration of a nitrogen atom is $1s^2\ 2s^2\ 2p^3$. Its atoms need to gain three electrons to achieve the noble gas configuration of neon. Nitrogen atoms do this by forming a triple covalent bond between two N atoms (see Figure 13.2).

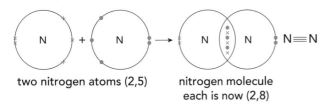

two nitrogen atoms (2,5)   nitrogen molecule
                                each is now (2,8)

Figure 13.2: The triple bonding in a nitrogen molecule, N_2.

The triple covalent bond is very strong. Its bond energy is almost 1000 kJ mol⁻¹. This bond is difficult to break and so nitrogen gas will only react under extreme conditions. For example, the nitrogen and oxygen in the air do react together during thunderstorms (Figure 13.3).

Figure 13.3: Nitrogen oxides are formed when lightning strikes.

The complete oxidation of the nitrogen gas takes place in three steps:

Step 1: Lightning provides the high activation energy needed for the oxidation of the unreactive nitrogen gas to form nitrogen(II) oxide:

$$N_2(g) + O_2(g) \rightarrow 2NO(g)$$
nitrogen(II) oxide

The nitrogen(II) oxide formed is then further oxidised by oxygen in the air to give nitrogen(IV) oxide, NO_2.

Step 2: $2NO(g) + O_2(g) \rightarrow 2NO_2(g)$
nitrogen(IV) oxide

Nitrogen(IV) oxide dissolves in water droplets in the air, and reacts with more oxygen, to form a dilute solution of nitric acid. The dilute acid falls to the Earth in rain:

Step 3: $2NO_2(g) + H_2O(l) + \frac{1}{2}O_2(g) \rightarrow 2HNO_3(aq)$
nitric acid

This sequence of reactions in the atmosphere forms part of the natural nitrogen cycle. In this way, nitrogen from unreactive, insoluble nitrogen gas can get into the soil in a soluble form that plants can absorb. The plants can then use the nitrate ions, NO_3^-, from the dilute nitric acid to make proteins. These proteins are essential for healthy growth of the plants.

Question

1 **a** Explain the lack of reactivity of nitrogen gas.

b There are three steps shown above in the complete oxidation of nitrogen gas.

Which row in the table shows the correct change in the oxidation number of nitrogen in each of the three steps?

	Step 1	Step 2	Step 3
A	−2 → +3	+2 → +4	+2 → +5
B	−3 → +2	+2 → +4	+4 → +6
C	0 → +2	0 → +4	0 → +6
D	0 → +2	+2 → +4	+4 → +5

c Looking at the three steps, decide which option describes what happens to the nitrogen in each of the three steps:

	Step 1	Step 2	Step 3
A	Reduction	Reduction	Reduction
B	Reduction	Oxidation	Oxidation
C	Oxidation	Oxidation	Oxidation
D	Oxidation	Oxidation	Reduction

Now share your answers to Question 1 with another learner, and discuss your reasoning. Refer to the transfer of electrons when explaining the answer to part **b**.

13.2 Ammonia and ammonium compounds

Ammonia, NH_3, is a very important compound of nitrogen. It is the only common alkaline gas. To test for ammonia gas, use damp red litmus paper. The litmus paper will turn blue in the alkaline gas.

In industry, scientists make ammonia on a large scale using the Haber process (for details of the process see Chapter 8).

$$N_2(g) + 3H_2(g) \rightleftharpoons 2NH_3(g)$$
nitrogen   hydrogen   ammonia

The bonding in ammonia is shown in Figure 13.4. You learned why the presence of a lone pair of electrons on the nitrogen atom causes ammonia molecules to have a pyramidal shape in Section 4.4.

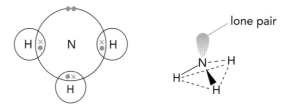

Figure 13.4: A dot-and-cross diagram showing the covalent bonding in an ammonia molecule and its triangular pyramidal shape. The shape is explained in Section 4.4.

You have also learned that nitrogen's lone pair of electrons can be donated to an H^+ ion from an acid, forming a co-ordinate (or dative) covalent bond (see Section 4.3 and Figure 13.5 below).

$$\left[\begin{array}{c} H \\ | \\ H-N\rightarrow H \\ | \\ H \end{array} \right]^+$$

Figure 13.5: The co-ordinate (dative) covalent bond is shown by the arrow that points from the donor atom (N) to the acceptor of the lone pair (H^+ ion).

The positive charge on the ammonium ion formed is spread over the whole ammonium ion. The charge is not concentrated on the hydrogen ion that accepted the lone pair of electrons. Chemists have found that all the N−H bonds in the NH_4^+ ion are the same length. This is evidence that all four covalent bonds in the NH_4^+ ion are equivalent and the positive charge is evenly spread around the ion.

Basicity of ammonia

When ammonia donates its lone pair of electrons to an H^+ ion, as described above, ammonia is acting as a base in this reaction. Remember from Section 8.6 that we can define Brønsted-Lowry bases as 'proton (or H^+ ion) acceptors':

$$NH_3(aq) + H^+(aq) \rightarrow NH_4^+(aq)$$
$$\text{ammonium ion}$$

Ammonia is an example of a weak base, as described in Section 8.6. In an aqueous solution of ammonia, an equilibrium mixture is established:

$$NH_3(aq) + H_2O(l) \rightleftharpoons NH_4^+(aq) + OH^-(aq)$$

The position of equilibrium lies well over to the left so there is a greater concentration of ammonia molecules in the solution than hydroxide ions. This makes the ammonia solution only weakly alkaline, unlike a strong base such as sodium hydroxide, which dissociates (splits up into aqueous ions) completely in solution.

If we heat an ammonium salt with a base, the ammonium ion, NH_4^+, produces ammonia gas, NH_3. We use this reaction to prepare ammonia gas in the laboratory. Ammonium chloride and calcium hydroxide, both in the solid state, are usually mixed together, then heated (see the apparatus in Figure 13.6).

$$2NH_4Cl(s) + Ca(OH)_2(s) \xrightarrow{\text{heat}}$$
$$CaCl_2(s) + 2H_2O(l) + 2NH_3(g)$$

This is an acid–base reaction, with NH_4^+ acting as an acid (proton, H^+, donor) and OH^- ions acting as a base (proton, H^+, acceptor).

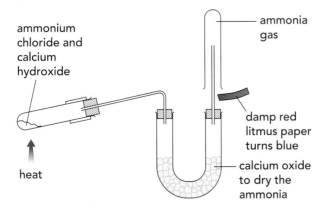

ammonium chloride and calcium hydroxide

heat

ammonia gas

damp red litmus paper turns blue

calcium oxide to dry the ammonia

Figure 13.6: Preparing ammonia gas from an ammonium salt, NH_4Cl, and a base, $Ca(OH)_2$.

We can use the acid–base reaction of an ammonium salt with a base as the basis of the test for ammonium ions. If an unknown compound contains NH_4^+ ions, it will give off ammonia when heated with a base. The ammonia given off will turn damp red litmus paper blue.

Question

2 **a** Give the formula of an ammonium ion.

b Discuss, with a partner, the difference in the H—N—H bond angles of an ammonium ion compared with an ammonia molecule. Reflect on each step you need to go through to arrive at your answer. Then make a list of the sequence.

c Write a balanced chemical equation, including state symbols, for the reaction of ammonia solution with dilute nitric acid.

d **i** Write a balanced chemical equation, including state symbols, for the reaction of solid ammonium sulfate with solid sodium hydroxide.

ii Discuss with a partner why the reaction in part **i** can be classified as an acid–base reaction.

13.3 Nitrogen oxides in the atmosphere

At the start of this chapter we explained why nitrogen gas is so unreactive. However, in the extreme conditions in a thunderstorm, lightning can trigger the reaction between nitrogen and oxygen to form gaseous nitrogen oxides: nitrogen(II) oxide, NO, and nitrogen(IV) oxide, NO_2.

A similar oxidation of nitrogen takes place at the high temperature inside a car engine. In the engine, a mixture of air (which is mainly nitrogen, 78%, and oxygen, 21%) and fuel is compressed and ignited by a spark. Under this high pressure and high temperature, nitrogen can form nitrogen oxides. These oxides of nitrogen are then released into the atmosphere through the car's exhaust fumes.

Nitrogen oxides pollute our atmosphere. They cause acid rain and photochemical smog.

Acid rain

You learned earlier that nitrogen(II) oxide, formed in lightning strikes, is oxidised to form nitrogen(IV) oxide in air:

$$2NO(g) + O_2(g) \rightleftharpoons 2NO_2(g)$$

This is followed by further oxidation to nitric acid when nitrogen(IV) oxide dissolves and reacts in water with oxygen:

$$NO_2(aq) + H_2O(l) + 1.5\ O_2(g) \rightarrow 2HNO_3(aq)$$

The water is often in the form of tiny droplets that make up clouds. The droplets get larger as the temperature drops when clouds rise. When heavy enough the droplets, containing dilute nitric acid, will fall as acid rain.

Dilute sulfuric acid is also found in acid rain. This comes from another pollutant called sulfur dioxide gas (or sulfur(IV) oxide). Nitrogen oxides, as well as causing acid rain directly, can also act as catalysts in the reactions that make dilute sulfuric acid in the atmosphere. NO and NO_2 catalyse the oxidation of sulfur dioxide gas, SO_2, during the formation of acid rain. The gas sulfur trioxide, SO_3, that is produced by this oxidation of SO_2, reacts with rainwater, forming dilute sulfuric acid:

$$SO_3(g) + H_2O(l) \rightarrow H_2SO_4(aq)$$

The reactions below show the catalytic activity of the nitrogen oxides:

$$SO_2(g) + NO_2(g) \rightarrow SO_3(g) + NO(g)$$

Then NO_2 is regenerated as NO reacts with oxygen in the air:

$$NO(g) + \tfrac{1}{2}O_2(g) \rightarrow NO_2(g)$$

This NO_2 molecule can then go on to oxidise another sulfur dioxide molecule. At the same time, the reaction also produces an NO molecule to make another NO_2 molecule. This will oxidise another sulfur dioxide molecule, and so on. Therefore, NO_2 effectively catalyses the oxidation of SO_2.

Photochemical smog

The oxides of nitrogen are also dangerous in the atmosphere because they react to make other pollutants. These other pollutants formed are called *secondary pollutants*. This is because they are not given off directly from human activity: for example, they are not vehicle exhaust gases or gases from power plants. Nitrogen oxides

are examples of *primary pollutants* as they are given off directly into the air from the source of pollution.

Other primary pollutants in exhaust fumes are volatile organic compounds (VOCs). These are largely unburnt hydrocarbons from fuel, and their oxidised products. The VOCs can react in sunlight with oxides of nitrogen to make peroxyacetyl nitrate (also called PAN). Its chemical formula can be written as $CH_3CO_3NO_2$. Sunlight provides the energy needed to start the reactions off in the atmosphere, so we call them photochemical reactions.

Figure 13.7: Photochemical smog hangs over Los Angeles in certain weather conditions. The word 'smog' is derived from the two words 'smoke' and 'fog'.

IMPORTANT

PAN is one of the harmful pollutants found in photochemical smog (Figure 13.7). PAN affects the lungs and eyes, and in high concentrations also affects plant-life.

Reducing the effects of nitrogen oxides

Nowadays, car exhaust systems are fitted with catalytic converters to help reduce the pollutants from motor vehicles (see Section 15.2). The reaction of pollutant gases inside the converter takes place on the surface of the hot catalyst, for example platinum. The nitrogen oxides are reduced to form harmless nitrogen gas, which is released from the vehicle's exhaust pipe.

$$2CO(g) + 2NO(g) \rightarrow 2CO_2(g) + N_2(g)$$

Question

3 **a** State one source of nitrogen oxides in our atmosphere that is:

- i natural
- ii human-made.

b i Explain why PAN is called a *secondary pollutant*.

ii Identify the type of pollution PAN contributes to.

iii State the condition needed to start off the reaction between VOCs and nitrogen oxides that produces PAN in the atmosphere.

c Discuss with a partner how nitrogen oxides are involved in the formation of atmospheric sulfur trioxide (SO_3). Then each write your own explanation, including equations.

d The following reaction takes place in a car's catalytic converter once it is warmed up:

$$2CO(g) + 2NO(g) \longrightarrow 2CO_2(g) + N_2(g)$$

Use oxidation numbers to explain which species is reduced and which is oxidised in the reaction.

REFLECTION

1 Work with another learner to discuss:

- a the lack of reactivity of nitrogen gas
- b the basicity of ammonia and the formation and structure of the ammonium ion
- c the displacement of ammonia from its ammonium salts.

2 Now summarise the role of nitrogen oxides in atmospheric pollution. Create a mind map, with 'Oxides of nitrogen' in its centre. Do you feel you understand more about atmospheric pollution now?

3 Make a list of the key words in this chapter so far and explain their meanings to another learner.

4 Work with another learner to decide which aspects of this chapter you enjoyed most and which you did not enjoy. Then discuss the reasons why.

SUMMARY

Nitrogen, N_2, is a very unreactive gas because of the high bond energy of the N≡N triple bond.
Ammonia, NH_3, is a common compound of nitrogen. Its molecules have a triangular pyramidal shape.
An ammonia molecule can act as a base, accepting an H^+ ion to form an ammonium ion, NH_4^+.
Ammonia gas is given off from ammonium salts by heating them with a base.
Nitrogen oxides are formed naturally during lightning strikes, when nitrogen gas is oxidised. These gaseous nitrogen oxides are also formed in internal combustion engines and become pollutants in the atmosphere, contributing to acid rain.

CONTINUED

Sulfur dioxide gas is the main cause of acid rain. In the atmosphere, the oxidation of sulfur dioxide to sulfur trioxide is catalysed by oxides of nitrogen.

PAN, peroxyacetyl nitrate, is a pollutant found in photochemical smog. It is formed by reactions between oxides of nitrogen and unburnt hydrocarbons and other VOCs (volatile organic compounds).

EXAM-STYLE QUESTIONS

1   Ammonia is made from its elements in the Haber process.

   a   Give the formula of ammonia.   [1]

   b   Write a balanced equation for the formation of ammonia in the Haber process.   [1]

   c   Explain how the ammonia molecule acts as a base when it dissolves in water. Include an equation in your answer.   [2]

   d   For the ammonium ion, give the following:

      i   formula   [1]

      ii   shape, including its bond angles.   [2]

   e   Give the formulae of the following ammonium salts:

      i   ammonium chloride   [1]

      ii   ammonium nitrate   [1]

      iii   ammonium sulfate   [1]

   f   Ammonium chloride reacts with calcium hydroxide when heated to produce ammonia gas.

      i   Is this reaction carried out using solids or solutions?   [1]

      ii   Write the balanced equation for this reaction.   [1]

      iii   Which of the following types of reaction is this an example of?

         A   Acid–base

         B   Combustion

         C   Redox

         D   Precipitation   [1]

      iv   Describe how you could test for ammonia gas.   [1]

[Total: 14]

2   Phosphorus is the element below nitrogen in Group 15 of the Periodic Table. Its atomic number is 15.

   a   Which molecule shows phosphorus in its lowest oxidation state?

      A P_4

      B H_3PO_4

      C H_3PO_2

      D PH_3 [1]

   b   Write the electronic configuration of a phosphorus atom.   [1]

CONTINUED

c   Suggest which element, phosphorus or nitrogen, has the higher first ionisation energy and explain your reasoning. [4]

d   The hydride of phosphorus is commonly called *phosphine*, PH_3. Suggest the shape of a molecule of phosphine, and predict the H—P—H bond angles, explaining your reasoning. [4]

e   Phosphorus, like nitrogen, can form a negatively charged ion if it reacts with a metal at high temperatures. With magnesium, its phosphide has the formula Mg_3P_2.

   i   Give the charge on the phosphide ion in magnesium phosphide. [1]

   ii   State which element has the same electronic configuration as the phosphide ion. [1]

   iii   Suggest the structure of magnesium phosphide. [1]

[Total: 13]

SELF-EVALUATION

After studying this chapter, complete a table like this:

I can	See section...	Needs more work	Almost there	Ready to move on
explain the lack of reactivity of nitrogen gas	13.1			
explain the basicity of ammonia, and the formation and structure of the ammonium ion	13.2			
explain the displacement of ammonia from its ammonium salts	13.2			
state the industrial importance of ammonia and nitrogen compounds derived from ammonia	13.2			
explain the natural and human-made occurrences of oxides of nitrogen and their catalytic removal from the exhaust gases of internal combustion engines	13.3			
explain why atmospheric oxides of nitrogen are pollutants, including their role in the formation of photochemical smog and the catalytic oxidation of atmospheric sulfur dioxide.	13.3			

> Chapter 14

Introduction to organic chemistry

LEARNING INTENTIONS

In this chapter you will learn how to:

- define the term hydrocarbon and describe how alkanes are simple hydrocarbons with no functional group
- deduce the molecular and / or empirical formula of a compound, given its structural, displayed or skeletal formula
- interpret, name and use the general, structural, displayed and skeletal formulae of the alkanes, alkenes, halogenoalkanes, alcohols (including primary, secondary and tertiary), aldehydes, ketones, carboxylic acids, esters, amines (primary only) and nitriles
- explain and use the following terminology associated with organic reactions and their mechanisms:
  - functional group
  - homolytic and heterolytic fission
  - free radical, initiation, propagation, termination
  - nucleophile, electrophile, nucleophilic, electrophilic
  - addition, substitution, elimination, hydrolysis, condensation
  - oxidation and reduction
  - explain and identify isomerism, including chiral centres and geometrical isomers
  - deduce possible isomers from a given molecular formula

CONTINUED

- describe, give bond angles and explain the shape of molecules in terms of their sp, sp^2 and sp^3 hybridised atomic orbitals, and their σ bonds and π bonds
- describe and explain the different types of structural isomerism and stereoisomerism.

BEFORE YOU START

1 Discuss with a partner which type of atoms form covalent bonds (metals or non-metals).

   Then work together to draw a dot-and-cross diagram of a carbon dioxide molecule.

2 Give the shape of a methane, CH_4, molecule and the H—C—H bond angles.

3 Work with a partner to think up a model to explain the meaning of 'electronegativity' to a younger person.

4 Which two of the following are true about a molecule of ethene, C_2H_4?

   A It contains one sigma (σ) bond and five pi (π) bonds

   B It contains five sigma (σ) bonds and one pi (π) bond

   C Three of the carbon atoms' atomic orbitals have become sp^2 hybridised

   D Four of the carbon atoms' atomic orbitals have become sp^3 hybridised

THE MOLECULES OF LIFE

Living things are made of atoms covalently bonded to form molecules of organic compounds (Figure 14.1). Almost all of these molecules of life are based on carbon compounds.

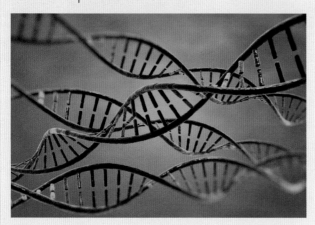

Figure 14.1: Organic compounds form the basis of all living things. Carbon atoms tend to form the 'backbone' of organic molecules: from the proteins in muscles and enzymes to the DNA (see above) that determines our characteristics.

Life is complicated and needs a great variety of different compounds. A great variety of organic compounds is possible because every carbon atom can bond with other carbon atoms to form chains and rings. We often find these chains and rings bonded to atoms of other elements, such as hydrogen, oxygen and nitrogen. This explains the millions of organic compounds that exist.

Note that not all carbon compounds are classified as organic compounds. Scientists classify the oxides of carbon and compounds containing carbonate and hydrogencarbonate ions as *inorganic* compounds.

Question for discussion

Discuss with another learner or group of learners:

- Carbohydrates (compounds of carbon, hydrogen and oxygen) can vary in size between relatively small molecules, such as glucose, $C_6H_{12}O_6$, to thousands of glucose molecules bonded together in giant polymers, such as starch and cellulose. How does the size of organic molecules change their properties? You might consider the process of digesting a starchy food to illustrate your answer.

14.1 Representing organic molecules

Figure 14.2 shows two types of three-dimensional (3D) diagram representing a selection of organic molecules. Chemists use various types of model for different purposes. The compounds shown are called *hydrocarbons*. Hydrocarbons are compounds of carbon and hydrogen *only*.

The colours used in the modelling of molecules are shown in Table 14.1.

We can represent organic molecules using different types of formula.

1 The *empirical formula* gives us the least detail. It tells us the simplest ratio of the different types of atoms present in the molecule. For example, an organic compound called *propene* has the empirical formula CH_2. This tells us that it has twice as many hydrogen atoms as carbon atoms in its molecules.

Colour ...	... used to represent
white	hydrogen
dark grey	carbon
red	oxygen
blue	nitrogen
yellow-green	fluorine
green	chlorine
orange-brown	bromine
brown	phosphorus
violet	iodine
pale yellow	sulfur
yellow ochre	boron
pink	lone pair electron clouds
green	π-bond electron clouds

Table 14.1: Colours used in molecular modelling in this text.

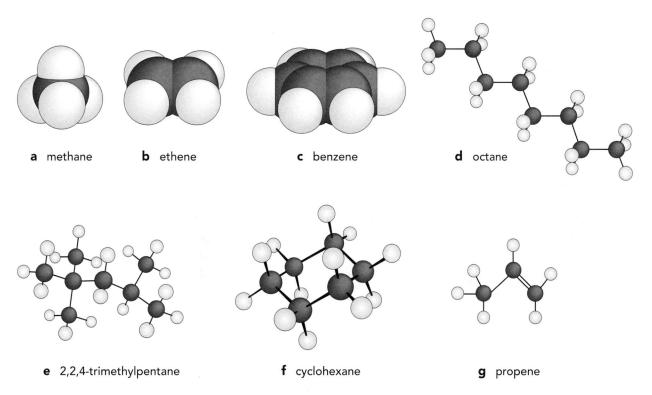

a methane   **b** ethene   **c** benzene   **d** octane

e 2,2,4-trimethylpentane   **f** cyclohexane   **g** propene

Figure 14.2: Examples of the variety of hydrocarbons. **a–c** These hydrocarbons are shown as space-filling models. Such models show the region of space occupied by the atoms and the surrounding electrons. **d–g** These hydrocarbons are shown as ball-and-stick models, which enable bonds between atoms to be seen clearly.

We can calculate empirical formulae from experimental data on the mass of each element in a sample of a compound. Then we can convert the masses to the number of moles of each element present, cancelled down to the simplest ratio.

2   The *molecular formula* shows us the actual numbers of each type of atom in a molecule. To find this we need to know the relative molecular mass of the compound. The relative molecular mass of propene is 42. We know that its empirical formula is CH_2. This CH_2 group of atoms has a relative mass of 14, as the relative atomic mass of C = 12 and H = 1. By dividing the relative molecular mass by the relative mass of the empirical formula ($\frac{42}{14} = 3$), we see that there must be ($3 \times CH_2$) atoms in a propene molecule. So its molecular formula is C_3H_6.

> ### KEY DEFINITIONS
>
> **structural formula:** the formula that shows how many, and the symbols of, atoms bonded to each carbon atom in an organic molecule.
>
> **displayed formula:** a 2D representation of an organic molecule, showing *all* its atoms (by their symbols) and their bonds (by short single, double or triple lines between the symbols).
>
> **skeletal formula:** a simplified displayed formula with all C and H atoms and C—H bonds removed.

3   Chemists can give more detail about a molecule by giving its **structural formula**. This tells us about the atoms bonded to each carbon atom in the molecule. The structural formula of propene is $CH_3HC{=}CH_2$ (also written as $CH_3CH{=}CH_2$, but the central H atom does not form a double bond).

This structural formula tells us how many hydrogen atoms are bonded to each carbon atom. In the case of propene, it also shows us that two of the carbon atoms in the molecule are joined by a double bond.

4   Carbon–carbon double bonds are shown in a structural formula. However, *all* the bonds within a molecule are shown in its **displayed formula**. We can think of this representation as a 2D, or flattened out, version of the 'ball-and-stick' models shown in Figure 14.2. The displayed formula of propene is shown in Figure 14.3.

Figure 14.3: The displayed formula of propene, showing all the bonds in the molecule.

A simplified version of the displayed formula is called the **skeletal formula**. It has all the symbols for carbon and hydrogen atoms removed, as well as the carbon to hydrogen bonds. The carbon to carbon bonds are left in place. Figure 14.4 shows the skeletal formula of propene.

Figure 14.4: The skeletal formula of propene.

All other atoms that are not carbon or hydrogen, and their bonds, are included in the skeletal formula of an organic molecule. You can see the displayed and skeletal formulae of an alcohol called butan-2-ol in Figure 14.5. Notice that the skeletal formula includes the H atom in an —OH group.

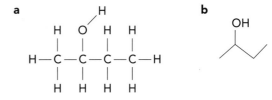

Figure 14.5: a The displayed formula of butan-2-ol. **b** The skeletal formula of butan-2-ol.

You can see the 'zig-zag' in the carbon chain shown in a skeletal formula in the 3D representations of hydrocarbons in Figure 14.2. You will see more detailed 3D displayed formulae later in this chapter, when we look at optical isomers (see Section 14.6). Figure 14.6 shows the 3D displayed formula of butan-2-ol.

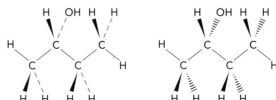

Figure 14.6: The 3D displayed formula of butan-2-ol. The 'wedge' bond is sticking out of the plane of the paper and the 'dashed-line' or 'open wedge' bond is sticking into the plane of the paper. This figure shows both conventions – either representation is acceptable.

5 With complex molecules, chemists sometimes find it useful to combine structural, 3D and skeletal formulae when representing a molecule. The molecule of cholesterol shown in Figure 14.7 is one such example.

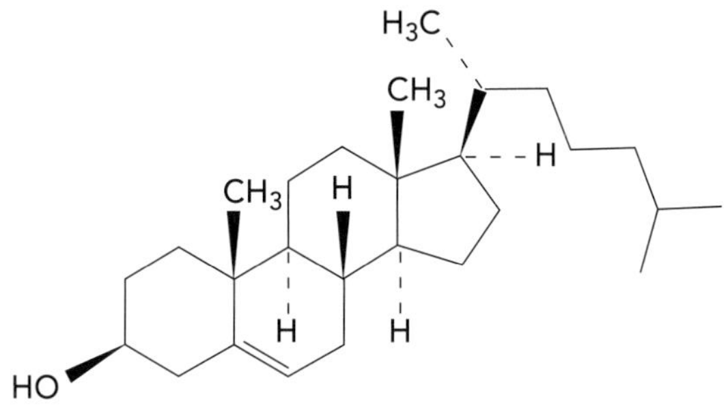

Figure 14.7: A useful way of combining structural, 3D and skeletal formulae.

Question

1 a i On analysis, a hydrocarbon was found to contain 0.72 g of carbon and 0.18 g of hydrogen. Calculate the empirical formula of the hydrocarbon.

   ii Further investigation showed that the relative molecular mass of the hydrocarbon was 30.

   Deduce its molecular formula.

b A compound contains the elements carbon, hydrogen and oxygen. Its empirical formula is CH_2O and its relative molecular mass is 60.

   Deduce the molecular formula of the compound.

c Draw the displayed formula of:

   i ethene (molecular formula C_2H_4)

   ii propane (molecular formula C_3H_8).

d i Draw the skeletal formula of pentane, a straight-chain hydrocarbon with a molecular formula of C_5H_{12}.

   ii Draw the structural formulae of the molecules shown in Figure 14.2, parts **d**, **e** and **f**.

Now share all your answers to Question 1 with a partner and correct the answers together. Ask your teacher if you are unsure or cannot agree on an answer.

14.2 Homologous series of organic compounds

There are many classes of related organic compounds called **homologous series**, some of which are shown in Table 14.2. Within each homologous series of compounds, all the compounds consist of molecules with a particular atom, or grouping of atoms, called a **functional group**. Different classes of compounds have different functional groups.

KEY DEFINITIONS

homologous series: a group of organic compounds having the same functional group, the same general formula and similar chemical properties.

functional group: an atom or group of atoms in an organic molecule which determines the characteristic chemical reactions.

general formula: a formula that represents a homologous series of compounds using letters and numbers; e.g. the general formula for the alkanes is C_nH_{2n+2}.

The functional group determines the characteristic chemical properties of the compounds that contain that specific functional group. The functional group in an alkene is the $C=C$ double bond. The functional group in a carboxylic acid is the $-COOH$ group.

The **general formulae** of some homologous series of compounds are given in Table 14.3. By substituting a number for n (or m) in the general formula, you get the molecular formula of a particular compound containing that functional group. Note that this formula assumes there is just one functional group present in the molecule.

14.3 Naming organic compounds

Table 14.2 shows the names of the first ten alkanes and the stems used in naming other molecules.

Chemists have a system of naming organic compounds that can be applied consistently. This means that they can communicate with each other clearly when referring to organic compounds.

Number of carbon atoms	Molecular formula of straight-chain alkane	Name of alkane	Stem used in naming
1	CH_4	methane	meth-
2	C_2H_6	ethane	eth-
3	C_3H_8	propane	prop-
4	C_4H_{10}	butane	but-
5	C_5H_{12}	pentane	pent-
6	C_6H_{14}	hexane	hex-
7	C_7H_{16}	heptane	hept-
8	C_8H_{18}	octane	oct-
9	C_9H_{20}	nonane	non-
10	$C_{10}H_{22}$	decane	dec-

Table 14.2: The stems used in naming simple **aliphatic** organic compounds that contain a hydrocarbon chain.

KEY DEFINITION

aliphatic compounds: straight-chain or branched-chain organic compounds, and also include cyclic organic compounds that do not contain benzene rings (see benzene in Figure 14.11).

The homologous series of hydrocarbons called alkanes provides the basis of the naming system. The stem of each name indicates how many carbon atoms are in the longest chain in one molecule of the compound.

We indicate the position of side-chains or functional groups by numbering the carbon atoms in the longest chain. The numbering starts at the end that produces the lowest possible numbers in the name (Figure 14.8).

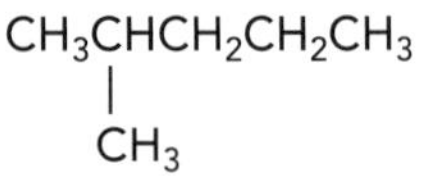

$$CH_3CHCH_2CH_2CH_3$$
$$\overset{|}{CH_3}$$

Figure 14.8: This is called 2-methylpentane, not 4-methylpentane. Its structural formula is $CH_3CH(CH_3)CH_2CH_2CH_3$.

Note that the hydrocarbon side-chain is shown in brackets in its structural formula. It is named by adding '-yl' to the normal alkane stem, in this case a methyl group. This type of group is called an alkyl group. If there is more than one of the same alkyl

side-chain or functional group, we indicate how many by inserting di- (for two), tri- (for three) or tetra- (for four) in front of its name. Figure 14.9 shows an example.

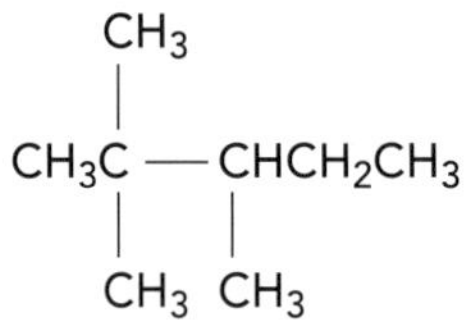

$$\overset{CH_3}{\underset{|}{}}$$
$$CH_3C — CHCH_2CH_3$$
$$\overset{|}{CH_3} \overset{|}{CH_3}$$

Figure 14.9: This is 2,2,3-trimethylpentane.

Note that adjacent *numbers* in a name have a comma between them, whereas numbers are separated from *words* by a hyphen.

If there is more than one type of alkyl side-chain, they are listed in the name in alphabetical order (Figure 14.10).

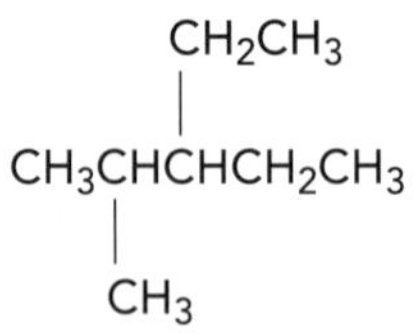

$$\overset{CH_2CH_3}{\underset{|}{}}$$
$$CH_3CHCHCH_2CH_3$$
$$\overset{|}{CH_3}$$

Figure 14.10: This is 3-ethyl-2-methylpentane. (The alkyl groups appear in its name in alphabetical order).

Table 14.3 shows some common homologous series together with their functional groups. It also shows some examples.

Homologous series and the structure of its functional group	General formula of the homologous series	An example from the homologous series	Structural formula of the example
alkenes 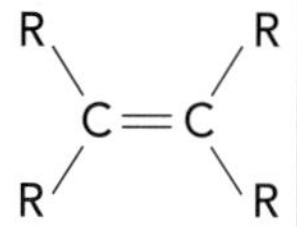 $\begin{array}{cc}R & R\\ \diagdown & \diagup\\ C=C\\ \diagup & \diagdown\\ R & R\end{array}$	C_nH_{2n}	ethene	$CH_2{=}CH_2$
halogenoalkanes $\quad R{-}X$ where X = F, Cl, Br, I	$C_nH_{2n+1}X$	chloromethane	CH_3Cl
alcohols $\qquad R{-}OH$	$C_nH_{2n+1}OH$	methanol	CH_3OH
aldehydes 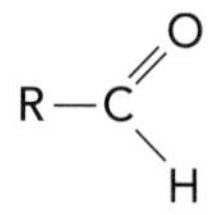 $\quad R{-}C{\diagup^O_{\diagdown H}}$	$C_nH_{2n+1}CHO$	ethanal	CH_3CHO
ketones 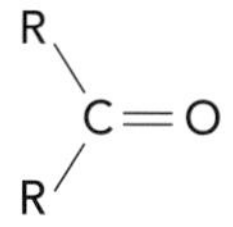 $\begin{array}{c}R\\ \diagdown\\ C=O\\ \diagup\\ R\end{array}$	$C_nH_{2n+1}COC_mH_{2m+1}$	propanone	CH_3COCH_3
carboxylic acids 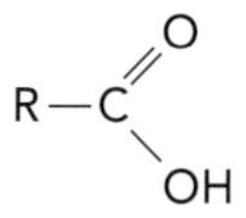 $\quad R{-}C{\diagup^O_{\diagdown OH}}$	$C_nH_{2n+1}COOH$	ethanoic acid	CH_3COOH
esters 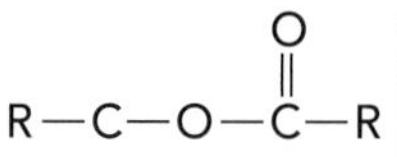 $\quad R{-}C{\overset{O}{\underset{\|}{}}}{-}O{-}C{-}R$	$C_nH_{2n+1}COOC_mH_{2m+1}$	propyl ethanoate	$CH_3COOC_3H_7$ or $CH_3COOCH_2CH_2CH_3$
amines $\qquad R{-}NH_2$	$C_nH_{2n+1}NH_2$	methylamine	CH_3NH_2
nitriles $\qquad R{-}C{\equiv}N$	$C_nH_{2n+1}CN$	ethanenitrile	CH_3CN

Table 14.3: Some common homologous series of organic compounds and their functional groups, general formulae, and named examples, with their structural formulae.

Table 14.4 shows the structural formula and skeletal formula of a compound from each of the homologous series shown in Table 14.3.

Question

2 **a** Draw the displayed formula of:

  i 2-methylbutane

  ii 3,5-diethylheptane

  iii 2,4,6-trimethyloctane.

b **i** What is the name of this hydrocarbon?

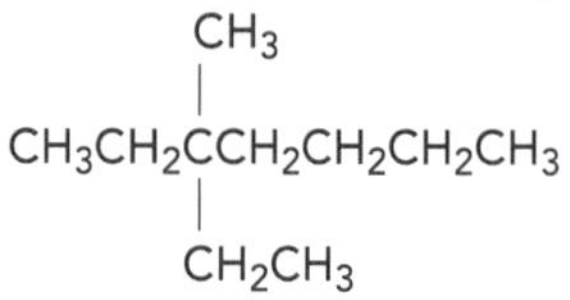

$$CH_3$$
$$|$$
$$CH_3CH_2CCH_2CH_2CH_2CH_3$$
$$|$$
$$CH_2CH_3$$

  ii Give the skeletal formula of the hydrocarbon molecule.

Now compare all your answers to Question 2 with those of others in a small group. Look at any differences in your answers. Then explain the steps in your thinking to each other to agree on the correct answer.

Homologous series	Name of example and its structural formula	Skeletal formula
alkenes	but-2-ene, $CH_3CH{=}CHCH_3$	
halogenoalkanes	2-chloropropane, $CH_3CHClCH_3$	
alcohols	butan-1-ol, $CH_3CH_2CH_2CH_2OH$	
aldehydes	butanal, $CH_3CH_2CH_2CHO$	
ketones	butanone, $CH_3COCH_2CH_3$	
carboxylic acids	butanoic acid, $CH_3CH_2CH_2COOH$	
esters	ethyl propanoate, $CH_3CH_2COOCH_2CH_3$	
amines	butylamine, $CH_3CH_2CH_2CH_2NH_2$	
nitriles	butanenitrile, $CH_3CH_2CH_2CN$	

Table 14.4: The structural and skeletal formula of examples from common homologous series.

In Table 14.3 we saw the names of compounds with common functional groups. We also use the numbering system where necessary to indicate the position of the functional group in a molecule. For some functional groups, no number is needed if the group can only be positioned at the end of a chain. Examples of this include carboxylic acids such as butanoic acid, C_3H_7COOH, and aldehydes, such as pentanal, C_4H_9CHO.

As well as alkyl groups, you will also have to recognise aryl groups. Aryl compounds contain at least one benzene ring. A benzene molecule has six carbon atoms arranged in a hexagon, with each carbon atom bonded to one hydrogen atom. You will look at benzene and related compounds in more detail in Chapter 25.

Figure 14.11 shows the displayed and skeletal formulae of benzene.

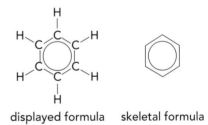

displayed formula   skeletal formula

Figure 14.11: Ways of representing benzene.

If only one alkyl group is bonded to a benzene ring, we do not have to include a number in the name. This is because all six carbon atoms in the ring are equivalent. However, at A Level, you will learn that with two or more alkyl groups we need to indicate their positions, as shown in Figure 14.12. (You do not need to recall this numbering for AS Level.)

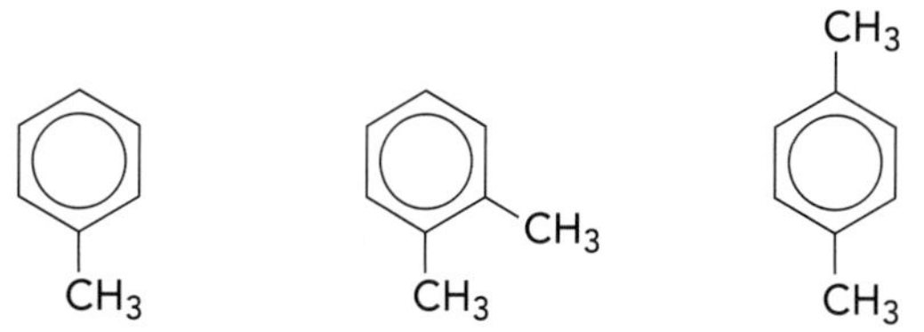

methylbenzene   1,2-dimethylbenzene   1,4-dimethylbenzene

Figure 14.12: Naming aryl compounds.

Question

3 **a** Using the skeletal formula of benzene in the formulae as shown in Figure 14.11, draw the displayed formula of:

  i   propylbenzene

  ii   1-ethyl-4-methylbenzene

  iii   1,3,5-triethylbenzene,

b Draw the displayed formula of 2-bromo-3,3-dichlorohexane.

c Which of the following is the structural formula of the aldehyde 3,5-dimethylhexanal?

  A $CH_3CH(CH_3)CH_2CH(CH_3)CH_2COOH$

  B $CH_3CH(CH_3)CH_2CH(CH_3)CHO$

  C $CH_3CH(CH_3)CH_2CH(CH_3)CH_2CHO$

  D $CH_3(CH_3)CH_2(CH_3)CH_2CHO$

REFLECTION

1 At this point, reflect on your understanding of the basics of organic chemistry covered so far in Chapter 14. This includes naming organic compounds and representing them by empirical, molecular, structural and displayed formulae.

2 You should also recognise the common functional groups.

3 Work with a partner to ask each other five questions about the work covered so far. What does this reveal about you as a learner?

4 Make a note of anything you are not sure about and think about things you could do to get a better understanding of these. Then you will be on your way to mastering organic chemistry.

14.4 Bonding in organic molecules

We can explain the ability of a carbon atom to bond to other carbon atoms, and the shapes of the molecules formed, by looking closely at the bonding involved.

Sigma (σ) bonds

Each carbon atom has six electrons, with an electronic configuration of $1s^2\ 2s^2\ 2p^2$. This means that carbon has four electrons in its outermost shell. By forming **single covalent bonds** with four other atoms, a carbon atom can gain the electronic configuration of the noble gas neon (see Section 4.2). These single covalent bonds are known as **sigma (σ) bonds**.

KEY WORDS

single covalent bond: a bond made up of a pair of electrons shared between two atoms.

sigma bond (σ-bond): a single covalent bond formed by the 'end-on' overlap of atomic orbitals.

The pair of electrons in a σ bond is found in a region of space (described as a lobe) between the nuclei of the two atoms sharing the electrons. The electrostatic attraction, between the negatively charged electrons and the two positively charged nuclei, bonds the atoms to each other (see Section 4.3).

In many organic compounds each carbon atom forms four σ bonds. The four bonding pairs of electrons (which are all areas of negative charge) around each carbon atom repel each other. They position themselves in a tetrahedral arrangement so that the bonding pairs are as far apart from each other as possible. The tetrahedral bond angle is 109.5° (see Section 4.4). Figure 14.13 shows the 3D formula of an ethane molecule. This gives an impression of the shape of an ethane molecule.

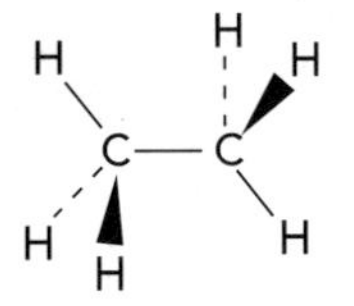

Figure 14.13: The bond angles are all close to 109.5° in an ethane molecule. The two carbon atoms, each forming four sigma bonds, are said to be sp³ hybridised (see Section 4.5).

Pi (π) bonds

KEY WORD

pi (π) bond: a covalent bond formed by 'sideways' overlap of p and p or p and d atomic orbitals.

Carbon can also form double and triple bonds between its atoms in organic molecules, as well as forming single bonds. A C=C double bond, as found in *alkenes* such as ethene, is made up of a σ bond and a **pi (π) bond**. The carbon atoms involved in the double bond will each form three σ bonds. This is an example of sp² hybridisation (see Section 4.5). This leaves each carbon atom with one spare outer electron in a 2p orbital. When these two p orbitals overlap they form a π bond. Figure 14.14 shows how the π bond is formed in ethene.

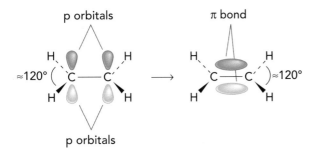

Figure 14.14: The overlap of two p orbitals results in a π bond. Ethene is described as a *planar* molecule. All the carbon and hydrogen atoms in the ethene molecule lie in the same plane. The two carbon atoms are said to be sp² hybridised (see Section 4.5).

The two lobes that make up the π bond lie above and below the plane of the atoms in an ethene molecule. This maximises overlap of the p orbitals. The carbon atoms involved in the double bond are each surrounded by three pairs of electrons in the σ bonds. These are all in the plane of the molecule and repel each other to give bond angles of about 120°.

You can read about the special case of π bonding in a benzene molecule in Section 25.1.

Carbon atoms can also form triple covalent bonds, C≡C. These are found in the homologous series of *alkynes*. The simplest example of an alkyne is ethyne, HC≡CH.

When forming a triple bond, the carbon atoms' p orbitals are sp hybridised (see Section 4.5). This leaves two electrons in different p atomic orbitals on each of the bonding carbon atoms. The p orbitals overlap, forming two π bonds, each containing two electrons.

The two lobes of one π bond lie above and below the plane of the atoms in the ethyne molecule (as in ethene). The two lobes of the other π bond lie in front of and behind the plane of the atoms in the ethyne molecule.

This maximises overlap of the p orbitals, which in effect form a cylinder of electron density around the two carbon atoms. The ethyne molecule is linear in shape, with all its atoms arranged in a straight line (Figure 14.15).

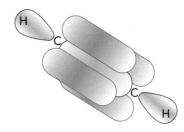

Figure 14.15: The overlap of four p orbitals resulting in two π bonds in ethyne. Ethyne is described as a *linear* molecule. The two carbon atoms and both hydrogen atoms in the ethyne molecule lie in a straight line. The two carbon atoms are said to be sp hybridised.

Question

4   a   Draw 3D formulae for:

    i   propane

    ii   propene

    iii   ethyne.

b i Join with a partner to discuss all the options in the questions below:

Which molecule is an example of carbon atoms adopting both sp^2 and sp^3 hybridisation?

A C_2H_2

B C_2H_4

C C_2H_6

D C_3H_6

ii For the three incorrect options in part **i**, decide on the type of hybridisation of carbon atomic orbitals in each molecule.

Swap your answers to Question 4 with another learner and mark each other's answers. Discuss your reasoning when your answers are not the same and arrive at an agreed answer. Show these agreed answers to your teacher if you are still in doubt.

14.5 Structural isomerism

We have seen how a compound's molecular formula tells us the number and type of each atom in one molecule of the compound. For example, a propene molecule, C_3H_6 (Figure 14.16), contains three carbon atoms and six hydrogen atoms:

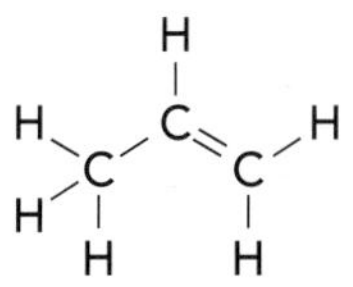

Figure 14.16: The displayed formula of propene, C_3H_6.

However, for a given molecular formula there may be different ways of arranging these atoms. This means different molecules can be formed, with different structures, resulting in different compounds. Such compounds with the same molecular formula but different structural formulae are called **structural isomers**. For example, the molecular formula propene, C_3H_6, could also describe cyclopropane (Figure 14.17).

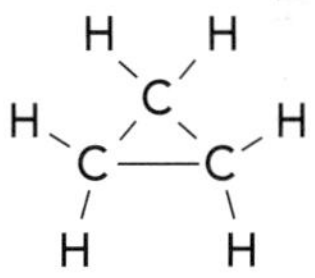

Figure 14.17: The displayed formula of another possible structure, called a structural isomer, of molecules with the formula C_3H_6. Cyclopropane is an example of a *cyclic* alkane. Its structural formula is $(CH_2)_3$.

> **KEY WORD**
>
> **structural isomers:** compounds with the same molecular formula but different structural formulae.

There are three types of structural isomerism:

1 position isomerism

2 functional group isomerism

3 chain isomerism.

Position isomerism

In position isomerism, it is the location of the functional group that varies in each isomer. An example is provided by the compound with the molecular formula $C_3H_6Br_2$. Its four possible isomers are shown in Figure 14.18.

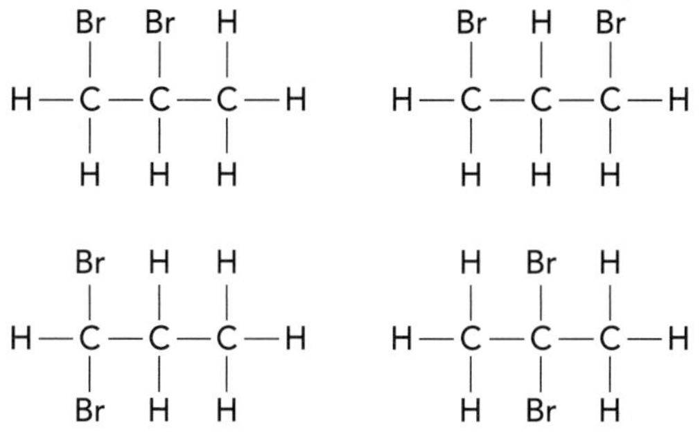

Figure 14.18: An example of position isomerism.

You need to take care when drawing the structural or displayed formula of different isomers not to repeat the same structure. Remember that there is free rotation about C—C single bonds. The three molecules shown in Figure 14.19 are all 1,2-dibromopropane; they are *not* three different isomers of $C_3H_6Br_2$.

Functional group isomerism

In functional group isomerism, there are different functional groups present. For example, given the molecular formula C_3H_8O we can draw both an alcohol and an ether (Figure 14.20).

These two isomers have different functional groups and so have very different chemical properties.

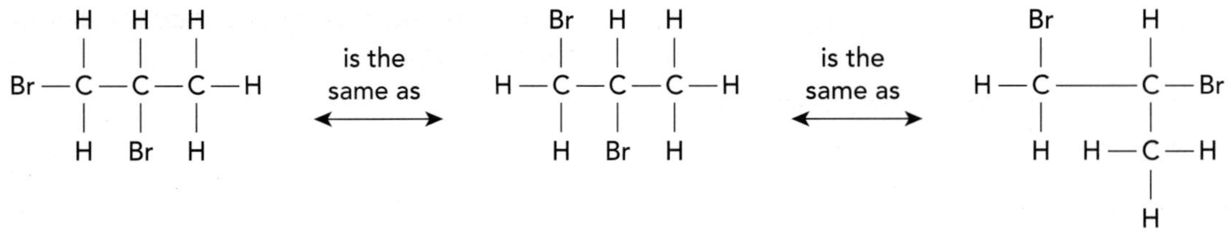

Figure 14.19: These are different ways of representing the *same molecule* because of free rotation about C—C single bonds.

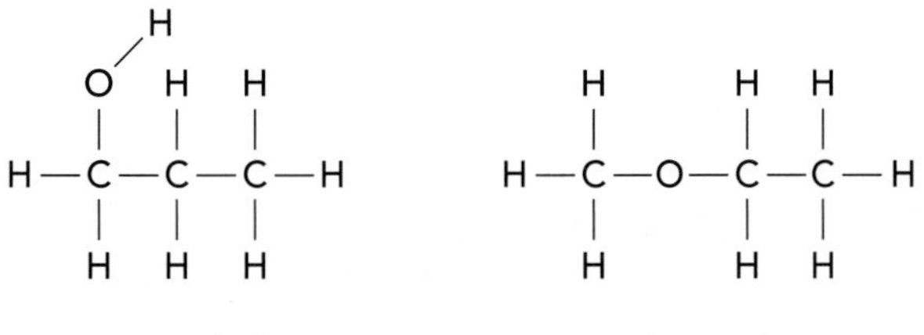

propan-1-ol   methoxyethane

Figure 14.20: An example of functional group isomerism.

Chain isomerism

Chain isomers differ in the structure of their carbon 'skeleton'. For example, butane and methylpropane are chain isomers, both with the molecular formula of C_4H_{10} (Figure 14.21).

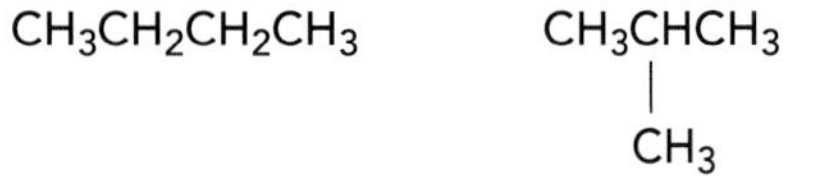

butane   methylpropane

Figure 14.21: An example of chain isomerism.

Question

5 **a** Name the four isomers in Figure 14.18.

b Draw the displayed formulae and name the structural isomers of C_3H_7Cl.

c Draw the displayed formulae and name the functional group isomers of C_3H_6O that are:

i an aldehyde

ii a ketone.

d Draw the displayed formula and name an isomer of C_3H_8O that could be used as an example of positional isomerism of one of the isomers in Figure 14.20.

e Draw the displayed formulae and give the names of the isomers of C_5H_{12}.

Check all your answers with a small group of other learners. Discuss any differences between your answers and agree on the best answer for each question.

14.6 Stereoisomerism

Stereoisomers are compounds whose molecules have the same atoms bonded to each other, but with different arrangements of the atoms in space.

There are two types of stereoisomerism:

1 geometrical (*cis*/*trans*) isomerism
2 optical isomerism.

KEY WORD

stereoisomers: compounds whose molecules have the same atoms bonded to each other in the same way, but with a different arrangement of atoms in space so that the molecules cannot be superimposed on each other.

Geometrical (*cis/trans*) isomerism

Unlike a C—C single bond, there is *no free rotation* about a C=C double bond. This can result in a different type of isomerism in unsaturated organic compounds. Figure 14.22 gives an example.

cis-1,2-dibromoethene   *trans*-1,2-dibromoethene

Figure 14.22: An example of geometrical (*cis/trans*) isomerism.

KEY WORDS

geometrical isomerism: displayed by unsaturated or ring compounds with the same molecular formula and order of atoms but different shapes. It arises because of a lack of free rotation about a double bond (due to the presence of a π (pi) bond – see Section 4.5) or a ring structure.

In *cis*-1,2-dibromoethene, both the Br atoms remain fixed on the same side of the C=C double bond as there is no free rotation about this bond because of the presence of a π (pi) bond. However, in *trans*-1,2-dibromoethene, the Br atoms are positioned across the C=C double bond. (Remember that the prefix 'trans-' means *across*.)

These two stereoisomers have different arrangements of the atoms in space, so they are different compounds with different physical properties. Stereoisomers can also have some different chemical properties. For example, they may react at different rates for the same reaction. Whenever we have unsaturated compounds with the structures shown in Figure 14.23, we can have this geometrical (*cis/trans*) type of isomerism.

Figure 14.23: These three arrangements can result in geometrical (*cis/trans*) isomerism because there is restricted rotation about the C=C double bond.

There is also geometrical (*cis/trans*) isomerism possible in *substituted cyclic compounds*. This is because of the limited rotation about C—C single bonds that make up the rings. We usually show the *cis*- and *trans*- isomers using a combination of skeletal and 3D formulae. For example, *cis*-3-methylcyclopentanol and *trans*-3-methylcyclopentanol:

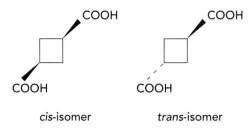

cis-3-methylcyclopentanol   *trans*-3-methylcyclopentanol

We can also show the two *cis/trans* isomers more clearly from a side view:

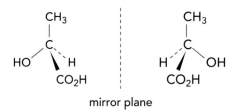

both —CH₃ and —OH groups point upwards (out of the paper)
cis-isomer

The —CH₃ group points upwards whereas the —OH group points downwards
trans-isomer

Another example is a substituted compound of cyclobutane, with two groups substituted into its four-membered ring. The two geometrical isomers below are called *cis*- and *trans*-cyclobutane-1,3-dicarboxylic acid:

cis-isomer   *trans*-isomer

In the *cis*-isomer, the two carboxylic acid groups are either both pointing above (as shown) or both below the ring of four carbon atoms. In the *trans*-isomer, one carboxylic acid group points above the ring and one below.

Optical isomerism

If a molecule contains a carbon atom that is bonded to four different atoms or groups of atoms, it can form two optical isomers. We can describe this carbon atom as an 'asymmetric' carbon atom because there is no plane of symmetry in its molecule. The two different optical isomers, called **enantiomers**, are mirror images of each other, and they cannot be superimposed (Figure 14.24). The carbon atom with the four different groups attached to it is called the **chiral centre** of the molecule.

mirror plane

Figure 14.24: This pair of molecules are optical isomers, referred to as enantiomers. Trying to superimpose the two isomers is like trying to superimpose your left hand on top of your right hand, with them both facing downwards: it can't be done.

KEY WORDS

enantiomers: a pair of optically active molecules whose mirror images cannot be superimposed.

chiral centre: a carbon atom with the four different atoms or groups of atoms attached. This allows optical isomers to exist.

PRACTICAL ACTIVITY 14.1

Modelling optical isomers

Using a molecular modelling kit, take a black carbon atom and attach four different coloured atoms to it. Then make another model molecule that is its mirror image using the same colours. Now try superimposing the two models so all the atoms match up. Can it be done?

Optical isomers differ in their effect on polarised light. Normal light is unpolarised. It can be thought of as fluctuating electric and magnetic fields, vibrating at right angles to each other in every possible direction. Passing this unpolarised light through a polariser results in polarised light, which vibrates in only one plane. A pair of optical isomers will rotate the plane of polarised light by equal amounts but in opposite directions. One will rotate the plane of polarised light clockwise and the other anticlockwise.

Organic molecules can contain more than one asymmetric carbon atom, i.e. more than one chiral centre. If there are two asymmetric carbon atoms, then each of its chiral centres will rotate the plane of polarised light. In this case, there will be four possible optical isomers.

As well as straight and branched chain molecules, *substituted cyclic molecules* can also have chiral centres in their ring structures. To decide where the chiral centres are, we still have to find any carbon atoms that are bonded to four different atoms or groups of atoms.

Look at this example of a substituted cyclohexane molecule:

In cyclohexane all the carbon atoms are bonded to two hydrogen atoms so there is no chiral centre. But when you start substituting other groups or atoms to replace hydrogen atoms, there is a possibility of asymmetric carbon atoms.

In the cyclic molecule shown we have a hydroxyl ($-OH$) group and an amine ($-NH_2$) group introduced into the ring. Let's consider the carbon atom bonded to the hydroxyl ($-OH$) group first. This carbon atom is also bonded to a hydrogen atom (not shown in the skeletal formula). The other two groups bonded to it, making up its four single bonds, are not the same. Imagine travelling around the ring in a clockwise direction from this carbon atom, you come to four carbon atoms, each bonded to two hydrogen atoms. Then you come to the carbon bonded to the $-NH_2$ group and one hydrogen atom, before arriving back where we started. We can think of this group as $-(CH_2)_4CHNH_2$. After that, travel around the ring in the opposite direction, an anti-clockwise direction, from same original carbon. This fourth bond from the carbon atom will be attached to a $-CHNH_2(CH_2)_4$ group, so the original carbon atom has four different groups or atoms bonded to it:

- an H atom
- the $-OH$ group
- the $-(CH_2)_4CHNH_2$ group
- the $-CHNH_2(CH_2)_4$ group.

Now you follow the same process starting from the carbon atom bonded to the $-NH_2$ group. You will find that this is also an asymmetric carbon atom. Therefore this cyclic molecule has *two chiral centres*.

Symmetrical substituted cyclic molecules will not have a chiral centre. Starting from the carbon atom(s) bonded to the group(s) substituted into the ring, you will find two identical groups 'going around' the ring in both the clockwise and the anticlockwise direction. Therefore, no carbon atom has four different groups attached to it.

Question

6 a i Draw the displayed formulae and label the *cis/trans* isomers of but-2-ene.

    ii Draw the *cis/trans* isomers of 1-bromo-2-chlorocyclobutane.

b The molecule CHBrClF exhibits optical isomerism. Draw the 3D displayed formulae of both optical isomers.

c i Which one of the following can have optical isomers?

    A $H_2C{=}CHCH_3$

    B $(CH_3)_2C{=}CHCHClCH_3$

    C $(CH_3)_3CBr$

    D $CH_3CH_2CH_2CHCl_2$

    ii Draw the displayed formula of your chosen answer and clearly label its chiral centre.

d Consider the two molecules below, methylcyclohexane and 2-methylcyclohexanone:

methylcyclohexane   2-methylcyclohexanone

Compare the number of chiral centres in each molecule and clearly label any chiral centres.

e Look back to the structure of the cholesterol molecule in Figure 14.7.

How many chiral centres are present in a cholesterol molecule?

    A 2   **C** 6

    B 4   **D** 8

14.7 Types of organic reaction and reaction mechanisms

Chemists find it useful to explain organic reactions by summarising the overall reaction in a series of steps called a **reaction mechanism**. Like all chemical reactions, organic reactions involve the breaking and making of chemical bonds. There are two ways in which covalent bonds can break:

- homolytic fission

- heterolytic fission.

> **KEY WORD**
>
> **reaction mechanism:** the series of steps that take place in the course of the overall reaction.

Homolytic fission

In this type of bond breaking, both the atoms at each end of the bond leave with one electron from the pair that formed the covalent bond. This is shown in Figure 14.25, using the simple example of a hydrogen chloride molecule.

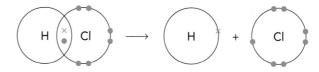

Figure 14.25: Homolytic fission of a covalent bond.

The species produced when a bond breaks homolytically are called *free radicals*. We can show the formation of free radicals by using an equation:

$$HCl \rightarrow H{\cdot} + Cl{\cdot}$$

H· and Cl· are free radicals. All free radicals have an unpaired electron (represented by the dot) and are very reactive.

You can read more about a free-radical reaction in Section 15.2.

This type of reaction involves the formation of the free radicals in an *initiation step*. This requires an input of energy to break a covalent bond, resulting in two free radicals.

The radicals formed can then attack reactant molecules, generating more free radicals. These reactions are called *propagation steps*. You can think of these as a chain reaction which only stops when free radicals react with each other.

Two free radicals reacting together will form a molecule, with no free radicals generated. We call this a *termination step*.

The three steps in a **free-radical reaction** are:

- initiation step: the formation of free radicals to start a reaction off

- propagation steps: steps in a mechanism that regenerate more free radicals

- termination step: the final step in a mechanism, when two free radicals meet and form a product molecule.

Heterolytic fission

The second type of bond breaking involves the 'uneven' breaking of a covalent bond. In heterolytic fission, the more electronegative atom takes both electrons in the covalent bond. Again, we can use hydrogen chloride to illustrate this (Figure 14.26).

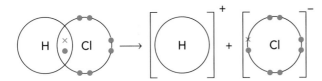

Figure 14.26: Heterolytic fission of a covalent bond.

We can show this type of bond breaking in an equation. A small curly arrow shows the movement of a pair of electrons:

$$H \overset{\frown}{-} Cl \longrightarrow H^+ + Cl^-$$

The heterolytic fission of a bond can involve a C—X bond, where X is an atom more electronegative than carbon.

For example:

$$H_3C \overset{\frown}{-} Br \longrightarrow CH_3^+ + Br^-$$

In this case, as the bond breaks, the Br atom takes both shared electrons, forming a bromide anion (a negatively charged ion). This leaves the methyl group one electron

short, resulting in the formation of a positively charged ion. This type of alkyl ion is called a **carbocation**. These positively charged carbocations often appear in reaction mechanisms (see Section 16.3).

There are three types of carbocations that you need to consider: primary, secondary and tertiary carbocations (Figure 14.27).

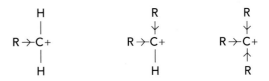

primary carbocation (least stable)   secondary carbocation   tertiary carbocation (most stable)

Key: where R = an alkyl group

Figure 14.27: Carbocations and their stability relative to each other.

Note that the carbon atom with the positive charge only has three covalent bonds, not the usual four, making it electron deficient. Any alkyl groups (e.g. $-CH_3$, $-C_2H_5$, $-C_3H_7$) attached to the positively charged carbon atom tend to be 'electron donating'. We say the alkyl groups have a positive **inductive effect**. The arrowheads on the bonds in Figure 14.27 are used to show the inductive effect of atoms or groups of atoms.

The alkyl groups 'push' electrons away from themselves, and reduce the charge density of the positive charge on the carbocation. This has the effect of spreading out the charge around the carbocation, making it energetically more stable. This means that a tertiary carbocation, with its *three* 'electron-donating' alkyl groups is the most energetically stable of the three types of carbocation.

> **IMPORTANT**
>
> The more alkyl groups adjacent to the positively charged carbon atom, the more stable the carbocation.

As a result of this, tertiary carbocations are more likely to form in reaction mechanisms than secondary carbocations, and primary carbocations are least favoured. This has effects on the products of some organic reactions, such as addition reactions to alkenes (see Section 15.3).

Carbocations are an example of a species called an **electrophile**.

> **KEY WORDS**
>
> **electrophile:** a species in organic chemistry that can act as an electron pair acceptor.
>
> **nucleophile:** species that can act as a donor of a pair of electrons.

When an electrophile accepts a pair of electrons, this results in the formation of a new covalent bond (see Section 15.3).

You will also meet **nucleophiles** when studying organic reactions and their mechanisms. These are electron-rich species, i.e. they carry a negative (–), or partial negative (δ–), charge.

When a nucleophile donates a pair of electrons, this leads to the formation of a new covalent bond with the electron-deficient atom under attack (see Section 18.4).

Question

7   a   Write an equation to show the homolytic fission of the Cl—Cl bond in a chlorine molecule, Cl_2.

   b   Write an equation to show the heterolytic fission of the C—Cl bond in chloromethane. Include a curly arrow in your answer.

   c   Which one of the following species is likely to act as a nucleophile?

   A H_2 **B** H^+ **C** OH^-

   d   Explain your answer to part **c**.

   e   Which one of the following species is likely to act as an electrophile?

   A H_2 **B** H^+ **C** OH^-

   f   Explain your answer to part **e**.

   g   Which of these carbocations is most likely to form as an intermediate in an organic reaction? Justify your answer.

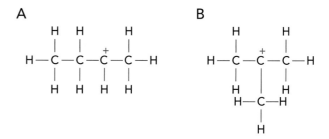

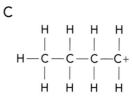

14.8 Types of organic reaction

Addition reactions involve the formation of a single product from two or more reactant molecules. An example is the addition reaction between an alkene and bromine (see Section 15.3):

$$C_2H_4 + Br_2 \rightarrow C_2H_4Br_2$$

Elimination reactions result in the removal of a small molecule from a larger reactant molecule. An example is the dehydration of an alcohol by concentrated sulfuric acid (see Section 17.3):

$$C_2H_5OH \xrightarrow{\text{conc. } H_2SO_4} C_2H_4 + H_2O$$

Condensation reactions involve a first step where addition takes place. This is followed by a second step where elimination occurs to form the final product. You will meet condensation reactions in Chapter 18 when you study carbonyl compounds.

KEY WORDS

addition reaction: an organic reaction in which two or more molecules combine to give a single product molecule.

elimination reaction: a reaction in which a small molecule, such as H_2O or HCl, is removed from an organic molecule.

condensation reaction: a reaction in which two organic molecules join together and in the process eliminate a small molecule, such as water or hydrogen chloride.

substitution reaction: a reaction that involves the replacement of one atom, or group of atoms, by another.

oxidation reaction: the addition of oxygen, removal of electrons or increase in oxidation number of a substance; in organic chemistry this refers to a reaction in which oxygen atoms are added to a molecule and/or hydrogen atoms are removed from a molecule.

reduction reaction: the removal of oxygen, addition of electrons or decrease in oxidation number of a substance; in organic chemistry it is the removal of oxygen atoms from a molecule and/or the addition of hydrogen atoms to a molecule.

free-radical substitution: the reaction in which halogen atoms substitute for hydrogen atoms in alkanes. The mechanism involves steps in which reactive free radicals are produced (initiation), regenerated (propagation) and consumed (termination).

Substitution reactions involve the replacement of one atom, or a group of atoms, by another. For example, the **free-radical substitution** of alkanes by chlorine in sunlight (see Section 15.2):

$$CH_4 + Cl_2 \xrightarrow{\text{UV light}} CH_3Cl + HCl$$

Here, an H atom in CH_4 has been replaced by a Cl atom.

Hydrolysis is the breakdown of a molecule by water. We can speed up this type of reaction by adding acid or alkali. For example, the hydrolysis of a halogenoalkane by water to give an alcohol (see Section 16.2):

$$C_2H_5Br + H_2O \rightarrow C_2H_5OH + HBr$$

Hydrolysis with alkali is faster, and gives slightly different products:

$$C_2H_5Br + NaOH \rightarrow C_2H_5OH + NaBr$$

Oxidation is defined as the loss of electrons from a species. However, in organic reactions it is often simpler to think of **oxidation reactions** in terms of the number of oxygen and / or hydrogen atoms before and after a reaction.

An example is the partial oxidation of ethanol to ethanal using acidified potassium dichromate(VI) solution (see Section 17.3):

$$C_2H_5OH + [O] \rightarrow CH_3CHO + H_2O$$

- before the reaction ethanol contains one O atom and six H atoms
- after the reaction ethanal contains one O atom and four H atoms.

In effect, the ethanol loses two H atoms, so we can say that ethanol has been oxidised.

Notice that we use [O] to simplify the chemical equation describing oxidation reactions. This is commonly used, but the equation must still be balanced: just like a normal equation. For example, in the complete oxidation of ethanol to ethanoic acid, using the reagents above but under harsher conditions (see Section 17.3):

$$C_2H_5OH + 2[O] \rightarrow CH_3COOH + H_2O$$

[O] represents an oxygen atom from the oxidising agent. The 2 in front of the [O] is needed to balance the equation for oxygen atoms.

For example, in the reduction of a ketone, using sodium tetrahydridoborate, $NaBH_4$ (see Section 18.3):

$$CH_3COCH_3 + 2[H] \rightarrow CH_3CH(OH)CH_3$$

Notice that we use [H] to simplify the chemical equation describing **reduction reactions**. [H] represents a hydrogen atom from the reducing agent. The 2 in front of the [H] is necessary to balance the equation for hydrogen atoms.

Question

8   Identify these reactions, choosing from the types of reaction described above:

a $C_3H_7I + H_2O \rightarrow C_3H_7OH + HI$

b $CH_3CHO + 2[H] \rightarrow CH_3CH_2OH$

c $C_2H_5Br \rightarrow C_2H_4 + HBr$

d $C_2H_4 + H_2O \rightarrow C_2H_5OH$

e $C_2H_6 + Cl_2 \rightarrow C_2H_5Cl + HCl$

REFLECTION

1   The ideas introduced in this chapter will all be revisited in later organic chemistry chapters. It will be useful for you to create a mind map now of the various ideas introduced. Put 'Organic chemistry' at the centre and label the links branching out to the new concepts. These could include 'functional groups', 'bonding', 'isomers', 'mechanisms', 'types of reaction'.

Your mind map will be useful to refer back to when studying the other organic chapters and when revising for exams.

2   Swap your mind map with another learner and discuss similarities and differences. Discuss the strengths and weaknesses in both mind maps.

Then explain to each other the process you both applied when constructing your mind map.

SUMMARY

We can represent an organic molecule, with increasing detail, by using its:
- empirical formula
- molecular formula
- structural formula
- displayed formula
- 3D displayed formula.

Functional groups give organic compounds their characteristic reactions.

Important functional groups include alkenes, alcohols, halogenoalkanes, aldehydes, ketones, carboxylic acids, esters, amines and nitriles.

The shapes of organic molecules can be explained by the σ and π bonds between carbon atoms, and the hybridisation of their atomic orbitals.

There are two types of isomer: structural isomers and stereoisomers.

Structural isomers have the same molecular formula but different structural formulae. We can group these into position, functional group or chain isomers.

Stereoisomers have the same molecular formula but different arrangement of their atoms in space.
- *Cis/trans* isomers arise because of the restricted rotation around a C=C double bond.
- Optical isomers contain a chiral centre (a carbon atom bonded to four different atoms or groups of atoms), resulting in mirror images of the molecule that cannot be superimposed.

EXAM-STYLE QUESTIONS

1 Which one of the following compounds does *not* need any numbers in its name? [1]

   A $CH_3CH{=}CHCH_3$

   B $CH_3COCH_2CH_3$

   C $CH_3CHBrCH_2CH_3$

   D $CH_3CHClCH_2CH_2Cl$

2 Which one of the molecules below contains a chiral centre? [1]

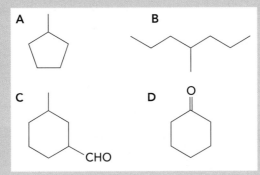

3 Methylpropane, $CH_3CH(CH_3)CH_3$, is commonly used in the petrochemical industry.

   a i   Name the homologous series that methylpropane belongs to. [1]

      ii   Give the molecular formula of methylpropane. [1]

      iii Give the empirical formula of methylpropane. [1]

      iv   Draw the displayed formula of methylpropane. [1]

      v   Draw the skeletal formula of methylpropane. [1]

   b Each carbon atom in methylpropane has hybridised atomic orbitals.

      i   What type of hybridisation is found in a molecule of methylpropane?

           A sp hybridisation

           B sp^2 hybridisation

           C sp^3 hybridisation

           D sp^4 hybridisation [1]

      ii   Give the bond angles found within a molecule of methylpropane. [1]

   c When methylpropane is passed over a hot aluminium oxide catalyst, it can be converted into *methylpropene*.

      i   To which homologous series of organic compounds does methylpropene belong? [1]

      ii   Methylpropene can be converted back into methylpropane by heating with hydrogen gas in the presence of a platinum / nickel catalyst:

$$H_2C{=}C(CH_3)CH_3 + H_2 \xrightarrow{\text{Pt / Ni}} CH_3CH(CH_3)CH_3$$

           What type of reaction best describes this reaction?

           A Oxidation

           B Elimination

           C Hydrolysis

           D Addition [1]

CONTINUED

d i Draw the displayed formula of a structural isomer of methylpropene. [1]

ii Give the empirical formula of both isomers. [1]

[Total: 13]

4 A carbon compound P has the percentage composition 85.7% carbon and 14.3% hydrogen. Its relative molecular mass was found to be 56.

a i Calculate its empirical formula. [4]

ii Calculate its molecular formula. [1]

b Write down the names and displayed formulae of all the non-cyclic isomers of compound P which have the following characteristics:

i straight chain [6]

ii branched chain. [2]

[Total: 13]

5 A chemist was investigating the best way to produce 1,2-dichloroethane. She devised two methods, I and II, of doing this.

I She reacted ethane with chlorine in the presence of UV light by the following reaction:

$$C_2H_6(g) + 2Cl_2(g) \rightarrow C_2H_4Cl_2(l) + 2HCl(g)$$

After doing this she found that 600 g of ethane gave 148.5 g of $C_2H_4Cl_2$.

a i Calculate how many moles of ethane there are in 600 g. [1]

ii Deduce how many moles of 1,2-dichloroethane would have been formed if the yield had been 100%. [1]

iii Calculate how many moles of 1,2-dichloroethane there are in 148.5 g. [1]

iv Calculate the percentage yield of 1,2-dichloroethane. [1]

II She reacted ethene with chlorine in the dark by the following reaction:

$$C_2H_4(g) + Cl_2(g) \rightarrow C_2H_4Cl_2(l)$$

b In this reaction 140 g of ethene gave 396 g of $C_2H_4Cl_2$.

Calculate the percentage yield for this reaction. Show your working. [3]

c There are isomers of the compound $C_2H_4Cl_2$.

Draw the displayed formulae of the isomers and name them. [4]

d Choose from:

A redox   D addition

B substitution   E hydrolysis

C elimination

to give the type of reaction for:

i reaction I [1]

ii reaction II. [1]

[Total: 13]

SELF-EVALUATION

After studying this chapter, complete a table like this:

I can	See section...	Needs more work	Almost there	Ready to move on
define the term hydrocarbon and describe what alkanes are	14.1			
interpret, name and use the general, structural, displayed and skeletal formulae of all the homologous series introduced in this chapter	14.1, 14.2, 14.3			
deduce the molecular and/or empirical formula of a compound, given its structural, displayed or skeletal formula	14.1			
explain the following terms: a functional group b homolytic and heterolytic fission c free radical d initiation e propagation f termination g nucleophile h electrophile i nucleophilic j electrophilic k addition l substitution m elimination n hydrolysis o condensation p oxidation q reduction	14.1, 14.7, 14.8			
describe and explain the shape of, and bond angles of, organic molecules in terms of their sp, sp^2 and sp^3 hybridised atomic orbitals, and their σ bonds and π bonds	14.4			
describe and explain the different types of structural isomerism and stereoisomerism.	14.5, 14.6			
explain and identify isomerism, including chiral centres and geometrical isomers	14.6			
deduce possible isomers from a given molecular formula	14.5, 14.6			

> Chapter 15
Hydrocarbons

LEARNING INTENTIONS

In this chapter you will learn how to:

- explain the general unreactivity of alkanes, and describe their complete and incomplete combustion

- explain the free-radical substitution of alkanes by chlorine and by bromine, as shown by their three-step mechanism

- suggest how cracking can be used to obtain more useful alkanes and alkenes of lower relative molecular mass from larger hydrocarbon molecules

- describe the environmental consequences of burning hydrocarbon fuels in vehicles and the removal of pollutants by catalytic converters

- describe the reactions of alkenes as shown by their addition, oxidation and polymerisation

- describe the mechanism of electrophilic addition in alkenes, and explain the inductive effects of alkyl groups on the stability of cations formed

- describe the difficulty of disposing of waste poly(alkene)s.

BEFORE YOU START

1 Here are four types of hybridisation of carbon atomic orbitals:

   only sp   only sp^2 only sp^3 sp^2 and sp^3

   Which do you find in the following molecules?

   a   ethane

   b   ethene

   c   propene.

2 a   Give the names of:

   i $CH_3CH_2CH(CH_3)CH_3$

   ii $CH_3CH_2CH_2CH{=}CH_2$

   b   Give the structural formulae of:

   i   2,3-dimethylhexane

   ii   pent-2-ene.

3 a   Are alkyl groups 'electron withdrawing' or 'electron donating' to their neighbouring carbon atom?

   b   Which type of carbocation is most energetically stable: primary, secondary or tertiary carbocation?

4 Working with a partner, discuss the difference between an electrophile and a nucleophile, and what we mean by a 'reaction mechanism'.

HYDROCARBONS IN USE

Crude oil (Figure 15.1) is our main source of hydrocarbons. Hydrocarbons are compounds containing carbon and hydrogen only. They provide us with fuels such as petrol, diesel and kerosene. Hydrocarbons are also the starting compounds used to make many new compounds, such as most of the plastics we use in everyday life.

Crude oil is a complex mixture of hydrocarbons. It contains alkanes, cycloalkanes and arenes (compounds containing benzene rings – see Chapter 25).

Cycloalkanes are saturated hydrocarbons in which there is a 'ring' consisting of three or more carbon atoms. Imagine the two carbon atoms at each end of a straight-chain alkane bonding to each other. These two carbon atoms could then only bond to two hydrogen atoms each, not three as in the straight-chain alkane. Cyclohexane, C_6H_{12}, is an

example (Figure 15.2). Note that a cycloalkane does not follow the general alkane formula, C_nH_{2n+2}.

Figure 15.1: Crude oil is extracted from porous seams of rock found beneath an impervious layer of rock within the Earth's crust.

CONTINUED

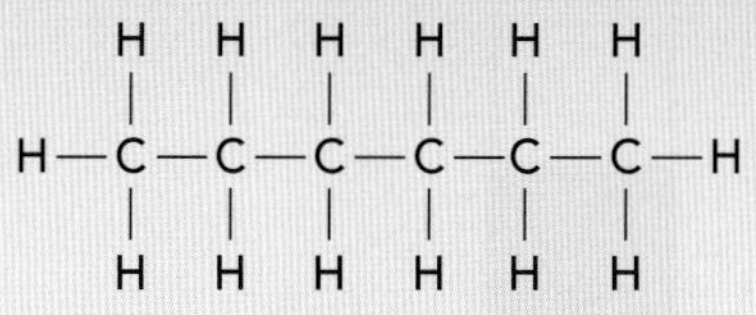

displayed formula of hexane

skeletal formula of hexane

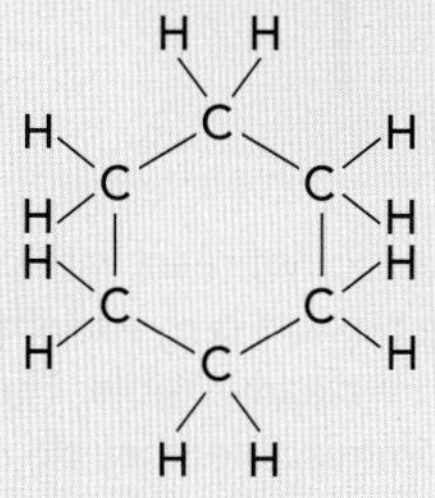

displayed formula of cyclohexane

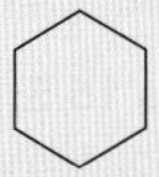

skeletal formula of cyclohexane

Figure 15.2: Hexane (C_6H_{14}) and cyclohexane (C_6H_{12}).

The crude oil is brought to the surface at oil wells and transported to an oil refinery. The actual composition of crude oil varies in different oilfields around the world.

At the refinery, the crude oil is processed into useful fuels. The first step is fractional distillation of the oil. This separates the wide range of different hydrocarbons into fractions. The hydrocarbons in each fraction will have similar boiling points. This is carried out in tall fractionating columns.

The oil-based compounds that are in high demand are the gasoline fraction (providing petrol) and the naphtha fraction (providing the starting compounds for making many other chemicals in industry).

Questions for discussion

Discuss with another learner or group of learners:

As you know, the supplies of crude oil are a finite resource and they are rapidly running out. One way to conserve the oil we have left is to switch from petrol and diesel cars to electric cars. Discuss the difficulties in making the switch to electric vehicles, as well as the benefits it will bring. Then feedback your main points to the rest of your group.

15.1 The homologous group of alkanes

The majority of compounds found in the mixture of hydrocarbons we call crude oil are alkanes. We met the first ten members of this homologous series in Table 14.2. The general formula for the alkanes is C_nH_{2n+2}. For example, the molecular formula of pentane, in which $n = 5$, is C_5H_{12} (Figure 15.3).

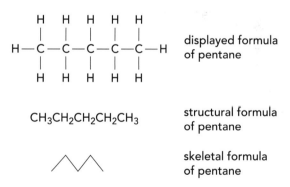

displayed formula of pentane

$CH_3CH_2CH_2CH_2CH_3$

structural formula of pentane

skeletal formula of pentane

Figure 15.3: Three different ways of representing pentane molecules.

Note that all the carbon–carbon bonds are single covalent bonds. The carbon atoms all display sp³ hybridisation (see Section 4.5). This means that alkanes have the maximum number of hydrogen atoms in their molecules, and are known as **saturated hydrocarbons** (Figure 15.4).

KEY WORDS

alkanes: saturated hydrocarbons with the general formula C_nH_{2n+2}

saturated hydrocarbon: compound of hydrogen and carbon only in which the carbon–carbon bonds are all single covalent bonds, resulting in the maximum number of hydrogen atoms in the molecule.

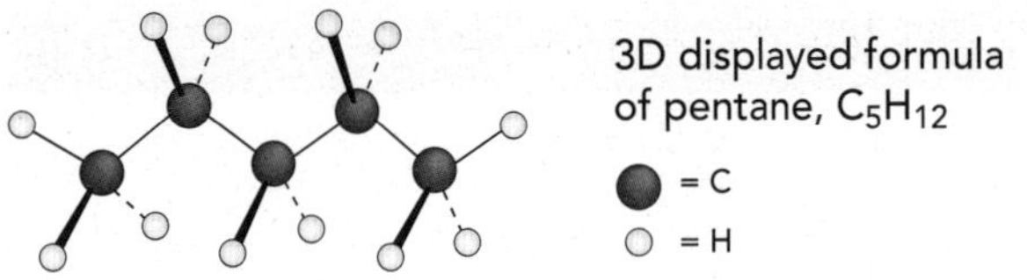

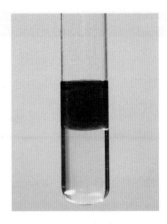

3D displayed formula
of pentane, C_5H_{12}

● = C
○ = H

Figure 15.4: The 3D displayed formula shows the tetrahedral arrangement of atoms around each carbon atom (approximate bond angles of 109.5°).

Figure 15.5: Non-polar alkanes do not react with polar compounds such as water. The hexane is dyed with iodine to make it coloured, so it is more clearly visible. The hexane and water in the test-tube are immiscible: they do *not* mix and they do *not* react with each other.

Question

1 a Eicosane is a straight-chain alkane whose molecules contain 20 carbon atoms.

    i What is the molecular formula of eicosane?

    ii Draw the skeletal formula of eicosane.

  b Draw the displayed formula and the skeletal formula of cyclopentane.

  c What is the general formula of cycloalkanes?

  d Give two differences between a molecule of cyclopentane and a molecule of pentane.

15.2 Reactions of alkanes

The alkanes are generally unreactive compounds. We can explain this by the very small difference in electronegativity between carbon and hydrogen. Their atoms share the pair of electrons in the single covalent bonds almost equally. Therefore, alkane molecules are non-polar, so they are not attacked by nucleophiles or electrophiles (Figure 15.5). They have no partial positive charges (δ+) on any of their carbon atoms to attract nucleophiles, neither do they have areas of high electron density to attract electrophiles (see Section 14.7).

However, the alkanes do react with oxygen in combustion reactions and also undergo substitution by halogens in sunlight. These reactions are covered in the following sections.

Combustion of alkanes

Alkanes are often used as fuels (Figure 15.6). We burn them for many reasons:

• to generate electricity in power stations,

• to heat our homes and cook our food

• to provide energy needed in industrial processes

• to provide fuel for ships, aeroplanes, trains, lorries, buses, cars and motorbikes.

Figure 15.6: Alkanes are useful fuels.

If we burn an alkane in plenty of oxygen, the alkane will undergo complete combustion. All the carbon will be oxidised fully to form carbon dioxide, and all the hydrogen will be oxidised to form water:

$$\text{alkane} + \text{oxygen} \xrightarrow{\text{complete combustion}} \text{carbon dioxide} + \text{water}$$

For example, octane is one of the alkanes in petrol that is burned inside the internal combustion engine in motor vehicles. Some of the octane will undergo complete combustion in a car engine:

$$2C_8H_{18} + 25O_2 \rightarrow 16CO_2 + 18H_2O$$
$$\text{octane} + \text{oxygen} \rightarrow \text{carbon dioxide} + \text{water}$$

The equation can also be written as:

$$C_8H_{18} + 12\tfrac{1}{2}O_2 \rightarrow 8CO_2 + 9H_2O$$

Pollution from burning hydrocarbon fuels

When the petrol or diesel is mixed with air inside a car engine, there is only a limited supply of oxygen. Under these conditions, not all the carbon in the hydrocarbon fuel is fully oxidised to carbon dioxide. Some of the carbon is only partially oxidised to form carbon monoxide (CO) gas. This is called *incomplete combustion*.

For example:

$$2C_8H_{18} + 17O_2 \xrightarrow{\text{incomplete combustion}} 16CO + 18H_2O$$
$$\text{octane} + \text{oxygen} \xrightarrow{\text{incomplete combustion}} \text{carbon monoxide} + \text{water}$$

or

$$C_8H_{18} + 8\tfrac{1}{2}O_2 \rightarrow 8CO + 9H_2O$$

Carbon monoxide is a toxic gas that bonds with the haemoglobin in your blood. The haemoglobin molecules can then no longer bond to oxygen and so cannot transport oxygen around your body. Victims of carbon monoxide poisoning will feel dizzy, then lose consciousness. If not removed from the toxic gas, the victim will die.

Carbon monoxide is odourless, so this adds to the danger. This is why faulty gas heaters in which incomplete combustion occurs can kill unsuspecting people in rooms with poor ventilation.

As well as releasing carbon monoxide, road traffic also releases acidic nitrogen oxides, mainly NO and NO_2. These contribute to the problem of acid rain (see Section 13.3). Acid rain can kill trees and aquatic animals in lakes (Figure 15.7). Acid rain also erodes limestone buildings and statues, as well as corroding metals, such as iron.

Figure 15.7: These trees have been badly damaged by acid rain.

In normal combustion, nitrogen gas in the air is not oxidised. However, in the very high temperatures in car engines, oxidation of nitrogen does take place. A variety of nitrogen oxides can be formed and released in the car's exhaust fumes (Figure 15.8). For example:

$$N_2(g) + O_2(g) \rightleftharpoons 2NO(g)$$
$$2NO(g) + O_2(g) \rightleftharpoons 2NO_2(g)$$

Figure 15.8: The vast numbers of cars on the roads pollute our atmosphere. Nitrogen oxides from traffic contribute to photochemical smog, as well as acid rain.

As well as toxic carbon monoxide and acidic nitrogen oxides, cars also release unburnt hydrocarbons, often referred to as volatile organic compounds (VOCs), into the air. Some of these are carcinogens (they cause cancers) and can form PAN, a contributor to photochemical smog (see Section 13.3).

Reducing traffic emissions

Motor vehicles can now be fitted with catalytic converters in their exhaust systems (Figure 15.9). Once warmed up, a catalytic converter can cause the following reactions to take place:

- the oxidation of carbon monoxide to form carbon dioxide

- the reduction of nitrogen oxides to form harmless nitrogen gas

- the oxidation of unburnt hydrocarbons to form carbon dioxide and water.

Unfortunately, catalytic converters can do nothing to reduce the amount of carbon dioxide (a greenhouse gas) given off in the exhaust gases of cars and trucks.

Figure 15.9: Catalytic converters reduce the pollutants from car exhausts. Precious metals, such as platinum, are coated on a honeycomb structure to provide a large surface area on which the reactions can occur.

The following equation describes the reaction between carbon monoxide and nitrogen monoxide. It takes place on the surface of the precious metal catalyst in a catalytic converter:

$$2CO + 2NO \rightarrow 2CO_2 + N_2$$

Some of the carbon monoxide gas can also be oxidised inside the hot catalytic converter:

$$2CO + O_2 \rightarrow 2CO_2$$

Note that more carbon dioxide is released in the process of removing carbon monoxide. Carbon dioxide is not a toxic gas, but it is still considered a pollutant because of its contribution to enhanced global warming, resulting in climate change.

Question

2 a Predict what would happen if octane was added to a solution of sodium hydroxide.

   b Explain your answer to part **a**.

   c Give the balanced symbol equations for:

      i the complete combustion of heptane, C_7H_{16}, giving carbon dioxide and water

      ii the incomplete combustion of methane, CH_4, giving carbon monoxide and water

      iii the incomplete combustion of nonane, C_9H_{20}, giving carbon monoxide and water.

   d i Name two pollutants from a car engine that can be oxidised in a catalytic converter.

      ii Name a pollutant that is reduced in a catalytic converter.

      iii Which pollutant from a car engine is not reduced by the use of a catalytic converter? What environmental problem does this pollutant contribute to?

Now swap your answers with another learner and compare your responses. Discuss any differences, and arrive at an agreed set of answers before looking up the correct answers online.

Substitution reactions of alkanes

The alkanes will undergo substitution reactions with halogens in sunlight.

Consider the reaction between ethane and chlorine in sunlight:

$$\underset{\text{ethane}}{C_2H_6} + Cl_2 \xrightarrow{\text{sunlight}} \underset{\text{chloroethane}}{CH_3CH_2Cl} + HCl$$

In this reaction, a hydrogen atom in the ethane molecule gets replaced by a chlorine atom. However, this type of reaction does not take place in darkness (Figure 15.10). So what role does the sunlight play in the mechanism of this substitution reaction?

Initiation step

The first step in the mechanism is the breaking of the Cl—Cl bond by energy from ultraviolet light in sunlight. This is called the **initiation step** in the mechanism:

$$Cl_2 \xrightarrow{\text{UV light}} 2Cl\cdot$$

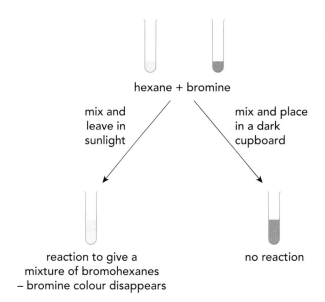

hexane + bromine

mix and leave in sunlight / mix and place in a dark cupboard

reaction to give a mixture of bromohexanes – bromine colour disappears

no reaction

Figure 15.10: A substitution reaction takes place between alkanes and bromine in sunlight, but there is no reaction in darkness.

As the Cl—Cl bond breaks, each chlorine atom takes one electron from the pair of electrons in the Cl—Cl bond. This is an example of homolytic fission of a covalent bond (see Section 14.7). Two Cl atoms are formed. These Cl atoms, each with an unpaired electron, are called *free radicals*.

KEY WORDS

initiation step: the first step in the mechanism of free-radical substitution of alkanes by halogens. It involves the breaking of the halogen–halogen bond using energy from ultra-violet light from the Sun.

propagation step: the second step in a free-radical mechanism in which the radicals formed can then attack reactant molecules generating more free radicals, and so on.

termination steps: the final steps in a free-radical mechanism in which two free radicals react together to form a product molecule.

Propagation steps

Free radicals are very reactive. They will attack the normally unreactive alkanes. A chlorine free radical will attack the ethane molecule:

$$CH_3CH_3 + Cl\cdot \rightarrow \cdot CH_2CH_3 + HCl$$

In this propagation step, a C—H bond in CH_3CH_3 breaks homolytically. An ethyl free radical, $\cdot CH_2CH_3$, is produced. This can then attack a chlorine molecule, forming chloroethane and regenerating a chlorine free radical:

$$\cdot CH_2CH_3 + Cl_2 \rightarrow CH_3CH_2Cl + Cl\cdot$$

Then the first propagation step can be repeated as the chlorine free radical can attack another ethane molecule. This forms the ethyl free radical, which regenerates another chlorine free radical, and so on.

The word 'propagation' usually refers to growing new plants. In this mechanism the substitution reaction progresses (grows) in a type of chain reaction.

This reaction is not really suitable for preparing specific halogenoalkanes, because we get a mixture of substitution products. In the reaction between ethane and chlorine, the products can include many different chloroalkanes. These can include 1,1-dichloroethane, 1,1,1 trichloroethane, 1,2-dichloroethane, 1,1,2-trichloroethane, 1,1,2,2-tetrachloroethane, and so on, as well as chloroethane. If there is enough chlorine present, we eventually get hexachloroethane (C_2Cl_6), This variety of chloroalkane products results from propagation steps in which a chlorine free radical attacks a chloroalkane already formed.

For example:

$$CH_3CH_2Cl + Cl\cdot \rightarrow \cdot CH_2CH_2Cl + HCl$$

This can then be followed by:

$$\cdot CH_2CH_2Cl + Cl_2 \rightarrow ClCH_2CH_2Cl + Cl\cdot$$
1,2-dichloroethane

The more chlorine gas in the reaction mixture to start with, the greater the proportions of chlorine atoms in the chloroalkane molecules formed.

Termination steps

Whenever two free radicals meet they will react with each other. A single molecule is the only product. As no free radicals are made that can carry on the reaction sequence, the chain reaction stops. Examples of **termination steps** include:

$$\cdot CH_2CH_3 + \cdot Cl \rightarrow ClCH_2CH_3$$
$$\cdot CH_2CH_3 + \cdot CH_2CH_3 \rightarrow CH_3CH_2CH_2CH_3$$
(butane, C_4H_{10})

- In the initiation step, we start with a molecule and get two free radicals formed.

- In each propagation step, we start with a molecule and a free radical and get a different molecule and a different free radical formed.

- In the termination steps, we start with two free radicals and end up with a molecule and no free radicals.

Overall, the reaction between alkanes and halogens, involving initiation, propagation and termination steps, is called free-radical substitution.

Question

3 Bromine can react with ethane to form bromoethane.

a What conditions are needed for the reaction between ethane and bromine to take place?

b What do we call this type of reaction?

c Write an equation to show the reaction of ethane and bromine to form bromoethane.

d Why is this reaction not a good way to prepare a pure sample of bromoethane?

e i Name the three steps in the mechanism of this reaction.

ii Write an equation to show the first step in the mechanism.

iii What type of bond breaking does this first step involve?

REFLECTION

1 At this point, reflect on your work done studying the 'alkanes'. Make a two-column table to record 'New things I know about the alkanes' / 'New things that I do not really understand yet'.

2 Discuss your table with a fellow learner and explain to each other exactly where your problems lie. If you can't sort out any of your difficulties together, ask your teacher to help.

15.3 The alkenes

We have looked at the nature of the double bond found in the hydrocarbons called *alkenes* in Section 14.4. Alkenes with one double bond per molecule have the general formula C_nH_{2n}. One example is ethene, C_2H_4. Whereas alkanes, which contain only single bonds, are described as saturated hydrocarbons, we describe alkenes as unsaturated hydrocarbons.

Oil refineries provide useful alkenes for the chemical industry. In the introduction to this chapter, we saw how crude oil is separated into fractions at a refinery. Oil companies find that the demand for each fraction differs. The lighter fractions, such as the gasoline fraction, are in high demand. So, chemical engineers convert some of the excess heavier fractions into lighter hydrocarbons. The large, less useful hydrocarbon molecules are broken down into smaller, more useful molecules. The process is called cracking.

KEY WORDS

unsaturated hydrocarbons: compounds of hydrogen and carbon only whose molecules contain carbon-to-carbon double bonds (or triple bonds).

cracking: the process in which large, less useful hydrocarbon molecules are broken down into smaller, more useful molecules in an oil refinery.

The larger hydrocarbon molecules are fed into a steel chamber that contains no oxygen, so combustion does not take place. The larger hydrocarbon molecules are heated to a high temperature and are passed over an aluminium oxide, Al_2O_3, catalyst (Figure 15.11).

When large alkane molecules are cracked, they form smaller alkane molecules and alkene molecules. One possible example of a cracking reaction is:

$$CH_3(CH_2)_8CH_3 \xrightarrow[\text{heat}]{Al_2O_3}$$
$$CH_3(CH_2)_4CH_3 + CH_2{=}CHCH_2CH_3$$
$$C_{10}H_{22} \xrightarrow[\text{heat}]{Al_2O_3} C_6H_{14} + C_4H_8$$

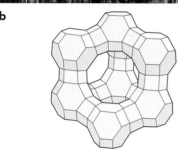

Figure 15.11: a A catalytic cracker occupies the bulk of the central part of this view of an oil refinery. **b** A computer graphic showing a catalyst used to crack hydrocarbons.

The low-molecular mass alkanes formed (C_6H_{14} in this example) make very useful fuels and are in high demand. However, the alkenes produced (C_4H_8 in this example) are also very useful. They are more reactive than the alkanes because of their double bonds. This makes them useful for the chemical industry as the starting compounds (feedstock) for making many new products. These include most plastics (see Section 15.5).

As well as the cracking of alkanes, alkenes can also be made by:

- elimination of a hydrogen halide (e.g. HCl) from a halogenoalkane by heating with ethanolic sodium hydroxide (see Section 16.4)

- dehydration of an alcohol by using a heated catalyst (e.g. aluminium oxide, Al_2O_3) or a concentrated acid (see Section 17.3).

Dehydration is the elimination of a water molecule from a reactant molecule.

Question

4   a   Name the first member of the homologous series of alkenes.

    b   Give the molecular formula of the alkene containing 18 carbon atoms and one C=C bond.

    c   Look at the equation for cracking given in the text. Write a word equation for this reaction.

    d   Write a balanced equation to show the cracking of nonane into heptane and ethene.

    e   Discuss and suggest why 'Alkenes are more reactive than alkanes'. Think about whether electrophiles or nucleophiles would attack alkenes and explain your choice.

Addition reactions of the alkenes

Most reactions of the alkenes are examples of addition reactions. In these reactions one of the two bonds in the carbon–carbon (C=C) double bond is broken and a new single bond is formed from each of the two carbon atoms.

The general addition reactions are shown in Figure 15.12.

Figure 15.12: General equations for addition reactions of the alkenes: **a** with a hydrogen halide, such as hydrogen bromide, and **b** with a halogen, such as chlorine.

Addition of hydrogen, $H_2(g)$

When hydrogen gas and an alkene are heated and passed over a finely divided platinum / nickel catalyst, the addition reaction produces an alkane:

$$CH_2{=}CH_2 + H_2 \xrightarrow[\text{heat}]{\text{Pt / Ni catalyst}} CH_3CH_3$$

ethene   ethane

> ### KEY WORD
>
> **hydrogenation:** the addition reaction of alkenes with hydrogen.

The addition reaction of alkenes with hydrogen is called **hydrogenation**, and is used in the manufacture of margarine (Figure 15.13).

Addition of hydrogen halides, HX(aq)

When an alkene is bubbled through a concentrated solution of a hydrogen halide (either HF, HCl, HBr or HI) at room temperature, the product is a halogenoalkane. For example:

$$CH_2{=}CH_2 + HBr \rightarrow CH_3CH_2Br$$

ethene   bromoethane

With longer, asymmetric alkenes there are always two possible products that could be formed.

For example, with propene:

$$CH_3CH{=}CH_2 + HBr \rightarrow CH_3CH_2CH_2Br$$

propene   1-bromopropane

and

$$CH_3CH{=}CH_2 + HBr \rightarrow CH_3CHBrCH_3$$

propene   2-bromopropane

> ### IMPORTANT
>
> Where two addition products are possible, the major product is the one that has the halogen atom bonded to the C=C carbon atom with the highest number of alkyl groups bonded to it.

In the two reactions of propene with HBr shown, the Br bonds to the central C atom to form the major product. The central C atom has two alkyl (methyl) groups

Figure 15.13: Unsaturated oils, such as sunflower oil, contain hydrocarbon chains with several carbon–carbon double bonds. These oils become partially saturated by reacting them with hydrogen, straightening their hydrocarbon chains. This raises the melting points of the oils, changing them from liquids to soft solids that can be spread easily.

bonded to it compared with the single alkyl (ethyl) group on the end C atom. Therefore, $CH_3CHBrCH_3$ is the major product.

We can explain why this happens by thinking back to the stability of the carbocations discussed in Section 14.7. Remember that each alkyl group tends to donate electrons along its bond to the positively charged carbon atom in the carbocation. The $CH_3CHBrCH_3$ is formed from a secondary carbocation intermediate, $CH_3C^+HCH_3$. In Section 14.7 we saw that a secondary carbocation is more stable than a primary carbocation, in this case $CH_3CH_2C^+H_2$. This is because the positive charge becomes less concentrated by the inductive effect of two alkyl groups rather than just one alkyl group. Therefore, the secondary carbocation **intermediate** is more readily formed in the course of the addition reaction.

> ### KEY WORD
>
> **intermediate:** a species, such as a carbocation, which is formed at a particular step of the reaction. Intermediates are stable enough to react with another substance but not stable enough to be a product. They often have a partial positive or negative charge.

The mechanism of electrophilic addition that follows shows how:

- a carbocation forms

- which is then attacked by a negative ion

- to give the final product of the addition reaction.

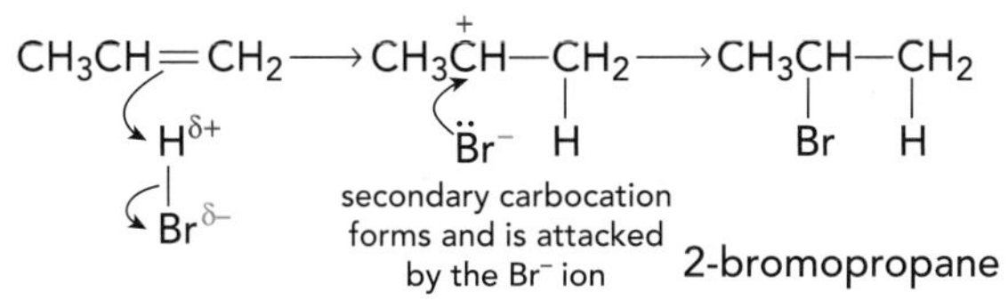

$$CH_3CH=CH_2 \longrightarrow CH_3\overset{+}{C}H-CH_2 \longrightarrow CH_3CH-CH_2$$

secondary carbocation forms and is attacked by the Br^- ion   2-bromopropane

Figure 15.14: The mechanism for the electrophilic addition of HBr to propene.

Addition of steam, $H_2O(g)$

Scientists in industry use the addition of steam to alkenes to make alcohols. They react steam and the gaseous alkene at a high temperature and pressure, in the presence of concentrated phosphoric acid, H_3PO_4, as the catalyst. When the alkene is ethene, the product is ethanol (Figure 15.15). However, the ethanol found in alcoholic drinks is always produced by the fermentation of glucose.

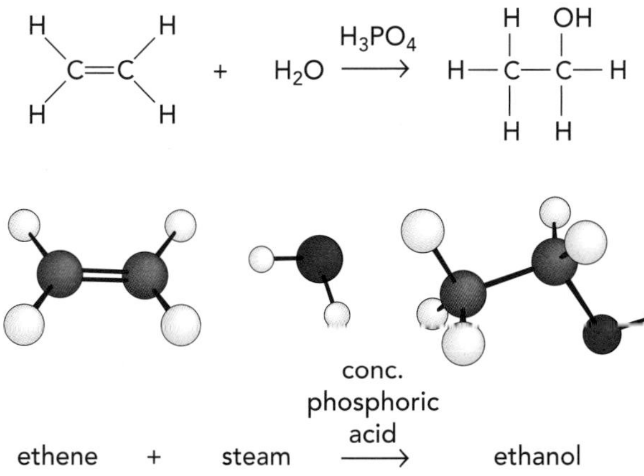

ethene   +   steam $\xrightarrow{\text{conc. phosphoric acid}}$ ethanol

Figure 15.15: The addition reaction between ethene and steam.

Addition of halogens, $X_2(aq)$

If we bubble an alkene through a solution of chlorine or bromine at room temperature, we again get an addition reaction. The colour of the halogen molecules in solution is removed in the course of the reaction (Figures 15.16 and 15.17).

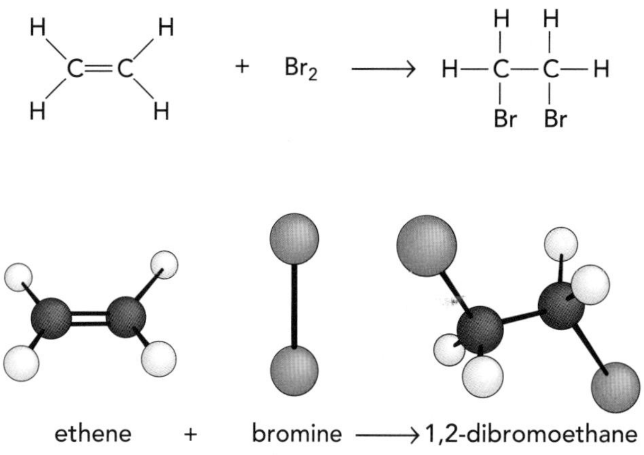

ethene   +   bromine $\longrightarrow$ 1,2-dibromoethane

Figure 15.16: The reaction between ethene and bromine.

The reactant $Cl_2(aq)$ is a very pale green solution, called *chlorine water*. Bromine water, $Br_2(aq)$, is orange or yellow, depending on the concentration of bromine water.

Bromine water is used to test for the presence of the $C=C$ bond in compounds. The compound to be tested is shaken with bromine water. If it is unsaturated, the bromine water will be decolorised.

Figure 15.17: The addition reaction used to test for an unsaturated compound.

The mechanism of electrophilic addition to alkenes

In Section 14.4 we saw how the double bond in ethene is formed from a σ (sigma) bond and a π (pi) bond.

There are four electrons in total in this double bond. So although ethene is a non-polar molecule, there is an area of high electron density around the C=C bond. This makes the alkenes open to attack by electrophiles (see Section 14.7).

Remember that an electrophile is an acceptor of a pair of electrons. HBr is a polar molecule because of the difference in electronegativity between the H atom and the Br atom. In a molecule of HBr, the H atom carries a partial positive charge and the Br atom carries a partial negative charge.

In the mechanism of addition, the H atom acts as the electrophile, accepting a pair of electrons from the C=C bond in the alkene. Look back to Figure 15.14.

But how can a non-polar molecule such as Br_2 act as an electrophile? As the bromine molecule and ethene molecules approach each other, the area of high electron density around the C=C bond repels the pair of electrons in the Br—Br bond away from the nearer Br atom. This makes the nearer Br atom slightly positive and the further Br atom slightly negative. Figure 15.18 shows the mechanism of electrophilic addition.

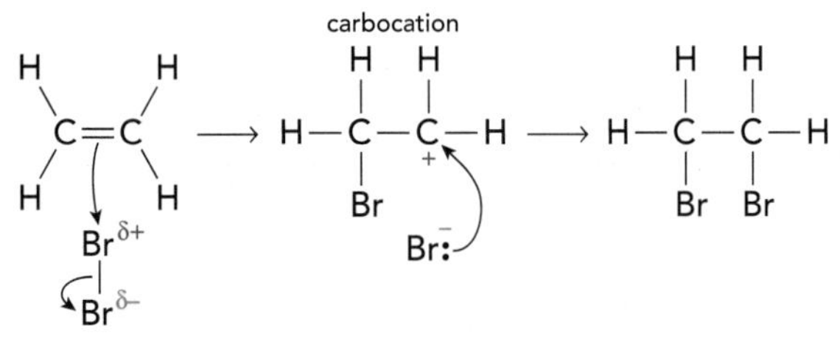

Figure 15.18: The mechanism of the electrophilic addition of bromine to ethene.

As the new bond between the C and Br atom forms, the Br—Br bond breaks heterolytically (see Section 14.7). The Br^- ion formed then attacks the highly reactive carbocation intermediate. So, one bromine atom bonds to each carbon atom, producing 1,2-dibromoethane.

Question

5   a   State the general conditions used in the reaction between an alkene and hydrogen.

 b   Name the product formed when propene reacts with chlorine.

 c   Ethanol can be used as a solvent. How is this ethanol made in industry?

 d   What will be formed when ethene gas is bubbled through a concentrated solution of hydrochloric acid?

 e   Define the term *electrophile*.

 f   Explain how a chlorine molecule can act as an electrophile in its reaction with an alkene.

 g   Discuss and then draw the mechanism for the reaction between ethene and chlorine.

15.4 Oxidation of the alkenes

Alkenes can be oxidised by acidified potassium manganate(VII) solution, $KMnO_4(aq)$, which is a powerful oxidising agent. The products formed will depend on the conditions chosen for the reaction. In Figure 15.18, the R, R^1 and R^2 are alkyl groups.

PRACTICAL ACTIVITY 15.1

Cold dilute acidified manganate(VII) solution

If an alkene is shaken with a dilute solution of acidified potassium manganate(VII), $KMnO_4(aq)$, at room temperature, the pale purple solution turns colourless. The alkene is converted into a diol, i.e. a compound with two alcohol (O—H) groups:

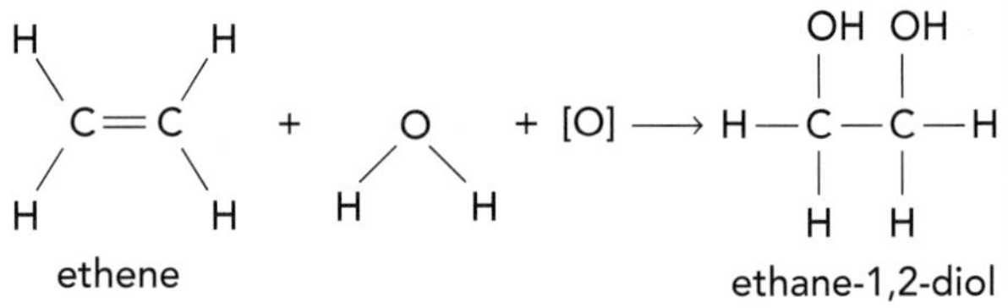

This reaction can be used as a test to find out whether a compound is unsaturated. However, the decolourisation of bromine water is a more commonly used test (see Section 15.3).

Hot concentrated acidified manganate(VII) solution, $KMnO_4$

Under these harsher conditions, the C=C double bond in the alkene is broken completely. The O—H groups in the diol formed initially are further oxidised to ketones, aldehydes, carboxylic acids or carbon dioxide gas.

The actual products depend on what is bonded to the carbon atoms in the C=C double bond.

Figure 15.19 shows the oxidation products from each type of group bonded to a carbon atom in the C=C bond.

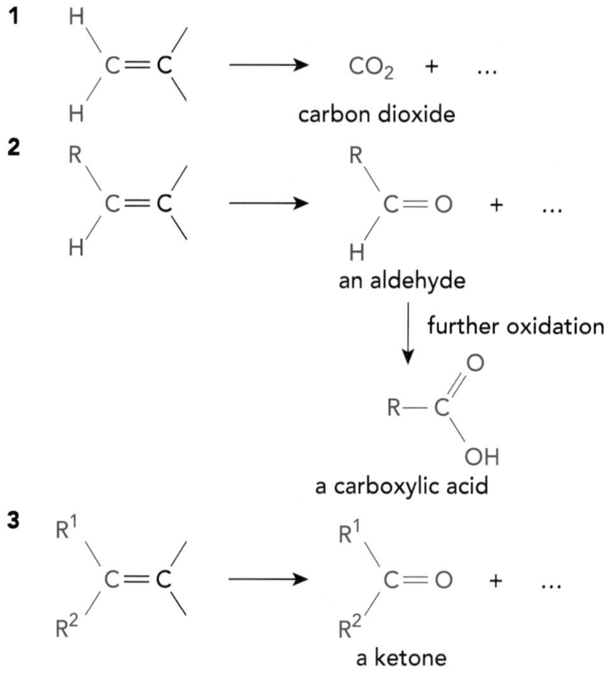

Figure 15.19: Oxidation of alkenes with hot, concentrated potassium manganate(VII) solution, $KMnO_4(aq)$.

To see what is formed when we heat 2-methylprop-1-ene with hot, concentrated acidified $KMnO_4(aq)$, look at equations 1 and 3 in Figure 15.19. The actual oxidation can be represented as:

$$(CH_3)_2C=CH_2 + 4[O] \rightarrow (CH_3)_2C=O + CO_2 + H_2O$$

2-methylpropene   propanone (a ketone)

We can use this reaction to determine the position of the double bond in larger alkenes. To do this we would need to identify the products of the oxidation reaction and work backwards to deduce the original alkene.

If, for example, carbon dioxide is given off in the oxidation, this tells us that the double bond was between the end two carbon atoms in the alkene.

We can summarise the oxidations under harsh conditions (using a hot, concentrated solution of potassium manganate(VII)) in three reactions.

1   If a carbon atom is bonded to two hydrogen atoms, we get oxidation to a CO_2 molecule.

$$H_2C=CH_2 \rightarrow CO_2 + CO_2$$

2   If a carbon atom is bonded to one hydrogen atom and one alkyl group, we get oxidation to a COOH (carboxylic acid) group.

$$RHC=CHR \rightarrow RCHO + RCHO \rightarrow$$
$$RCOOH + RCOOH$$

3   If a carbon atom is bonded to two alkyl groups, we get oxidation to a C=O (ketone) group.

$$R^1R^2C=CR^3R^4 \rightarrow R^1R^2C=O + R^3R^4C=O$$

Question

6   a   Draw the displayed formula of the organic product formed when propene is oxidised by a cold solution of acidified potassium manganate(VII).

Name the compound.

b   Draw the displayed formula of the organic product formed when but-2-ene is oxidised by a cold solution of acidified potassium manganate(VII).

Name the compound.

c   Methylbut-2-ene is heated with concentrated acidified potassium manganate(VII) solution.

i   Draw the displayed formulae of the products and name them.

ii   Write a balanced chemical equation for this reaction, using [O] to show oxygen atoms involved.

Compare your answers to Question 6 with another learner. Use your combined answers to create a mark scheme showing where each mark could be awarded.

15.5 Addition polymerisation

Probably the most important addition reaction of the alkenes forms the basis of much of the plastics industry. Molecules of ethene, as well as other unsaturated compounds, can react with each other under the right conditions to form polymer molecules.

A **polymer** is a long-chain molecule made up of many repeating units. The small, reactive molecules that react together to make the polymer are called **monomers**. Up to 10 000 ethene monomers can bond together to form the polymer chains of poly(ethene). Poly(ethene) is commonly used to make carrier bags.

KEY WORDS

polymer: a long-chain molecule made up of many repeating units derived from the monomers.

monomers: small molecules that react together to make long chain molecules (polymers).

We can show the polymerisation reaction of ethene as:

$$n\mathrm{C_2H_4} \rightarrow \left[\mathrm{C_2H_4}\right]_n$$

ethene   poly(ethene)

or by using the displayed formulae:

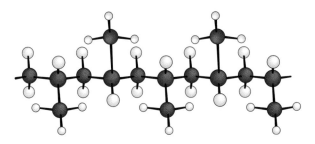

n is very large, e.g. up to 10 000

The section of the polymer shown in the brackets is the repeat unit of the polymer.

The reaction is called **addition polymerisation**. As in other addition reactions of the alkenes, it involves the breaking of the π bond in each C=C bond. Then the monomers link together.

KEY WORD

addition polymerisation: the reaction of many monomers containing at least one double C=C bond to form the long-chain polymers as the only product.

Other alkenes and substituted alkenes also polymerise to make polymers with different properties. Examples of other poly(alkenes) include poly(propene) and poly(chloroethene).

We can show the polymerisation of propene as:

$$n\mathrm{C_3H_6} \rightarrow \left[\mathrm{C_3H_6}\right]_n$$

or, using structural formulae:

$$n\mathrm{H_2C{=}CHCH_3} \rightarrow \left[\mathrm{H_2CCH(CH_3)}\right]_n$$

propene   poly(propene)

The polymer chain has methyl ($-\mathrm{CH_3}$) groups sticking out from the carbon skeleton of the poly(propene). We can show this as in Figure 15.20.

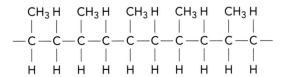

Figure 15.20: This shows a regular arrangement of the methyl groups along the poly(propene) polymer chain.

We can also represent the polymer by showing part of its structure using a 3D displayed formula, as shown in Figure 15.21.

Figure 15.21: A 3D displayed formula of a small section of the poly(propene) molecule.

Question

7   Which one of the following statements is correct?

Discuss all the options with a partner, and explain why each is either correct or incorrect.

A   Poly(propene) and poly(ethene) will both decolorise bromine water.

B   Poly(ethene) is a saturated hydrocarbon.

C   Poly(propene) will melt at a lower temperature than propene.

D   The polymerisation of ethene is an example of an electrophilic substitution reaction.

More about addition polymers

We can also use substituted alkenes, such as chloroethene, as monomers:

$$n\mathrm{H_2C{=}CHCl} \rightarrow \left[\mathrm{H_2C{-}CHCl}\right]_n$$

chloroethene   poly(chloroethene)

The $\text{+H}_2\text{C—CHCl+}$ section of the polymer chain is the called the **repeat unit** of poly(chloroethene) (Figure 15.22).

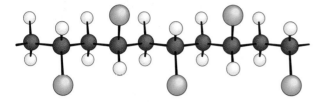

Figure 15.22: A 3D displayed formula of a small section of the poly(chloroethene) molecule. Its common name is PVC, as the old name for chloroethene was vinyl chloride.

In poly(alkenes) and substituted poly(alkenes) made of one type of monomer, the repeat unit is the same as the monomer except that the C=C double bond is changed to a C—C single bond.

Notice that, as in any other addition reaction of the alkenes, addition polymerisation yields only *one* product.

IMPORTANT

Remember that:

- the section of the polymer chain shown inside the square brackets by its structural or displayed formula is called its *repeat unit*
- addition polymerisation is characterised by:
  - monomers which are unsaturated, e.g. contain a C=C double bond
  - the polymer being the only product of the reaction.

Disposal of poly(alkene) plastics

Plastics are widely used in many aspects of everyday life. However, the large-scale use of poly(alkene)s has created a problem when we come to dispose of them.

During their life, one of the most useful properties of poly(alkene)s is their lack of reactivity.

As poly(alkene)s are effectively huge alkane molecules, they are resistant to chemical attack. So they can take hundreds of years to decompose when dumped in landfill sites, taking up valuable space. They are non-biodegradable. Therefore, throwing away poly(alkenes) creates rubbish that will pollute the environment for centuries (Figure 15.23).

Figure 15.23: A beach littered with poly(alkene) plastic waste.

Burning plastic waste

One way to solve this problem would be to burn the poly(alkene)s and use the energy released to generate electricity. As we have seen in Section 15.2, if hydrocarbons burn in excess oxygen, the products are carbon dioxide and water. This solution would not help combat global warming, but would help to conserve our supplies of fossil fuels that currently generate most of our electricity. However, we have also seen that toxic carbon monoxide is produced from the incomplete combustion of hydrocarbons.

Another problem is the difficulty recycling companies have in separating other plastic waste from the poly(alkene)s. This happens when objects have just been thrown away and not been sorted according to their recycling code. Also, if poly(chloroethene) waste is burnt, acidic hydrogen chloride gas will be given off, as well as toxic compounds called dioxins. Acidic gases should be neutralised before releasing the waste gases into the atmosphere. Very high temperatures should be used in incinerators to break down any toxins.

15.6 Tackling questions on addition polymers

In your exam, you might be asked to:

1 deduce the repeat unit of a polymer obtained from a given unsaturated monomer

2 identify the monomer(s) present in a given section of a polymer molecule.

Deducing the repeat unit of an addition polymer for given monomer(s)

If you are given a monomer with a C=C double bond, simply turn the double bond into a C—C single bond and show the bonds either side of the two C atoms that would continue the chain:

Identifying the monomer(s) present in a given section of an addition polymer molecule

First of all, you should split the polymer chain into its repeat units.

With an addition polymer, you then need to put the C=C double bond back into the monomer:

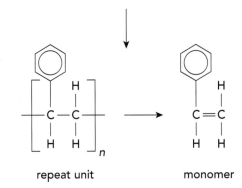

Question

8 Tetrafluoroethene, C_2F_4, is the monomer for the polymer PTFE, which is used in the non-stick coating on pans.

  a State what PTFE stands for.

  b Give the name of the type of reaction used to form PTFE.

  c Write a chemical equation to show the formation of PTFE from C_2F_4.

  d Draw the structure of the repeat unit in PTFE.

  e How could poly(alkene) waste be used to conserve fossil fuels?

  f Why would your answer to part **e** add to the problem of enhanced global warming?

  g A waste batch of poly(ethene) pellets was burnt in an inefficient industrial incinerator. Name a toxic gas that would be released.

  h Name the monomer used to make this polymer:

REFLECTION

1   Working as a pair, each write a question and its mark scheme. One of you should devise an assessment of the free-radical substitution of an alkane, while the other assesses the electrophilic addition to an alkene. You can use the Exam-style Questions in this coursebook to help with the style of your question and on-line answers to write a typical mark scheme. However, your question and answers should be your own work.

   Then try to answer each other's questions, giving your answers back for your partner to mark using their mark scheme.

2   Use this exercise to give you an idea of your understanding of the key reactions of alkanes and alkenes. What have you learned from the activity?

SUMMARY

Alkanes are saturated hydrocarbons with the general formula C_nH_{2n+2}.

Alkanes are relatively unreactive as they are non-polar. Most reagents are polar and do not usually react with non-polar molecules.

Alkanes are widely used as fuels. When they burn completely they produce carbon dioxide and water. However, they produce toxic carbon monoxide gas when they burn in a limited supply of oxygen, e.g. in a car engine.

Cracking of the less useful fractions from the fractional distillation of crude oil produces a range of more useful alkanes with lower molecular masses, as well as alkenes.

Chlorine atoms or bromine atoms can substitute for hydrogen atoms in alkanes in the presence of ultraviolet light, producing halogenoalkanes. This is called a free-radical substitution reaction. The Cl—Cl or Br—Br bond undergoes homolytic fission in ultraviolet light, producing reactive Cl· or Br· free radicals. This initiation step is followed by propagation steps involving a chain reaction which regenerates the halogen free radicals. Termination steps occur, when two free radicals combine.

Alkenes are unsaturated hydrocarbons with one carbon–carbon double bond consisting of a σ bond and a π bond. Their general formula is C_nH_{2n}.

Alkenes are more reactive than alkanes because they contain a π bond. The characteristic reaction of the alkenes is addition, which occurs across the π bond:
*   ethene produces ethane when heated with hydrogen gas over a platinum / nickel catalyst: this is called *hydrogenation*
*   ethene produces 1,2-dibromoethane when reacted with bromine water at room temperature
*   ethene produces chloroethane when reacted with hydrogen chloride gas at room temperature
*   ethene produces ethanol when reacted with steam, in the presence of concentrated H_3PO_4 catalyst.

The mechanism of the reaction of bromine with ethene is electrophilic addition. Electrophiles accept a pair of electrons from an electron-rich atom or centre, in this case the π bond. A carbocation intermediate is formed after the addition of the first bromine atom. This rapidly reacts with a bromide ion to form 1,2-dibromoethane.

CONTINUED

Mild oxidation of alkenes by cold, dilute acidified manganate(VII) solution gives a diol. However, a hot, concentrated acidified manganate(VII) solution will break the C=C bond and give two oxidation products. Identifying the two products formed will indicate the position of the C=C bond in the original alkene.

Alkenes produce many useful polymers by addition polymerisation. For example, poly(ethene) is made from $CH_2=CH_2$, and poly(chloroethene) is made from $CH_2=CHCl$.

The disposal of poly(alkene) plastic waste is difficult, as much of it is chemically inert and non-biodegradable. When burnt, waste plastics may produce toxic products, such as hydrogen chloride from PVC, poly(chloroethene).

EXAM-STYLE QUESTIONS

1   2-Methylpentane, 3-ethylpentane and 2,3-dimethylbutane are alkanes.

　a   For each one give:

　　i   its molecular formula [3]

　　ii   its structural formula [3]

　　iii   its displayed formula [3]

　　iv   its skeletal formula. [3]

　b   Give the general formula that is used to represent alkanes. [1]

　c   Two of the alkanes in this question are isomers of each other.
　　Identify which two and identify the type of isomerism they show. [2]

　d   Using terms from part **a** of this question, define isomers. [2]

　e   Name the alkane whose structural formula is
　　$CH_3CH(CH_3)CH_2CH(CH_3)_2$ [1]

[Total: 18]

2   a   Alkanes are saturated hydrocarbons. Explain the words
　　saturated and *hydrocarbons*. [2]

　b   Alkanes are generally unreactive. Explain why this is so. [2]

　c   Write balanced symbol equations for the complete combustion of:

　　i   methane [2]

　　ii   ethane. [2]

[Total: 8]

3   Use the passage below and your own knowledge to answer the questions that follow.

Methane reacts with bromine to give bromomethane and hydrogen bromide. The mechanism for the reaction is called free-radical substitution and involves homolytic fission of chemical bonds. The reaction proceeds via initiation, propagation and termination steps.

　a   Name the mechanism by which bromine reacts with methane. [1]

　b   Write a balanced symbol equation for this reaction. [2]

CONTINUED

c Bonds break in this reaction. What type of bond breaking is involved? [1]

d Explain the essential conditions that are required for this reaction. [2]

e For this reaction, write down an equation for:

    i an initiation step [2]

    ii a propagation step [2]

    iii a termination step. [2]

[Total: 12]

4 In a similar reaction to the one in Question 3, 1.50 g of ethane reacts with chlorine. 1.29 g of chloroethane is formed.
(A_r values: H = 1.0, C = 12.0, Cl = 35.5)

Calculate:

a the number of moles of ethane that were used [2]

b the number of moles of chloroethane that were formed [2]

c the percentage yield [2]

d the number of grams of chloroethane that would have formed if the percentage yield had been 60.0%. [2]

[Total: 8]

5 Propene, *cis*-pent-2-ene and *trans*-pent-2-ene are alkenes.

a For each one give:

    i its molecular formula [3]

    ii its structural formula [3]

    iii its displayed formula [3]

    iv its skeletal formula. [3]

b Give the general formula that is used to represent alkenes. [1]

c Two of these alkenes are isomers of each other.

Identify which two. [1]

d Explain why it is *not* possible to change one of these two isomers into the other at room temperature. [2]

e Give displayed formulae and the names of the four alkenes with molecular formula C_4H_8. [8]

f 3-Methylpent-2-ene has two *cis/trans* isomers.

Draw and name the two isomers. [3]

[Total: 27]

6 a Alkenes are unsaturated hydrocarbons. Explain the word *unsaturated*. [1]

b Describe the bonding between the two carbon atoms in ethene. [2]

c Describe and draw the shape of an ethene molecule, labelling all bond angles. [2]

d Explain the meaning of the term *functional group*. Which functional group is present in all alkenes? [2]

CONTINUED

e Describe a simple chemical test to determine whether an unknown hydrocarbon is unsaturated.

Describe the result if the test is positive. [2]

[Total: 9]

7 Use the passage below and your own knowledge to answer the questions that follow.

Ethene reacts with bromine to give 1,2-dibromoethane as the only product. The mechanism for the reaction is electrophilic addition and involves heterolytic fission of chemical bonds. The bromine molecules behave as electrophiles in this reaction.

a Name the mechanism by which bromine reacts with ethene. [1]

b Write a balanced symbol equation for this reaction. [2]

c Bonds break in this reaction. Give the type of bond breaking involved. [1]

d Show the mechanism of the reaction as fully as you can, including curly arrows. [5]

e Which substance behaves here as an electrophile? Explain what is meant by the term *electrophile*. [2]

[Total: 11]

8 In a similar reaction to the reaction described in Question 7, 2.80 g of ethene react with chlorine. 8.91 g of dichloroethane are formed.
(A_r values: H = 1.0, C = 12.0, Cl = 35.5)

Calculate:

a the number of moles of ethene that were used [2]

b the number of moles of dichloroethane that were formed [2]

c the percentage yield [2]

d the number of grams of dichloroethane that would have formed if the percentage yield had been 80.0%. [2]

[Total: 8]

9 This question is about the reactions of alkenes with hot, concentrated acidified potassium manganate(VII) solution.

a **i** Give two effects that a hot, concentrated solution of acidified potassium manganate(VII) have on an alkene molecule. [2]

ii State how this reaction is useful to chemists. [1]

b An alkene is known to be either but-1-ene or but-2-ene. When heated with concentrated acidified potassium manganate(VII) solution, bubbles of carbon dioxide gas were given off.

Name the alkene. [1]

c Pent-2-ene is heated with concentrated acidified potassium manganate(VII) solution.

i Draw the displayed formulae of the products and name them. [3]

ii Write a balanced chemical equation for this reaction, using [O] to show oxygen atoms involved. [1]

[Total: 8]

SELF-EVALUATION

After studying this chapter, complete a table like this:

I can	See section...	Needs more work	Almost there	Ready to move on
explain the general unreactivity of alkanes, and describe their complete and incomplete combustion	15.1, 15.2			
explain the free-radical substitution of alkanes by chlorine and by bromine, as shown by their mechanism	15.2			
suggest how cracking can be used to obtain more useful alkanes, and alkenes, of lower relative molecular mass from larger hydrocarbon molecules	15.3			
describe the environmental consequences of burning hydrocarbon fuels in vehicles and the removal of pollutants by catalytic converters	15.2			
describe the reactions of alkenes as shown by their addition, oxidation and polymerisation	15.3, 15.4, 15.5, 15.6			
describe the mechanism of electrophilic addition in alkenes, and explain the inductive effects of alkyl groups on the stability of cations formed	15.3			
describe the difficulty of disposing of waste poly(alkene)s.	15.5			

Chapter 16
Halogenoalkanes

LEARNING INTENTIONS

In this chapter you will learn how to:

- write equations for the main reactions that can produce halogenoalkanes, including the reagents and conditions used

- write equations for the reactions of halogenoalkanes when they undergo:

  - nucleophilic substitution, such as hydrolysis, formation of nitriles, and the formation of primary amines by reaction with ammonia

  - elimination of hydrogen bromide (for example, from 2-bromopropane)

- describe and explain the S_N1 and S_N2 mechanisms of nucleophilic substitution in halogenoalkanes

- interpret the different reactivities of halogenoalkanes.

BEFORE YOU START

1 Which statement below describes what happens when a covalent bond breaks heterolytically?

When the bond breaks …

A one of the atoms takes both the electrons in the bond, and becomes negatively charged

B one of the atoms takes both the electrons in the bond, and becomes positively charged

C both atoms take one electron each from the bond, forming free radicals

D both atoms take one electron each from the bond, with one atom becoming a free radical, and the other a positive ion.

2 Discuss with a partner how substitution and elimination reactions differ. Write a sentence explaining the difference. Then look back to Chapter 14 to illustrate your answer with two chemical equations.

3 Describe the test and result to positively identify a bromide ion.

4 Working with a partner, define *nucleophile*.

USES OF HALOGENOALKANES

Halogenoalkanes are used in many industrial chemical processes. Halogenoalkanes are formed from elements such as fluorine and chlorine but, unlike these elements, many halogenoalkanes are relatively unreactive under normal conditions. This leads to their use as flame retardants and anaesthetics.

You might have heard of one of the first anaesthetics, chloroform. Its systematic name is trichloromethane ($CHCl_3$). Nowadays, if you require an anaesthetic, you may receive a gas known as 'halothane'. Its systematic name is 2-bromo-2-chloro-1,1,1-trifluoroethane.

$$F-C-C-Br$$

with F, Cl on top and F, H on bottom of the two carbons

One of the essential properties of an anaesthetic (Figure 16.1) is chemical inertness (lack of reactivity), and each halothane molecule contains three very strong C—F bonds that are difficult to break. This makes halothane inert (very unreactive) and safe to use in the aqueous environment inside the body.

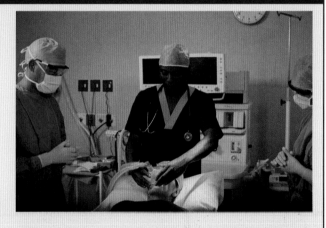

Figure 16.1: An anaesthetist putting a patient to sleep before an operation.

However, under other conditions, such as high in the Earth's stratosphere, some halogenoalkanes react in completely different ways.

CFCs are chlorofluorocarbons. Chemists refer to them as chlorofluoroalkanes. When scientists developed these new compounds in the 1930s, people could see no drawbacks to using the new 'wonder compounds'. They are all chemically inert. They are not flammable and are not toxic. These

CONTINUED

properties made volatile CFCs useful as aerosol propellants, solvents and as the refrigerants inside fridges. They were also used as blowing agents for polymers such as expanded polystyrene.

However, CFCs have caused a serious environmental issue. They have damaged the ozone layer in the upper atmosphere. The ozone layer is a thin layer of gas that protects the Earth by absorbing harmful UV radiation arriving from the Sun.

It turns out that CFCs are unreactive in normal conditions, but high up in the atmosphere they become totally different. The CFCs can persist in the atmosphere for about a hundred years. The UV light from the Sun breaks the C—Cl bonds in the CFC molecules. This releases highly reactive chlorine atoms, called chlorine free radicals. These chlorine free radicals react with ozone molecules. In a sequence of chain reactions, chemists estimate that each chlorine free radical can destroy a million ozone molecules.

Governments have been working on the problem, and most industrialised countries have now banned the use of CFCs (Figure 16.2). Chemists developed new compounds for fridges and aerosols, such as hydrofluorocarbons (HFCs): for example, CH_2FCF_3. These non-chlorinated compounds break down more quickly once released into the air because of the presence of hydrogen in their molecules. This means that they never rise in the atmosphere as far as the ozone layer. There is now evidence that the ozone layer is recovering from the effects of CFCs. The hole in the ozone layer is slowly closing up.

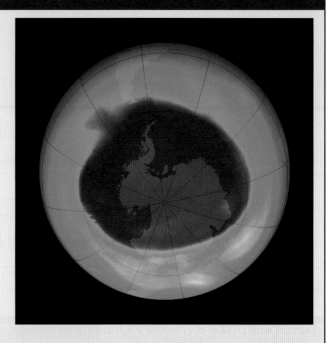

Figure 16.2: Banning the use of CFCs has meant that the hole in the ozone layer over Antarctica is now getting smaller.

Question for discussion

Discuss with another learner or group of learners:

- Discuss how the passage above about the use of halogenoalkanes demonstrates how some scientific developments can have both good and bad effects on society and the environment.

16.1 Making halogenoalkanes

Very few halogenoalkanes are found in nature. Most are made in chemical reactions between other organic compounds and a halogen or halide compound.

The main reactions are:

- the free-radical substitution of alkanes by chlorine, Cl_2, or bromine, Br_2, in ultraviolet light:

$$C_2H_6 + Cl_2 \xrightarrow{\text{UV light}} C_2H_5Cl + HCl$$

(For more details, see Section 15.2)

- the electrophilic addition of an alkene with a halogen, X_2, or a hydrogen halide, $HX(g)$, at room temperature:

$$C_2H_4 + Br_2 \rightarrow C_2H_4Br_2$$

(For more details, see Section 15.3)

- substitution of an alcohol. For example, by reactions:

  - with HX (or with KX and H_2SO_4 or H_3PO_4 to make HX),

    $$CH_3CH_2OH + HCl \rightarrow CH_3CH_2Cl + H_2O$$

  - with PCl_3 and heat:

    $$3C_2H_5OH + PCl_3 \xrightarrow{\text{heat}} 3C_2H_5Cl + H_3PO_3$$

- with PCl_5 at room temperature:

$$C_2H_5OH + PCl_5 \rightarrow C_2H_5Cl + HCl + POCl_3$$

- or with $SOCl_2$:

$$C_2H_5OH + SOCl_2 \rightarrow C_2H_5Cl + HCl + SO_2$$

The chloroethane made in the reactions above is classified as a primary halogenoalkane, as the chlorine is bonded to a carbon atom that is bonded to just one alkyl group (a methyl group in this case). We can also make halogenoalkanes where the carbon atom adjacent to the halogen atom is bonded to two alkyl groups, called secondary halogenoalkanes. Tertiary halogenoalkanes have three alkyl groups on the adjacent carbon atom.

16.2 Nucleophilic substitution reactions

We can think of the halogenoalkanes as alkanes that have one or more hydrogen atoms replaced by halogen atoms.

Remember that the halogens are the elements in Group 17 of the Periodic Table, namely fluorine (F), chlorine (Cl), bromine (Br) and iodine (I).

The simplest halogenoalkanes, whose molecules contain just one halogen atom, will have the general formula $C_nH_{2n+1}X$, where X is F, Cl, Br or I. The halogen atom has a huge effect on the reactivity of the halogenoalkanes compared with that of the alkanes. The halogenoalkanes are more reactive because of the polar nature of the covalent bond between the carbon

and halogen atom unlike the non-polar bonds in alkane molecules. The carbon bonded to the halogen carries a partial positive charge, and the halogen a partial negative charge.

Substitution reactions with aqueous alkali, OH⁻(aq)

When an aqueous solution of sodium hydroxide is heated with a halogenoalkane, a nucleophilic substitution reaction takes place. The halogen atom in the halogenoalkane is replaced by an —OH, hydroxyl group, so the organic product formed is an alcohol:

$$\underset{\text{bromoethane}}{CH_3CH_2Br} + NaOH \rightarrow \underset{\text{ethanol}}{CH_3CH_2OH} + NaBr$$

We can also show this equation as:

$$CH_3CH_2Br + OH^- \rightarrow CH_3CH_2OH + Br^-$$

The aqueous hydroxide ion behaves as a nucleophile here, because it is donating a pair of electrons to the carbon atom bonded to the halogen in the halogenoalkane. This is why the reaction is called a *nucleophilic substitution*.

KEY WORD

nucleophilic substitution: the mechanism of the organic reaction in which a nucleophile attacks a carbon atom carrying a partial positive charge ($\delta+$). This results in the replacement of an atom carrying a partial negative charge ($\delta-$) by the nucleophile.

PRACTICAL ACTIVITY 16.1

Hydrolysis of a halogenoalkane

The reaction is carried out under reflux in the laboratory. This lets us heat the reaction mixture without evaporating off the volatile organic compounds in the reaction flask. The apparatus is shown in Figure 16.3.

Similar reactions occur with other halogenoalkanes, but the reaction rates differ. We can investigate the rate of hydrolysis using aqueous silver nitrate solution. The water in the silver nitrate solution acts as the nucleophile, and again an alcohol is

CONTINUED

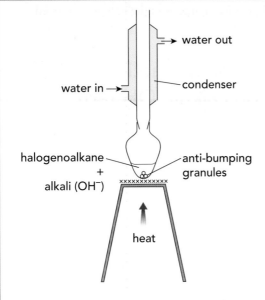

Figure 16.3: Reflux apparatus for hydrolysis of a halogenoalkane.

formed. The reaction is called *hydrolysis* (meaning 'breakdown by water'):

$$CH_3CH_2Br + H_2O \rightarrow CH_3CH_2OH + H^+ + Br^-$$

It is a very similar reaction to the reaction that takes place with aqueous alkali.

However, the hydrolysis with water occurs more slowly than with the hydroxide ion, $OH^-(aq)$. This is because the negatively charged hydroxide ion is a more effective nucleophile than a neutral water molecule. This is due to the fact that, in water, the oxygen atom in H_2O only carries partial negative charge ($\delta-$), whereas in the hydroxide ion, OH^-, the oxygen atom carries a full negative charge.

From the equation above, you can see that a halide ion, in this case the bromide ion, Br^-, is produced in the reaction.

In Section 12.3 we used silver nitrate solution to test for halide ions. Remember that:

- aqueous chlorides give a white precipitate (silver chloride),

- bromides give a cream precipitate (silver bromide)

- iodides produce a pale yellow precipitate (silver iodide).

The water in the silver nitrate solution will hydrolyse the halogenoalkane.

Observing this reaction, we can time how long it takes for test-tubes containing the halogenoalkanes and aqueous silver nitrate solution to become opaque.

Conclusion

We find that:

- the fastest nucleophilic substitution reactions take place with the iodoalkanes

- the slowest nucleophilic substitution reactions take place with the fluoroalkanes.

The substitution reaction involves the breaking of the carbon–halogen bond. The bond energies in Table 16.1 help us to explain the rates of reaction:

Bond	Bond energy / kJ mol⁻¹
C—F	467 (strongest bond)
C—Cl	346
C—Br	290
C—I	228 (weakest bond)

Table 16.1: Bond energy values of the carbon–halogen bonds.

Notice that the C—I bond is the weakest, so it is broken most easily. When the C—I bond breaks, it forms an I⁻ ion during the substitution reaction. The bond breaks heterolytically, with the iodine atom taking both the electrons in the C—I bond.

This is shown clearly in an ionic equation:

$$CH_3CH_2I + OH^- \rightarrow CH_3CH_2OH + I^-$$
$$\text{iodoethane} \qquad\qquad \text{ethanol}$$

> **IMPORTANT**
>
> The trend in the reactivity of the halogenoalkanes is shown below:
>
> Fluoroalkanes   least reactive
>
> Chloroalkanes
>
> Bromoalkanes
>
> Iodoalkanes   most reactive

There is more about the mechanism of nucleophilic substitution in Section 16.3.

Substitution with cyanide ions, CN⁻ (in ethanol)

In this reaction the nucleophile is the cyanide, CN^-, ion. To carry out the reaction, a solution of potassium cyanide, KCN, in ethanol (known as an ethanolic solution of potassium cyanide) is made up. This is then heated under reflux with the halogenoalkane.

An ionic equation for this reaction is:

$$CH_3CH_2Br + CN^- \rightarrow CH_3CH_2CN + Br^-$$
bromoethane   propanenitrile

Notice that the reaction with the cyanide ion adds an *extra carbon atom* to the original halogenoalkane carbon chain. In this case, bromoethane is converted to propanenitrile.

Sometimes in industry, chemists need to make a new compound with one more carbon atom than the best available organic raw material (the starting compound). Therefore, if we can convert the starting compound to a halogenoalkane, we can then reflux with ethanolic KCN to make a nitrile. We now have an intermediate nitrile with the correct number of carbon atoms.

We will consider nitriles and their subsequent conversion to carboxylic acids and amines again in Chapter 18.

Substitution with ammonia, NH₃ (in ethanol)

If we heat a halogenoalkane with an excess of ammonia dissolved in ethanol under pressure, an amine is formed.

$$CH_3CH_2Br + NH_3 \rightarrow CH_3CH_2NH_2 + HBr$$
bromoethane   ethylamine

Here the nucleophile is the ammonia, NH_3, molecule. The organic product, ethylamine, is a primary amine, as the nitrogen atom is attached to only one alkyl group. If the ammonia is not in excess, we get a mixture of amine products. This is because the primary amine product will act as a nucleophile itself and will attack halogenoalkane molecules, forming secondary amines, and so on. The secondary amine formed above would be $(CH_3CH_2)_2NH$, called *diethylamine*.

You can read more about amines in Chapter 27.

Question

Work with another learner to discuss and answer these questions:

1.   a   Name the reactants you would use to produce 1,2-dichloropropane.

     b   Why does the hydrolysis of a halogenoalkane happen more quickly with $OH^-(aq)$ ions than with water molecules?

     c   Explain why silver nitrate solution can be used to investigate the rate of hydrolysis of the halogenoalkanes. Include ionic equations for the formation of the precipitates.

     d   Why can ammonia and amine molecules act as nucleophiles?

     e   When ammonia is reacted with an excess of a halogenoalkane, a mixture of amines can be formed.

        If we start with an excess of 1-bromopropane, give the structural formula and name of the *tertiary* amine formed.

Compare your answers with those of another pair. Discuss and amend any errors you come across together.

16.3 Mechanism of nucleophilic substitution in halogenoalkanes

Many of the reactions of halogenoalkanes are nucleophilic substitutions. In these reactions, the nucleophile attacks the carbon atom bonded to the halogen. Remember from Chapter 14 that nucleophiles are donors of an electron pair, and are attracted to electron-deficient atoms.

The carbon–halogen bond is polarised because the halogen is more electronegative than carbon. So the halogen draws the pair of electrons in the bond away from the carbon atom, nearer to itself. Therefore, the carbon atom carries a positive charge (shown in Figure 16.4).

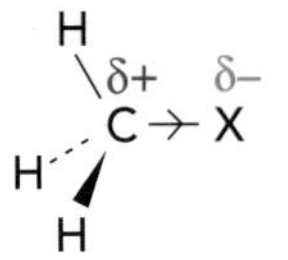

Figure 16.4: The carbon–halogen bond is polarised.

The halogen atom is replaced by the nucleophile in the substitution reaction.

There are two possible mechanisms that can operate in the nucleophilic substitution reactions of halogenoalkanes. The actual mechanism is determined by the structure of the halogenoalkane involved in the reaction.

Mechanism for primary halogenoalkanes (S_N2)

In primary halogenoalkanes containing one halogen atom, the halogen atom is bonded to a carbon atom, which is itself bonded to one other carbon atom and two hydrogen atoms. This means that the carbon atom bonded to the halogen is attached to only one alkyl group. For example, 1-chloropropane, $CH_3CH_2CH_2Cl$, is a primary halogenoalkane. In this case, the carbon atom bonded to the chlorine atom is attached to *one* alkyl group, an ethyl group.

In Section 16.2 we looked at the hydrolysis of bromoethane, another primary halogenoalkane. Figure 16.5 shows the mechanism for that reaction.

The OH^- ion donates a pair of electrons to the δ+ carbon atom, forming a new covalent bond. At the same time, the C—Br bond is breaking. The Br atom takes both the electrons in the bond. This is an example of **heterolytic fission** of a covalent bond (see Section 14.7). The Br atom leaves the halogenoalkane as a Br^- ion.

This mechanism is called an S_N2 **mechanism**. The 'S' stands for substitution and the 'N' stands for nucleophilic. The '2' tells us that the rate of the reaction, which is determined by the slow step in the mechanism (see Section 22.1), involves two reacting species. Experiments show us that the rate depends on both the concentration of the halogenoalkane and the concentration of the hydroxide ions present.

> ## KEY WORDS
>
> **heterolytic fission:** the breaking of a covalent bond in which one atom takes both electrons from the bond, forming a negative ion, and leaving behind a positive ion.
>
> **S_N2 mechanism:** the steps in a nucleophilic substitution reaction in which the rate of the reaction (which is determined by the slow step in the mechanism) involves two reacting species, e.g. in the hydrolysis of a *primary* halogenoalkane.

Mechanism for tertiary halogenoalkanes (S_N1)

In a tertiary halogenoalkane, the carbon atom bonded to the halogen atom is also bonded to three other carbon atoms (alkyl groups). For example, 2-bromo-2-methylpropane is a tertiary halogenoalkane. The carbon atom bonded

intermediate as
C—OH forms and
C—Br breaks

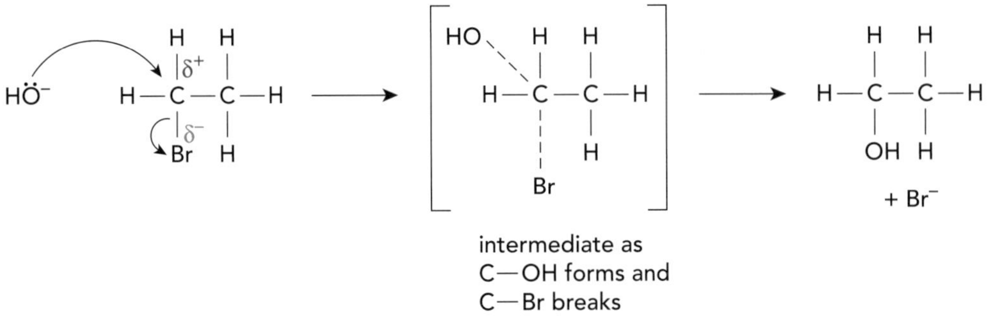

Figure 16.5: The mechanism of nucleophilic substitution in a primary halogenoalkane.

to the bromine atom is attached to *three* alkyl groups, all methyl groups. The structure of this tertiary halogenoalkane is shown in Figure 16.6.

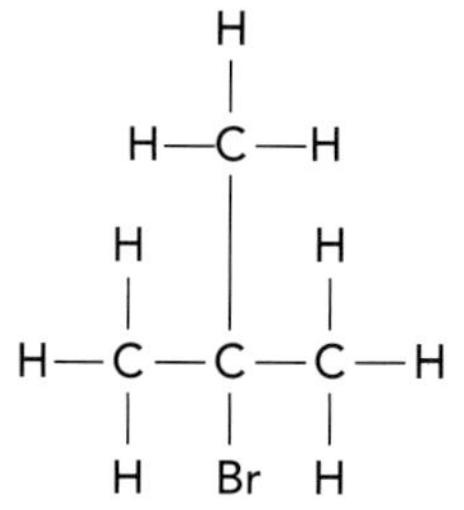

Figure 16.6: A tertiary halogenoalkane, 2-bromo-2-methylpropane.

A tertiary halogenoalkane reacts with a hydroxide ion by a two-step mechanism. The first step in the mechanism is the breaking of the carbon–halogen bond. This forms a tertiary carbocation (see Section 14.7). Then the tertiary carbocation is attacked immediately by the hydroxide ion (Figure 16.7).

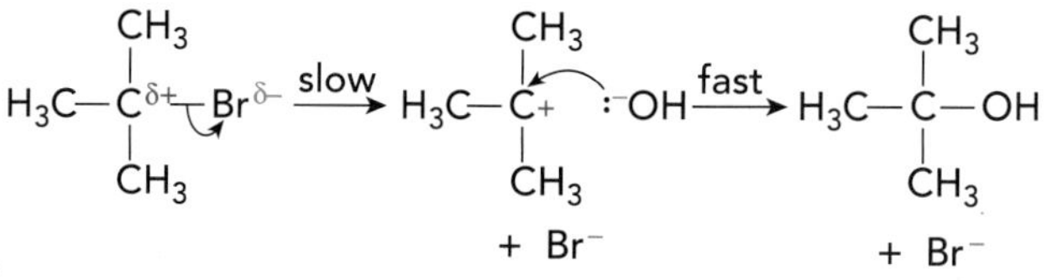

Figure 16.7: The mechanism of nucleophilic substitution in a tertiary halogenoalkane.

This mechanism is known as an S_N1 **mechanism**. The '1' tells us that the rate of the reaction only depends on one reagent, in this case the concentration of the

halogenoalkane, as shown in the first (*slow*) step of the mechanism.

Once again, this breaking of the C—Br bond is an example of heterolytic fission.

The Br^- ion forms again, as in the S_N2 mechanism, but in this mechanism a carbocation ion forms. This does not happen with primary halogenoalkanes. This is because tertiary carbocations are more stable than primary carbocations. This is due to the **positive inductive effect** of the alkyl groups attached to the carbon atom bonded to the halogen (see Section 14.5). Alkyl groups tend to release electrons to atoms attached to them. So a tertiary carbocation has three alkyl groups donating electrons towards the positively charged carbon atom, reducing its charge density. This makes it more stable than a primary carbocation, which just has one alkyl group releasing electrons (Figure 16.8).

The S_N1 mechanism and the S_N2 mechanism are both likely to play a part in the nucleophilic substitution of secondary halogenoalkanes.

KEY WORDS

S_N1 **mechanism:** the steps in a nucleophilic substitution reaction in which the rate of the reaction (which is determined by the slow step in the mechanism) involves only the organic reactant, e.g. in the hydrolysis of a *tertiary* halogenoalkane.

positive inductive effect: the release (pushing away) of electrons from an organic group, such as an alkyl group, towards the rest of the molecule.

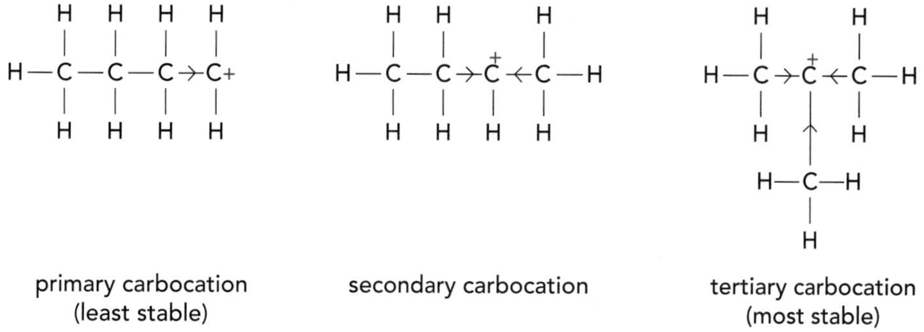

Figure 16.8: The trend in the stability of primary, secondary and tertiary carbocations.

Question

2 **a** Show the mechanism, including appropriate curly arrows, for the hydrolysis of 1-chloropropane, $CH_3CH_2CH_2Cl$, by alkali.

Explain what is happening in this mechanism to another learner.

b Draw the structure (displayed formula) of 2-chloro-2-methylbutane.

c Show the mechanism for the hydrolysis of 2-chloro-2-methylbutane by an alkali.

16.4 Elimination reactions

Halogenoalkanes also undergo elimination reactions. An elimination reaction involves the loss of a small molecule from the original organic molecule. In the case of halogenoalkanes, this small molecule is a hydrogen halide, such as HCl or HBr.

The reagent used in these elimination reactions is ethanolic sodium hydroxide, heated with the halogenoalkane:

$$CH_3CH_2Br + NaOH(ethanol) \xrightarrow{heat} CH_2{=}CH_2 + H_2O + NaBr$$

bromoethane ⟶ ethene

The original bromoethane molecule has lost an H atom and a Br atom. We can think of it as HBr being

eliminated from the halogenoalkane. The ethanolic OH^- ion acts as a base, accepting an H^+ ion from the halogenoalkane to form water.

The C—Br bond breaks heterolytically, forming a Br^- ion and leaving an alkene as the organic product.

Notice the importance of the conditions used in organic reactions:

> **IMPORTANT**
>
> If we use NaOH(ethanol), an *elimination* reaction occurs and an *alkene* is one of the products.
> *but*
> If we use NaOH(aq), a *nucleophilic substitution* reaction occurs and an *alcohol* is one of the products.

Question

3 **a** Write a balanced equation for the reaction of 2-bromopropane with ethanolic sodium hydroxide.

b Name the organic product.

c Discuss with a partner another elimination reaction with a different bromoalkane that would give the same products as in part **a**.

Write a balanced equation for this reaction.

> **REFLECTION**
>
> **1** Show the mechanism for the hydrolysis of 1-chlorobutane by an aqueous alkali, such as sodium hydroxide solution, NaOH(aq).
>
> Work as a pair:
>
> - listen to your partner explain this mechanism to you
>
> - assess each other's understanding of the S_N2 and S_N1 mechanisms for the hydrolysis of primary and tertiary halogenoalkanes.
>
> **2** Reflect together on all the knowledge you need to understand and explain the mechanisms of the hydrolysis of a primary halogenoalkane and a tertiary halogenoalkane by an alkali. Make a list of the essential knowledge to answer an exam question on S_N2 and S_N1 mechanisms.

SUMMARY

If one or more of the hydrogen atoms in an alkane molecule are replaced by halogen atoms, the compound is called a *halogenoalkane*.

Iodoalkanes are the most reactive halogenoalkanes, whereas fluoroalkanes are the least reactive. We explain this by the trend in the bond strength of the carbon–halogen bonds. The C—F bond is the strongest bond, and the C—I bond is the weakest bond. So the C—I bond is most easily broken during its reactions.

Halogenoalkanes are attacked by nucleophiles. This happens because the carbon bonded to the halogen carries a partial positive charge ($\delta+$), due to the higher electronegativity of the halogen. So halogenoalkanes can undergo nucleophilic substitution.

Suitable nucleophiles include aqueous alkali, $OH^-(aq)$, cyanide, CN^-, and ammonia, NH_3.

The reaction with OH^- ions (or with water) is known as hydrolysis, and an alcohol is formed as the organic product.

Halogenoalkanes will also undergo elimination reactions when heated with ethanolic sodium hydroxide, forming alkenes as the organic product.

EXAM-STYLE QUESTIONS

1   What type of reaction best describes the heating of chloroethane with ethanolic sodium hydroxide solution?

   A   addition   **B**   elimination

   C   hydrolysis   **D**   substitution   **[1]**

2   Which one of the following is a tertiary halogenoalkane?

   A $CHBr_3$ **B** $CH_3CH_2CH_2Br$

   C $(CH_3)_2CHCHBrCH_3$ **D** $(CH_3)_2CBrCH_2CH_3$ **[1]**

3   Which one of the following will form a carbocation in the mechanism of nucleophilic substitution?

   A $CH_3CH_2CH_2Cl$ **B** $(CH_3)_2CBrCH_3$

   C CH_3CH_2Cl **D** CH_3Br **[1]**

4   When a solution of potassium cyanide in ethanol is heated under reflux with 1-chloropropane, what is the organic product of the reaction called?

   A   butanenitrile   **B**   1-chloropropanenitrile

   C   ethanenitrile   **D**   propanenitrile   **[1]**

5   1-Bromobutane will undergo reactions when heated, as shown by reactions A and B.

$$CH_3CH_2CH_2CH_2Br$$

A   B

$$CH_3CH_2CH_2CH_2OH \qquad CH_3CH_2CH{=}CH_2$$

   a   For reactions A and B, give the reagents used in each case.   **[2]**

   b   Reaction A was repeated using 1-iodobutane instead of 1-bromobutane. Explain any difference in the rate of reaction observed.   **[2]**

CONTINUED

    c   Name the type of organic reaction shown in A.   [1]

    d   Draw the mechanism for reaction A.   [3]

    e   Reaction A was repeated with 2-bromo-2-methylpropane instead of 1-bromobutane.

        i   Name the organic compound formed.   [1]

        ii   The mechanism of the reaction with 2-bromo-2-methylpropane differs from the mechanism of reaction A.

          Describe how the mechanisms differ.   [2]

    f   Name the type of reaction shown in B.   [1]

    g   If reaction B was repeated with 2-bromobutane, deduce the other organic products that can form as well as the product shown above.   [2]

                                                       [Total: 14]

6   Bromochlorodifluoromethane has been used in fire extinguishers. However, its breakdown products were found to be toxic.

    a   Draw the displayed formula of bromochlorodifluoromethane.   [1]

    b CF_3CH_2F is being introduced as a replacement for various CFCs in refrigerants and aerosols.

        Deduce the name of this compound.   [1]

                                                       [Total: 2]

SELF-EVALUATION

After studying this chapter, complete a table like this:

I can	See section...	Needs more work	Almost there	Ready to move on
write equations for the main reactions that can produce halogenoalkanes, to include the reagents and conditions used	16.1			
write equations for the reactions of halogenoalkanes when they undergo nucleophilic substitution, such as hydrolysis, the formation of nitriles, and the formation of primary amines by their reaction with ammonia	16.2			
write equations for the reactions of halogenoalkanes when they undergo elimination of a hydrogen halide by ethanolic sodium hydroxide	16.4			
describe and explain the S_N1 and S_N2 mechanisms of nucleophilic substitution in halogenoalkanes	16.3			
interpret the different reactivities of halogenoalkanes.	16.2			

> Chapter 17

Alcohols, esters and carboxylic acids

LEARNING INTENTIONS

In this chapter you will learn how to:

- explain the acidity of alcohols compared with water

- recall the reactions (reagents and conditions) by which alcohols can be produced

- recall the reactions of alcohols in combustion, substitution to give halogenoalkanes, reaction with sodium, oxidation to carbonyl compounds and carboxylic acids, and dehydration to alkenes

- classify hydroxy compounds into primary, secondary and tertiary alcohols

- suggest characteristic distinguishing reactions, e.g. mild oxidation

- describe the acid and base hydrolysis of esters

CONTINUED

- describe the formation of carboxylic acids from alcohols, aldehydes and nitriles

- describe the reactions of carboxylic acids in the formation of:

  - salts, by the use of reactive metals, alkalis or carbonates

  - alkyl esters, by reaction with alcohols

  - primary alcohols, by reduction using $LiAlH_4$.

BEFORE YOU START

1   Which statement below describes what happens to an organic compound when it is reduced and then oxidised?

   A   It loses hydrogen, then loses oxygen

   B   It gains hydrogen, then gains oxygen

   C   It gains hydrogen, then loses oxygen

   D   It loses hydrogen, then gains oxygen

2   Discuss with a partner how to complete these general equations:

   a   acid + base $\rightarrow$

   b   acid + metal $\rightarrow$

   c   acid + carbonate $\rightarrow$

3   a   Give the skeletal formula for:

      i   propan-2-ol

      ii   butanone

      iii   ethanal

      iv   ethanoic acid.

   b   Give the displayed formula for:

      i   ethyl ethanoate

      ii   pentanenitrile.

4   a   Discuss with another learner what happens to an organic molecule during hydrolysis and dehydration.

   b   Discuss the Brønsted–Lowry theory to explain strong and weak acids.

MAKING ETHANOL AS A BIOFUEL

Ethanol, C_2H_5OH, is the most widely used of the homologous series of alcohols. The sugar extracted from crops such as sugar cane and sugar beet can be fermented with yeast to make ethanol (Figure 17.1). Ethanol is a 'biofuel' and burns with a clean flame. This process is becoming increasingly important as our supplies of crude oil run out and cleaner, easier to produce biofuels are needed to take the place of petrol and diesel.

Figure 17.1: The sugar extracted from sugar cane can be fermented with yeast to make ethanol.

The industrial production of ethanol uses ethene as a reactant. As you saw in the introduction to Chapter 15, we get ethene by the cracking of fractions from crude oil. The ethene reacts with steam, using a catalyst of phosphoric(V) acid, H_3PO_4, to make ethanol (see Section 15.3):

$$C_2H_4 \quad + \quad H_2O \xrightarrow{\ H_3PO_4\ } \quad C_2H_5OH$$

ethene   steam   ethanol

This is a relatively cheap, continuous process, especially for countries with their own reserves of crude oil. But ethanol made this way still costs more than petrol, as well as using up our remaining oil reserves.

Brazil is one country that has started making ethanol on a large scale. However, they do not use ethene. They start with sugar extracted from sugar cane. The sugar solution is fermented in a batch process with yeast to produce ethanol as fuel for cars. The fermentation only needs a warm temperature to take place.

The ethanol made needs to be distilled from the reaction mixture. This requires energy but more sugar cane (or sugar beet in colder climates) can be grown each year. So ethanol made this way is a renewable biofuel, unlike fossil fuels.

The ethanol itself can be used in cars with adapted engines or in normal cars as a mixture with petrol.

But the environment could really benefit if we start using more ethanol as a fuel. The huge volume of carbon dioxide given off from fossil fuels is causing global climate change. But carbon dioxide is also given off during the fermentation of sugar, as well as when ethanol burns:

$$C_2H_5OH + 3O_2 \rightarrow 2CO_2 + 3H_2O$$

However, the carbon dioxide released into the atmosphere is offset by carbon dioxide absorbed during photosynthesis as sugar cane grows:

$$6CO_2 + 6H_2O \rightarrow C_6H_{12}O_6 + 6O_2$$

Questions for discussion

Discuss with another learner or group of learners:

* It is difficult to achieve 100% carbon-neutrality, a perfect balance between CO_2 released and CO_2 absorbed. This might be because fossil fuels are often used in manufacturing fertilisers, harvesting and transporting the crops for processing, and distributing the ethanol.

  Discuss in small groups how we could make ethanol biofuel even more environmentally friendly. Make a list of suggestions to share with the whole group.

17.1 The homologous series of alcohols

Alcohols are organic molecules containing the hydroxyl group, OH. With one hydroxyl group substituted into an alkane molecule, the general formula is $C_nH_{2n+1}OH$.

The alcohols are named by adding '-anol' to the alkane stem. For example, CH_3OH is called *methanol*.

Classifying alcohols

For alcohol molecules with three or more carbon atoms, the position of the hydroxyl group is shown by inserting a number to indicate which carbon atom is bonded to the —OH group. Figure 17.2 gives some examples.

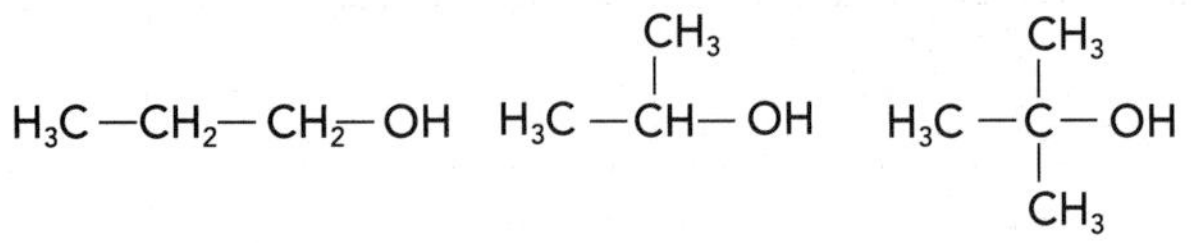

propan-1-ol **primary alcohol**   propan-2-ol **secondary alcohol**   2-methylpropan-2-ol **tertiary alcohol**

Figure 17.2: Note that the numbering to show the position of the —OH group in an alcohol starts from the end of the molecule that gives the smaller number.

Propan-1-ol is classified as a **primary alcohol**. The carbon atom bonded to the —OH group is attached to one other carbon atom (alkyl group). Propan-2-ol is a **secondary alcohol** as the carbon atom bonded to the —OH group is attached to two other carbon atoms (alkyl groups). With three alkyl groups attached, 2-methylpropan-2-ol is an example of a **tertiary alcohol**.

There are also alcohols with more than one —OH group. We came across an example in Section 15.4 when an alkene is oxidised to form a 'diol', ethane-1,2-diol. Its structural formula is $HOCH_2CH_2OH$. Both the hydroxy groups are bonded to a —CH_2 group, so both are classified as primary. On the other hand, a diol such as propane-1,2-diol, $HOCH_2CH(OH)CH_3$, has one primary and one secondary —OH group within its molecules.

Properties of alcohols

The alcohols have higher boiling points than expected when compared with other organic molecules with similar relative molecular masses. Even methanol,

the alcohol with the lowest molar mass, is a liquid at room temperature. This occurs because of hydrogen bonding between alcohol molecules (see Section 4.8). Hydrogen bonding also explains why the smaller alcohol molecules are so miscible (mix and dissolve well) in water.

Comparing the acidity of alcohols and water

Once dissolved in water, ethanol molecules do not dissociate (split up) to any great extent, although there is a very small **degree of dissociation**:

$$C_2H_5OH(aq) \rightleftharpoons C_2H_5O^-(aq) + H^+(aq)$$
ethanol   ethoxide ion

The position of equilibrium lies well over to the left, favouring the undissociated C_2H_5OH molecules. Even compared to the dissociation of water molecules:

$$H_2O(l) \rightleftharpoons H^+(aq) + OH^-(aq)$$

the concentration of $H^+(aq)$ ions is much lower. So we can say that ethanol is a weaker acid than water: its molecules are less likely to dissociate and form H^+ ions. This is because of the electron-donating alkyl (ethyl) group bonded to the negatively charged oxygen atom in the ethoxide ion. The positive inductive effect of the ethyl group (see Section 27.1) has the effect of concentrating more negative charge on this oxygen atom. So the ethoxide ion more readily accepts an H ion than the hydroxide ions, OH^-, from the dissociation of water. The hydroxide ion only has a hydrogen atom bonded to its negatively charged oxygen, and no alkyl groups.

KEY WORDS

primary alcohol: an alcohol in which the carbon atom bonded to the —OH group is attached to one other carbon atom (or alkyl group).

secondary alcohol: an alcohol in which the carbon atom bonded to the —OH group is attached to two other carbon atoms (or alkyl groups).

tertiary alcohol: an alcohol in which the carbon atom bonded to the —OH group is attached to three other carbon atoms (or alkyl groups).

Question

1 a   Explain how hydrogen bonds arise:

   i   between ethanol molecules

   ii   between ethanol and water molecules.

   b   Explain why ethanol mixes with water in all proportions but hexan-1-ol is less miscible with water.

   c   Give the structural formula of 2-methylbutan-2-ol, and classify it as a primary, secondary or tertiary alcohol.

   d   i   Give the structural difference that makes an alcohol a weaker acid than water.

      ii   Suggest which type of alcohol is the weakest acid:

         A   a primary alcohol

         B   a secondary alcohol

         C   a tertiary alcohol

         D   no difference

   Working as a pair, with your book closed, explain to your partner why ethanol is a weaker acid than water. Then listen while your partner talks about why water is a stronger acid than ethanol.

   Finish by opening the book and checking how you did.

17.2 Reactions to make alcohols

Alcohols do occur in nature, for example, in rotting fruit that undergoes fermentation. There are also plenty of ways that chemists can produce alcohols. Here is a summary of the reactions you need to know:

- electrophilic addition of steam, $H_2O(g)$, to an alkene, using a concentrated phosphoric(V) acid, H_3PO_4, catalyst (see Section 15.3):

$$C_2H_4 + H_2O \xrightarrow{H_3PO_4} C_2H_5OH$$
    ethene   steam   ethanol

- oxidation of alkenes with cold, dilute, acidified potassium manganate(VII) to form a diol (see Section 15.4). Remember that we can use the symbol [O] to represent oxygen provided by an oxidising agent in organic reactions:

$$C_2H_4 + H_2O + [O] \rightarrow HOCH_2CH_2OH$$
                          ethane-1.2-diol

- nucleophilic substitution (hydrolysis in this case) of a halogenoalkane by heating with NaOH(aq) (see Section 16.2):

$$CH_3CH_2Br + NaOH \rightarrow CH_3CH_2OH + NaBr$$
    bromoethane   ethanol

- reduction of an aldehyde (to form a primary alcohol) or of a ketone (to form a secondary alcohol) using a reducing agent, such as $NaBH_4$ or $LiAlH_4$ (see Section 18.3):

$$CH_3CH_2CHO + 2[H] \rightarrow CH_3CH_2CH_2OH$$
    propanal   propan-1-ol

$$CH_3COCH_3 + 2[H] \rightarrow CH_3CH(OH)CH_3$$
    propanone   propan-2-ol

- reduction of a carboxylic acid using $NaBH_4$ or $LiAlH_4$ (see Section 17.4):

$$CH_3COOH + 4[H] \rightarrow CH_3CH_2OH + H_2O$$
    ethanoic acid   ethanol

or $H_2(g)$ / Ni and heat

- hydrolysis of an ester by heating with a dilute acid or alkali (see Section 17.3):

  - with acid

$$CH_3COOCH_2CH_3 + H_2O \underset{}{\overset{H^+(aq)}{\rightleftharpoons}}$$
$$CH_3COOH + CH_3CH_2OH$$

  - with alkali

$$CH_3COOCH_2CH_3 + NaOH \rightarrow$$
$$CH_3COO^-Na^+ + CH_3CH_2OH$$

17.3 Reactions of the alcohols

Combustion

When ignited, the alcohols react with oxygen in the air (Figure 17.3). The products of complete combustion are carbon dioxide and water.

alcohol + oxygen → carbon dioxide + water

For example, ethanol burns with a clean blue flame in a good supply of air:

$$C_2H_5OH + 3O_2 \rightarrow 2CO_2 + 3H_2O$$
    ethanol

Figure 17.3: The fuel called 'gasohol' is a mixture of ethanol and petrol.

Substitution to form a halogenoalkane

In this substitution reaction with a hydrogen halide, such as hydrogen chloride, the —OH group in the alcohol is replaced by a halogen atom. This produces a halogenoalkane.

IMPORTANT

The general equation is:

alcohol + hydrogen halide →
                    halogenoalkane + water

For example:

$CH_3CH_2OH + HCl \rightarrow CH_3CH_2Cl + H_2O$
ethanol   chloroethane

The dry hydrogen chloride gas for this reaction can be made *in situ* (in the reaction vessel). Sodium chloride and concentrated sulfuric acid are used for this:

$NaCl + H_2SO_4 \rightarrow NaHSO_4 + HCl$

PRACTICAL ACTIVITY 17.1

Halogenation of an alcohol

The alcohol is heated under reflux (see apparatus in Section 16.2) with the reactants to make the halogenoalkane. The halogenoalkane made can then be distilled off from the reaction mixture and collected as oily droplets under water (Figure 17.4).

Figure 17.4: Bromoethane being distilled off following the reaction between ethanol and hydrogen bromide. The white solid visible in the pear-shaped flask is sodium bromide (crystals). The sodium bromide reacts with concentrated sulfuric or phosphoric(V) acid to make the hydrogen bromide needed for the reaction.

For a substitution reaction with hydrogen bromide, the HBr can be made using potassium bromide and concentrated phosphoric (or sulfuric) acid.

The nucleophilic substitution by the halide ion takes place after the —OH group has accepted an H^+ ion from the acid. This makes the C—O bond in the alcohol easier to break, and water is given off.

Sulfur dichloride oxide, $SOCl_2$, can also be used to substitute a chlorine atom into an alcohol molecule, as shown below:

$$C_2H_5OH + SOCl_2 \rightarrow C_2H_5Cl + HCl + SO_2$$

Note that in this reaction the two by-products of the reaction (HCl and SO_2) are both gases. These gases escape from the reaction mixture. The halogenoalkane is formed, without the need to heat the reaction mixture.

We can also use phosphorus halides to provide the halogen atoms for this substitution reaction with alcohols.

For chloroalkanes we can use solid phosphorus(V) chloride, PCl_5:

$$C_2H_5OH + PCl_5 \rightarrow C_2H_5Cl + HCl + POCl_3$$

The release of acidic hydrogen chloride gas from this reaction can be used as a test for the hydroxyl group. You can see acidic steamy fumes from the HCl gas produced.

Phosphorus(III) chloride can also be used to halogenate an alcohol, but this reaction does require heating.

$$3C_2H_5OH + PCl_3 \xrightarrow{heat} 3C_2H_5Cl + H_3PO_3$$

For bromoalkanes and iodoalkanes, we can make the phosphorus(III) halide, PBr_3 or PI_3, needed for the reaction. Red phosphorus and bromine or iodine are warmed with the alcohol.

For example:

$$3C_2H_5OH + PI_3 \xrightarrow{heat} 3C_2H_5I + H_3PO_3$$
iodoethane

Question

2 a Starting with an alkene, give the reactants and conditions needed to produce:

   i propanol

   ii propane-1,2-diol.

b Write a balanced equation for the complete combustion of:

   i propan-1-ol

   ii butan-1-ol.

c i Write a balanced equation to show the reaction between ethanol and hydrogen bromide.

   ii What are the reagents and conditions used for this reaction?

   iii What do we call this type of reaction?

Now go through your answers to Question 2 with a fellow learner and discuss any differences. Then check against the actual answers.

Reaction with sodium metal

In the reaction with hydrogen halides, the C—O bond in the alcohol breaks as it loses its —OH group. However, in some other reactions the O—H bond in the alcohol breaks. The reaction with sodium metal is an example:

$$2C_2H_5OH + 2Na \rightarrow 2C_2H_5O^-Na^+ + H_2$$
ethanol   sodium   sodium ethoxide   hydrogen

The reaction is similar to sodium's reaction with water, but less vigorous. In both cases hydrogen gas is given off and a basic ionic compound is formed. With ethanol, if the excess ethanol is allowed to evaporate off after the reaction, a white crystalline solid is left. This is sodium ethoxide.

Other alcohols react in a similar way with sodium. For example, propan-1-ol would produce sodium propoxide plus hydrogen gas.

> **IMPORTANT**
>
> In general:
>
> alcohol + sodium → sodium alkoxide + hydrogen

We find that the longer the hydrocarbon chain in the alcohol, the less vigorous the reaction with sodium metal (Figure 17.5).

Figure 17.5: Sodium reacting with ethanol. The pink colour is from a colourless phenolphthalein indicator that has been added to the ethanol, showing the basic nature of the sodium ethoxide formed in the ethanol.

Question

3 Lithium reacts with alcohols in a similar way to sodium.

A small piece of lithium metal is dropped onto a watch-glass containing propan-1-ol.

a Describe what you would observe.

b Name the products of the reaction.

c Suggest what difference you would see if you used sodium instead of lithium in this reaction.

Esterification

Another reaction that involves the breaking of the O—H bond in alcohols is **esterification**, i.e. the making of esters. An esterification reaction can take place between an alcohol and a carboxylic acid. It can be classified as a condensation reaction.

IMPORTANT

The general equation is:

$$\text{carboxylic acid} + \text{alcohol} \underset{}{\overset{\text{strong acid}}{\rightleftharpoons}} \text{ester} + \text{water}$$

KEY WORD

esterification: a reaction of a carboxylic or acyl chloride with an alcohol (or phenol) to produce an ester and a small molecule (water or a salt such as NaCl).

REFLECTION

1 At this point, review your knowledge of the reactions of the alcohols covered so far in this chapter. Go back to Section 17.2 'Reactions to make alcohols' and look at each chemical equation since then, covering the products with a sheet of paper. Try to complete each equation on your sheet of paper, checking your answers as you go along. How did you do?

2 If you know the *type* of reaction taking place it is a lot easier to identify the products formed. Discuss with a partner any strategies you have found useful to help remember organic equations.

PRACTICAL ACTIVITY 17.2

Alcohol plus carboxylic acid

For esterification to take place, the carboxylic acid and alcohol are heated under reflux with a strong acid catalyst (usually concentrated sulfuric acid, but also phosphoric(V) acid). The reaction is reversible, so an equilibrium mixture can be established with all the reactants and products shown in the general equation present.

The esters formed usually have sweet, fruity smells.

Here is an example of an esterification reaction:

$$C_2H_5OH + CH_3C\overset{O}{\underset{OH}{\diagup}} \underset{H_2SO_4}{\rightleftharpoons} CH_3C\overset{O}{\underset{OC_2H_5}{\diagup}} + H_2O$$

ethanol   ethanoic acid   ethyl ethanoate   water

The ester formed is called ethyl ethanoate.

But what would be the name of the ester formed if ethanol was reacted with propanoic acid?

Would it be propyl ethanoate or ethyl propanoate?

The answer is ethyl propanoate. That's because the first part of an ester's name comes from the alcohol: in this case ethanol, giving 'ethyl …'. The second part comes from the carboxylic acid, in this case propanoic acid, giving '… propanoate'. This makes 'ethyl propanoate' as the name of the ester formed (Figure 17.6).

$$CH_3CH_2COOH + C_2H_5OH \overset{H_2SO_4}{\rightleftharpoons}$$
propanoic acid   ethanol

$$CH_3CH_2COOC_2H_5 + H_2O$$
ethyl propanoate   water

Figure 17.6: Esters contribute to the complex mixture of substances blended in a perfume. They are also present naturally in fruits, and we use them in artificial flavourings and as solvents, e.g. in nail varnish remover.

Hydrolysis of esters

IMPORTANT

Esters can be hydrolysed by heating under reflux with either an acid or a base.

Refluxing with an acid, such as dilute sulfuric acid, simply reverses the preparation of the ester from an alcohol and a carboxylic acid. The reaction is reversible and an equilibrium mixture is established. In acid hydrolysis, there are always both reactants (ester + water) and products (carboxylic acid + alcohol) present after the reaction.

The equation for the acid hydrolysis of the ester ethyl ethanoate is:

$$H_3C-C\overset{O}{\underset{O-CH_2CH_3}{\diagup}} + H_2O \underset{H^+(aq)}{\rightleftharpoons} H_3C-C\overset{O}{\underset{O-H}{\diagup}} + CH_3CH_2OH$$

However, when an ester is refluxed with an alkali (a soluble base), such as aqueous sodium hydroxide, it is fully hydrolysed. Unlike acid hydrolysis, this is *not* a reversible reaction, so all the ester present can be broken down by excess alkali. An alcohol and the sodium salt of the carboxylic acid are formed.

The equation for the base hydrolysis of ethyl ethanoate is:

$$H_3C-C\overset{O}{\underset{O-CH_2CH_3}{\diagup}} + NaOH \longrightarrow H_3C-C\overset{O}{\underset{O^-Na^+}{\diagup}} + CH_3CH_2OH$$
                                                sodium
                                                ethanoate

Question

4   a   Name the ester formed in each of the following reactions :

     i   butan-1-ol + ethanoic acid

     ii   ethanol + hexanoic acid

     iii   pentan-1-ol and methanoic acid.

   b   Write the structural formula of each ester formed in part **a**.

Dehydration

Alcohols can also undergo elimination reactions in which water is lost, and in this case, alkenes are formed. As the small molecule removed from the alcohol molecule is H_2O, this reaction is also known as **dehydration**.

$$\text{alcohol} \xrightarrow[\text{heat}]{\text{catalyst}} \text{alkene} + \text{water}$$

The reaction takes place when alcohol vapour is passed over a hot catalyst of aluminium oxide powder. Pieces of porous pot or pumice, as well as a concentrated acid, also catalyse the reaction.

For example:

$$C_2H_5OH \xrightarrow[\text{heat}]{Al_2O_3\text{catalyst}} CH_2{=}CH_2 + H_2O$$

Figure 17.7 shows how you would collect the ethene gas formed.

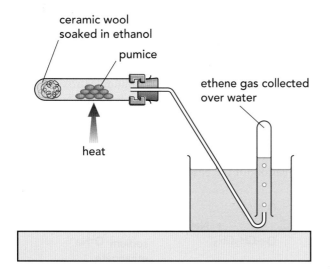

Figure 17.7: The dehydration of ethanol to give ethene.

Question

5   Concentrated sulfuric acid or phosphoric acid can be used to catalyse the dehydration of an alcohol.

The alcohol and concentrated acid are heated to about 170 °C. The concentrated acid does not change chemically during the reaction.

a   Write an equation showing the dehydration of ethanol using concentrated sulfuric acid.

b   If propan-1-ol was used instead of ethanol, name the organic product formed.

Oxidation

In Section 17.1 we saw how alcohols can be classified as primary, secondary or tertiary. For most of their reactions, the class of alcohol makes no difference to the type of products formed. In organic chemistry, we can usually generalise for the whole homologous series. However, when alcohols are oxidised, primary, secondary and tertiary alcohols each behave differently.

> ### IMPORTANT
>
> Primary and secondary alcohols can be oxidised by potassium dichromate(VI) solution, $K_2Cr_2O_7$, acidified with dilute sulfuric acid.
> Tertiary alcohols are not oxidised by acidified potassium dichromate(VI) solution.

The *orange* colour of acidified potassium dichromate(VI) solution is caused by the dichromate(VI) ions, $Cr_2O_7{}^{2-}$(aq). When the dichromate(VI) ions behave as an oxidising agent, the ions themselves are reduced. They become chromium(III) ions, Cr^{3+}(aq), which form a *green* solution. The reaction mixture needs to be warmed before the oxidation takes place.

The product formed when you attempt to oxidise an alcohol can be used to distinguish between primary, secondary and tertiary alcohols.

With tertiary alcohols, a mixture of the tertiary alcohol, dilute sulfuric acid and potassium dichromate(VI) solution remains orange when warmed. *No reaction* takes place.

A secondary alcohol, such as propan-2-ol, will be oxidised to form a *ketone*. In this case propanone is formed and the reaction mixture turns green:

$$\underset{\underset{H}{|}}{\overset{\overset{OH}{|}}{H_3C{-}C{-}CH_3}} + [O] \longrightarrow \underset{\text{propanone}}{\overset{\overset{O}{\|}}{H_3C{-}C{-}CH_3}} + H_2O$$

> ### KEY WORD
>
> **dehydration:** reaction in which water is removed from a larger molecule.

Remember that simplified oxidation equations use [O] to show the oxygen added from the oxidising agent (see Section 14.8).

With a primary alcohol, such as ethanol, the alcohol is oxidised to an *aldehyde*. Ethanol is oxidised to ethanal:

$$CH_3CH_2OH + [O] \longrightarrow \underset{\text{ethanal}}{H_3C-\overset{\overset{\textstyle O}{\|}}{C}-H} + H_2O$$

PRACTICAL ACTIVITY 17.3

Distinguishing tertiary alcohols

Given three unknown alcohols, one primary, one secondary and one tertiary, it is easy to distinguish the tertiary alcohol. Figure 17.8 shows the results of warming each class of alcohol with a solution of acidified potassium dichromate(VI).

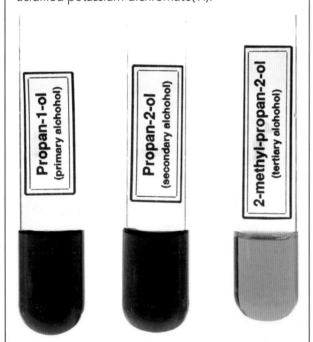

Figure 17.8: Before warming with the labelled alcohol, each of these tubes contained orange acidified potassium dichromate(VI) solution. After warming, the orange dichromate(VI) ions have been reduced to green chromium(III) ions by the primary and secondary alcohols. This shows that both the primary and secondary alcohols have been oxidised, but the tertiary alcohol, 2-methylpropan-2-ol, has not.

The ethanal formed can be further oxidised to form ethanoic acid, a carboxylic acid. This is achieved by refluxing with excess acidified potassium dichromate(VI):

$$\underset{\text{ethanal}}{H_3C-\overset{\overset{\textstyle O}{\|}}{C}-H} + [O] \longrightarrow \underset{\text{ethanoic acid}}{H_3C-\overset{\overset{\textstyle O}{\|}}{C}-OH}$$

Question

Working with a partner, discuss and answer these questions:

6   Propan-1-ol can be oxidised to propanal, CH_3CH_2CHO, and then further oxidised to propanoic acid, CH_3CH_2COOH.

   a   Give the reagents and conditions that should be used to oxidise propan-1-ol to propanal.

   b   Write a balanced chemical equation for this oxidation. Represent oxygen from the oxidising agent as [O].

   c   Give the reagents and conditions that should be used to oxidise propan-1-ol to propanoic acid.

   d   Write a balanced chemical equation for this oxidation. Again, show oxygen from the oxidising agent as [O].

17.4 Carboxylic acids

Reactions that form carboxylic acids

We have already seen how primary alcohols can be oxidised to aldehydes, which are then further oxidised to form carboxylic acids. The primary alcohol is refluxed with acidified potassium chromate(VI) solution (or acidified potassium manganate(VII) solution.

Carboxylic acids are also made from nitriles, $R-C{\equiv}N$. When a nitrile is refluxed with dilute hydrochloric acid, hydrolysis occurs. The $-C{\equiv}N$ group at the end of the hydrocarbon chain is converted to the $-COOH$ group, forming a carboxylic acid (see Section 18.4).

For example:

$$CH_3CH_2CN + HCl + 2H_2O \rightarrow$$
$$CH_3CH_2COOH + NH_4Cl$$

propanenitrile   propanoic acid

Reacting as typical acids

Carboxylic acids are described as weak acids because their molecules do not dissociate (ionise) completely when added to water. However, a small proportion of the molecules do dissociate. The carboxylic acid molecules then release $H^+(aq)$ ions. The solutions made have a pH value less than 7. For example, ethanoic acid forms aqueous hydrogen ions and ethanoate ions in water:

$$CH_3COOH(aq) \rightleftharpoons CH_3COO^-(aq) + H^+(aq)$$

ethanoic acid   ethanoate ion

You can learn more about the dissociation of carboxylic acids in Chapter 26.

The presence of excess $H^+(aq)$ ions in solutions of carboxylic acids means that they undergo all the usual reactions of acids. They react with:

- alkalis to form a salt and water:

$$CH_3COOH + NaOH \rightarrow CH_3COONa + H_2O$$

- reactive metals to form a salt and hydrogen gas:

$$2CH_3COOH + Mg \rightarrow (CH_3COO)_2Mg + H_2$$

- carbonates to form a salt, water and carbon dioxide gas:

$$2CH_3COOH + K_2CO_3 \rightarrow$$
$$2CH_3COOK + H_2O + CO_2$$

The salts formed in the three reactions above are called sodium ethanoate, magnesium ethanoate and potassium ethanoate, respectively.

Reduction of carboxylic acids

Carboxylic acids can be reduced to their corresponding primary alcohol by using the reducing agent lithium tetrahydridoaluminate, $LiAlH_4$, in dry ether at room temperature. The liquid ether is dried because $LiAlH_4$ reacts violently with any water present.

In the simplified reduction equation, you can use the symbol [H] to represent the hydrogen atoms from the reducing agent. Remember that in organic chemistry, you can think of reduction as the addition of hydrogen atoms.

So, for ethanoic acid being reduced to ethanol, we can show the reaction as:

$$CH_3COOH + 4[H] \rightarrow CH_3CH_2OH + H_2O$$

Question

7   a   Describe how would you make ethanoic acid from ethanenitrile.

    b   Write a balanced equation, using structural formulae for the organic compounds, to show the formation of:

       i   sodium methanoate, using sodium hydroxide as one of the reactants

       ii   potassium ethanoate, using potassium metal as one of the reactants

       iii   lithium propanoate, using lithium carbonate as one of the reactants.

    c   Name and give the formula of the reducing agent used to convert carboxylic acids to primary alcohols.

REFLECTION

1   Make a mind map to summarise the oxidation and reduction of alcohols. Label the links with the reaction conditions needed. Ensure you include how alcohols are formed, as well as the products made when alcohols themselves are oxidised and reduced.

    Check your mind maps with a partner and revise your own if necessary. What did your partner particularly notice about your mind map?

2   Reflect on the use of the symbols [O] and [H] in organic reactions. Discuss with your partner how these symbols help you to identify the products of reduction and oxidation and make organic chemistry easier to understand.

SUMMARY

The complete combustion of alcohols forms carbon dioxide and water.
A nucleophilic substitution reaction takes place between alcohols and hydrogen halides to form halogenoalkanes.
Alcohols react with sodium metal to give sodium alkoxides and hydrogen gas.
An alcohol will react with a carboxylic acid, in the presence of a strong acid catalyst, to form an ester and water.
Esters can be hydrolysed by an acid or by a base. Acid hydrolysis is a reversible reaction but base hydrolysis is not reversible.
Elimination of water from an alcohol produces an alkene; the reaction is called *dehydration*. Dehydration may be carried out by passing alcohol vapour over heated pumice, porous pot or aluminium oxide, or by using a concentrated acid catalysts.
A primary alcohol can be oxidised to an aldehyde by heating the alcohol gently with acidified potassium dichromate(VI) (and distilling out the aldehyde as it forms: see Section 18.2). The primary alcohol can be further oxidised to a carboxylic acid by refluxing the alcohol with excess acidified potassium dichromate(VI).
A secondary alcohol can be oxidised to a ketone by heating the alcohol with acidified potassium dichromate(VI).
Acidified potassium dichromate(VI) changes colour from orange to green when it oxidises a primary or secondary alcohol. However, tertiary alcohols cannot be oxidised by refluxing with acidified potassium dichromate(VI).
Carboxylic acids can be formed from the oxidation of primary alcohols or aldehydes by refluxing with excess potassium dichromate(VI) and dilute sulfuric(VI) acid. They can also be made by refluxing nitriles with dilute hydrochloric acid.
Carboxylic acids are weak acids that react with reactive metals, alkalis or carbonates to form carboxylate salts.
The carboxylic acids can be reduced by $LiAlH_4$ in dry ether, to form primary alcohols.

EXAM-STYLE QUESTIONS

1   Which one of these reactions will produce a primary alcohol?   [1]

   A   acid hydrolysis of a nitrile

   B   elimination of a halogenoalkane by ethanolic sodium hydroxide

   C   neutralisation of a carboxylic acid

   D   reduction of an aldehyde

2   What is the organic product when alcohol vapour is passed over hot aluminium oxide?   [1]

   A   an aldehyde   **B**   an alkene

   C   a carboxylic acid   **D**   a ketone

3   Pentan-2-ol, butan-1-ol and 2-methylpropan-2-ol are alcohols.

   a   For each one:

      i   give its molecular formula   [3]

      ii give its structural formula   [3]

CONTINUED

    iii give its displayed formula [3]

    iv give its skeletal formula [3]

    v state whether it is a primary, secondary or tertiary alcohol. [3]

  b Give the general formula that is used to represent alcohols. [1]

  c Two of the alcohols in this question are isomers of each other.

    Identify which two and name the type of isomerism they show. [2]

  d Name the alcohol whose structural formula is $CH_3CH_2COH(CH_3)_2$. [1]

[Total: 19]

4 Write a balanced chemical equation for each of the following processes. Structural or displayed formulae should be used for all organic substances.

  a Making ethanol, using ethene as feedstock. Include the formula of the catalyst used. [2]

  b The complete combustion of ethanol in oxygen. [2]

  c The dehydration of butan-2-ol when passed over hot Al_2O_3.

    Suggest three equations, one for each of the three possible products. [3]

  d The reaction of ethanoic acid with ethanol.

    Name the catalyst used, the type of reaction and the products. [4]

[Total: 11]

5 Primary and secondary alcohols can be oxidised by heating with a mixture of potassium dichromate(VI) and dilute sulfuric(VI) acid.

A primary alcohol can be oxidised to two different products, depending on the conditions used.

A secondary alcohol forms one product when oxidised.

Tertiary alcohols cannot be oxidised.

  a Write the chemical formula of potassium dichromate(VI). [1]

  b Using a primary alcohol of your choice as an example:

    i give the displayed formulae of the two products it could be oxidised to [2]

    ii state the conditions needed to give each product [2]

    iii state which homologous series each product belongs to [2]

    iv write a balanced chemical equation for each reaction (the convention [O] may be used for the oxidising agent). [2]

  c Using a secondary alcohol of your choice as an example:

    i give the displayed formula of the product it could be oxidised to [2]

    ii state which homologous series the product belongs to [1]

    iii write a balanced chemical equation for the reaction (the convention [O] may be used for the oxidising agent). [1]

  d Explain why tertiary alcohols are resistant to oxidation. [1]

[Total: 14]

SELF-EVALUATION

After studying this chapter, complete a table like this:

I can	See section...	Needs more work	Almost there	Ready to move on
explain the acidity of alcohols compared with water	17.1			
write equations for the reactions we can use to produce alcohols, to include reagents and conditions	17.2			
write equations for the reactions of alcohols in their combustion, substitution, reaction with sodium, oxidation to carbonyl compounds and carboxylic acids, and dehydration to alkenes	17.3			
classify hydroxy compounds into primary, secondary and tertiary alcohols	17.1			
suggest characteristic distinguishing reactions, e.g. mild oxidation	17.3			
describe the acid and base hydrolysis of esters	17.3			
describe the formation of carboxylic acids from alcohols, aldehydes and nitriles	17.4			
describe the reactions of carboxylic acids in the formation of salts, alkyl esters and primary alcohols.	17.4			

> # Chapter 18
Carbonyl compounds

LEARNING INTENTIONS

In this chapter you will learn how to:

- describe:

    - the formation of aldehydes from the oxidation of primary alcohols

    - the formation of ketones from the oxidation of secondary alcohols

    - the reduction of aldehydes and ketones, e.g. using $NaBH_4$ or $LiAlH_4$

    - the reaction of aldehydes and ketones with HCN (hydrogen cyanide) and KCN (potassium cyanide)

- describe the mechanism of the nucleophilic addition reactions of hydrogen cyanide with aldehydes and ketones

- describe the detection of carbonyl compounds by the use of 2,4-dinitrophenylhydrazine (2,4-DNPH) reagent

- distinguish between aldehydes and ketones by testing with Fehling's and Tollens' reagents

- describe the reaction of CH_3CO- compounds with alkaline aqueous iodine to give tri-iodomethane, CHI_3, and a carboxylate ion, $RCOO^-$

- devise a synthetic route (series of reactions) using any of the reactions from Chapters 14–18 to make a named organic product

CONTINUED

- deduce the presence of a CH₃CH(OH)— group in an alcohol from its reaction with alkaline aqueous iodine to form tri-iodomethane

- analyse an infrared spectrum of a simple molecule to identify functional groups .

BEFORE YOU START

1   Which equation below describes what happens when a ketone is reduced?

   A $CH_3COCH_3 + 2[H] \rightarrow CH_3CH(OH)CH_3$

   B $CH_3CHO + 2[H] \rightarrow CH_3CH_2OH$

   C $CH_3COCH_3 + H_2 \rightarrow CH_3CH(OH)CH_3$

   D $CH_3COCH_3 + H_2O \rightarrow CH_3CH(OH)CH_3 + [O]$

2   Describe the first step in the reaction mechanism when OH⁻(aq) is mixed with CH_3CH_2Cl.

3   Draw the displayed formula of your choice to represent:

   a   a primary alcohol

   b   a secondary alcohol

   c   a tertiary alcohol.

4   Discuss what happens in these addition reactions:

   a   bromine reacts with ethene

   b   ethene forms poly(ethene).

USING ALDEHYDES AND KETONES

Aromatic carbonyl compounds have very distinctive, almond-like odours. Benzaldehyde is used to make almond essence, the flavouring used in some cakes and puddings. Benzaldehyde is also a component of the mixtures that make up the smells and flavours of many fruits such as mangoes, cherries, apricots, plums and peaches. The structures of heptan-2-one and benzaldehyde are shown in Figure 18.1.

More complex aldehydes and ketones also occur in common smells and flavours, such as the lemony odour of citronella candles. Citronella candles can be used to repel mosquitoes. The common name for the aldehyde responsible for the smell is *citronellal*. Chemists can extract (take out) this

aldehyde from lemongrass and citronella grass. The structural formula of citronellal, with the aldehyde function group in bold, is:

$CH_3C(CH_3)$=$CHCH_2CH_2CH(CH_3)CH_2$**CHO**

Questions for discussion

Discuss with another learner or group of learners:

- Carry out some research to find the name and structure of the aldehyde responsible for the sweet smell of vanilla.

- Then discuss the difference between the structures of molecules of aldehydes and ketones.

CONTINUED

- Finish by each drawing the skeletal formula of citronellal, then compare each other's efforts.

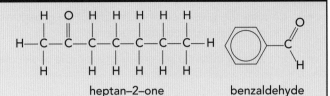

heptan–2–one benzaldehyde

Figure 18.1: a Heptan-2-one, a ketone, is responsible for the smell of blue cheese. **b** Benzaldehyde, an aldehyde, contributes to the flavours of many fruits and nuts. You can see the structures of heptan-2-one and benzaldehyde above from their displayed formulae.

18.1 The homologous series of aldehydes and ketones

You briefly looked at aldehydes and ketones, the main classes of carbonyl compounds, in Chapter 17.

IMPORTANT

Remember that:

- aldehydes can be formed from the oxidation of primary alcohols

- ketones can be formed from the oxidation of secondary alcohols (see Section 18.2).

In aldehydes, the carbon atom in the carbonyl group, $>C=O$, is bonded to a carbon atom and a hydrogen atom. In other words, the carbonyl group is positioned at the end of a carbon chain.

In ketones, the carbonyl group is attached to two other carbon atoms. Tables 18.1 and 18.2 give examples from the start of these homologous series.

Name	Structural formula
methanal	HCHO
ethanal	CH_3CHO
propanal	CH_3CH_2CHO
butanal	$CH_3CH_2CH_2CHO$
pentanal	$CH_3CH_2CH_2CH_2CHO$

Table 18.1: The names of aldehydes are derived from the name of the equivalent alkane, with the '-e' at the end of the name replaced by '-al'. Note that numbers are not needed when naming aldehydes, as the carbonyl group is always at the end of the carbon chain.

Name	Structural formula
propanone	CH_3COCH_3
butanone	$CH_3COCH_2CH_3$
pentan-2-one	$CH_3COCH_2CH_2CH_3$
pentan-3-one	$CH_3CH_2COCH_2CH_3$

Table 18.2: Ketones are named by replacing the '-e' at the end of the alkane with '-one'. However, in ketone molecules that are larger than butanone we also need to indicate the position of the carbonyl group.

Question

1 a Name the following compounds:

    i $CH_3CH_2CH_2CH_2CH_2CHO$

    ii $CH_3CH_2CH_2CH_2CH_2CH_2COCH_3$

  b Draw the displayed formula of:

    i   methanal

    ii propanal

    iii pentan-3-one.

  c Draw the skeletal formula of the compounds listed in part **a**.

Now compare your answers to Question 1 with another learner and discuss any differences. Then check against the correct answers.

18.2 Preparation of aldehydes and ketones

Preparing aldehydes

The general equation for the reaction in which an aldehyde is made from a primary alcohol is:

> **IMPORTANT**
>
> primary alcohol + oxygen atom from oxidising agent → aldehyde + water

For example:

$$CH_3CH_2CH_2OH + [O] \rightarrow CH_3CH_2CHO + H_2O$$

propan-1-ol   propanal

The oxidising agent used is a solution of potassium dichromate(VI), which is orange, acidified with dilute sulfuric acid. To make the aldehyde, the primary alcohol is heated gently with acidified dichromate solution. The reaction mixture turns green as the orange dichromate ions, $Cr_2O_7{}^{2-}(aq)$, are reduced to green $Cr^{3+}(aq)$ ions.

PRACTICAL ACTIVITY 18.1

Oxidation of a primary alcohol

The acidified oxidising agent is added one drop at a time to the warm *primary* alcohol. The aldehyde made is distilled off as it forms in the reaction vessel. This method works because the aldehyde product will always have a lower boiling point than the alcohol reactant. If the aldehyde is not distilled off as soon as it is formed, further heating with acidified dichromate solution will oxidise the aldehyde produced to a carboxylic acid. The apparatus used to prepare a sample of ethanal is shown in Figure 18.2.

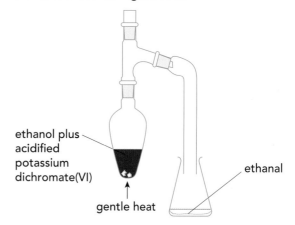

ethanol plus acidified potassium dichromate(VI)

gentle heat

ethanal

Figure 18.2: Distilling off and collecting the aldehyde, ethanal, formed in the mild oxidation of a primary alcohol, ethanol. The aqueous ethanal formed smells like rotting apples.

Preparing ketones

The general equation for making a ketone is:

> **IMPORTANT**
>
> secondary alcohol + oxygen atom from oxidising agent → ketone + water

For example:

$$CH_3CH(OH)CH_3 + [O] \rightarrow CH_3COCH_3 + H_2O$$

propan-2-ol   propanone

Once again, the oxidising agent used is a solution of potassium dichromate(VI), acidified with dilute sulfuric acid.

PRACTICAL ACTIVITY 18.2

Oxidation of a secondary alcohol

To produce a ketone, the acidified oxidising agent must be heated with a *secondary* alcohol. The reaction mixture in the flask will change from orange to green.

Unlike aldehydes, the ketone formed cannot be further oxidised, even if you heat the reaction mixture under reflux and add excess oxidising agent. Therefore, we do not need to distil off the ketone product immediately.

Question

2 a i Write a balanced equation for the oxidation of ethanol to ethanal, using [O] to represent an oxygen atom from the oxidising agent.

    ii Give practical details to explain how you would use the reaction described in part **a i** to prepare and collect a sample of ethanal.

  b i Write a balanced equation for the oxidation of butan-2-ol to butanone, using [O] to represent an oxygen atom from the oxidising agent.

    ii What do you observe in the reaction vessel if the oxidising agent used in part **b i** is potassium dichromate(VI) solution, acidified with dilute sulfuric acid, and the reaction mixture is heated?

    iii Discuss each option to complete the following statement with another learner, and agree on the correct answer:

The butanone does not have to be distilled off as it forms in the reaction vessel because …

A … it cannot be oxidised to a carboxylic acid.

B … it has a higher boiling point than butan-2-ol.

C … it is easier to filter it off from the reaction mixture.

D … it could be reduced back to butan-2-ol when heated.

18.3 Reduction of aldehydes and ketones

Chemical reduction of an aldehyde or ketone produces an alcohol:

IMPORTANT

aldehyde + reducing agent → primary alcohol

ketone + reducing agent → secondary alcohol

The reducing agent used is usually an aqueous alkaline solution of sodium tetrahydridoborate, $NaBH_4$, or lithium tetrahydridoaluminate, $LiAlH_4$, in dry ether.

The reduction reaction is carried out by either:

- warming the aldehyde or ketone with an aqueous alkaline solution of sodium tetrahydridoborate, or

- adding lithium tetrahydridoaluminate dissolved in a dry ether, such as diethyl ether, at room temperature. The organic solvent has to be dry because lithium tetrahydridoaluminate is a more powerful reducing agent than sodium tetrahydridoborate and reacts vigorously in water.

In the same way that we have used the symbol [O] in organic oxidation equations, we use the symbol [H] in reduction equations. [H] represents a hydrogen atom from the reducing agent. Look at the equations below used to summarise these reduction reactions:

$$CH_3CHO + 2[H] \rightarrow CH_3CH_2OH$$
ethanal   ethanol

$$CH_3COCH_3 + 2[H] \rightarrow CH_3CH(OH)CH_3$$
propanone   propan-2-ol

Question

3 a Write a balanced equation for the reaction that takes place when propanal is warmed with an aqueous alkaline solution of sodium tetra-hydridoborate, using the symbol [H] to represent a hydrogen atom from the reducing agent.

  b Name the product formed in the reduction reaction if pentan-3-one is added to lithium tetrahydridoaluminate in dry ether.

Compare your answers with those of another learner to arrive at two agreed answers.

18.4 Nucleophilic addition with HCN

The addition reactions we have met so far have involved electrophilic addition across the C=C double bond in alkene molecules (see Section 15.3).

Aldehydes and ketones also both undergo addition reactions with hydrogen cyanide, HCN. In these reactions, addition of HCN takes place across the C=O bond. However, the attack is by a nucleophile, not an electrophile.

We can show this using the **nucleophilic addition** reaction of the aldehyde propanal when heated with HCN. The HCN is generated *in situ* (in the reaction vessel) by the reaction of potassium cyanide, KCN, and dilute sulfuric acid.

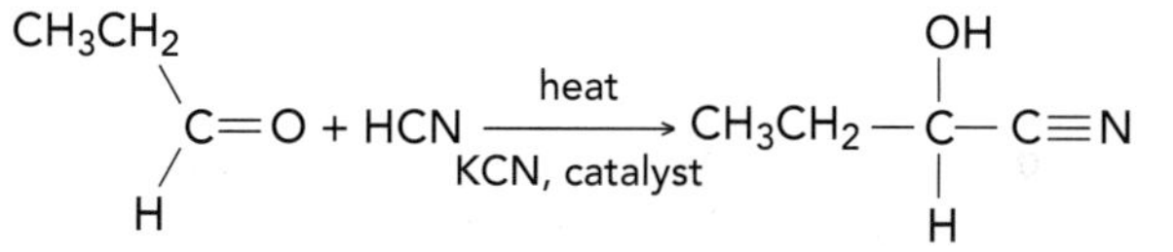

propanal   2-hydroxybutanenitrile

Note that a carbon atom has been added to the propanal molecule by the addition of the nitrile group ($-C\equiv N$). This is a useful reaction for chemists making new compounds as it increases the length of the carbon chain in the original aldehyde molecule by one carbon atom.

> **IMPORTANT**
>
> The nitrile group ($-C\equiv N$) can then be easily hydrolysed to a carboxylic acid.

You can carry out the hydrolysis of the nitrile group by refluxing with dilute hydrochloric acid:

$$-C\equiv N + HCl + 2H_2O \rightarrow -COOH + NH_4Cl$$

a nitrile   a carboxylic acid

You can also hydrolyse the nitrile group by refluxing with dilute alkali, such as sodium hydroxide solution. In this reaction a sodium salt of the carboxylic acid, $-COO^-Na^+$, is formed. Therefore, if you want to produce the carboxylic acid, $-COOH$, the products are treated with a strong acid, such as dilute sulfuric acid.

Mechanism of nucleophilic addition

The carbonyl group, >C=O, in aldehydes and ketones is polarised due to the high electronegativity of the oxygen atom. The electrons in the C=O bond are drawn nearer to the O atom, giving it a partial negative charge, and leaving the C atom with a partial positive charge. This makes the carbonyl C atom open to attack by a nucleophile, such as the cyanide ion, CN^-.

Note that the actual negative charge on a cyanide ion is on the carbon atom, not the nitrogen atom.

Step 1:

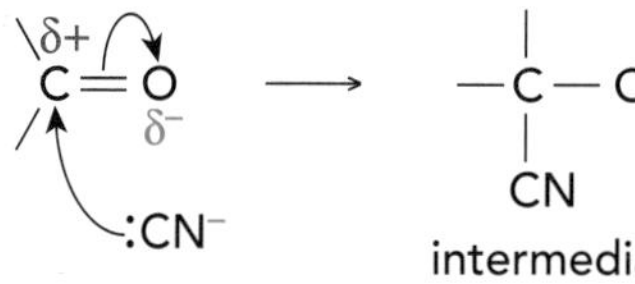

The negatively charged intermediate formed in the first step in the mechanism is highly reactive and quickly reacts with an aqueous H^+ ion. The hydrogen ion could be from HCN, from dilute acid or from water present in the reaction mixture. This forms the **2-hydroxynitrile** product.

> **KEY WORDS**
>
> **nucleophilic addition:** the mechanism of the reaction in which a nucleophile attacks the carbon atom in a carbonyl group and addition across the C=O bond occurs, e.g. aldehydes or ketones reacting with hydrogen cyanide.
>
> **2-hydroxynitrile:** the product from the nucleophilic addition of hydrogen cyanide to a carbonyl compound. For example, RRC(OH)CN from a ketone or RHC(OH)CN from an aldehyde, where R is an alkyl group.

Step 2:

$$-\overset{\displaystyle |}{\underset{\displaystyle |}{C}}-\overset{..}{\underset{..}{O}}:^- \quad H-CN \longrightarrow -\overset{\displaystyle |}{\underset{\displaystyle |}{C}}-OH \;+\; :CN^-$$

CN   CN

2-hydroxynitrile

All aldehydes and ketones form '2-hydroxynitriles' when they undergo nucleophilic addition. This is because the OH (hydroxyl) group will always be on the adjacent carbon atom to the nitrile group.

However, starting with the aldehyde methanal, HCHO, the hydroxynitrile formed in its nucleophilic addition with HCN would be called hydroxyethanenitrile. In this case there is no need to insert the '2' at the start of its name as the OH group could only possibly bond to the single carbon atom next to the nitrile group.

Question

4 Working with a partner, answer these questions together:

a Name the organic product that would be formed in the nucleophilic addition of HCN to:

     i ethanal

     ii propanone.

b Use diagrams and curly arrows to describe the mechanism of the reaction in part **a i**.

18.5 Testing for aldehydes and ketones

Testing for the carbonyl group

The reaction of an aldehyde or ketone with 2,4-dinitrophenylhydrazine is an example of a

---

PRACTICAL ACTIVITY 18.3

Testing with 2,4-DNPH

We can easily test for the presence of a carbonyl group in an aldehyde or ketone by adding a solution of 2,4-dinitrophenylhydrazine (often abbreviated to 2,4-DNPH). If an aldehyde or ketone is present, a *deep-orange precipitate* is formed (Figure 18.3).

The structure of 2,4-dinitrophenylhydrazine is:

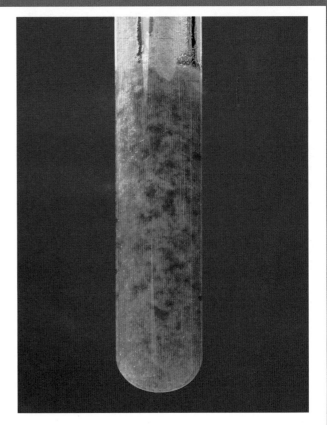

The precipitate formed can be purified by recrystallisation and its melting point can be measured experimentally. The identity of the precipitated compound can then be found by referring to melting point data. From this, we can identify the specific aldehyde or ketone used in the test.

Figure 18.3: The orange precipitate formed from 2,4-DNPH in a test with propanone, a ketone.

---

condensation reaction. In a condensation reaction, two molecules join together and, in the process, eliminate a small molecule, in this case water. The equation for the reaction of ethanal with 2,4-DNPH is:

2,4-dinitrophenylhydrazine

atoms lost in condensation reaction to form water

a 2,4-dinitrophenylhydrazone

Other classes of organic compound that also contain the carbonyl group, $>C{=}O$ (such as carboxylic acids and esters), do not form precipitates with 2,4-DNPH.

Distinguishing between aldehydes and ketones

As we saw in Section 18.2, aldehydes can be further oxidised to form carboxylic acids, but ketones cannot be oxidised easily. We can use this difference to distinguish between an aldehyde and a ketone in simple chemical tests. The two most common tests involve mild oxidation using Tollens' reagent or Fehling's solution.

PRACTICAL ACTIVITY 18.4

Testing with Tollens' reagent

Tollens' reagent is an aqueous solution of silver nitrate in excess ammonia solution, sometimes called *ammoniacal silver nitrate solution*. The silver ions, Ag^+, in the solution act as a mild oxidising agent. When warmed, the Ag^+ ions will oxidise an aldehyde to form a carboxylate ion.

Under the alkaline conditions in the test, any carboxylic acid formed is immediately neutralised to the carboxylate ion, $-COO^-$, as H^+ is removed from $-COOH$ and a salt is formed.

In the redox reaction with an aldehyde, the Ag^+ ions themselves are reduced to silver atoms. The silver atoms form a 'mirror' on the inside of the tube, giving a positive test for an aldehyde (Figure 18.4).

There will be *no change observed* when a ketone is warmed with Tollens' reagent as no redox reaction takes place. It remains a colourless mixture in the test-tube.

Figure 18.4: The 'before' and 'after' observations when Tollens' reagent is warmed with an aldehyde, such as ethanal, CH_3CHO.

PRACTICAL ACTIVITY 18.5

Testing with Fehling's solution

Fehling's solution is an alkaline solution containing copper(II) ions. When warmed with an aldehyde, the Cu^{2+} ions act as an oxidising agent. The aldehyde is oxidised to a carboxylate ion while the Cu^{2+} ions are reduced to Cu^+ ions. The clear blue Fehling's solution turns an opaque red / orange colour as a precipitate of copper(I) oxide forms throughout the solution (Figure 18.5).

As with Tollens' reagent, ketones are not oxidised in this test, so there is no change. The Fehling's solution remains blue when warmed.

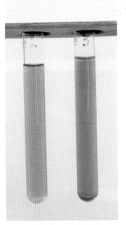

Figure 18.5: 'The 'before' and 'after' observations when Fehling's solution is warmed with an aldehyde, such as ethanal, CH_3CHO.

Question

5 The melting points of the derivatives of the reaction between 2,4-DNPH and various aldehydes and ketones are shown in the table.

Product of reaction between 2,4-DNPH and...	Melting point / °C
ethanal	168
propanal	155
butanal	126
propanone	126
butanone	116

a   Describe your observations when each of the carbonyl compounds in the table is mixed with 2,4-DNPH.

b   A derivative was formed between 2,4-DNPH and an unknown carbonyl compound.

   i   The melting point of the derivative was 126 °C. Deduce what this result tells you.

   ii   The unknown carbonyl compound formed an orange precipitate when warmed with Fehling's solution. Name the unknown compound.

   iii   Describe and explain the different results obtained when the compound named in part **b ii** is warmed with Tollens' reagent in a test-tube and then the same test is performed on butanone.

c   Write a half-equation to show silver ions acting as an oxidising agent in a positive test for an aldehyde.

d   Write a half-equation to show copper(II) ions acting as an oxidising agent in a positive test for an aldehyde.

REFLECTION

At this point, join another learner to discuss and reflect on your progress so far in this chapter.

1   Do you know how to prepare aldehydes and ketones?

2   Can you write equations for their reduction and the oxidation of aldehydes?

3   What about explaining the mechanism of nucleophilic addition, as well as testing for aldehydes and ketones?

4   Discuss with a partner the thought processes you need to go through to construct the mechanism for the nucleophilic condensation reaction between ethanal and HCN.

18.6 Reactions to form tri-iodomethane

Tri-iodomethane (iodoform) forms as a yellow precipitate with methyl ketones, i.e. compounds containing the CH_3CO- group (Figure 18.6). Note that ethanal, CH_3CHO, an aldehyde, also contains the CH_3CO- group. Chemists use the appearance of the yellow precipitate as evidence of the CH_3CO- group in an unknown compound.

The reagent used is an alkaline solution of iodine, which is warmed together with the substance being tested.

Figure 18.6: The yellow precipitate of tri-iodomethane forming.

The reaction involves two steps:

1 the carbonyl compound is halogenated: the three hydrogen atoms in the CH_3 methyl group are replaced by iodine atoms
2 the intermediate is hydrolysed to form the yellow precipitate of tri-iodomethane, CHI_3 (Figure 18.6).

When separated from the reaction mixture, the yellow crystals of tri-iodomethane can be positively identified by their melting point of 119 °C.

Here, R is an alkyl group in a methyl ketone:

Step 1	**Step 2**
I_2, NaOH(aq) halogenation	NaOH(aq) hydrolysis

$$RCOCH_3 \longrightarrow RCOCI_3 \longrightarrow RCOO^-Na^+ + CHI_3$$
a methyl ketone   tri-iodomethane

Testing for the $CH_3CH(OH)-$ group

The tri-iodomethane test can also be used to identify the presence of a secondary alcohol, with the hydroxy group (−OH) on the carbon atom next to a methyl group. This $CH_3CH(OH)-$ group is firstly oxidised by the alkaline iodine solution. This oxidation forms a methyl ketone, $RCOCH_3$, which then reacts via the two steps shown at the bottom of the first column. The products of the reaction are the yellow tri-iodomethane precipitate, CHI_3, and the sodium salt of a carboxylic acid, $RCOO^-Na^+$.

Question

Work with a partner, if possible, to discuss your reasoning as you answer the questions below together:

6   a   i   When propanone is warmed with alkaline iodine solution, a yellow precipitate is formed. Name and draw the displayed formula of the yellow precipitate.

ii   Give the structural formulae of the organic products formed in both steps of the reaction in part **i**.

b   Explain, naming any organic products formed, why ethanol gives a positive test (yellow precipitate) when warmed with alkaline iodine solution.

c   Which of these compounds will give a yellow precipitate when treated with alkaline aqueous iodine?

A   butanone
B   butanal
C   pentan-3-one
D   pentan-2-one
E   ethanal
F   methanol

At this point in the Coursebook you have finished the organic reactions needed for the AS Level course. You can be asked to devise a synthetic route (a series of reactions) to make a named product using any of the reactions in Chapters 14 to 18. A useful summary of these reactions is given in Table 29.4 found in Section 29.3. You can also try Question 8 at the end of this chapter as an example of devising synthetic routes.

18.7 Infrared spectroscopy

In **infrared spectroscopy** a sample being analysed is irradiated (exposed to radiation) with electromagnetic waves in the infrared region of the electromagnetic spectrum. The machine used is called a *spectrophotometer*. It detects the intensity of the wavelengths of infrared radiation that passes through the sample.

This analytical technique is particularly useful for organic chemists because all organic molecules absorb radiation in the infrared range of wavelengths. The energy absorbed corresponds to changes in the vibration of the bonds between atoms. The bonds can vibrate by stretching, bending and twisting. They have a natural frequency at which they vibrate. If we irradiate the molecules with energy that corresponds to this frequency, it stimulates larger vibrations and energy is absorbed. This is called the **resonance frequency** of that vibration.

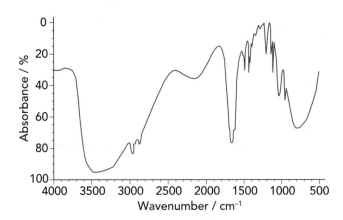

Figure 18.7: The infrared spectrum of ethylamine, $CH_3CH_2NH_2$. Note that the percentage absorbance and the wavenumbers on the axes both get smaller in magnitude along each axis.

> **KEY WORDS**
>
> **infrared spectroscopy:** a technique for identifying compounds based on the change in vibrations of particular atoms when infrared radiation of specific frequencies is absorbed.
>
> **resonance frequency:** the frequency of absorption of radiation which stimulates larger vibrations in bonds to allow the absorption of energy.

Each type of vibration will absorb characteristic wavelengths of infrared radiation. Scientists often express these as the reciprocal of the wavelength, in a unit called *wavenumbers* (measured in cm^{-1}).

We cannot be too specific when quoting the characteristic absorption frequency of a bond: the nature of the rest of the molecule shifts the energy absorbed in each particular molecule. However, we can say, for example, that the amine group ($-NH_2$) absorbs in the range 3300 to 3500 cm^{-1}.

Therefore, we can identify the presence (or absence) of different functional groups from the absorbance pattern on an infrared spectrum. Look at the infrared spectrum of ethylamine in Figure 18.7.

We can use the characteristic infrared spectrum of an unknown compound to identify it by 'fingerprinting' from a database of known spectra. Some characteristic absorption ranges of common bonds and the functional groups containing the bonds are shown in Table 18.3.

Bond	Functional groups containing the bond	Characteristic infrared absorption range (in wavenumbers) / cm^{-1}
C—O	hydroxy, ester	1040–1300
C=C	aromatic compound, alkene	1500–1680
C=O	amide	1640–1690
	carbonyl, carboxyl	1670–1740
	ester	1710–1750
C≡N	nitrile	2200–2250
C—H	alkane	2850–2950
N—H	amine, amide	3300–3500
O—H	carboxyl	2500–3000
	hydroxy	3200–3600

Table 18.3: Some characteristic infrared absorbance bands.

The values needed to answer questions will usually be given to you. You can see that absorption bands overlap considerably. That is why we need to use a variety of techniques, such as NMR, infrared spectroscopy and mass spectrometry, to work out the structure of a new organic compound (see Chapter 29).

As well as their wavenumber bands, particular absorbances have characteristic widths (broad or sharp peaks) and intensities (strong or weak) on the infrared spectrum. For example, the presence of hydrogen bonding makes the absorbance of the O—H bonds in alcohols and carboxylic acids broad. By contrast, the C=O bond in carbonyl groups has a strong, sharp absorbance peak.

Look at the infrared spectra of ethanol, ethanoic acid and ethyl ethanoate shown in Figures 18.8–18.10.

Using the data in Table 18.3, note the broad bands between 3200 and 3600 cm^{-1} in Figures 18.8 and 18.9 arising from the O—H groups involved in hydrogen bonding in the alcohol and in the carboxylic acid. Contrast the width of these peaks with the sharp peak between 1710 and 1750 cm^{-1} of the carbonyl group in the ester, ethyl ethanoate, in Figure 18.10.

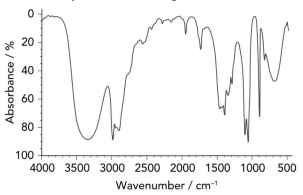

Figure 18.8: The infrared spectrum of ethanol, CH_3CH_2OH.

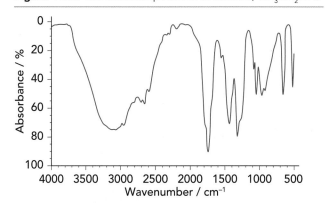

Figure 18.9: The infrared spectrum of ethanoic acid, CH_3COOH.

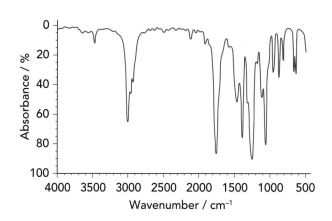

Figure 18.10: The infrared spectrum of ethyl ethanoate, $CH_3COOCH_2CH_3$.

Question

7 Look at the two infrared spectra below:

A

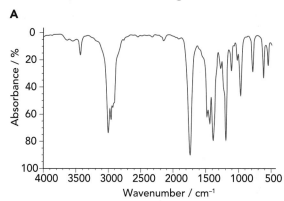

B

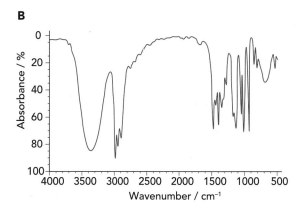

Figure 18.11: Infrared spectra for Question 7.

a Which one of the infrared spectra is that of butanone and which one is of butan-2-ol?

b Explain your reasoning in part **a**.

REFLECTION

1   Now share your answers to Question 7 with another learner and discuss your thinking in interpreting the infrared spectra in Q7. Then discuss and analyse the spectra in Figures 18.8, 18.9 and 18.10.

2   Look at the table at the end of this chapter and judge whether you need to:

- read through a topic again to make sure you really understand it

- seek more guidance on a topic, even after going over it again.

SUMMARY

Aldehydes and ketones contain the carbonyl group, $>C{=}O$:   • in aldehydes, the carbonyl group is bonded to one other carbon atom and a hydrogen atom   • in ketones, the carbonyl group is bonded to two other carbon atoms.
The names of aldehydes are derived from the name of the alkane with the '-e' at the end replaced by '-al'.   Similarly, ketones are named with the '-e' replaced by '-one'.
Carbonyl compounds are readily reduced by aqueous $NaBH_4$ or $LiAlH_4$ dissolved in dry ether: • reduction of an aldehyde forms a primary alcohol   • reduction of a ketone produces a secondary alcohol.
Aldehydes are readily oxidised under mild conditions to carboxylic acids. Ketones are not oxidised under mild conditions.
The polar nature of the carbonyl group in aldehydes and ketones enables them to undergo nucleophilic addition by reacting with the cyanide ions (CN^-) from HCN. The product is a 2-hydroxynitrile.
The reagent 2,4-dinitrophenylhydrazine (2,4-DNPH) can be used to identify the presence of a carbonyl group in an aldehyde or ketone. It produces an orange precipitate. The melting point of the product is used to identify particular aldehydes and ketones.
As aldehydes are readily oxidised, they may be distinguished from ketones on warming with suitably mild oxidising reagents: • with aldehydes, Tollens' reagent produces a silver mirror inside a warmed test-tube and Fehling's solution turns from a blue solution to a red / orange precipitate when warmed   • with ketones, there is no oxidation reaction, so no changes are observed when ketones are warmed with Tollens' reagent or Fehling's solution.
Chemists can use alkaline iodine solution to test for: • methyl ketones (and ethanal)   • ethanol or secondary alcohols with an adjacent methyl group.   A yellow precipitate of tri-iodomethane is formed in a positive test.
Infrared spectroscopy helps to identify organic compounds by their absorption of energy in the infrared range of wavelengths, matching their spectrum to a database of known infrared spectra.

EXAM-STYLE QUESTIONS

1 **a** Name the following compounds:

    i CH_3COCH_3 [1]

    ii $CH_3CH_2CH_2OH$ [1]

    iii CH_3CHO [1]

    iv $CH_3CH(OH)CH_3$ [1]

    v $CH_3COCH_2CH_3$ [1]

    vi CH_3CH_2CHO [1]

  b Which of the compounds in part **a** are alcohols and which are carbonyl compounds?   [1]

  c Which of the carbonyl compounds in part **a** are aldehydes and which are ketones?   [1]

  d Two of the compounds in part **a** could be made by oxidising two of the others.

    i Identify these four compounds, stating which could be made from which.   [4]

    ii State the reagents and conditions you would use to carry out each oxidation and write a balanced chemical equation for each oxidation. [O] can be used in the oxidation equations.   [4]

  e Ethanol could be made by the reduction of one of the compounds in part **a**.

    i Identify which compound this is.   [1]

    ii State the reagent you would use to carry out the reduction.   [1]

    iii Write a balanced chemical equation for the reduction. [H] can be used in reduction equations.   [1]

                                    [Total: 19]

2 **a** Name the reagent you would add to an unknown compound to test if it contains a carbonyl group.   [1]

  b Describe what you would see if the unknown compound did contain a carbonyl group.   [1]

  c Describe why it would be useful to find the melting point of the product of this test.   [1]

                                    [Total: 3]

3 **a** Draw the skeletal formulae of:

    i pentan-2-one   [1]

    ii pentan-3-one   [1]

    iii pentanal.   [1]

  b Describe the results you would expect to see if pentan-3-one and pentanal were separately treated with Tollens' reagent. Where a reaction takes place, name the organic product and name the type of reaction that takes place.   [4]

                                    [Total: 7]

CONTINUED

4   Ethanol can be made from ethanal using sodium tetrahydridoborate(III) as a reducing agent.

   a   Give the formula of sodium tetrahydridoborate(III).   [1]

   b   The reaction mechanism proceeds in a similar way to the steps in the reaction of ethanal with HCN, but the initial attack is by the H^- ion instead of the CN^- ion. The intermediate then gains an H^+ ion from a water molecule to form the product, ethanol.

   Using your knowledge of the reaction between ethanal and HCN, suggest the name of the mechanism to reduce ethanal. Then describe the mechanism as fully as you can, using curly arrows to show the movement of electron pairs.   [7]

   [Total: 8]

5   A compound, X, has the following percentage composition:

   66.7% carbon, 11.1% hydrogen and 22.2% oxygen.

   a   Calculate the empirical formula of X.   [3]

   b   The relative molecular mass of X is 72. Calculate the molecular formula.   [1]

   c   Give the structural formulae and names of the three isomers of X that are carbonyl compounds.   [3]

   d   Explain how you could identify X using chemical means.   [5]

   [Total: 12]

6   An alcohol has the molecular formula C_3H_8O. When warmed with an alkaline solution of iodine it forms a yellow precipitate.

   a   Name the yellow precipitate.   [1]

   b   Draw the displayed formula of the alcohol.   [1]

   c   The first stage in the reaction of the alcohol with alkaline iodine solution is an oxidation reaction. Name the organic product of this first stage.   [1]

   d   There are four isomeric alcohols with the formula C_4H_9OH.

   i   Name the four isomeric alcohols.   [1]

   ii   Classify each one as a primary, secondary or tertiary alcohol.   [1]

   iii   Which of the four isomeric alcohols will give a yellow precipitate when warmed with an alkaline solution of iodine?   [1]

   [Total: 6]

7   Use data from the table below of characteristic infrared absorptions in organic molecules to answer the following question.

Bond	Location	Wavenumber / cm^{-1}
C—O	alcohols, esters	1000–1300
C=O	aldehydes, ketones, carboxylic acids, esters	1680–1750
O—H	hydrogen bonded in carboxylic acids	2500–3300 (broad)
N—H	primary amines	3100–3500
O—H	hydrogen bonded in alcohols, phenols	3230–3550
O—H	free	3580–3670

CONTINUED

One of the three spectra labelled **A** to **C** below is produced when ethanal is analysed in an infrared spectrophotometer:

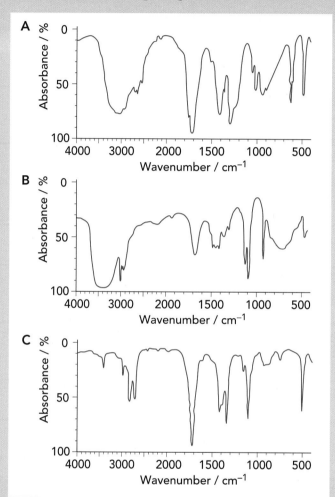

a   Consider the three spectra above to decide which one is most likely to be produced by ethanal? [1]

b   Give three reasons for your choice. [3]

[Total: 4]

8   Ethene can be obtained by cracking large hydrocarbons found in crude oil. Suggest how ethene can be converted into the following compounds, stating the reagents and conditions needed.

a   ethylamine [2]

b   ethanal [4]

c   propanoic acid [4]

[Total: 10]

SELF-EVALUATION

After studying this chapter, complete a table like this:

I can	See section...	Needs more work	Almost there	Ready to move on
describe the formation of aldehydes from the oxidation of primary alcohols and the formation of ketones from the oxidation of secondary alcohols	18.2			
describe the reduction of aldehydes and ketones, e.g. using $NaBH_4$ or $LiAlH_4$, and the reaction of aldehydes and ketones with HCN and KCN	18.3			
describe the mechanism of the nucleophilic addition reactions of hydrogen cyanide with aldehydes and ketones	18.4			
describe the detection of carbonyl compounds by the use of 2,4-dinitrophenylhydrazine (2,4-DNPH) reagent	18.5			
distinguish between aldehydes and ketones by testing with Fehling's solution and Tollens' reagent	18.5			
describe the reaction of CH_3CO- compounds with alkaline aqueous iodine to give tri-iodomethane, CHI_3, and a carboxylate ion, $RCOO^-$	18.6			
deduce the presence of a $CH_3CH(OH)-$ group in an alcohol from its reaction with alkaline aqueous iodine to form tri-iodomethane	18.6			
analyse an infrared spectrum of a simple molecule to identify functional groups	18.7			
devise a synthetic route (series of reactions) using any of the reactions from Chapters 14–18 to make a named organic product.	Chapters 14–18			

P1.1 Introduction

The analytical skills of chemists are still important despite the development of new increasingly rapid and sensitive instrumental techniques (Figure P1.1) (see Chapter 30). Your practical skills make an important contribution to the grade you achieve in your chemistry qualification.

Figure P1.1: Chemist performing a titration.

Review of practical knowledge and understanding

In scientific investigations, we are often interested in finding out how one variable affects another. For example, we might want to investigate a precipitation reaction to find out how the concentration of a reactant affects the rate at which the precipitate forms. You might have seen the reaction between sodium thiosulfate and dilute hydrochloric acid, which is a commonly investigated precipitation reaction. Sulfur is the precipitate formed:

$$Na_2S_2O_3(aq) + 2HCl(aq) \rightarrow$$
$$2NaCl(aq) + S(s) + H_2O(l) + SO_2(g)$$

This type of investigation involves changing only the variable under investigation (in this case the concentration of a reactant) and keeping all other relevant variables constant. We can judge the effect of changing the concentration by devising a way to measure how quickly the precipitate forms, such as timing how long it takes for the solution to become opaque.

We now have the question we are investigating and the structure of the investigation in terms of its key variables:

> **KEY WORDS**
>
> **independent variable:** the variable under investigation for which we choose different values.
>
> **dependent variable:** the variable we measure to judge the effect of changing the independent variable.
>
> **control variables:** variables (other than the dependent and independent variables) that must be kept the same during an experiment.

In a precipitation reaction, how does the concentration of a reactant affect the rate of precipitation (as measured by the time it takes for the solution to become opaque)?

- The **independent variable** is the one under investigation. This is changed systematically and we can choose different values (in this case, the concentration of reactant).

- The **dependent variable** is the one we measure to judge the effect of changing the independent variable (in this case, the time it takes for the solution to become opaque).

- The **control variables** are those that we must keep constant to ensure a fair test is carried out (in this case, we should control the temperature and total volume of reactants used).

Note that we can express the question in this type of investigation generally as:

> ***How does the independent variable affect the dependent variable?***

When asked to plan and / or carry out an investigation, it is important that you state the question under investigation clearly. You also need to list the independent, dependent and control variables before you start writing down your proposed method or planning how to record and present your results.

The type of variable under investigation will determine whether you display the data collected in a table, as a line graph or as a bar chart.

To decide which type of graph to draw, you need to know the difference between numerical value within the range of results – and categoric continuous variables – which are described using words. We can assume that

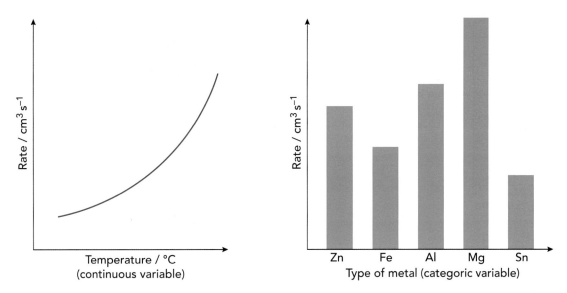

Figure P1.2: A continuous independent variable → a line graph; a categoric independent variable → a bar chart.

the dependent variable is continuous, as it measures the effect of varying the independent variable. Then if the independent variable is continuous, we draw a line graph. If the independent variable is categoric, we draw a bar chart. So if you investigate the effect of temperature on rate of reaction, the data can be presented as a line graph. If you investigate the rate of different metals reacting with dilute acid, the data can be presented as a bar chart (as there are no values between those chosen for the independent variable). See the graphs in Figure P1.2.

When sitting a Practical Skills examination, you will need to follow instructions to carry out an investigation into an unknown substance or mixture of substances. Always read through all of the instructions before carrying out the tests. Testing for unknown substances will require you to describe your observations in detail. You will be able to refer to tables of tests for cations, anions and gases (see Appendix 3) to draw your conclusions.

You will also carry out a quantitative task (based on measurements) as well as a qualitative task (based on observations). Examples of problems that need you to collect quantitative data could be a titration (a volumetric analysis) or an enthalpy change experiment.

The quantitative task will require you to read scales on measuring instruments such as burettes, measuring cylinders, gas syringes and balances. For instruments with an analogue scale, such as a burette, you should be able to read measurements to within half the value

of the fine line divisions on the scale. So a burette with fine line divisions every $0.10\ cm^3$ should be read to the nearest $0.05\ cm^3$. A thermometer with fine line divisions every 1 °C should be read to the nearest 0.5 °C (see Figure P1.3).

However, if a measuring instrument has very fine calibration (tightly grouped marks), it should be read to the nearest calibrated mark.

Useful definitions to know, because you may need to decide upon or recognise these in a task, are:

- **Range**: the minimum and maximum values for the independent or the dependent variable. For example, in the rate of precipitation investigation, the range of the independent variable (the concentration) might be $0.2\ mol\ dm^{-3}$ to $1.0\ mol\ dm^{-3}$.

- **Interval**: the difference chosen between consecutive values of the independent variable. For example, in the rate of precipitation investigation you might choose to test concentrations of 0.2, 0.4, 0.6, 0.8 and $1.0\ mol\ dm^{-3}$, giving an interval of $0.2\ mol\ dm^{-3}$.

- **Anomalous result**: a result that does not follow an established pattern.

- **Precise results**: results in which each set of repeat readings are grouped closely together.

- **Accurate results**: results that reflect the true value of a quantity.

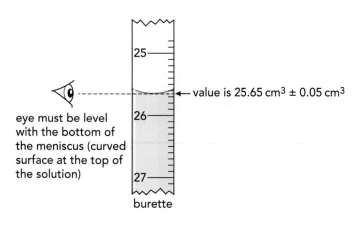

eye must be level with the bottom of the meniscus (curved surface at the top of the solution)

value is 25.65 cm³ ± 0.05 cm³

burette

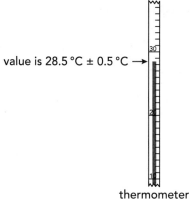

value is 28.5 °C ± 0.5 °C →

thermometer

Figure P1.3: Taking readings from a magnified burette scale and a thermometer with an analogue scale.

Question

1 A learner was investigating how temperature affects the rate of a reaction between magnesium and dilute hydrochloric acid. The learner decided to measure the volume of gas given off in 30 seconds for different temperatures of acid. She decided to use temperatures of 10, 20, 30, 40 and 50 °C.

    a   Name the independent variable.

    b   Name the dependent variable.

    c   List two control variables.

    d   Give the range of the independent variable.

    e   What is the value of the interval chosen for the independent variable?

    f   Which type of graph would you use to display the results of a different investigation to find out how different transition metal oxides affect the rate of a reaction?

P1.2 Manipulation, measurement and observation

In order to address a Practical Skills examination, you will need to master the expectations set out throughout this chapter.

Expectations

Successful collection of data and observations

You should be able to:

- set up apparatus correctly
- follow instructions given in the form of written instructions or diagrams
- use the apparatus to collect an appropriate quantity of data or observations, including subtle differences in colour, solubility or quantity of materials
- make measurements using pipettes, burettes, measuring cylinders, thermometers and other common laboratory apparatus.

Quality of measurements or observations

You should be able to:

- make accurate and consistent measurements and observations.

Decisions relating to measurements or observations

You should be able to:

- decide how many tests or observations to perform
- make measurements that span a range and have a distribution appropriate to the experiment
- decide how long to leave experiments running before making readings
- identify where repeated readings or observations are appropriate
- replicate readings or observations as necessary
- identify where confirmatory tests are appropriate and the nature of such tests
- choose reagents to distinguish between given ions.

Points to remember

- When describing a liquid or solution that is not coloured and is transparent, always use the word 'colourless'. Some people make the mistake of just writing 'clear' – but a solution of copper(II) sulfate is clear (i.e. transparent) but blue in colour.

- A solution that appears white and opaque in a chemical test probably contains a fine suspension of a white precipitate: for example, when using lime water to test for carbon dioxide gas.

- When carrying out a titration, you should repeat the test until you have two titres that are within 0.1 cm³ of each other. Ideally you should be aiming for two concordant titres with the same values – but judging the end-point can be tricky. That is why we carry out repeat sets of each test in many investigations – to make our results more accurate by reducing experimental error. You can read more about sources of error in Section P1.4.

- In a titration, the first titre measured is always a rough value to establish approximately where the actual end-point lies. When obtaining subsequent values, you should be able to add the solution from the burette one drop at a time near the end-point.

- Sometimes a result is clearly incorrect. For example, it might be very different from the others in a repeat set of readings or does not follow a well-established pattern in a series of tests. If you have time, try it again. If not, discard it: do *not* include it in your calculation of the mean; ignore the anomalous point when drawing a line of best fit on a graph.

- When plotting a line graph of the data collected, a minimum of five values of the independent variable (which is plotted along the horizontal axis) must be recorded to be confident of any pattern observed.

- Note that it is possible to have precise results that are not particularly accurate. For example, if you measure the mass of a product formed three times and the results are all the same, they are precise. However, if the balance was not set to zero for any of the measurements, the mass will not be accurate.

Question

2   a   A learner carried out a titration four times and got results for the titre of 13.25, 12.95, 12.65 and then 12.65 cm³. What is the most accurate value of the titre to use in any calculations?

   b   What do we call a mixture of water and fine particles of an insoluble solid dispersed throughout the liquid?

   c   Describe any similarities and differences you observe when looking at a test-tube of dilute sulfuric acid and a test-tube of 0.05 mol dm⁻³ copper(II) sulfate solution.

   d   Name the white precipitate formed in the test for carbon dioxide gas.

   e   In Question 1 in Section P1.1, name a piece of apparatus the learner could use to measure:

     i   the independent variable

     ii   the dependent variable.

P1.3 Presentation of data and observations

Expectations

Recording data or observations

You should be able to:

- present numerical data, values or observations in a single table of results

- draw up the table in advance of taking readings or making observations so that you do not have to copy up your results

- include in the table of results, if necessary, columns for raw data, for calculated values and for analyses or conclusions

- use column headings that include both the quantity and the unit and that conform to accepted scientific conventions

- record raw readings of a quantity to the same degree of precision and observations to the same level of detail.

Display of calculation and reasoning

You should be able to:

- show your working in calculations, and the key steps in your reasoning

- use the correct number of significant figures for calculated quantities.

Data layout

You should be able to:

- choose a suitable and clear method to present the data, e.g. tables, graphs or a mixture of presentation methods

- select which variables to plot and decide whether a graph should be drawn as a straight line or a curve

- plot appropriate variables on clearly labelled *x*- and *y*-axes

- choose sensible scales for graph axes

- plot all points or bars to an appropriate accuracy

- follow the Association for Science Education (ASE) recommendations for putting lines on graphs (see the 'Points to remember' referring to graphs, below).

Points to remember

- There are certain conventions to observe when designing and drawing a table to use to record your experimental data. Generally, the independent variable goes in the first column and the dependent variable goes in the second column. Sometimes, if space on the page is an issue, a table can be organised horizontally. In this case, the independent variable again goes first but at the start of the first row in the table, with the dependent variable beneath it, not next to it as in a conventional table.

- When recording quantitative data you will often need columns for repeat results and calculations of the mean. This is achieved by subdividing the column for the dependent variable into the required number of columns. For example, in the rate of precipitation investigation described at the beginning of this chapter, the table to record three repeat readings and their means would be organised as:

Concentration / mol dm⁻³	Time for reaction mixture to turn opaque / s			
	1st test	2nd test	3rd test	Mean

- Note that the headings in the table have their units included. You then do not need to record the units for each entry you make in the table.

- On graphs, always plot the independent variable along the horizontal (*x*-)axis and the dependent variable up the vertical (*y*-)axis.

- Draw the lines in tables and graphs in pencil, labelling the axes as in the corresponding table headings, including their units.

- In the table above, there could be an extra column on the right-hand side for values of the reciprocal of the mean time taken for the reaction mixture to become opaque (headed '$\frac{1}{\text{time}}$'). This could be plotted on a graph of $\frac{1}{\text{time}}$ against concentration to see how the rate of reaction varies with temperature (as rate is proportional to $\frac{1}{\text{time}}$, so the greater the time, the slower the rate). See the graphs in Figure P1.4.

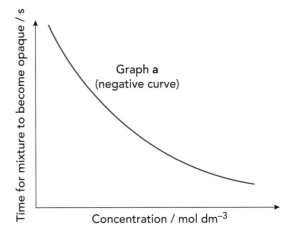

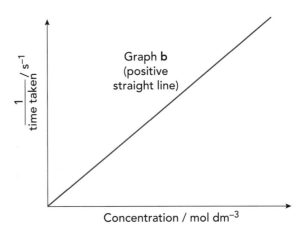

Figure P1.4: Graphs that could be drawn from the data in a table using concentrations and mean times.

- The labelled axes must be longer than half the size of the graph grid in both directions, selecting a sensible scale (e.g. 1, 2, 5 or 10 units per 20 mm square on the grid: not 3 units).

- Each point should be plotted as a small, neat x or + with a sharp pencil. The line drawn through the points should not be 'dot-to-dot' but should be a line of best fit. This should be either drawn with a ruler for a straight line or a smooth free-hand line for a curve. Think of the best-fit line as the 'average' line though the points.

- Always show your working out in calculations.

- Only give answers produced by calculation to correspond to the number of significant figures of the least accurate experimental data used. So, if calculating a concentration using titre volumes such as 15.35 cm^3, then the value of the concentration of the unknown solution can be given to 4 significant figures (e.g. 1.244 or 0.9887 mol dm^{-3}). However, if the known concentration of one of the reactants is given to three significant figures (e.g. 0.0250 mol dm^{-3} or 0.200 mol dm^{-3}), then the calculated concentration could be given to three significant figures.

- When recording qualitative descriptions in a table, if there is 'no change visible', write that and do not just put in a dash.

Question

3 In an experiment to find the enthalpy change of a reaction between two solutions, the mass of solutions mixed together was 50.0 g and the temperature increased by 7.5 °C. The following equation is used:

   energy transferred = mass ×
        specific heat capacity × change in temperature

   where the specific heat capacity of the solutions was taken as 4.18 J g^{-1} °C^{-1}.

   a Calculate the energy transferred in joules (J) to an appropriate number of significant figures.

   b Explain the number of significant figures chosen in part **a**.

P1.4 Analysis, conclusions and evaluation

Expectations

Interpretation of data or observations and identifying sources of error

You should be able to:

- describe the patterns and trends shown by tables and graphs

- describe and summarise the key points of a set of observations

- find an unknown value by using co-ordinates or intercepts on a graph

- calculate other quantities from data, or calculate the mean from replicate (repeat) values, or make other appropriate calculations

- determine the gradient of a straight-line graph

- evaluate the effectiveness of control variables

- identify the most significant sources of error in an experiment

- estimate, quantitatively, the uncertainty in quantitative measurements

- express such uncertainty in a measurement as an actual or percentage error

- show an understanding of the distinction between systematic errors and random errors.

Drawing conclusions

You should be able to:

- draw conclusions from an experiment, giving an outline description of the main features of the data, considering whether experimental data support a given hypothesis, and making further predictions

- draw conclusions from interpretations of observations, data and calculated values

- make scientific explanations of the data, observations and conclusions that have been described.

Suggesting improvements

You should be able to:

- suggest modifications to an experimental arrangement that will improve the accuracy of the experiment or the accuracy of the observations that can be made

- suggest ways in which to extend the investigation to answer a new question

- describe such modifications clearly in words or diagrams.

Points to remember

- To measure the gradient (slope) of a straight line on a graph, choose two points on the line at least half as far apart as its total length. Then construct a right-angled triangle, as shown in Figure P1.5. The gradient tells us the rate of change of y (the dependent variable) per unit change of x (the independent variable):

$$\text{gradient} = \frac{\text{change in } y}{\text{change in } x}$$

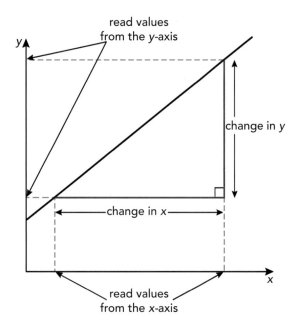

Figure P1.5: Finding the gradient of a straight-line graph. Choosing to construct a large triangle reduces the percentage error in the values read from the axes, which are then used to calculate the gradient.

- When evaluating the quality of the data collected, there are two types of error to consider: *random errors* and *systematic errors*. Whenever we carry out an experiment, there are always errors involved. They might be due to the person carrying out the experiment not reading the scale on a measuring instrument correctly or choosing a measuring instrument with an inappropriate scale. These examples of human error are equally likely to make the values of data too high or too low, so they are called **random errors**. Repeating tests and taking the mean value helps to reduce the effect of random errors.

- However, other errors can result in consistently high or low values being recorded. These are called **systematic errors**. Examples would be reading the volume of liquid in a burette to the upper level of the liquid instead of to the bottom of the meniscus. It should be noted though that these consistently high measurements of volume would not result in an incorrect value for the titre, because the final volume is subtracted from the initial volume. Not ensuring the measuring instrument is correctly set on zero is another example of a systematic error. If this is not corrected during an investigation, it can result in consistently high or low masses being measured on balances. Other systematic errors can be caused by errors when planning an investigation. This might result in data being collected that does not really answer the question under investigation. For example, a control variable might not be kept constant or taken into account, or the dependent variable chosen might not be a true measure of the effect of varying the independent variable. An error such as this will make the data collected invalid (incorrect).

- You will have to estimate the error that is found in reading scales, as described at the beginning of this chapter. In your evaluation of the experiment you should discuss the effect that these measurement errors might have on the validity of the data and the conclusions you can draw from them. In the example of a thermometer with 1 °C calibration marks, you can quote values to the nearest 0.5 °C. The actual effect of this margin of error on confidence levels will depend on the magnitude of the temperature being measured. When reading a low temperature of, say, 5.0 °C, plus or minus 0.5 °C will have a bigger effect than when reading a higher temperature, such as 92.5 °C. For this reason it is best to quote percentage errors, worked out using the equation:

$$\text{percentage error} = \frac{\text{margin of error}}{\text{actual or mean measurement}} \times 100\%$$

KEY WORDS

random errors: errors that are due to chance changes in the experiment or by the experimenter. They are equally likely to make the values of data too high or too low.

systematic errors: errors due to data being inaccurate in a consistent way. Systematic errors are often caused by errors in the experimental procedure or equipment.

WORKED EXAMPLE

1   What is the percentage error in the case of the two temperatures 5 °C and 92.5 °C?

Solution

For the reading of 5 °C the percentage error will be:

$$\frac{0.5 \times 100}{5} = 10\%$$

whereas for 92.5 °C the percentage error is:

$$\frac{0.5 \times 100}{92.5} = 0.54\%$$

So there is a significant error in reading 5 °C compared with reading 92.5 °C.

- In enthalpy change investigations, you often have to measure temperature differences. You can do this by subtracting the final temperature from the initial temperature. In this case, using the thermometer just described, the error would be plus or minus 1 °C, as the two 0.5 °C margins of error in both readings should be added together. In this case, you should suggest increasing the temperature change. For example, when evaluating enthalpies of combustion of alcohols by heating water in a copper calorimeter, you could use a smaller volume of water to heat. However, this change would have to be balanced against the increase in percentage error in measuring the smaller volume of water, to see which gives the least percentage error overall.

- You might need to suggest how to make your data from an experiment more accurate. For example, in the rate of precipitation investigation, you could improve the accuracy of judging the time for the reaction to reach a certain point in each test carried out. Whereas judging the moment when a pencil mark can no longer be seen through the reaction mixture is subjective, you could use a light source and light meter to make more objective judgements. You could stop the timer when the level of light passing through the reaction mixture drops to the same level as measured by the light meter in each test. This will make your repeat (or replicate) data more precise and improve the accuracy of your results.

- Your evaluation might lead beyond suggestions to change the method to ideas to investigate new questions. For example, when evaluating the rate of precipitation, you will have tried to control the temperature: probably by ensuring that both the solutions mixed started at the same temperature. However, if the reaction is exothermic, this might cause the temperature to change between the different concentrations investigated. This could lead to a new investigation to compare the energy transferred in a precipitation reaction at different concentrations. The question could be phrased as 'How does the concentration of a reactant solution affect the … energy transferred in the reaction?'.

- When drawing conclusions from investigations involving the manipulation of variables, you should refer to your graph when commenting on the relationship between the independent and dependent variables. You can explain your findings using the data and your scientific knowledge and understanding.

- When drawing conclusions from qualitative tests to identify an unknown substance, where possible, try to carry out or suggest a further confirmatory test for the same substance (see Appendix 3).

- Any hypotheses you test can only be refuted (disproved) by a practical investigation you carry out. They *cannot* be proved because of the limitations of your investigation. So hypotheses can only be 'supported' by the data collected. Say that your hypothesis predicts that the rate of reaction increases with increasing concentration, with a justification using collision theory, and then show how data collected from your investigation *supports* this. You cannot say whether this relationship is true beyond the range of concentrations tested. There might be a point using higher concentrations where increasing the concentration of one reactant will start to have less, or even no, effect on the rate. This could be because there is such an excess of one reactant that the rate of collisions with the other reactant particles is not affected by further increases of concentration. This would now give you another idea to test!

Question

4 **a** A learner measured the average rate of a reaction by timing how long it took to collect $20\ cm^3$ of the gas liberated in the reaction. What calculation would the learner do to work out the mean (average) rate in $cm^3\ s^{-1}$?

b The learner finds that the rate of a reaction is directly proportional to the concentration of a reactant, X.

i Sketch a graph to show this relationship.

ii Explain how to work out the gradient of the line on the graph.

iii If the learner changed the concentration of X from $0.50\ mol\ dm^{-3}$ to $0.25\ mol\ dm^{-3}$, what would happen to the rate of reaction?

c Explain the quantitative relationship that the learner found in this investigation using your scientific knowledge and understanding.

SUMMARY

In your practical examination, you will be expected to collect, record and analyse data so that you can answer questions related to the two or three activities. You will need to develop the following practical skills.

Manipulation, measurement and observation:
- successfully collect data and observations by setting up and carrying out experiments efficiently and safely
- make precise and accurate measurements, as well as detailed observations
- make decisions relating to measurements or observations, including the choice of equipment, the range and interval of measurements, and the recognition of anomalous results.

Presentation of data and observations:
- record data or observations in tables and display data using appropriate graphs
- display calculations and reasoning in tables and logical sequences.

Analysis, conclusions and evaluation:
- interpret data or observations and identify sources of error, recognising systematic or random errors and working out their significance
- draw conclusions based on scientific knowledge and understanding
- suggest improvements that can be made to improve the quality and validity of data collected.

EXAM-STYLE QUESTIONS

1 A learner investigated the ease with which various metal carbonates decompose on heating. She decided to heat equal masses of each carbonate and time how long it took for the carbon dioxide given off to turn limewater in a test-tube cloudy.

a **i** Name the independent variable in the investigation. [1]

ii Name the dependent variable. [1]

iii Name the control variable described at the start of this question. [1]

CONTINUED

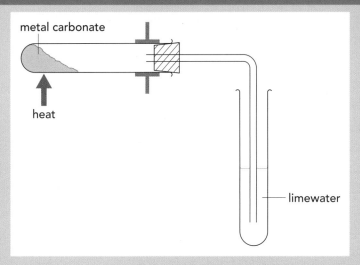

b   The learner decided to repeat the test on each of five metal carbonates provided three times.

    i   State why it is a good idea to collect replicate data in investigations.   [1]

    ii   Draw a table that the learner could fill in as the investigation was carried out.   [3]

c   i   The test-tube contained 10 cm³ of limewater. The learner measured this volume in a 10 cm³ measuring cylinder with calibration marks every 0.1 cm³. Give the margin of error when reading this scale. State the percentage error in measuring the volume of limewater for this investigation.   [2]

    ii   Explain what is likely to be the greatest source of error in this investigation.   [2]

d   Give the type of graph the learner should use to display the data from the investigation.   [1]

[Total: 12]

2   The rate of the following reaction between hydrogen peroxide (H_2O_2) and iodide ions can be monitored using sodium thiosulfate and starch indicator:

$$2H^+(aq) + H_2O_2(aq) + 2I^-(aq) \rightarrow 2H_2O(l) + I_2(aq)$$

A mixture of starch solution, potassium iodide solution, sulfuric acid and sodium thiosulfate is made. This mixture can then be reacted with varying concentrations of 10-volume hydrogen peroxide, made by making measured volumes of the peroxide solution up to 25 cm³ with distilled water. When the hydrogen peroxide solution is added to the original mixture containing starch in a flask, the time for the contents of the flask to turn a blue / black colour can be measured.

CONTINUED

This procedure, using a range of volumes of hydrogen peroxide, can determine how the concentration of hydrogen peroxide affects the rate of the reaction shown above. Here is a set of results obtained from one such investigation.

Volume of hydrogen peroxide used / cm³	Time, t, for blue / black colour to appear / s	
1	300	
2	200	
4	90	
6	60	
8	44	
10	37	
12	28	

a   A learner wants to use these results to draw a graph that will show how the concentration of hydrogen peroxide affects the rate of reaction. Record the heading and values that the learner could use to complete the third column of the table (to 2 significant figures).   [3]

b   Give the name of the piece of measuring equipment they would use to make up the volumes of hydrogen peroxide solution to 25 cm³.   [1]

c   The learner was provided with a stopclock (measuring to the nearest second) to measure the time taken for the solution to turn blue / black. They then asked for a stopwatch measuring to one-hundredth of a second. The teacher said that would not be necessary. Explain the teacher's response.   [2]

d   The original mixture was made up using a solution of 40 cm³ of 0.10 mol dm⁻³ potassium iodide. Calculate the number of moles of iodide ions in the reaction mixture.   [2]

e   Describe the role of the sodium thiosulfate in this investigation.   [3]

[Total: 11]

CONTINUED

3 You have to identify an unknown compound, **X**.

Test	Observations made
To a 1 cm depth of **X** solution in a test tube, add the same volume of aqueous dilute ammonia solution. Then use a dropping pipette to add concentrated ammonia solution to the mixture in the test tube.	White ppt No change to ppt
To 1 cm depth of **X** solution in a boiling tube, add aqueous sodium hydroxide and aluminium foil. Then heat the tube carefully.	A gas is given off that turns damp red litmus paper blue.
To a 1 cm depth of **X** solution in a test tube, add the same volume of dilute hydrochloric acid.	No change
Carefully heat the solid **X** in the test tube provided. Note that two gases are released.	A brown gas is given off (nitrogen dioxide is a brown gas). The mixture of gases re-lights a glowing splint. The solid remains white as it is heated.

a From the results of the tests above, and the Tables of Qualitative Analysis notes in Appendix 3 at the back of the book, identify the cation present in **X**. [1]

b Suggest how to confirm the cation present in **X**, giving the predicted observations. [2]

c Suggest the identity of **X**. [1]

[Total: 4]

> # Chapter 19
Lattice energy

LEARNING INTENTIONS

In this chapter you will learn how to:

- define and use the terms *enthalpy change of atomisation* and *lattice energy*

- define and use the term *first electron affinity*

- explain the factors affecting the electron affinities of the elements

- describe and explain the trends in the electron affinities of the Group 16 and Group 17 elements

- construct and use Born–Haber cycles for ionic solids

- carry out calculations involving Born–Haber cycles

- explain the effect of ionic charge and ionic radius on the magnitude (big or small) of the lattice energy

- define and use the terms *enthalpy change of hydration* and *enthalpy change of solution*

- construct and use an energy cycle involving enthalpy change of solution, lattice energy and enthalpy changes of hydration

CONTINUED

- carry out calculations using an energy cycle involving enthalpy change of solution, lattice energy and enthalpy changes of hydration

- explain the effect of ionic charge and ionic radius on the magnitude (big or small) of the enthalpy change of hydration

- describe and explain qualitatively the trend in the thermal stability of the nitrates and carbonates in Group 2 including the effect of ionic radius on the polarisation of the large anion

- describe and explain qualitatively the variation in solubility and enthalpy change of solution of the hydroxides and sulfates in Group 2 in terms of relative magnitudes of enthalpy change of hydration and the lattice energy.

BEFORE YOU START

1 Work with another learner to draw a fully labelled reaction pathway diagram (energy profile diagram) for an endothermic reaction.

 Explain to another learner how this diagram shows that the reaction is endothermic.

2 Explain to another learner how to find the enthalpy change of combustion of an alcohol by experiment. Then ask the other learner to explain to you how to reduce experimental errors in the experiment that you chose.

3 Take it in turns to explain these terms to another learner: *crystal lattice*; *bond energy*; *enthalpy change*; *activation energy*; *standard conditions*; *standard enthalpy change of formation*.

4 Work with another learner to write equations which represent:

 a the enthalpy change of formation of calcium carbonate

 b the enthalpy change of combustion of ethane

 c the enthalpy change of neutralisation of sulfuric acid by sodium hydroxide.

5 Take turns in challenging a partner to write precise definitions of the enthalpy changes that are represented by the symbols $\Delta H_r^{\ominus}$, $\Delta H_f^{\ominus}$, $\Delta H_{neut}^{\ominus}$ and $\Delta H_c^{\ominus}$.

 Check your definitions with those in Chapter 6 of the coursebook.

6 Explain to another learner the difference between average bond energies and exact bond energies.

7 Explain Hess's law to another learner.

8 Ask another learner to select a combustion reaction from a textbook. Explain to the other learner how to construct an enthalpy cycle to calculate the enthalpy change of combustion for this reaction. Then reverse the process: you choose a simple reaction involving compounds and the other learner explains how to construct an enthalpy cycle to calculate the enthalpy change of reaction.

9 Ask another learner to select an example of an enthalpy cycle from Chapter 6 of the coursebook. Explain to the other learner exactly how to calculate the required enthalpy change (remember to take note of the stoichiometry of the reaction). Then reverse the process: you choose an enthalpy cycle and the other learner explains.

INVESTIGATING THE STRUCTURE OF CRYSTALS

When water waves hit a barrier with a narrow slit in the middle of it, the waves behind the slit appear to be curved. We say that the waves have been diffracted. The electrons in a crystal lattice can act like a slit and X-rays can be diffracted by the crystal.

Figure 19.1: The X-ray diffraction pattern appears as a series of spots. We can determine the structure of a crystal from the position of the spots.

When a beam of X-rays of one particular wavelength falls on a crystal, some X-rays pass straight through the crystal but others are absorbed. The absorbed X-rays cause some electrons to become 'excited' and move to higher energy levels. When these electrons return to a lower energy level X-rays are re-emitted ('reflected' again). These re-emitted X-rays are scattered in an orderly manner. The scattered X-rays give rise to an interference pattern of spots which are recorded on a photographic plate (Figure 19.1). The X-ray diffraction pattern is related to the pattern of the electrons in the solid and the density of the electrons. A mathematical analysis of the X-ray pattern was first carried out by William Henry Bragg and William Lawrence Bragg (Figure 19.2). From this analysis they were able to deduce the pattern of electron density in the solid and hence identify the relative positions of the electrons and atoms. These maps are similar to geographical contour maps (maps showing similar heights joined by curved lines). From these maps it is possible to construct an accurate model of the solid. Bond lengths can be determined to an accuracy of better than 1%.

Figure 19.2: William Henry Bragg developed X-ray diffraction to determine the structures of simple crystals. Dorothy Hodgkin developed the method further to determine the structure of penicillin and insulin.

The calculations involved in translating the diffraction pattern into a model of the crystal structure are extremely complicated. To determine even a simple structure such as sodium chloride requires a lot of mathematical knowledge and many complex calculations.

Questions for discussion

Discuss with another learner or group of learners:

- Suggest why the position of H atoms in compounds is not usually determined by X-ray diffraction.

- The first crystal structure to be determined by X-ray crystallography was zinc sulfide. This was done over 100 years ago. The crystal structures of some proteins and DNA were determined 50 years later than this. Suggest why it took so much longer to determine the crystal structures of proteins and DNA.

19.1 Defining lattice energy

When ions combine to form an ionic solid, there is a huge release of energy. The reaction is highly exothermic. The energy given out when ions of opposite charges come together to form a crystalline lattice is called the **lattice energy**, $\Delta H_{\text{latt}}^{\ominus}$.

Lattice energy is the enthalpy change when 1 mole of an ionic compound is formed from its gaseous ions under standard conditions.

You can see equations describing the lattice energy of sodium chloride and magnesium chloride here.

$$Na^+(g) + Cl^-(g) \rightarrow NaCl(s) \qquad \Delta H_{\text{latt}}^{\ominus} = -787 \text{ kJ mol}^{-1}$$

$$Mg^{2+}(g) + 2Cl^-(g) \rightarrow MgCl_2(s) \qquad \Delta H_{\text{latt}}^{\ominus} = -2526 \text{ kJ mol}^{-1}$$

Note that:

- it is the *gaseous* ions that combine to form the ionic solid

- the lattice energy is always exothermic: the value of $\Delta H_{\text{latt}}^{\ominus}$ is always negative, because the definition specifies the bonding together of ions, not the separation of ions.

> ## KEY WORD
>
> **lattice energy, $\Delta H_{\text{latt}}^{\ominus}$**: the energy change when 1 mole of an ionic compound is formed from its gaseous ions under standard conditions. Strictly speaking, the values given usually refer to the lattice enthalpy rather than the lattice energy but the difference is usually not significant

The large exothermic value of the lattice energy shows that the ionic lattice is very stable with respect to its gaseous ions. The more exothermic the lattice energy, the stronger the ionic bonding in the lattice.

It is impossible to determine the lattice energy of a compound by a single direct experiment. We can, however, calculate a value for $\Delta H_{\text{latt}}^{\ominus}$ using several experimental values and an energy cycle called a Born–Haber cycle. To do this, we first need to introduce two more types of enthalpy change.

Note that the quantity we have defined as lattice energy is more accurately called the lattice *enthalpy*. However,

the term 'lattice energy' is commonly applied to lattice enthalpy as well. Lattice energy is the internal energy change when 1 mole of an ionic compound is formed from its gaseous ions at 298 K. Lattice enthalpy values are very close to the corresponding lattice energy values.

> ## IMPORTANT
>
> Remember that the enthalpy change for lattice energy ΔH_{latt} is always negative.

Question

1 a Give values for the standard conditions of temperature and pressure.

   b Write equations describing the lattice energy of:

   i   magnesium oxide

   ii potassium bromide

   iii sodium sulfide.

19.2 Enthalpy change of atomisation and electron affinity

Enthalpy change of atomisation

> ## KEY DEFINITION
>
> **standard enthalpy change of atomisation, $\Delta H_{\text{at}}^{\ominus}$**: the enthalpy change when 1 mole of gaseous atoms is formed from its element under standard conditions

The **standard enthalpy change of atomisation** of lithium relates to the equation:

$$Li(s) \rightarrow Li(g) \qquad \Delta H_{\text{at}}^{\ominus} = +161 \text{ kJ mol}^{-1}$$

The standard enthalpy change of atomisation of chlorine relates to the equation:

$$\frac{1}{2} Cl_2(g) \rightarrow Cl(g) \qquad \Delta H_{\text{at}}^{\ominus} = +122 \text{ kJ mol}^{-1}$$

Values of $\Delta H_{\text{at}}^{\ominus}$ are always positive (endothermic). This is because energy must be supplied to break the bonds holding the atoms in the element together.

Question

2 **a** The bond energy of the chlorine molecule is $+244$ kJ mol^{-1}. Why is the standard enthalpy change of atomisation half this value?

    b Write equations, including state symbols, that represent the enthalpy change of atomisation of:

      i oxygen

      ii barium

      iii bromine.

    c What is the numerical value of the enthalpy change of atomisation of helium? Explain your answer.

Electron affinity

The energy change occurring when a gaseous non-metal atom accepts one electron is called the *electron affinity*. The symbol for electron affinity is EA.

KEY DEFINITIONS

first electron affinity, EA$_1$: the enthalpy change when 1 mole of electrons is added to 1 mole of gaseous atoms to form 1 mole of gaseous ions with a single negative charge under standard conditions.

second electron affinity, EA$_2$: the enthalpy change when 1 mole of electrons is added to 1 mole of gaseous 1– ions to form 1 mole of gaseous 2– ions under standard conditions.

The **first electron affinity, EA$_1$**, is the enthalpy change when 1 mole of electrons is added to 1 mole of gaseous atoms to form 1 mole of gaseous ions with a single negative charge under standard conditions.

Equations representing the first electron affinity of chlorine and sulfur are:

$$Cl(g) + e^- \rightarrow Cl^-(g) \qquad EA_1 = -348 \text{ kJ mol}^{-1}$$

$$S(g) + e^- \rightarrow S^-(g) \qquad EA_1 = -200 \text{ kJ mol}^{-1}$$

Note that:

- the change is from gaseous atoms to gaseous 1– ions

- the enthalpy change for the first electron affinity, EA$_1$ is generally exothermic: EA$_1$ is negative.

When an element forms an ion with more than one negative charge, we must use successive electron affinities (this is rather like the successive ionisation energies we used in Section 2.2). The first, second and third electron affinities have symbols EA$_1$, EA$_2$ and EA$_3$.

The equations representing the first and second electron affinities of oxygen are:

first electron affinity:

$$O(g) + e^- \rightarrow O^-(g) \qquad EA_1 = -141 \text{ kJ mol}^{-1}$$

second electron affinity:

$$O^-(g) + e^- \rightarrow O^{2-}(g) \qquad EA_2 = +798 \text{ kJ mol}^{-1}$$

Note that **second electron affinities** are always endothermic (EA$_2$ is positive), and so are third electron affinities.

The overall enthalpy change in forming an oxide ion, O^{2-}, from an oxygen atom is found by adding together the first and second electron affinities:

$$O(g) + 2e^- \rightarrow O^{2-}(g) \qquad \begin{aligned} EA_1 + EA_2 \\ = (-141) + (+798) \\ = +657 \text{ kJ mol}^{-1} \end{aligned}$$

Trends in electron affinities

There is less experimental data about electron affinities compared with ionisation energies. For some atoms the variation in the experimental data is considerable. Generally, electron affinities for non-metal atoms get more negative (more exothermic) across a period with a maximum at Group 17 but the pattern is not always clear. There is no clear pattern in electron affinities down many groups apart from Groups 16 and 17. Table 19.1 shows that here, there is a trend to less negative (less exothermic) electron affinities as you go down the group, apart from the first member in the group.

Electron affinity / kJ mol^{-1}			
C = −122.3	N = 0 (±19)	O = −141.1	F = −328.0
		S = −200.4	Cl = −348.8
		Se = −195	Br = −324.6
		Te = −190	I = −295.4

Table 19.1: Selected electron affinities.

The value of the first electron affinity depends on the attraction between the added electron and the positively charged nucleus. The stronger the attraction, the greater the amount of energy released. These factors influencing the value of the electron affinity for Group 16 and 17 elements are the same as those relating to first ionisation energy:

- The greater the nuclear charge, the greater the attractive force between the nucleus and the outer electrons. So chlorine, with a greater nuclear charge than sulfur, will tend to attract an electron more readily. This means that more energy is released when a chlorine atom gains an electron.

- The further away the outer shell electrons are from the positive nuclear charge, the less the attractive force between the nucleus and the outer shell electrons is. Since the number of electron shells (and the atomic radius) increases down Groups 16 and 17, the electron affinity decreases going from chlorine to bromine to iodine.

- The greater the number of electron shells, the greater the power of inner shell electrons to shield the outer shell electrons from the nuclear charge. This also helps to decrease the electron affinity as you go from chlorine to iodine.

> **IMPORTANT**
>
> Fluorine does not fit the trend. The electron affinity of a fluorine atom is lower than that of a chlorine atom because the atomic radius of the fluorine atom is very small. The high electron density causes a greater repulsion between the electrons within the atom. This greatly reduces the attractive effect between the incoming electron and the nucleus.

Question

3 a   Suggest why the second and third electron affinities are always endothermic.

b   The first electron affinity of sulfur is -200 kJ mol^{-1}. The second electron affinity of sulfur is $+640$ kJ mol^{-1}. Calculate a value for the enthalpy change
$$S(g) + 2e^- \rightarrow S^{2-}(g)$$

c   Write equations representing:
   i   the first electron affinity of iodine
   ii the second electron affinity of sulfur.

d   Explain the trend in the first electron affinities going from sulfur to tellurium.

19.3 Born–Haber cycles

Components of the Born–Haber cycle

We have seen how we can apply Hess's law in energy cycles to work out enthalpy changes (Section 6.4). A *Born–Haber cycle* is a particular type of energy cycle used to calculate lattice energy. In simple terms it can be represented by Figure 19.3.

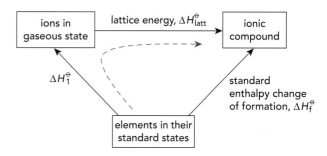

Figure 19.3: A simple energy cycle that can be used to calculate lattice energy. The dashed line shows the two-step route: using Hess's law, $\Delta H_1^{\ominus} + \Delta H_{\text{latt}}^{\ominus} = \Delta H_f^{\ominus}$

We can determine the lattice energy of a compound if we know:

- its enthalpy change of formation, $\Delta H_f^{\ominus}$

- the enthalpy changes involved in changing the elements from their standard states to their gaseous ions, $\Delta H_1^{\ominus}$.

According to Hess's law, Figure 19.3 shows that:
$$\Delta H_1^{\ominus} + \Delta H_{\text{latt}}^{\ominus} = \Delta H_f^{\ominus}$$

Rearranging this equation we get:
$$\Delta H_{\text{latt}}^{\ominus} = \Delta H_f^{\ominus} - \Delta H_1^{\ominus}$$

> **IMPORTANT**
>
> When constructing Born–Haber cycles, remember:
>
> 1   atomise metal →
>   ionise metal →
>   atomise non-metal →
>   ionise non-metal →
>
> 2   for ionising metals you use ionisation energies and for ionising non-metals you use electron affinities.

The enthalpy change $\Delta H_1^{\ominus}$ involves several steps.

Taking lithium fluoride as an example, the relevant enthalpy cycle can be written to show these steps (Figure 19.4).

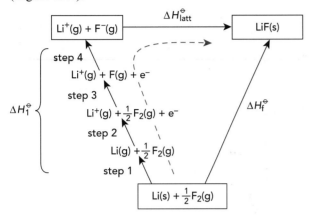

Figure 19.4: An energy cycle that can be used to calculate the lattice energy of lithium fluoride. The dashed line shows the two-step route.

The enthalpy changes needed to calculate $\Delta H_1^{\ominus}$ are as follows.

Step 1: Convert solid lithium to gaseous lithium atoms: the enthalpy change required is the enthalpy change of atomisation of lithium, $\Delta H_{at}^{\ominus}$.

$$\text{Li(s)} \rightarrow \text{Li(g)} \qquad \Delta H_{at}^{\ominus} = +161 \text{ kJ mol}^{-1}$$

Step 2: Convert gaseous lithium atoms to gaseous lithium ions: the enthalpy change required is the first ionisation energy of lithium, IE_1 (see Section 2.2).

$$\text{Li(s)} \rightarrow \text{Li(g)} + e^- \qquad IE_1 = +520 \text{ kJ mol}^{-1}$$

Step 3: Convert fluorine molecules to fluorine atoms: the enthalpy change required is the enthalpy change of atomisation of fluorine, $\Delta H_{at}^{\ominus}$.

$$\tfrac{1}{2}\text{F}_2(\text{g}) \rightarrow \text{F(g)} \qquad \Delta H_{at}^{\ominus} = +79 \text{ kJ mol}^{-1}$$

Step 4: Convert gaseous fluorine atoms to gaseous fluoride ions: the enthalpy change required is the first electron affinity of fluorine, EA_1.

$$\text{F(g)} + e^- \rightarrow \text{F}^-(\text{g}) \qquad EA_1 = -328 \text{ kJ mol}^{-1}$$

Step 5: By adding all these values together, we get a value for $\Delta H_1^{\ominus}$. We can then calculate the lattice energy using Hess's law.

The enthalpy change of formation of lithium fluoride is -617 kJ mol^{-1}.

We now have all the information we need to calculate the lattice energy.

Calculating lattice energies

Applying Hess's law to find the lattice energy of lithium fluoride:

$$\Delta H_{latt}^{\ominus} = \Delta H_f^{\ominus} - \Delta H_1^{\ominus}$$

We know that:

$$\Delta H_1^{\ominus} = \Delta H_{at}^{\ominus} [\text{Li}] + IE_1 [\text{Li}] + \Delta H_{at}^{\ominus} [\text{F}] + EA_1 [\text{F}]$$

Putting in the figures:

$$\Delta H_1^{\ominus} = (+161) + (+520) + (+79) + (-328) = +432$$

$$\Delta H_{latt}^{\ominus} = (-617) - (+432) = -1049 \text{ kJ mol}^{-1}$$

Note: take care to account for the signs of the enthalpy changes. The values of the enthalpy changes of formation and the overall electron affinity may be negative or positive.

Question

4 **a** Write equations to represent:

  i the first ionisation energy of caesium

  ii the third ionisation energy of aluminium

  iii the enthalpy change of formation of calcium oxide

  iv the enthalpy change of formation of iron(III) chloride.

b Calculate the lattice energy for sodium chloride, given that:

$$\Delta H_f^{\ominus} [\text{NaCl}] = -411 \text{ kJ mol}^{-1}$$

$$\Delta H_{at}^{\ominus} [\text{Na}] = +107 \text{ kJ mol}^{-1}$$

$$\Delta H_{at}^{\ominus} [\text{Cl}] = +122 \text{ kJ mol}^{-1}$$

$$IE_1[\text{Na}] = +496 \text{ kJ mol}^{-1}$$

$$EA_1[\text{Cl}] = -348 \text{ kJ mol}^{-1}$$

The Born–Haber cycle as an energy level diagram

We can show the Born–Haber cycle as an energy level diagram (Figure 19.5). This is the best, and clearest, type of diagram for a Born–Haber cycle. You should therefore choose to draw this type of diagram to show a Born–Haber cycle.

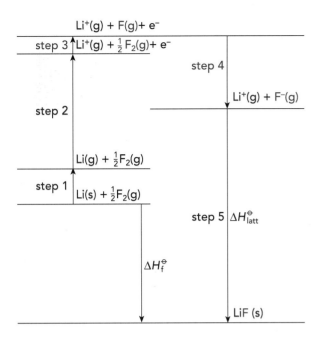

Figure 19.5: Born–Haber cycle for lithium fluoride.

To draw the cycle, you:

- start by putting down the elements in their standard state on the left-hand side
- add the other enthalpy changes in the order of steps 1 to 4 shown in Figure 19.5
- complete the cycle by adding the enthalpy change of formation and lattice energy.

Note: the arrows going upwards represent an increase in energy ($\Delta H^{\ominus}$ is positive) and the arrows going downwards represent a decrease in energy ($\Delta H^{\ominus}$ is negative).

> **IMPORTANT**
>
> When constructing Born–Haber cycles, remember that the elements go near the bottom on the left-hand side and you atomise and ionise the metal first then atomise and ionise the non-metal.

Question

5 **a** Draw a fully labelled Born–Haber cycle for potassium bromide, naming each step.

   b State the name of the enthalpy changes represented by the following equations:

   i $I_2(s) \rightarrow I(g)$

   ii $N(g) + e^- \rightarrow N^-(g)$

iii $Sr(s) + Cl_2(g) \rightarrow SrCl_2(s)$

iv $Cd^{2+}(g) + 2Cl^-(g) \rightarrow CdCl_2(s)$

The Born–Haber cycle for magnesium chloride

The Born–Haber cycle for magnesium chloride is shown in Figure 19.6.

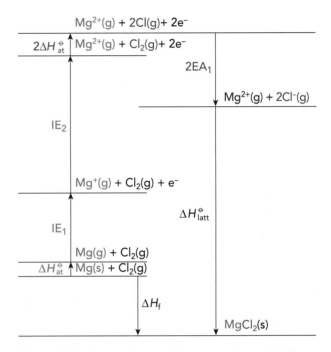

Figure 19.6: Born–Haber cycle for magnesium chloride.

There are a few differences between this cycle and the one for lithium fluoride.

1 The magnesium ion is Mg^{2+}, so the first and the second ionisation energies need to be taken into account:

$Mg(g) \rightarrow Mg^+(g) + e^-$ $IE_1 = +736 \text{ kJ mol}^{-1}$

$Mg^+(g) \rightarrow Mg^{2+}(g) + e^-$ $IE_2 = +1450 \text{ kJ mol}^{-1}$

2 There are two chloride ions in $MgCl_2$, so the values of the enthalpy change of atomisation and the first electron affinity of chlorine must be multiplied by 2.

$Cl_2(g) \rightarrow 2Cl(g)$ $2\Delta H^{\ominus}_{at} = 2 \times (+122)$
                                            $= +244 \text{ kJ mol}^{-1}$

$2Cl(g) + 2e^- \rightarrow 2Cl^-(g)$ $2EA_1 = 2 \times (-348)$
                                                  $= -696 \text{ kJ mol}^{-1}$

In order to calculate the lattice energy, we need some additional information:

$$\Delta H_f^{\ominus} [MgCl_2] = -641 \text{ kJ mol}^{-1}$$

$$\Delta H_{at}^{\ominus} [Mg] = +148 \text{ kJ mol}^{-1}$$

According to Hess's law:

$$\Delta H_{latt}^{\ominus} = \Delta H_f^{\ominus} - \{\Delta H_{at}^{\ominus} [Mg] + IE_1 [Mg] + IE_2 [Mg] + 2\Delta H_{at}^{\ominus} [Cl] + 2EA_1 [Cl]\}$$

$$\Delta H_{latt}^{\ominus} = (-641) - \{(+148) + (+736) + (+1450) + 2 \times (+122) + 2 \times (-348)\}$$

$$\Delta H_{latt}^{\ominus} = (-641) - (+1882) = -2523 \text{ kJ mol}^{-1}$$

Question

6   Draw fully labelled Born–Haber cycles for:

   a   MgO

   b   Na₂O

Constructing a Born–Haber cycle for aluminium oxide

> **Note:** this section about the Born–Haber cycle for Al_2O_3 is extension work. You will only be asked to construct and do calculations involving ions with one or two positive or negative charges.

Aluminium oxide, Al_2O_3, contains two aluminium ions (Al^{3+}) and three oxide ions (O^{2-}).

- In order to form 1 mole of gaseous Al^{3+} ions from 1 mole of Al(s), we apply the following sequence of enthalpy changes:

$$Al(s) \xrightarrow{\Delta H_{at}^{\ominus}} Al(g) \xrightarrow{IE_1} Al^+(g) \xrightarrow{IE_2} Al^{2+}(g) \xrightarrow{IE_3} Al^{3+}(g)$$
+326 kJ mol⁻¹   +577 kJ mol⁻¹   +1820 kJ mol⁻¹   +2740 kJ mol⁻¹

- In order to form 1 mole of gaseous O^{2-} ions from oxygen molecules, we apply the following sequence of enthalpy changes:

$$\frac{1}{2} O_2(g) \xrightarrow{\Delta H_{at}^{\ominus}} O(g) \xrightarrow{EA_1} O^-(g) \xrightarrow{EA_2} O^{2-}(g)$$
+249 kJ mol⁻¹   −141 kJ mol⁻¹   +798 kJ mol⁻¹

Question

> **Note:** Question 7 is extension content.

7   a   Draw a Born–Haber cycle for aluminium oxide.

   b   Calculate a value for the lattice energy of aluminium oxide using the data under the arrows in the sequences above and given that $\Delta H_f^{\ominus} [Al_2O_3] = -1676 \text{ kJ mol}^{-1}$. Remember that there are 2 moles of Al^{3+} ions and 3 moles of O^{2-} ions in 1 mole of Al_2O_3.

Factors affecting the value of lattice energy

Lattice energy arises from the electrostatic force of attraction of oppositely charged ions when the crystalline lattice is formed. The size and charge of these ions can affect the value of the lattice energy.

Lattice energy and ion size

As the size of the ion increases, the lattice energy becomes less exothermic. This applies to both anions and cations. Figure 19.7 shows that:

- for any given anion, e.g. F^-, the lattice energy gets less exothermic as the size of the cation increases from Li^+ to Cs^+

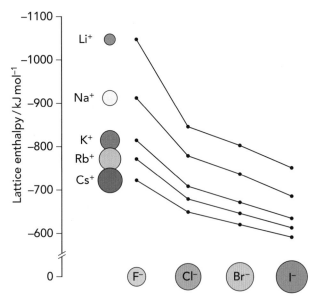

Figure 19.7: Lattice energies of the Group 1 halides.

for any given cation, e.g. Li^+, the lattice energy gets less exothermic as the size of the anion increases from F^- to I^-.

Ions with the same ionic charge have a lower charge density if their radius is larger. This is because the same charge is spread out over a larger volume. A lower charge density results in weaker electrostatic forces of attraction in the ionic lattice. Sodium fluoride has a less exothermic lattice energy than lithium fluoride. This reflects the lower charge density on sodium ions compared with lithium ions.

Lattice energy and the charge on ions

The lattice energy becomes more exothermic as the ionic charge increases.

We can see this by comparing lithium fluoride, LiF, with magnesium oxide, MgO. These compounds have the same arrangement of ions in their lattice structure. The cations Li^+ and Mg^{2+} have similar sizes. The anions F^- and O^{2-} are fairly similar in size (although they are much larger than the cations). The major physical difference between LiF and MgO is the ionic charge. This affects the lattice energy:

$$\Delta H^{\ominus}_{latt} [LiF] = -1049 \text{ kJ mol}^{-1}$$

$$\Delta H^{\ominus}_{latt} [MgO] = -3923 \text{ kJ mol}^{-1}$$

Magnesium oxide has a greater lattice energy than lithium fluoride. The doubly charged Mg^{2+} and O^{2-} ions in magnesium oxide attract each other more strongly than the singly charged ions of the same size in LiF. For ions of similar size, the greater the ionic charge, the higher the charge density. This results in stronger ionic bonds being formed.

IMPORTANT

The value of the lattice energy depends on the size of the ions and the charge on the ion. The lattice energy is higher if the ionic charge is greater and the ionic radius is smaller.

Questions

8 a For each pair of compounds, suggest which will have the most exothermic lattice energy.
   i   KCl and BaO (ionic radii are similar)
   ii MgI_2 and SrI_2
   iii CaO and NaCl (ionic radii are similar).

b Place the following compounds in order of increasingly exothermic lattice energy. Explain your answer.
   LiF   MgO   RbCl

Note: Question 9 is extension content.

9 Learners taking Physics A Level learn that the electrostatic force between two charged particles is proportional to $\dfrac{Q_1 \times Q_2}{r^2}$ where Q_1 and Q_2 are the charges on the particles and r is the distance between the centres of the particles.

Use this relationship to explain why:

a magnesium oxide has a greater lattice energy than lithium fluoride

b lithium fluoride has a greater lattice energy than potassium bromide.

10 Which one of these equations for the calculation of the lattice energy of sodium oxide, Na_2O, is correct?

A $\Delta H^{\ominus}_{latt} = \Delta H^{\ominus}_{f} - \{\Delta H^{\ominus}_{at} [Na] + IE_1 [Na] + \Delta H^{\ominus}_{at} [O] + EA_1 [O] + EA_2 [O]\}$

B $\Delta H^{\ominus}_{latt} = \Delta H^{\ominus}_{f} - \{2\Delta H^{\ominus}_{at} [Na] + 2IE_1 [Na] + \Delta H^{\ominus}_{at} [O] + 2EA_1\}$

C $\Delta H^{\ominus}_{latt} = \Delta H^{\ominus}_{f} - \{2\Delta H^{\ominus}_{at} [Na] + 2IE_1 [Na] + EA_1 [O] + EA_2 [O]\}$

D $\Delta H^{\ominus}_{latt} = \Delta H^{\ominus}_{f} - \{2\Delta H^{\ominus}_{at} [Na] + 2IE_1 [Na] + \Delta H^{\ominus}_{at} [O] + EA_1 [O] + EA_2 [O]\}$

Ion polarisation

In our model of an ionic lattice, we have thought of the ions as being spherical in shape. This is not always the case. In some cases, the positive charge on the cation in an ionic lattice may attract the electrons in the anion towards it. This results in a distortion of the electron cloud of the anion and the anion is no longer spherical (Figure 19.8). We call this distortion

Figure 19.8: Ion polarisation. A small highly charged cation can distort the shape of the anion.

ion polarisation. The ability of a cation to attract electrons and distort an anion is called the **polarising power** of the cation.

KEY WORDS

ion polarisation: the distortion of the electron cloud of an anion by a neighbouring cation. The distortion is greatest when the cation is small and highly charged.

polarising power (of a cation): the ability of a cation to attract the electron cloud of an anion and distort it.

Factors affecting ion polarisation

The degree of polarisation of an anion depends on:

- the charge density of the cation
- the ease with which the anion can be polarised: its polarisability.

An anion is more likely to be polarised if:

- the cation is small
- the cation has a charge of 2+ or 3+
- the anion is large
- the anion has a charge of 2– or 3–.

A small highly charged cation such as Fe^{3+} can attract electrons and distort a larger anion to such an extent that the bond formed has a considerable amount of covalent character. Pure ionic bonding and pure covalent bonding are extremes. Many ionic compounds have some covalent character due to ion polarisation. Many covalent compounds have some degree of charge separation, i.e. they are polar, due to bond polarisation (see Chapter 4).

Question

11 a   Explain why a cation with a smaller ionic radius has a higher charge density.

   b   Which one of the following ions will be the best polariser of the large nitrate ion? Explain your answer.

   Cs^+ Li^+ Na^+ K^+

   c   Which one of these ions will be most polarised by a Mg^{2+} ion? Explain your answer.

   Br^- Cl^- F^- I^-

The thermal stability of Group 2 carbonates and nitrates

The Group 2 carbonates decompose to their oxides and carbon dioxide on heating. For example:

$$CaCO_3(s) \xrightarrow{\text{heat}} CaO(s) + CO_2(g)$$

Table 19.2 shows the decomposition temperature and enthalpy change of reaction, $\Delta H_r^\ominus$, for some Group 2 carbonates.

Group 2 carbonate	Decomposition temperature / °C	Enthalpy change of reaction / kJ mol^{-1}
magnesium carbonate	540	+117
calcium carbonate	900	+176
strontium carbonate	1280	+238
barium carbonate	1360	+268

Table 19.2: Enthalpy change of reaction values for the decomposition of some Group 2 carbonates.

The relative ease of thermal decomposition is shown by the values of the enthalpy changes of reaction. The more positive the enthalpy change, the more stable the carbonate relative to its oxide and carbon dioxide. You can also see this in the decomposition temperatures: the further down the group, the higher the temperature required to decompose the carbonate (see Section 11.4).

So, the relative stabilities of these carbonates increase down the group in the order:

$BaCO_3 > SrCO_3 > CaCO_3 > MgCO_3$.

We can explain this trend using ideas about ion polarisation:

- the carbonate ion has a relatively large ionic radius so it is easily polarised by a small highly charged cation
- the Group 2 cations increase in ionic radius down the group:

  $Mg^{2+} < Ca^{2+} < Sr^{2+} < Ba^{2+}$

- the smaller the ionic radius of the cation, the better it is at polarising the carbonate ion (Figure 19.9)

- so the degree of polarisation of the carbonate ion by the Group 2 cation follows the order

  $Mg^{2+} > Ca^{2+} > Sr^{2+} > Ba^{2+}$

- the greater the polarisation of the carbonate ion, the easier it is to weaken a carbon–oxygen bond in the carbonate and form carbon dioxide and the oxide on heating.

Figure 19.9: Magnesium ions are better polarisers of carbonate ions than calcium ions.

A similar pattern is observed with the thermal decomposition of Group 2 nitrates: these decompose to form the oxide, nitrogen dioxide and oxygen. For example:

$$2Mg(NO_3)_2(s) \rightarrow 2MgO(s) + 4NO_2(g) + O_2(g)$$

The order of stability with respect to the products is in the order:

$$Ba(NO_3)_2 > Sr(NO_3)_2 > Ca(NO_3)_2 > Mg(NO_3)_2$$

The difference in thermal stability of Group 2 carbonates can be analysed by comparing Born–Haber cycles involving the lattice energies of calcium carbonate and calcium oxide. The unequal changes in the lattice energies of the Group 2 carbonates and the Group 2 oxides as the cation size increases can be related to the increasing thermal stability down the group.

Question

12 Use ideas about ion polarisation to explain why magnesium nitrate undergoes thermal decomposition at a much lower temperature than barium nitrate.

19.4 Enthalpy changes in solution

When an ionic solid dissolves in water, the crystal lattice breaks up and the ions separate. It needs a large amount of energy to overcome the attractive forces between the ions. How does this happen, even when the water is not heated? We will answer this question in this section.

Enthalpy change of solution

The **standard enthalpy change of solution**, $\Delta H_{sol}^{\ominus}$, is the energy absorbed or released when 1 mole of an ionic solid dissolves in sufficient water to form a very dilute solution.

> **KEY WORD**
>
> **standard enthalpy change of solution, $\Delta H_{sol}^{\ominus}$:** the energy absorbed or released when 1 mole of an ionic solid dissolves in sufficient water to form a very dilute solution under standard conditions.

The enthalpy changes of solution for magnesium chloride and sodium chloride are described by the equations below:

$$MgCl_2(s) + aq \rightarrow MgCl_2(aq) \quad \Delta H_{sol}^{\ominus} = -55 \text{ kJ mol}^{-1}$$

or

$$MgCl_2(s) + aq \rightarrow Mg^{2+}(aq) + 2Cl^-(aq)$$
$$\Delta H_{sol}^{\ominus} = -55 \text{ kJ mol}^{-1}$$

$$NaCl(s) + aq \rightarrow NaCl(aq) \quad \Delta H_{sol}^{\ominus} = +3.9 \text{ kJ mol}^{-1}$$

or

$$NaCl(s) + aq \rightarrow Na^+(aq) + Cl^-(aq)$$
$$\Delta H_{sol}^{\ominus} = +3.9 \text{ kJ mol}^{-1}$$

Note that:

- the symbol for enthalpy change of solution is $\Delta H_{sol}^{\ominus}$

- the symbol 'aq' represents the very large amount of water used

- enthalpy changes of solution can be positive (endothermic) or negative (exothermic)

- a compound is likely to be soluble in water only if $\Delta H_{sol}^{\ominus}$ is negative or has a small positive value; substances with large positive values of $\Delta H_{sol}^{\ominus}$ are relatively insoluble.

Question

13 a Write equations to represent the enthalpy change of solution of:

    i potassium sulfate

    ii zinc chloride.

b The enthalpies of solution of some metal halides are given below. What do these values tell you about the relative solubilities of these four compounds?

sodium chloride, $\Delta H^{\ominus}_{sol} = +3.9$ kJ mol^{-1}

silver chloride, $\Delta H^{\ominus}_{sol} = +65.7$ kJ mol^{-1}

sodium bromide, $\Delta H^{\ominus}_{sol} = -0.6$ kJ mol^{-1}

silver bromide, $\Delta H^{\ominus}_{sol} = +84.5$ kJ mol^{-1}

'Soluble' and 'insoluble' are only relative terms. We think of magnesium carbonate as being insoluble because only 0.6 g of the salt dissolves in every dm^3 of water. No metallic salts are absolutely insoluble in water. Even lead carbonate, which is regarded as insoluble, dissolves to a very small extent: 0.00017 g dissolves in every dm^3 of water. If salts were completely insoluble, they could not have a value for $\Delta H^{\ominus}_{sol}$.

PRACTICAL ACTIVITY 19.1

Enthalpy change of solution by experiment

SAFETY: Only carry out this activity in the presence of a teacher after safety aspects have been explained.

The enthalpy change of solution of sodium hydroxide can be found using a polystyrene cup as a calorimeter. We use known amounts of solute and solvent with the solvent in excess to make sure that all the solute dissolves.

Procedure

1 Weigh an empty polystyrene cup.

2 Pour 100 cm^3 of water into the cup and weigh the cup and water.

3 Record the steady temperature of the water with a thermometer reading to at least the nearest 0.2 °C.

4 Add a few pellets of sodium hydroxide (corrosive!) which have been stored under dry conditions.

5 Keep the mixture stirred continuously with a thermometer and record the temperature at fixed intervals, e.g. every 20 seconds.

6 Keep recording the temperature for 5 minutes after the maximum temperature has been reached.

7 Weigh the cup and its contents to calculate the mass of sodium hydroxide which dissolved.

Specimen results and calculations

mass of polystyrene cup	= 23.00 g
mass of polystyrene cup + water	= 123.45 g
mass of water	= 100.45 g
mass of cup + water + sodium hydroxide	= 124.95 g
mass of sodium hydroxide that dissolved	= 1.50 g
initial temperature of water	= 18.0 °C
final temperature of water	= 21.6 °C
temperature rise	= +3.6 °C

From the results, 1.50 g of sodium hydroxide dissolved in 100.45 cm^3 (100.45 g) of water and produced a temperature change of +3.6 °C.

energy change, q (in J) = $-$ mass of water (in g) $\times$ specific heat capacity $\times$ temperature change (in °C)

$= -(100.45 \times 4.18 \times 3.6)$

$= -1511.57$ J $= -1.5$ kJ (to 2 significant figures)

The energy change for 1.5 g sodium hydroxide is -1.5 kJ

The enthalpy change for 1.0 mole of sodium hydroxide ($M_r = 40$ g mol^{-1})

is $-\dfrac{40}{1.5} \times 1.5$ kJ $= -40$ kJ

$\Delta H^{\ominus}_{sol} = -40$ kJ mol^{-1}

In this experiment, we are assuming that the specific heat capacity of the solution is the same as the specific heat capacity of water. The heat losses in this experiment, however, are likely to be considerable because the sodium hydroxide takes some time to dissolve. This means that the reaction mixture has a longer period of cooling.

Enthalpy change of hydration

The lattice energy for sodium chloride is -788 kJ mol^{-1}. This means that we need to supply (at least) $+788 \text{ kJ mol}^{-1}$ to overcome the forces of attraction between the ions. But $\Delta H_{sol}^{\ominus}$ [NaCl] is only $+3.9 \text{ kJ mol}^{-1}$. Where does the energy needed to separate the ions come from? The answer is that it comes from the strong attraction between the ions and the water molecules.

When an ionic solid dissolves in water, bonds are formed between water molecules and the ions. These bonds are called ion–dipole bonds. Water is a polar molecule. The $\delta-$ oxygen atoms in water molecules are attracted to the positive ions in the ionic compound. The $\delta+$ hydrogen atoms in water molecules are attracted to the negative ions in the ionic compound (Figure 19.10).

The energy released in forming ion–dipole bonds is sufficient to compensate for the energy that must be put in to separate the anions and cations that are bonded together in the crystal lattice.

> ### KEY WORD
>
> ion–dipole bond: the bond formed between an ion and a polar compound such as water. The negative end of the dipole (on the oxygen atom of water) bonds with a positive ion. The positive end of the dipole (on the hydrogen atoms of water) bonds with a negative ion.

The energy released when gaseous ions dissolve in water is called the standard enthalpy change of hydration.

The enthalpy change of hydration, $\Delta H_{hyd}^{\ominus}$, is the enthalpy change when 1 mole of a specified gaseous ion dissolves in sufficient water to form a very dilute solution.

> ### KEY DEFINITION
>
> standard enthalpy change of hydration, $\Delta H_{hyd}^{\ominus}$: the enthalpy change when 1 mole of a specified gaseous ion dissolves in sufficient water to form a very dilute solution under standard conditions.

The enthalpy changes of hydration for calcium ions and chloride ions are described by the equations below:

$$Ca^{2+}(g) + aq \rightarrow Ca^{2+}(aq) \qquad \Delta H_{hyd}^{\ominus} = -1650 \text{ kJ mol}^{-1}$$

$$Cl^-(g) + aq \rightarrow Cl^-(aq) \qquad \Delta H_{hyd}^{\ominus} = -364 \text{ kJ mol}^{-1}$$

Note:

- the symbol for enthalpy change of hydration is $\Delta H_{hyd}^{\ominus}$

- the enthalpy change of hydration is always exothermic

- the value of $\Delta H_{hyd}^{\ominus}$ is more exothermic for ions with the same charge but smaller ionic radii, e.g. $\Delta H_{hyd}^{\ominus}$ is more exothermic for Li^+ than for Na^+. The charge density is greater for lithium than for sodium because the ionic radius of Li^+ is smaller and there is less shielding than for Na^+. This effect is greater than the effect of increased nuclear charge present in Na^+. Water is a polar molecule. So ion–dipole attractions between water and Li^+ are stronger than ion–dipole attractions between water and Na^+.

- the value of $\Delta H_{hyd}^{\ominus}$ is more exothermic for ions with the same radii but a larger charge, e.g. $\Delta H_{hyd}^{\ominus}$ is more exothermic for Mg^{2+} than for Li^+. The charge density is greater for magnesium than for lithium because the charge on Mg^{2+} is greater for the same size of atom. There are also a greater number of positive charges in the nucleus. So ion–dipole attractions between water and Mg^{2+} are stronger than ion–dipole attractions between water and Li^+.

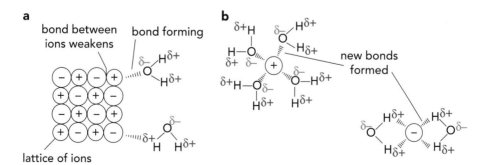

Figure 19.10: a Water molecules forming ion–dipole bonds with an ionic compound. **b** Hydrated ions in solution.

Questions

14 a Why is the enthalpy change of hydration always exothermic?

b Write equations to represent:
  i the hydration of a sodium ion
  ii the hydration of a chloride ion.

c Draw diagrams to show:
  i four water molecules hydrating a magnesium ion
  ii two water molecules hydrating a bromide ion.
  Show the dipole on each water molecule.

d Explain why the value of $\Delta H^{\ominus}_{\mathrm{hyd}}$ for magnesium ions is much more exothermic than $\Delta H^{\ominus}_{\mathrm{hyd}}$ for potassium ions.

15 Name the changes associated with the equations below:

a $KBr(s) + aq \rightarrow KBr(aq)$ (for 1 mole of KBr)

b $K^+(g) + aq \rightarrow K^+(aq)$ (for 1 mole of K^+ ions)

c $K^+(g) + Br^-(g) \rightarrow KBr(s)$ (for 1 mole of KBr)

d $Br^-(g) + aq \rightarrow Br^-(aq)$ (for 1 mole of Br^- ions)

Calculating enthalpy changes in solution

We can calculate the enthalpy change of solution or the enthalpy change of hydration by constructing an energy cycle and using Hess's law (Figure 19.11).

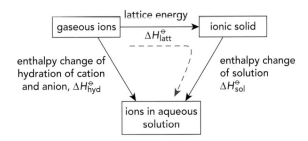

Figure 19.11: An energy cycle involving lattice energy, enthalpy change of hydration and enthalpy change of solution.

We can see from this energy cycle that:

$$\Delta H^{\ominus}_{\mathrm{latt}} + \Delta H^{\ominus}_{\mathrm{sol}} = \Delta H^{\ominus}_{\mathrm{hyd}}$$

Note that the $\Delta H^{\ominus}_{\mathrm{hyd}}$ values for both anions and cations are added together to get the total value of $\Delta H^{\ominus}_{\mathrm{hyd}}$. We can use this energy cycle to calculate:

- the value of $\Delta H^{\ominus}_{\mathrm{sol}}$
- the value of $\Delta H^{\ominus}_{\mathrm{hyd}}$

REFLECTION

1 Work with another learner to make a list of differences between the standard enthalpy change of hydration and standard enthalpy change of solution.

2 Work with another learner to list and define each of the different enthalpy changes that you need in order to calculate the lattice energy of an ionic compound. When constructing a Born–Haber cycle, what is the best order for these enthalpy changes?
Did you leave out any enthalpy changes? If so, what strategies will you take in order to remember these?
What processes did you go through to produce this order?

WORKED EXAMPLE

1 Determine the enthalpy change of solution of sodium fluoride using the following data:

- lattice energy = −902 kJ mol⁻¹

- enthalpy change of hydration of sodium ions = −406 kJ mol⁻¹

- enthalpy change of hydration of fluoride ions = −506 kJ mol⁻¹

Solution

Step 1: Draw the energy cycle (Figure 19.12)

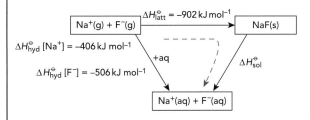

Figure 19.12: An energy cycle to determine $\Delta H_{sol}^{\ominus}$ of NaF.

Step 2: Rearrange the equation and substitute the figures to find $\Delta H_{sol}^{\ominus}$.

$$\Delta H_{latt}^{\ominus} + \Delta H_{sol}^{\ominus} = \Delta H_{hyd}^{\ominus}$$

so

$$\Delta H_{sol}^{\ominus} = \Delta H_{hyd}^{\ominus} - \Delta H_{latt}^{\ominus}$$
$$\Delta H_{sol}^{\ominus} [NaF] = (-406) + (-506) - (-902)$$
$$\Delta H_{sol}^{\ominus} [NaF] = -10 \text{ kJ mol}^{-1}$$

An energy level diagram for this energy cycle is shown in Figure 19.13.

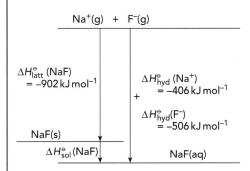

Figure 19.13: An energy level diagram to determine $\Delta H_{sol}^{\ominus}$ + of NaF.

2 Determine the enthalpy change of hydration of the chloride ion using the following data.

- lattice energy of lithium chloride = −846 kJ mol⁻¹

- enthalpy change of solution of lithium chloride = −37 kJ mol⁻¹

- enthalpy change of hydration of lithium ion = −519 kJ mol⁻¹

Solution

Step 1: Draw the energy cycle (Figure 19.14).

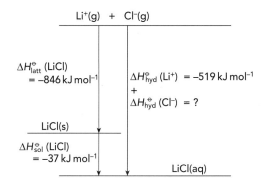

Figure 19.14: An energy cycle to determine $\Delta H_{hyd}^{\ominus}$ [Cl⁻].

Step 2: Rearrange the equation and substitute the figures to find $\Delta H_{hyd}^{\ominus}$ [Cl⁻].

$$\Delta H_{latt}^{\ominus} + \Delta H_{sol}^{\ominus} = \Delta H_{hyd}^{\ominus} [Li^+] + \Delta H_{hyd}^{\ominus} [Cl^-]$$

so

$$\Delta H_{hyd}^{\ominus} [Cl^-] = \Delta H_{latt}^{\ominus} + \Delta H_{sol}^{\ominus} - \Delta H_{hyd}^{\ominus} [Li^+]$$
$$\Delta H_{hyd}^{\ominus} [Cl^-] = (-846) + (-37) - (-519)$$
$$\Delta H_{hyd}^{\ominus} [Cl^-] = -364 \text{ kJ mol}^{-1}$$

Question

16 a Draw an energy cycle to calculate the enthalpy of hydration of magnesium ions when magnesium chloride dissolves in water.

b Calculate the enthalpy of hydration of magnesium ions given that:
$$\Delta H_{latt}^{\ominus} [MgCl_2] = -2592 \text{ kJ mol}^{-1}$$
$$\Delta H_{sol}^{\ominus} [MgCl_2] = -55 \text{ kJ mol}^{-1}$$
$$\Delta H_{hyd}^{\ominus} [Cl^-] = -364 \text{ kJ mol}^{-1}$$

The solubility of Group 2 sulfates

Table 19.3 shows the solubility in water of some Group 2 sulfates. The solubility decreases as the radius of the metal ion increases. We can explain this variation in solubility in terms of the relative values of enthalpy change of hydration and the corresponding lattice energy.

Compound	Solubility / mol dm^{-3}
magnesium sulfate	1.83
calcium sulfate	4.66×10^{-2}
strontium sulfate	7.11×10^{-4}
barium sulfate	9.43×10^{-6}

Table 19.3: Solubilities in water of some Group 2 sulfates.

Change in hydration enthalpy down the group

- Smaller ions (with the same charge) have greater enthalpy changes of hydration

- so the enthalpy change of hydration decreases (gets less exothermic) in the order:

$$Mg^{2+} > Ca^{2+} > Sr^{2+} > Ba^{2+}$$

- this decrease is relatively large down the group and it depends entirely on the increase in the size of the cation, as the anion is unchanged (it is the sulfate ion in every case).

Change in lattice energy down the group

- Lattice energy is greater if the ions (with the same charge) forming the lattice are small

- so the lattice energy decreases in the order: $Mg^{2+} > Ca^{2+} > Sr^{2+} > Ba^{2+}$

- the lattice energy is also inversely proportional to the sum of the radii of the anion and cation

- the sulfate ion is much larger than the Group 2 cations

- so the sulfate ion contributes a relatively greater part to the change in the lattice energy down the group

- so the decrease in lattice energy is relatively smaller down the group and it is determined more by the size of the large sulfate ion than the size of the cations.

Difference in enthalpy change of solution of Group 2 sulfates

Earlier in this section we saw that substances that have a very low solubility in water are likely to have $\Delta H_{sol}^{\ominus}$ with a high positive (endothermic) value. As a rough guide, the higher the positive value of $\Delta H_{sol}^{\ominus}$ the less soluble the salt.

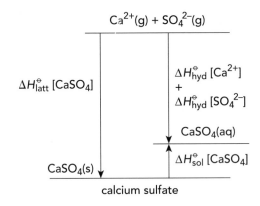

calcium sulfate

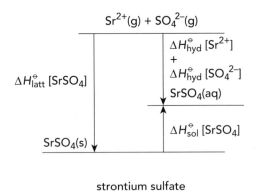

strontium sulfate

Figure 19.15: Enthalpy cycles comparing the enthalpy change of solution of calcium sulfate and strontium sulfate.

We have seen that:

- the lattice energy of the sulfates decreases (gets less exothermic) by relatively smaller values down the group

- the enthalpy change of hydration decreases (gets less exothermic) by relatively larger values down the group

- so applying Hess's law, the value of $\Delta H^{\ominus}_{sol}$ gets more endothermic down the group (Figure 19.15)

- so the solubility of the Group 2 sulfates decreases down the group.

Question

17 a Draw an enthalpy cycle as an energy level diagram showing the relationship between lattice energy, enthalpy change of solution and enthalpy change of hydration for barium sulfate.

$\Delta H^{\ominus}_{sol}$ [$BaSO_4$] is very endothermic.

b Explain why magnesium sulfate is more soluble than barium sulfate by referring to the relative values of the lattice energies and enthalpy changes of hydration.

SUMMARY

The lattice energy ($\Delta H^{\ominus}_{latt}$) is the energy change when gaseous ions come together to form 1 mole of a solid lattice (under standard conditions).

The standard enthalpy change of atomisation ($\Delta H^{\ominus}_{at}$) is the enthalpy change when 1 mole of gaseous atoms is formed from the element in its standard state under standard conditions.

The first electron affinity (EA_1) is the enthalpy change when 1 mole of electrons is added to 1 mole of gaseous atoms to form 1 mole of gaseous ions with a single negative charge under standard conditions.

A Born–Haber cycle is a type of enthalpy cycle (Hess cycle) that includes lattice energy, enthalpy change of formation and relevant electron affinities, enthalpy changes of atomisation and enthalpy changes of ionisation.

The thermal stability of the carbonates and nitrates of Group 2 elements depends on the degree to which the Group 2 cation is able to polarise the larger anion:
- smaller cations have a higher charge density and are better polarisers of a given anion
- larger anions are more polarised by a given cation.

The standard enthalpy change of solution ($\Delta H^{\ominus}_{sol}$) is the enthalpy change when 1 mole of an ionic solid dissolves in sufficient water to form a very dilute solution. $\Delta H^{\ominus}_{sol}$ may be exothermic or endothermic.

The enthalpy change of hydration ($\Delta H^{\ominus}_{hyd}$) is the enthalpy change when 1 mole of gaseous ions dissolves in sufficient water to form a very dilute solution. $\Delta H^{\ominus}_{hyd}$ is always exothermic.

Hess's law can be applied to construct energy cycles to determine enthalpy changes of solution and enthalpy changes of hydration.

The decrease in solubility of Group 2 sulfates down the group can be explained in terms of the relative values of the enthalpy change of hydration and the corresponding lattice energy.

EXAM-STYLE QUESTIONS

1 The table shows the enthalpy changes needed to calculate the lattice energy of potassium oxide, K_2O.

Type of enthalpy change	Value of enthalpy change / kJ mol^{-1}
first ionisation energy of potassium	+418
first electron affinity of oxygen	−141
second electron affinity of oxygen	+798
enthalpy change of formation of K_2O	−361
enthalpy change of atomisation of potassium	+89
enthalpy change of atomisation of oxygen	+249

a Copy the incomplete Born–Haber cycle shown below. On the lines A to E of your copy of the Born–Haber cycle, write the correct symbols relating to potassium and oxygen. **[5]**

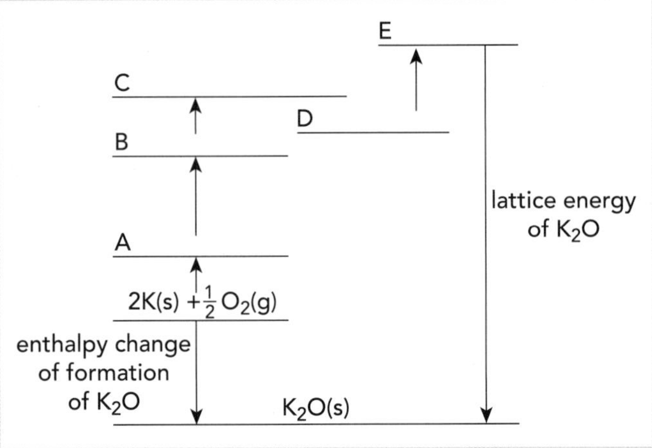

b Use the data in the table above to calculate the lattice energy of potassium oxide. **[2]**

c Describe how, and explain why, the lattice energy of sodium oxide differs from that of potassium sulfide, K_2S. **[4]**

d Explain why the second electron affinity of oxygen has a positive value. **[1]**

[Total: 12]

2 The lattice energy of sodium chloride can be calculated using the following enthalpy changes:

- enthalpy change of formation of sodium chloride
- enthalpy changes of atomisation of sodium and chlorine

IMPORTANT

Learn a mental check list to help you construct Born–Haber cycles:

- have I included the enthalpy of formation?
- have I included both enthalpies of atomisation?
- have I converted all atoms into ions of the correct charge?
- have I considered how many moles of each ion are in 1 mole of the compound?

The last two points get forgotten most often, especially the final one. This final point is important in Question 1, parts **a** and **b**, Question 3, part **b ii**, and Question 4, part **c**.

CONTINUED

- first ionisation energy of sodium
- first electron affinity of chlorine.

a Define the terms:

   i first ionisation energy [3]

   ii enthalpy change of atomisation. [2]

b Draw and label a Born–Haber cycle to calculate the lattice energy of sodium chloride. [4]

c Explain why the lattice energy of sodium chloride has a value that is lower than the lattice energy of lithium chloride. [2]

[Total: 11]

3 a Draw an energy cycle to show the dissolving of magnesium iodide in water. [5]

b The table shows the values for all but one of the enthalpy changes relevant to this cycle.

Enthalpy change	Value/kJ mol^{-1}
lattice energy	−2327
enthalpy change of hydration of Mg^{2+} ion	−1920
enthalpy change of hydration of I^- ion	−314

   i Define *enthalpy change of hydration*. [2]

   ii Use the values in the table to calculate the value for the enthalpy change of solution of magnesium iodide. [3]

c Draw a diagram to show how water molecules are arranged around a magnesium ion. [2]

d Explain why the enthalpy change of hydration of a magnesium ion is more exothermic than the enthalpy change of hydration of a sodium ion. [3]

[Total: 15]

4 The lattice energy of magnesium bromide, $MgBr_2$, can be calculated using the enthalpy changes shown in the table.

Type of enthalpy change	Value / kJ mol^{-1}
first ionisation energy of magnesium	+736
second ionisation energy of magnesium	+1450
first electron affinity of bromine	−325
enthalpy change of formation of $MgBr_2$	−524
enthalpy change of atomisation of magnesium	+150
enthalpy change of atomisation of bromine	+112

CONTINUED

a State the meaning of the terms:

   i lattice energy [2]

   ii second ionisation energy. [3]

b Draw and label a Born–Haber cycle to calculate the lattice energy of magnesium bromide. [4]

c Calculate the lattice energy of magnesium bromide. [2]

[Total: 11]

5 a For each of the following pairs of compounds, state, with reasons, which one you would expect to have the higher lattice energy.

   i NaCl and KBr [2]

   ii KCl and SrS. [2]

b In some crystal lattices, some of the ions are polarised.

   i State the meaning of the term *ion polarisation*. [2]

   ii Explain why a magnesium ion is better than a sodium ion at polarising an iodide ion. [2]

   iii Use ideas about ion polarisation to explain why barium carbonate is more stable to thermal decomposition than magnesium carbonate. [3]

[Total: 11]

6 The diagram shows the enthalpy changes when sodium chloride is dissolved in water.

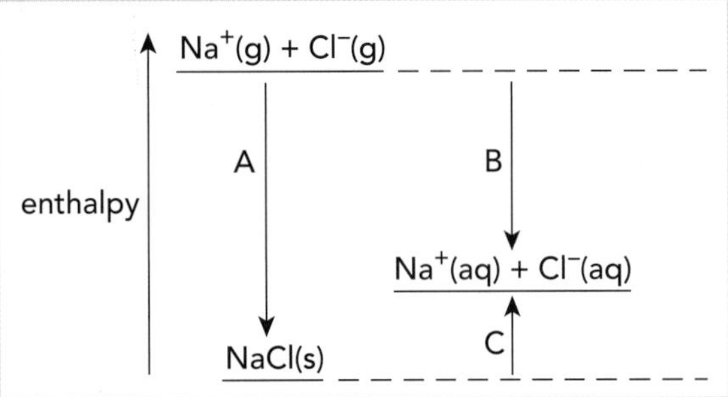

a Define the following terms:

   i enthalpy change of solution [2]

   ii enthalpy change of hydration. [2]

b Write symbol equations that describe the following:

   i enthalpy change of solution of sodium chloride [2]

   ii enthalpy change of hydration of the chloride ion. [2]

c Name the enthalpy changes labelled A, B and C. [3]

d Draw the water molecules around magnesium ions and sulfate ions in a solution of magnesium sulfate. [3]

e Explain, in terms of differences of lattice energies and enthalpy changes of hydration, why magnesium sulfate is more soluble in water than calcium sulfate. [5]

[Total: 19]

SELF-EVALUATION

After studying this chapter, complete a table like this:

I can	See section...	Needs more work	Almost there	Ready to move on
define and use the terms *enthalpy change of atomisation* and *lattice energy*	19.1, 19.2			
define and use the term *first electron affinity*	19.2			
explain the factors affecting the electron affinities of the elements	19.2			
describe and explain the trends in the electron affinities of the Group 16 and Group 17 elements	19.2			
construct and use Born–Haber cycles for ionic solids	19.3			
carry out calculations involving Born–Haber cycles	19.3			
explain the effect of ionic charge and ionic radius on the magnitude (big or small) of the lattice energy	19.3			
define and use the terms *enthalpy change of hydration* and *enthalpy change of solution*	19.4			
construct and use an energy cycle involving enthalpy change of solution, lattice energy and enthalpy changes of hydration	19.4			
carry out calculations using an energy cycle involving enthalpy change of solution, lattice energy and enthalpy changes of hydration	19.4			
explain the effect of ionic charge and ionic radius on the magnitude (big or small) of the enthalpy change of hydration	19.4			
describe and explain qualitatively, the trend in the thermal stability of the nitrates and carbonates in Group 2, including the effect of ionic radius on the polarisation of the large anion	19.4			
describe, and explain qualitatively, the variation in solubility and enthalpy change of solution of the hydroxides and sulfates in Group 2 in terms of relative magnitudes of enthalpy change of hydration and the lattice energy.	19.4			

> Chapter 20
Electrochemistry

LEARNING INTENTIONS

In this chapter you will learn how to:

- predict the identity of the substance liberated during electrolysis from:

    - the state of electrolyte (molten or aqueous)

    - the position of the ions (in the electrolyte) in the redox series (electrode potential)

    - the concentration of the ions in the electrolyte

- state and apply the relationship $F = Le$ between the Faraday constant, F, the Avogadro constant, L, and the charge on the electron, e

- calculate:

    - the quantity of charge passed during electrolysis using $Q = It$

    - the mass and / or volume of substance liberated during electrolysis

- describe the determination of a value of the Avogadro constant by an electrolytic method

- define the terms:

    - standard electrode (reduction) potential

    - standard cell potential

CONTINUED

- describe the standard hydrogen electrode

- describe methods used to measure the standard electrode potentials of:

  - metals or non-metals in contact with their ions in aqueous solution

  - ions of the same element in different oxidation states

- calculate a standard cell potential by combining two standard electrode potentials

- use standard cell potential to:

  - deduce the polarity of each electrode and hence explain / deduce the direction of electron flow in the external circuit of a simple cell

  - predict the feasibility of a reaction

- deduce from standard electrode potential values the relative reactivity of elements, compounds and ions as oxidising agents or reducing agents

- construct redox equations using the relevant half-equations

- predict qualitatively how the value of an electrode potential varies with the concentration of the aqueous ion

- use the Nernst equation $E = E^{\ominus} + \dfrac{0.059}{z} \log_{10} \dfrac{[\text{oxidised species}]}{[\text{reduced species}]}$ to predict quantitatively how the value of an electrode potential varies with the concentration of the aqueous ions.

BEFORE YOU START

1   Explain to another learner the meaning of the terms *reversible reaction*, *equilibrium* and *Le Chatelier's principle*.

2   Make a list of the factors that affect an equilibrium reaction. Choose an equilibrium reaction from Chapter 8 in the coursebook and work with another learner to suggest how these factors affect the position of that particular equilibrium.

3   Work with another learner. Take it in turns to explain the meaning of the terms *electrolysis*, *anode*, *cathode*, *electrolyte*, *anion* and *cation*. If you do not agree or are not sure, check with a textbook or the internet.

4   Make a list of compound ions (e.g. MnO_4^-, SO_3^{2-}) or compounds (e.g MnO_2). Share this list with another learner, then deduce the oxidation number of the metal in the ion or more electropositive non-metal in the compound. Compare your answers with the other learner.

5   Take turns in challenging another learner to define these terms: *redox*, *oxidation*, *reduction*, *disproportionation*, *oxidation number*, *oxidising agent* and *reducing agent*. If you do not agree or are not sure, check your answers with the definitions given in the coursebook.

6   Explain to another learner the meaning of the terms *Avogadro constant*, *standard conditions* and *mole*.

CONTINUED

7   Ask another learner to write down an unbalanced ion–electron equation (half equation) from Appendix 2 of the coursebook but without including the electron(s), e.g. $O_2 + 4H^+ \rightarrow 2H_2O$. The equation can be written either as shown or reversed. You then have to balance the equation. Do this by adding electrons to one or other side of the equation so that it balances. Then reverse the process: you select the equation and the other learner balances it. Continue until you are sure that you can balance these equations.

GETTING RID OF THE POISONS

Figure 20.1: This land has been contaminated by poisonous ions such as cadmium ions and cyanide ions. We can use electrochemistry to remove these ions.

In many places in the world, the land once occupied by old chemical industries, gasworks or fertiliser factories cannot be built on. This is because the ground is polluted with poisonous substances such as cadmium ions, Cd^{2+}, copper ions, Cu^{2+}, or cyanide ions, CN^- (Figure 20.1). Some countries have laws to prevent these 'brown field sites' from being used until the poisons have been removed. Electrochemistry can be used to remove some of these pollutants from the soil (Figure 20.2).

The surface of soil particles can be positively or negatively charged. Sometimes both charges are present on the surface of a single particle. The surface of negatively charged soil particles can attract positive ions such as Cd^{2+} or Cu^{2+} and hold them in place by ionic bonding. These harmful positive ions can be removed by ion exchange (the swapping of one ion by another). The process works like a battery in reverse.

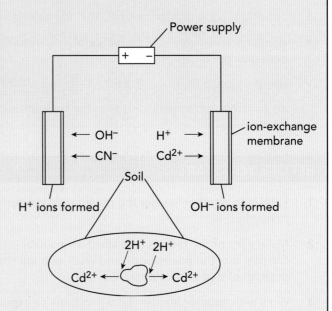

Figure 20.2: Exchanging ions in the soil by an electrochemical method.

*   Electrical energy from a power supply is passed through a chemical cell, which is made part of the soil. In practice, several pairs of electrodes are used.

*   The electrodes contain an ion-exchange membrane on the outside of an acid electrolyte, which circulates throughout the electrode.

CONTINUED

- The electrical energy breaks down water to OH^- ions at the cell cathode and H^+ ions at the cell anode.

- The OH^- ions and H^+ ions from this reaction pass through the water between the soil particles to the opposite electrodes.

- Some of the H^+ ions replace metal cations such as Cd^{2+} on the surface of the soil particles and some of the OH^- ions replace anions such as CN^-. When this happens, the Cd^{2+} and CN^- ions are released from the surface of the soil particles and go into solution.

- The Cd^{2+} ions move to the negative electrode and the CN^- ions move to positive electrode. These poisonous ions are then removed in the circulating electrolyte.

Questions for discussion

Discuss with another learner or group of learners:

- Suggest an advantage and disadvantage of this electrochemical process.

- Work with another learner to do some research using books or the internet to find out why cyanide ions are so poisonous and why nitrate ions, although present in fertilisers, are not good for the environment.

- Suggest why so many 'brown field sites' still exist in the world. Someone stated that 'the number of these polluted brown field sites is almost certain to increase in great number'. Suggest why this is not necessarily true.

20.1 Redox reactions revisited

In Chapter 7, you learned to construct equations for redox reactions from relevant half-equations. You also used the concept of oxidation numbers to show whether a particular reactant has been oxidised or reduced during a chemical reaction.

Electrons may be gained or lost in redox reactions.

- The species (atom, ion or molecule) losing electrons is being oxidised. It acts a reducing agent.

- The species gaining electrons is being reduced. It acts an oxidising agent.

Make sure that you can do Questions 1 and 2 before continuing with this chapter. Refer back to Chapter 7 if you need some help.

Questions

1   In each of the chemical reactions **a** to **c**:
   i   Which species gains electrons?
   ii Which species loses electrons?
   iii Which species is the oxidising agent?
   iv Which species is the reducing agent?

a $CuCl_2 + Fe \rightarrow FeCl_2 + Cu$
b $Cu + Br_2 \rightarrow Cu^{2+} + 2Br^-$
c $PbO_2 + SO_2 \rightarrow PbSO_4$

2   Construct full redox equations from the following pairs of half-equations.
   a   The reaction of iodide ions with hydrogen peroxide:
   $$I^- \rightarrow \tfrac{1}{2} I_2 + e^-$$
   $$H_2O_2 + 2H^+ + 2e^- \rightarrow 2H_2O$$
   b   The reaction of chloride ions with acidified manganese(IV) oxide:
   $$Cl^- \rightarrow \tfrac{1}{2} Cl_2 + e^-$$
   $$MnO_2 + 4H^+ + 2e^- \rightarrow Mn^{2+} + 2H_2O$$
   c   The reaction of acidified MnO_4^- ions with Fe^{2+} ions:
   $$Fe^{2+} \rightarrow Fe^{3+} + e^-$$
   $$MnO_4^- + 8H^+ + 5e^- \rightarrow Mn^{2+} + 4H_2O$$

20.2 Electrolysis

Electrolytic cells

Electrolysis is the decomposition of a compound into its elements by an electric current. It is often used to extract metals that are high in the reactivity series. These metals cannot be extracted by heating their ores with carbon. Electrolysis is also used to produce non-metals such as chlorine and to purify some metals. Electrolysis is generally carried out in an electrolysis cell (Figure 20.3).

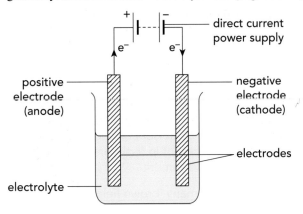

Figure 20.3: The main parts of an electrolysis cell. The actual structure of the cell will vary according to the element extracted. The e⁻ shows the direction of travel of the electrons around the external circuit.

In the electrolysis cell:

- the **electrolyte** is the compound that is decomposed. It is either a molten ionic compound or a concentrated aqueous solution of ions

- the **electrodes** are rods, made from either carbon (graphite) or metal, which conduct electricity to and from the electrolyte

  - the **anode** is the positive electrode

  - the **cathode** is the negative electrode

- the power supply must be direct current.

KEY WORDS

electrolysis: the decomposition of an ionic compound when molten or in aqueous solution by an electric current.

electrolyte: a molten ionic compound or an aqueous solution of ions that is decomposed during electrolysis.

electrode: a rod of metal or carbon (graphite) which conducts electricity to or from an electrolyte.

cathode: the negative electrode (where reduction reactions occur).

anode: the positive electrode (where oxidation reactions occur).

Question

3 a Why does an ionic compound have to be molten to undergo electrolysis?

b Give two properties of graphite that make it a suitable material for use as an electrode. Explain your answers.

Redox reactions in electrolysis

IMPORTANT

During electrolysis, reduction occurs at the cathode because ions gain electrons from the cathode, and oxidation occurs at the anode because ions lose electrons to the anode.

During electrolysis, the positive ions (cations) move to the cathode. When they reach the cathode they gain electrons from the cathode. For example:

$$Cu^{2+} + 2e^- \rightarrow Cu$$

$$2H^+ + 2e^- \rightarrow H_2$$

Gain of electrons is reduction. Reduction always occurs at the cathode.

If metal atoms are formed, they may be deposited as a layer of metal on the cathode. Alternatively, they may form a molten layer in the cell. If hydrogen gas is formed, it bubbles off.

The negative ions (anions) move to the anode. When they reach the anode they lose electrons to the anode. For example:

$$2Cl^- \rightarrow Cl_2 + 2e^-$$

$$4OH^- \rightarrow O_2 + 2H_2O + 4e^-$$

Loss of electrons is oxidation. Oxidation always occurs at the anode.

Electrolysis is a redox reaction. For example, when molten zinc chloride is electrolysed the electrode reactions are:

cathode: $Zn^{2+} + 2e^- \rightarrow Zn$ (reduction)

anode: $2Cl^- \rightarrow Cl_2 + 2e^-$ (oxidation)

The electron loss at the anode balances the electron gain at the cathode. Overall, the reaction is:

$$ZnCl_2 \rightarrow Zn + Cl_2$$

Question

4   a   Explain why cations move towards the cathode during electrolysis.

   b   When lead iodide, PbI_2, is electrolysed, the following reactions occur:

$$Pb^{2+} + 2e^- \rightarrow Pb \text{ and } 2I^- \rightarrow I_2 + 2e^-$$

   i   Which of these equations describes the reaction at the cathode? Explain your answer.

   ii   State the ox. no. change of each iodide ion in the reaction

$$2I^- \rightarrow I_2 + 2e^-$$

20.3 Quantitative electrolysis

The mass of substance deposited during electrolysis

The mass of a substance produced at an electrode during electrolysis is proportional to:

- the time over which a constant electric current passes

- the strength of the electric current.

Combining current and time, we get the relationship:

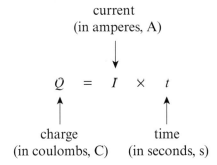

The mass of a substance produced at (or removed from) an electrode during electrolysis is proportional to the quantity of electricity (in coulombs) which passes through the electrolyte.

We can express the quantity of electricity in terms of a unit called the faraday (symbol F). One faraday is the quantity of electric charge carried by 1 mole of electrons

or 1 mole of singly charged ions. Its value is 96 500 C mol^{-1} (to 3 significant figures). So the relationship between the Faraday and the Avogadro constant is $F = Le$ where e is the charge on an electron.

During the electrolysis of silver nitrate solution, silver is deposited at the cathode:

$$Ag^+(aq) \quad + \quad e^- \quad \rightarrow \quad Ag(s)$$
$$1 \text{ mol} \qquad\qquad 1 \text{ mol} \qquad 1 \text{ mol}$$

One faraday of electricity (96 500 C) is required to deposit 1 mole of silver.

During the electrolysis of copper(II) sulfate solution, copper is deposited at the cathode:

$$Cu^{2+}(aq) \quad + \quad 2e^- \quad \rightarrow \quad Cu(s)$$
$$1 \text{ mol} \qquad\qquad 2 \text{ mol} \qquad 1 \text{ mol}$$

The equation shows that you need 2 moles of electrons to produce 1 mole of copper from Cu^{2+} ions. So it requires two faradays of electricity ($2 \times 96\,500$ C) to deposit 1 mole of copper.

During the electrolysis of molten sodium chloride, chlorine is produced at the anode:

$$2Cl^-(aq) \quad \rightarrow \quad Cl_2(g) \quad + \quad 2e^-$$
$$2 \text{ mol} \qquad\qquad 1 \text{ mol} \qquad 2 \text{ mol}$$

The equation shows that 2 moles of electrons are released when 1 mole of chlorine gas is formed from 2 moles of Cl^- ions. So it requires two faradays of electricity ($2 \times 96\,500$ C) to produce 1 mole of Cl_2.

During the electrolysis of an aqueous solution of sulfuric acid or aqueous sodium sulfate, oxygen is produced at the anode:

$$4OH^-(aq) \rightarrow O_2(g) + 2H_2O(l) + 4e^-$$

The equation shows that 4 moles of electrons are released when 1 mole of oxygen gas is formed from 4 moles of OH^- ions. So it requires 4 faradays of electricity ($4 \times 96\,500$ C) to produce 1 mole of O_2.

Calculating amount of substance produced during electrolysis

We can use the value of F to calculate:

- the mass of substance deposited at an electrode
- the volume of gas produced at an electrode.

WORKED EXAMPLES

1 Calculate the mass of lead deposited at the cathode during electrolysis when a current of 1.50 A flows through molten lead(II) bromide for 20.0 min.

(A_r value: [Pb] = 207; F = 96 500 C mol^{-1})

Solution

Step 1: Write the half-equation for the reaction.

$Pb^{2+} + 2e^- \rightarrow Pb$

Step 2: Find the number of coulombs required to deposit 1 mole of product at the electrode.

2 moles of electrons are required per mole of Pb formed:

$= 2F$

$= 2 \times 96\ 500$

$= 193\ 000$ C mol^{-1}

Step 3: Calculate the charge transferred during the electrolysis.

$Q = I \times t$

$= 1.50 \times 20 \times 60$

$= 1800$ C

Step 4: Calculate the mass by simple proportion using the relative atomic mass.

193 000 C deposits 1 mole Pb, which is 207 g Pb

so 1800 C deposits $\frac{1800}{193000} \times 207$

$= 1.93$ g Pb

2 Calculate the volume of oxygen produced at r.t.p. when a concentrated aqueous solution of sulfuric acid, H_2SO_4, is electrolysed for 30.0 min using a current of 0.50 A.

(F = 96 500 C mol^{-1}; 1 mole of gas occupies 24.0 dm^3 at r.t.p.)

Solution

Step 1: Write the half-equation for the reaction.

$4OH^-(aq) \rightarrow O_2(g) + 2H_2O(l) + 4e^-$

Step 2: Find the number of coulombs required to produce 1 mole of gas.

4 moles of electrons are released per mole of O_2 formed:

$= 4F$

$= 4 \times 96\ 500$

$= 386\ 000$ C mol^{-1}

Step 3: Calculate the charge transferred during the electrolysis.

$Q = I \times t$

$= 0.50 \times 30 \times 60$

$= 900$ C

Step 4: Calculate the volume by simple proportion using the relationship 1 mole of gas occupies 24.0 dm^3 at r.t.p.

386 000 C produces 1 mole O_2, which is 24 dm^3 O_2

so 900 C produces $\frac{900}{386000} \times 24.0$

$= 0.0560$ dm^3 O_2 at r.t.p.

Questions

5 Calculate the mass of silver deposited at the cathode during electrolysis when a current of 1.80 A flows through an aqueous solution of silver nitrate for 45.0 min.

(A_r value: [Ag] = 108; F = 96 500 C mol^{-1})

6 Calculate the volume of hydrogen produced at r.t.p. when a concentrated aqueous solution of sulfuric acid is electrolysed for 15.0 min using a current of 1.40 A.

(F = 96 500 C mol^{-1}; 1 mole of gas occupies 24.0 dm^3 at r.t.p.)

7 Calculate the volume of oxygen produced at r.t.p. when a concentrated aqueous solution of sodium sulfate is electrolysed for 55.0 min using a current of 0.70 A.

(F = 96 500 C mol^{-1}; 1 mole of gas occupies 24.0 dm^3 at r.t.p.)

Calculating the Avogadro constant by an electrolytic method

The Avogadro constant, L, is the number of specified particles in 1 mole (see Section 3.4).

We can use an electrolytic method to find a value for the Avogadro constant by calculating the charge associated with 1 mole of electrons.

$$L = \frac{\text{charge on 1 mole of electrons}}{\text{charge on 1 electron}}$$

We can calculate the charge on the electron by experiment. The results show us that the charge on the electron is approximately 1.60×10^{-19} C.

PRACTICAL ACTIVITY 20.1

Finding the charge on 1 mole of electrons

The charge on 1 mole of electrons can be found from a simple electrolytic experiment. The apparatus for this is shown in Figure 20.4.

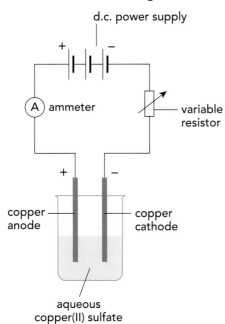

Figure 20.4: Apparatus for calculating the mass of copper deposited during the electrolysis of aqueous copper(II) sulfate.

Procedure

- weigh the pure copper anode and pure copper cathode separately
- arrange the apparatus as shown in Figure 20.4; the variable resistor is used to keep the current constant (about 0.2 amps)
- pass a constant electric current for a measured time interval (e.g. 40 minutes exactly)
- remove the cathode and anode and wash and dry them with distilled water and then with propanone
- reweigh the cathode and anode.

The cathode increases in mass because copper is deposited. The anode decreases in mass because the copper goes into solution as copper ions. The decrease in mass of the anode is measured. This is preferred because the copper does not always 'stick' to the cathode very well.

A sample calculation is shown below, using a current of 0.20 A for 34 min.

CONTINUED

- mass of anode at start of the experiment $= 56.53$ g
- mass of anode at end of experiment $= 56.40$ g
- mass of copper removed from anode $= 0.13$ g
- quantity of charge passed $Q = L \times t$
$$= 0.20 \times 34 \times 60$$
$$= 408 \text{ C}$$

To deposit 0.13 g of copper requires 408 C, so to deposit 1 mole of copper (63.5 g) requires $\frac{63.5}{0.13} \times 408$ C

But the equation for the electrolysis shows that 2 moles of electrons are needed to produce 1 mole of copper:

$$Cu^{2+} + 2e^- \rightarrow Cu$$

The charge on 1 mole of electrons $= \frac{63.5}{0.13} \times 408 \times \frac{1}{2}$

$$= 99\,646 \text{ C}$$

If the charge on one electron is 1.60×10^{-19} C,

$$L = \frac{99\,646}{1.60 \times 10^{-19}} = 6.2 \times 10^{23} \text{ mol}^{-1} \text{ (to 2 significant figures)}$$

This is in good agreement with the accurate value of 6.02×10^{23} mol^{-1}.

Questions

8 A learner passed a constant electric current of 0.15 A through a solution of silver nitrate, using pure silver electrodes, for 45 min exactly. The mass of the anode decreased by 0.45 g. Use this data to calculate the charge on a mole of electrons.

(A_r value: [Ag] = 108)

9 An accurate value of the Faraday constant is 96 485 C mol^{-1}. An accurate value for the charge on one electron is 1.6022×10^{-19} C. Use these values to calculate a value of the Avogadro constant to 5 significant figures.

20.4 Electrode potentials

Introducing electrode potentials

KEY WORD

electrode potential, E: the voltage measured for a half-cell compared with another half-cell.

A redox equilibrium exists between two chemically related species that are in different oxidation states. For example, when a copper rod is placed in contact with an aqueous solution of its ions the following equilibrium exists:

$$Cu^{2+}(aq) + 2e^- \rightleftharpoons Cu(s)$$

There are two opposing reactions in this equilibrium.

- Metal atoms from the rod entering the solution as metal ions. This leaves electrons behind on the surface of the rod. For example:

$$Cu(s) \rightarrow Cu^{2+}(aq) + 2e^-$$

- Ions in solution accepting electrons from the metal rod and being deposited as metal atoms on the surface of the rod. For example:

$$Cu^{2+}(aq) + 2e^- \rightarrow Cu(s)$$

The redox equilibrium is established when the rate of electron gain equals the rate of electron loss.

For unreactive metals such as copper, if this equilibrium is compared with the equilibrium set up by other metals, the equilibrium set up by copper lies further over to the right.

$$Cu^{2+}(aq) + 2e^- \rightleftharpoons Cu(s)$$

$Cu^{2+}(aq)$ ions are therefore relatively easy to reduce. They gain electrons readily to form copper metal.

For reactive metals such as vanadium, the equilibrium lies further over to the left.

$$V^{2+}(aq) + 2e^- \rightleftharpoons V(s)$$

$V^{2+}(aq)$ ions are therefore relatively difficult to reduce. They gain electrons much less readily by comparison.

The position of equilibrium differs for different combinations of metals placed in solutions of their ions.

When we place a metal into a solution of its ions, we establish an electric potential (voltage) between the metal and the metal ions in solution. We cannot measure this potential directly. But we can measure the difference in potential between the metal / metal ion system and another system. We call this value the **electrode potential**, *E*. Electrode potential is measured in volts. The system we use for comparison is the *standard hydrogen electrode*.

Scientists think the absolute electrical potentials that we cannot measure are caused by the formation of an electrical double layer when an element is placed in a solution of its ions. For example, when zinc is placed in a solution containing zinc ions, a tiny number of zinc atoms on the surface of the metal are converted to zinc ions, which go into solution. This leaves an excess of electrons on the surface of the zinc. The solution around the metal now has excess Zn^{2+} ions. Some of these cations near the surface of the zinc are attracted to its surface. So an electrical double layer is formed. This build-up of charge causes an electric potential (voltage) between the metal and the metal ions in solution (Figure 20.5).

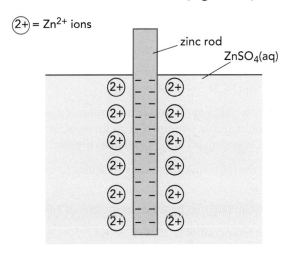

Figure 20.5: The separation of charge when a zinc rod is placed in a solution of Zn^{2+} ions results in an electrical double layer.

The standard hydrogen electrode

The standard hydrogen electrode is one of several types of half-cell that can be used as reference electrodes. Figure 20.6 shows a standard hydrogen electrode.

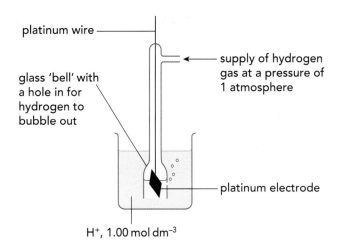

Figure 20.6: The standard hydrogen electrode.

This electrode consists of:

- hydrogen gas at 101 kPa pressure, in equilibrium with H^+ ions of concentration 1.00 mol dm⁻³

- a platinum electrode covered with platinum black in contact with the hydrogen gas and the H^+ ions.

The platinum black is finely divided platinum. This allows close contact of hydrogen gas and H^+ ions in solution so that equilibrium between H_2 gas and H^+ ions is established quickly. The platinum electrode is inert so it does not take part in the reaction.

We measure standard electrode potential $E^\ominus$ values for all half-cells relative to this electrode. When connected to another half-cell, the value read on the voltmeter gives the standard electrode potential for that half-cell.

The half-equation for the hydrogen electrode can be written:

$$2H^+(aq) + 2e^- \rightleftharpoons H_2(g)$$

or

$$H^+(aq) + e^- \rightleftharpoons \tfrac{1}{2}H_2(g)$$

The way that you balance the half-equation makes no difference to the value of $E^\ominus$. The equation does not affect the tendency for the element to gain electrons.

Electrode potential and redox reactions

Electrode potential values give us an indication of how easy it is to reduce a substance.

Note that:

- By convention, the electrode potential refers to the reduction reaction. So the electrons appear on the left-hand side of the half-equation. For example:

  $Al^{3+}(aq) + 3e^- \rightleftharpoons Al(s)$

- The more positive (or less negative) the electrode potential, the easier it is to reduce the ions on the left. So the metal on the right is relatively unreactive and is a relatively poor reducing agent. For example:

  $Ag^+(aq) + e^- \rightleftharpoons Ag(s)$ voltage = +0.80 V

- The more negative (or less positive) the electrode potential, the more difficult it is to reduce the ions on the left. So the metal on the right is relatively reactive and is a relatively good reducing agent. For example:

  $Zn^{2+}(aq) + 2e^- \rightleftharpoons Zn(s)$ voltage = −0.76 V

Question

10 Refer to the list of electrode potentials below to answer parts **a** to **d**.

$Ag^+(aq) + e^- \rightleftharpoons Ag(s)$	voltage = +0.80 V
$Co^{2+}(aq) + 2e^- \rightleftharpoons Co(s)$	voltage = −0.28 V
$Cu^{2+}(aq) + 2e^- \rightleftharpoons Cu(s)$	voltage = +0.34 V
$Pb^{2+}(aq) + 2e^- \rightleftharpoons Pb(s)$	voltage = −0.13 V
$Zn^{2+}(aq) + 2e^- \rightleftharpoons Zn(s)$	voltage = −0.76 V

  a Which metal in the list is the best reducing agent?

  b Which metal ion in the list is most difficult to reduce?

  c Which metal in the list is most reactive?

  d Which metal ion in the list is the easiest to reduce?

20.5 Combining half-cells

KEY WORD

half-cell: one half of an electrochemical cell which either donates electrons to or receives electrons from an external circuit when connected to another half-cell.

Figure 20.7: The Cu^{2+} / Cu half-cell.

In order to measure the electrode potential relating to the half-equation

$Cu^{2+}(aq) + 2e^- \rightarrow Cu(s)$

we place a pure copper rod in a solution of $Cu^{2+}(aq)$ ions (for example copper(II) sulfate solution). This Cu^{2+} / Cu system is called a **half-cell** (Figure 20.7).

We use the following standard conditions to make the half-cell:

- the $Cu^{2+}(aq)$ ions have a concentration of 1.00 mol dm^{-3}

- the temperature is 25 °C (298 K)

- the rod must be pure copper.

If we connect two half-cells together, we have made an electrochemical cell. We can measure the voltage between these two half-cells. Figure 20.8 shows a Cu^{2+} / Cu half-cell connected to a Zn^{2+} / Zn half-cell to make a complete electrochemical cell.

Half-cells are connected together using:

- wires connecting the metal rods in each half-cell to a high-resistance voltmeter. The electrons flow round this external circuit from the metal with the more negative (or less positive) electrode potential to the metal with the less negative (or more positive) electrode potential

• a salt bridge to complete the electrical circuit allowing the movement of ions between the two half-cells so that ionic balance is maintained. A salt bridge does *not* allow the movement of electrons.

A salt bridge can be made from a strip of filter paper (or other inert porous material) soaked in a saturated solution of potassium nitrate.

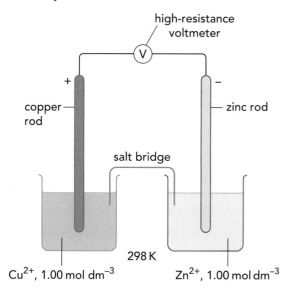

Figure 20.8: One type of electrochemical cell is made by connecting a Cu^{2+} / Cu half-cell to a Zn^{2+} / Zn half-cell. The voltage generated by this cell is +1.10 V.

The voltages for the half-cells in Figure 20.8 can be represented by the following half-equations:

$Cu^{2+}(aq) + 2e^- \rightleftharpoons Cu(s)$ voltage = +0.34 V

$Zn^{2+}(aq) + 2e^- \rightleftharpoons Zn(s)$ voltage = −0.76 V

The relative values of these voltages tell us that Zn^{2+} ions are more difficult to reduce than Cu^{2+} ions. So Cu^{2+} ions will accept electrons from the Zn^{2+} / Zn half-cell and zinc will lose electrons to the Cu^{2+} / Cu half-cell.

Half-equations can be used to show us the contents of half-cells. A half-cell does not have to be a metal / metal ion system. We can construct half-cells for any half-equation written. For example:

$Fe^{3+}(aq) + e^- \rightleftharpoons Fe^{2+}(aq)$

$Cl_2(g) + 2e^- \rightleftharpoons 2Cl^-(aq)$

$MnO_4^-(aq) + 8H^+(aq) + 5e^- \rightleftharpoons Mn^{2+}(aq) + 4H_2O(l)$

Note that the oxidised species (having the higher oxidation number) is always written on the left-hand side and the reduced form on the right-hand side.

Question

11 a Suggest why aqueous silver nitrate is not used in a salt bridge when connecting a half-cell containing Zn and 1.00 mol dm⁻³ $ZnCl_2(aq)$ to another half-cell.

    b Write half-equations for the reactions taking place in the half-cells below. Write each equation as a reduction (electrons on the left-hand side of the equation).

        i Cr^{2+} / Cr^{3+}

        ii Br_2 / $2Br^-$

        iii $O_2 + H_2O$ / OH^- (make sure that you balance the equation)

        iv $VO^{2+} + H_2O$ / $VO_2^+ + H^+$ (make sure that you balance the equation)

Standard electrode potential

The position of equilibrium of a reaction may be affected by changes in the concentration of reagents, temperature and pressure of gases. The voltage of an electrochemical cell will also depend on these factors, so we should use standard conditions when comparing electrode potentials. These are:

• concentration of ions at 1.00 mol dm⁻³

• a temperature of 25 °C (298 K)

• any gases should be at a pressure of 1 atmosphere (101 kPa)

• the value of the electrode potential of the half-cell is measured relative to the standard hydrogen electrode.

Under these conditions, the electrode potential we measure is called the **standard electrode potential**. This has the symbol, $E^{\ominus}$. It is spoken of as 'E standard'. These are sometimes referred to as standard reduction potentials because they refer to the reduction reaction (addition of electrons).

> **KEY DEFINITION**
>
> **standard electrode potential:** the voltage produced when a standard half-cell (ion concentration 1.00 mol dm⁻³ at 298 K) is connected to a standard hydrogen electrode under standard conditions.

The standard electrode potential for a half-cell is the voltage measured under standard conditions with a standard hydrogen electrode as the other half-cell.

Measuring standard electrode potentials

There are three main types of half-cell whose $E^\ominus$ value can be obtained when connected to a standard hydrogen electrode:

- metal / metal ion half-cell
- non-metal / non-metal ion half-cell
- ion / ion half-cell.

Half-cells containing metals and metal ions

Figure 20.9 shows how to measure the $E^\ominus$ value for a Cu^{2+} / Cu half-cell. The Cu^{2+} / Cu half-cell is connected to a standard hydrogen electrode and the voltage measured. The voltage is +0.34 V. The copper is the positive terminal (positive pole) of the cell and the hydrogen electrode is the negative terminal. The two half-equations are:

$$Cu^{2+}(aq) + 2e^- \rightleftharpoons Cu(s) \qquad E^\ominus = +0.34 \text{ V}$$
$$H^+(aq) + e^- \rightleftharpoons \tfrac{1}{2}H_2(g) \qquad E^\ominus = 0.00 \text{ V}$$

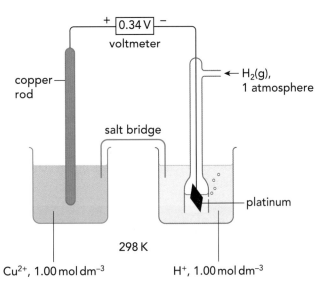

Figure 20.9: Measuring the standard electrode potential of a Cu^{2+} / Cu half-cell.

- The $E^\ominus$ values show us that Cu^{2+} ions are easier to reduce than H^+ ions (they have a more positive $E^\ominus$ value).

- Cu^{2+} ions are more likely to gain electrons than H^+ ions.

- So Cu^{2+} ions will accept electrons from the H^+ / H_2 half-cell and H_2 will lose electrons to the Cu^{2+} / Cu half-cell.

Figure 20.10 shows how to measure the $E^\ominus$ value for a Zn^{2+} / Zn half-cell. The voltage of the Zn^{2+} / Zn half-cell is −0.76 V. The zinc is the negative terminal (negative pole) of the cell and the hydrogen electrode is the positive terminal. The two half-equations are:

$$H^+(aq) + e^- \rightleftharpoons \tfrac{1}{2}H_2(g) \qquad E^\ominus = 0.00 \text{ V}$$
$$Zn^{2+}(aq) + 2e^- \rightleftharpoons Zn(s) \qquad E^\ominus = -0.76 \text{ V}$$

- The $E^\ominus$ values show us that Zn^{2+} ions are more difficult to reduce than H^+ ions (they have a more negative $E^\ominus$ value).

- Zn^{2+} ions are less likely to gain electrons than H^+ ions.

- So Zn will lose electrons to the H^+ / H_2 half-cell and H^+ ions will gain electrons from the Zn^{2+} / Zn half-cell.

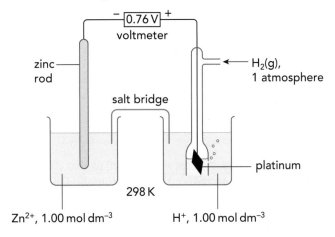

Figure 20.10: Measuring the standard electrode potential of a Zn^{2+} / Zn half-cell.

From these two examples, we can see that:

- Reduction takes place at the positive terminal of the cell. For example, in the Zn^{2+} / Zn; H^+ / H_2 cell:

$$H^+(aq) + e^- \rightleftharpoons \tfrac{1}{2}H_2(g)$$

- Oxidation takes place at the negative terminal of the cell. For example, in the Zn^{2+} / Zn: H^+ / H_2 cell:

$$Zn(s) \rightleftharpoons Zn^{2+}(aq) + 2e^-$$

Question

12 a Write half-equations for the three reactions taking place in the half-cells shown on the left in Figure 20.11.

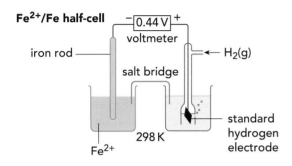

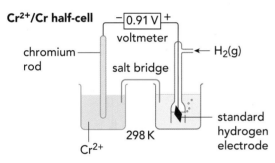

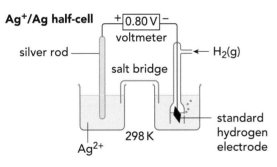

Figure 20.11: Measuring standard electrode potentials.

b What are the standard electrode potentials for these half-cell reactions?

c List all the necessary conditions in each cell.

Half-cells containing non-metals and non-metal ions

In half-cells that do not contain a metal, electrical contact with the solution is made by using platinum wire or platinum foil as an electrode. The redox equilibrium is established at the surface of the platinum. The platinum electrode is inert and so plays no part in the reaction.

The platinum must be in contact with both the element and the aqueous solution of its ions.

Figure 20.12 shows a Cl_2 / Cl^- half-cell connected to a standard hydrogen electrode. The voltage of the Cl_2 / Cl^- half-cell is +1.36 V. So the Cl_2 / Cl^- half-cell forms the positive terminal of the cell and the hydrogen electrode is the negative terminal. The two half-equations are:

$$\frac{1}{2}Cl_2(g) + e^- \rightleftharpoons Cl^-(aq) \qquad E^\ominus = +1.36 \text{ V}$$
$$H^+(aq) + e^- \rightleftharpoons \frac{1}{2}H_2(g) \qquad E^\ominus = 0.00 \text{ V}$$

- The $E^\ominus$ values show us that Cl_2 molecules are easier to reduce than H^+ ions (they have a more positive $E^\ominus$ value).

- Cl_2 molecules are more likely to gain electrons than H^+ ions.

- So Cl_2 molecules will gain electrons from the H^+ / $\frac{1}{2}H_2$ half-cell and H_2 molecules will lose electrons to the $\frac{1}{2}Cl_2$ / Cl^- half-cell.

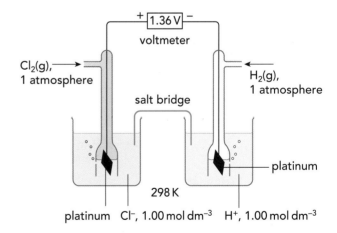

Figure 20.12: Measuring the standard electrode potential of a Cl_2 / Cl^- half-cell.

Questions

13 a Look at Figure 20.13. Write a half-equation for the half-cell on the left-hand side.

b What is the $E^\ominus$ value for this half-cell?

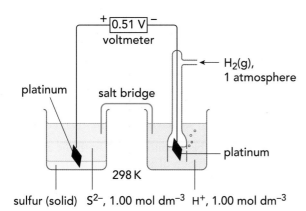

Figure 20.13: Measuring the standard electrode potential of an S / S^{2-} half-cell.

14 Draw a diagram to show how you would measure the standard electrode potential for the half-cell:

$$\frac{1}{2} I_2 + e^- \rightleftharpoons I^-(aq)$$

Include the actual $E^\ominus$ value of +0.54 V on your diagram.

Half-cells containing ions of the same element in different oxidation states

Half-cells can contain two ions of different oxidation states derived from the same element. For example, a mixture of Fe^{3+} and Fe^{2+} ions can form a half-cell using a platinum electrode. In this type of half-cell, the concentration of each ion present is 1.00 mol dm^{-3}. Figure 20.14 shows the set-up for a cell used to measure the standard electrode potential of the Fe^{3+} / Fe^{2+} half-cell.

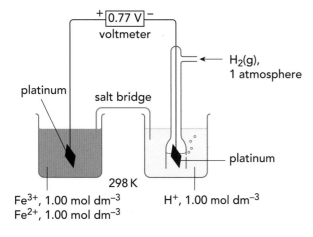

Figure 20.14: Measuring the standard electrode potential of the Fe^{3+} / Fe^{2+} half-cell.

The voltage of this half-cell is +0.77 V.

$$Fe^{3+}(aq) + e^- \rightleftharpoons Fe^{2+}(aq) \qquad E^\ominus = +0.77 \text{ V}$$

Some reactions involve several ionic species. For example:

$$MnO_4^-(aq) + 8H^+(aq) + 5e^- \rightleftharpoons Mn^{2+}(aq) + 4H_2O(l)$$

The H$^+$ ions are included because they are essential for the conversion of MnO$_4^-$ (manganate(VII) ions) to Mn^{2+} ions.

So the half-cell contains:

- 1.00 mol dm^{-3} MnO$_4^-$(aq) ions
- 1.00 mol dm^{-3} Mn^{2+}(aq) ions
- 1.00 mol dm^{-3} H$^+$(aq) ions.

Figure 20.15 shows the set-up of a cell used to measure the standard electrode potential of the MnO$_4^-$ / Mn^{2+} half-cell.

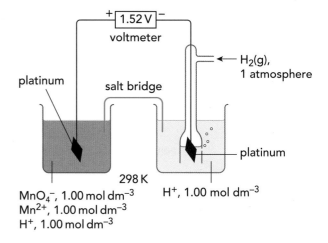

Figure 20.15: Measuring the standard electrode potential of the MnO$_4^-$ / Mn^{2+} half-cell.

Questions

15 What is the $E^\ominus$ value for the half-cell on the left-hand side of Figure 20.15?

16 Why is platinum used in preference to other metals in half-cells where the reaction does not involve a metallic element?

17 Show, with the aid of a diagram, how you would measure the $E^\ominus$ value for the half-cell shown by the equation:

$$VO^{2+} + 2H^+ + e^- \rightleftharpoons V^{3+} + H_2O$$

20.6 Using $E^{\ominus}$ values

Using $E^{\ominus}$ values to predict cell voltages

We can use $E^{\ominus}$ values to calculate the voltage of an electrochemical cell made up of two half-cells, even when neither of them is a standard hydrogen electrode. The voltage measured is the difference between the $E^{\ominus}$ values of the two half-cells. We call this value the **standard cell potential**.

> ### KEY DEFINITION
>
> **standard cell potential:** the difference in standard electrode potential between two specified half cells.

For the electrochemical cell shown in Figure 20.16, the two relevant half-equations are:

$$Ag^+(aq) + e^- \rightleftharpoons Ag(s) \qquad E^{\ominus} = +0.80 \text{ V}$$
$$Zn^{2+}(aq) + 2e^- \rightleftharpoons Zn(s) \qquad E^{\ominus} = -0.76 \text{ V}$$

The voltage of this cell is $+0.80 - (-0.76) = +1.56$ V (Figure 20.17).

Note that in order to calculate the cell voltage, we always subtract the less positive $E^{\ominus}$ value from the more positive $E^{\ominus}$ value.

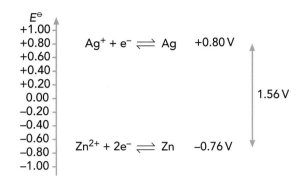

Figure 20.17: The difference between +0.80 V and −0.76 V is +1.56 V.

The $E^{\ominus}$ value for the Ag^+ / Ag half-cell is more positive than for the Zn^{2+} / Zn half-cell. So the Ag^+ / Ag half-cell is the positive pole and the Zn^{2+} / Zn half-cell is the negative pole of the cell.

For the electrochemical cell shown in Figure 20.18, the relevant half-equations are:

$$Fe^{3+}(aq) + e^- \rightleftharpoons Fe^{2+}(aq) \qquad E^{\ominus} = +0.77 \text{ V}$$
$$Cu^{2+}(aq) + 2e^- \rightleftharpoons Cu(s) \qquad E^{\ominus} = +0.34 \text{ V}$$

The voltage of this cell is $+0.77 - (+0.34) = +0.43$ V.

The $E^{\ominus}$ value for the Fe^{3+} / Fe^{2+} half-cell is more positive than for the Cu^{2+} / Cu half-cell. So the Fe^{3+} / Fe^{2+} half-cell is the positive pole and the Cu^{2+} / Cu half-cell is the negative pole of the cell.

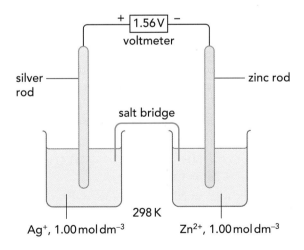

Figure 20.16: An Ag^+ / Ag, Zn^{2+} / Zn electrochemical cell.

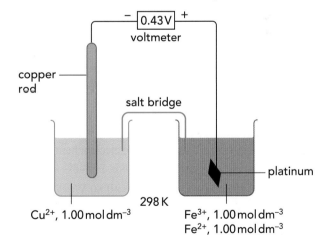

Figure 20.18: A Cu^+ / Cu, Fe^{3+} / Fe^{2+} electrochemical cell.

Write down two half-reactions and their standard electrode potentials from Appendix 2 of this coursebook. Start by choosing simple examples. Share this example with another learner. Both of you will now draw and label a diagram of the electrochemical cell that can be made by coupling these half-reactions. Compare your diagram with the other learner and find a similar diagram in the coursebook to check if you were correct.

What could you do to try and improve your drawing / labelling?

Questions

18 **a** Draw a diagram of an electrochemical cell consisting of a Cr^{3+} / Cr half-cell and a Cl_2 / Cl^- half-cell.

  b Use the data in Appendix 2 to calculate the cell voltage.

  c Which half-cell is the positive pole?

19 **a** Draw a diagram of an electrochemical cell consisting of a Mn^{2+} / Mn half-cell and a Pb^{2+} / Pb half-cell.

  b Use the data in Appendix 2 to calculate the cell voltage.

  c Which half-cell is the positive pole?

$E^\ominus$ values and the direction of electron flow

We can deduce the direction of electron flow in the wires in the external circuit by comparing the $E^\ominus$ values for the two half-cells which make up the electrochemical cell. For example, in Figure 20.16 these voltages are:

$$Ag^+(aq) + e^- \rightleftharpoons Ag(s) \qquad E^\ominus = +0.80 \text{ V}$$

$$Zn^{2+}(aq) + 2e^- \rightleftharpoons Zn(s) \qquad E^\ominus = -0.76 \text{ V}$$

The relative values of these voltages tell us that Zn^{2+} ions are more difficult to reduce than Ag^+ ions. So:

- Zn metal will lose electrons to the Ag^+ / Ag half-cell

- Ag^+ ions will accept electrons from the Zn^{2+} / Zn half-cell.

The electrons move through the wires in the external circuit. They do not travel through the electrolyte solution.

So the electron flow is from the Zn^{2+} / Zn half-cell to the Ag^+ / Ag half-cell. In other words, the flow is from the negative pole to the positive pole. It may help you to remember that the more *positive* pole attracts the *negative* electrons.

1 The positive pole of a cell is the half-cell which has the less negative or more positive $E^\ominus$ value.

2 The direction of electron flow through the external circuit is from the half-cell with the more negative (less positive) value of $E^\ominus$ to the half-cell with the less negative (or more positive) value of $E^\ominus$.

In the electrochemical cell in Figure 20.18, the electrons move in the external circuit from the Cu^{2+} / Cu half-cell to the Fe^{3+} / Fe^{2+} half-cell.

$$Fe^{3+}(aq) + e^- \rightleftharpoons Fe^{2+}(aq) \qquad E^\ominus = +0.77 \text{ V}$$

$$Cu^{2+}(aq) + 2e^- \rightleftharpoons Cu(s) \qquad E^\ominus = +0.34 \text{ V}$$

The negative pole of this cell is provided by the Cu^{2+} / Cu half-cell. This because the Cu^{2+} / Cu half-cell is better at losing electrons than the Fe^{3+} / Fe^{2+} half-cell.

Question

20 State the direction of the electron flow in the electrochemical cells represented by the following pairs of half-equations. Use the data in Appendix 2 to help you.

  a $F_2 + 2e^- \rightleftharpoons 2F^-$ and $Mn^{2+} + 2e^- \rightleftharpoons Mn$

  b $Sn^{4+} + 2e^- \rightleftharpoons Sn^{2+}$ and $I_2 + 2e^- \rightleftharpoons 2I^-$

  c $Cr_2O_7^{2-} + 14H^+ + 6e^- \rightleftharpoons 2Cr^{3+} + 7H_2O$ and $Cu^{2+} + 2e^- \rightleftharpoons Cu$

  d $Ni^{2+} + 2e^- \rightleftharpoons Ni$ and $Fe^{3+} + 3e^- \rightleftharpoons Fe$

Using $E^{\ominus}$ values to predict if a reaction will occur

Standard electrode potential values, $E^{\ominus}$, give us a measure of how easy or difficult it is to oxidise or reduce a species. We can compare the oxidising and reducing powers of elements and ions by comparing the $E^{\ominus}$ values for their half reactions.

Figure 20.19 compares the oxidising and reducing powers of selected elements and ions. The $E^{\ominus}$ values are listed in order of increasingly negative values. For each half-equation, the more oxidised form is on the left and the more reduced form is on the right.

- The more positive the value of $E^{\ominus}$, the greater the tendency for the half-equation to proceed in the forward direction.

- The less positive the value of $E^{\ominus}$, the greater the tendency for the half-equation to proceed in the reverse direction.

- The more positive the value of $E^{\ominus}$, the easier it is to reduce the species on the left of the half-equation.

- The less positive the value of $E^{\ominus}$, the easier it is to oxidise the species on the right of the half-equation.

We can make an electrochemical cell from the two half-cells:

$$Cu^{2+}(aq) + 2e^- \rightleftharpoons Cu(s) \qquad E^{\ominus} = +0.34 \text{ V}$$

$$Zn^{2+}(aq) + 2e^- \rightleftharpoons Zn(s) \qquad E^{\ominus} = -0.76 \text{ V}$$

When these two half-cells are connected together, a reaction takes place in each of the half-cells. The $E^{\ominus}$ values can be used to predict whether the reaction happening in each half-cell is a reduction (i.e. forward direction) reaction, or an oxidation (i.e. backwards direction) reaction. If the reactions happening in each half-cell are combined, we can produce an ionic equation for the reaction that takes place in the electrochemical cell as a whole.

Cu^{2+} has a greater tendency to gain electrons than Zn^{2+}, so the chemical reaction that proceeds in this half-cell is in the forward direction:

$$Cu^{2+}(aq) + 2e^- \rightarrow Cu(s)$$

Zn has a greater tendency to lose electrons than Cu. This means the chemical reaction that proceeds in this half-cell is in the reverse direction:

$$Zn(s) \rightarrow Zn^{2+}(aq) + 2e^-$$

We can combine these two half-equations to show the direction of the reaction in the electrochemical cell as a whole.

$$Zn(s) + Cu^{2+}(aq) \rightarrow Zn^{2+}(aq) + Cu(s)$$

This is the reaction taking place in the electrochemical cell. But it is also the reaction that takes place if a piece of zinc metal is placed directly into a 1.00 mol dm⁻³ solution of Cu^{2+} ions. A reaction is said to be **feasible** if it is likely to occur. The reaction between zinc metal and copper ions is feasible.

> ### KEY WORD
>
> **feasible:** likely to take place, e.g. a reaction is likely to be feasible if $E^{\ominus}_{cell}$ has a positive value.

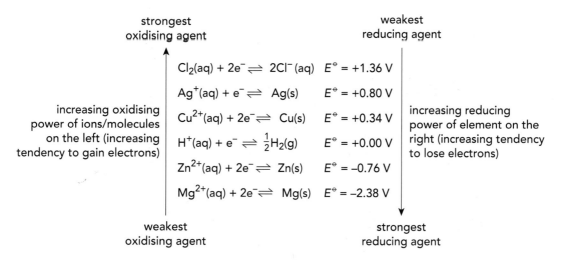

Figure 20.19: Standard electrode potentials for some oxidising and reducing agents.

Figure 20.20: As predicted by the $E^\ominus$ values, zinc reacts with Cu^{2+} ions but copper does not react with Zn^{2+} ions.

IMPORTANT

1 When two half-cells are joined, the half-cell with the more positive value of $E^\ominus$ accepts electrons more readily and the reaction proceeds in the forward direction.

2 A redox reaction occurs in the direction where the better oxidising agent reacts with the better reducing agent.

WORKED EXAMPLE

3 Will chlorine oxidise Fe^{2+} ions to Fe^{3+} ions?

Solution

- Write down the two half-equations with the more positive $E^\ominus$ value first.

$$\tfrac{1}{2}Cl_2(g) + e^- \rightleftharpoons Cl^-(aq) \qquad E^\ominus = +1.36 \text{ V}$$
$$Fe^{3+}(aq) + e^- \rightarrow Fe^{2+}(aq) \qquad E^\ominus = +0.77 \text{ V}$$

- Identify the stronger oxidising agent and the stronger reducing agent.

If the forward reaction is feasible, the reverse reaction (between Cu metal and zinc ions) is *not* feasible. If a piece of copper metal is placed directly into a 1.00 mol dm^{-3} solution of Zn^{2+} ions, no reaction takes place.

We can predict whether a reaction is likely to occur by referring to a list of half-reactions with their $E^\ominus$ values listed in descending order from most positive to most negative (see Figure 20.20). When we select two half-equations, the direction of the reaction is given by a clockwise pattern (reactant, product, reactant, product) starting from the top left as shown in Figure 20.21 for the cell made from the two half-cells Cu^{2+} / Cu and Zn^{2+} / Zn.

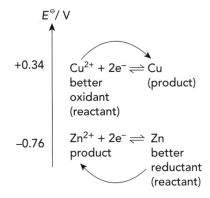

Figure 20.21: A reaction occurs in a direction so that the stronger oxidising agent reacts with the stronger reducing agent.

The following Worked examples shows how we can use $E^\ominus$ values to predict whether a reaction occurs or not.

Cl_2 is the better oxidising agent. This is because the more positive value of $E^\ominus$ indicates that Cl_2 molecules are more likely to accept electrons than are Fe^{3+} ions.

Fe^{2+} is the better reducing agent. This is because the more negative value of $E^\ominus$ indicates that Fe^{2+} ions are more likely to release electrons than are Cl^- ions.

- The stronger oxidising agent reacts with the stronger reducing agent, meaning that the reaction is feasible.

CONTINUED

- The top reaction goes in the forward direction and the bottom reaction goes in the reverse direction:

$$\tfrac{1}{2} Cl_2(g) + e^- \rightleftharpoons Cl^-(aq)$$

$$Fe^{2+}(aq) \rightleftharpoons Fe^{3+}(aq) + e^-$$

- Combine the two half-equations:

$$\tfrac{1}{2} Cl_2(g) + Fe^{2+}(aq) \rightarrow Cl^-(aq) + Fe^{3+}(aq)$$

This reaction is feasible. The prediction made using $E^\ominus$ values is correct, this reaction takes place in a suitable electrochemical cell, or when

Cl_2 gas is bubbled into a 1.00 mol dm^{-3} solution of Fe^{2+} ions.

This means that this reaction:

$$Cl^-(aq) + Fe^{3+}(aq) \rightarrow \tfrac{1}{2} Cl_2(g) + Fe^{2+}(aq)$$

is *not* feasible. If a 1.00 mol dm^{-3} solution of Fe^{3+} ions is added to a 1.00 mol dm^{-3} solution of Cl^- ions, no reaction takes place. This prediction has been made using $E^\ominus$ values, and it is correct.

$E^\ominus$ values are a very powerful tool for predicting which redox reactions are feasible, and which ones are not feasible.

WORKED EXAMPLE

4   Will iodine, I_2, oxidise Fe^{2+} ions to Fe^{3+} ions?

Solution

- Give the two half-equations, with most positive $E^\ominus$ value first.

$$Fe^{3+}(aq) + e^- \rightleftharpoons Fe^{2+}(aq) \qquad E^\ominus = +0.77 \text{ V}$$

$$\tfrac{1}{2} I_2(aq) + e^- \rightleftharpoons I^-(aq) \qquad E^\ominus = +0.54 \text{ V}$$

- Identify the stronger oxidising agent and the stronger reducing agent.

Fe^{3+} is the better oxidising agent. It is more likely to accept electrons than I_2 molecules.

I^- is the better reducing agent. It is more likely to release electrons than Fe^{2+} ions.

- I_2 is a relatively weaker oxidising agent and Fe^{2+} is a relatively weaker reducing agent. So the reaction is *not* feasible. (The reaction that is feasible is the reaction between Fe^{3+} ions and I^- ions.)

WORKED EXAMPLE

5   Will hydrogen peroxide, H_2O_2, reduce acidified manganate(VII) ions, MnO_4^-, to Mn^{2+} ions?

Solution

- Write down the two half-equations with the more positive $E^\ominus$ value first.

$$MnO_4^-(aq) + 8H^+(aq) + 5e^-$$
$$\rightleftharpoons Mn^{2+}(aq) + 4H_2O(l) \quad E^\ominus = +1.52 \text{ V}$$

$$O_2(g) + 2H^+(aq) + 2e^-$$
$$\rightleftharpoons H_2O_2(aq) \quad E^\ominus = +0.68 \text{ V}$$

- Identify the stronger oxidising agent and the stronger reducing agent.

The system $MnO_4^- + H^+$ is the better oxidising agent. It is more likely to accept electrons than the system $O_2 + 2H^+$.

Figure 20.22: If the KMnO$_4$(aq) is acidified, would it be safe to do this in an open lab or would chlorine gas be produced? You will answer this question in Question 21, part **a**.

CONTINUED

H_2O_2 is the better reducing agent. It is more likely to release electrons than Mn^{2+} ions.

- The stronger oxidising agent reacts with the stronger reducing agent, so the reaction is feasible.

- The top reaction goes in the forward direction and the bottom reaction goes in the reverse direction:

$$MnO_4^-(aq) + 8H^+(aq) + 5e^- \rightleftharpoons Mn^{2+}(aq) + 4H_2O(l)$$

$$H_2O_2(aq) \rightleftharpoons O_2(g) + 2H^+(aq) + 2e^-$$

- Balance the electrons, so that ten electrons are involved in each half-equation:

$$2MnO_4^-(aq) + 16H^+(aq) + 10e^- \rightleftharpoons 2Mn^{2+}(aq) + 8H_2O(l)$$

$$5H_2O_2(aq) \rightleftharpoons 5O_2(g) + 10H^+(aq) + 10e^-$$

- Combine the two half-equations:

$$2MnO_4^-(aq) + 6H^+(aq) + 5H_2O_2(aq) \rightleftharpoons 2Mn^{2+}(aq) + 8H_2O(l) + 5O_2(g)$$

Note that 10 H^+ ions have been cancelled from each side.

We can use the relative voltage of the half-cells to predict whether a reaction takes place without considering which species is the best oxidant or reductant. The procedure is given in Worked examples 6 and 7.

WORKED EXAMPLES

6 Will bromine oxidise silver to silver ions?

Solution

Step 1: Write the equation for the suggested reaction.

$$\tfrac{1}{2}Br_2 + Ag \rightarrow Br^- + Ag^+$$

Step 2: Write the two half-equations:

$$\tfrac{1}{2}Br_2 + e^- \rightleftharpoons Br^-$$

$$Ag \rightleftharpoons Ag^+ + e^-$$

Step 3: Include the value of $E^\ominus$ for each half-reaction but reverse the sign of the half-equation showing oxidation (loss of electrons). This is because the data book values are always for the reduction reaction.

$$\tfrac{1}{2}Br_2 + e^- \rightleftharpoons Br^- \qquad E^\ominus = +1.07 \text{ V}$$

$$Ag \rightleftharpoons Ag^+ + e^- \qquad E^\ominus = -0.80 \text{ V}$$

Step 4: Add the two voltages. This is because we are combining the two half-equations.

$$= +1.07 + (-0.80)$$

$$= +0.27 \text{ V}$$

Step 5: If the value of the sum of the two voltages is positive the reaction will occur as written. If the value of the sum of the two voltages is negative the reaction will *not* occur.

In this case the sum of the two voltages is positive so bromine will oxidise silver to silver ions.

7 Will iodine oxidise silver to silver ions?

Solution

Step 1: Write the equation for the suggested reaction.

$$\tfrac{1}{2}I_2 + Ag \rightarrow I^- + Ag^+$$

Step 2: The two half-equations are:

$$\tfrac{1}{2}I_2 + e^- \rightleftharpoons I^-$$

$$Ag \rightleftharpoons Ag^+ + e^-$$

Step 3: Write the $E^\ominus$ values, with the sign reversed for the oxidation reaction.

$$\tfrac{1}{2}I_2 + e^- \rightleftharpoons I^- \qquad E^\ominus = +0.54 \text{ V}$$

$$Ag \rightleftharpoons Ag^+ + e^- \qquad E^\ominus = -0.80 \text{ V}$$

Step 4: Add the two voltages.

$$= +0.54 + (-0.80)$$

$$= -0.26 \text{ V}$$

Step 5: The sum of the two voltages is negative, so iodine will not oxidise silver to silver ions.

Questions

21 Use the data in Appendix 2 to predict whether or not the following reactions are feasible. If a reaction does occur, write a balanced equation for it.

   a Can MnO_4^- ions oxidise Cl^- ions to Cl_2 in acidic conditions?

   b Can MnO_4^- ions oxidise F^- ions to F_2 in acidic conditions?

   c Can H^+ ions oxidise V^{2+} ions to V^{3+} ions?

   d Can H^+ ions oxidise Fe^{2+} ions to Fe^{3+} ions?

22 Suggest a suitable reagent that can carry out each of the following oxidations or reductions. Use the data in Appendix 2 to help you.

   a The reduction of Zn^{2+} ions to Zn.

   b The oxidation of Br^- ions to Br_2

   c The reduction of acidified SO_4^{2-} ions to SO_2

   d The oxidation of Cl^- ions to Cl_2

23 Use the cell voltage method described in Worked examples 6 and 7 above to answer Question 21, parts **a** to **d**.

$E^\ominus$ values and oxidising and reducing agents

> **IMPORTANT**
>
> Remember that oxidising agents accept electrons from another species and reducing agents donate electrons to another species.

Look back at Figure 20.19. Note the following as the values of $E^\ominus$ for each of these reduction reactions gets more negative.

- The species on the left of the equation become weaker oxidising agents. They accept electrons less readily.

- The species on the right of the equation become stronger reducing agents. They release electrons more readily.

Cu will not reduce Zn^{2+} ions to Zn. So how can we reduce Zn^{2+} ions? The answer is to react the Zn^{2+} ions with a stronger reducing agent, which should have an $E^\ominus$ value more negative than the $E^\ominus$ value for Zn^{2+} / Zn. In Figure 20.19, we see that the half-equation Mg^{2+} / Mg has a more negative $E^\ominus$ value. So Mg is a suitable reducing agent.

$$Zn^{2+}(aq) + 2e^- \rightleftharpoons Zn(s) \qquad E^\ominus = -0.76 \text{ V}$$

$$Mg^{2+}(aq) + 2e^- \rightleftharpoons Mg(s) \qquad E^\ominus = -2.38 \text{ V}$$

Zn^{2+} is the better oxidising agent. It is more likely to accept electrons than Mg^{2+} ions. Mg is the better reducing agent. It is more likely to release electrons than Zn.

Nitric acid is a good oxidising agent, but it will not oxidise chloride ions to chlorine. So how can we oxidise Cl^- ions? The answer is to react the Cl^- ions with a stronger oxidising agent, which should have an $E^\ominus$ value more positive than the $E^\ominus$ value for Cl_2 / Cl^-. The half-equation

$$MnO_4^-(aq) + 8H^+(aq) + 5e^- \rightleftharpoons Mn^{2+}(aq) + 4H_2O(l)$$

provides a suitable oxidising agent.

This half-equation has a more positive $E^\ominus$ value than that for the Cl_2 / Cl^- half-equation. So acidified MnO_4^- ions are a suitable oxidising agent to oxidise chloride ions to chlorine (see Figure 20.22).

$$MnO_4^-(aq) + 8H^+(aq) + 5e^- \rightleftharpoons Mn^{2+}(aq) + 4H_2O(l)$$
$$E^\ominus = +1.52 \text{ V}$$

$$\tfrac{1}{2} Cl_2(g) + e^- \rightleftharpoons Cl^-(aq) \qquad E^\ominus = +1.36 \text{ V}$$

Acidified MnO_4^- is the better oxidising agent. It is more likely to accept electrons than Cl_2 molecules. Cl^- is the better reducing agent. It is more likely to release electrons than Mn^{2+}.

We can explain the relative oxidising abilities of the halogens in a similar way. The standard electrode potentials for the halogens are:

$$\tfrac{1}{2} F_2 + e^- \rightleftharpoons F^- \qquad\qquad E^\ominus = +2.87 \text{ V}$$

$$\tfrac{1}{2} Cl_2 + e^- \rightleftharpoons Cl^- \qquad\qquad E^\ominus = +1.36 \text{ V}$$

$$\tfrac{1}{2} Br_2 + e^- \rightleftharpoons Br^- \qquad\qquad E^\ominus = +1.07 \text{ V}$$

$$\tfrac{1}{2} I_2 + e^- \rightleftharpoons I^- \qquad\qquad E^\ominus = +0.54 \text{ V}$$

Based on these $E^\ominus$ values, as we go down Group 17 from F_2 to I_2, the oxidising ability of the halogen decreases and the ability of halide ions to act as reducing agents increases (Figure 20.23).

Figure 20.23: Aqueous chlorine displaces bromine from a solution of potassium bromide. We can use $E^{\ominus}$ values to explain why a halogen higher in Group 17 displaces a halogen lower in the group from a solution of its halide ions.

Questions

24 Use the $E^{\ominus}$ values for the halogens to explain the following:

a   why bromine can oxidise an aqueous solution of iodide ions

b   why bromine does not react with chloride ions.

25 Use the data in Appendix 2 to answer these questions.

a   Of the ions Ag^+, Cr^{2+} and Fe^{2+}, which one needs the strongest reducing agent to reduce it to metal atoms?

b   Of the atoms Ag, Cr and Fe, which one needs the strongest oxidising agent to oxidise it to an ion?

REFLECTION

1   Write down two half-reactions and their standard electrode potentials from Appendix 2 of this coursebook. Start by choosing simple examples. Ask another learner to deduce the electrode potential of the cell and then work together to construct a balanced equation for the reaction. Then reverse the roles: you choose the half-reactions and the other learner deduces the electrode potential. Carry on like this until you are both sure that you understand the processes involved.

2   What processes did you go through to calculate the cell potential and balance the equations? What did you learn about yourself as worked through this?

How does the value of $E^{\ominus}$ vary with ion concentration?

In Chapter 8 we saw that the position of an equilibrium reaction is affected by changes in concentration, temperature and pressure. Redox equilibria are no different. When we compare the voltage of a standard half-cell, X, with a standard hydrogen electrode, we are measuring $E^{\ominus}$ for the half-cell X. If we change the concentration or temperature of half-cell X, the electrode potential also changes. Under these non-standard conditions we use the symbol E for the electrode potential.

What happens to the electrode potential when we change the concentration of ions in a half-cell? Let us take an example of a metal / metal ion equilibrium:

$$Zn^{2+}(aq) + 2e^- \rightleftharpoons Zn(s) \qquad E^{\ominus} = -0.76 \text{ V}$$

- If $[Zn^{2+}]$ is greater than 1.00 mol dm^{-3}, the value of E becomes less negative / more positive (for example −0.61 V).

- If $[Zn^{2+}]$ is less than 1.00 mol dm^{-3}, the value of E becomes more negative / less positive (for example, −0.80 V).

We can apply Le Chatelier's principle to redox equilibria. If we increase the concentration of the species on the left of the equation, the position of equilibrium will shift to the right. So the value of E becomes more positive / less negative.

If two different ions are present in the half-cell, we have to consider both ions.

Let us take the equilibrium between Fe^{3+} ions and Fe^{2+} ions as an example.

$$Fe^{3+} + e^- \rightleftharpoons Fe^{2+} \qquad E^{\ominus} = +0.77 \text{ V}$$
$$1.00 \text{ mol dm}^{-3} \qquad 1.00 \text{ mol dm}^{-3}$$

- If $[Fe^{3+}]$ is greater than 1.00 mol dm^{-3} (keeping $[Fe^{2+}] = 1.00 \text{ mol dm}^{-3}$) the value of E becomes more positive (for example +0.85 V).

- If $[Fe^{3+}]$ is less than 1.00 mol dm^{-3} (keeping $[Fe^{2+}] = 1.00 \text{ mol dm}^{-3}$) the value of E becomes less positive (for example +0.70 V).

- If $[Fe^{2+}]$ is greater than 1.00 mol dm^{-3} (keeping $[Fe^{3+}] = 1.00 \text{ mol dm}^{-3}$) the value of E becomes less positive (for example +0.70 V).

- If $[Fe^{2+}]$ is less than 1.00 mol dm^{-3} (keeping $[Fe^{3+}] = 1.00 \text{ mol dm}^{-3}$) the value of E becomes more positive (for example +0.85 V).

You can see from the information above that if we increase the concentration of both the Fe^{3+} and Fe^{2+} ions, these effects may cancel each other out.

How can we predict whether or not a given reaction will occur under non-standard conditions? The answer is that if the $E^{\ominus}$ values of the two half-reactions involved differ by more than 0.30 V, then the reaction predicted by values is highly likely to occur. So chlorine is likely to oxidise Fe^{2+} ions even if the conditions are not standard. This is because the difference in their $E^{\ominus}$ values is 0.59 V, which is considerably greater than 0.30 V.

$$\tfrac{1}{2}Cl_2(g) + e^- \rightleftharpoons Cl^-(aq) \qquad E^{\ominus} = +1.36 \text{ V}$$
$$Fe^{3+}(aq) + e^- \rightleftharpoons Fe^{2+}(aq) \qquad E^{\ominus} = +0.77 \text{ V}$$

We cannot, however, predict with confidence whether the reaction between MnO_4^- ions and Cl_2 will take place if the conditions are too far from standard.

$$MnO_4^-(aq) + 8H^+(aq) + 5e^- \rightleftharpoons Mn^{2+}(aq) + 4H_2O(l)$$
$$E^{\ominus} = +1.52 \text{ V}$$
$$\tfrac{1}{2}Cl_2(g) + e^- \rightleftharpoons Cl^-(aq) \qquad E^{\ominus} = +1.36 \text{ V}$$

This is because the difference in $E^{\ominus}$ values is 0.16 V, which is considerably smaller than 0.30 V.

The figure of 0.30 V given here to help us to tell if a reaction will still occur under non-standard conditions is a rough guide only. If $E^{\ominus}$ values differ by less than 0.30 V, non-standard conditions may result in an unexpected outcome.

Question

26 The half-cell $Cr_2O_7^{2-} + 14H^+ + 6e^- \rightleftharpoons 2Cr^{3+} + 7H_2O$ has an $E^{\ominus}$ value of +1.33 V.

   a   Suggest how the value of $E^{\ominus}$ changes if the other species are kept at 1.00 mol dm^{-3} but:

      i $[Cr_2O_7^{2-}]$ is increased

      ii $[H^+]$ is decreased

      iii $[Cr^{3+}]$ is increased.

   b   What effect would each of these concentration changes have on the strength of the acidified $Cr_2O_7^{2-}$ solution as an oxidising agent?

   c   What conditions would you use to make a solution of $Cr_2O_7^{2-}$ as strong an oxidising agent as possible?

   d   Use Le Chatelier's principle to explain your answer to part **c**.

The Nernst equation

If we consider a cell made up from a silver / silver ion electrode and a copper / copper(II) ion electrode, the reaction taking place is:

$$Cu(s) + 2Ag^+(aq) \rightleftharpoons Cu^{2+}(aq) + 2Ag(s) \quad E^{\ominus} = +0.46 \text{ V}$$

This equation relates to standard conditions for the concentrations of the ions (1.00 mol dm^{-3}). If we change the concentration of the silver ions, the cell is no longer standard, so we use the symbol E_{cell}. The graph, Figure 20.24, shows how the value of E_{cell} changes with the concentration of silver ions. Note that we have plotted the value of E_{cell} against the logarithm of the silver ion concentration.

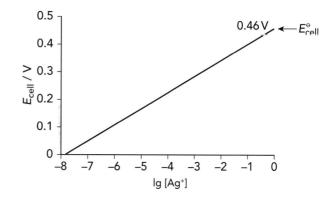

Figure 20.24: Increasing the concentration of silver ions in the cell reaction $Cu(s) + 2Ag^+(aq) \rightleftharpoons Cu^{2+}(aq) + 2Ag(s)$ makes the value of E_{cell} more positive.

The effect of concentration and temperature on the value of E_{cell} can be deduced using the Nernst equation. For a given electrode, e.g. a Cu(s) / Cu^{2+}(aq) electrode, the relationship is:

$$E = E^{\ominus} + \frac{RT}{zF} \ln \frac{[\text{oxidised form}]}{[\text{reduced form}]}$$

where

E is the electrode potential under non-standard conditions

$E^{\ominus}$ is the standard electrode potential

R is the gas constant, 8.31, in J K^{-1} mol^{-1}

T is the kelvin temperature

z is the number of electrons transferred in the reaction

F is the value of the Faraday constant in C mol^{-1}

ln is the natural logarithm

[oxidised] refers to the concentration of the oxidised form in the half-equation.

Fortunately for us, for a metal / metal ion electrode, we can simplify this equation in three ways:

- The natural logarithm, ln, is related to log to the base 10 by the relationship

  $\ln x = 2.303 \log_{10} x$

- At standard temperature the values of R, T and F are constant

- The equation then becomes

  $$E = E^{\ominus} + \frac{0.059}{z} \log_{10} \frac{[\text{oxidised species}]}{[\text{reduced species}]}$$

So for the reaction Fe^{3+}(aq) + e$^-$ $\rightleftharpoons$ Fe^{2+}(aq) in which the concentration of Fe^{3+}(aq) is 0.50 mol dm^{-3} and the concentration of Fe^{2+}(aq) is 1.0 mol dm^{-3}

IMPORTANT

The form of the Nernst equation that you are expected to know is

$$E = E^{\ominus} + \frac{0.059}{z} \log_{10} \frac{[\text{oxidised species}]}{[\text{reduced species}]}$$

Fe^{3+}(aq) is the oxidised form, Fe^{2+}(aq) is the reduced form and $z = 1.0$

Substituting into the Nernst equation we have:

$$E = E^{\ominus} + \frac{0.059}{1} \log_{10} \frac{[0.50]}{[1.0]}$$

- For a metal / metal ion electrode, e.g.

  Cu^{2+}(aq) + 2e $\rightleftharpoons$ Cu(s)

  the reduced form is the metal.

- Note that the concentration of the metal does not change. So the ratio $\frac{[\text{oxidised species}]}{[\text{reduced species}]}$ can be written [oxidised form], e.g. [Cu^{2+}(aq)]

- This means that the relationship becomes:

  $$E = E^{\ominus} + \frac{0.059}{z} \log_{10} [\text{oxidised form}]$$

Note that if the temperature is not 25 °C the full form of the Nernst equation must be used.

Question

27 a Calculate the value of the electrode potential at 298 K of a Ni(s) / Ni^{2+}(aq) electrode that has a concentration of Ni^{2+}(aq) ions of 1.5 mol dm^{-3}. $E^{\ominus} = -0.25$ V.

WORKED EXAMPLE

8 Calculate the value of the electrode potential at 298 K of a Cu(s) / Cu^{2+}(aq) electrode that has a concentration of Cu^{2+}(aq) ions of 0.001 mol dm^{-3}. $E^{\ominus} = +0.34$ V

Solution

Substituting the values in the relationship:

$$E = E^{\ominus} + \frac{0.059}{z} \log_{10} [\text{Cu}^{2+}(\text{aq})]$$

$$E = +0.34 + \frac{0.059}{2} \log_{10} (0.001)$$

$$E = +0.34 - 0.089 = +0.25 \text{ V}$$

Note how $\log_{10}$ [oxidised form] changes the sign of the second term in the equation:

- If the concentration is 1 mol dm^{-3}, $\log_{10}$ [oxidised form] is 0 and $E = E^{\ominus}$.

- If the concentration is less than 1 mol dm^{-3}, $\log_{10}$ [oxidised form] is negative and E is less positive than $E^{\ominus}$.

- If the concentration is greater than 1 mol dm^{-3}, $\log_{10}$ [oxidised form] is positive and E is more positive than $E^{\ominus}$.

b Calculate the electrode potential of a silver / silver ion electrode, $Ag(s) / Ag^+(aq)$, at 298 K when the concentration of $Ag^+(aq)$ ions is 0.0002 mol dm^{-3}. $E^\ominus = +0.80$ V.

IMPORTANT

If both oxidised and reduced species in solution have the same concentration, the ratio $\frac{\text{[oxidised species]}}{\text{[reduced species]}}$ is 1 and since $\log_{10}(1) = 0$, $E = E^\ominus$. Note that this applies to any concentration, e.g. 0.05 mol dm^{-3} oxidised species and 0.05 mol dm^{-3} reduced species.

Feasibility predictions based on $E^\ominus$ don't always work!

The feasibility of a reaction based on $E^\ominus$ values is no guarantee that a reaction will proceed quickly. It only tells us that a reaction is possible, and that the reverse reaction does not occur. Some reactions are feasible, but they proceed so slowly that they do not seem to be taking place. Take, for example, the lack of reactivity of zinc with cold water. Remember that water contains H^+ ions. The relevant half-equations are:

$$H^+(aq) + e^- \rightleftharpoons \tfrac{1}{2} H_2(g) \qquad E^\ominus = 0.00 \text{ V}$$
$$Zn^{2+}(aq) + 2e^- \rightleftharpoons Zn(s) \qquad E^\ominus = -0.76 \text{ V}$$

Even when the low concentration of H^+ ions is taken into account, $E^\ominus$ values predict that a reaction should occur. The rate of reaction between zinc and water, however, is extremely slow. It is the rate of reaction rather than the value of $E^\ominus$ which is determining the lack of reactivity.

Questions

28 A half-cell containing Sn in 1.00 mol dm^{-3} Sn^{2+} ions is connected to another half-cell containing Zn in 1.00 mol dm^{-3} Zn^{2+} ions.

$$Zn^{2+}(aq) + 2e^- \rightleftharpoons Zn(s) \qquad E^\ominus = -0.76 \text{ V}$$
$$Sn^{2+}(aq) + 2e^- \rightleftharpoons Sn(s) \qquad E^\ominus = -0.14 \text{ V}$$

Which one of the following is the value of E when the concentration of both the $Zn^{2+}(aq)$ ions and $Sn^{2+}(aq)$ are changed to 0.1 mol dm^{-3}?

A −0.062 V   **C** −0.90 V
B +0.62 V   **D** −1 V

29 An industrial process relies on a reaction that is impractically slow under normal conditions. How might you try to solve this problem? Use your knowledge of reaction rates to suggest several different approaches.

30 Describe two limitations to using $E^\ominus$ values to predict the feasibility of a reaction.

20.7 More about electrolysis

In Section 20.3 we studied the electrolysis of molten sodium chloride. During electrolysis:

- cations (positive ions) move towards the cathode where they gain electrons; gain of electrons is reduction

- anions (negative ions) move towards the anode where they lose electrons; loss of electrons is oxidation.

In this section we shall find out how the nature of the electrolyte and the concentration of aqueous electrolytes affects the products of electrolysis.

Electrolysis of molten electrolytes

When pure molten ionic compounds containing two simple ions are electrolysed, a metal is formed at the cathode and a non-metal at the anode. Some examples are shown in Table 20.1.

Compound electrolysed	Cathode product	Anode product
aluminium oxide	aluminium	oxygen
magnesium bromide	magnesium	bromine
sodium chloride	sodium	chlorine
zinc iodide	zinc	iodine

Table 20.1: The products formed at the cathode and anode when some molten salts are electrolysed.

Let us take the electrolysis of molten zinc chloride as an example.

At the cathode, the metal ions gain electrons and are reduced to the metal.

$$Zn^{2+} + 2e^- \rightarrow Zn$$

At the anode, the non-metal ions lose electrons and are oxidised to a non-metal.

$$2Cl^- \rightarrow Cl_2 + 2e^-$$

Electrolysis of aqueous solutions

Aqueous solutions of electrolytes contain more than one cation and more than one anion. For example, an aqueous solution of sodium chloride contains Na^+, Cl^-, H^+ and OH^- ions. The H^+ and OH^- ions arise from the ionisation of water:

$$H_2O \rightleftharpoons H^+ + OH^-$$

So, which ions are **discharged** during the electrolysis of aqueous solutions?

KEY WORD

discharged: ions changed into atoms or molecules.

Among other things this depends on:

- the relative electrode potential of the ions
- the concentration of the ions.

Electrolysis products and electrode potentials

When an aqueous ionic solution is electrolysed using inert electrodes, there is usually only one product obtained at each electrode. The ease of discharge of cations at the cathode is related to their electrode potentials. Figure 20.25 shows some half-reactions and their electrode potentials.

The cation that is most easily reduced is discharged at the cathode. So the cation in the half-equation with the most positive $E^{\ominus}$ value will be discharged.

When a concentrated aqueous solution of sodium chloride (1.00 mol dm^{-3}) is electrolysed, H^+ ions and Na^+ ions are present in the solution. Hydrogen rather than sodium is formed at the cathode because H^+ ions are more easily reduced than Na^+ ions.

$$H^+ + e^- \rightleftharpoons \tfrac{1}{2} H_2 \qquad E^{\ominus} = 0.00 \text{ V}$$
$$Na^+(aq) + e^- \rightleftharpoons Na(s) \qquad E^{\ominus} = -2.71 \text{ V}$$

IMPORTANT

Remember the three things which decide the product at an electrode:

1. Is the electrolyte molten or an aqueous solution?

2. Are the discharge potentials of the competing ions, e.g. OH^- and Cl^-, in the electrochemical series (discharge series) similar or significantly different?

3. Is the concentration of the relevant ions high or low?

$E^{\ominus}/$ V

+0.80	$Ag^+(aq) + e^-$	$\rightleftharpoons Ag(s)$
+0.34	$Cu^{2+}(aq) + 2e^-$	$\rightleftharpoons Cu(s)$
0.00	$H^+(aq) + e^-$	$\rightleftharpoons \tfrac{1}{2}H_2(g)$
−0.13	$Pb^{2+}(aq) + 2e^-$	$\rightleftharpoons Pb(s)$
−0.76	$Zn^{2+}(aq) + 2e^-$	$\rightleftharpoons Zn(s)$
−2.38	$Mg^{2+}(aq) + 2e^-$	$\rightleftharpoons Mg(s)$
−2.71	$Na^+(aq) + e^-$	$\rightleftharpoons Na(s)$

increasing ease of discharge of cation at cathode

Figure 20.25: The ease of discharge of ions at a cathode in electrolysis is related to the electrode potential of the ions.

When a concentrated aqueous solution of copper(II) sulfate (1.00 mol dm^{-3}) is electrolysed, H^+ ions and Cu^{2+} ions are present in the solution. Copper rather than hydrogen is formed at the cathode because Cu^{2+} ions are more easily reduced than H^+ ions.

$$Cu^{2+}(aq) + 2e^- \rightleftharpoons Cu(s) \qquad E^{\ominus} = +0.34 \text{ V}$$
$$H^+ + e^- \rightleftharpoons \tfrac{1}{2} H_2 \qquad E^{\ominus} = 0.00 \text{ V}$$

At the anode, using platinum electrodes, the ease of discharge of anions follows the order:

$$SO_4^{2-}(aq), NO_3^-(aq), Cl^-(aq), OH^-(aq), Br^-(aq), I^-(aq)$$

increasing ease of discharge, increasing ease of oxidation

When a concentrated aqueous solution of sodium sulfate (1.00 mol dm^{-3} Na_2SO_4) is electrolysed, OH^- ions and SO_4^{2-} ions are present in the solution. Hydroxide ions are discharged at the anode because OH^- ions are more easily oxidised than SO_4^{2-} ions. The OH^- ions are oxidised to oxygen, which bubbles off at the anode.

$$4OH^-(aq) \rightarrow O_2(g) + 2H_2O(l) + 4e^-$$

When a concentrated aqueous solution of sodium iodide (1.00 mol dm^{-3}) is electrolysed, I^- ions and OH^- ions are present in the solution. Iodide ions are discharged at the anode because I⁻ ions are more easily oxidised than OH⁻ ions.

$$I^-(aq) \rightarrow \tfrac{1}{2} I_2(aq) + e^-$$

Note that in the discussion above, we have used standard electrode potentials. If conditions are standard, the concentration of the aqueous solution is 1.00 mol dm^{-3} with respect to the ionic compound dissolved in water. But the concentration of hydrogen and hydroxide ions in solution is very low. We saw in Section 20.6 that we can use electrode potential values to predict whether or not a reaction will occur under non-standard conditions. As long as the difference in electrode potentials is greater than 0.30 V, we can be fairly sure that the predictions will be correct.

Questions

31 An aqueous solution of sodium sulfate, Na_2SO_4, is electrolysed using carbon electrodes.

  a Explain why hydrogen is formed at the cathode and not sodium.

  b Write a half-equation for the reaction occurring at the anode.

32 Predict the electrolysis products at the anode and cathode when the following are electrolysed:

  a molten aluminium iodide

  b a concentrated aqueous solution of magnesium chloride

  c a concentrated aqueous solution of sodium bromide

  d molten zinc oxide.

Electrolysis products and solution concentration

When aqueous solutions are electrolysed, the ions are rarely present at concentrations of 1.00 mol dm^{-3}. In Section 20.6 we saw that the value of E changes with the concentration of the ion. An ion, Z, higher in the discharge series may be discharged in preference to one below it if Z is present at a relatively higher concentration than normal. For this to be possible, the E values of the competing ions are usually less than 0.30 V different from each other.

When a concentrated solution of sodium chloride is electrolysed, chloride ions are discharged at the anode in preference to hydroxide ions. This is because chloride ions are present in a much higher concentration than hydroxide ions. The chloride ions fall below the hydroxide ions in the discharge series.

But what happens when we electrolyse an extremely dilute solution of sodium chloride?

We find that oxygen, rather than chlorine, is formed at the anode. This is because the relatively lower concentration of Cl⁻ ions allows OH⁻ ions to fall below Cl⁻ ions in the discharge series. In reality, the electrolysis of a dilute aqueous solution of sodium chloride gives a mixture of chlorine and oxygen at the anode. The proportion of oxygen increases, the more dilute the solution.

Question

33 A concentrated aqueous solution of hydrochloric acid is electrolysed.

  a Write half-equations to show the reactions at:

   i the cathode

   ii the anode.

  b A very dilute solution of hydrochloric acid is electrolysed. What substance or substances are formed at the anode? Explain your answer.

REFLECTION

1 Make a list of the relationships (equations) between the various physical quantities that you have come across in this chapter, e.g. electric current, electrode potential, etc. Give the unit of each of these physical quantities.

2 Compare your list with that of another learner. Which of these relationships (equations) do you need more help with understanding? How will you get this help?

SUMMARY

During electrolysis, reduction occurs at the cathode (negative electrode) because ions gain electrons from the cathode and oxidation occurs at the anode (positive electrode) because ions lose electrons to the anode.

A metal is formed at the cathode and a non-metal at the anode when molten metal salts are electrolysed. Hydrogen may be formed at the cathode and oxygen at the anode when dilute aqueous solutions of metal salts are electrolysed.

The relationship between the Faraday constant (F), the Avogadro constant (L) and the charge on an electron (e) is given by $F = Le$.

The quantity of charge, in coulombs, passed during electrolysis is found by multiplying the current, in amps, by time, in seconds: $Q = It$.

A standard hydrogen electrode is a half-cell in which hydrogen gas at a pressure of 101 kPa bubbles through a solution of 1.00 mol dm^{-3} H$^+$(aq) ions.

The standard electrode potential of a half-cell ($E^\ominus$) is the voltage of the half-cell under standard conditions compared with a standard hydrogen electrode.

The direction of electron flow in a simple cell is from the half-cell that has the more negative (or less positive) electrode potential to the half-cell that has the less negative (or more positive) electrode potential.

A particular redox reaction will occur if the $E^\ominus$ of the half-equation involving the species being reduced is more positive than the $E^\ominus$ of the half-equation of the species being oxidised.

The Nernst equation shows the relationship between the concentration of aqueous ions in each half-cell and the electrode potential:

$$E = E^\ominus + \frac{0.059}{z} \log_{10} \frac{[\text{oxidised form}]}{[\text{reduced form}]}$$

EXAM-STYLE QUESTIONS

1   The diagram shows an electrochemical cell designed to find the standard electrode potential for zinc.

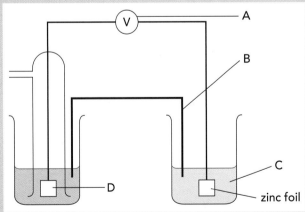

    a   Name the apparatus labelled A and give a characteristic it should have.   **[2]**

    b **i**   Name part B and give its two functions.   **[3]**

        ii   Describe how part B can be prepared.   **[2]**

CONTINUED

c Name C. [2]

d Name part D and give its two functions. [3]

e Give the three standard conditions for the measurement of a standard electrode potential. [3]

[Total: 15]

2 The diagram shows an electrochemical cell involving two metal / metal ion systems.

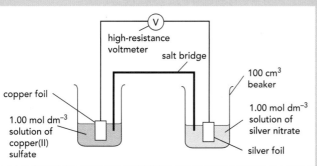

The standard electrode potentials for the half-cells are:

$$Ag^+ + e^- \rightleftharpoons Ag \qquad E^\ominus = +0.80 \text{ V}$$
$$Cu^{2+} + 2e^- \rightleftharpoons Cu \qquad E^\ominus = +0.34 \text{ V}$$

a Calculate a value for the cell voltage. Show your working. [2]

b Write the balanced ionic equation for the overall cell reaction. [2]

c In this reaction:

   i Name the substance that is oxidised. Explain your answer. [1]

   ii Name the substance that is reduced. Explain your answer. [1]

   iii State the direction in which the electrons flow. Explain your answer. [2]

d The contents of the Cu^{2+} / Cu half-cell are diluted with water. The contents of the Ag^+ / Ag half-cell are kept the same. State what effect this will have on the value of the cell voltage, E. Explain your answer. [3]

[Total: 11]

3 a Define the term *standard electrode potential*. [3]

b Draw a labelled diagram to show how the standard electrode potential of a half-cell containing chlorine gas and chloride ions can be measured. [5]

c Write a half-equation for this half-cell. [1]

d The standard electrode potential of a Cl_2 / Cl^- half-cell is +1.36 V. This Cl_2 / Cl^- half-cell was connected to a standard half-cell containing solid iodine in equilibrium with iodide ions. The standard electrode potential of an I_2 / I^- half-cell is +0.54 V.

   i Calculate the standard cell voltage for this cell. [1]

   ii Write the balanced ionic equation for the overall cell reaction. [2]

[Total: 12]

CONTINUED

4 **a** In the presence of acid, the manganate(VII) ion is a powerful oxidising agent. The half-equation for its reduction in acid solution is:

$$MnO_4^-(aq) + 8H^+(aq) + 5e^- \rightleftharpoons Mn^{2+}(aq) + 4H_2O(l) \qquad E^\ominus = +1.51 \text{ V}$$

   i Explain why the presence of an acid is necessary for the $MnO_4^-(aq)$ to function as an oxidising agent. **[1]**

   ii Give two reasons for the $MnO_4^-(aq)$ acting as an oxidising agent in acidic solution. **[2]**

   b Iodide ions are oxidised to iodine according to the half-cell equation:

$$\tfrac{1}{2}I_2(aq) + e^- \rightleftharpoons I^-(aq) \qquad E^\ominus = +0.54 \text{ V}$$

   i Explain why an acidified solution of manganate(VII) ions can be used to oxidise iodide ions to iodine. **[5]**

   ii Write the balanced equation for this reaction. **[2]**

   [Total: 10]

5 Liquid bromine is added to an aqueous solution of potassium iodide. The following reaction takes place.

$$Br_2(l) + 2I^-(aq) \rightarrow 2Br^-(aq) + I_2(aq) \qquad E^\ominus \text{ cell} = +0.53 \text{ V}$$

   a Write two half-equations for this reaction. **[2]**

   b Draw a labelled diagram to show two linked half-cells that could be used to measure the standard cell potential for this reaction. **[7]**

   c The standard cell potential for this reaction is +0.53 V. State whether the position of equilibrium favours the reactants or the products. Explain your answer. **[4]**

   d The standard electrode potentials for a number of half-equations are shown below:

$$Fe^{3+}(aq) + e^- \rightleftharpoons Fe^{2+}(aq) \qquad E^\ominus = +0.77 \text{ V}$$

$$I_2(aq) + 2e^- \rightleftharpoons 2I^-(aq) \qquad E^\ominus = +0.54 \text{ V}$$

$$Ni^{2+}(aq) + 2e^- \rightleftharpoons Ni(s) \qquad E^\ominus = -0.25 \text{ V}$$

$$Pb^{4+}(aq) + 2e^- \rightleftharpoons Pb^{2+}(aq) \qquad E^\ominus = +1.69 \text{ V}$$

   Give the name of an atom or ion in this list that will reduce iodine to iodide ions. Explain your answer. **[4]**

   [Total: 17]

6 The list below gives the standard electrode potentials for five half-reactions.

$$Cu^{2+}(aq) + 2e^- \rightleftharpoons Cu(s) \qquad E^\ominus = +0.34 \text{ V}$$

$$Fe^{2+}(aq) + 2e^- \rightleftharpoons Fe(s) \qquad E^\ominus = -0.44 \text{ V}$$

$$Fe^{3+}(aq) + e^- \rightleftharpoons Fe^{2+}(aq) \qquad E^\ominus = +0.77 \text{ V}$$

$$I_2(aq) + 2e^- \rightleftharpoons 2I^-(aq) \qquad E^\ominus = +0.54 \text{ V}$$

$$Zn^{2+}(aq) + 2e^- \rightleftharpoons Zn(s) \qquad E^\ominus = -0.76 \text{ V}$$

CONTINUED

a Define *standard electrode potential*. [3]

b Give the name of the species in the list which is:

  i the strongest oxidising agent [1]

  ii the strongest reducing agent. [1]

c A cell was set up as shown below.

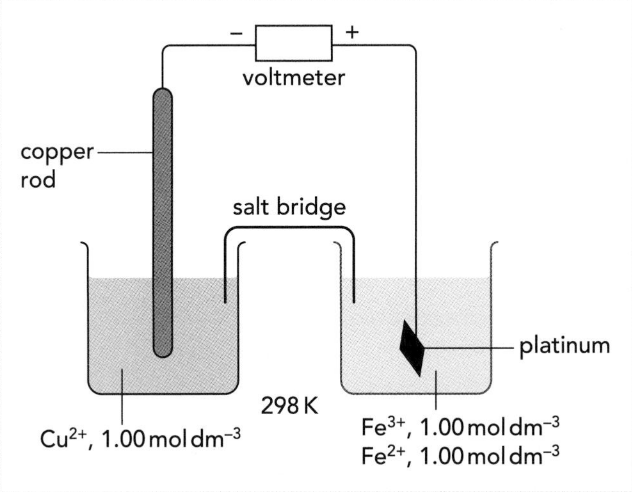

  i Calculate the standard cell potential of this cell. [1]

  ii State the direction of the electron flow in the external circuit. Explain your answer. [2]

  iii Write an equation for the complete cell reaction. [2]

d The concentration of copper(II) ions in the left-hand electrode was increased from 1.00 mol dm^{-3} to 1.30 mol dm^{-3}. The concentration of ions in the right-hand cell was not changed.

  i State the effect of this change on the E value of the Cu^{2+} / Cu half-cell. [1]

  ii State the effect of this change on the E value for the complete electrochemical cell. [1]

  iii Explain why the direction of the cell reaction is unlikely to be altered by this change in concentration. [1]

  [Total: 13]

7 An electric current of 1.04 A was passed through a solution of dilute sulfuric acid for 6.00 min.

The volume of hydrogen produced at r.t.p. was 43.5 cm^3.

a Calculate the number of coulombs of charge transferred during the experiment. [1]

b Calculate the number of coulombs of charge required to liberate 1 mole of hydrogen gas. ($F = 96\,500$ C mol^{-1}) [2]

CONTINUED

c In another experiment, copper(II) sulfate was electrolysed using copper electrodes. Copper was deposited at the cathode.

  i Write a half-equation for this reaction. [1]

  ii A learner conducted an experiment to calculate a value for the Faraday constant, F. An electric current of 0.300 A was passed through the solution of copper(II) sulfate for exactly 40 minutes. 0.240 g of copper was deposited at the cathode. Use this information to calculate a value for F. Express your answer to 3 significant figures. (A_r value: [Cu] = 63.5) [3]

  iii The charge on one electron is approximately 1.60×10^{-19} C. Use this information and your answer to part **ii** to calculate a value for the Avogadro constant. [2]

  [Total: 9]

8 An aqueous solution of silver nitrate is electrolysed.

  a **i** Explain why silver rather than hydrogen is produced at the cathode. [2]

  ii Write an equation for the reaction occurring at the cathode. [1]

  b **i** Write an equation for the reaction occurring at the anode. [1]

  ii Deduce whether the anode reaction is an oxidation or reduction reaction. Explain your answer. [1]

  c Explain why the silver nitrate solution becomes acidic during this electrolysis. [3]

  d Calculate the mass of silver deposited at the cathode when the electrolysis is carried out for exactly 35 min using a current of 0.18 A. (A_r[Ag] = 108; F = 96 500 C mol^{-1}) [3]

  [Total: 11]

9 The reaction taking place in an electrochemical cell under standard conditions is

$$Fe^{2+}(aq) + Ag^+(aq) \rightarrow Fe^{3+}(aq) + Ag(s)$$

  a Write two half-equations for this reaction. For each, state whether oxidation or reduction is occurring. [2]

  b The standard electrode potential for the half-cell containing $Fe^{2+}(aq)$ and $Fe^{3+}(aq)$ is +0.77 V.

  i Use the relationship $E = E^{\ominus} + \dfrac{0.059}{Z} \log_{10} \dfrac{\text{[oxidised form]}}{\text{[reduced form]}}$

  to calculate the electrode potential at 298 K if the concentration of $Fe^{2+}(aq)$ is 0.02 mol dm^{-3} and the concentration of $Fe^{3+}(aq)$ is 0.1 mol dm^{-3}. [3]

  ii Use the relationship above to explain why the standard electrode potential for the half-cell containing $Fe^{2+}(aq)$ and $Fe^{3+}(aq)$ is always +0.77 V if there are equimolar concentrations of $Fe^{2+}(aq)$ and $Fe^{3+}(aq)$. [2]

CONTINUED

c The standard electrode potential for the half-cell containing $Ag^+(aq)$ and $Ag(s)$ is +0.80 V.

Calculate the electrode potential at 298 K if the concentration of $Ag^+(aq)$ is 0.05 mol dm^{-3}. [2]

d Use your results to parts **b i** and **c** to predict whether the reaction $Fe^{2+}(aq) + Ag^+(aq) \rightarrow Fe^{3+}(aq) + Ag(s)$ is likely to occur at the concentrations $Fe^{2+}(aq)$ 0.05 mol dm^{-3}, $Fe^{3+}(aq)$ 0.1 mol dm^{-3} and $Ag^+(aq)$ 0.05 mol dm^{-3}. Explain your answer. [4]

[Total: 13]

10 Concentrated aqueous sodium chloride can be electrolysed in the laboratory using graphite electrodes.

a Write the formulae for all the ions present in an aqueous solution of sodium chloride. [2]

b Write half-equations to show the reactions at:

i the anode (positive electrode) [1]

ii the cathode (negative electrode). [1]

c Explain why the reaction at the anode is classed as oxidation. [1]

d After a while, the solution near the cathode becomes very alkaline. Explain why. [3]

e The chlorine produced at the anode can react with warm concentrated sodium hydroxide:

$$Cl_2 + 6NaOH \rightarrow 5NaCl + NaClO_3 + 3H_2O$$

Deduce the oxidation number changes per atom of chlorine when

i Cl_2 is converted to NaCl [1]

ii Cl_2 is converted to $NaClO_3$. [1]

f Give the systematic name for the compound $NaClO_3$. [1]

[Total: 11]

SELF-EVALUATION

After studying this chapter, complete a table like this:

I can	See section...	Needs more work	Almost there	Ready to move on
predict the identity of the substance liberated during electrolysis from the state of electrolyte (molten or aqueous)	20.2, 20.3			
predict the identity of the substance liberated during electrolysis from the position of the ions (in the electrolyte) in the redox series (electrode potential)	20.4			
predict the identity of the substance liberated during electrolysis from the concentration of the ions in the electrolyte	20.7			
state and apply the relationship, $F = Le$, between the Faraday constant, F, the Avogadro constant, L, and the charge on the electron, e	20.3			
calculate the quantity of charge passed during electrolysis using $Q = It$	20.3			
calculate the mass and / or volume of substance liberated during electrolysis	20.3			
describe the determination of a value of the Avogadro constant by an electrolytic method	20.3			
define the terms *standard electrode (reduction) potential* and *standard cell potential*	20.5, 20.6			
describe the standard hydrogen electrode	20.4			
describe methods used to measure the standard electrode potentials of metals or non-metals in contact with their ions in aqueous solution	20.5			
describe methods used to measure the standard electrode potentials of ions of the same element in different oxidation states	20.5			
calculate a standard cell potential by combining two standard electrode potentials	20.6			
use standard cell potential to deduce the polarity of each electrode and the direction of electron flow in the external circuit of a simple cell	20.6			

CONTINUED

I can	See section...	Needs more work	Almost there	Ready to move on
use standard cell potential to predict the feasibility of a reaction.	20.6			
deduce from standard electrode potential values the relative reactivity of elements, compounds and ions as oxidising agents or reducing agents	20.6			
construct redox equations using the relevant half-equations	20.6			
predict qualitatively how the value of an electrode potential varies with the concentration of the aqueous ion	20.6			
use the Nernst equation to predict quantitatively how the value of an electrode potential varies with the concentration of the aqueous ions	20.6			

> Chapter 21
Further aspects of equilibria

LEARNING INTENTIONS

In this chapter you will learn how to:

- define and use the terms *conjugate acid* and *conjugate base*
- define mathematically the terms pH, K_a, pK_a and K_w and use them in calculations
- calculate $[H^+(aq)]$ and pH values for strong acids, strong alkalis and weak acids
- define a buffer solution and explain how a buffer solution can be made
- explain how buffer solutions control pH, using chemical equations in these explanations
- describe and explain the uses of buffer solutions, including the role of HCO_3^- in controlling pH in the blood
- calculate the pH of buffer solutions, given appropriate data

- describe and use the term *solubility product*, K_{sp}

- write an expression for K_{sp}

- calculate K_{sp} from concentrations and vice versa

- describe and use the common ion effect to explain the different solubility of a compound in a solution containing a common ion

- perform calculations using K_{sp} values and concentration of a common ion

- state what is meant by the term *partition coefficient*, K_{pc}

- calculate and use a partition coefficient for a system in which the solute is in the same physical state in the two solvents

- understand the factors affecting the numerical value of a partition coefficient in terms of the polarities of the solute and the solvents used.

BEFORE YOU START

1 Write down the definition of a *Brønsted–Lowry acid* and *Brønsted–Lowry base*. Compare your definitions with those of another learner.

2 Work with another learner. Take it in turns to explain the meaning of the terms: *equilibrium*, *equilibrium constant*, *dissociation*, *strong acid*, *strong base*, *weak acid*, *weak base*, *neutralisation*. If you do not agree with each other or are both not sure, check with a textbook or the internet.

3 Make a list of strong acids and weak acids and strong bases and weak bases. Compare your lists with the rest of the class.

4 Get another learner to select a weak acid from Table 21.2. You then both write an equilibrium expression for this acid. Note that the process is the same as for writing equilibrium expressions for K_c that you used in Chapter 8. The only difference is you put K_a instead of K_c.

5 Explain to another learner why the equation $H^+ + OH^- \rightarrow H_2O$ applies to any acid–alkali reaction.

6 Write a paragraph describing how to carry out an experiment to find the enthalpy change of neutralisation of an acid by an alkali. Share your ideas with the rest of the class.

7 Work with another learner. Take it in turns to explain the meaning of the terms: *solute*, *solution*, *salt*, *sparingly soluble*, *polarisation*, *non-polar*, *enthalpy change*, *hydration*. If you do not agree or are not sure, check with a textbook or the internet.

GETTING RID OF THE HARDNESS

Figure 21.1: In a hard water area, enough limescale is formed in water pipes, kettles and boilers in your house to fill a small bucket!

When you add soap solution to a bottle of water and shake it, soap bubbles may form. We say that the sample of water is 'soft'. If a greasy solid (scum) forms on the surface of the water and the water looks milky, we say that the water is 'hard' (Figure 21.1). Hard water is caused by dissolved calcium hydrogencarbonate, magnesium hydrogencarbonate or magnesium sulfate. The scum is an insoluble compound of calcium or magnesium ions with the long-chain carboxylic acids present in soap.

When hard water is boiled, the soluble hydrogencarbonates change to insoluble carbonates:

$$Ca(HCO_3)_2(aq) \rightarrow CaCO_3(s) + H_2O(l) + CO_2(g)$$

Carbonates of calcium and magnesium can build up in kettles, boilers and water pipes and cause many problems. There are several ways of softening hard water. One way is to use an ion-exchange resin to remove calcium ions. The resin consists of an insoluble polymer which is packed in a column. The polymer contains negatively charged SO_3^- groups along its chain. We can represent these as RSO_3^-, where R is part of the polymer chain. If we wash the resin with sodium chloride, the sodium ions are attracted to the SO_3^- groups. When the ion-exchange resin is connected to the water supply coming into the house, the calcium or magnesium ions in the hard water are exchanged for the sodium ions in an equilibrium reaction.

$$2RSO_3^-Na^+(s) + Ca^{2+}(aq) \rightleftharpoons R_2(SO_3^-)_2Ca^{2+}(s) + 2Na^+(aq)$$

The position of equilibrium is in favour of the products. So the positive calcium ions form ionic bonds with the negative charges on the resin and the sodium ions are released. The sodium ions are soluble in hot water, so no solid is formed on boiling the water.

Questions for discussion

Discuss with another learner or group of learners:

* Work with another learner to make a list of the disadvantages of hard water.

* Use textbooks or the internet to find out some other ways of making the water softer.

* Use the ion-exchange equation shown above to suggest how you could convert the resin back to its original form.

21.1 Conjugate acids and conjugate bases

In Chapter 8, we considered acids and bases in terms of the Brønsted–Lowry theory. Acids are proton donors and bases are proton acceptors.

In a reaction at equilibrium, products are being converted to reactants at the same rate as reactants are being converted to products. The reverse reaction can also be considered in terms of the Brønsted–Lowry theory of acids and bases.

Consider the reaction:

$$NH_3(g) + H_2O(l) \rightleftharpoons NH_4^+(aq) + OH^-(aq)$$

In the reverse reaction, the NH_4^+ ion donates a proton to the OH^- ion. So NH_4^+ is acting as an acid and OH^- is acting as a base.

$$\underset{\text{base}}{NH_3(g)} + \underset{\text{acid}}{H_2O(l)} \rightleftharpoons \underset{\text{acid}}{NH_4^+(aq)} + \underset{\text{base}}{OH^-(aq)}$$

H⁺ donated

If a reactant is linked to a product by the transfer of a proton we call this pair a **conjugate pair**. Consider the following reaction:

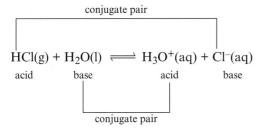

Looking at the forward reaction:

Cl^- is the conjugate base of the acid HCl

H_3O^+ is the conjugate acid of the base H_2O.

Looking at the reverse reaction:

HCl is the conjugate acid of the base Cl^-

H_2O is the conjugate base of the acid H_3O^+.

In a conjugate pair, the acid has one proton more than its conjugate base.

The conjugate pairs for the equilibrium between ammonia and water to form ammonium ions and hydroxide ions are:

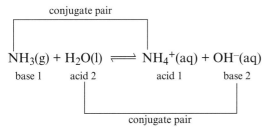

The idea of conjugate acids and bases is sometimes called the acid 1 / base 1, acid 2 / base 2 concept.

KEY DEFINITION

conjugate pair (acid-base): an acid-base pair on each side of an acid–base equilibrium equation that are related to each other by the difference of a hydrogen ion, e.g. the acid in the forward reaction and the base in the backward reaction.

Question

1 a Identify the acid and the base on the right-hand side of these equilibria.

i $HClO_2 + HCOOH \rightleftharpoons ClO_2^- + HCOOH_2^+$

ii $H_2S + H_2O \rightleftharpoons HS^- + H_3O^+$

b Identify the acid on the right-hand side of this equation which is conjugate with the base on the left-hand side.

$CH_3NH_2 + H_2O \rightleftharpoons CH_3NH_3^+ + OH^-$

The ionic product of water, K_w

Water is able to act as either an acid (by donating protons, H^+) or a base (by accepting protons). In pure water, the following equilibrium exists.

$$H_2O(l) + H_2O(l) \rightleftharpoons H_3O^+(aq) + OH^-(aq)$$

We can simplify this equation by writing hydroxonium ions, H_3O^+, as simple hydrogen ions, H^+:

$$H_2O(l) \rightleftharpoons H^+(aq) + OH^-(aq)$$

The equilibrium expression for this reaction is:

$$K_c = \frac{[H^+(aq)][OH^-(aq)]}{[H_2O(l)]}$$

IMPORTANT

Remember that one use of square brackets is to indicate the concentration of the substance inside the brackets.

The extent of ionisation of water is very low. The concentration of hydrogen ions and hydroxide ions in pure water (and hence the value of K_c) is extremely small. Because of this, we can regard the concentration of water as being constant.

We can therefore incorporate this into the value of K_c. The equilibrium expression then becomes:

$$K_w = [H^+][OH^-]$$

K_w is called the **ionic product of water**. Its value at 298 K is 1.00×10^{-14} mol^2 dm^{-6}.

We can use this equation to find the hydrogen ion concentration in pure water; for simplicity we will now omit the state symbol (aq). For each molecule of water that ionises, one H^+ ion and one OH^- ion are produced.

$$[H^+] = [OH^-]$$

We can rewrite the equilibrium expression

$$K_w = [H^+][OH^-]$$

as:

$$K_w = [H^+]^2$$

Rearranging this equation to find the hydrogen ion concentration $[H^+]$ in pure water:

$$[H^+] = \sqrt{K_w} = \sqrt{1.00 \times 10^{-14}} = 1.00 \times 10^{-7}\ \text{mol dm}^{-3}$$

> **KEY DEFINITION**
>
> **ionic product of water**, K_w: the equilibrium constant for the ionisation of water. $K_w = [H^+][OH^-]$

21.2 pH calculations

We know that the lower the hydrogen ion concentration, the higher the pH. The pH values of some familiar aqueous solutions are shown in Table 21.1.

The range of possible hydrogen ion concentrations in different solutions is very large. It can range from 10^{-15} mol dm^{-3} to 10 mol dm^{-3}. In order to overcome the problem of dealing with a wide range of numbers, the Danish chemist Søren Sørensen introduced the pH scale.

pH is defined as the negative logarithm to base 10 of the hydrogen ion concentration. In symbols this is written:

$$pH = -\log_{10}[H^+]$$

Note:

- the negative sign is introduced to make the pH values positive in most cases

- the logarithms used are to the base 10 (not to the base e), so make sure that when doing calculations, you press the 'log' or 'lg' button on your calculator (*not* the 'ln' button)

- we can use this equation to convert $[H^+]$ to pH or pH to $[H^+]$

Solution	pH
hydrochloric acid (1.00 mol dm^{-3})	0.0
stomach 'juices' (contains HCl(aq))	1.0–2.0
lemon juice	2.3
vinegar	3
coffee	around 5
rainwater (normal)	5.7
saliva	6.3–6.8
fresh milk	around 6.5
pure water	7.0
sea water	around 8.5
milk of magnesia	10
soapy water (cheap soap!)	11
bench sodium hydroxide (1.00 mol dm^{-3})	14

Table 21.1: pH values of some familiar aqueous solutions.

Calculating pH values from $[H^+]$

Here is an example of the use of logarithms to calculate pH from hydrogen ion concentrations.

Use your own calculator to check that you can get the correct answer. Try it several times. If you cannot get this answer (3.27) check with your calculator's instruction booklet, or find your teacher or a member of your teaching group to work with to solve this problem.

> **WORKED EXAMPLE**
>
> 1 Calculate the pH of a solution whose H^+ ion concentration is 5.32×10^{-4} mol dm^{-3}.
>
> **Solution**
>
> $$pH = -\log_{10}[H^+]$$
> $$= -\log_{10}(5.32 \times 10^{-4})$$
> $$= 3.27$$

Question

2 Calculate the pH of the following solutions:

   a $[H^+] = 3.00 \times 10^{-4}$ mol dm^{-3}

   b $[H^+] = 1.00 \times 10^{-2}$ mol dm^{-3}

   c $[H^+] = 4.00 \times 10^{-8}$ mol dm^{-3}

   d $[H^+] = 5.40 \times 10^{-12}$ mol dm^{-3}

   e $[H^+] = 7.80 \times 10^{-10}$ mol dm^{-3}

You should notice that the solutions in Question 2, parts **c**, **d** and **e**, are alkalis. They all have pH values greater than 7. Even though they are alkalis, they each have a small concentration of H$^+$ ions, and this concentration is used to calculate the pH. They each have a small concentration of H$^+$ ions because $H_2O \rightleftharpoons H^+ + OH^-$ is an equilibrium. Even when there is an excess of OH$^-$ ions, there is still a small concentration of H$^+$ ions. In the same way, the solutions in Question 2, parts **a** and **b**, have a small concentration of OH$^-$ ions, even though the solutions are acids.

Calculating [H⁺] from pH

Here is an example of the use of logarithms to calculate hydrogen ion concentration from pH. Use your own calculator to check that you get the correct answers.

Question

3 Calculate the concentration of hydrogen ions in solutions having the following pH values:

   a pH 2.90

   b pH 3.70

   c pH 11.2

   d pH 5.40

   e pH 12.9

The pH of strong acids

Monobasic acids contain only one replaceable hydrogen atom per molecule. Strong monobasic acids such as hydrochloric acid are completely ionised in solution. It follows from this that the concentration of hydrogen ions in solution is approximately the same as the concentration of the acid (Figure 21.2). (We assume here that the concentration of H$^+$ ions we get from the ionisation of water molecules is very small compared with the concentration of H$^+$ ions we get from the acid.)

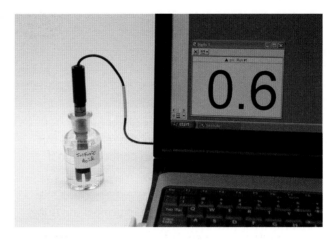

Figure 21.2: A pH electrode allows us to determine pH accurately.

- pH of 0.1 mol dm^{-3} HCl is $-\log (1 \times 10^{-1}$ mol dm$^{-3}) = $ pH 1

- pH of 0.01 mol dm^{-3} HCl is $-\log (1 \times 10^{-2}$ mol dm$^{-3}) = $ pH 2

- pH of 0.001 mol dm^{-3} HCl is $-\log (1 \times 10^{-3}$ mol dm$^{-3}) = $ pH 3

WORKED EXAMPLE

2 Calculate the hydrogen ion concentration of a solution whose pH is 10.5.

   Solution

   $$pH = -\log_{10} [H^+]$$
   $$[H^+] = 10^{-pH}$$
   $$= 10^{-10.5}$$
   $$= 3.16 \times 10^{-11} \text{ mol dm}^{-3}$$

   Use your own calculator to check that you can get the correct answer. Try it several times. If you cannot get this answer (3.16×10^{-11}), check with your calculator's instruction booklet, or ask your teacher or a member of your teaching group to work with you to solve this problem.

Diluting the acid ten times reduces the value of the H$^+$ ion concentration to one-tenth and increases the pH by a value of one.

Calculating the pH of strong bases

> **IMPORTANT**
>
> The ionic product for water is given by the equation $K_w = [H^+][OH^-]$. You can rearrange this to calculate the hydroxide ion concentration if you know K_w and $[H^+]$.

Note: You will not be expected to remember anything about the basic dissociation constant K_b.

Strong bases, such as sodium hydroxide, ionise completely in solution. The concentration of hydroxide ions in a solution of sodium hydroxide is therefore approximately the same as the concentration of the sodium hydroxide.

To calculate the pH of a solution of strong base we need to know:

- the concentration of OH^- ions in solution
- the equilibrium expression for the ionisation of water:
- $K_w = [H^+][OH^-]$
- the value of K_w for water.

As $K_w = [H^+][OH^-]$

$$[H^+] = \frac{K_w}{[OH^-]}$$

We can calculate the $[H^+]$ and then calculate the pH.

WORKED EXAMPLE

3 Calculate the pH of a solution of sodium hydroxide of concentration $0.0500 \text{ mol dm}^{-3}$.

$K_w = 1.00 \times 10^{-14} \text{ mol}^2 \text{ dm}^{-6}$ (at 298 K)

Solution

Step 1: Write the expression relating $[H^+]$ to K_w and $[OH^-]$

$$[H^+] = \frac{K_w}{[OH^-]}$$

Step 2: Substitute the values into the expression to calculate $[H^+]$.

$$[H^+] = \frac{1.00 \times 10^{-14}}{0.0500}$$

$$= 2.00 \times 10^{-13} \text{ mol dm}^{-3}$$

Step 3: Calculate the pH.

$$pH = -\log_{10}[H^+]$$
$$= -\log_{10}(2.00 \times 10^{-13})$$
$$= 12.7$$

A quick way to get the same answer is to:

- find $-\log_{10}[OH^-]$ (here $-\log_{10}[OH^-] = -\log_{10}(0.0500) = 1.3$)
- subtract this value from 14 (in this example $14 - 1.3 = 12.7$).

This works because $-\log_{10}[H^+] - \log_{10}[OH^-] = 14$.

Question

4 Find the pH of the following strong acids and strong bases:

a 1.00 mol dm^{-3} HNO_3

b $0.500 \text{ mol dm}^{-3}$ HNO_3

c an aqueous solution containing $3.00 \text{ g HCl per dm}^3$

d $0.00100 \text{ mol dm}^{-3}$ KOH ($K_w = 1.00 \times 10^{-14} \text{ mol}^2 \text{ dm}^{-6}$)

e an aqueous solution containing 0.200 g of NaOH per dm^3 ($K_w = 1.00 \times 10^{-14} \text{ mol}^2 \text{ dm}^{-6}$)

21.3 Weak acids: using the acid dissociation constant, K_a

K_a and pK_a

We can apply the equilibrium law (see Section 8.3) to aqueous solutions of weak acids and weak bases. For example, when ethanoic acid dissolves in water the following equilibrium results:

$$CH_3COOH(aq) + H_2O(l) \rightleftharpoons H_3O^+(aq) + CH_3COO^-(aq)$$

We can simplify this equation to:

$$\underset{\text{ethanoic acid}}{CH_3COOH(aq)} \rightleftharpoons H^+(aq) + \underset{\text{ethanoate ion}}{CH_3COO^-(aq)}$$

The equilibrium expression for this reaction is:

$$K_a = \frac{[H^+][CH_3COO^-]}{[CH_3COOH]}$$

K_a is called the **acid dissociation constant**. At 298 K, the value of K_a for the dissociation of ethanoic acid is 1.74×10^{-5} mol dm^{-3}.

The units of K_a are determined in the same way as for K_c (see Section 8.3). For the dissociation of a monobasic acid the units are mol dm^{-3}.

We can write the general formula for a monobasic acid as HA. The balanced equation for the partial ionisation of this weak acid is:

$$HA(aq) \rightleftharpoons H^+(aq) + A^-(aq)$$

The general equilibrium expression applying to a monobasic acid then becomes:

$$K_a = \frac{[H^+][A^-]}{[HA]}$$

> ### KEY DEFINITION
>
> **acid dissociation constant, K_a**: the equilibrium constant for the dissociation of a weak acid.
>
> $$K_a = \frac{[H^+][A^-]}{[HA]}$$

Figure 21.3: Friedrich Ostwald (1853–1932) was a German chemist who developed the idea of 'degree of dissociation' of weak acids and bases. He was one of the most well-known physical chemists of his day. But strangely enough, he didn't accept the atomic theory until 1906.

The value of K_a indicates the extent of dissociation of the acid (Figure 21.3).

- A high value for K_a (for example, 40 mol dm^{-3}) indicates that the position of equilibrium lies to the right. The acid is almost completely ionised.

- A low value for K_a (for example, 1.0×10^{-4} mol dm^{-3}) indicates that the position of equilibrium lies to the left. The acid is only slightly ionised and exists mainly as HA molecules and comparatively few H$^+$ and A$^-$ ions.

As K_a values for many acids are very low, we can use pK_a **values** to compare their strengths.

$$pK_a = -\log_{10}K_a$$

Table 21.2 shows the range of values of K_a and pK_a for various acids. Note that the less positive the value of pK_a, the more strongly acidic is the acid.

KEY WORD

pK_a values: values of K_a expressed as a logarithm to base 10.

$$pK_a = -\log_{10}K_a$$

IMPORTANT

Remember that a small 'p' in front of a symbol related to acids and bases means the negative logarithm (to the base 10).
So pH is $-\log_{10}[H^+]$ and p$K_a = -\log_{10}K_a$.

Question

5 a Write equilibrium expressions for the following reactions:

  i $C_6H_5COOH(aq) \rightleftharpoons H^+(aq) + C_6H_5COO^-(aq)$

  ii $HCO_3^-(aq) \rightleftharpoons H^+(aq) + CO_3^{2-}(aq)$

  iii $NH_4^+(aq) \rightleftharpoons H^+(aq) + NH_3(aq)$

  b Look at Table 21.2. For the following acids or ions (shown in the left-hand column), work out which species in the equilibrium are Brønsted–Lowry acids and which are their conjugate bases:

  i hydrated Fe^{3+} ion

  ii nitric(III) acid

  iii carbonic acid

  iv hydrogensilicate ion

Acid or ion	Equilibrium in aqueous solution	K_a / mol dm^{-3}	pK_a
nitric acid	$HNO_3 \rightleftharpoons H^+ + NO_3^-$	about 40	−1.4
sulfuric(IV) acid	$H_2SO_3 \rightleftharpoons H^+ + HSO_3^-$	1.5×10^{-2}	1.82
hydrated Fe^{3+} ion	$[Fe(H_2O)_6]^{3+} \rightleftharpoons H^+ + [Fe(H_2O)_5(OH)]^{2+}$	6.0×10^{-3}	2.22
hydrofluoric acid	$HF \rightleftharpoons H^+ + F^-$	5.6×10^{-4}	3.25
nitric(III) acid	$HNO_2 \rightleftharpoons H^+ + NO_2^-$	4.7×10^{-4}	3.33
methanoic acid	$HCOOH \rightleftharpoons H^+ + HCOO^-$	1.6×10^{-4}	3.80
benzoic acid	$C_6H_5COOH \rightleftharpoons H^+ + C_6H_5COO^-$	6.3×10^{-5}	4.20
ethanoic acid	$CH_3COOH \rightleftharpoons H^+ + CH_3COO^-$	1.7×10^{-5}	4.77
propanoic acid	$CH_3CH_2COOH \rightleftharpoons H^+ + CH_3CH_2COO^-$	1.3×10^{-5}	4.89
hydrated Al^{3+} ion	$[Al(H_2O)_6]^{3+} \rightleftharpoons H^+ + [Al(H_2O)_5(OH)]^{2+}$	1.0×10^{-5}	5.00
carbonic acid	$CO_2 + H_2O \rightleftharpoons H^+ + HCO_3^-$	4.5×10^{-7}	6.35
silicic acid	$SiO_2 + H_2O \rightleftharpoons H^+ + HSiO_3^-$	1.3×10^{-10}	9.89
hydrogencarbonate ion	$HCO_3^- \rightleftharpoons H^+ + CO_3^{2-}$	4.8×10^{-11}	−10.3
hydrogensilicate ion	$HSiO_3^- \rightleftharpoons H^+ + SiO_3^{2-}$	1.3×10^{-12}	−11.9
water	$H_2O \rightleftharpoons H^+ + OH^-$	1.0×10^{-14}	−14.0

Table 21.2: Acid dissociation constants, K_a, for a range of acids, for aqueous solutions in the region of 0.0–0.01 mol dm^{-3}.

Calculating K_a for a weak acid

We can calculate the value of K_a for a weak acid if we know:

- the concentration of the acid

- the pH of the solution.

From the general equation:

$$HA(aq) \rightleftharpoons H^+ + A^-$$

we can see that for each molecule of HA that ionises, one H^+ ion and one A^- ion are produced. (This assumes that we ignore the H^+ ions we get from the ionisation of water.)

$$[H^+] = [A^-]$$

We can rewrite the equilibrium expression

$$K_a = \frac{[H^+][A^-]}{[HA]}$$

as

$$K_a = \frac{[H^+]^2}{[HA]}$$

In order to calculate the value of K_a we make two assumptions:

- We ignore the concentration of hydrogen ions produced by the ionisation of the water molecules present in the solution. This is reasonable because the ionic product of water (1.00×10^{-14} mol^2 dm^{-6}) is negligible compared with the values for most weak acids (see Table 21.2).

- We assume that the ionisation of the weak acid is so small that the concentration of undissociated HA molecules present at equilibrium is approximately the same as that of the original acid.

Worked example 4 shows how to calculate the value of K_a using the pH and the concentration of the weak acid.

WORKED EXAMPLE

4   Calculate the value of K_a for methanoic acid. A solution of 0.010 mol dm^{-3} methanoic acid, HCOOH, has a pH of 2.90.

Solution

Step 1: Convert pH to $[H^+]$.

$$[H^+] = 10^{-2.90}$$

$$= 1.26 \times 10^{-3} \text{ mol dm}^{-3}$$

CONTINUED

Step 2: Write the equilibrium expression.

$$K_a = \frac{[H^+]^2}{[HA]} \text{ or } K_a = \frac{[H^+][A^-]}{[HA]}$$

Step 3: Enter the values into the expression and calculate the answer.

$$K_a = \frac{(1.26 \times 10^{-3})^2}{(0.010)}$$

$$= 1.59 \times 10^{-4} \text{ mol dm}^{-3}$$

Question

6   a   Calculate the value of K_a for the following acids:

   i   0.0200 mol dm^{-3} 2-aminobenzoic acid, which has a pH of 4.30

   ii   0.0500 mol dm^{-3} propanoic acid, which has a pH of 3.10

   iii 0.100 mol dm^{-3} 2-nitrophenol, which has a pH of 4.10

   b   Calculate pK_a values for each of the acids in part **a**.

Calculating the pH of a weak acid

We can calculate the pH value (or $[H^+]$) of a weak acid if we know:

- the concentration of the acid

- the value of K_a for the acid.

Again, we make the same assumptions about the concentration of hydrogen ions produced by the ionisation of water and the equilibrium concentration of the weak acid. The value of the pH calculated will not be significantly affected by these factors unless we require great accuracy (for example, calculating pH to the third decimal place).

Worked example 5 shows how to calculate pH from the value of K_a and concentration of the weak acid.

WORKED EXAMPLE

5   Calculate the pH of 0.100 mol dm^{-3} ethanoic acid, CH$_3$COOH.

(K_a = 1.74 × 10^{-5} mol dm^{-3})

Solution

Step 1: Write the equilibrium expression for the reaction.

$$CH_3COOH(aq) \rightleftharpoons H^+(aq) + CH_3COO^-(aq)$$

$$K_a = \frac{[H^+]^2}{[HA]} \text{ or } K_a = \frac{[H^+]^2}{[CH_3COOH]}$$

Step 2: Enter the values into the expression.

$$1.74 \times 10^{-5} = \frac{[H^+]^2}{[0.100]}$$

Step 3: Rearrange the equation.

$$[H^+]^2 = 1.74 \times 10^{-5} \times 0.100 = 1.74 \times 10^{-6}$$

Step 4: Take the square root.

$$[H^+] = \sqrt{1.74 \times 10^{-6}} = 1.32 \times 10^{-3} \text{ mol dm}^{-3}$$

Step 5: Calculate pH.

$$pH = -\log_{10}[H^+]$$
$$= -\log_{10}(1.32 \times 10^{-3})$$
$$= 2.88 \text{ (to 3 significant figures)}$$

Question

7   Use the data from Table 21.2 to work out the pH values of the following solutions:

a   0.0200 mol dm^{-3} aqueous benzoic acid

b   0.0100 mol dm^{-3} hydrated aluminium ions

c   0.100 mol dm^{-3} aqueous methanoic acid.

21.4 Buffer solutions

What is a buffer solution?

A **buffer solution** is a solution in which the pH does not change significantly when small amounts of acids or alkalis are added. A buffer solution is used to keep pH (almost) constant.

KEY DEFINITION

buffer solution: a solution that minimises changes in pH when moderate amounts of acid or base are added.

A buffer solution is either a weak acid and its conjugate base or a weak base and its conjugate acid, which minimises any change in pH when an acid or alkali is added.

One type of buffer solution is a mixture of a weak acid and one of its salts. An example is an aqueous mixture of ethanoic acid and sodium ethanoate. Mixtures of ethanoic acid and sodium ethanoate in different proportions act as buffers between pH values of 4 and 7. We can understand how a buffer solution works by referring to the equilibria involved (Figure 21.4).

Ethanoic acid is a weak acid. So it stays mostly in the un-ionised form (CH$_3$COOH) and only gives rise to a low concentration of ethanoate ions in solution:

$$\underset{\text{ethanoic acid}}{CH_3COOH(aq)} \rightleftharpoons H^+(aq) + \underset{\text{ethanoate ion}}{CH_3COO^-(aq)}$$

Sodium ethanoate is fully ionised in aqueous solution:

$$\underset{\text{sodium ethanoate}}{CH_3COONa(s)} + aq \rightarrow Na^+(aq) + \underset{\text{ethanoate ion}}{CH_3COO^-(aq)}$$

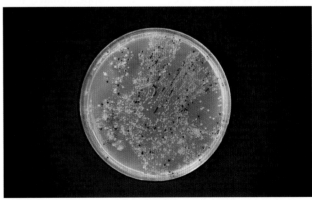

Figure 21.4: The pH of this agar plate for growing bacteria is kept constant by using a buffer solution. The buffer solution is added into the agar jelly used to make the plate.

The buffer solution contains relatively high concentrations of both CH_3COOH and CH_3COO^-. We say that there are *reserve supplies* of the acid (CH_3COOH) and its conjugate base (CH_3COO^-). The pH of a buffer solution depends on the ratio of the concentration of the acid and the concentration of its conjugate base. If this does not change very much, the pH changes very little.

In the buffer solution ethanoic acid molecules are in equilibrium with hydrogen ions and ethanoate ions:

$$CH_3COOH(aq) \rightleftharpoons H^+(aq) + CH_3COO^-(aq)$$

relatively high concentration of ethanoic acid   relatively high concentration of ethanoate ions

We can use this equation to explain how buffer solutions work.

An increase in hydrogen ion concentration would greatly lower the pH of water, but when H^+ ions are added to the buffer solution:

- addition of H^+ ions shifts the position of equilibrium to the left because H^+ ions combine with CH_3COO^- ions to form more CH_3COOH until equilibrium is re-established

- the large reserve supply of CH_3COO^- ensures that the concentration of CH_3COO^- ions in solution does not change significantly

- the large reserve supply of CH_3COOH ensures that the concentration of CH_3COOH molecules in solution does not change significantly

- so the pH does not change significantly.

An increase in hydroxide ion concentration would greatly increase the pH of water, but when OH^- ions are added to the buffer solution:

- the added OH^- ions combine with H^+ ions to form water

- this reduces the H^+ ion concentration

- the position of equilibrium shifts to the right

- so CH_3COOH molecules ionise to form more H^+ and CH_3COO^- ions until equilibrium is re-established

- the large reserve supply of CH_3COOH ensures that the concentration of CH_3COOH molecules in solution does not change significantly

- the large reserve supply of CH_3COO^- ensures that the concentration of CH_3COO^- ions in solution does not change significantly

- so the pH does not change significantly.

In unpolluted regions of the Earth, rainwater has a pH of 5.7. This is because carbon dioxide dissolves in the rainwater to form a dilute solution of the weak acid carbonic acid, H_2CO_3. This acid and its conjugate base, HCO_3^-, act as a buffer solution. It minimises changes in pH if very small amounts of acid or alkali are added to the rainwater. But in regions where there is pollution caused by the emission of acidic oxides of nitrogen and sulfur, the pH of the rainwater falls to around 4. The rainwater can no longer act as a buffer because the concentrations of the H_2CO_3 and HCO_3^- are not high enough to cope with the large amounts of acidic pollution involved.

No buffer solution can cope with the excessive addition of acids or alkalis. If very large amounts of acid or alkali are added, the pH will change significantly.

Buffer solutions that resist changes in pH in alkaline regions are usually a mixture of a weak base and its conjugate acid. An example is a mixture of aqueous ammonia with ammonium chloride.

Aqueous ammonia is a weak base, so there is only a low concentration of ammonium ions in ammonia solution:

$$NH_3(aq) + H_2O(l) \rightleftharpoons NH_4^+(aq) + OH^-(aq)$$

Ammonium chloride is fully ionised in aqueous solution. This supplies the reserve supplies of the conjugate acid, NH_4^+.

$$NH_4Cl(aq) \rightleftharpoons NH_4^+(aq) + Cl^-(aq)$$

Question

8 A mixture of 0.500 mol dm^{-3} aqueous ammonia and 0.500 mol dm^{-3} ammonium chloride acts as a buffer solution.

   a Explain how this buffer solution minimises changes in pH on addition of

     i dilute hydrochloric acid

     ii dilute sodium hydroxide.

   b Explain why dilute aqueous ammonia alone will not act as a buffer solution.

Calculating the pH of a buffer solution

We can calculate the pH of a buffer solution if we know:

- the K_a of the weak acid
- the equilibrium concentration of the weak acid and its conjugate base (salt).

To do the calculation, we use the equilibrium expression for the particular reaction.

We can make the numbers easier to deal with in calculations involving buffer solutions by using logarithms throughout. So instead of using the expression:

$$[H^+] = K_a \times \frac{[\text{acid}]}{[\text{salt}]}$$

we can use the expression:

$$pH = pK_a + \log_{10} \frac{[\text{salt}]}{[\text{acid}]}$$

IMPORTANT

Remember that in the expression

$$[H^+] = K_a \times \frac{[\text{acid}]}{[\text{salt}]}$$

for the buffer solution

$$HCOOH \rightleftharpoons HCOO^- + H^+$$

- the salt contains the $HCOO^-$
- $HCOO^-$ and $HCOOH$ are a conjugate pair.

WORKED EXAMPLE

6 Calculate the pH of a buffer solution containing 0.600 mol dm^{-3} propanoic acid and 0.800 mol dm^{-3} sodium propanoate.

(K_a propanoic acid = 1.35×10^{-5} mol dm^{-3})

Solution

Step 1: Write the equilibrium expression.

$$K_a = \frac{[H^+][C_2H_5COO^-]}{[C_2H_5COOH]}$$

Step 2: Rearrange the equilibrium expression to make [H$^+$] the subject.

$$[H^+] = \frac{K_a \times [C_2H_5COOH]}{[C_2H_5COO^-]}$$

Note that in this expression, the ratio determining [H$^+$], and hence pH, is the ratio of the concentration of the acid to the salt (conjugate base).

Step 3: Substitute the data given.

$$[H^+] = 1.35 \times 10^{-5} \times \frac{0.600}{0.800}$$

$$= 1.01 \times 10^{-5} \text{ mol dm}^{-3}$$

Step 4: Calculate the pH.

$$pH = -\log_{10}[H^+]$$
$$= -\log_{10}(1.01 \times 10^{-5})$$
$$= -(-4.99)$$
$$= 4.99$$

Questions

9 a Calculate the pH of the following buffer solutions:

   i   0.0500 mol dm^{-3} methanoic acid and 0.100 mol dm^{-3} sodium methanoate.

   (K_a of methanoic acid = 1.60×10^{-4} mol dm^{-3})

   ii 0.0100 mol dm^{-3} benzoic acid and 0.0400 mol dm^{-3} sodium benzoate.

   (K_a of benzoic acid = 6.3×10^{-5} mol dm^{-3})

   b How many moles of sodium ethanoate must be added to 1.00 dm^3 of 0.100 mol dm^{-3} ethanoic acid to produce a buffer solution of pH 4.90?

   (K_a of ethanoic acid = 1.74×10^{-5} mol dm^{-3})

Tip: first find the hydrogen ion concentration, then rearrange the equilibrium expression to make [(sodium) ethanoate] the subject of the expression.

10 What is the pH of a buffer solution made by mixing 100 cm^3 of 0.1 mol dm^{-3} methanoic acid with 50 cm^3 0.1 mol dm^{-3} sodium methanoate?

K_a (HCOOH) = 1.6×10^{-4}

A pH 4.1

B pH 3.8

C pH 4.5

D pH 3.5

Making a buffer solution

We make buffer solutions by adding a solution of a weak acid to its conjugate base or a weak base to its conjugate acid until we get the pH that is required. The more concentrated the acid and conjugate base, the more effective is the buffer solution at preventing a change in pH.

1 Put 50 cm^3 of 0.1 mol dm^{-3} ethanoic acid in a small beaker.

2 Add a spatula-ful of sodium ethanoate and stir with a glass rod until the sodium ethanoate dissolves.

3 Add a few drops of universal indicator solution to give a definite colour and determine the pH using the indicator colour chart. (Alternatively, use a pH meter.)

4 Label the beaker 'buffer solution'.

5 To a second beaker add 1 drop of 1.0 mol dm^{-3} hydrochloric acid and 50 cm^3 distilled water.

6 Add a few drops of universal indicator solution and then dilute the solution very gradually with more distilled water until you get the same pH as the pH of the buffer solution. You may need to add more indicator to get the same colour intensity as the buffer solution.

7 Label the beaker 'unbuffered solution'.

8 Add one drop of 0.1 mol dm^{-3} sodium hydroxide to each of the beakers. Observe what happens. Add a further drop of sodium hydroxide one at a time, to each of the beakers. Which solution is best at resisting pH change?

Uses of buffer solutions

Buffer solutions play an important part in many industrial processes, including electroplating, the manufacture of dyes and in the treatment of leather. They are also used to make sure that pH meters record the correct pH.

Many animals depend on buffers to keep a constant pH in various parts of their bodies. In humans, the pH of the blood is kept between 7.35 and 7.45 by a number of different buffers in the blood:

* hydrogencarbonate ions, HCO_3^-

* haemoglobin and plasma proteins

* dihydrogenphosphate ($H_2PO_4^-$) and hydrogenphosphate (HPO_4^{2-}) ions.

The pH of the blood is often checked by doctors as it can give information which helps identify problems in the workings of the body (Figure 21.5).

The cells in our body produce carbon dioxide as a product of aerobic respiration (the oxidation of glucose to provide energy). Carbon dioxide combines with water in the blood to form a solution containing hydrogen ions.

$$CO_2(aq) + H_2O(aq) \rightleftharpoons H^+(aq) + HCO_3^-(aq)$$

hydrogencarbonate ion

This reaction is catalysed by the enzyme carbonic anhydrase. When the blood passes through the small blood vessels around our lungs, hydrogencarbonate ions are rapidly converted to carbon dioxide and water. The carbon dioxide escapes into the lungs.

The production of H$^+$ ions, if left unchecked, would lower the pH of the blood and cause 'acidosis'. This may disrupt some body functions and eventually lead to coma. The equilibrium between carbon dioxide and hydrogencarbonate is the most important buffering system in the blood.

If the H$^+$ ion concentration increases:

* the position of this equilibrium shifts to the left

* H$^+$ ions combine with HCO_3^- ions to form carbon dioxide and water until equilibrium is restored

* this reduces the concentration of hydrogen ions in the blood and helps keep the pH constant.

If the H$^+$ ion concentration decreases:

* the position of this equilibrium shifts to the right

* some carbon dioxide and water combine to form H$^+$ and HCO_3^- ions until equilibrium is restored

* this increases the concentration of hydrogen ions in the blood and helps keep the pH constant.

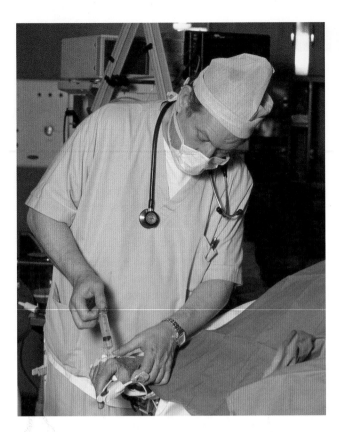

Figure 21.5: Anaesthetists monitor the pH of a patient's blood.

21.5 Equilibrium and solubility

In Chapter 4 we learned that most ionic compounds dissolve in water. In Chapter 19 we related solubility to enthalpy change of solution. Some ionic compounds, however, are insoluble or only slightly soluble in water. But even 'insoluble' ionic compounds may dissolve to a very small extent in water. Solubility is generally quoted as the number of grams or number of moles of compound needed to saturate 100 g or 1 kg of water at a given temperature. We say that a solution is saturated when no more solute dissolves in it.

- Sodium chloride is regarded as a soluble salt: a saturated solution contains 36 g per 100 g of water.

- Lead(II) chloride is regarded as an insoluble salt: a saturated solution contains 0.99 g per 100 g of water.

Solubility product

An equilibrium is established when an undissolved ionic compound is in contact with a saturated solution of its ions. The ions move from the solid to the saturated solution at the same rate as they move from the solution to the solid (Figure 21.6).

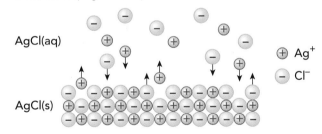

Figure 21.6: An equilibrium is established between solid silver chloride and its saturated solution. The water molecules are not shown.

Question

11 a One of the buffers in blood plasma is a mixture of dihydrogenphosphate ions ($H_2PO_4^-$) and hydrogenphosphate ions (HPO_4^{2-}).

   i Identify the conjugate acid and base in this buffer.

   ii Write a balanced equation for the equilibrium between these two ions.

b Some proteins in the blood can act as buffers. The equation below shows a simplified equilibrium equation for this reaction. (Pr = protein)

$$HPr \rightleftharpoons H^+ + Pr^-$$

Explain how this system can act as a buffer to prevent the blood getting too acidic.

> ### KEY DEFINITION
>
> **solubility product, K_{sp}:** the product of the concentrations of each ion in a saturated solution of a sparingly soluble salt at 298 K, raised to the power of their relative concentrations

When solid silver chloride dissolves, it is in contact with saturated silver chloride solution and the following equilibrium is set up:

$$AgCl(s) \rightleftharpoons Ag^+(aq) + Cl^-(aq)$$

The equilibrium expression relating to this equation is:

$$K_c = \frac{[Ag^+(aq)]\,[Cl^-(aq)]}{[AgCl(s)]}$$

For any solid, the concentration of the solid phase remains constant and can be combined with the value of K_c.

So we can write this equilibrium expression as:

$$K_{sp} = [Ag^+(aq)]\,[Cl^-(aq)]$$

K_{sp} is called the **solubility product**. Values are quoted at 298 K.

$$K_{sp} = [C^{y+}(aq)]^a\,[A^{x-}(aq)]^b$$

where a is the number of C^{y+} cations in one formula unit of the compound and b is the number of A^{x-} anions in one formula unit of the compound.

So for Fe_2S_3 (which contains Fe^{3+} ions and S^{2-} ions) the equilibrium is:

$$Fe_2S_3(s) \rightleftharpoons 2Fe^{3+}(aq) + 3S^{2-}(aq)$$

and the equilibrium expression is:

$$K_{sp} = [Fe^{3+}(aq)]^2\,[S^{2-}(aq)]^3$$

The idea of solubility product only applies to ionic compounds that are slightly soluble.

The units of solubility product depend on the number of each type of ion present in solution. You can work the units out in the same way as for general equilibrium expressions (see Section 8.3), but you don't have to do any cancelling. For example, for the expression:

$$K_{sp} = [Mg^{2+}(aq)] \times [OH^-(aq)]^2$$
$$= \text{mol dm}^{-3} \times (\text{mol dm}^{-3})^2$$
$$= \text{mol}^3 \text{ dm}^{-9}$$

The idea of solubility product is only useful for sparingly soluble salts. The smaller the value of K_{sp} the lower is the solubility of the salt. Some values of K_{sp} are given in Table 21.3.

Compound	K_{sp} / (mol dm^{-3})$^{a+b}$
AgCl	1.8×10^{-10}
Al(OH)$_3$	1.0×10^{-32}
BaCO$_3$	5.5×10^{-10}
BaSO$_4$	1.0×10^{-10}
CaCO$_3$	5.0×10^{-9}
CoS	2.0×10^{-26}
CuS	6.3×10^{-36}
Fe(OH)$_2$	7.9×10^{-16}
Fe$_2$S$_3$	1.0×10^{-88}
HgI$_2$	2.5×10^{-26}
Mn(OH)$_2$	1.0×10^{-11}
PbCl$_2$	1.6×10^{-5}
Sb$_2$S$_3$	1.7×10^{-93}
SnCO$_3$	1.0×10^{-9}
Zn(OH)$_2$	2.0×10^{-17}
ZnS	1.6×10^{-23}

Table 21.3: Some values of solubility product at 298 K.

Question

12 a Write equilibrium expressions for the solubility products of the following:

   i Fe(OH)$_2$

   ii Fe$_2$S$_3$

   iii Al(OH)$_3$

   b State the units of solubility product for each of the compounds in part **a**.

Solubility product calculations

You may be asked to calculate the solubility product of a compound from its solubility, or you may be asked to calculate the solubility of a compound from its solubility product. An example of each of these types of calculation is shown in Worked examples 7 and 8.

WORKED EXAMPLES

7 Calculating solubility product from solubility.

A saturated solution of magnesium fluoride, MgF_2, has a solubility of 1.22×10^{-3} mol dm^{-3}. Calculate the solubility product of magnesium fluoride.

Solution

Step 1: Write down the equilibrium equation.

$$MgF_2(s) \rightleftharpoons Mg^{2+}(aq) + 2F^-(aq)$$

Step 2: Calculate the concentration of each ion in solution.

When 1.22×10^{-3} mol dissolves to form 1 dm^3 of solution the concentration of each ion is:

$$[Mg^{2+}] = 1.22 \times 10^{-3} \text{ mol dm}^{-3}$$

$$[F^-] = 2 \times 1.22 \times 10^{-3} \text{ mol dm}^{-3}$$
$$= 2.44 \times 10^{-3} \text{ mol dm}^{-3}$$

(The concentration of F^- is $2 \times 1.22 \times 10^{-3}$ mol dm^{-3} because each formula unit contains $2 \times F^-$ ions.)

Step 3: Write down the equilibrium expression.
$$K_{sp} = [Mg^{2+}] [F^-]^2$$

Step 4: Substitute the values.
$$K_{sp} = (1.22 \times 10^{-3}) \times (2.44 \times 10^{-3})^2$$
$$= 7.26 \times 10^{-9}$$

Step 5: Add the correct units.

$$(\text{mol dm}^{-3}) \times (\text{mol dm}^{-3})^2 = \text{mol}^3 \text{ dm}^{-9}$$

Answer $= 7.26 \times 10^{-9}$ mol^3 dm^{-9}

8 Calculating solubility from solubility product.

Calculate the solubility of copper(II) sulfide in mol dm^{-3}.

(K_{sp} for CuS $= 6.3 \times 10^{-36}$ mol^2 dm^{-6})

Solution

Step 1: Write down the equilibrium equation.
$$CuS(s) \rightleftharpoons Cu^{2+}(aq) + S^{2-}(aq)$$

Step 2: Write the equilibrium expression in terms of one ion only.

From the equilibrium equation $[Cu^{2+}] = [S^{2-}]$

So $K_{sp} = [Cu^{2+}] [S^{2-}]$ becomes $K_{sp} = [Cu^{2+}]^2$

Step 3: Substitute the value of K_{sp}.
$$(6.3 \times 10^{-36}) = [Cu^{2+}]^2$$

Step 4: Calculate the concentration.

In this case we take the square root of K_{sp}.

$$[Cu^{2+}] = \sqrt{K_{sp}}$$

$$[Cu^{2+}] = \sqrt{6.3 \times 10^{-36}} = 2.5 \times 10^{-18} \text{ mol dm}^{-3}$$

Question

13 a Calculate the solubility product of the following solutions:

    i a saturated aqueous solution of cadmium sulfide, CdS (solubility = 1.46×10^{-11} mol dm^{-3})

    ii a saturated aqueous solution of calcium fluoride, CaF_2, containing 0.0168 g dm^{-3} CaF_2

b Calculate the solubility in mol dm^{-3} of zinc sulfide, ZnS.

(K_{sp} = 1.6×10^{-23} mol^2 dm^{-6})

c Calculate the solubility of silver carbonate, Ag_2CO_3.

(K_{sp} = 6.3×10^{-12} mol^3 dm^{-9})

Tip: you have to divide by 4, then take the cube root. Can you see why? You should have a cube root button on your calculator ($\sqrt[3]{\ }$).

Predicting precipitation

We can use the solubility product to predict whether precipitation will occur when two solutions are mixed. For example, will we get a precipitate when we mix a solution of barium chloride, $BaCl_2$, with a very dilute solution of sodium carbonate?

Both barium chloride and sodium carbonate are soluble salts, but barium carbonate is relatively insoluble. We must consider the equilibrium for the insoluble salt dissolving in water:

$$BaCO_3(s) \rightleftharpoons Ba^{2+}(aq) + CO_3^{2-}(aq)$$

The solubility product is given by:

$$K_{sp} = [Ba^{2+}][CO_3^{2-}] = 5.5 \times 10^{-10}\ mol^2\ dm^{-6}$$

If $[Ba^{2+}][CO_3^{2-}]$ is greater than $5.5 \times 10^{-10}\ mol^2\ dm^{-6}$ a precipitate will form.

If $[Ba^{2+}][CO_3^{2-}]$ is less than $5.5 \times 10^{-10}\ mol^2\ dm^{-6}$ no precipitate will form (see worked example 9).

> **IMPORTANT**
>
> Remember that solubility product is only relevant for salts which are sparingly (very slightly) soluble. The concept cannot be used for soluble salts such as sodium chloride. Remember that soluble salts include salts of Group I elements, all nitrates and ammonium salts and many sulfates. Halides are generally soluble except for lead(II) halides and silver halides.

The common ion effect

The **common ion effect** is the reduction in the solubility of a dissolved salt achieved by adding a solution of a compound that has an ion in common with the dissolved salt. This often results in precipitation (Figure 21.7).

Figure 21.7: The shell of this nautilus is composed mainly of calcium carbonate. The nautilus adjusts conditions so shell material is formed when the concentration of calcium ions and carbonate ions in seawater are high enough to precipitate calcium carbonate.

> **KEY WORD**
>
> **common ion effect:** the reduction of the solubility of a dissolved salt by adding a compound that has an ion in common with the dissolved salt, e.g. addition of sodium chloride to a solution of very slightly soluble lead(II) chloride.

An example of the common ion effect can be seen when we add a solution of sodium chloride to a saturated solution of silver chloride and silver chloride precipitates. Why is this?

> **WORKED EXAMPLE**
>
> 9 Will a precipitate form if we mix equal volumes of solutions of $1.00 \times 10^{-4}\ mol\ dm^{-3}$ Na_2CO_3 and $5.00 \times 10^{-5}\ mol\ dm^{-3}$ $BaCl_2$?
>
> **Solution**
>
> $[CO_3^{2-}] = 5.00 \times 10^{-5}\ mol\ dm^{-3}$
>
> $[Ba^{2+}] = 2.50 \times 10^{-5}\ mol\ dm^{-3}$
>
> $[Ba^{2+}][CO_3^{2-}] = (2.50 \times 10^{-5}) \times (5.00 \times 10^{-5})$
>
> $\qquad\qquad\quad = 1.25 \times 10^{-9}\ mol^2\ dm^{-6}$
>
> This value is greater than the solubility product, so a precipitate of barium carbonate forms.

In a saturated solution of silver chloride in water, we have the following equilibrium:

$$AgCl(s) \rightleftharpoons Ag^+(aq) + Cl^-(aq)$$

We now add a solution of sodium chloride:

- the chloride ion is common to both sodium chloride and silver chloride
- the added chloride ions shift the position of equilibrium to the left
- silver chloride is precipitated.

The addition of the common ion, Cl^-, has reduced the solubility of the silver chloride because its solubility product has been exceeded. When $[Ag^+][Cl^-]$ is greater than the K_{sp} for silver chloride, a precipitate will form.

The solubility of an ionic compound in aqueous solution containing a common ion is less than its solubility in water.

For example, the solubility of barium sulfate, $BaSO_4$, in water is 1.0×10^{-5} mol dm^{-3} and the solubility of barium sulfate in 0.100 mol dm^{-3} sulfuric acid, H_2SO_4, is only 1.0×10^{-9} mol dm^{-3}.

We can explain the lower solubility in sulfuric acid by referring to the solubility product of barium sulfate:

$$K_{sp} = [Ba^{2+}][SO_4^{2-}] = 1.0 \times 10^{-10} \text{ mol}^2 \text{ dm}^{-6}$$

If we ignore the very small amount of $SO_4^{2-}(aq)$ from the barium sulfate then $[SO_4^{2-}]$ is 0.1 mol dm^{-3} (from the sulfuric acid). This gives:

$$1.0 \times 10^{-10} = [Ba^{2+}] \times [0.1]$$

$$[Ba^{2+}] = 1.0 \times 10^{-9} \text{ mol dm}^{-3}$$

Questions

14 a Thallium(I) chloride is a salt that is sparingly soluble in water. When hydrochloric acid is added to a saturated solution of thallium(I) chloride, a precipitate is formed. Explain why a precipitate is formed.

b Calcium sulfate is a sparingly soluble salt that can be made by mixing solutions containing calcium and sulfate ions. A 0.00100 mol dm^{-3} solution of aqueous calcium chloride, $CaCl_2$, is mixed with an equal volume of 0.00100 mol dm^{-3} solution of aqueous sodium sulfate, Na_2SO_4.

i Calculate the concentration of calcium and sulfate ions when equal volumes of these solutions of calcium chloride and sodium sulfate are mixed.

ii Will a precipitate of calcium sulfate form? (K_{sp} of calcium sulfate = 2.0×10^{-5} mol^2 dm^{-6})

15 Which one of these is the correct numerical value for the solubility product for bismuth sulfide Bi_2S_3? Solubility of $Bi_2S_3 = 3.6 \times 10^{-8}$ mol dm^{-3}.

A 6.53×10^{-36}

B 1.30×10^{-39}

C 7.77×10^{-15}

D 4.35×10^{-36}

21.6 Partition coefficients

The principle of partition of a *solute* between two solvents helps us to understand more fully how we separate the components in a mixture in chromatography (see Section 30.1). Let us consider ammonia dissolved in two immiscible solvents. Immiscible solvents are solvents that do not dissolve in each other and so form two separate layers (Figure 21.8).

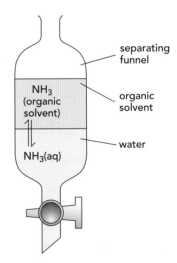

Figure 21.8: Ammonia (the solute) dissolves in both the solvents, water and the organic solvent. A state of dynamic equilibrium is established.

A separating funnel is shaken with the organic solvent and an aqueous solution of ammonia. The ammonia is soluble in both solvents so when the mixture is left to settle, a dynamic equilibrium is established. At this point, ammonia molecules are moving from the aqueous layer to the organic layer at the same rate as they are moving from the organic layer to the aqueous layer:

$$NH_3(aq) \rightleftharpoons NH_3(\text{organic solvent})$$

We can calculate a value for the equilibrium constant (see Section 8.3). We call this the **partition coefficient,** K_{pc}. The partition coefficient is the equilibrium constant that relates the concentration of a solute partitioned between two immiscible solvents at a particular temperature.

WORKED EXAMPLE

10 100 cm³ of a 0.100 mol dm⁻³ solution of ammonia in water at 20 °C was shaken with 50 cm³ of an organic solvent and left in a separating funnel for equilibrium to be established.

A 20.0 cm³ portion of the aqueous layer was run off and titrated against 0.200 mol dm⁻³ dilute hydrochloric acid. The end-point was found to be 9.40 cm³ of acid.

What is the partition coefficient of ammonia between these two solvents at 20 °C?

Solution

The alkaline ammonia solution is neutralised by dilute hydrochloric acid:

$$NH_3(aq) + HCl(aq) \rightarrow NH_4Cl(aq)$$

1 mole of ammonia reacts with 1 mole of the acid. In the titration we used:

$$\frac{9.40}{1000} \times 0.200 \text{ moles of HCl}$$

$$= 1.88 \times 10^{-3} \text{ moles}$$

This reacts with ammonia in the ratio 1 : 1 so there must be 1.88×10^{-3} moles of NH_3 in the 20.0 cm³ portion titrated.

Therefore, in the 100 cm³ aqueous layer there are

$$1.88 \times 10^{-3} \times \frac{100}{20.0} \text{ mol}$$

$$= 9.40 \times 10^{-3} \text{ mol}$$

The number of moles of ammonia in the organic layer must be equal to the initial number of moles of ammonia minus the amount left in the aqueous layer at equilibrium.

- initial number of moles of ammonia

$$= 0.100 \times \frac{100}{1000} = 0.0100 \text{ mol}$$

- final number of moles of ammonia in organic layer

$$= 0.0100 - 9.40 \times 10^{-3} \text{ mol}$$

$$= 6.00 \times 10^{-4} \text{ mol}$$

Now we need to change the numbers of moles of ammonia in each layer into concentrations (i.e. the number of moles in 1000 cm³ or 1 dm³) to substitute into the equilibrium expression for the partition coefficient, K_{pc}.

- concentration of ammonia in 100 cm³ of the aqueous layer

$$= 9.40 \times 10^{-3} \times \frac{1000}{100}$$

$$= 0.094 \text{ mol dm}^{-3}$$

- concentration of ammonia in 50 cm³ of the organic solvent

$$= 6.00 \times 10^{-4} \times \frac{1000}{50}$$

$$= 0.012 \text{ mol dm}^{-3}$$

The expression for the partition coefficient, K_{pc} is:

$$K_{pc} = \frac{[NH_3(\text{organic solvent})]}{[NH_3(aq)]}$$

$$= \frac{0.012}{0.094} \text{ (no units)}$$

$$= 0.13$$

- This value is less than 1, which shows us that ammonia is more soluble in water than in the organic solvent.

What affects the value of K_{pc}?

The value of K_{pc} depends on the relative solubilities of the solute in the two solvents used in the partitioning. Solubility depends on the strength of the intermolecular bonds between the solute and the solvent. This in turn depends on the polarity of the molecules of solute and solvent. For example, ammonia is a polar molecule that forms hydrogen bonds with water. So ammonia is very soluble in water. Ammonia is less soluble in organic solvents such as trichloromethane ($CHCl_3$) because the bonding between ammonia and the solvent is permanent dipole–permanent dipole, which is weaker than hydrogen bonding. So the partition coefficient:

$$K_{pc} = \frac{[NH_3(CHCl_3)]}{[NH_3(aq)]}$$

is less than 1 because the concentration of ammonia in $CHCl_3$ is less than the concentration of ammonia in water.

Iodine is a molecular element and will not dissolve very well in water. In order for it to dissolve, iodine–water bonds need to be formed. This is unlikely because the hydrogen bonding between water molecules is one of the strongest intermolecular forces. The iodine cannot disrupt the hydrogen bonded structure of water. Iodine dissolves in organic solvents such as cyclohexane. Both are non-polar molecules. Iodine forms instantaneous dipole–induced dipole bonds with cyclohexane.

IMPORTANT

Iodine does appear to dissolve in water to a very small extent. This is due to the equilibrium

$$I_2 + H_2O \rightleftharpoons IO^- + I^- + 2H^+$$

The position of equilibrium is well over to the left. The iodine itself is not soluble but the ions formed are and so the iodine appears to dissolve very slightly. Note that solutions of iodine in the laboratory are made up by dissolving iodine in potassium iodide. The ion I_3^- is formed, which is soluble in water.

So iodine is more soluble in organic solvents than in water and the partition coefficient:

$$K_{pc} = \frac{[I_2(C_6H_{12})]}{[I_2(aq)]}$$

is greater than 1 because the concentration of iodine in C_6H_{12} is greater than the concentration of iodine in water.

In general, for a solute X partitioned between two solvents, A and B, the equilibrium expression is given by:

$$K_{pc} = \frac{[X(\text{solvent A})]}{[X(\text{solvent B})]}$$

The solute X should be in the same physical state and molecular state in both solvents, e.g. in Worked example 10, ammonia is present as NH_3 in solution.

Partition coefficients and paper chromatography

In paper chromatography, the different partition coefficients of the components in a mixture correspond to their relative solubilities in the two solvents. In Worked example 10, the relative solubility of ammonia in water is greater than in the organic solvent. In paper chromatography, the mobile phase is the solvent chosen. The other solvent is the water trapped in the paper's structure, which is the stationary phase. Figure 21.9 shows solute molecules partitioned between the mobile phase and a stationary liquid phase on a solid support.

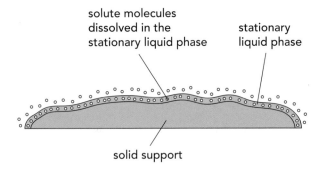

Figure 21.9: Partition chromatography. The mobile phase moves over the stationary liquid phase, carrying solute particles with it. The filter paper is the solid support in paper chromatography.

The solutes in the mixture being separated are partitioned to different extents between the solvents in the mobile and stationary phases. The greater the relative solubility in the mobile phase, the faster the rate of movement as the mobile phase passes over the stationary phase.

a Calculate the concentration of BDA in the water layer after shaking.

b Calculate the concentration of BDA in the ether layer after shaking.

c Determine the value of the partition coefficient, K_{pc}.

Question

16 A solution of butanedioic acid (BDA) in ether contains 0.034 mol of BDA in 20 cm³ of ether. This solution is shaken with 50 cm³ of water. The mass of BDA extracted into the water layer after shaking was 0.032 mol.

REFLECTION

1 Without looking at the coursebook, write down a list of all the mathematical expressions that are relevant to this chapter. Compare them with those of another learner and then with those given in the coursebook.

Which expressions did you find difficult to remember. or even forget completely? What will you do to try to remember them better?

2 Work with another learner and take it in turns to explain these terms to each other: solubility product; buffer solution; partition coefficient; conjugate acid.

What problems did you encounter while explaining these terms? How can you overcome these problems?

SUMMARY

pH is a measure of the hydrogen ion concentration: $pH = -\log_{10}[H^+(aq)]$
K_a is the dissociation constant for an acid. It is the equilibrium constant for the dissociation of a weak acid, $$K_a = \frac{[H^+](aq)[A^-(aq)]}{[HA(aq)]}$$
Acid strengths can be compared using pK_a values: $pK_a = -\log_{10}K_a$
The ionic product for water, $K_w = [H^+(aq)][OH^-(aq)] = 1.00 \times 10^{-14}$ mol² dm⁻⁶
A buffer solution is a mixture of a weak acid and its conjugate base or a weak base and its conjugate acid.
The pH of a buffer solution can be calculated by using the equilibrium concentrations of the weak acid and its conjugate base and the K_a value of the weak acid.
The solubility product, K_{sp}, is the equilibrium expression showing the equilibrium concentrations of the ions in a saturated solution of a sparingly soluble salt taking into account the relative number of each ion present.

CONTINUED

The addition of a common ion to a saturated solution of a sparingly soluble salt (e.g. adding a concentrated solution of (sodium) chloride to a saturated solution of silver chloride) causes precipitation of the sparingly soluble salt.

The partition coefficient, K_{pc}, is the equilibrium constant which relates the concentration of a solute partitioned between two immiscible solvents at a particular temperature.

$$K_{pc} = \frac{[X(\text{solvent A})]}{[X(\text{solvent B})]}$$

EXAM-STYLE QUESTIONS

1 a Write general expressions for the terms:

    i   pH   [1]

    ii K_w [1]

    iii K_a [1]

  b Calculate the pH of 0.004 00 mol dm^{-3} HCl(aq). Show your working.   [2]

  c Calculate the pH of 0.004 00 mol dm^{-3} butanoic acid(aq).
    ($K_a = 1.51 \times 10^{-5}$ mol dm^{-3})   [3]

  d 0.25 mol of sodium hydroxide is dissolved in 2.00 dm^3 of water.
    Calculate the concentration and pH of the sodium hydroxide solution.
    ($K_w = 1.00 \times 10^{-14}$ mol^2 dm^{-6})   [3]

                [Total: 11]

2 a Calculate the pH of a solution containing 0.100 mol dm^{-3} ethanoic acid and 0.100 mol dm^{-3} sodium ethanoate?
    (K_a of CH$_3$COOH = 1.74×10^{-5} mol dm^{-3})   [3]

  b How many moles of sodium ethanoate must be added to 2.00 dm^3 of
    0.0100 mol dm^{-3} ethanoic acid to produce a buffer solution of pH 5.40?   [5]

  c Explain why the pH of a solution containing 0.100 mol dm^{-3} ethanoic acid
    and 0.100 mol dm^{-3} sodium ethanoate does not change significantly
    when a small amount of hydrochloric acid is added.   [3]

                [Total: 11]

3 Copper(I) bromide, CuBr, is a sparingly soluble salt. ($K_{sp} = 3.2 \times 10^{-8}$ mol^2 dm^{-6})

  a Define the terms:

    i   solubility product   [2]

    ii common ion effect   [2]

  b Calculate the solubility of CuBr in:

    i   pure water   [2]

    ii an aqueous solution of 0.0100 mol dm^{-3} sodium bromide.   [1]

    iii Explain the difference in your answers to part **b**, **i** and **ii**.   [2]

                [Total: 9]

IMPORTANT

1 You have to know how to calculate the pH of three different types of solution:

- a strong acid
- a weak acid
- a buffer.

Each of these requires a different approach. Practise them until you always choose the correct method for each one.

2 In Question 1 part **d**, rearrange the expression for K_w to work out the OH$^-$ ion concentration.

CONTINUED

4   A buffer solution consists of 6.00 g of ethanoic acid (CH_3COOH) and 12.3 g of sodium ethanoate (CH_3COONa) in 200 cm^3 of aqueous solution. (A_r values: H = 1.0, C = 12.0, O = 16.0, Na = 23.0; K_a for CH_3COOH = 1.74×10^{-5} mol dm^{-3})

   a   Calculate the concentration of ethanoic acid in the buffer.   [2]

   b   Calculate the concentration of sodium ethanoate in the buffer.   [2]

   c   Calculate the pH of the buffer solution.   [2]

   d   Using this solution as an example, explain why the pH of a buffer solution changes very little when small amounts of hydrogen ions or hydroxide ions are added to it.   [3]

   e   Explain how the carbon dioxide / hydrogencarbonate buffer helps control blood pH.   [3]

[Total: 12]

5   A saturated solution of copper(I) sulfide, Cu_2S, contains 1.91×10^{-12} g of Cu_2S dissolved in 1 dm^3 of water. (A_r values: Cu = 63.5, S = 32.1)

   a   Write an equilibrium expression for the solubility product of copper(I) sulfide.   [1]

   b   Calculate the value of the solubility product of copper(I) sulfide, stating the units.   [5]

   c   Copper(II) chromate has a solubility of 1.9×10^{-3} mol dm^{-3} in water. Copper(II) sulfate has a solubility of 1.4×10^{-1} mol dm^{-3} in water. What will you observe when 10 cm^3 of an aqueous solution of 0.0100 mol dm^{-3} copper(II) sulfate is added to an equal volume of a saturated solution of copper(II) chromate. Explain your answer.   [3]

[Total: 9]

6   a   Deduce the pH of 0.25 mol dm^{-3} HCl(aq).   [1]

   b   Deduce the pH of 0.0500 mol dm^{-3} sodium hydroxide. ($K_w = 1.00 \times 10^{-14}$ mol^2 dm^{-6})   [2]

   c   When dissolved in an organic solvent, hydrogen chloride reacts with hydrogen iodide.

   $$HCl + HI \rightleftharpoons H_2Cl^+ + I^-$$

   i   Explain which reactant is the acid and which is the base.   [2]

   ii Identify which of the products is a conjugate acid and which is the conjugate base of the substances you identified in part i.   [1]

   d   Propanoic acid is a weak acid. A 0.0500 mol dm^{-3} solution of propanoic acid has a pH of 3.1. Calculate the value of K_a for propanoic acid. Show all your working.   [4]

[Total: 10]

SELF-EVALUATION

After studying this chapter, complete a table like this:

I can	See section...	Needs⌒ more work	Almost there	Ready to move on
define and use the terms *conjugate acid* and *conjugate base*	21.1			
define mathematically the terms pH, K_a, pK_a and K_w and use them in calculations	21.1, 21.2, 21.3			
calculate [H^+(aq)] and pH values for strong acids, strong alkalis and weak acids	21.2			
define a *buffer solution* and explain how a buffer solution can be made	21.3, 21.4			
explain how buffer solutions control pH, using chemical equations in these explanations	21.4			
describe and explain the uses of buffer solutions, including the role of HCO_3^- in controlling pH in the blood	21.4			
calculate the pH of buffer solutions, given appropriate data	21.4			
describe and use term *solubility product*, K_{sp}	21.5			
write an expression for K_{sp}	21.5			
calculate K_{sp} from concentrations and vice versa	21.5			
describe and use the common ion effect to explain the different solubility of a compound in a solution containing a common ion	21.5			
perform calculations using K_{sp} values and concentration of a common ion	21.5			
state what is meant by the term *partition coefficient*, K_{pc}	21.6			
calculate and use a partition coefficient for a system in which the solute is in the same physical state in the two solvents	21.6			
understand the factors affecting the numerical value of a partition coefficient in terms of the polarities of the solute and the solvents used.	21.6			

> Chapter 22
Reaction kinetics

LEARNING INTENTIONS

In this chapter you will learn how to:

- define and explain the terms *rate equation*, *order of reaction*, *overall order of reaction*, *rate constant*, *half-life*, *rate-determining step* and *intermediate*

- construct and use rate equations of the form rate = $k[A]^m[B]^n$ for which m and n are 0, 1 or 2

- deduce the order of a reaction from concentration–time graphs or from experimental data relating to the initial rate method or half-life method

- interpret experimental data in graphical form, including concentration–time and rate–concentration graphs

- calculate initial rates using concentration data

- construct rate equations

CONTINUED

- demonstrate that the half-life of a first-order reaction is independent of concentration

- use the half-life of a first-order reaction in calculations

- calculate the numerical value of a rate constant by using initial rates and the rate equation

- calculate the numerical value of a rate constant by using the half-life and the equation

$$k = \frac{0.693}{t_{\frac{1}{2}}}$$

- suggest a multistep reaction mechanism that is consistent with the rate equation and the equation for the overall reaction

- predict the order that would result from a given reaction mechanism and rate-determining step

- deduce a rate equation given a reaction mechanism and rate-determining step for a given reaction

- identify an intermediate or catalyst from a given reaction mechanism

- identify the rate-determining step from a rate equation and a given reaction mechanism

- describe catalysts as homogeneous or heterogeneous

- describe heterogeneous catalysis in terms of adsorption of reactants, bond weakening and desorption of products (with reference to iron in the Haber process and palladium, platinum and rhodium in the catalytic removal of oxides of nitrogen from the exhaust gases of car engines)

- describe homogeneous catalysis in terms of being used in one step and reformed in a later step (with reference to atmospheric oxides of nitrogen in the oxidation of atmospheric sulfur dioxide and Fe^{2+} or Fe^{3+} in the I^- / $S_2O_3^{2-}$ reaction).

- Describe qualitatively the effect of temperature on the rate constant and therefore on rate of reaction.

BEFORE YOU START

1. Work with another learner. Take it in turns to explain to each other the meaning of the terms: *rate of reaction, frequency, effective collisions, non-effective collisions.*

2. Write a paragraph using ideas about colliding particles to explain the effect of increasing the concentration of a reactant on the rate of reaction and decreasing the temperature on the rate of reaction. Share your ideas with another learner.

3. Work with a group of other learners to suggest three different methods of monitoring the rate of a reaction.

4. Write a paragraph about how catalysts increase the rate of a chemical reaction. Check your answers with other learners or with the coursebook.

5. Sketch a reaction pathway diagram for an endothermic reaction in the presence and absence of a catalyst. Check your diagram with another learner or with the coursebook.

6. Explain to another learner how you can find the rate of reaction at any one time from a graph of volume of gas (*y*-axis) against time (*x*-axis). Then ask the other learner to draw and explain the shape of the graph obtained by plotting the loss in mass of the reaction mixture with time for the reaction

$$CaCO_3 + 2HCl \rightarrow CaCl_2 + H_2O + CO_2$$

STUDYING VERY FAST REACTIONS

Fifty years ago, chemists were becoming excited about monitoring very fast reactions in milliseconds. The complete course of some very fast reactions can be monitored using stopped-flow spectrophotometry. In this technique, very small volumes of reactants are driven at high speed into a mixing chamber. From here they go to an observation cell, where the progress of the reaction is monitored (usually by measuring the transmission of ultraviolet radiation through the sample). A graph of rate of reaction against time can be generated automatically.

At the same time, physicists were developing and experimenting with lasers that produce a beam of radiation of a single wavelength and produce pulses of radiation which last only a few picoseconds (1 picosecond = 10^{-12} s) (Figure 22.1). This led to the possibility of studying even faster light-dependent reactions that involve the formation of free radicals, e.g. the reaction of chlorine with methane in the presence of light.

In order to investigate a light-dependent reaction, the laser light is separated into two pulses. We can use the time delay between the pulses to get information about the reaction. One of the first uses of this new technology by chemists was to investigate the dissociation of iodine molecules dissolved in a solution of tetrachloromethane. After the first pulse of light, it takes 50 picoseconds for the iodine molecules to dissociate (break up) into iodine atoms. The iodine atoms then recombine to form iodine molecules. The rate of recombination of the iodine atoms into iodine molecules was lower than predicted. This led the scientists to suggest that a solvent cage of tetrachloromethane around the iodine was reducing the rate of the reaction. Some iodine atoms were escaping from the solvent cage but the molecules did not. Carrying out the experiment with higher frequency (higher energy) light increased this difference. The scientists suggested that more iodine atoms escaped from the solvent cage because more iodine atoms were formed.

Questions for discussion

Discuss with another learner or group of learners:

* Sketch a graph of the laser experiment to show the change in absorption (y-axis) of the iodine with time. Assume that the absorption is proportional to the number of iodine atoms in the mixture.

* Suggest why the results of the experiment were controversial at the time.

* To what extent do chemists depend on physicists and mathematicians?

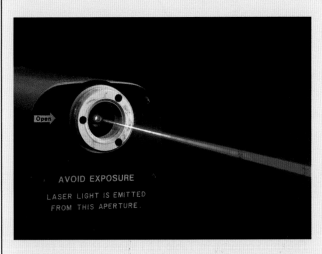

AVOID EXPOSURE
LASER LIGHT IS EMITTED
FROM THIS APERTURE.

Figure 22.1: Lasers such as this can be used to study how molecules break apart and rearrange themselves.

22.1 Factors affecting reaction rate

In Chapter 9 you learned why reaction rate is increased when:

* the concentrations of the reactants are increased

* the temperature is increased

* a catalyst is added to the reaction mixture.

In this chapter you will review the definition of the rate of reaction, and find out about:

* quantitative aspects of reaction rates

* how the data gathered from experiments on rates of reaction can be used to confirm possible reaction mechanisms

* more about how catalysts speed up reaction rates.

22.2 Rate of reaction

Defining rate of reaction

We calculate *rate of reaction* by measuring a decrease in concentration of a particular reactant or an increase in concentration of a particular product over a period of time.

$$\text{rate of reaction} = \frac{\text{change in concentration}}{\text{time taken for this change}}$$

Units of concentration are usually expressed in mol dm^{-3}, units of time are usually expressed in seconds, so the units of rate of reaction are normally mol dm^{-3} s^{-1}. For very slow reactions, you may see the units of rates expressed as mol dm^{-3} min^{-1} or mol dm^{-3} h^{-1}.

In Chapter 9 we showed how the rate of reaction can be calculated by using tangents to the curve. In this chapter we will analyse the shape of the curves obtained in greater depth and show how the information obtained from experiments on rate of reaction can be used to give information consistent with a proposed reaction mechanism.

22.3 Rate equations

The rate constant and rate equations

The units of rate of reaction are mol dm^{-3} s^{-1}.

In Chapter 9 we studied the rate of isomerisation of cyclopropane to propene.

$$\text{H}_2\text{C} \underset{\text{H}_2\text{C}}{\overset{}{\diagdown}} \text{CH}_2(g) \longrightarrow \text{CH}_3\text{CH}{=}\text{CH}_2(g)$$

cyclopropane   propene

The progress of this reaction can be followed by measuring the decrease in concentration of cyclopropane or increase in concentration of propene. Table 22.1 shows the change of cyclopropane concentration at 500 °C. The measurements were all made at the same temperature because reaction rate is affected markedly by temperature.

A graph of rate of reaction against concentration of cyclopropane (Figure 22.2) shows us that the rate is directly proportional to the concentration of cyclopropane. So, if the concentration of cyclopropane

[cyclopropane] / mol dm^{-3}	Rate / mol dm^{-3} s^{-1}	$\dfrac{\text{Rate}}{\text{[cyclopropane]}}$ / s^{-1}
1.50	1.00×10^{-3}	6.67×10^{-4}
1.00	6.67×10^{-4}	6.67×10^{-4}
0.50	3.30×10^{-4}	6.60×10^{-4}

Table 22.1: Rates of conversion of cyclopropane to propene at different concentrations of cyclopropane.

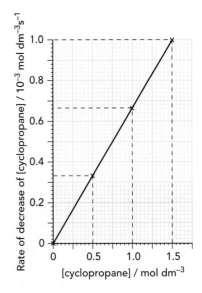

Figure 22.2: The rate of decrease of cyclopropane. Note how the gradient ($\frac{\text{rate}}{\text{concentration}}$) is constant.

is doubled, the rate of reaction is doubled. If the concentration of cyclopropane falls by one-third, the rate of reaction falls by one-third.

The third column in Table 22.1 shows that the rate of the reaction is proportional to cyclopropane concentration (within the limits of experimental error). This is shown by the fact that the rate divided by concentration is constant.

We can express this mathematically as:

rate of reaction = $k \times$ [cyclopropane]

The proportionality constant, k, is called the **rate constant**.

KEY WORD

rate constant: the proportionality constant, k, in a rate equation, e.g. rate = k[NO]^2.

Reaction number	Stoichiometric equation	Rate equation
1	$H_2(g) + I_2(g) \rightarrow 2HI(g)$	rate $= k[H_2][I_2]$
2	$NO(g) + CO(g) + O_2(g) \rightarrow NO_2(g) + CO_2(g)$	rate $= k[NO]^2$
3	$2H_2(g) + 2NO(g) \rightarrow 2H_2O(g) + N_2(g)$	rate $= k[H_2][NO]^2$
4	$BrO_3^-(aq) + 5Br^-(aq) + H^+(aq) \rightarrow 3Br_2(aq) + 3H_2O(l)$	rate $= k[BrO_3^-][Br^-][H^+]^2$

Table 22.2: Rate equations for some reactions.

The overall expression (rate of reaction $= k \times$ [cyclopropane]) is the **rate equation** for this particular reaction. Rate equations are generally written without the $\times$ sign.

For example:

rate $= k[\text{cyclopropane}]$

Rate equations can only be determined from experimental data. They cannot be found from the stoichiometric equation.

Some experimentally determined rate equations are shown in Table 22.2.

You can see from reaction 1 that the rate of reaction is proportional to the concentration of both H_2 and I_2; however, in reaction 2, CO and O_2 do not appear in the rate equation, even though they are present in the stoichiometric equation. Similarly in reactions 3 and 4 there is no relationship between the rate equation and the stoichiometry of the chemical equation.

In order to find the rate equation, we have to conduct a series of experiments. Using reaction 3 from Table 22.2 as an example:

- First, find how the concentration of $H_2(g)$ affects the rate by varying the concentration of $H_2(g)$, while keeping the concentration of NO(g) constant.

The results show that the rate is proportional to the concentration of hydrogen (rate $= k_1[H_2]$)

- Then find how the concentration of NO(g) affects the rate by varying the concentration of NO(g) while keeping the concentration of $H_2(g)$ constant.

The results show that the rate is proportional to the square of the concentration of NO (rate $= k_2[NO]^2$).

Combining the two rate equations we get the overall rate equation:

rate $= k[H_2][NO]^2$

The rate equations for some reactions may include compounds that are not present in the chemical equation.

> **KEY WORD**
>
> **rate equation:** an equation showing the relationship between the rate constant and the concentrations of the species that affect the rate of reaction.

Question

1   Write rate equations for each of the following reactions:

a   cyclopropane $\rightarrow$ propene

where rate is proportional to the concentration of cyclopropane

b $2HI(g) \rightarrow H_2(g) + I_2(g)$

where rate is proportional to the square of the hydrogen iodide concentration

c $C_{12}H_{22}O_{11}(g) + H_2O(l) \xrightarrow{H^+} 2C_6H_{12}O_6(aq)$

where rate is proportional to the concentration of $C_{12}H_{22}O_{11}$ and to the concentration of H^+ ions

d $2HgCl_2(aq) + K_2C_2O_4(aq) \rightarrow$
$\qquad\qquad Hg_2Cl_2(s) + 2KCl(aq) + 2CO_2(g)$

where rate is proportional to the concentration of $HgCl_2$ and to the square of the concentration of $K_2C_2O_4$

e $CH_3COCH_3 + I_2 \xrightarrow{H^+} CH_3COCH_2I + HI$

where rate is proportional to the concentration of CH_3COCH_3 and to the concentration of H^+ ions, but the concentration of I_2 has no effect on the rate.

Order of reaction

The order of a reaction shows how the concentration of a reactant affects the rate of reaction.

The **order of reaction** with respect to a particular reactant is the power to which the concentration of that reactant is raised in the rate equation.

For example, for a rate equation involving only one particular reactant, the order is the power of the concentration shown in the rate equation. For reaction 2 in Table 22.2, the rate equation is rate = $k[NO]^2$ and so the order is 2 with respect to [NO].

When you are writing about order of reaction, you must distinguish carefully between the order with respect to a particular reactant and the overall order of reaction. Taking reaction 3 in Table 22.2 as an example:

$$rate = k[H_2][NO]^2$$

We say that this reaction is:

- first order with respect to H_2 (as rate is proportional to $[H_2]^1$)

- second order with respect to NO (as rate is proportional to $[NO]^2$)

- third order overall (as the sum of the powers is $1 + 2 = 3$).

In general terms, for a reaction A + B → products, the rate equation can be written in the form:

$$rate of reaction = k[A]^m[B]^n$$

In this equation:

- [A] and [B] are the concentrations of the reactants

- m and n are the orders of the reaction

- the values of m and n can be 0, 1, 2, 3 or rarely higher

- when the value of m or n is 0 we can ignore the concentration term because any number to the power of zero = 1.

KEY WORD

order of reaction: the power to which the concentration of the reactant is raised in the rate equation. If a rate is directly proportional to concentration, it is first order – if the rate is directly proportional to the square of the concentration, it is second order. The overall order of reaction is the sum of these powers.

Orders of reaction are not always whole numbers. A few reactions have fractional orders. For example, the reaction:

$$CH_3CHO(g) \rightarrow CH_4(g) + CO(g)$$

has an overall order of 1.5. The rate equation for this reaction is:

$$rate = k[CH_3CHO]^{1.5}$$

Many reactions involving free radicals have fractional orders of reaction.

IMPORTANT

When discussing order of reaction, make sure that you state what the order refers to, e.g. first order with respect to hydrogen; second order overall.

Question

2 For each of the reactions **a** to **e** in Question 1, state:

   i   the order of reaction with respect to each reactant

   ii the overall order of reaction.

Units of k

The units of k vary according to the form of the rate equation.

IMPORTANT

Remember that the units of rate are usually mol dm^{-3} *but* the units of the rate constant must be worked out from the rate equation in the form

$$k = \frac{mol\ dm^{-3}}{units\ for\ the\ product\ of\ the\ concentration\ terms}$$

Question

3 State the units of k corresponding to each of the following rate equations:

   a   rate = $k[NO]^2$

   b   rate = $k[NH_3]^0$

   c   rate = $k[BrO_3^-][Br^-][H^+]^2$

   d   rate = $k[cyclopropane]$

WORKED EXAMPLES

1 State the units of k for the following equation:
$H_2(g) + I_2(g) \rightarrow 2HI(g)$

Step 1: Write the rate equation.

$\text{rate} = k[H_2][I_2]$

Step 2: Rearrange the equation in terms of k.

$$k = \frac{\text{rate}}{[H_2][I_2]}$$

Step 3: Substitute the units.

$$k = \frac{\text{mol dm}^{-3}\,\text{s}^{-1}}{(\text{mol dm}^{-3}) \times (\text{mol dm}^{-3})}$$

Step 4: Cancel mol dm^{-3}

$$k = \frac{\cancel{\text{mol dm}^{-3}}\,\text{s}^{-1}}{(\text{mol dm}^{-3}) \times \cancel{(\text{mol dm}^{-3})}}$$

Step 5: Units of k.

units of $k = \text{s}^{-1}\,\text{mol}^{-1}\,\text{dm}^3 = \text{dm}^3\,\text{mol}^{-1}\,\text{s}^{-1}$

- when writing the units on one line, the indices on the bottom change sign
- we usually put the unit with the positive index first
- don't forget the s^{-1} arising from the units of rate.

2 State the units of k for the following equation:
$2H_2(g) + 2NO(g) \rightarrow 2H_2O(g) + N_2(g)$

Step 1: Write the rate equation.

$\text{rate} = k[H_2][NO]^2$

Step 2: Rearrange the equation in terms of k.

$$k = \frac{\text{rate}}{[H_2][NO]^2}$$

Step 3: Substitute the units.

$$k = \frac{\text{mol dm}^{-3}\,\text{s}^{-1}}{(\text{mol dm}^{-3}) \times (\text{mol dm}^{-3})^2}$$

Step 4: Cancel mol dm^{-3}.

$$k = \frac{\cancel{\text{mol dm}^{-3}}\,\text{s}^{-1}}{\cancel{(\text{mol dm}^{-3})} \times (\text{mol dm}^{-3})^2}$$

Step 5: Units of k.

units of $k = \text{s}^{-1}\,\text{mol}^{-2}\,\text{dm}^6$
$= \text{dm}^6\,\text{mol}^{-2}\,\text{s}^{-1}$

22.4 Which order of reaction?

We can identify the order of a reaction in three ways:

- plot a graph of reaction rate against concentration of reactant
- plot a graph of concentration of reactant against time
- deduce successive half-lives from graphs of concentration against time.

Graphs of reaction rate against concentration

A graph of reaction rate against concentration tells us whether a reaction is zero, first, second or third order with respect to a particular reactant (or overall). It is very rare to obtain an order with respect to a particular reactant higher than second order. Figure 22.3 shows the shapes of the graphs expected for different orders of reaction.

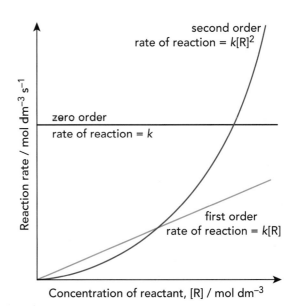

Figure 22.3: Zero-, first- and second-order reactions: how changes in the concentration of a reactant affect the reaction rate.

We shall now look at some examples of zero-, first- and second-order reactions.

Zero-order reaction

$$2NH_3(g) \xrightarrow{\text{hot tungsten}} N_2(g) + 3H_2(g)$$

The rate equation derived from experiments is:

rate = $k[NH_3]^0$

The plot of reaction rate against concentration is a horizontal straight line (see Figure 22.3). The reaction rate does not change with concentration. For a zero-order reaction, k is numerically equal to the reaction rate:

rate = k

This is because any number to the power of zero = 1.

First-order reaction

$$2N_2O(g) \xrightarrow{\text{gold}} 2N_2(g) + O_2(g)$$

The rate equation derived from experiments is:

rate = $k[N_2O]^1$

This is usually written as:

rate = $k[N_2O]$

The plot of reaction rate against concentration is an inclined straight line going through the origin (see Figure 22.3). The rate is directly proportional to the concentration of N_2O. So doubling the concentration of N_2O doubles the rate of reaction.

Second-order reaction

$$NO_2(g) + CO(g) \rightarrow NO(g) + CO_2(g)$$

The rate equation derived from experiments is:

rate = $k[NO_2]^2$

The plot of reaction rate against concentration is an upwardly curved line (see Figure 22.3).

In this case, reaction rate is directly proportional to the square of the concentration of $NO_2(g)$. When the concentration of $NO_2(g)$ doubles, the rate of reaction increases four-fold. If we consider the second-order rate equation as written above, we can see that this is true by comparing the rates at two different concentrations, 1 mol dm^{-3} and 2 mol dm^{-3}.

rate at 1 mol dm^{-3} = $k(1)^2 = 1k$

rate at 2 mol dm^{-3} = $k(2)^2 = 4k$

Question

4 Draw sketch graphs of reaction rate against concentration of the reactant in bold for each of the following reactions:

a **NO**(g) + CO(g) + O$_2$(g) → NO$_2$(g) + CO$_2$(g)

for which the rate equation is: rate = $k[NO]^2$

b **2HI**(g) $\xrightarrow{\text{gold}}$ H$_2$(g) + I$_2$(g)

for which the rate equation is: rate = k

Note: the catalyst influences the order here: the order is *not* the same as for the uncatalysed reaction.

c **(CH$_3$)$_3$CCl** + OH$^-$ → (CH$_3$)$_3$COH + Cl$^-$

for which the rate equation is: $k[(CH_3)_3CCl]$

Graphs of concentration of reactant against time

Figure 22.4 shows how we can distinguish between zero-, first- and second-order reactions by plotting a graph of concentration against time.

For a zero-order reaction, the graph is a descending straight line. The rate of reaction is the slope (gradient) of the graph. The reaction proceeds at the same rate whatever the concentration of the reactant.

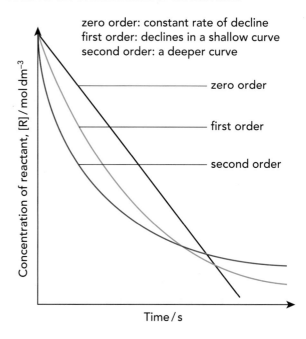

zero order: constant rate of decline
first order: declines in a shallow curve
second order: a deeper curve

zero order

first order

second order

Concentration of reactant, [R] / mol dm^{-3}

Time / s

Figure 22.4: Zero-, first- and second-order reactions: how changes in the concentration of a reactant affect the time taken for a reaction to proceed.

For first- and second-order reactions, the graph is a curve. The curve for the second-order reaction is much deeper than for a first-order reaction. It also appears to have a relatively longer 'tail' as it levels off. We can also distinguish between these two curves by determining successive half-lives of the reaction.

Question

5 For each of the reactions **a** to **c** in Question 4, draw a sketch graph to show how the concentration of the bold reactant changes with time.

Half-life and reaction rates

Half-life, $t_{\frac{1}{2}}$, is the time taken for the concentration of a **limiting reactant** to fall to half of its initial value.

Figure 22.5 shows how half-life is measured for the cyclopropane to propene reaction that we studied earlier. Three successive half-lives are shown. Table 22.3 shows the values of the successive half-lives obtained from Figure 22.5.

You can see that the successive half-lives have values that are fairly close to each other (17.0, 17.3, 16.7). The mean half-life is 17.0 minutes for this reaction. We can tell that this reaction is first order because the successive half-lives are more or less constant. In a first-order

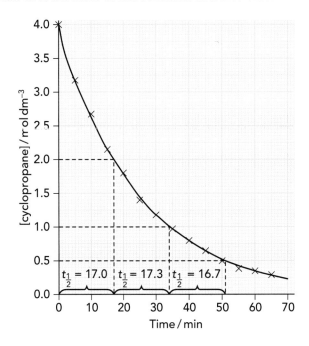

Figure 22.5: Measurement of half-life for cyclopropane isomerisation.

Δ[cyclopropane] / mol dm⁻³	Half-life / min
4.00 to 2.00	17.0
2.00 to 1.00	34.3 – 17.0 = 17.3
1.00 to 0.50	51.0 – 34.3 = 16.7

Table 22.3: A constant half-life indicates a first-order reaction.

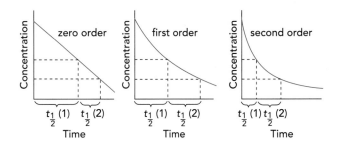

Figure 22.6: The half-life of zero-, first- and second-order reactions can be determined from graphs of concentration against time.

reaction like this, the half-life is independent of the original concentration of reactant. This means that whatever the starting concentration of cyclopropane, the half-life will always be 17 minutes.

We can distinguish zero-, first- and second-order reactions from their successive half-lives (Figure 22.6).

- A zero-order reaction has successive half-lives which decrease with time.

- A first-order reaction has a half-life which is constant.

- Second-order reactions have successive half-lives which increase with time. (This also applies to reactions with a higher order for a particular reactant but we will not be discussing these.)

KEY DEFINITION

half-life, $t_{\frac{1}{2}}$: the time taken for the amount (or concentration) of the limiting reactant in a reaction to decrease to half its initial value.

KEY WORD

limiting reactant: the reactant which is not in excess. The reaction will stop when the limiting reactant is all used up.

IMPORTANT

For the half-life method, you will only be expected to do calculations for first-order reactions.

Question

6 Benzenediazonium chloride, $C_6H_5N_2Cl$, decomposes at room temperature:

$C_6H_5N_2Cl(aq) + H_2O(l) \rightarrow$
$\qquad C_6H_5OH(aq) + N_2(g) + HCl(aq)$

a Describe how this reaction can be monitored.

b Using the data in the table, plot a graph of concentration of $C_6H_5N_2Cl$ against time.

Time / s	$[C_6H_5N_2Cl]$ / 10^{-4} mol dm^{-3}
0	5.8
200	4.4
400	3.2
600	2.5
800	1.7
1000	1.2
1200	0.8
1400	0.5
1600	0.3

c From your graph, find the value of two successive half-lives.

d Use the values of these half-lives to deduce the order of the reaction.

22.5 Calculations involving the rate constant, k

Calculating k from initial concentrations and initial rate

In the presence of hydrogen ions, hydrogen peroxide, H_2O_2, reacts with iodide ions to form water and iodine:

$$H_2O_2(aq) + 2I^-(aq) + 2H^+(aq) \rightarrow 2H_2O(l) + I_2(aq)$$

The rate equation for this reaction is:

$$\text{rate of reaction} = k[H_2O_2][I^-]$$

The progress of the reaction can be followed by measuring the initial rate of formation of iodine. Table 22.4 shows the rates of reaction obtained using various initial concentrations of each reactant.

The procedure for calculating k is shown below, using the data for experiment 1.

Step 1: Write out the rate equation.

$$\text{rate of reaction} = k[H_2O_2][I^-]$$

Step 2: Rearrange the equation in terms of k

$$k = \frac{\text{rate}}{[H_2O_2][I^-]}$$

Step 3: Substitute the values

$$k = \frac{3.50 \times 10^{-6}}{(0.0200) \times (0.0100)}$$

$$k = 1.75 \times 10^{-2} \text{ dm}^3 \text{ mol}^{-1} \text{ s}^{-1}$$

Note: the concentration of hydrogen ions is ignored because $[H^+]$ does not appear in the rate equation. The reaction is zero order with respect to $[H^+]$.

Experiment	$[H_2O_2]$ / mol dm^{-3}	$[I^-]$ / mol dm^{-3}	$[H^+]$ / mol dm^{-3}	Initial rate of reaction / mol dm^{-3} s^{-1}
1	0.0200	0.0100	0.0100	3.50×10^{-6}
2	0.0300	0.0100	0.0100	5.30×10^{-6}
3	0.0050	0.0200	0.0200	1.75×10^{-6}

Table 22.4: Rates of reaction obtained using different initial concentrations of H_2O_2, I^- ions and H^+ ions.

Calculating *k* from half-life

For a first-order reaction, half-life is related to the rate constant by the expression:

$t_{\frac{1}{2}} = \dfrac{0.693}{k}$, where $t_{\frac{1}{2}}$ is the half-life, measured in s.

We can rewrite this in the form:

$k = \dfrac{0.693}{t_{\frac{1}{2}}}$

So, for the first-order reaction cyclopropane to propene, for which the half-life is 17.0 min, we:

- convert minutes to seconds

- then substitute the half-life into the expression:

$t = 0.693$

$k = \dfrac{0.693}{t_{\frac{1}{2}}} = \dfrac{0.693}{17.0 \times 60}$

$= 6.79 \times 10^{-4} \text{ dm}^3 \text{ mol}^{-1} \text{ s}^{-1}$

This value is very close to the ones quoted in Table 22.1. Rate constants for zero- and second-order reactions can also be calculated from half-lives but the calculations are more complex.

We can also use the expression $k = \dfrac{0.693}{t_{\frac{1}{2}}}$ to calculate the half-life of a first-order reaction if we know the rate constant.

WORKED EXAMPLE

3 Methanol reacts with hydrochloric acid at 25 °C. The products are chloromethane and water.

$CH_3OH(aq) + HCl(aq) \rightarrow CH_3Cl(g) + H_2O(l)$

Equimolar amounts of methanol and hydrochloric acid are mixed at 25 °C. The progress of the reaction is followed by:

- taking a small sample of the reaction mixture from time to time, then

- titrating each sample with a standard solution of sodium hydroxide.

The data obtained are shown in Table 22.5.

CONTINUED

Time / min	[HCl] / mol dm^{-3}	[CH$_3$OH] / mol dm^{-3}
0	1.84	1.84
200	1.45	1.45
400	1.22	1.22
600	1.04	1.04
800	0.91	0.91
1000	0.81	0.81
1200	0.72	0.72
1400	0.66	0.66
1600	0.60	0.60
1800	0.56	0.56
2000	0.54	0.54

Table 22.5: Data for the reaction between methanol and hydrochloric acid.

Step 1: Draw a graph of concentration (of hydrochloric acid) against time (Figure 22.7).

Step 2: Draw tangents to the curve at various places corresponding to a range of concentrations.
In Figure 22.7 the tangent drawn corresponds to [HCl] = 1.04 mol dm^{-3}.

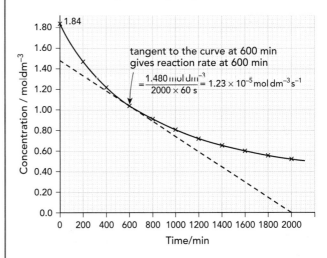

Figure 22.7: The concentration of both hydrochloric acid and methanol fall at the same rate as time passes.

CONTINUED

Step 3: For each tangent drawn, calculate the gradient and then the rate of reaction. In Figure 22.7, the rate corresponding to [HCl] = 1.04 mol dm^{-3} is $\frac{1.480}{2000 \times 60}$ = 1.23 × 10^{-5} mol dm^{-3} s^{-1} (multiply by 60 to convert minutes to seconds)

Table 22.6 shows the rates corresponding to five different concentrations of hydrochloric acid.

Time / min	Concentration / mol dm^{-3}	Rate from graph / mol dm^{-3} min^{-1}	Rate from graph / mol dm^{-3} s^{-1}
0	1.84	2.30 × 10^{-3}	3.83 × 10^{-5}
200	1.45	1.46 × 10^{-3}	2.43 × 10^{-5}
400	1.22	1.05 × 10^{-3}	1.75 × 10^{-5}
600	1.04	0.74 × 10^{-3}	1.23 × 10^{-5}
800	0.91	0.54 × 10^{-3}	0.90 × 10^{-5}

Table 22.6: Values calculated for the reaction between methanol and hydrochloric acid.

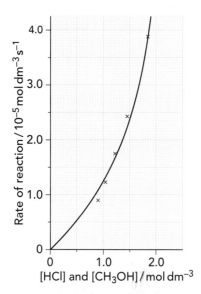

Figure 22.8: A graph showing how changes of concentration in hydrochloric acid or methanol affect the rate of reaction. The curve shows that the reaction is likely to be second order.

CONTINUED

Step 4: Plot a graph of rate of reaction against concentration.

Figure 22.8 shows a plot of rate against the concentration of [HCl] or [CH$_3$OH]. We have included the [CH$_3$OH] because if you look at the data in Table 22.5, you will see that the concentration of CH$_3$OH is decreasing at the same rate as the decrease in concentration of HCl.

Figure 22.8 shows an upward curve. This indicates that the reaction is second order. But second order with respect to what? As the concentrations of both HCl and CH$_3$OH are decreasing at the same rate, either of these may be second order. The possibilities are:

- rate = k[CH$_3$OH] [HCl]

- rate = k[CH$_3$OH]^2

- rate = k[HCl]^2

Further experiments would have to be carried out to confirm one or other of these possibilities. The only thing we can be sure of is that the reaction is second order overall.

Question

7 **a** Use the data from experiments 2 and 3 in Table 22.4 to calculate the rate constant for the following reaction.

$$H_2O_2(aq) + 2I^-(aq) + 2H^+(aq) \rightarrow 2H_2O(l) + I_2(aq)$$

The rate equation for this reaction is: rate of reaction = k[H$_2$O$_2$] [I$^-$]

b Use the formula $t_{\frac{1}{2}} = \frac{0.693}{k}$ to calculate a value for the rate constant of a reaction which is first order and has a half-life of 480 s.

c A first-order reaction has a rate constant of 9.63 × 10^{-5} s^{-1}. Calculate a value for the half-life of this reaction.

The effect of temperature on the rate constant

In Chapter 9, when studying the Boltzmann distribution curve, we learned that at higher temperatures a greater proportion of the molecules have energy greater than the activation energy. So the rate of reaction increases at higher temperatures. The rate constant, k, and therefore the rate of reaction, is proportional to the fraction of molecules with energy equal to or greater than the activation energy. So the rate constant increases as the temperature increases.

Figure 22.9a shows the effect of increasing temperature on rate of reaction. For every 10 °C rise in temperature, the rate of reaction approximately doubles. The exact relationship between temperature and the rate constant is given by the equation:

$$\ln k = \ln A - \frac{E_A}{RT}$$

where:

$\ln k$ is the natural logarithm of the rate constant

A is a constant related to the frequency of collisions and the orientation in which the molecules collide

E_A is the activation energy

R is the gas constant

T is the temperature in kelvin

You do not have to learn this equation but it is useful for an understanding of how temperature affects the rate constant.

A varies very little with temperature so can be thought of as being constant. E_A and R are also constants. So a graph of $\ln k$ against $\frac{1}{T}$ should give a straight line of gradient $\frac{-E_A}{R}$ (Figure 22.9b).

22.6 Deducing order of reaction from raw data

We can use any of the methods mentioned in Section 22.3 to determine the order of a reaction. In this section we shall look in detail at some more complex examples.

Using data from the course of a reaction

For this method, we carry out one or more experiments with known initial concentrations of reactants and follow the course of the reaction until it is complete (or nearly complete).

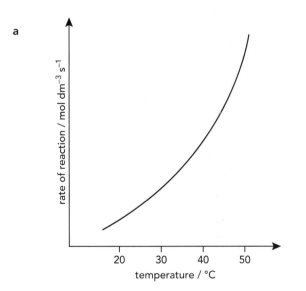

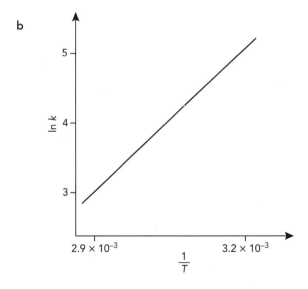

Figure 22.9: The effect of increasing temperature on **a** rate of reaction **b** rate constant.

The steps in analysing the data are as follows.

Step 1: Plot a graph to show how the concentration of a particular reactant (or product) changes with time.

Step 2: Take tangents at various points along the curve which correspond to particular concentrations of the reactant.

Step 3: Calculate the slope (gradient) at each concentration selected. The rate of reaction is calculated from the slope of the graph.

Step 4: Plot a graph of rate of reaction against concentration.

Using initial rates

The initial rates method is often used when the rate of reaction is slow.

- Carry out several experiments with different known initial concentrations of each reactant.
- Measure the initial rates of reaction by either:
  - taking the tangent of the curve at the start of each experiment, or
  - measuring the concentration of a reactant or product soon after the experiment has started.
- For each reactant, plot a graph of initial rate against concentration of that particular reactant.

WORKED EXAMPLE

4   Nitrogen(V) oxide, N_2O_5, decomposes to nitrogen(IV) oxide and oxygen.

$$2N_2O_5(g) \rightarrow 4NO_2(g) + O_2(g)$$

Table 22.7 shows how the initial rate of reaction varies with the initial concentration of N_2O_5.

Initial concentration, $[N_2O_5]$ / mol dm^{-3}	Initial rate / 10^{-5} mol dm^{-3} s^{-1}
3.00	3.15
1.50	1.55
0.75	0.80

Table 22.7: Data for the decomposition of nitrogen(V) oxide.

A graph of the data (Figure 22.10) shows that the initial rate of reaction is directly proportional to the initial concentration of N_2O_5.

rate of reaction $\propto [N_2O_5] = k[N_2O_5]$

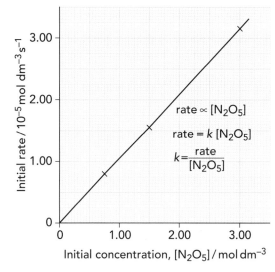

Figure 22.10: The initial rate of decomposition of nitrogen(V) oxide is directly proportional to the initial concentration.

Question

8   Suggest how the experiment for the reaction between methanol and hydrochloric acid might be re-designed to obtain evidence for the effect of changing the HCl concentration while controlling the CH_3OH concentration.

WORKED EXAMPLE

5 The equation below describes the reaction of propanone with iodine. Hydrogen ions catalyse this reaction.

$$CH_3COCH_3 + I_2 \xrightarrow{H^+} CH_3COCH_2I + HI$$

The progress of the reaction can be followed by using a colorimeter. The brown colour of the iodine fades as the reaction proceeds (Figure 22.11). The experimental results are shown in Table 22.8.

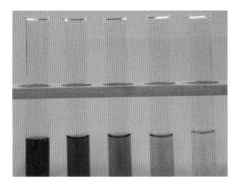

Figure 22.11: The rate of reaction between propanone and iodine can be followed by the loss of colour of the reaction mixture as the reaction proceeds.

Note that:

- the data is from real experiments, so experimental errors have to be taken into account

- the hydrogen ions have been provided by the hydrochloric acid.

In this method, we see how changing the concentration of each reactant in turn affects the rate of reaction. In order to make a fair comparison, we must make sure that the concentrations of the other reactants are kept constant.

Compare experiments 1 and 2 (propanone and iodine concentrations are constant):

- doubling the concentration of H^+ ions from 0.625 to 1.25 mol dm^{-3} doubles the rate of reaction

- the reaction is first order with respect to H^+ ions.

Compare experiments 1 and 3 (hydrochloric acid and iodine concentrations are constant):

- doubling the concentration of propanone from 0.25×10^{-3} to 0.50×10^{-3} mol dm^{-3} doubles the rate of reaction

- the reaction is first order with respect to propanone.

Compare experiments 1 and 4 (hydrochloric acid and propanone concentrations are constant):

- doubling the concentration of iodine from 0.625×10^{-3} to 1.25×10^{-3} mol dm^{-3} has no effect on the rate of reaction.

- the reaction is zero order with respect to iodine.

Experiment	[HCl] / mol dm^{-3}	[propanone] / 10^{-3} mol dm^{-3}	[iodine] / 10^{-3} mol dm^{-3}	Initial rate / 10^{-6} mol dm^{-3} s^{-1}
1	1.25	0.50	1.25	10.9
2	0.625	0.50	1.25	5.4
3	1.25	0.25	1.25	5.1
4	1.25	0.50	0.625	10.7

Table 22.8: Experimental results for the reaction of propanone with iodine at varying aqueous concentrations.

Questions

9 **a** State the order of reaction for the decomposition of nitrogen(V) oxide.

  b Use the data for 3.00 mol dm^{-3} N$_2$O$_5$ in Table 22.7 to calculate a value for the rate constant for this decomposition.

10 **a** Write the rate equation for the acid-catalysed reaction of iodine with propanone.

  b Use your rate equation and the information in Table 22.8 (experiment 1) to calculate a value for the rate constant for this reaction.

22.7 Kinetics and reaction mechanisms

The rate-determining step

In Worked example 5 you saw that for the reaction:

$$CH_3COCH_3 + I_2 \xrightarrow{H^+} CH_3COCH_2I + HI$$

the iodine did not appear in the rate equation but the H^+ ions did.

- A reactant that appears in the chemical equation may have no effect on reaction rate.

- A substance that is not a reactant in the chemical equation can affect reaction rate.

In organic chemistry, you have met the idea that reactions occur in a number of steps. We call this the *reaction mechanism*. These steps do not take place at the same rate. The overall rate of reaction depends on the slowest step. We call this the **rate-determining step**. If the concentration of a reactant appears in the rate equation, then that reactant (or substances that react together to form it) appears in the rate-determining step. If a substance does not appear in the overall rate equation it does *not* take part in the rate-determining step. So, for the reaction between propanone and iodine, H^+ ions are involved in the rate-determining step but iodine is not.

> **KEY WORD**
>
> **rate-determining step:** the slowest step in a reaction mechanism.

Verifying possible reaction mechanisms

We can use kinetic data to confirm proposed reaction mechanisms. It is important to realise that the mechanism is not deduced from the kinetic data. The kinetic data simply show us that a proposed reaction mechanism is possible.

Various mechanisms have been proposed for the reaction

$$CH_3COCH_3 + I_2 \xrightarrow{H^+} CH_3COCH_2I + HI$$

Figure 22.12 shows one proposed mechanism.

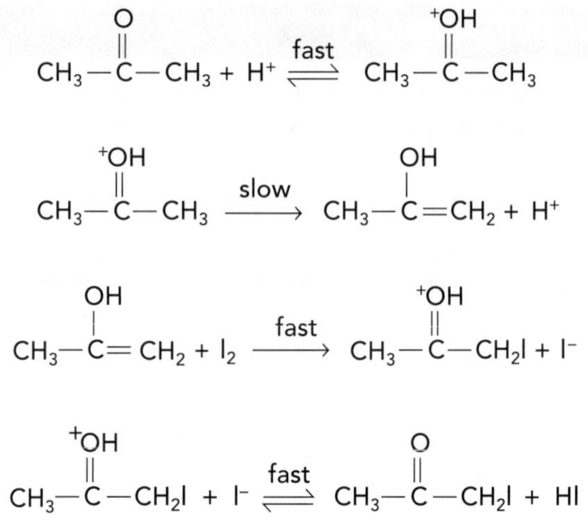

Figure 22.12: Propanone molecules rapidly accept hydrogen ions to form an intermediate that slowly forms propen-2-ol. This reacts rapidly with iodine to give the products.

The rate equation for this reaction is

$$rate = k[CH_3COCH_3][H^+]$$

We could not have deduced this reaction mechanism from the rate equation. But the mechanism is consistent with the rate equation.

The slow step (the rate-determining step) does not involve either propanone or hydrogen ions directly. However, the intermediate with the formula

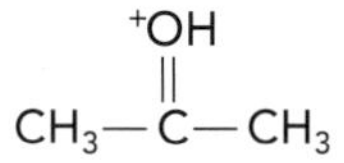

$$CH_3-\overset{\overset{+OH}{\|}}{C}-CH_3$$

is derived from substances that react together to form it (propanone and hydrogen ions). So both $[CH_3COCH_3]$ and $[H^+]$ appear in the rate equation.

The reaction between iodine and the intermediate $CH_3C(OH)=CH_2$ is fast and iodine molecules are not involved in the mechanism until after the rate-determining step. So the rate of reaction does not depend on the concentration of iodine.

In Section 22.6 we saw that the rate equation for the reaction

$$2N_2O_5(g) \rightarrow 4NO_2(g) + O_2$$

is rate = $k[N_2O_5]$. Figure 22.13 shows a suggested mechanism for this reaction. The rate equation suggests that a single N_2O_5 molecule is involved in the rate-determining step. This fits in with the proposed mechanism that suggests that the decomposition of N_2O_5 to form NO_2 and NO_3 is the slow step. The steps

in the first step – each molecule breaks down, they don't collide in pairs

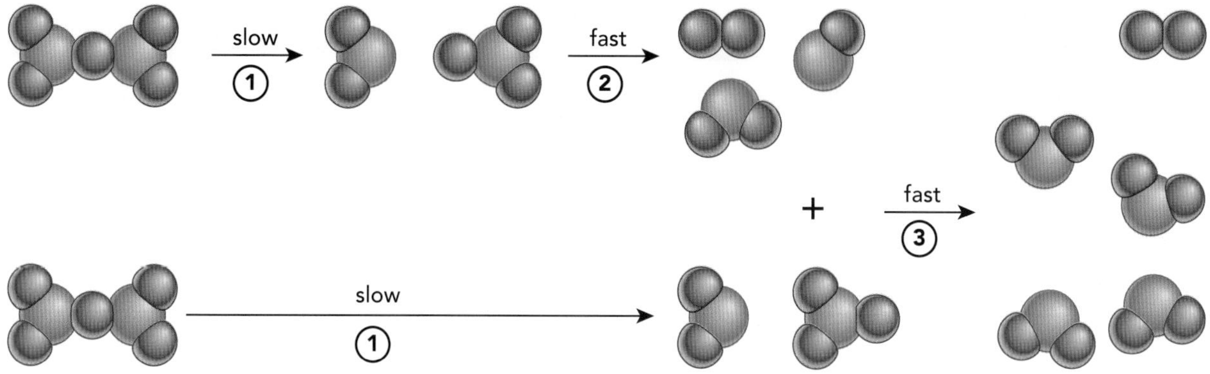

Reaction steps: (1) $N_2O_5 \xrightarrow{\text{slow}} NO_2 + NO_3$

(2) $NO_2 + NO_3 \xrightarrow{\text{fast}} NO + NO_2 + O_2$

(3) $NO + NO_3 \xrightarrow{\text{fast}} 2NO_2$

(note that two molecules of N_2O_5 need to have reacted for subsequent steps to be completed)

Figure 22.13: The rate equation tells us that the decomposition of individual molecules of nitrogen(V) oxide is the rate-determining step. The subsequent reactions are very much faster by comparison, and do not influence the overall rate. Try to match the reaction steps with the illustrations to get a picture of what is happening.

that follow the slow step are relatively fast and so have no effect on reaction rate.

If there is only a single species (atom, ion or molecule) in the rate-determining step we call the reaction *unimolecular*. If two species (which can be the same or different) are involved in the rate-determining step, we say that the reaction is *bimolecular*. Mechanisms that involve a trimolecular step are rare. This is because it is unlikely that three species will collide at the same time.

Question

11 An acidified solution of hydrogen peroxide reacts with iodide ions.

$H_2O_2(aq) + 2H^+(aq) + 2I^-(aq) \rightarrow 2H_2O(l) + I_2(aq)$

The rate equation for this reaction is

rate $= [H_2O_2][I^-]$

The mechanism that follows has been proposed for this reaction.

$H_2O_2 + I^- \xrightarrow{\text{slow}} H_2O + IO^-$

$H^+ + IO^- \xrightarrow{\text{fast}} HIO$

$HIO + H^+ + I^- \xrightarrow{\text{fast}} I_2 + H_2O$

Explain why this mechanism is consistent with the rate equation.

> **IMPORTANT**
>
> Remember that the overall stoichiometry of a chemical equation does not tell us anything about the reaction mechanism. A suggested mechanism should be consistent with the rate equation *not* the stoichiometric equation.

Predicting the order of a reaction from reaction mechanisms

We can predict the order of reaction from a given reaction mechanism if we know the intermediates present in the rate-determining step (or substances that react together to form the intermediate). Take, for example, the reaction of propanone with bromine in alkaline solution.

$CH_3COCH_3 + Br_2 + OH^- \rightarrow$
$\qquad\qquad\qquad CH_3COCH_2Br + H_2O + Br^-$

The reaction mechanism is shown in Figure 22.14.

REFLECTION

1 Write a list of the different methods of determining the order of a reaction. For each method, give details of exactly how you do the calculations. Compare your list with that of another learner. What processes did you go through to produce these details?

2 Which of these topic areas did you find most challenging: constructing a rate equation; calculating rate of reaction or rate constants; answering questions about reaction mechanisms? What strategies are needed in order to improve your understanding of this topic area?

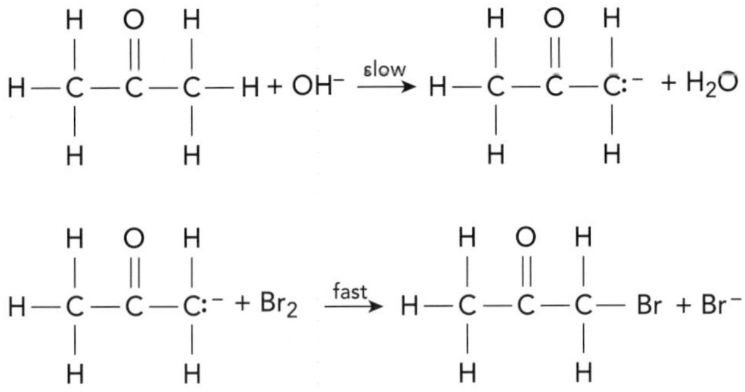

Figure 22.14: The reaction mechanism for the bromination of propanone in alkaline conditions.

The rate-determining step in this reaction is the slow step. The slow step involves one molecule of propanone and one hydroxide ion, so only these two species appear in the rate equation. The reaction is second order overall, first order with respect to propanone and first order with respect to hydroxide ions.

$$\text{rate} = k[CH_3COCH_3]\,[OH^-]$$

Bromine does not appear in the rate equation, as it takes part in a fast step after the rate-determining step.

Question

12 The reaction $2NO(g) + Cl_2(g) \rightarrow 2NOCl(g)$ is carried out in a sealed tube.

At the start of the experiment, the concentration of both NO and Cl_2 was 0.01 mol dm^{-3}.

The reaction is second order with respect to NO and first order with respect to Cl_2.

Which one of these represents the rate of reaction when the concentration of NO falls to 0.005 mol dm^{-3}?

A $k \times (0.005)^2 \times (0.0025)$

B $k \times (0.005) \times (0.0075)$

C $(0.005)^2 \times (0.0075)$

D $k \times (0.005)^2 \times (0.0075)$

22.8 Catalysis

In Chapter 9 you saw that catalysts increase the rate of a chemical reaction. They do this by providing an alternative pathway for the reaction with lower activation energy. Many transition element compounds are catalysts (Figure 22.15).

We can divide catalysts into two main classes.

- **Homogeneous catalysis** occurs when the catalyst is in the same phase as the reaction mixture. For example: hydrogen ions catalyse the hydrolysis of esters.

  $$CH_3COOC_2H_5(aq) + H_2O(l) \xrightleftharpoons{H^+(aq)} CH_3COOH(aq) + C_2H_5OH(aq)$$

  In this reaction the reactants, products and catalyst are all in the aqueous phase.

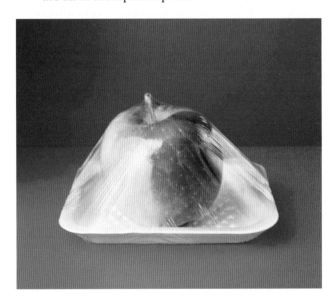

Figure 22.15: Addition polymers are produced using metallocene catalysts such as $[(C_5H_5)_2ZrCH_3]^+$. The strength and puncture resistance of this polymer film have made it popular for food packaging.

- **Heterogeneous catalysis** occurs when the catalyst is in a different phase to the reaction mixture. For example, the decomposition of aqueous hydrogen peroxide is catalysed by manganese(IV) oxide.

$$2H_2O_2(aq) \xrightarrow{MnO_2(s)} 2H_2O(l) + O_2(g)$$

The manganese(IV) oxide is in the solid phase, whereas the hydrogen peroxide is in aqueous solution.

> **KEY DEFINITIONS**
>
> **homogeneous catalysis:** the type of catalysis in which the catalyst and reactants are in the same phase. For example, sulfuric acid catalysing the formation of an ester from an alcohol and carboxylic acid.
>
> **heterogeneous catalysis:** the type of catalysis in which the catalyst is in a different phase to the reactants. For example, iron in the Haber process.

Homogeneous catalysis

Homogeneous catalysis often involves changes in oxidation number of the ions involved in catalysis. For example, small amounts of iodide ions catalyse the decomposition of hydrogen peroxide. In the catalysed reaction, iodide ions, I^-, are first oxidised to iodate(I) ions, IO^-. The IO^- ions then react with further molecules of hydrogen peroxide and are reduced back to iodide ions.

$$H_2O_2(aq) + I^-(aq) \rightarrow H_2O(l) + IO^-(aq)$$

$$H_2O_2(aq) + IO^-(aq) \rightarrow H_2O(l) + I^-(aq) + O_2(g)$$

The overall equation is:

$$2H_2O_2(aq) \xrightarrow{I^-} 2H_2O(l) + O_2(g)$$

Ions of transition elements are often good catalysts because of their ability to change oxidation number.

Examples of homogeneous catalysis

> **IMPORTANT**
>
> Most examples of homogeneous catalysis involve redox reactions.

The iodine–peroxodisulfate reaction

Peroxodisulfate (persulfate) ions, $S_2O_8^{2-}$, oxidise iodide ions to iodine. This reaction is very slow.

$$S_2O_8^{2-}(aq) + 2I^-(aq) \rightarrow 2SO_4^{2-}(aq) + I_2(aq)$$

The peroxodisulfate and iodide ions both have a negative charge. In order to collide and react, these ions need considerable energy to overcome the repulsive forces when like charges approach each other. $Fe^{3+}(aq)$ ions catalyse this reaction. The catalysis involves two redox reactions.

PRACTICAL ACTIVITY 22.1

SAFETY: Only carry out this activity in the presence of a teacher after safety aspects have been explained.

Examples of catalysts

1 Homogeneous catalysis

    a   Put 10 cm³ of 0.5 mol dm⁻³ sodium potassium tartrate in a 250 cm³ beaker.

    b   Add 10 cm³ 2.0 mol dm⁻³ hydrogen peroxide and stir.

    c   Warm the beaker carefully and note any signs of a reaction.

    d   Stop heating then add 1 cm³ of 0.1 mol dm⁻³ cobalt chloride.

    e   Describe the result.

2 Heterogeneous catalysis

    a   To each of 6 test-tubes add 2 cm³ 2.0 mol dm⁻³ hydrogen peroxide.

    b   Add very small portions (end of a spatula) of each of the following to separate test-tubes.

        i MnO_2

        ii Cu_2O

        iii MgO

        iv Fe_2O_3

        v Al_2O_3

    c   Describe the results and suggest the common features of the oxides with catalytic power.

- Reaction 1: reduction of Fe^{3+} ions to Fe^{2+} ions by I^- ions:

$$2Fe^{3+}(aq) + 2I^-(aq) \rightarrow 2Fe^{2+}(aq) + I_2(aq)$$

- Reaction 2: oxidation of Fe^{2+} ions back to Fe^{3+} by $S_2O_8^{2-}$ ions:

$$2Fe^{2+}(aq) + S_2O_8^{2-}(aq) \rightarrow 2Fe^{3+}(aq) + 2SO_4^{2-}(aq)$$

In both reactions 1 and 2, positively charged iron ions react with negatively charged ions. As ions with unlike charges are attracted to each other, these reactions are more likely to occur than direct reaction between $S_2O_8^{2-}$ and I^- ions.

You should notice that it doesn't matter what the order is of the two reactions. The oxidation of Fe^{2+} ions to Fe^{3+} by $S_2O_8^{2-}$ ions could happen first:

$$2Fe^{2+}(aq) + S_2O_8^{2-}(aq) \rightarrow 2Fe^{3+}(aq) + 2SO_4^{2-}(aq)$$

followed by

$$2Fe^{3+}(aq) + 2I^-(aq) \rightarrow 2Fe^{2+}(aq) + I_2(aq)$$

This reaction is catalysed by $Fe^{3+}(aq)$ and it is also catalysed by $Fe^{2+}(aq)$.

Figure 22.16 shows an energy level profile for the catalysed and the uncatalysed reactions. Note that the catalysed reaction has two energy 'humps' because it is a two-stage reaction.

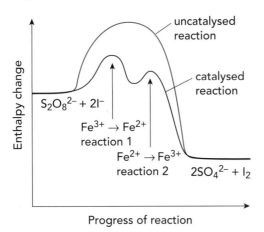

Figure 22.16: Energy level profiles for the catalysed and uncatalysed reactions of peroxodisulfate ions with iodide ions.

In order for this catalysis to work, the standard electrode potentials for the reactions involving the catalyst must lie between the electrode potentials involving the two reactants (Figure 22.17).

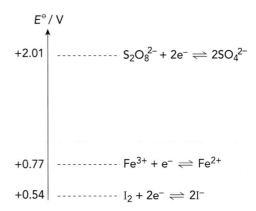

Figure 22.17: The electrode potential diagram for the catalysis of the reaction $S_2O_8^{2-} + 2I^- \rightarrow 2SO_4^{2-} + I_2$.

The use of electrode potentials in this way only predicts that the catalysis is possible. It does not give any information about the rate of reaction.

Oxides of nitrogen and acid rain

Sulfur dioxide is produced when we burn fossil fuels containing sulfur. When sulfur dioxide escapes into the atmosphere, it contributes to acid rain. One of the steps in the formation of acid rain is the oxidation of sulfur dioxide to sulfur trioxide.

$$SO_2(g) + \frac{1}{2}O_2(g) \rightarrow SO_3(g)$$

This oxidation is catalysed by a wide variety of mechanisms. Nitrogen(IV) oxide present in the atmosphere from a variety of sources (see Section 13.3) can catalyse the oxidation of sulfur dioxide. The nitrogen(IV) oxide is re-formed by reaction with atmospheric oxygen.

$$SO_2(g) + NO_2(g) \rightarrow SO_3(g) + NO(g)$$

$$NO + \frac{1}{2}O_2 \rightarrow NO_2(g)$$

Question

13 a State which pairs of substances **i** to **iv** below might catalyse the reaction:

$$S_2O_8^{2-}(aq) + 2I^-(aq) \rightarrow 2SO_4^{2-}(aq) + I_2(aq)$$

Explain your answer.

i	$Ni^{2+}(aq) / Ni(s)$	$E^\ominus = -0.25$ V
ii	$Mn^{3+}(aq) / Mn^{2+}(aq)$	$E^\ominus = +1.49$ V
iii	$Ce^{4+}(aq) / Ce^{3+}(aq)$	$E^\ominus = +1.70$ V
iv	$Cu^{2+}(aq) / Cu^+(aq)$	$E^\ominus = +0.15$ V

b Describe in terms of oxidation number change, which species are being oxidised and which are being reduced in these equations:

i $SO_2(g) + NO_2(g) \rightarrow SO_3(g) + NO(g)$

ii $NO + \frac{1}{2}O_2 \rightarrow NO_2(g)$

Heterogeneous catalysis

Heterogeneous catalysis often involves gaseous molecules reacting at the surface of a solid catalyst. The mechanism of this catalysis can be explained using the theory of adsorption. Chemical adsorption (also called chemisorption) occurs when molecules become bonded to atoms on the surface of a solid. Transition elements such as nickel are particularly good at chemisorbing hydrogen gas. Figure 22.18 shows the process of adsorption of hydrogen onto a nickel surface.

You must be careful to distinguish between the words adsorb and absorb. *Adsorb* means to bond to the surface of a substance. *Absorb* means to move right into the substance: rather like a sponge absorbs water.

The stages in adsorption of hydrogen onto nickel are:

* hydrogen gas diffuses to the surface of the nickel

* the hydrogen is physically adsorbed onto the surface: weak forces link the hydrogen molecules to the nickel

* the hydrogen becomes chemically adsorbed onto the surface: this causes stronger bonds to form between the hydrogen and the nickel

* this causes weakening of the hydrogen–hydrogen covalent bond.

When a reaction on the catalyst surface is complete, the bonds between the products and the catalyst weaken so much that the products break away from the surface. This is called desorption.

Examples of heterogeneous catalysis

Iron in the Haber process

Particular conditions of temperature and pressure are required to form ammonia from nitrogen and hydrogen (see Section 13.2). The reaction is catalysed by iron. The catalyst works by allowing hydrogen and nitrogen molecules to come close together on the surface of the iron. They are then more likely to react. Figure 22.19 shows the five steps in this heterogeneous catalysis.

1 **Diffusion**: nitrogen gas and hydrogen gas diffuse to the surface of the iron.

2 **Adsorption**: the reactant molecules are chemically adsorbed onto the surface of the iron. The bonds formed between the reactant molecules and the iron are:

* strong enough to weaken the covalent bonds within the nitrogen and hydrogen molecules so the atoms can react with each other

* weak enough to break and allow the products to leave the surface.

> **KEY WORDS**
>
> **adsorption (in catalysis):** the first stage in heterogeneous catalysis where reactant molecules form bonds with atoms on the catalyst surface.
>
> **desorption:** the last stage in heterogeneous catalysis. The bonds holding the molecule(s) of product(s) to the surface of the catalyst are broken and the product molecules diffuse away from the surface of the catalyst.

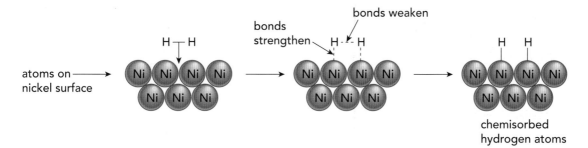

Figure 22.18: The adsorption of hydrogen onto a nickel surface.

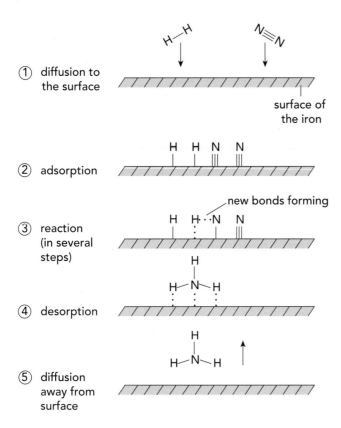

Figure 22.19: A possible mechanism for catalysis in the Haber process.

3 **Reaction**: the adsorbed nitrogen and hydrogen atoms react on the surface of the iron to form ammonia.

4 **Desorption**: the bonds between the ammonia and the surface of the iron weaken and are eventually broken.

5 **Diffusion**: ammonia diffuses away from the surface of the iron.

IMPORTANT

For the mechanism of heterogeneous catalysis remember the order:

    adsorption → old bonds breaking and
    new bonds forming → desorption

Transition elements in catalytic converters

Catalytic converters are fitted to car exhausts to reduce the amount of harmful nitrogen oxides escaping into the atmosphere. Once warmed up, the catalyst speeds up the conversion of nitrogen oxides to harmless nitrogen gas and the conversion of poisonous carbon monoxide to carbon dioxide. Unburned hydrocarbons from car engines may also reduce the nitrogen oxides in a catalytic reaction. Simplified equations for the overall reaction are:

$$2NO(g) + CO(g) \rightarrow N_2(g) + CO_2(g)$$

and

$$2NO_2(g) + 4CO(g) \rightarrow N_2(g) + 4CO_2(g)$$

The 'honeycomb' structure inside the catalytic converter contains small beads coated with platinum, palladium or rhodium. These act as heterogeneous catalysts. Possible steps in the catalytic process include:

- adsorption of nitrogen oxides and carbon monoxide onto the catalyst surface

- weakening of the covalent bonds within the nitrogen oxides and carbon monoxide

- formation of new bonds between

  - adjacent nitrogen atoms (to form nitrogen molecules)

  - carbon monoxide and oxygen atoms to form carbon dioxide

- desorption of nitrogen molecules and carbon dioxide molecules from the surface of the catalyst.

Question

14 a Describe in general terms what is meant by *desorption*.

  b Nickel acts as a catalyst for the hydrogenation of alkenes. For example:

$$CH_2\text{=}CH_2 + H_2 \xrightarrow{Ni} CH_3\text{—}CH_3$$

Suggest how nickel catalyses this reaction by referring to the processes of adsorption, reaction on the metal surface and desorption.

  c In catalytic converters, rhodium catalyses the reduction of nitrogen(II) oxide, NO, to nitrogen. Draw diagrams to suggest:

    i how NO is adsorbed onto the surface of the rhodium metal

    ii how nitrogen is formed.

REFLECTION

1 Work with another learner. Choose one aspect of catalysis, e.g. how homogeneous catalysts work or a specific catalytic reaction. Without looking at a textbook, work together to write a paragraph about this aspect of catalysis.

2 Was there anything that the other learner suggested that you could learn from? Did you have any ideas that they could learn from as well?

SUMMARY

The general form of the rate equation is: rate $= k[A]^m[B]^n$, where:

- k is the rate constant
- [A] and [B] are the concentrations of those reactants that affect the rate of reaction
- m is the order of the reaction with respect to A and n is the order of reaction with respect to B.

The order of reaction can be determined from graphs of reaction rate against concentration.

The half-life of a first-order reaction may be used in calculations to find the first-order rate constant using the relationship:

$$t_{\frac{1}{2}} = \frac{0.693}{k}$$

The rate-determining step is the slowest step in a reaction mechanism. The rate-determining step determines the overall rate of reaction.

The order of reaction with respect to a particular reactant shows how many molecules of that reactant are involved in the rate-determining step of a reaction.

The order of a reaction can be predicted from a given reaction mechanism knowing the rate-limiting step.

Homogeneous catalysis occurs when a catalyst and the reactants are in the same phase.

Heterogeneous catalysis occurs when a catalyst is in a different phase from the reactants.

The mechanism of heterogeneous catalysis involves the processes of adsorption, reaction and desorption.

EXAM-STYLE QUESTIONS

1 The rate of reaction between butanone and iodine is studied. In this experiment, iodine is in excess. The concentration of butanone is measured at various time intervals. The results are shown in the table below.

Time / min	0	10	20	30	40	50	60	80	100	120
[butanone] / mol dm^{-3}	0.080	0.055	0.035	0.024	0.015	0.010	0.007	0.003	0.001	0.001

    a   Plot these data on a suitable graph.   [3]

CONTINUED

b Demonstrate that this data is consistent with the reaction being first order with respect to butanone. [2]

c Find the gradient of your graph when the butanone concentration is:

   i   0.070 mol dm^{-3} [1]

   ii   0.040 mol dm^{-3} [1]

   iii   0.010 mol dm^{-3} [1]

d Use your answers to part **c** to plot a suitable graph to show rate of reaction (on the vertical axis) against concentration (on the horizontal axis). [3]

e Explain how the graph you plotted in part **d** is consistent with the reaction being first order with respect to butanone. [2]

[Total: 13]

2 The reaction

$$A + B + C \rightarrow ABC$$

is zero order with respect to one reactant, first order with respect to another reactant and second order with respect to another reactant.

a i Explain what is meant by the term *order of reaction* with respect to a given reactant. [2]

   ii Use the data in the table below to deduce the order with respect to each of the reactants, A, B and C.

Experiment	[A] / mol dm^{-3}	[B] / mol dm^{-3}	[C] / mol dm^{-3}	Rate / mol dm^{-3} s^{-1}
1	0.100	1.00	1.00	0.00783
2	0.200	1.00	1.00	0.00802
3	0.300	1.00	1.00	0.00796
4	1.00	0.100	1.00	0.00008
5	1.00	0.200	1.00	0.00031
6	1.00	0.300	1.00	0.00073
7	1.00	1.00	0.100	0.00078
8	1.00	1.00	0.200	0.00158
9	1.00	1.00	0.300	0.00236

[9]

b i Write the rate equation for this reaction. [1]

   ii State the overall order of the reaction. [1]

   iii Calculate the value of the rate constant using experiment 6. Include the units in your answer. [3]

c Suggest a possible mechanism consistent with the rate equation you have proposed and the chemical equation

$$A + B + C \rightarrow ABC$$ [3]

[Total: 19]

IMPORTANT

Questions **1 a**, **4 b** and **6 a** all require you to plot a graph. Make sure that you do the following:

- the axes (e.g. 0–120 minutes and 0–0.080 mol dm^{-3}) take up more than half of the graph paper you use

- label the axes sensibly so that plotting is easy; for example, if on your time axis, one large square = 10 minutes, you are less likely to make plotting mistakes

- plot points precisely with a sharp pencil

- draw a smooth curve through the points, with care.

These skills are all essential and should be practised every time you plot a graph.

CONTINUED

3   The rate equation for the reaction between iodine and propanone is:

$$\text{rate} = k[CH_3COCH_3][H^+][I_2]^0$$

   a   State the order of reaction with respect to iodine.   [1]

   b   State the overall order of reaction.   [1]

   c   i   Define the term *half-life*.   [1]

       ii In an experiment, a large excess of iodine is reacted with a small
           concentration of propanone in the presence of $H^+(aq)$. The
           concentration of propanone is measured at regular time intervals.
           Explain what happens to the value of the half-life of the propanone
           concentration as the concentration of propanone decreases.   [1]

   d   Copy the sketch graph. Plot additional points at
       10-second intervals up to 50 s. Join all the points with
       a smooth curve.   [4]

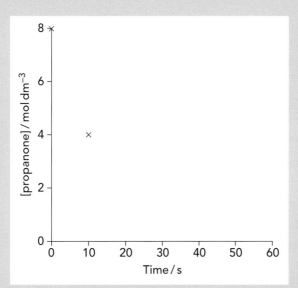

   e   Explain the term *rate-determining step*.   [2]

   f   Suggest a possible mechanism for the rate-determining step for the
       reaction between iodine and propanone.   [3]

                                                                                          [Total: 13]

4   The decomposition of hydrogen peroxide, H_2O_2, to oxygen and water is
    catalysed by manganese(IV) oxide.

   a   Define the term *catalyst*.   [2]

   b   The results for the decomposition of a sample of hydrogen
       peroxide are shown in the table.

Time / min	0	1	2	3	4	5	6	7	8
$[H_2O_2]$ / mol dm^{-3}	1.60	1.04	0.61	0.40	0.25	0.16	0.10	0.06	0.04

CONTINUED

    i Draw a graph of concentration of hydrogen peroxide (vertical axis) against time (horizontal axis).

       Draw a curve of best fit. [3]

    ii Use your graph to determine the half-life of the reaction. Show your working. [2]

    iii Use your graph to find the rate of reaction after 2 min. [4]

  c **i** Give the rate equation for the reaction. Explain your answer. [3]

    ii Use your answer to part **b iii** to calculate the value of the rate constant, k, and give the units. [3]

    iii Using your rate equation, find the rate of reaction when $[H_2O_2] = 2$ mol dm^{-3}. [2]

                                               [Total: 19]

5 Peroxodisulfate ions, $S_2O_8^{2-}$, react with iodide ions in aqueous solution to form iodine and sulfate ions.

$$S_2O_8^{2-}(aq) + 2I^-(aq) \rightarrow 2SO_4^{2-}(aq) + I_2(aq) \qquad \textbf{equation 1}$$

The initial rates of reaction are compared by timing how long it takes to produce a particular amount of iodine using four different initial concentrations of $S_2O_8^{2-}$. The results are shown in the table.

$[S_2O_8^{2-}]$ / mol dm^{-3}	Initial rate of reaction / s^{-1}
0.0200	4.16×10^{-3}
0.0150	3.12×10^{-3}
0.0120	2.50×10^{-3}
0.0080	1.70×10^{-3}

  a Plot a suitable graph to calculate rate of reaction. [3]

  b Deduce the order of reaction with respect to peroxodisulfate ions. Explain your answer. [2]

  c The reaction is first order with respect to iodide ions. Use this information and your answer to part **b** to write the overall rate equation for the reaction. [1]

  d The reaction between peroxodisulfate ions and iodide ions is slow. The reaction can be speeded up by adding a few drops of Fe^{3+}(aq) ions. The following reactions then take place:

$$2I^-(aq) + 2Fe^{3+}(aq) \rightarrow I_2(aq) + 2Fe^{2+}(aq) \qquad \textbf{equation 2}$$
$$2Fe^{2+}(aq) + S_2O_8^{2-}(aq) \rightarrow 2Fe^{3+}(aq) + 2SO_4^{2-}(aq) \qquad \textbf{equation 3}$$

    i Identify the type of catalysis occurring here. Explain your answer. [2]

    ii By referring to equations 1, 2 and 3 above, suggest why Fe^{3+}(aq) ions catalyse the reaction between peroxodisulfate ions and iodide ions. [4]

                                               [Total: 12]

CONTINUED

6 The rate of reaction between butanone and iodine is studied. In this experiment, butanone is in excess. The concentration of iodine is measured every 10 minutes for 1 hour. The results are shown in the table.

Time / min	0	10	20	30	40	50	60
$[I_2]$ / mol dm^{-3}	0.060	0.051	0.041	0.032	0.022	0.012	0.003

  a Plot these data on a suitable graph. [3]

  b Show from the graph that these data are consistent with the reaction being zero order with respect to iodine. [1]

  c The balanced chemical equation for the reaction is

$$CH_3CH_2COCH_3 + I_2 \rightarrow CH_3CH_2COCH_2I + HI$$

  Suggest whether or not this reaction could occur in a single step. Explain your answer. [2]

  d The rate equation for the reaction is rate = $k[CH_3CH_2COCH_3]$

  Explain the different meanings of the balanced chemical equation and the rate equation. [4]

  [Total: 10]

7 Nitrogen oxides can be removed from the exhaust gases of a car engine by using a catalytic converter. Many catalytic converters contain metals such as platinum and rhodium. These act as heterogeneous catalysts.

  a i State what is meant by the term *heterogeneous catalysis*. [2]

   ii Explain in general terms how heterogeneous catalysts work. [4]

  b Nitrogen(IV) oxide and carbon monoxide from car exhausts can react in a catalytic converter.

$$NO_2(g) + CO(g) \rightarrow NO(g) + CO_2(g)$$

  The rate equation for this reaction is rate = $k[NO_2]^2$

  Suggest a two-step reaction mechanism for this reaction that is consistent with this rate equation. [2]

  c Nitrogen(IV) oxide is formed when nitrogen(II) oxide reacts with oxygen.

$$2NO(g) + O_2(g) \rightarrow 2NO_2(g)$$

  The table shows the data obtained from a series of experiments to investigate the kinetics of this reaction.

Experiment	[NO] / mol dm^{-3}	[O$_2$] / mol dm^{-3}	Initial rate / mol dm^{-3} s^{-1}
1	0.00100	0.00300	21.3
2	0.00100	0.00400	28.4
3	0.00300	0.00400	256

   i Deduce the order of reaction with respect to each reactant. In each case, show your reasoning. [4]

   ii Deduce the rate equation for this reaction. [1]

   iii State the units of the rate constant, k, for this reaction. [1]

   [Total: 14]

CONTINUED

8 Bromate(V) ions react with bromide ions in acidic solution to form bromine.

$$BrO_3^-(aq) + 5Br^-(aq) + 6H^+(aq) \rightarrow 3Br_2(aq) + 3H_2O(l)$$

a   Suggest two methods of following the progress of this reaction. For each method explain your answer.   **[4]**

b   The initial rates of reaction were compared using the initial concentrations of reactants shown in the table.

Experiment	$[BrO_3^-]$ / mol dm^{-3}	$[Br^-]$ / mol dm^{-3}	$[H^+]$ / mol dm^{-3}	Relative rate of formation of bromine
1	0.040	0.20	0.24	1
2	0.040	0.20	0.48	4
3	0.080	0.20	0.48	8
4	0.040	0.10	0.48	2

i   Deduce the order of reaction with respect to each reactant. In each case, show your reasoning.   **[6]**

ii   Deduce the rate equation for this reaction.   **[1]**

iii   State the units of the rate constant, k, for this reaction.   **[1]**

c.   Describe and explain in terms of the Boltzmann distribution curve and collisions between particles, the effect of temperature on the rate constant of this reaction.   **[4]**

[Total: 16]

SELF-EVALUATION

After studying this chapter, complete a table like this:

I can	See section...	Needs more work	Almost there	Ready to move on
define and explain the terms *rate equation, order of reaction, overall order of reaction, rate constant, half-life, rate-determining step* and *intermediate*	22.1, 22.2, 22.3, 22.4			
construct and use rate equations of the form rate = $k[A]^m[B]^n$ for which m and n are 0, 1 or 2	22.4			
deduce the order of a reaction from concentration–time graphs or from experimental data relating to the initial rate method or half-life method	22.4			
interpret experimental data in graphical form, including concentration–time and rate–concentration graphs	22.4			
calculate initial rate using concentration data	22.5			
construct rate equations	22.3			

CONTINUED

I can	See section...	Needs more work	Almost there	Ready to move on
demonstrate that the half-life of a first-order reaction is independent of concentration	22.6			
use the half-life of a first-order reaction in calculations	22.4			
calculate the numerical value of a rate constant by using initial rates and the rate equation	22.5			
calculate the numerical value of a rate constant by using the half-life and the equation $k = \dfrac{0.693}{t_{\frac{1}{2}}}$	22.5			
suggest a multistep reaction mechanism that is consistent with the rate equation and the equation for the overall reaction	22.7			
predict the order that would result from a given reaction mechanism and rate-determining step	22.7			
deduce a rate equation given a reaction mechanism and rate-determining step for a given reaction	22.7			
identify an intermediate or catalyst from a given reaction mechanism	22.7, 22.8			
identify the rate-determining step from a rate equation and a given reaction mechanism	22.7			
describe catalysts as homogeneous or heterogeneous	22.8			
describe heterogeneous catalysis in terms of adsorption of reactants, bond weakening and desorption of products (with reference to iron in the Haber process and palladium, platinum and rhodium in the catalytic removal of oxides of nitrogen from the exhaust gases of car engines)	22.8			
describe homogeneous catalysis in terms of being used in one step and reformed in a later step (with reference to atmospheric oxides of nitrogen in the oxidation of atmospheric sulfur dioxide and Fe^{2+} or Fe^{3+} in the I^- / $S_2O_3^{2-}$ reaction).	22.8			
Describe qualitatively the effect of temperature on the rate constant and therefore on rate of reaction.				

> Chapter 23
Entropy and Gibbs free energy

LEARNING INTENTIONS

In this chapter you will learn how to:

- define the term *entropy* as being the number of possible arrangements of the particles and their energy in a given system

- predict and explain the sign of the entropy changes that occur during a change in state, during a temperature change and during a reaction in which there is a change in the number of gaseous molecules

- calculate the entropy change for a reaction using standard entropy values of the reactants and products

- perform calculations using the Gibbs equation $\Delta G^{\ominus} = \Delta H^{\ominus} - T\Delta S^{\ominus}$

- determine if a reaction is feasible by referring to the sign of $\Delta G^{\ominus}$

CONTINUED

- predict the effect of temperature change on the feasibility of a reaction when given standard enthalpy and entropy changes

- predict the feasibility of a reaction using the equation $\Delta G^\ominus = -nFE^\ominus_{cell}$.

BEFORE YOU START

1   Work with another learner. Take it in turns to explain to each other the meaning of the chemical terms: *surroundings, system, feasible, bond rotation, bond stretching*.

2   Explain Hess's law to another learner.

3   Write a paragraph explaining why it is important to take the state (solid, liquid or gas) into account when you are carrying out calculations involving enthalpy changes. Share your ideas with the rest of the class.

4   Ask another learner to select an example of a chemical reaction involving at least one compound as a reactant. Explain to the other learner exactly how to calculate the enthalpy change of this reaction (remember to take note of the stoichiometry of the reaction). Then reverse the process: you choose the reaction and the other learner explains.

5   Explain to another learner how to calculate the standard cell potential, $E^\ominus_{cell}$, for the cell reaction:

$$Fe^{3+} + I^- \rightarrow Fe^{2+} + \frac{1}{2}I_2$$

WHY DO RUBBER BANDS HAVE ELASTIC PROPERTIES?

Entropy can be thought of as a measure of randomness or disorder. The second law of thermodynamics states that the total entropy increases in all processes that take place by themselves (spontaneous changes). In other words, reactions go in the direction of more disorder.

Some rubbery polymers show an amazing elastic behaviour. Natural rubber is a polymer that can be stretched up to six times its original length. But it still returns to its original length when the pulling force is removed.

A polymer chain with freely rotating bonds, i.e. single bonds, can be coiled into thousands of different shapes all having similar energy. The natural shape of the chain (random unstretched coils) has the highest entropy. The most *unlikely* shape is a perfectly ordered straight chain.

For stretching to take place, the molecules must have some freedom to move and the polymer must have weak intermolecular forces between the chains. When we stretch an elastic band, we straighten out the chain by applying a force. This can be easily done with a very small force since it only involves rotation of the bonds rather than stretching the bonds (Figure 23.1).

So why does the elastic go back to a random coil when the stretching force is removed? It is because *entropy* rather than energy is the important factor in a spontaneous change. The stretched form has lower entropy because the polymer chains are more ordered (less random). So when the stretching force is removed, the rubber goes back to the form with greater entropy (more randomness). Remember from the second law of thermodynamics that processes go in the direction of more disorder!

CONTINUED

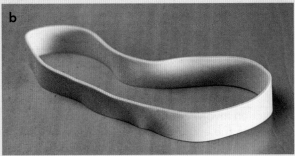

Figure 23.1: In diagram **a** the polymer chains are stretched and have low entropy. In diagram **b** the polymer chains are unstretched and have high entropy.

Question for discussion

Read the following paragraph about rubber production.

Natural rubber is produced from the latex (white sap) of various types of tree. The latex is removed by making a slit in the trunk and collecting the latex. The latex is then coagulated with the help of methanoic acid and sodium metabisulfite. Ammonia and sodium sulfite are often added as preservatives. Phosphates are sometimes added as well. Sulfuric acid used in the process of 'curing' the rubber can also be reduced to hydrogen sulfide gas. The rubber sheets are dried near where the rubber is produced, either in the air or often using a 'smokehouse' where wood or another fuel is burned to help dry the sheets. The rubber is then washed with plenty of water.

Discuss with another learner or group of learners:

*   What environmental problems can arise during the production of rubber?

23.1 Introducing entropy

KEY DEFINITIONS

entropy: the number of possible arrangements of the particles and their energy in a given system.

surroundings (in enthalpy changes): anything other than the chemical reactants and products, e.g. solvent, reaction vessel.

Entropy is a measure of the dispersal of energy at a specific temperature. Entropy can also be thought of as a measure of the randomness or disorder of a system. The higher the randomness or disorder, the greater the entropy of the system. A system is the part under investigation. In chemistry, this is the chemical reaction itself, i.e. reactants being converted to products.

The system of magnesium reacting with sulfuric acid in a test-tube to form magnesium sulfate and hydrogen releases energy to the surroundings.

The **surroundings** include:

*   the solvent (in this case water)

*   the air around the test-tube

*   the test-tube itself

*   anything dipping into the test-tube (e.g. a thermometer).

Changes that tend to continue to happen naturally are called *spontaneous changes*. Once started, a spontaneous change will carry on. When a spark is applied, methane gas reacts with oxygen in a spontaneous reaction to form carbon dioxide and water. The reaction is spontaneous because the methane continues to burn in the oxygen until either the methane or oxygen is completely used up. For a reaction to be spontaneous, it does not need to happen rapidly. Many spontaneous reactions are slow or need an input of energy to start them.

Entropy can also be thought of as a dispersal of energy, either from the system to the surroundings or from the surroundings to the system. The system becomes energetically more stable when it becomes more disordered.

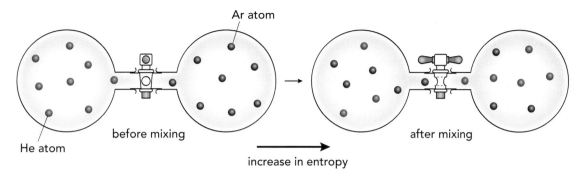

Figure 23.2: The spontaneous mixing of helium atoms (●) with argon atoms (●).

23.2 Chance and spontaneous change

Diffusion

If you spill a few drops of perfume in a closed room with no air draughts, the smell spreads gradually throughout the room. The molecules in the perfume vapour, which are responsible for the smell, move randomly in straight lines until they collide with air molecules, other perfume molecules or with the walls of the room. After collision, the perfume molecules change direction. This process of random movement and random collisions of molecules is called *diffusion*. The reason molecules in a vapour diffuse is because of the laws of chance and probability.

We can make a model to show how, during a spontaneous process, the entropy of the system increases. Figure 23.2 shows a system of two flasks connected by a stopcock. One flask contains helium and the other contains argon. These gases do not react.

When the stopcock is opened, the gas atoms move spontaneously by diffusion. After mixing, the gases are mixed up and there is more disorder than before mixing. The entropy has increased.

Diffusion and number of ways

We can show that the molecules in a vapour diffuse by chance. We do this by thinking about the probability of finding them at one place at any one time. Consider the simplified model shown below.

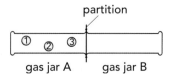

The three molecules in gas jar A cannot move into gas jar B.

In this model we assume:

- there are only a few molecules in gas jar A
- there are no other particles present
- the molecules move randomly and change directions when they collide.

After we remove the partition, the molecules can move randomly not only within gas jar A but also into gas jar B. There are three molecules and two places in which they can be (gas jar A and gas jar B). The possible ways of arranging the molecules after removing the partition are shown in Figure 23.3.

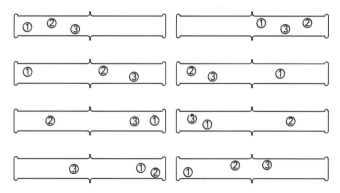

Figure 23.3: The eight possible arrangements of molecules after removing the partition between the gas jars.

There are eight different ways of arranging the three molecules between two gas jars. We can express this as:

number of molecules

$$2 \times 2 \times 2 = 2^3 = 8$$

two gas jars

Each of these ways is equally likely (equally probable). So the chance that all the molecules will stay in gas jar A is 1 in 8. Similarly, the chance that all three molecules will move over to gas jar B is 1 in 8. The molecules diffuse because there are more ways of them being spread out than remaining in the same place.

If we started with five molecules in gas jar A, the number of different ways of arranging the molecules is $2^5 = 32$. If we scaled this up to the numbers of gas molecules that we might find in a container in the laboratory, the number of ways of arranging the molecules is extremely large. For example, for a million molecules between two gas jars, it would be $2^{1\,000\,000}$, a number that is too large for your calculator to deal with. Diffusion happens because there is an strong likelihood of it taking place as a result of the large number of ways of arranging the molecules. The idea of the 'number of ways' of arranging either molecules or the energy within molecules affects whether the changes that take place are the ones that are most likely to happen. This applies to chemical reactions as well as to physical processes such as diffusion.

IMPORTANT

Entropy is greater if:

- there are more ways of arranging the energy in a molecule or atom
- there are more ways of arranging the molecules or atoms in a given volume.

Question

1   a   For this question, refer back to Figure 23.3. If there are four molecules in the gas jar on the left, how many ways of arranging the molecules are there when the partition is removed?

   b   What is the probability of finding all four molecules in the right-hand gas jar?

   c   Which of the following changes are likely to be spontaneous?

   i   sugar dissolving in water

   ii   the smell from an open bottle of aqueous ammonia diffusing throughout a room

   iii   water turning to ice at 10 °C

   iv   ethanol vaporising at 20 °C

   v   water mixing completely with cooking oil

   vi   limestone (calcium carbonate) decomposing at room temperature.

Comparing entropy values

To make any comparison of entropy values fair, we must use standard conditions. These standard conditions are the same as those used for ΔH:

- a pressure of 10^5 Pa
- a temperature of 298 K (25 °C)
- each substance involved in the reaction is in its normal physical state (solid, liquid or gas) at 10^5 Pa and 298 K.

Under these conditions, and for a mole of substance, the unit of standard molar entropy, $S^{\ominus}$, is J K^{-1} mol^{-1}. Standard molar entropy is the entropy of one mole of substance in its standard state. The symbol $\ominus$ indicates that the entropy is at standard conditions.

Table 23.1 shows some values for some standard molar entropies.

Substance	$S^{\ominus}$ / J K^{-1} mol^{-1}
diamond(s)	2.4
graphite(s)	5.7
calcium(s)	41.4
lead(s)	64.8
calcium oxide(s)	39.7
calcium carbonate(s)	92.9
mercury(l)	76.0
bromine(l)	151.6
methanol(l)	239.7
water(l)	69.9
carbon monoxide(g)	197.6
hydrogen(g)	130.6
helium(g)	126.0
ammonia(g)	192.3
oxygen(g)	205.0
carbon dioxide(g)	213.6

Table 23.1: Standard molar entropy values of some solids, liquids and gases. The states are shown as state symbols after each substance.

The values of all standard molar entropies are positive. Remember that elements have positive standard molar entropy values. Do not mix entropies up with enthalpies: the elements in their standard states have *enthalpy* values of zero.

Figure 23.4: a A diamond has a very low entropy value because it is a solid element with atoms regularly arranged. b Bromine has a high entropy value because it tends to spread out.

The entropy values are compared to a theoretically perfect crystal. The third law of thermodynamics states that 'All perfect crystals have the same entropy at a temperature of absolute zero'. The nearest we can get to this is a perfect diamond weighing 12 g cooled to as low a temperature as possible.

From the values in the table and other data we can make some generalisations:

- Gases generally have much higher entropy values than liquids, and liquids have higher entropy values than solids (see Figure 23.4). There are exceptions to this. For example, calcium carbonate (solid) has a higher entropy value than mercury (liquid).

- Simpler substances with fewer atoms have lower entropy values than more complex substances with a greater number of atoms. For example, for calcium oxide, CaO, $S^\ominus = 39.7$ J K^{-1} mol^{-1}, but for calcium carbonate, CaCO$_3$, $S^\ominus = 92.9$ J K^{-1} mol^{-1}. Carbon monoxide, CO, has a lower entropy value than carbon dioxide, CO$_2$.

- For similar types of substances, harder substances have a lower entropy value. For example, diamond has a lower entropy value than graphite and calcium has a lower entropy value than lead.

- For a given substance, the entropy increases as a solid melts and then changes to a vapour (see Figure 23.5). For example, the molar entropy of ice just below its melting point is 48.0 J K^{-1} mol^{-1}.

The molar entropy for water is 69.9 J K^{-1} mol^{-1}, but just above its boiling point, the value increases to 188.7 J K^{-1} mol^{-1}. There is a gradual increase in entropy as the temperature of a substance is increased. Increasing the temperature of a solid makes the molecules, atoms or ions vibrate more. Increasing the temperature of a liquid or gas increases the entropy because it increases the disorder of the particles. When a substance melts or vaporises, there is a large increase in entropy because there is a very large increase in the disorder of the particles.

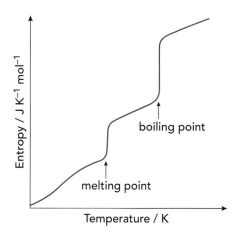

Figure 23.5: The change in entropy as a substance melts and then boils.

When a solid changes to a liquid

The regularly arranged lattice of particles close together in the solid changes to an irregular arrangement of particles, which are close together but rotate and slide over each other in the liquid.

When a liquid changes to a vapour

The irregular arrangement of particles in the liquid which are close together and rotating changes to an irregular arrangement of particles which are free to move around rapidly because they are far apart from each other.

> **IMPORTANT**
>
> Note that when a gas condenses to a liquid or a liquid changes to a solid, the entropy *decreases* because the particles are going from a more disordered state to a more ordered state. There are also fewer ways of arranging the energy in a solid.

When a solid dissolves in a solvent, the entropy generally increases. In the solid, the particles are ordered and can only vibrate. The entropy is low. When dissolved in a solvent to form a dilute solution, the particles are spread out from each other and can move randomly from place to place. The entropy is high because not only are the particles spread out more but also the number of ways of arranging the energy is greater. So, there is generally an increase in entropy on dissolving. Conversely, when a salt crystallises from a solution, the entropy decreases because some of the random mobile particles in the solution are becoming ordered particles in the crystal.

> **IMPORTANT**
>
> Care must be taken when discussing the entropy change of solution. For concentrated aqueous solutions of salts which have highly charged ions, there may be a considerable order in the solvent due to several hydration layers around these ions.

Question

2 Explain the difference in the entropy of each of the following pairs of substances in terms of their state and structure.

   a $Br_2(l)$ ($S^\ominus = 151.6$ J K^{-1} mol^{-1}) and $I_2(s)$ ($S^\ominus = 116.8$ J K^{-1} mol^{-1})

   b $H_2(g)$ ($S^\ominus = 130.6$ J K^{-1} mol^{-1}) and $CH_4(g)$ ($S^\ominus = 186.2$ J K^{-1} mol^{-1})

   c $Hg(l)$ ($S^\ominus = 76.00$ J K^{-1} mol^{-1}) and $Na(s)$ ($S^\ominus = 51.20$ J K^{-1} mol^{-1})

   d $SO_2(g)$ ($S^\ominus = 248.1$ J K^{-1} mol^{-1}) and $SO_3(l)$ ($S^\ominus = 95.60$ J K^{-1} mol^{-1})

Entropy changes in reactions

In a chemical reaction, if we compare the entropies of the reactants and products, we can try to explain the magnitude of the entropy change and whether or not it increases or decreases. We will assume that gases have high entropy and solids have low entropy. If there is a change in the number of gaseous molecules in a reaction, there is likely to be a significant entropy change. This is because high values of entropy are associated with gases. The more gas molecules, there are, the greater the number of ways of arranging them and the higher the entropy. For example, in the reaction:

$$CaCO_3(s) \rightarrow CaO(s) + CO_2(g)$$

there is an increase in entropy of the system because a gas is being produced (high entropy) but the reactant, calcium carbonate, is a solid (low entropy).

In the reaction $2N_2O_5(g) \rightarrow 4NO_2(g) + O_2(g)$

we should expect an increase of entropy of the system because there is a greater number of moles of gas molecules in the products (5 molecules) than in the reactants (2 molecules). In addition, there are two different product molecules but only one type of reactant molecule. This also contributes to a greater disorder in the products compared with the reactants. The system becomes energetically more stable when it becomes more disordered.

In the reaction $N_2(g) + 3H_2(g) \rightarrow 2NH_3(g)$

we should expect a decrease in the entropy of the system because there is a reduction in the number of gas molecules as the reaction proceeds. So the entropy change of the system is negative. The reactants, hydrogen and nitrogen, are more stable than the product, ammonia.

Question

3   For each of the following reactions, suggest whether the entropy of the reactants or the products will be greater or whether it is difficult to decide. Explain your answers.

a $NH_3(g) + HCl(g) \rightarrow NH_4Cl(s)$

b $S(s) + O_2(g) \rightarrow SO_2(g)$

c $2Mg(s) + CO_2(g) \rightarrow 2MgO(s) + C(s)$

d $2Li(s) + Cl_2(g) \rightarrow 2LiCl(s)$

e $H_2O(g) + C(s) \rightarrow H_2(g) + CO(g)$

f $2HI(g) \rightarrow H_2(g) + I_2(g)$

g $2K(s) + 2H_2O(l) \rightarrow 2KOH(aq) + H_2(g)$

h $MgCO_3(s) \rightarrow MgO(s) + CO_2(g)$

23.3 Calculating entropy changes

Entropy changes in exothermic and endothermic reactions

Energy can be transferred from the system to the surroundings (exothermic change) or from the surroundings to the system (endothermic change). The surroundings are so large that when energy exchange takes place there is such a small change in temperature or pressure that we can ignore this.

- For an exothermic reaction, the energy released to the surroundings increases the number of ways of arranging the energy. This is because the energy goes into rotation and translation (movement from place to place) of molecules in the surroundings. So there is likely to be an increase in entropy and an increased probability of the chemical change occurring spontaneously. In other words, the reaction becomes more feasible.

- For an endothermic reaction, the energy absorbed from the surroundings decreases the number of ways of arranging the energy. So there is likely to be a decrease in entropy and a decreased probability of the chemical change occurring spontaneously.

Total entropy change

> **IMPORTANT**
>
> You do not have to know the equation
> $$\Delta S^{\ominus}_{total} = \Delta S^{\ominus}_{system} + \Delta S^{\ominus}_{surroundings}$$
> for your examination, but this section is useful for a general understanding of entropy.

We can use entropy values to predict whether a chemical reaction will occur spontaneously or not. When a chemical reaction takes place there is a change in entropy because the reactants and products have different entropy values. The symbol for standard entropy change is $\Delta S^{\ominus}$. The total entropy change involves both the system and the surroundings. For the system (reactants and products), we write the entropy change as $\Delta S^{\ominus}_{system}$. For the surroundings we write the entropy change as $\Delta S^{\ominus}_{surroundings}$.

The total entropy change is given by:

$$\Delta S^{\ominus}_{total} = \Delta S^{\ominus}_{system} + \Delta S^{\ominus}_{surroundings}$$

If the total entropy change increases, the entropy change is positive, e.g. $\Delta S^{\ominus}_{total}$ is +40 J K^{-1} mol^{-1}. The reaction will then occur spontaneously. We say that the reaction is *feasible*.

If the total entropy change decreases, the entropy change is negative, e.g. $\Delta S^{\ominus}_{total}$ is −40 J K^{-1} mol^{-1}. The reaction is then *not* likely to occur.

Calculating the entropy change of the system

> **KEY WORD**
>
> **system:** the reactants and products of a chemical reaction.

In order to calculate the entropy change of a **system**, we use the relationship:

$$\Delta S^{\ominus}_{system} = \Sigma S^{\ominus}_{products} - \Sigma S^{\ominus}_{reactants}$$

The symbol 'Σ' means 'the sum of'. So, to calculate $\Delta S^{\ominus}_{system}$ we add the entropy values of the products and the entropy values of the reactants separately, then take away the sum of the reactants from the sum of the products.

Note:

1 We need to take account of the stoichiometry of the equation (as we did in calculations involving $\Delta H^{\ominus}$).

2 When looking up entropy values in tables of data, we need to choose the data for the correct state, solid, liquid or gas.

WORKED EXAMPLES

1 Calculate the entropy change of the system for the reaction:

$$2Ca(s) + O_2(g) \rightarrow 2CaO(s)$$

Solution

The standard entropy values are:

$S^{\ominus} [Ca(s)] = 41.40 \text{ J K}^{-1} \text{ mol}^{-1}$

$S^{\ominus} [O_2(g)] = 205.0 \text{ J K}^{-1} \text{ mol}^{-1}$

$S^{\ominus} [CaO(s)] = 39.70 \text{ J K}^{-1} \text{ mol}^{-1}$

$\Delta S^{\ominus}_{\text{system}} = \Sigma S^{\ominus}_{\text{products}} - \Sigma S^{\ominus}_{\text{reactants}}$

$= 2 \times S^{\ominus} [CaO(s)] - \{2 \times S^{\ominus} [Ca(s)] + S^{\ominus} [O_2(g)]\}$

$= 2 \times 39.70 - \{(2 \times 41.40) + 205.0\}$

$= 79.40 - 287.8$

$\Delta S^{\ominus}_{\text{system}} = -208.4 \text{ J K}^{-1} \text{ mol}^{-1}$

The negative value for the entropy change shows that the entropy of the system has decreased. We know, however, that calcium reacts spontaneously with oxygen. So the entropy of the surroundings must also play a part because the total entropy change must be positive for the reaction to be feasible.

2 Calculate the entropy change of the system for the reaction:

$$CH_4(g) + 2O_2(g) \rightarrow CO_2(g) + 2H_2O(g)$$

Solution

The standard entropy values are:

$S^{\ominus} [CH_4(g)] = 186.2 \text{ J K}^{-1} \text{ mol}^{-1}$

$S^{\ominus} [O_2(g)] = 205.0 \text{ J K}^{-1} \text{ mol}^{-1}$

$S^{\ominus} [CO_2(g)] = 213.6 \text{ J K}^{-1} \text{ mol}^{-1}$

$S^{\ominus} [H_2O(g)] = 188.7 \text{ J K}^{-1} \text{ mol}^{-1}$

$\Delta S^{\ominus}_{\text{system}} = \Sigma S^{\ominus}_{\text{products}} - \Sigma S^{\ominus}_{\text{reactants}}$

$= \{S^{\ominus} [CO_2(g)] + 2 \times S^{\ominus} [H_2O(g)]\} - \{S^{\ominus} [CH_4(g)] + 2 \times S^{\ominus} [O_2(g)]\}$

$= \{213.6 + (2 \times 188.7)\} - \{186.2 + (2 \times 205.0)\}$

$= 591.0 - 596.2$

$\Delta S^{\ominus}_{\text{system}} = -5.2 \text{ J K}^{-1} \text{ mol}^{-1}$

The negative value for the entropy change shows that the entropy of the system has decreased slightly. We know, however, that methane burns in oxygen once it is ignited. So the entropy of the surroundings must also play a part in the overall entropy change.

Question

4 Calculate the standard entropy change of the system in each of the following reactions using the standard molar entropy values given here.

(Values for $S^{\ominus}$ in J K^{-1} mol^{-1}: $Cl_2(g) = 165.0$, $Fe(s) = 27.30$, $Fe_2O_3(s) = 87.40$, $H_2(g) = 130.6$, $H_2O(l) = 69.90$, $H_2O_2(l) = 109.6$, $Mg(s) = 32.70$, $MgO(s) = 26.90$, $Na(s) = 51.20$, $NaCl(s) = 72.10$, $NH_4NO_3(s) = 151.1$, $N_2O(g) = 219.7$, $O_2(g) = 205.0$

a $2H_2O_2(l) \rightarrow 2H_2O(l) + O_2(g)$

b $NH_4NO_3(s) \rightarrow N_2O(g) + 2H_2O(g)$

c $2Mg(s) + O_2(g) \rightarrow 2MgO(s)$

d $2Na(s) + Cl_2(g) \rightarrow 2NaCl(s)$

e $3Mg(s) + Fe_2O_3(s) \rightarrow 3MgO(s) + 2Fe(s)$

Calculating the entropy change of the surroundings

IMPORTANT

You do not have to know the equation $\Delta S^{\ominus}_{\text{surroundings}} = \dfrac{-\Delta H^{\ominus}_{\text{reaction}}}{T}$ for your examination but the equation is useful for a general understanding of entropy.

Many chemical reactions are accompanied by large enthalpy changes. These enthalpy changes change the number of ways of arranging the energy in the surroundings. So, in many chemical reactions, the value of the entropy changes in the surroundings cannot be ignored.

The entropy change of the surroundings is calculated using the relationship:

$$\Delta S^{\ominus}_{surroundings} = \frac{-\Delta H^{\ominus}_{reaction}}{T}$$

where

- $\Delta H^{\ominus}_{reaction}$ is the standard enthalpy change of the reaction

- T is the temperature in kelvin. At standard temperature, this value is 298 K.

Note:

1 When performing calculations to find $\Delta S^{\ominus}_{surroundings}$ the value of $\Delta H^{\ominus}_{reaction}$ in kJ mol^{-1} should be multiplied by 1000. This is because entropy changes are measured in units of joules per kelvin per mole.

2 The negative sign in front of $\Delta H^{\ominus}_{reaction}$ is part of the equation and not the sign of the enthalpy change. If the enthalpy change is negative, the whole $\frac{-\Delta H^{\ominus}_{reaction}}{T}$ term becomes positive.

WORKED EXAMPLES

Note: These examples are extension questions but they give you useful practice in converting kJ to J for $\Delta H^{\ominus}_{reaction}$, which is necessary later on in this chapter.

3 Calculate the entropy change of the surroundings for the reaction:

$$2Ca(s) + O_2(g) \rightarrow 2CaO(s)$$
$$\Delta H^{\ominus}_{reaction} = -1270.2 \text{ kJ mol}^{-1}$$

Solution

Step 1: Convert the enthalpy change into J mol^{-1} by multiplying by 1000.

$$-1270.2 \times 1000 = -1\,270\,200 \text{ J mol}^{-1}$$

Step 2: Apply the relationship.

$$\Delta S^{\ominus}_{surroundings} = \frac{-\Delta H^{\ominus}_{reaction}}{T}$$
$$= \frac{-(-1\,270\,200)}{298}$$
$$= +4262.4 \text{ J K}^{-1} \text{ mol}^{-1}$$

4 Calculate the entropy change of the surroundings for the reaction:

$$CH_4(g) + 2O_2(g) \rightarrow CO_2(g) + 2H_2O(g)$$
$$\Delta H^{\ominus}_{reaction} = -890.3 \text{ kJ mol}^{-1}$$

Solution

Step 1: Convert the enthalpy change into J mol^{-1} by multiplying by 1000.

$$-890.3 \times 1000 = -890\,300 \text{ J mol}^{-1}$$

Step 2: Apply the relationship.

$$\Delta S^{\ominus}_{surroundings} = \frac{-\Delta H^{\ominus}_{reaction}}{T}$$
$$\frac{-(-890\,300)}{298}$$
$$- +2987.6 \text{ J K}^{-1} \text{ mol}^{-1}$$

Question

5 Calculate the entropy change of the surroundings in each of the following reactions. Assume that the value of ΔH does not change with temperature.

   a $C(s) + O_2(g) \rightarrow CO_2(g)$ $\qquad \Delta H^{\ominus}_{reaction} = -393.5$ kJ mol^{-1}, carried out at 0 °C

   b $2C(s) + N_2(g) \rightarrow C_2N_2(g)$ $\qquad \Delta H^{\ominus}_{reaction} = +307.9$ kJ mol^{-1}, carried out at 300 °C

   c $H_2(g) + F_2(g) \rightarrow 2HF(g)$ $\qquad \Delta H^{\ominus}_{reaction} = -271.1$ kJ mol^{-1}, carried out at standard temperature

   d $Si(s) + 2H_2(g) \rightarrow SiH_4(g)$ $\qquad \Delta H^{\ominus}_{reaction} = +34.30$ kJ mol^{-1}, carried out at −3 °C

Calculating total entropy change

> **Note:** This section about total entropy change is extension material. You will not be examined on it but it does give you a useful insight into how the surroundings are important in driving the direction of a reaction.

The total entropy change is given by:

$$\Delta S^{\ominus}_{\text{total}} = \Delta S^{\ominus}_{\text{system}} + \Delta S^{\ominus}_{\text{surroundings}}$$

We can also write this as:

$$\Delta S^{\ominus}_{\text{total}} = \Delta S^{\ominus}_{\text{system}} - \frac{\Delta H^{\ominus}_{\text{reaction}}}{T}$$

The total entropy changes for the examples given above for the reactions of calcium with oxygen and the combustion of methane are calculated by simply adding the entropy change of the system to the entropy change of the surroundings.

You can see that in both Worked examples 5 and 6, the large positive entropy change of the surroundings more than compensates for the negative entropy change of the system. The total entropy change is positive and the reactions are feasible.

WORKED EXAMPLES

5 Calculate the total entropy change for the reaction:

$$2Ca(s) + O_2(g) \rightarrow 2CaO(s)$$

$$\Delta S^{\ominus}_{\text{system}} = -208.4 \text{ J K}^{-1} \text{ mol}^{-1}$$

$$\Delta S^{\ominus}_{\text{surroundings}} = +4262.4 \text{ J K}^{-1} \text{ mol}^{-1}$$

Solution

$$\Delta S^{\ominus}_{\text{total}} = \Delta S^{\ominus}_{\text{system}} + \Delta S^{\ominus}_{\text{surroundings}}$$

$$= -208.4 + 4262.4$$

$$\Delta S^{\ominus}_{\text{total}} = +4054.0 \text{ J K}^{-1} \text{ mol}^{-1}$$

6 Calculate the total entropy change for the reaction:

$$CH_4(g) + 2O_2(g) \rightarrow CO_2(g) + 2H_2O(g)$$

$$\Delta S^{\ominus}_{\text{system}} = -5.2 \text{ J K}^{-1} \text{ mol}^{-1}$$

$$\Delta S^{\ominus}_{\text{surroundings}} = +2987.6 \text{ J K}^{-1} \text{ mol}^{-1}$$

CONTINUED

Solution

$$\Delta S^{\ominus}_{\text{total}} = \Delta S^{\ominus}_{\text{system}} + \Delta S^{\ominus}_{\text{surroundings}}$$

$$= -5.2 + 2987.6$$

$$\Delta S^{\ominus}_{\text{total}} = +2982.4 \text{ J K}^{-1} \text{ mol}^{-1}$$

Question

6 Calculate the total standard entropy change in each of the following reactions using the standard molar entropy values given here.

Values for $S^{\ominus}$ in J K^{-1} mol^{-1}: C(graphite) = 5.700, $C_2N_2(g)$ = 242.1, $C_3H_8(g)$ = 269.9, $CO_2(g)$ = 213.6, $H_2(g)$ = 130.6, $H_2O(l)$ = 69.90, $H_2S(g)$ = 205.7, $N_2(g)$ = 191.6, $O_2(g)$ = 205.0, $P(s)$ = 41.10, $P_4O_{10}(s)$ = 228.9, $S(s)$ = 31.80

a $S(s) + H_2(g) \rightarrow H_2S(g)$

$$\Delta H^{\ominus}_{\text{reaction}} = -20.6 \text{ kJ mol}^{-1}$$

b $2C(\text{graphite}) + N_2(g) \rightarrow C_2N_2(g)$

$$\Delta H^{\ominus}_{\text{reaction}} = +307.9 \text{ kJ mol}^{-1}$$

c $4P(s) + 5O_2(g) \rightarrow P_4O_{10}(s)$

$$\Delta H^{\ominus}_{\text{reaction}} = -2984.0 \text{ kJ mol}^{-1}$$

d $C_3H_8(g) + 5O_2(g) \rightarrow 3CO_2(g) + 4H_2O(l)$

$$\Delta H^{\ominus}_{\text{reaction}} = -2219.2 \text{ kJ mol}^{-1}$$

Entropy in equilibrium reactions

In equilibrium reactions, both products and reactants are present. How can the total entropy change be positive in both directions? There is an additional increase in disorder and so an increase in entropy associated with this mixing.

Figure 23.6 shows how the increase in entropy changes as a reaction progresses, starting either from pure reactants or pure products to reach equilibrium. As mixing proceeds, the rate of increasing disorder decreases as more and more NO_2 molecules are formed from N_2O_4. At some stage in the reaction, the rate of the forward reaction equals the rate of the backward reaction. Equilibrium has been reached. The same argument applies to the reverse reaction.

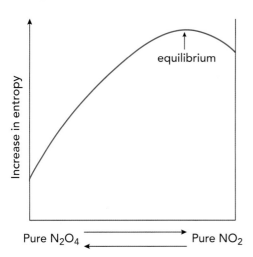

Figure 23.6: The total entropy change, $\Delta S^{\ominus}_{\text{total}}$, when N_2O_4 is converted to an equilibrium mixture of NO_2 and N_2O_4 and NO_2 is converted to the same equilibrium mixture.

At the position of equilibrium, the total entropy change of the forward reaction equals the total entropy change of the backward reaction, and under standard conditions the overall entropy change is zero.

Entropy and temperature

The entropy change of the surroundings is given by

$$\Delta S^{\ominus}_{\text{surroundings}} = \frac{-\Delta H^{\ominus}_{\text{reaction}}}{T}$$

If we carry out reactions at temperatures above standard temperature, an increase in temperature makes the entropy change of the surroundings less negative or more positive. If we carry out reactions at temperatures below standard temperature, a decrease in temperature makes the entropy change of the surroundings more negative or less positive. In both these cases we make the assumption that $\Delta H^{\ominus}_{\text{reaction}}$ does not change significantly

with temperature. In reality, $\Delta H^{\ominus}_{\text{reaction}}$ does change slightly with temperature, but we can often disregard this change.

We can see how increasing the temperature affects the ability of zinc carbonate to undergo thermal decomposition by comparing the entropy changes at 298 K and 550 K. However, we have to take into account both the surroundings and the system. We assume that neither the standard molar entropies nor the enthalpy change of formation changes with temperature.

$$ZnCO_3(s) \rightarrow ZnO(s) + CO_2(g)$$
$$\Delta H^{\ominus}_{\text{reaction}} = +72.3 \text{ kJ mol}^{-1}$$

For this reaction $\Delta S^{\ominus}_{\text{system}} = +174.8 \text{ J K}^{-1} \text{ mol}^{-1}$ (the same for both temperatures).

Reaction at 298 K

$$\Delta S^{\ominus}_{\text{surroundings}} = \frac{-72\,300}{298}$$
$$= -242.6 \text{ J K}^{-1} \text{ mol}^{-1}$$
$$\Delta S^{\ominus}_{\text{total}} = +174.8 - 242.6 \text{ J K}^{-1} \text{ mol}^{-1}$$
$$\Delta S^{\ominus}_{\text{total}} = -67.8 \text{ J K}^{-1} \text{ mol}^{-1}$$

Reaction at 550 K

$$\Delta S^{\ominus}_{\text{surroundings}} = \frac{-72\,300}{550}$$
$$= -131.5 \text{ J K}^{-1} \text{ mol}^{-1}$$
$$\Delta S^{\ominus}_{\text{total}} = +174.8 - 131.5 \text{ J K}^{-1} \text{ mol}^{-1}$$
$$\Delta S^{\ominus}_{\text{total}} = +43.3 \text{ J K}^{-1} \text{ mol}^{-1}$$

You can see that at 298 K the total entropy change is negative, so the reaction does not occur at this temperature. At 550 K the total entropy change is positive, so the reaction is spontaneous at this temperature.

- When the total entropy change in a reaction shows a large increase, e.g. +200 J K^{-1} mol^{-1}, the reaction can be regarded as going to completion. It is definitely spontaneous.

- When the total entropy change shows a large decrease, e.g. −600 J K^{-1} mol^{-1}, we can deduce that there is very little likelihood of a reaction occurring.

Question

7 The decomposition of calcium carbonate

$$CaCO_3(s) \rightarrow CaO(s) + CO_2(g)$$

does not take place at room temperature.

a Explain in terms of entropy changes why heating the calcium carbonate to a high temperature increases the likelihood of this reaction taking place.

b In a closed system at high temperature, the reactants and products are in equilibrium.

$$CaCO_3(s) \rightleftharpoons CaO(s) + CO_2(g)$$

i Explain the meaning of the term *closed system*.

ii Explain, in terms of entropy changes, what happens when the pressure on this system is increased.

iii What is the value of the standard total entropy change at equilibrium?

23.4 Entropy, enthalpy changes and Gibbs free energy

For an exothermic reaction such as:

$$CH_4(g) + 2O_2(g) \rightarrow CO_2(g) + 2H_2O(g)$$
$$\Delta H^\ominus_{reaction} = -890.3 \text{ kJ mol}^{-1}$$

the entropy change of the system is negative. But the large negative value of the enthalpy change more than compensates for the negative entropy change of the system. This is because it causes the term $-\dfrac{-\Delta H^\ominus_{reaction}}{T}$ to have a high positive value. So the total energy change is positive and the reaction, once started, is spontaneous. In highly exothermic reactions, where the value of $\Delta H^\ominus_{reaction}$ is large and negative, the enthalpy change is the driving force of the reaction.

In endothermic reactions, the entropy term tends to be more important. The term $-\dfrac{-\Delta H^\ominus_{reaction}}{T}$ has a negative value. If the value of $\Delta S^\ominus_{system}$ and $\Delta S^\ominus_{surroundings}$ are both negative, then the reaction will *not* be spontaneous. However, if the value of $\Delta S^\ominus_{system}$ is positive and large enough, it can compensate for the negative value of the

$\Delta S^\ominus_{surroundings}$ so that $\Delta S^\ominus_{total}$ becomes positive. The reaction is spontaneous.

Chemists are usually interested in the system of reactants and products rather than having to consider the energy changes with the surroundings. Fortunately for us, there is a way in which we can take account of both system and surroundings in a more straightforward way. This involves a quantity called **Gibbs free energy** or, more simply, *free energy*. It can also be called Gibbs energy or Gibbs function, G (Figure 23.7).

Figure 23.7: Gibbs free energy is named after American scientist Josiah Willard Gibbs, who applied the concept of entropy and 'applied energy' changes to chemical reactions and physical processes.

23.5 Gibbs free energy

What is Gibbs free energy?

In determining whether a chemical reaction is likely to be spontaneous, we use the quantity Gibbs free energy change, ΔG. The Gibbs free energy change is given by the relationship:

$$\Delta G = -T\Delta S_{\text{total}}$$

We can also write the expression without having to consider the entropy changes of the surroundings. This expression is called the *Gibbs equation*.

$$\Delta G^{\ominus} = \Delta H^{\ominus}_{\text{reaction}} - T\Delta S^{\ominus}_{\text{system}}$$

where T is the temperature in kelvin.

Gibbs free energy is a useful concept because it includes both enthalpy change and entropy change.

To make any comparison of Gibbs free energy values fair, we must use standard conditions. These standard conditions are the same as those used for ΔH and ΔS:

- pressure of 10^5 Pa

- temperature of 298 K (25 °C)

- each substance involved in the reaction is in its normal physical state (solid, liquid or gas) at 10^5 Pa and 298 K.

The *standard molar Gibbs free energy of formation* is the free energy change that accompanies the formation of one mole of a compound from its elements in their standard state.

The symbol for standard molar Gibbs free energy of formation is $\Delta G^{\ominus}_{\text{f}}$. The units are kJ mol^{-1}.

For example:

$$\text{Mg(s)} + \frac{1}{2}\text{O}_2\text{(g)} \rightarrow \text{MgO(s)} \qquad \Delta G^{\ominus}_{\text{f}} = -569.4 \text{ kJ mol}^{-1}$$

Derivation

Gibbs free energy can easily be derived from the equation relating total entropy to the entropy changes of system and surroundings.

As:

$$\Delta S^{\ominus}_{\text{total}} = \Delta S^{\ominus}_{\text{system}} + \frac{\Delta H^{\ominus}}{T}$$

Multiplying by $-T$: $-T\Delta S^{\ominus}_{\text{total}} = -T\Delta S^{\ominus}_{\text{system}} + \Delta H^{\ominus}$

The term $-T\Delta S^{\ominus}_{\text{system}} + \Delta H^{\ominus}$ is equivalent to the Gibbs free energy change of the reaction system $\Delta G^{\ominus}$.

So $-T\Delta S^{\ominus}_{\text{total}} = \Delta G^{\ominus}$ and so $\Delta G^{\ominus} = \Delta H^{\ominus} - T\Delta S^{\ominus}_{\text{system}}$

Gibbs free energy and spontaneous reactions

> **IMPORTANT**
>
> The words *spontaneous* and *feasible* both have meanings of 'likely to happen'. We use the word feasible for chemical reactions. The word spontaneous is a more general term and applies to physical processes such as diffusion and dissolving as well.

For a reaction to be feasible (spontaneous), $\Delta S^{\ominus}_{\text{total}}$ must be positive. The value of T is always positive on the absolute (kelvin) temperature scale. So applying these signs to the relationship $\Delta G^{\ominus} = -TS^{\ominus}_{\text{total}}$, the value of ΔG must be negative for a reaction to be spontaneous. So, when a feasible (spontaneous) reaction occurs at constant temperature and pressure, the value of the Gibbs free energy is negative. If the value of ΔG is positive, the reaction is not feasible.

Applying the equation $\Delta G^{\ominus} = \Delta H^{\ominus} - T\Delta S^{\ominus}_{\text{system}}$

> **IMPORTANT**
>
> In calculations involving the equation
>
> $\Delta G^{\ominus} = \Delta H^{\ominus} - T\Delta S^{\ominus}_{\text{system}}$
>
> don't forget to multiply the value of $\Delta H^{\ominus}$ by 1000 if $\Delta H^{\ominus}$ is in kJ. This is because the units of $\Delta S^{\ominus}$ are in joules per kelvin per mole.

We can calculate the Gibbs free energy change for a reaction if we know:

- the entropy change of the system in J K^{-1} mol^{-1}

- the enthalpy change of the system in J mol^{-1}; we may have to multiply the value of the enthalpy change by 1000 to convert from kJ mol^{-1}

- the temperature: under standard conditions, this is 298 K.

WORKED EXAMPLE

7 Calculate the Gibbs free energy change for the decomposition of zinc carbonate at 298 K.

$$ZnCO_3(s) \rightarrow ZnO(s) + CO_2(g)$$
$$\Delta H_r^\ominus = +71.0 \text{ kJ mol}^{-1}$$

Values for $S^\ominus$ in J K^{-1} mol^{-1}:
$CO_2(g) = +213.6$, $ZnCO_3(s) = +82.4$, $ZnO(s) = +43.6$

Solution

Step 1: Convert the value of $\Delta H^\ominus$.
$$\Delta H^\ominus = 71.0 \times 1000 = 71\ 000 \text{ J mol}^{-1}$$

Step 2: Calculate $\Delta S^\ominus_{system}$.
$$\Delta S^\ominus_{system} = \Sigma S^\ominus_{products} - \Sigma S^\ominus_{reactants}$$
$$= S^\ominus[ZnO(s)] + S^\ominus[CO_2(g)] - S^\ominus[ZnCO_3(s)]$$
$$= 43.6 + 213.6 - 82.4$$
$$\Delta S^\ominus_{system} = +174.8 \text{ J K}^{-1} \text{ mol}^{-1}$$

Step 3: Calculate $\Delta G^\ominus$.
$$\Delta G^\ominus = \Delta H^\ominus_{reaction} - T\Delta S^\ominus_{system}$$
$$= 71\ 000 - 298 \times (+174.8)$$
$$\Delta G^\ominus = +18\ 909.6 \text{ J mol}^{-1}$$
$$= +18.9 \text{ kJ mol}^{-1} \text{ (to 3 significant figures)}$$

As the value of $\Delta G^\ominus$ is positive, the reaction is not spontaneous at 298 K.

Temperature change and reaction spontaneity

For a reaction to be spontaneous, ΔG must be negative. The temperature can influence the spontaneity of a reaction. We can deduce this by considering the Gibbs free energy as a combination of two terms in the relationship:

$$\Delta G = \underbrace{\Delta H_{reaction}}_{\text{first term}} - \underbrace{T\Delta S_{system}}_{\text{second term}}$$

Questions

8 Calculate the standard Gibbs free energy of reaction in each of the following, using the standard molar entropy values given. Express your answers to 3 significant figures in kJ mol^{-1}, and in each case state whether or not the reaction is spontaneous under standard conditions.

Values for $S^\ominus$ in J K^{-1} mol^{-1}: $Ag_2CO_3(s) = 167.4$, $Ag_2O(s) = 121.3$, $CH_4(g) = 186.2$, $Cl_2(g) = 165$, $CO_2(g) = 213.6$, $H_2(g) = 130.6$, $HCl(g) = 186.8$, $H_2O(l) = 69.9$, $Mg(s) = 37.2$, $MgCl_2(s) = 89.6$, $Na(s) = 51.2$, $Na_2O_2(s) = 95.0$, $O_2(g) = 205.0$

a $H_2(g) + Cl_2(g) \rightarrow 2HCl(g)$
$$\Delta H_r^\ominus = -184.6 \text{ kJ mol}^{-1}$$

b $CH_4(g) + 2O_2(g) \rightarrow CO_2(g) + 2H_2O(l)$
$$\Delta H_r^\ominus = -890.3 \text{ kJ mol}^{-1}$$

c $2Na(s) + O_2(g) \rightarrow Na_2O_2(s)$
$$\Delta H_r^\ominus = -510.9 \text{ kJ mol}^{-1}$$

d $Mg(s) + Cl_2(g) \rightarrow MgCl_2(s)$
$$\Delta H_r^\ominus = -641.3 \text{ kJ mol}^{-1}$$

e $Ag_2CO_3(s) \rightarrow Ag_2O(s) + CO_2(g)$
$$\Delta H_r^\ominus = +167.5 \text{ kJ mol}^{-1}$$

9 Methanol reacts with hydrogen bromide.
$$CH_3OH(l) + HBr(g) \rightarrow CH_3Br(g) + H_2O(l)$$
$$\Delta H_r^\ominus = -46 \text{ kJ mol}^{-1}$$

Which one of these values is the correct value of ΔG for this reaction at 25 °C?

Standard molar entropy values (in J mol^{-1}K^{-1}) are:

$CH_3OH(l) = 239.7$, $HBr(g) = 98.6$,
$CH_3Br(g) = 246.3$, $H_2O(l) = 69.9$

A -82.4 kJ mol^{-1} C -52.6 kJ mol^{-1}
B -39.4 kJ mol^{-1} D $+43.0$ kJ mol^{-1}

Assuming that the value of $\Delta H_{reaction}$ does not change much with temperature, we can see that the value of $T\Delta S_{system}$ may influence the value of ΔG.

For an exothermic reaction, the first term ($\Delta H_{reaction}$) has a negative value.

- If the value of ΔS_{system} is positive, the second term ($-T\Delta S_{system}$) is negative and the reaction will be spontaneous because both $\Delta H_{reaction}$ and $-T\Delta S_{system}$ are negative. So ΔG is negative.

- If the value of ΔS_{system} is negative, the second term is positive to overcome the negative value of $\Delta H_{reaction}$ and make ΔG positive. So the reaction is less likely to be spontaneous at a higher temperature. This mirrors what we know about the effect of temperature on equilibrium: for an exothermic reaction, a higher temperature shifts the position of the equilibrium in favour of the reactants. The reaction is likely to be spontaneous if the temperature is low because $\Delta H_{reaction}$ is more likely to have a greater negative value than the positive value of the second term. So ΔG is negative. If the temperature is very high, the second term may be positive enough to shift the position of equilibrium in favour of the reactants.

For an endothermic reaction, the first term ($\Delta H_{reaction}$) has a positive value.

- If the value of ΔS_{system} is negative, the second term is positive. The reaction will not occur because both terms are positive, making the value of ΔG positive.

- If the value of ΔS_{system} is positive, the second term is negative. The reaction is unlikely to be spontaneous if the temperature is low because $\Delta H_{reaction}$ is more likely to have a greater positive value than the negative value of the second term. So ΔG is positive. If the temperature is very high, the second term may be negative enough to overcome the positive value of $\Delta H_{reaction}$ and make ΔG negative. So the reaction is more likely to be spontaneous at a higher temperature. This mirrors what we know about the effect of temperature on equilibrium: for an endothermic reaction, a higher temperature shifts the position of equilibrium in favour of the products.

We can see the effect of temperature on the spontaneity of the reaction if we rework Worked example 7 at a temperature of 1200 K.

Comparing Gibbs free energy values

Table 23.2 shows some values for some standard molar Gibbs free energy changes of formation.

You learned in Chapter 6 that the standard enthalpy change of an element is zero. Similarly, the standard Gibbs free energy change of formation of an element is zero. Many compounds in the solid state have high negative values of Gibbs free energy change of formation. Many gases and liquids have standard Gibbs free energy change values that are negative but many others, such as ethene, have positive values. The standard Gibbs free energy change of formation also depends on the state. For example, $\Delta G_f^{\ominus}$ [$H_2O(l)$] is -237.2 kJ mol^{-1} but $\Delta G_f^{\ominus}$ [$H_2O(g)$] is -228.6 kJ mol^{-1}.

23.6 Gibbs free energy calculations

Gibbs free energy change of reaction

> **IMPORTANT**
>
> Note that for any type of enthalpy change, e.g. enthalpy change of formation, or enthalpy change of reaction, you can get a corresponding Gibbs free energy change, e,g. $\Delta G_f^{\ominus}$ or $\Delta G_{reaction}^{\ominus}$. The Gibbs free energy change you will be using will usually be the Gibbs free energy change of formation.

WORKED EXAMPLE

8   Calculate the Gibbs free energy change for the decomposition of zinc carbonate at 1200 K.

$ZnCO_3(s) \rightarrow ZnO(s) + CO_2(g)$ $\Delta H_r^{\ominus} = +71.0$ kJ mol^{-1}

Values for $S^{\ominus}$ in J K^{-1} mol^{-1}: $CO_2(g) = +213.6$, $ZnCO_3(s) = +82.4$, $ZnO(s) = +43.6$

Solution

$\Delta H_r^{\ominus} = +71.0$ kJ mol^{-1}

$\Delta S_{system}^{\ominus} = +174.8$ J K^{-1} mol^{-1}

$\Delta G^{\ominus} = \Delta H_{reaction}^{\ominus} - T\Delta S_{system}^{\ominus}$

$= 71\,000 - 1200 \times (+174.8)$

$= 71\,000 - 209\,760$

$\Delta G^{\ominus} = -139$ kJ mol^{-1}

As the value of $\Delta G^{\ominus}$ is negative, the reaction is spontaneous at 1200 K.

The *standard Gibbs free energy change of reaction* is the Gibbs free energy change when the amounts of the reactants shown in the stoichiometric equation react under standard conditions to give products. The reactants and products must be in their standard states.

The method of calculating Gibbs free energy change of reaction uses an energy cycle similar to the enthalpy cycles you used to calculate the enthalpy change of reaction in Chapter 6 (see Figure 23.8).

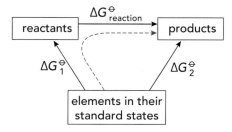

Figure 23.8: A free energy cycle for calculating the standard Gibbs free energy of reaction. The dashed line shows the indirect (two-step) route.

Using the same ideas as in Hess's law, we see that:

$$\Delta G_2^\ominus = \Delta G_1^\ominus + \Delta G_{\text{reaction}}^\ominus$$

So: $\Delta G_{\text{reaction}}^\ominus = \Delta G_2^\ominus - \Delta G_1^\ominus$

Another way of writing this is:

$$\Delta G_{\text{reaction}}^\ominus = \Sigma\Delta G_{\text{products}}^\ominus - \Sigma\Delta G_{\text{reactants}}^\ominus$$

IMPORTANT

If you are doing a calculation to find $\Delta G_{\text{reaction}}^\ominus$, you do not have to draw an energy cycle unless asked. Just use $\Sigma\Delta G_{\text{reaction}}^\ominus = \Sigma\Delta G_{\text{products}}^\ominus - \Sigma\Delta G_{\text{reactants}}^\ominus$

To calculate the Gibbs free energy change of reaction from an energy cycle like this, we use the following procedure:

- write the balanced equation at the top

- draw the cycle with the elements at the bottom

- draw in all arrows making sure that they go in the correct directions

- calculate $\Delta G_{\text{reaction}}^\ominus = \Delta G_2^\ominus - \Delta G_1^\ominus$ taking into account the number of moles of reactants and products.

Substance	$\Delta G_f^\ominus$ / kJ mol^{-1}	Substance	$\Delta G_f^\ominus$ / kJ mol^{-1}
carbon(s)	0	water(l)	−237.2
calcium(s)	0	methanol(l)	−166.4
bromine(l)	0	chlorobenzene(l)	+93.6
helium(g)	0	water(g)	−228.6
calcium oxide(s)	−604.0	ethane(g)	+68.2
calcium carbonate(s)	−1128.8	ammonia(g)	−16.5
magnesium oxide(s)	−569.4	magnesium ion, Mg^{2+}(aq)	−454.8
zinc sulfide(s)	−201.3	carbonate ion, CO_3^{2-}(aq)	−527.9

Table 23.2: Standard molar Gibbs free energy changes of some solids, liquids, gases and aqueous ions. The states are shown as state symbols after each substance.

WORKED EXAMPLE

9   Draw a Gibbs free energy cycle to calculate the standard Gibbs free energy change of decomposition of sodium hydrogen-carbonate.

$$2NaHCO_3(s) \rightarrow Na_2CO_3(s) + CO_2(g) + H_2O(l)$$

The relevant Gibbs free energy values are:

$\Delta G_f^\ominus [NaHCO_3(s)] = -851.0 \text{ kJ mol}^{-1}$

$\Delta G_f^\ominus [Na_2CO_3(s)] = -1044.5 \text{ kJ mol}^{-1}$

$\Delta G_f^\ominus [CO_2(g)] = -394.4 \text{ kJ mol}^{-1}$

$\Delta G_f^\ominus [H_2O(l)] = -237.2 \text{ kJ mol}^{-1}$

> **CONTINUED**

Solution

The Gibbs free energy cycle is shown in Figure 23.9.

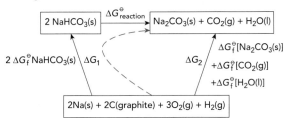

Figure 23.9: The free energy cycle for the decomposition of sodium hydrogencarbonate. The dashed line shows the two-step route.

$$\Delta G^{\ominus}_{\text{reaction}} = \Delta G^{\ominus}_2 - \Delta G^{\ominus}_1$$

$$\Delta G^{\ominus}_{\text{reaction}} = \Delta G^{\ominus}_f [\text{Na}_2\text{CO}_3(\text{s})] + \Delta G^{\ominus}_f [\text{CO}_2(\text{g})]$$
$$+ \Delta G^{\ominus}_f [\text{H}_2\text{O(l)}] - 2 \times \Delta G^{\ominus}_f [\text{NaHCO}_3(\text{s})]$$

$$= (-1044.5) + (-394.4) + (-237.2) - \{2 \times (-851.0)\}$$

$$= -1676.1 - (-1702)$$

$$= +25.9 \text{ kJ}$$

The value of $\Delta G^{\ominus}_{\text{reaction}}$ is positive. So under standard conditions, the reaction is not spontaneous. However, $\Delta G^{\ominus}_{\text{reaction}}$ does vary with temperature. At a higher temperature the reaction is spontaneous.

> **WORKED EXAMPLE**

10 Calculate the standard Gibbs free energy change of the reaction between hydrogen and oxygen.

$$2\text{H}_2(\text{g}) + \text{O}_2(\text{g}) \rightarrow 2\text{H}_2\text{O(l)}$$

(The relevant Gibbs free energy value is: $\Delta G^{\ominus}_f [\text{H}_2\text{O(l)}] = -237.2 \text{ kJ mol}^{-1}$)

Note that the values of $\Delta G^{\ominus}_f$ for both hydrogen and oxygen are zero, as they are elements in their standard states.

Solution

$$\Delta G^{\ominus}_{\text{reaction}} = \Delta G^{\ominus}_{\text{products}} - \Delta G^{\ominus}_{\text{reactants}}$$
$$\Delta G^{\ominus}_{\text{reaction}} = 2 \times \Delta G^{\ominus}_f [\text{H}_2\text{O(l)}] - $$
$$\{2 \times \Delta G^{\ominus}_f [\text{H}_2(\text{g})] + \Delta G^{\ominus}_f [\text{O}_2(\text{g})]\}$$
$$= 2 \times (-273.2) - 0 + 0$$
$$\Delta G^{\ominus}_{\text{reaction}} = -546.4 \text{ kJ}$$

The value of $\Delta G^{\ominus}_{\text{reaction}}$ is negative. So under standard conditions, the reaction is spontaneous.

Gibbs free energy and work

Gibbs free energy change can be thought of as part of the enthalpy change that is needed to do work. If we rearrange the equation $\Delta G = \Delta H - T\Delta S$ as $\Delta H = \Delta G + T\Delta S$, we can regard the $+T\Delta S$ part as being the energy unavailable to do work because it is involved with the disorder of the system (Figure 23.10). The ΔG part is free energy that is available to do work, e.g. driving the charge in electrochemical cells.

Gibbs free energy change and direction of chemical change

Gibbs free energy of formation is a measure of the stability of a compound. The more negative the value of $\Delta G^{\ominus}_f$, the greater the stability of the compound. It is unlikely to decompose. If $\Delta G^{\ominus}_f$ is positive, the compound is likely to be unstable with respect to its elements. For example:

$$\tfrac{1}{2}\text{H}_2(\text{g}) + \tfrac{1}{2}\text{I}_2(\text{s}) \rightarrow \text{HI(g)} \qquad \Delta G^{\ominus}_f[\text{HI(g)}] = +1.7 \text{ kJ mol}^{-1}$$

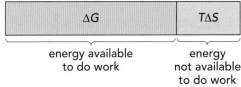

Figure 23.10: The enthalpy change of a reaction at constant temperature can be split into two parts.

The Gibbs free energy change of reaction is also a measure of the feasibility of a reaction. Reactions with negative values of $\Delta G^{\ominus}_{\text{reaction}}$ are likely to be feasible (spontaneous), whereas those with positive values are less likely to be spontaneous.

- When a system is in chemical equilibrium and the amounts of products and reactants balance, the value of $\Delta G^{\ominus}_{\text{reaction}}$ is zero ($\Delta G^{\ominus}_{\text{reaction}} = 0$).

- The products predominate if the value of $\Delta G^{\ominus}_{reaction}$ has a fairly low negative value, e.g. −10 kJ mol⁻¹.

- The reactants predominate if the value of $\Delta G^{\ominus}_{reaction}$ has a slightly positive value, e.g. +10 kJ mol⁻¹.

- The reaction can be regarded as complete if the value of $\Delta G^{\ominus}_{reaction}$ is high and negative, e.g. −60 kJ mol⁻¹.

- The reaction can be regarded as not being feasible (spontaneous) at all if the value of $\Delta G^{\ominus}_{reaction}$ is high and positive, e.g. +60 kJ mol⁻¹.

Question

10 Calculate the standard Gibbs free energy change of reaction in each of the following using the standard molar values for Gibbs free energy change given here. In each case, comment on whether the reaction is spontaneous or not, under standard conditions.

Values for $G^{\ominus}$ in kJ mol⁻¹: $C_3H_8(g) = -23.4$, $CO_2(g) = -394.4$, $Fe_2O_3(s) = -742.2$, $H_2O(l) = -273.2$, $H_2O_2(l) = -120.4$, $MgO(s) = -569.4$, $NaCl(s) = -384.2$, $NH_4NO_3(s) = -184.0$, $N_2O(g) = +104.2$

a $2H_2O_2(l) \rightarrow 2H_2O(l) + O_2(g)$

b $NH_4NO_3(s) \rightarrow N_2O(g) + 2H_2O(g)$

c $2Mg(s) + O_2(g) \rightarrow 2MgO(s)$

d $C_3H_8(g) + 5O_2(g) \rightarrow 3CO_2(g) + 4H_2O(l)$

e $3Mg(s) + Fe_2O_3(s) \rightarrow 3MgO(s) + 2Fe(s)$

Gibbs free energy change and standard electrode potential

In Chapter 20 we learned that the standard electrode potential, $E^{\ominus}_{cell}$, can be used to determine whether a reaction is feasible or not.

- If the value of $E^{\ominus}_{cell}$ is zero then the reaction is in an equilibrium where the products and reactants are balanced. The position of equilibrium is neither to the right nor to the left.

- If the value of $E^{\ominus}_{cell}$ is about +0.1 V, there are more products than reactants.

- If the value of $E^{\ominus}_{cell}$ is about −0.1 V, there are more reactants than products.

- If the value of $E^{\ominus}_{cell}$ is more positive than about +0.6 V the reaction goes to completion.

- If the value of $E^{\ominus}_{cell}$ is more negative than about −0.6 V there is no reaction or minimal reaction.

Since the values of $E^{\ominus}_{cell}$ and $\Delta G^{\ominus}$ both tell us about whether a reaction is feasible or not, there must be a relationship between them.

This relationship is:

$$\Delta G^{\ominus} = -nFE^{\ominus}_{cell}$$

where:

$\Delta G^{\ominus}$ is the standard Gibbs free energy in J mol⁻¹

n is the number of moles of electrons transferred in the cell reaction

F is the charge on a mole of electrons in C mol⁻¹ (this is the Faraday, 96 500 C mol⁻¹)

$E^{\ominus}_{cell}$ is the standard cell potential.

> **IMPORTANT**
>
> Note that when you apply the equation $\Delta G^{\ominus} = -nFE^{\ominus}_{cell}$, the units of $\Delta G^{\ominus}$ are in J mol⁻¹ (*not* kJ mol⁻¹). This is because the equation is derived from a relationship between entropy, enthalpy change and temperature and the units of entropy are J mol⁻¹.

> **WORKED EXAMPLE**
>
> **11** Calculate the standard free energy change for the reaction of magnesium with zinc ions and state whether the reaction is feasible.
>
> $Mg(s) + Zn^{2+}(aq) \rightarrow Mg^{2+}(aq) + Zn(s)$
>
> $Mg^{2+}(aq) + 2e^- \rightleftharpoons Mg(s)$ $E^{\ominus}_{cell} = -2.38$ V
>
> $Zn^{2+}(aq) + 2e^- \rightleftharpoons Zn(s)$ $E^{\ominus}_{cell} = -0.76$ V
>
> **Solution**
>
> **Step 1:** Calculate the value of $E^{\ominus}_{cell}$.
>
> $E^{\ominus}_{cell} = -0.76 + (+2.38) = +1.62$ V
>
> **Step 2:** Note the number of electrons transferred = 2
>
> **Step 3:** Substitute the values into the expression:
>
> $\Delta G^{\ominus} = -nFE^{\ominus}_{cell}$
>
> $\Delta G^{\ominus} = -2 \times 96\ 500 \times +1.62 = -313$ kJ mol⁻¹
>
> So the reaction is feasible. It will go to completion since the value of $\Delta G^{\ominus}$ is large and negative.

Question

11 Calculate the Gibbs free energy for these reactions and state, giving a reason for the position of equilibrium for the reaction.

a $Sn(s) + Pb^{2+}(aq) \rightarrow Sn^{2+}(aq) + Pb(s)$

$Sn^{2+}(aq) + 2e^- \rightleftharpoons Sn(s)$ $E^\ominus = -0.14$ V

$Pb^{2+}(aq) + 2e^- \rightleftharpoons Pb(s)$ $E^\ominus = -0.13$ V

b $Fe^{3+}(aq) + Ag(aq) \rightarrow Fe^{2+}(aq) + Ag^+(aq)$

$Fe^{3+}(aq) + e^- \rightleftharpoons Fe^{2+}(s)$ $E^\ominus = +0.77$ V

$Ag^+(aq) + e^- \rightleftharpoons Ag(s)$ $E^\ominus = +0.80$ V

c $Ce(s) + Al^{3+}(aq) \rightleftharpoons Ce^{3+}(aq) + Al(s)$

$Ce^{3+}(aq) + 3e^- \rightleftharpoons Ce(s)$ $E^\ominus = -2.33$ V

$Al^{3+}(aq) + 3e^- \rightleftharpoons Al(s)$ $E^\ominus = -1.66$ V

d   Predict the feasibility of the reactions in parts **a**, **b** and **c**, using the equation $\Delta G^\ominus = -nFE^\ominus_{cell}$

REFLECTION

1   Without looking at the coursebook, make a list of the equations relating to ΔS and ΔG that you have learned during this chapter. Compare your list to that made by another learner.

Which equations did you have most difficulty remembering? What strategies will you employ to help you remember them?

2   Discuss with another learner the three different equations that give information about the feasibility of a reaction.

What problems did you encounter while describing these methods? How did it help to have two of you discussing the problem?

SUMMARY

Entropy, S, is the number of possible arrangements of the particles and their energy in a given system.
A spontaneous change or feasible reaction involves an increase in total entropy (ΔS is positive). If a reaction is *not* feasible, there is a decrease in entropy (ΔS is negative).
The entropy increases as a substance changes state from solid to liquid to gas or dissolves to form a solution.
A knowledge of the structures and states of reactants and products helps us make generalisations about whether or not the entropy of the reactants is greater than the entropy of the products.
The entropy change in the system is given by $\Delta S_{system} = \Sigma \Delta S_{products} - \Sigma \Delta S_{reactants}$
Gibbs free energy can be calculated using the Gibbs equation $\Delta G^\ominus = \Delta H^\ominus_{reaction} - T\Delta S^\ominus_{system}$
The Gibbs free energy change of a reaction can be calculated from Gibbs free energy changes of formation using the relationship $\Delta G^\ominus_{reaction} = \Sigma \Delta G^\ominus_{products} - \Sigma \Delta G^\ominus_{reactants}$
A reaction is feasible if the sign of ΔG is negative.
The feasibility of a reaction can be predicted using the equation $\Delta G^\ominus = -nFE^\ominus_{cell}$

EXAM-STYLE QUESTIONS

1   Graphite and diamond are both forms of carbon. Their standard molar entropies are:

   $\Delta S^{\ominus}_{graphite} = 5.70\ J\ K^{-1}\ mol^{-1}, \Delta S^{\ominus}_{diamond} = 2.40\ J\ K^{-1}\ mol^{-1}$

   a i   Suggest why the standard molar entropy of graphite is greater than that of diamond.   **[2]**

   ii Calculate the entropy change of the process $C_{graphite} \rightarrow C_{diamond}$ at 298 K.   **[1]**

   iii Explain why you would be unlikely to make diamonds from graphite at atmospheric temperature and pressure.   **[1]**

   b   Graphite reacts with oxygen to form carbon dioxide. Suggest whether the entropy of the products is greater or less than the entropy of the reactants? Explain your answer.   **[2]**

   [Total: 6]

2   **a**   When ethanol undergoes combustion, carbon dioxide and water are formed.

   $C_2H_5OH(l) + 3O_2(g) \rightarrow 2CO_2(g) + 3H_2O(l)$

   Calculate the standard entropy change for this reaction.

   Values for $S^{\ominus}$ in J K^{-1} mol^{-1}: $C_2H_5OH(l) = 160.7, CO_2 = 213.6$, $H_2O(l) = 69.90, O_2(g) = 205.0$ **[6]**

   b   Calculate the Gibbs free energy for this reaction.

   Values for $\Delta G^{\ominus}_f$ in kJ mol^{-1}: $C_2H_5OH(l) = -174.9, CO_2 = -394.4$, $H_2O(l) = -237.2$ **[3]**

   c   Use your answers from parts **a** and **b** to calculate the value of the enthalpy change at 298 K.   **[3]**

   [Total: 12]

3   At 0 °C ice changes to water.

   $H_2O(s) \rightarrow H_2O(l)$ $\Delta H^{\ominus} = +6.01\ kJ\ mol^{-1}$

   a   Explain why the entropy change of the system is positive.   **[2]**

   b   Some water is heated until it boils. Compare and contrast the entropy change while the water is being heated to the entropy change when the water boils. Explain any differences.   **[4]**

   c   Water and bromine are both liquids. The standard molar entropy of water is 69.9 J K^{-1} mol^{-1}. The standard molar entropy of bromine is 174.9 J K^{-1} mol^{-1}. Suggest why these values are different even though they are both liquids.   **[4]**

   d   When 2 g of potassium chloride is dissolved in 50 cm^3 water, the entropy of the system increases. A further 2 g of potassium chloride is added. The entropy still increases but by a smaller amount. Explain this difference.   **[4]**

   [Total: 14]

4   Barium carbonate decomposes when heated.

   $BaCO_3(s) \rightarrow BaO(s) + CO_2(g)$

CONTINUED

a Use your knowledge of Hess cycles from Chapter 6 to calculate the enthalpy change of this reaction.
Express your answer to three significant figures.

$$\Delta H_f^\ominus [BaCO_3(s)] = -1216.0 \text{ kJ mol}^{-1}$$

$$\Delta H_f^\ominus [BaO(s)] = -553.5 \text{ kJ mol}^{-1}$$

$$\Delta H_f^\ominus [CO_2(g)] = -393.5 \text{ kJ mol}^{-1}$$ [2]

b Use your answer to part **a** and the data below to calculate ΔS_{system} for this reaction under standard conditions.
Express your answer to three significant figures.

$$\Delta S^\ominus [BaCO_3(s)] = +112.1 \text{ J K}^{-1} \text{ mol}^{-1}$$

$$\Delta S^\ominus [BaO(s)] = +70.40 \text{ J K}^{-1} \text{ mol}^{-1}$$

$$\Delta S^\ominus [CO_2(g)] = +213.6 \text{ J K}^{-1} \text{ mol}^{-1}$$ [5]

c Calculate the value of the Gibbs free energy for this reaction at 298 K.

$$\Delta G_f^\ominus [BaCO_3(s)] = -1137.6 \text{ J K}^{-1} \text{ mol}^{-1}$$

$$\Delta G_f^\ominus [BaO(s)] = -525.1 \text{ J K}^{-1} \text{ mol}^{-1}$$

$$\Delta G_f^\ominus [CO_2(g)] = -394.4 \text{ J K}^{-1} \text{ mol}^{-1}$$ [2]

d Suggest whether or not this reaction is feasible at 298 K.
Explain your answer. [1]

e Calculate the temperature at which this reaction has a total entropy value of zero. [4]

[Total: 14]

5 a For each of the following changes, state whether the entropy of the system decreases or increases.
In each case, explain your answer in terms of the order or disorder of the particles.

i $NaCl(s) + aq \rightarrow Na^+(aq) + Cl^-(aq)$ [5]

ii $H_2O(g) \rightarrow H_2O(l)$ [3]

b The table shows the formula, state and standard molar entropies of the first five straight-chain alkanes.

Alkane	$CH_4(g)$	$C_2H_6(g)$	$C_3H_8(g)$	$C_4H_{10}(g)$	$C_5H_{12}(l)$
$\Delta S^\ominus$ / J K^{-1} mol^{-1}	186.2	229.5	269.9	310.1	261.2

i Describe and explain the trend in the standard molar entropies of these alkanes. [4]

ii Estimate the value of the standard molar entropy of the straight-chain alkane with the formula C_6H_{14}. [1]

[Total: 13]

6 a i Define *standard free energy change of formation*. [2]

ii Write a balanced equation to represent the standard free energy change of formation of ethane. Include state symbols in your answer. [2]

CONTINUED

b The standard free energy change of formation of ethane is -32.9 kJ mol^{-1}. The standard entropy change of the system for this reaction is -173.7 J K^{-1} mol^{-1}.

  i State the relationship between standard free energy change of formation, standard entropy change of the system and the enthalpy change. [1]

  ii Explain why the reaction can be feasible, even though the value of the standard entropy change of the system is negative. [3]

c Ethane undergoes combustion to form carbon dioxide and water.

$$C_2H_6(g) + 3\tfrac{1}{2}O_2(g) \rightarrow 2CO_2(g) + 3H_2O(l)$$

Calculate the free energy change of combustion for this reaction.

Values for $\Delta G_f^{\ominus}$ in kJ mol^{-1}: $C_2H_6(g) = -32.9$, $CO_2(g) = -394.4$, $H_2O(l) = -237.2$ [3]

[Total: 11]

7 Calcium carbonate decomposes when heated to form calcium oxide and carbon dioxide.

$$CaCO_3(s) \rightarrow CaO(s) + CO_2(g)$$

a Calculate the entropy change of the system for this reaction.

Values for $S^{\ominus}$ in J K^{-1} mol^{-1}: $CaCO_3(s) = +92.9$, $CaO(s) = +39.7$, $CO_2(g) = +213.6$ [2]

b Calculate the enthalpy change for this reaction.

Values for $\Delta H_f^{\ominus}$ in kJ mol^{-1}: $CaCO_3(s) = -1206.9$, $CaO(s) = -635.1$, $CO_2(g) = -393.5$ [2]

c Use your answers to parts **a** and **b** to calculate the Gibbs free energy change of this reaction at 298 K. [5]

d Explain why the reaction is not spontaneous at 298 K even though the entropy change of the system has a positive value. [3]

[Total: 12]

8 Water is formed when hydrogen burns in oxygen.

$$2H_2(g) + O_2(g) \rightarrow 2H_2O(l) \qquad\qquad \Delta H_f^{\ominus} = -561.6 \text{ kJ mol}^{-1}$$

a Calculate the entropy change of the system for this reaction.

Values for $S^{\ominus}$ in J K^{-1} mol^{-1}: $H_2(g) = +130.6$, $O_2(g) = +205.0$, $H_2O(g) = +69.9$ [3]

b Use your answer to part **a** and the information at the start of the question to calculate a value for the Gibbs free energy change of this reaction. [5]

c Suggest whether or not this reaction is feasible at room temperature. Explain your answer. [1]

d Use your answer to part **b** to suggest a value for the standard Gibbs free energy of formation of $H_2O(l)$. Explain your answer. [2]

[Total: 11]

CONTINUED

9 Manganate(VII) ions, $MnO_4^-(aq)$, oxidise $Fe^{2+}(aq)$ ions.

$$MnO_4^-(aq) + 5Fe^{2+}(aq) + 8H^+(aq) \rightarrow 5Fe^{2+}(aq) + Mn^{2+}(aq) + 4H_2O(l)$$

a i Deduce the value of $E^{\ominus}_{cell}$ for this reaction.

$MnO_4^-(aq) + 8H^+(aq) + 5e^- \rightleftharpoons Mn^{2+}(aq) + 4H_2O(l)$ $E^{\ominus} = +1.52$ V

$Fe^{3+}(aq) + e^- \rightleftharpoons Fe^{2+}(aq)$ $E^{\ominus} = +0.77$ V **[1]**

ii Explain how you know that this reaction is feasible. **[1]**

b Nickel is added to aqueous manganese(II) ions. A learner suggested that the following reaction should take place.

$$Ni(s) + Mn^{2+}(aq) \rightarrow Ni^{2+}(aq) + Mn(s)$$

The value of $E^{\ominus}_{cell}$ for this reaction is −0.94 V.

i Calculate the Gibbs free energy for this reaction.
($F = 96\ 500$ C mol^{-1}) **[3]**

ii Use this value to deduce the feasibility of this reaction, the position of equilibrium and the relative value of K_c (high or low). **[2]**

c Cadmium reacts with copper(II) ions in aqueous solution:

$$Cd(s) + Cu^{2+}(aq) \rightarrow Cd^{2+}(aq) + Cu(s)$$

i Calculate the Gibbs free energy for this reaction.
Values for $G^{\ominus}_f$ in kJ mol^{-1}: $Cu^{2+}(aq) = +65.5$, $Cd^{2+}(aq) = -77.6$ **[2]**

ii Deduce the value of $E^{\ominus}_{cell}$ for this reaction.
($F = 96\ 500$ C mol^{-1}) **[3]**

[Total: 12]

SELF-EVALUATION

I can	See section...	Needs more work	Almost there	Ready to move on
define the term *entropy* as being the number of possible arrangements of the particles and their energy in a given system	23.1			
predict and explain the sign of the entropy changes that occur during a change in state, during a temperature change and during a reaction in which there is a change in the number of gaseous molecules	23.2			
calculate the entropy change for a reaction using standard entropy values of the reactants and products	23.2, 23.3			
perform calculations using the Gibbs equation $\Delta G^{\ominus} = \Delta H^{\ominus} - T\Delta S^{\ominus}$	23.5, 23.6			
determine if a reaction is feasible by referring to the sign of $\Delta G^{\ominus}$	23.5			
predict the effect of temperature change on the feasibility of a reaction when given standard enthalpy and entropy changes	23.5			
predict the feasibility of a reaction using the equation $\Delta G^{\ominus} = -nFE^{\ominus}_{cell}$	23.6			

Chapter 24

Transition elements

LEARNING INTENTIONS

In this chapter you will learn how to:

- explain what is meant by a *transition element*

- describe how transition elements have variable oxidation states, behave as catalysts, form complex ions and form coloured ions

- state the electronic configuration of a first-row transition element and of its ions

- describe the tendency of transition elements to have variable oxidation states

- describe and explain the use of $MnO_4^- / C_2O_4^{2-}$, MnO_4^- / Fe^{2+} and Cu^{2+} / I^- as examples of redox systems (see also Chapter 20)

- predict, using $E^\ominus$ values, the feasibility of redox reactions involving transition metal compounds

- define the terms *ligand* and *complex*

- describe and explain the reactions of transition elements with ligands to form complexes, and describe the shapes and bond angles of complexes

CONTINUED

- describe the types of stereoisomerism (*cis/trans* and optical isomerism) shown by complexes, including those with bidentate ligands

- explain qualitatively how ligand exchange may occur

- describe the term stability constant, K_{stab}, of a complex ion, and write an expression for the stability constant of a complex

- explain ligand exchange in terms of stability constants

- sketch the general shape of atomic d orbitals

- describe the splitting of degenerate d orbitals into two energy levels in octahedral and tetrahedral complexes

- explain the origin of colour in transition element complexes

- describe, in qualitative terms, the effects of different ligands on the absorption of light, and hence the colour of a complex.

BEFORE YOU START

Working in your group, answer these questions:

1   Write down the electronic configuration of:

    a   a titanium (Ti) atom

    b   a Ti^{2+} ion.

2   The oxidation number of manganese can vary. What is its oxidation number in the following compounds?

    a MnO_2

    b MnO_4^-

3   Draw a dot-and-cross diagram to show the bonding in an ammonium ion, NH_4^+. Only include the outer shell electrons.

4   Using the standard electrode potentials in Appendix 2, explain why magnesium (Mg) can displace silver ions (Ag^+) from a solution of silver nitrate.

5   Work with a partner to write a general set of rules to derive the expression for the equilibrium constant, K_c, for a reaction such as:

    $mA(aq) + nB(aq) \rightleftharpoons pC(aq) + qD(aq)$

FIGHTING CANCER

Most cancers are associated with abnormal DNA replication. During DNA replication, the double helix 'unwinds' to form the template for a new strand. When the process goes wrong, this can produce mutations or can accelerate out of control. This results in cancerous tumours that can grow rapidly and interfere with normal cells. Finding ways to fight cancers remains one of the main areas of medical research today.

Cis-platin is an anti-cancer drug, first used in chemotherapy in the 1970s. The drug is a compound of platinum, a transition element. Molecules of cis-platin are made up of platinum(II) ions, with dative bonds to two chloride ions and two ammonia molecules. The bonds are arranged around the central Pt^{2+} ion in a flat, square planar shape. Its structure is shown in Figure 24.1.

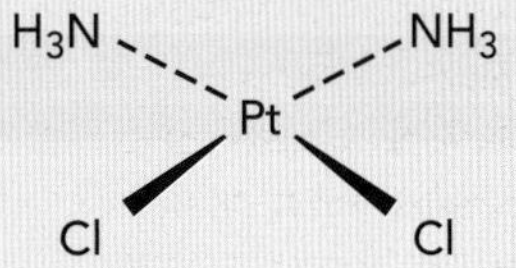

Figure 24.1: The square planar shape of cis-platin.

The cis-platin can be taken by patients in solution and can pass through cell membranes and into the nucleus of the cell. There it can form a new platinum complex that can form a bridge within a DNA strand. This 'bridging' can also take place to a lesser extent between the two strands in DNA.

With the platinum complex inserted into the strands, replication is disrupted, so the cell dies. If fast-growing tumour cells are treated with cis-platin, the tumour shrinks and the cancer goes into remission. This means that the signs and symptoms of the cancer disappear.

However, cis-platin can also interfere with DNA replication in normal healthy cells. Therefore, how effective it is in fighting cancer depends on the balance between the death of healthy cells and the death of cancerous cells. The cis-platin particularly affects fast-growing cells. So, the production of white blood cells in bone marrow can be disrupted. This can leave patients open to infectious diseases that would be no problem for a healthy person.

Cis-platin can also cause hair loss, kidney damage, and a range of other side-effects, such as hearing loss. Yet, despite the discovery of many more complex, modern drugs, cis-platin is still used to treat a variety of cancers. It is often used as part of a combined programme of drugs.

Questions for discussion

Carry out some research to find out more details of how cis-platin makes the 'bridges' in DNA to disrupt replication.

Working with another learner or group of learners:

* Discuss the use of drugs to treat life-threatening diseases, despite the side-effects that the drugs themselves can cause.

24.1 What is a transition element?

The transition elements are found in the d block of the Periodic Table, between Groups 2 and 13. However, not all d-block elements are classified as transition elements.

> **IMPORTANT**
>
> A transition element is a d-block element that forms one or more stable ions with an incomplete d sub-shell.

We do *not* define scandium (Sc) and zinc (Zn) as transition elements.

- Scandium, with the electronic configuration [Ar] $3d^1 4s^2$, forms only one ion, Sc^{3+}. This 3+ ion has no electrons in its 3d sub-shell: the electronic configuration of Sc^{3+} is just its argon core, [Ar].

- Zinc, with the electronic configuration [Ar] $3d^{10} 4s^2$, forms only one ion, Zn^{2+}. This 2+ ion has a complete 3d sub-shell: the electronic configuration of Zn^{2+} is [Ar] $3d^{10}$.

So neither scandium nor zinc forms an ion with an incomplete d sub-shell.

In this chapter we will be looking at the transition elements in the first row of the d block. These are the metals titanium (Ti) through to copper (Cu), according to the definition above.

Electronic configurations

Atoms of transition elements

Table 24.1 shows the electronic configurations of the atoms in the first row of the transition elements. In atoms of the transition elements, the 4s sub-shell is normally filled and the rest of the electrons occupy orbitals in the 3d sub-shell. However, chromium and copper atoms are the exceptions.

Chromium atoms have just one electron in the 4s sub-shell. The remaining five electrons are arranged in the 3d sub-shell so that each of its five orbitals is occupied by one electron.

Copper atoms also have just one electron in the 4s sub-shell. The remaining ten electrons are arranged in the 3d sub-shell so that each orbital is filled by two electrons.

Element	Electronic configuration
titanium (Ti)	$1s^2\ 2s^2\ 2p^6\ 3s^2\ 3p^6\ 3d^2\ 4s^2$
vanadium (V)	$1s^2\ 2s^2\ 2p^6\ 3s^2\ 3p^6\ 3d^3\ 4s^2$
chromium (Cr)	$1s^2\ 2s^2\ 2p^6\ 3s^2\ 3p^6\ 3d^5\ 4s^1$
manganese (Mn)	$1s^2\ 2s^2\ 2p^6\ 3s^2\ 3p^6\ 3d^5\ 4s^2$
iron (Fe)	$1s^2\ 2s^2\ 2p^6\ 3s^2\ 3p^6\ 3d^6\ 4s^2$
cobalt (Co)	$1s^2\ 2s^2\ 2p^6\ 3s^2\ 3p^6\ 3d^7\ 4s^2$
nickel (Ni)	$1s^2\ 2s^2\ 2p^6\ 3s^2\ 3p^6\ 3d^8\ 4s^2$
copper (Cu)	$1s^2\ 2s^2\ 2p^6\ 3s^2\ 3p^6\ 3d^{10}\ 4s^1$

Table 24.1: Electronic configurations of the first row of transition elements.

Ions of transition elements

The transition elements are all metals. In common with all metals, their atoms tend to lose electrons so they form positively charged ions. However, each transition metal can form more than one positive ion. For example, the common ions of copper are Cu^+ and Cu^{2+}. We say that the transition metals have *variable oxidation states*. The resulting ions are often different colours.

Look at the ions of vanadium in their different oxidation states (Figure 24.2).

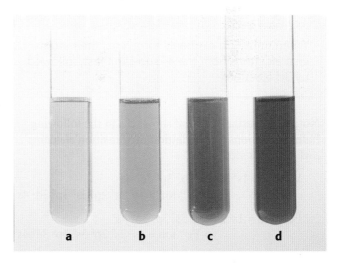

Figure 24.2: Vanadium and its oxidation states: **a** a solution containing VO_2^+ ions, **b** a solution containing VO^{2+} ions, **c** a solution containing V^{3+} ions, **d** a solution containing V^{2+} ions.

Table 24.2 shows the most common oxidation states of the first row of the transition elements.

Element	Most common oxidation states
titanium (Ti)	+3, +4
vanadium (V)	+2, +3, +4, +5
chromium (Cr)	+3, +6
manganese (Mn)	+2, +4, +6, +7
iron (Fe)	+2, +3
cobalt (Co)	+2, +3
nickel (Ni)	+2
copper (Cu)	+1, +2

Table 24.2: Common oxidation states of the transition elements.

It is the similarity in the energy of the 3d and 4s atomic orbitals that make these variable oxidation numbers possible. Because there are variable oxidation states, the names of compounds containing transition elements must have their oxidation number included, e.g. manganese(IV) oxide, MnO_2, and cobalt(II) chloride, $CoCl_2$.

IMPORTANT

When transition elements form ions, their atoms lose electrons from the 4s sub-shell first, followed by 3d electrons.

Notice the partially filled d sub-shells in the following examples of ions (see definition of transition element earlier in this section):

V atom = $1s^2 \, 2s^2 \, 2p^6 \, 3s^2 \, 3p^6 \, 3d^3 \, 4s^2$
$\rightarrow V^{3+}$ ion = $1s^2 \, 2s^2 \, 2p^6 \, 3s^2 \, 3p^6 \, 3d^2 \, 4s^0$

Fe atom = $1s^2 \, 2s^2 \, 2p^6 \, 3s^2 \, 3p^6 \, 3d^6 \, 4s^2$
$\rightarrow Fe^{3+}$ ion = $1s^2 \, 2s^2 \, 2p^6 \, 3s^2 \, 3p^6 \, 3d^5 \, 4s^0$

Cu atom = $1s^2 \, 2s^2 \, 2p^6 \, 3s^2 \, 3p^6 \, 3d^{10} \, 4s^1$
$\rightarrow Cu^{2+}$ ion = $1s^2 \, 2s^2 \, 2p^6 \, 3s^2 \, 3p^6 \, 3d^9 \, 4s^0$

The most common oxidation state is +2, usually formed when the atom of a transition element loses its two 4s electrons.

The maximum oxidation number of the transition elements at the start of the row involves all the 4s and 3d electrons in the atoms. For example, vanadium's maximum oxidation state is +5, involving its two 4s electrons and its three 3d electrons.

At the end of the row, from iron onwards, the +2 oxidation state becomes most common as 3d electrons become increasingly harder to remove as the nuclear charge increases across the period.

The higher oxidation states of the transition elements are found in complex ions or in compounds formed with oxygen or fluorine. Common examples are the chromate(VI) ion, CrO_4^{2-}, and the manganate(VII) ion, MnO_4^-.

Question

1 a State the electronic configurations of each of the following atoms and ions:

   i Ti

   ii Cr

   iii Co

   iv Fe^{3+}

   v Ni^{2+}

   vi Cu^+

   b Explain why scandium (which forms only one ion, Sc^{3+}) and zinc (which forms only one ion, Zn^{2+}) are *not* called transition elements.

   c Explain why the maximum oxidation state of manganese is +7.

   d Look back at the different oxidation states of vanadium shown in Figure 24.2. State the oxidation state of the vanadium in each test-tube **a–d**.

   e Zirconium (Zr) is in the second row of transition elements beneath titanium in the Periodic Table. Its electronic configuration is [Kr] $4d^2 \, 5s^2$, where [Kr] represents the electronic configuration of krypton, the noble gas with atomic number 36.

      i Predict the maximum stable oxidation state of zirconium and explain your answer.

      ii Give the formula of the oxide of zirconium, assuming zirconium exhibits the oxidation state given in part **e i**.

Swap your answers to Question 1 with another learner and find any differences. Discuss the differences and explain your reasoning to each other before agreeing on a final answer. Now mark your answers together against the correct ones provided.

24.2 Physical and chemical properties of the transition elements

The transition elements commonly have physical properties that are typical of most metals:

- they have high melting points
- they have high densities
- they are hard and rigid, and so are useful as construction materials
- they are good conductors of electricity and heat
- they have variable oxidation states
- they behave as catalysts
- they form complex ions (see Section 24.1)
- they form coloured ions (see Section 24.1).

Redox reactions

We have seen how the transition elements can exist in various oxidation states. When a compound of a transition element is treated with a suitable reagent, the oxidation state of the transition element can change in the reaction.

Whenever a reaction involves reactants that change their oxidation states, the reaction is a redox reaction. Redox reactions involve the transfer of electrons. Remember that a species (atom, molecule or ion) is reduced when its oxidation state is reduced. The oxidation state changes to a lower value. An oxidation state is lowered when a species gains electrons, and, when it is being reduced, it acts as an oxidising agent.

Example 1

In the half-equation:

$$Fe^{3+}(aq) + e^- \rightarrow Fe^{2+}(aq)$$

pale yellow   pale green

Fe^{3+} has been reduced to Fe^{2+} by gaining one electron. In the equation above, Fe^{3+} is acting as an oxidising agent, an electron acceptor.

For this reaction to happen, another half-equation is needed in which the reactant loses one or more electrons. The full reaction needs a reducing agent, an electron donor.

In Chapter 20 we saw how we can use standard electrode potential values, $E^\ominus$, to predict whether or not such reactions could possibly take place.

Another half-equation we could consider combining with the reduction of Fe^{3+} half-equation is:

$$MnO_4^-(aq) + 8H^+(aq) + 5e^- \rightarrow Mn^{2+}(aq) + 4H_2O(l)$$

purple   pale pink

Here the MnO_4^- ion is also acting as an oxidising agent, an electron acceptor.

Both half-equations are written below as they appear in tables of data showing standard electrode potentials:

$$Fe^{3+}(aq) + e^- \rightarrow Fe^{2+}(aq) \qquad E^\ominus = +0.77 \text{ V}$$

$$MnO_4^-(aq) + 8H^+(aq) + 5e^-$$
$$\rightarrow Mn^{2+}(aq) + 4H_2O(l) \qquad E^\ominus = +1.52 \text{ V}$$

So the question is: Can Fe^{3+} ions oxidise Mn^{2+} to MnO_4^- ions, or can MnO_4^- ions in acid solution oxidise Fe^{2+} ions to Fe^{3+} ions? In other words, which is the more powerful oxidising agent, Fe^{3+} ions or MnO_4^- ions?

The magnitude of the positive values provides a measure of the tendency of the half-equations to proceed to the right-hand side. The values show us that $MnO_4^-(aq)$ is more likely to accept electrons and proceed in the forward direction, changing to $Mn^{2+}(aq)$, than $Fe^{3+}(aq)$ is to accept electrons and change to $Fe^{2+}(aq)$. $MnO_4^-(aq)$ is a more powerful oxidising agent than $Fe^{3+}(aq)$. Therefore, $MnO_4^-(aq)$ ions are capable of oxidising $Fe^{2+}(aq)$ ions to form $Fe^{3+}(aq)$. So the top half-equation proceeds in the reverse direction.

We can now combine the two half-cells to get the overall reaction. Note that the sign of the Fe^{3+}/Fe^{2+} half-cell has changed by reversing its direction. The Fe^{2+}/Fe^{3+} equation also has to be multiplied by 5 so that the electrons on either side of the equation cancel out when we add the half-equations together. This does not affect the value of $E^\ominus$.

Combining the two half-equations:

$$5Fe^{2+}(aq) \rightarrow 5Fe^{3+}(aq) + 5e^- \qquad E^\ominus = -0.77 \text{ V}$$

$$+ MnO_4^-(aq) + 8H^+(aq) + 5e^-$$
$$\rightarrow Mn^{2+}(aq) + 4H_2O(l) \qquad E^\ominus = +1.52 \text{ V}$$

$$\overline{MnO_4^-(aq) + 5Fe^{2+}(aq) + 8H^+(aq)}$$
$$\rightarrow Mn^{2+}(aq) + 5Fe^{3+}(aq) + 4H_2O(l) \qquad E^\ominus = +0.75 \text{ V}$$

The relatively large positive value of $E^\ominus$ (+0.75 V) tells us that the reaction is likely to proceed in the forward direction as written.

PRACTICAL ACTIVITY 24.1

Redox titration

We can use the reaction above to calculate the amount of iron (Fe²⁺ ions) in a sample, such as an iron tablet, by carrying out a titration.

- A known volume (e.g. 25 cm³) of an unknown concentration of $Fe^{2+}(aq)$ is placed in a conical flask.

- A solution of a known concentration of potassium manganate(VII) is put in a burette.

- The potassium manganate(VII) solution is titrated against the solution containing $Fe^{2+}(aq)$ in the conical flask.

- During the reaction of $MnO_4^-(aq)$ with $Fe^{2+}(aq)$ in the flask, the purple colour of the manganate(VII) ions is removed. The end-point is reached when the $Fe^{2+}(aq)$ ions have all reacted and the first permanent purple colour appears in the conical flask. This is when the $MnO_4^-(aq)$ ions become *in excess* in the reaction mixture (Figure 24.3).

Figure 24.3: Manganate(VII) ions can be used to determine the percentage of Fe^{2+} in an iron tablet.

You can achieve a more accurate result for the mass of Fe^{2+} in a solution by using dichromate(VI) ions, $Cr_2O_7^{2-}(aq)$, to oxidise it in a titration. This is because compounds such as potassium dichromate(VI) can be prepared to a higher degree of purity than potassium manganate(VII). In a titration with $Fe^{2+}(aq)$ and dichromate(VI), we need an indicator of the end-point that will be oxidised as soon as the $Fe^{2+}(aq)$ has all reacted.

The half-equation and value for $E^{\ominus}$ for the use of dichromate as an oxidising agent is:

$$Cr_2O_7^{2-}(aq) + 14H^+(aq) + 6e^-$$
$$\rightarrow 2Cr^{3+}(aq) + 7H_2O(l) \quad E^{\ominus} = +1.33 \text{ V}$$

WORKED EXAMPLE

1 0.420 g of iron ore were dissolved in acid, so that all of the iron present in the original ore was then present as $Fe^{2+}(aq)$. The solution obtained was titrated against 0.0400 mol dm⁻³ $KMnO_4(aq)$. The titre was 23.50 cm³.

a Calculate the number of moles of MnO_4^- in the titre.

Solution to part a

Use the equation:

$n = V \times c$

where n = number of moles, V = volume of solution in dm³ and c = concentration.

$n = \dfrac{23.50}{1000} \times 0.0400$

$= 0.000\,940$ mol

CONTINUED

b Calculate the number of moles of Fe^{2+} in the solution.

Solution to part b

The equation for the reaction in the titration is:

$$5Fe^{2+} + MnO_4^- + 8H^+ \rightarrow 5Fe^{3+} + Mn^{2+} + 4H_2O(l)$$

number of moles of $Fe^{2+} = 5 \times 0.000\,940$
$$= 0.004\,70 \text{ mol}$$

c Calculate the mass of iron in the solution (A_r of iron is 55.8).

Solution to part c

moles of Fe = moles of $Fe^{2+} = 0.004\,70$ mol

mass of Fe $= n \times A_r$
$$= 0.004\,70 \times 55.8$$
$$= 0.262 \text{ g}$$

d Calculate the percentage mass of iron in the 0.420 g of iron ore.

Solution to part d

percentage mass of iron $= \dfrac{0.262}{0.420} \times 100\%$
$$= 62.4\%$$

Example 2

Another example of a redox titration is the reaction of manganate(VII) ions with ethanedioate ions, $C_2O_4^{2-}$. The ethanedioate ion is derived from ethanedioic acid, formerly known as oxalic acid. The ethanedioate ions can be oxidised by potassium manganate(VII) in an acidic solution. A similar titration to the one above can be carried out to find the unknown concentration of ethanedioate ions (toxic) in a solution or to standardise potassium manganate(VII) solution (when the sodium ethanedioate solution needs to be warmed before titrating).

The half-equation for the oxidation of ethanedioate ions is:

$$C_2O_4^{2-}(aq) \rightarrow 2CO_2(g) + 2e^-$$
$$+3 \qquad\qquad +4$$

As we have just seen, the reduction of manganate(VII) ions to manganese(II) is:

$$MnO_4^-(aq) + 8H^+(aq) + 5e^- \rightarrow Mn^{2+}(aq) + 4H_2O(l)$$
$$+7 \qquad\qquad\qquad\qquad +2$$

Combining the two half-equations to get the full redox equation we need to multiply the ethanedioate ions half-equation by 5, and multiply the manganate(VII) half-equation by 2. This will ensure that the 10 electrons cancel out on either side of the full equation:

Combining the two half-equations we get the full redox equation:

$$5C_2O_4^{2-}(aq) \rightarrow 10CO_2(g) + 10e^-$$
$$+ 2MnO_4^-(aq) + 16H^+(aq) + 10e^-$$
$$\rightarrow 2Mn^{2+}(aq) + 8H_2O(l)$$
$$\overline{2MnO_4^-(aq) + 5C_2O_4^{2-}(aq) + 16H^+(aq)}$$
$$\rightarrow 2Mn^{2+}(aq) + 10CO_2(g) + 8H_2O(l)$$

Note from the redox equation that, in a titration calculation, the manganate(VII) ion reacts with the ethanedioate ion in the ratio 2 : 5.

This reaction is an example of autocatalysis, as the $Mn^{2+}(aq)$ ions formed act as a catalyst for reaction. The transition elements and their ions can act as catalysts because they can vary their oxidation state in the course of a reaction, accepting or losing electrons, and then reverting back to their original state. They can also accept pairs of electrons into vacant d orbitals forming dative bonds with ligands.

Example 3

In this final redox example, we can consider the reaction of copper(II) ions with iodide ions in aqueous solution. We can add the two half-equations together if we multiply the Cu^{2+} / Cu^+ half-equation by 2 in order to cancel out the electrons:

$$2Cu^{2+} + 2e^- \rightarrow 2Cu^+$$
$$+ 2I^- \rightarrow I_2 + 2e^-$$
$$\overline{2Cu^{2+} + 2I^- \rightarrow 2Cu^+ + I_2}$$

If we add *excess* iodide ions to a solution of $Cu^{2+}(aq)$ ions, we get iodine forming in solution and a precipitate of copper(I) iodide:

$$2Cu^{2+}(aq) + 4I^-(aq) \rightarrow 2CuI(s) + I_2(aq) \qquad \text{equation 1}$$

We can use this reaction to find the concentration of copper(II) ions in a solution. The formation of iodine in the reaction mixture means that we can use starch indicator to judge an accurate end-point in a titration experiment.

With excess iodide ions added to the copper(II) solution, we can add sodium thiosulfate solution of a known concentration from a burette to the reaction mixture in a flask. The aqueous iodine, $I_2(aq)$, formed in the reaction mixture reacts with the thiosulfate ions added:

$$I_2(aq) + 2S_2O_3^{2-}(aq) \rightarrow 2I^-(aq) + S_4O_6^{2-}(aq) \qquad \text{equation 2}$$

The brownish colour of the solution gets lighter as the iodine is used up. Now we can add the starch solution, which turns blue / black with the remaining $I_2(aq)$ in the flask, to help us get a sharp end-point. Then titrate slowly until the blue / black colour disappears when all the iodine has reacted, noting the reading on the burette.

So, knowing the number of moles of thiosulfate ions added in the titration, from equation 2 we can deduce that half that number of moles of $I_2(aq)$ must have been formed in equation 1. So, the number of moles of $Cu^{2+}(aq)$ that we started with in equation 1 must be twice that of the $I_2(aq)$, i.e. the same number of moles as the thiosulfate ions added in the titration. From this we can calculate the concentration of the $Cu^{2+}(aq)$ ions in the initial copper(II) solution (i.e. the number of moles in 1 dm³ or 1000 cm³).

WORKED EXAMPLE

2 A 25.00 cm³ of copper(II) sulfate solution of unknown concentration reacted with excess potassium iodide solution. The reaction mixture was then titrated against 0.0850 mol dm⁻³ sodium thiosulfate solution, using a starch indicator. The titre was 15.40 cm³ when the blue / black colour disappeared.

Calculate the concentration of the copper(II) sulfate solution.

Solution

First, calculate the number of moles of thiosulfate ions, $S_2O_3^{2-}(aq)$, in the titre.

Use the equation:

$$n = V \times c$$

where n = number of moles, V = volume of solution in dm³ and c = concentration.

$$n = \frac{15.40}{1000} \times 0.0850 \text{ mol of thiosulfate ions}$$

Working backwards from the two equations (as explained above this worked example):

$$2Cu^{2+}(aq) + 4I^-(aq) \rightarrow 2CuI(s) + I_2(aq)$$

$$I_2(aq) + 2S_2O_3^{2-}(aq) \rightarrow 2I^-(aq) + S_4O_6^{2-}(aq)$$

we can deduce that the number of moles of copper(II) ions in the original solution is the same as the number of moles of thiosulfate ions in the titre

$$\text{i.e. } \frac{15.40}{1000} \times 0.0850 \text{ mol}$$

Therefore, we can calculate the concentration (c) of the 25.00 cm³ of copper(II) sulfate solution by re-arranging the equation $n = V \times c$ to

$$c = \frac{n}{V}$$

$$= \frac{15.40}{1000} \times 0.0850 \text{ divided by } \frac{25.00}{1000}$$

$$= 0.0524 \text{ mol dm}^{-3} \text{ (to 3 significant figures)}$$

Question

2 a Write two half-equations for the reactions that take place when $Fe^{2+}(aq)$ is oxidised by dichromate(VI) ions.

b Combine the two half-equations and write the equation for the oxidation of $Fe^{2+}(aq)$ by dichromate(VI) ions.

c Work out the $E^{\ominus}$ value of the cell made when the two half-cells in part **a** are connected and the reaction in part **b** takes place. Discuss and explain what this value predicts about the likelihood of $Fe^{2+}(aq)$ being oxidised by dichromate(VI) ions.

d How many moles of $Fe^{2+}(aq)$ can 1 mole of dichromate(VI) oxidise?

e In a titration, 25.0 cm³ of a solution containing $Fe^{2+}(aq)$ ions was completely oxidised by 15.30 cm³ of 0.001 00 mol dm⁻³ potassium dichromate(VI) solution.

   i Calculate the number of moles of potassium dichromate(VI) in 15.30 cm³ of 0.001 00 mol dm⁻³ solution?

   ii Calculate how many moles of Fe^{2+} were present in the 25.0 cm³ of solution.

   iii Calculate the concentration of the $Fe^{2+}(aq)$ in the flask at the start of the titration.

24.3 Ligands and complex formation

In the section above on redox reactions, we learned about the oxidation of Fe^{2+}(aq) ions. When these ions are in solution the Fe^{2+} ion is surrounded by six water molecules. Each water molecule bonds to the central Fe^{2+} ion by forming a dative (co-ordinate) bond from the oxygen atom into vacant orbitals on the Fe^{2+} ion (Figure 24.4). The water molecules are called **ligands** and the resulting ion is called a **complex ion**. Its formula is written as $[Fe(H_2O)_6]^{2+}$. The shape of a complex with six ligands is octahedral.

All ligands can donate an electron pair to a central transition metal ion. The **co-ordination number** of a

complex is the number of co-ordinate (dative) bonds to the central metal ion.

Some ligands can form two co-ordinate (dative) bonds from each ion or molecule to the transition metal ion. These are called **bidentate ligands**, as shown in Figure 24.6. Most ligands, such as water and ammonia, form just one co-ordinate (dative) bond and are called **monodentate ligands**.

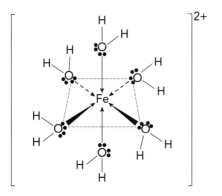

Figure 24.4: $[Fe(H_2O)_6]^{2+}$; the complex ion formed between an Fe^{2+} ion and six water molecules. It is called a hexaaquairon(II) ion.

KEY WORDS

ligand: a molecule or ion with one or more lone pairs of electrons which form dative covalent bonds to a central transition element atom or ion.

complex ion: a central transition metal ion surrounded by ligands, bonded to the central ion by dative (also called co-ordinate) covalent bonds.

co-ordination number: the number of co-ordinate bonds formed by ligands with a transition element ion in a complex.

bidentate ligand: a ligand that forms two co-ordinate (or dative) bonds to the central transition metal ion in a complex.

monodentate ligand: a ligand forming one co-ordinate bond with a transition element ion in a complex.

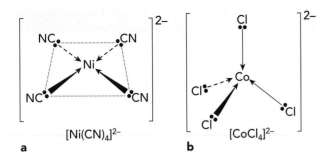

a $[Ni(CN)_4]^{2-}$

b $[CoCl_4]^{2-}$

Figure 24.5: The complex ion formed between a transition metal ion and a larger ligand can only fit four, not six, ligands around the central ion. These are arranged in either a square planar shape (as in **a** $[Ni(CN)_4]^{2-}$) or a tetrahedral shape (as in **b** $[CoCl_4]^{2-}$).

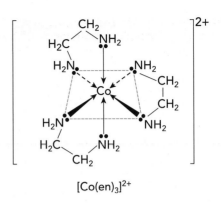

$[Co(en)_3]^{2+}$

Figure 24.6: $[Co(en)_3]^{2+}$ is an example of a complex ion containing the bidentate ligand $NH_2CH_2CH_2NH_2$ (abbreviated to 'en'). Another common bidentate ligand is the ethanedioate ion, $C_2O_4^{2-}$ (abbreviated to 'ox') e.g. in $[Fe(ox)_3]^3$.

Name of ligand	Formula	Example of complex	Co-ordination number	Shape of complex
water	H_2O	$[Fe(H_2O)_6]^{2+}$	6	octahedral (see Figure 24.4)
ammonia	NH_3	$[Co(NH_3)_6]^{3+}$	6	octahedral
chloride ion	Cl^-	$[CoCl_4]^{2-}$	4	tetrahedral (see Figure 24.5b)
cyanide ion	CN^-	$[Ni(CN)_4]^{2-}$	4	square planar (see Figure 24.5a)
hydroxide ion	OH^-	$[Cr(OH)_6]^{3-}$	6	octahedral
thiocyanate ion	SCN^-	$[FeSCN]^{2+}$ or $[Fe(SCN)(H_2O)_5]^{2+}$	6	octahedral
ethanedioate ion (abbreviated to 'ox' – oxalate – in the formulae of complexes)	$^-OOC—COO^-$	$[Mn(ox)_3]^{3-}$	6	octahedral
1,2-diaminoethane (abbreviated to 'en' in the formulae of complexes)	$NH_2CH_2CH_2NH_2$	$[Co(en)_3]^{3+}$	6	octahedral (see Figure 24.6)

Table 24.3: Some common ligands and their complexes.

A few transition metal ions (e.g. copper(I), silver(I), gold(I)) form linear complexes with ligands. The co-ordination number in these complexes is 2 (Figure 24.7).

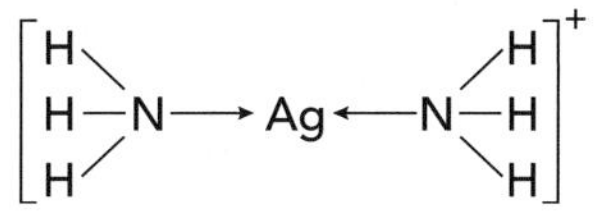

$$\begin{bmatrix} H \\ H-N \rightarrow Ag \leftarrow N-H \\ H \end{bmatrix}^+ \begin{matrix} H \\ \\ H \end{matrix}$$

Figure 24.7: The diamminesilver(I) cation has a linear structure.

Table 24.3 shows some common ligands. Note that the charge on a complex is simply the sum of the charges on the central metal ion and on each ligand in the complex. Some complexes will carry no charge, e.g. $Cu(OH)_2(H_2O)_4$.

$EDTA^{4-}$ ions can act as ligands. A single $EDTA^{4-}$ ion can form six co-ordinate bonds to a central transition metal ion to form an octahedral complex. It is an example of a *polydentate* ligand called a *hexadentate* ligand.

Question

3 a State the oxidation number of the transition metal in each of the following complexes:

   i $[Co(NH_3)_6]^{3+}$

   ii $[Ni(CN)_4]^{2-}$

   iii $[Cr(OH)_6]^{3-}$

   iv $[Co(en)_3]^{3+}$

   v $Cu(OH)_2(H_2O)_4$

b Give the formula of a complex formed between Ni^{2+} and $EDTA^{4-}$.

c Which ligands in Table 24.3 are bidentate?

Stereoisomerism in transition metal complexes

In Chapter 14 we learned about two types of stereoisomerism: *geometric* and *optical* isomerism.

> **KEY WORD**
>
> **geometric isomers:** molecules or ions with the same molecular formula and same bonds between their atoms but which cannot be superimposed on each other, due to some lack of rotation around their bonds; these are also known as *cis/trans* isomers.

The presence of a double bond in 1,2-dibromoethene means that two **geometrical isomers** (*cis/trans* isomers) are possible. Geometric isomerism is also possible in transition metal complexes, where no double bond exists. In this case, the term 'geometric isomerism' refers to complexes with the same molecular formula but different geometrical arrangements of their atoms. Examples are any square planar complexes with the general formula $[M(A)_2(B)_2]$, where M is the transition element, and A and B are its surrounding ligands. *Cis-* and *trans*-platin are geometric isomers (Figure 24.8). In *cis*-platin, the chlorine atoms are next to each other in the square complex but in *trans*-platin, they are diagonally opposite.

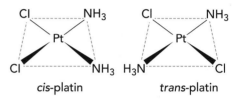

Figure 24.8: The geometrical isomers, *cis*-platin and *trans*-platin.

Cis-platin has been used as an anti-cancer drug. It acts by binding to sections of the DNA in cancer cells, preventing cell division (see the 'Fighting cancer' section at the start of Chapter 24). *Trans*-platin does not have the same beneficial medical effects.

The properties of geometrical isomers can be different. Differences in electronegativity of the atoms in ligands forming the dative bonds to the central transition metal ion can result in *polar and non-polar complexes*. For example, the *cis*-isomer will have two identical groups on one side of any square planar complex. So any difference in electronegativity between the two pairs of isomers will cause an imbalance of charge, making a *polar* complex. The atoms with the higher electronegativity have a stronger pull on the electrons in the dative bonds and will carry a partial negative charge. However, the trans-isomer will have identical ligands directly opposite each other at the corners of the square planar complex. So the pull on the electrons in the dative bonds to the central metal ion are perfectly balanced. This means that the charge is balanced and results in a *non-polar* complex.

Octahedral complexes, with the general formula $[M(A)_4(B)_2]$, can also display geometric isomerism. An example is the cobalt(II) complex ion, $[Co(NH_3)_4(H_2O)_2]^{2+}$ (see Figure 24.9).

Again, the *cis*-isomer is a slightly polar complex, whereas the *trans*-isomer is non-polar. The imbalance

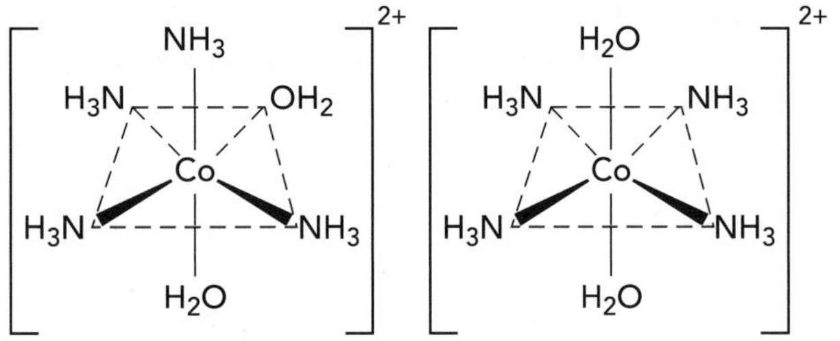

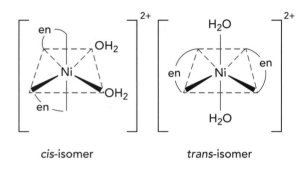

Figure 24.9: The *cis-* and *trans-* isomers of $[Co(NH_3)_4(H_2O)_2]^{2+}$

of charge in *cis*-isomer results from the asymmetric shape of the *cis*-$[Co(NH_3)_4(H_2O)_2]^{2+}$ isomer and the difference in electronegativity between the oxygen and nitrogen atoms bonded to the central cobalt(II). The side of the complex with the water ligands will be partially negative as oxygen is more electronegative than the nitrogen in the ammonia ligands. The differences in electronegativity still apply in the *trans*-$[Co(NH_3)_4(H_2O)_2]^{2+}$ isomer but its symmetical arrangement ensures the charge in the complex is spread evenly around the complex.

Stereoisomerism is also commonly shown by octahedral (six co-ordinate) complexes associated with bidentate ligands. An example is the complex containing nickel as the transition metal and 1,2-diaminoethane ($NH_2CH_2CH_2NH_2$) as the bidentate ligand (Figure 24.10).

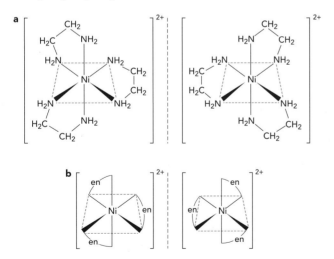

Figure 24.10: The two non-superimposable optical isomers of $[Ni(NH_2CH_2CH_2NH_2)_3]^{2+}$: **a** the full structure, **b** a simplified structure with 'en' representing a molecule of 1,2-diaminoethane.

The two isomers are stereoisomers because the two different molecules are *mirror images* of each other and cannot be superimposed. They are optical isomers, differing only in their ability to rotate the plane of polarised light in opposite directions.

The complex ion consisting of nickel(II) bonded to two bidentate 1,2-diaminoethane (en) ligands and two monodentate ligands, such as water or chloride ions, can form both geometric (*cis*/*trans*) isomers and optical isomers. Look at the *cis*- and *trans*-isomers of $[Ni(H_2NCH_2CH_2NH_2)_2(H_2O)_2]^{2+}$ in Figure 24.11, simplified to $[Ni(en)_2(H_2O)_2]^{2+}$.

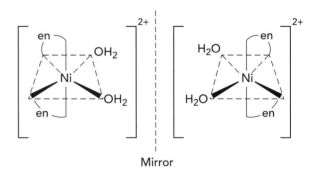

Figure 24.11: The geometric, *cis*- and *trans*- isomers of $[Ni(H_2NCH_2CH_2NH_2)_2(H_2O)_2]^{2+}$

Of the two *cis*- and *trans*- isomers of $[Ni(en)_2(H_2O)_2]^{2+}$ only the *cis*- isomer is optically active, with its two non-superimposable mirror images. The symmetrical nature of the *trans*-isomers of $[Ni(en)_2(H_2O)_2]^{2+}$ means that its mirror images can be superimposed so they do not display optical isomerism. Look at the optical isomers of $[Ni(en)_2(H_2O)_2]^{2+}$ in Figure 24.12.

Mirror

Figure 24.12: The non-superimposable, optical isomers of *cis*-$[Ni(en)_2(H_2O)_2]^{2+}$

Question

4 a Cobalt forms a complex with the simplified structure:

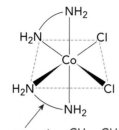

the curve represents —CH₂—CH₂—

    i   Give the co-ordination number of this complex.

    ii   Draw the stereoisomer of this complex.

    iii Explain why this is a stereoisomer.

  b i   Draw the two geometrical isomers of $[Ni(CN)_2(Cl)_2]^{2-}$. Label the *cis*-isomer and the *trans*-isomer.

    ii Deduce the overall polarity of the *trans*-isomer of $[Ni(CN)_2(Cl)_2]^{2-}$.

Discuss your answers to Question 4, and your reasoning, with a partner.

Substitution of ligands

Copper complexes

The ligands in a complex can be exchanged, wholly or partially, for other ligands. This is a type of substitution reaction. It happens if the new complex formed is more stable than the original complex.

The complexes of copper(II) ions can be used to show ligand substitution reactions, also called ligand exchange reactions.

Whenever we write $Cu^{2+}(aq)$ we are really referring to the complex ion $[Cu(H_2O)_6]^{2+}$. This ion gives a solution of copper sulfate its blue colour. On adding sodium hydroxide solution, we see a light blue precipitate forming.

Two water ligands are replaced by two hydroxide ligands in the reaction:

$[Cu(H_2O)_6]^{2+}(aq) + 2OH^-(aq) \rightarrow$
blue solution $Cu(OH)_2(H_2O)_4(s) + 2H_2O(l)$
                              pale blue precipitate

If you now add concentrated ammonia solution, the pale blue precipitate dissolves and we get a deep blue solution:

$Cu(OH)_2(H_2O)_4(s) + 4NH_3(aq) \rightarrow$
pale blue precipitate

               $[Cu(NH_3)_4(H_2O)_2]^{2+}(aq) + 2H_2O(l) + 2OH^-(aq)$
               deep blue solution

The first reaction can also be achieved by adding concentrated ammonia solution to copper sulfate solution drop by drop or by adding a dilute solution of ammonia. The pale blue precipitate formed will then dissolve and form the deep blue solution when excess ammonia is added. The structure of $[Cu(NH_3)_4(H_2O)_2]^{2+}(aq)$ is shown in Figure 24.13.

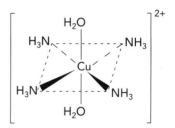

Figure 24.13: The octagonal structure of $[Cu(NH_3)_4(H_2O)_2]^{2+}(aq)$

Water ligands in $[Cu(H_2O)_6]^{2+}$ can also be exchanged for chloride ligands if we add concentrated hydrochloric acid drop by drop. A yellow solution forms, containing the complex ion $[CuCl_4]^{2-}$:

$[Cu(H_2O)_6]^{2+}(aq) + 4Cl^-(aq) \rightarrow [CuCl_4]^{2-}(aq) + 6H_2O(l)$
  blue solution   yellow solution

The mixture of blue and yellow solutions in the reaction mixture gives it a greenish colour (Figure 24.14).

Cobalt complexes

Aqueous cobalt(II) compounds also form complex ions. Whenever we write $Co^{2+}(aq)$, we are referring to the complex ion $[Co(H_2O)_6]^{2+}$. This ion gives an aqueous solution of cobalt(II) sulfate its pink colour. On adding sodium hydroxide solution, we see a blue precipitate of cobalt(II) hydroxide forming, which turns red when warmed if the alkali is in excess.

$[Co(H_2O)_6]^{2+}(aq) + 2OH^-(aq) \rightarrow$
    pink solution $Co(OH)_2(H_2O)_4(s) + 2H_2O(l)$
                                   blue precipitate

start here

$[CuCl_4]^{2-}$
this complex forms on
adding concentrated HCl

$[Cu(H_2O)_6]^{2+}$
the well-known blue Cu^{2+}
complex with water

$[Cu(NH_3)_4(H_2O)_2]^{2+}$
this dark blue complex forms
on adding concentrated NH_3

Figure 24.14: The equations for the changes are:

$[Cu(H_2O)_6]^{2+} + 4Cl^- \rightleftharpoons [CuCl_4]^{2-} + 6H_2O$

$[Cu(H_2O)_6]^{2+} + 4NH_3 \rightleftharpoons [Cu(NH_3)_4(H_2O)_2]^{2+} + 4H_2O$

Water ligands in $[Co(H_2O)_6]^{2+}$ can also be exchanged for ammonia ligands if we add concentrated aqueous ammonia drop by drop.

$[Co(H_2O)_6]^{2+}(aq) + 6NH_3(aq) \rightarrow$
pink solution $\qquad [Co(NH_3)_6]^{2+}(aq) + 6H_2O(l)$
$\qquad\qquad\qquad\qquad$ brown solution

The brown cobalt(II) complex ion is oxidised by oxygen in the air to $[Co(NH_3)_6]^{3+}(aq)$, a cobalt(III) complex ion.

Adding concentrated hydrochloric acid drop by drop to an aqueous solution of cobalt(II) ions results in the formation of a blue solution containing the tetrahedral complex $[CoCl_4]^{2-}(aq)$.

$[Co(H_2O)_6]^{2+}(aq) + 4Cl^-(aq) \rightarrow [CoCl_4]^{2-}(aq) + 6H_2O(l)$
pink solution $\qquad\qquad\qquad$ blue solution

Aqueous cobalt(II) ions usually form tetrahedral complexes with monodentate anionic ligands such as Cl^-, SCN^- and OH^-.

Question

5 **a** Blue cobalt chloride paper gets its blue colour from $[CoCl_4]^{2-}$ ions.

Give the oxidation number of the cobalt in this complex.

b Blue cobalt chloride paper is used to test for water. If water is present, the paper turns pink as a complex forms between the cobalt ion and six water ligands (Figure 24.15).

Write an equation to show the ligand substitution reaction that takes place in a positive test for water.

c Which equation correctly describes the reaction of hydrated copper(II) ions with concentrated hydrochloric acid?

A $[Cu(H_2O)_6]^{2+}(aq) + 4Cl^-(aq) \rightarrow$
$\qquad\qquad\qquad [CuCl_4]^{2-}(aq) + 6H_2O(l)$

B $[Cu(H_2O)_6]^{2+}(aq) + 6Cl^-(aq) \rightarrow$
$\qquad\qquad\qquad [CuCl_6]^{4-}(aq) + 6H_2O(l)$

C $[Cu(H_2O)_6]^{2+}(aq) + 2Cl^-(aq) \rightarrow$
$\qquad\qquad\qquad [CuCl_2]^{2-}(aq) + 6H_2O(l)$

D $[Cu(H_2O)_6]^{2+}(aq) + 4Cl^-(aq) \rightarrow$
$\qquad\qquad\qquad [Cu(H_2O)_2Cl_4]^{2-}(aq) + 4H_2O(l)$

Discuss with a partner the thought processes you go through to deduce the oxidation number of the central transition element in a complex (Question 5**a**). Working together, list the sequence of steps that another learner could follow.

Discuss the option you chose in Question 5**c**, explaining why you think the three other options are incorrect.

Figure 24.15: A positive test for the presence of water using anhydrous cobalt chloride paper.

Stability constants

Aqueous solutions of transition element ions are hydrated. They are complex ions with water molecules acting as ligands, forming dative (coordinate) bonds to the central metal ion.

Different ligands form complexes with different stabilities. For example, when we add concentrated aqueous ammonia to an aqueous solution of copper(II) sulfate, the ammonia ligands displace water ligands in a stepwise process.

$$[Cu(H_2O)_6]^{2+}(aq) + NH_3(aq) \rightleftharpoons \\ [Cu(NH_3)(H_2O)_5]^{2+}(aq) + H_2O(l)$$

$$[Cu(NH_3)(H_2O)_5]^{2+}(aq) + NH_3(aq) \rightleftharpoons \\ [Cu(NH_3)_2(H_2O)_4]^{2+}(aq) + H_2O(l)$$

As we increase the concentration of ammonia, this process continues until four of the water molecules are replaced by ammonia molecules. The solution formed is a deep blue colour. The overall ligand substitution reaction is:

$$\underset{\text{blue solution}}{[Cu(H_2O)_6]^{2+}} + 4NH_3(aq) \rightleftharpoons \\ \underset{\text{deeper blue solution}}{[Cu(NH_3)_4(H_2O)_2]^{2+}(aq)} + 4H_2O(l)$$

We can think of this exchange of ligands in terms of competing equilibria of the forward and backward reactions. The position of equilibrium lies in the direction of the more stable complex. In this case, the complex with ammonia as a ligand is more stable than the complex with just water as a ligand. If we dilute the complex with water, the position of equilibrium shifts to the left and a complex with more water molecules as ligands forms.

The stability of the complex is expressed in terms of the equilibrium constants for ligand displacement.

This is called the **stability constant**. Usually an overall stability constant, K_{stab}, is given rather than the stepwise constants. The method for writing equilibrium expressions for stability constants is similar to the one we used for writing K_c (see Section 21.1). So for the equilibrium:

$$[Cu(H_2O)_6]^{2+} + 4Cl^-(aq) \rightleftharpoons [CuCl_4]^{2-}(aq) + 6H_2O(l)$$

the expression for the stability constant is:

$$K_{stab} = \frac{[[CuCl_4]^{2-}(aq)]}{[Cu(H_2O)_6]^{2+}[Cl^-(aq)]^4}$$

> **KEY WORD**
>
> **stability constant, K_{stab}:** the equilibrium constant for the formation of a complex ion in a solvent from its constituent ions or molecules.

Note:

- water does not appear in the equilibrium expression because it is in such a large excess that its concentration is regarded as being constant

- the units for the stability constant are worked out in the same way as for the units of K_c (see Section 8.3). For example, in the above case:

$$K_{stab} = \frac{[[CuCl_4]^{2-}(aq)]}{[Cu(H_2O)_6]^{2+}[Cl^-(aq)]^4}$$

$$\frac{[[CuCl_4]^{2-}(aq)]}{[Cu(H_2O)_6]^{2+}[Cl^-(aq)]^4} \qquad \frac{(mol\,dm^{-3})}{(mol\,dm^{-3}) \times (mol\,dm^{-3})^4}$$

$$= dm^{12}\,mol^{-4}$$

Stability constants are often given on a $\log_{10}$ scale. When expressed on a $\log_{10}$ scale, they have no units (see Table 24.4).

Stability constants can be used to compare the stability of any two ligands. The values quoted usually give the stability of the complex relative to the aqueous ion where the ligand is water.

> **IMPORTANT**
>
> The higher the value of the stability constant, the more stable the complex.

Table 24.4 gives some values of stability constants for various copper(II) complexes relative to their aqueous ions.

Ligand	$\log_{10} K_{stab}$
chloride, Cl^-	5.6
ammonia, NH_3	13.1
2-hydroxybenzoate	16.9
1,2-dihydroxybenzene	25.0

Table 24.4: The stability constants of some complexes of copper.

From Table 24.4 you can see that, in general, complexes with bidentate ions (2-hydroxybenzoate and 1,2-dihydroxybenzene) have higher stability constants than those with monodentate ligands.

We can use the values of the stability constants to predict the effect of adding different ligands to complex ions. For example, the addition of excess ammonia to the complex $[CuCl_4]^{2-}(aq)$ should result in the formation of a dark blue solution of the ammonia complex. That is because the stability constant of the ammonia complex is higher than that of the chloride complex. The position of equilibrium is shifted to the right in the direction of the more stable complex.

Addition of excess 1,2-dihydroxybenzene to the dark blue ammonia complex results in the formation of a green complex with 1,2-dihydroxybenzene. This is because the stability constant with the 1,2-dihydroxybenzene is much higher than that for ammonia. You can see from Table 24.4 that the log of K_{stab} for 1,2-dihydroxybenzene is 25.0, so the actual value of K_{stab} is 10 raised to the power 25, compared to the actual value for ammonia of 10 raised to the power 13.1. This shows that the copper complex with 1.2-dihydroxybenzene is much more stable than the complex ion formed with ammonia. These values of K_{stab} predict that there will be hardly any of the copper complex with ammonia left in the equilibrium mixture shown in the equation below:

WORKED EXAMPLE

3   When concentrated hydrochloric acid is added to copper(II) sulfate solution, the aqueous solution formed contains $[CuCl_4]^{2-}$ and $[Cu(H_2O)_4]^{2+}$ complex ions.

   a   Write the expression for the stability constant for $[CuCl_4]^{2-}$ in an aqueous solution.

   Solution

   First of all write the chemical equation for the ligand exchange equilibrium mixture formed in the reaction:

   $[Cu(H_2O)_4]^{2+}(aq) + 4Cl^-(aq) \rightleftharpoons [CuCl_4]^{2-}(aq) + 4H_2O$

   Then write the expression for K_{stab}. (Remember that products go on the top line and reactants on the bottom line in equilibrium expressions, and that H_2O is not included)

   $$K_{stab} = \frac{[[CuCl_4]^{2-}(aq)]}{[Cu(H_2O)_6^{2+}][Cl^-(aq)]^4}$$

   b   Work out the units of K_{stab} for the expression in part **a**.

   Solution

   Substitute the unit of concentration ($mol\ dm^{-3}$) into your equilibrium expression from part **a** in this question. Then cancel out the units.

   $$\frac{(mol\ dm^{-3})}{(mol\ dm^{-3})(mol\ dm^{-3})^4} = dm^{12}\ mol^{-4}$$

CONTINUED

c   Using Table 24.4, explain the proportions of the two copper(II) complex ions present in the equilibrium mixture.

Solution

As the value of $\log_{10}K_{stab}$ for the chloride ion is given in the table as 5.6, this shows that the actual value of K_{stab} is 10 raised to the power of 5.6 i.e. a very large number. This shows that the concentration of products in the equilibrium expression, in this case the $[CuCl_4]^{2-}$ ions, is much greater than the concentration of the reactant $[Cu(H_2O)_6]^{2+}$ ions.

d   When concentrated ammonia solution is added to copper(II) chloride, explain what you would see happen, using Table 24.4.

Solution

As the K_{stab} value for the copper(II) complex with ammonia is a much larger value than that of the complex with chloride ions, the ammonia molecules will displace the chloride ions from the $[CuCl_4]^{2-}$ complex, forming a more stable complex of $[Cu(NH_3)_4(H_2O)_2]^{2+}$. This will turn the (greenish) yellow solution of the chloride complex a deep blue colour.

e   The exchange of ligands occurs step-by-step as successive ligands are replaced. For example the second step in the exchange of water ligands for chloride ion ligands is shown by this equation:

$$[Cu(H_2O)_5Cl]^+(aq) + Cl^-(aq) \rightleftharpoons Cu(H_2O)_4Cl_2(aq) + H_2O(l)$$

It was found for this reaction that when a 0.15 mol dm^{-3} solution of the complex ion $[(Cu(H_2O)_5Cl]^+$ was mixed with 0.15 mol dm^{-3} hydrochloric acid, the equilibrium concentration of the $Cu(H_2O)_4Cl_2(aq)$ complex was 0.10 mol dm^{-3}.

i   Write an expression for the stability constant for this ligand exchange reaction.

Solution

$$K_{stab} = \frac{[Cu(H_2O)_4Cl_2(aq)]}{[Cu(H_2O)_5Cl]^+(aq)] \times [Cl^-(aq)]}$$

ii   Calculate the value for K_{stab} for the reaction giving the units.

Solution

Work out the concentration of each of the ions at equilibrium:

	$[Cu(H_2O)_5Cl]^+(aq)$	$Cl^-(aq)$	$Cu(H_2O)_4Cl_2(aq)$
At start	0.15 mol dm^{-3}	0.15 mol dm^{-3}	0
At equilibrium	$(0.15 - 0.10)$ mol dm^{-3}	$(0.15 - 0.10)$ mol dm^{-3}	0.10 mol dm^{-3}

Then substitute the concentrations at equilibrium into the expression for K_{stab} in **e i**:

$$K_{stab} = \frac{0.10 \text{ mol dm}^{-3}}{0.05 \text{ mol dm}^{-3} \times 0.05 \text{ mol dm}^{-3}}$$

$$= 40 \text{ dm}^3 \text{ mol}^{-1}$$

Question

6 **a** Write expressions for the stability constants for the following reactions:

  i $[PtCl_4]^{2-}(aq) + 2NH_3(aq) \rightleftharpoons$
        $PtCl_2(NH_3)_2(aq) + 2Cl^-(aq)$

  ii $[Cr(H_2O)_6]^{3+}(aq) + 2Cl^-(aq) \rightleftharpoons$
        $[Cr(H_2O)_4Cl_2]^+(aq) + 2H_2O(l)$

  iii $[Ni(H_2O)_6]^{2+}(aq) + 4NH_3(aq) \rightleftharpoons$
        $[Ni(NH_3)_4(H_2O)_2]^{2+}(aq) + 4H_2O(l)$

 b An iron(III) ion, Fe^{3+}, in aqueous solution has six water molecules bonded to it as ligands.

  i Draw the structure of this ion.

  ii When thiocyanate ions, SCN^-, are added to an aqueous solution of iron(III) ions, the solution turns red and one water molecule is replaced by a thiocyanate ion.

    Use the concept of stability constants to explain why the reaction occurs.

  iii Deduce the formula of the ion forming the red solution.

  iv The stability constant for aqueous Fe^{3+} ions with SCN^- as a ligand is $891\ dm^3\ mol^{-1}$. The stability constant for aqueous Fe^{3+} ions with fluoride ions, F^-, as a ligand is $2 \times 10^5\ dm^3\ mol^{-1}$. A solution containing fluoride ions is added to the red solution.

    Would you expect to observe any changes? Explain your answer.

Now share and discuss your answers to Question 6 with another learner. Agree on a final set of answers before checking them against the answers provided.

The colour of complexes

You will have now seen the striking colours of complexes containing transition metal ions. But how do these colours arise?

White light is made up of all the colours of the visible spectrum. When a solution containing a transition metal ion in a complex appears coloured, part of the visible spectrum is absorbed by the solution.

The colour we see is called the complementary colour, made up of light with frequencies not absorbed. For example, copper(II) ions absorb light from the red end of the spectrum, so the complementary colour seen is a pale blue (called cyan). Here is a list of complementary pairs of colours:

red	cyan
yellow	blue
green	magenta

You should be aware that mixing light of different frequencies does not produce the same colour as mixing different colours of paint.

However, that still doesn't explain why part of the spectrum is absorbed by transition metal ions. To answer this question, we must look in more detail at the d orbitals in the ions (Figure 24.16).

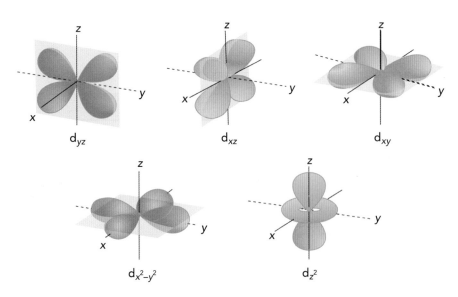

Figure 24.16: The degenerate d orbitals in a transition metal atom.

The five d orbitals in an isolated transition metal atom or ion are described as **degenerate orbitals**, meaning they are all at the same energy level.

In the presence of ligands, a transition metal ion is not isolated. The dative (or co-ordinate) bonding from the ligands causes the five d orbitals in the transition metal ion to split into two sets. The two sets of orbitals are described as **non-degenerate orbitals** as they are at slightly different energy levels (see Figure 24.17).

In a complex with six ligands, the ligands are arranged in an octahedral shape around the central metal ion. The lone pairs donated by the ligands into the transition metal ion repel electrons in the two $d_{x^2-y^2}$ and d_{z^2} orbitals shown in Figure 24.17 more than those in the other three d orbitals. This happens because these two d orbitals line up with the dative (co-ordinate) bonds in the complex's octahedral shape. As the electrons in the $d_{x^2-y^2}$ and d_{z^2} orbitals are closer to the bonding electrons in the octahedral arrangement, the repulsion between electrons increases. Therefore, the d orbitals are split, with these two d orbitals at a slightly higher energy level than the d_{yz}, d_{xz} and d_{xy} orbitals.

Look at the left-hand side of Figure 24.17.

A Cu^{2+} ion has an electronic configuration of $[Ar]\,3d^9$. Figure 24.17 shows how the nine d electrons are distributed between the non-degenerate orbitals formed in a complex with ligands. The difference in the energy between the non-degenerate d orbitals is labelled ΔE.

ΔE corresponds to part of the visible spectrum of light. So, when light shines on the solution containing the $[Cu(H_2O)_6]^{2+}$ complex, an electron absorbs this amount of energy. It uses this energy to jump into the higher of the two non-degenerate energy levels. In copper complexes, the rest of the visible spectrum that passes through the solution makes it appear blue in colour.

The exact energy difference (ΔE) between the non-degenerate d orbitals in a transition metal ion is affected by many factors. One of these factors is the identity of the ligands that surround the transition metal ion. As you have seen, a solution containing $[Cu(H_2O)_6]^{2+}$ is a light blue, whereas a solution containing $[Cu(NH_3)_4(H_2O)_2]^{2+}$ is a very deep shade of blue. The colour change arises because the presence of the ammonia ligands causes the d orbitals to split by a different amount of energy. This means that the size of ΔE changes and this results in a slightly different amount of energy being absorbed by electrons jumping up to the higher orbitals. Therefore, a different colour is absorbed from visible light, so a different colour is seen.

In tetrahedral complexes, such as $[CoCl_4]^{2-}$, the splitting of the d orbitals is different (Figure 24.18). The bonding pairs of electrons from four ligands line up with the d_{yz}, d_{xz} and d_{xy} orbitals of the transition metal ion. Unlike the octahedral arrangement, the $d_{x^2-y^2}$ and d_{z^2} orbitals in a tetrahedral complex lie between the metal–ligand

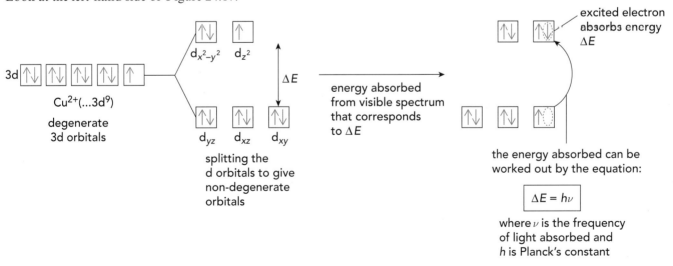

Figure 24.17: The splitting of the 3d orbitals in the octahedral $[Cu(H_2O)_6]^{2+}$ complex ion.

bonds. So there is less repulsion between electrons in $d_{x^2-y^2}$ or d_{z^2} orbitals and the lone pairs of bonding electrons donated by the ligands. Therefore, when the d orbitals split in this case, the $d_{x^2-y^2}$ or d_{z^2} are at a lower, more stable energy level than the d_{yz}, d_{xz} and d_{xy} orbitals.

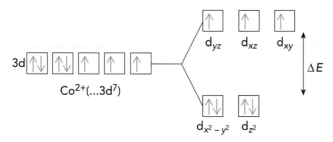

Figure 24.18: The splitting of the 3d orbitals in the tetrahedral $[CoCl_4]^{2-}$ complex ion.

Question

7 **a** What do we mean by *degenerate atomic orbitals*?

   b Explain why an octahedral complex of a transition element is coloured.

   c Draw the non-degenerate 3d orbitals in a Ni^{2+} ion on a diagram similar to Figure 24.18. The electrons should be shown in the configuration that gives the lowest possible energy.

   d A solution of Sc^{3+} ions is colourless. Suggest a reason for this.

   e A solution of Zn^{2+} ions is colourless. Suggest a reason for this.

   f Make a brief PowerPoint presentation to explain the difference in the splitting of the 3d atomic orbitals in the two copper(II) complexes, $[Cu(H_2O)_6]^{2+}$ and $[CuCl_4]^{2-}$.

REFLECTION

1 Working with a partner, each write a question and mark scheme. One of you devise an assessment of the reactions of transition elements with ligands to form complexes, and describe the shapes and bond angles of complexes, together with the types of stereoisomerism (*cis/trans* and optical isomerism) shown by complexes. The other person can assess the use of $MnO_4^- / C_2O_4^{2-}$, MnO_4^- / Fe^{2+} and Cu^{2+} / I^- as examples of redox systems.

   You can use your coursebook Exam-style questions to help with the style of your question, and on-line answers to write a typical mark scheme. However, your questions and answers should be your own work.

2 Then try to answer each other's questions, giving your answers back for your partner to mark using their mark scheme.

3 Use this exercise to give you an idea of your level of understanding about transition element complexes and redox reactions. What have you learned from the activity?

SUMMARY

Each of the transition elements forms at least one ion with a partially filled d orbital. They are metals with similar physical and chemical properties.

When a transition element is oxidised, it loses electrons from the 4s sub-shell first and then the 3d sub-shell to form a positively charged ion.

Transition elements can exist in several oxidation states.

Many reactions involving transition elements are redox reactions. Some redox reactions are used in titrations to determine concentrations.

CONTINUED

| A ligand is a molecule or ion with one or more lone pairs of electrons available to donate to a transition metal ion. |
| Transition elements form complexes by combining with ligands. Ligands bond to transition metal ions by one or more dative (co-ordinate) bonds. |
| Ligands can be exchanged for other ligands in a complex. This can result in a change of colour. |
| Some transition element complexes exist as geometrical (*cis/trans*) isomers, e.g. *cis*- and *trans*-platin; others, especially those associated with bidentate ligands with co-ordination number 6, may exist as optical isomers. |
| Ligand exchange can be described in terms of competing equilibria. |
| The stability constant, K_{stab}, of a complex ion is the equilibrium constant for the formation of the complex ion in a solvent from its constituent ions or molecules. |
| The higher the value of the stability constant, the more stable is the complex ion formed. |
| Transition metal compounds are often coloured because of d orbital splitting, caused by ligands. |
| The splitting is different in octahedral and tetrahedral complexes. Different ligands will split the d orbitals by different amounts, resulting in differently coloured complexes. |

EXAM-STYLE QUESTIONS

1 Define the following terms:

    a transition element   **[1]**

    b ligand   **[1]**

    c complex ion.   **[2]**

                                                              [Total: 4]

2 Use sub-shell notation ($1s^2\ 2s^2\ 2p^6$, etc.) to give the electronic configurations of the following:

    a an Fe atom   **[1]**

    b a Co^{2+} ion   **[1]**

    c a Ti^{3+} ion.   **[1]**

                                                              [Total: 3]

3 **a** Give the formulae of two iron compounds in which iron has different oxidation states. Give the oxidation states of the iron in each compound. **[4]**

    b Explain why complexes of iron compounds are coloured.   **[3]**

                                                             [Total: 7]

4 Write balanced ionic equations and describe the observations for the reactions that occur when:

    a sodium hydroxide solution is added to a solution containing $[Cu(H_2O)_6]^{2+}(aq)$ **[2]**

    b excess concentrated ammonia solution is added to a solution containing $[Cu(H_2O)_6]^{2+}(aq)$.   **[3]**

                                                             [Total: 5]

CONTINUED

5 The half-cell reactions given below are relevant to the questions that follow.

$$Cl_2 + 2e^- \rightarrow 2Cl^- \qquad\qquad E^\ominus = +1.36 \text{ V}$$

$$Fe^{3+} + e^- \rightarrow Fe^{2+} \qquad\qquad E^\ominus = +0.77 \text{ V}$$

$$MnO_4^- + 8H^+ + 5e^- \rightarrow Mn^{2+} + 4H_2O \quad E^\ominus = +1.51 \text{ V}$$

$$SO_4^{2-} + 4H^+ + 2e^- \rightarrow SO_2 + 2H_2O \quad E^\ominus = +0.17 \text{ V}$$

In order to standardise a solution of $KMnO_4$, a learner weighed out 5.56 g of $FeSO_4.7H_2O$ and dissolved it in sulfuric acid. She then made it up to a total volume of 250 cm³ with distilled water. She took 25.0 cm³ portions of this solution, and added 10 cm³ of 2.00 mol dm⁻³ sulfuric acid to cach. She then titrated these solutions against the potassium manganate(VII) solution. The average titre was 21.20 cm³.

a Using the electrode potentials, explain why she used sulfuric acid and not hydrochloric acid in her titrations. **[4]**

b Calculate the concentration of the iron(II) sulfate solution. **[3]**

c i Write the full ionic equation for the reaction between the manganate(VII) solution and the iron(II) sulfate. **[2]**

   ii Describe how the learner knows that she has reached the end-point for the reaction. **[1]**

d Calculate the concentration of the manganate(VII) solution. **[2]**

e If the learner passed sulfur dioxide gas through 25.0 cm³ of the manganate(VII) solution, calculate the volume of gas that would be required to completely decolorise the manganate(VII).
(1 mol of gas occupies 24.0 dm³ at room temperature and pressure) **[5]**

[Total: 17]

6 Copper forms complexes with chloride ions and with ammonia.

$\log_{10} K_{stab}$ for aqueous Cu^{2+} ions with Cl^- as a ligand is 2.80

$\log_{10} K_{stab}$ for aqueous Cu^{2+} ions with NH_3 as a ligand is 4.25

a A few drops of hydrochloric acid are added to blue aqueous copper(II) sulfate.

   i Copy and complete the equation for this reaction.

   $$[Cu(H_2O)_6]^{2+}(aq) + \underline{} \rightleftharpoons [CuCl_4]^{2-}(aq) + \underline{}$$
   light blue   yellow-green **[2]**

   ii Describe and explain what happens when excess water is then added to the reaction mixture in part **i**. **[3]**

   iii Explain what happens in terms of ligand exchange, when concentrated aqueous ammonia is added to the reaction mixture from part **ii**. **[2]**

b Aqueous copper ions form a complex with 1,2-diaminoethane, $NH_2CH_2CH_2NH_2$. They also form a complex with 1,3-diaminopropane $NH_2CH_2CH_2CH_2NH_2$.

   $\log_{10} K_{stab}$ for aqueous Cu^{2+} ions with 1,2-diaminoethane as a ligand is 20.3

   $\log_{10} K_{stab}$ for aqueous Cu^{2+} ions with 1,3-diaminopropane as a ligand is 17.7

CONTINUED

i Name the type of ligands that 1,2-diaminoethane and 1,3-diaminopropane are. Explain your answer. **[2]**

ii Identify which one of these ligands forms a more stable complex. Explain your answer. **[1]**

iii 1,2-diaminoethane can be abbreviated as 'en'.

A complex of nickel ions, Ni^{2+}, with 1,2-diaminoethane is octahedral in shape with a co-ordination number of 6.

Draw the structures of the two stereoisomers of this complex. **[4]**

[Total: 14]

SELF-EVALUATION

After studying this chapter, complete a table like this:

I can	See section...	Needs more work	Almost there	Ready to move on
explain what we mean by a *transition element* and describe how transition elements have variable oxidation states, behave as catalysts, form complex ions, and form coloured ions	24.1, 24.2			
state the electronic configuration of a first-row transition element and of its ions and describe the tendency of transition elements to have variable oxidation states	24.2			
describe and explain the use of $MnO_4^- / C_2O_4^{2-}$, MnO_4^- / Fe^{2+} and Cu^{2+} / I^- as examples of redox systems and predict, using $E^\ominus$ values, the feasibility of redox reactions involving transition metal compounds	24.2			
define the terms *ligand* and *complex* and explain the reactions of transition elements with ligands to form complexes, describing the shapes and bond angles of complexes	24.3			
describe the types of stereoisomerism (*cis/trans* and optical isomerism) shown by complexes, including those with bidentate ligands	24.3			
explain qualitatively how ligand exchange may occur and describe the term stability constant, K_{stab}, of a complex ion, and write an expression for the stability constant of a complex	24.3			
sketch the general shape of atomic d orbitals and describe the splitting of degenerate d orbitals into two energy levels in octahedral and tetrahedral complexes	24.3			
explain the origin of colour in transition element complexes and describe, in qualitative terms, the effects of different ligands on the absorption of light, and hence the colour of a complex.	24.3			

Benzene and its compounds

CONTINUED

- describe the mechanism of electrophilic substitution in arenes and the effect of the delocalisation of electrons in such reactions, as well as the directing effects of electron-donating and electron-withdrawing groups on further substitutions

- interpret the difference in reactivity between benzene and chlorobenzene

- predict whether halogenation will occur in the side-chain or in the benzene ring in arenes, depending on reaction conditions

- apply knowledge relating to position of substitution in the electrophilic substitution of arenes and aryl compounds, such as phenol

- describe the reactions (reagents and conditions) by which phenol can be prepared

- describe the reactions of phenol with bases, and with Na(s)

- describe the nitration, and the bromination, of phenol's aromatic ring and compare these reactions with those of benzene

- explain the acidity of phenol and the relative acidities of water, phenol and ethanol

- apply knowledge of the reactions of phenol to those of other phenolic compounds, such as naphthol.

BEFORE YOU START

Working in your group, answer these questions:

1   The bond angles around a carbon atom in which its atomic orbitals are sp^2 hybridised is likely to be:

    A   90°   B   109.5°   C   120°   D   180°

2   How many electrons are involved in a pi (π) bond?

    A   1   B   2   C   3   D   4

3   Describe the reaction mechanism when HBr is reacted with ethene, $CH_2{=}CH_2$.

4   Discuss with a partner how you would name this compound:

    CH₃ — Cl (benzene ring with CH3 and Cl substituents)

5   Discuss what happens in the substitution reaction that takes place between either chloroethane and NaOH or chloroethane and HCN.

BENZENE

Benzene is a colourless, volatile liquid that has been used by chemists since the 1800s. It works well as a solvent for other organic compounds, but is immiscible (does not mix) with water.

At one time, chemists used it with few precautions. However, we know now that it is highly toxic, and is described as a carcinogen (a cancer-causing agent). It is particularly hazardous as it can be absorbed through the skin.

Experiments in the 19th century showed that the formula of benzene was C_6H_6. But the chemists working around 1860 were still struggling to work out its structure.

Working as a pair, can you come up with a straight-chain structure for C_6H_6, with each carbon forming four bonds and each hydrogen one bond?

It was at that time that a German chemist called Friedrich August Kekulé had a fortunate dream. As you have just done, he was working the problem of benzene's structure. He grew tired and dozed off and dreamt that the benzene molecules were snakes! One of the snakes bit its own tail, forming a circle. When Kekulé woke up, he claimed that his dream inspired him to propose the structure shown in Figure 25.1

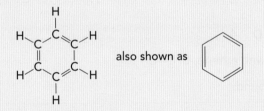

Figure 25.1: The Kekulé structure of benzene.

You can find out how later chemists developed Kekulé's structure to match their observations in Section 25.1.

Figure 25.2: This is a vanilla orchid. Its seed pods contain a substance called vanillin.

Compounds based on benzene are found widely in nature, such as vanillin in vanilla (Figure 25.2).

Vanillin molecules are based on a benzene ring, as represented by the hexagon with a circle inside in the structure shown below. Vanillin is used to flavour foods such as ice cream and chocolate. Its structure is:

Questions for discussion
Working with another learner or group of learners:

- Carry out some research to find out how the dream of another chemist, Dmitri Mendeleev, led to the design of the Periodic Table in 1869.

- Suggest a theory about the way the human brain works to explain the role of dreams in scientific discoveries.

25.1 The benzene ring

The 'benzene ring' is a particularly important functional group found in many organic compounds. A benzene ring is a hexagon made of six carbon atoms bonded together in a particular way. Benzene rings are found in many compounds that are commercially important: for example, as medicines, dyes and plastics.

Organic hydrocarbons containing one or more benzene rings are called **arenes**. In general, compounds of benzene are known as *aryl compounds* or aromatic compounds; an example is chlorobenzene, which is one of the halogenoarenes.

> **KEY WORD**
>
> **arene:** hydrocarbon containing one or more benzene rings.

As you read in the section above, in Kekulé's structure the hexagonal ring contained three double C=C bonds. This is reflected in benzene's name, which has the same ending as the alkenes.

As chemists developed analytical techniques, however, they found out that the benzene molecule was a planar, perfectly symmetrical molecule. Kekulé's structure would suggest three shorter double C=C bonds and three longer C—C single bonds in the ring. This would produce a distorted hexagonal shape, not the perfect hexagonal arrangement of carbon atoms in benzene's actual molecules. Figure 25.3 shows how we represent benzene's skeletal formula.

Figure 25.3: The skeletal formula of benzene. It can also be used in displayed formulae of aryl compounds, as in the figure below Figure 25.2, showing the structure of vanillin.

We can now measure actual bond lengths. This was impossible in the 19th century when Kekulé worked. Table 25.1 shows that the bond length of the carbon–carbon bonds in benzene lies between the values for C—C single bonds and C=C double bonds.

The chemistry of benzene also suggests that the Kekulé structure is incorrect. If there were three C=C bonds in benzene it would undergo addition reactions in the same way as the alkenes (see Section 15.3). However,

Bond	Bond length / nm
C—C	0.154
C=C	0.134
carbon to carbon bond in benzene	0.139

Table 25.1: Comparing bond lengths.

this is not the case. For example, ethene will decolorise bromine water on mixing at room temperature, but benzene needs much harsher conditions.

The actual structure of benzene can be explained by considering the bonding in the molecule. Each of the six carbon atoms in the hexagonal ring is sp^2 hybridised (see Section 4.5), sharing:

- one pair of electrons with one of its neighbouring carbon atoms

- one pair of electrons with its other neighbouring carbon atom

- one pair of electrons with a hydrogen atom.

These are three σ (sigma) bonds. These covalent bonds are a pair of electrons found mainly between the nuclei of the atoms bonded to each other. Each carbon atom with sp^2 hybrised atomic orbitals forms three σ bonds: so that leaves one electron spare on each of the six carbon atoms in benzene. Each carbon atom contributes its one spare electron to a π (pi) bond (see Section 4.5).

However, the π bonds formed by benzene are not the same as the π bonds in an alkene C=C bond (see Section 4.5). In an alkene, a π bond helps to bond one pair of carbon atoms to each other; but in benzene six spare p orbital electrons are spread over all six carbon atoms in the hexagonal ring. The six electrons in the π bonds are said to be *delocalised*.

The π bonding in benzene is formed by the overlap of carbon p atomic orbitals, one from each of the six carbon atoms. To achieve maximum overlap, the benzene molecule must be planar. The lobes of the p orbitals overlap to form a ring of delocalised electrons above and below the plane of the carbon atoms in the benzene molecule. This is shown in Figure 25.4.

Naming aryl compounds

You saw how to name aryl compounds with alkyl side-chains in Section 14.3. Some aryl compounds have

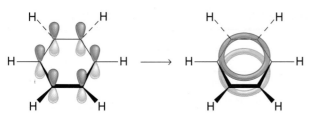

overlap of p orbitals produces a ring of delocalised electrons above and below the plane of benzene's carbon atoms

Figure 25.4: The π bonding in benzene. The three bond angles around each of the sp² hybridised carbon atoms are 120°.

functional groups that are substituted directly into the benzene ring in place of a hydrogen atom.

You need to know the names of the compounds in Table 25.2.

Question

1 **a** Give the number of electrons involved in the π bonding system in a benzene molecule.

   b State the type of atomic orbital that the electrons in part **a** come from.

   c Explain what we mean by the term *delocalised electrons* in benzene.

   d Compare the π bonding in benzene with the π bonding in hex-3-ene.

   e Draw the displayed or skeletal formula of:

   i 1,3,5-tribromobenzene

   ii 1,3-dichloro-5-nitrobenzene.

   f Name the molecules below:

   i   OH
        CH₃

   ii   Br
        Cl
        Cl

Choose a partner and discuss your answers to Question 1 part **d** together. Then write a mark scheme for this question showing what each mark is given for.

Compare your mark scheme with those produced by other pairs of learners.

Skeletal formula of aryl compound	Name
Cl	chlorobenzene
NO₂	nitrobenzene
OH	phenol
OH Br Br Br	2,4,6-tribromophenol: note the numbering of the carbon atoms in the benzene ring to describe the position of each substituted group (see Section 14.3)
NH₂	phenylamine

Table 25.2: The names of some aryl compounds. The phenyl group in a substituted benzene compound can be written as C_6H_5; e.g. the structural formula of phenylamine is $C_6H_5NH_2$.

25.2 Reactions of arenes

Most reactions of benzene and other arenes maintain the highly stable delocalised ring of π bonding electrons intact. This occurs by substituting an atom, or group of atoms, for one or more hydrogen atoms attached to the benzene ring. Addition reactions into the benzene ring would disrupt the 'aromatic stabilisation' achieved by the complete delocalisation in the ring. The initial attack is usually by an electrophile, which is attracted to the high electron density around the benzene ring.

Electrophilic substitution with chlorine or bromine

Benzene will react with bromine in the presence of an anhydrous aluminium bromide catalyst. The substitution reaction is:

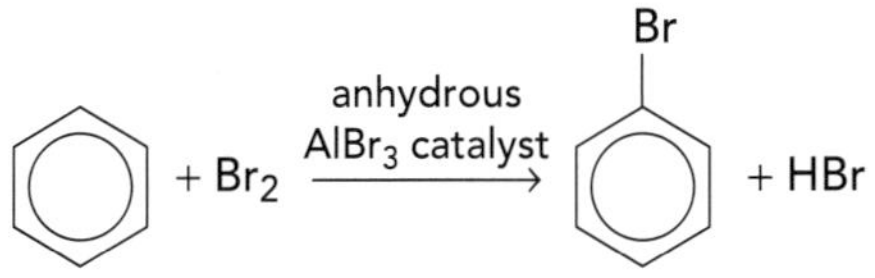

At first sight, the electrophile that starts the attack on benzene is not obvious. The electrophile is created when an aluminium bromide molecule polarises a bromine molecule. The Br_2 molecule forms a dative (co-ordinate) bond with aluminium bromide by donating a lone pair of electrons from one of its bromine atoms into an empty 3p orbital in the aluminium. This draws electrons from the other bromine atoms in the Br_2 molecule, making it partially positive, and creating the electrophile.

We can think of the electrophile as a Br^+ cation:

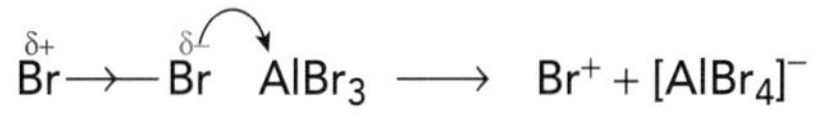

The Br^+ cation and the 'electron-rich' benzene ring are attracted to each other, as the mechanism of **electrophilic substitution** below shows. Remember that the curly arrows show the movement of a pair of electrons:

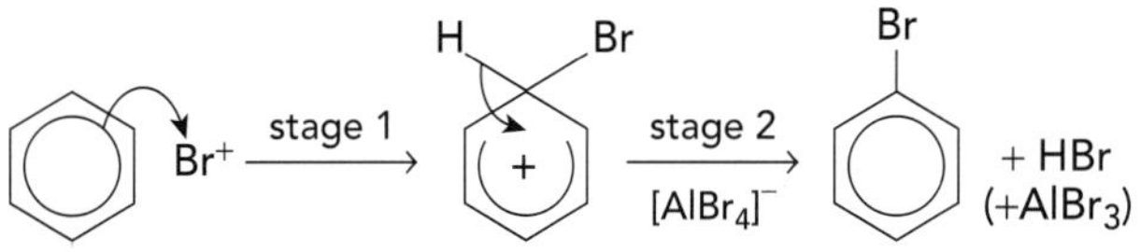

A similar reaction happens when chlorine gas is bubbled through benzene at room temperature in the presence of a catalyst, such as aluminium chloride. The products of this electrophilic substitution are chlorobenzene and hydrogen chloride. The catalysts in these reactions, $AlBr_3$ and $AlCl_3$, are known as *halogen carriers*.

> **KEY WORD**
>
> **electrophilic substitution:** the replacement of an atom by another atom or group of atoms after initial attack by an electron-deficient species.

When we halogenate methylbenzene or other alkylarenes, the halogen atom substitutes into the benzene ring at positions 2 or 4. These positions are 'activated' by any *electron-donating* groups bonded directly to the benzene ring (see Table 25.4 at the end of the chapter).

Other examples of benzene compounds that are activated in these positions are phenol (C_6H_5OH) and phenylamine ($C_6H_5NH_2$).

So when we react methylbenzene with chlorine gas, using an anhydrous aluminium chloride catalyst, two products can be made:

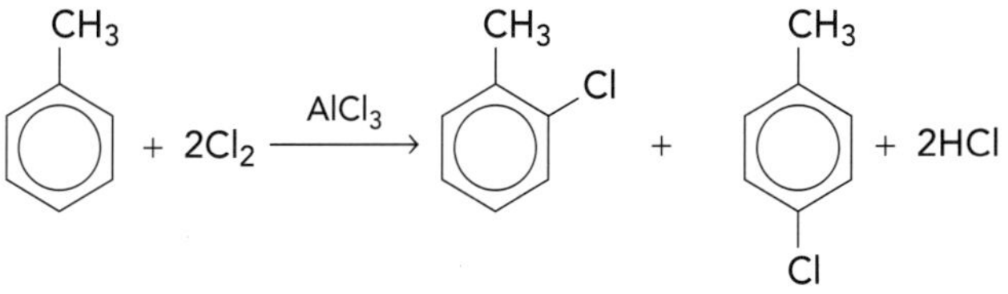

If *excess* chlorine gas is bubbled through, we can form 2,4-dichloromethylbenzene, 2,6-dichloromethylbenzene and 2,4,6-trichloromethylbenzene. (Remember that the 2 and 6 positions in substituted arenes are equivalent.)

The carbon–halogen bond in halogenoarenes is stronger than the equivalent bond in a halogenoalkane, making the halogenoarenes much less reactive. This is because one of the lone pairs on the halogen atom overlaps slightly with the π bonding system in the benzene ring. This gives the carbon–halogen bond in a halogenoarene a partial double bond character.

Notice that the methyl side-chain off the benzene ring is not affected under the conditions used in the reaction above. However, we learned in Section 15.2 that chlorine will react with alkanes in the presence of ultraviolet (UV) light or strong sunlight. This reaction of the alkanes is a free-radical substitution reaction. So, if the chlorine gas is passed into boiling methylbenzene in the presence of UV light, the following reaction takes place:

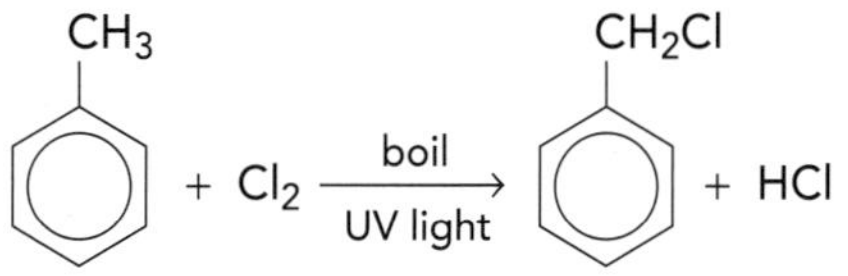

Note that there is no substitution into the benzene ring under these conditions.

In excess chlorine, eventually all three of the hydrogen atoms on the methyl side-chain will be replaced by chlorine atoms.

Question

2 a Write the equation for the reaction of chlorine with benzene in the presence of an aluminium chloride catalyst.

   b Name this type of mechanism for the reaction in part **a**.

   c Draw the mechanism of the reaction in part **a**, with Cl^+ as the attacking species and using curly arrows to show the movement of electron pairs.

   d Draw the displayed formula of the 'tri-substituted' halogenoarene produced if methylbenzene is added to excess bromine at room temperature in the presence of aluminium bromide.

   e Suggest how the reaction in part **d** would differ if the methylbenzene and bromine were boiled in the presence of UV light.

   f Name the mechanism of the reaction in part **e**.

Nitration of benzene

The nitration of benzene is another example of an electrophilic substitution. Nitration refers to the introduction of the $-NO_2$ group into a molecule. In this reaction the electrophile is the NO_2^+ ion, known as the nitronium ion (or nitryl cation). This is made from a mixture of concentrated nitric acid and concentrated sulfuric acid:

$$HNO_3 + 2H_2SO_4 \rightarrow NO_2^+ + 2HSO_4^- + H_3O^+$$

This 'nitrating mixture' is refluxed with benzene at between 25 °C and 60 °C to make nitrobenzene:

The *mechanism* of the electrophilic substitution in this nitration is:

In stage 1 in the mechanism, the electrophile, NO_2^+, is attracted to the high electron density of the π bonding system in benzene. A pair of electrons from the benzene ring is donated to the nitrogen atom in NO_2^+, and forms a new covalent bond. At this point, benzene's delocalised ring of electrons is disrupted. There are now four π bonding electrons and a positive charge spread over five carbon atoms.

However, the full delocalised ring is restored in stage 2 when the C—H bond breaks heterolytically (see Section 14.7). Both electrons in the C—H covalent bond go into nitrobenzene's π bonding system, and hydrogen leaves as an H^+ ion. There are now six electrons spread over the six carbon atoms, so the chemical stability of the benzene ring is retained in this substitution reaction.

In order to predict the products of further substitution into the benzene ring of the nitrobenzene formed, we must consider the '*directing effect*' of the nitro group. Further nitration of the nitrobenzene produces 1,3-dinitrobenzene and 1,3,5-trinitrobenzene. Unlike the electron-donating methyl group in methylbenzene (which activates the 2 and 4 positions in the benzene ring), the $-NO_2$ group is *electron-withdrawing*. This type of group (which includes $-COOH$) *deactivates* the 2 and 4 positions in the benzene ring. Therefore, when there is a nitro group bonded to the benzene ring, further substitutions are directed to the 3 and 5 positions (see Table 25.4 at the end of the chapter).

Question

3 a Copy and complete the two equations below, which can both be used to show the nitration of methylbenzene:

   i $C_6H_5CH_3 + NO_2^+ \rightarrow$ ____ + ____

   ii $C_6H_5CH_3 + HNO_3 \xrightarrow{H_2SO_4}$ ____ + ____

   iii Name the possible mono-substituted products in parts **i** and **ii**.

   iv 2,4-dinitromethylbenzene and 2,4,6-trinitromethylbenzene are formed on further nitration of methylbenzene.

   Draw the displayed formula of each compound.

   b Benzene also undergoes electrophilic substitution when refluxed with fuming sulfuric acid for several hours. This is called *sulfonation*. The electrophile is the SO_3 molecule and the product formed is benzenesulfonic acid, $C_6H_5SO_3H$.

i Suggest which atom in the SO_3 molecule accepts an electron pair in the mechanism of sulfonation.

ii Write an equation in the style of part **a** **i** for the sulfonation of benzene to form benzenesulfonic acid.

Discuss and sketch with a partner the mechanism of sulfonation in part **b** above. If you get stuck, work with another group before displaying your suggested mechanism.

Alkylation (or acylation) of benzene (Friedel–Crafts reactions)

Friedel–Crafts reactions, named after the chemists who first discovered them, are a third example of electrophilic substitution into the benzene ring.

Sometimes chemists need to change the structure of an arene in order to make a new product. Examples include the manufacture of detergents or the reactants needed to make plastics, such as poly(phenylethene), commonly known as polystyrene. They can use a Friedel–Crafts reaction to substitute a hydrogen in the benzene ring for an alkyl group, such as a methyl ($—CH_3$) or an ethyl ($—C_2H_5$) group:

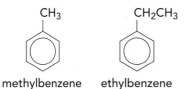

methylbenzene   ethylbenzene

The same type of reaction can also be used to introduce an acyl group into a benzene ring. An acyl group contains an alkyl group and a carbonyl ($C=O$) group:

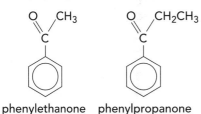

phenylethanone   phenylpropanone

KEY WORD

Friedel–Crafts reaction: the electrophilic substitution of an alkyl or acyl group into a benzene ring.

IMPORTANT

Friedel–Crafts reactions result in the introduction of a side-chain into a benzene ring.

Friedel–Crafts reactions are also called *alkylation* or *acylation reactions*.

For example:

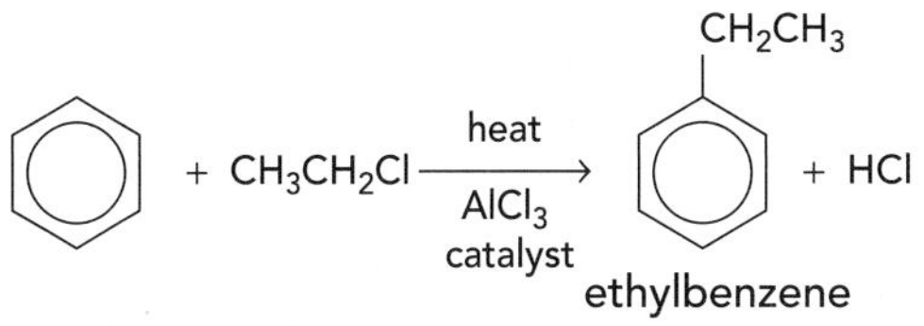

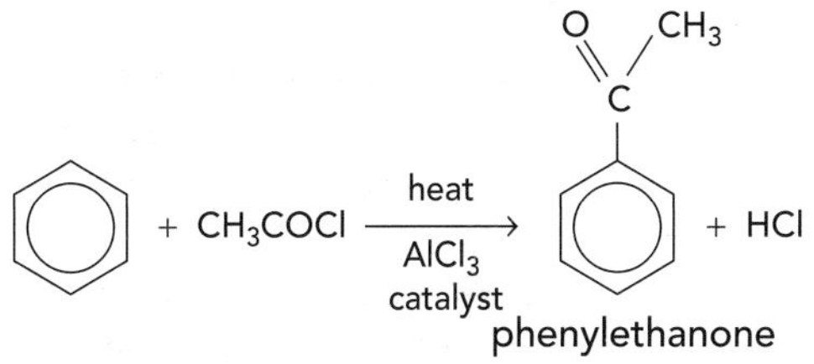

The mechanisms for Friedel–Crafts reactions involve attack on the benzene ring by an electrophile. In these reactions, the electrophile carries a positive charge on a carbon atom, so there is attack by a carbocation.

The electrophile is formed by adding an aluminium chloride catalyst to:

- a halogenoalkane, to make an alkylbenzene, *or*

- an acyl chloride, to make an acylbenzene.

This creates the carbocation electrophile to attack the benzene in the first step of the two mechanisms below.

In alkylation

The alkylation of benzene, substituting an alkyl chain into the benzene ring, can be described by this three-step mechanism:

Step 1:

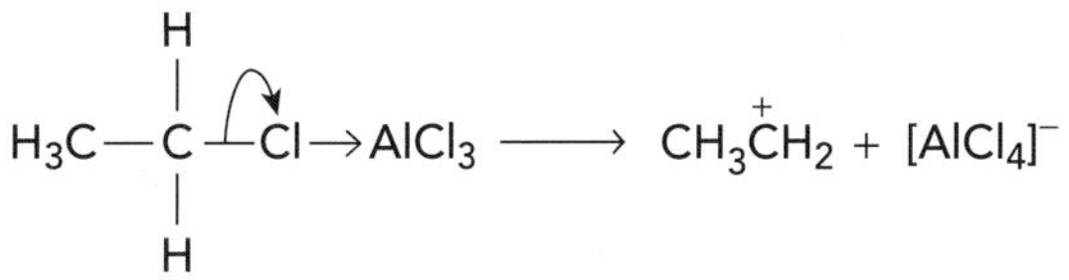

The arrow between Cl and $AlCl_3$ represents a coordinate (dative covalent) bond.

The carbocation electrophile made then attacks the benzene ring:

Step 2:

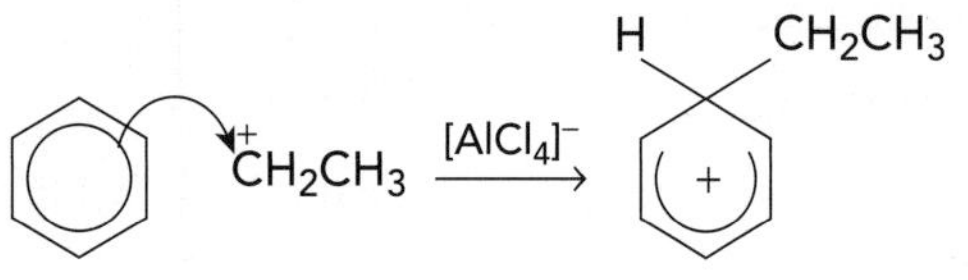

The aluminium chloride catalyst is regenerated in the final step:

Step 3:

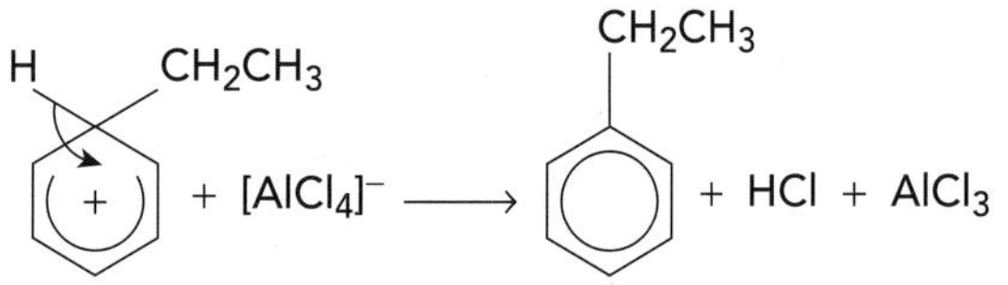

Further alkylation of the benzene ring can take place as the reaction proceeds.

In acylation

The acylation of benzene, substituting an acyl group into the benzene ring, can be described by this three-step mechanism:

Step 1:

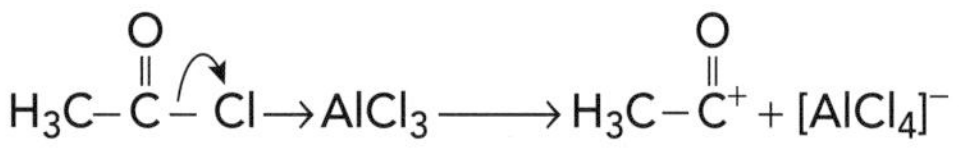

ethanoyl chloride

Again, the electrophile made then attacks the benzene ring:

Step 2:

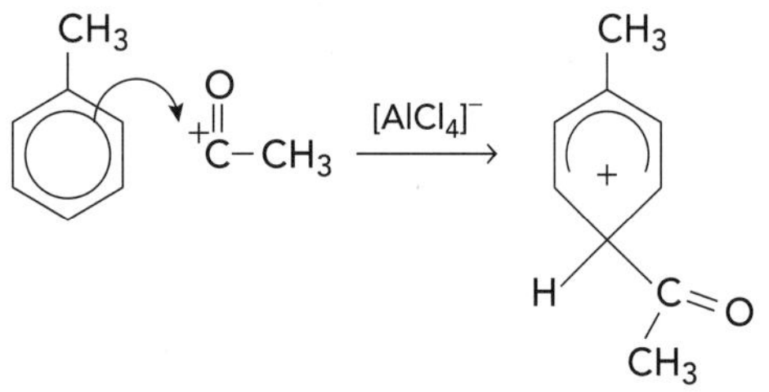

Then the aluminium chloride catalyst is regenerated in the final step:

Step 3:

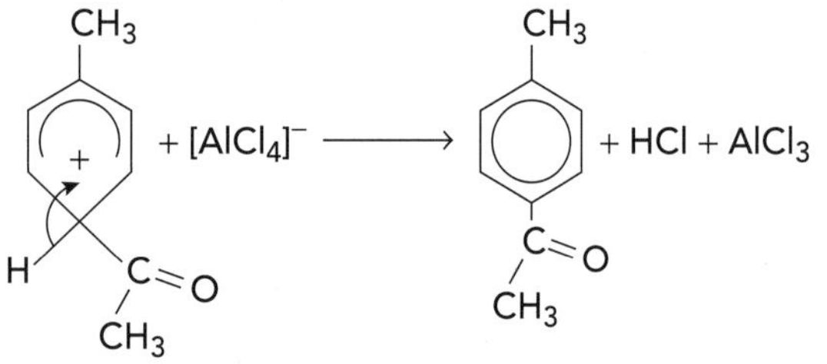

Oxidation of the side-chain in arenes

The presence of the benzene ring in an alkylarene, such as methylbenzene, can affect the characteristic reactions of its alkyl side-chain. For example, alkanes are not usually oxidised by a chemical oxidising agent such as potassium manganate(VII).

However, in alkylarenes, the alkane side-chain is oxidised to form a carboxylic acid. For example, methylbenzene produces benzoic acid when *refluxed* with alkaline potassium manganate(VII), and then acidified with dilute sulfuric acid:

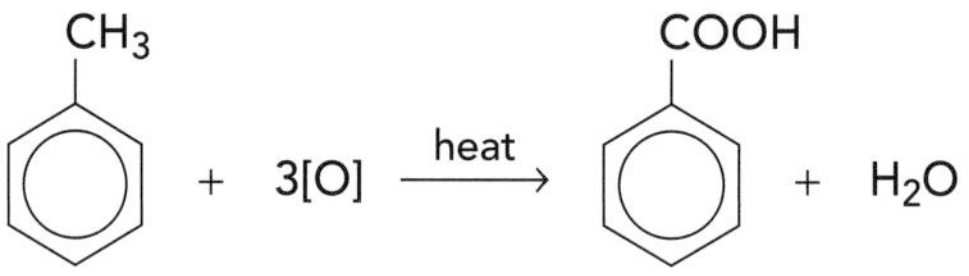

Hydrogenation

Unusually, the hydrogenation reaction is similar to an alkene's reaction with hydrogen. The unsaturated alkene becomes saturated as an alkane is formed. The reaction is carried out by heating the alkene with hydrogen gas and a nickel or platinum catalyst.

The same reaction takes place with benzene. The benzene is hydrogenated and is converted to cyclohexane. With methylbenzene, the product is methylcyclohexane:

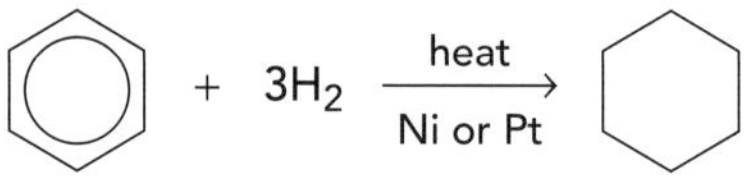

benzene (C_6H_6)   cyclohexane (C_6H_{12})

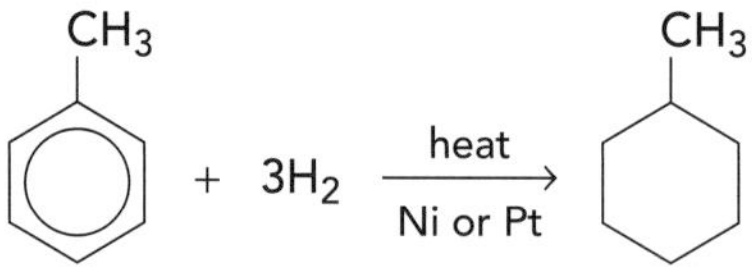

methylbenzene ($C_6H_5CH_3$)   cyclomethylbenzene ($C_6H_{11}CH_3$)

Question

4 a Copy and complete the two equations, which can be used to show the alkylation and acylation of benzene to produce the mono-substituted products.

  i $C_6H_6 + CH_3CH_2CH_2Cl \rightarrow$ _____ + _____

  ii $C_6H_6 + CH_3CH_2CH_2CH_2COCl \rightarrow$
  _____ + _____

b i Name the mono-substituted organic product in part **a i**.

  ii Name the class of compound formed in part **a ii**.

c Hexylbenzene is refluxed with alkaline potassium manganate(VII) and then acidified with dilute sulfuric acid. The same experiment is carried out but using hexane and the oxidising agent.

  Compare what would happen in these experiments.

d i Give the reagents and conditions needed to convert benzene into cyclohexane.

  ii Which type of reaction classifies the reaction in part **d i**?

  A addition

  B condensation

  C elimination

  D substitution

  Discuss your reasoning with another learner.

REFLECTION

At this point, reflect on the work you have covered so far on benzene and its reactions. After looking back, work with a partner to take turns asking each other short, quick questions.

Then discuss how you both feel about your progress so far in this chapter.

25.3 Phenol

Phenol, C_6H_5OH, is a crystalline solid that melts at 43 °C. It is used to manufacture a wide range of products (Figure 25.5). Its structure is:

Figure 25.5: Phenol and its derivatives are used to make a variety of consumer goods.

The melting point of phenol is relatively high for an aryl compound of its molecular mass because of hydrogen bonding between its molecules. However, the large non-polar benzene ring makes phenol only slightly soluble in water, as it disrupts hydrogen bonding with water molecules.

We can prepare phenol by reacting phenylamine, $C_6H_5NH_2$, with nitric(III) acid, HNO_2, using ice to keep the temperature below 10 °C. The reaction gives an unstable diazonium salt. We then warm the diazonium salt in the aqueous solution to produce phenol. The equations are given below.

- Prepare nitric(III) acid (nitrous acid) in a test-tube, using sodium nitrate(III) and dilute hydrochloric acid:

$$NaNO_2 + HCl \rightarrow \underset{\text{nitric(III) acid}}{HNO_2} + NaCl$$

- Then add the phenylamine:

benzenediazonium chloride

- The diazonium salt formed is unstable and will decompose easily on warming with water, giving off nitrogen gas, N_2:

$$\underset{\text{diazonium salt}}{C_6H_5N_2^+Cl^-} + H_2O \rightarrow \underset{\text{phenol}}{C_6H_5OH} + HCl + N_2$$

You can read more about diazonium salts and their use in the dye industry in Chapter 27.

The acidity of phenol

Phenol is weakly acidic, losing an H^+ ion from its hydroxyl group:

$$C_6H_5OH(aq) \rightleftharpoons C_6H_5O^-(aq) + H^+(aq)$$

phenol   phenoxide ion

The position of this equilibrium lies well over to the left-hand side.

The strength of acids can be compared by looking at their pK_a values. The values for phenol, water and ethanol are shown in Table 25.3. Remember: the higher the value of pK_a, the weaker the acid (see Section 21.3).

Weak acid	Dissociation in water	pK_a at 25 °C
phenol	$C_6H_5OH(aq) \rightleftharpoons$ $C_6H_5O^-(aq) + H^+(aq)$	10.0
water	$H_2O(l) \rightleftharpoons$ $H^+(aq) + OH^-(aq)$	14.0
ethanol	$C_2H_5OH(aq) \rightleftharpoons$ $C_2H_5O^-(aq) + H^+(aq)$	16.0

Table 25.3: Comparing the acidity of phenol, water and ethanol.

IMPORTANT

Phenol is a stronger acid than water and ethanol. Ethanol is less acidic than phenol and water.

We can explain the order of acidity by looking at the conjugate bases formed on the right-hand side of the equations in Table 25.3. The phenoxide ion, $C_6H_5O^-(aq)$, has its negative charge spread over the whole ion as one of the lone pairs on the oxygen atom overlaps with the delocalised π bonding system in the benzene ring.

phenoxide ion, with negative charge spread over the whole ion

ethoxide ion, with negative charge concentrated on the oxygen

This delocalisation reduces the charge density of the negative charge on the phenoxide ion compared with $OH^-(aq)$ or $C_2H_5O^-(aq)$. Therefore $H^+(aq)$ ions are not as strongly attracted to the phenoxide ion as they are to hydroxide or ethoxide ions. This makes phenoxide ions less likely to re-form the undissociated phenol molecules than hydroxide ions are to form water molecules, and ethoxide ions are to form ethanol molecules.

Alternatively, we can explain the greater acidity of phenol by saying that phenol ionises to form a more stable negative ion than water or ethanol, with its charge spread out. This stability means that the ionisation of phenol is more likely to happen. This results in the position of equilibrium in the phenol equation in Table 25.3 lying further to the right-hand side: so a higher proportion of phenol molecules donate an H^+ ion than in the dissociation equations for water and ethanol.

Ethanol is a weaker acid than water because of the electron-donating alkyl (ethyl) group attached to the oxygen atom in the ethoxide ion. This has the effect of concentrating more negative charge on this oxygen atom, which more readily accepts an H^+ ion. This explains why the position of equilibrium lies further to the left-hand side, favouring the undissociated ethanol molecules.

Question

5   Discuss your reasoning with another learner before writing your answers to parts **a** and **b**.

     a   Place the following molecules in order of their acidity, starting with the most acidic:

         CH_3COOH C_6H_5OH HCl C_3H_7OH H_2O

     b   Would you expect methanol to be more or less acidic than phenol?

         Explain your answer.

     c   **i**   Name the three reactants mixed to prepare a diazonium chloride salt.

           ii   Give the conditions used for the reaction in **c** part **i**.

25.4 Reactions of phenol

We can divide the reactions of phenol into those involving the hydroxyl group, —OH, and those involving substitution into the benzene ring.

Breaking of the O—H bond in phenol

Although phenol is only slightly soluble in water, it dissolves well in an alkaline solution. As you have just learned, phenol is a weak acid so it will react with an alkali to give a salt plus water:

$$\text{C}_6\text{H}_5\text{OH} + \text{NaOH} \longrightarrow \text{C}_6\text{H}_5\text{O}^-\text{Na}^+ + \text{H}_2\text{O}$$

The salt formed, sodium phenoxide, is soluble in water.

Molten phenol reacts vigorously with sodium metal, giving off hydrogen gas and again forming sodium phenoxide:

$$2\,\text{C}_6\text{H}_5\text{OH} + 2\text{Na} \longrightarrow 2\,\text{C}_6\text{H}_5\text{O}^-\text{Na}^+ + \text{H}_2$$

Substitution into the benzene ring of phenol

Compared with benzene, phenol reacts more readily with electrophiles. The overlap of one of the lone pairs of electrons on the oxygen atom in the —OH group with the π bonding system increases the electron density of the benzene ring in phenol. This makes phenol's benzene ring more open to attack from electron-deficient electrophiles than benzene itself. The electron-donating —OH group 'activates' the benzene ring, directing substitution to positions 2, 4 and 6 (see Table 25.4, at the end of this chapter).

PRACTICAL ACTIVITY 25.1

Bromination of phenol

Phenol undergoes similar reactions to benzene, but phenol does so under milder conditions. For example, bromine water will not react with benzene at room temperature. To produce bromobenzene we need pure bromine (not a solution) and an aluminium bromide catalyst.

However, bromine water reacts readily with phenol. Phenol decolorises the orange bromine solution and forms a white precipitate of 2,4,6-tribromophenol (see Figure 25.6).

$$\text{C}_6\text{H}_5\text{OH} + 3\text{Br}_2 \longrightarrow \text{C}_6\text{H}_2\text{Br}_3\text{OH} + 3\text{HBr}$$

2,4,6-tribromophenol

Similar reactions happen between phenol and chlorine or iodine.

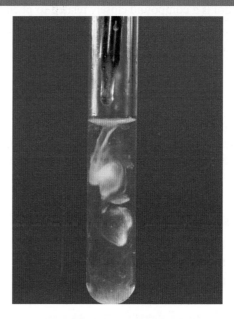

Figure 25.6: Bromine water is added to aqueous phenol from a dropper to form 2,4,6-tribromophenol.

CONTINUED

This activation of the benzene ring is also shown in the nitration of phenol. With benzene, we need a mixture of concentrated nitric acid and sulfuric acid to reflux with benzene between 25 °C and 60 °C for nitration to take place (see Section 25.2).

However, the activated ring in phenol readily undergoes nitration with dilute nitric acid at room temperature:

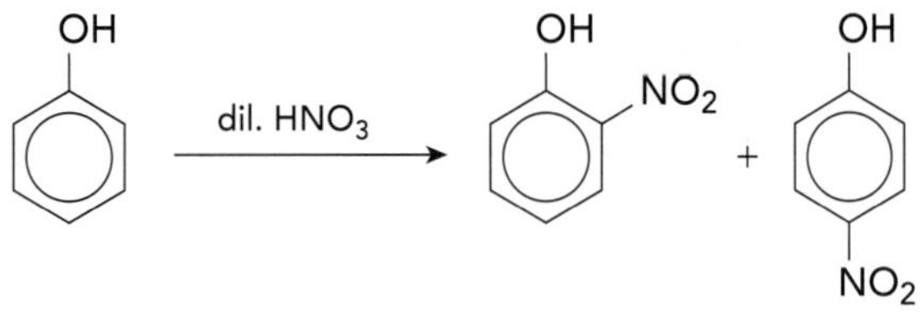

If we use concentrated nitric acid, we get 2,4,6-trinitrophenol formed, shown below:

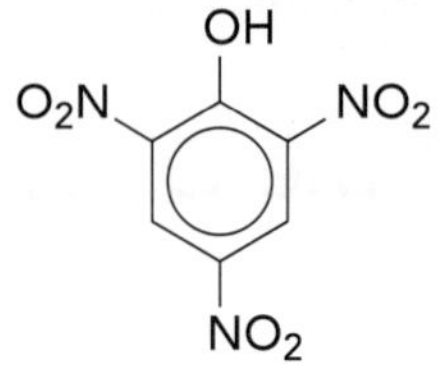

A phenolic compound

1-Naphthol is a compound closely related to phenol:

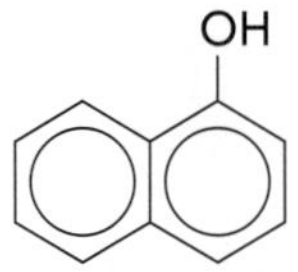

1-naphthol

The electron donating —OH group in 1-naphthol activates the benzene ring that it is bonded to. This makes the ring more open to electrophilic substitution, directing attack to the 2 and/or 4 positions.

Question

6　a　Place these molecules in order of ease of nitration, with the most reactive first:

C_6H_6　$C_6H_5CH_3$　C_6H_5COOH　C_6H_5OH

b　i　Write a balanced equation to show the reaction when excess chlorine is bubbled through aqueous phenol at room temperature.

　　ii　How would the reaction conditions differ from those in part b i if you wanted to make chlorobenzene from benzene and chlorine?

c　Predict the reactions of excess 1-naphthol with each of the following, and draw one of the organic products formed in each case.

　　i　potassium hydroxide solution

　　ii　sodium metal

　　iii　bromine water

　　iv　dilute nitric acid

Compare your answers with a partner and discuss any differences. Then check against the answers provided.

REFLECTION

1　Draw a mind map with 'BENZENE' at its centre to summarise what you have learned in Chapter 25, labelling links clearly. Swap your map with a partner and compare your efforts.

2　Discuss with a friend which, if any, parts of Chapter 25 that you need to:

- read through again to make sure you really understand all the new terms introduced in organic chemistry

- seek more guidance on, even after going over it again yourself or with a friend.

SUMMARY

The benzene molecule, C_6H_6, is symmetrical, with a planar hexagonal shape.
Arenes have considerable energetic stability because of the six delocalised π bonding electrons that lie above and below the plane of the benzene ring.
The main mechanism for the reactions of arenes is electrophilic substitution. This enables arenes to retain their delocalised π electrons. Hydrogen atoms on the benzene ring may be replaced by a variety of other atoms or groups, including halogen atoms and nitro ($-NO_2$) groups, as well as alkyl or acyl groups in Friedel–Crafts reactions.
Despite the name ending in -ene, arenes do not usually behave like alkenes. Arenes typically undergo electrophilic substitution, whereas alkenes undergo electrophilic addition.
Sometimes the presence of the benzene ring affects the usual reactions of its side-chain, e.g. methylbenzene is oxidised by refluxing with alkaline potassium manganate(VII) to form benzoic acid.
When the $-OH$ group is joined directly to a benzene ring, the resulting compound is called a *phenol*.
Phenols are weakly acidic, but are more acidic than water and alcohols. The acidity of phenol is due to delocalisation of the negative charge on the phenoxide ion into the π bonding electron system on the benzene ring.
When reacted with sodium hydroxide, phenol forms a salt (sodium phenoxide) plus water. The reaction of sodium metal with phenol produces sodium phenoxide and hydrogen gas.
The $-OH$ group enhances the reactivity of the benzene ring towards electrophiles. The $-OH$ group is said to activate the benzene ring. For example, bromine water is decolorised by phenol at room temperature, producing a white precipitate of 2,4,6-tribromophenol.
Table 25.4 summarises the positions activated by different substituents in a benzene ring:

Substituent groups in the benzene ring that direct the in-coming electrophile to attack the 2, 4 and / or 6 positions. These groups activate attack by electrophiles (because they tend to donate electrons into the benzene ring).	Substituent groups in the benzene ring that direct the in-coming electrophile to attack the 3 and / or 5 positions. These groups de-activate attack by electrophiles (because they tend to withdraw electrons from the benzene ring).
$-NH_2$	$-NO_2$
$-OH$	$-COR$
$-R$	$-CHO$
$-Cl$	$-COOH$

Table 25.4: Summary of positions attacked in electrophilic substitution into substituted benzene compounds, where R = alkyl group.

EXAM-STYLE QUESTIONS

1 a   Give the empirical formula of benzene.   [1]
   b   Give the molecular formula of benzene.   [1]
   c   i   Draw the full displayed formula of the Kekulé structure
           of benzene, showing all atoms and using double bonds
           and single bonds.   [1]
       ii Draw the skeletal formulae for the Kekulé and the delocalised
           structures of benzene.   [2]

                                                                              [Total: 5]

2 Benzene reacts with bromine.
   a   Write a balanced chemical equation for this reaction.   [1]
   b   Name the catalyst used.   [1]
   c   Describe the visual observations you could make during the reaction.   [2]
   d   Benzene will also react with halogenoalkanes. This is called a
       Friedel–Crafts reaction.
       i   Using 1-chloropropane, write the formula of the catalyst
           needed to start the reaction with benzene.   [1]
       ii Write the formula of the electrophile in this
           Friedel–Crafts reaction.   [1]
       iii Name the organic product of this reaction.   [1]
       iv There are three steps in the mechanism of this Friedel–Crafts
           reaction. Draw the three steps in the mechanism to show the
           formation of the electrophile, the attack on the benzene ring
           by the electrophile and the formation of the products
           of the reaction (to include the regeneration of the catalyst).   [4]

                                                                             [Total: 11]

3 Phenol is an aryl compound.
   a   i   Give the molecular formula of phenol.   [1]
       ii Give the empirical formula of phenol.   [1]
   b   Molten phenol reacts with sodium metal.
       Give one observation and write a balanced chemical equation
       for the reaction.   [2]
   c   Phenol reacts with sodium hydroxide solution.
       Name the type of reaction and write a balanced chemical
       equation for the reaction.   [2]
   d   The reactions in parts b and c both give the same organic product.
       Name this product.   [1]
   e   Phenol reacts with bromine water.
       Give the name of the product, two visual observations and
       a balanced chemical equation. Then comment on how this shows
       that phenol is more reactive than benzene.   [7]

CONTINUED

f Contrast the molecules of phenol and benzene to explain why phenol is more reactive than benzene. Your answer must include reference to the model used for the arrangement of electrons. **[4]**

[Total: 18]

4 Benzene can be nitrated to give nitrobenzene.

a Name the mechanism for this reaction. **[2]**

b The species attacking benzene in the reaction is NO_2^+.

How is NO_2^+ generated in the reaction mixture? Name the substances used and give a chemical reaction leading to the formation of NO_2^+. **[3]**

c Give a suitable temperature for this reaction. **[1]**

d Use curly arrows to draw the mechanism of how benzene reacts with NO_2^+ to produce nitrobenzene. **[3]**

e The structure of a common household substance is given below:

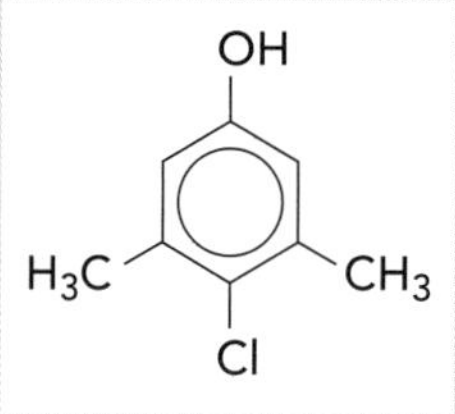

i Give the molecular formula of the compound. **[1]**

ii When bromine water is added to a solution of the compound, it is decolorised. Suggest two structures for the product of the reaction. **[2]**

[Total: 12]

5 a Describe the bonding in benzene. Include a description of the model used for the arrangement of electrons in the molecule. **[5]**

b Cyclohexene decolorises bromine water whereas benzene has no effect on bromine water.

Explain the difference in reactivity towards bromine water. **[5]**

[Total: 10]

SELF-EVALUATION

After studying this chapter, complete a table like this:

I can	See section...	Needs more work	Almost there	Ready to move on
interpret, name and use the general, structural, displayed and skeletal formulae of benzene and simple aryl compounds, and describe and explain the shape of, and bond angles in, benzene molecules in terms of σ and π bonds	25.1			
describe the reactions of arenes, such as benzene and methylbenzene, in substitution reactions with chlorine, and also with bromine; nitration; Friedel–Crafts alkylation and acylation; complete oxidation of the side-chain to give a benzoic acid; hydrogenation of the benzene ring to form a cyclohexane ring	25.2			
describe the mechanism of electrophilic substitution in arenes and the effect of the delocalisation of electrons in such reactions	25.2			
interpret the difference in reactivity between benzene and chlorobenzene	25.2			
predict whether halogenation will occur in the side-chain or in the benzene ring in arenes, depending on reaction conditions	25.2			
apply knowledge of the 'directing effect' relating to position of substitution in the electrophilic substitution of aryl compounds, such as nitrobenzene and phenol (see Table 25.4)	25.2, Summary			
describe the reactions (reagents and conditions) by which phenol can be prepared and its reactions with bases, and with Na(s)	25.3			
describe the nitration, and the bromination, of phenol's aromatic ring and compare these reactions with those of benzene	25.4			
explain the acidity of phenol and the relative acidities of water, phenol and ethanol	25.3			
apply knowledge of the reactions of phenol to those of other phenolic compounds, such as naphthol.	25.4			

> Chapter 26

Carboxylic acids and their derivatives

LEARNING INTENTIONS

In this chapter you will learn how to:

- explain the relative acidity of carboxylic acids and of chlorine-substituted ethanoic acids

- describe how some carboxylic acids, such as methanoic acid and ethanedioic acid, can be further oxidised

- describe the reactions of carboxylic acids in the preparation of acyl chlorides

- describe the hydrolysis of acyl chlorides

- describe the reactions of acyl chlorides with alcohols, phenols, ammonia and primary or secondary amines

- explain the relative ease of hydrolysis of acyl chlorides, alkyl chlorides (chloroalkanes) and aryl chlorides (chloroarenes)

- describe the condensation (addition–elimination) mechanism for the reactions of acyl chlorides.

BEFORE YOU START

Working in your group, answer these questions:

1 Discuss with a partner which is the stronger acid: chloric(I) acid (HClO) with a K_a of 3.7×10^{-8} mol dm^{-3}, or hydrocyanic acid (HCN) with a K_a of 4.9×10^{-10} mol dm^{-3}. Then explain how the K_a value enables you to decide.

2 Using an arrowhead and the symbols for a partial negative charge and a partial positive charge, add labels to both of the following bonding pairs of atoms: $C=O$, $C-Cl$

3 Which row in Table 26.1 correctly describes one use of a curly arrow in a mechanism?

	Starts at	Points to
A	a + charge	a − charge
B	an electron	a covalent bond
C	a pair of electrons	a δ+ carbon atom
D	a nucleus	a hydrogen atom

Table 26.1

4 Which *two* processes take place in a condensation reaction?

A elimination followed by substitution   B hydrolysis followed by addition

C dehydration followed by elimination   D addition followed by elimination

TRANS-FATTY ACIDS

In general, when we get carboxylic acids from the hydrolysis of oils or fats, they are called 'fatty acids'. They usually contain an even number of carbon atoms and form unbranched chains (Figure 26.1). For example, octadecanoic acid contains 18 carbon atoms. Its structural formula is $CH_3(CH_2)_{16}COOH$. Its skeletal formula is shown as:

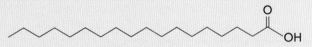

Figure 26.1: The skeletal formula of a fatty acid.

We call fatty acids with one $C=C$ double bond 'monounsaturated'. We describe them as 'polyunsaturated' if they contain more than one $C=C$ double bond. Each double bond will give rise to *cis/trans* isomers (see Section 24.3).

Octadec-9-enoic acid is a common monounsaturated fatty acid we get from plant seeds. Its molecules have eighteen carbon atoms and one $C=C$ double bond. Figure 26.2 shows the skeletal formulae of its *cis*- and *trans*-isomers.

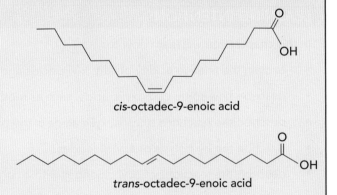

cis-octadec-9-enoic acid

trans-octadec-9-enoic acid

Figure 26.2: The *cis*- and *trans*-isomers of octadec-9-enoic acid.

CONTINUED

You can see that the *trans*-isomer has straight chains whereas the *cis*-isomer is bent. This means that the *trans*-fatty acids can pack together better and so have the higher melting points.

Trans-fatty acids are associated with health risks due to their use in foodstuffs, such as biscuits and pastry. Plant oils are turned into 'spreadable' margarines by heating the oils with hydrogen using a nickel or platinum catalyst. This addition reaction saturates some of the double bonds, straightening out the chains in their molecules. The hydrogenation process also converts *cis*-isomers into *trans*-isomers, which increases their melting points. *Trans*-fatty acids are particularly associated with fast foods that are prepared by frying in these partially hydrogenated oils.

Researchers have found links between the amount of *trans*-fats consumed and an increased risk of

heart disease and strokes. The *trans*-fats appear to increase the amount of low-density lipoprotein (LDLs) cholesterol (known as 'bad' cholesterol) and lowers the amount of high-density lipoproteins (HDLs) the 'good' cholesterol associated with health benefits. Disturbing the balance in your blood between LDLs and HDLs can result in arteries furring up and narrowing, causing circulatory problems. This can result in high blood pressure, strokes and heart disease.

Questions for discussion

Discuss with another learner or group of learners:

- why do the makers of margarines often use *trans*-fatty acids to make their products?

- how does consuming too much affect your body?

- how can we reduce our intake of foods containing *trans*-fatty acids?

26.1 The acidity of carboxylic acids

Carboxylic acids display the typical reactions of all acids due to the presence of excess $H^+(aq)$ ions in their aqueous solutions (see Section 21.3). For example, they react with bases to form a salt and water. Their salts are called *carboxylates*. The carboxylate salt formed by the reaction of ethanoic acid with sodium hydroxide is called sodium ethanoate, $CH_3COO^-Na^+$.

The carboxylic acids are weak acids. The majority of their molecules are undissociated in water.

For example:

$$CH_3COOH(aq) \rightleftharpoons CH_3COO^-(aq) + H^+(aq)$$
ethanoic acid   ethanoate ion

The position of this equilibrium lies well over to the left-hand side. The dissociation constant, K_a, of ethanoic acid at 25 °C is 1.7×10^{-5} mol dm⁻³ (see Section 21.3).

IMPORTANT

Remember that the smaller the value of K_a, the weaker the acid.

The carboxylic acids are stronger acids than alcohols. This is explained by:

- the O—H bond in the carboxylic acid is weakened by the carbonyl group, C=O.

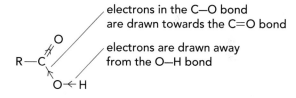

electrons in the C—O bond are drawn towards the C=O bond

electrons are drawn away from the O—H bond

- The carboxylate ion is stabilised by the delocalisation of electrons around the —COO⁻ group. This delocalisation spreads out the negative charge on the carboxylate ion, reducing its charge density. This makes it less likely to bond with an $H^+(aq)$ ion to re-form the undissociated acid molecule with its —COOH group.

negative charge is spread over the whole — COO⁻ group (the bond lengths of both carbon–oxygen bonds are equal)

As we have already seen in Section 25.3, phenol (C_6H_5OH) is a stronger acid than ethanol. However, phenol ($K_a = 1.0 \times 10^{10}$ mol dm⁻³) is a weaker acid than ethanoic acid, CH_3COOH ($K_a = 1.7 \times 10^{-5}$ mol dm⁻³) and benzoic acid, C_6H_5COOH ($K_a = 6.3 \times 10^{-5}$ mol dm⁻³).

We find that electron-withdrawing groups bonded to the carbon atom next to the —COOH group make the acid stronger.

There are two reasons for this:

- electron-withdrawing groups further weaken the O—H bond in the undissociated acid molecule

- electron-withdrawing groups extend the delocalisation of the negative charge on the —COO⁻ group of the carboxylate ion, further increasing the stabilisation of the —COO⁻ group, and making it less likely to bond with an H⁺(aq) ion.

Chlorine atoms are an example of an electron-withdrawing group. The dissociation constants (K_a) of ethanoic acid and its three chloro-substituted derivatives are shown in Table 26.2.

Acid	K_a at 25 °C / mol dm⁻³
ethanoic acid, CH_3COOH	1.7×10^{-5}
chloroethanoic acid, $CH_2ClCOOH$	1.3×10^{-3}
dichloroethanoic acid, $CHCl_2COOH$	5.0×10^{-2}
trichloroethanoic acid, CCl_3COOH	2.3×10^{-1}

Table 26.2: The larger the value of K_a, the stronger the acid.

Trichloroethanoic acid, CCl_3COOH, has three strongly electronegative Cl atoms all withdrawing electrons from the —COOH group, weakening the O—H bond more than the other acids in Table 26.2. Once the O—H bond is broken, the resulting anion is also stabilised more effectively as the negative charge is further spread out by its three electron-withdrawing Cl atoms, making it less attractive to H⁺(aq) ions. This makes the CCl_3COOH the strongest of the acids listed in Table 26.2 as it has most Cl atoms (see Figure 26.3).

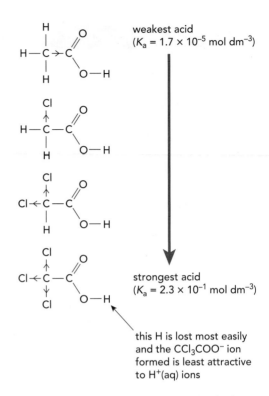

weakest acid
($K_a = 1.7 \times 10^{-5}$ mol dm⁻³)

strongest acid
($K_a = 2.3 \times 10^{-1}$ mol dm⁻³)

this H is lost most easily and the CCl_3COO^- ion formed is least attractive to H⁺(aq) ions

Figure 26.3: The trend in the acid strength of ethanoic acid and its chloro-substituted derivatives.

Ethanoic acid is the weakest acid in Table 26.2, as the methyl group is electron donating. This has the opposite effect to electron-withdrawing groups:

- it strengthens the O—H bond in the acid's —COOH group

- it donates negative charge towards the —COO⁻ group of the carboxylate ion, concentrating its negative charge, and making it more likely to accept an H⁺(aq) ion.

Question

Working in a pair or a small group, discuss Question 1 below together before writing down your answers.

1 a Place the following acids in order of strength, starting with the strongest acid.

   CH_3CH_2COOH CH_3CCl_2COOH
   $CH_3CHClCOOH$

   b Explain why ethanoic acid is a stronger acid than ethanol.

   c Predict which would be the stronger acid: methanoic acid or ethanoic acid. Explain your reasoning.

26.2 Oxidation of two carboxylic acids

You saw in Chapter 17 that primary alcohols can be oxidised by heating with acidified potassium dichromate(VI) solution to form aldehydes and then further oxidation produces carboxylic acids (see Section 18.2). The carboxylic acids prepared are not usually oxidised any further.

However, *methanoic acid* (HCOOH) is a stronger reducing agent than other carboxylic acids, so it can undergo further oxidation (Figure 26.4).

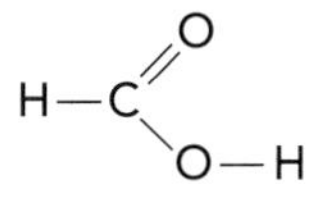

Figure 26.4: The displayed formula of methanoic acid.

This involves the oxidising agent breaking down the methanoic acid molecule, forming *carbon dioxide*. This oxidation can be carried out even by warming with mild oxidising agents, such as the Fehling's or Tollens' reagents used to distinguish between aldehydes and ketones (see Section 18.5).

In a positive test for an aldehyde, the Cu^{2+} ion in Fehling's solution is reduced to the Cu^+ ion, which precipitates out as red copper(I) oxide. When methanoic acid is oxidised by Fehling's solution, the same positive test result is obtained. With Tollens' reagent, the silver ion present, Ag^+, is reduced to silver metal, Ag, when it oxidises methanoic acid (also as in the positive test for an aldehyde).

The half-equation for the oxidation of methanoic acid can be written in terms of electron transfer to an oxidising agent as:

$$HCOOH \xrightarrow{oxidation} CO_2 + 2H^+(aq) + 2e^-$$

Oxidation no. of carbon: $+2$ ... $+4$

or in terms of the addition of oxygen from an oxidising agent as:

$$HCOOH + [O] \rightarrow CO_2 + H_2O$$

This oxidation of methanoic acid will also occur with stronger oxidising agents such as acidified solutions of potassium manganate(VII) (decolorising the purple solution) or potassium dichromate(VI) (turning the orange solution green).

Another common example of a carboxylic acid that can be oxidised by these stronger oxidising agents is *ethanedioic acid* (a dicarboxylic acid). Its molecular formula is $H_2C_2O_4$. Its structural formula is HOOCCOOH or $(COOH)_2$, and its displayed formula is shown in Figure 26.5.

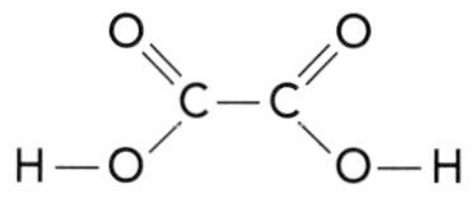

Figure 26.5: The displayed formula of ethanedioic acid.

A solution of ethanedioic acid (with sulfuric acid added) can be used in titrations to standardise a solution of potassium manganate(VII). As with methanoic acid, the oxidation results in the formation of carbon dioxide and water. The solid ethanedioic acid can be weighed out accurately to make a standard solution of known concentration. This is warmed in a conical flask and the potassium manganate(VII) solution to be standardised is run in from a burette. The end-point of the titration is identified when the addition of a drop of the purple manganate(VII) solution turns the solution pink. This happens when all the ethanedioic acid has been oxidised.

The balanced ionic equation for this redox reaction is:

$$2MnO_4^- + 6H^+ + 5H_2C_2O_4 \rightarrow 2Mn^{2+} + 10CO_2 + 8H_2O$$

The manganese(II) ions formed catalyse the reaction. This is an example of autocatalysis, in which one of the products of the reaction acts as a catalyst for that reaction.

Question

2   a   Carboxylic acids can be prepared by refluxing a primary alcohol with a strong oxidising agent.

Why is methanoic acid never prepared by refluxing methanol with acidified potassium dichromate(VI) solution?

b   Look back at the two half-equations for the oxidation of methanoic acid.

Write two similar equations representing the oxidation of ethanedioic acid.

c   i   In a titration between ethanedioic acid and potassium manganate(VII) solutions, ethanedioic acid is heated in its conical flask before adding the potassium manganate(VII) solution from the burette. Suggest why.

ii In an experiment to standardise a solution of potassium manganate(VII), 25.0 cm³ of a standard solution of 0.0500 mol dm⁻³ ethanedioic acid was fully oxidised by a titre of 8.65 cm³ of potassium manganate(VII) solution.

Calculate the concentration of the potassium manganate(VII) solution.

REFLECTION

This activity helps you to reflect on your understanding of redox reactions, half-equations and titration calculations.

Discuss with a partner whether or not you both feel that you have a good understanding of redox reactions, half-equations and titration calculations. Are you confident in all three areas or not? Think about the skills and thought processes you need to master these areas. This will help you identify where any problems lie.

If necessary, look back to Chapters 1, 7 and 24 to revise redox reactions, half-equations and titration calculations. How will you use the skills and thought processes you discussed with your partner when revising these chapters?

26.3 Acyl chlorides
Preparing acyl chlorides

An **acyl chloride** is similar in structure to a carboxylic acid but the hydroxyl group, —OH, has been replaced by a Cl atom. The displayed formula of ethanoyl chloride is shown in Figure 26.6.

KEY WORD

acyl chloride: reactive organic compounds, characterised by the functional group, —COCl.

The structural formula of ethanoyl chloride is written as CH_3COCl.

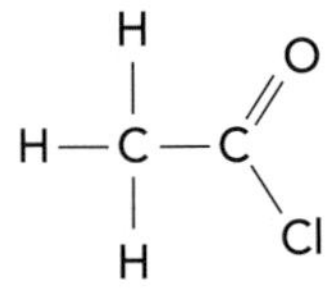

ethanoyl chloride

Figure 26.6: Ethanoyl chloride is the acyl chloride derived from ethanoic acid.

We can prepare acyl chlorides from their corresponding carboxylic acid using solid phosphorus(V) chloride, liquid phosphorus(III) chloride or liquid sulfur dichloride oxide ($SOCl_2$).

With phosphorus(V) chloride

$$CH_3COOH + PCl_5 \rightarrow CH_3COCl + POCl_3 + HCl$$

No special conditions are required for this reaction.

With phosphorus(III) chloride

$$3CH_3COOH + PCl_3 \rightarrow 3CH_3COCl + H_3PO_3$$

Heat is required for this reaction to take place.

With sulfur dichloride oxide

$$CH_3COOH + SOCl_2 \rightarrow CH_3COCl + SO_2 + HCl$$

No special conditions are required for this reaction.

You can observe steamy white fumes when hydrogen chloride gas given off. The third reaction, with $SOCl_2$, is the one reaction to produce the acyl chloride as the *only* liquid product, as both SO_2 and HCl are gases.

Question

3 Write a balanced equation, using structural formulae for the organic compounds, and state any conditions necessary, to show the formation of:

a propanoyl chloride from a suitable carboxylic acid and $SOCl_2$

b methanoyl chloride from a suitable carboxylic acid and PCl_3

c butanoyl chloride from a suitable carboxylic acid and PCl_5.

Check your answers to Question 3 against those of another learner, making sure all your equations are balanced, before looking at the answers provided.

Reactions of acyl chlorides

Many useful compounds can be synthesised from carboxylic acids. However, the synthetic reactions can be difficult to carry out because carboxylic acids are relatively unreactive. One way round this is to first convert the carboxylic acid into an acyl chloride. Acyl chlorides are *much* more reactive than carboxylic acids.

As we saw in Section 18.2, an acyl chloride is similar in structure to a carboxylic acid, with the —OH group replaced by a Cl atom. So the —COOH functional group becomes the —COCl group. The structural formula of acyl chlorides can be written as ROCl, where R is an alkyl or aryl group. For example, propanoyl chloride can be written as CH_3CH_2COCl.

The structural formulae of benzoic acid and its derivative benzoyl chloride are shown in Figure 26.7.

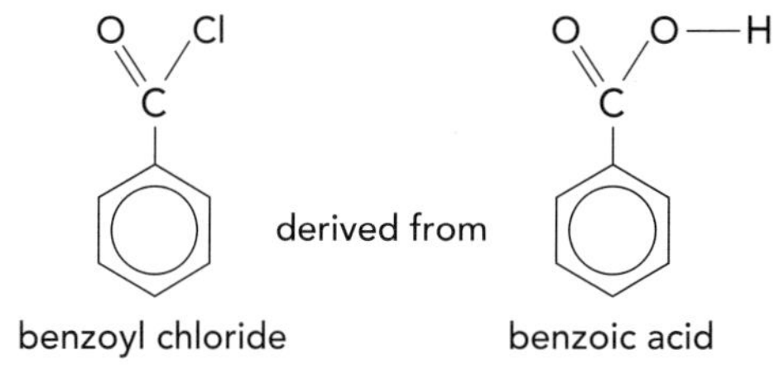

benzoyl chloride   derived from   benzoic acid

Figure 26.7: Benzoyl chloride is the acyl chloride derived from benzoic acid.

Acyl chlorides are reactive compounds. The carbonyl carbon has electrons drawn away from it by the Cl atom as well as by its O atom as both are strongly electronegative atoms. This gives the carbonyl carbon a relatively large partial positive charge and makes it particularly open to attack from nucleophiles. Remember that nucleophiles can donate a lone pair of electrons to an electron-deficient carbon atom in the mechanism of a reaction.

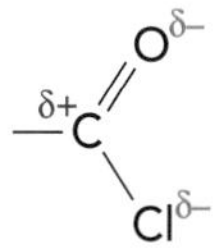

The acyl chlorides are reactive liquids. When they react with nucleophiles the C—Cl bond breaks and white fumes of hydrogen chloride, HCl, are given off.

Note that HZ contains either an oxygen or nitrogen atom with a lone pair of electrons that can be donated. HZ can therefore act as a nucleophile.

Also note that in the reactions with ammonia and amines, the HCl gas formed reacts quickly with the ammonia / amines to form salts. Ammonia will form $NH_4^+Cl^-$, primary amines form $RNH_3^+Cl^-$ and secondary amines form $R_2NH_2^+Cl^-$. This means that you see far less of the white HCl fumes given off than with water, alcohols or phenols.

Reaction with water

Figure 26.8 shows the *mechanism of hydrolysis*, showing the initial attack by a water molecule, acting as a nucleophile, followed by the elimination of a molecule of hydrogen chloride.

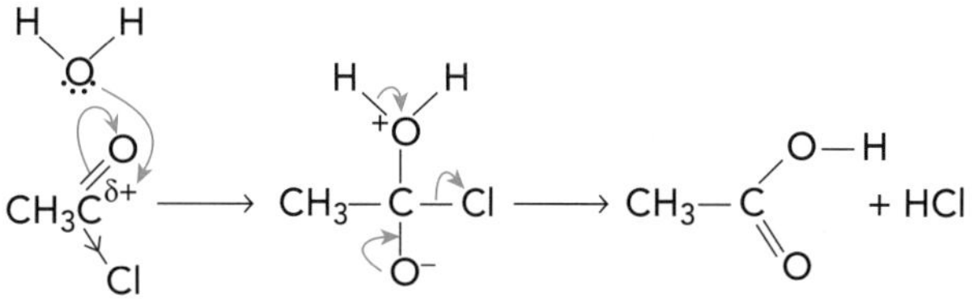

Figure 26.8: The condensation (addition–elimination) mechanism of hydrolysis of ethanoyl chloride.

The hydrolysis can be classified as a condensation reaction, as there is an initial *addition* reaction of water across the C=O bond, followed by *elimination* of a small molecule, in this case HCl.

This reaction is far more vigorous than the hydrolysis of chloroalkanes (see Section 16.2). The hydrolysis of chloroalkanes needs a strong alkali, such as aqueous sodium hydroxide, to be refluxed with the chloroalkane to hydrolyse it. The nucleophile needed to hydrolyse a chloroalkane is the negatively charged hydroxide ion, OH^-.

However, a neutral water molecule is sufficient to hydrolyse an acyl chloride quickly at room temperature. This difference is due to the carbon bonded to the chlorine atom in a chloroalkane not being as strongly δ+ as the carbon atom in an acyl chloride. Remember that in an acyl chloride, the carbon bonded to the chlorine atom is also attached to an oxygen atom. So the carbonyl carbon has two strongly electronegative atoms pulling electrons away from it. Therefore, the attack by the nucleophile is much more rapid.

Aryl chlorides or chloroarenes, such as chlorobenzene, C_6H_5Cl, will *not* undergo hydrolysis. The carbon atom bonded directly to the chlorine atom is part of the delocalised π bonding system of the benzene ring. A lone pair of electrons from the Cl atom tends to overlap with the delocalised p electrons in the benzene ring. This causes the C—Cl bond to have some double bond character, making it stronger and more difficult to break, so hydrolysis does not occur.

> **IMPORTANT**
>
> The ease of hydrolysis, starting with the compounds most readily broken down, is:
>
> acyl chloride > chloroalkane > aryl chloride or chloroarene

Question

4 a In its reaction with a nucleophile, explain why an acyl chloride reacts faster than an alcohol.

b Name the products of the hydrolysis of propanoyl chloride.

c i Place the following compounds in order of ease of hydrolysis, starting with the most reactive.

   C_6H_5Cl CH_3CH_2COCl $CH_3CH_2CH_2Cl$

   ii Explain your answer to part **i**.

   iii If a reaction occurs with water, what will you see in part **i**?

Reaction with alcohols and with phenol

When acyl chlorides react with alcohols and phenol they form esters (and HCl). The reactions happen more quickly than the reactions of alcohols or phenol with carboxylic acids. The acyl chloride reactions also go to completion and do not form an equilibrium mixture like the reactions with carboxylic acids. Therefore acyl chlorides are useful in the synthesis of esters in the chemical industry.

Ethanoyl chloride will react vigorously with ethanol to form an ester:

ethanoyl chloride   ethanol   ethyl ethanoate

> **PRACTICAL ACTIVITY 26.1**
>
> ### Hydrolysis of acyl chlorides
>
> Water is a suitable nucleophile to attack an acyl chloride molecule.
>
> A lone pair of electrons on the oxygen atom in a water molecule initiates the attack on the δ+ carbonyl carbon atom. The reaction produces a carboxylic acid and hydrogen chloride gas. It is an example of a hydrolysis reaction, i.e. the breakdown of a compound by water.
>
> For example:
>
> $CH_3CH_2COCl + H_2O \rightarrow CH_3CH_2COOH + HCl$
> propanoyl chloride   propanoic acid
>
> The acyl chloride can be added to water using a dropping pipette. The reaction is immediate and white fumes of HCl are observed rising from the liquid.

With phenol, the reaction with an acyl chloride proceeds if warmed. There is no reaction between phenol and carboxylic acids, so acyl chlorides must be used if you want to make phenyl esters. The reaction takes place in the presence of a base. The initial reaction between phenol and the base creates the phenoxide ion, $C_6H_5O^-$. The negatively charged phenoxide ion acts as the nucleophile to attack the carbonyl carbon in the acyl chloride:

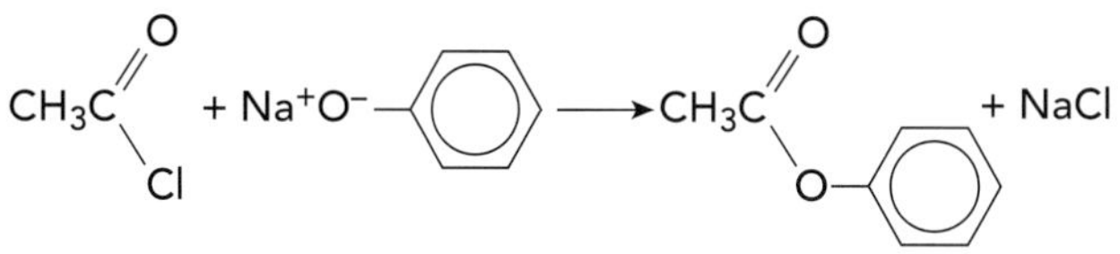

ethanoyl chloride   sodium phenoxide   phenyl ethanoate

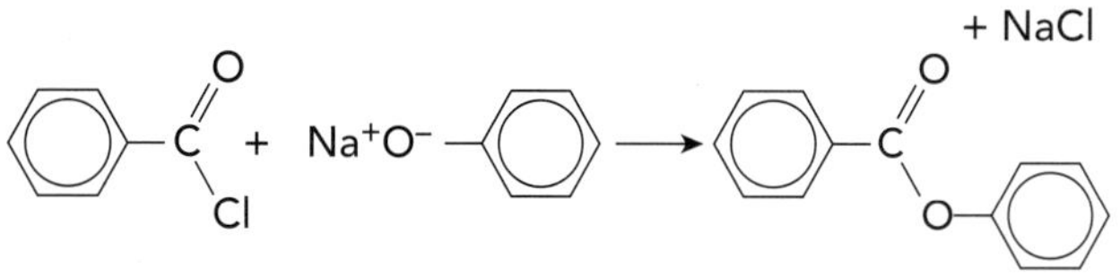

benzoyl chloride   sodium phenoxide   phenyl benzoate

Reaction with ammonia and amines

Ammonia (NH_3) acts as the nucleophile in the usual nucleophilic addition–elimination reaction of acyl chlorides. The concentrated ammonia is added at room temperature and the reaction is vigorous:

$$CH_3COCl + NH_3 \rightarrow CH_3CONH_2 + HCl$$
ethanamide

followed by:

$$HCl + NH_3 \rightarrow NH_4^+Cl^-$$

The organic product is an amide ($R—CONH_2$), in which the Cl atom in the acyl chloride is replaced by an $—NH_2$ group. The mechanism of the reaction with ammonia is shown in Figure 26.9:

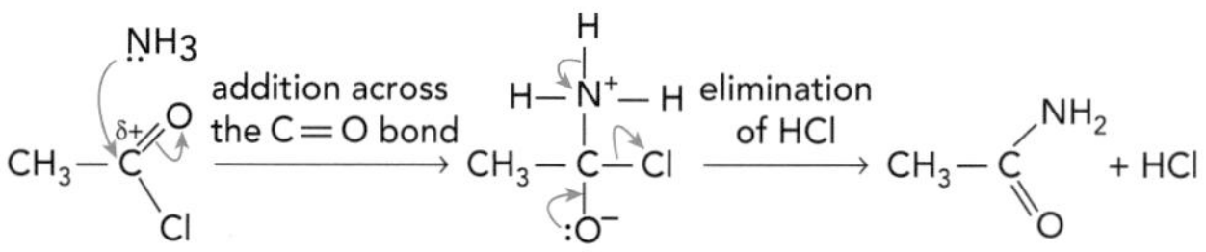

Figure 26.9: Mechanism of the nucleophilic addition–elimination of an acyl chloride with ammonia.

Primary amines ($R—NH_2$) can also act as nucleophiles as they contain nitrogen atoms with a lone pair of electrons. This lone pair of electrons is available to attack the carbonyl carbon atom in acyl chlorides.

The reaction of an acyl chloride with an amine is vigorous and the organic product is a substituted amide.

For example, with a primary amine such as methylamine:

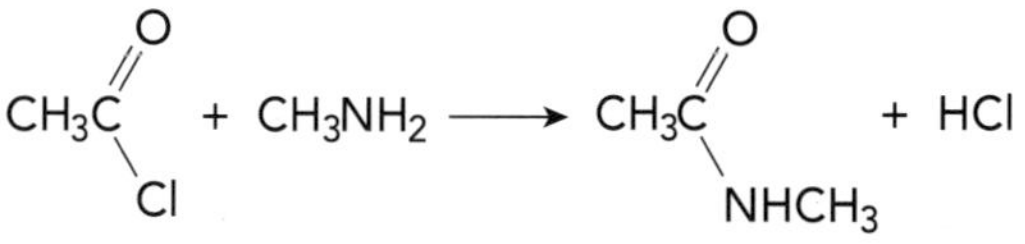

N-methylethanamide

The *mechanism* of the nucleophilic condensation (addition–elimination) reactions of acyl chlorides with amines follows the same steps as the hydrolysis with water in Figure 26.8 earlier in this section, and the reaction with ammonia above (Figure 26.9). You can imagine the primary amine as an ammonia molecule with one of its H atoms replaced by an alkyl group.

Look at Figure 26.10.

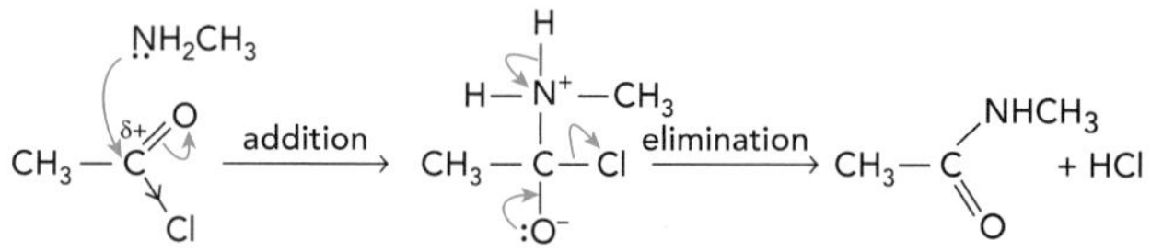

Figure 26.10: The nucleophilic condensation (addition–elimination) mechanism of ethanoyl chloride reacting with a primary amine.

With secondary amines (R^1R^2NH), such as dimethylamine, the reaction is similar:

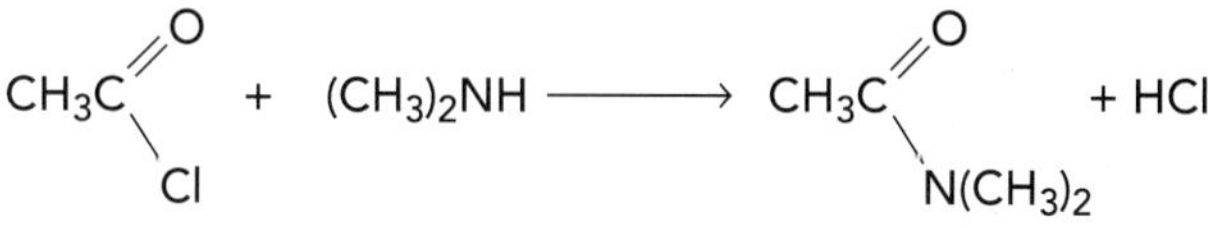

In both the reactions with amines shown above, most of the HCl is not given off as white fumes. As with ammonia, most of the HCl undergoes an acid–base reaction with unreacted amine to form a white organic ammonium salt. With methylamine, we get $CH_3NH_3^+Cl^-$, and with dimethylamine $(CH_3)_2NH_2^+Cl^-$ is formed.

For example:

$$CH_3NH_2 + HCl \rightarrow CH_3NH_3^+Cl^-$$
base   acid   salt

Question

5 a Using an acyl chloride as a starting compound in each case, name the reactants you would use to make:

  i   ethyl ethanoate

  ii methyl butanoate

  iii phenyl benzoate.

b Copy and complete the following equation:

$$CH_3CH_2COCl + CH_3CH_2CH_2NH_2 \rightarrow$$

_____ + _____

REFLECTION

1 Working with a partner, discuss the mechanism of nucleophilic addition–elimination in the reaction between ethanoyl chloride and dimethylamine. Then try showing the mechanism using curly arrows.

2 Now discuss which nuceophile you would expect to be most effective: ammonia, a primary amine or a secondary amine. Think about the inductive effect of alkyl groups.

3 Talk together about how you go about drawing mechanisms and how they help to make sense of organic reactions.

4 Discuss if there are any parts of Chapter 26 that you need to:

  • read through again to make sure you really understand

  • seek more guidance on, even after going over it again.

Use the checklist in the Summary to help you reflect.

SUMMARY

Carboxylic acids are weak acids. Their strength is increased if the carbon atom next to the —COOH group has electron-withdrawing atoms, such as chlorine, bonded to it.
Acyl chlorides (RCOCl) are made by reacting carboxylic acids with PCl_5, PCl_3 or $SOCl_2$.
Acyl chlorides react with amines to give substituted amides. Acyl chlorides are more reactive than their corresponding carboxylic acids.
Acyl chlorides are reactive liquids. They are easily hydrolysed by water, forming a carboxylic acid while giving off white fumes of hydrogen chloride.
Acyl chlorides also react with alcohols and phenols to give esters.
The ease of hydrolysis of chloro compounds is largely determined by the size of the partial positive charge on the carbon in the C—Cl bond and its strength. So acyl chlorides are more reactive with water than alkyl chlorides (halogenoalkanes), which are more reactive the hydrolysis-resistant aryl chlorides (halogenoarenes).

EXAM-STYLE QUESTIONS

1   Acyl chlorides and carboxylic acids can both be used to prepare esters.

   a **i** Give the reagents and conditions required to make ethyl ethanoate directly from a carboxylic acid. **[3]**

       ii Write an equation to show the formation of ethyl ethanoate in part **a i**. **[1]**

   b **i** Give the reagents and conditions required to make phenyl benzoate from an acyl chloride. **[3]**

       ii Write an equation to show the formation of phenyl benzoate in part **b i**. **[1]**

       iii Describe what you see happen in this reaction. **[1]**

   c Describe two advantages that acyl chlorides have over carboxylic acids in the preparation of esters in industry. **[2]**

[Total: 11]

2   **a** Draw the displayed formula of butanoyl chloride. **[1]**

   b **i** Give the name and formula of a reagent that can be used to prepare butanoyl chloride from butanoic acid. **[2]**

       ii Write a balanced equation for the reaction in part **b i**. **[1]**

       iii Butanoic acid is a weaker acid than 2-chlorobutanoic acid. Explain why. **[2]**

       iv Draw the skeletal formula of 2-chlorobutanoic acid. **[1]**

       v Name a chloro-substituted butanoic acid that is a stronger acid than 2-chlorobutanoic acid. **[1]**

       vi Explain the relative ease of hydrolysis for the compounds chlorobenzene, butanoyl chloride, and 1-chlorobutane. **[4]**

[Total: 12]

SELF-EVALUATION

After studying this chapter, complete a table like this:

I can	See section...	Needs more work	Almost there	Ready to move on
explain the relative acidity of carboxylic acids and of chlorine-substituted ethanoic acids	26.1			
describe how some carboxylic acids, such as methanoic acid and ethanedioic acid, can be further oxidised	26.2			
describe the reactions of carboxylic acids in the preparation of acyl chlorides	26.3			
describe the hydrolysis of acyl chlorides	26.3			
describe the reactions of acyl chlorides with alcohols, phenols, ammonia and primary or secondary amines	26.3			
describe the condensation (addition–elimination) mechanism for the reactions of acyl chlorides	26.3			
explain the relative ease of hydrolysis of acyl chlorides, alkyl chlorides and halogenoarenes (aryl chlorides).	26.3			

> Chapter 27
Organic nitrogen compounds

LEARNING INTENTIONS

In this chapter you will learn how to:

- describe the formation of:

    - alkyl amines (by the reaction of ammonia with halogenoalkanes or the reduction of amides with $LiAlH_4$ or the reduction of nitriles with $LiAlH_4$ or H_2 / Ni)

    - phenylamine (by the reduction of nitrobenzene with tin / concentrated HCl, followed by NaOH(aq))

- describe and explain the basicity of amines, and the relative basicities of ammonia, ethylamine and phenylamine

CONTINUED

- describe the reaction of phenylamine:

  - with aqueous bromine

  - with nitric(III) acid to give the diazonium salt and phenol, followed by the coupling of benzenediazonium chloride and phenol to make a dye

- identify the azo group and describe the formation of other azo dyes

- describe the formation of amides from the reaction between R^1NH_2 and R^2COCl, and the hydrolysis of amides by aqueous alkali or acid

- explain why amides are weaker bases than amines

- describe the acid / base properties of amino acids and the formation of zwitterions, including the isoelectric point

- describe the formation of amide (peptide bonds) between amino acids to give di- and tripeptides

- describe simply the process of electrophoresis and the effect of pH, using peptides and amino acids as examples.

BEFORE YOU START

Working in your group, answer these questions:

1 Which one of the following is the best definition of a Brønsted–Lowry base?

    A proton acceptor   **B** H^+ donor   **C** lone pair acceptor   **D** electrophile

2 Which one of the following best describes the inductive effect of an alkyl group?

    A proton accepting   **B** proton donating   **C** electron accepting   **D** electron donating

3 Discuss with a partner what effect:

    a the ethyl group ($-C_2H_5$) has on the benzene ring in ethylbenzene

    b the nitro group ($-NO_2$) has on the benzene ring in nitrobenzene.

4 Which one of the following reactions can be classified as 'hydrolysis'?

    A $C_2H_5Br + NaOH \rightarrow C_2H_5OH + NaBr$

    B $C_2H_5OH \xrightarrow{\text{conc. } H_2SO_4} C_2H_4 + H_2O$

    C $C_2H_4 + Br_2 \rightarrow C_2H_4Br_2$

    D $CH_3COCH_3 + 2[H] \rightarrow CH_3CHOHCH_3$

COLOURFUL CHEMISTRY

In 1856 William Henry Perkin was only 18 years old when he made a remarkable discovery – by accident! William was studying chemistry and was given the task of making quinine, a drug used to treat malaria. After one of his experiments with coal tar, his beaker was filled with a black sticky mess. Another failure, he assumed. However, when he tried to wash the beaker with alcohol, he found that the gooey mess dissolved to form a beautiful, rich purple-coloured solution.

Instead of disposing of the solution, he was so thrilled with the colour that he decided to dye a piece of silk with it. When the silk was dry he found that the dye did not wash out in water, and the colour did not fade in sunlight. Perkin had made the first synthetic dye.

After that he formed a company to market the new dye and continued his research to make more new colours of dye.

Figure 27.1 shows what the main structure in the dye was later found to be.

Now we have thousands of synthetic dyes to choose from and the vast majority contain nitrogen atoms, like the original synthetic dye. You can read more

about 'azo dyes' and how we can prepare them in Section 27.2. Figure 27.2 shows a few examples of azo dyes.

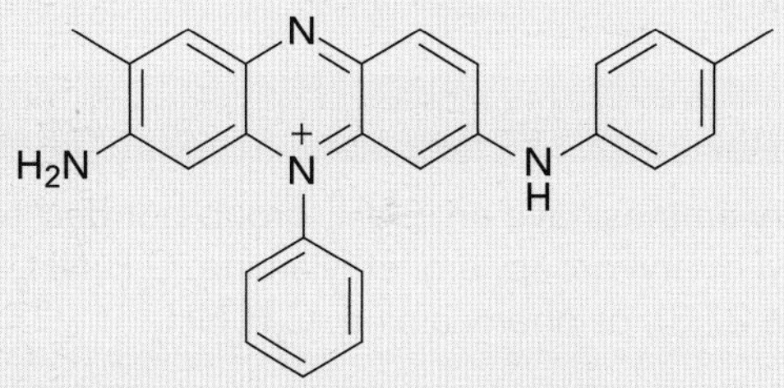

Figure 27.1: The skeletal formula of the main compound in William Perkin's original synthetic dye (mauve).

Questions for discussion

Working with another learner or group of learners:

- Discuss the role of chance in scientific discoveries.

- Carry out some research to find two more examples where chemical discoveries were made by chance.

- Look at the azo dyes in Figure 27.2. Which group of atoms in the azo dyes, besides the benzene rings, are found in all the structures?

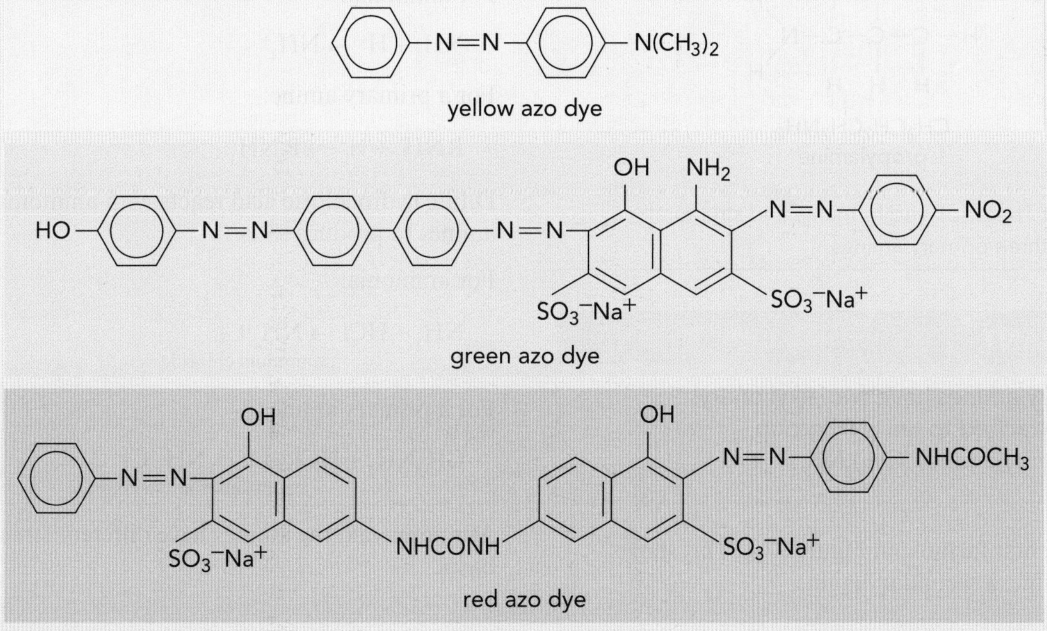

yellow azo dye

green azo dye

red azo dye

Figure 27.2: The structures of differently coloured azo dyes.

27.1 Amines

Classes of amines

There are three classes of amine: primary, secondary and tertiary.

> **IMPORTANT**
>
> *Primary amines* have an $—NH_2$ group bonded to an alkyl or aryl group, e.g. ethylamine, $C_2H_5NH_2$ (Figure 27.3), or phenylamine, $C_6H_5NH_2$.

Note that some primary amines do not have the $—NH_2$ group at the end of an alkyl chain. We indicate the position of the $—NH_2$ group on the hydrocarbon chain by numbering from the nearest end of the molecule. In these cases we refer to the $—NH_2$ group as the 'amino' group, e.g. $CH_3CH_2CH(NH_2)CH_2CH_2CH_3$ is called 3-aminohexane.

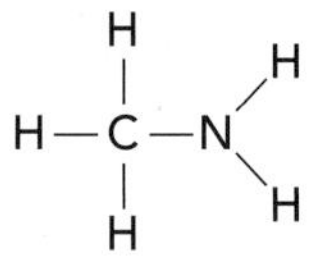

CH_3NH_2
methylamine

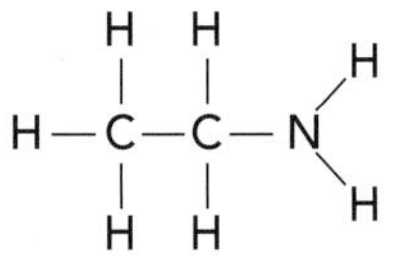

$CH_3CH_2NH_2$
ethylamine

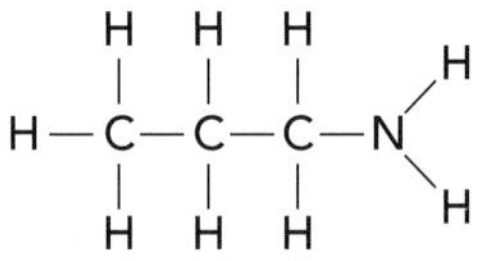

$CH_3CH_2CH_2NH_2$
propylamine

Figure 27.3: The displayed formulae and structural formulae of three primary amines.

> **IMPORTANT**
>
> *Secondary amines* have two alkyl or aryl groups attached to an >NH group, e.g. dimethylamine, $(CH_3)_2NH$.

Look at the first formula in Figure 27.4. This shows dimethylamine, a secondary amine.

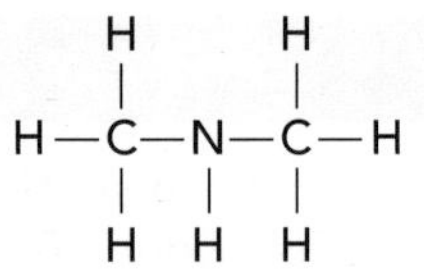

CH_3NHCH_3 or $(CH_3)_2NH$
dimethylamine
(a secondary amine)

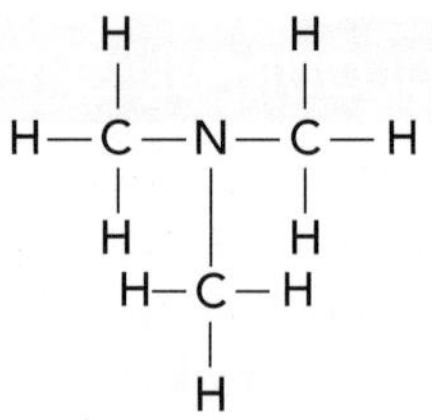

$(CH_3)_3N$
trimethylamine
(a tertiary amine)

Figure 27.4: A secondary amine and a tertiary amine.

Tertiary amines have three alkyl or aryl groups attached to the same nitrogen atom, e.g. trimethylamine, $(CH_3)_3N$ (shown in Figure 27.4). However, at this level, we will only be looking at the reactions of primary and secondary amines.

The basicity of amines

We can think of the amines as substituted ammonia (NH_3) molecules. For example, a primary amine is an ammonia molecule with one of its H atoms replaced by an alkyl or aryl group. Ammonia and the amines act as bases because of the lone pair of electrons on the nitrogen atom. Remember that a base is a proton (H^+ ion) acceptor. The nitrogen atom donates its lone pair to an H^+ ion, forming a co-ordinate (dative) bond.

For ammonia:

$$NH_3 + H^+ \rightarrow NH_4^+$$

For a primary amine:

$$RNH_2 + H^+ \rightarrow RNH_3^+$$

Dilute hydrochloric acid reacts with ammonia and with amines to produce salts.

For ammonia:

$$NH_3 + HCl \rightarrow NH_4^+Cl^-$$
ammonium chloride

For a primary amine:

$$CH_3NH_2 + HCl \rightarrow CH_3NH_3^+Cl^-$$
methylammonium chloride

Ammonia and the amines have different strengths as bases.

The strength of ammonia and amines as bases depends on the availability of the lone pair of electrons on their N atom to bond with an H^+ ion.

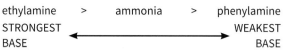

ethylamine > ammonia > phenylamine

STRONGEST BASE ⟵⟶ WEAKEST BASE

Let us consider ammonia, ethylamine and phenylamine as examples. We find that the strongest base of the three is ethylamine, followed by ammonia and, finally, phenylamine.

Ethylamine is a stronger base than ammonia because the ethyl group is electron-donating: it has a positive inductive effect (see Figure 27.5). By releasing electrons to the N atom, the ethyl group makes the lone pair more readily available to bond with an H^+ ion than it is in ammonia. Ammonia just has three H atoms bonded to the N atom, and no alkyl groups.

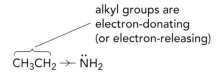

alkyl groups are electron-donating (or electron-releasing)

$CH_3CH_2 \rightarrow \ddot{N}H_2$

Figure 27.5: Ethylamine is a stronger base than ammonia.

However, ammonia is a stronger base than phenylamine because one of the p orbitals on the nitrogen atom in phenylamine overlaps with the π bonding system in the benzene ring. This causes the lone pair of the N atom in phenylamine to be delocalised into the benzene ring. This then makes the lone pair less available to form a co-ordinate (dative) bond with an H^+ ion than it is in ammonia (see Figure 27.6).

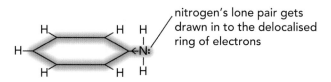

nitrogen's lone pair gets drawn in to the delocalised ring of electrons

Figure 27.6: Phenylamine is a very weak base.

Question

1 a Name the following compounds:

i $CH_3CH_2CH_2CH_2CH_2NH_2$

ii $(CH_3CH_2CH_2)_2NH$

iii $C_2H_5NH_3^+Cl^-$

b Discuss and predict whether diethylamine is a stronger or weaker base than ethylamine. Explain your reasoning.

27.2 Formation of amines

1 In Chapter 16 you learned how bromoethane undergoes nucleophilic substitution with ammonia to form a mixture of amines. In order to prepare ethylamine (while avoiding the formation of secondary and tertiary amines we use excess hot ethanolic ammonia under pressure:

$$CH_3CH_2Br + NH_3 \rightarrow CH_3CH_2NH_2 + HBr$$
ethylamine

Hydrogen bromide, HBr, which could react with the ethylamine, is removed by the excess ammonia. It forms ammonium bromide, NH_4Br. The excess ammonia also reduces the chances of bromoethane being attacked by ethylamine, as ethylamine is also a nucleophile.

However, if your aim is to prepare a secondary amine, we can start with a halogenoalkane and a primary amine and react them, again in ethanol, heated in a sealed tube, under pressure. For example:

$$CH_3CH_2NH_2 + CH_3CH_2Br \rightarrow$$
$$(CH_3CH_2)2NH + HBr$$

The secondary amine formed in this example is named diethylamine.

2 We also learned in Chapter 16 about the formation of nitriles by reacting a halogenoalkane with the CN^- ion. To carry out the reaction, a solution of potassium cyanide, KCN, in ethanol is heated under reflux with the halogenoalkane:

$$CH_3Br + CN^- \xrightarrow{heat} CH_3CN + Br^-$$
bromomethane   ethanenitrile

Note that we start with bromomethane, not bromoethane, as the cyanide group adds a carbon atom to the alkyl group.

We can then reduce (add hydrogen to) the ethanenitrile to make ethylamine.

The nitrile vapour and hydrogen gas are passed over a nickel catalyst, or $LiAlH_4$ (lithium tetrahydridoaluminate) in dry ether can be used for the reduction:

$$CH_3CN + 4[H] \rightarrow \underset{\text{ethylamine}}{CH_3CH_2NH_2}$$

3 We can also use $LiAlH_4$ in dry ether to reduce amides to amines.

So the carbonyl group, $>C=O$, in the ethanamide will be reduced to ethylamine:

$$\underset{\text{ethanamide}}{CH_3CONH_2} + 4[H] \rightarrow \underset{\text{ethylamine}}{CH_3CH_2NH_2} + H_2O$$

Preparing phenylamine

Phenylamine is made by reducing nitrobenzene. This reduction is carried out by heating nitrobenzene under reflux with tin (Sn) and concentrated hydrochloric acid. The organic product in the acidic reaction mixture is the ion $C_6H_5N^+H_3$, which is then converted to phenylamine, $C_6H_5NH_2$, by adding sodium hydroxide solution. The reduction can be summarised as:

$$\text{⬡—NO}_2 + 6[H] \longrightarrow \text{⬡—NH}_2 + 2H_2O$$

The phenylamine is separated from the reaction mixture by steam distillation (Figure 27.7).

Figure 27.7: Steam generated in the conical flask is passed into the reaction mixture in the pear-shaped flask and phenylamine is distilled off and collected.

Question

2 **a** **i** Give the reagents and conditions needed to make butylamine from butanenitrile.

   ii Name the bromoalkane that can be used to make the butanenitrile in part **a i**.

   iii Name two types of organic compound that can be reduced by $LiAlH_4$ to form an alkylamine.

b **i** Give the name and structural formula of the arylamine formed when 2-nitrophenol reacts with tin and concentrated hydrochloric acid.

   ii State the type of reaction 2-nitrophenol undergoes in part **b i**.

Now share your answers to Question 2 with another learner and discuss any differences before checking against the answers provided.

Reactions of phenylamine

Phenylamine with aqueous bromine

The reaction of aqueous bromine with phenylamine is similar to the reaction of aqueous bromine with phenol (see Section 25.4): a white precipitate is formed. The nitrogen in the —NH_2 group in phenylamine has a lone pair of electrons that can be delocalised into the benzene ring so that the π bonding system extends to include the C—N bond. The extra electron density in the benzene ring makes it more readily attacked by electrophiles. Remember that the 2, 4 and 6 positions around the benzene ring are activated when electron-donating groups, such as —NH_2 or —OH, are attached to the ring:

$$\text{⬡—NH}_2 + 3Br_2 \longrightarrow \text{Br⬡Br, Br} + 3HBr$$

2,4,6-tribromophenylamine

Using phenylamine to make dyes

Phenylamine is an important compound in the synthesis of dyes.

PRACTICAL ACTIVITY 27.1

Making an azo dye

The first step in making an azo dye is the reaction between phenylamine and nitric(III) acid (nitrous acid), HNO_2, to give a diazonium salt.

Nitric(III) acid is unstable, so it has to be made in the test-tube. Then the phenylamine is added. We can make the nitric(III) acid using sodium nitrate(III) (sodium nitrite), $NaNO_2$, and dilute hydrochloric acid:

$$NaNO_2 + HCl \rightarrow \underset{\text{nitric(III) acid}}{HNO_2} + NaCl$$

The first step in the synthesis of a dye is the production of benzenediazonium chloride:

$$\underset{\text{benzenediazonium chloride}}{\text{⬡}-NH_2 + HNO_2 + HCl \longrightarrow \text{⬡}-\overset{+}{N}\equiv NCl^- + 2H_2O}$$

Note that the positive charge on the diazonium ion ($C_6H_5N_2^+$) is on the nitrogen atom bonded to the benzene ring, shown with four bonds in the equation above.

In the second step, the diazonium ion reacts with an alkaline solution of phenol in a **coupling reaction**:

$$\underset{\text{an azo dye}}{\text{⬡}-\overset{+}{N}\equiv NCl^- + \text{⬡}-OH \longrightarrow \text{⬡}-N=N-\text{⬡}-OH + HCl}$$

KEY WORD

coupling reaction: the reaction between a diazonium salt and an alkaline solution of phenol (or similar compound) to make an azo dye.

Figure 27.8: The azo dye (also called a diazonium dye) forms in a coupling reaction between the diazonium ion and an alkaline solution of phenol.

Explaining the steps in making an azo dye

Step 1: The reaction between nitrous acid and phenylamine is called **diazotisation**.

$$\underset{\text{diazonium ion}}{\text{⬡}-NH_2 + HNO_2 + H^+ \longrightarrow \text{⬡}-\overset{+}{N}\equiv N + 2H_2O}$$

KEY WORD

diazotisation: the reaction between phenylamine and nitrous acid (HNO_2) to give a diazonium salt in the first step in preparing an azo dye.

The reaction mixture must be kept below 10 °C using ice. This is because the diazonium ion is unstable and will decompose easily, giving off nitrogen gas, N_2, at higher temperatures.

Step 2: In the coupling reaction, the positively charged diazonium ion acts as an electrophile. It substitutes into the benzene ring of phenol at the 4 position, directly opposite the —OH group.

$$\text{⬡}-\overset{+}{N}\equiv N + \underset{\text{phenol}}{\text{⬡}-OH} \longrightarrow$$

$$\underset{\text{the azo group}}{\text{⬡}-N=N-\text{⬡}-OH + H^+}$$

The orange dye formed is called an azo dye, or diazonium dye.

> **KEY WORD**
>
> **azo dyes:** coloured compounds formed on the addition of phenol (or another aryl compound) to a solution containing a diazonium ion.

Its delocalised π bonding system extends between the two benzene rings through the —N=N— azo group, which acts like a bridge between the two rings. This makes the azo dye, called 4-hydroxyphenylazobenzene, very stable (an important characteristic of a good dye). The azo dye forms immediately on addition of the alkaline solution of phenol to the solution containing the diazonium ion (Figure 27.8).

By using alternative aryl compounds to phenol, such as $C_6H_5N(CH_3)_2$, we can make a range of brightly coloured dyes. For example, Figure 27.9 shows a molecule of a compound used as a yellow dye.

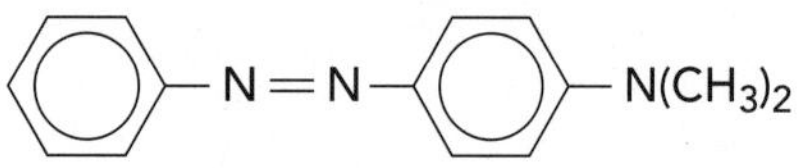

Figure 27.9: A molecule of a yellow azo dye. Instead of phenol, C_6H_5OH, the reactant used in the coupling reaction is $C_6H_5N(CH_3)_2$.

Question

3 a i Discuss which would be more readily attacked by an electrophile: benzene or phenylamine. Then write an explanation of your answer.

   ii Write a general equation to show the equation for the reaction of phenylamine with excess of an electrophile, represented as X^+.

  b i Explain why the reaction of phenylamine to make the diazonium ion is carried out below 10 °C.

   ii Write a balanced equation to show how nitric(III) acid (nitrous acid) is made for the reaction in part **b i** to take place.

   iii Show the two steps that would be used to make the yellow dye shown in Figure 27.9, starting from phenylamine.

   Discuss with another learner how you both tackled Question 3.

27.3 Amino acids

Amino acids are an important group of compounds that all contain:

- the basic amino group (—NH_2), and
- the acidic carboxylic acid group (—COOH).

This makes the amino acids amphoteric, as they can behave as both an acid and a base.

One type of amino acid has the —NH_2 group bonded to the carbon atom next to the —COOH group. These 2-aminocarboxylic acids are the 'building blocks' that make up proteins. There are about 20 of these naturally occurring amino acids.

The general structure of an amino acid (2-aminocarboxylic acid) molecule is shown in Figure 27.10.

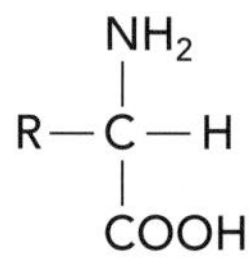

Figure 27.10: The general structure of an amino acid (a 2-aminocarboxylic acid).

The general structural formula of an amino acid (2-aminocarboxylic acid) is $RCH(NH_2)COOH$.

The R group is the part of the amino acid that can vary in different amino acids. The simplest amino acid is glycine (systematic name aminoethanoic acid) in which R is an H atom:

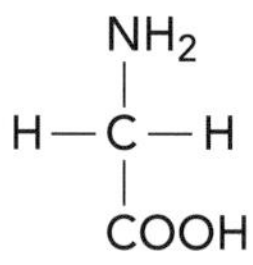

glycine (aminoethanoic acid)

Alanine (systematic name 2-aminopropanoic acid) is an amino acid in which the R group is the methyl group, —CH_3.

The R group can be:

- acidic (e.g. it contains another carboxylic acid group, —COOH group),
- basic (e.g. it contains another amine group, —NH_2 group), or
- neutral (e.g. when R is an alkyl group).

Reactions of amino acids

Amino acids will undergo most reactions of amines and carboxylic acids. However, each molecule can interact within itself due to its basic —NH$_2$ group and its acidic —COOH group:

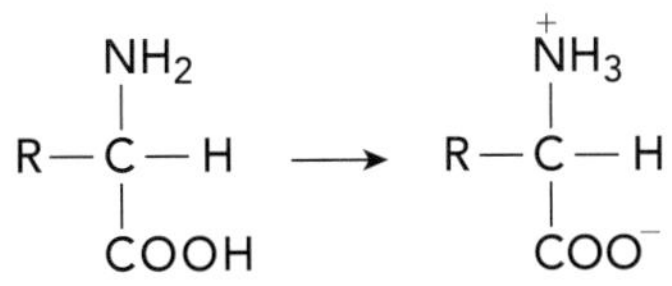

The ion is called a zwitterion (from the German 'zwei' meaning 'two') as it carries two charges: one positive (—NH$_3^+$) and one negative (—COO$^-$). The ionic nature of the zwitterions gives amino acids relatively strong intermolecular forces of attraction. They are crystalline solids that are soluble in water.

A solution of amino acids in water contains zwitterions that have both acidic and basic properties (i.e. they are amphoteric). They will resist changes in pH when small amounts of acid or alkali are added to them. Solutions that do this are called buffer solutions (see Section 21.4).

If the pH is lowered by adding acid, the —COO$^-$ part of the zwitterion will accept an H$^+$ ion, re-forming the undissociated —COOH group. This leaves a positively charged ion:

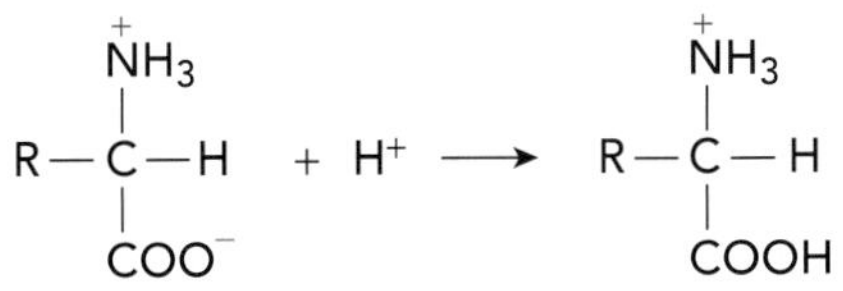

If the pH is raised by adding a base, the —NH$_3^+$ part of the zwitterion will donate an H$^+$ ion to the hydroxide ion (H$^+$ + OH$^-$ → H$_2$O), re-forming the amine —NH$_2$ group. This leaves a negatively charged ion:

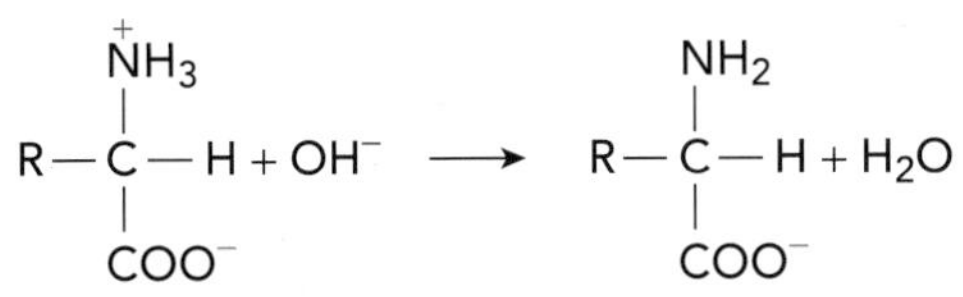

By adjusting the pH by small amounts, we can reach a point where neither the positive nor negative ions shown above dominate, so the amino acid has no charge overall. This pH is called the **isoelectric point** of an amino acid.

The isoelectric point can be found by measuring the pH value of the amino acid solution when it is not attracted to either a positive electrode or a negative electrode (see 'Electrophoresis' in Section 27.6).

Question

4 a i Which one of these general formulae represents amino acids, such as alanine and valine?

   A RCH$_2$CH(NH$_2$)COOH

   B RCH(N=NH$_2$)COOH

   C RCH(NH$_3$Cl)COOH

   D RCH(NH$_2$)COOH

   ii Explain why all amino acids are solids at 20 °C.

   b i Draw the displayed formula of the 2-aminocarboxylic acid called serine, in which the R group is HO—CH$_2$—.

   ii Draw the structure of the zwitterion of serine.

   iii Draw the structure of the ion of serine present in acidic conditions.

   iv Draw the structure of the ion of serine present in alkaline conditions.

   v Discuss with a partner what we mean by the *isoelectric point* of serine.

27.4 Peptides

Amino acid molecules can also react with each other. The acidic —COOH group in one amino acid molecule reacts with the basic —NH$_2$ group in another molecule. When two amino acids react together, the resulting molecule is called a **dipeptide**.

KEY WORDS

isoelectric point: the pH value at which there is no overall charge on a particular amino acid in its aqueous solution.

dipeptide: a compound formed from the condensation reaction between two amino acids. The —COOH group of one amino acid reacts with the —NH$_2$ group of another amino acid.

peptide link

a dipeptide

Note that the shaded area is the **amide bond** between the two amino acids. An amide bond between two amino acid molecules is also called a peptide bond or peptide link. The reaction is a condensation reaction, as a small molecule, in this case water, is eliminated when the reactant molecules join together.

You can see that the dipeptide product still has an amine group, $-NH_2$, at one end and a carboxylic acid group, $-COOH$, at the other end. Therefore the reaction can continue, to form a **tripeptide** initially, and then ever-longer chains of amino acids. The longer molecules are known as polypeptides, and then proteins as they become even longer sequences of amino acids (see Chapter 28).

KEY WORDS

amide bond: the group of atoms, made up of a carbonyl group and an amine group ($-CONH-$), that join together the amino acids in peptides and proteins.

tripeptide: a compound made by combining three amino acids.

Question

5 The R groups in the amino acids alanine and valine are $-CH_3$ and $(CH_3)_2HC-$, respectively.
  a Draw the structures of both these amino acids.
  b Give an equation to show the formation of a dipeptide made from alanine and valine.

27.5 Reactions of the amides

The amide group is represented in structural formulae by $-CONH_2$. For example, ethanamide can be shown as CH_3CONH_2.

Its displayed formula is:

ethanamide

Unlike the basic amines that you learned about at the start of this chapter, the amides are *neutral* compounds. The presence of the electron-withdrawing oxygen atom in the amide group means that the lone pair on the nitrogen atom of an amide is not available to donate to electron-deficient species, such as H^+ ions.

Preparing an amide

The acyl chlorides are more reactive compounds than the carboxylic acids they are made from (see Section 26.3) and they are used for synthesising other useful compounds, such as amides.

Ethanamide can be made by reacting ethanoyl chloride with concentrated ammonia solution:

$$CH_3COCl + NH_3 \rightarrow CH_3CONH_2 + HCl$$

A primary amine, such as ethylamine, reacts with an acyl chloride to produce a substituted amide:

$$C_3H_7COCl + C_2H_5NH_2 \rightarrow C_3H_7CONHC_2H_5 + HCl$$

Both these reactions occur at room temperature, releasing white fumes of hydrogen chloride as soon as the reactants are added together. If there is an excess of the amine, it will react with the HCl formed to make its salt. For example, in the previous reaction ethylamine will form ethylammonium chloride, $C_2H_5NH_3^+Cl^-$.

The italic letter N is used in naming substituted amides to denote which alkyl (or aryl) group or groups are bonded to the nitrogen atom. For example, in N-ethylbutanamide, $C_3H_7CONHC_2H_5$, the ethyl (C_2H_5-) group has replaced an H atom in the amide group. If the H atom on the nitrogen in this molecule is replaced by another alkyl or aryl group, two *N*s are used in the name, e.g. $C_3H_7CON(C_2H_5)_2$ is called *N,N*-diethylbutanamide.

Hydrolysis of amides

The characteristic —CONH— group in substituted amides links the two hydrocarbon sections of their molecules together. This amide link can be broken by hydrolysis with an acid or an alkali. The amide is refluxed with, for example, hydrochloric acid or sodium hydroxide solution, to hydrolyse it:

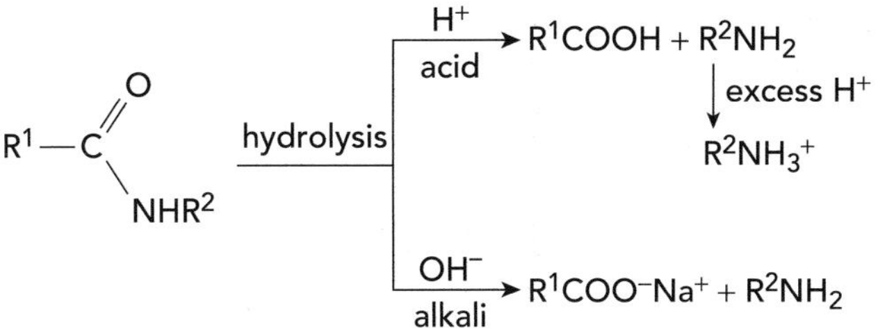

The products of hydrolysis of a substituted amide with acid are a carboxylic acid (R^1COOH) and a primary amine (R^2NH_2). The amine formed will react with excess acid in the reaction vessel to make its ammonium salt, e.g. $R^2NH_3^+Cl^-$ with excess hydrochloric acid.

With an alkali, such as aqueous sodium hydroxide, the products are the sodium salt of the carboxylic acid ($R^1COO^-Na^+$) and the primary amine (R^2NH_2).

If we reflux an unsubstituted amide ($RCONH_2$) with acid, the products are the corresponding carboxylic acid and ammonia. The ammonia in solution reacts with excess acid to make an ammonium salt. With an alkali, the products are the salt of the carboxylic acid and ammonia.

Question

6 **a** Write an equation to show the formation of the following compounds using an acid chloride:

    i propanamide

    ii *N*-ethylpropanamide.

  b Write an equation to show the hydrolysis of:

    i butanamide by refluxing with dilute hydrochloric acid

    ii *N*-ethylbutanamide by refluxing with aqueous sodium hydroxide.

Compare your answers to Question 6 with those of another learner, and discuss any differences before you check against the answers provided.

27.6 Electrophoresis

How electrophoresis works

Electrophoresis is used extensively in biochemical analysis. It can be used to separate, identify and purify proteins. We can use it with the amino acids and peptides obtained when a protein is hydrolysed.

> **KEY WORD**
>
> **electrophoresis:** the separation of ions placed in an electric field between a positive and a negative electrode.

The analytical technique of electrophoresis is based on separating ions placed in an electric field.

> **IMPORTANT**
>
> If a sample is placed between two oppositely charged electrodes:
>
> - positively charged ions will move towards the negatively charged electrode
> - negatively charged ions will move towards the positively charged electrode.

The sample is placed on absorbent paper or a gel supported on a glass plate. A buffer solution carries the ions along.

The rate at which the ions move towards the oppositely charged electrode depends, among other things, on the size and charge on the ions. Larger ions will move more slowly; highly charged ions will move more quickly.

Therefore the ions are separated as the electric field is applied. You get a series of lines or bands on the paper or gel once a locating agent is applied. Sometimes ultraviolet light is used to show the bands up. The series of bands is called an *electropherogram* (Figure 27.11).

Let us consider a simple example of how a mixture of three amino acids undergoes separation. Amino acid A could have a side-chain that is positively charged in a certain buffer solution, amino acid B could be neutral and amino acid C could be negatively charged (Figure 27.12).

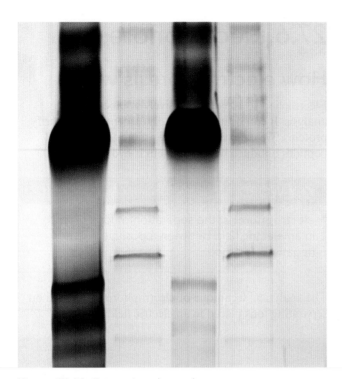

Figure 27.11: Comparing electropherograms.

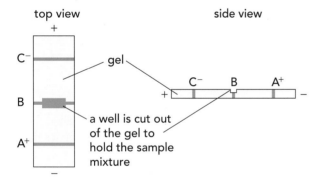

Figure 27.12: The principle of gel electrophoresis.

At a pH of 7, the amino acid species present in samples of A, B and C are shown in Figure 27.13.

The chemical structures in Figure 27.13 show why we need to control the pH with a buffer solution in electrophoresis. In Section 27.3, we saw how amino acids react in acidic and alkaline conditions to form ions. The charge on the ions depends on the pH. Therefore pH will affect the movement of ions during electrophoresis.

When separating a mixture of proteins, they are usually first treated with a chemical that makes them all negatively charged. A dye can also be added. All the proteins then migrate in the same direction towards the positive electrode, but larger proteins move more slowly.

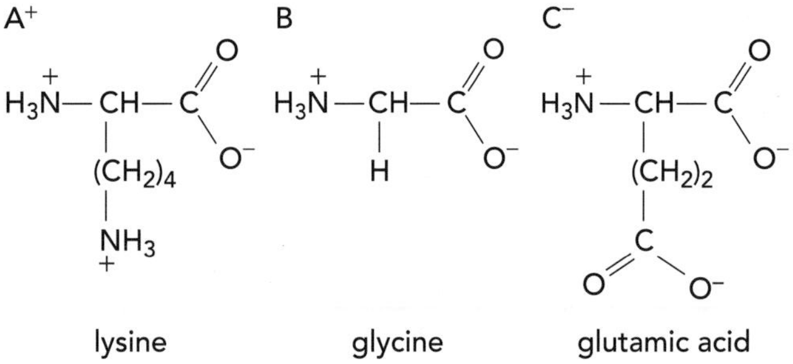

Figure 27.13: The charge on amino acids depends on the pH of the solution.

Question

7   A mixture of three amino acids is separated by gel electrophoresis.

The three amino acids are glycine, valine and phenylalanine (Figure 27.14):

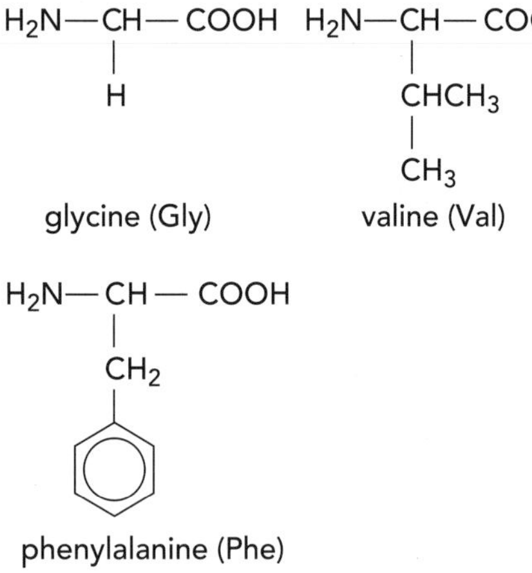

$$H_2N—CH—COOH \quad H_2N—CH—COOH$$

glycine (Gly)   valine (Val)

phenylalanine (Phe)

Figure 27.14: Three amino acids to be separated by electrophoresis.

a   The electrophoresis is carried out in a buffer solution of pH 10. Draw the ions present in these alkaline conditions.

b   i   Draw a sketch of the electropherogram you would expect (viewed from above), labelling the amino acids as Gly, Val and Phe.

ii   Explain your answer to part **b i**.

c   An amino acid at its isoelectric point is placed between the positive and negative electrodes and a voltage is applied. Describe the movement of the amino acid.

REFLECTION

1   Work as a pair to:

- explain how we can make an azo dye from phenylamine

- assess each other's understanding of the steps involved.

2   Look at the displayed formulae of the amino acids shown in this chapter. Choose three examples and show the displayed formula of a tripeptide they could form together.

Reflect on your progress in Chapter 27: decide which aspects have you found most interesting / most difficult / most enjoyable. Then discuss with your partner the reasons for your choices, and assess your overall progress.

SUMMARY

Primary amines contain the —NH_2 group.
Ethylamine is prepared either by reducing ethanenitrile, e.g. with hydrogen gas using a nickel catalyst, or by treating bromoethane with an excess of hot, ethanolic ammonia.
Phenylamine is prepared by reducing nitrobenzene using tin and concentrated hydrochloric acid, then adding NaOH (aq).
Like ammonia, amines behave as bases. Because of the lone pair of electrons on their nitrogen atom, they can readily accept protons (H^+ ions), reacting to form salts.
Ethylamine is a stronger base than ammonia because of the electron-releasing ethyl group.
Phenylamine is a weaker base than ammonia because the lone pair on the N atom of phenylamine is delocalised into the benzene ring.
Phenylamine reacts with nitric(III) acid (nitrous acid) below 10 °C, to form benzenediazonium chloride and water; this reaction is called diazotisation.
Diazonium salts react with other aryl compounds (such as phenol) to form dyes; this is known as a coupling reaction. Diazonium dyes are commercially important.
The stability of diazonium dyes arises from the extensively delocalised π bonding electron system that covers their benzene rings and the azo bridge —N≡N— between them.
Amino acids (2-aminocarboxylic acids) have the general formula $RCH(NH_2)COOH$, where R may be H, CH_3 or another organic group.
The amino group of an amino acid interacts with the acid group to form a zwitterion.
Amino acids react with both acids and bases to form salts.
The isoelectric point of an amino acid is the pH value at which there is no overall charge on that amino acid in its aqueous solution.

CONTINUED

Two amino acids react together in a condensation reaction, bonding together by an amide (peptide) bond to form a dipeptide and water. Three amino acids form a tripeptide, and repetition of this condensation reaction many times leads to the formation of polypeptides and proteins.

Amides are prepared by reacting acyl chlorides with ammonia or amines.

Amides can be hydrolysed by aqueous alkali or acid. With aqueous alkali the products are the salt of a carboxylic acid and a primary amine. With acid hydrolysis the products are a carboxylic acid and a primary amine.

Electrophoresis uses an electric field to separate ions in a mixture. It is used widely in analysing the sequence of amino acids in proteins.

EXAM-STYLE QUESTIONS

1   Ethylamine and phenylamine are two organic nitrogen compounds. Both compounds are basic.

   a   Draw the displayed formula of each compound, including lone pairs.   **[2]**

   b   Write a balanced symbol equation for the reaction between one of these compounds and an acid to form a salt.   **[2]**

   c   Identify the structural feature of each compound that accounts for the basicity.   **[1]**

                   [Total: 5]

2   Phenylamine can be made using nitrobenzene as starting material.

   a   Name this type of reaction.   **[1]**

   b   Give the reagents that are used to bring about this change.   **[2]**

   c   Write a balanced symbol equation for this reaction. The conventions [O] or [H] may be used if necessary.   **[2]**

                   [Total: 5]

3   Phenylamine reacts with nitric(III) acid (nitrous acid) to form a diazonium salt.

   a   State which two reagents you would use to prepare the nitric(III) acid.   **[2]**

   b   State the essential conditions for the reaction.   **[1]**

   c   Give the displayed formula of the diazonium salt.   **[3]**

   d   Write a balanced symbol equation for this reaction.   **[2]**

                   [Total: 8]

4   The diazonium salt formed in Question 3 reacts with phenol to form a useful substance, X.

   a   Give the essential conditions for the reaction.   **[2]**

   b   Give the displayed formula of X.   **[2]**

   c   Write a balanced symbol equation for this change.   **[1]**

   d   Suggest a possible use for X.   **[1]**

                   [Total: 6]

CONTINUED

5 The formulae of two amino acids, glycine (Gly) and alanine (Ala), are given here: glycine is H_2NCH_2COOH and alanine is $H_2NCH(CH_3)COOH$.

   a **i** Give the systematic names of both amino acids. **[2]**

        ii Draw their skeletal formulae. **[2]**

   b Alanine can exist as two stereoisomers.

        i Draw these two stereoisomers, showing how they differ in their spatial arrangements. **[2]**

        ii Explain why glycine does not have stereoisomers. **[2]**

                          [Total: 8]

6 Both glycine and alanine are amphoteric.

   a Explain the term *amphoteric*. **[1]**

   b Explain the structural features of both glycine and alanine that enable them to be amphoteric. **[4]**

   c **i** Amino acids form zwitterions. Using glycine as an example, explain the term *zwitterion*. **[1]**

        ii State and explain two physical properties of amino acids that can be explained by the existence of zwitterions. **[4]**

   d Draw the two different dipeptides that can be formed when alanine and glycine react together through a condensation reaction. **[4]**

                          [Total: 14]

7 The structure of a certain tripeptide is shown here:

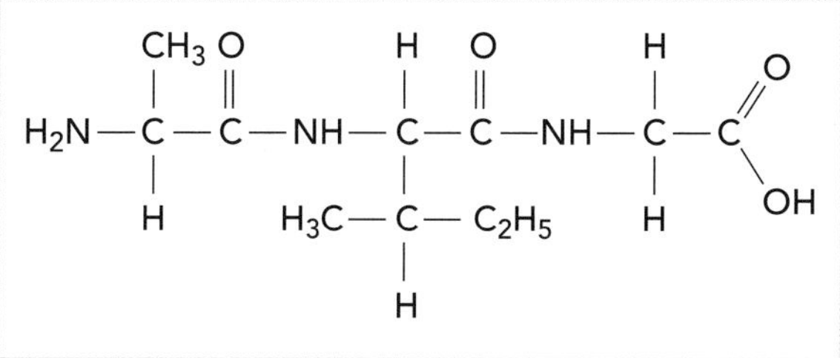

   a **i** Draw the displayed formulae of the three amino acids that make up the tripeptide. **[3]**

        ii Identify which of these amino acids has two chiral carbon atoms. **[1]**

   b This tripeptide can be split up into the three amino acids by refluxing with aqueous hydrochloric acid.

        i Which bond is broken in this reaction? **[1]**

        ii This reaction can be described as hydrolysis. Suggest why, using a diagram. **[3]**

        iii Name the method commonly used to separate mixtures of amino acids. **[1]**

        iv Explain how the method to separate amino acids works. **[5]**

                          [Total: 14]

SELF-EVALUATION

After studying this chapter, complete a table like this:

I can	See section...	Needs more work	Almost there	Ready to move on
describe the formation of alkyl amines and phenylamine	27.2			
describe and explain the basicity of amines, and the relative basicities of ammonia, ethylamine and phenylamine	27.1			
describe the reaction of phenylamine with aqueous bromine, and with nitric(III) acid to give the diazonium salt and water, followed by the coupling of benzenediazonium chloride and phenol to make a dye	27.2			
identify the azo group and describe the formation of other azo dyes	27.2			
describe the formation of amides from the reaction between R^1NH_2 and R^2COCl, and the hydrolysis of amides by aqueous alkali or acid	27.5			
explain why amides are weaker bases than amines	27.5			
describe the acid / base properties of amino acids and the formation of zwitterions, including the isoelectric point	27.3			
describe the formation of amide (peptide bonds) between amino acids to give di- and tripeptides	27.4			
describe simply the process of electrophoresis and the effect of pH, using peptides and amino acids as examples.	27.6			

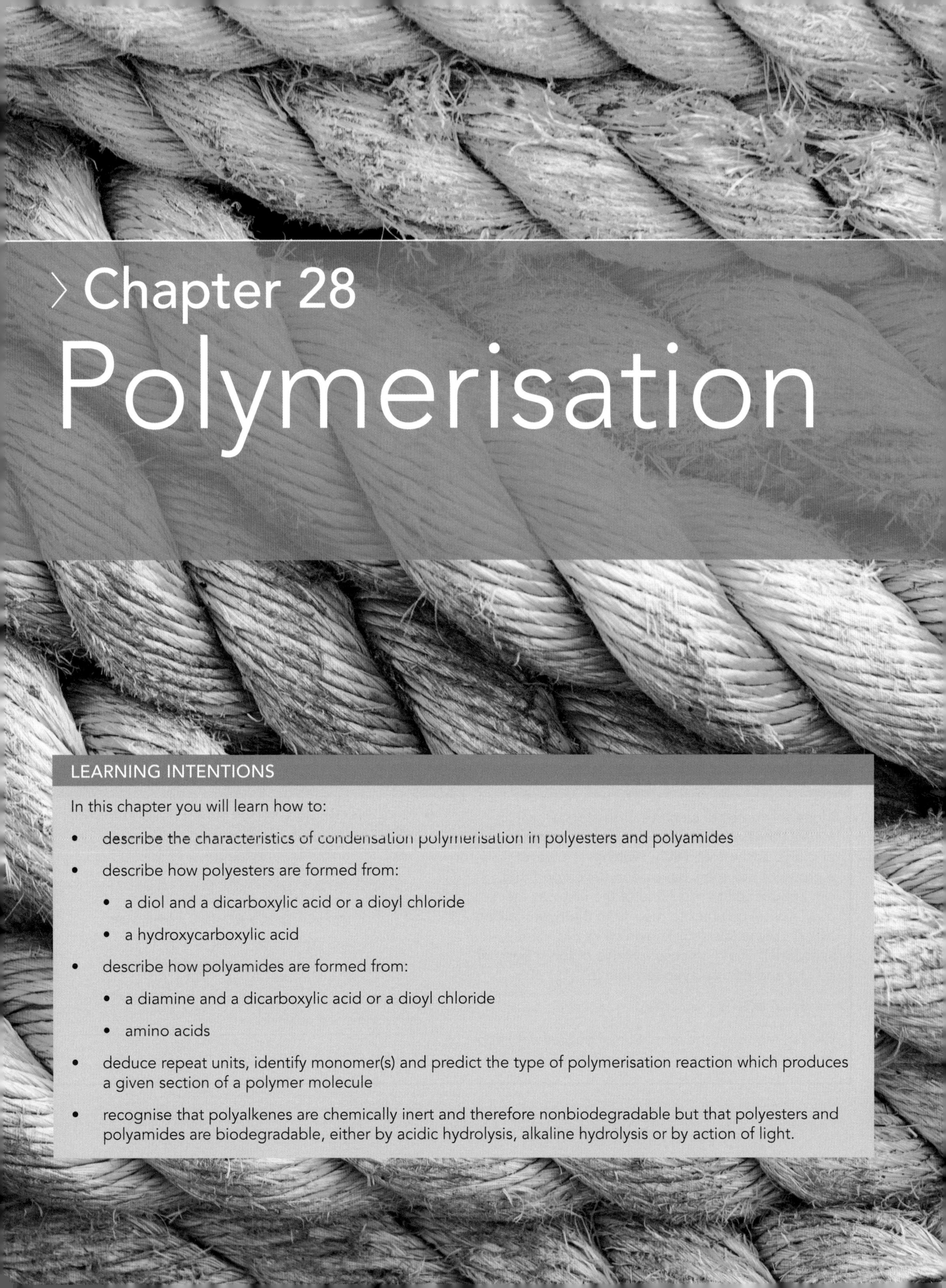

> # Chapter 28
> # Polymerisation

LEARNING INTENTIONS

In this chapter you will learn how to:

- describe the characteristics of condensation polymerisation in polyesters and polyamides

- describe how polyesters are formed from:

  - a diol and a dicarboxylic acid or a dioyl chloride

  - a hydroxycarboxylic acid

- describe how polyamides are formed from:

  - a diamine and a dicarboxylic acid or a dioyl chloride

  - amino acids

- deduce repeat units, identify monomer(s) and predict the type of polymerisation reaction which produces a given section of a polymer molecule

- recognise that polyalkenes are chemically inert and therefore nonbiodegradable but that polyesters and polyamides are biodegradable, either by acidic hydrolysis, alkaline hydrolysis or by action of light.

BEFORE YOU START

Working in your group, answer these questions:

1   Give the structural formula of:

   a   but-2-ene

   b   methanoic acid

   c   2-aminopropanoic acid

   d   phenylamine

   e   propanoyl chloride.

2   Write an equation to represent the polymerisation of ethene, $H_2C\!=\!CH_2$.

3   Copy and complete this equation to show the polymerisation of 2–chloro-1,3-butadiene, a synthetic rubber. Use square brackets around the polymer's repeat unit:

   $$nH_2C\!=\!CClCH\!=\!CH_2 \rightarrow \ \ldots\ldots\ldots\ldots\ldots$$

   where n is a very large number.

4   Here is a section of an addition polymer:

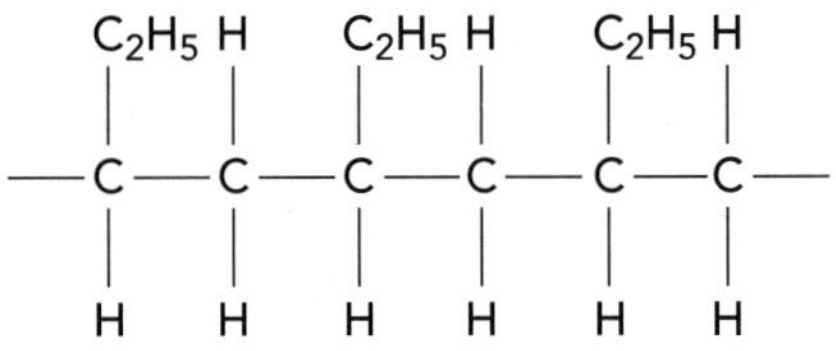

   Draw the displayed formula of its monomer.

CONDUCTING POLYMERS

Most polymers are electrical insulators, which makes them very useful for making the casings of plugs, sockets and light switches. However, a group of polymers have been developed that can conduct electricity. One of the first was the poly(alkyne) polymer formed from the hydrocarbon called ethyne (also still known by its old name, acetylene). The molecular formula of this monomer is C_2H_2 and its displayed formula is:

   $H\!-\!C\!\equiv\!C\!-\!H$

We can represent the formation of poly(ethyne) from its ethyne monomers as shown in Figure 28.1.

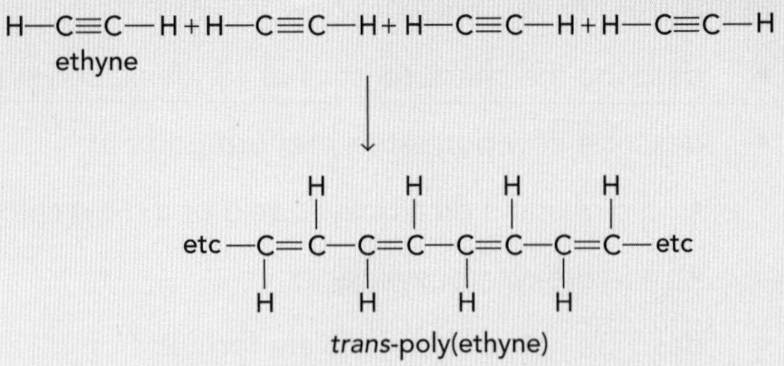

Figure 28.1: The polymerisation of ethyne (acetylene) to form a conducting polymer.

CONTINUED

As drawn in Figure 28.1, the poly(ethyne) is in the *trans*-configuration rather than the *cis*-form of the polymer. Figure 28.2 below shows how to represent the skeletal formulae of both forms. A polymer chain with a mixture of *cis*- and *trans*-sections can be made by varying the reaction conditions.

In Figure 28.1 you can see the alternate double and single carbon–carbon bonds in poly(ethyne). This can conduct electricity because its π bonding spreads continuously down the whole length of each polymer chain. The overlapping p orbitals on neighbouring carbon atoms result in long bands of delocalised electrons, above and below the plane of the atoms. These delocalised electrons are free to move along the length of the polymer chains (see Sections 5.4 and 25.1).

Lots of research has been carried out to produce other conducting polymers with extended π bonding systems. Poly(ethyne) and some other examples are shown by their skeletal formulae in Figure 28.2.

Conducting polymers usually have other substances, such as iodine, added to improve their electrical conductivity. This is called *doping*. They have a number of advantages over the metal conductors that they can potentially replace. They do not corrode, are much less dense, and can be shaped more easily. For example, they can be made into thin sheets to make flat panels that light up. They can also now be used in LED lighting. They are also ideal in situations where saving weight is important.

trans-poly(ethyne)   cis-poly(ethyne)

poly(1,6-heptadiyne)   poly(phenylene)   poly(pyrrole)

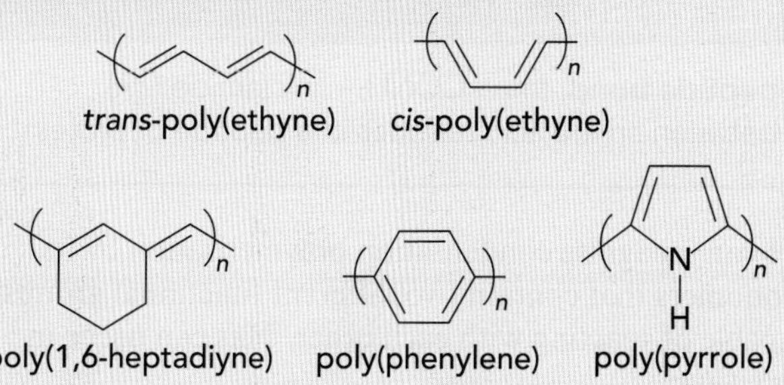

Figure 28.2: Some examples of conducting polymers: note the alternate double and single carbon–carbon bonds.

Questions for discussion

Working with another learner or group of learners:

- Suggest how poly(ethyne) can conduct electricity, using your knowledge of π bonding.

- Sketch a diagram to show how you visualise the extended π bonding system in poly(ethyne).

- Suggest some uses of poly(ethyne) where saving weight is important.

28.1 Condensation polymerisation

In Chapter 27 we saw how amino acids can react together to form peptides. The reaction is called a *condensation reaction*. We can think of it as an addition reaction (in which reactant molecules bond to each other), followed by an elimination reaction (in which a small molecule is released).

For example, the following equation shows how three amino acid molecules can react to make a tripeptide:

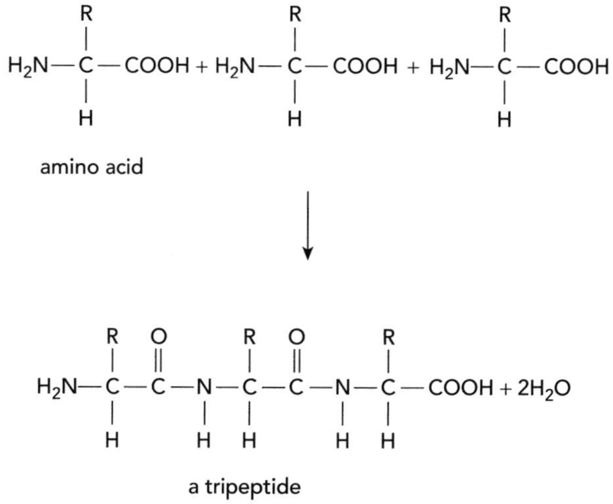

A large protein molecule, formed by condensation polymerisation, can contain thousands of amino acid monomers. As each amino acid monomer joins the chain, an amide bond (or **peptide bond**) forms, and an H_2O molecule is also produced (see Section 27.4).

> **KEY WORD**
>
> **peptide bond:** the —CONH— link (amide link) between amino acid residues in a peptide or protein.

We can recognise condensation polymerisation by its monomers that contain two different functional groups capable of reacting with each other. This can occur in two ways:

- the two different functional groups are found within the same molecule, as in amino acids. Each amino acid monomer molecule has a basic —NH_2 functional group and an acidic —COOH functional group

- the two different functional groups are found in two different molecules. For example, nylon 6,6 is made from two different monomers: one monomer has two —NH_2 functional groups, and the other monomer has two —COOH functional groups.

Condensation polymerisation also leads to the formation of small molecules, such as H_2O or HCl.

Question

Discuss the following questions with another learner:

1 a Which of these monomers form addition polymers (see Section 15.5) and which form condensation polymers?

    i $NH_2CH(CH_3)COOH$

    ii $H_2C{=}CHC_6H_5$

    iii $H_2C{=}CHCOOH$

    iv NH_2CH_2COOH

    v $CH_3CH(OH)COOH$

  b Explain how you made your decisions in part **a**.

  c i Write an equation to show the polymerisation reaction between propene molecules, $H_2C{=}CHCH_3$.

    ii What type of polymerisation reaction is shown in part **c i**?

    iii What is the repeat unit of poly(propene)?

  d What type of polymerisation reaction results in the formation of poly(peptides) and protein polymers?

REFLECTION

At the start of this chapter so far, what have you found difficult? What did you find easy to do?

Reflect on any areas you would like to improve. Are you unsure about any of the work you have studied on addition and condensation polymerisation? If so, read through the work again, and look back to the polymer work in Chapters 15 and 27 then ask for help if anything is still not clear.

28.2 Synthetic polyamides

Nylons

Chemists have used condensation polymerisation to make synthetic **polyamides** since the 1930s. Nylon is a polyamide. Nylon can be made from a variety of monomers, but all nylons are made in reactions between the amine group (—NH_2) and a carboxylic acid (—COOH) or the more reactive acyl chloride group (—COCl).

> **KEY WORD**
>
> **polyamides:** polymers made in the condensation polymerisation reaction between a diamine and a dicarboxylic acid (or a dioyl chloride) or between amino acids.

For example, 1,6-diaminohexane reacts with hexanedioic acid to make nylon 6,6:

amide link or peptide link

Figure 28.4: The monomers, 1,4-diaminobenzene and benzene-1,4-dicarboxylic acid, or benzene-1,4-dioyl chloride, that react together to make the polymer Kevlar®.

Figure 28.3: Climbers rely on nylon's elasticity and high tensile strength to minimise the effects of a fall.

The numbers used in nylon 6,6 refer to the number of carbon atoms in each monomer unit.

Hexanedioyl dichloride, $ClOC(CH_2)_4COCl$, can be used as a more reactive, but more expensive, monomer than hexanedioic acid.

Nylon's low density, its strength and its elasticity make it a very useful fibre in the clothing industry. These properties also make it ideal for climbing ropes (Figure 28.3).

During the manufacturing process, the nylon is forced out of nozzles and pulled into long fibres. This is called *cold drawing*. It lines up the nylon polymer chains along the length of the fibre. Strong hydrogen bonds form between neighbouring chains, accounting for nylon's high tensile strength and elasticity.

Kevlar®

Kevlar is a polyamide containing benzene rings. It is very strong, but flexible. It is also resistant to fire and abrasion. It has these properties because of its structure.

The monomers that make Kevlar are an aryl diamine and an aryl dicarboxylic acid or dioyl chloride (Figure 28.4).

PRACTICAL ACTIVITY 28.1

Making nylon

Place a shallow layer of aqueous 1,6-diaminohexane in a very small beaker. Carefully add a solution of decanedioyl dichloride which will float on top of the aqueous layer of the diamine. Using a pair of tweezers slowly draw out a long, thin thread of nylon 6,10 from the boundary between the two immiscible layers where the nylon polymer is forming.

The formula and structure of Kevlar are shown in Figure 28.5. The long, linear polymer chains of Kevlar can line up next to each other in a regular pattern. This results in extensive hydrogen bonding between the polymer chains of Kevlar.

The exceptional properties of Kevlar have also led to its use in making bullet-proof vests, ropes, fire-protective clothing (as used by Formula 1 racing drivers) and modern 'leathers' worn by motorcycle riders. The polymer is also used to reinforce other materials, such as the rubber in tyres.

Instead of using diamino and dicarboxylic acid monomers, it is also possible to make synthetic polymers from monomers that contain both amino and carboxylic acid groups with the same monomer. These monomers will react together in a similar way to the condensation polymerisation seen in nylons and Kevlar to form polyamides.

Question

2   Different types of nylon are identified by the number of carbon atoms in each of its monomers, with the diamine quoted first, followed by the dicarboxylic acid.

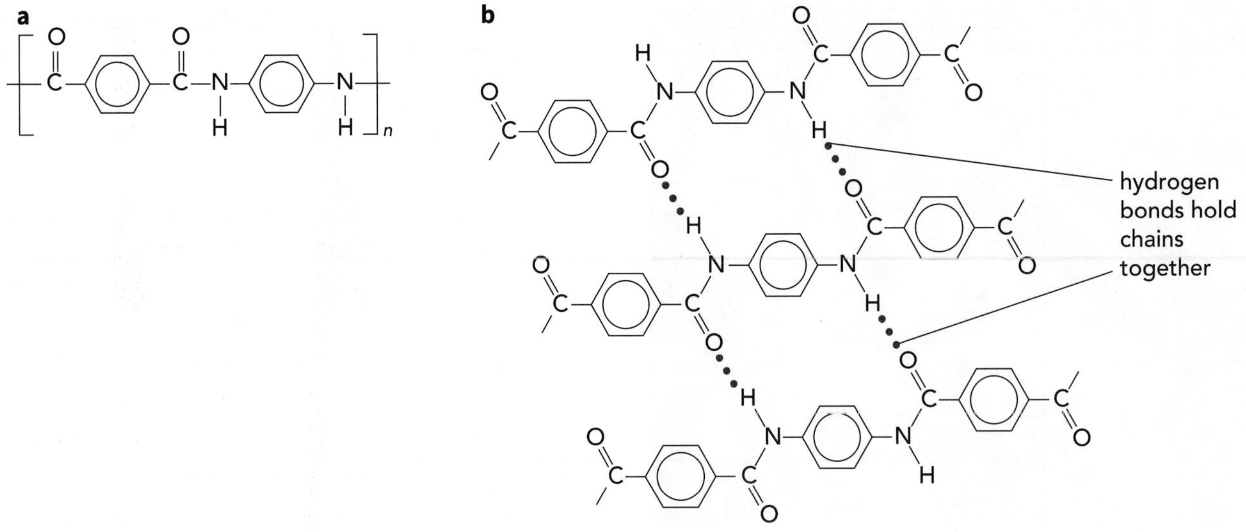

Figure 28.5: a The formula showing the repeat unit of Kevlar. **b** The hydrogen bonding between chains of the polyamide (shown by three red dots). The latest tennis rackets contain Kevlar, where its low density and strength are important. The wings of fighter jets can also be made of Kevlar.

a Draw the skeletal formula of each monomer used to make nylon 6,10.

b Use the skeletal formulae in part **a** to draw an equation showing the condensation polymerisation to make nylon 6,10 from a diamine and a dicarboxylic acid.

c **i** Draw the skeletal formula of an alternative monomer to the dicarboxylic acid drawn in part **a** to make nylon 6,10.

   ii What would be the other product of the polymerisation reaction using the alternative monomer?

d **i** Draw the displayed formula of Kevlar using its repeat unit in square brackets and *n* to represent a very large number.

   ii Explain in terms of structure and intermolecular forces why Kevlar is such a strong material.

REFLECTION

Make a table with two columns and place the parts of Question 2 in either the 'Questions that I found easy' or 'Questions that I struggled to answer' columns.

Compare your table with others in the group; help each other with any issues, and identify any problems that you need further support with.

28.3 Biochemical polyamides

Proteins are made from amino acids

Proteins have their monomers bonded to each other via amide bonds (or peptide bonds). This means that polypeptides and proteins are types of polyamide.

The amino acids found in proteins are called α-amino acids (Figure 28.6). The names of the amino acids found in proteins can be written in a shorthand form containing three letters. For example, Ala is alanine, Try is tryptophan and Gln is glutamine.

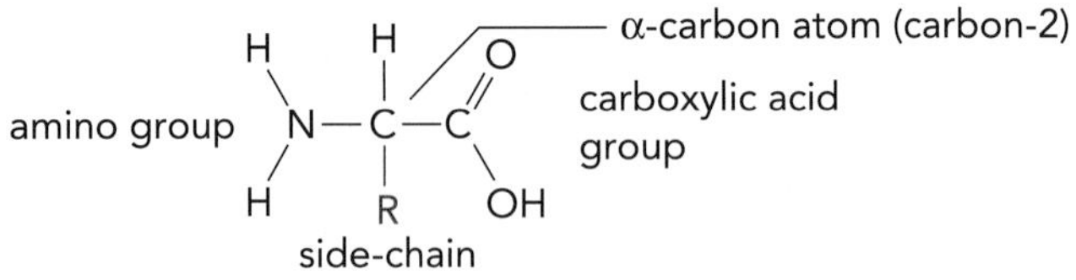

Figure 28.6: The generalised structure of an amino acid, highlighting the key features.

Type of side-chain	Example	Structure
non-polar	alanine (Ala)	$NH_2-\overset{\overset{\displaystyle H}{\mid}}{\underset{\underset{\displaystyle CH_3}{\mid}}{C}}-COOH$
	valine (Val)	$NH_2-\overset{\overset{\displaystyle H}{\mid}}{\underset{\underset{\displaystyle CH}{\mid}}{C}}-COOH$ $CH_3\ CH_3$
polar	serine (Ser)	$NH_2-\overset{\overset{\displaystyle H}{\mid}}{\underset{\underset{\displaystyle CH_2OH}{\mid}}{C}}-COOH$
electrically charged (acidic or basic)	aspartic acid (Asp)	$NH_2-\overset{\overset{\displaystyle H}{\mid}}{\underset{\underset{\displaystyle CH_2COOH}{\mid}}{C}}-COOH$
	lysine (Lys)	$NH_2-\overset{\overset{\displaystyle H}{\mid}}{\underset{\underset{\displaystyle (CH_2)_4NH_2}{\mid}}{C}}-COOH$

Table 28.1: Examples of the three different classes of side-chains (in red) in the amino acids found in proteins.

The 20 different amino acids that cells use to build proteins are distinguished by their side-chains (R groups). The side-chains can be classified as non-polar, polar or electrically charged (acidic or basic). Table 28.1 shows some examples.

Proteins are condensation polymers

In Section 27.3 you learned that the $-NH_2$ group of one amino acid can react with the $-COOH$ of another amino acid to form a dipeptide by a condensation reaction. The links between individual units of the polymer are called amide bonds (or peptide bonds). Additional amino acids can then react to form a tripeptide, a tetrapeptide, and so on. Eventually a polypeptide, containing many peptide bonds, is formed.

A polypeptide chain may contain 50 to 2000 amino acids. An amino acid unit within a polypeptide chain is called an **amino acid residue**. We draw the amino acid sequence in a polypeptide starting from the end that has a free $-NH_2$ group (the N-terminal end).

> **KEY WORD**
>
> **amino acid residue:** the individual units of the amino acids that make up a polypeptide or protein.

$$NH_2-\boxed{}-CONH-...-\boxed{}-CONH-\boxed{}-COOH$$

Proteins may contain one or more polypeptide chains. Each protein has its own, unique function because each protein has its own, unique 3D shape.

The primary structure of a polypeptide or protein is the order in which the amino acids are linked together. The primary structure of one of the polypeptide chains of insulin is shown in Figure 28.7.

The structure of a protein:

- is written with the amino acids numbered from the N-terminal end

- determines the way that the protein can fold to form its unique shape

- is held together by covalent bonds. These bonds are found within amino acid residues, and between the residues as amide (or peptide) bonds.

Question

3 a Name and give the formulae of the two functional groups present in all amino acids.

b Name an example of an amino acid with a non-polar side-chain.

c Draw a diagram of two molecules of serine to show the formation of hydrogen bonds between the $-OH$ groups of the side-chain (see Table 28.1).

d Which one of the following shows the structural formula of the amide (or peptide) bond that links amino acid monomers together in a polypeptide or a protein?

A $-CONH-$

B $-CONH_2-$

C $-COONH-$

D $-COONH_2-$

e State what is meant by the term *amino acid residue*.

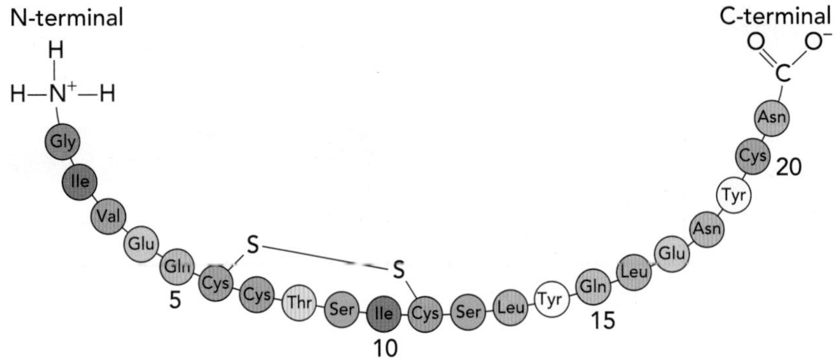

Figure 28.7: The primary sequence of the insulin A chain, a short polypeptide of 21 amino acids. Notice the —S—S— link (disulfide bridge) between two amino acid residues. This helps maintain the shape of the polypeptide.

Polyesters

Polyesters are another type of condensation polymer. As you learned in Chapter 17, esters are made by reacting carboxylic acids with alcohols:

carboxylic acid + alcohol → ester + water

> **KEY WORD**
>
> **polyester:** polymer whose monomers are bonded to each other via the ester link, COO.

Therefore, *poly*esters can be made by reacting dicarboxylic acids with diols, e.g. propanedioic acid and ethane-1,2-diol. The most common polyester fibre is Terylene®.

Terylene is made from benzene-1,4-dicarboxylic acid and ethane-1,2-diol. The conditions required are a catalyst such as antimony(III) oxide and heat:

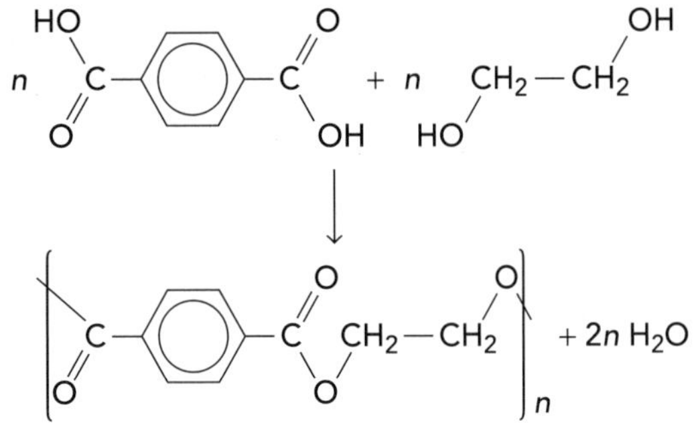

Poly(lactic acid), PLA, is another polyester. However, PLA is made using just one monomer, lactic acid. Its systematic name is 2-hydroxypropanoic acid. The monomer contains the carboxylic acid and alcohol (hydroxyl) groups within each molecule:

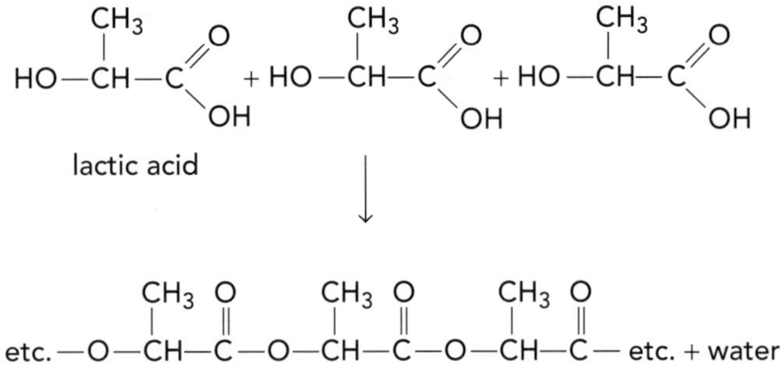

The ester group bonding each repeat unit together in the chain is shown in a structural formula as —COO—.

Question

Work as a pair on this question:

4 **a** Draw the repeat unit of the polyester, PLA (shown above).

  b Draw the repeat unit of Terylene.

> **REFLECTION**
>
> Reflect on the process you went through to determine the repeat unit. Are you confident you can go through the same process for other polymers?

28.4 Degradable polymers

The disposal of polymer waste, much of it made up of poly(alkene)s, is an ever-increasing problem worldwide. Poly(alkene)s, such as poly(ethene) and poly(propene), are chemically inert because their polymer chains are non-polar, saturated hydrocarbons, like giant alkane molecules. This makes them non-biodegradable.

However, chemists have developed degradable polymers that do break down when they are discarded. The use of degradable polymers is becoming more common as people become aware of the issues related to the disposal of poly(alkene)s as a result of their lack of reactivity (see Section 15.5, 'Disposal of poly(alkene) plastics').

Two of the developments to help solve the disposal problem are *biodegradable polymers* and *photodegradable polymers* (Figure 28.8).

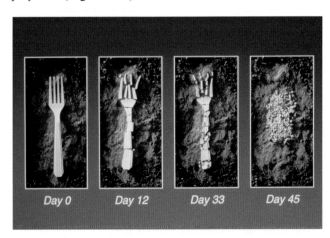

Figure 28.8: Chemists are developing plastics that can be broken down by microorganisms in soil or by light.

Biodegradable polymers

Some polymers, when buried for many years, eventually become brittle and break down into smaller pieces that can be decomposed naturally by microorganisms in soil. If the surface area of the polymer being buried could be increased, then it could degrade much more quickly. Scientists have developed polymers that contain small amounts of starch granules that the bacteria and fungi in moist soil can break down. So the polymer is broken into smaller pieces, with a larger surface area for decomposition to occur faster. Other polymers are now made from monomers derived directly from plant materials, such as PLA, which soil microorganisms can digest easily.

In polyamides, such as nylon, the amide bonds, —CO—NH—, between the repeat units can be broken down over time. This occurs by hydrolysis in the hot, acidic conditions found in land-fill waste dumps with rotting vegetation.

You can see the hydrolysis reaction of an amide in Section 27.5, in which carboxylic acids and amines are formed. In hot, acidic conditions the products of hydrolysis of a polyamide are its original diamine and dicarboxylic acid monomers or the original aminocarboxylic acid monomer. The amine (—NH$_2$) groups will react with any excess acid to make their ammonium salts.

With an excess of alkali, such as aqueous sodium hydroxide, the sodium salts of the original dicarboxylic acid monomers (plus the diamine monomers) will form. If the polyamide was made from an aminocarboxylic acid, then the sodium salt of the amino acid will form, for example, H$_2$N—R—COO$^-$Na$^+$.

In polyesters, the ester links (—COO—) are similarly broken down by acid hydrolysis, forming alcohols and carboxylic acids (see Section 17.3).

The polyester PLA, whose raw material is starch from crops such as corn, is now being used as a biodegradable alternative to oil-based polymers. The ester links can be hydrolysed in acidic conditions to break down the polymer chains when used items containing polyesters are dumped in land-fill sites. Alcohol and carboxylic acids will be the products of the acid hydrolysis of polyesters.

> **IMPORTANT**
>
> Because they will undergo hydrolysis, this makes both polyamides and polyesters biodegradable, unlike the nonbiodegradable polyalkenes.

Photodegradable polymers

Polymer chains also have been designed that incorporate carbonyl groups ($>C=O$) at intervals down their length. These carbonyl groups absorb energy from the ultraviolet region of the electromagnetic spectrum. This causes the bonds in the region of the carbonyl group to weaken and break down. As the polymer breaks into smaller fragments, the polymer will biodegrade much more quickly if it is not chemically inert. Polyamides and polyesters both contain carbonyl groups.

There is some debate as to whether photodegradable polymers are better for the environment or not. In a landfill site, the polymer waste is often buried under other rubbish and eventually soil, so there is no light available to trigger the breakdown of the polymer chains. They also make recycling polymers problematic, as they could weaken a recycled mixture of different polymers when it is put to a new use.

REFLECTION

Reflect on the problems that plastic waste is causing on our planet. Discuss the issues in small groups.

Present your findings to the other groups, and together make suggestions on how we can tackle the issues raised.

In your group again, reflect on any ways in which you could improve future presentations.

28.5 Polymer deductions

You may encounter a variety of different problems about polymers to solve, such as:

1   predict the type of polymerisation reaction for a given monomer or pair of monomers

2   deduce the repeat unit of a polymer obtained from a given monomer or pair of monomers

3   deduce the type of polymerisation reaction that produces a given section of a polymer molecule

4   identify the monomer(s) from a given section of a polymer molecule.

Predicting the type of polymerisation reaction for given monomer(s)

Addition polymers

Given a monomer that contains the $C=C$ double bond, it will undergo addition polymerisation. Many addition polymers are made using one type of monomer, e.g. poly(propene) from propene monomers. (However, co-polymers can also be produced by using more than one type of unsaturated monomer, e.g. with $H_2C=CH_2$ and $H_2C=CHCOOH$ in the reaction mixture). See Section 15.5 to remind yourself about tackling questions on addition polymers.

Condensation polymers

When identifying monomers used in condensation polymerisation, look out for the presence of two functional groups that will react with each other, giving off a small molecule in the reaction. These two functional groups can be in the same molecule, as in the case of poly(lactic acid) in Section 28.3, or at either end of two different monomers, as in nylon 6,6 in Section 28.3. The functional groups involved in condensation polymerisation are usually:

*   amines ($-NH_2$) and carboxylic acids ($-COOH$) producing a polyamide and H_2O

*   amines ($-NH_2$) and acyl chlorides ($-COCl$) producing a polyamide and HCl

*   carboxylic acids ($-COOH$) and alcohols ($-OH$) producing a polyester and H_2O

*   acyl chlorides ($-COCl$) and alcohols ($-OH$) producing a polyester and HCl.

Deducing the repeat unit of a polymer for given monomer(s)

Addition polymers

If you are given a monomer with a $C=C$ double bond, simply turn the double bond into a $C-C$ single bond and show the bonds either side of the two C atoms that would continue the chain:

monomer   repeat unit

Condensation polymers

If you are given monomers with two reactive functional groups, draw the product formed when two monomers react together. Then take off the atoms at both ends that would be lost if another two monomers were to react with those groups:

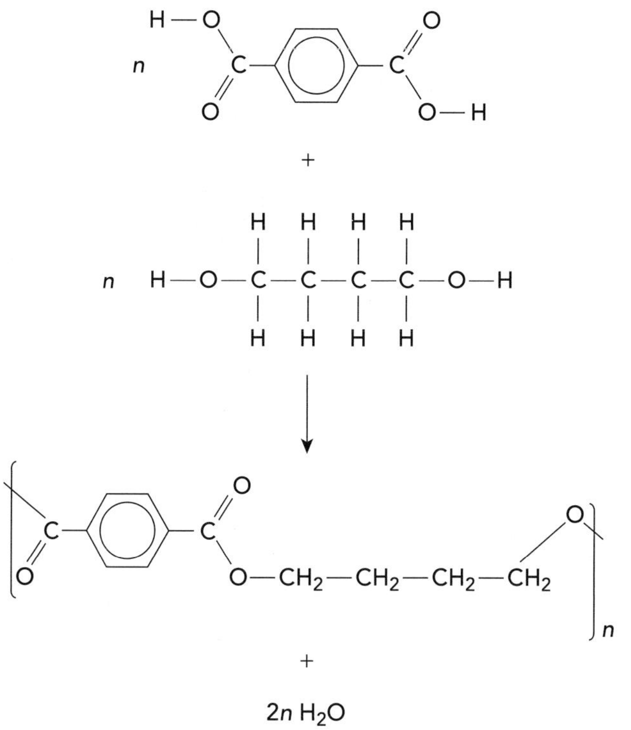

+

+

$2n\ H_2O$

Deducing the type of polymerisation reaction for a given section of a polymer chain

Addition polymers

Polymers resulting from addition polymerisation will have repeat units with no functional groups in the actual chain of carbon atoms that forms the 'backbone' of the polymer. Poly(phenylethene) is an example:

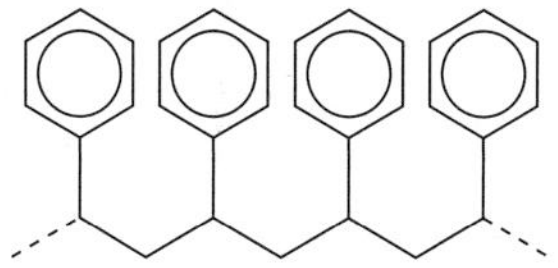

poly(phenylethene)

Note that functional groups may be present on the side-chains, such as the nitrile group, —CN. However, the 'backbone' in addition polymers usually consists of a chain of carbon atoms.

Condensation polymers

Polymers resulting from condensation polymerisation will have amide links (—CONH—) or ester links (—COO—) in the 'backbone' of the polymer chain. For example:

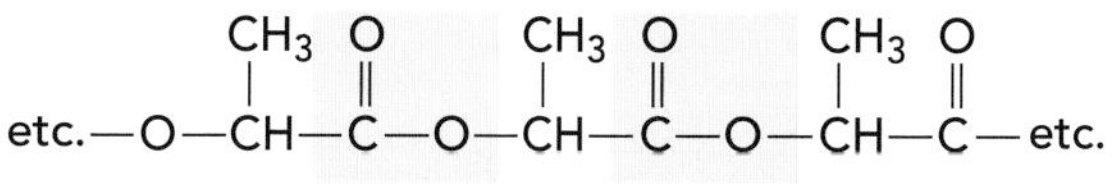

Identifying the monomer(s) present in a given section of a polymer chain

This is an extension of the approach above. Having decided whether the polymer was made in an addition or a condensation polymerisation, you can then split the polymer chain into its repeat units.

Addition polymers

With an addition polymer, you need to put the C=C double bond back into the monomer:

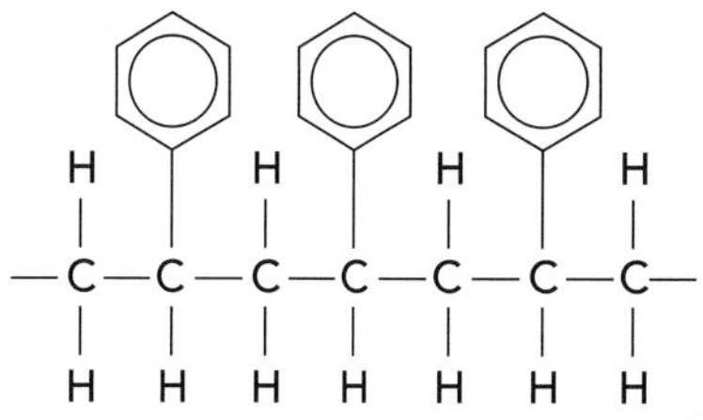

part of addition polymer

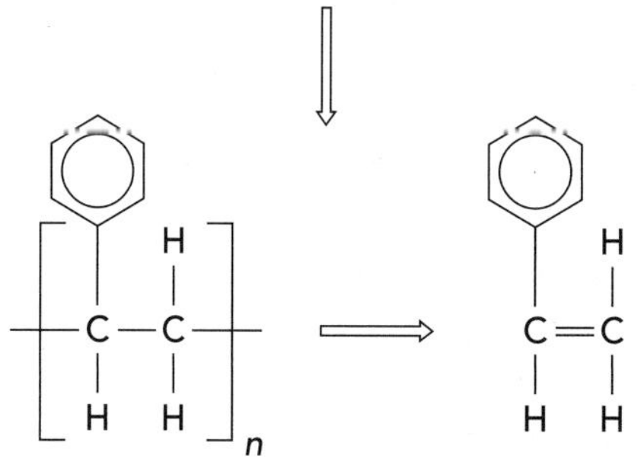

repeat unit   monomer

Condensation polymers

With condensation polymers, you need to identify the atoms from the small molecules given off in the polymerisation reaction and replace them on the reactive functional groups in the monomers.

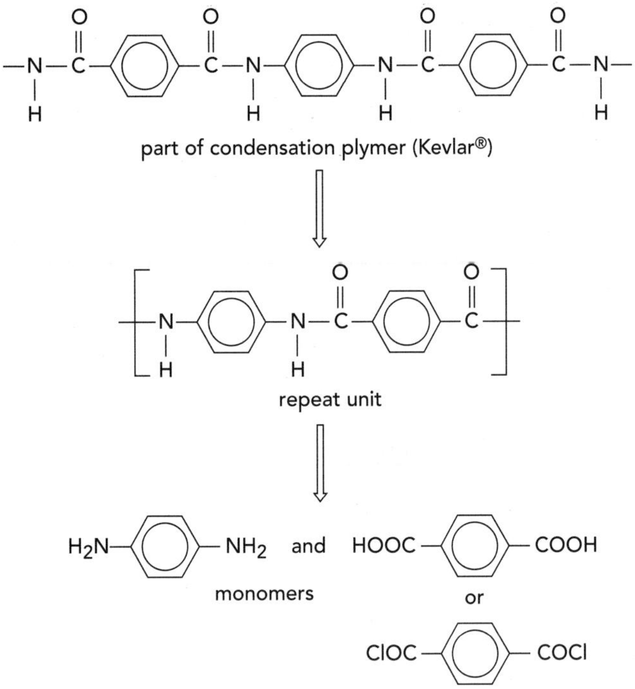

part of condensation plymer (Kevlar®)

repeat unit

H_2N—◯—NH_2 and $HOOC$—◯—$COOH$

monomers

or

$ClOC$—◯—$COCl$

Question

5 a What type of polymerisation reaction formed the polymer shown below?

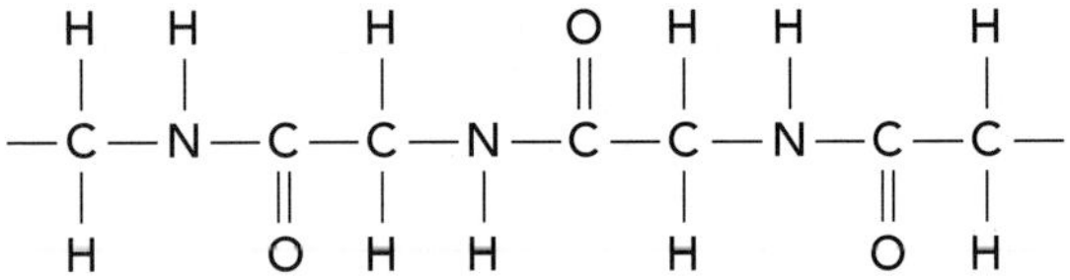

b Draw the displayed formula of the single monomer used to make the polymer shown in part a.

Compare your answers with another learner and discuss the thought process you went through to arrive at your answers. Then check them against the answers provided and seek help if you are unsure.

SUMMARY

Polymers are very large molecules that are built up from a very large number of small molecules known as monomers.
Remember from Chapter 15 that addition polymerisation occurs when an unsaturated monomer, such as an alkene, bonds to itself in an addition reaction. Poly(ethene), poly(propene), poly(chloroethene) and poly(phenylethene) are all common addition polymers.
Condensation polymerisation involves the loss of a small molecule (usually water or hydrogen chloride) in the reaction between two monomer molecules. Both polyesters and polyamides are formed by condensation polymerisation.
Polyamides are formed by condensation polymerisation between an amine group and a carboxylic acid group. These groups may be in the same monomer or on different monomers. Nylon 6,6 is formed in a condensation polymerisation between 1,6-diaminohexane and hexanedioic acid.
Condensation polymerisation between the amino and carboxylic acid groups in amino acids produces a polypeptide or protein. The links between the repeat units in these polymers are called *amide bonds*, also known as peptide bonds.
The polyester called Terylene is formed by condensation polymerisation of benzene-1,4-dicarboxylic acid with ethane-1,2-diol. H_2O is the small molecule eliminated in the reaction.
The amino acids molecules that react to form proteins contain a carboxylic acid, an amino group and a side-chain (represented by R) all attached to the same carbon atom. They have the general formula $NH_2CH(R)COOH$.
Proteins and polypeptides can be hydrolysed by refluxing in a strong acid, such as HCl(aq), forming amino acids (2-aminocarboxylic acids).
Polyesters and polyamides are biodegradable by acidic or alkaline hydrolysis and by the action of light, breaking their ester or amide links between their monomers in the polymer chains.

EXAM-STYLE QUESTIONS

1 a Explain the term *condensation polymer*. [2]

b Kevlar is a condensation polymer that is used for making bullet-proof vests.

Here are two monomers that could be used for making Kevlar:

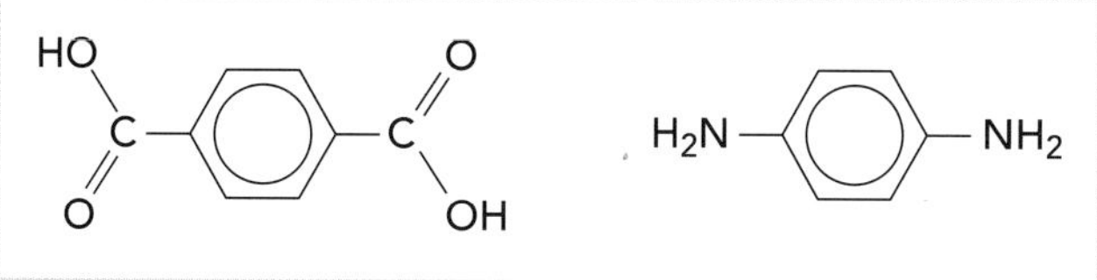

i Explain the term *monomer*. [1]

ii Give the structure of Kevlar, showing its repeat unit. [2]

iii Name the type of condensation polymer that Kevlar is classified as. [1]

c Explain how the chains of Kevlar are held together to make it such a strong material. [3]

[Total: 9]

2 Polyesters are condensation polymers.

a Give the structures of two monomers that could be used to make a polyester. [2]

b Give the structure of the polyester formed from these two monomers. [2]

[Total: 4]

3 a Glycine is an amino acid with the formula H_2NCH_2COOH.

i Give the systematic name for glycine. [1]

ii Give the structure of the polymer that could be formed from glycine, showing at least two repeat units. [2]

iii Name the linkage between the repeat units. [1]

iv State what type of attractive force forms between the chains of poly(glycine). [1]

b 3-Hydroxypropanoic acid is capable of forming polymers.

i Give the structure of 3-hydroxypropanoic acid. [1]

ii Give the structure of the polymer formed from this acid, showing at least two repeat units. [2]

iii Name the linkage present in the polymer. [1]

iv State what type of attractive force forms between chains of poly(3-hydroxypropanoic acid). [1]

[Total: 10]

CONTINUED

4 Sections of some polymers are shown below. For each polymer:
   i   identify the repeat unit
   ii give the structures of the monomers used to make each polymer.

   a   [3]

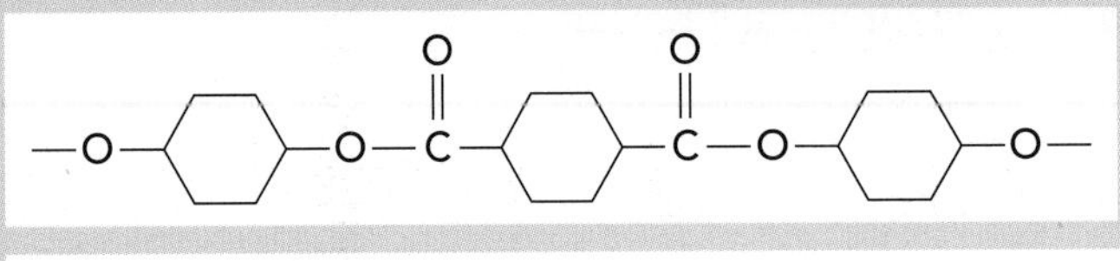

   b   [3]

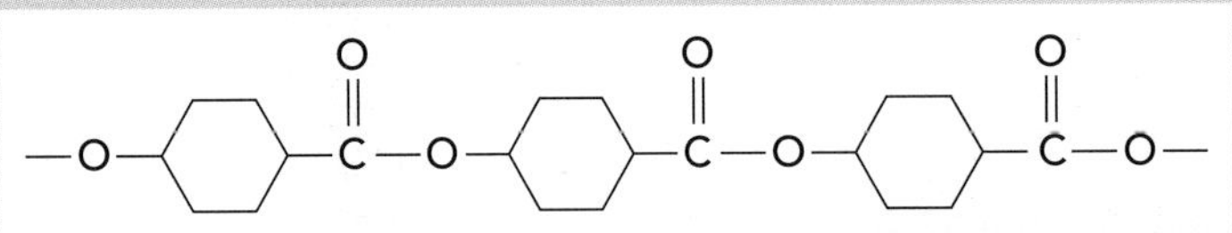

   c   [2]

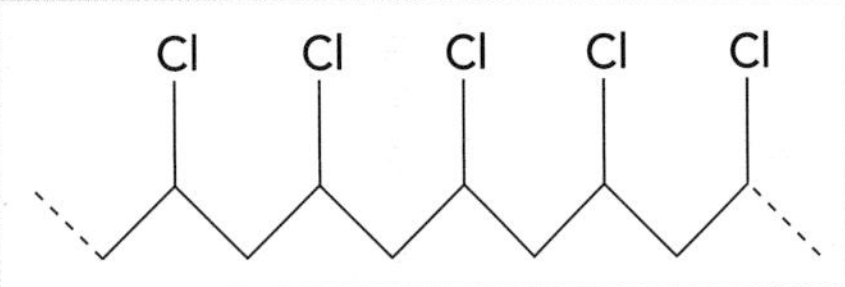

   d   [3]

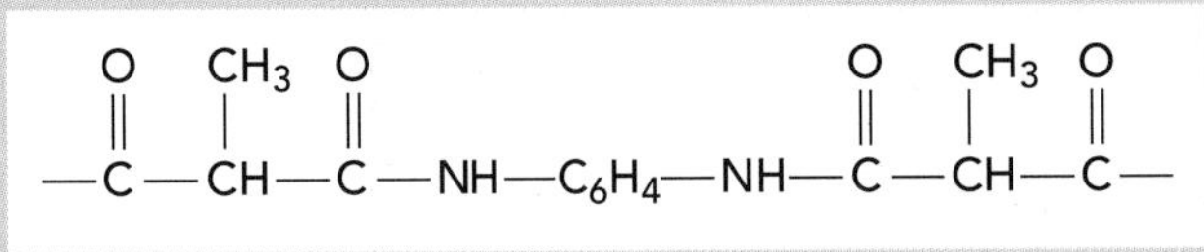

   e   [2]

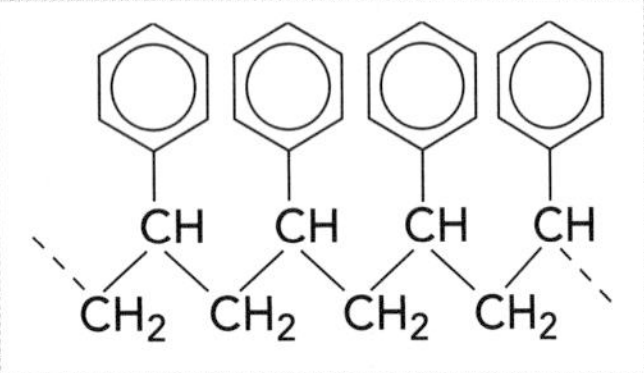

                                                                    [Total: 13]

5 Give the structures of the polymers formed from the monomers given below,
   showing at least two repeat units. For each polymer identify the following:
   i   the repeat unit
   ii   the type of linkage present
   iii the attractive force between the polymer chains.

   a   [3]

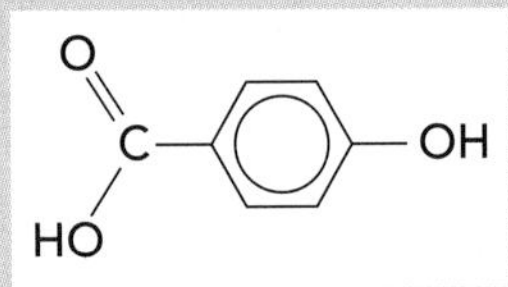

   b   [3]

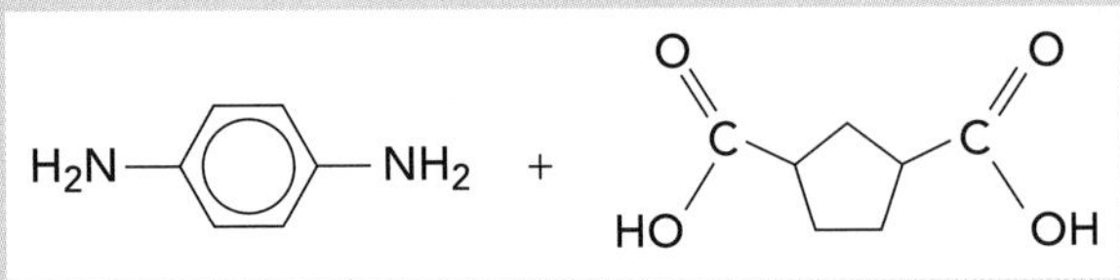

                                                                     [Total: 6]

CONTINUED

6 **a** Explain the term *biodegradable*. [2]

  b Explain how the production of biodegradable polymers has lessened the impact of polymers on the environment. [3]

  c Poly(L-lactic acid) is a biodegradable polymer. Give two uses of poly(L-lactic acid) and explain how its properties make it suitable for each use. [4]

[Total: 9]

SELF-EVALUATION

After studying this chapter, complete a table like this:

I can	See section...	Needs more work	Almost there	Ready to move on
describe the characteristics of condensation polymerisation in polyesters and polyamides	28.1, 28.2			
describe how polyesters are formed from: **a** a diol and a dicarboxylic acid or a dioyl chloride **b** a hydroxycarboxylic acid	28.3			
describe how polyamides are formed from: **a** a diamine and a dicarboxylic acid or a dioyl chloride **b** amino acids	28.3			
deduce repeat units, identify monomer(s) and predict the type of polymerisation reaction which produces a given section of a polymer molecule	28.4, 28.5			
recognise that polyalkenes are chemically inert and therefore nonbiodegradable but that polyesters and polyamides are biodegradable, either by acidic hydrolysis, alkaline hydrolysis or by action of light.	28.4			

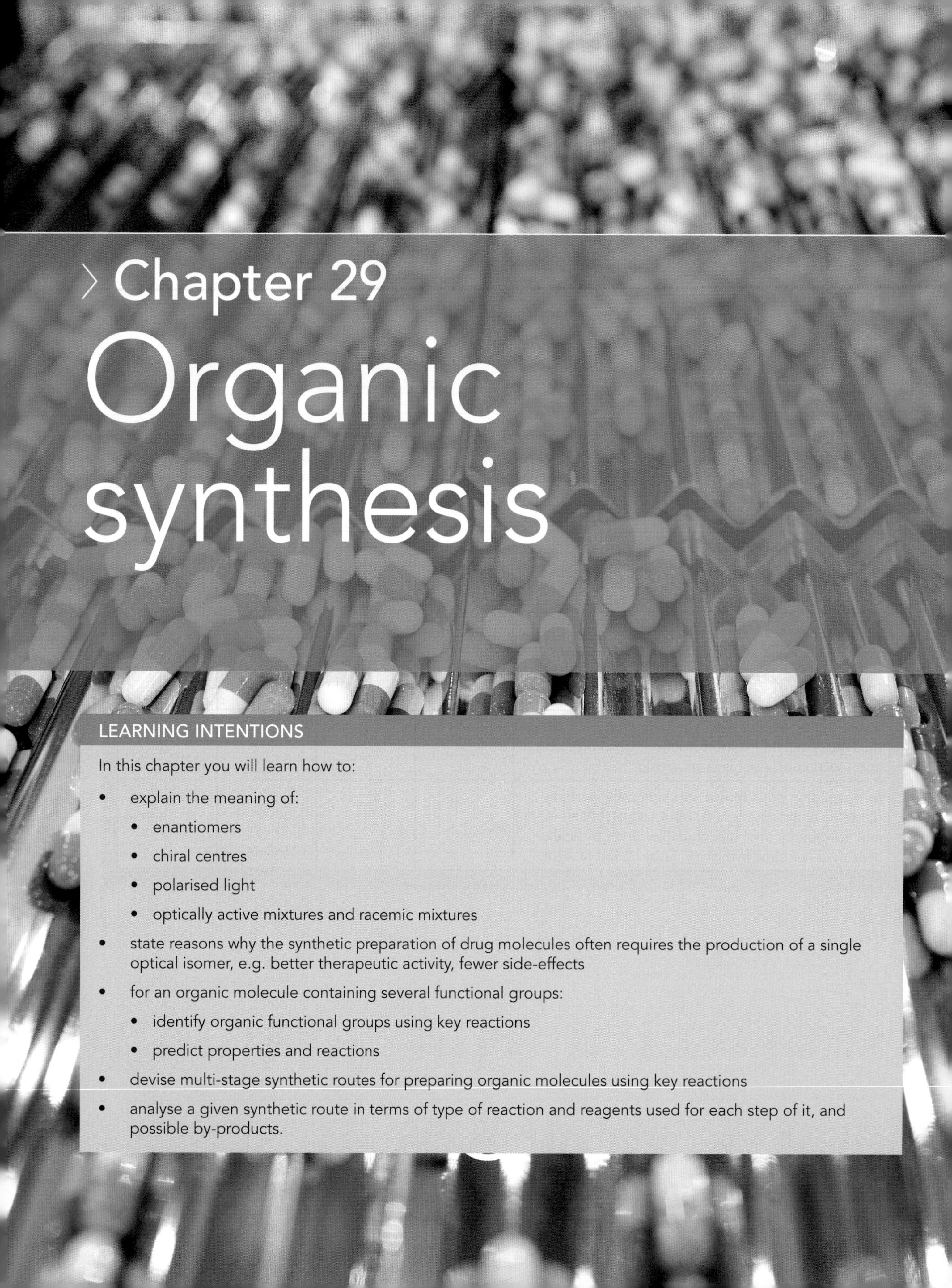

Chapter 29

Organic synthesis

LEARNING INTENTIONS

In this chapter you will learn how to:

- explain the meaning of:
    - enantiomers
    - chiral centres
    - polarised light
    - optically active mixtures and racemic mixtures
- state reasons why the synthetic preparation of drug molecules often requires the production of a single optical isomer, e.g. better therapeutic activity, fewer side-effects
- for an organic molecule containing several functional groups:
    - identify organic functional groups using key reactions
    - predict properties and reactions
- devise multi-stage synthetic routes for preparing organic molecules using key reactions
- analyse a given synthetic route in terms of type of reaction and reagents used for each step of it, and possible by-products.

BEFORE YOU START

Working in a small group:

1   Discuss what we mean by *optical isomerism.*

2   Describe the structural feature of a molecule that displays optical isomerism.

3   Draw a molecule that will exhibit optical isomerism and swap with a partner to draw its optical isomer.

4   Working with a partner, take turns to describe the following types of reaction to each other, giving an example to show what happens in the reaction:

    a   addition

    b   condensation

    c   hydrolysis

    d   substitution.

Look back to Chapter 14 if you are having trouble with the tasks above.

DESIGNING A DRUG

Figure 29.1: Chemists around the world work in large teams to model, develop and test new medicinal drugs.

How do we go about designing new molecules to fight diseases? One way is to identify the structural features the new drug will need to stop particular bacteria or viruses working (Figure 29.1). The structural features may be associated with the active site on a particular enzyme needed for an essential function of the pathogen (the disease-causing organism). Once these structural features have been identified, we can then predict the shape of a molecule that would fit into, and then block, the active site.

The functional groups present are also very important to ensure the drug can bind into the active site effectively. The intermolecular bonds formed between the drug and its target molecule could involve hydrogen bonding, ionic attraction, dipole–dipole forces, and instantaneous dipole–induced dipole forces (see Chapter 4).

Computers are now used to judge the fit between a potential drug molecule and a receptor site on its target molecule. Such 'molecular modelling' has greatly speeded up the process of designing new medicines. The interactions and fit of a potential medicine with a biological receptor molecule can be studied before the medicine is ever made in the lab. Before molecular modelling became available, the synthesis of a new medicine involved far more trial and error, with chemists having to prepare many more possible medicines for testing.

This type of research was used in the fight against AIDS in the late 1980s and 1990s. Scientists using X-ray crystallography (a method in which a sample is irradiated with X-rays and the pattern is analysed by computer) worked out the shape of HIV protease in 1988 (Figure 29.2). Knowing its structure made the search for drugs to fight AIDS much quicker and cheaper than traditional trial-and-error methods.

CONTINUED

Figure 29.2: A 'ribbon diagram' showing the symmetrical HIV protease molecule, with its active site in the centre of the molecule.

This enzyme plays an important role when the virus becomes infectious. Researchers realised that if a molecule could be discovered that could block its active site, this might be one step on the route to

finding a cure for AIDS. Knowing the molecule that the enzyme worked on (its substrate), researchers were able to construct similar molecules on the computer screen to fit the active site.

In less than eight years, pharmaceutical companies had developed three new anti-viral drugs for people with HIV / AIDS and the death rate from AIDS dropped significantly. These inhibitors are now one part of a cocktail of drugs that can be used to treat the disease.

Question for discussion

Discuss with another learner or group of learners how molecular modelling has helped in the search for new and improved medicinal drugs. Think about:

- the method used to determine the structure of HIV protease

- how anti-viral drugs work

- the time and costs involved.

29.1 Chirality in pharmaceutical synthesis

The pharmaceutical industry is constantly searching for new drugs. Research chemists have discovered that most of these drugs contain at least one chiral centre (see Section 14.6). Remember that a molecule containing a carbon atom bonded to four different atoms or groups of atoms can exist as two non-superimposable mirror images. The carbon atom is called a *chiral centre*. These two mirror-image isomers are called *enantiomers* and they will be optically active. They differ only in their ability to rotate the plane of polarised light to the left or to the right, and in their potential biological activity (and hence their effectiveness as medicines).

Using conventional organic reactions to make the desired product will yield a 50 : 50 mixture of the two enantiomers. We call this a **racemic mixture**. Although the physical and chemical properties of the enantiomers will be identical, each differs in its biological (or pharmaceutical) activity, i.e. the effect the drug has on the body. For example, naproxen is a drug used to treat the pain caused by arthritis (see Figure 29.3). One of its enantiomers will ease the pain but the other can cause liver damage.

KEY WORD

racemic mixture: a mixture containing equal amounts of a pair of enantiomers.

As another example of the need to separate the enantiomers from a racemic mixture, one enantiomer of a drug used to treat tuberculosis (TB) is effective, whereas the other can cause blindness.

IMPORTANT

Chemists ideally need a single pure enantiomer to put in their drug product.

Note that about 80% of new drugs patented are single enantiomers.

Using pure enantiomers will be beneficial as it:

- reduces the patient's dosage by half as the pure enantiomer is more potent, i.e. has better therapeutic activity (thereby cutting the cost of production)

- minimises the risk of side-effects (thereby protecting patients from further problems and protecting drug companies from possible legal action for damages if serious side-effects do occur).

At this point, you can also refer to the 'Fighting cancer' section at the start of Chapter 24, which looks at the drug *cis*-platin.

29.2 Preparing pure enantiomers for use as drugs

Optical resolution

This method involves chemists following a traditional synthetic route to make the compound, resulting in a racemic (50 : 50) mixture. Then they separate the two enantiomers in a process called *optical resolution*. This involves using a pure enantiomer of another optically active compound (called a chiral auxiliary) that will react with one of the isomers in the mixture. The new product formed will now have different properties and so can be separated by physical means. For example, their solubility in a given solvent will differ so the unwanted enantiomer and the new product can be separated by fractional crystallisation. The new product is then converted back to the desired enantiomer in a simple reaction (e.g. by adding dilute alkali).

The crystallisation is repeated many times to ensure purity. This method is difficult, time-consuming, uses extra reagents and involves the disposal of half the original racemic mixture.

Large volumes of organic solvents (often harmful to the environment) are used in the process. However, chemists are now using supercritical carbon dioxide as a solvent, which is much safer. At 31 °C and 73 atmospheres pressure, CO_2 is a suitable non-polar solvent for many drug derivatives in the racemic resolution process. The solubility of the derivatives can be changed simply by varying the density of the solvent. The solvent, which is non-toxic, is easily removed by reducing the pressure and then recycling it to use in the process again.

We can also use high-performance liquid chromatography (HPLC) to separate a racemic mixture, as long as the stationary medium (i.e. the solid that packs the column) is itself optically active.

Using optically active starting materials

This technique uses starting materials that are themselves optically active and in the same orientation as the desired product. These are often naturally occurring compounds such as carbohydrates or L-amino acids. The biochemist will choose from this 'chiral pool'. The synthetic route is designed to keep any intermediates and the final product formed in the same enantiomeric form. As a result, there is no need to carry out the costly separation process needed when a racemic mixture is produced.

Chiral catalysts

If possible, the most efficient way to prepare a pure enantiomer is to use a chiral catalyst.

Chemists are also developing new chiral catalysts that ensure only one specific enantiomer is formed in a reaction. The benefits of these catalysts are that only small quantities are needed and they can be used over and over again, although the catalyst itself can be expensive. A ruthenium (Ru) organometallic catalyst is used in the production of naproxen, a drug to treat arthritis (see Figure 29.3).

Often scientists need a combination of optical resolution and chiral synthesis in the production of a pharmaceutically active, pure enantiomer.

The pharmaceutical industry can also use enzymes to promote stereoselectivity and produce single-enantiomer products. The specific shape and the nature of the molecular interactions at the active site of an enzyme (a biological catalyst) ensure that only one enantiomer will be formed, as in living things. The enzymes are often immobilised (fixed in place) on inert supports. This enables the reactants to be passed over them without the need to separate the product from the enzymes after the reaction.

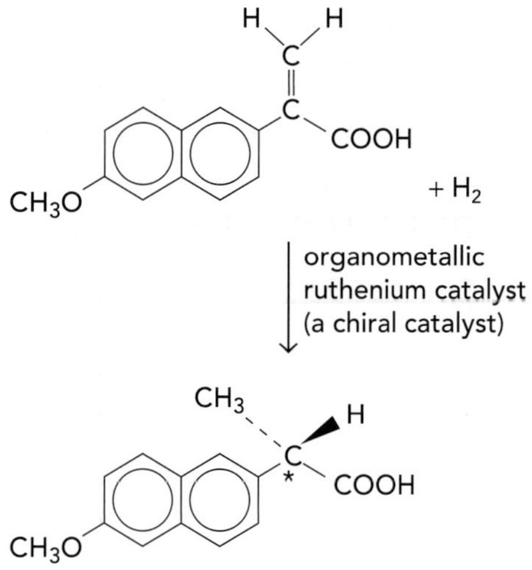

Figure 29.3: The chiral catalyst (an organometallic ruthenium compound) ensures only the desired enantiomer is formed: in this case, the naproxen enantiomer that is effective in treating arthritis. The chiral centre in naproxen is marked with an asterisk. The marked carbon atom is also known as an 'asymmetric carbon'.

However, it can be expensive isolating enzymes from living things. Using whole organisms, such as bacteria, can reduce this cost. In recent times, synthetic enzymes designed for a particular synthesis have also been made. Therefore, a search for a suitable enzyme from the limited pool available from natural sources is not always necessary.

Overall, using an enzyme process might take longer to develop than a conventional synthetic route, but in the long run the benefits generally outweigh the disadvantages. There are fewer steps needed in the synthesis route, resulting in a 'greener' process.

Question

Discuss these questions in a small group before writing your answers.

1 a Why are pure enantiomers rather than racemic mixtures the better option for use as pharmaceutical drugs from the point of view of:

  i a patient

  ii a pharmaceutical company?

 b Why are modern chiral catalyst-based processes, or using enzymes, for manufacturing pure enantiomers more sustainable (environmentally friendly) than traditional synthetic routes used by the pharmaceutical industry?

 c Find out why the drug thalidomide resulted in legal action against its manufacturer.

29.3 Synthetic routes

When research chemists want to make a new compound, they usually work backwards from the desired compound to create a series of reactions, starting with a compound extracted from a commonly available raw material. In

---

REFLECTION

1   Reflect on how a molecule containing two chiral centres could have no effect on plane-polarised light. Discuss your reasoning with a partner.

2   Discuss with a partner your ideas about why pairs of enantiomers differ in their effectiveness as drugs. Think about the role of active sites in how enzymes work.

3   Are you satisfied that you understand the terms and issues regarding the use of enantiomers in medicinal drugs? If not, it is a good idea to revise the basics of stereoisomerism in Chapter 14, and read through the start of this chapter again, making notes about any points you need support with.

4   What other learning strategies will you use when looking back at Chapter 14?

industry, common starting materials are hydrocarbons from crude oil and its refining, and compounds extracted from plants, such as esters from vegetable oils.

You will need some of the skills of a research chemist when tackling questions that involve:

- predicting the reactions of complex molecules you have never seen before, containing more than one functional group
- suggesting a series of reactions to make a given compound from a given starting compound.

In order to be successful in answering these questions, you will need to be familiar with all the reactions and conditions of each homologous series mentioned in the syllabus.

The flow chart in Figure 29.4 is a summary of some of the most useful reactions you need to know. However, you could be asked about others, so it is a good idea to make your own summary spider charts for all the reactions in Chapters 15 to 18, and 25 to 28.

For example, for Chapter 16 write the word 'Halogenoalkane' in a box and draw arrows radiating

out from the box to the products made in their reactions, labelling the arrows with other reactants and the reaction conditions. Displaying these on a wall and using different colours will help you remember them.

Suppose we want to convert ethene to ethanoic acid. A possible route is to convert ethene to ethanol, which is then oxidised to ethanoic acid. Alternatively, ethene could be converted to bromoethane, which is then hydrolysed to ethanol, and this is oxidised to ethanoic acid. This second alternative involves an extra reaction step. You should usually try to complete a synthesis in as few steps as possible. Remember that material is lost at each stage when preparing organic compounds. Reaction yields seldom approach 100%.

You also need to recall the reactions of benzene and its related compounds. Figure 29.5 provides you with a summary of reactions involving aromatic compounds. You can try copying and displaying the reaction summaries (from Figures 29.4 and 29.5) where you will look at them regularly: this will help you to learn the reactions and their conditions.

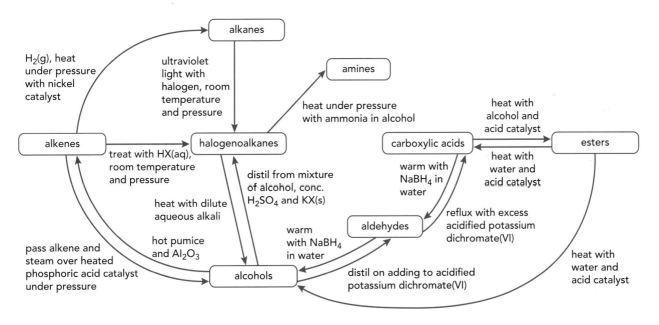

Figure 29.4: Some of the important organic reactions you need to remember for both the AS and A Level courses.

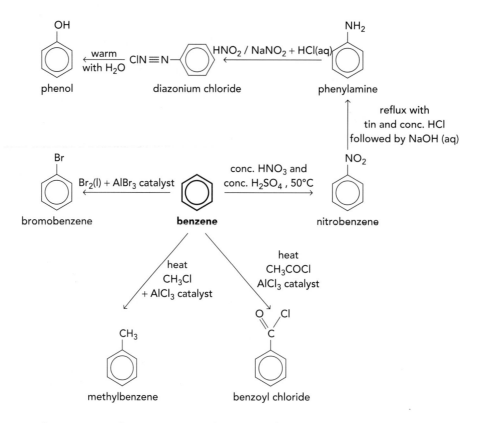

Figure 29.5: Summary of reactions involving aromatic (aryl) compounds needed for the A Level course.

Question

2 Show a sequence of reactions to plan how the following conversions can be made in two- or three-step syntheses.

Include the conditions required for each reaction.

(Start by drawing the structural formulae of the initial and final compounds).

a ethene to ethylamine.

b benzaldehyde to ethyl benzoate.

c 1-bromobutane to butanoic acid.

d butan-2-one to 2-aminobutane.

REFLECTION

Join another learner to reflect on how well you tackled these four problems. Discuss the thought processes you used when solving each problem.

Which problem did you find easiest and which was most difficult? Think about why some problems are easier than others and what you need to do to successfully design synthetic routes.

Adding carbon atoms

Sometimes the starting compound from a raw material does not have enough carbon atoms in its molecules to make the desired product. An extra carbon atom can be added by adding the nitrile functional group, $-C\equiv N$. Remember that these can be made from halogenoalkanes:

$$RBr + HCN \xrightarrow{\text{reflux with ethanolic KCN}} RC\equiv N + HBr$$

where R is an alkyl group, so $RC\equiv N$ has an extra carbon atom.

The $RC\equiv N$ molecule can be either hydrolysed to make a carboxylic acid (by refluxing with dilute hydrochloric acid) or reduced to make an amine (by adding $LiAlH_4$ in dry ether).

We can add an alkyl or acyl side-chain to a benzene ring by carrying out a Friedel–Crafts reaction, which is another useful reaction when planning synthetic routes.

For example:

$$C_6H_6 + CH_3CH_2Cl \xrightarrow{AlCl_3 \text{ catalyst}} C_6H_5CH_2CH_3 + HCl$$
$$\text{benzene} \qquad\qquad\qquad\qquad \text{ethylbenzene}$$

Question

3 a Name the functional groups in the molecules of:

   i   aspirin

   ii paracetamol.

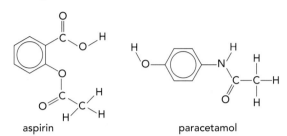

aspirin   paracetamol

   b i Both the molecules in part **a** are broken
         down when refluxed with dilute hydrochloric
         acid. Write equations for the reactions of
         aspirin and paracetamol with H$_2$O.

      ii Give the name of the type of reaction in **b i**.

   c Name the organic products A to D in the
      synthetic route below:

   C$_2$H$_5$COOC$_3$H$_7$

      ↓ boil with NaOH(aq)

      A

      ↓ add excess HCl(aq)

      B

      ↓ add PCl$_5$

      C

      ↓ add conc. ammonia

      D

   d i   Devise a three-stage synthetic route to
          convert benzene into benzenediazonium
          chloride.

      ii Suggest how you would convert the
          benzenediazonium chloride into an
          orange dye.

      iii Which one of the following formulae is the
          correct formula of a benzenediazonium
          cation?

          A   C$_6$H$_4$H$^+$N≡N

          B   C$_6$H$_5$N≡N$^+$

          C   C$_6$H$_5$N$^+$=N

          D   C$_6$H$_5$N$^+$≡N

REFLECTION

Reflect on the chemistry of aryl compounds
with a partner. Do you find their reactions more
difficult to understand and remember than other
organic reactions?

Discuss with a partner any ways you have found
useful to help recall organic reactions and the
conditions they need. Share your ideas with
another pair.

SUMMARY

Both natural biochemical compounds and modern medicinal drugs contain chiral molecules. Generally, only
one of the enantiomers of a drug is beneficial to living organisms and the other isomer may have undesirable
effects. The beneficial isomer has the appropriate shape and pattern of intermolecular forces to interact with a
receptor molecule in a living organism.

Chemists are now producing drugs containing single enantiomers rather than a racemic mixture of isomers.
This enables the dose to be halved, improves biological / pharmacological activity (behaviour of molecule in an
organism), reduces side-effects, and minimises litigation against manufacturers.

Recognising the functional groups in a given organic molecule enables us to predict its reactions.

Knowing the reactions of the different functional groups in organic reactions enables us to devise synthetic
routes to make given compounds.

EXAM-STYLE QUESTIONS

1   A sample of lactic acid, $CH_3CH(OH)COOH$, was extracted from a natural source and found to be optically active.

It was then subjected to two reactions, as shown below.

$$CH_3CH(OH)COOH \xrightarrow{\text{Step A}} CH_3COCOOH \xrightarrow{\text{Step B}} CH_3CH(OH)COOH$$
sample 1   sample 2

Sample 1 was optically active but sample 2 was not optically active.

a   i   Give the systematic name for lactic acid. [1]

ii The structure of one optical isomer of the lactic acid is:

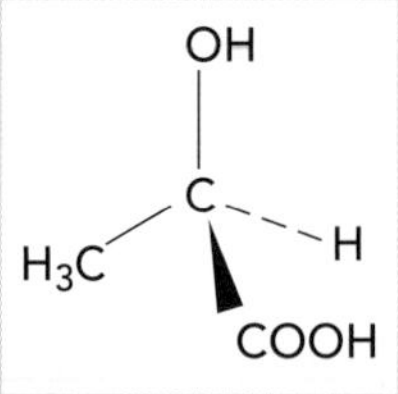

Draw the other optical isomer. [1]

iii Explain why lactic acid can form optical isomers. [1]

b   i   Give the reagents and conditions necessary for step A. [2]

ii Give the balanced equation for the reaction. [2]

c   i   Give the reagents and conditions necessary for step B. [2]

ii Give the balanced equation for the reaction. [2]

d   i   Give the mechanism for step B. The first step involves nucleophilic attack on the carbon of the ketone group by an H^- ion from $NaBH_4$. [5]

ii Explain why sample 2 does not show any optical activity: it does not rotate the plane of polarised light. [3]

e   i   Explain why lactic acid can be polymerised. [2]

ii State the type of polymerisation reaction that this an example of. [1]

iii Draw the repeat unit of poly(lactic acid). [1]

[Total: 23]

2   Explain how 2-aminopropanoic acid can be prepared from lactic acid in two steps. You should give the reagents and conditions necessary plus balanced symbol equations for the reactions taking place.

[Total: 9]

3   The structure of the compound known as thalidomide can be shown as:

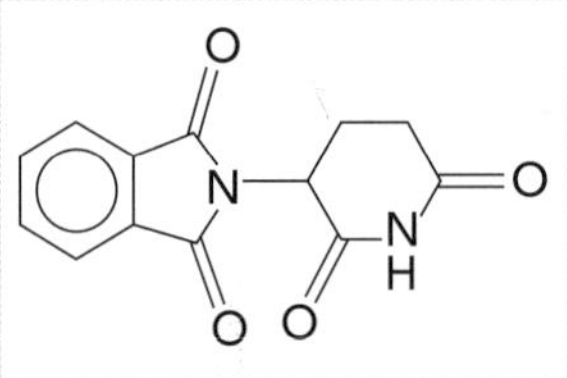

a   Copy the molecule and label the chiral centre on your drawing. [1]

b   Name two functional groups found in a molecule of thalidomide. [2]

CONTINUED

   c Suggest the type of reaction that might change the molecule into an alcohol and any reagents needed.   **[2]**

   d Explain why the chirality of drugs has been such an important issue in the pharmaceutical industry, giving one benefit to patients and one benefit to pharmaceutical companies of using pure enantiomers.   **[3]**

                      [Total: 8]

4   The flow charts below show how poly(ethene) can be obtained by two different routes.

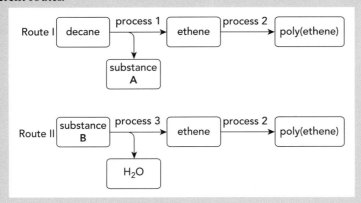

   a i Identify substance A and give the equation for the reaction taking place in process 1.   **[3]**

      ii Give the term used to describe process 1.   **[1]**

   b i Name substance B and give the equation for the reaction taking place in process 3.   **[3]**

      ii Give the term used to describe process 3.   **[1]**

                      [Total: 8]

SELF-EVALUATION

After studying this chapter, complete a table like this:

I can	See section...	Needs more work	Almost there	Ready to move on
explain the meaning of *enantiomers*, *chiral centres*, *polarised light*, *optically active mixtures* and *racemic mixtures*	29.1			
state reasons why the synthetic preparation of drug molecules often requires the production of a single optical isomer, e.g. better therapeutic activity, fewer side-effects	29.2			
for an organic molecule containing several functional groups: a identify organic functional groups using key reactions b predict properties and reactions	29.3			
devise multi-stage synthetic routes for preparing organic molecules using key reactions.	29.3			

Chapter 30

Analytical chemistry

LEARNING INTENTIONS

In this chapter you will learn how to:

- explain and use the term 'R_f value' in thin-layer chromatography

- explain and use *retention time* in gas–liquid chromatography, and interpret gas–liquid chromatograms to find the percentage composition of a mixture

- analyse a carbon-13 NMR spectrum of a simple molecule to deduce the different environments of the carbon atoms present and the possible structures for the molecule

- predict the number of peaks in a carbon-13 NMR spectrum for a given molecule

- analyse and interpret a proton NMR spectrum of a simple molecule to deduce the different types of proton present, the relative numbers of each type of proton present, the number of non-equivalent protons adjacent to a given proton, and the possible structures for the molecule

- predict the chemical shifts (δ) and splitting patterns of the signals in an NMR spectrum, given the molecule

- in obtaining an NMR spectrum, describe the use of tetramethylsilane, TMS, as the standard for chemical shift measurements, and the need for deuterated solvents, e.g. $CDCl_3$

- describe the identification of O—H and N—H protons by proton exchange using D_2O.

BEFORE YOU START

The analytical techniques introduced in this chapter are used together with mass spectrometry (Chapter 3) and infrared spectroscopy (Chapter 18).

Working in a group of five, choose *one* of the following topics to teach the rest of the group how to use a mass spectrum to deduce:

1   the relative molecular mass of an organic compound

2   the number of carbon atoms in a molecule using the $[M + 1]$ peak

3   the number of chlorine and bromine atoms in a molecule using the $[M + 2]$ peak

4   the structure of an organic molecule from its fragmentation pattern on a mass spectrum

5   how we use infrared spectroscopy to identify organic compounds.

USING NMR

NMR spectroscopy (see Section 30.4) is an analytical tool used extensively to find out the structures of biological macromolecules, such as proteins and nucleic acids. As well as identifying the different types of ^1H atoms present, more sophisticated data can give, for example, the distance between atoms in macromolecules. Large amounts of data are collected and analysed by computer programs to reveal the shape of the molecules under investigation.

Figures 30.1, 30.2 and 30.3 show images obtained from NMR analysis of protein molecules made up from over 100 amino acid residues (see Section 28.3). These images are called *ribbon diagrams*.

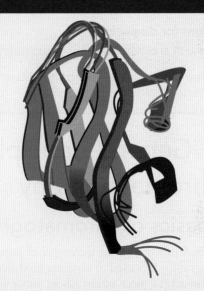

Figure 30.2: A protein made up of 153 amino acid residues.

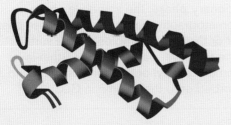

Figure 30.1: A protein made up of 106 amino acid residues.

This type of NMR analysis takes place in solution, so it is particularly useful for medical research. Many human proteins exist in solution in the body so we can mimic the interactions that take place in cells or in the bloodstream.

Ribbon diagrams were developed in the 1980s, with Jane Richardson's hand-drawn images published in the Journal *Advances in Protein Chemistry* (Figure 30.4).

At present, these useful images are computer generated, sometimes with areas of the protein shown using the ball-and-stick model to add extra detail.

CONTINUED

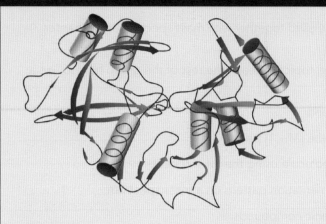

Figure 30.3: Another computer-generated image of an enzyme of pepsin containing over 300 amino acid residues.

Questions for discussion

Discuss with another learner or group of learners:

- What are the benefits of using ribbon diagrams when investigating proteins?

Figure 30.4: Jane Richardson is known as 'The mother of the ribbon diagrams'. She was born in 1941 and heads a research group at Duke University in America, where she has worked since 1970. Ribbon diagrams are also referred to as 'Richardson diagrams'.

- Carry out some research to find out more about the scientist Jane Richardson: her life and her work. Decide together on a way to present your findings to the rest of the group.

30.1 General principles of chromatography

The basics of chromatography

You will be familiar with the technique of paper chromatography. It is used to separate mixtures as a solvent moves up a piece of absorbent paper.

We call the solvent the **mobile phase**, and water trapped between the cellulose fibres of the paper is the **stationary phase**. The substances in the mixture will have different affinities for the solvent and for the water, and so they move at different rates over the paper. Look at Figure 30.5.

The R_f values (retardation factors) of substances are calculated as shown in Figure 30.6. The conditions must be identical to those quoted in the R_f data table, e.g. the same temperature and the same solvent used.

KEY WORDS

mobile phase: the solvent used in chromatography, which moves along the paper, thin layer of aluminium oxide, or column containing liquid supported on a solid.

stationary phase: the immobile phase in chromatography that the mobile phase passes over or through. Examples are the surface of the thin-layer particles in TLC (thin-layer chromatography) or the non-volatile liquid adsorbed onto the column in GLC.

Coloured substances can be seen directly on the paper but others are sprayed with a chemical that forms coloured compounds on the chromatogram. For example, amino acids can be revealed as bluish spots by ninhydrin spray.

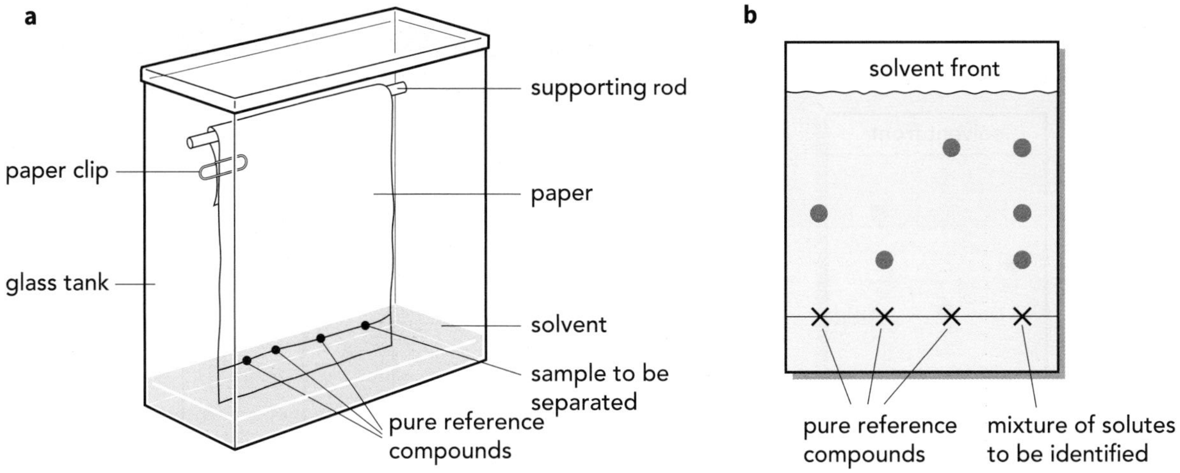

a

b

Figure 30.5: **a** Paper chromatography. **b** The chromatogram produced. Components of the mixture can be identified by comparison with pure reference compounds or by calculating R_f **values** (see Figure 30.6) and comparing these values with those in tables of data.

> **KEY WORD**
>
> R_f **value (retention factor)**: in paper chromatography (or TLC), the ratio of the distance travelled by a specific component to the distance travelled by the solvent front.

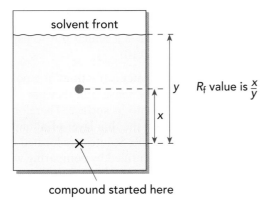

Figure 30.6: How to calculate R_f values, which are then compared with reference values obtained under identical conditions.

Partition coefficients in chromatography

The principle of partition of a solute between two solvents (see Section 21.6) helps us to understand more fully how the components in a mixture are separated in chromatography.

In paper chromatography the different partition coefficients of the components in a mixture correspond to their relative solubilities in the two solvents. The mobile phase is the solvent chosen. The other solvent is the water trapped in the paper's structure, which is the stationary phase. Figure 30.7 shows solute molecules partitioned between the mobile phase and a stationary liquid phase on a solid support.

The solutes in the mixture being separated are partitioned to different extents between the solvents in the mobile and stationary phases. The greater the relative solubility in the mobile phase, the faster the rate of movement as the mobile phase passes over the stationary phase.

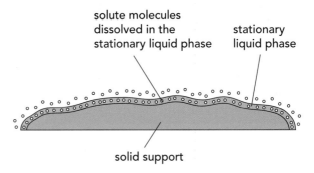

Figure 30.7: Partition paper chromatography. The mobile phase (solvent) moves over the stationary liquid phase (water trapped between the paper fibres), carrying solute particles with it. The filter paper is the solid support in paper chromatography.

Question

1 Look at this paper chromatogram:

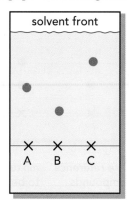

Figure 30.8: Paper chromatogram for Question 1.

a The solvent used was ethanol. Which sample of ink, A, B or C, has the greatest relative solubility in ethanol?

b Work out the R_f value of the ink whose partition coefficient in ethanol and water lies between the values of the other two inks.

Share your answers to Question 1 with another learner and explain your reasoning to each other. Then mark each other's answers using the answers provided.

30.2 Thin-layer chromatography

In thin-layer chromatography, referred to as TLC, the stationary phase is a solid that adsorbs the solute molecules under investigation onto its surface (Figure 30.9).

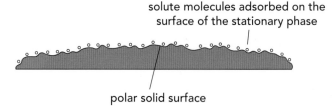

Figure 30.9: Adsorption thin-layer chromatography. The mobile phase moves over the stationary solid phase.

The solid stationary phase is usually alumina (Al_2O_3), which is made into a slurry with water and spread onto a microscope slide. This is then put into an oven, where it dries out into a solid white coating on the glass. A

PRACTICAL ACTIVITY 30.1

Making a thin-layer chromatogram

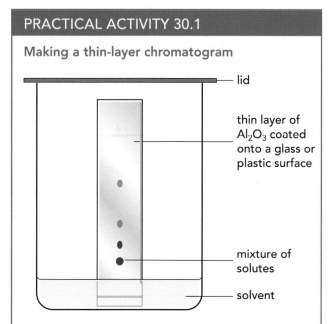

Figure 30.10: Thin-layer chromatography.

You can measure the distance from the baseline (the centre of the original mixture) to the solvent front (the height the solvent front rises to). Then measure the distance between the baseline and the centre of each solute. Using this information, you can then calculate the R_f values of the solutes.

---

chromatogram is then made in a similar way to paper chromatography (Figure 30.10).

Polar molecules have a greater attraction for a polar solid used as the stationary phase, and they are adsorbed more strongly onto its surface. Therefore, they travel more slowly up the thin layer of aluminium oxide, and separation occurs. Solutes are located on the chromatogram and identified by comparing with standard known substances or by calculating R_f values.

Note that although TLC is normally described as adsorption chromatography, some partitioning does occur if water is present. Dried aluminium oxide can become rehydrated. When this happens, water also acts as a partitioning stationary phase together with the adsorbing stationary solid phase.

TLC is quicker than paper chromatography and can be used on smaller samples, making it useful in forensic science, where it can be used to identify drugs and explosive residues.

For example, when forensic scientists use TLC to analyse a substance that is suspected to be cannabis, the stationary phase is silicon dioxide (silica) sprayed with silver nitrate solution, which is then dried. The mobile phase is the non-polar solvent methylbenzene.

Question

2 a TLC can separate mixtures of components. What do we call the mechanism of separation usually at work in TLC?

   b A mixture of propanone and hexane was separated on a TLC chromatogram using aluminium oxide as the stationary phase and methylbenzene as the solvent. Which substance would you expect to rise further up the chromatogram? Discuss your reasoning with another learner, then write down your answer.

30.3 Gas–liquid chromatography

In gas–liquid chromatography (GLC), a gaseous sample under investigation enters a long column.

> ### IMPORTANT
>
> The column contains the stationary phase and the sample is moved through by an inert carrier gas. In a mixture, the components will move through the column at different rates.

This method can be used with gases, and volatile liquids or solids (as they must be in the form of a vapour).

The apparatus is shown in Figure 30.10.

The stationary phase is a non-volatile liquid that has a high boiling point. This is often a long-chain, non-polar hydrocarbon, bonded onto a solid support, e.g. small particles of silica packed tightly into a column.

The mobile phase is an inert (unreactive) 'carrier' gas, such as helium or nitrogen.

The tiny solid particles in the column have a very large surface area over which partitioning can occur, resulting in excellent separation.

The more non-polar components in the mixture have a greater relative interaction with the non-polar liquid on the solid particles (stationary phase). Therefore, they are carried through the column more slowly than components whose molecules are more polar.

The detector at the end of the column records **retention times**, i.e. how long it takes each component to pass through the column.

> ### KEY WORD
>
> **retention time:** the time taken for a compound to travel through a chromatography column in GLC.

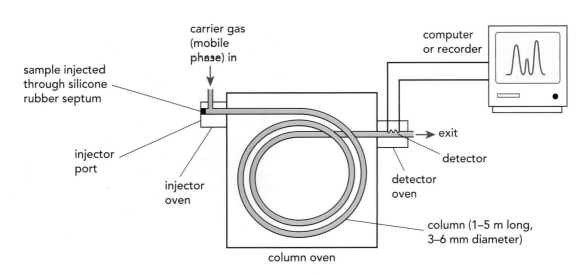

Figure 30.11: Gas–liquid chromatography (GLC). The oven maintains a constant temperature, higher than the boiling point of the components in the mixture to be analysed.

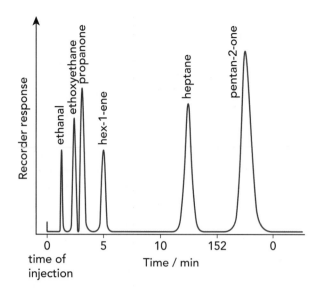

Figure 30.12: A gas chromatogram from a mixture of volatile organic compounds.

As in all chromatography, the conditions must be controlled in order to make comparisons with published databases. The chromatogram must be obtained using the same carrier gas, flow rate of gas, stationary phase and temperature that were used when the standard data was obtained.

Figure 30.12 shows a chromatogram obtained using GLC.

Analysis by gas–liquid chromatography does have some limitations. For example, similar compounds will have similar retention times. Also, if a newly discovered compound is detected, it will not have a match in the computer's database of retention times.

Determination of the percentage composition of a mixture by GLC

For quantitative analysis, the component peaks are first identified and then the area of each is measured. The peaks are roughly triangular in shape so their area is approximately:

$\frac{1}{2} \times \text{base} \times \text{height}$ (i.e. the area of a triangle)

The GLC machine usually measures the area of the peak automatically and can print the results with the chromatogram. If the peaks are very narrow or have similar base widths, then peak height may be used instead of peak area to estimate the proportion of components in a mixture.

For this method:

- the chromatogram must show peaks for all the components in the mixture

- all the components of the mixture must be separated

- the detector must respond equally to the different components so that peak area is directly proportional to the component concentration.

The amount of each component in a mixture is found by expressing it as a percentage of the sum of the areas under all the peaks.

For example, for a mixture of three esters A, B and C:

(approx.) % of ester A

$= \dfrac{\text{peak area (or height) of A}}{\text{sum of the areas (or heights) of A, B and C}} \times 100$

GLC is used to test for steroids in competing athletes and to test the fuels used in Formula One motor racing (Figure 30.13). It is also used for medical diagnosis in analysing blood samples. With GLC, it is possible to determine the percentages of dissolved oxygen, nitrogen, carbon dioxide and carbon monoxide in blood samples as small as 1.0 cm^3.

GLC is often combined with mass spectrometry to separate then rapidly identify the components of a mixture.

Figure 30.13: GLC is used to check that the components in the fuel used in Grand Prix cars conform to strict regulations.

Question

3 **a** For GLC separations explain:

  i how retention time is measured

  ii how the areas under the component peaks are used.

  b State what you can use as an approximate measure of the proportion of a component in a mixture from a GLC chromatogram which produces sharp peaks.

30.4 Proton (¹H) nuclear magnetic resonance

How NMR works

Nuclear magnetic resonance (**NMR**) spectroscopy is a widely used analytical technique for organic compounds. NMR uses the fact that the nucleus of each hydrogen atom in an organic molecule behaves like a tiny magnet. The nucleus of a hydrogen atom consists of a single proton. This proton can spin. The spinning motion of the positively charged proton causes a very small magnetic field to be set up.

In NMR we put the sample to be analysed in a magnetic field. The hydrogen nuclei (protons) either line up with the field or, by spinning in the opposite direction, line up against the magnetic field (Figure 30.14).

There is a tiny difference in energy between the oppositely spinning ¹H nuclei. This difference corresponds to the energy carried by waves in the radiowave range of the electromagnetic radiation spectrum. In NMR spectroscopy, the nuclei 'flip' between the two energy levels (Figure 30.15). Only atoms whose mass number is an odd number, e.g. ¹H or ¹³C, absorb energy in the range of frequencies that is analysed.

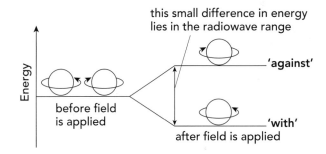

Figure 30.15: Hydrogen (¹H) nuclei will absorb energy in the radiowave range when they 'flip' from the lower energy level, lining up with the applied magnetic field, to the higher energy level, lining up against it.

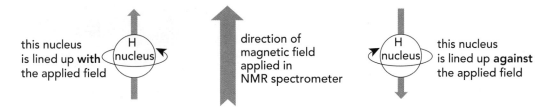

Figure 30.14: Hydrogen (¹H) nuclei will line up with or against a magnetic field.

The size of the gap between the nuclear energy levels varies slightly, depending on the location of other atoms in the molecule (the molecular environment). Therefore, NMR can be used to identify ^{1}H atoms in different parts of a molecule.

You will find this easier to understand by looking at an example. If we look at a molecule of methanol, CH_3OH, we can see that there are ^{1}H atoms in two different molecular environments. We have ^{1}H atoms in both the —CH_3 group and the —OH group. The energy absorbed by the ^{1}H atoms in —CH_3 is different from the energy absorbed by the ^{1}H atom in —OH.

In NMR spectroscopy, we vary the magnetic field as that is easier than varying the wavelength of radio waves. As the magnetic field is varied, the ^{1}H nuclei in different molecular environments flip at different field strengths. The different field strengths are measured relative to a reference compound, which is given a value of zero. The standard compound chosen is tetramethylsilane (**TMS**).

TMS is chosen because it is an inert, volatile liquid that mixes well with most organic compounds. Also, its formula is $Si(CH_3)_4$, so all its H atoms are equivalent (i.e. they are all in the same molecular environment). So, importantly, TMS only gives one sharp absorption, called a peak, and this peak is at a higher frequency than most other protons (Figure 30.16). All other absorptions are measured by their shift away from the sharp TMS peak on the NMR spectrum. This is called the *chemical shift* (δ), and is measured in units of parts per million (ppm).

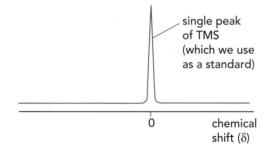

Figure 30.16: The standard TMS peak used as a reference on NMR spectra.

> ### KEY WORD
>
> **TMS:** an abbreviation for tetramethylsilane, $Si(CH_3)_4$, the standard compound used in NMR spectroscopy, providing the peak to measure chemical shifts relative to its given value of zero

Question

Discuss the following questions in a small group before writing your answers.

4 **a** Explain why tetramethylsilane (TMS) is used as a standard in NMR spectroscopy.

   b In NMR we use solvents such as tetrachloromethane to prepare samples for the machine (Figure 30.17).

   i Give the molecular formula of tetrachloromethane.

   ii Suggest why tetrachloromethane is used as a solvent when preparing samples for NMR analysis.

   iii Solvents that contain deuterium, D, are also used as solvents in NMR. Deuterium is the ^{2}H isotope of hydrogen. A substance in which ^{1}H is replaced by ^{2}H is said to be *deuterated*. Suggest why the deuterated solvent $CDCl_3$ would be used instead of $CHCl_3$.

Figure 30.17: Samples dissolved in a solvent in narrow tubes ready for NMR analysis.

Low-resolution NMR

A low-resolution NMR spectrum shows a single peak for each *non-equivalent* hydrogen atom; an example is shown in Figure 30.18.

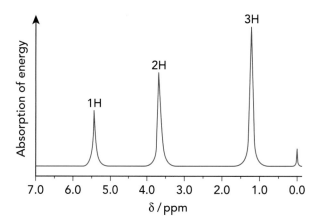

Figure 30.18: The low-resolution NMR spectrum of ethanol, CH_3CH_2OH.

Note how the zero reference point on the x-axis, chemical shift (δ), is on the right of the spectrum and the shift increases in value going left.

There are three peaks on ethanol's low-resolution NMR spectrum. These correspond to the ^1H atoms in —OH, —CH$_2$— and —CH$_3$.

Note how the heights of the three peaks vary. The area under each peak tells us the relative number of equivalent ^1H atoms responsible for that particular chemical shift. The largest peak will be from the —CH$_3$ hydrogen atoms, the middle peak from the —CH$_2$— hydrogen atoms and the smallest peak from the —OH hydrogen. The relative areas under the peaks are shown on the NMR spectrum by the labels 1H, 2H and 3H (see Figure 30.17).

The type of H atom present can be checked against tables of data (Table 30.1) if you are using NMR to identify unknown organic compounds.

Using Table 30.1 we can see that:

- the peak at about 1.2 ppm is caused by the —CH$_3$ hydrogen atoms (range 0.9–1.7 ppm)

- the peak at about 3.7 ppm corresponds to —CH$_2$— hydrogen atoms (range 3.2–4.0 ppm)

- the peak at about 5.4 ppm is due to the —OH hydrogen atom.

Question

Discuss your answers to parts **a–f** together with a partner, taking turns to explain your reasoning to each other.

5 Predict the number of peaks and the relative areas under each peak, where appropriate, on the low-resolution proton NMR spectrum of:

   a methanol, CH_3OH

   b benzene, C_6H_6

   c chloroethane, C_2H_5Cl

   d propan-1-ol

   e propan-2-ol

   f propanone.

Which spectra did you find most difficult? Why?

Which spectra were easiest?

Now check your answers against those provided to see if you were correct.

High-resolution NMR

As you can see in Table 30.1, the chemical shifts are given over ranges, and the ranges for different types of hydrogen atoms do overlap. In some molecules where there is heavy shielding of the hydrogen nuclei by lots of electrons in surrounding atoms, peaks are shifted beyond their usual range. In such cases high-resolution NMR is useful.

High-resolution NMR gives us more information to interpret. Peaks that appear as one 'signal' on a low-resolution NMR spectrum are often revealed to be made up of a cluster of closely grouped peaks. This is because the magnetic fields generated by spinning nuclei interfere slightly with those of neighbouring nuclei.

This interference is called spin–spin coupling. The exact **splitting pattern** of a peak depends on the number of hydrogen atoms on the adjacent carbon atom or atoms.

IMPORTANT

The number of signals a peak splits into = $n + 1$ where n is the number of ^1H atoms on the adjacent carbon atom.

KEY WORD

splitting pattern: the series of peaks that main signals are divided into in high-resolution NMR.

Environment of proton	Example	Chemical shift range δ / ppm
alkane	—CH₃, —CH₂—, >CH—	0.9–1.7
alkyl next to C=O	CH₃—C=O, —CH₂—C=O, >CH—C=O	2.2–3.0
alkyl next to aromatic ring	CH₃—Ar, —CH₂—Ar, >CH—Ar	2.3–3.0
alkyl next to electronegative atom	CH₃—O, —CH₂—O, —CH₂—Cl	3.2–4.0
attached to alkene	=CHR	4.5–6.0
attached to aromatic ring	H—Ar	6.0–9.0
aldehyde	HCOR	9.3–10.5
alcohol	ROH	0.5–6.0
phenol	Ar—OH	4.5–7.0
carboxylic acid	RCOOH	9.0–13.0
alkyl amine	R—NH—	1.0–5.0
aryl amine	Ar—NH₂	3.0–6.0
amide	RCONHR	5.0–12.0

Table 30.1: Note: δ values for O—H and N—H protons can vary depending on solvent and concentration. Ar is used to represent an aromatic ring.

We can use the high-resolution NMR spectrum of ethanol to illustrate this 'n + 1 rule'. The 'n + 1 rule' will help you to interpret splitting patterns (Figure 30.19).

- The —CH₃ peak is split into three because there are two ¹H atoms on the adjacent —CH₂— group.

  $n + 1 = 3$ (as $n = 2$)

  This splitting pattern is called a *triplet*.

- The —CH₂— peak is split into four because there are three ¹H atoms on the adjacent —CH₃ group.

  $n + 1 = 4$ (as $n = 3$)

  This splitting is called a *quartet*.

- The —OH peak is not usually split as its ¹H atom is constantly being exchanged with the ¹H atoms of other ethanol molecules and any water present. This results in one average peak being produced.

Table 30.2 shows the relative intensities and distribution of the splitting patterns you are likely to meet.

Figure 30.20 shows another high-resolution NMR spectrum. You should try to interpret it by following these steps:

Step 1: Use δ values (chemical shift in ppm) to identify the environment of the equivalent protons (¹H atoms) present at each peak (remembering the peak at zero is the TMS standard reference peak).

Step 2: Look at the relative areas under each peak to determine how many of each type of non-equivalent protons (¹H atoms) are present.

Step 3: Apply the n + 1 rule to the splitting patterns to see which protons (¹H atoms) are on adjacent carbon atoms in the unknown molecule.

Step 4: Put all this information together to identify the unknown molecule.

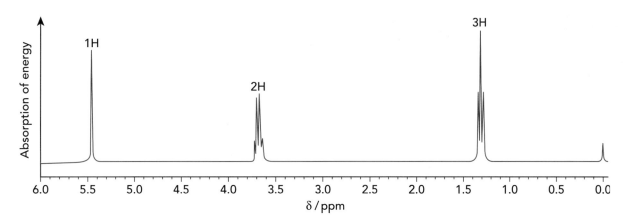

Figure 30.19: The high-resolution NMR spectrum of ethanol, showing the splitting pattern in two of the peaks. The area under each series of peaks still represents the number of equivalent ^1H atoms in the molecule, as in low-resolution NMR.

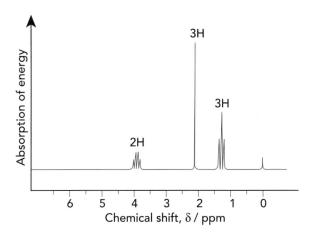

Figure 30.20: The high-resolution NMR spectrum of an unknown ester in a glue. (See the Worked example on the next page.)

Number of adjacent ^1H atoms	Splitting pattern: using the $n + 1$ rule, the peak will be split into …	Relative intensities in the splitting pattern	Observed on the NMR spectrum as …
0	1 peak, called a singlet	1	
1	2 peaks, called a doublet	1:1	
2	3 peaks, called a triplet	1:2:1	
3	4 peaks, called a quartet	1:3:3:1	

Table 30.2: Splitting patterns in high-resolution NMR spectra.

WORKED EXAMPLE

1   An ester is used as a solvent in a glue. A chemist was given a sample of the ester to analyse. The NMR spectrum of the ester is shown in Figure 30.20. Identify the ester.

Solution

Step 1: Identify possibilities for the three major peaks that appear at chemical shifts of 1.3, 2.2 and 3.9 ppm. Using Table 30.1, these could be:

1.3 ppm	$R—CH_3$, $R—CH_2—$, $R_2{>}CH—$
2.2 ppm	possibly $H_3C—CO—$, $RCH_2CO—$ or $R_2CH—CO—$
3.9 ppm	$O—CH_3$, $O—CH_2R$, $O—CHR_2$

Step 2: Use the relative numbers of each type of proton (^{1}H atom), labelling each major peak to narrow down possibilities.

1.3 ppm, labelled 3H, so could be $R—CH_3$

2.2 ppm, labelled 3H, so could be $H_3C—CO—$

3.9 ppm, labelled 2H, so could be $O—CH_2R$

Step 3: By applying the $n + 1$ rule to the splitting patterns we can see which protons (^{1}H atoms) are on adjacent carbon atoms.

1.3 ppm, labelled 3H and split into triplet, so $R—CH_3$ would be next to a C atom bonded to *two* ^{1}H atoms (2 + 1 = 3, triplet) i.e. R = $—CH_2—$.

2.2 ppm, labelled 3H and a singlet, so $H_3C—CO—$ would be next to a C atom with *no* ^{1}H atoms attached (0 + 1 = 1, singlet). It could well be that the carbonyl carbon, $—CO—$, is also bonded to an $—O—$ atom, as in an ester, i.e. $H_3C—COOR$.

3.9 ppm, labelled 2H and split into a quartet, $O—CH_2R$ would be next to a C atom bonded to three ^{1}H atoms (3 + 1 = 4, quartet), i.e. R = $—CH_3$.

Step 4: Putting this information together we get the ester ethyl ethanoate, $CH_3COOCH_2CH_3$.

Question

If possible, work as a small group to discuss and answer this question.

6   A pathologist was given a sample of a white tablet to identify. In order to complete her report, the pathologist received an NMR spectrum of the sample (Figure 30.21a) and information from the police that the tablets involved were either aspirin or paracetamol. The displayed formulae of both drugs are also shown in Figure 30.21b.

   a   Using this information, identify the drug in the white tablet. Explain your answer.

   b   Sketch the NMR spectrum you would expect to see if the other drug had undergone NMR analysis. Label each peak with its relative area and the type of proton (^{1}H) that caused it.

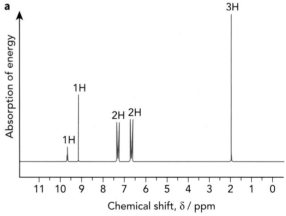

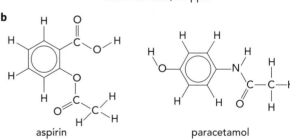

Figure 30.21: a NMR analysis of the unknown drug sample. **b** Structures of aspirin and paracetamol.

Identifying the —OH or —NH signal in an NMR spectrum

The —OH signal in the high-resolution NMR spectrum of ethanol appears as a single peak. As we have seen earlier in this section, the peak is not split by the ^{1}H atoms (protons) on the neighbouring —CH$_2$— group. The reason for this is that the —OH proton exchanges very rapidly with protons in any traces of water (or acid) present, as follows:

$$CH_3CH_2OH + HOH \rightleftharpoons CH_3CH_2OH + HOH$$

The hydrogen atoms involved in this reversible proton exchange have been coloured red and blue. The exchange takes place so rapidly that the signal for the —OH protons becomes a single peak. This exchange also happens in amines and amides which contain the —NH— group.

Table 30.3 shows the chemical shift ranges for the different —OH and —NH— signals.

As you can see from Table 30.1, these ranges overlap with the chemical shifts of other types of proton. The signals can also appear outside the quoted ranges under certain conditions, e.g. choice of solvent or concentration. This makes NMR spectra difficult to interpret.

Different —OH and —NH— protons	Range of chemical shift (δ) / ppm
in alcohols, R—OH protons	0.5–6.0
in phenols, arene —OH protons	4.5–7.0
in carboxylic acids, R—COOH protons	9.0–13.0
in amines, —NH—	1.0–5.0
in aryl amines, arene—NH$_2$	3.0–6.0
in amides, —CONH—	5.0–12.0

Table 30.3: Chemical shift ranges for —OH and —NH— protons in different molecular environments.

However, there is a technique for positively identifying —OH or —NH— groups in a molecule. Their peaks 'disappear' from the spectra if you add a small amount of deuterium oxide, D$_2$O, to the sample. The deuterium atoms (^{2}H) in D$_2$O, called 'heavy water', exchange reversibly with the protons in the —OH or —NH— groups.

For example:

$$—OH + D_2O \rightleftharpoons —OD + HOD$$
$$—NH—CO— + D_2O \rightleftharpoons —ND—CO— + HOD$$

The deuterium atoms do not absorb in the same region of the electromagnetic spectrum as protons (^{1}H atoms). This makes the —OH or —NH— signal disappear from the NMR spectrum. By checking against the peaks in the original NMR spectrum without D$_2$O, we can tell if the —OH or —NH— groups are present in the sample. The ^{1}H atom in the —OH or —NH— group is referred to as a 'labile' proton.

Question

7 a Look back at Figure 30.19.
The high-resolution NMR spectrum shown is from a sample of ethanol containing traces of water.
Describe how the NMR spectrum would differ if D$_2$O had been added to the sample of ethanol.

   b Look back at Question 6. How would repeating the NMR analysis using a solvent of D$_2$O help the pathologist distinguish between aspirin and paracetamol?

Did Questions 6 and 7 reveal any areas of proton NMR analysis that you need more practise on? You can try Exam-style Questions 2–5 to interpret more ^{1}H NMR spectra.

30.5 Carbon-13 NMR spectroscopy

In addition to proton NMR, carbon-13 NMR is another analytical tool used frequently by organic chemists. The vast majority of carbon atoms in any organic compound will be the carbon-12 isotope. This isotope has an even mass number (12). Therefore, it has no signal on an NMR spectrum, as NMR only works with atoms with an odd mass number (such as ^{1}H, as we have already seen).

However, about 1% of the carbon atoms in any sample of an organic compound will be the carbon-13 isotope. These ^{13}C nuclei will interact with the magnetic field applied in NMR analysis, so any organic compound can produce an NMR spectrum.

Typical carbon-13 NMR shifts are shown in Table 30.4. As in proton NMR, the chemical shifts are measured

> **IMPORTANT**
>
> Carbon-13 NMR produces a spectrum with different chemical shifts for non-equivalent carbon atoms in a molecule.

with reference to the TMS (tetramethylsilane) peak at 0 ppm on the spectrum (see Section 30.4).

Analysis of carbon-13 NMR spectra is similar to that of proton NMR, looking to match different chemical shifts to characteristic molecular environments. However, the signals produced in carbon-13 NMR appear as discrete vertical lines on the spectra. You do not find the complication of the splitting patterns caused by the protons in ^{1}H atoms within the molecules. Take care in interpreting the carbon-13 NMR spectra because the heights of the lines are not usually proportional to the number of equivalent ^{13}C atoms present.

Hybridisation of carbon atom	Environment of carbon atom	Example structures	Chemical shift range (δ) / ppm
sp^3	alkyl	CH_3-, CH_2-, $-CH<$, $>C<$	0–50
sp^3	next to alkene / arene	$-C-C=C$, $-C-\bigcirc$	25–50
sp^3	next to carbonyl / carboxyl	$-C-COR$, $-C-CO_2R$	30–65
sp^3	next to halogen	$C-X$	30–60
sp^3	next to oxygen	$C-O$	50–70
sp^2	alkene or arene	$>C=C<$, (benzene ring)	110–160
sp^2	carboxyl	$R-COOH$, $R-COOR$	160–185
sp^2	carbonyl	$R-CHO$, $R-CO-R$	190–220
sp	nitrile	$R-C\equiv N$	100–125

Table 30.4: Typical ^{13}C chemical shift values (δ) relative to TMS = 0. Note that chemical shifts are typical values and can vary slightly depending on the solvent, the concentration and substituents present.

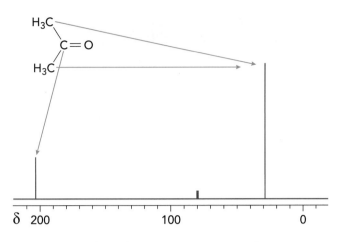

Figure 30.22: The carbon-13 NMR spectrum of propanone.

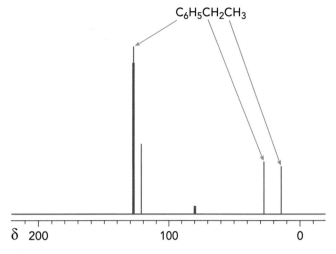

Figure 30.23: The carbon-13 NMR spectrum of ethylbenzene.

The solvent used to prepare samples for ^{13}C NMR analysis is $CDCl_3$. This accounts for the small signal near 80 ppm that can be ignored when interpreting a spectrum, as it is caused by the atoms of ^{13}C in the solvent molecules.

Figure 30.22 shows the ^{13}C NMR spectrum for propanone, $(CH_3)_2CO$.

Note that there are only two peaks: one for the carbon atom in the carbonyl group, $>C{=}O$, and the other for the carbon atoms in the methyl groups, $-CH_3$. Although there are two $-CH_3$ groups in propanone, they are equivalent and so appear as only a single peak (just as equivalent H atoms do in proton NMR).

Figure 30.23 shows another example; the carbon-13 NMR spectrum of ethylbenzene, $C_6H_5CH_2CH_3$.

The carbon atoms in the benzene ring are almost equivalent but will be affected to slightly different extents by the presence of the ethyl group in the molecule. Hence the series of lines clustered between 130 and 120 ppm.

Question

8   a   Look at the series of lines clustered between 130 and 120 ppm in Figure 30.23.

   i   One line is separated slightly from the main cluster.

   Explain which carbon atom in ethylbenzene is most likely to have produced that signal.

   ii   Predict how many lines make up the tightly clustered grouping of the tallest line on the ^{13}C spectrum.

   Explain your reasoning.

   b   Predict the number and location of signal lines in the carbon-13 NMR spectrum of benzene, C_6H_6.

   c   Explain the number of signal peaks you would expect to see in the carbon-13 NMR spectrum of:

   i   propan-1-ol

   ii   propan-2-ol.

REFLECTION

Compare your answers in Question 8 with those of another learner. Do you have any differences that you need to discuss? Try to reach an agreed set of answers before checking against the answers provided.

Which parts of Chapter 30 did you enjoy most / find most difficult / find easiest? Talk with your partner about your reasons why.

SUMMARY

Chromatography separates mixtures of substances for identification. In chromatography, the mobile phase moves the components of a mixture through or over the stationary phase. Separation occurs by the transfer of the components to the stationary phase by:

- partition between two liquids (due to the different solubility of solutes in the mobile phase and stationary phase), or

- partition between a gas and a liquid, or

- adsorption on a solid surface.

The stationary phase may be solid or liquid; the mobile phase may be liquid or gas.

In paper and thin-layer chromatography (TLC) the components of a mixture are identified by their R_f values.

In gas–liquid chromatography (GLC), the components of a mixture are identified by their retention times; the amount of each component is found by measuring the area under each peak (estimates can be made from narrow or sharp peak heights).

The proton NMR spectrum of a compound provides detailed information about the structure of the compound. In particular, the spectrum for the protons, ^1H, in a compound can provide a complete determination of the compound's structure.

Protons in different chemical environments produce signals at different chemical shifts. The chemical shift (δ) provides information about the proton's environment.

Protons on neighbouring carbon atoms cause signals to be split. The splitting pattern establishes which groups of protons are on adjacent carbon atoms. The '$n + 1$' rule predicts the splitting pattern.

Protons on OH and NH can be identified by the addition of D_2O to the NMR sample, which collapses the peak due to an –OH or an –NH– proton.

Carbon-13 NMR can also help to determine the structure of organic molecules.

A combination of techniques, such as infrared (see Chapter 18), NMR and mass spectroscopy (see Chapter 3) must be used to confirm the structure of newly discovered compounds.

EXAM-STYLE QUESTIONS

1   The gas–liquid chromatogram for a mixture of organic compounds is shown below.

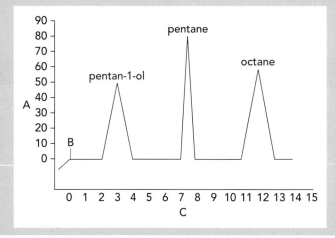

CONTINUED

a   Give the correct labels for A, B and C.   [3]

b   Calculate the percentage of pentan-1-ol in the mixture.   [6]

c   Give an explanation for the different retention times.   [3]

d   i   Describe how the chromatogram would change if the liquid
        in the stationary phase was much more polar.   [1]

    ii Explain your answer.   [2]

e   Describe why gas–liquid chromatography is useful in testing for
    anabolic steroids in the blood of athletes.   [2]

f   Suggest why the use of gas–liquid chromatography linked to a
    mass spectrometer is such a useful analytical technique.   [2]

g   Suggest why it is difficult to separate dyes using gas–liquid
    chromatography.   [2]

                                                               [Total: 21]

When answering Questions 2–5, you will need to use the values in
Table 30.1.

2   Compound B has the composition 62.1% carbon, 10.3% hydrogen
    and 27.6% oxygen.

    Its mass spectrum and ^{1}H NMR spectrum are shown below.

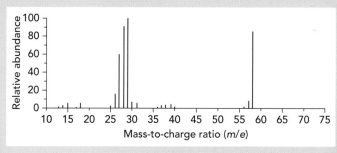

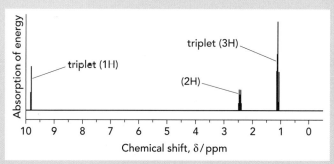

a   Calculate the empirical formula of B.   [2]

b   From the mass spectrum, find the molecular mass of B and hence
    its molecular formula.   [2]

c   i   Draw displayed formulae for the possible isomers of B which
        contain a carbonyl group, >C=O.   [2]

    ii Use the ^{1}H NMR spectrum of B to decide which isomer is B.   [1]

    iii Explain your reasoning.   [3]

d   Deduce what caused the peak at δ = 1.1 ppm, and why it is split
    into a triplet in the ^{1}H NMR spectrum of B.   [2]

CONTINUED

  e Predict the number of signal lines present on the carbon-13 NMR spectrum of:

    i compound B, stating the origin of each line [2]

    ii the isomer of compound B identified in your answer to part **c i**, stating the origin of each line. [2]

                                                  [Total: 16]

3 Arene C has the composition 90.6% carbon and 9.4% hydrogen.

Its mass spectrum and ^1H NMR spectrum are shown below.

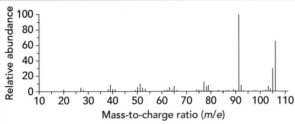

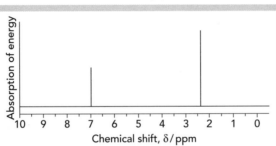

  a Calculate the empirical formula of C. [2]

  b From the mass spectrum, find the molecular mass of C and hence its molecular formula. [2]

  c **i** Draw displayed formulae for the possible aryl (aromatic) isomers of C. [4]

    ii When C is treated with chlorine in the presence of $AlCl_3$ it undergoes electrophilic substitution. In this reaction one of the hydrogen atoms bonded directly to the benzene ring is replaced with one chlorine atom, and one single aromatic product is formed. Consider this evidence and the NMR spectrum of C to decide which isomer is C. [5]

  d Explain the main features of the ^1H NMR spectrum of C. [4]

                                                  [Total: 17]

4 Compound D has the composition 77.8% carbon, 7.41% hydrogen and 14.8% oxygen.

Its mass spectrum and ^1H NMR spectrum are shown below.

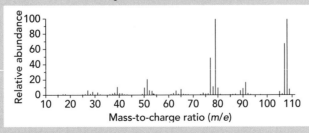

CONTINUED

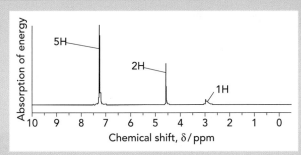

a Calculate the empirical formula of D. [2]

b From the mass spectrum, find the molecular mass of D
   (ignoring the ^{13}C peak) and hence its molecular formula. [2]

c i   Draw displayed formulae for five possible isomers of D
       that contain a benzene ring. [5]

   ii Use the ^1H NMR spectrum of D to deduce which isomer is D. [1]

   iii Explain why you chose this isomer. [3]

d Explain why there are three main peaks on the NMR spectrum of D,
   and identify the protons responsible for the peak at 7.3 ppm. [2]

[Total: 15]

5 Compound E has the composition 69.8% carbon, 11.6% hydrogen
   and 18.6% oxygen. Its mass and ^1H NMR spectra are shown below.

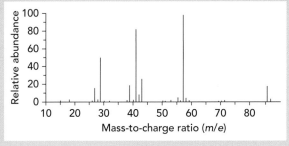

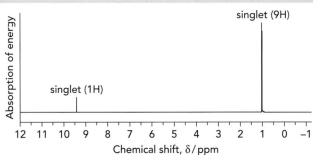

a Calculate the empirical formula of E. [2]

b From the mass spectrum, find the molecular mass of E
   (ignoring the ^{13}C peak) and hence its molecular formula. [2]

c Compound E reacts with 2,4-dinitrophenylhydrazine to give
   a yellow-orange precipitate.

   Draw displayed formulae for the seven possible isomers of E. [7]

CONTINUED

d Compound E gives a silver mirror with Tollens' reagent.
Identify the functional group in E. [3]

e Use the ^{1}H NMR spectrum to identify E.
Explain your reasoning. [4]

[Total: 18]

SELF-EVALUATION

I can	See section...	Needs more work	Almost there	Ready to move on
explain and use the term 'R_f value' in thin-layer chromatography	30.1, 30.2			
explain and use *retention time* in gas–liquid chromatography, and interpret gas–liquid chromatograms to find the percentage composition of a mixture	30.3			
analyse a carbon-13 NMR spectrum of a simple molecule to deduce the different environments of the carbon atoms present and the possible structures for the molecule	30.5			
predict the number of peaks in a carbon-13 NMR spectrum for a given molecule	30.5			
analyse and interpret a proton NMR spectrum of a simple molecule to deduce: **a** the different types of proton present **b** the relative numbers of each type of proton present **c** the number of non-equivalent protons adjacent to a given proton **d** the possible structures for the molecule	30.4			
predict the chemical shifts (δ) and splitting patterns of the signals in an NMR spectrum, given the molecule	30.4			
in obtaining an NMR spectrum, describe the use of tetramethylsilane, TMS, as the standard for chemical shift measurements, and the need for deuterated solvents, e.g. $CDCl_3$	30.4			
describe the identification of O—H and N—H protons by proton exchange using D_2O.	30.4			

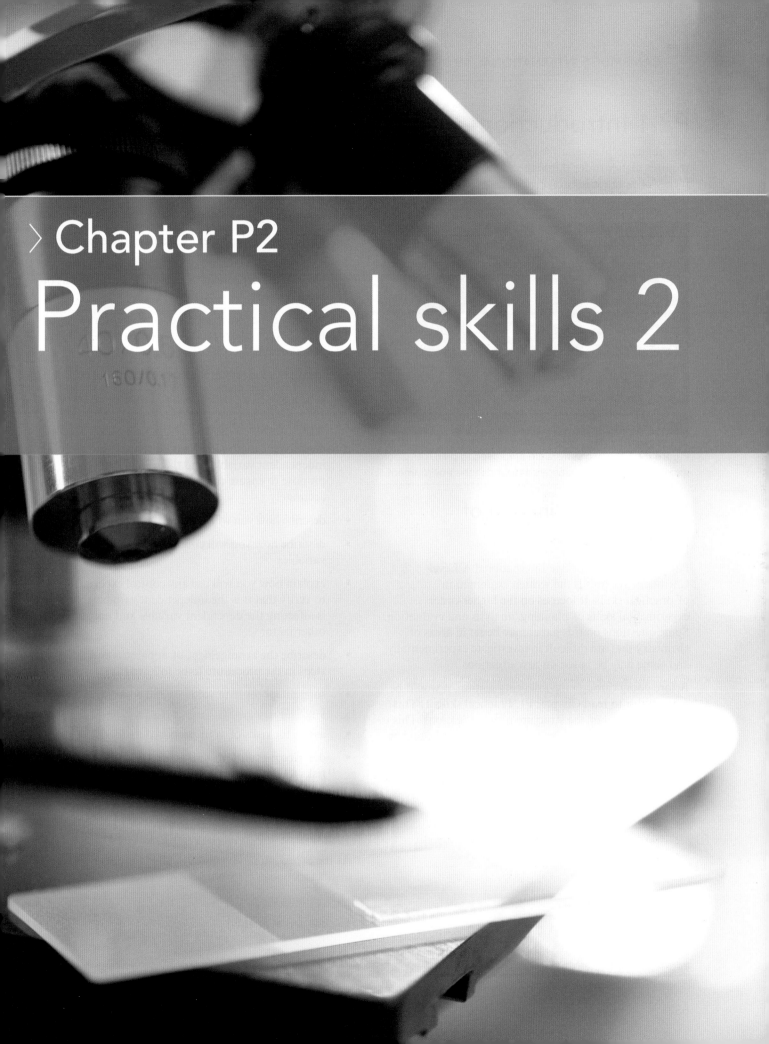

> Chapter P2
Practical skills 2

P2.1 Introduction

The ability to plan, analyse and evaluate practical work requires higher-order thinking skills. You will need plenty of practice in carrying out tasks requiring these skills as you progress through your course (Figure P2.1).

Figure P2.1 Many chemists are employed to plan, carry out and evaluate tests on substances found in the environment.

Written examination of practical skills

Paper 5 in the Cambridge International A Level Chemistry syllabus is the written examination of practical skills. It focuses on the higher-order experimental skills of planning, analysis and evaluation. Some questions on this paper may be set in areas of chemistry that are difficult to investigate experimentally and some may be based on new situations.

Before going through the following section, it would be a good idea to read Chapter P1, Practical skills 1. This will remind you of the structure of investigations. This is essential to understand before you can apply the higher-order practical skills tested in Paper 5.

P2.2 Planning

Expectations

Defining the problem

You should be able to:

- identify the independent variable in the experiment or investigation

- identify the dependent variable in the experiment or investigation

- formulate the aim in terms of a prediction or hypothesis, and express this in words or in the form of a predicted graph

- identify the variables that are to be controlled.

Methods

You should be able to:

- describe the method to be used to vary the independent variable, and the means that you propose to ensure that you have measured its values accurately

- describe how you will measure the dependent variable

- describe how you will control each of the other key variables

- explain how you will use any control experiments to verify that it is the independent variable that is affecting the dependent variable and not some other factor

- describe the arrangement of apparatus and the steps in the procedure to be followed

- suggest appropriate volumes and concentrations of reagents

- assess the risks of your proposed methods

- describe precautions that should be taken to keep risks to a minimum

- draw up tables for data that you might wish to record

- describe how the data might be used in order to reach a conclusion.

As the expectations above show, all plans contain two distinct sections:

- defining the problem

- the actual method.

Defining the problem

The question generally begins with a stem, which will contain information relevant to the plan and the aim of the investigation. The context of the task to be covered may or may not be familiar to you, but the stem will contain all the detail required.

Almost invariably, a prediction is required and, together with an explanation of the basis of the prediction, they form a hypothesis to test. For example, in a question about rate of reaction, you might make a quantitative prediction, such as the direct proportionality between the rate and concentration. Here, the supporting explanation would need to be given in terms of the doubling of the frequency of particle collisions as a result of doubling the concentration. The planning question might also ask you to give a supporting sketch graph.

You will have to specify the independent and the dependent variables. You might also have to consider the need to control other variables.

In a 'rate' exercise, the independent variable might be the concentration of a reactant or the temperature. The measured rate of the reaction at different values of the independent variable is the dependent variable. Alternative ways of measuring the rate of reaction, such as the time to collect a set volume of gas (giving average rates) or the monitoring of gas released over time (then calculating the initial gradient of lines on a graph to measure initial rates), are acceptable.

Methods

When creating a method, you should produce one that can be followed by another learner without the need to ask any extra questions. This means that fine detail is required and nothing should be left out just because you think it is 'obvious'.

The question might provide further information that builds on the stem, but you are expected to have experience of basic laboratory apparatus. The best way to achieve this is to follow a programme of experimental work throughout the course. This also has the advantage of promoting the understanding of concepts underlying the practical work.

Basic techniques, such as titrations, standard solution production and rate measurement, should be thoroughly understood in detail. You also need to be aware of the various methods of measuring volume and mass available in a laboratory. For example, an experiment involving the production and collection of a gas, such as the effect of heat on nitrates, would require you to be aware that gas syringes usually have a maximum capacity of 100 cm³. An alternative method to collect the gas over water in a burette would allow for the collection of only 50 cm³. This example shows how it is important to perform meaningful practical work in order to prepare for Paper 5. There is no substitute for familiarity in handling real apparatus.

On occasion, you could be asked to draw a diagram of the apparatus to be used. You need to be able to represent the apparatus in a simple and understandable format. It is essential that each piece of equipment can be easily recognised in the diagram. Practice drawing sessions are a very good idea.

Relevant calculations are an almost routine requirement, and these must be logically presented, step by step.

The preparation of a standard solution of a solid acid, such as ethanedioic acid, requires the calculation of the mass to be dissolved in a chosen volumetric flask in order to produce the required concentration. The described procedure should indicate that the solid needs to be dissolved completely in distilled water before adding the solution to the volumetric flask (see Figure P2.2). You should make clear how you can ensure that all of this solution is transferred successfully to the volumetric flask. For example, you would rinse any solution stuck on the inside of the original container into the volumetric flask using distilled water. Once in the volumetric flask, the solution is made up to the required mark, and must then be thoroughly mixed.

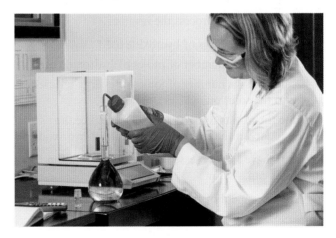

Figure P2.2 Volumetric flasks are used to make up standard solutions of known concentration accurately.

You are expected to calculate the amounts of substance used to suit the volume or size of the apparatus that you specify. For example, if the plan involves collecting a gas from the decomposition of a carbonate in a 100 cm³ gas syringe, the calculated mass of the solid to be heated should be such as to produce slightly less than 100 cm³ of the gas.

An important part of any plan is the collection and presentation of results. Any processing of the results must be specified, and the figures obtained should also be presented as the 'derived results'. The derived results may then be processed in order to confirm or deny (falsify) the original prediction or hypothesis. This processing may involve calculating means of repeat readings and the graphical presentation of results.

The recorded results are those collected from the various steps taken in carrying out the procedure. For example, in an exercise to find the enthalpies of solution of Group 1 hydroxides, the necessary results columns to be recorded are:

- the name or nature of the hydroxide
- the mass of a weighing bottle
- the mass of the weighing bottle and a sample of the hydroxide
- the initial temperature of the water
- the final temperature of the solution.

If you plan to repeat any tests to get replicate results, extra columns must be added to the results table. Each column should have the correct units: for example, represented as either ' / g' or '(g)' for any mass.

The next stage is to process the results:

1 calculate the mass of hydroxide used
2 calculate the number of moles of hydroxide used
3 calculate the number of joules of energy released into the solution
4 use the results to parts **2** and **3** to deduce the standard enthalpy change per mole of hydroxide.

All plans have to be assessed for risk. Examination questions can ask for:

- an assessment of the risks involved in a particular experiment
- how to deal with the risks
- both of the above.

In an exercise to determine the enthalpy of neutralisation of hydrochloric acid (the question will tell you that this is 'harmful') and sodium hydroxide (which is 'corrosive'), you could be asked about a suitable precaution. Alternatively, an experiment on solubility may have hot water as a possible hazard. If a toxic gas is formed, as in the decomposition of Group 2 nitrates, the investigation should be carried out in a fume hood.

Points to remember

- When planning an investigation, your method must be ordered in a logical sequence. Therefore, you might prefer to make some rough notes at the back of the examination paper before writing a bullet-pointed list or flow chart that explains exactly how you would carry out the investigation. These could include diagrams of the assembled apparatus instead of complicated written explanations of the set-up.

- When describing how to vary your independent variable, make sure that you consider how to measure its values accurately. For example, in a rate of precipitation investigation, when varying the concentration of a solution, you might choose to measure volumes of water and solution using volumetric pipettes and fillers rather than just using a measuring cylinder (see Figure P2.3). You should also be familiar with the volumes and masses of reagents that are reasonable to use in normal everyday laboratory work. For example, a volume of 15 cm³ of solution would be suitable for an experiment in a boiling tube but not in a 250 cm³ conical flask.

- When deciding how to measure the dependent variable, you should also consider accuracy: how you intend to measure its 'true' value. In a rate of precipitation investigation, you might choose to carry out the reaction in a conical flask on top of a piece of paper with a pencil mark drawn on it. You could then time how long it takes for the pencil mark to be no longer visible when viewed from above the flask. This will involve a subjective judgement by the observer. If you have done an experiment like this before, you will know just how difficult it is to decide the exact moment when you can no longer see through the solution. So including a very accurate timing device, reading to one-thousandth of a second, would not be appropriate for this method.

- You might also be required to sketch the axes you would use to graph the data collected and describe how you would use the data to draw a conclusion.

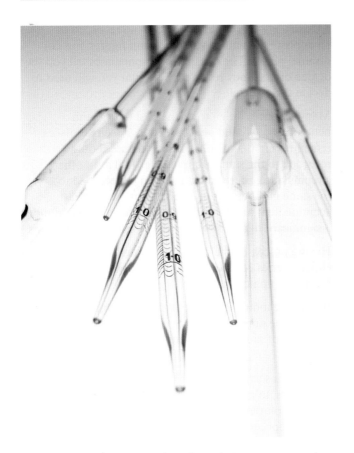

Figure P2.3 Volumetric and graduated pipettes are used to transfer accurate volumes of liquid. Volumetric pipettes give greater accuracy than graduated pipettes, due to the single line to measure to on the thin section above the bulge.

Question

1 In an experiment to determine the formula of an oxide of copper, the copper oxide was reduced by hydrogen gas. The hydrogen was passed over the oxide of copper in a boiling tube with a hole near its end. The excess hydrogen was burnt off at this hole. The copper oxide was placed inside the boiling tube, which was clamped in a horizontal position, in a porcelain boat and heated strongly.

a Name the products of the reaction.

b Draw a labelled diagram of the apparatus.

c Make a list of the measurements you would make to find the formula of the oxide of copper.

d Show how you would work out, using the measurements, the mass contained in the oxide of copper of:

   i copper

   ii oxygen

e The experiment was carried out by ten groups of learners, each with a different initial mass of the oxide of copper. Sketch a graph with the line you would expect to enable you to work out the formula.

P2.3 Analysis, conclusions and evaluation

Expectations

Dealing with data

You should be able to:

- identify the calculations and means of presentation of data that are necessary to be able to draw conclusions from provided data

- use calculations to enable simplification or explanation of data

- use tables and graphs to draw attention to the key points in quantitative data, including the variability of data.

Evaluation

You should be able to:

- identify anomalous values in provided data and suggest appropriate means of dealing with such anomalies

- within familiar contexts, suggest possible explanations for anomalous readings

- identify the extent to which provided readings have been adequately replicated, and describe the adequacy of the range of data provided

- use provided information to assess the extent to which selected variables have been effectively controlled.

Conclusions

You should be able to:

- draw conclusions from an investigation, providing a detailed description of the key features of the data and analyses, and considering whether experimental data supports a given hypothesis

- make detailed scientific explanations of the data, analyses and conclusions that you have described

- make further predictions, ask informed and relevant questions and suggest improvements.

P2.4 The three remaining skills

The three remaining skills are Dealing with data, Evaluation and Conclusions. You should revise Section P1.4 before reading the following advice.

Dealing with data

In a written practical paper, you will often be presented with some data, usually in a table, derived from an experiment. The details of the experiment will be given to you, and then you will be asked to process the data and produce a system that incorporates all the results and allows not only correct patterns to become apparent but also detects anomalous results. The tabulated results will be the measured quantities of the processes carried out in a laboratory.

For example, in an experiment to confirm the formula of zinc iodide by reacting excess zinc with iodine, the measurements would be:

- mass of an empty test-tube

- mass of the test-tube and zinc powder

- mass of the test-tube, zinc powder and iodine

- mass of the test-tube and excess of zinc.

From these you would calculate:

- the mass of zinc used

- the mass of iodine that reacted with that mass of zinc.

These results would be tabulated, possibly alongside the original data, with each column showing the appropriate units and an expression to show how the values were calculated.

All calculations should be correct and recorded to an appropriate number of significant figures and / or decimal places. The question will sometimes tell you the degree of accuracy required, but often you will need to decide this yourself.

Many balances weigh to the nearest 0.01 g, and hence masses should be recorded to 2 decimal places, remembering that whole number masses should be recorded to the same accuracy, e.g. 4.00 g. In other circumstances, derived data should be recorded to the same number of significant figures as the least accurate item of supplied data. Where you are in doubt, 3 significant figures is appropriate for most calculations.

Having processed the raw data, the next step involves either a series of calculations to be averaged or some form of graphical plot.

In the zinc iodide experiment already discussed, the ratio of the number of moles of iodine to the number of moles of zinc can be used to produce a series of ratios.

These ratios can then either be averaged, excluding any anomalies, to produce an appropriate result, or a graph could be plotted of the two molar values. In this case, the appropriate gradient of the line would indicate the formula of zinc iodide. For example, if you plot the number of moles of zinc on the x-axis and the number of moles of iodine on the y-axis, the gradient of the line on the graph should be 2. This shows that the formula of zinc iodide is ZnI_2.

The first step in plotting a graph is an appropriate choice of scales for the two axes, with the independent variable along the x-axis (the horizontal axis). When choosing a suitable scale, it is useful to remember that the plotted points should be spread over at least half of each axis.

You must decide whether or not the origin (0,0) is a point on your graph. Whether or not to include the origin will usually be clear from the nature of the results. For example, if the concentration of a reactant is shown to affect the rate of a reaction, it is reasonable to assume that if the reactant were absent the reaction would not occur, so the rate would be zero when the concentration was zero. The origin can then provide a further useful point to be plotted. Chosen scales should be easily readable, but errors are counted if unhelpful scales are used. For example, the division of each of the two-centimetre squares on the graph grid into three makes accurate plotting very difficult.

Each of the plotted points can best be shown as a small x or +, made with a hard, sharp, pencil.

Most plotted points will show a clear trend, indicating whether the graph should be a straight line or a curve; a straight line is the more usual. The plotted points must first be assessed to identify any anomalous points. If any anomalous points are identified, they should be clearly labelled as such. The line of best fit is then drawn, either as a curve or straight line. This line may not pass through all, or indeed any, of the plotted points. As a rough guide, an equal number of points should lie on the left of the line and on the right of the line, producing an 'average' line.

Evaluation

You can approach the evaluation of a set of results in a number of ways. The aim of any experiment is to draw an appropriate conclusion, either to verify a relationship or to establish a new relationship. This is accomplished by looking at the nature of the results and the quality of the experiment itself.

When anomalous results are identified, they should be clearly labelled as such. The source of the anomaly will often need to be identified and will usually fall into one of two categories: either a positive or a negative deviation from the general trend.

In a reaction involving the reduction of a metal oxide, the anomaly might arise because the reduction was incomplete, leading to a larger than expected mass of metal. The excess mass is the unreacted oxide.

If the reaction involves the thermal decomposition of hydrated iron(II) sulfate, two opposite errors are possible:

- insufficient heating: this will cause the residual mass to be too great

- overheating: this will cause the residual mass to be too small.

The former result corresponds to the incomplete removal of the water of crystallisation, whereas the latter relates to the decomposition of the iron(II) sulfate into iron oxide.

You may be called upon to consider whether the actual experimental data under consideration is of high enough quality to produce reliable results, and appropriate improvements may be requested. If the results provide poor support for a conclusion, it may be that further repeats are needed, or that the range of results needs to be extended.

Apparatus may need to considered from two viewpoints:

- is it appropriate?

- is it accurate?

In the measurement of volume, burettes and pipettes are more accurate than measuring cylinders, but if the volume to be measured is large, a measuring cylinder could be perfectly adequate.

An experiment measuring a small temperature change in an enthalpy exercise often involves volumes of the order of 25 cm^3 to 50 cm^3 and a typical temperature change of the order of 5 °C to 10 °C, using a thermometer accurate to the nearest degree. In this case, the volumes could safely be measured with a measuring cylinder, as the percentage error of the temperature change will be greater than that of the measuring cylinder.

The volumes measured during titrations are about as accurate as simple exercises can be. If these are involved in an experiment the source of any error is likely to be elsewhere.

Measuring small volumes or masses generally produces high percentage errors, whichever item of simple laboratory apparatus is used. As an example, an experiment to investigate the rate of reaction between hydrochloric acid and magnesium by measuring the volume of hydrogen produced requires less than 0.10 g of magnesium if the gas produced is to be collected in a 100 cm^3 syringe. This is a very small mass of magnesium. Using a typical balance accurate to 0.01 g would give a 10% error and consequently the accuracy of the syringe is of negligible significance. The error in measuring the mass of the magnesium will be the greatest percentage error.

Conclusions

The conclusion of an exercise draws upon the key features of data collected and the subsequent analyses. Usually the data given will support a given hypothesis. However, it must be clearly understood that data that do not support an initial suggestion might also have to be considered.

In the magnesium / acid reaction, processing could involve plotting a graph of rate against the relative concentration of the acid. Inspection of the graph would allow a deduction to be made about the order with respect to [H^+] in the rate equation. This conclusion would then be considered in the light of an original hypothesis. This, in turn, could lead to further predictions and experiments (see Section P1.4 in Chapter P1).

If the experiment is considered to be too approximate, suggested improvements to the exercise might be requested.

Points to remember

Calculations involving data collected may ask for the mean, median, mode, percentage loss or percentage gain.

- To calculate the mean, add up the individual values in a set and divide by the number of values. Take care not to quote the mean to an unrealistic number of significant figures. The mean should reflect the precision of the measurements from which it was calculated.

- The median is the middle result when all the results are put in order of magnitude.

- The mode is the most common value.

- Percentage loss or gain is calculated by dividing the actual loss or gain by the original value, then multiplying by 100.

The interval of the independent variable should be consistent when planning an investigation. However, additional values can be selected to look more closely where a pattern seems to change (e.g. the gradient of a line changes on a graph of your results) or to extend the limits of your original range below its minimum value or above its maximum value. For example, you might decide to test a much lower dilution of 0.01 mol dm^{-3} when investigating the effect of concentration on the rate of reaction. This would enable you to test if the trend you see within your original range of data continues as expected.

Question

2 a   In the experiment described in Question 1, a learner weighed a mass of 11.35 g of the oxide of copper on a balance reading to the nearest 0.05 g. What was the percentage error in this measurement?

   b   Another group of learners carrying out the same experiment found that their sample of the oxide of copper contained 13.24 g of copper and 3.26 g of oxygen. What is the most likely formula of the oxide of copper? (Relative atomic mass of Cu = 63.5; O = 16.0.)

   c   Nine out of the ten groups who tackled the experiment obtained results consistent with those of the group described in part **b**. The other group's measurements resulted in a ratio that suggested the formula of the oxide was Cu_2O.

   i   What do we call their result when plotted on a class graph of moles of oxygen against moles of copper?

   ii   How would you deal with this result when drawing the line of best fit?

   iii   Give a possible explanation for the Cu_2O result obtained.

SUMMARY

In the written practical examination, you will be tested on your skills of planning, analysis and evaluation.

The planning skill can be split into two sections.

a   Defining the problem, where you should:

- identify the independent variable, the dependent variable, and the variables that are to be controlled in the experiment or investigation

- formulate a prediction or hypothesis, and

b   Describing a method.

CONTINUED

The analysis and evaluation skills include:

- using calculations to simplify or explain data

- using tables and graphs to interpret data

- identifying and dealing with anomalous data

- considering the precision of data

- assessing the control of variables in tests.

- making detailed explanations of the data, analyses and conclusions

- making further predictions, asking questions and suggesting improvements.

EXAM-STYLE QUESTIONS

1   Diffusion in a gas is the random motion of particles involved in the net movement of a substance from an area of high concentration to an area of low concentration. The process of diffusion also takes place in solution. Medical scientists are interested in the rate of diffusion of pharmaceutical compounds through tumours. They can model the factors that affect the rate of diffusion of these drugs by conducting investigations using coloured compounds (to model the drugs) and gelatin, a jelly-like substance (to model the tumours).

The kinetic energy of particles depends on their mass and the speed they travel at. So at a given temperature, large particles will travel slower on average than smaller particles.

Imagine that you are a member of a research team trying to find out how the rate of diffusion through gelatin depends on the relative molecular mass (M_r) of a drug.

a   i   Predict how you think that the rate of diffusion will be affected as the relative molecular mass of a drug increases. Explain your reasoning. [2]

ii   Sketch your prediction on a graph, including any relevant units. [2]

b   In the experiment you are about to plan, identify:

i   the independent variable [1]

ii   the dependent variable. [1]

CONTINUED

c   The research team can make thin discs of gelatin to cover the central area of Petri dishes, leaving space around the edge of each disc to place a solution of the coloured dyes under investigation.

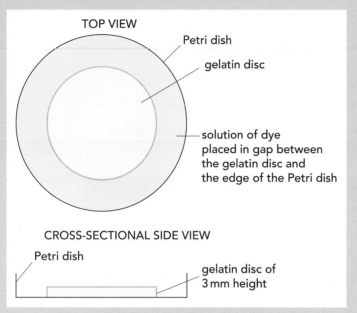

TOP VIEW
— Petri dish
— gelatin disc
— solution of dye placed in gap between the gelatin disc and the edge of the Petri dish

CROSS-SECTIONAL SIDE VIEW
Petri dish
gelatin disc of 3 mm height

You have been given five coloured powders of dyes, labelled A to E, to test. These have relative molecular masses of 486, 534, 686, 792 and 886, respectively. You are also provided with a stopclock / watch and a ruler with a millimetre scale. You can also use any other common laboratory apparatus needed to complete the investigation. The diffusion is a slow process and the team carry out some trial runs to get a rough idea how quickly the dyes diffuse through the gelatin. They decide to monitor the experiment for 72 hours.

Consider the information above and describe how you would carry out the experiment, making sure that you include:

- how to ensure the same number of dye molecules is used in each test

- how to ensure that the Petri dish is kept under the same conditions throughout all of the experiments to measure the rate of diffusion

- how to produce reliable results.   [6]

d   Two of the dyes are classified as 'harmful' and are hazardous if absorbed through the skin or are inhaled. State any precautions you would take to minimise the risk.   [2]

e   Draw a table with headings that show clearly the data you would record when carrying out your experiments and any values you would need to calculate in order to construct a graph to check your prediction in part **a**. The headings must include the appropriate units. Ensure that the table covers all the detail relating to the five dyes listed in part **c**.   [2]

[Total: 16]

Appendix 1

The Periodic Table of the Elements

key

atomic number
atomic symbol
name
relative atomic mass

Period	Group 1	2	3	4	5	6	7	8	9	10	11	12	13	14	15	16	17	18
1	1 **H** hydrogen 1.0																	2 **He** helium 4.0
2	3 **Li** lithium 6.9	4 **Be** beryllium 9.0											5 **B** boron 10.8	6 **C** carbon 12.0	7 **N** nitrogen 14.0	8 **O** oxygen 16.0	9 **F** fluorine 19.0	10 **Ne** neon 20.2
3	11 **Na** sodium 23.0	12 **Mg** magnesium 24.3											13 **Al** aluminium 27.0	14 **Si** silicon 28.1	15 **P** phosphorus 31.0	16 **S** sulfur 32.1	17 **Cl** chlorine 35.5	18 **Ar** argon 39.9
4	19 **K** potassium 39.1	20 **Ca** calcium 40.1	21 **Sc** scandium 45.0	22 **Ti** titanium 47.9	23 **V** vanadium 50.9	24 **Cr** chromium 52.0	25 **Mn** manganese 54.9	26 **Fe** iron 55.8	27 **Co** cobalt 58.9	28 **Ni** nickel 58.7	29 **Cu** copper 63.5	30 **Zn** zinc 65.4	31 **Ga** gallium 69.7	32 **Ge** germanium 72.6	33 **As** arsenic 74.9	34 **Se** selenium 79.0	35 **Br** bromine 79.9	36 **Kr** krypton 83.8
5	37 **Rb** rubidium 85.5	38 **Sr** strontium 87.6	39 **Y** yttrium 88.9	40 **Zr** zirconium 91.2	41 **Nb** niobium 92.9	42 **Mo** molybdenum 95.9	43 **Tc** technetium –	44 **Ru** ruthenium 101.1	45 **Rh** rhodium 102.9	46 **Pd** palladium 106.4	47 **Ag** silver 107.9	48 **Cd** cadmium 112.4	49 **In** indium 114.8	50 **Sn** tin 118.7	51 **Sb** antimony 121.8	52 **Te** tellurium 127.6	53 **I** iodine 126.9	54 **Xe** xenon 131.3
6	55 **Cs** caesium 132.9	56 **Ba** barium 137.3	57–71 lanthanoids	72 **Hf** hafnium 178.5	73 **Ta** tantalum 180.9	74 **W** tungsten 183.8	75 **Re** rhenium 186.2	76 **Os** osmium 190.2	77 **Ir** iridium 192.2	78 **Pt** platinum 195.1	79 **Au** gold 197.0	80 **Hg** mercury 200.6	81 **Tl** thallium 204.4	82 **Pb** lead 207.2	83 **Bi** bismuth 209.0	84 **Po** polonium –	85 **At** astatine –	86 **Rn** radon –
7	87 **Fr** francium –	88 **Ra** radium –	89–103 actinoids	104 **Rf** rutherfordium –	105 **Db** dubnium –	106 **Sg** seaborgium –	107 **Bh** bohrium –	108 **Hs** hassium –	109 **Mt** meitnerium –	110 **Ds** darmstadtium –	111 **Rg** roentgenium –	112 **Cn** copernicium –	113 **Nh** nihonium –	114 **Fl** flerovium –	115 **Mc** moscovium –	116 **Lv** livermorium –	117 **Ts** tennessine –	118 **Og** oganesson –

lanthanoids

57 **La** lanthanum 138.9	58 **Ce** cerium 140.1	59 **Pr** praseodymium 140.9	60 **Nd** neodymium 144.4	61 **Pm** promethium –	62 **Sm** samarium 150.4	63 **Eu** europium 152.0	64 **Gd** gadolinium 157.3	65 **Tb** terbium 158.9	66 **Dy** dysprosium 162.5	67 **Ho** holmium 164.9	68 **Er** erbium 167.3	69 **Tm** thulium 168.9	70 **Yb** ytterbium 173.1	71 **Lu** lutetium 175.0

actinoids

89 **Ac** actinium –	90 **Th** thorium 232.0	91 **Pa** protactinium 231.0	92 **U** uranium 238.0	93 **Np** neptunium –	94 **Pu** plutonium –	95 **Am** americium –	96 **Cm** curium –	97 **Bk** berkelium –	98 **Cf** californium –	99 **Es** einsteinium –	100 **Fm** fermium –	101 **Md** mendelevium –	102 **No** nobelium –	103 **Lr** lawrencium –

> Appendix 2

Selected standard electrode potentials

Electrode reaction	$E^{\ominus}/V$	Electrode reaction	$E^{\ominus}/V$
$Ag^+ + e^- \rightleftharpoons Ag$	$+0.80$	$Mn^{2+} + 2e^- \rightleftharpoons Mn$	-1.18
$Br_2 + 2e^- \rightleftharpoons 2Br^-$	$+1.07$	$MnO_4^- + 8H^+ + 5e^- \rightleftharpoons Mn^{2+} + 4H_2O$	$+1.52$
$Ca^{2+} + 2e^- \rightleftharpoons Ca$	-2.87	$Ni^{2+} + 2e^- \rightleftharpoons Ni$	-0.25
$Cl_2 + 2e^- \rightleftharpoons 2Cl^-$	$+1.36$	$NO_3^- + 2H^+ + e^- \rightleftharpoons NO_2 + H_2O$	$+0.81$
$ClO^- + H_2O + 2e^- \rightleftharpoons Cl^- + 2OH^-$	$+0.89$	$NO_3^- + 10H^+ + 8e^- \rightleftharpoons NH_4^+ + 3H_2O$	$+0.87$
$Cr^{2+} + 2e^- \rightleftharpoons Cr$	-0.91	$O_2 + 4H^+ + 4e^- \rightleftharpoons 2H_2O$	$+1.23$
$Cr^{3+} + 3e^- \rightleftharpoons Cr$	-0.74	$O_2 + 2H_2O + 4e^- \rightleftharpoons 4OH^-$	$+0.40$
$Cr_2O_7^{2-} + 14H^+ + 6e^- \rightleftharpoons 2Cr^{3+} + 7H_2O$	$+1.33$	$Pb^{2+} + 2e^- \rightleftharpoons Pb$	-0.13
$Cu^+ + e^- \rightleftharpoons Cu$	$+0.52$	$PbO_2 + 4H^+ + 2e^- \rightleftharpoons Pb^{2+} + 2H_2O$	$+1.47$
$Cu^{2+} + e^- \rightleftharpoons Cu^+$	$+0.15$	$Sn^{2+} + 2e^- \rightleftharpoons Sn$	-0.14
$Cu^{2+} + 2e^- \rightleftharpoons Cu$	$+0.34$	$Sn^{4+} + 2e^- \rightleftharpoons Sn^{2+}$	$+0.15$
$F_2 + 2e^- \rightleftharpoons 2F^-$	$+2.87$	$SO_4^{2-} + 4H^+ + 2e^- \rightleftharpoons SO_2 + 2H_2O$	$+0.17$
$Fe^{2+} + 2e^- \rightleftharpoons Fe$	-0.44	$S_2O_8^{2-} + 2e^- \rightleftharpoons 2SO_4^{2-}$	$+2.01$
$Fe^{3+} + e^- \rightleftharpoons Fe^{2+}$	$+0.77$	$S_4O_6^{2-} + 2e^- \rightleftharpoons 2S_2O_3^{2-}$	$+0.09$
$Fe^{3+} + 3e^- \rightleftharpoons Fe$	-0.04	$V^{2+} + 2e^- \rightleftharpoons V$	-1.20
$2H^+ + 2e^- \rightleftharpoons H_2$	0.00	$V^{3+} + e^- \rightleftharpoons V^{2+}$	-0.26
$2H_2O + 2e^- \rightleftharpoons H_2 + 2OH^-$	-0.83	$VO^{2+} + 2H^+ + e^- \rightleftharpoons V^{3+} + H_2O$	$+0.34$
$H_2O_2 + 2H^+ + 2e^- \rightleftharpoons 2H_2O$	$+1.77$	$VO_2^+ + 2H^+ + e^- \rightleftharpoons VO^{2+} + H_2O$	$+1.00$
$I_2 + 2e^- \rightleftharpoons 2I^-$	$+0.54$	$VO_3^- + 4H^+ + e^- \rightleftharpoons VO^{2+} + 2H_2O$	$+1.00$
$K^+ + e^- \rightleftharpoons K$	-2.92	$Zn^{2+} + 2e^- \rightleftharpoons Zn$	-0.76
$Mg^{2+} + 2e^- \rightleftharpoons Mg$	-2.38		

> Appendix 3

Qualitative analysis notes

1 Reactions of aqueous cations

Cation	Reaction with	
	NaOH(aq)	NH$_3$(aq)
aluminium, Al^{3+}(aq)	white precipitate soluble in excess	white precipitate insoluble in excess
ammonium, NH$_4^+$(aq)	no precipitate NH$_3$ produced on heating	–
barium, Ba^{2+}(aq)	faint white precipitate is nearly always observed unless reagents are pure	no precipitate
calcium, Ca^{2+}(aq)	white precipitate with high [Ca^{2+}(aq)]	no precipitate
chromium(III), Cr^{3+}(aq)	grey-green precipitate soluble in excess	grey-green precipitate insoluble in excess
copper(II), Cu^{2+}(aq)	pale blue precipitate insoluble in excess	pale blue precipitate soluble in excess giving dark blue solution
iron(II), Fe^{2+}(aq)	green precipitate turning brown on contact with air insoluble in excess	green precipitate turning brown on contact with air insoluble in excess
iron(III), Fe^{3+}(aq)	red-brown precipitate insoluble in excess	red-brown precipitate insoluble in excess
magnesium, Mg^{2+}(aq)	white precipitate insoluble in excess	white precipitate insoluble in excess
manganese(II), Mn^{2+}(aq)	off-white precipitate rapidly turning brown on contact with air insoluble in excess	off-white precipitate rapidly turning brown on contact with air insoluble in excess
zinc, Zn^{2+}(aq)	white precipitate soluble in excess	white precipitate soluble in excess

2 Reactions of anions

Ion	Reaction
carbonate, CO_3^{2-}(aq)	CO_2 liberated by dilute acids
chloride, Cl^-(aq)	gives white precipitate with Ag^+(aq) (soluble in NH_3(aq))
bromide, Br^-(aq)	gives cream precipitate with Ag^+(aq) (partially soluble in NH_3(aq))
iodide, I^-(aq)	gives yellow precipitate with Ag^+(aq) (insoluble in NH_3(aq))
nitrate, NO_3^-(aq)	NH_3 liberated on heating with OH^-(aq) and Al foil
nitrite, NO_2^-(aq)	NH_3 liberated on heating with OH^-(aq) and Al foil; NO liberated by dilute acids (colourless NO → (pale) brown NO_2 in air)
sulfate, SO_4^{2-}(aq)	gives white precipitate with Ba^{2+}(aq) (insoluble in excess dilute strong acids)
sulfite, SO_3^{2-}(aq)	SO_2 liberated on warming with dilute acids; gives white precipitate with Ba^{2+}(aq) (soluble in excess dilute strong acids)
thiosulfate, $S_2O_3^{2-}$(aq)	gives white precipitate slowly with H^+

3 Tests for gases

Gas	Test and test result
ammonia, NH_3	turns damp red litmus paper blue
carbon dioxide, CO_2	gives a white precipitate with limewater (precipitate dissolves with excess CO_2)
hydrogen, H_2	'pops' with a lighted splint
oxygen, O_2	relights a glowing splint

4 Test for an element in aqueous solution

Element	Test and test result
iodine, I_2	gives blue-black colour on addition of starch solution

> Glossary

Command words

Below are the Cambridge International syllabus definitions for Command words which may be used in exams. The information in this section is taken from the Cambridge International syllabus (9701) for examination from 2022. You should always refer to the appropriate syllabus document for the year of your examination to confirm the details and for more information. The syllabus document is available on the Cambridge International website at www.cambridgeinternational.org.

Analyse: examine in detail to show meaning, identify elements and the relationship between them

Calculate: work out from given facts, figures or information

Compare: identify / comment on similarities and / or differences

Consider: review and respond to given information

Contrast: identify / comment on differences

Deduce: conclude from available information

Define: give precise meaning

Demonstrate: show how or give an example

Describe: state the points of a topic / give characteristics and main features

Determine: establish an answer using the information available

Discuss: write about issue(s) or topic(s) in depth in a structured way

Evaluate: judge or calculate the quality, importance, amount, or value of something

Examine: investigate closely, in detail

Explain: set out purposes or reasons / make the relationships between things evident / provide why and / or how and support with relevant evidence

Give: produce an answer from a given source or recall / memory

Identify: name / select / recognise

Justify: support a case with evidence / argument

Predict: suggest what may happen based on available information

Show (that): provide structural evidence that leads to a given result

Sketch: make a simple drawing showing the key features

State: express in clear terms

Suggest: apply knowledge and understanding to situations where there are a range of valid responses in order to make proposals / put forward considerations

Key words

acid: a proton (H^+ ion) donor (Brønsted-Lowry definition)

acid–base indicator: a compound that has two different ranges of colours depending on the pH of the solution in which it is placed. It changes colour over a narrow range of pH values

acid dissociation constant, K_a: the equilibrium constant for the dissociation of a weak acid

$$K_a = \frac{[H^+][A^-]}{[HA]}$$

activation energy, E_A: the minimum energy that colliding particles must possess to break bonds to start a chemical reaction

acyl chloride: reactive organic compounds, characterised by the functional group, —COCl

addition polymerisation: the reaction of many monomers containing at least one double C=C bond to form the long-chain polymers as the only product

addition reaction: an organic reaction in which two (or more) molecules combine to give a single product

adsorption (in catalysis): the first stage in heterogeneous catalysis where reactant molecules form bonds with atoms on the catalyst surface

aliphatic compounds: straight-chain or branched-chain organic compounds, and also include cyclic organic compounds that do not contain benzene rings.

alkaline earth metals: elements in Group 2 of the Periodic Table

alkanes: saturated hydrocarbons with the general formula C_nH_{2n+2}

allotrope: different crystalline or molecular forms of the same element e.g. graphite and diamond are allotropes of carbon

alloy: a mixture of two or more metals or a metal with a non-metal

amide bond: the group of atoms, made up of a carbonyl group and an amine group (—CONH—), that join together the amino acids in peptides and proteins

amino acid residue: the individual units of the amino acids that make up a polypeptide or protein

amphoteric: able to behave as both an acid and as a base. Aluminium oxide is an amphoteric oxide because it reacts with both acids such as hydrochloric acid and bases such as sodium hydroxide to form salts

anhydrous: containing no water of crystallisation

anion: a negatively charged ion

anode: the positive electrode (where oxidation reactions occur)

arene: hydrocarbon containing one or more benzene rings

atom: the smallest part of an element that can take part in a chemical change. Every atom contains protons in its nucleus and electrons outside the nucleus. Most atoms have neutrons in the nucleus. The exception is the isotope of hydrogen $_1^1H$

atomic number: the number of protons in the nucleus of an atom. Also called the proton number. Remember that in writing isotopic symbols, $_y^xA$, this is the figure which is subscript.

atomic orbitals: regions of space outside the nucleus that can be occupied by a maximum of two electrons. Orbitals are named s, p, d and f. They have different shapes

atomic radius: the covalent atomic radius is half the distance between the nuclei of two covalently bonded atoms of the same type. This is not the only type of atomic radius but it gives us the best data when comparing the elements across a period

average bond energy: the average energy needed to break a specific covalent bond averaged from a variety of molecules in the gaseous state, e.g. the average O—H bond energy in ethanol, water and other compounds

Avogadro constant, L: the number of defined particles (atoms, ions, molecules or electrons) in a mole of those particles. Its numerical value is 6.02×10^{23}

azo dyes: coloured compounds formed on the addition of phenol (or another aryl compound) to a solution containing a diazonium ion

base: a proton (H^+ ion) acceptor (Brønsted–Lowry definition)

bidentate ligand: a ligand that forms two co-ordinate (or dative) bonds to the central transition metal ion in a complex

Boltzmann distribution: a graph showing the number of molecules with a particular kinetic energy plotted against the kinetic energy. The exact shape of the curve varies with temperature. The curve shows that only a very small proportion of the molecules have very high energies

bond energy: the energy required to break one mole of a particular covalent bond in the gaseous state. The units of bond energy are kilojoules per mole, $kJ\,mol^{-1}$

bond length: the distance between the nuclei of two covalently bonded atoms

bond polarity: the partial separation of charge when two different atoms are joined by a covalent bond. This results in an unequal attraction for the bonding pair of electrons

Brønsted–Lowry acid: a proton (H^+ ion) donor

Brønsted–Lowry base: a proton (H^+ ion) acceptor

buckminsterfullerene: a simple molecular structure of carbon, with formula C_{60}. The molecule has the shape of a football (soccer ball). The carbon atoms are arranged at the corners of 20 hexagons and 12 pentagons. The bonds where two hexagons join are shorter than the bonds between the hexagons and the pentagons

buffer solution: a solution that minimises changes in pH when moderate amounts of acid or base are added

carbocation: an alkyl group with a single positive charge on one of its carbon atoms. It is formed in reaction mechanisms, e.g. CH_3^+

catalysis: the increase in rate of a chemical reaction brought about by the addition of particular substances which are not used up in the reaction

catalyst: a substance that increases the rate of a chemical reaction but is chemically unchanged at the end of the reaction. It provides a different mechanism of reaction which has a lower activation energy

cathode: the negative electrode (where reduction reactions occur)

cation: a positively charged ion

chiral centre: a carbon atom with the four different atoms or groups of atoms attached. This allows optical isomers to exist

closed system: a system in which matter is not lost or gained, e.g. gases in a closed jar

collision theory: in order for particles to react when they collide, they must have sufficient energy and collide in the correct orientation

common ion effect: the reduction of the solubility of a dissolved salt by adding a compound that has an ion in common with the dissolved salt, e.g. addition of sodium chloride to a solution of very slightly soluble lead(II) chloride

complex ion: a central transition metal ion surrounded by ligands, bonded to the central ion by dative (also called co-ordinate) covalent bonds

compound ion: an ion containing more than one type of element, e.g. OH^-, and PO_4^{3-}

condensation reaction: a reaction in which two organic molecules join together and in the process eliminate a small molecule, such as water or hydrogen chloride

condensation: the change in state when a vapour changes to a liquid

conjugate pair (acid–base): an acid–base pair on each side of an acid–base equilibrium equation that are related to each other by the difference of a hydrogen ion, e.g. the acid in the forward reaction and the base in the backward reaction

control variables: variables (other than the dependent and independent variables) that must be kept the same during an experiment

co-ordinate bond: the sharing of a pair of electrons between two atoms where both the electrons in the bond come from the same atom. Also called a dative covalent bond

co-ordination number: the number of co-ordinate bonds formed by ligands with a transition element ion in a complex

coupling reaction: the reaction between a diazonium salt and an alkaline solution of phenol (or similar compound) to make an azo dye

covalent bond: the electrostatic attraction between the nuclei of two atoms and a shared pair of electrons

cracking: the process in which large, less useful hydrocarbon molecules are broken down into smaller, more useful molecules in an oil refinery

degenerate orbitals: atomic orbitals in the same energy level in a given sub-shell

degree of dissociation: the extent to which a molecule of an acid ionises in a solvent to produce H^+ ions or the extent to which a base produces OH^- ions in a solvent

dehydration: a reaction in which water is removed from a larger molecule

delocalised electrons: electrons that are not associated with any particular atom. In metals, the delocalised electrons move throughout the metallic structure between the metal ions when a voltage is applied. (In the molecule benzene, the delocalised electrons have a more limited movement)

dependent variable: the variable we measure to judge the effect of changing the independent variable

desorption: the last stage in heterogeneous catalysis. The bonds holding the molecule(s) of product(s) to the surface of the catalyst are broken and the product molecules diffuse away from the surface of the catalyst

diazotisation: the reaction between phenylamine and nitrous acid (HNO_2) to give a diazonium salt in the first step in preparing an azo dye

dipeptide: a compound formed from the condensation reaction between two amino acids. The —COOH group of one amino acid reacts with the —NH_2 group of another amino acid

discharged: ions changed into atoms or molecules

displayed formula: a 2D representation of an organic molecule, showing *all* its atoms (by their symbols) and their bonds (by short single, double or triple lines between the symbols)

disproportionation: the simultaneous oxidation and reduction of the same species in a chemical reaction

dot-and-cross diagram: a diagram showing the arrangement of the outer-shell electrons in an ionic or covalent element or compound. The electrons are shown as dots or crosses to show their origin

double covalent bond: two shared pairs of electrons bonding two atoms together

dynamic equilibrium: reactants are being converted to products at the same rate as products are being converted back to reactants

effective collisions: collisions of particles which lead to bond breaking and a chemical reaction

electrode: a rod of metal or carbon (graphite) which conducts electricity to or from an electrolyte

electrode potential, *E*: the voltage measured for a half-cell compared with another half-cell

electrolysis: the decomposition of an ionic compound when molten or in aqueous solution by an electric current

electrolyte: a molten ionic compound or an aqueous solution of ions that is decomposed during electrolysis

electron: negatively charged particle found in orbitals outside the nucleus of an atom. It has negligible mass compared with a proton

electron deficient: an atom or molecule that has less than its usual share of electrons

electronegativity: the power of a particular atom that is covalently bonded to another atom to attract the bonding pair of electrons towards itself

electronic configuration: a way of representing the arrangement of the electrons in atoms showing the principal quantum shells, the sub-shells and the number of electrons present, e.g. $1s^2\ 2s^2\ 2p^3$. The electrons may also be shown in boxes

electrophile: a species in organic chemistry that can act as an electron pair acceptor

electrophilic substitution: the replacement of an atom by another atom or group of atoms after initial attack by an electron-deficient species

electrophoresis: the separation of ions placed in an electric field between a positive and a negative electrode

electrovalent bond: another name for an ionic bond

element: a substance containing only one type of atom. All the atoms in an element have the same proton number

elimination reaction: a reaction in which a small molecule, such as H_2O or HCl, is removed from an organic molecule

empirical formula: the simplest whole number ratio of the elements present in one molecule or formula unit of the compound, e.g. the empirical formula of ethanoic acid is CH_3O

enantiomers: a pair of optically active molecules whose mirror images cannot be superimposed

endothermic reaction: heat energy is absorbed during a reaction. The value of ΔH is positive

energy levels: each electron in an atom has its particular average amount of energy. The further away the electron is from the nucleus, the more energy it has. Each principal energy level (symbol n) corresponds to an electron shell at a certain distance from the nucleus. Energy levels are split up into sub-levels which are given the names s, p, d, etc.

enthalpy change, ΔH: the heat energy transferred during a chemical reaction

entropy: the number of possible arrangements of the particles and their energy in a given system

equilibrium constant, K_c or K_p: a constant which is calculated from the equilibrium expression for a reaction. It can be in terms of concentrations, K_c, or partial pressures, K_p

equilibrium expression: a simple relationship that links K_c to the equilibrium concentrations, or K_p to the equilibrium partial pressures, of reactants and products and the stoichiometric equation

equilibrium reaction: a reaction that does not go to completion and in which reactants and products are present in fixed concentration ratios

esterification: a reaction of a carboxylic or acyl chloride with an alcohol (or phenol) to produce an ester and a small molecule (water or a salt such as NaCl)

eutrophication: an environmental problem caused by fertilisers leached from fields into rivers and lakes

exact bond energy: the energy needed to break a specific covalent bond in a named molecule in the gaseous state, e.g. the O—H bond in water. Also called the bond dissociation energy or bond enthalpy

exothermic reaction: heat energy is released during a reaction. The value of ΔH is negative

Faraday constant: the charge (in coulombs) carried by one mole of electrons or one mole of singly charged ions

feasible: likely to take place, e.g. reaction is likely to be feasible if $E^{\ominus}_{cell}$ has a positive value

first electron affinity, EA_1: the enthalpy change when one mole of electrons is added to one mole of gaseous atoms to form 1 mole of gaseous ions with a single negative charge under standard conditions

first ionisation energy, IE_1: the energy needed to remove one mole of electrons from one mole of atoms of an element in the gaseous state to form one mole of gaseous ions

formula unit: the simplest formula for a covalent giant structure or an ionic giant structure e.g. SiO_2, $MgCl_2$

fragmentation: breaking up of a covalent compound during mass spectrometry into smaller positively charged species, e.g. CH_3^+

free radical: a species with one (or sometimes more than one) unpaired electron

free-radical reaction: a 'three-step' reaction that starts with the production of reactive atoms or molecules with an unpaired electron. The second step regenerates free radicals. Then the reaction finishes with two free radicals meeting to form a molecule

free-radical substitution: the reaction in which halogen atoms substitute for hydrogen atoms in alkanes. The mechanism involves steps in which reactive free radicals are produced (initiation), regenerated (propagation) and consumed (termination)

Friedel–Crafts reaction: the electrophilic substitution of an alkyl or acyl group into a benzene ring

functional group: an atom or group of atoms in an organic molecule which determines the characteristic chemical reactions

general formula: a formula that represents a homologous series of compounds using letters and numbers; e.g. the general formula for the alkanes is C_nH_{2n+2}

geometrical isomerism: displayed by unsaturated or ring compounds with the same molecular formula and order of atoms but different shapes. It arises because of a lack of free rotation about a double bond (due to the presence of a π (pi) bond) or a ring structure

geometric isomers: molecules or ions with the same molecular formula and same bonds between their atoms but which cannot be superimposed on each other, due to some lack of rotation around their bonds; these are also known as *cis/trans* isomers

giant molecular structure / giant covalent structure: structures having a three-dimensional network of covalent bonds throughout the whole structure

Gibbs free energy: the energy change that takes into account both the entropy change of a reaction and the enthalpy change. This is shown by the Gibbs equation:

$$\Delta G^{\ominus} = \Delta H^{\ominus}_{\text{reaction}} - T\Delta S^{\ominus}_{\text{system}}$$

half-cell: one half of an electrochemical cell which either donates electrons to or receives electrons from an external circuit when connected to another half-cell

half-equation: an equation which shows either oxidation or reduction only. These are sometimes called ion–electron equations, because you need to balance the equation by including the correct number of electrons. Example: $Al^{3+} + 3e^- \rightarrow Al$

half-life, $t_{\frac{1}{2}}$: the time taken for the amount (or concentration) of the limiting reactant in a reaction to decrease to half its initial value

halogens: the Group 17 elements

Hess's law: the enthalpy change in a chemical reaction is independent of the route by which the chemical reaction takes place as long as the initial and final conditions and states of reactants and products are the same for each route

heterogeneous catalysis: the type of catalysis in which the catalyst is in a different phase to the reactants. For example, iron in the Haber process

heterolytic fission: the breaking of a covalent bond in which one atom takes both electrons from the bond, forming a negative ion, and leaving behind a positive ion

homogeneous catalysis: the type of catalysis in which the catalyst and reactants are in the same phase. For example, sulfuric acid catalysing the formation of an ester from an alcohol and carboxylic acid

homologous series: a group of organic compounds having the same functional group, the same general formula and similar chemical properties

hydrated compound: compound which contains a definite number of moles of water in their structure (water of crystallisation)

hydrocarbon: organic compound made up of hydrogen and carbon only

hydrogenation: the addition reaction of alkenes with hydrogen

hydrogen bond: the strongest type of intermolecular force but weaker than covalent bonds. It is a strong type of pd-pd force

hydrolysis: the breakdown of a compound by water. Hydrolysis is also used to describe the breakdown of a substance by dilute acids or alkali

2-hydroxynitrile: the product from the nucleophilic addition of hydrogen cyanide to a carbonyl compound. For example, RRC(OH)CN from a ketone or RHC(OH)CN from an aldehyde, where R is an alkyl group

ideal gas: a gas whose volume varies in proportion to the temperature and in inverse proportion to the pressure. Noble gases such as helium and neon approach ideal behaviour because of their low intermolecular forces

immiscible: two liquids that do not dissolve in each other, so form two separate layers, such as oil and water

independent variable: the variable under investigation for which we choose different values

inductive effect: the uneven sharing of electrons along a covalent bond. Electron-donating species, such as an alkyl group, are said to have a positive inductive effect, whereas electron-withdrawing species, such as an oxygen atom, have a negative inductive effect

ineffective collisions: the particles collide without sufficient kinetic energy to react. Collisions may also be ineffective because, although the molecules collide with enough energy, the reactive parts are not close enough to each other

infrared spectroscopy: a technique for identifying compounds based on the change in vibrations of particular atoms when infrared radiation of specific frequencies is absorbed

initiation step: the first step in the mechanism of free-radical substitution of alkanes by halogens. It involves the breaking of the halogen–halogen bond using energy from ultra-violet light from the Sun

Instantaneous dipole-induce dipole forces (id-id forces): the weakest intermolecular attractive force. It results from temporary instantaneous dipoles induced in both polar and non-polar molecules. These forces are also called

intermediate: a species, such as a carbocation, which is formed at a particular step of the reaction. Intermediates are stable enough to react with another substance but not stable enough to be a product. They often have a partial positive or negative charge

intermolecular forces: the weak forces between molecules

ion–dipole bond: the bond formed between an ion and a polar compound such as water. The negative end of the dipole (on the oxygen atom of water) bonds with a positive ion. The positive end of the dipole (on the hydrogen atoms of water) bonds with a negative ion

ionic bonding: the electrostatic attraction between oppositely charged ions (cations and anions)

ionic equation: a balanced equation showing only those ions, atoms or molecules taking part in the reaction. Spectator ions are not shown. Ionic equations are often written for reactions involving a change in oxidation state

ionic product of water, K_w: the equilibrium constant for the ionisation of water $K_w = [H^+][OH^-]$

ion polarisation: the distortion of the electron cloud of an anion by a neighbouring cation. The distortion is greatest when the cation is small and highly charged

isoelectric point: the pH value at which there is no overall charge on a particular amino acid in its aqueous solution

isotope: atoms of the same element with different mass numbers. They have the same number of protons but a different number of neutrons. Note that the word 'atom' is essential in this definition

kinetic theory: the theory that particles in gases and liquids are in constant movement. The kinetic theory can be used to explain the effect of temperature and pressure on the volume of a gas as well as rates of chemical reactions

lattice: a regularly repeating arrangement of atoms, molecules or ions in three dimensions throughout the whole crystal structure

lattice energy, $\Delta H_{latt}^{\ominus}$: the energy change when one mole of an ionic compound is formed from its gaseous ions under standard conditions. Strictly speaking, the values given usually refer to the lattice enthalpy rather than the lattice energy but the difference is usually not significant

Le Chatelier's principle: if one or more factors that affect a dynamic equilibrium is changed, the position of equilibrium moves to minimise this change

ligand: a molecule or ion with one or more lone pairs of electrons which form dative covalent bonds to a central transition element atom or ion

limiting reactant: the reactant which is not in excess. The reaction will stop when the limiting reactant is all used up

lone pairs (of electrons): pairs of electrons in the outer shell of an atom not involved in bonding

mass number: the number of protons + neutrons in an atom. Also called the nucleon number

metallic bonding: the electrostatic attraction between positive ions and delocalised electrons

mobile phase: the solvent used in chromatography, which moves along the paper, thin layer of aluminium oxide, or column containing liquid supported on a solid

molar gas volume: the volume occupied by one mole of any gas at room temperature and pressure (r.t.p.). One mole of gas occupies 24.0 dm^3 at r.t.p.

molar mass: the mass of a mole of substance in grams

mole: the amount of substance which contains 6.02×10^{23} specified particles (atoms, molecules, ions or electrons)

molecular formula: the formula that shows the number and type of each atom in a molecule, e.g. the molecular formula for ethanol is C_2H_6O

molecular ion: the ion that is formed by the loss of an electron from the original complete molecule during mass spectrometry. This gives us the relative molecular mass of an unknown compound

mole fraction: the number of moles of a particular gas in a mixture of gases divided by the total number of moles of all the gases in the mixture. So for a mixture of gases r, s and t:

$$\text{mole fraction of gas } r = \frac{\text{mol } r}{\text{mol } r + \text{mol } s + \text{mol } t}$$

monodentate ligand: a ligand forming one co-ordinate bond with a transition element ion in a complex

monomers: small molecules that react together to make long chain molecules (polymers)

nanotube: fullerene of hexagonally arranged carbon atoms like a single layer of graphite bent into the form of a cylinder

neutralisation: the reaction of an acid with an alkali to form a salt and water

neutron: uncharged particle in the nucleus of an atom, with the same relative mass as a proton

NMR: an abbreviation for 'nuclear magnetic resonance', a type of spectroscopy used to determine the identity and structure of organic compounds

non-degenerate orbitals: groups of atomic orbitals in the same sub-shell that have slightly different amounts of energy (splitting of orbitals)

nucleophile: species that can act as a donor of a pair of electrons

nucleophilic addition: the mechanism of the reaction in which a nucleophile attacks the carbon atom in a carbonyl group and addition across the C=O bond occurs, e.g. aldehydes or ketones reacting with hydrogen cyanide

nucleophilic substitution: the mechanism of the organic reaction in which a nucleophile attacks a carbon atom carrying a partial positive charge (δ+). This results in the replacement of an atom carrying a partial negative charge (δ−) by the nucleophile

order of reaction: the power to which the concentration of each reactant is raised in the rate equation. If a rate is directly proportional to concentration, it is first order – if the rate is directly proportional to the square of the concentration, it is second order. The overall order of reaction is the sum of these powers

oxidation: the loss of electrons from an atom, ion or molecule

oxidation number (oxidation state): a number given to an atom or ion in a compound that describes how oxidised or reduced it is

oxidation reaction: the addition of oxygen, removal of electrons or increase in oxidation number of a substance; in organic chemistry this refers to a reaction in which oxygen atoms are added to a molecule and / or hydrogen atoms are removed from a molecule

oxidising agent: a substance which brings about oxidation by removing electrons from another atom or ion

PAN: organic pollutant made by reactions with nitrogen oxides, in sunlight, causing photochemical smog

partial pressure: the pressure exerted by a particular gas A in a mixture of gases, A, B, C, etc. i.e. $\dfrac{p_A}{p_A + p_B + p_C}$

partition coefficient, K_{pc}: the ratio of the concentrations of a solute in two different immiscible solvents in contact with each other when equilibrium has been established (immiscible solvents are solvents which do not mix)

peptide bond: the —CONH— link (amide link) between amino acid residues in a peptide or protein

periodicity: the repeating patterns in the physical and chemical properties of the elements across the periods of the Periodic Table

permanent dipole–permanent dipole forces (pd–pd forces): attractive intermolecular forces which result from permanent dipoles in molecules

photochemical reactions: reactions started by energy from ultraviolet light (for example, from the Sun)

pi bond (π-bond): a covalent bond formed by 'sideways' overlap of p and p or p and d atomic orbitals

pK_a values: values of K_a expressed as a logarithm to base 10.

$$pK_a = -\log_{10} K_a$$

polar bonds: the electron pair in the bond is drawn towards the atom with the larger electronegativity, making one end of the molecule slightly positive compared with the other

polarising power (of a cation): the ability of a cation to attract the electron cloud of an anion and distort it

polyamides: polymers made in the condensation polymerisation reaction between a diamine and a dicarboxylic acid (or a dioyl chloride) or between amino acids

polyester: polymer whose monomers are bonded to each other via the ester link, COO

polymer: a long-chain molecule made up of many repeating units derived from the monomers

positive inductive effect: the release (pushing away) of electrons from an organic group, such as an alkyl group, towards the rest of the molecule

primary alcohol: an alcohol in which the carbon atom bonded to the —OH group is attached to one other carbon atom (or alkyl group)

propagation step: the second step in a free-radical mechanism in which the radicals formed can then attack reactant molecules generating more free radicals, and so on

proton: positively charged particle in the nucleus of the atom

racemic mixture: a mixture containing equal amounts of a pair of enantiomers

random errors: errors that are due to chance changes in the experiment or by the experimenter. They are equally likely to make the values of data too high or too low

rate constant: the proportionality constant, k, in a rate equation, e.g. rate = $k\,[NO]^2$

rate-determining step: the slowest step in a reaction mechanism

rate equation: an equation showing the relationship between the rate constant and the concentrations of the species that affect the rate of reaction

rate of reaction: the change in the amount or concentration of a particular reactant or product per unit time

reaction kinetics: the study of rates of chemical reactions

reaction mechanism: the series of steps that take place in the course of the overall reaction

reaction pathway diagram: shows the relative enthalpies of the reactants (on the left) and the products (on the right) and the enthalpy change as an arrow. It may also include the activation energy

real gas: a gas that does not obey the ideal gas law, especially at low temperatures and high pressures

redox reaction: a reaction in which oxidation and reduction take place at the same time

reducing agent: a substance which brings about reduction by donating (giving) electrons to another atom or ion

reduction reaction: the removal of oxygen, addition of electrons or decrease in oxidation number of a substance; in organic chemistry it is the removal of oxygen atoms from a molecule and / or the addition of hydrogen atoms to a molecule

reduction: the gain of electrons by an atom, ion or molecule

relative atomic mass, A_r: the weighted average mass of atoms in a given sample of an element compared to the value of the unified atomic mass unit

relative formula mass, M_r: the weighted average mass of one formula unit compared to the value of the unified atomic mass unit

relative isotopic abundance: the proportion of one particular isotope in a mixture of isotopes usually expressed as a percentage. The heights of the peaks in a mass spectrum show the proportion of each isotope present

relative isotopic mass: the mass of a particular atom of an isotope compared to the value of the unified atomic mass unit

relative molecular mass, M_r: the weighted average mass of a molecule in a given sample of that molecule compared to the value of the unified atomic mass unit

repeat unit: the smallest group of atoms that when linked successively make up the whole polymer chain (apart from the two end units)

resonance frequency: the frequency of absorption of radiation which stimulates larger vibrations in bonds to allow the absorption of energy

retention time: the time taken for a compound to travel through a chromatography column in GLC

reversible reaction: a reaction in which products can be changed back to reactants by reversing the conditions

R_f value (retention factor): in paper chromatography (or TLC), the ratio of the distance travelled by a specific component to the distance travelled by the solvent front

salt: a substance formed when an acid reacts with a metal, an alkali, a metal oxide or a carbonate

saturated hydrocarbon: compound of hydrogen and carbon only in which the carbon–carbon bonds are all single covalent bonds, resulting in the maximum number of hydrogen atoms in the molecule

saturated solution: a solution which can dissolve no more solute at a particular temperature (in the presence of undissolved solute)

secondary alcohol: an alcohol in which the carbon atom bonded to the —OH group is attached to two other carbon atoms (or alkyl groups)

second electron affinity, EA_2: the enthalpy change when 1 mole of electrons is added to 1 mole of gaseous 1– ions to form 1 mole of gaseous 2– ions under standard conditions

shielding: the ability of inner shell electrons to reduce the effect of the nuclear charge on outer shell electrons

sigma bond (σ-bond): a single covalent bond formed by the 'end-on' overlap of atomic orbitals

single covalent bond: a bond made up of a pair of electrons shared between two atoms

skeletal formula: a simplified displayed formula with all C and H atoms and C—H bonds removed

S_N1 mechanism: the steps in a nucleophilic substitution reaction in which the rate of the reaction (which is determined by the slow step in the mechanism) involves only the organic reactant, e.g. in the hydrolysis of a *tertiary* halogenoalkane

S_N2 mechanism: the steps in a nucleophilic substitution reaction in which the rate of the reaction (which is determined by the slow step in the mechanism) involves two reacting species, e.g. in the hydrolysis of a *primary* halogenoalkane

solubility product, K_{sp}: the product of the concentrations of each ion in a saturated solution of a sparingly soluble salt at 298 K, raised to the power of their relative concentrations

solute: a substance which dissolves in a solvent to form a solution

solution concentration: the amount of solute (in moles) dissolved in a stated volume of solution (usually in 1.00 dm^3)

solvent: a substance which dissolves a solute to form a solution

specific heat capacity, c: the energy needed to raise the temperature of 1 g of a substance by 1 °C (by 1 K)

spectator ions: ions present in a reaction mixture which do not take part in the reaction

spin-pair repulsion: a pair of electrons in the same orbital repel each other because they have the same charge. Pairing the spinning electrons so they spin in opposite directions reduces the repulsion. The repulsion is more than that of single electrons in separate orbitals. That is why the electrons in the p and d orbitals go into separate orbitals before being paired up

splitting pattern: the series of peaks that main signals are divided into in high-resolution NMR

stability constant, K_{stab}: the equilibrium constant for the formation of a complex ion in a solvent from its constituent ions or molecules

standard cell potential: the difference in standard electrode potential between two specified half cells

standard conditions: a pressure of 101 kPa and temperature of 298 K, shown by $^\ominus$

standard electrode potential: the voltage produced when a standard half-cell (ion concentration 1.00 mol dm^{-3} at 298 K) is connected to a standard hydrogen electrode under standard conditions

standard enthalpy change of atomisation, $\Delta H_{at}^\ominus$: the enthalpy change when one mole of gaseous atoms is formed from its element under standard conditions

standard enthalpy change of combustion, $\Delta H_c^\ominus$: the enthalpy change when one mole of a substance is burnt in excess oxygen under standard conditions

standard enthalpy change of formation, $\Delta H_f^\ominus$: the enthalpy change when one mole of a compound is formed from its elements under standard conditions

standard enthalpy change of hydration, $\Delta H_{hyd}^\ominus$: the enthalpy change when one mole of a specified gaseous ion dissolves in sufficient water to form a very dilute solution under standard conditions

standard enthalpy change of neutralisation, $\Delta H_{neut}^\ominus$: the enthalpy change when one mole of water is formed by the reaction of an acid with an alkali under standard conditions

standard enthalpy change of reaction, $\Delta H_r^\ominus$: the enthalpy change when the amounts of reactants shown in the stoichiometric equation react to give products under standard conditions

standard enthalpy change of solution, $\Delta H_{sol}^\ominus$: the energy absorbed or released when one mole of an ionic solid dissolves in sufficient water to form a very dilute solution under standard conditions

state symbol: in a chemical equation a symbol (sign) placed after each reactant and product in a chemical equation to indicate whether they are solid (s), liquid (l), gas (g) or in aqueous solution (aq)

stationary phase: the immobile phase in chromatography that the mobile phase passes over or through. Examples are the surface of the thin-layer particles in TLC (thin-layer chromatography) or the non-volatile liquid absorbed onto the column in GLC

stereoisomers: compounds whose molecules have the same atoms bonded to each other in the same way, but with a different arrangement of atoms in space so that the molecules cannot be superimposed on each other. (Superimposed means that however you turn the isomer, the atoms are never in exactly the same place – like your hands)

stoichiometry: the mole ratios of reactants and products shown in the balanced equation, e.g. the equation: $2Na + Cl_2 \rightarrow 2NaCl$, the stoichiometry is $2(Na) : 1(Cl_2) : 2(NaCl)$

strong acids and bases: acid and bases which dissociate completely in solution

structural formula: the formula that shows how many, and the symbols of, atoms bonded to each carbon atom in an organic molecule

structural isomers: compounds with the same molecular formula but different structural formulae

sub-shells (subsidiary quantum shells): regions of the principal quantum shells where electrons exist in defined areas associated with particular amounts of energy. They are named s, p, d, etc.

substitution reaction: a reaction that involves the replacement of one atom, or group of atoms, by another

successive ionisation energies: the energy required in each step to remove the first electron, then the second, then the third, and so on, from a gaseous atom or ion. Note: you should be able to write equations for each of these steps, e.g.

1st ionisation energy: $Li(g) \rightarrow Li^+(g) + e^-$

2nd ionisation energy: $Li^+(g) \rightarrow Li^{2+}(g) + e^-$

3rd ionisation energy: $Li^{2+}(g) \rightarrow Li^{3+}(g) + e^-$

surroundings (in enthalpy changes): anything other than the chemical reactants and products, e.g solvent, reaction vessel

system: the reactants and products of a chemical reaction

systematic errors: errors due to data being inaccurate in a consistent way. Systematic errors are often caused by errors in the experimental procedure or equipment

termination steps: the final steps in a free-radical mechanism in which two free radicals react together to form a product molecule

tertiary alcohol: an alcohol in which the carbon atom bonded to the —OH group is attached to three other carbon atoms (or alkyl groups)

thermal decomposition: the breakdown of a compound by heat into two or more different substances

thermal stability: the resistance of a compound to breakdown by heating

titre: in a titration, the final burette reading minus the initial burette reading

TMS: an abbreviation for tetramethylsilane, $Si(CH_3)_4$, the standard compound used in NMR spectroscopy, providing the peak to measure chemical shifts relative to its given value of zero

tripeptide: a compound made by combining three amino acids

triple covalent bond: three shared pairs of electrons bonding two atoms together

unified atomic mass unit: one twelfth of the mass of a carbon-12 atom

unsaturated hydrocarbons: compounds of hydrogen and carbon only whose molecules contain carbon-to-carbon double bonds (or triple bonds)

van der Waals' forces: weak forces of attraction between molecules involving either instantaneous (id–id) or permanent dipole- permanent dipole forces (pd–pd) (including hydrogen bonding). The expression covers all types of intermolecular forces

vaporisation: the change in state when a liquid changes to vapour

vapour pressure: the pressure exerted by a vapour in equilibrium with a liquid

vigorous: a reaction that has a rapid rate of reaction

volatility: the ease with which a substance evaporates. A volatile substance will evaporate at a low temperature

water of crystallisation: a specific number of moles of water associated with a crystal structure

weak acids and bases: acid and bases which dissociate partially (incompletely) in solution

> Index

A

acid, 191
  strong acids, 194
  weak acid *vs.* strong acid, 195–6
  weak acids, 194
acid dissociation constant, K_a, 445
acid rain, 277, 307, 482
acid–base equilibria, 190–6
acid–base indicator, 197–8
acid–base titrations, 196–201
acidity of alcohols *vs.* water, 338
activation energy, E_A, 136
actual yield moles, 52
acyl chlorides, 562
  preparation, 562
  reactions, 563–5
acylation, *see* Friedel-Crafts reactions
addition polymerisation, 316
addition reactions, 297
adsorption (in catalysis), 483
alcohols, 339
  carboxylic acids, 345–6
  homologous series of alcohols, 338
  primary, 338
  properties, 338
  reactions
    combustion, 339–40
    dehydration, 344
    esterification, 342–3
    hydrolysis of esters, 343
    oxidation, 344–5
    sodium metal, 341–2
    substitution to form halogenoalkane, 340–1
  secondary, 338
  tertiary, 338
aldehydes
  homologous series, 352
  preparation of, 353
  reduction of, 354
  uses, 351
  vs. ketones, 357–8

aliphatic compounds, 286
alkaline earth metals, 249
alkanes, 286, 305
  combustion, 306–7
  homologous group, 305–6
  reactions, 306
  substitution reactions, 308–10
alkenes, 310
  addition reactions, 311–13
  electrophilic addition to, 313–14
  oxidation of, 314–15
  poly(alkene) plastics disposal, 317
alkylation, *see* Friedel-Crafts reactions
allotropes, 122
alloy, 121
amide bond, 578, 591
amines
  basicity of, 572–3
  classes of, 572
  formation of, 573–6
  reactions, 578–9
amino acid residue, 591
amino acids, 576–7
ammonia, NH_3, 275
amphoteric, 237
analytical chemistry
  carbon-13 NMR spectroscopy, 624–5
  gas liquid chromatography, 615–17
  principles of chromatography, 612–14
  proton (^{1}H) nuclear magnetic resonance
    high-resolution NMR, 619–22
    identifying the —OH or —NH signal, 623
    low-resolution NMR, 619
  thin-layer chromatography, 614–15
anhydrous compound, 40–1
anions, 77
  reactions, 644
anode, 6, 406
aqueous cations, reactions of, 643

arenes, 543
  electrophilic substitution, 545–6
  oxidation of side-chain in, 548
  reactions of, 544–9
aromatic compounds, *see* aryl compounds
aryl compounds, 543–4
atom, 4
  electronic configuration of, 24–5
  electrons in, 14–30
  elements and, 4
  simple electronic structure, 17
  structure of, 4–7
  transition elements, 519
atomic number (Z), 7
atomic orbitals, 22–3
atomic radius, 27
  periodic patterns, 228–30
atomic structure, 1–10
average bond energy, 146
Avogadro constant, 47
  mole and, 46–7
Avogadro number, *see* Avogadro constant
Avogadro's hypothesis, 65
azo dyes, 571, 576
  using phenylamine, 574–6

B

base, 191
  strong bases, 195
  weak bases, 195
benzene, 542
  alkylation (acylation) of, 547–8
  Kekulé structure of, 542
  nitration of, 546
benzene ring, 543–4
bidentate ligand, 525
bimolecular reaction, 479
biodegradable polymers, 593
biofuel, 337
Boltzmann distribution, 219
bond breaking (endothermic), 145
bond dissociation energy, 145
bond energy, 83

＞ Acknowledgements

The authors and publishers acknowledge the following sources of copyright material and are grateful for the permissions granted. While every effort has been made, it has not always been possible to identify the sources of all the material used, or to trace all copyright holders. If any omissions are brought to our notice, we will be happy to include the appropriate acknowledgements on reprinting.

Thanks to the following for permission to reproduce images:

Cover Cybrain/GI; **Chapter 1:** Mehau Kulyk/SPL/GI; Bettmann/GI; Ibm Research/SPL; Bettmann/GI; Print Collector/GI; **Chapter 2:** Eric Heller/GI; Georgy Shafeev/SPL/GI; **Chapter 3:** Ted Horowitz/GI; Mikulas1/GI; Tek Image/SPL; Dea/Chomon/GI; Charles D. Winters/SPL; Andrew Lambert Photography/SPL; Cuhrig/GI; David Acaster; Martyn F. Chillmaid/SPL; Barry Winiker/GI; David Acaster; Spl/GI; **Chapter 4:** Andrzej Wojcicki/GI; MarkMirror/GI; Kevin Schafer/GI; Charles D. Winters/SPL; Cerae/GI; Roberto De Gugliemo/GI; Andrew Lambert Photography/SPL; Videophoto/GI; Teresa Short/GI; Roman_slavik/GI; Spl/GI; **Chapter 5:** Chaofann/GI; [N]okia/GI; Bigjo5/GI; Ds70/GI; SPL/GI; Science Picture Co/GI; **Chapter 6:** 8213erika/GI; Marie-Ange Ostré/GI; [ ] Meadows/GI; **Chapter 7:** Zenobillis/GI; Westend61/GI; MediaWorldImages/Alamy; Charles D. Winters/SPL(x2); [Chap]ter 8: Fitopardo.com/GI; Claver Carroll/GI; David Acaster; Shaen Adey/GI; Eskaylim/GI; Samohin/GI; [Andre]w Lambert Photography/SPL; Mtreasure/GI; **Chapter 9:** Ibreakstock/Shutterstock; Michael Dunning/GI; [Phot]oCosmicos/GI; Martyn F. Chillmaid/SPL; Andrew Lambert Photography/SPL; Giphotostock/SPL; [Scie]ncephotos/Alamy; **Chapter 10:** Lawrence Lawry/GI; Print Collector/GI; John Freeman/GI; Andrew Lambert [Pho]tography/SPL(x2); Phil Degginger/Alamy; David R. Frazier Photolibrary,Inc/Alamy; Andrew Lambert [Pho]tography/SPL; **Chapter 11:** Nemoris/GI; Gert Kromhout/Stocktrek Images/GI; Portland Press Herald/GI; [A]ndrew Lambert Photography/SPL/GI; Lester V. Bergman/GI(x3); Andrew Lambert Photography/SPL(x2); **Chapter 12:** Giorez/GI; Pacific Press/GI; Andrew Lambert Photography/SPL(x3); **Chapter 13:** Ralph Wetmore/GI; Geography Photos/GI; Nancy Newell/GI; Claver Carroll/GI; **Chapter 14:** LeManna/GI; Svisio/GI; **Chapter 15:** Doranjclark/GI; Anankkml/GI; Andrew Lambert Photography/SPL; PhotoAlto/James Hardy/GI; Xxmmxx/GI; Construction Photography/Avalon/GI; Raymond Reuter/GI; Paul Rapson/SPL; Seyfettinozel/GI; Martyn F. Chillmaid/SPL; Daniela Dirscherl/GI; **Chapter 16:** Lphl Phat'hn Mali Waly/GI; Laflor/GI; Nasa/GI; **Chapter 17:** PathomP/GI; Isitsharp/GI; Saeed Khan/GI; Andrew Lambert Photography/SPL(x2); Dan Dalton/GI; Andrew Lambert Photography/SPL; **Chapter 18:** ArtesiaWells/GI; PicturePartners/GI; Andrew Lambert Photography/SPL(x4); **Chapter 19:** Alfred Pasieka/SPL/GI; Omikron/SPL; Science & Society Picture Library/GI; Keystone/GI; **Chapter 20:** Extreme Media/GI; Photofusion/GI; Andrew Lambert Photography/SPL(x4); **Chapter 21:** Roberto/GI; Goldfinch4ever/GI; Martin Shields/GI; Ullstein bild Dtl/GI; Anyaivanova/GI; Bsip/GI; Douglas Faulkner/GI; **Chapter 22:** Eerik/GI; Madsci/GI; Roger Norris; Chris Ryan/GI; **Chapter 23:** Richard Newstead; Frank Bean/GI; Image Source/GI; Andrew Brookes/GI; Spl/SPL; Bettmann/GI; **Chapter 24:** DKart/GI; Andrew Lambert Photography/Spl(x6); **Chapter 25:** Sol de Zuasnabar Brebbia/GI; Imnature/GI; Bsip/GI; Andrew Lambert Photography/SPL; **Chapter 26:** Jens Schwarz/GI; **Chapter 27:** Nuno Valadas/GI; Andrew Lambert Photography/SPL(x2); R.A. Longuehaye/SPL; **Chapter 28:** Ditto/GI; Freemixer/GI; Roger Ressmeyer/GI; **Chapter 29:** Zorazhuang/GI; Sanjeri/GI; **Chapter 30:** Anyaivanova/GI; Photo by Jared Lazarus, used with permission of Duke University; Speedpix/Alamy; Colin Cuthbert/SPL; Kot2626/GI; TrichopCMU/GI; Nicolas/GI; CasarsaGuru; Huntstock,Inc/GI; Tek Image/SPL/GI.

Key: GI= Getty Images, SPL= Science Photo Library, Alamy = Alamy Stock Photo